# Race, Gender, Sexuality, and Social Class

## Second Edition

*For my daughters, Gillian and Alana,*
*who have taught me more than any book could.*

**⊛SAGE** | **50** YEARS

**SAGE** was founded in 1965 by Sara Miller McCune to support the dissemination of usable knowledge by publishing innovative and high-quality research and teaching content. Today, we publish more than 850 journals, including those of more than 300 learned societies, more than 800 new books per year, and a growing range of library products including archives, data, case studies, reports, conference highlights, and video. SAGE remains majority-owned by our founder, and after Sara's lifetime will become owned by a charitable trust that secures our continued independence.

Los Angeles | London | New Delhi | Singapore | Washington DC

# RACE, GENDER, SEXUALITY, AND SOCIAL CLASS

## Dimensions of Inequality and Identity

### SECOND EDITION

**SUSAN J. FERGUSON**
*Grinnell College*

**Editor**

Los Angeles | London | New Delhi
Singapore | Washington DC

Los Angeles | London | New Delhi
Singapore | Washington DC

FOR INFORMATION:

SAGE Publications, Inc.
2455 Teller Road
Thousand Oaks, California 91320
E-mail: order@sagepub.com

SAGE Publications Ltd.
1 Oliver's Yard
55 City Road
London EC1Y 1SP
United Kingdom

SAGE Publications India Pvt. Ltd.
B 1/I 1 Mohan Cooperative Industrial Area
Mathura Road, New Delhi 110 044
India

SAGE Publications Asia-Pacific Pte. Ltd.
3 Church Street
#10-04 Samsung Hub
Singapore 049483

Printed in the United States of America

ISBN 978-1-4833-7495-6

This book is printed on acid-free paper.

Acquisitions Editor:   Jeff Lasser
Editorial Assistant:   Alexandra Croell
eLearning editor:   Robert Higgins
Production Editor:   Laura Barrett
Copy Editor:   Paula L. Fleming
Typesetter:   C&M Digitals (P) Ltd.
Proofreader:   Alison Syring
Cover Designer:   Rose Storey
Marketing Manager:   Erica DeLuca

SUSTAINABLE FORESTRY INITIATIVE
Certified Chain of Custody
Promoting Sustainable Forestry
www.sfiprogram.org
SFI-01268

SFI label applies to text stock

15 16 17 18 19 10 9 8 7 6 5 4 3 2 1

# CONTENTS

## Theories of Difference

## PART II   IDENTITIES MATTER: THE SOCIAL CONSTRUCTION AND EXPERIENCES OF RACE, GENDER, SEXUALITY, AND SOCIAL CLASS          147

### Identity Formation

### Identities and Social Interaction

## Identity Construction and Stigma Management

# PART III  SOCIAL INSTITUTIONS
# AND THE PERPETUATION OF INEQUALITY     289

## The Family

## Education

# TABLE OF CONTENTS BY THEME/TOPIC

## Gender

## Intersectionality

## Social Inequality/Social Stratification

## Social Inequality and Schools

## Social Inequality and the Family

*Prejudices, it is well known, are most difficult to eradicate from
the heart whose soil has never been loosened or fertilized by education;
they grow there, firm as weeds among rocks.*

Emily Brontë

# PREFACE

As I write this preface, I am watching my younger daughter attempt to build a snowperson with the new, wet snow that has fallen. She is struggling, trying to get the three sections to fit on top of each other without collapsing. As a parent, I want to go outside and make suggestions about how it could be done better. Another part of my parenting side knows that a considerable amount of learning requires struggling with the materials at hand until you can make sense of them yourself. I decide to leave her alone to try, and try again, to figure out the best way to get the snow to hold together. Eventually, by late in the afternoon, a wonderful snowperson begins to appear beneath her mittens, and Alana goes in search of something to use as a nose.

This anecdote is a metaphor for how I see my anthologies and student learning. I provide you with much of the material: key writings from significant scholars, larger theoretical frameworks, discussion questions, exercises, and resources for further learning. However, you will need to struggle with this material a bit until the concepts of social inequality and of race, gender, sexuality, and social class make sense to you. The effort you put into studying this material is well worth the energy you expend, because you will have a deeper understanding of your own identities and of more general social inequities. This knowledge also will give you some tools to enact social change in order to lessen injustices in our society.

This anthology, *Race, Gender, Sexuality, and Social Class: Dimensions of Inequality and Identity,* began six years ago when I was asked to design a new reader in this area. I spent two years researching the field, reading hundreds of articles and books and designing and teaching a new course, "Identities and Inequalities," until I came up with the right combination of readings for this text. When I am designing a course for my students at Grinnell College, I want them to read the primary works by the top scholars in the field. Lynn Weber, Patricia Hill Collins, Erik Olin Wright, Joan Acker, Abby Ferber, Evelyn Nakano Glenn, Matthew Desmond, Mustafa Emirbayer, Doug Massey, and Joe Feagin, just to name a few, are all important names in the study of race, gender, and social class. Their writings and the writings of many other eminent scholars make up the readings in this volume.

My review of the literature also revealed that this subject comprises not just one field of scholarship; instead, race, class, and gender studies are informed by multiple areas of analysis, including the studies of social stratification, social inequality, race and ethnicity, gender studies, and intersectionality. Moreover, it is an area of study that keeps evolving over time. For example, social stratification, one of the oldest areas of inquiry in sociology, studies how societies hierarchically sort and rank people based on their social statuses. Social thinkers such as Émile Durkheim,

Karl Marx, and Max Weber were concerned with social differentiation and social stratification in their earliest writings. As time progressed, the field of social stratification morphed into courses on social inequality, a field that studies the inequities of distributing scarce and valuable resources to those different social status groups. Move further forward in time, and the area of race, class, and gender developed to address social inequality not just in terms of social class but also in terms of these other social categories. Margaret Andersen and Patricia Hill Collins's classic reader, *Race, Class, and Gender: An Anthology,* first published in 1992, responded to this new pedagogical area.

Now, over twenty years later, the field is moving away from discussions of discrete categorical identities toward a more intersectional and nuanced understanding of how social categories work together to create situations of privilege and difference. People are multiply situated and experience their race and ethnicity through the lenses of their social class, gender, and other identities. The experiences of a middle-class African American female are vastly different from those of a white, middle-class male. These differences are not due simply to their race or to their gender but to how their race simultaneously interacts with both their social class and their gender.

This book explores how these differences are shaped and maintained over time. I want students to understand these core sociological concepts of race, ethnicity, gender, sexuality, and social class and when and why these categories of difference were constructed. I also show how these social categories shape our identities and experiences by providing us with privilege or putting us at a disadvantage. Thus, one purpose of this book is to introduce key concepts and social categories of difference and to establish how these social categories integrate into our lived experiences. Another goal of this anthology is to investigate how these social categories are part of larger social structures and institutions that systemically define and affect social behavior. For example, how are social class and race-ethnicity embedded in the institution of education? How do gender, sexuality, and race-ethnicity affect families? Social categories contribute to relationships of power in society that can result in discrimination and other forms of social inequality and oppression. This book examines multiple cases that explain why these situations occur and how we can change them.

## AUDIENCE FOR RACE, GENDER, SEXUALITY, AND SOCIAL CLASS

This anthology can be used in undergraduate and graduate-level courses on social stratification; social inequality; race and ethnicity; gender and women's studies; and race, class, and gender. It also can be used as a reader in introductory sociology courses. An anthology lends itself to the flexibility of topics and order that a teacher might want to use as a framework for her or his class. While there are many fine collections on race, class, and gender, I incorporate more intersectionality, use more cutting-edge scholarship, and provide an analysis of social inequality at both the micro level of the individual and at the macro level of society. Although in their most recent revisions, other competing books have begun to add readings that address intersectionality, none of these readers is fully integrated. This anthology, on the other hand, takes an intersectional approach to topics as much as possible.

Moreover, many race, class, and gender texts focus only on minority groups or others who are oppressed rather than on those with privilege. Or, they discuss racial diversity by looking only at African Americans. Furthermore, while in general, race and gender tend to be addressed well in a number of anthologies, many of these fall short on discussions of social class. Other differences, such as disability and sexuality, could be better incorporated, as well. *Race, Gender, Sexuality, and Social Class* does not focus on specific racial-ethnic subgroups as an organizing principle but instead arranges its contents around key themes and topic areas, and it includes pieces that investigate whiteness. In addition, this anthology includes readings that examine the middle and upper classes, not just the lower socioeconomic groups. No reader can do it all, but in *Race, Gender, Sexuality, and Social Class:*

*Dimensions of Inequality and Identity,* many of the shortcomings found elsewhere are addressed.

## MAJOR FEATURES OF THE BOOK

The distinguishing characteristics of this book are many. First, this anthology has five major parts that frame the scholarship on social inequality and identity. Each of these parts contains an introductory essay to introduce students to the readings and the important concepts and themes. The first is Part I, "Introduction to Race, Gender, Sexuality, and Social Class: Concepts, History, and Theories of Difference." In addition to defining the critical terms, some readings in Part I provide a historical context for understanding contemporary issues of race, gender, sexuality, and social class. Part II investigates the micro level of identity and is titled "Identities Matter: The Social Construction and Experiences of Race, Gender, Sexuality, and Social Class." This part focuses on identity formation, identities and social interaction, and identity construction and stigma management. Part III, "Social Institutions and the Perpetuation of Inequality," examines six social institutions and how they affect identity and maintain or challenge social inequality. Readings explore current topics in the family, schools, the economy, health care, media, and government. Part IV, "Power and Privilege Unmasked," looks at how power is distributed in society, the theories that explain this distribution, and examples of discrimination. Part V, "Empowerment and Social Change," turns our attention to how individuals, communities, and larger social structures can effect social change.

The 60 readings in this anthology contain some of the most compelling, relevant, and cutting-edge scholarship available. And, as mentioned previously, the list of authors included reads like a *Who's Who* of scholars studying social inequality. The readings focus primarily on the United States, but several make connections to global social inequality. The readings are carefully edited to a length that makes them accessible, but they are not too short for readers to comprehend the issue at hand. Each reading is preceded by a brief headnote that introduces the author, the context of the reading, and the main points. Please note that each reading retains its endnotes, but all references have been moved to the end of the book.

## SPECIAL PEDAGOGICAL FEATURES

This anthology incorporates a number of special pedagogical features that will enable the instructor and the student to get more out of the material. These features include part introductions, headnotes, and discussion questions.

*Alternative Table of Contents:* To help scholars and teachers organize the diverse readings around particular topics or themes, an alternative table of contents has been provided.

*Part Introductions:* At the beginning of each of the five parts, I have included an overview essay that introduces the major concepts and themes of that part. This essay also briefly introduces the readings and explains their pertinence.

*Headnotes:* At the beginning of each reading, I have written a brief headnote that introduces the reading, the author(s), and their affiliations. The headnote also provides a context for the piece and gives information on the source of the reading.

*Discussion Questions:* Discussion questions appear at the end of each reading to help students review the main points and apply the reading.

## ANCILLARIES

Additional ancillary materials further support and enhance the learning goals of this book. These ancillary materials include the following:

### Instructor Teaching Site: www.sagepub.com/ferguson

The new, password-protected instructor teaching site provides one integrated source for all instructor materials, including the following key components for each chapter:

*Test Bank (Microsoft Word):* This Word test bank offers a diverse set of test questions and answers for each chapter of the book. Multiple-choice, true/false, short-answer, and essay questions for every chapter help instructors assess students' progress and understanding.

*PowerPoint Slides:* Chapter-specific slide presentations offer assistance with lecture and review preparation by highlighting essential content, features, and artwork from the book.

*Course Syllabi:* Sample syllabi—for semester, quarter, and online classes—provide suggested models for instructors to use when creating the syllabi for their courses.

*Chapter Exercises and Activities:* These lively and stimulating ideas for use in and out of class reinforce active learning. The activities apply to individual or group projects.

*Video Links:* Carefully selected, web-based video resources feature relevant interviews, lectures, personal stories, inquiries, and other content for use in independent or classroom-based explorations of key topics.

*Web Resources:* These links to relevant websites direct both instructors and students to additional resources for further research on important chapter topics.

**Student Study Site: www.sagepub.com/ferguson**

The open-access student study site provides a variety of additional resources to build on the students' understanding of the book content and extend their learning beyond the classroom. The website includes the following:

*eFlashcards:* These study tools reinforce students' understanding of key terms and concepts that have been outlined in the chapters.

*Web Quizzes:* Flexible self-quizzes allow students to independently assess their progress in learning course material.

*Video Links:* Carefully selected, web-based video resources feature relevant interviews, lectures, personal stories, inquiries, and other content for use in independent or classroom-based explorations of key topics.

*Web Resources:* These links to relevant websites direct both instructors and students to additional resources for further research on important chapter topics.

*Glossary:* A glossary is available to help students with the terminology found in the readings.

## ACKNOWLEDGMENTS

This book project has benefited greatly from the insights of many students and scholars, beginning with my two phenomenal undergraduate research assistants, Nicole Baker '10 and Allison Brinkhorst '11. Nicole and Allison, both advanced sociology majors, read all the early drafts of the readings, responded to them with a student's eye, and made suggestions for different selections. I also thank two student secretaries, Elizabeth Buehler and Amelia Rudberg, who found books and articles in the library or online, copied manuscripts, and typed up references. The students in my fall 2011 seminar, "Identities and Inequalities," also read several of the readings and provided me with feedback. I am especially appreciative of my sociology and Grinnell College colleagues, who read and commented on parts of the manuscript and who kept cheering me on as I began getting closer to my deadline. Thank you, Janet Carl, Peter Hart-Brinson, Chris Hunter, Maxwell Leung, and Kaelyn Wiles. Since the publication of the first edition, two more seminar classes have read the manuscript and provided me with feedback. I want to give a special shout-out to these Grinnell students who continually push my thinking and teaching around these issues of inequality and identity.

At SAGE Publications, I principally thank my former sociology editor, David Repetto, who initiated the discussion of this project with me and provided support at several key points along the way. My current sociology editor, Jeff Lasser, also has provided incredible support. Also at SAGE Publications are editorial assistant Alexandra Croell;

production editor Laura Barrett; copy editor Paula L. Fleming; and designer Rose Storey. I also thank Rashawn Ray, who worked on the pedagogical features of the book.

Sage was very thorough in sending the manuscript out for review at different developmental stages, and the feedback I received from the anonymous reviewers was immeasurable. For the first edition, my gratitude extends to the following reviewers: Travis Plowman, College of Saint Rose–Albany; Rashawn Ray, University of Maryland; Michael O'Connor, Hawkeye Community College; Megan Burke, Illinois Wesleyan University; Ben Chappell, University of Kansas; Ann Wagner, Nipissing University; Catherine Collier, Western Washington University; Mikaila Mariel Lemonik Arthur, Rhode Island College; and Richard Perry, Wake Technical Community College. And for the second edition, I appreciate the comments and suggestions from:

Becky J. Starnes,  Austin Peay State University

Carmen I. Aponte,  School of Social Work, Michigan State University

Pamela E Guess, UTC

Wendy M. Christensen, William Paterson University

Deden Rukmana, Savannah State University

Candy Pettus, Orange Coast College

Judy Berglund, Western Illinois University

Linda Scola, Bethune-Cookman University

Bernard F. Matt, Wilmington College—Cincinnati Branch

Ana Villalobos, Brandeis University

Michael D. Grimes, Louisiana State University

B. Dana Kivel, CSU Sacramento

Sam Erevbenagie Usadolo, University of Fort Hare

# ABOUT THE EDITOR

**Susan J. Ferguson** is professor of sociology at Grinnell College, where she has taught for over twenty-two years. Ferguson regularly teaches introduction to sociology courses, and her critically acclaimed anthology, *Mapping the Social Landscape: Readings in Sociology* (McGraw-Hill, 2013), is used in introductory classes around the country. Ferguson also teaches courses on the family and the sociology of health and illness, as well as a new seminar on social inequality and identity. Ferguson has published in all of these areas, including the research collection *Breast Cancer: Society Shapes an Epidemic* (with co-editor Anne Kasper, Palgrave, 2000) and *Shifting the Center: Understanding Contemporary Families* (McGraw-Hill, 2011). In addition, Ferguson is general editor for "Contemporary Family Perspectives," which is a series of research monographs and short texts on the family (SAGE Publications).

Ferguson, who grew up in a working-class family in Colorado, still considers the Rocky Mountains her spiritual home. A first-generation college student, Ferguson was able to attend college with the help of scholarships, work study, and financial loans. She majored in political science and Spanish and completed certificates of study in women's studies and Latin American studies. After working for a large research grant sponsored by the U.S. Agency for International Development, Ferguson entered graduate school and completed her master's degree in sociology at Colorado State University and her Ph.D. in sociology at the University of Massachusetts at Amherst. Her areas of study are gender, family, women's health, and pedagogy, but her primary enthusiasm is teaching.

# PART I

# INTRODUCTION TO RACE, GENDER, SEXUALITY, AND SOCIAL CLASS
## Concepts, History, and Theories of Difference

This introductory part of the anthology *Race, Gender, Sexuality, and Social Class: Dimensions of Inequality and Identity* introduces students to studies of social stratification, social inequality, and intersectionality. These sociological areas help us to better understand the social categories of race, social class, gender, and sexuality and why these categories were created in the first place. These social categories are key variables or axes of difference in U.S. society. *Social stratification* refers to a hierarchy of social strata or groups and the allocation of social resources to those distinct groups. Stratification systems distribute scarce and valuable resources to people of different social statuses in a given society. Thus, we can have racial stratification systems, gender stratification systems, and social class stratification systems, each overlapping and functioning within the same society. The inequality that results from this distribution of social rewards and valuable resources is referred to as *social inequality*. Some groups in society tend to receive more of what society values (for example, wealth, power, education, prestige) than other groups. As Dill and Zambrana state in Reading 12, social inequality is

"institutionalized patterns of unequal control over and distribution of a society's valued goods and resources, such as land, property, money, employment, education, healthcare, and housing" (p. 121). Scholars study social stratification and social inequality to better comprehend how social categories are constructed as difference and how resources are distributed in terms of race, gender, sexuality, and social class.

Intersectionality is a theoretical perspective that argues we should not study these social categories in isolation. Instead, we need to study how people experience multiple social categories at once. That is to say, instead of just looking at a working-class Latina's social class status or racial-ethnic identity, we can ask how her social categories affect her access to social rewards in the United States. Every individual in society is multiply situated in this way; we all have identities and social statuses based on our gender, sexuality, race-ethnicity, and social class. Using an intersectional lens enables scholars to see how these social categories play out at the individual level of identity and lived experience and also how these social categories are intermeshed at the structural or systemic levels of society. The interweaving of these social positions can create opportunities or barriers for the individual. They also can create institutional forms of discrimination. This introduction explores these concepts and contains 14 readings divided into three subsections: "Concepts," "History," and "Theories of Difference."

## CONCEPTS

The first three readings in this section, "Concepts"—by Weber; Desmond and Emirbayer; Crawley, Foley, and Shehan; and Wendell—define race, gender, sexuality, and social class. The scholars explore how and why these categories of difference are constructed and what purposes these concepts serve in the larger society. These scholars challenge essentialist and biological understandings of these social categories and argue instead that these categories are social constructions; they are created and defined in particular social, cultural, and political contexts. Lynn Weber's reading, "Defining Contested Concepts" (Reading 1), provides an excellent introduction to the study of race, gender, sexuality, and social class. Weber illustrates her conceptualization of these terms and the systems of inequality that surround them using examples and personal stories. The second reading, by Matthew Desmond and Mustafa Emirbayer, "What Is Racial Domination?" provides an introduction to the field of race studies. Desmond and Emirbayer first define the concept of race and explain how it relates to the concepts of ethnicity and nationality. They then examine racism and the conditions of racial domination. As is proposed in the Weber reading, Desmond and Emirbayer argue succinctly that the concept of race is tied to social inequality and power.

While Desmond and Emirbayer focus on race, racism, and racial domination, the third reading, by Sara Crawley, Lara Foley, and Constance Shehan, investigates gender, sex, and sexuality. In this reading, "Creating a World of Dichotomy: Categorizing Sex and Gendering Cultural Messages," Crawley, Foley, and Shehan break apart and analyze the relationships between the concepts of sex and gender.

They show how essentialist views of gender are problematic and how gender is instead real, learned, and sociohistorical. They also investigate how gender is embodied, or, better said, how bodies are expected to look and behave in a gendered way. One main emphasis of their writing is the gender binary, or how U.S. society has created the dichotomous gender categories of masculinity and femininity and reified them in gender norms, gender performances, and the social construction of sexuality. Race-ethnicity, sexuality, and social class all can affect these gendered meanings and performances.

The fourth reading in "Concepts," by Susan Wendell ("The Social Construction of Disability"), argues that disability is a social construction. Wendell contends that, even though we attempt to define disability through bodily function and appearance, the meaning of both mental and physical disabilities varies according to history, law, and social context. Not too long ago, we defined left-handedness, pregnancy, and even homosexuality as physical or mental disabilities. These constructions have been challenged and changed. Perhaps that is one of the most important reasons why we need to define and examine the social constructions of these terms. If these concepts are *social* categories and not ontological, we can change them. We have to understand these specific social constructions in order to challenge why they exist and whom they benefit in society. For instance, defining pregnancy as a disability benefits which groups of people? Defining certain races of people as problematic benefits which groups of people?

Disability, race, gender, sexuality, and social class shape individual identity, social interaction, and one's everyday life. But they are much more than just individual markers of identity. As Lynn Weber argues in "Defining Contested Concepts," race, gender, sexuality, and social class reflect patterns of social relationships: social relationships that involve power and can create social inequality. Weber argues that "race, class, gender, and sexuality are social systems, patterns of social relationships among people that are complex, pervasive, variable, persistent, severe, and power based . . . [They] are systems of oppression" (p. 6). Moreover, every social situation is affected by these patterns of relating in terms of race, gender, and social class. Thus, scholars like Weber, Desmond and Emirbayer, and Crawley and colleagues see race, gender, sexuality, and social class as complex social systems that inform all social life. They are upheld by dominant ideologies that are resistant to change (for example, the myth of meritocracy, color-blind racism, patriarchy), but these social systems are not immutable; they can and have changed over time and across different regional locations and cultural milieu. These social categories can provide one with opportunities or privileges in society, or they can create barriers and oppression. One's social location or place in society is determined by one's positions on the race, social class, and gender hierarchies. (Part II of this anthology, "Identities Matter," explores the impact these social categories have on the individual level.)

## HISTORY

The second section in this introduction to *Race, Gender, Sexuality, and Social Class* is titled "History" because the four readings found here study the historical origins of social class, gender, race, and sexuality. This historical context is important because, as the scholarship illustrates, each of these concepts develops at a particular point in Western history. While social class and gender arose earlier and are used to mutually reinforce each other, the concept of race developed later and also complements and strengthens social class hierarchies, while notions of sexuality have been advanced most recently. Reading 5 in the history section, titled "Rethinking the Paradigm: Class," is by Gerda Lerner. Lerner's comprehensive research exemplifies well how the historic origins of social class are embedded in notions of gender and sexuality. In particular, Lerner argues that "every major historical development in the formation of classes . . . depended on the regulation of women's reproduction and on limiting their direct access to economic power" (p. 55). Therefore, to fully understand social class and social class inequality, we have to examine how social class is experienced differently by men and women as well as by people of different races, nationalities, and ages.

Reading 6 in "History" is by Tukufu Zuberi, who, like Lerner, provides students with a historical lens to better understand the history of racial domination. In "Racial Domination and the Evolution of Racial Classification," Zuberi demonstrates that the history of race is tied to social class interests and to the subjugation of people's labor by the ruling elites. Zuberi's and Lerner's works complement each other; both show the expansion of racial and gender domination as key components of the development of Western economic ascendancy and expansion. The third reading in the historical section is by Michael Polgar, an associate professor of sociology at Penn State University. After teaching with this anthology, Polgar wrote this piece specifically for this collection. In it, Polgar argues that Jews are more than a religious group or an ethnic group. In order to promote understanding of this argument, he reviews the history of Jewish practice in the United States and how sociologists understand Jewish cultural assimilation. Polgar also examines anti-Judaic and anti-Semitic discrimination and how Jews have been active in countering prejudice against multiple racial-ethnic groups in the United States. "Ethno-Religious Dimensions of Jewish Cultures" (Reading 7) is more contemporary, and it looks at the history of Judaism in the United States during the 20th century. Polgar also analyzes ethnic identity, cultural assimilation, and anti-Semitism in the United States and how Jewish service organizations have worked to lessen prejudice. Similar to Polgar's contemporary analysis, Jonathan Ned Katz's reading, "The Invention of Heterosexuality" (Reading 8), provides a more recent history of when the terms *heterosexual* and *homosexual* started being used in the United States. These social constructions developed at a particular historical time in the late 19th and early 20th centuries to serve certain social class and economic interests.

## THEORIES OF DIFFERENCE

The third and last section in this introduction is titled "Theories of Difference," and it refers to the various social theories that attempt to explain social differences and inequalities, including the theories of Marxism, feminism, social constructionism, and intersectionality. The six readings in this section enable students to recognize some of these different theoretical perspectives and how each theory explains social categories and social inequality. The first two readings, by Erik Olin Wright (Reading 9) and Joan Acker (Reading 10), each look at Marxist explanations of social class and capitalism. Wright provides an introduction to Marxism in his reading, "Foundations of Class Analysis: A Marxist Perspective," while Acker expands on Wright's analysis of social class by incorporating the social categories of race and gender in her piece, "Is Capitalism Gendered and Racialized?"

The next two readings, by Evelyn Nakano Glenn (Reading 11) and Bonnie Thornton Dill and Ruth Enid Zambrana (Reading 12), introduce the theories of social constructionism and intersectionality. While some earlier scholars have addressed these theories in their readings, including Weber (Reading 1), Crawley and colleagues (Reading 3), and Wendell (Reading 4), Glenn illustrates how the social construction of race and the social construction of gender should be compared and integrated. Glenn argues that racial formation theories and the social construction of gender share similar processes of representation, micro-interaction, and social structure. Bonnie Thornton Dill and Ruth Enid Zambrana, in their reading "Critical Thinking About Inequality: An Emerging Lens," take this integration further by providing an introduction to intersectionality. According to Dill and Zambrana, an "intersectional analysis begins with the experiences of groups that occupy multiple social locations and finds approaches and ideas that focus on the complexity rather than the singularity of human experience" (p. 121). Intersectionality is characterized by four theoretical interventions: "(1) Placing the lived experiences and struggles of people of color and other marginalized groups as a starting point for the development of theory; (2) Exploring the complexities not only of individual identities but also the group identity . . . ; (3) Unveiling the ways inter-connected domains of power organize and structure inequality and oppression; and (4) Promoting social justice and social change . . ." (p. 123).

The final two readings in "Theories of Difference" add to earlier scholars' arguments that explain social inequality. Pem Davidson Buck in "Whiteness by Any Other Color Is Still Whiteness" (Reading 13) pushes our thinking on the social construction of race as discussed by Desmond and Emirbayer (Reading 2) and by Zuberi (Reading 6). Buck argues that whiteness supports racial domination because of its links to understandings of citizenship and to notions of the state. In particular, Buck contends that the United States, as a nation-state, is sustained by whiteness and other constructions of race. Similarly, Ellen Samuels, in "My Body, My Closet: Invisible Disability and the Limits of Coming-Out Discourse" (Reading 14), pushes our thinking on bodies and sexuality as discussed by Crawley and colleagues (Reading 3) by using feminism and queer theory. Specifically, Samuels uses the analogy of the coming-out discourse in queer studies and applies it to her understanding of disability. Samuels also examines how the visibility or invisibility of a social category affects the meaning and interpretation of difference.

## SUMMARY

Part I of the anthology contains 14 readings, grouped into three sections that introduce students to the concepts of race, gender, sexuality, social class, and disability. All are considered to be social categories or categories of difference because they affect social stratification systems and social inequality. The first section introduces concepts of race, sex and gender, and disability. These social categories affect people at the individual level of identity and social interaction, and they also are part of social hierarchies that distribute wealth and power in society. The readings in the second section establish the historical origins of many of these terms and explicate the larger political and economic structures that have benefited from the concepts of race, gender, social class, and sexuality. The third section of this introduction presents social theories that attempt to explain various types of social inequality, including Marxism, feminism, social constructionism, and intersectionality.

# 1

# DEFINING CONTESTED CONCEPTS

LYNN WEBER

*This first reading is by Lynn Weber, a professor of psychology and women's studies at the University of South Carolina. Weber, a well-known scholar of the American social class system and of gender studies and intersectionality, argues that race, social class, gender, and sexuality are all social systems that, while they change over time and across cultures, persist to preserve the privilege of some groups over that of others. This excerpt is taken from Weber's 2009 book,* Understanding Race, Class, Gender, and Sexuality: A Conceptual Framework; *it introduces readers to these concepts and how they are used by some societal groups to sustain their power and social control.*

To analyze race, class, gender, and sexuality, it is necessary to characterize what we mean by the terms. But because their meanings are in fact contested and often obscured, defining these social systems is not a simple task. This reading offers working definitions of key terms, discusses some of the processes that operate to obscure these systems, and describes social arenas in which they are manifested differently—in political, economic, and ideological institutions.

Race, class, gender, and sexuality are social systems, patterns of social relationships among people that are

*Source:* Weber, Lynn. 2010. "Defining Contested Concepts" in *Understanding Race, Class, Gender, and Sexuality: A Conceptual Framework.* Second Edition. New York: Oxford University Press. By permission of Oxford University Press, USA.

| | | |
|---|---|---|
| 1. | *Complex* | Intricate and interconnected |
| 2. | *Pervasive* | Widespread throughout all societal domains—for example, in |
| | | • families and communities, religion, education, the economy |
| | | • government, the law and criminal justice, the media |
| 3. | *Variable* | changing, always transforming |
| 4. | *Persistent* | prevailing over time and across places |
| 5. | *Severe* | serious in their consequences for social life |
| 6. | *Power Based* | hierarchical, stratified (ranked), centered in power— |
| | | • benefiting and providing options and resources for some by |
| | | • harming and restricting options and resources for others |

## Race, Class, Gender, and Sexuality as Complex Social Systems

Stated otherwise, race, class, gender, and sexuality are systems of oppression. *Oppression* exists when one group has historically gained power and control over valued assets of a society (e.g., wealth, information, and political power) by exploiting the labor and lives of other groups and then by using those assets to secure its position of power into the future. In exploitative relationships, the welfare of one group of people—the exploiters, the dominant group—*depends* on the poverty and efforts of another—the exploited, the subordinate group. Exploitation is thus a *power relationship* resulting from and reinforcing the unequal distribution of productive assets in society (Wright 2008). The unequal distribution of society's valued opportunities and resources is repeatedly reinforced in daily life, and its fundamental unfairness is masked in a pervasive belief system—an ideology, a set of stereotypes—that

interprets the inequalities as a "natural" outcome of each group's presumed superior or inferior traits.

When we first meet people, we often try to get an idea of who they are by asking questions that situate them in time and place, as well as in meaningful social categories. We ask "Where are you from?" often meaning geographic location, and "What do you do?" often meaning work or occupation. But we actually use these questions as indicators of more important social and cultural experiences and background that we associate with time, place, and work. When we meet people, we also situate them in other critical social locations—race, class, gender, and sexuality— that are powerfully embedded in all our institutions, that touch every aspect of life, and that suggest other commonalities of experience and background. *Social location* refers to an individual's or a group's social "place" in the race, class, gender, and sexuality hierarchies, as well as in other critical social hierarchies such as age, ethnicity, and nation.

Although the meaning and experience of race, class, gender, and sexuality change over time and place, they also have a persistence and resilience that leads people to believe that they will always be with us. Perhaps the central principle undergirding these hierarchies and the primary reason they persist over time is that they are intersecting systems of *power relationships*. One way of defining power is the capacity to achieve one's aims despite resistance. Groups remain dominant in a system over time because their position enables them to continue no matter what the will or aims of others might be: They have power. Lani Guinier and Gerald Torres (2002) describe the ways these systems operate, much like a zero-sum game. Games have winners and losers, and the powerful are those who have the advantage on three fronts, the three faces of power:

- The power to design or manipulate the rules
- The power to win the game through force or competition
- The power that winners have to name the game, to tell the story about the game, its significance, and why they won—in modern slang, to spin the story

Who makes the rules that give some groups privilege? Those with power in our political, economic, and ideological systems. Who wins the game? Those whom the rules have advantaged. Who gets to put the spin on the game—who names the game and interprets its outcome? The winners.

## Heterosexism: An Example

Heterosexism, like racism, classism, and sexism, is a system of power relations. Heterosexuals set the laws and acceptable practices governing adult intimate life ("the rules"), the advantages that go to those who follow the rules ("the winners"), and the rationale for the hierarchy that justifies the unequal treatment ("the spin"). In our culture, heterosexual marriage was long ago established as the standard and legally privileged status against which all other ways of conducting adult intimate life are measured ("the rules"). Advantages accrue to those who conform ("the winners"): the right to marry, to adopt children, to receive survivor benefits from Social Security, to file taxes as married couples, to receive health insurance from a spouse's employer, to inherit from one's partner, and to claim a legal family connection in medical emergencies. To be sure, significant changes have taken place in the legal status of gay people (e.g., twenty states, the District of Columbia, and many municipalities now prohibit employment discrimination on the basis of sexual orientation) and in public attitudes about alternative sexualities, especially among the young (Arthur Levitt Public Affairs Center 2006; Badgett et al. 2008). Still, most people who depart from the sexual standards set by those in power are denied full citizenship rights, making it difficult for them to create and to maintain families at all.

These restrictions, however, do not affect all gay, lesbian, bisexual, or transgender people in the same way. Some middle- and upper-class White men and women, for example, have more political, economic, and social resources to construct families in spite of legal obstacles and social disapproval. Class and race privilege give White upper-middle-class, educated gay men and women the options of suing if employers discriminate; of living without spousal insurance; of establishing estates with the help of estate attorneys who can find other tax shields for their monies; of traveling to other cities, states, or countries that may allow adoption or marriage and paying the costs incurred; of living well without a partner's Social Security.

The rationale for the unequal treatment of gay, lesbian, bisexual, and transgender people is provided in the interpretation that the powerful place on them by defining them variously as "other," "deviant," "sexual predators," "sinners," as less than fully human—not deserving of full citizenship status ("the spin"). And because they are defined as not "normal," gay, lesbian, bisexual, and transgender people have only recently begun to appear in popular culture texts—books, videos, films, television shows, advertisements—in ways that are less stereotypical, as was the case in such popular TV shows as *Will and Grace* or *Ugly Betty* (Gay and Lesbian Alliance Against Defamation [GLAAD] 2009). The advertising industry has even coined a term, *gay vague*, for ads constructed to appeal to gay consumers—a market estimated to have had $690 billion in buying power in 2007—without overtly challenging heterosexual dominance (HarrisInteractive 2009; Wilke and Applebaum 2001).

This third arena of power, "the spin," is carried out in the world of ideas through the media, the knowledge experts, and the image makers. These sources provide us with explanations and interpretations intended to help us make sense of our everyday lives, including hierarchies of power and privilege, and thereby either help to create and reinforce or to challenge and transform the systems of race, class, gender, and sexuality. They can encourage us to feel comfortable with harsh treatment of some people by presenting a pervasive belief system—an ideology, a set of stereotypes—that interprets the treatment as a "natural" outcome of a group's presumed inferior traits.

## WHY RACE, CLASS, GENDER, AND SEXUALITY?

When we examine these four systems of social inequality—race, class, gender, and sexuality—and recognize their interrelationships as the previous example of heterosexism's interaction with race, class, and gender suggests, you might ask which of the four is most important. And what of other forms of oppression? By focusing on these four dimensions, I do not intend to suggest that these are the only hierarchical dimensions of inequality that matter in social life. People face oppression along many other dimensions— disability, region, nation, ethnicity— and those patterns of relationships are also hierarchical and intersect with race, class, gender, and sexuality. In different times and places, and with regard to particular issues, they may carry more significance than the four dimensions examined here.

But race, class, gender, and sexuality are given priority for several reasons:

- ... In the United States, race, class, gender, and sexuality each have such a significant history as powerful organizers of social hierarchy that they are deeply embedded in our most important institutions: law and justice, education, religion, family, economy.

- Subordinate groups have struggled in large-scale social movements of resistance against these oppressions in legal, educational, religious, family, economic, and other institutions for many years. As a consequence, each of these inequalities is quite visible in the public consciousness now in the United States. In recent years, for example, the persistent and rapidly growing social movements of gays, lesbians, bisexuals, and transgender people for social power and self-determination have precipitated significant social change and enhanced attention from the political, religious, and other realms . . . .

- Given the visibility and the fundamental importance of these dimensions at this time in the United States, this analysis of race, class, gender, and sexuality and its extended application to education in the United States should give you the tools—the conceptual framework and the questions to ask—to analyze other dimensions of inequality, as well.

The primary purpose of my research is to deepen our understanding of the intersections of race, class, gender, and sexuality and to demonstrate how to analyze those intersections in specific times and places. But the framework should encourage you to look beyond the most clearly visible dimensions of inequality in any arena, to look for more subtle expressions of power dynamics, and to seek out the structures and mechanisms that undergird oppression in all areas of society.

## PROCESSES THAT OBSCURE RACE, CLASS, GENDER, AND SEXUALITY

Race, class, gender, and sexuality shape everyone's life every day. Yet these systems are often hard to see, to understand, even to define. In U.S. society, these constructs are typically defined by referring to social groups selected for unequal treatment and ranked according to

- **Race:** Ancestry and selected physical characteristics, such as skin color, hair texture, and eye shape[1]

- **Class:** Position in the economy; in the distribution of wealth, income, and poverty; in the distribution of power and authority in the workforce

- **Sex/Gender:** Biological and anatomical characteristics attributed to males and females (sex); culturally and socially structured relationships between women and men (gender)

- **Sexual Orientation:** Sex of partners in emotional-sexual relationships

Yet these definitions tend to reify the categories, to make them seem universal, seem tied to a presumably stable biology, rigid and unchanging—characteristics quite the opposite of the way the framework in this reading presents them. One of the challenges of my research is to present a more complex picture of these systems and their intersections so that we can see their persistence and significance in shaping social life and their shifting nature over time and space.

In fact, the reasons that these intersecting systems of oppression are so difficult to understand and to define are contained in the very nature of the systems themselves:

> Every social situation is affected by societywide historical patterns of race, class, gender, and sexuality that are not necessarily apparent to the participants and that are experienced differently depending on the race, class, gender, and sexuality of the people involved.

Typically, the beneficiaries of long-standing patently unfair practices that routinely reinforce social injustice, such as giving special preference in college and law school admissions to the sons and daughters of wealthy alumni, do not come away viewing the practices as unfair, do not associate them with affirmative action, and may in fact view them as fair and even desirable practices (Crosby and Stockdale 2007; Karabel 2005; Sturm and Guinier 1996). To those who occupy positions of privilege, that is, who benefit from the existing social arrangements, the fact that their privilege is dependent on the unfair exclusion of or direct harm to others is obscured, unimportant, practically invisible.

Although I remember, for example, when my all-White girls' high school desegregated in the 1960s, the event meant very little to me at the time. I had never even seen the segregated African American schools whose inferior conditions had made school desegregation such an important goal in the African American community. But for my new African American schoolmates, the unfairness of racial segregation was painfully apparent, and being the first African Americans to attend my school was most certainly a critical life event for them.

Systemic patterns of inequality can also be obscure to those disadvantaged by them because they lack access to information and resources that dominant groups control. So, at the same time that I experienced my high school's integration as a non-event because of my racial privilege, I became aware of the significant restrictions on my life imposed by my gender.

I rode to school on a bus with other students from my end of town who had gone to elementary school with me. The bus stopped at the three small Catholic girls' high schools and the single large Catholic boys' high school. Every day on the bus, my good friend Mickey O'Hara and I, who had competed with each other academically in elementary school, compared notes about what we were learning in high school. As the days, weeks, and years went on, it became clear that Mickey was being taught much more than I. The boys in college prep courses went further in math, read more in English, had more science. They scored better on standardized tests. They had better facilities, books, and teachers. Why? In large part because each parish was required to contribute money to the boys' high school for each boy in the parish who attended the school. And for the girls? Nothing. So the girls' schools ran on tuition alone; the boys' ran on subsidies from the parishes—a fact I didn't learn until years later. My brother's education cost my parents far less and provided him much more, a discrepancy that few saw as troublesome because the school system was organized to prepare boys to provide materially for their families and to prepare girls to have children and to raise them in two-parent, heterosexual nuclear families.

These assumptions about the fundamental aims of our education—to learn to enact gender-specific roles in heterosexual marriages and in the labor market—were profound. They shaped every aspect of our lives—from proms to course content, from sports to labs. The girls' schools provided the homecoming queens and the cheerleaders; the boys' school, the athletes. The girls' schools provided the home economics and typing labs; the boys' school, the physics course.

So in my position as a girl in a gender-stratified school system, I had been aware of many of the differences in education between the boys' and the girls' schools but was unaware of the funding practices that supported them and would have been unable to do much about the practices even if I had known. Likewise, law school applicants who lack class and family privilege may never know or may be unable to change the fact that their chances for admission were reduced by the preferences given to the children of alumni. People often come away from a discriminatory practice not knowing whether or how the discrimination took place—even when they are the victims of the injustice. Even though those who suffer the unfairness are more likely to see it, we all participate in discriminatory systems *with and without* knowing that or how we have done so.

### The dominant ideologies of a "color-blind," "gender-blind," and "sexually restrained" society obscure oppression and its history.

The dominant ideology (belief system), particularly about race and gender but also about social class and sexuality, that pervades the media and dominates public policy is that the United States is or should be a "gender-blind," "race-blind," "classless," and "sexually restrained" society. These ideologies are presented as "neutral" perspectives suggesting that a "gender-blind" or "postgender" or "race-blind" or "postracial" society is the preferred outcome of any social policy that seeks to address pervasive inequalities—the goal to strive for—as well as the way that policies designed to achieve equity should operate. Although on their surface these ideologies sound much like the arguments made by antiracists in the civil rights movement of the 1960s, they are currently aimed at obscuring the privilege that accompanies Whiteness and maleness rather than at seeking to transform them from an identity of social superiority to one of social responsibility (Bonilla-Silva 2003; McDermott and Samson 2005).

We do not hear the term *class-blind* used in public discourse because the dominant ideology of class differs from race and gender ideology. The classless ideology does not assert that even though classes are biologically determined, we should strive not to attend to them—as it does with race and gender. Although it recognizes great differences in income, wealth, and other valuable resources, it asserts that classes—either as biological groups or as social groups in a relation of oppression and conflict with one another—simply do not exist. Instead, economic positions in the United States are presumed to be earned in a free and open "meritocratic" society in which hard work and talent pay off—the land of the

American Dream. And it is those differences in hard work and talent—not oppression—that are offered as the core causes of the obvious, extreme economic differences present in the population.

The dominant ideology of sexuality is one of restraint, with the alleged sexual practices of the heterosexual majority taken as the moral norm against which the sexual orientation and practices of people who are gay, lesbian, bisexual, and transgender[2] are seen as deviant and dangerous. The dominant ideology of sexuality is not that we should be blind to differences, that they should not matter or do not exist, but rather that they should be denied, contained, or ignored—neither discussed in public nor condoned. The military's former policy toward homosexuals of "don't ask, don't tell," implemented in 1994, captures the dominant ideology of sexual restraint well: "We won't ask and you shouldn't tell, because if you tell you will be punished."

Think about these ideologies. Why would we use *denial* and *blindness* as bases for social policy and the assessment of moral rightness? To do so implies that we seek not to see and therefore, not to know. It suggests that ignorance is a preferred foundation for social policy—an anti-intellectual stance that has no valid place in the modern academy, where we seek knowledge, truth, and wisdom.

Yet these stances on race, class, gender, and sexuality prevail for at least two basic reasons:

- **Because members of privileged groups are not disadvantaged and, in fact, benefit from these systems, people in these groups find dismissing the claims of oppressed groups as unreal relatively easy.**

- **In our education and in mass media, we do not systematically learn about the totality of the experiences of subordinate groups.**

The experiences of oppressed groups are either excluded or distorted in our society by being presented in limited and stereotyped ways: gays, lesbians, bisexuals, and transgender people solely as people who engage in particular sexual acts or wear sex-inappropriate clothes; African Americans as slaves or protesters in the civil rights movement in the 1960s, as sports heroes and music stars, and as welfare moms and criminals; Latino/as as illegal aliens swelling the schools and welfare rolls; Native Americans as unassimilable, alcoholic reservation dwellers benefiting from gambling-driven windfalls; hard-working Asian Americans as clannishly living in Chinatowns and overcoming all obstacles to rise to educational and employment heights, especially in math and science. In short, we typically learn of these groups only as they can be seen to present "problems" or threats to the dominant group or as exceptions to the "normal" way of life.

We rarely learn of the common ground in our experiences or of the ways that the lives and struggles of oppressed groups can and have benefited the entire society. The Civil Rights Act of 1964, for example, although fought for and won primarily by African Americans, expanded protections against discrimination to women, religious minorities, and all racial groups. In a similar vein, Lani Guinier and Gerald Torres (2002) compare the experiences of women and people of color to the miner's canary. Miners used to take a canary into the mines with them to signal whether or not the air was safe to breathe. If the canary thrived, the atmosphere was safe. If the canary became sick or died, the atmosphere was toxic.

Members of oppressed groups—people of color, poor and working classes, women, gays, lesbians, bisexuals, and transgender people—are like the canary: They signal when the atmosphere is not healthy. When oppressed groups experience high death rates from lack of access to medical care; high infant mortality rates; increasing high school dropout rates; declining college, graduate, and professional school attendance rates; high unemployment and poverty rates; and declining standardized test scores, something is wrong with the atmosphere— not with the canary. Trying to "fix" the canary or blaming the toxic atmosphere on the canary makes the atmosphere no less toxic to everyone in it. Learning about the atmosphere through the experience of the canary, we can develop a broader and healthier assessment of societal processes that affect us all—international relations, family life, and the workings of the economy, of education, of religion.

**These systems are never perfectly patterned; some people have experiences that defy the overall patterns.**

In my high school, some students in the college preparatory track never went to college; some home economics students did. But rags-to-riches stories, popular in America, are always more complex than we are often led to believe. For example, in "A Darker Shade of Crimson: Odyssey of a Harvard Chicano," Ruben Navarrette, Jr., a twenty-four-year-old Mexican American man, tells of how he went from valedictorian of his class in a school system with a 50 percent dropout rate for Hispanics to Harvard University and then to the University of California Los Angeles graduate school in education. He describes the guilt, pain, and isolation he felt in graduate school:

> White student colleagues smile at me as they tell me, implicitly, that people like my parents, like my old friends, like the new girlfriend back home whose immeasurable love is sustaining me, are incompetent and unintelligent and unmotivated and hopeless. They wink and nod at me, perhaps taking comfort that I am different from the cultural caricature that they envision when they hear the word "Chicano." (Navarrette 1997:278)

So even though a pervasive pattern of oppression exists, individual exceptions also exist. And these exceptions tend to reinforce the views of dominant groups that the system is not oppressive but is indeed open and fair, because those who have benefited from the current arrangements have difficulty seeing the ways in which the exclusion of others has made their inclusion in the successful mainstream possible.

**These systems are not immutable; they change over time and vary across different regional locations and different cultural milieus.**

Race, class, gender, and sexuality are not fixed systems or traits of individuals. Because they are negotiated and contested every day in social relationships, they change over time and in different places. Many of the working-class White girls who were my high school classmates, for example, did not attend college immediately after high school but attended college later, in the 1970s and 1980s, after marrying and having children. Changing economic conditions no longer allowed their husbands to be the sole support of the family; changing family conditions meant that many of their marriages ended in divorce; and changing education and labor market conditions meant that there were significantly increased opportunities for women. Thus what race, class, gender, and sexuality meant for the lives of White, heterosexual, working-class women had changed considerably from the 1960s to the 1980s.

**Because of the pervasive, persistent, and severe nature of oppressive systems, people resist subordination and in their resistance can develop positive skills, talents, and abilities. These skills fortify them to survive and to challenge more effectively the very system designed to limit their opportunities to use their skills, talents, and abilities.**

The fact that no parish resources were sent to the all-girls schools in my community meant, for example, that the parishes could funnel all their resources into the education of their boys—to fortify their ability to succeed and to bolster the economic base of the patriarchal nuclear family. Yet because we were segregated, I was able to play leadership roles and participate in activities that girls in coeducational schools mostly could not play. In much the same way, segregated African American schools, Native American reservation schools, and barrio schools—typically inferior in resources, per-pupil expenditures, physical facilities, and teacher preparation—have become fertile ground for the development of future leaders and activists who effectively challenge the systems themselves.

Because members of oppressed groups can withstand oppression and may even succeed while facing it, dominant group members often take that success to mean that the oppression either does not exist or is not severe. But it is not the oppression itself that creates the success that some people experience: It is the human will to resist oppression and overcome obstacles that makes this success possible. Resistance

in individual and collective forms pressures the dominant system to change and transform over time. If anything, because so many people are willing to resist, President Obama was able to connect powerfully to a wide cross-section of America. He asked people to believe that their resistance could bring about fundamental change, and his many new strategies of reaching people (employing the Internet, text messaging, organizer training, etc.) engaged a decisive segment of the United States in resistance to the status quo.

## DOMAINS, INSTITUTIONS, AND LEVELS OF OPPRESSION

### Domains and Associated Institutions

Relationships of dominance and subordination along race, class, gender, and sexuality lines are produced, reinforced, challenged, and changed in many arenas or social domains. Although historically employed to characterize the domains of class oppression (cf. Vanneman and Weber Cannon 1987), three broad domains—the ideological, the political, and the economic—also represent useful ways of seeing the societal context for other forms of oppression. Each domain has associated with it certain *social institutions*—patterns of social relationships that are intended to accomplish the goals of the particular domain. And relations of dominance and subordination are structured within the institutions associated with each of the three major domains of society:

• *Ideological Domain*. The media, arts, religion, and education represent institutions whose primary purpose is *ideological*—producing and distributing ideas and knowledge about society and its people, why society is organized the way it is, what people need to know in order to function in society. Control over ideological institutions enables dominant groups to shape public images and cultural beliefs about both dominant and subordinate groups. Some refer to negative group images, for example, of "welfare queens," as *controlling images* to highlight their intended purpose of restricting the lives and options of subordinate groups, in this case poor African American women (Collins 2000; Hancock 2004).

- *Political Domain.* The government, law, civil and criminal justice, the police, and the military represent institutions whose primary purpose is *political*—creating and enforcing the laws and government structures that define citizens' and non-citizens' rights, responsibilities, and privileges. Through control over these institutions, dominant groups exert direct control over the behavior of others.

- *Economic Domain.* The major industries (e.g., finance, health care, manufacturing, housing, transportation, and communication) and work represent institutions whose primary emphasis is *economic*—producing and distributing society's valued goods and services. Control over material goods and resources such as wealth, jobs, wages and benefits, health care, day care, and education makes dominant groups more c_____ in community life.

*domains - makes sense*

Each of these domains and the institutions associated with them are organized to reinforce and reproduce the prevailing social hierarchies of race, class, gender, and sexuality—by producing and disseminating ideas that justify these inequalities, by concentrating government power and social control mechanisms among dominant groups, and by unequally distributing society's valued material and social resources to Whites, the middle and upper classes, men, heterosexuals, and U.S. citizens.

Although most institutions have a primary purpose, none of the major social institutions relates solely to a single domain of oppression—ideological, political, or economic. Just as race, class, gender, and sexuality are interconnected dimensions of oppression, so are social institutions intertwined with one another. If we think again about the realm of sports, for example, sports are:

- *Ideological:* Ideas about "winners and losers," fair play, and a "level playing field" often serve as a basis for defining how groups should be treated, punished, and rewarded.

- *Political:* Many connections between the powerful in society—especially among men—are first forged in sports teams in kindergarten through twelfth grade (K–12) and in college (Messner 1992). Sports also become overtly political arenas, as when, for example, the International Olympic Committee tied its decision to allow Beijing to host the Olympics in 2008 to demands for greater human rights in China (Human Rights Watch 2008).

- *Economic:* Over the past forty years, as manufacturing has declined, many municipalities around the country have turned to tourism and recreation, including professional sports teams, to improve the economies of urban areas. Large colleges and universities commit millions of dollars to sports promotion to increase revenues, to satisfy alumni, and to increase donations. And some of the richest people in America are sports professionals (e.g., Tiger Woods, Phil Mickelson, LeBron James) and team owners.

Education, too, although primarily an ideological institution, is deeply implicated in the economic and political domains because it certifies people for different social locations within them.

Society's expenditures on schooling are justified on economic grounds as preparing and sorting people for different positions in the capitalist economic system as owners, managers, professionals, laborers, and—for those who drop out or otherwise fail—as society's underclass. As the costs of higher education have risen dramatically in recent years, students are increasingly viewed as consumers who must be "sold" on the "product" that any given institution offers and who must be "satisfied" in order to keep their "business." Some have even sued schools for failure to educate them. Advocates for rural and inner-city K–12 schools are challenging school funding formulas that most often rely on local property taxes and heavily advantage affluent suburban areas. For example, when its supreme court ruled that the state's constitution merely obligated it to provide students a "minimally adequate" education, a South Carolina citizens' coalition proposed a constitutional amendment to require the state to level out the gross inequities in funding across its districts in order to provide all students with a high-quality education (see www.Good byeMinimallyAdequate.com).

And because of the ideological and economic importance of education, the state is deeply involved in legislating the structure of education. Social movements seeking to challenge the fundamental basis of the social order often begin with and emanate from schools. Take, for example, the historical equity movements surrounding school desegregation, students with disabilities, gender equity (Title IX), and affirmative action.

## Cross-Cutting Institutions

Some institutions have no single focus and uniformly cross cut all dimensions—for example, the *family*. The family is a social institution whose purpose is to meet people's basic psychological, emotional, and physical needs. And even though emotional support, love, and nurturance take place in families, families also serve as sites where inequality is reproduced in the ideological, political, and economic realms:

• *Ideological*: Families are places where the ideas that bolster and justify the dominant power structure are reinforced daily in an intimate setting. Conservative politicians and political interest groups, for example, have used the term *family values* to refer to the political values that serve the interests of nuclear, heterosexual, White, middle- and upper-class Christian families: values that serve to reinforce the dominant power structure.

• *Political*: Families are places where the public authority and power of middle- and upper-class White male heterosexuals is reinforced daily in a variety of ways. When a man rapes or otherwise sexually assaults the child of a neighbor, for example, the violation is typically seen as a crime and is often pursued in the criminal justice system. When, however, the same man, particularly if he is middle or upper class, rapes or otherwise sexually assaults his own daughter, the rape is more often not challenged at all, is treated as an issue for social services, or is dealt with in therapy. The public power of men

(including their greater economic power) gives them power in the family, making it especially difficult for women and children to successfully challenge the abuse of that power either in the family or in the criminal justice system.

• *Economic*: Families are places where goods and services are distributed to reinforce the economic power of dominant groups. The family wage, a wage large enough to enable a man to provide for his entire family, was extended at the beginning of industrialization to White men to lure them away from family farms and into factory work but was never extended to men of color. It also served as a mechanism for exerting control over women both by denying them access to wage work and by justifying lower wages to women (Hartmann 1997). Current tax laws determining what part of income earned by individual workers will be retained by the state is set by their family status—married, heterosexual couples pay one rate, unmarried individuals pay another rate, and deductions and tax credits accrue to parents with dependent children. . . .

## SOCIAL RELATIONS OF CONTROL

Maintaining their position of control over subordinate groups is a primary task for dominant groups. To do so, they must structure:

• **Ideology so that exploitation is explained, justified, and rationalized and comes to be seen as a natural, normal, and acceptable part of social life**

• **The polity so that the state supports and enforces the exploitative relations**

• **The economy so that the exploitative relations continue, so that the poverty and labor of the exploited enhances the welfare of the exploiters**

### Internalized Oppression

The very fact that society continues without major disruption every day serves as a testimony not only to the power of dominant groups to effectively control the ideological, political, and material resources that subordinate groups need to shift the balance of power but also to the persuasive power of dominant ideologies to convince subordinate group members that the current social hierarchies are acceptable and cannot be changed (cf. Mullings 1994). Two processes of *internalized oppression* are at work:

- *Self-Negation*: Subordinate group members sometimes restrict their own lives because they believe the negative views and limits imposed on their group by the dominant ideology. When subordinate group members internalize oppression, they do not challenge the social order and may even exhibit self-destructive patterns such as drug abuse, family violence, or depression. In more subtle ways, for example, a woman who fails to put herself up for consideration for a promotion at work because she believes that she is less capable or less suited for management than her male counterparts has internalized the socially constructed, controlling images of women.

- *Negation of Others*: Subordinate group members sometimes restrict the lives of other members of oppressed groups or of their own group because they believe the negative views of and limits imposed on another subordinate group or their own group. When working-class Latinos, for example, accept negative images of Latinas as sexually promiscuous and treat them as sexual objects, the Latinos reinforce the larger structural patterns of race, class, gender, and sexuality dominance. When women managers fail to promote other women because they believe that women are less capable than men, they also reinforce structures of race, class, gender, and sexuality dominance, the same structures that have restricted their own lives.

## Resistance

But people also resist oppression. Even though each of these social institutions is organized to reproduce the current social hierarchy and is thus a structure of oppression; strong forces of resistance occur within each. The resistance occurs at both the *macro social level of community and society* and at the *micro level of the individual and the family*. Ever since the beginning of our public education system, for example, various groups have established alternative schools—religious schools, other private schools, single-sex schools, African American schools, bilingual schools, and home schools, to name a few—to resist the dominant culture's organization of education and to produce students who have different ideas about the social order. And because education is a primary institution charged with the socialization of the young, it holds a key to the future stability of the social order. Education is thus a critical site for resistance to all forms of oppression: racism, sexism, classism, and heterosexism, as well as oppression resulting from religious, ethnic, national, political, age, and disability status.

A major focus of the civil rights, women's rights, gay and lesbian rights, and poor people's movements has been educational system reform—for example, through school desegregation; through battles over the gender, race, and sexuality content of school texts and curricula; through struggles for access for students with disabilities; through bilingual education; and through poor (mostly rural and inner city) school districts' challenges to school funding formulas based on property values.

Resistance also occurs at the micro level of the individual and the family, when individuals develop an alternative consciousness insist on self-definition and self-valuation, and refuse to incorporate negative images of their groups. An alternative consciousness is often nurtured in a community of resistance, such as a racial ethnic community, a community of workers, a gay and lesbian community, a religious community, or a women's community. And increasingly today, those communities of resistance are created and sustained through the use of advanced technologies such as the Internet and cell phones, which facilitate communication across vast reaches of time and space.

When groups publicly resist oppression, individuals within them can participate in the development of a positive definition of self in the face of dominant culture oppression. When, for example, gay, lesbian, bisexual, and transgender people acknowledge their sexual orientation at work, they often face ostracism, hostility, lost opportunities for promotions, and even loss of their jobs. At the same time, however, by living their lives openly—something heterosexuals take for granted—they also contradict the denial and silence that enables dominant culture distortions about their lives to persist and to operate against them. In valuing themselves in this way, gays, lesbians, bisexuals, and transgender people contribute to an environment in which others are better able to do the same. This process is one of *empowerment,* "a process aimed to consolidating, maintaining, or changing the nature and distribution of power in a particular social context" (Morgen and Bookman 1988:4). Processes of oppression and resistance and empowerment exist in dynamic relation to one another: Each is in a continuous process of changing to adapt to the shifts in the other.

## DISCUSSION QUESTIONS

1. Discuss how domination and subordination along race, social class, gender, and sexuality lines become structured by institutions within the three domains: the ideological, the economic, and the political.
2. Using examples from Weber's life or your own, explain how the "intersecting systems" of race,

social class, gender, and sexuality support the domination of one group over another group by obscuring or denying this power relationship and its resulting inequities.

## NOTES

1. *Ethnicity,* a concept closely related to race, is conceived as shared culture based on nationality/ national origin, language, religion, and, by some definitions, also race. I address ethnicity in the context of race because the Black-White divide in the United States has most powerfully shaped the terrain on which ethnic groups—people of color (Asians, Latinos, Arabs, Natives) and Whites (Irish, Italians, Jews, Poles)—have historically been viewed and treated (cf., Brodkin 2004; Ignatiev 1995; Perlman 2005).
2. *Transgender* is a term increasingly used by people whose gender expression (e.g., masculine, feminine) is deemed inappropriate for their biological sex (e.g., male, female). As Leslie Feinberg (1996:xi) states, "Because it is our entire spirit—the essence of who we are—that doesn't conform to narrow gender stereotypes many people who in the past have been referred to as cross-dressers, transvestites, drag queens, and drag kings today define themselves as trans*gender.*"

# 2

# WHAT IS RACIAL DOMINATION?

MATTHEW DESMOND

MUSTAFA EMIRBAYER

*This second reading is an excerpt from Matthew Desmond and Mustafa Emirbayer's 2009 article, "What Is Racial Domination?" Desmond is assistant professor of sociology and social studies at Harvard University, and Emirbayer is professor of sociology at the University of Wisconsin–Madison. Together they have coauthored a number of books on racial issues in America. In this reading, Desmond and Emirbayer explain why race and racism are still a part of contemporary social life. They define both concepts and illustrate different explanations for and misunderstandings about race and racism.*

## WHAT IS RACE?

You do not come into this world African or European or Asian; rather, this world comes into you. As literally hundreds of scientists have argued, you are not born with a race in the same way you are born with fingers, eyes, and hair. Fingers, eyes, and hair are natural creations, whereas race is a social fabrication (Duster 2003; Graves 2001). We define race as *a symbolic category, based on phenotype or ancestry and constructed according to specific social and historical* contexts, that is misrecognized as a natural category. This definition deserves to be unpacked.

### Symbolic Category

A symbolic category belongs to the realm of ideas, meaning-making, and language. It is something actively created and recreated by human beings rather than pregiven, needing only to be labeled. Symbolic categories mark differences between grouped people or things. In doing so, they actually

*Source:* Desmond, Matthew and Mustafa Emirbayer. "What is Racial Domination?" *Du Bois Review: Social Science Research on Race*, Volume 6, Issue 02 (2009), pp. 335–355. Copyright © 2009 W.E.B. Du Bois Institute for African and African American Research. Reprinted with permission of Cambridge University Press.

bring those people or things into existence (Bourdieu 2003). For example, the term "Native American" is a symbolic category that encompasses all peoples indigenous to the land that is known, today, as the United States. But the term "Native American" did not exist before non–Native Americans came to the Americas. Choctaws, Crows, Iroquois, Hopis, Dakotas, Yakimas, Utes, and dozens of other people belonging to indigenous tribes existed. The term "Native American" flattens under one homogenizing heading the immensely different histories, languages, traditional beliefs, and rich cultural practices of these various tribes. In naming different races, racial categories create different races.

Such insights into the importance of the symbolic have not always been appreciated. Consider, for example, Oliver Cromwell Cox's hypothesis "that racial exploitation and race prejudice developed among Europeans with the rise of capitalism and nationalism, and that because of the worldwide ramifications of capitalism, all racial antagonisms can be traced to the policies and attitudes of the leading capitalist people, the [W]hite people of Europe and North America" (1948:322). Though few scholars today would agree fully with Cox's reduction, many continue to advance structuralist claims, filtering racial conflict through the logic of class conflict (e.g., Reich 1981), regarding racial formation as a political strategy (e.g., Marx 1998), or concentrating on the legal construction of racial categories (e.g., Haney-López 1996). Helpful as they are, structuralist accounts often treat race as something given and accepted—that is, as a "real" label that attaches itself to people (Bonilla-Silva 1997) or as an imposed category that forms racial identity (Marx 1998)—and thereby overlook how actors create, reproduce, and resist systems of racial classification . . . .

### Phenotype or Ancestry

Race also is based on phenotype or ancestry. A person's phenotype is her or his physical appearance and constitution, including skeletal structure, height, hair texture, eye color, and skin tone. A person's ancestry is her or his family lineage, which often includes tribal, regional, or national affiliations. The symbolic category of race organizes people into bounded groupings based on their phenotype, ancestry, or both. It is difficult to say which matters more, phenotype or ancestry, in determining racial membership in the United States. In some settings, ancestry trumps phenotype; in others, the opposite is true.

Recent immigrants often are pigeonholed in one of the dominant racial categories because of their phenotype; however, many resist this classification because of their ancestry. For instance, upon arriving in the United States, many first generation West Indian immigrants, quite familiar with racism against African Americans, actively resist the label "Black." Despite their efforts, many are considered African American because of their dark skin (that is, they "look" Black to the American eye). The children of West African immigrants, many of whom are disconnected from their parents' ancestries, more readily accept the label "Black" (Waters 1999). And many individuals with mixed heritage often are treated as though they belonged only to one "race."

Some people, by contrast, rely on their phenotype to form a racial identity, though they are often grouped in another racial category based on their ancestry. Susie Guillory Phipps, a blond-haired blue-eyed woman who always considered herself "White," discovered, upon glancing at her birth certificate while applying for a passport, that her native state, Louisiana, considered her "Black." The reason was that Louisiana grouped people into racial categories according to the "one thirty-second rule," a rule that stated that anyone who was one thirty-second Black—regardless of what they looked like—was legally "Black." In 1982, Susie Guillory Phipps sued Louisiana for the right to be White. She lost. The state genealogist discovered that Phipps was the great-great-great-great-grandchild of a White Alabama plantation owner and his Black mistress and, therefore—although all of Phipps's other ancestors were White—she was to be considered "Black." (This outlandish law was finally erased from the books in 1983.) In this case, Phipps's ancestry (as identified by the state) was more important in determining her race than her phenotype (Davis 1991).

## Social and Historical Contexts

Racial taxonomies are bound to their specific social and historical contexts. The racial categories that exist in America may not exist in other parts of the globe. In South Africa, racial groups are organized around three dominant categories: White, Black, and "Coloured." During apartheid, the Coloured category was designed to include all "mixed-race" people (Sparks 2006). More recently, the Black category has been expanded to include all groups oppressed under apartheid, not only those of African heritage but also those of Indian descent and (as of 2008) Chinese South Africans. In Brazil, five racial categories are employed in the official census: *Branco* (White), *Pardo* (Brown), *Preto* (Black), *Amarelo* (Asian), and *Indígena* (Indigenous). However, in everyday usage, many Brazilians identify themselves and one another through several other racial terms—including *moreno* (other type of brown), *moreno claro* (light brown), *negro* (another type of black), and *claro* (light)—which have much more to do with the tint of one's skin than with one's ancestry (Stephens 1999; Telles 2004). Before racial language was outlawed by the Communist regime, Chinese racial taxonomies were based first and foremost on blood purity, then on hair, then odor, then brain mass, then finally—and of least importance— skin color, which, according to the taxonomy, was divided into no less than ten shades (Dikőtter 1992). And in Japan, a group called the Burakamin is considered to be unclean and is thought to constitute a separate race, although it is impossible to distinguish someone with Burakamin ancestry from the rest of the Japanese population (Eisenstadt 1998; Searle-Chatterjee and Sharma 1994).

Cross-national comparisons, then, reveal that systems of racial classification vary greatly from one country to the next. Racial categories, therefore, are *place-specific*, bound to certain geographic and social contexts. They also are *time-specific*, changing between different historical eras. As a historical product, race is quite new. Before the sixteenth century, race, as we know it today, did not exist. During the Middle Ages, prejudices were formed and wars waged against "other" people, but those "other" people were not categorized or understood as people of other races. Instead of the color line, the primary social division in those times was that between "civilized" and "uncivilized." The racial categories so familiar to us only began to calcify around the beginning of the nineteenth century, a mere two hundred years ago (Gossett 1965; Smedley 1999). In fact, the word, "race," has a very recent origin; it only obtained its modern meaning in the late eighteenth century (Hannaford 1996).

But racial domination survives by covering its tracks, by erasing its own history. It encourages us to think of the mystic boundaries separating, say, West from East, White from Black, Black from Asian, or Asian from Hispanic, as timeless separations, as divisions that have always been and will always be. We would be well served to remember, with Stuart Hall, that we must grapple with "the historical specificity of race in the modern world" (1980:308) to gain an accurate understanding of racial phenomena. In the American context, the "Indian" was invented within the context of European colonization, as indigenous peoples of the Americas were lumped together under one rubric to be killed, uprooted, and exploited. Whiteness and Blackness were invented as antipodes within the context of English, and later American, slavery. More than any other institution, slavery would dictate the career of American racism: Blackness became associated with bondage, inferiority, and social death; Whiteness with freedom, superiority, and life. The Mexican American was invented within the context of the colonization of Mexico. At the end of the nineteenth century, the Asian American was invented as a response to immigration from the Far East. Whiteness expanded during the early years of the twentieth century as new immigrants from Southern, Central, and Eastern Europe transformed themselves from "lesser Whites" to, simply, "Whites." All the while, White supremacy was legitimated by racial discourses in philosophy, literature, and science. By the middle of the twentieth century, the racial categories so familiar to us today were firmly established. Although the second half of the twentieth century brought great changes in the realm of race—including the rise of the Civil Rights Movement and the fall of Jim Crow—the racial categories that emerged in America over the previous 300 years remained, for the most part, unchallenged. Americans, White and non-White alike, understood themselves as raced, and, by and large, accepted the dominant racial classification even if they refused to accept the terms of racial inequality.

### Misrecognized as Natural

The last part of the definition we have been unpacking has to do with a process of naturalization. This word signifies a metamorphosis of sorts, where something created by humans is mistaken as something dictated by nature. Racial categories are naturalized when these symbolic groupings—the products of specific historical contexts—are wrongly conceived as natural and unchangeable. We misrecognize race as natural when we begin to think that racial cleavages and inequalities can be explained by pointing to attributes somehow inherent in the race itself (as if they were biological) instead of understanding how social powers, economic forces, political institutions, and cultural practices have brought about these divisions.

Naturalized categories are powerful; they are the categories through which we understand the world around us. Such categories divide the world along otherwise arbitrary lines and make us believe that there is nothing at all arbitrary about such a division. What is more, when categories become naturalized, alternative ways of viewing the world begin to appear more and more impossible. Why, we might ask, should we only have five main racial groups? Why not ninety-five? Why should we divide people according to their skin color? Why not base racial divisions according to foot size, ear shape, teeth color, arm length, or height? Why is ancestry so important? Why not base our racial categories on regions—North, South, East, and West? One might find these suggestive questions silly, and, indeed, they are. But they are no sillier than the idea that people should be sorted into different racial groups according skin color or blood composition. To twist Bourdieu's phrase, we might say, *when it comes to race, one never doubts enough* (1998 [1994]:36).

The system of racial classification at work in America today is not the only system imaginable, nor is it the only one that has existed in the young life of the United States. Race is far from fixed; rather, its forms, depending on the social, economic, political, and cultural pressures of the day, have shifted and fluctuated in whimsical and drastic ways over time (Duster 2001). Indeed, today's multiracial movement is challenging America's dominant racial categories (which remained relatively stable during the latter half of the twentieth century) as people of mixed heritage are refusing to accept as given the state's racial classification system (DaCosta 2007). Race is social through and through. Thus, we can regard race as a *well-founded fiction*. It is a fiction because it has no natural bearing, but it is nonetheless well founded since most people in society provide race with a real existence and divide the world through this lens.

## ETHNICITY AND NATIONALITY

The categories of ethnicity and nationality are intrinsically bound up with race. Ethnicity refers to a shared lifestyle informed by cultural, historical, religious, and/or national affiliations. Nationality is equated with citizenship, membership in a specific politically delineated territory controlled by a government (cf. Weber 1946). Race, ethnicity, and nationality are overlapping symbolic categories that influence how we see the world around us, how we view ourselves, and how we divide "us" from "them." The categories are mutually reinforcing insofar as each category educates, upholds, and is informed by the others. This is why these three categories cannot be understood in isolation from one another (Loveman 1999). For example, if someone identifies as ethnically Norwegian, which, for them, might include a shared lifestyle composed of Norwegian history and folklore, language, cultural rituals and festivals, and food, they may also reference a nationality, based in the state of Norway, as well as a racial group, White, since nearly all people of Norwegian descent would be classified as White by American standards. Here, ethnicity is informed by nationality (past or present) and signifies race.

Ethnicity often carves out distinctions and identities within racial groups. Ten people can be considered Asian American according to our modern racial taxonomy; however, those ten people might have parents or grandparents that immigrated to the United States from ten different countries, including Thailand, Vietnam, Cambodia, Singapore, China, South Korea, North Korea, Japan, Indonesia, and Laos. They might speak different languages, uphold different traditions, worship different deities, enjoy different kinds of food, and go through different experiences. What is more, many Asian countries have histories of conflict (such as China and Japan, North and South Korea). Accordingly, we cannot assume that a Chinese American and a Japanese American have similar lifestyles or see the world through a shared vision simply because they are both classified as "Asian" under American racial rubrics. Therefore, just as race, ethnicity, and nationality cannot be separated from one another, neither can all three categories be collapsed into one (cf. Brubaker et al., 2004).

Race and ethnicity (as well as nationality) are both marked and made. They are *marked* through America's racial taxonomy, as well as global ethnic taxonomy, which seek to divide the world into distinct categories. In this case, race and ethnicity impose themselves on you. They are *made* through a multiplicity of different practices—gestures, sayings, tastes, ways of walking, religious convictions, opinions, and so forth. In this case, you perform race or ethnicity. Ethnicity is a very fluid, layered, and situational construct. One might feel very American when voting, very Irish when celebrating St. Patrick's Day, very Catholic when attending Easter mass, very "New Yorker" when riding the subway, and very Northern when visiting a relative in South Carolina (Waters 1990). Race, too, can be performed to varying degrees. One might act "very Black" when celebrating Kwanzaa with relatives but may repress one's Blackness while in a business meeting with White colleagues. Race as performance is "predicated on actions, on the things one does in the world, on how one behaves. "As anthropologist John Jackson Jr. notes, "You are not Black because you are (in essence) Black; you are Black . . . because of how

you act—and not just in terms of one field of behavior (say, intellectual achievement in school) but because of how you juggle and combine many differently racialized class(ed) actions (walking, talking, laughing, watching a movie, standing, emoting, partying) in an everyday matrix of performative possibilities" (2001:171, 188). Because racial domination attaches to skin color, a dark-skinned person can never completely escape its clutches simply by acting "not Black." But that person may choose one saying over another, one kind of clothing over another, one mode of interaction over another, because she believes such an action makes her more or less Black (cf. Johnson 2003). This is why we claim that race and ethnicity are ascribed and achieved, both marked and made . . . .

In some instances, non-Whites may perform ethnicity in order to resist certain racial classifications (as when African migrants teach their children to speak with an accent so they might avoid being identified as African Americans); in other instances, they might, in an opposite way, attempt to cleanse themselves of all ethnic markers (be they linguistic, religious, or cultural in nature) to avoid becoming victims of discrimination or stigmatization. Either way, their efforts may prove futile since those belonging to dominated racial groups have considerably less ethnic agency than those belonging to the dominant—and hence normalized—group.

One reason why race and ethnicity are relatively decoupled for White Americans but bound tightly together for non-White Americans is found in the history of the nation's immigration policies and practices. Until the late nineteenth century, immigration to America was deregulated and encouraged (with the exception of Chinese exclusion laws); however, at the turn of the century, native-born White Americans, who blamed immigrants for the rise of urban slums, crime, and class conflict, began calling for immigration restrictions. Popular and political support for restrictions swelled and resulted in the development of a strict immigration policy, culminating in the Johnson-Reed Act of 1924. America's new immigration law, complete with national quotas and racial restrictions on citizenship, would fundamentally realign the country's racial taxonomy. "The national origins system classified Europeans as nationalities and assigned quotas in a hierarchy of desirability," writes historian Mae Ngai in *Impossible Subjects: Illegal Aliens and the Making of Modern America.* "[B]ut at the same time the law deemed all Europeans to be part of a White race, distinct from those considered to be not [W]hite. Euro-American identities turned both on ethnicity—that is, a nationality-based cultural identity that is defined as capable of transformation and assimilation—and on a racial identity defined by [W]hiteness" (2004:7). Non-Whites, on the other hand, were either denied entry into the United States (as was the case for Asian migrants) or were associated with illegal immigration through harsh border control policies (as was the case for Mexicans). Indeed, the immigration laws of the 1920s applied the newly formed concept of "national origin" only to European nations; those classified as members of the "colored races" were conceived as bereft of a country of origin. The result, Ngai observes, was that "unlike Euro-Americans, whose ethnic and racial identities became uncoupled during the 1920s, Asians' and Mexicans' ethnic and racial identities remained conjoined" (2004:7–8).

The history of America's immigration policy underscores the intimate conception between race, ethnicity, citizenship, and national origin. Racial categories often are defined and changed by national lawmakers, as citizenship has been extended or retracted depending on one's racial ascription. The U.S. justice system has decided dozens of cases in ways that have solidified certain racial classifications in the law. During the nineteenth and twentieth centuries, legal cases handed down rulings that officially recognized Japanese, Chinese, Burmese, Filipinos, Koreans, Native Americans, and mixed-race individuals as "not White." In 1897, a Texas federal court ruled that Mexicans were legally "White." And Indian Americans, Syrians, and Arabians have been capriciously classified as both "White" and "not White" (Haney-López 1996). Briefly examining how the legal definitions of White and non-White have changed over the years demonstrates the incredibly unstable and fluid nature of racial categories. It also shows how our legal system helps to construct race. For instance,

the "prerequisite cases" that determined people's race in order to determine their eligibility for U.S. citizenship resulted in poisonous symbolic consequences. Deemed worthy of citizenship, White people were understood to be upstanding, law-abiding, moral, and intelligent. Conversely, non-White people, from whom citizenship was withheld, were thought to be base, criminal, untrustworthy, and of lesser intelligence. For most of America's history, courts determined race, and race determined nationality; thus, nationality can only be understood within the context of U.S. racial and ethnic conflict (Loury 2001; Shklar 1991).

## FIVE FALLACIES ABOUT RACISM

According to the Southern Poverty Law Center (2005), there are hundreds of active hate groups across the country. These groups are mostly found in the Southern states—Texas, Georgia, and South Carolina have over forty active groups per state—but California ranks highest in the nation, housing within its borders fifty-three groups. For some people, hate groups epitomize what the essence of racism amounts to: intentional acts of humiliation and hatred. While such acts undoubtedly are racist in nature, they are but the tip of the iceberg. To define racism only through extreme groups and their extreme acts is akin to defining weather only through hurricanes. Hurricanes are certainly a type of weather pattern—a harsh and brutal type—but so too are mild rainfalls, light breezes, and sunny days. Likewise, racism is much broader than violence and epithets. It also comes in much quieter, everyday-ordinary forms (cf. Essed 1991 [1984]).

Americans are deeply divided over the legacies and inner workings of racism, and a large part of this division is due to the fact that many Americans understand racism in limited or misguided ways (Alba et al., 2005). We have identified five fallacies, recurrent in many public debates, fallacies one should avoid when thinking about racism.

(1) *Individualistic Fallacy.*—Here, racism is assumed to belong to the realm of ideas and prejudices. Racism is only the collection of nasty thoughts

that a "racist individual" has about another group. Someone operating with this fallacy thinks of racism as one thinks of a crime and, therefore, divides the world into two types of people: those guilty of the crime of racism ("racists") and those innocent of the crime ("non-racists") (Wacquant 1997). Crucial to this misconceived notion of racism is intentionality. "Did I intentionally act racist? Did I cross the street because I was scared of the Hispanic man walking toward me, or did I cross for no apparent reason?" Upon answering "no" to the question of intentionality, one assumes one can classify one's own actions as "nonracist," despite the character of those actions, and go about his or her business as innocent.

This conception of racism simply will not do, for it fails to account for the racism that is woven into the very fabric of our schools, political institutions, labor markets, and neighborhoods. Conflating racism with prejudice, as Herbert Blumer (1958) pointed out fifty years ago, ignores the more systematic and structural forms of racism; it looks for racism within individuals and not institutions. Labeling someone a "racist" shifts our attention from the social surroundings that enforce racial inequalities and miseries to the individual with biases. It also lets the accuser off the hook—"He is a racist; I am not"—and treats racism as aberrant and strange, whereas American racism is rather normal. Furthermore, intentionality is in no way a prerequisite for racism. Racism is often habitual, unintentional, commonplace, polite, implicit, and well meaning (Brown et al., 2003). Thus, racism is located not only in our intentional thoughts and actions; it also thrives in our unintentional thoughts and habits, as well as in the social institutions in which we all are embedded (Bonilla-Silva 1997; Feagin et al., 2001).

(2) *Legalistic Fallacy.*—This fallacy conflates *de jure* legal progress with *de facto* racial progress. One who operates under the legalistic fallacy assumes that abolishing racist laws (racism in principle) automatically leads to the abolition of racism writ large (racism in practice). This fallacy will begin to crumble after a few moments of critical reflection. After all, we would not make the same mistake when it comes to other criminalized acts: Laws against theft do not mean that one's car will never be stolen. By

way of tangible illustration, consider *Brown v. Board of Education*, the landmark case that abolished *de jure* segregation in schools. The ruling did not lead to the abolition of *de facto* segregation: fifty years later, schools are still drastically segregated and drastically unequal (Neckerman 2007; Oaks 2005). In fact, some social scientists have documented a nationwide movement of educational resegregation, which has left today's schools even more segregated than those of 1954.

(3) *Tokenistic Fallacy.*—One guilty of the tokenistic fallacy assumes that the presence of people of color in influential positions is evidence of the eradication of racial obstacles. Although it is true that non-Whites have made significant inroads to seats of political and economic power over the course of the last fifty years, a disproportionate number remain disadvantaged in these arenas (Alexander 2006). Exceptions do not prove the rule. We cannot, in good conscience, ignore the millions of African Americans living in poverty and, instead, point to Oprah Winfrey's millions as evidence for economic equality. Rather, we must explore how Winfrey's financial success can coexist with the economic deprivation of millions of Black women. We need to explore, in historian Thomas Holt's words, how the "simultaneous idealization of Colin Powell," or, for that matter, Barack Obama, "and demonization of blacks as a whole . . . is replicated in much of our everyday world" (2000:6) . . . .

(4) *Ahistorical Fallacy.*—This fallacy renders history impotent. Thinking hindered by the ahistorical fallacy makes a bold claim: Most U.S. history—namely, the period of time when this country did not extend basic rights to people of color (let alone classify them as fully human)—is inconsequential today. Legacies of slavery and colonialism, the eradication of millions of Native Americans, forced segregation, clandestine sterilizations and harmful science experiments, mass disenfranchisement, race-based exploitation, racist propaganda distributed by the state caricaturing Asians, Blacks, and Hispanics, racially motivated abuses of all kinds (sexual, murderous, and dehumanizing)—all of this, purport those operating under the ahistorical fallacy, are too far removed to matter to those living in

the here-and-now. This idea is so erroneous it is difficult to take seriously. Today's society is directed, constructed, and molded by—indeed grafted onto—the past (Ngai 2004; Winant 2001). And race, as we have already seen, is a historical invention.

A "soft version" of the ahistorical fallacy might admit that events in the "recent past"—such as the time since the Civil Rights Movement or the attacks on September 11—matter while things in the "distant past"—such as slavery or the colonization of Mexico—have little consequence. But this idea is no less fallacious than the "hard version," since many events in America's "distant past"—especially the enslavement and murder of millions of Africans—are the *most* consequential in shaping present-day society. In this vein, consider the question French historian Marc Bloch poses to us: "But who would dare to say that the understanding of the Protestant or Catholic Reformation, several centuries removed, is not far more important for a proper grasp of the world today than a great many other movements of thought or feeling, which are certainly more recent, yet more ephemeral" (1953:41)?

(5) *Fixed Fallacy.*—Those who assume that racism is fixed—that it is immutable, constant across time and space—partake in the fixed fallacy. Since they take racism to be something that does not develop at all, those who understand racism through the fixed fallacy are often led to ask questions such as: "Has racism increased or decreased in the past decade?" And because practitioners of the fixed fallacy usually take as their standard definition of racism only the most heinous forms—racial violence, for example—they confidently conclude that, indeed, things have gotten better.

It is important and useful to trace the career of American racism, analyzing, for example, how racial attitudes or measures of racial inclusion and exclusion have changed over time, and many social scientists have developed sophisticated techniques for doing so (e.g., Bobo 2001; Schuman et al., 1997). But the question, "Have things gotten better or worse?," is legitimate *only* after we account for the morphing attributes of racism. We cannot quantify racism like we can quantify, say, birthrates. The nature of "birthrate" does not fluctuate over time; thus, it makes

sense to ask, "Are there more or less births now than there were fifty years ago?" without bothering to analyze if and how a birthrate is different today than it was in previous historical moments. American racism, on the other hand, assumes different forms in different historical moments. Although race relations today are informed by those of the past, we cannot hold to the belief that twenty-first-century racism takes on the exact same form as twentieth-century racism. And we certainly cannot conclude that there is "little or no racism" today because it does not resemble the racism of the 1950s. (Modern-day Christianity looks very different, in nearly every conceivable way, than the Christianity of the early church. But this does not mean that there is "little or no Christianity" today.) So, before we ask, "Have things gotten better or worse?," we should ponder the essence of racism today, noting how it differs from racism experienced by those living in our parents' or grandparents' generation. And we should ask, further, to quote Holt again, "What enables racism to reproduce itself after the historical conditions that initially gave it life have disappeared" (2000:20)?

## RACIAL DOMINATION

We have spent a significant amount of time talking about what racial domination is not but have yet to spell out what it is. We can delineate two specific manifestations of racial domination: institutional racism and interpersonal racism. *Institutional racism* is systemic White domination of people of color, embedded and operating in corporations, universities, legal systems, political bodies, cultural life, and other social collectives. The word "domination" reminds us that institutional racism is a type of power that encompasses the *symbolic power* to classify one group of people as "normal" and other groups of people as "abnormal"; the *political power* to withhold basic rights from people of color and marshal the full power of the state to enforce segregation and inequality; the *social power* to deny people of color full inclusion or membership in associational life; and the *economic power* that privileges Whites in terms of job placement, advancement, wealth, and property accumulation.

Informed by centuries of racial domination, institutional racism withholds from people of color opportunities, privileges, and rights that many Whites enjoy. Social scientists have amassed a significant amount of evidence documenting institutional racism, evidence that demonstrates how White people—strictly because of their Whiteness—reap considerable advantages when buying and selling a house, choosing a neighborhood in which to live, getting a job and moving up the corporate ladder, securing a first-class education, and seeking medical care (Massey 2007; Quillian 2006). That Whites accumulate more property and earn more income than members of minority populations, possess immeasurably more political power, and enjoy greater access to the country's cultural, social, medical, legal, and economic resources are well documented facts (e.g., Oliver and Shapiro 1997; Western 2006). While Whites have accumulated many opportunities due to racial domination, people of color have suffered disaccumulation (Brown et al., 2003). Thus, if we talk about "Hispanic poverty," then we must also talk about White affluence; if we speak of "Black unemployment," then we must also keep in mind White employment; and if we ponder public policies for people of color, then we must also critically examine the public policies that directly benefit White people.

Below the level of institutions—yet directly informed by their workings—we find *interpersonal racism*. This is racial domination manifest in everyday interactions and practices. Interpersonal racism can be overt; however, most of the time, interpersonal racism is quite covert: it is found in the habitual, commonsensical, and ordinary practices of our lives. Our racist attitudes, as Lillian Smith remarked in *Killers of the Dream*, easily "slip from the conscious mind deep into the muscles" (1994 [1949]:96). Since we are disposed to a world structured by racial domination, we develop racialized dispositions—some conscious, many more unconscious and somatic—that guide our thoughts and behaviors. We may talk slowly to an Asian woman at the farmer's market, unconsciously assuming that she speaks poor English; we may inform a Hispanic man at a corporate party that someone has spilled their punch, unconsciously assuming that he is a janitor; we may ask to change seats if an Arab American man

sits next to us on an airplane. Miniature actions such as these have little to do with one's intentional thoughts; they are orchestrated by one's practical sense, one's habitual knowhow, and informed by institutional racism . . . .

## Intersecting Modes of Domination

Racial domination does not operate inside a vacuum, cordoned off from other modes of domination. On the contrary, it *intersects* with other forms of domination—those based on gender, class, sexuality, religion, nationhood, ability, and so forth. The notion that there is a monolithic "Arab American experience," "Asian American experience," or "White experience"—experiences somehow detached from other pieces of one's identity—is nothing but a chimera. Researchers have labeled such a notion "racial essentialism," for such a way of thinking boils down vastly different human experiences into a single "master category": race (Harris 2000). When we fail to account for these different experiences, we create silences in our narratives of the social world and fail to explain how overlapping systems of advantage and disadvantage affect individuals' opportunity structures, lifestyles, and social hardships. The idea of intersectionality implies that we cannot understand the lives of poor White single mothers or gay Black men by examining only one dimension of their lives—class, gender, race, or sexuality. Indeed, we must explore their lives in their full complexity, examining how these various dimensions come together and structure their existence. When we speak of racial domination, then, we must always bear in mind the ways in which it interacts with masculine domination (or sexism), heterosexual domination (or homophobia), class domination (poverty), religious persecution, disadvantages brought on by disabilities, and so forth (Collins 2000; Crenshaw 1990).

In addition, we should not assume that one kind of oppression is more important than another or that being advantaged in one dimension of life somehow cancels out other dimensions that often result in disadvantage. While it is true that poor Whites experience many of the same hardships as poor Blacks, it is not true that poverty somehow de-Whitens poor Whites. In other words, though they are in a similarly precarious economic position as poor Blacks, poor Whites still experience race-based privileges, while poor Blacks are oppressed not only by poverty but also by racism. In a similar vein, well-off people of color cannot "buy" their way out of racism. Despite their economic privilege, middle- and upper-class non-Whites experience institutional and interpersonal racism on a regular basis (Feagin 1991). But how, exactly, should we conceptualize these intersecting modes of domination? Many scholars have grappled with this question (e.g., Walby 2007; Yuval-Davis 2006), and we do so here, if only in the most provisional way.

The notion of intersectionality is perhaps as old as the social problems of racial, masculine, and class domination, but in recent memory it was popularized by activists who criticized the feminist and civil rights movements for ignoring the unique struggles of women of color. The term itself is credited to critical race scholar Kimberlé Crenshaw (1989), who imagined society as divided every which way by multiple forms of inequality. For Crenshaw, society resembled an intricate system of crisscrossing roads—each one representing a different social identity (e.g., race, gender, class, religion, age); one's unique social position (or structural location) could be identified by listing all the attributes of one's social identity and pinpointing the nexus (or intersection) at which all those attributes coalesced. This conception of intersectionality has been the dominant one for many years, leading scholars to understand overlapping modes of oppression as a kind of "matrix of domination" (Collins 2000) . . . .

We believe a more analytically sophisticated and politically useful rendering of intertwined oppressions is Myra Marx Ferree's model of "interactive intersectionality" (cf. Prins 2006; Walby 2007). In this version, overlapping social identities are best understood, not as a collection of "points of intersection," but as a "figuration" (as Elias would have it) or "field" (as Bourdieu would) of shifting, deeply-dimensioned, and "mutually constituted *relationships*. This means "intersection of gender and race' is not any number of specific *locations* occupied by individuals or groups (such as Black women) but a

*process* through which 'race' takes on multiple 'gendered' meanings for particular women and men . . . . In such a complex system, gender is not a dimension limited to the organization of reproduction or family, class is not a dimension equated with the economy, and race is not a category reduced to the primacy of ethnicities, nations, and borders, but all of the processes that systematically organize families, economies, and nations, are co-constructed along with the meanings of gender, race, and class that are presented in and reinforced by these institutions separately and together" (Ferree 2009:85).

The best metaphor for intersecting modes of oppression, therefore, may not be that of crisscrossing roads but of a web or field of relations within which struggles over opportunities, power, and privileges take place (cf. Bourdieu 1996 [1992]; Emirbayer 1997). The implication of this new theoretical development is that if we focus strictly on race and ignore other sources of social inequality (such as class and gender), not only will we be deaf to the unique experiences of certain members of society—their voices drowned out by our violent and homogenizing categorization—but we will also (and always) fundamentally misunderstand our object of analysis: race itself. Intersectional analysis of the type that breaks with old modes of thinking (e.g., society as a "matrix of domination") and adopts a thoroughly relational perspective on multiple modes of oppression (e.g., "interactive intersectionality") is not an option but a *prerequisite* for fully understanding the nature of racial identity and racial domination.

## DISCUSSION QUESTIONS

1. Discuss Desmond and Emirbayer's definition of race as a social construct. What is the authors' argument about race as a "symbolic category" based on phenotype and ancestry?
2. Discuss the ways in which racial classifications have shifted in the United States depending upon social, economic, political, and cultural conditions at different points in our history. Use the examples in this reading and from any others.

# 3

# CREATING A WORLD OF DICHOTOMY

## Categorizing Sex and Gendering Cultural Messages

SARA L. CRAWLEY

LARA J. FOLEY

CONSTANCE L. SHEHAN

*The third reading in this introductory section is by Sara L. Crawley, Lara J. Foley, and Constance L. Shehan, all sociologists who study gender. This excerpt is taken from their 2008 book, <u>Gendering Bodies</u>, and it provides a thorough overview of the concepts of and explanations for sex and gender. Sociologists often distinguish between sex (biological attributes of femaleness and maleness) and gender (the social and cultural meanings of femininity and masculinity). The authors' work here is primarily concerned with how cultural messages about gender often determine the gendered experiences of bodies, and thus the social (cultural) becomes intertwined with the physical world and gets demarcated on our bodies.*

With the courage to confront, understand, and redefine our incorrigible propositions, we can begin to discover new scientific knowledge and to construct new realities in everyday life (Kessler and McKenna 1978:167).

In U.S. culture, we commonly assume that our physiological bodies (in particular notions of femaleness or maleness and presumptions about physical size, strength, and reproductive capacities) determine our social roles. Here we argue that this is a premature conclusion. There is no necessary relationship between one's capacity to produce ova or sperm (or lack of capacity to produce either) and acting "ladylike" or "manly." We too commonly

*Source:* Crawley, Sara L., Lara, J. Foley, and Constance L. Shehan. 2008. "Creating a World of Dichotomy: Categorizing Sex and Gendering Cultural Messages." In *Gendering Bodies*. Reproduced with permission of Rowman & Littlefield Publishing Group, Inc. in the format Textbook via Copyright Clearance Center.

assume that social expectations come from bodily necessity. In our everyday lives we are so practiced at conforming the uses of our bodies to gendered expectations that we assume our comfort with those practices comes from nature. In this reading, we wish to reverse the casual direction and turn that commonsense argument on its head. We argue that *cultural messages*[1] that form our expectations and "rules" about gender determine the gendered experiences of our bodies—our *embodied knowledge*, and that these messages and our resulting gendered practices help to shape our physical bodies as well. Thus, social messages and physical ("natural") bodies are inextricably inseparable. There is no physical body separate from social practices (which originate from gendered messages). There is no social experience separable from physical bodies. The imprint of physical propensities and social experiences exists in each person. In essence, the social world and the physical world co-construct gendered bodies . . . .

## Gender Does Not Exist, but It Is Real

Gender is a bit of a conundrum. On the one hand, *social constructionism* suggests that the differences between women and men that we identify as significant (i.e., femininity and masculinity) are products of the social world, not nature. So, like laws, U.S. currency, and the Western calendar, gender is a system of organizing that Western cultures have devised to organize and make sense of our lives. (All cultures use gender as an organizing system, but may not all use the system in exactly the same ways.) Importantly, because gender is "done" by us rather than innate within us, we can decide whether and how to allow the organization of gender to affect us in the future, if we choose to be attentive to its effects. Social constructionism stands in sharp contrast to the essentialist notion of biological determinism. *Essentialism* is the notion that there is an enduring truth to be found if only we look hard enough. For example, to believe that a real difference between women and men resides in the body is an essentialist belief. This belief is the basis of evolutionary theory or *biological*

*determinism*—the notion that women and men have been bred to be different animals, adapting to evolutionary functional necessities. Social constructionism is the response to evolutionary theory that argues that what we understand as "appropriately" feminine and masculine are social evaluations, not physical necessities, and are based on social organization, not physiological adaptation. Clearly,. we lean much more strongly in the direction of social constructionism.

On the other hand, gender inequality exists (as do inequalities based on race, class, sexuality, age, and ability, among others). That is, there are a number of very measurable, and hence seemingly real, social disadvantages experienced by people who are not members of the dominant group (e.g., income and wealth inequality, unequal access to jobs, unequal representation in politics, etc.). Hence, even though socially constructed phenomena are not "real" in terms of being an innate part of our bodies, they are real in their effects on our lives and life chances (and in many ways their effects may leave a mark on our bodies as well).

So, while it seems clear that gender is socially constructed, it seems equally clear that the effects of gender are quite real. As a result, we argue that *gender does not exist* (in nature) *but it is real* (in terms of real consequences, including various structural inequalities, physical violence, etc.). In this way, we can remain attentive to both the theoretical perspectives that understand gender as constructed, as well as the material effects that the system of gender has on the lives of real people. In other words, we see both the theoretical relevance of gender theory and the practical application of gendered experiences in the lives of actual people.

A social constructionist perspective on social problems argues that people live in two worlds simultaneously (and inseparably): the physical world and the symbolic world (Loseke 1999). We only know the physical world through the interpretations that we make of it, and conversely, there is no world of meaning outside of our physical place in the world—in the body.

We see gender and *embodied knowledge* (knowledge of self and others via experiences of one's body) in the same way. Gender exists in both the world of language, images, and interactions (which always have significance attached) and the physical practices and experiences of the body (Paechter 2003, 2006). Every use of the body has meaning. Every meaning and interpretation is experienced through the body. Hence, each body is an ever-developing process that begins with a physiological basis but on which constant social intervention makes its mark (Shilling 1993; Turner 1996). Therefore, we will never ask the question: Is it nature *or* nurture? We always understand gendered experiences as a combination of both physiological experience and social interpretation.

Nonetheless, we suggest that the physical effects of social practices are far more flexible than has been popularly imagined. The sizes and shapes of bodies are a result of social practices (e.g., nutrition, dieting, fitness, surgical alteration, contraceptive practices, female and male circumcision), just as social practices are designed to meet physical needs (e.g., food preparation and distribution, creating and obtaining shelter, sanitary practices) (Cashmore 2005; Connell 2002; Lorber 1994). Therefore, we are attentive to cultural messages and social practices. Like Lorber (1994), we see gender as something that most of us first *believe* to be true of bodies and that we then *find* selectively in the world of social practice. Lorber writes, "Gendered people do not emerge from physiology or hormones but from the exigencies of social order, from the need for reliable division of the work of food production and the social (not physical) reproduction of new members" (19).

In other words, although our physiological bodies emerge from nature, gender—as a part of social organization—defines what is "appropriate" in the uses of our bodies. Lorber continues, "I am not saying that physical differences between male and female bodies don't exist, but that these differences are socially meaningless until social practices transform them into social facts" (18).

To suggest that gender is a social construction is to argue that there are "rules" (which originate in cultural messages) of appropriate behavior for women and men, and that those rules do not inhere in nature (that is, they do not originate from within our bodies), but they are mandated by social participation. In other words, "we" made them up—what we consider appropriate comes from the social world. Much like laws, the "rules" of gender have developed *over time through social participation*. While these rules of behavior are based on expectations about bodies (femaleness or maleness), they rarely have to do with bodily capacities. For example, it is traditional for men to open doors for women. However, there is no physiological reason for this expectation. Women and men both have hands with opposable thumbs such that door opening is generally not problematic (unless a particular person has a physical difference, such as being wheelchair bound). Genitalia are not commonly used in the opening of doors. Hence, there is no necessary reason to expect that maleness or femaleness renders one a better door opener. Nonetheless, the tradition of door opening is based on a social expectation about female and male bodies. This example demonstrates how the "rules" of appropriate gender behavior are more about gender performance than physiological necessity. They are more about what we expect of female or male people than about what female or male bodies require or can accomplish physically.

To suggest that gender—the rules of "appropriate" participation—is socially constructed is not to suggest that gender expectations are not serious. Gender is serious business. If you have broken the rules, you will know about it. Your peers, mentors, families, friends, authority figures, and sometimes even strangers will indicate it to you with more or less formalized types of sanctions: perhaps by giving you a nasty look, making an unpleasant remark, or beating you up or arresting you. Oftentimes if you have broken the rules, you will feel it intuitively or viscerally; even without comment or response from another person (because these rules are so practiced you already know what response to expect).

Additionally, recognizing gender as a social construction does not suggest that physiology and the social world are fully separable. Indeed, the overarching argument throughout this book is that, while gender is socially constructed, it is so "real," serious, and pervasive as to change the way in which we experience our bodies and the ways we use our bodies—over time resulting in changes to physical capacities (e.g., strength, size, proportion).

But to further shore up our argument, we can demonstrate that gender is socially constructed because *gender expectations change over time and across cultures.* While some gendered system has always historically existed in the United States, what is considered appropriately masculine or feminine has changed considerably over just the past 50 years. For example, Feinberg (1996) reports that in the 1950s in Albany, New York, a person could have been arrested for dressing inappropriately for one's gender (sometimes called cross-dressing). The law required each person to be wearing at least three pieces of gender-appropriate clothing. Feinberg reports that this law was primarily applied to arrest people who attended lesbian and gay bars, above all drag queens and butch women, who she reports were regularly beaten and raped by the police. Given that cross-dressing performances, such as drag queen and drag king performances, are common in most major cities today, and that celebrities such as David Bowie, RuPaul, Boy George, k.d. lang, Dennis Rodman, Ellen DeGeneres, and Marilyn Manson, among others, have become famous while gender bending (nonconforming in terms of styles of dress and fashion) since the 1950s example above, we can say that expectations about gender performances have changed and are changing. Similarly, the once common notion of the stay-at-home mom as the core of the (white) nuclear family (as seen in the television shows *Leave It to Beaver* and *Father Knows Best*) has shifted considerably out of economic necessity in the twenty-first century to the extent that it is much more likely today than in the past to expect mothers to work (Coontz 1992). In actuality throughout U.S. history the notion of a stay-at-home mom was only reserved for economically privileged, mostly white families. Women of color, especially immigrant women, have always been expected to work, even in extremely arduous jobs—such as domestic labor and immigrant farming.

In the nineteenth century, during the U.S. transition to capitalist industrialism, an ideology referred to as the *cult of true womanhood* (Welter 1978) emerged. It reflected the movement of economic work out of the home and into separate workplaces. The division between public and private worlds prescribed a division of labor by gender, with men following production out of the home and women remaining in the home to tend to reproductive issues. The home became the proper sphere for women's interests and influence. This gendered division of labor was accompanied by new beliefs about women's "natural superiority" as caregivers and moral custodians of the home. This ideology of women's true place, although aspired to by families of all social classes, was not easily attainable. Many families depended on the paid labor of women and could not afford to have them sitting "idle" at home. Thus, the cult of true womanhood functioned as a class ideology. It was a way for white, middle-class families to distinguish themselves from people of color and working-class white people. However, even for white middle-class wives, the cult of true womanhood restricted life options to home and family. So, notions of appropriate femininity (including expectations of physical strength of female bodies) have always been a matter of context and have shifted across time and social strata.

Further, notions of appropriate behavior for female and male people differ considerably across cultures and religious traditions. With the renewed sensationalism in the U.S. media during the Second Gulf War about Muslim women in Iraq and Afghanistan wearing *burquas,* and the various interpretations of this practice, it is clear that clothing imperatives differ greatly between the United States and other countries. Beyond mere clothing imperatives, other cultures allow for gender switching or gender ambiguity in ways to which U.S. culture provides no recognizable parallels. For example, Brown (1997) writes about the existence of "Two Spirit People" among some Native American cultures who he argues occupy six different gender positions, some of which are not analogous to any gender position in Western cultures. Additionally, Young (2000) writes about "women who become men" in rural Albania—female-bodied people who become "sworn virgins" and legitimately live their lives and dress as men in Albanian culture. Again, this form of gender switching has no legitimated and recognized parallel in the United States. So, while we regularly take current- day notions of masculinity and femininity as normative—a given—in our everyday lives, it need not be so . . . .

## Why Only Two?
## Understanding Dualisms and Typifications

Before understanding how gender works, we need to first examine two important attributes about Western thought—dualistic thinking and typification. Both dualistic thinking and typification create the categorization system that allows us to believe in the naturalness of femaleness and maleness.[2]

In Western cultures, we tend to practice *dualistic thinking* (Bordo 1986; Jay 1981; Sprague 1997). In other words, we tend to think in terms of two options (i.e., either/or). That is, we utilize the most simple category system—one or the other. Common sense tells us there are "two sides to every argument" or "two sides of a coin." Of course, we could think of coins as continuous circles or arguments as having an unlimited number of complex sides (5? 27?). But we commonly refer to most issues in terms of simple dualisms or binaries. Some examples are as follows: right/wrong, white/black, man/woman, straight/gay, citizen/alien, rational/emotional, abstract/concrete, public/private, up/down, high/low, divine/mortal, capitalist/worker, masculine/feminine. Not only do we conceptualize in terms of dualisms, but we imagine them as polar opposites—mutually exclusive categories with no gray area in between.

While this practice may seem innocent enough, there are at least two particular problems with dualistic thinking. First, thinking in terms of two and only two possible options masks the complexity of the world. Imagine trying to describe all the variety of flowers in terms of one type or the other. Can you describe trees in terms of two options? Let's assume all trees can be described as deciduous (those that shed their leaves once a year) or evergreens. If someone giving you directions were to tell you to turn left at the deciduous tree, would you have any idea to which tree they were referring? Categorizing in terms of twos greatly reduces the variability with which we can describe the world—and falsely so. It too narrowly focuses our attention to very limited criteria. Not only can we not describe wide variety, but we are continually focused on the simple categories created.

The second problem with dualisms is that we rarely create equal and opposite options within our dualisms. We tend to think hierarchically. That is, we rank the options. Rational is imagined as better than emotional. Even space is understood hierarchically—up is better than down; high is better than low. Of course, in many ways this is nonsensical. Exactly how up is "up" enough? If high is better than low, how do we know how high is high? Is four feet off the ground "high" or "low"? Is it "high" if the other option is two feet off the ground? Or is it that high is good but higher is always better? Clearly the ideas of high and low are relative and never provide enough information to fully understand a complex situation. Nonetheless, we use this dualism to be somehow informative.

Gender expectations fall into Western practices of thinking dualistically (Bem 1993; Kessler and McKenna 1978); Lorber 1996). We think in terms of masculine = male and feminine = female. We often think this is linked to expectations of "natural" reproduction. Interestingly, we do not categorize based on actual reproductive capacity—those who can reproduce (the fertiles) and those who cannot (the nonfertiles) (Kessler and McKenna 1978). Perhaps we avoid this dualism because it is not readily apparent upon sight exactly who falls into each group. After all, the nonfertiles would be comprised of the very young (not yet fertile) and the old (beyond fertile age), as well as some younger adults who simply will never be fertile. Similarly, the gender binary is based on presumptions about the clothed, visible body—presumptions about genitalia and reproductive capacity (Kessler 1998; West and Zimmerman 1987) . . . .

In addition to dualistic thinking, we tend to think categorically using what Schutz (1970) calls *typification,* or the idea that human thought is the process of categorizing—the process of linking objects abstractly into categories such that we can think in terms of what is typical. So while desks can come in a variety of styles comprised of a variety of materials, when one thinks of "desk," one has a mental picture of the thing that is typical of desk. Indeed, language is categorical.

You do not have to be thinking of a particular desk (your desk, for example) to imagine "desk" as a type of thing that is used in typical ways. The word d-e-s-k is a marker for that typical thing into which a wide variety of actual objects fall. Typifications are abstract notions that group physical objects into manageable categories (Zerubavel 1996). If you could not typify, you would have to figure out each object that you encounter as if it were new to you each time you encounter it. For Schutz, typifications are useful and necessary. Without the ability to typify, language itself would not exist. So typifications are very efficient and useful in the development of language.

Of course, people are objects about which typifications can be applied. When applied to people, typifications may be thought of by the more familiar term *stereotypes*. Stereotyping is the use of common-sense (often discriminatory) assumptions about groups of people to make predictions about characteristics of an individual. Indeed, as physical objects, people are readily stereotyped based on visual cues of the physical body.

There are some qualities of typifications that make it problematic to apply them to people. First, typifications are acquired in the everyday world of interaction. That is, they develop through our interactions into what we call common sense—the collections of our experiences within a culture. In other words, our typifications are not based on scientific measurement and testing, but rather on acting and interacting within our culture, specifically that part of our culture that is most familiar to us. So what you believe is true or typical is based only on the biases of your own cultural experiences.

Also, the existing category system blinds us to other possibilities. Once we have developed notions of the typical, we focus our attention on the typical, not the aberration, often even when the aberration is common. That is, rather than upset our category system, we simply call that thing that doesn't fit "atypical" ("Oh, that's not typical!") and dismiss it . . . .

## Heteronormativity and the Gender Box Structure

Our binary notions of "typical" bodies suggest our rules for interaction have a basis in the "natural" body. True to our Western intellectual origins, these so-called "natural" bodies are also understood in hierarchical ways. We see male bodies (and hence men) as strong, tall, powerful, and aggressive; and female bodies (and hence women) as small, petite, elegant, and in need of protection. In our culture, the male body is understood as physically better than the female body—that is, we see males as "naturally physically superior" to females. This means that we as a culture do not understand the ability to give birth to human life as strength or an indicator of any sort of physical superiority; it is attributed to the "weak" female body.

Notice that all this discussion relies on typification—generalized ideas about everyone falling into the groups "women" and "men." Whereas we know that not all men are stronger than all women and that not all men are taller than all women, we typify "women" as small and "men" as tall and ignore any evidence to the contrary. If we notice the differences, we have to amend our categories, and that is often too challenging.

*Heteronormativity* is the belief that institutionalized heterosexuality should be the standard for legitimate intimate relationships (Ingraham 1996:169). Within the heteronormative paradigm, sex, gender, and sexual orientation are ideologically fused and are assumed to be based on innate characteristics of the body, rather than social prescriptions (Butler 1990; Kessler 1998; Kessler and McKenna 1978; Lorber 1996; West and Zimmerman 1987). That is, they are presumed to be "natural" and reliant on whether one has a penis or a vagina (which has historically been understood as lack of a penis [de Beauvoir 1952; Kessler 1998]). So in practice, when we see a person (or even imagine the sight of someone, for example, when interacting virtually via the Internet), we first attribute biological sex (femaleness or maleness) to that person, then implicitly apply expectations for gendered behavior (modes of dress, uses of the body) and heterosexual practices (coupling with an "opposite" partner). That is, we typify each person or "place them in a box"—the female box or the male box (Figure 3.1).

Two points are particularly pertinent in this figure. First, notice that sex, gender, and sexual orientation

FIGURE 3.1    Gender Box Structure. Binary gender messages in the social world tell us to typify each person as either "female" or "male" and apply assumptions about bodies, gender, and sexual orientation.

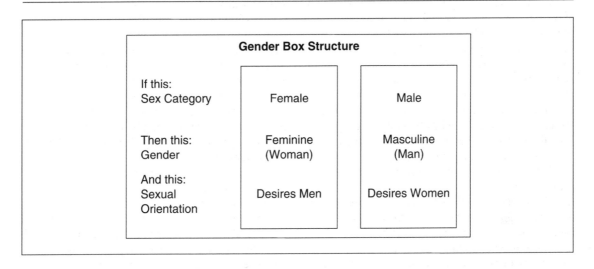

are fused and assumed to be attached to biological bodies. So, if we believe we know the sex of the person, we also believe we know the gender and sexual orientation of the person. Second, notice that there is a space between the boxes where presumably no one can exist. That is, this is an instance of Western dualistic thought that provides for two and only two options that are understood as mutually exclusive (not overlapping). In other words, we understand all people to fit in either one box or the other. Anyone not fitting in these boxes is understood as "unnatural," "not normal," aberrant, an outlier. And so we "throw them out"—place them outside the realm of our acknowledgment or understanding. Like all dualisms, this box structure is far too narrowly focused to accurately and colorfully describe the human diversity that we know to exist. We know people who do not fit our typifications; we just choose not to figure them into our categories. And, like all dualisms, we implicitly create a hierarchy in which to have a penis (be masculine, be the "active" sexual participant) is understood as better than to have no penis (be feminine, be the "passive" sexual recipient).

    . . . We argue that the gender box structure is both unnecessary and inaccurate in understanding

and describing human experience. Far greater diversity of humanity exists than is imagined and described by heteronormative paradigms. We provide an alternative theory of how gender works shortly . . . .

    Are all girls feminine and all boys masculine? . . . In your everyday experience of the world, you are likely to say no. Each of us knows people who do not readily fit the prescriptions of femininity or masculinity, whether by conscious or seemingly unconscious choice. We know men who enjoy cooking and women who are Marines, and so forth. In fact, not all people who may be considered normatively masculine or feminine engage in masculine or feminine activities all the time. For example, if a woman is good at ice hockey, does that make her masculine? If a man is changing a diaper, does that make him feminine? Perhaps you might say, "It's not fair to question someone's identity just because they are good at sports or because they care for their children!" But isn't that how we assign those identities in the first place? If a man is good at sports, we see him as masculine. If a woman is good at sports, we see her as "pretty good for a girl." Or perhaps we even question whether she is a *real* girl by suggesting she is lesbian. If a woman is changing a diaper, we assume she is enacting her nurturing "nature." If a man is changing a diaper, we avoid seeing him as feminine; rather we say he's a good dad even though nurturing activities are supposed to be related to femininity. Hence, we fall back into the box structure typifications. Yet we know many female-bodied people who are good athletes and male-bodied people who care for children. What we argue, then, is that via the gender box structure, *we understand activities as gendered and then we encourage or discourage people with certain presumed genitalia to or form participating.* We think of sports as typically masculine and cooking as typically feminine[3] and then typify people who do them. Anyone can play ice hockey. Anyone can cook. Yet we make significance out of who does what, when, and how. More importantly, there is a performance style to playing sports and cooking that suggests a "realness" to our understandings of gender assignments . . . .

We use typifications to think about sexuality also. Is it true that all people are heterosexual? No, quite a large number of people identify as homosexual, some of whom have received a good bit of celebrity in the last 10 years via television and popular culture. It is very likely that you know someone who does not identify as heterosexual. Is it true that all people are either heterosexual or homosexual (another Western binary)? No, there are people who identify as bisexual. Does bisexual mean always preferring women and men at all times? Does it imply serial monogamy (my current partner is x but future partners could be x or y)? Does it mean sexually voracious—or wanting sex all the time with any willing partner? Bisexuality is often understood as a problematic category because it does not easily align with binary notions of homo or hetero and confuses the "naturalness" of binary biological sex urges, and hence becomes politically confusing to those who prefer neat categories (Rust 1995). Do you believe that someone can have attractions to females and males throughout their entire lives? Many people report just that.

Additionally, do people always identify in one of those categories for their entire lives? What is the defining characteristic of someone's "real" sexual orientation? Sexual practices? Whom they desire? How they choose to self-identify? This, in fact, is the classic question in studies of sexual orientation opened by Kinsey's (1948, 1953) famous studies in which he asserted that a great deal of the U.S. population could be labeled bisexual based on reports of his participants of same-sex sexual practices, desires, or identities.[4] If sexual orientation is an essentially true characteristic about people, how do we determine the "true" orientation of each of us?

Let's assume sexuality is based on with whom you have had sexual contact. If a female-bodied person currently identifies as lesbian but had sex with men until age 30, is she lesbian or bisexual? If a person has never had sex with anyone (i.e., the person is a "virgin"), can they have a sexual orientation?

Perhaps sexuality is based on how people identify themselves. If a man identifies as heterosexual but occasionally has sex with men, is he straight or gay? This scenario is apparently much more common than common-sense knowledge would have predicted, or Kinsey's study (1948) would not have caused such lengthy discussion both in and out of the academy. If you said he's gay, then you've admitted that your definition of someone's sexuality is as salient as that person's definition. In other words, identity is co-constructed between a person and the social context in which others label that person. If someone identifies as heterosexual and engages in a three-some with both a male and female partner, is that person bisexual by definition? If you answered no to this and "gay" to the previous question, you have just contradicted your own theory of sexuality.

Perhaps you imagine the answer lies in whom the person desires. So, if the male person who occasionally has sex with another man does not express desire for him ("It's just sex—a way to get off."), is that not "gay" sex? What if the two men are having sex for the voyeuristic enjoyment of a female person: are all three heterosexual? If a female person has always been married heterosexually but secretly dreams of sex with women, is she "really" lesbian—even if she only has sex with her heterosexually married partner?

Sexuality is not nearly as clear-cut as we imagine it. Life experiences and sexual histories of individuals are not continuously consistent over time. Sexual practices, identities, and desires often do not align consistently: some people report desire without sexual contact, or contact without desire, or identities that do not match practices (Schwartz and Rutter 1998). Interestingly, in U.S. culture, the notion of sexual orientation is not based strictly on an individual's characteristics, but on the sex of their partner. Further, this notion of sexuality has not been the definition of appropriate sexuality throughout time or across cultures—that is, it is a socially constructed notion of sexuality (Katz 1995; Rubin 2003; Weeks 2003). Katz (1995) writes that our notion of "heterosexuality" is a modern invention originating in the second half of the nineteenth century. It appeared in the dictionary after the word "homosexual" appeared in the dictionary. Prior to this time frame, various notions of sexuality existed. Of course, same-sex sexual practices have been recorded throughout history, but the ways in which people have understood them have changed considerably. Halperin (1989) writes of Ancient Greek cultures in which sexual prerogative was defined by citizenship (land ownership) such that to be a citizen meant that one could have sexual relations with any noncitizen (female or male). Hence, the notion of "orientation" was nonsensical to Ancient Greeks. Further, in current cultures in other areas of the world, if a man is having anal sex with another man, it does not automatically imply that both men are understood as gay. Almaguer (1993) writes that in some subcultures in northern Mexico, the active partner is *activo* or masculine, and hence not stigmatized; whereas the partner who allows himself to be penetrated is *pasivo* and stigmatized as feminine (essentially made a woman). In the United States, some men secretly engage in sex with other men while considering themselves to be heterosexual (Humphreys 1970; King 2005). The slang term for this practice is "on the down low." A significant concern about this practice is that many of these men have female partners or wives to whom they do not reveal their (often unprotected) sexual interactions with men, hence risking HIV infection for their unsuspecting female partners (King 2005).[5]

So notions of sexual practices, sexual identities, gendered activities, and gendered participation in the world are much fuzzier than the dichotomous box structure would predict. Although people regularly use these typifications of gender and sexuality, the dichotomous box structure simply does not describe the vast variability of experiences and practices in the world. But what about so-called biological sex? Can that be dichotomous?

## What About Nature?

Isn't it true that all people are born unambiguously female or male? No, a significant portion of the human population (estimated at 1.7% of live births) are born *intersexed*—that is, born with various ambiguities of genital appearance or chromosomal or hormonal differences (Blackless et al. 2000; Fausto-Sterling 2005:51).[6] In other words, some people do not fit into the dichotomous standard of femaleness or maleness, based on some genital, chromosomal, or hormonal difference (Fausto-Sterling 2000; Kessler 1998). The works of Anne Fausto-Sterling and Suzanne Kessler demonstrate to us how the "problem" of intersexuality is a problem of normative categories, not a problem of bodies or intersexed people themselves.

Kessler documents the process of twentieth-century medical practice in the United States that has come to define genital difference as "abnormal" or even "deviant" and in need of surgical change in *intersexed* children. During the so-called progress of twentieth-century medical science, doctors began making surgical changes to "fix" the genitals of intersexed infants that could not be clearly assigned a sex category. In other words, a sex category (female or male) was chosen for the child and normative-appearing genitals surgically constructed based on the greatest likeness the doctors felt could be achieved (based on medical abilities of the particular time). The medical premise for such changes was that intersexed bodies were "abnormal" or "a mistake" of nature that medical science proposed to "fix." Having surgically and hormonally "fixed" these so-called aberrant bodies, doctors were purported to have made these children "normal" so they might fit into the "biological" order of femaleness and maleness. In essence, doctors were purporting to make these ambiguous bodies into "normal" women and men (Kessler 1998) . . . .

Unfortunately, these doctors' protocols left little concern for the sexual pleasure of the surgically altered children when they reached adulthood or any consideration of the possibility of sexual pleasure outside the penile-vaginal penetrative model. Hence, any loss of sensation from surgical intervention was considered irrelevant to the medical necessity of knowing gender from birth. Additionally, no latitude was given to allowing the child self-definition. It was not until the early 1990s that adult intersexed persons began to advocate for a change to the treatment of intersexed babies, favoring self-elective surgeries later in life (if at all). The Intersex Society of North America,[7] an advocacy and information-providing organization originated by Cheryl Chase, emerged in the early 1990s to advocate self-determination to the American Medical Association. Only in very recent years has the medical establishment seemed willing to listen.

In addition to Kessler's work, there is a large body of literature from transgendered or transsexual people who testify to not fitting into the heteronormative box structure and, hence, the social problematic of the category system itself (Bornstein 1994; Crawley and Broad 2004; Feinberg 1996). *Transsexual* (a term generally reserved for those who have undertaken some form of surgical alteration of the body) and *transgendered* (a broader term that denotes anyone who defines themselves as not fitting the requisite body/gender dualism prescribed by heteronormativity) people challenge the preeminence of the body's determination of the person or psyche. If we take seriously the earnest reports of adult transsexuals and transgendered people that their bodies need to be made to conform to fit their own gender expectations (i.e., making some genital surgical changes such that the body matches the person they wish to display), we must recognize that genitals are not the origin of psyche or self.[8] Indeed, the very idea that a person can "change sex" surgically or hormonally (or both) suggests that bodies (and, thus, sex itself) are malleable. If we can surgically change sexes, how fixed or original, then, can biology be? And, how useful is bodily appearance in predicting sex? . . .

Fausto-Sterling (1986, 2000) supports our argument that so-called biological sex is more a continuum than a dichotomy, by recognizing that there remains no accurate, consistent, and reliable measure of so-called biological sex. That's right, *there is no specific, distinct measure that will consistently determine maleness or femaleness for all persons.* We have already shown that genital appearance is not a useful test. Sex chromosomes come in more interesting combinations than just XX = female and XY = male, with varying results, some of which are not physically transparent. Hormones are the least well understood component of all. While decades of research have *assumed* that testosterone influences male aggression and estrogen makes people want to cuddle babies, much of this research has not questioned the relationship of hormones to maleness and femaleness. Testosterone and estrogen have been typed as "sex hormones" for little reason, according to Fausto-Sterling (2000), since all bodies possess both kinds of hormones and both function in many ways to affect the body far beyond one's sex organs. She writes:

> Why, then, have hormones always been strongly associated with the idea of sex, when, in fact, "sex hormones" apparently affect organs throughout the entire body and are not specific to either gender? The brain, lungs, bones, blood vessels, intestine, and liver (to give a partial list) all use estrogen to maintain proper growth and development . . . . Researchers accomplished this feat by defining as sex hormones what are, in effect, multi-site chemical growth regulators, thus rendering their far-reaching, non-sexual roles in both male and female development nearly invisible. (147)

Most importantly, Fausto-Sterling offers the critique that scientists' social presumptions about bodies originate in the gender box structure that has far too narrowly focused scientific study and, hence, our interpretation of its results. To paraphrase Lorber's (1993) important article, "Believing Is Seeing," first we believed in gender, then we found it in bodies (578) . . . .

## The Gender Feedback Loop

We propose a new diagram that we call the gender feedback loop that we believe describes the lived experience of individuals much better than the heteronormative box structure. Rather than suggest that the human population fits into one of two "natural" boxes, we assert that each person experiences a feedback loop of ideas about bodies and what are deemed appropriate gender expressions that entice each of us to behave as expected. Mapping out her argument for the social embodiment of gender, Connell (2002) agrees with our argument for a gender feedback loop when she writes:

Bodies are both objects of social practice and agents in social practice. The same bodies, at the same time, are both . . . . There is a loop, circuit, linking bodily processes and social structures. In fact, there is a tremendous number of such circuits. They occur in historical time, and change over time. They add up to the historical process in which society is embodied, and bodies are drawn into history. (47)

This loop ultimately confirms itself by encouraging each of us to produce the gender expression expected of us, which we incorrectly read as "only natural." Throughout this reading we explain the

**Figure 3.2**   Gender Feedback Loop: Performance/Surveillance/Resistance. Through gender performance and public surveillance, people put gender messages into action using the body, often confirming and sometimes disrupting those messages in aconstant feedback loop.

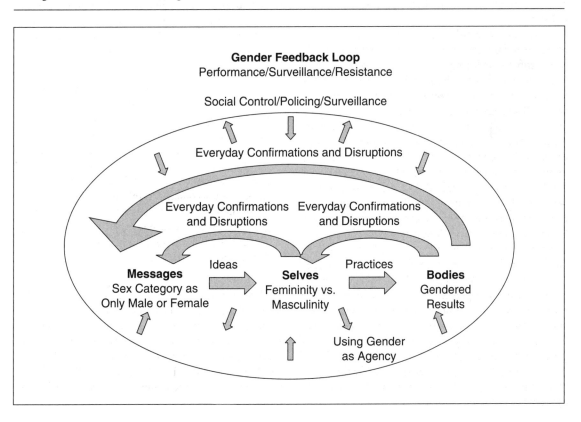

details of our argument, but let us take a moment to summarize the argument here.

If this figure looks daunting, it is not surprising. The figure is complex because the operation of gender in our worlds is complex. So here we walk you through the details, adding some crib notes to the figure (see Figure 3.2). The figure begins with gendered messages or ideas from our culture that we "inherit" in a sense from previous generations, so, to some extent, the messages are not something we each invent. The messages are notions about how the world exists and are based in the current historical moment in which we have been using science to understand the world around us for about a couple of hundred years. The messages come to us from our families, churches, schools, peers, and media outlets and tell us that there are only two options for biological sex—male or female—and that sex is determinant of the kind of person we are to be in the world. The messages then are a set of ideas that suggest to us how to think about our "selves"— about what is "appropriately" masculine or feminine. They produce expectations for each of our individual selves, which cause us to engage in body practices or gender performances, both of which shore up our ideas about self and our beliefs in the naturalness of gendered practices.

Of course, you are a thinking person. You do not always do exactly as you are told. The arrows looping back to "messages" and "selves" show us that our interactions help to confirm and sometimes change (although usually very modestly) our ideas about self or the cultural messages themselves. Hence, the entire process is a feedback loop of the interplay of personal thought and social interaction for each person. The oval surrounding the figure suggests that all of these experiences exist in an environment of social conformity in interaction in which we are encouraged by others and the social setting to act in conformist ways. Although we are given these conformist instructions and we may often follow them, we also resist as individuals and as groups. So the experience is not so much a linear one of conforming to fit appropriately into boxes, but rather a swirling, interactive one of gendered messages, self- measurement and assessment, and

finding ways for each of us to conform to certain ideals and also to exercise some latitude to become individuals. All this happens in social interaction with others and is constantly changing but continually referring to messages that pre-existed each of us. Hence, the process is complex, ongoing, interactive, and occurring in real time in every social situation.

## DISCUSSION QUESTIONS

1. How do Crawley, Foley, and Shehan support their claim that we have "embodied knowledge" because the physical experience of our bodies cannot be separated from cultural and social practices?
2. Were gender a "natural" binary system, it would be invariable over time and place, yet it is not. Discuss the significance of this idea as a refutation to the overall argument being made in this reading.
3. How does "dualistic thinking" serve to exclude many elements of sexuality that have in recent decades, to the contrary, become front-and-center talking points in the gay movement?

## NOTES

1. Here we reference the work of Michel Foucault (1977, 1980). We use the terms *messages* or *cultural messages* in much the same way that he uses *discourses,* or in the way Dorothy Smith (1987) uses the term *relations of ruling* to imply a discursive form of power as social control.
2. Here, although we are describing closely the important work of Kessler and McKenna (1978), we cite Schutz's notion of *typification,* rather than Garfinkel's notion of *attribution* as Kessler and McKenna do. We do so consciously. Although we concede that Garfinkel's (1967) legendary discussion of Agnes was likely the original "queer theory" in that he was the first to take seriously the idea that binary sex (or "sexual status" as he put it) is a socially constructed reality, we feel Schutz's concept of typification is more accessible to a

broader audience than Garfinkel's attribution and more useful for theorizing how gender works than ethnomethodology's goal of only describing lived realities.

3. Interestingly, cooking is understood as masculine and appropriate for males if the person who is cooking is paid well for the skill. So, according to the typification, "being a chef" is typically understood as appropriate for men, whom we expect to be highly paid, whereas "cooking" is a feminine thing women do for free on an everyday basis for their families.

4. While Kinsey is often heralded as the father of sexology, the scientific study of human sexuality, other lesser-known writers and scholars were studying these same issues (although perhaps not on such a grand scale) at the same time as Kinsey (see Hohman and Schaffner 1947), and even a decade before Kinsey (see Bromley and Britten 1938).

5. We find it unfortunate that the national discussion of being "on the down low" seems to target primarily black men as those who engage in clandestine sex with other men. As documented famously by Laud Humphreys' *Tea Room Trade* in 1970, this practice is neither new nor specific to black men.

6. The term *hermaphrodite* was formerly used to describe intersexed people, but is now considered a derogatory term.

7. See the Intersex Society of North America's website: http://www.isna.org.

8. Even among transsexuals there is disagreement about the degree to which gender is innate. Some transsexuals argue that gender is a very original, if not genetic, component of their personhood, and that therefore gender is more fixed than sex and can be understood in binary ways (Feinberg 1996; Green 2004). There are other transsexuals who argue that gender and sex are historically situated and should not be viewed as inflexible or binary (Bornstein 1994; Rubin 2003; Stone 1991). Often these are diametrically opposed arguments. Nonetheless, most agree that the ability to reconstruct sexual bodies to live as another sex suggests that your genital body at birth does not predict your gender or sexual orientation as the gender box structure would anticipate.

# 4

# THE SOCIAL CONSTRUCTION OF DISABILITY

SUSAN WENDELL

*Susan Wendell is professor emerita of women's studies at Simon Fraser University, British Columbia. In this excerpt from her 1996 book,* The Rejected Body: Feminist Philosophical Reflections on Disability, *Wendell introduces us to the social construction of disability. Similar to arguments made in the previous reading by Crawley, Foley, and Shehan, Wendell argues that the biological dimensions of disability are linked to the social construction of disability. Moreover, this social construction is influenced by a number of social factors, including physical illness and injury, the pace of life, culture, and the social organization of society.*

In earlier research, I argued that neither impairment nor disability can be defined purely in biomedical terms, because social arrangements and expectations make essential contributions to impairment and disability, and to their absence. In this reading, I develop that argument further. I maintain that the distinction between the biological reality of a disability and the social construction of a disability cannot be made sharply, because the biological and the social are interactive in creating disability. They are interactive not only in that complex interactions of social factors and our bodies affect health and functioning, but also in that social arrangements can make a biological condition more or less relevant to almost any situation. I call the interaction of the biological and the social to create (or prevent) disability "the social construction of disability." . . .

I see disability as socially constructed in ways ranging from social conditions that straightforwardly create illnesses, injuries, and poor physical functioning, to subtle cultural factors that determine

*Source:* Wendell, Susan. "The Social Construction of Disability." In *The Rejected Body: Feminist Philosophical Reflections on Disability.* Copyright © 1996 Taylor and Francis Group LLC–Books. Reprinted with permission.

standards of normality and exclude those who do not meet them from full participation in their societies. I could not possibly discuss all the factors that enter into the social construction of disability here, and I feel sure that I am not aware of them all, but I will try to explain and illustrate the social construction of disability by discussing what I hope is a representative sample from a range of factors.

## SOCIAL FACTORS THAT CONSTRUCT DISABILITY

First, it is easy to recognize that social conditions affect people's bodies by creating or failing to prevent sickness and injury. Although, since disability is relative to a person's physical, social, and cultural environment, none of the resulting physical conditions is necessarily disabling, many do in fact cause disability given the demands and lack of support in the environments of the people affected. In this direct sense of damaging people's bodies in ways that are disabling in their environments, much disability is created by the violence of invasions, wars, civil wars, and terrorism, which cause disabilities not only through direct injuries to combatants and noncombatants, but also through the spread of disease and the deprivations of basic needs that result from the chaos they create. In addition, although we more often hear about them when they cause death, violent crimes such as shootings, knifings, beatings, and rape all cause disabilities, so that a society's success or failure in protecting its citizens from injurious crimes has a significant effect on its rates of disability.[1]

The availability and distribution of basic resources such as water, food, clothing, and shelter have major effects on disability, since much disabling physical damage results directly from malnutrition and indirectly from diseases that attack and do more lasting harm to the malnourished and those weakened by exposure. Disabling diseases are also contracted from contaminated water when clean water is not available. Here too, we usually learn more about the deaths caused by lack of basic resources than the (often life-long) disabilities of survivors.

Many other social factors can damage people's bodies in ways that are disabling in their environments, including (to mention just a few) tolerance of high-risk working conditions; abuse and neglect of children; low public safety standards; the degradation of the environment by contamination of air, water, and food; and the overwork, stress, and daily grinding deprivations of poverty. The social factors that can damage people's bodies almost always affect some groups in a society more than others because of racism, sexism, heterosexism, ageism, and advantages of class background, wealth, and education.[2]

Medical care and practices, traditional and Western-scientific, play an important role in both preventing and creating disabling physical damage. (They also play a role in defining disability . . . .) Lack of good prenatal care and dangerous or inadequate obstetrical practices cause disabilities in babies and in the women giving birth to them. Inoculations against diseases such as polio and measles prevent quite a lot of disability. Inadequate medical care of those who are already ill or injured results in unnecessary disablement. On the other hand, the rate of disability in a society increases with improved medical capacity to save the lives of people who are dangerously ill or injured in the absence of the capacity to prevent or cure all the physical damage they have incurred. Moreover, public health and sanitation measures that increase the average lifespan also increase the number of old people with disabilities in a society, since more people live long enough to become disabled.

The *pace of life* is a factor in the social construction of disability that particularly interests me, because it is usually taken for granted by nondisabled people, while many people with disabilities are acutely aware of how it marginalizes or threatens to marginalize us. I suspect that increases in the pace of life are important social causes of damage to people's bodies through rates of accident, drug and alcohol abuse, and illnesses that result from people's neglecting their needs for rest and good nutrition. But the pace of life also affects disability as a second form of social construction, the social construction of disability through expectations of performance.[3]

When the pace of life in a society increases, there is a tendency for more people to become disabled, not only because of physically damaging consequences of efforts to go faster, but also because fewer people can meet expectations of "normal" performance; the physical (and mental) limitations of those who cannot meet the new pace become conspicuous and disabling, even though the same limitations were inconspicuous and irrelevant to full participation in the slower-paced society. Increases in the pace of life can be counterbalanced for some people by improvements in accessibility, such as better transportation and easier communication, but for those who must move or think slowly, and for those whose energy is severely limited, expectations of pace can make work, recreational, community, and social activities inaccessible . . . .

Expectations of performance are reflected, because they are assumed, in the social organization and physical structure of a society, both of which create disability. Societies that are physically constructed and socially organized with the unacknowledged assumption that everyone is healthy, non-disabled, young but adult, shaped according to cultural ideals, and, often, male, create a great deal of disability through sheer neglect of what most people need in order to participate fully in them.

Feminists talk about how the world has been designed for the bodies and activities of men. In many industrialized countries, including Canada and the United States, life and work have been structured as though no one of any importance in the public world, and certainly no one who works outside the home for wages, has to breast-feed a baby or look after a sick child. Common colds can be acknowledged publicly, and allowances are made for them, but menstruation cannot be acknowledged and allowances are not made for it. Much of the public world is also structured as though everyone were physically strong, as though all bodies were shaped the same, as though everyone could walk, hear, and see well, as though everyone could work and play at a pace that is not compatible with any kind of illness or pain, as though no one were ever dizzy or incontinent or simply needed to sit or lie down. (For instance, where could you rest for a few minutes in a supermarket if you needed to?) Not only the architecture, but the entire physical and social organization of life tends to assume that we are either strong and healthy and able to do what the average young, non-disabled man can do or that we are completely unable to participate in public life.

A great deal of disability is caused by this physical structure and social organization of society. For instance, poor architectural planning creates physical obstacles for people who use wheelchairs, but also for people who can walk but cannot walk far or cannot climb stairs, for people who cannot open doors, and for people who can do all of these things but only at the cost of pain or an expenditure of energy they can ill afford. Some of the same architectural flaws cause problems for pregnant women, parents with strollers, and young children. This is no coincidence. Much architecture has been planned with a young adult, non-disabled male paradigm of humanity in mind. In addition, aspects of social organization that take for granted the social expectations of performance and productivity, such as inadequate public transportation (which I believe assumes that no one who is needed in the public world needs public transportation), communications systems that are inaccessible to people with visual or hearing impairments, and inflexible work arrangements that exclude part-time work or rest periods, create much disability.

When public and private worlds are split, women (and children) have often been relegated to the private, and so have the disabled, the sick, and the old. The public world is the world of strength, the positive (valued) body, performance and production, the non-disabled, and young adults. Weakness, illness, rest and recovery, pain, death, and the negative (devalued) body are private, generally hidden, and often neglected. Coming into the public world with illness, pain, or a devalued body, people encounter resistance to mixing the two worlds; the split is vividly revealed. Much of the experience of disability and illness goes underground, because there is no socially acceptable way of expressing it and having the physical and psychological experience acknowledged. Yet acknowledgement of this experience is exactly what is required for creating accessibility in the public world. The more a society regards disability as a private matter, and people with disabilities as belonging in the private sphere, the more disability it creates by failing to make the public sphere accessible to a wide range of people.

Disability is also socially constructed by the failure to give people the amount and kind of help they need to participate fully in all major aspects of life in the society, including making a significant contribution in the form of work. Two things are important to remember about the help that people with disabilities may need. One is that most industrialized societies give non-disabled people (in different degrees and kinds, depending on class, race, gender, and other factors) a lot of help in the form of education, training, social support, public communication and transportation facilities, public recreation, and other services. The help that non-disabled people receive tends to be taken for granted and not considered help but entitlement, because it is offered to citizens who fit the social paradigms, who by definition are not considered dependent on social help. It is only when people need a different kind or amount of help than that given to "paradigm" citizens that it is considered help at all, and they are considered socially dependent. Second, much, though not all, of the help that people with disabilities need is required because their bodies were damaged by social conditions, or because they cannot meet social expectations of performance, or because the narrowly conceived physical structure and social organization of society have placed them at a disadvantage; in other words, it is needed to overcome problems that were created socially.

Thus disability is socially constructed through the failure or unwillingness to create ability among people who do not fit the physical and mental profile of "paradigm" citizens. Failures of social support for people with disabilities result in inadequate rehabilitation, unemployment, poverty, inadequate personal and medical care, poor communication services, inadequate training and education, poor protection from physical, sexual, and emotional abuse, minimal opportunities for social learning and interaction, and many other disabling situations that hurt people with disabilities and exclude them from participation in major aspects of life in their societies . . . .

## CULTURAL CONSTRUCTION OF DISABILITY

Culture makes major contributions to disability. These contributions include not only the omission of experiences of disability from cultural representations of life in a society, but also the cultural stereotyping of people with disabilities, the selective stigmatization of physical and mental limitations and other differences (selective because not all limitations and differences are stigmatized, and different limitations and differences are stigmatized in different societies), the numerous cultural meanings attached to various kinds of disability and illness, and the exclusion of people with disabilities from the cultural meanings of activities they cannot perform or are expected not to perform.

The lack of realistic cultural representations of experiences of disability not only contributes to the "Otherness" of people with disabilities by encouraging the assumption that their lives are inconceivable to non-disabled people but also increases non-disabled people's fear of disability by suppressing knowledge of how people live with disabilities. Stereotypes of disabled people as dependent, morally depraved, superhumanly heroic, asexual, and/or pitiful are still the most common cultural portrayals of people with disabilities (Kent 1988; Dahl 1993). Stereotypes repeatedly get in the way of full participation in work and social life. For example, Francine Arsenault, whose leg was damaged by childhood polio and later by gangrene, describes the following incident at her wedding:

> When I got married, one of my best friends came to the wedding with her parents. I had known her parents all the time I was growing up; we visited in each other's homes and I thought that they knew my situation quite well.
>
> But as the father went down the reception line and shook hands with my husband, he said, "You know, I used to think that Francine was intelligent, but to put herself on you as a burden like this shows that I was wrong all along. (Arsenault 1994:6)

Here the stereotype of a woman with a disability as a helpless, dependent burden blots out, in the friend's father's consciousness, both the reality that Francine simply has one damaged leg and the probability that her new husband wants her for her other qualities. Moreover, the man seems to take for granted that the new husband sees Francine in the same stereotyped way (or else he risks incomprehension or rejection), perhaps because he counts on the cultural assumptions about people with disabilities. I think both the stigma of physical "imperfection" (and possibly the additional stigma of having been damaged by disease) and the cultural meanings attached to the disability contribute to the power of the stereotype in situations like this. Physical "imperfection" is more likely to be thought to "spoil" a woman than a man by rendering her unattractive in a culture where her physical appearance is a large component of a woman's value; having a damaged leg probably evokes the metaphorical meanings of being "crippled," which include helplessness, dependency, and pitifulness.[4] Stigma, stereotypes, and cultural meanings are all related and interactive in the cultural construction of disability . . . .

The power of culture alone to construct a disability is revealed when we consider bodily differences—deviations from a society's conception of a "normal" or acceptable body—that, although they cause little or no functional or physical difficulty for the person who has them, constitute major social disabilities. An important example is facial scarring, which is a disability of appearance only, a disability constructed totally by stigma and cultural meanings.[5] Stigma, stereotypes, and cultural meanings are also the primary components of other disabilities, such as mild epilepsy and not having a "normal" or acceptable body size . . . .

I believe that in thinking about the social construction of disability we need to strike a balance between, on the one hand, thinking of a body's abilities and limitations as given by nature and/or accident, as immutable and uncontrollable, and, on the other hand, thinking of them as so constructed by society and culture as to be controllable by human thought, will, and action. We need to acknowledge that social justice and cultural change can eliminate a great deal of disability while recognizing that there may be much suffering and limitation that they cannot fix.

## SOCIAL DECONSTRUCTION OF DISABILITY

In my view, then, disability is socially constructed by such factors as social conditions that cause or fail to prevent damage to people's bodies; expectations of performance; the physical and social organization of societies on the basis of a young, non-disabled, "ideally shaped," healthy adult male paradigm of citizens; the failure or unwillingness to create ability among citizens who do not fit the paradigm; and cultural representations, failures of representation, and expectations. Much, but perhaps not all, of what can be socially constructed can be socially (and not just intellectually) deconstructed, given means and the will.

A great deal of disability can be prevented with good public health and safety standards and practices, but also by relatively minor changes in the built environment that provide accessibility to people with a wide range of physical characteristics and abilities. Many measures that are usually regarded as helping or accommodating people who are now disabled, such as making buildings and public places wheelchair accessible, creating and respecting parking spaces for people with disabilities, providing American Sign Language translation, captioning, and Telephone Devices for the Deaf, and making tapes and Descriptive Video services available for people who are visually impaired, should be seen as preventive, since a great deal of disability is created by building and organizing environments, objects, and activities for a too-narrow range of people. Much more could be done along the same lines by putting people with a wide variety of physical abilities and characteristics in charge of deconstructing disability. People with disabilities should be in charge, because people without disabilities are unlikely to see many of the obstacles in their environment. Moreover, they are likely not to see them *as obstacles* even when they are pointed out, but rather as "normal" features of the built environment that present difficulties for "abnormal" people . . . .

Attitudes that disability is a personal or family problem (of biological or accidental origin), rather than a matter of social responsibility, are cultural contributors to disability and powerful factors working against social measures to increase ability. The attitude that disability is a personal problem is manifested when people with disabilities are expected to overcome obstacles to their participation in activities by their own extraordinary efforts. The public adoration of a few disabled heroes who are believed to have "overcome their handicaps" against great odds both demonstrates and contributes to this expectation. The attitude that disability is a family matter is manifested when the families of people with disabilities are expected to provide whatever they need, even at great personal sacrifice by other family members. Barbara Hillyer describes the strength of expectations that mothers and other caregivers will do whatever is necessary to "normalize" the lives of family members, especially children, with disabilities—not only providing care, but often doing the work of two people to maintain the illusion that there is nothing "wrong" in the family (Hillyer 1993).

These attitudes are related to the fact that many modern societies split human concerns into public and private worlds. Typically, those with disabilities and illnesses have been relegated to the private realm, along with women, children, and the old. This worldwide tendency creates particularly intractable problems for women with disabilities, since they fit two "private" categories, they are often kept at home, isolated and overprotected (Driedger and Gray 1992). In addition, the confinement of people with disabilities in the private realm exploits women's traditional caregiving roles in order to meet the needs of people with disabilities (Hillyer 1993), and it hides the need for measures to make the public realm accessible to everyone.

There also seem to be definite material advantages for some people (people without disabilities who have no disabled friends or relatives for whom they feel responsible) to seeing disability as a biological misfortune, the bad luck of individuals, and a personal or family problem. Accessibility and creating ability cost time, energy, and/or money. Charities for people with disabilities are big businesses that employ a great many non-disabled professionals; these charities depend upon the belief that responding to the difficulties faced by people with disabilities is superogatory for people who are not members of the family—not a social responsibility to be fulfilled through governments, but an act of kindness. Moreover, both the charities and most government bureaucracies (which also employ large numbers of non-disabled professionals) hand out help which would not be needed in a society that was planned and organized to include people with a wide range of physical and mental abilities. The potential resistance created by these vested interests in disability should not be underestimated . . . .

It seems that the cultural constructions of disability, including the ignorance, stereotyping, and stigmatization that feed fears of disability, have to be at least partly deconstructed before disability can be seen by more people as a set of social problems and social responsibilities. Until that change in perspective happens, people with disabilities and their families will continue to be given too much individual responsibility for 'overcoming' disabilities, expectations for the participation of people with disabilities in public life will be far too low, and social injustices that are recognized now (at least in the abstract), such as discrimination against people with disabilities, will be misunderstood.

## Discussion Questions

1. Discuss the various ways in which disability is socially constructed, using examples from this reading.
2. What are the social and cultural factors that largely determine what we label *disability*? How is disability treated in the United States?

## NOTES

1. For example, a friend who recently spent time in the spinal cord ward of a hospital in a major U.S. city discovered that many people in the ward had been shot.
2. For a discussion of the interactions of race, age, income, education, and marital status in the rates of work disability among women in the United States, see Russo and Jansen 1988.
3. For a discussion of how people with disabilities and those who care for them are affected by social expectations of pace, see Hillyer 1993, chapter 4, "Productivity and Pace."
4. For more on the cultural meanings of disabilities and illnesses, see Sontag 1977 and 1988; Fine and Asch 1988; Kleinman 1988; Morris 1991.
5. For a first-person account of living with facial scarring, see Grealy 1994.

# 5

# RETHINKING THE PARADIGM

*Class*

GERDA LERNER

*This reading by Gerda Lerner is the first of four readings that provide historical context to our understanding of race-ethnicity, social class, gender, and sexuality in the United States. History helps us to see when certain social categories were created, for what purpose, and for whose benefit. Lerner, a well-known feminist historian, is the Robinson-Edwards Professor of History, emerita, at the University of Wisconsin–Madison. This excerpt is from Lerner's 1997 book,* <u>Why History Matters: Life and Thought</u>, *in which she argues that social class is historically tied to the commodification and control of women's sexual and reproductive capacities. According to Lerner, we cannot understand social class without a gendered lens, because patriarchal practices such as marriage often uphold social class, property interests, and the generational transfer of wealth.*

No theoretical framework for conceptualizing the situation of women can be constructed without taking race as well as class fully into consideration. I will here attempt to discuss the way both concepts can be transformed by putting them into an interactive framework, and how such re-definition has transformational power.

When I began to write this essay, more than ten years ago, I still thought of class in Marxist terms as the relation of men to the means of production. I wanted to show how and why this definition did not fit women and did not do justice to their class position. As I continued to work through the historical material I realized that this definition of class also did not fit men adequately. To my amazement I arrived at a much more radical re-definition of class than I had initially intended. The essay reflects the growth and changes in my thought. I hope to take the reader through the evidence as I was taken and show her/him why my redefinition is preferable to the old way of thinking about the subject.

I will argue the following propositions:

*Class in its historical origins was not and is not now a separate construct from gender; rather class was and is expressed in generic terms. This means:*

1. The commodification of women's sexual and reproductive capacities formed one of the major sources for the creation of private property, on which class is based. Historically, class was constructed out of gender relations, which advantaged men over women.

2. Classes were formed and maintained by gendered marriage arrangements and inheritance practices.

3. Class must always be defined differently for men and women and has historically always been different for men and women. Men and women never belong to the same class in the same way. Class describes multilayered locations, relations and experiences, differing according to sex, race, nationality and stage in the life cycle.[1]

To elaborate on these propositions I will briefly discuss their origins in the Ancient Near East and, focusing on points 2 and 3, give examples from medieval Europe and then show the continuity of these organizing principles in the development of early capitalism. I distinguish between class formation and class maintenance as two different processes in which elites pursue different strategies.

1. The commodification of women's sexual and reproductive capacities formed one of the basic sources for the accumulation of private property on which class is based. Historically, class was constructed out of gender relations which advantaged men over women.

Patriarchy is a system, created by men and women in a process which in the Ancient Near East took nearly 1500 years (*ca.* 2100–*ca.* 600 B.C.). Patriarchy is not a historically unchanging social construct, but rather all historically known economic and social systems have incorporated the basic principles of patriarchy. Historians must study the ways in which the application of these patriarchal principles have changed over time, how they have been constructed and institutionalized at different periods and how and why they have so long remained invisible.

In its earliest form patriarchy appeared as the archaic state. Long before its formation in the 2nd millennium B.C. gender had already been created and defined.[2] Gender—the different roles and behavior deemed appropriate to each of the sexes—was expressed in values, customs, and social roles. During the long period that led to the establishment of patriarchally organized archaic states, gender definitions became institutionalized in laws, the organization of hierarchies and in religion. Gender was also expressed in leading metaphors that shaped the culture and entered the explanatory systems of Western civilization.

The sexuality of women, consisting of their sexual and their reproductive capacities and services, was commodified, even prior to the creation of archaic states. The development of agriculture in the Neolithic age fostered the inter-tribal "exchange of women," not only as a means of avoiding incessant warfare by the cementing of marriage alliances, but also because societies with more women could produce more children. In contrast to the economic needs of hunting/gathering societies, agriculturists could use the labor of children to increase production and accumulate surpluses. The first gender-defined social role for women was to be those who were exchanged in marriage transactions. For men, the obverse gender role was to be those who do the exchanging or define the terms of the exchanges. As a result of such widespread practices, men had rights in women which women did not have in men. Women themselves became a resource, acquired by men, much as the land was acquired by men.[3]

After the establishment of class societies, women of elite groups shared in their husbands' power in their gender-defined role of "deputy-husband."[4] Fulfilling this role meant that elite women, in the temporary absence of their husbands, could substitute for them in their public functions. Such women also provided connections and linkages between elite families and alternately represented their fathers' and their husbands' interests. They had considerable power and privileges, but their power depended on their attachment to elite men and was based on their satisfactory performance in rendering these men sexual and reproductive services. If a woman failed to meet these demands, she was quickly replaced and thereby lost all her privileges and standing. The wife as "deputy-husband" appears as early as 1790 B.C. in royal documents from the mesopotamian city of Mari. They detail the activities of Queen Shibtu, who, in the absence of her husband during warfare, reigned as his deputy, but who had to follow his orders to select from among captive women he sent home a number of the most attractive for his harem.[5]

2. Classes were formed and maintained by gendered marriage arrangements and inheritance practices.

From the inception of class structures, class was formed *genderically*. That is, some men accumulated land and wealth and controlled the reproduction of the females under their tutelage in such a way that ownership of resources was not threatened. But property accumulation, by itself, does not lead to class formation. *What turns property into class is a set of institutional practices that perpetuate property holdings within a small elite and assure the maintenance of this propertied elite over time.* The main instruments for this process are homogamy and gendered inheritance practices.

It is worth noting how crucial marriage settlements were to the stabilization of classes. Homogamy, the practice of restricting marriages to people within the same propertied group, assures the continuity of property holdings within that group. If men could marry beneath their own group, their property would not increase in marriage and quickly be depleted through the demands of impoverished kin. To secure homogamous marriages the propertied must control the sexuality of their children, but particularly that of their daughters. Homogamy is further reinforced by inheritance arrangements that assure patrilineal control over property.

In the Ancient Near East, homogamy and gendered inheritance practices developed simultaneously and in support of each other. Among the propertied group, marriages were contracted by negotiations between the fathers of bride and groom. The father of the bride received a bride price from the father of the groom. This bride price was offset by a somewhat smaller "settlement" or dowry, given by the father of the bride to the groom after the marriage had been consummated.

Bride price and dowry were material binders of the promise of the bride's virginity. If the bride turned out not to be a virgin at marriage, the bride price was returned and no dowry was given. If the bride was a virgin and the marriage was consummated, the dowry was given to the husband in usufruct, but it was understood that it or its equivalent would be returned to the donor should the marriage fail. Thus the couple had a joint property interest in the success of the marriage. At the death of the husband, the dowry constituted the main source of the widow's support. On her death, it was given to her sons as heirs. Thus, marital property passed from men to men *through* women.

In elite families the bride price received for a daughter frequently enabled the bride's family to secure more financially advantageous marriages for their sons, thus improving the family's economic position. This arrangement again helped to consolidate class formation within the elite.

At the very inception of patriarchy, Babylonian wives of the propertied classes had many civic and economic rights, even some rights in regard to decisions about their children. They could sign contracts, buy and sell land and slaves, and transact business in their own right. But their sexuality was strictly regulated. Thus, female adultery was punishable by death, whereas male adultery was not even considered a crime. Men could take second and third wives and use slave women for sexual services without any societal censure.

For the upper classes judicious management of the bride price and upwardly mobile marriages of sons guaranteed that property would stay and grow within the kin group. The acquisition of slaves would further improve the family's wealth, for female slaves produced textiles, which were a major export item, and their children could be sold or hired out profitably. The product of the commodification of women's sexuality—bride price, sales price and children—was appropriated by men.

If a family had a surplus of daughters they could and did designate one or more of them as priestesses. The dowry a priestess brought to the temple would revert back to her family upon her death, thus furthering the family's class position by not scattering its wealth to other families through marriage.

In Babylonian families of middle or lower range, where usually the only available property consisted of land, the bride price received for a daughter was essential in order to marry off the son. When no daughters were available, the couple often resorted to adoption of a girl. If marriage arrangements for daughters were unfavorable or impossible, the family would go into debt to hold on to its land. If a husband or father could not pay his debt, his wife and children could be used as pawns, becoming debt slaves to the creditor. These conditions were so firmly established by 1750 B.C. that Hammurabic law made a decisive improvement in the lot of debt slaves, by limiting their terms of service to three years, where as earlier it had been for life. The improvement in the lot of debt slaves coincided with a hardening of the conditions of slaves acquired by conquest.

For lower-class families the sexuality of their daughters became their one tangible and negotiable asset if their land failed to produce subsistence. Daughters were bartered for a favorable bride price, if and when possible; they could serve—together with their brothers—as debt slaves, and they might, with luck, become concubines. To the very poor, who had no movable property or land, marriage transactions for profit were not possible, but during bad times the daughters of the poor were sold into marriage or prostitution in order to advance the economic interests of their families.

We see here how the patrician or upper class was formed genderically and maintained through gendered marriage and inheritance practices; how the middling class or burghers maintained their position in the hierarchy through sexual politics; and how the lower classes, peasants and slaves, used male sexual privileges to maintain their precarious class position.

If we look at medieval Europe, we find similar processes of class formation on the basis of gendered family arrangements at work. This can best be discerned by studying the changes in marriage patterns and property arrangements among the warrior aristocracy, usually occurring when simpler forms of tribal organization gave way to more hierarchically organized states, led by a king and his bureaucrats. In western Europe, in the Frankish kingdom, the shift from Merovingian rule (481–751) to Carolingian society (768–884) offers a good vantage point for comparison. In England in the time prior to and past the Norman conquest (1066 A.D.) we find a comparable process.

The transition from tribe- and kinship-focused social organization to bureaucratic, hierarchical states occurred in western European countries somewhat earlier than it did in England, but with similar results for women. Clovis I, the first of the Merovingian line, after assassinating his rivals, made himself King of the Franks in 481 A.D. and expanded his realm by annexation of the disintegrating provinces of Roman Gaul. After his death Frankish royal power was weakened through the division of his land among his four sons and it remained weak under succeeding Merovingian rulers. Following upon the ascension of Charlemagne as King of the Franks in 768, the expansion of his realm through wars of annexation resulted in the creation of the Frankish Empire, and the crowning of Charlemagne as Holy Roman Emperor in 800. During his reign close cooperation between Church and state centralized power and strengthened the authority of both institutions.

By comparing conditions for women in the Frankish kingdom and in England we can observe a similar process of development: as royal power and Church power became bureaucratically institutionalized in national states, opportunities narrowed for women and their sexuality was more rigidly controlled than previously. Their access to property became more limited and their control of property weakened. Society increasingly viewed them as lifelong dependents of their fathers or their husbands, celebrated their role as mothers, nurturers and domestic care-givers, but restricted their public and political roles. These generalizations hold mostly for aristocratic women. Peasant and serf women were not as dramatically affected by these social changes.[6]

As in Anglo-Saxon England, so in Europe, polygamy, concubinage and forced marriage of widows by male kin were wide-spread among the nobility early in the Christian era. King Clovis's Salic law, issued between 507 and 511, was based on Germanic law, which valued women highly as child-bearers. Later Merovingian law codes also incorporated Roman law, which placed a married woman entirely under her husband's power.[7]

The Merovingian nobility increased and consolidated its wealth, i.e., it became a class, by conducting homogamous marriages and by manipulating the marriages of dependents so as to keep as far as possible the inheritance of land intact. Marriages were contracted without regard to the wishes or inclinations of the couple. Daughters were frequently forced into marriages by raw power and physical chastisement.

The marriage settlement was made by an exchange of gifts and a contract. The bride gift similar to the Mesopotamian bride price was given by the groom's kin to the male kin of the bride and was then wholly or in part turned over to the bride, to provide economic security for her in case she was repudiated. The betrothal followed and was considered binding, even if it was made when the bride was a child, which was often the case. Young women were strictly bound by the betrothal, but young men could repudiate it with ease, by forfeiting the bride gift. At the time of marriage, the bride's parents gave her a dowry, which would later serve as her dower in case of widowhood. Under Merovingian law, the husband controlled the wife's property. Wives were obliged to produce male heirs; failure to do so was always regarded as the wife's fault. She could be divorced; the marriage could be annulled; she could be set aside or imprisoned. Bride gift and dowry formed the basis of the widow's share of the estate, which was to provide her maintenance and that of her dependent children, but at her death it went either to her sons or to the male members of her family of origin. Note that here, too, as in the Ancient Near East, wealth passed from men to men *through* women.

Over time, the economic independence of women improved under Merovingian rule. A husband managed the wife's property, but he could not alienate it without her consent. Some women were given land and real property and gradually, under the influence of Roman law, daughters were able to claim an equal share with their brothers in their inheritances.

Some Merovingian women could escape forced marriage, by entering a quasi-marriage (similar to a common law marriage of later periods) without the consent of their parents. Such an arrangement, in which an unmarried woman lived with a man of her choice, deprived her of any economic rights in case her male partner abandoned her. Her parents could also deny her an inheritance. Still, such arrangements were socially recognized as valid marriages and the children were considered legitimate. It is significant from the point of view of tracing the connection between marriage regulation and class formation that in both Roman and Germanic laws unions of free and unfree partners were forbidden and punished with severe sanctions. The dilution of boundaries between free people and slaves threatened the foundation of class formation and was therefore to be avoided. Yet, noblemen often circumvented or ignored laws against the marriages of free persons to slaves, by offering land to free women who were willing to marry the slaves in their realm. Since by such marriages the free women became the lord's retainers, contributing their labor to his household, narrow economic interests prevailed over larger class interests.[8]

The conditions of widows were better under Merovingian law than under Roman, under which she remained a lifelong legal minor. As a widow she had all her husband's rights and became head of the household, which included having guardianship of minor children. She had to give up these rights when she remarried, in which case she also lost her dower rights . . . .

The situation of the lower orders, free peasants, serfs and slaves, was characterized by their dependence on their lords. Although they had life-long tenancy of their huts and fields, they were bound to the manor and its lord. Peasant women were obliged to get the lord's permission for marriage, but were otherwise free to choose the particular man they wanted. Male and female peasants had to pay the lord a marriage tax, known as *merchet*. Serfs could not contract marriage outside of the lord's realm. Free peasants and serfs owed military and economic tribute to their lords, usually in the form of several days' free labor each week. Since these obligations always included the labor of their wives and children, the nobility as a class directly profited from the marriages of their serfs and peasants.[9]

Within their own class, peasant women enjoyed greater equality with their men than did women of the nobility. Women made essential contributions to the family economy by weaving, spinning, and raising livestock, and their labor was highly regarded both by their men and their lords. Peasant women could improve their status by upwardly mobile marriages and even slave women could rise from concubine to legitimate wife.[10] Still, lower-class women had to bear the typical class burden of women: neither virginity nor married status protected them from the sexual exploitation of their masters. The nobleman routinely assumed and took advantage of his sexual prerogatives. Lower-class women routinely were subject to the demand for sexual services on the part of their masters and had few defenses against sexual assault.

It is also worth noting that when the peasantry began to evolve as a class out of serfdom, peasants began to adopt primogeniture or ultimogeniture (inheritance of the land by the youngest son), with daughters getting goods and tools for their dowry. This is another example of the way in which gendered inheritance, disadvantaging women, functions to create class.

If we now turn, for comparison, to pre-Conquest Anglo-Saxon England, we find a tribal social organization. Warriors acquired land by conquest or by donations to them by a chief or king whose vassal they became. In exchange for their military obligations to that chief, they administered the land and distributed resources to the men and women in their kin group and under their tutelage. Individuals and kin groups advanced in rank by allying with higher-ranking groups through marriages and vassalage.

Marriages were constituted by the payment of a bride price, a gift exchange and, later, by contract. But the contract could be broken by mutual consent and even by the woman alone. A married woman who had a lover, had the option of arranging for a consensual divorce. Her lover would abduct her, pay the husband a fine and buy him a new wife. Married women were entitled to the property they had brought into the marriage and could bequeath it to children of both sexes. Women could ask for a divorce and have it granted. When widowed, Anglo-Saxon wives received half of their husbands' property, if the marriage had produced children. If the marriage had been childless, the widow got only a child's portion of the inheritance. In either event, the widow was placed under male guardianship and was often forced to remarry. Concubinage among nobles was widespread, which offered an opportunity for lower-class (peasant) women to rise by way of sexual liaisons. Concubines became members of a man's household and their children could inherit, if their father so desired it.[11]

After the Norman Conquest, state power was consolidated, as kings created more royal bureaucracies, and kinship no longer was the chief determinant of advancement. In a development similar to what we have observed in the Carolingian Frankish realm, the legal status of women declined, as did the ability of lower-class women to be upwardly mobile through marriages and sexual unions. After the Conquest, bride price was gradually transformed so that most or all of it was now given to the bride, as a fund which would later supply her widow's portion, but the money remained under her husband's control during his lifetime.[12] By the end of the Anglo-Saxon period the buying of wives seemed to have abated, divorce initiated by women was no longer possible, and female adultery was severely punished. Married women still could engage in property transactions, but only with the consent of their husbands.[13]

In the pre-Conquest period nobles not only negotiated the marriages of their daughters and sisters, but also had the right to negotiate marriages of the widows of their vassals. Anglo-Saxon kings had the right to force widows to marry a man of the king's choosing. After the Conquest, widows were no longer subject to male guardianship and were able to avoid forced marriage. Henry I (reigned 1100–1135) declared that he would not force a widow to remarry and that she could have her dower, but collected fines from the widows for this prerogative. Henry II (reigned 1154–1189) also collected fines from widows both for their use of their dower, and if they refused remarriage.[14]

The concept of the legitimacy of children has long been an important aspect of class formation. By regulating the sexuality of daughters and wives, men can control the legitimacy of their descendants. Patriarchal marriage definitions based on the virginity of brides and the absolute fidelity of wives ensure the paternity of the householder and with it the legitimacy of his sons and heirs. By privileging legitimate offspring over illegitimate, the householder can keep his property from being divided among too large a pool of children. The law codes of the Ancient Near East gave fathers the right to legitimize the children of concubines or slaves by a certain public declaration, thus disadvantaging the children of the first or legitimate wife.[15] In effect this prerogative would have been used mostly if a man sexually tired of his first wife and wished to please or pacify a second or third wife. Women never had this power. This is another instance of the institutionalization of men's control over female reproduction, which made her privileges dependent on the satisfactory performance of her sexual services to her husband.

As we have seen, males of the upper nobility in early medieval Europe enjoyed sexual privileges similar to those of Babylonian men. Merovingian nobles could declare the sons of their second or third wives or even those of a slave concubine to be legitimate heirs.

In its turn the Church of Rome used sexual control over women and men as a primary means for its own consolidation of power. As Christianity advanced in England and on the Continent, the Church sought to assert its control over the regulation of marriages. Beginning in the 9th century the Church gradually secured the abolition of polygamy and gained control over marriage rituals, and insisted, above all, upon the indissolubility of marriages. Secular Carolingian legislation outlawed divorce and brought marriage practices more firmly under Church control. Indissoluble monogamous marriage upgraded the position of wives, but it also increased wife abuse and weakened the economic power of women. With the downgrading of quasi-marriages the road to upward mobility of lower-class women through sexual liaisons was closed.[16]

The success of the Church in winning control over marriage rituals also increased its ability to enforce rules of legitimacy. Any privileges extended to bastard children and their mothers were strongly opposed by the Church. It insisted on the inheritance rights of "legitimate" children (those stemming from a monogamous marriage) over "illegitimate" children (those stemming from concubinage and extramarital relations), who were to be disinherited. The firmer lines drawn between legitimate and illegitimate heirs tended to strengthen class formation in the nobility and to sharpen class divisions.

Concubinage proved to be most resistant to reform efforts and continued into the 11th century. In the Merovingian period the Church began a systematic campaign for celibacy of the clergy, by insisting that married men who became clerics must abandon their wives and cease having sexual intercourse. In the Carolingian period, the Church, now transformed into a *Reichskirche* (state church), became more tightly organized, and better able to enforce internal discipline. Clerics were forbidden to live with women other than close blood relatives, and thousands of priests' concubines and their children were cast out and abandoned. The aim was the institution of a celibate clergy, which would benefit the Church by keeping its priesthood free from temptation toward the acquisition and holding of property. A celibate clergy free of personal property would not put family interest above the interests of the Church. This aim was not fully realized until the reform campaigns in the 11th century. Noble families, instead of enriching individual priests, would now have an incentive to leave their property to the Church. The connection between sexual regulation and economic power is evident: in enforcing the celibacy of the clergy, the Church vastly increased its landed property until it held nearly half of the land in Western Europe.

In the process of the consolidation of Church power, the division between male and female religious sharpened. The secure monopoly of the Church over education enhanced the position of the educated male clergy, while restricting the role of the female religious. By the middle of the 12th century double monasteries, ruled over by female abbesses, had virtually disappeared. Total enclosure of female religious and their supervision by priests had become the norm. The study of Latin by nuns, which had been widespread in the early Middle Ages, became the exception.

Similar to developments in the Church, the consolidation of secular power in nation-states was based, at least in part, on curtailment of the rights of women. Although marital and spousal rights varied greatly by region, we can generalize that by the 12th century women's property and dower rights were more closely circumscribed, their rights as widows curtailed, and a number of economic rights which they had enjoyed in the earlier centuries now restricted.[17] . . .

From the early Renaissance on, the growth of capitalism was supported by the marriage market. As usual, the relatively favorable conditions for women in the early phases of the new economic system gradually became more restricted and disadvantageous. In the 14th century, women could hold membership in about a third of the existing guilds in Paris and in other European cities and were listed in a broad range of craft guilds, but by the 17th century they were excluded from membership in most of the guilds. Even in formerly predominantly female occupations, such as brewing, weaving and work in the silk industry, women were gradually prohibited from using new technologies or new materials. Increasing regulation and gendered restrictions confined women to the least profitable work and technological advances and increased specialization worked to their disadvantage.[18]

As women's autonomous occupations shrank, their dependence on making a prudent and advantageous marriage intensified. The plight of women who through their own actions or because of the folly of a father made imprudent marriages or failed to get married at all is vividly reflected in the fictional literature of the 18th and 19th centuries. Not until the second half of the 19th century would women be able to choose careers and lifestyles that would give them economic independence apart from and outside of marriage.

As one historian has observed:

> Rules concerning married women's property have always functioned to facilitate the transmission of significant property from male to male; entitlements of women have been to provide them with subsistence for themselves and minor children who are dependent upon them. Men want women to have enough to survive . . . but not enough to exercise the power that comes with a significant accumulation of property.[19]

Thus, the medieval widow would lose her dower property if she remarried or committed fornication (1285). A wife lost her dower if she eloped or committed adultery. Eighteenth- century British and U.S. law hedged widows' dower rights as had medieval law. And even in the 20th century, divorced wives can lose alimony, trust funds or pension benefits if they remarry.[20]

A detailed consideration of European and British inheritance laws and customs in the 17th and 18th centuries is beyond the scope of this essay, but certain patterns can be noted. There is general agreement by historians that for aristocratic families, marriages consistently were instruments for improving the landholdings of the family dynasty and for enhancing the family's power. Thus, the prudent management of marriages served the interest of class formation. Class maintenance, on the other hand, demanded the development of strategies which would guarantee that land would not be dispersed among too many heirs and that favorable marriage alliances could be contracted with offspring of the rising middle class. Male inheritance and primogeniture had served to keep land together; now trust and marriage settlements were developed to assure that younger children, sons and daughters disadvantaged by primogenture, would have some share in the family income so as to enable them to make upwardly mobile marriages. Eileen Spring has argued persuasively that the purposes of the "strict settlement," an inheritance settlement made at the time of the eldest son's marriage, which came into extensive use in the 17th century and provided for inheritance in the male line, was to preserve estates, patrilineally and in the interests of patriarchy. The over-all effect of changing patterns of marriage arrangements was a "decline of women's rights over land."[21]

In the same period the rising middle class, wealthy professional and businessmen, married into the gentry and followed the gentry mode of class formation by buying land and holding on to it through gendered marriage and inheritance arrangements that strengthened male control over land and wealth.

As we can see, there is a continuity over several millennia in the way gender relations interconnect with class formation and maintenance of class status. Every major historical development in the formation of classes—slavery in the Ancient Near East; the formation of states in the early Middle Ages; the emergence of nation-states; the consolidation of Church power; the rise of bourgeois capitalism—depended on the regulation of women's reproduction and on limiting their direct access to economic power . . . .

From the 16th to the 19th century, peasant populations in Europe and England gradually were transformed into industrial workers. During this early stage of industrialization before the factory system, peasant households became part of the "putting-out" system, whereby merchant-capitalists supplied raw materials and tools to the rural workers and marketed their finished products, paying them a pittance. Conditions in the cottage industries broke the power of peasant patriarchs to control the marriages and lives of their children. It also undermined the modicum of financial independence peasant women had been able to gain by selling the products of their domestic labor—eggs, butter, yarn, wool—in local markets. Since family labor, not land, provided the basis of the family's survival, young men and women could found new households, new units of labor, without regard to their parents' wishes. The essence of the putting-out system was the unlimited supply of cheap labor provided by the peasants and their families. With substandard pay for labor, only the

work of the entire family could provide the equivalent of one living wage. The self-exploitation of home-industry workers was ensured by their not being paid a wage, but rather, as independent producers, being paid for their product. Child labor became a survival necessity for rural workers. The work of women and children in home industry thus subsidized the profits and capital accumulation on which industrialization was based. We find the same system in different form operating in the early 19th century in the cities of the eastern United States.

It is tempting to think of the exploited home-industrial workers as belonging to the same class, men, women and children. The merchant-capitalist contracted with the male householder for work performed by the entire family. Wife and children thus functioned as unpaid hired help of the father. But the home-weaver's wife, in addition to her own labor as a weaver or spinner, also had to provide the family with children, whose labor in turn could make the difference between starvation and family survival. The reproductive and household labor of women of this class was, as usual everywhere, unpaid, a double burden for the already overburdened woman. When increased fertility led to an oversupply of rural labor and with it a lowering of pay standards, further pauperization ensued. Poor peasants were turned into landless peasants; rural cottage workers became an industrial proletariat.

In the period of mature capitalism, in the 19th and the early 20th century, the continuation of the upper and middle classes depended, as it had earlier, on homogamy and gendered inheritance practices. The passage of women's property-rights legislation in the later half of the 19th century improved the economic position of middle-class wives. But class stability increasingly rested on the gendered availability of another resource crucial to the success of industrialization: education.

I have shown elsewhere that women were systematically educationally disadvantaged in every known patriarchal society, always with the exception of a small group of elite women, whose education served to advance the interests of their kin group in case of the absence of suitable male heirs.[22] Still, as long as informal, household-based education in skills and trades prepared young people for future occupations, gender differences in access to education did not matter very much. But with the rise of capitalism access to education became a precondition for economic success, especially after entry into politics, professions and technical training depended on university training. Universities had, from their inception in the 11th century, been closed to women. In Europe, in England and in the United States, women's primary and secondary education also lagged far behind that of men, as did their literacy rates.

The systematic under-education of women constituted, in the first place, a maldistribution of resources, which benefited males in every class. Family resources were spent on the education of sons and were withheld from daughters, which constitutes a tangible economic advantage for sons. By it, women were denied economic opportunities that might maintain them independent of marriage. Married women who faced the need for self- or family support were forced into the lowest-paying jobs by their educational deprivation. Thus, the issue of access to education became, for women, the primary and earliest demand in their search for emancipation . . . .

The general connection between access to education and class can be stated as follows: Throughout historical time education was, above all, a class privilege. But it also was a male gender privilege, which served to maintain class . . . .

From its inception in slavery, class dominance took different forms for men and women: men were primarily exploited as workers; women were always exploited as workers, as providers of sexual services and as reproducers. The historical record of every slave society offers evidence for this generalization. The sexual exploitation of lower-class women by upper-class men can be shown in antiquity, under feudalism, in the middle-class households of 19th and 20th-century Europe, in the complex sex/race relations between women of the colonized countries and their male colonizers—it is ubiquitous and pervasive. For women, sexual exploitation is the very mark of class exploitation.

Class for men was first and foremost based on their relation to the means of production: those who owned the means of production could dominate those who did not. The owners of the means of production also acquired the commodity of female sexual services, both from women of their own class and from women of the subordinate classes. Additionally, men were entitled to the domestic and child-rearing services of women in exchange for women's economic maintenance. This labor-for-maintenance arrangement, which characterizes slavery, continued for women through all historic changes in economic systems, from ancient slavery to modern capitalism. In Ancient Mesopotamia, in classical antiquity and in slave societies, dominant males also acquired, as property, the product of the reproductive capacity of subordinate women—children, to be worked, traded, married off or sold as slaves, as the case might be.

For women, class is mediated through their sexual ties to a man. It is through the man that women have access to or are denied access to the means of production and to resources. It is through their sexual behavior that they gain access to class. "Respectable women" gain access to class through their fathers and husbands, but breaking the sexual rules can at once declass them. "Sexual deviance" marks a woman as "not respectable," which in fact consigns her to the lowest class status possible. We find the first institutional vestige of this definition in Middle Assyrian Law # 40 (recorded 1500–1100 B.C.), which prescribes the dress of women. The law distinguished between women who are sexually attached to one man—wives and daughters of burghers and free men, concubine wives accompanied by their mistress and married hierodules (temple servants)—and those who are not—harlots, slave women and unmarried hierodules. The former are permitted to appear in public veiled, the latter are forbidden to wear the veil. The law imposes severe penalties on female violators and equally severe penalties on males who fail to denounce and prosecute female violators. Since the penalties are public and enforced by the courts, we can assumed that the enforcing of visible class distinctions among women was considered an important aspect of public policy . . . . From that period forward, that distinction—between sexually respectable and not respectable women—will indeed determine women's class position.

Women who withheld heterosexual services from men, such as single women, nuns, lesbians, were for many centuries in a precarious position. Such women connected to class through the dominant man in their family of origin and through him gained access to resources. In some historical periods, convents and other enclaves created some sheltered space, in which such women could function and retain their respectability. But the vast majority of single women were, by definition, marginal and dependent on the protection of male kin.

As for those women who insisted on being in charge of their own sexuality and reproduction, they were declassed and marked as deviant. Beginning with the prostitutes in the Assyrian state, who were publicly marked by being denied the right to veil, sexually deviant women were identified by their clothing, their location and by surveillance throughout the centuries. Whether they were actresses, entertainers, peddlers or prostitutes, they were objects of persecution, regulation and discrimination. It is only late in the 20th century that these sexual regulations for women have ceased to have absolute prescriptive power.

The possibility of choosing singleness without severe economic loss did not exist for most women until the development of mature capitalism, which allowed them direct access to employment and economic independence. But we need to keep in mind that even today single, self-supporting women are economically disadvantaged compared with their brothers, by operating in a gender-defined and gender-segmented labor market . . . .

The formation of the working classes—skilled workers, unskilled workers and the underclass of occasional workers—also proceeded along gender lines. While both female and male workers under capitalism had access to resources only by way of hiring out their labor power, men struggled and succeeded in defining their rights of access along patriarchal lines. The concept of "the family wage," a wage sufficient to support a family, shored up the creation of a sex-segregated labor market in which women's wages were permanently fixed at well below the wages of men. Trade-union struggles, until the 1930s in the United States, continued to preserve male privileges in the labor market. Gender-specific job definitions, which relegated women to lower-paying, lower-skilled jobs, reinforced these patterns.

In addition, working-class husbands, as "heads of households," had rights over whatever property the household could accumulate. The fact that working-class fathers and husbands could collect and spend the earnings of their daughters and wives illustrates this point. Working-class housewives supplemented their husbands' earnings or substituted for them in times of economic crises by bartering, homemade production of clothing, by taking in boarders or other people's washing. Finally, women were disadvantaged and more heavily burdened than men by their unpaid household and reproductive labor.

The "invisibility" of housework, its repetitiveness and its ahistoricity has made it easy to overlook it as a serious factor in considering the class position of women. Housework is seldom taken into consideration when class is the subject of discussion.

Regardless of period, regardless of rank and economic position, women's domestic service obligations prevailed over their work, their careers, their ambitions. Whatever class their occupation may have assigned them to, by being women they were also unpaid servants. Working women have a double burden; they have not one job, but two. While this is quite true, it does not adequately explain the situation of women.

It is true that if one adds housework and childcare work to the paid labor of women, women work far longer hours than men do. But the relation between their paid and unpaid work is not merely additive; their unpaid service work degrades their status and pay in the workforce. The large wage differential between service jobs held by men (for example, garbage collector, building maintenance worker) and those held by women (child-care worker, domestic worker) illustrates this point.[23]

The examples above show that class is *always different for men and women*. Any class theory which regards economic oppression as structurally different from sexual oppression can neither explain the persistence of social inequalities nor offer adequate solutions. Economic oppression and exploitation are based as much on the commodification of female sexuality and the appropriation by men of women's labor power and her reproductive power as they are on the direct economic acquisition of resources and persons. The traditional concept of "class" is inadequate to describe the economic/social relations of *both men and women*. What is needed is a concept that illuminates the actual "relations of ruling" in society, a reconceptualization of "class" in the light of gender differences.

*Class or "location in the ranking order of hierarchical societies" consists of various sets of relations whereby people gain access to a variety of resources and privileges. These include economic resources, land, political power, education, technology and access to the formal and informal networks through which societies organize power. Power, in patriarchal societies, has always been maintained through gender and/or "racial" dominance.* Various groups in the societies are given partial advantages over other subordinated groups, in order to keep them in line with a system that distributes access to resources and privileges in an unequal way. That is the true structural underpinning of hierarchical governance, whatever form it may take . . . .

*Class is not only a set of relations whereby people gain access to resources and privileges, but it is a set of relations dependent on other power relations among people.* Each person is, so to speak, enmeshed in a variety of relationships all expressive of various aspects of that person's existence. The network of relations defines the person's location on a ranking order of hierarchies in such a way that the person can be at various levels of ranking for different aspects of his/her existence. For example, a black man can be the deacon of his church (high rank and status); a man with a high-school education (middle rank in access to jobs and resources); a highly respected basketball player (high status within a special network); a janitor in a hospital (relatively low rank and income); a tyrannical husband and father. Clearly, a concept of class dealing only with economics cannot do justice to this man's position in society . . . .

Finally, a holistic re-definition of class would move away from all vertical, horizontal and two- or three-dimensional models. Class is not and never has been static.

*Class is a process over time through which hierarchical relations are created and maintained in such a way*

*as to give some men power and privilege over women and other men by their control over material resources, sexual and reproductive services, education and knowledge. Such control over others is maintained by a complex weave of social relations among the dependent groups, which offer each group some advantages over other groups, sufficient to keep each group within the dominance system, subordinate to the top elite.*

Class is constructed and maintained genderically; class is constructed racially as well. The relationships are not additive, but interdependent and mutually reinforcing. People derive racial and sexual benefits from class and, in turn, class oppression is expressed in different ways for members of different races and sexes.

## DISCUSSION QUESTIONS

1. According to Lerner, how has social class formation and the maintenance of class status been gendered over millennia?
2. Historically, how has marriage been the primary site for the gendering of social class, advantaging men over women? Describe the institutional practices of different historical periods that illustrate how social class is formed and maintained by gender within marriage arrangements and inheritance practices.

## NOTES

1. My theoretical speculations are based on empirical data gathered in my historical work on women, especially the two volumes Women and History: Vol. I: The Creation of Patriarchy (New York: Oxford University Press, 1986); Vol. II: The Creation of Feminist Consciousness: From the Middle Ages to 1870 (New York: Oxford University Press, 1993).
2. The discussion of conditions in the Ancient Near East is based on a broad range of primary and secondary sources cited in my *Creation of Patriarchy*. See esp. chaps. 1–3.
3. Claude Meillassoux, "From Reproduction to Production: A Marxist Approach to Economic Anthropology," *Economy and Society*, no. 1 (1972):93–105, and "The

Social Organisation of the Peasantry: The Economic Basis of Kinship," *Journal of Peasant Studies* I, no. 1 (1973); John Moore, "The Exploitation of Women in Evolutionary Perspective," *Critique of Anthropology* III, nos. 9–10 (1977): 83–100 . . . .

4. I prefer to use the term coined by Laurel Thatcher Ulrich in her excellent book, *Good Wives: Image and Reality in the Lives of Women in Northern New England: 1650–1750* (New York: Oxford University Press, 1980), p. 9.

5. The incident is detailed in Lerner, *Creation of Patriarchy*, pp. 70–71.

6. My generalizations are based on Suzanne Fonay Wemple, *Women in Frankish Society: Marriage and the Cloister, 500 to 900* (Philadelphia: University of Pennsylvania Press, 1985); Susan Mosher Stuard (ed.), *Women in Medieval Society* (Philadelphia: University of Pennsylvania Press, 1976); Jacques Le Goff, *Time, Work & Culture in the Middle Ages* (Chicago: University of Chicago Press, 1980); David Herlihy, *Opera Muliebra: Women and Work in Medieval Europe* (New York: McGraw-Hill, 1990).

7. Under Germanic law a woman's *Wergeld*, the sum the family would receive if she were to be killed, was set at twice the amount of that for a man. Reference to Merovingian law: Wemple, *Women in Frankish Society*, p. 31.

8. Wemple, *Women in Frankish Society*, p.72.

9. Chris Middleton, "Peasants, Patriarchy and the Feudal Mode of Production in England: Feudal Lords and the Subordination of Peasant Women," *The Sociological Review* 29, no. 1 (Feb. 1981):137–54; information on tax, p. 143.

10. Wemple details the practice of polygyny in the Merovingian royal family through three generations . . . . Concubinage was also common among the Merovingian nobility (pp. 38–41). Chart, pp. xii–xiii . . . .

11. General information on the "warrior aristocracy" is based on Joan Kelly, "Family and Society," in Joan Kelly, *Women, History and Theory: The Essays of Joan Kelly* (Chicago: University of Chicago Press, 1984), pp. 100–155; Bonnie S. Anderson and Judith P. Zinsser, *A History of Their Own*, 2 vols. (New York: Harper & Row, 1988), I, 119–50.

12. W. G. Runciman, "Accelerating Social Mobility: The Case of Anglo-Saxon England," *Past & Present*, No. 104 (August 1984):3–30, pp. 7, 26. See also Goody cited above, p. 27.

13. Klinck, "Anglo-Saxon Women and the Law," p. 118.

14. Janet Senderowitz Loengard, "'Of the Gift of Her Husband': English Dower and Its Consequences," in Julius Kirshner and Suzanne F. Wemple (eds.), *Women of the Medieval World: Essays in Honor of John H. Mundy* (Oxford: Basil Blackwell, 1985), pp. 233–34. Also Anderson and Zinsser, *A History of Their Own*, I, 325.

15. The story of Abraham, his legitimate wife Sarah, and their "bonds-woman" Hagar (Gen. 21:1–21) reflects marriage customs prevalent in surrounding Ancient Near East societies. The infertile couple, Abraham and Sarah, accept as their own son the son of Hagar by Abraham. But then the story deviates sharply from Babylonian practice. Through a miracle, Sarah, in ripe old age, bears a son; she feels herself mocked by Hagar and, at Sarah's insistence, Abraham banishes Hagar and her son Ishmael into the desert. God saves both from death, but the family line is carried forward only by Isaac, the offspring of the legitimate wife. This may be considered a strong divine endorsement of a new concept—the primacy of the rights of legitimate sons.

16. Jo-Ann McNamara and Suzanne Wemple, "Marriage and Divorce in the Frankish Kingdom," in Stuard, *Women in Medieval Society*, pp. 95–124, and Wemple, *Women in Frankish Society*, chap. 6.

17. Shifts and changes in dowry and women's property rights have been thoroughly analyzed in Marion A. Kaplan, *The Marriage Bargain: Women and Dowries in European History* (New York: Harrington Park Press, 1985; originally published by Haworth Press, 1985). See esp. Diane Owen Hughes, "From Brideprice to Dowry in Mediterranean Europe," *ibid.*, pp. 13–58.

18. Anderson and Zinsser, *A History of Their Own* I, 376–73; 406–9.

19. Susan Staves, *Married Women's Separate Property in England, 1660–1833* (Cambridge: Harvard University Press, 1990), p. 35.

20. *Ibid.*, p. 37.

21. Eileen Spring, *Law, Land & Family: Aristocratic Inheritance in England, 1300–1800* (Chapel Hill: University of North Carolina Press, 1993), citation p. 93. Spring revises earlier interpretations which regarded marriage settlements as more favorable to women.

22. Lerner, *Feminist Consciousness*, chap. 2.

23. Alice Kessler-Harris, *A Woman's Wage: Historical Meaning & Social Consequences* (Lexington: University Press of Kentucky, 1990), chap. 4.

# 6

# Racial Domination and the Evolution of Racial Classification

## Tukufu Zuberi

*While the previous reading by Gerda Lerner examines the intersections between social class and gender in a historical context, this reading focuses on the historical construction of race. Tukufu Zuberi, a sociologist, is the Lasry Family Professor of Race Relations at the University of Pennsylvania. Zuberi also is well known for his social history research on the popular television show History Detectives (PBS). This excerpt is taken from Zuberi's 2001 book,* Thicker Than Blood: How Racial Statistics Lie, *in which he shows how the construction of race was used by scientists and later by statisticians to support a number of political constructions of race.*

Beginning in the fifteenth century, Europeans experienced a flood of new contacts with peoples in faraway lands. European notions about the nature of the world were turned on their heads by "new knowledge" gleaned about plants, animals, and peoples in places such as Africa, Asia, and the Americas. European scientists attempted to fit this mass of new information into a logical framework that explained the world they lived in and the world they wanted. Race became a particularly important "scientific" notion. African colonialism and enslavement were two important moments in this process of racialization.

*Source:* Tukufu Zuberi, "Racial Domination and the Evolution of Racial Classification," in *Thicker than Blood: How Racial Statistics Lie.* Copyright © 2001. Reprinted by permission of University of Minnesota Press.

The concept of race is rooted in the fifteenth-century expansion of European nations.[1] The advent of racial slavery and colonialism marked a turning point in how physical differences were viewed. Orlando Patterson remarks that "there is nothing notably peculiar about the institution of slavery. It has existed from before the dawn of human history right down to the twentieth century, in the most primitive of human societies and in the most civilized."[2] However, the white supremacy that accompanied the racialization of slavery in the Americas has not existed since the dawn of human history, and it continues to exert a peculiar influence today. The same can be said of colonialism. The racialization of colonization and slavery was historically unique, and its consequences have been lasting.

Most of the people enslaved throughout the Mediterranean before the seizure of Constantinople in 1453 were of European origin. There were African slaves as well, but slavery had not been racialized.[3] Between the fifteenth and sixteenth centuries, the European Christian rulers of Cyprus, Crete, and Sicily created the world's most profitable sugar plantations using a slave labor pool made up of Turks, Russians, Bulgarians, Greeks, and Africans.[4] These plantations were not governed by Roman slave codes, so they provided an opportunity for a new ethic of enslavement, and by the middle of the fifteenth century Cyprus had become the largest slave market in the Mediterranean.[5]

The victory of the Ottoman Turks over the Christians gradually pushed the Mediterranean sugar industry west to Spain and Portugal, and then to the Atlantic islands off the coast of West Africa, including the Azores, Madeira, the Canaries, Cape Verde, Fernando Po, São Tomé, and Príncipe. The supply of people for enslavement was plentiful and close at hand in sub-Saharan Africa, and the plantations were very profitable. The combination of African slaves and European capital became a model of success in Spain, Portugal, and Italy.

Gold- and slave-hungry explorers colonized the Atlantic islands with the blessing and backing of state and religious leaders. The pope granted his approval of the practice between 1442 and 1456 with a series of papal bulls. And, in 1460, the Portuguese royal authorities licensed expeditions to contractors who, upon paying a fee, were given commercial rights to exploit areas of their "discovery." Portuguese adventurers such as Infante Henrique received state and church approval for colonization and enslavement of indigenous peoples. Henrique visited North Africa briefly three times; however, he sponsored several expeditions that established trading posts and connections along the African coast and islands. "As a royal prince he was perfectly prepared to combine raids on the African coast with systematic work on island colonization" from his bases at Sagres in the Algarve.[6]

The soil and climate of the Atlantic islands were favorable to sugar cultivation.[7] This was especially true for São Tomé and Príncipe, which lay close to the equator. In the sixteenth century, São Tomé and Príncipe became major sugar plantations stocked with enslaved Africans. This early shift in the demography of the enslaved population was the historical precursor to the racialization of enslavement.

The colonial occupation of islands off the west coast of Africa is the historical precedent for the racialization of enslavement of African-origin populations. The colonization of these African islands coincided with Dias's demonstration to Europe in 1488 that the Cape of Good Hope was the end of the African continent. While the creation of racialized plantation slavery first developed off the west coast of Africa, the state structures for racialized colonial rule in Africa developed in the Cape.

The European settlers came from developing states that experienced numerous wars in which plunder was a natural part. As the more powerful northwestern European states, like England and France, began to transform the weaker nations into economic satellites within Europe, they also initiated the process of transforming parts of Africa and Asia into economic satellites externally.[8] As Magubane observes in South Africa, the "Dutch settlers had come from developing capitalist states that had been forged after numberless wars, in which ferocious plunder was normal."[9] Between Africa and Europe, in the four centuries before colonial rule was dominant, the principal items of plunder were men and women. Europeans shipped enslaved Africans to European-dominated markets for profit. East Africa served as the point of departure for the other slave trade in Africans, the Arab slave trade. In the beginning, these colonial and slave experiences were typical expansions, with religion, fame, and economic gain as the sole driving forces. The same justification for dominating the weaker parts of Europe drove the expansion to Asia and Africa. The ideological justification was simple profit.

Two types of economic systems developed among European colonizers during the fifteenth and sixteenth centuries. The first was a diversified, self-sufficient economy of small farmers living off the land on which they toiled. The second was the export economy of large-scale plantations producing staple articles such as sugar.[10] It is the second type of colony that became the basis for the racialization of slave labor off the coast of Africa and in the Americas.

By the end of the sixteenth century, settler colonialism had become institutionalized and spread in southern Africa. European colonization required the appropriation of land, a settling population as well as domination of a local majority, and the transformation of indigenous institutions into European constructs. As in all colonial situations, the settlers had to determine how a small and foreign minority could rule over an indigenous majority. Direct colonial rule was the initial response to the problem of administering non-European colonial subjects.[11] European law was to rule the land, and both the colonized and the colonizers could ignore indigenous institutions. All would be required to submit and conform to these laws, but only Europeanized (or "civilized") natives would have access to European rights.

Indirect colonial rule was the mode of domination over a semifree peasantry. In this context of restricted freedom, the community possessed land, and domination of the market was restricted to the products of labor; the indigenous population owned land and labor. The colonial authority dominated the market relationships in the political and civil life of the colonized. Indigenous customary law was used to regulate non-market relationships in the family and community of the dominated population.

The reality of indirect and direct colonial rule suggests that different colonial systems did not constitute radical breaks from what came before colonization; the social and economic practices of the epoch were themselves a complex product of things old and new. Although an ideological offspring of direct domination of the initial settlement of a colony, indirect rule was born of, and bore within it, a series of connections to direct colonial rule.

European settler colonies have different histories of racial and ethnic stratification. In South Africa racial tensions stem from European colonization, the enslavement of both Africans from other areas in Africa and Asians, and the spatial displacement of the native indigenous African population through colonization. The racial conflicts in the United States stem from racial tensions that began with a century and a half of race-specific policies such as enslavement and the colonization of Native Americans. In Brazil, the European settlers from Portugal initiated the racial tensions by colonization and enslavement first of the indigenous Native American populations and later the African-origin population.

Walter Rodney argued in his book *How Europe Underdeveloped Africa* that "the first significant thing about the internationalization of trade in the fifteenth century was that Europeans took the initiative and went to other parts of the world."[12] Europe exclusively established itself as the major power in the trade among Africa, Europe, and the Americas and became a formidable contender for control over the Pacific as well.[13] European interests owned the majority of the world's seagoing vessels that could travel the Atlantic from continent to continent, and they controlled the financing of the trade between these continents. The superiority of their ships and cannons gave Europeans control over trade across the Atlantic trade routes.

As part of the Spanish Empire since the rule of Hapsburg Charles V, the Dutch who occupied the seven northern provinces of the Low Countries fought for independence in the latter part of the sixteenth century.[14] The Dutch East India Company destroyed Portuguese domination in the Indian Ocean in the first decade of the seventeenth century. The Portuguese may have been the trailblazers, but the Dutch delivered Africa into the hands of the western European world-trading system. African incorporation into this trading system generated sufficient momentum to lead to European domination of the African continent and the Americas. The Americas illustrate how Europeans racialized colonialism and enslavement.

The European slave trade of Africans to the Americas began in 1502 with the Spanish. The end of the trade did not come until the 1850s in Brazil and Cuba. The racialization of America began with the dehumanization of the Native American population. In the New World, Native Americans became the first source of slave labor for the building up of plantations.[15] As in the Cape Colony, the European settlers and the indigenous Americans struggled for control of the land and the bodies of the colonized. In the sixteenth century, Portuguese settlements enslaved Native Americans ten to fifteen times as often as Africans. With the introduction of new diseases from Europe and Africa, the excessive demand for labor, and changes and limitations in their diet, Native Americans declined rapidly in number.[16] This demographic collapse was an additional stimulation to the European slave trade in Africans.

The Native American population decline stimulated by European contact affected Africa as well as America. It was not surprising that the Europeans turned to Africans as a replacement for Native American slaves. Africa's American diaspora was born. The need to justify the grand scale of African enslavement also came into play. Thus began the racialization of enslavement and the antiblack discourse on race.

Slavery was an accepted institution in Africa before the development of the European or Arab slave trades.[17] Consequently, commerce in slaves was not foreign to Africa. In Africa, slavery as an institution tended to be domestic and with few exceptions never developed into the large-scale plantation slavery that dominated the Atlantic islands under the Portuguese. This changed as the Portuguese explorers and traders established themselves on the sub-Saharan coast of Africa. The Portuguese slave trade stimulated an increase

in the demand for African slaves. This demand transformed the market conditions in Africa and increased the African dependence on the slave trade. These changes occurred simultaneously with the Spanish conquest of the Caribbean islands and the Portuguese settlement of the Brazilian subcontinent, creating the American market for enslaved Africans.

In most cases Europeans did not invade Africa and enslave Africans; however, they did create the demand for slaves and promoted internal conflict through indirect military pressure by introducing military technology and political manipulation. At first, enslavement resulted primarily from the political-economic strategies of African kings and leaders. The African elite attempted to increase the size of their kingdoms by increasing the number of dependent subjects, entourages of clients, subjects, kin, serfs, and slaves. As these royal efforts became intertwined with international commerce with Europe, the search for dependents became a search for slaves, and eventually the slave trade dominated internal African markets.

The African diaspora in the Americas resulted primarily from the enslavement of Africans by Europeans. The literature on this enslavement is extensive, and I will not attempt to describe or summarize it. However, it is important to note that the arrival of Africans in the Americas in the sixteenth, seventeenth, eighteenth, and nineteenth centuries became a central thread in the racialization of the Americas— at once a challenge to the idea of democracy and an important part of their economic histories and social developments.

Portugal took possession of the eastern coastline of South America in the early sixteenth century. The Portuguese Empire claimed the region during expeditions to the East Indies and, like the Dutch in the Cape Colony, had no plans for immediate development. However, it did not take long for the Portuguese to transport their experience in the islands off the coast of West Africa to their new American colonies.[18] They brought sugar experts from the Madeira and Sáo Tomé plantations. This effort resulted in the first slave plantation system in the Americas and quickly outpaced the Atlantic islands in the production of sugar.

By the seventeenth century, the northeast provinces of Pernambuco and Bahia had the most profitable sugar plantations in the world. Northeastern Brazil dominated the European sugar market. The trade in the enslaved and sugar gave the Portuguese a prize place in the New World market.

The Dutch had become deeply involved in the European slave trade as sugar producers and traders in enslaved Africans.[19] After establishing the Dutch West India Company, they took control of the Portuguese settlement of Pernambuco in 1630. By the 1640s, after they had captured the Portuguese El Mina fortress on the Gold Coast and the Angolan coastal region, the Dutch were a major colonial actor in the creation of Africa's American diaspora. Like the Dutch in South Africa when confronted by a superior European force, the Portuguese sought refuge in the domination of indigenous populations. To compensate for their defeats, the Portuguese increased Native American enslavement and their own settlement activities in the interior of the continent.

The Dutch exported the sugar plantation economy to the West Indies and expanded access to the sugar market within France and England. As Klein noted, "In the 1640s, Dutch planters with Pernambuco experience arrived in Barbados as well as Martinique and Guadeloupe to introduce modern milling and production techniques. Dutch slavers provided the credit to the local planters to buy African slaves, while Dutch West Indian freighters hauled the finished sugar to the refineries in Amsterdam."[20] However, Dutch settlers themselves proved decisive in the efforts to expand the sugar plantation system to the islands. The Portuguese had firmly implanted in Brazil their lessons of slave plantations from the Atlantic islands off the coast of West Africa. The extension of these methods to the Lesser Antillean islands and from the Amazonian estuary to Florida was carried forward by French and English settlers. After decimating the Carib population, European settlers were able to import first indentured servants and then slaves to establish profitable slave plantation economies.

These developments did not destroy the importance of the Brazilian sugar industry or its oppressive system of enslavement. By 1645, the Portuguese had recaptured their lost territory in Brazil and, by 1648, had recovered the colonial outpost in Angola and their islands in the Gulf of Guinea. They apparently never stopped resisting Dutch rule in the interior. The Portuguese were able to regain control of the European slave trade south of the equator; however, the Dutch continued to dominate north of the equator. Although Brazil never regained its sugar and slave monopoly, it was able to return to its exclusive dependence on African slave labor and continue to play a leading role in the production of sugar.

The Dutch West India Company successfully extended the slave plantation system in the Americas, and it benefited greatly from English and French dependence on supplies of slaves and technology. However, France and England did not allow their American settlers to become totally dependent on Dutch merchants. English and French companies competed with the Dutch in the European slave trade. This competition was in part responsible for the wars among the Netherlands, England, and France between 1652 and 1713.

The eighteenth century witnessed the opening of the slave trade to a host of individual merchants. African communities organized themselves to meet the growing demand for slaves resulting from the expansion of the slave plantation system in the Americas. Britain, France, Spain, Portugal, the Netherlands, and Denmark all thrived from their commercial activities with the settler colonies in the Americas. The expansion of new sugar plantations increased the ratio of enslaved Africans to the "free" Europeans and fostered a new industrial discipline using the gang system on rice, coffee, and cotton plantations.[21] The United States was unique in that the sugar-plantation system arrived later than it did in other areas of the Americas, close to the end of the enslavement period. Thus, not as many enslaved Africans entered the United States as they did Brazil and the Caribbean. However, as in Brazil, enslavement in the United States became a racialized system. The settlers considered Africans to be natural slaves, indigenous Americans to be noble natives, and other Europeans as potential citizens. The problem of race was born.

## RACE AND THE PROBLEM OF FREEDOM

The African diaspora, like the European diaspora, began during a time of great change and social transformation. The European Renaissance suggested a new freedom for the European spirit and body. However, it also suggested a newfound freedom to colonize and enslave Africans, Asians, and American Indians. The European world knew of these slaves, but they were slaves that came from various other regions and populations. The European Renaissance coincided with the rise of racialized enslavement and colonization.

The nineteenth century was the era of transformation in the status of the enslaved African-origin populations.[22] These transformations began in Haiti at the turn of the previous century and ended in Brazil on May 13, 1888. A succession of revolts and wars swept away the systems of enslavement in the Americas and the Caribbean islands. Slavery was anathema to both the new industrial capitalism and the liberal democratic state. However, the result of emancipation—the transition from enslavement to free labor—exposed the contradiction of applying the idea of the liberal democratic state in a racially stratified society. The justification of racial stratification was an important means of evading the issue of persistent racial differences in societies that claimed to be democratic.

The transformation of enslaved Africans into wage laborers was not unique; it had a precedent in the transformation of European-origin agricultural workers into an industrial working class in the northern United States and Europe. Yet, the enslaved were by definition chattel, unlike the agricultural workers, and emancipation included the transition of the African-origin population to freedom.

The end of African enslavement accompanied the colonization of Asia and Africa, the expansion of colonization in the Americas, and state formation in nations such as the United States and Brazil. European settlers, dressed in their revolutionary clothing, sought to secure their freedom from the kings in Britain and Portugal and simultaneously the right to deny that freedom to the African and indigenous American populations.[23] The United States was the first of the racially stratified societies to gain independence from the mother country in Europe. And as Judge Higginbotham reminds us: "From the perspective of the black masses, the Revolution merely assured the plantation owners of their right to continue the legal tyranny of slavery."[24] In Brazil, Prince Regent Pedro and the merchants of Rio de Janeiro proclaimed independence in 1822. However, the slave trade continued well into the 1850s, and emancipation did not come until 1888. These developments required new justifications of racial stratification.

In 1794, France abolished slavery in her colonies and "apprenticed" the formerly enslaved people of Guadeloupe and Santo Domingo.[25] In 1802, Napoleon Bonaparte overthrew the abolition decree and forced the African-origin population into a battle for freedom and independence. The army of Toussaint l'Ouverture defeated Napoleon's troops, forcing the French to withdraw from Santo Domingo. Santo Domingo became independent Haiti, and the price of maintaining the enslavement of Africans in the Americas increased substantially.

Haiti was an exception in the transition to freedom among the formerly enslaved: it was a state formed by the enslaved as a result of war with the oppressors. The formerly enslaved were not emancipated; they were liberated. The Haitian revolution of 1792–1804 was the clearest manifestation of the rejection of African enslavement. After this the history of African emancipation was to be a different story entirely.

As Jay R. Mandle notes: "Everywhere in plantation America, with the exception of Haiti, the momentous transformation that the ending of slavery seemed to promise turned out to be far less than revolutionary. The slave-owning classes, by and large, were able to accomplish the transition from being what Gavin Wright calls labor lords to becoming landlords and, in the process, continue in their former role as the dominant class in society."[26] The ideas of freedom and equality were inconsistent with the economic and social system envisioned by the designers of emancipation and reconstruction. Several examples illustrate the illusion of freedom offered by emancipation. In 1838, the British emancipated all the enslaved under the British flag. As had been the case with the French, for the British Empire emancipation meant the replacement of enslavement with apprenticeship. Discussing the problems of the transition to freedom in Jamaica, Thomas C. Holt writes: "Apprenticeship was a halfway covenant in which the relationship between the planter and the worker was much the same as that between master and slave for forty and one-half hours of the work week, but during the balance of the week they were to assume the respective statuses of employer and employee freely negotiating conditions of work and wages."[27]

In the final year of the apprenticeship system, Holt notes, colonial administrations in the West Indies developed policies to restrict the freedom of the "freedmen." His citation of an administrator captures these inconsistencies:

> Given the demographic imbalances in the colonies, the "natural" effect of complete emancipation would be a general desertion of the estates to cultivate food crops. Eventually the growth of population might right this imbalance, but the plantations would be destroyed in the meantime. Thus the government must interdict the freedmen's natural—and, one might add, rational—proclivity to abandon the plantations.[28]

In 1865, the United States emancipated the enslaved African-origin population,[29] and racial enslavement was replaced with other forms of social and economic marginalization. As Du Bois notes:

> It must be remembered and never forgotten that the civil war in the South which overthrew Reconstruction was a determined effort to reduce black labor as nearly as possible to a condition of unlimited exploitation and build a new class of capitalists on this foundation. The wage of the Negro worker, despite the war amendments, was to be reduced to the level of bare subsistence by taxation, peonage, caste, and every method of discrimination. This program had to be carried out in open defiance of the clear letter of the law.[30]

Brazil was the first country in the Americas to institute the slave plantation system, yet it was one of the last states to end its support of the European slave trade. Official Brazilian opposition to the slave trade coincided with a return to the rebellions of the enslaved in 1800, the 1820s, and the 1830s.[31] In 1831, Brazil signed an antislaving treaty with Great Britain, effectively ending the legal European slave trade to Brazil by 1852.[32]

In 1871, Viscount Rio Branco successfully proposed the "law of the free womb," which manumitted children born to enslaved women when they reached the age of majority. The bill was approved by the Brazilian parliament as the Rio Branco Law. On May 13, 1888, Princess Regent Isabel signed the Golden Law abolishing slavery throughout Brazil. With the Golden Law, legal enslavement in the Americas ended, and the last large African-origin population in the Americas was emancipated.

Following emancipation in São Paulo, as in the United States and Jamaica, the planter elite created a postemancipation system of racial stratification to secure their interest. European-origin populations replicated this pattern throughout the Americas, and it continues to exert an influence on racial interactions. As in other postemancipation societies, because of their size and place in the economy the Brazilian freedmen (or *libertos*) were in a position to negotiate the terms of their labor and the political order of the day. In response the planters attempted to Europeanize Brazil. As George Reid Andrews observed:

> Far from doing away with "distinctions of class and race," as the black Republicans of Campinas had hoped, the Republic would cement landowner rule and then embark on a national campaign to "Europeanize" Brazil, a campaign in which the "whitening" of the national population, and the replacement of African racial heritage with European, would assume a prominent role.[33]

A similar policy was implemented in the United States.

In the West Indies, the United States, and Brazil, emancipation was part of a process that transformed labor conditions but did not end domination by the European settler elite. There were limits to the freedom of the "freedmen" after emancipation. Being freed did not translate into equality or justice . . . .

Rather than put an end to the racial hierarchy, emancipation became the next phase in racial stratification. The contradictions between freedom and domination needed to be reconciled. The intellectual justification of racial stratification began with the idea of the Great Chain of Being but continued with the adaptation of the evolutionary ideas of Darwin.

## The Evolution of Racial Classification

The racialization of social and economic stratification required the classification of human beings by their physical characteristics. The physical classification of human populations took on added meaning during the process of racial colonization and slavery. Both racial slavery and colonialism required a dehumanizing discourse. One of the first intellectual articulations of this discourse was the Great Chain of Being. The classical idea of the Great Chain of Being ranked all creation, including the Creator, hierarchically. The chain of Being classified creation from inanimate objects upward through lowly animals, women, and men, to God. In the European mind, the use of the Chain of Being to support and justify the enslavement of Africans was obvious.[34]

The Chain of Being maintained that humans shared a close affinity with beasts. It followed, therefore, that the lowest human beings were closely related to the highest animals. Given the belief in Europe that the ape was the highest animal, it followed that the lowest group of human beings would be apelike. The economic desire to justify the enslavement of Africans played an important role in shaping the eighteenth-century opinion among some European scholars that Africans were just above the ape on the Great Chain of Being.

The chain ranged from simple to very complex beings. Common descent was not critical to this idea. Stratification within a particular race and among different races was the work of the Creator. With European colonialism came knowledge of the "technologically primitive" populations of the Americas, Africa, Asia, and Oceania. Not only were

there inferior races within Europe, but races inferior to those were found among peoples of color.

The idea of a radical hierarchy assumed a class hierarchy. Both colonialism and enslavement are class relationships, and the idea of a racial hierarchy justified the existence of these relationships in the past. The idea of the primitive African was key in discussions of the Great Chain. The Dutch settlers originally referred to the Khoikhoi as Hottentots.[35] The African "Hottentots" became a common reference to the bottom of the human population.[36] Eighteenth- and nineteenth-century intellectuals commonly referred to Hottentots as the lowest of the savage races.

Ideologies and social theories of racial hierarchy supported European colonization.[37] "Race" identified various forms of religious and social differences. That some people were less advanced technologically or militarily than others was seen as the will of God, the consequences of environment, or the outcome of differences in moral character. Within Europe the idea of the Great Chain of Being led British colonists in seventeeth-century Ulster to attempt to enslave the Irish. This attempt failed, but soon afterward Africans were successfully enslaved in Virginia, the Carolinas, and Georgia.

The racial theories of the seventeenth and eighteenth centuries were grounded in the notion of "divine providence" and justified the enslavement of Africans and the colonization of the Americas, Asia, and Africa. The theories held that God had ordained that Europe should rule the world, and various religious leaders were willing to give decrees to this effect.[38]

Justifying racial stratification was essential for the system of enslavement to exist in the Americas. Enslavement is a form of domination. Domination and its companions exploitation and marginalization refer to social relationships in which one population benefits as the others suffers. The degree of suffering can vary from society to society; however, the degree to which the dominant class depends on the exploited population does not determine the extent to which the exploited are marginalized. The dominant class's partial dependence may entail the destruction of the exploited class. This has been the case in the interaction of several indigenous Caribbean populations with European settler populations.[39] Or the dominant class's more general dependence may entail coexistence with the exploited population, as in the case of South Africa and Brazil, for example. This continuum of domination allows us to avoid extremist arguments without sacrificing the force of the idea of domination. The various degrees of dominant-exploited and dominant-marginalized relationships may be placed on a continuum ranging from a point prior to equality to one just the other side of extermination or genocide. Domination needs justification in an age of democracy. As racially stratified societies entered the twentieth century, they needed to justify this domination. Social Darwinism and eugenics provided the first scientific justification of continued racial stratification by "democratic" societies.

The nineteenth-century justifications of racial stratification are rooted in the eighteenth- century development of evolutionary theory in biology and social statistics. The shift from natural history to biology gave new life to old ideas of racial hierarchy. When the Great Chain of Being no longer carried the weight of legitimacy, science came to the rescue, beginning with the theories of evolution. The Swedish natural historian Carolus Linnaeus led the way, formulating the first scientific classification of human populations . . . .

Linnaeus's system was thought to be crude and inadequate, and refinements followed in Johann Friedrich Blumenbach's *On the Natural Variety of Mankind* (1775). Linnaeus's system was based on anatomical and cultural characteristics. Using only anatomical (morphological) characteristics, Blumenbach divided human beings into five categories: American, Caucasian, Ethiopian, Malay, and Mongolian. His five races became identified with the skin colors red, white, black, brown, and yellow. He maintained that all human beings belonged to one species and that his categories merely signaled breaks in a continuum. Blumenbach's work both clashed with and complemented the work of many naturalists of the time, but it was singularly important in challenging the legitimacy of the Great Chain of Being . . . .

Many other individuals, particularly Jean-Baptiste de Monet de Lamarck, played key roles in the development of European theories of evolution and race. As Charles Darwin himself noted, Lamarck was one of the first naturalists to formulate "the doctrine that all species, including man, are descended from other species."[40] Lamarck argued that evolution occurred through the inheritance of *acquired* characteristics, not natural ones . . . .

The worldview of the seventeenth century, as envisioned by Thomas Hobbes, presented human existence as *bellum omnium contra omnes*, a war of all against all. In 1798 Thomas R. Malthus applied the Hobbesian worldview in his population perspective, linking the issue of survival to population growth and the competition for natural resources.[41] Malthus was the first to argue scientifically for population control, by showing that populations grew geometrically whereas resources grew only arithmetically. He argued that population growth had to be kept in check lest misery and poverty become the predominant conditions in society. Because the competition for resources was natural, he contended that the poor and the powerless constituted a natural social occurrence. Attempts by society to help the poor would simply add to the problem, by increasing their numbers, and so should be abandoned. Poverty was a fact of nature and a product of God's will.

At the same time Malthus emphasized personal responsibility as the operative factor in the competition for natural resources. The poor were poor because of their individual characteristics, not because of their social position or the society they lived in. Governmental intervention in the natural workings of the economy thus was bound to fail. The distribution of rewards within society reflected individual accomplishment rather than historical and social circumstances; to engineer a change within society by welfare or any type of "wealth transfer" would lead to more misery and would be an act against nature and God.

Malthus was concerned that Europe in general and Britain in particular maintain a naturally strong and healthy people.[42] For Malthus, the issue of civilization versus barbarism was the most important distinction among and within societies. In his view, the population problem was one of moral discipline and probity.

Malthus's ideas had a profound impact on the way people viewed population problems in society. It is too easy, however, to overstate his influence in the formation of the idea of race. The doctrine of colonialism did not wait upon Malthus's arrival, nor was the racism to come simply a result of Malthus's *Essay on the Principle of Population*. In fact, racism was not a result of conflict between the very dissimilar peoples of Europe (whites) and those of the rest of the world (people of color); rather, it was conceived in the class systems of Europe . . . . Joseph Arthur de Gobineau, himself a count, argued that the nobility descended from superior progenitors and were therefore the only ones capable of ruling. The poor came from inferior progenitors and were thus politically incompetent.

Even before Malthus, states in the Americas were firmly grounded in the notions of European racial superiority.[43] The wars with the indigenous American population and the proslavery practices and arguments of politicians and propagandists made the idea of racial inferiority a living fact, one that was supported by the moral order of European people and "God." Europeans declared themselves owners and governors of the lands of nonwhite, "heathen" Others, and when they met with resistance, they were "forced into lawful war" in the name of preserving civilization and upholding righteousness. The colonial and slave practices of the era in which Gobineau lived required this new source of legitimacy.

However, Malthus's ideas were critical in the development of evolutionary thought . . . .

It is through Malthus's theoretical connection to Darwin that he had a critical impact on scholarly perspectives of ranking differences such as race . . . .

In 1859 Darwin fundamentally challenged Lamarck's argument with the publication of *On the Origin of Species by Means of Natural Selection, or the Preservation of Favored Races in the Struggle for Life*. Darwin's reading of Malthus's *Essay on the Principle of Population* alerted him to the struggle for existence that was, in his view, responsible for natural selection through competition. Darwin went a step further than Malthus did by applying the principle of natural selection to every living thing.[44]

Darwin's work was another blow to the religious theories of race based on the Great Chain of Being. The morphological view of species—that they are fixed in form and structure—dovetails with the assumptions of the Great Chain of Being that the Creator designs each form of life. Darwin disagreed with this morphological view. He argued that species formed populations of diverse individuals who adapted to different environments in such a way that their successors' characteristics would change through natural selection. Species did not progress and become better; they became diverse . . . .

Darwin's theory of natural selection holds that one species evolves into another. With this revolutionary idea, debates about the human races were radically altered. Writers began to argue that if man evolved from apelike ancestors and there were no "white" apes, then the white race is the most evolved. Thus, the races of color, which Europeans considered culturally and spiritually more primitive, were closer to the nonhuman progenitor (the ape), and the white populations of Europe represented the latest and highest form of evolutionary progress.

Pioneered by the English sociologist Herbert Spencer in the late nineteenth century, Social Darwinism became the dominant theory of sociological thought and played an important role in the prevailing ideology of racism. Like Darwin, Spencer viewed Malthus's population perspective as the principal force in evolution. Unlike Darwin, however, Spencer based his view of evolution on Lamarck.

Social scientists tended to think that Darwin's theory of natural selection mirrored contemporary social processes.[45] The same competitive individualism lay at the root of laissez-faire capitalism and became the key to economic development and progress . . . .

Spencer argued that the evolutionary laws applicable in the physical world paralleled those guiding human cultural developments. Civilization moved from the homogeneous to the heterogeneous, from the undifferentiated to the differentiated,[46] racial, social, and cultural differences represented various *stages* of evolution. At the turn of the twentieth century, Social Darwinism was extremely influential, and Spencer was one of the most popular academics in the world.[47]

## DISCUSSION QUESTIONS

1. According to Zuberi, how and when did colonialism and slavery become racialized so that racial hierarchy assumed a class hierarchy in America?
2. How was the racialization of social and economic stratification supported by scientific thought in the 19th century? Discuss some of the key thinkers of the 19th century whose ideas served to confer legitimacy on racial classifications and, ultimately, class stratification by race.

## NOTES

1. Oliver C. Cox, *Caste, Class and Race: A Study in Social Dynamics* (New York: Doubleday, 1948), 322–45.
2. Orlando Patterson, *Slavery and Social Death: A Comparative Study* (Cambridge, Mass.: Harvard University Press, 1982), vii.
3. Abdul Sheriff, *Slaves, Spices and Ivory in Zanzibar: Integration of an East African Commercial Empire into the World Economy, 1770–1873* (Dar es Salaam: Tanzania Publishing House, 1987).
4. Robin Blackburn, *The Making of New World Slavery: From the Baroque to the Modern, 1492–1800* (London: Verso, 1997), 77–78.
5. Blackburn, *The Making of New World Slavery,* 35.
6. Ibid., 99–112.
7. Drake, *Black Folk Here and There,* 2:234–36; Blackburn, *The Making of New World Slavery,* 111.
8. Walter Rodney, *How Europe Underdeveloped Africa* (Washington, D.C.: Howard University Press, 1981).
9. Bernard Makhosezwe Magubane, *The Political Economy of Race and Class in South Africa* (New York: Monthly Review Press, 1990), 29.
10. Eric Williams has noted that "[u]nder certain circumstances slavery has some obvious advantages. In the cultivation of crops like sugar, cotton and tobacco, where the cost of production is appreciably reduced on larger units, the slave owner, with his large-scale production and his organized slave gang, can make more profitable use of the land than the small farmer or peasant proprietor . . . . (Eric Williams, *Capitalism and Slavery* [Chapel Hill: University of North Carolina

Press, 1944], 6–7). See also Magubane, *The Political Economy of Race and Class in South Africa,* 4–5.
11. For an excellent summary and discussion of the difference between direct and indirect rule, see Mahmood Mamdani, *Citizen and Subject: Contemporary Africa and the Legacy of Late Colonialism* (Princeton: Princeton University Press, 1996), 16–18.
12. Rodney, *How Europe Underdeveloped Africa,* 75. The arrival of Africans in the Americas may well have begun before the arrival of Europeans. Recent research, such as on the Olmec stone heads of Mexico, is suggestive of the pre-Columbus contact of Africans and Americans. However, if African boats did reach America and American boats did reach Africa, research has yet to establish that they developed two-way links. Africans and Native Americans did not develop international trade. See: Leo Wiener, *Africa and the Discovery of America* (Philadelphia: Innes and Sons, 1920); and Ivan Van Sertima, *They Came before Columbus* (New York: Random House, 1977).
13. Rodney, *How Europe Underdeveloped Africa,* 75–82.
14. J. D. Fage, *A History of Africa,* 3d ed. (New York: Routledge, 1995), 244–47; Herbert S. Klein, *African Slavery in Latin America and the Caribbean* (Oxford: Oxford University Press, 1986), 45–50.
15. Williams, *Capitalism and Slavery,* 7–9; Blackburn, *The Making of New World Slavery,* 166–67; Forbes, *Africans and Native Americans,* 26–64.
16. Russell Thornton, *American Indian Holocaust and Survival: A Population History since 1492* (Norman: University of Oklahoma Press, 1987), 44–56.
17. The existence and nature of slavery in Africa before and during the European slave trade continues to be a debated issue. See the classic article by Walter Rodney, "African Slavery and Other Forms of Social Oppression on the Upper Guinea Coast in the Context of the Atlantic Slave Trade," *Journal of African History* 7 (1966):431–43.
18. Klein, *African Slavery in Latin America and the Caribbean,* 38–39.
19. Fage, *A History of Africa,* 244–52; Klein, *African Slavery in Latin American and the Caribbean,* 45–50.
20. Klein, *African Slavery in Latin America and the Caribbean,* 49.
21. Fogel, *Without Consent or Contract,* 23–25; Klein, *African Slavery in Latin America and the Caribbean,* 66.
22. See Thomas C. Holt, "'An Empire over the Mind': Emancipation, Race, and Ideology in the British West

Indies and the American South," in *Region, Race, and Reconstruction: Essays in Honor of C. Vann Woodward*, ed. J. Morgan Kousser and James M. McPherson (New York: Oxford University Press, 1982), 283–313.

23. See Leon Higginbotham, Jr., *In the Matter of Color: Race and the American Legal Process: The Colonial Period* (Oxford: Oxford University Press, 1978), 371–89.

24. Higginbotham, *In the Matter of Color*, 371.

25. See C. L. R. James, *The Black Jacobins: Toussaint l'Ouverture and the San Domingo Revolution* (New York: Random House, 1963).

26. Jay R. Mandle, "Black Economic Entrapment after Emancipation in the United States," in *The Meaning of Freedom: Economics, Politics, and Culture after Slavery*, ed. Frank McGlynn and Seymour Dreshler (Pittsburgh: University of Pittsburgh Press, 1992), 69.

27. Thomas C. Holt, *The Problem of Freedom, Race, Labor, and Politics in Jamaica and Britain, 1832–1938* (Baltimore: Johns Hopkins University Press, 1992), 56–57.

28. Holt, "'An Empire over the Mind,'" 304.

29. Prior to this date several northern states in the United States abolished slavery as a legal institution: Vermont in 1777, Pennsylvania and Massachusetts in 1780; also, in 1784 Rhode Island and Connecticut began to dismantle their systems of slavery.

30. W. E. B. Du Bois, *Black Reconstruction in America, 1860–1880* (1935; reprint, New York: Atheneum, 1992), 670.

31. João José Reis, *Slave Rebellion in Brazil: The Muslim Uprising of 1835 in Bahia*, trans. Arthur Brakel (Baltimore: Johns Hopkins University Press, 1993), chapter 2.

32. George Reid Andrews, *Blacks and Whites in São Paulo, Brazil, 1888–1988* (Madison: University of Wisconsin Press, 1991), 32–42.

33. Andrews, *Blacks and Whites in São Paulo, Brazil*, 42–53.

34. As Jordan observes, "Though other people, most notably the Indians, were enslaved by Europeans, slavery was typically a Negro-white relationship. This fact in itself inevitably meant that the Negro would not be accorded a high place when Europeans set about arranging the varieties of men on a grand scale. No one thought of the Great Chain of Being as originating in differences in power or social status between human groups; to do so would have been to

blaspheme the Creator. However, this did not prevent the idea of the Chain of Being from being applied to social relationships" (ibid., 227).

35. Leonard Thompson, *A History of South Africa* (New Haven: Yale University Press, 1995), 58; Wesseling, *Divide and Rule*, 264.

36. For some examples of how the term *Hottentot* was used in speech and writing, see the quotations in Bernard M. Magubane, *The Making of a Racist State: British Imperialism and the Union of South Africa, 1875–1910* (Trenton, N.J.: Africa World Press, 1996).

37. See St. Clair Drake, *Black Folk Here and There: An Essay in History and Anthropology* (Los Angeles: University of California, Center for Afro American Studies, 1987), vol. 2, chapters 4, 6, and 7.

38. Eric Williams, *Capitalism and Slavery* (Chapel Hill: University of North Carolina Press, 1944), 3–4; Mahmood Mudimbe, *The Invention of Africa: Gnosis, Philosophy, and the Order of Knowledge* (Bloomington: Indiana University Press, 1988), 20, 51–54; Robin Blackburn, *The Making of New World Slavery: From the Baroque to the Modern, 1492–1800* (London: Verso, 1997), 103.

39. See Clark Spencer Larsen, et al., "Population Decline and Extinction in La Florida," in *Disease and Demography in the Americas*, ed. John W. Verano and Douglas H. Ubelaker (Washington, D.C.: Smithsonian Institution Press, 1992), 25–39.

40. Charles Darwin, *On the Origin of Species by Means of Natural Selection, or the Preservation of Favored Races in the Struggle for Life* (1859; reprint, New York; Modern Library, 1995), 3.

41. He did so in the anonymously published *An Essay on the Principle of Population as It Affects the Future Improvement of Society, with Remarks on the Speculations of Mr. Goodwin, M. Condorcet and Other Writers* (London: J. Johnson, 1798). Malthus's work served three related purposes: it elaborated a theory of natural selection; it disputed the radical progressivism of Godwin and Condorcet; and it presented a systematic opposition to legislative changes (then proposed) in the Poor Laws in Great Britain that would make welfare payments proportional to family size . . . .

42. However, he doubted the efficacy of attempts at selective breeding. For example, Malthus doubted Condorcet's idea of "organic perfectibility." . . . (Malthus, *An Essay on the Principle of Population*, 170–71).

43. Jordan, *White over Black*, chapters 1 and 2; and Drake, *Black Folk Here and There*, chapter 7.

44. Charles Darwin, *Autobiography and Selected Letters*, ed. Francis Darwin (1887; reprint, New York: Dover Press, 1958), 42–43.

45. Richard Hofstadter, *Social Darwinism in American Thought* (Boston: Beacon Press, 1944), 143–69.

46. Herbert Spencer, *Principles of Sociology* (1885; reprint, New York: D. Appleton, 1901–1907), 1:95, 432–34, 550–56, 614–22, 757, 764; 2:242–43; 3:331.

47. J. S. Haller, *Outcasts from Evolution: Scientific Attitudes of Racial Inferiority, 1859–1900* (Urbana: University of Illinois Press, 1971), 128, 153.

# 7

# ETHNO-RELIGIOUS DIMENSIONS OF JEWISH CULTURES

## MICHAEL POLGAR

*This third reading in the historical section is by Michael Polgar, an associate professor of sociology at Penn State University. After teaching with this anthology, Polgar wrote this piece specifically for this collection. In it, Polgar argues that Jews are more than a religious group or an ethnic group. In order to advance the understanding of this argument, he reviews the history of Jewish practice in the United States and how sociologists understand Jewish cultural assimilation. Polgar also examines anti-Judaic and anti-Semitic discrimination and how Jews have been active in countering prejudice against multiple racial-ethnic groups in the United States.*

## INTRODUCTION

Jewish people are more than either an ethnic or a religious group, rather Jews are both at the same time (Goldscheider 2002). Judaism as a religion is also sometimes described as a civilization which includes history, literature, languages, organizations, standards, values, and spiritual ideals (Kaplan 1967). Leading sociologists help us to move beyond simplistic or narrow conceptions of cultural groups and memberships, conceiving of each person belonging to multiple intersecting social groups, each cultural group as being internally heterogeneous, and each form of oppression intersecting with others (Collins 2013). Orlando Patterson's insightful description of African American within-group cultural diversities is helpful in this respect: it is often accurate and descriptive to use the term "ethno-racial group" (Patterson 2013).

Adapting this hyphenated terminology to Judaism, we also may conceive of and describe Jewish people, in the United States and throughout the world, as belonging to a variety of "ethno-religious groups." This multidimensional view of both ethnicity and

*Source:* Polgar, Michael. 2015. "Ethno-Religious Dimensions of Jewish Cultures." (Unpublished manuscript).

religion can describe Jewish and other ethno-religious groups at multiple and intersecting levels, in terms of both social structure and culture (Kotler-Berkowitz 2005). American Jews in particular are both ethnically and religiously defined. In the words of leading historian David Sarna (2004), Jews in the United States are an "ethnic church."

Jewish people often claim similarities of tribal or ethnic lineage. This is done ritually when observant Jews regularly and ritually trace heritage to patriarchs (and sometimes also matriarchs) in liturgy (worship), scripture (Torah), and many forms of prayer. In practice, Jewish people inherit culture through communities and membership in a tribe through matrilineal decent. Jews affirm culture through ritual practices (religious participation), as well as through language (Hebrew and Yiddish, among others), diet, traditional garments, and other forms of individual and social behavior. There are all kinds of Jewish cultural groups and many ongoing debates about which Jewish cultural traditions are most important or necessary (Boyarin and Boyarin 1997). Many modern Jews exercise "ethnic options" in practicing religion and (symbolic) ethnicity, as do many other U.S.-based modern ethnic groups (Waters 1990, 2009). Jews have become more populous in the diaspora that is outside of Israel. Orthodoxy and even religiosity among Jews, as among other religious groups, is far from universal.

Jewish people generally divide culturally, distinguishing more ancient Mediterranean (Sephardic or Spanish) from more modern European or German (Ashkenazi) cultures. Hebrew and Yiddish languages (along with modern European customs) are developed in both Sephardic and Ashkenazi traditions. Yiddish and reform Judaism were brought to the USA through German and other European immigrations (Sarna 2004). Sephardic Jewry is less common in the United States, associated with more ancient, mid-eastern, and southern-European cultures (Gilbert 2001). The Zionist movement, with origins in Europe that run from the turn of the 20th century until Israel was founded in 1948, realizes the promise of the Torah and helps create the modern State of Israel. The state of Israel ensures that Jewry always has a homeland in its historic Mesopotamian location (National Foreign Assessment Center 1981). The population of modern Jewry is concentrated in certain nations, with 81% living in two roughly equal parts in the United States or Israel. More than half of 13.8 million Jews live in what is called the diaspora, outside of the state of Israel. Jews live in many nations, with an additional 16% living in 16 nations that are home to sizable Jewish populations (DellaPergola 2014).

Jewish leaders in sociology have proposed intellectual foundations for sociology of Jewry, taking as its objective study of the collective social group which shares expected actions "in support of what are considered to be Jewish values" (Klausner 1987). Jewry so defined has been classified at times and places as a nation, a nationality, a people, and a religious civilization. Collective actions by members of these social groupings define Jewish societies. From a sociological standpoint, having a Jewish orientation or "acting Jewish" is important for defining the boundaries of community and sometimes also as an accounting for being "special" or even "chosen." "Being" (essentially) Jewish (being born of Jewish heritage and claiming Jewish identity by lineage) is less certain, since direct descent from Abraham to modern Jewry may be considered largely fictive (Ibid). We are indeed one human family. At the same time, modernization of Jewish civilization, like modernization generally, is an important object for the sociology of Jewry (Goldscheider 1987).

In sociological terms, individual membership in Jewish groupings may be considered "*ascribed*" to members of Jewry (by birth, matrilineal decent, and thus ethnic origins). Other memberships and indeed strong Jewish identification among existing members may also be "achieved" by and through social actions, including marriage and religious conversion. People who *achieve* (or better "advance") our own Jewishness can and do so through religious conversion or through ritual practices, such as bar- or bat-mitzvot (coming of age ceremonies). Increasingly frequent inter-faith marriages involving Jews sometimes (but not always) involve conversions, sometimes to Judaism (Lazerwitz 1995).

## Streams of Jewish Practice in 20th c. USA

In the history of 20th century American Judaism (Sarna 2004), we see the development of three and soon four *movements* or *streams* within Jewish ethno-religious culture. Sarna specifically avoids calling these group variations "denominations," as commonly done within Christianity and Protestantism, since all four streams identify singularly and primarily as Jewish, not as a separate or distinct religion. Jewish movements or streams include reform, conservative, orthodox, and later reconstructionist Judaism (Gilbert 2001). Each stream of Judaism has had its own home seminary (eventually becoming a larger institutional religious training system with schools) for Jewish (and rabbinical) education. Early versions of Jewish movements in the United States were partly identified with their national origins (e.g., the German American and English origins of the reform movement and Eastern European origins of orthodoxy). Conservative and orthodox streams were partially developed based on the strengths and needs of U.S. immigrant populations, as well as charismatic rabbinical leaders (Sarna 2004).

Jewish people, though heterogeneous living in various ethno-religious groups, identify and are seen as one group, described as Jewry, united in a common civilization through social practices. A modern (fourth) stream of Judaism which is the reconstructive movement views Judaism as a civilization (Kaplan 1967). Jews are certainly not unique among religious groups in this respect; "civilization" is not a uniquely Jewish quality or conceptualization. However, after histories of oppression, including anti-Semitism and especially the Holocaust (Gilbert 2000), Jews and other religious minorities have been portrayed as "more ethnic," sometimes as special or exceptional (Michels 2010), and even as separate racial groups. Crises stemming from ethnocentrism and discrimination can have a powerful effect on group identities, spurring group identity movements, social solidarity, and at certain historical moments social action, such as a "war on prejudice" (Svonkin 1997).

The history of Judaism in the United States, particularly in the 20th century, has been intertwined and sometimes consistent with American social and economic developments and ideals, infused with patterns of migration, assimilation, and economic mobility, contrasting old and new worlds. Too many old world "policies" (Russian pogroms and German Nazi crimes in particular) created or enforced discrimination, hardship, and persecution including genocide, forcing Jews and other immigrants to find new freedom and opportunity within the borders and shores of other nations including the United States (Gilbert 2001). In this modern diaspora, especially in the "new world," Jewish life and political culture has emphasized pluralism and tolerance, leading to a "new pluralism" in the late 20th century (Goren 1999).

Modern Jews are not bound to identify with or practice in one or only one stream of Judaism. Research finds that not all Jews in the United States are affiliated with a single synagogue and/or movement (advocates and other adherents complain that too many U.S. Jews are unaffiliated). Research also finds that some Jews, like Christians and others, change identification among different movements, with greater numbers accruing in reform movement and fewer in orthodoxy (Lazerwitz 1998). This lack of identification and internal ambiguity among Jewish populations often raises concerns about the health and continuity of American Jewry as a whole.

## Cultural Assimilation: Modernization Makes New Jews

Assimilation to new nations, languages, and cultures is not always simply a positive, progressive, and one-way process. Contemporary sociologists have found reasons to elaborate a theoretically simple and transformative path of assimilation, modifying "straight-line" to "bumpy-line" analogies to summarize this ongoing and inter-generational cultural process (Alba and Nee 1997). Jewish cultural assimilation has been required if not forced in many historical contexts. Like assimilation for many cultural groups, national and ethnic assimilation has become (in modern American contexts) an iconic and well-known combination of declining cultural distinctions and blurring boundaries (e.g., dissolving differences between Jews and more general ethnic categories of Americans) (Alba 2006). This means that Jews are considered culturally not-so-different, much like others groups who gain collective status in the United States, middle-class and culturally usual, though still maintaining unique (different) cultural identities and practices. While some groups have experienced cultural assimilation across "bright-line" differences (recognizable changes from very "different" cultures), Jews have blended in without having to lose all ethnic identity. One result is that Jewish Americans may not always feel the need to choose or take sides in a newly pluralistic ethno-religious world, where both Passover and Easter can be celebrated (or at least recognized). Even so, dietary laws and differences in religious calendars can create distinctions and even some conflicts among groups and individuals.

The present and future of ethno-racial and -religious differences is a source of sociological study and debate. Sociologists describe a recent "twilight (declining significance) of ethnicity" in which we are seeing assimilation as the culmination of a historical process starting after World War II (Alba 2014). Some Jews in the modern United States have grown up or become "mainstream," modern, or even "whiter" in the context of larger-scale economic improvements (what President Reagan called "rising tides") in social class status (Brodkin 1998). Jewish people in the contemporary United States have had more cultural, economic, and ethnic options than ever before.

For some modern Jews, Judaism has become *symbolic* ethnicity and religion (Gans 1979, 1994). Symbolic ethnicity involves optional uses of a few distinctive practices or habits in diet or dress (e.g., bagels) instead of a complete cultural identity involving religion and language (e.g., orthodoxy), with many Jews identifying or practicing "Jewishly" mainly or only through these cultural choices. Like white ethnics more generally, "choosing" ethnic options in a time of blurred ethnic boundaries is associated with a symbolic form of ethnicity (Waters 1990). The ease of ethnic options can blind us to the historical and sometimes contemporary costs of ethnic or racial identification (Waters 2009). Ultimately, this can both dilute the strength of ethnic identification with culture (hence declining significance) and also prevent people from recognizing the harm of externally imposed racial and ethnic identification and the consequent need for anti-discriminatory policies and practices.

Jewish public health in the United States also is a recent concern. Research exploring cultural differences and inequalities in health is important in general, although religious variations have not yet been a primary concern in the growing health disparities scholarship (Smedley, Stith, and Nelson 2003). Jewish health is comparable to health in other U.S. white ethnicities, though not as favorably as might be imagined. Controlling for socio-economic status, research finds Jews have lower self-rated health, similar to African Americans, when compared to other ethnic white populations (Kotler-Berkowitz 2005). The density of co-ethnic ties (relationships or social networks among Jews) tends to reduce this disparity.

## ANTI-JUDAISM AND ANTI-SEMITISM, INCLUDING THE HOLOCAUST

There are many chapters in the worldwide history of anti-Semitism that illustrate Jewish ethno-religious dimensions of inequality. Anti-Semitism, and anti-Judaism more specifically, has a much long history in the older and larger world beyond the United States (Fein 1987). Multiple historic periods of historic anti-Judaism in many nations and eras are well documented. For modern societies, anti-Judaism culminates with the Holocaust of 1933-45 and the subsequent documentation of Nazi war crimes (Gilbert 2000). Americans, British, French, and Russian jurists established the truth of these atrocities at the Nuremburg trials (Dodd and Bloom 2007). The Holocaust clouds the history of modern Europe, using religious and racialized persecution of Jews and other enemies of Nazis, scapegoats for economic failures in Germany (Michman 1995). Holocaust studies in the United States have been extensive but were slow to develop until the latter half of the 20th century.

The Holocaust is one of multiple historical examples of "human wrongs," including slavery, terror, and other attempts at genocide (Fein 1979, 2007). It is not the only example of these criminal injustices, nor is the Holocaust the only historical persecution of large numbers of Jews. However, it is a horrific chapter in the history of humanity, one of several "unnatural" episodes of violence (unlike war and combat) with no comparative behavior among other species (Fein 2007). Unfortunately, holocaust education remains necessary, as trivialization and denial have been a part of a more general assault on Holocaust memory (Rosenfeld 1988, 2001).

Sociology texts include uneven coverage of the Holocaust and anti-Judaism more generally (Fein 1979). While most informed people agree that prejudice against any ethno-religious or racial group is morally objectionable and that these forms of discrimination are illegal, historical work questions how to interpret the considerable ebbs and flows in modern American experiences of anti-Semitism (Gerber 1986). Certainly there was more anti-Judaism in the United States during the 1920s and 1930s, and less during the 1950s and 1960s (Sarna 2004; Gerber 1986). After the Second World War, reinforcing the popular ideal of successful cultural assimilation through American immigrant opportunities and experiences, patterns of Jewish social mobility were celebrated, especially in comparison to earlier and less tolerant cultural histories of Jews and many other immigrant and minority groups (Michels 2010).

Public opinion research shows a wide variety of progressive (but not universal) attitudinal changes during the latter half of the 20th century. Research finds modern and recent improvements in public attitudes towards Jews (Chelsea and Greg 2009; Rosenfield 1982). Public opinion does not show equivalent or positively improving attitudes towards all groups (including Muslims), nor does it show universally improved attitudes towards African Americans and people of color generally (Krysan 2000; Krysan and Lewis 2004).

Decreasing rates of public intolerance does not mean that anti-Semitism and racism have slowly or simply "gone away" as populations become more tolerant. Civil and human rights are won through protest and public education; many people with racial or ethnic privilege have hidden and still hide behind mythic attitudes of "color-blindness" (Bonilla-Silva 2014). Structural inequalities still remain at the heart of racism and other forms of ethnocentrism (Bonilla-Silva 1997). Old and new dimensions of prejudice and intolerance have evolved to take new and multiple forms, requiring ongoing work to increase tolerance, equality, and freedom.

## WAR ON PREJUDICE: JEWISH SOCIAL ACTION

While the post-war period through the mid-1960s has been called "the Golden Era" of American Jewry (Goren 1999), this happy retrospection can obscure the important work against prejudice and discrimination done by multiple progressive organizations, including Jewish social action groups and allies. The *intergroup relations movement* included social scientists and Jewish service organizations to fight a battle on bigotry, at times tagged a "war on prejudice," from the 1940s into the 1960s (Svonkin 1997). One important result has been a community (or human) relations movement which continues to involve organizations of all faiths and origins across the United States. Jewish organizations played a leading role in defining this anti-prejudice movement, supporting social action with social sciences, including work by leading scholars who came to the United States from Europe in the context of Nazi persecution. The Anti-Defamation League (ADL) of B'nai B'rith joined with the American Jewish Committee (AJC) and the American Jewish Congress (all secular agencies) to advance civil rights and fight prejudice and discrimination within the National Community Relations Advisory Council (Ibid). No longer struggling for survival or self-defense, Jewish social action turned towards more general efforts for a culturally pluralistic and egalitarian nation.

While scholars and opinion-shapers in the media joined the war on prejudice, anti-Semitism work evolved into appeals for tolerance more generally (Svonkin 1997). Scholars defined the social psychology of prejudice and many diverse popular media campaigns promoted intergroup relations through education. "American All-Immigrants All" was one inclusive promotion, in contrast to vitriolic and hateful propaganda from earlier and less tolerant generations. Educational films and television spots reminded viewers that we were all human, bringing popular stars (from Lucille Ball to Frank Sinatra) to the screen to support this ongoing war on prejudice, with CBS portraying the first American Passover in 1955.

Multicultural education, now popularized in educational kits like the "Teaching Tolerance" education campaign by the Southern Poverty Law Center of Alabama, is effective for many groups and goals, and especially helpful for white students (Martin 2014). "Multicultural" is a modern form of what was called "intercultural" education. The "mother" of this educational movement is Rachel Davis Dubois, who established a Bureau for this purpose in 1934 (Svonkin 1997). Human and intergroup relations education was initially designed for educational use, and then spread thorough the general population for use in occupational and professional training. Jewish agencies initially supported this process, though keeping a "low profile" so it was not seen as a "Jewish enterprise." National inter-group relations conferences were developed during the 1950s and multicultural education has expanded tremendously into the 21st century. These developments took place in parallel with an evolution in public attitudes towards race and ethnicity.

The first advanced scientific research on racial attitudes shows that U.S. public opinions on race and ethnicity evolved from "color caste" (Myrdal, Sterner, and Rose 1944) to "color blind," starting during the Second World War. The paths towards tolerance and acceptance of black and other racially or ethnically defined groups of people in the United States was built (not granted) by social action and after a long history of oppression. While inequalities persist and white privilege has not disappeared, scholars document changes in attitudes that have supported systemic racism and oppression. Attitudinal changes are documented along dimensions of social distance along with racial beliefs, principles, policies, and conflicts (Krysan 2012a).

The most drastic changes in racial and ethnic attitudes are documented among whites, who (as a group) have had the most potential for progress. Few can justify biologically based prejudice and discrimination through racially caste systems, especially in the wake of the racism and Holocaust, but many are slow to support "amalgamation" of different groups. White attitudes changed more progressively during the civil rights era, dovetailing with the end of legal segregation and Jim Crow, though showing some groups remained socially distant (Krysan 2012b). Blacks and others became an "activated public" who mobilized public opinion in support of both progressive attitudes and egalitarian policies (Lee 2002). Modern research shows that many white attitudes have shifted from biologically to culturally-based forms prejudice but still remain less than fully inclusive (Krysan 2012c). Still, both white and black attitudes about race and ethnicity are heterogeneous and related to class privilege (Hochschild 1995). Since the new millennium, sociological scholars have increasingly identified facets of racial attitudes, finding that variations in social context affect the risk of disrespect (Anderson 2011) and critiquing ideas of "color-blindness" (Bonilla-Silva 2014).

At the same time, socio-economic inequalities have long been combined with racialized oppression. Sociologists recognize that many lasting forms of oppression have affected black and other populations of color, from the historical development of racial slavery oppressing people of color who were often of African origin (Zuberi 2001). The most unjust inequalities of group and tribe have based on misunderstandings and misuses of racial classification, like slavery, American Jim Crow laws, and South African Apartheid. Jewish people of many national and racial origins seem to have had economic success in historical comparison. Even so, Jewish cultures were economically oppressed, even enslaved, at different and earlier points in the historical record. Within Jewish populations there has been and still remain economic inequalities. These economic and social forces not only made life difficult for historical Jewish groups, it forced a historically extended exodus of Jewish populations, "unsettling" the tribe from its various roots in middle-eastern (Sephardic) locations and later European (including Russian) or Ashkenazi cultures (Konner 2003).

## CONCLUSION: ETHNIC OPTIONS WITHIN AND AMONG JEWISH COMMUNITIES

In crafting a research agenda for studying Jewry through the social sciences, we should reconsider and reconceptualize three recurring, uncertain, and cumulative arguments about Jewish past and present (Goldscheider 2002). First, many Jews have become more secular and assimilated during modern times. Second, Jews have become less ethnically distinctive, but this loss of minority status has opened opportunities and reduced constraints associated with prejudice and discrimination. Third (and subsequently), some Jewish communities outside of Israel appear to have weakened as a result of these modern developments, so that there is a "vanishing Jewish diaspora" with various uncertain Jewish communities.

The sociological challenge to these arguments is that, even during times of assimilation, which can create what Alba (2006) terms blurred ethnic boundaries, many modern Jewish communities and institutions have developed or renewed cultural strengths. Jewish communities are diverse and powerful, some large and cohesive, and Jews are comfortable as citizens of many nations and of the world. New expressions of Judaism and Jewish civilization fill many aspects of culture and many parts of the world.

The vitality and diversity of Jewish life is good news for social scientists and others who have worried about varied consequences of anti-Judaism, not to mention concerns about cultural drift or change in the diverse ethno-religious streams and forms of Judaism. The fact remains that many (though not all) Jewish streams and populations have achieved social status through high levels of education and consequently less social stress. Structural social mobility and cohesion seem to help continuity of the tribe (Gilbert 2001; Sarna 2004).

While inequalities in society remain a challenge to all, Jewish survival and resilience in the century after the Holocaust are a lesson to follow. Wars against prejudice combined with civil rights movements and the war on poverty to help future generations. Holocaust studies, while troubled by denials and anti-Semitism, advanced the cause of human rights worldwide. We remember and continue, we learn and reflect, and we do not allow the injustices of past or present intolerance recur.

## DISCUSSION QUESTIONS

1. Why and how are streams of Jewish culture characterized as ethno-religious groups?
2. Describe how inequalities and differences have been related to Jewish assimilation, anti-Judaism, and Jewish involvement in the "war on prejudice."

# 8

# THE INVENTION OF HETEROSEXUALITY

JONATHAN NED KATZ

*This last reading in the historical section is a classic piece by Jonathan Ned Katz, director of Ourhistory.org. Similar to other readings in this section, Katz illustrates well that the concepts of homosexuality and heterosexuality were constructed at a particular time in history to demarcate changing social relations. This excerpt is taken from a 1990 journal article published in the* Socialist Review. *Katz argues that our perception of sexuality in the United States is ahistorical and that we need to see how constructions of sexuality evolve as changes occur in the larger economy and as medicalization and the scientific study of human behavior alter our understanding of sexuality.*

Heterosexuality is as old as procreation, ancient as the lust of Eve and Adam. That first lady and gentleman, we assume, perceived themselves, behaved, and felt just like today's heterosexuals. We suppose that heterosexuality is unchanging, universal, essential, ahistorical.

Contrary to that common sense conjecture, the concept of heterosexuality is only one particular historical way of perceiving, categorizing, and imagining the social relations of the sexes. Not ancient at all, the idea of heterosexuality is a modern invention, dating to the late nineteenth century. The heterosexual belief, with its metaphysical claim to eternity, has a particular, pivotal place in the social universe of the late nineteenth and twentieth centuries that it did not inhabit earlier. This essay traces the historical process by which the heterosexual idea was created as ahistorical and taken-for-granted . . . .

By not studying the heterosexual idea in history, analysts of sex, gay and straight, have continued to

*Source:* ©Jonathan Ned Katz, co-director, OutHistory.org, author of *Love Stories: Sex Between Men Before Homosexuality* (University of Chicago Press, 2001).

privilege the "normal" and "natural" at the expense of the "abnormal" and "unnatural." Such privileging of the norm accedes to its domination, protecting it from questions. By making the normal the object of a thoroughgoing historical study we simultaneously pursue a pure truth and a sex-radical and subversive goal: we upset basic preconceptions. We discover that the heterosexual, the normal, and the natural have a history of changing definitions. Studying the history of the term challenges its power.

Contrary to our usual assumption, past Americans and other peoples named, perceived, and socially organized the bodies, lusts, and intercourse of the sexes in ways radically different from the way we do. If we care to understand this vast past sexual diversity, we need to stop promiscuously projecting our own hetero and homo arrangement. Though lip-service is often paid to the distorting, ethnocentric effect of such conceptual imperialism, the category heterosexuality continues to be applied uncritically as a universal analytical tool. Recognizing the time-bound and culturally specific character of the heterosexual category can help us begin to work toward a thoroughly historical view of sex . . . .

## BEFORE HETEROSEXUALITY: EARLY VICTORIAN TRUE LOVE, 1820–1860

In the early nineteenth-century United States, from about 1820 to 1860, the heterosexual did not exist. Middle-class white Americans idealized a True Womanhood, True Manhood, and True Love, all characterized by "purity"—the freedom from sensuality.[1] Presented mainly in literary and religious texts, this True Love was a fine romance with no lascivious kisses. This ideal contrasts strikingly with late-nineteenth and twentieth century American incitements to a hetero sex.[2]

Early Victorian True Love was only realized within the mode of proper procreation, marriage, the legal organization for producing a new set of correctly gendered women and men. Proper womanhood, manhood, and progeny—not a normal male-female eros—was the main product of this mode of engendering and of human reproduction.

The actors in this sexual economy were identified as manly men and womanly women and as procreators, not specifically as erotic beings or heterosexuals. Eros did not constitute the core of a heterosexual identity that inhered, democratically, in both men and women. True Women were defined by their distance from lust. True Men, though thought to live closer to carnality, and in less control of it, aspired to the same freedom from concupiscence.

Legitimate natural desire was for procreation and a proper manhood or womanhood; no heteroerotic desire was thought to be directed exclusively and naturally toward the other sex; lust in men was roving. The human body was thought of as a means toward procreation and production; penis and vagina were instruments of reproduction, not of pleasure. Human energy, thought of as a closed and severely limited system, was to be used in producing children and in work, not wasted in libidinous pleasures.

The location of all this engendering and procreative labor was the sacred sanctum of early Victorian True Love, the home of the True Woman and True Man—a temple of purity threatened from within by the monster masturbator, an archetypal early Victorian cult figure of illicit lust. The home of True Love was a castle far removed from the erotic, exotic ghetto inhabited most notoriously then by the prostitute, another archetypal Victorian erotic monster . . . .

## LATE VICTORIAN SEX-LOVE: 1860–1892

Heterosexuality and "Homosexuality" did not appear out of the blue in the 1890s. These two eroticisms were in the making from the 1860s on. In late Victorian America and in Germany, from about 1860 to 1892, our modern idea of an eroticized universe began to develop, and the experience of a heterolust began to be widely documented and named . . . .

In the late nineteenth-century United States, several social factors converged to cause the eroticizing of consciousness, behavior, emotion, and identity that became typical of the twentieth-century Western middle class. The transformation of the family from producer to consumer unit resulted in a change in family members' relation to their own bodies; from being an instrument primarily of work, the human body was integrated into a new economy, and began more commonly to be perceived as a means of consumption and pleasure. Historical work has recently begun on how the biological human body is differently integrated into changing modes of production, procreation, engendering, and pleasure so as to alter radically the identity, activity, and experience of that body.[3]

The growth of a consumer economy also fostered a new pleasure ethic. This imperative challenged the early Victorian work ethic, finally helping to usher in a major transformation of values. While the early Victorian work ethic had touted the value of economic production, that era's procreation ethic had extolled the virtues of human reproduction. In contrast, the late Victorian economic ethic hawked the pleasures of consuming, while its sex ethic praised an erotic pleasure principle for men and even for women.

In the late nineteenth century, the erotic became the raw material for a new consumer culture. Newspapers, books, plays, and films touching on sex, "normal" and "abnormal," became available for a price. Restaurants, bars, and baths opened, catering to sexual consumers with cash. Late Victorian entrepreneurs of desire incited the proliferation of a new eroticism, a commoditized culture of pleasure.

In these same years, the rise in power and prestige of medical doctors allowed these upwardly mobile professionals to prescribe a healthy new sexuality. Medical men, in the name of science, defined a new ideal of male-female relationships that included, in women as well as men, an essential, necessary, normal eroticism. Doctors, who had earlier named and judged the sex-enjoying woman a "nymphomaniac," now began to label women's *lack* of sexual pleasure a mental disturbance, speaking critically, for example, of female "frigidity" and "anesthesia."[4]

By the 1880s, the rise of doctors as a professional group fostered the rise of a new medical model of Normal Love, replete with sexuality. The new Normal Woman and Man were endowed with a healthy libido. The new theory of Normal Love was the modern medical alternative to the old Cult of True Love. The

doctors prescribed a new sexual ethic as if it were a morally neutral, medical description of health. The creation of the new Normal Sexual had its counterpart in the invention of the late Victorian Sexual Pervert. The attention paid the sexual abnormal created a need to name the sexual normal, the better to distinguish the average him and her from the deviant.

## HETEROSEXUALITY: THE FIRST YEARS, 1892–1900

In the periodization of heterosexual American history suggested here, the years 1892 to 1900 represent "The First Years" of the heterosexual epoch, eight key years in which the idea of the heterosexual and homosexual were initially and tentatively formulated by U.S. doctors. The earliest-known American use of the word "heterosexual" occurs in a medical journal article by Dr. James G. Kiernan of Chicago, read before the city's medical society on March 7, 1892, and published that May, portentous dates in sexual history.[5] But Dr. Kiernan's heterosexuals were definitely not exemplars of normality. Heterosexuals, said Kiernan, were defined by a mental condition, "physical hermaphroditism." Its symptoms were "inclinations to both sexes." These heterodox sexuals also betrayed inclinations "to abnormal methods of gratification," that is, techniques to ensure pleasure without procreation. Dr. Kiernan's heterogeneous sexuals did demonstrate "traces of the normal sexual appetite" (a touch of procreative desire). Kiernan's normal sexuals were implicitly defined by a monolithic other-sex inclination and procreative aim. Significantly, they still lacked a name.

Dr. Kiernan's article of 1892 also included one of the earliest known uses of the word homosexual in American English. Kiernan defined "Pure homosexuals" as persons whose "general mental state is that of the opposite sex." Kiernan thus defined homosexuals by their deviance from a gender norm. His heterosexuals displayed a double deviance from both gender and procreative norms.

Though Kiernan used the new words heterosexual and homosexual, an old procreative standard and a new gender norm coexisted uneasily in his thought.

His word heterosexual defined a mixed person and compound urge, abnormal because they want only included procreative and non-procreative objectives, as well as same-sex and different-sex attractions.

That same year, 1892, Dr. Krafft-Ebing's influential *Psychopathia Sexualis* was first translated and published in the United States.[6] But Kiernan and Krafft-Ebing by no means agreed on the definition of the heterosexual. In Krafft-Ebing's book, "hetero-sexual" was used unambiguously in the modern sense to refer to an erotic feeling for a different sex. "Homo-sexual" refered unambiguously to an erotic feeling for a "same sex." In Krafft-Ebing's volume, unlike Kiernan's article, heterosexual and homosexual were clearly distinguished from a third category, a "psycho-sexual hermaphroditism," defined by impulses toward both sexes.

Krafft-Ebing hypothesized an inborn "sexual instinct" for relations with the "opposite sex," the inherent "purpose" of which was to foster procreation. Krafft-Ebing's erotic drive was still a reproductive instinct. But the doctor's clear focus on a different-sex versus same-sex sexuality constituted a historic, epochal move from an absolute procreative standard of normality toward a new norm. His definition of heterosexuality as other-sex attraction provided the basis for a revolutionary, modern break with a centuries-old procreative standard.

It is difficult to overstress the importance of that new way of categorizing. The German's mode of labeling was radical in referring to the biological sex, masculinity or femininity, and the pleasure of actors (along with the procreant purpose of acts). Krafft-Ebing's heterosexual offered the modern world a new norm that came to dominate our idea of the sexual universe, helping to change it from a mode of human reproduction and engendering to a mode of pleasure. The heterosexual category provided the basis for a move from a production-oriented, procreative imperative to a consumerist pleasure principle—an institutionalized pursuit of happiness . . . .

Only gradually did doctors agree that heterosexual referred to a normal, "other-sex" eros. This new standard-model heterosex provided the pivotal term for the modern regularization of eros that paralleled similar attempts to standardize masculinity and femininity, intelligence, and manufacturing.[7] The idea of heterosexuality as the master sex from which all others deviated was (like the idea of the master race) deeply authoritarian. The doctors' normalization of a sex that was hetero proclaimed a new heterosexual separatism—an erotic apartheid that forcefully segregated the sex normals from the sex perverts. The new, strict boundaries made the emerging erotic world less polymorphous—safer for sex normals. However, the idea of such creatures as heterosexuals and homosexuals emerged from the narrow world of medicine to become a commonly accepted notion only in the early twentieth century. In 1901, in the comprehensive *Oxford English Dictionary*, "heterosexual" and "homosexual" had not yet made it.

## THE DISTRIBUTION OF THE HETEROSEXUAL MYSTIQUE: 1900–1930

In the early years of this heterosexual century the tentative hetero hypothesis was stabilized, fixed, and widely distributed as the ruling sexual orthodoxy: The Heterosexual Mystique. Starting among pleasure-affirming urban working-class youths, southern blacks, and Greenwich Village bohemians as defensive subculture, heterosex soon triumphed as dominant culture.[8]

In its earliest version, the twentieth-century heterosexual imperative usually continued to associate heterosexuality with a supposed human "need," "drive," or "instinct" for propagation, a procreant urge linked inexorably with carnal lust as it had not been earlier. In the early twentieth century, the falling birth rate, rising divorce rate, and "war of the sexes" of the middle class were matters of increasing public concern. Giving vent to heteroerotic emotions was thus praised as enhancing baby-making capacity, marital intimacy, and family stability. (Only many years later, in the mid-1960s, would hetero-eroticism be distinguished completely, in practice and theory, from procreativity and male-female pleasure sex justified in its own name.)

The first part of the new sex norm—hetero— referred to a basic gender divergence. The "oppositeness" of the sexes was alleged to be the basis for a universal, normal, erotic attraction between males and females. The stress on the sexes' "oppositeness," which harked back to the early nineteenth century, by no means simply registered biological differences of females and males. The early twentieth-century focus on physiological and gender dimorphism reflected the deep anxieties of men about the shifting work, social roles, and power of men over women, and about the ideals of womanhood and manhood. That gender anxiety is documented, for example, in 1897, in *The New York Times'* publication of the Reverend Charles Parkhurst's diatribe against female "andromaniacs," the preacher's derogatory, scientific-sounding name for women who tried to "minimize distinctions by which manhood and womanhood are differentiated."[9] The stress on gender difference was a conservative response to the changing social-sexual division of activity and feeling which gave rise to the independent "New Woman" of the 1880s and eroticized "Flapper" of the 1920s.

The second part of the new hetero norm referred positively to sexuality. That novel, upbeat focus on the hedonistic possibilities of male-female conjunctions also reflected a social transformation—a revaluing of pleasure and procreation, consumption and work in commercial, capitalist society. The democratic attribution of a normal lust to human females (as well as males) served to authorize women's enjoyment of their own bodies and began to undermine the early Victorian idea of the pure True Woman—a sex–affirmative action still part of women's struggle. The twentieth-century Erotic Woman also undercut nineteenth-century feminist assertions of women's moral superiority, cast suspicions of lust on women's passionate romantic friendships with women, and asserted the presence of a menacing female monster, "the lesbian."[10] . . . .

In the perspective of heterosexual history, this early twentieth century struggle for the more explicit depiction of an "opposite-sex" eros appears in a curious new light. Ironically, we find sex-conservatives, the social-purity advocates of censorship and repression, fighting against the depiction not just of sexual perversity but also of the new normal heterosexuality. That a more open depiction of normal sex had to be defended against forces of propriety confirms the claim that heterosexuality's predecessor, Victorian True Love, had included no legitimate eros . . . .

## THE HETEROSEXUAL STEPS OUT: 1930–1945

In 1930, in *The New York Times,* heterosexuality first became a love that dared to speak its name. On April 30th of that year, the word "heterosexual" is first known to have appeared in *The New York Times Book Review.* There, a critic described the subject of André Gide's *The Immoralist* proceeding "from a heterosexual liaison to a homosexual one." The ability to slip between sexual categories was referred to casually as a rather unremarkable aspect of human possibility. This is also the first known reference by *The Times* to the new hetero/homo duo.[11]

The following month the second reference to the hetero/homo dyad appeared in *The New York Times Book Review,* in a comment on Floyd Dell's *Love in the Machine Age.* This work revealed a prominent antipuritan of the 1930s using the dire threat of homosexuality as his rationale for greater heterosexual freedom. *The Times* quoted Dell's warning that current abnormal social conditions kept the young dependent on their parents, causing "infantilism, prostitution and homosexuality." Also quoted was Dell's attack on the "inculcation of purity" that "breeds distrust of the opposite sex." Young people, Dell said, should be "permitted to develop normally to heterosexual adulthood." "But," *The Times* reviewer emphasized, "such a state already exists, here and now." And so it did. Heterosexuality, a new gender-sex category, had been distributed from the narrow, rarified realm of a few doctors to become a nationally, even internationally cited aspect of middle-class life.[12] . . .

## HETEROSEXUAL HEGEMONY: 1945–1965

The "Cult of Domesticity" following World War II—the reassociation of women with the home, motherhood, and child-care; men with fatherhood and wage work outside the home—was a period in which the predominance of the hetero norm went almost unchallenged, an era of heterosexual hegemony. This was an age in which conservative mental-health professionals reasserted the old link between heterosexuality and procreation. In contrast, sex-liberals of the day strove, ultimately with success, to expand the heterosexual ideal to include within the boundaries of normality a wider-than-ever range of nonprocreative, premarital, and extra-marital behaviors. But sex-liberal reform actually helped to extend and secure the dominance of the heterosexual idea, as we shall see when we get to Kinsey.

The post-war sex-conservative tendency was illustrated in 1947, in Ferdinand Lundberg and Dr. Marnia Farnham's book, *Modern Woman: The Lost Sex.* Improper masculinity and femininity were exemplified, the authors decreed, by "engagement in heterosexual relations . . . with the complete intent to see to it that they do not eventuate in reproduction."[13] Their procreatively defined heterosex was one expression of a post-war ideology of fecundity that, internalized and enacted dutifully by a large part of the population, gave rise to the post-war baby boom.

The idea of the feminine female and masculine male as prolific breeders was also reflected in the stress, specific to the late 1940s, on the homosexual as sad symbol of "sterility"—that particularly loaded term appears incessantly in comments on homosex dating to the fecund forties.

In 1948, in *The New York Times Book Review*, sex liberalism was in ascendancy. Dr. Howard A. Rusk declared that Alfred Kinsey's just- published report on *Sexual Behavior in the Human Male* had found "wide variations in sex concepts and behavior." This raised the question: "What is 'normal' and 'abnormal'?" In particular, the report had found that "homosexual experience is much more common than previously thought," and "there is often a mixture of both homo and hetero experience."[14]

Kinsey's counting of orgasms indeed stressed the wide range of behaviors and feelings that fell within the boundaries of a quantitative, statistically accounted heterosexuality. Kinsey's liberal reform of the hetero/homo dualism widened the narrow, old hetero category to accord better with the varieties of social experience. He thereby contradicted the older idea of a monolithic, qualitatively defined, natural procreative act, experience, and person.[15]

Though Kinsey explicitly questioned "whether the terms 'normal' and 'abnormal' belong in a scientific vocabulary," his counting of climaxes was generally understood to define normal sex as majority sex. This quantified norm constituted a final, society-wide break with the old, qualitatively defined reproductive standard. Though conceived of as purely scientific, the statistical definition of the normal as the-sex-most-people-are-having substituted a new, quantitative moral standard for the old, qualitative sex ethic—another triumph for the spirit of capitalism.

Kinsey also explicitly contested the idea of an absolute, either/or antithesis between hetero and homo persons. He denied that human beings "represent two discrete populations, heterosexual and homosexual." The world, he ordered, "is not to be divided into sheep and goats." The hetero/homo division was not nature's doing: "Only the human mind invents categories and tries to force facts into separated pigeon-holes. The living world is a continuum."[16]

With a wave of the taxonomist's hand, Kinsey dismissed the social and historical division of people into heteros and homos. His denial of heterosexual and homosexual personhood rejected the social reality and profound subjective force of a historically constructed tradition which, since 1892 in the United States, had cut the sexual population in two and helped to establish the social reality of a heterosexual and homosexual identity.

On the one hand, the social construction of homosexual persons has led to the development of a powerful gay liberation identity politics based on an ethnic group model. This has freed generations of women and men from a deep, painful, socially induced sense of shame, and helped to bring about a society-wide liberalization of attitudes and responses to homosexuals.[17] On the other hand, contesting the notion of homosexual and heterosexual persons was one early, partial resistance to the limits of the hetero/homo construction. Gore Vidal, rebel son of Kinsey, has for years been joyfully proclaiming:

there is no such thing as a homosexual or a heterosexual person. There are only homo- or heterosexual acts. Most people are a mixture of impulses if not practices, and what anyone does with a willing partner is of no social or cosmic significance.

So why all the fuss? In order for a ruling class to rule, there must be arbitrary prohibitions. Of all prohibitions, sexual taboo is the most useful because sex involves everyone . . . we have allowed our governors to divide the population into two teams. One team is good, godly, straight; the other is evil, sick, vicious.[18]

Though Vidal's analysis of our "wacky division" is persuasive, we may now go one step further and question not only the division into hetero and homo persons but the hetero/homo division itself . . . .

## HETEROSEXUALITY QUESTIONED: 1965–1982

By the late 1960s, anti-establishment counterculturalists, fledgling feminists, and homosexual-rights activists had begun to produce an unprecedented critique of sexual repression in general, of women's sexual repression in particular, of marriage and the family—and of some forms of heterosexuality. This critique even found its way into *The New York Times*.

In March 1968, in the theater section of that paper, freelancer Rosalyn Regelson cited a scene from a satirical review brought to New York by a San Francisco troup:

a heterosexual man wonders inadvertently into a homosexual bar. Before he realizes his mistake, he becomes involved with an aggressive queen who orders a drink for him. Being a broadminded liberal and trying to play it cool until he can back out of the situation gracefully, he asks, "How do you like being a, ah, homosexual?" To which the queen drawls drily, "How do you like being, ah, whatever it is you are?"

Regelson continued:

The middle-class liberal, challenged today on many fronts, finds his last remaining fixed value, his

heterosexuality, called into question. The theater . . . recalls the strategies he uses in dealing with this ultimate threat to his world view.[19]

Just a few weeks later, in March 1968, *Times* critic Clive Barnes reviewed Paddy Chayefsky's new play, *The Latent Heterosexual*. In this play, a middle-aged and extremely effeminate writer discovered that "his homosexuality was . . . merely a cover-up for his fears of impotence." The play, said the ever-earnest Barnes, "makes a serious point."[20] In the perspective of heterosexual history, Chayefsky's holding out hope of hetero hapiness for even the most unlikely homosexual queen is a document of heterosexuality on the defensive. Chayefsky's portrayal of latent heterosexuality triumphing against all odds was nervous propaganda for a norm increasingly challenged by feminists, counterculturalists, homosexualists, and those advanced other-sex lovers aware of something radically wrong in the house of heterosex . . . .

## HETEROSEXUAL HISTORY: OUT OF THE SHADOWS

Our brief survey of the heterosexual idea suggests a new hypothesis. Rather than naming a conjunction old as Eve and Adam, heterosexual designates a word and concept, a norm and role, an individual and group identity, a behavior and feeling, and a peculiar sexual-political institution particular to the late nineteenth and twentieth centuries.

Because much stress has been placed here on heterosexuality as word and concept, it seems important to affirm that heterosexuality (and homosexuality) came into existence before it was named and thought about. The formulation of the heterosexual idea did not create a heterosexual experience or behavior; to suggest otherwise would be to ascribe determining power to labels and concepts. But the titling and envisioning of heterosexuality did play an important role in consolidating the construction of the heterosexual's social existence. Before the wide use of the word heterosexual, I suggest, women and men did not mutually lust with the same profound, sure sense of normalcy that followed the distribution of "heterosexual" as universal sanctifier.

According to this proposal, women and men make their own sexual histories. But they do not produce their sex lives just as they please. They make their sexualities within a particular mode of organization given by the past and altered by their changing desire, their present power and activity, and their vision of a better world. That hypothesis suggests a number of good reasons for the immediate inauguration of research on a historically specific heterosexuality.[21]

The study of the history of the heterosexual experience will forward a great intellectual struggle still in its early stages. This is the fight to pull heterosexuality, homosexuality, and all the sexualities out of the realm of nature and biology into the realm of the social and historical. Feminists have explained to us that anatomy does not determine our gender destinies (our masculinities and femininities). But we've only recently begun to consider that *biology does not settle our erotic fates*. The common notion that biology determines the object of sexual desire, or that physiology and society together cause sexual orientation, are determinisms that deny the break existing between our bodies and situation and our desiring. Just as the biology of our hearing organs will never tell us why we take pleasure in Bach or delight in Dixieland, our female or male anatomies, hormones, and genes will never tell us why we yearn for women, men, both, other, or none. That is because desiring is a self-generated project of individuals within particular historical cultures. Heterosexual history can help us see the place of values and judgments in the construction of our own and others' pleasures, and to see how our erotic tastes—our aesthetics of the flesh—are socially institutionalized through the struggle of individuals and classes.

The study of heterosexuality in time will also help us to recognize the vast *historical diversity of sexual emotions and behaviors*—a variety that challenges the monolithic heterosexual hypothesis. John D'Emilio and Estelle Freedman's *Intimate Matters: A History of Sexuality in America* refers in passing to numerous substantial changes in sexual activity and feeling: for example, the widespread use of contraceptives in the nineteenth century, the twentieth-century incitement of the female orgasm, and the recent sexual conduct changes by gay men in response to the AIDS epidemic. It's now a commonplace of family history that people in particular classes feel and behave in substantially different ways under different historical conditions.[22] Only when we stop assuming an invariable essence of heterosexuality will we begin the research to reveal the full variety of sexual emotions and behaviors.

The historical study of the heterosexual experience can help us *understand the erotic relationships of women and men in terms of their changing modes of social organization*. Such modal analysis actually characterizes a sex history well underway.[23] This suggests that the erosgender-procreation system (the social ordering of lust, femininity and masculinity, and baby-making) has been linked closely to a society's particular organization of power and production. To understand the subtle history of heterosexuality we need to look carefully at correlations between (1) society's organization of eros and pleasure; (2) its mode of engendering persons as feminine or masculine (its making of women and men); (3) its ordering of human reproduction; and (4) its dominant political economy. This General Theory of sexual Relativity proposes that substantial historical changes in the social organization of eros, gender, and procreation have basically altered the activity and experience of human beings within those modes.[24]

A historical view locates heterosexuality and homosexuality in time, helping us distance ourselves from them. This distancing can help us formulate new questions that clarify our long-range sexual-political goals: what has been and is the social function of sexual categorizing? Whose interests have been served by the division of the world into heterosexual and homosexual? Do we dare not draw a line between those two erotic species? Is some sexual naming socially necessary? Would human freedom be enhanced if the sex-biology of our partners if lust was of no particular concern, and had no name? In what kind of society could we all more freely explore our desire and our flesh?

As we move toward [the future] . . . a new sense of the historical making of the heterosexual and homosexual suggests that these are ways of feeling, acting, and being with each other that we can together unmake and radically remake according to our present desire, power, and our vision of a future political-economy of pleasure.

## DISCUSSION QUESTIONS

1. How does Katz challenge the taken-for-granted assumption that heterosexuality is both natural and ahistorical? In answering this question, mention the historical texts he cites that help explain the emergence of the concept of heterosexuality.

2. Explain how Katz posits the emergence of the idea of heterosexuality alongside the development of the consumer society. What are the historical factors he cites to support this claim?

## NOTES

1. Barbara Welter, "The Cult of True Womanhood: 1820–1860," *American Quarterly*, vol. 18 (Summer 1966); Welter's analysis is extended here to include True Men and True Love.

2. Some historians have recently told us to revise our idea of sexless Victorians: their experience and even their ideology, it is said, were more erotic than we previously thought. Despite the revisionists, I argue that "purity" was indeed the dominant, early Victorian, white, middle-class standard. For the debate on Victorian sexuality see John D'Emilio and Estelle Freedman, *Intimate Matters: A History of Sexuality in America* (New York: Harper & Row, 1988), p. xii.

3. See, for example, Catherine Gallagher and Thomas Laqueur, eds., "The Making of the Modern Body: Sexuality and Society in the Nineteenth Century," *Representations*, no. 14 (Spring 1986) (republished, Berkeley: University of California Press, 1987).

4. This reference to females reminds us that the invention of heterosexuality had vastly different impacts on the histories of women and men. It also differed in its impact on lesbians and heterosexual women, homosexual and heterosexual men, the middle class and working class, and on different religious, racial, national, and geographic groups.

5. Dr. James G. Kiernan, "Responsibility in Sexual Perversion," *Chicago Medical Recorder*, vol. 3 (May 1892), pp. 185–210.

6. R. von Kraffi-Ebing, *Psychopathia Sexualis, with Especial Reference to Contrary. Sexual Instinct: A Medico-Legal Study*, trans. Charles Gilbert Chaddock (Philadelphia: F.A. Davis, 1892), from the 7th and revised German ed. Preface, November 1892.

7. For the standardization of gender, see Lewis Terman and C. C. Miles, *Sex and Personality, Studies in Femininity and Masculinity* (New York: McGraw Hill, 1936). For the standardization of intelligence, see Lewis Terman, *Stanford-Binet Inteligence Scale* (Boston: Houghton Mifflin, 1916). For the standardization of work, see "scientific management" and "Taylorism" in Harry Braverman, *Labor and Monopoly Capital: The Degradation of Work in the Twentieth Century* (New York: Monthly Review Press, 1974).

8. See D'Emilio and Freedman, *Intimate Matters*, pp. 194–201, 231, 241, 295–96; Ellen Kay Trimberger, "Feminism, Men, and Modern Love: Greenwich Village, 1900–1925," in *Powers of Desire: The Politics of Sexuality*, eds. Ann Snitow, Christine Stansell, Sharon Thompson (New York: Monthly Review Press, 1983), pp. 131–52; Kathy Peiss, "'Charity Girls' and City Pleasures: Historical Notes on Working Class Sexuality, 1880–1920," in *Powers of Desire*, pp. 74–87; and Mary P. Ryan, "The Sexy Saleslady: Psychology, Heterosexuality, and Consumption in the Twentieth Century," in her *Womanhood in America*, 2nd ed. (New York: Franklin Watts: 1979), pp. 151–82.

9. [Rev. Charles Parkhurst], "Woman. Calls Them Andromaniacs. Dr. Parkhurst So Characterizes Certain Women Who Passionately Ape Everything That Is Mannish. Woman Divinely Preferred. Her Supremacy Lies in Her Womanliness, and She Should Make the Most of It—Her Sphere of Best Usefulness the Home," *The New York Times*, May 23, 1897, p. 16:1.

10. See Lisa Duggan, "The Social Enforcement of Heterosexuality and Lesbian Resistance in the 1920s," in *Class, Race, and Sex: The Dynamics of Control*, ed. Amy Swerdlow and Hanah Lessinger (Boston: G. K. Hall, 1983), pp. 75–92; Rayna Rapp and Ellen Ross, "The Twenties Backlash: Compulsory Heterosexuality,

the Consumer Family, and the Waning of Feminism," in Swerdlow and Lessinger; Christina Simmons, "Companionate Marriage and the Lesbian Threat," *Frontiers*, vol. 4, no. 3 (Fall 1979), pp. 54–59; and Lillian Faderman, *Surpassing the Love of Men* (New York: William Morrow, 1981).

11. Louis Kronenberger, review of André Gide, *The Immoralist*, *New York Times Book Review*, April 20, 1930, p. 9.

12. Henry James Forman, review of Floyd Dell, *Love in the Machine Age* (New York: Farrar & Rinehart), *New York Times Book Review*, September 14, 1930, p. 9.

13. Ferdinand Lundberg and Dr. Marnia F. Farnham, *Modern Woman, the Lost Sex* (NY: Harper, 1947).

14. Dr. Howard A. Rusk, *New York Times Book Review*, January 4, 1948, p. 3.

15. Alfred Kinsey, Wardell B. Pomeroy, Clyde E. Martin, *Sexual Behavior in the Human Male* (Philadelphia: W. B. Saunders, 1948), pp. 199–200.

16. Kinsey, *Sexual Behavior*, pp. 637, 639.

17. See Steven Epstein, "Gay Politics, Ethnic Identity: The Limits of Social Constructionism," *Socialist Review* 93/93 (1987), pp. 9–54.

18. Gore Vidal, "Someone to Laugh at the Squares With" [Tennessee Williams], *New York Review of Books,* June 13, 1985; reprinted in his *At Home: Essays, 1982–1988* (New York: Random House, 1988). p. 48.

19. Rosalyn Regelson, "Up the Camp Staircase," *The New York Times*, March 3, 1968, Section II, p. 1:5.

20. Clive Barnes, *The New York Times*, March 22, 1968, p. 52:1. Barnes lavishly praised Zero Mostel's acting of Chayefsky's "fag poet": "It is the humor of the shriekingly heterosexual actor pretending camp, with grotesquely exaggerated mannerisms that are funny simply through their very distance from reality."

21. In addition to those already cited in these notes, a few writers have begun the historicizing of heterosexuality. In 1987, Gmp in London published *Heterosexuality*, a collection of essays by gay men and lesbians edited by Gillian E. Hanscombe and Martin Humphries; the essay by Jon Ward on "The Nature of Heterosexuality" is the most relevant to historical analysis . . . .

22. D'Emilio and Freedman, *Intimate Matters*, pp. 57–63, 268, 356.

23. Ryan, *Womanhood;* John D'Emilio, "Capitalism and Gay Identity," in *Powers of Desire*, pp. 100–13; Jeffrey Weeks, *Coming Out: Homosexual Politics in Britain from the Nineteenth Century to the Present* (London: Quarter Books, 1977); D'Emilio and Freedman, *Intimate Matters*; Katz, "Early Colonial Exploration, Agriculture, and Commerce: The Age of Sodomitical Sin, 1607–1740," *Gay/Lesbian Almanac*, pp. 23–65.

24. This tripartite system is intended as a revision of Gayle Rubin's pioneering work on the social-historical organization of eros and gender. See "The Traffic in Women: Notes on the Political-Economy of Sex," in *Toward an Anthropology of Women*, ed. Rayna R. Reiter (New York: Monthly Review Press, 1975), pp. 157–210, and "Thinking Sex: Notes for a Radical Theory of the Politics of Sexuality," in *Pleasure and Danger: Exploring Female Sexuality*, ed. Carole S. Vance (Boston: Routledge & Kegan Paul, 1984), pp. 267–329.

# 9

# FOUNDATIONS OF CLASS ANALYSIS

## A Marxist Perspective

ERIK OLIN WRIGHT

*This reading by Erik Olin Wright is the first of six readings in the "Theories of Difference" section of Part I. Wright, professor of sociology at the University of Wisconsin–Madison, is a recent president of the American Sociological Association (ASA). Wright is considered to be a brilliant social theorist whose work has challenged sociologists to reexamine the foundations of Marxism as an explanation of social life. Wright lays out his understanding of social class analysis from an analytical Marxist perspective in the reading excerpted here. This piece was originally published in a 2001 research anthology,* Reconfigurations of Class and Gender, *edited by Janeen Baxter and Mark Western.*

If "class" is the answer, what is the question? The word "class" is deployed in a wide range of explanatory contexts in sociology, and, depending on that explanatory context, different concepts of class may be needed. Three broad kinds of questions are particularly common for which the word "class" figures centrally in the answer. First, the word "class" sometimes figures in the answers to questions such as "How do people locate themselves within a social structure of inequality?" Class is one of the possible answers to the question. In this case, the concept would be defined something like "a social category sharing a common set of subjectively salient attributes within a system of stratification." Second, class is offered as part of the answer to the question "What explains inequalities in economically defined standards of living?" Here, typically, the concept of class would not be defined by subjectively salient attributes of a social location but rather by the relationship of people to income-generating resources or assets of

*Source:* Wright, Erik Olin. "Foundations of Class Analysis: A Marxist Perspective." In *Reconfigurations of Class and Gender,* edited by Janeen Baxter and Mark Western. Copyright © 2001 by the Board of Trustees of the Leland Stanford Jr. University. All rights reserved. Used with the permission of Stanford University Press, www.sup.org.

various sorts. Third, class plays a central role in answering the question "What sorts of struggles have the potential to transform capitalist economic oppressions in an emancipatory direction?" This is the distinctively Marxist question. Marxists may share with Weberians the second question concerning the explanation of economic inequalities, and, as we will see, the Marxist concept of class shares much with the Weberian concept in terms of its role in explaining such inequality. Marxists may also use the concept of class in the account of people's subjective understandings of their location in systems of stratification, as in the first question. However, it is the third question that imparts to the Marxist concept of class a distinctive explanatory and normative agenda. It suggests a concept of class that is not simply defined in terms of relations to economic resources but that elaborates these relations in terms of mechanisms of economic oppression. The problem of specifying the theoretical foundations of the concept of class, therefore, crucially depends on what explanatory work the concept is called on to do.

In these terms, the concept of class has greater explanatory ambitions within the Marxist tradition than in any other tradition of social theory, and this, in turn, places greater burdens on its theoretical foundations. In its most ambitious form, classical historical materialism argued that class—or very closely linked concepts such as "mode of production" or "the economic base"—constituted the primary explanation of the epochal trajectory of social change as well as social conflicts located within concrete time and place, and of the macro-level institutional form of the state along with the micro-level subjective beliefs of individuals. Expressions such as "class struggle is the motor of history" and "the executive of the modern state is but a committee of the bourgeoisie" captured this ambitious claim of explanatory primacy for the concept of class.

Most Marxist scholars today have pulled back significantly from the grandiose explanatory claims of historical materialism (if not necessarily from its explanatory aspirations). Few today defend stark versions of "class primacy." Nevertheless, it remains the case that class retains a distinctive centrality within the Marxist tradition and is called on to do much more arduous explanatory work than in other theoretical traditions. Indeed, a good argument can be made that this, along with a specific orientation to radically egalitarian normative principles, is a large part of what defines the remaining distinctiveness and vitality of the Marxist tradition as a body of thought, particularly within sociology. It is for this reason that I have argued that "Marxism as class analysis" defines the core agenda of Marxist sociology (see Wright, Levine, and Sober 1992: chap. 8).

The task of this reading is to lay out the central analytical foundations of the concept of class in a way that is broadly consistent with the Marxist tradition. This is a tricky business, for within Marxism there is no consensus on any of the core concepts of class analysis. What defines the tradition is more a loose commitment to the importance of class analysis for understanding the conditions for challenging capitalist oppressions and the language within which debates are waged— what Alvin Gouldner (1970) aptly called a "speech community"—than a precise set of definitions and propositions. Any claims about the analytical foundations of Marxist class analysis that I make, therefore, will reflect my specific stance within that tradition rather than an authoritative account of "Marxism" in general or of the work of Karl Marx in particular.

I proceed in the following manner. First, I lay out a series of conceptual elements that underlie the kind of Marxist class analysis that I have pursued. Many of these elements apply, perhaps with some rhetorical modification, to Weberian-inspired class analysis as well as Marxist, although as a package they reflect the background assumptions characteristic of the Marxist agenda. Some of the points I make here may be quite obvious, but nevertheless I think it is useful to lay these out step by step. Second, I specify what I feel is the core common explanatory claim of class analysis in both the Marxist and the Weberian tradition. Third, I identify what I believe to be the distinctive hallmark of the Marxist concept, which differentiates from its Weberian cousins and anchors the broader theoretical claims and agenda of Marxist class analysis. This involves, above all, elaborating the specific causal mechanisms through which Marxists claim that class relations generate social effects. Finally, I briefly lay out what I see as the advantages of the Marxian-inspired form of class analysis.

## CONCEPTUAL ELEMENTS

Five conceptual elements need to be clarified in order to give specificity to the Marxist approach to class analysis: (1) the concept of social relations of production, (2) the idea of class as a specific form of such relations, (3) the problem of the forms of variation of class relations, (4) the meaning of a "location" within class relations, and (5) the distinction between micro and macro levels of class analysis.

### Relations of Production

Any system of production requires the deployment of a range of assets or resources or factors of production: tools, machines, land, raw materials, labor power, skills, information, and so forth. This deployment can be described in technical terms as a production function—so many inputs of different kinds are combined in a specific process to produce an output of a specific kind. The deployment can also be described in social relational terms: The individual actors that participate in production have different kinds of rights and powers over the use of the inputs and over the results of their use. Rights and powers over resources, of course, are attributes of social relations, not descriptions of the relationship of people to things as such: To have rights and powers with respect to land defines one's social relationship to other people with respect to the use of the land and the appropriation of the fruits of using the land productively. The sum total of these rights and powers constitutes the "social relations of production."

### Class Relations as a Form of Relations of Production

When the rights and powers of people over productive resources are unequally distributed—when some people have greater rights/powers with respect to specific kinds of productive resources than do others—these relations can be described as class relations. The classic contrast in capitalist societies is between owners of means of production and owners of labor power since "owning," is a description of rights and powers with respect to a resource deployed in production.

Let us be quite precise here: The rights and powers in question are not defined with respect to the ownership or control of things in general but only of resources or assets insofar as they are deployed in production. A capitalist is not someone who owns machines but someone who owns machines, deploys those machines in a production process, hires owners of labor power to use them, and appropriates the profits from the use of those machines. A collector of machines is not, by virtue of owning those machines, a capitalist. To count as a class relation, it is therefore not sufficient that there be unequal rights and powers over the sheer physical use of a resource. There must also be unequal rights and powers over the appropriation of the results of that use. In general, this implies appropriating income generated by the deployment of the resource in question.

### Variations in Class Relations

Different kinds of class relations are defined by the kinds of rights and powers that are embodied in the relations of production. For example, in some systems of production, people are allowed to own the labor power of other people. When the rights accompanying such ownership are absolute, the class relation is called "slavery." When the rights and powers over labor power are jointly owned by the laborer and someone else, the class relation is called "feudalism."[1] In capitalist societies, in contrast, such absolute or shared ownership of other people is prohibited.

Because of the specific role that class analysis played in historical materialism, Marxists have traditionally limited the range of variation of types of class relations to a very few abstract forms, slavery, feudalism, and capitalism being the main types. Once the restrictions of historical materialism are relaxed, the basic concept of class relations allows for a much richer array of variations. The rights and powers that constitute "ownership" can be decomposed, with different rights and powers going to different actors. Just as feudalism is characterized by a decomposition of rights and powers over labor power—some belonging to feudal lords, others to serfs—so too can there be a decomposition of the rights and powers over means of production. Government restrictions on workplace practices, union representation on boards of directors, code-termination schemes, employee stock option, delegations of power to managerial hierarchies, and so on all constitute various ways in which the property rights and powers embodied in the idea of "owning the means of production" are decomposed and redistributed. Such redistribution of rights and powers constitutes a form of variation in class relations. To be sure, such systems of redistributed rights and powers are complex and move class relations away from the simple, abstract form of perfectly polarized relations. One of the objectives of class analysis is to understand the consequences of these forms of variation of class relations. Such complexity, however, is still complexity in the form of class relations, not some other sort of social relation, since the social relations still govern the unequal rights and powers of people over economically relevant assets.

The sum total of the class relations in a given unit of analysis can be called the "class structure" of that unit of analysis. One can thus speak of the class structure of a firm, of a city, of a country, and perhaps of the world. A class structure generally does not consist of a single type of class relation. Typically, a variety of forms of class relations are combined in various ways, further adding to the complexity of class structures.[2]

### Class Locations Within Class Relations

"Class locations" can be understood as the social positions occupied by individuals—and, in some contexts, families—within class relations. Again, these class locations need not be polarized—locations in which there is an absolute disjuncture between the rights and powers of the different locations within relations. A characteristic feature of many class structures is the existence of what I have termed "contradictory locations within class relations." The claim of a class analysis of such social locations is that the specific pattern of rights and powers over productive resources that are combined in a given location defines a set of real and significant causal processes. Contradictory locations are like a chemical compound

in which its properties can best be explained by uncovering the specific way in which different elements—different rights and powers with respect to the various assets used in production—are combined rather than treating such locations as unitary, one-dimensional categories.

### Micro- and Macro-Class Analysis

The micro level of class analysis attempts to understand the ways in which class impacts on individuals. At its core is the analysis of the effects of class locations on various aspects of individual lives. Analyses of labor market strategies of unskilled workers or political contributions of corporate executives would be examples of micro-level class analysis as long as the rights and powers of these actors over economic resources figured in the analysis. The macro level of analysis centers on the effects of class structures on the unit of analysis in which they are defined. The analysis of how the international mobility of capital constrains the policy options of states, for example, constitutes a macro-level investigation of the effects of a particular kind of class structure on states.

## THE EXPLANATORY CLAIMS: THE FUNDAMENTAL METATHESIS OF CLASS ANALYSIS

The fundamental metathesis of class analysis is that class, understood in the way described here, has systematic and significant consequences for both the lives of individuals and the dynamics of institutions. One might say "class counts" as a slogan. At the micro level, whether one sells one's labor power on a labor market, whether one has the power to tell other people what to do in the labor process, whether one owns large amounts of capital, whether one possesses a legally certified valuable credential, and so on have real consequences in the lives of people. At the macro level, it is consequential for the functioning of a variety of institutions whether the rights over the allocation and use of means of production are highly concentrated in the hands of a few people, whether certain of these rights have been appropriated by public authority or remain privately controlled, whether there are significant barriers to the acquisition of different kinds of assets by people who lack them, and so on. To say that class counts, then, is to claim that the distribution of rights and powers over the basic productive resources of the society have significant, systematic consequences.

What, then, are the specific mechanisms through which these effects are generated? By virtue of what are class relations, as defined here, explanatory? At the most general and abstract level, the causal processes embedded in class relations help explain two kinds of proximate effects: what people get and what they have to do to get what they get. The first of these concerns, above all, the distribution of income. The class analysis claim is, therefore, that the rights and powers that people have over productive assets constitute a systematic and significant determinant of their standards of living: What you have determines what you get. The second of these causal processes concerns, above all, the distribution of economic activities. Again, the class analysis thesis is that the rights and powers over productive assets constitute a systematic and significant determinant of the strategies and practices in which people engage to acquire their income: whether they have to pound the pavement looking for a job, whether they make decisions about the allocation of investments around the world, whether they have to worry about making payments on bank loans to keep a farm afloat, and so on. What you have determines what you have to do to get what you get. Other kinds of consequences that are linked to class—voting patterns, attitudes, friendship formation, health, and so on—are second-order effects of these two primary processes.

These are not trivial claims. It could be the case, for example, that the distribution of the rights and powers of individuals over productive resources has relatively little to do with their income or economic activities. Suppose that the welfare state provided a universal basic income to everyone sufficient to sustain a decent standard of living. In such a society, what people get would be significantly, although not entirely, decoupled from what they own. Similarly, if the world became like a continual lottery in which there was virtually no stability either within or across generations to the distribution of assets, then, even if it were still the case that relations to such assets statically mattered for income, it might make sense to say that class did not matter very much. Or, suppose that the central determinant of what you had to do to get what you get was race or sex or religion and that ownership of economically relevant assets was of marginal significance in explaining anyone's economic activities or conditions. Again, in such a society, class might not be very explanatory (unless, of course, the main way in which gender or race affects these outcomes was by allocating people to class positions on the basis of their race and gender). The sheer fact of inequalities of income or of domination and subordination within work is not proof that class counts; what has to be shown is that the rights and powers of people over productive assets have a systematic bearing on these phenomena.

## MARXIST CLASS ANALYSIS

As formulated above, there is nothing uniquely Marxist about the explanatory claims of class analysis. "What people get" and "what people have to do to get what they get" sounds very much like "life chances." Weberian class analysts would say very much the same thing. It is for this reason that there is a close affinity between Marxist and Weberian concepts of class (although less affinity in the broader theoretical frameworks within which these concepts figure or in the explanatory reach class is thought to have).

What makes class analysis distinctively Marxist is the account of specific mechanisms that are seen as generating these two kinds of consequences. Here the pivotal concepts are exploitation and domination. These are the conceptual elements that anchor the Marxist concept of class in the distinctive Marxist question of class analysis.

Exploitation is a complex and challenging concept. It is meant to designate a particular form of interdependence of the material interests of people, namely, a situation that satisfies three criteria:[3]

1. *The inverse interdependent welfare principle*: The material welfare of exploiters causally depends on the material deprivations of the exploited.

2. *The exclusion principle*: This inverse interdependence of welfares of exploiters and exploited depends on the exclusion of the exploited from access to certain productive resources.

3. *The appropriation principle*: Exclusion generates material advantage to exploiters because it enables them to appropriate the labor effort of the exploited.

Exploitation is thus a diagnosis of the process through which the inequalities in incomes are generated by inequalities in rights and powers over productive resources: The inequalities occur, at least in part, through the ways in which exploiters, by virtue of their exclusionary rights and powers over resources, are able to appropriate surplus generated by the effort of the exploited. If the first two of these principles are present, but not the third, economic oppression may exist, but not exploitation. The crucial difference is that in non-exploitative economic oppression, the privileged social category does not itself need the excluded category. While their welfare does depend on the exclusion, there is no ongoing interdependence of their activities. In the case of exploitation, the exploiters actively need the exploited: Exploiters depend on the effort of the exploited for their own welfare.

This deep interdependence makes exploitation a particularly explosive form of social relation for two reasons. First, exploitation constitutes a social relation that simultaneously pits the interests of one group against another and that requires their ongoing interactions. Second, it confers on the disadvantaged group a real form of power with which to challenge the interests of exploiters. This is an important point. Exploitation depends on the appropriation of labor effort. Because human beings are conscious agents, not robots, they always retain significant levels of real control over their expenditure of effort. The extraction of effort within exploitative relations is thus always to a greater or lesser extent problematic and precarious, requiring active institutional devices for its reproduction. Such devices can become quite costly to exploiters in the form of the costs of supervision, surveillance, sanctions, and so on. The ability to impose such costs constitutes a form of power among the exploited.

Domination is a simpler idea. It identifies one dimension of the interdependence of the activities within production itself rather than simply the interdependence of material interests generated by those activities. Here the issue is that, by virtue of the relations into which people enter as a result of their rights and powers that they have over productive resources, some people are in a position to control the activities of others—to direct them, to boss them, to monitor their activities, to hire and fire them, or to advance or deny them credit.[4] The Marxist class analysis thesis, therefore, is not simply that "what you have determines what you have to do to get what you get" but, rather, "what you have determines the extent to which you are dominated or dominating when you do what you have to do to get what you get."

In Weberian class analysis, just as much as in Marxist class analysis, the rights and powers that individuals have over productive assets define the material basis of class relations. However, for Weberian-inspired class analysis, these rights and powers are consequential primarily because of the ways they shape life chances, most notably life chances within market exchanges, rather than the ways they structure patterns of exploitation and domination. Control over resources affects bargaining capacity within processes of exchange, and this in turn affects the results of such exchanges, especially income. Exploitation and domination are not centerpieces of this argument.

This suggests the contrast between Marxist and Weberian frameworks of class analysis illustrated in Figure 9.1. Both Marxist and Weberian class analysis differ sharply from simple gradational accounts of class in which class is itself directly identified within inequalities in income since both begin with the problem of the social relations that determine the access of people to economic resources. In a sense, therefore, Marxist and Weberian definitions of class in capitalist society share the same definitional criteria. Where they differ is in the theoretical elaboration and specification of the implications of this common set of criteria: The Marxist model sees two causal paths being systematically generated by these relations—one operating through market exchanges and the other through the process of production itself—whereas the Weberian model traces only one causal path; and the Marxist model elaborates the mechanisms of these causal paths in terms of exploitation and domination as well as bargaining capacity within exchange, whereas the Weberian model deals only with the last of these. In a sense, then, the Weberian strategy of class analysis is contained within the Marxist model.

Of course, any Weberian can include an analysis of class-based domination and exploitation within any specific sociological inquiry. One of the charms of the Weberian analytical framework is that it is entirely permissive about the inclusion of additional causal processes. Such an inclusion, however, represents the importation of Marxist themes into the Weberian model; the model itself does not imply any particular importance to these issues. Frank Parkin (1979) once made a well-known quip in a book about class theory: "Inside every neo-Marxist is a Weberian struggling to get out." The argument presented here suggests a complementary proposition: "Inside every leftist neo-Weberian is a Marxist struggling to stay hidden."

## THE PAYOFF: WHAT ARE THE ADVANTAGES OF THE MARXIST STRATEGY OF CLASS ANALYSIS?

Elaborating the concept of class in terms of exploitation and domination clearly facilitates its analytical relevance to the agenda embedded in the distinctive

**FIGURE 9.1**    Three Models of Social Class Analysis.

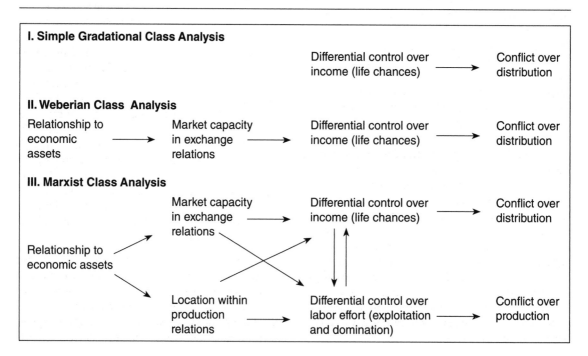

Marxist question: "What sorts of struggles have the potential to challenge and transform capitalist economic oppressions in an emancipatory direction?" Class struggles have this potential because of the way class relations shape the interests and capacities of actors with respect to those oppressions. Saying this, of course, does not define the conclusion of the Marxist agenda but only its starting point. It does not prejudge the problem of what social conditions enable or impede such struggles or determine their effectiveness, of how class struggles are linked to other kinds of social conflicts, whether class compromises are possible within such struggles, or even of the historically possible extent to which capitalist economic oppressions can be eliminated. I am claiming, however, that the answer to these questions is facilitated when class is understood in terms of exploitation and domination.

However, what if one is not particularly interested in the foundational Marxist question? What if one believes that emancipatory transformations of capitalism, however morally attractive, are utopian fantasies? Or, even more critically, what if one believes that capitalism is not especially oppressive? If one rejects the relevance of the Marxist question, does this necessarily imply a complete rejection of the Marxist conceptualization of class as well? I think not. There are a number of reasons that elaborating the concept of class in terms of exploitation and domination has theoretical payoffs beyond the specific normative agenda of Marxist class analysis itself:

1. *Linking exchange and production.* The Marxist logic of class analysis affirms the intimate link between the way in which social relations are organized within exchange and within production. This is a substantive, not a definitional, point: The social relations that organize the rights and powers of individuals with respect to productive resources systematically shape their location both within exchange relations and within the process of production itself. This does not mean, of course, that there is no independent variation of exchange and production, but it does imply that this variation is structured by class relations.

2. *Conflict.* One of the standard claims about Marxist class analysis is that it foregrounds conflict within class relations. Indeed, a conventional way of describing Marxism in sociological textbooks is to see it as a variety of "conflict theory." This characterization, however, is not quite precise enough, for conflict is certainly a prominent feature of Weberian views of class as well. The distinctive feature of the Marxist account of class relations in these terms is not simply that it gives prominence to class conflict but that it understands conflict as generated by inherent properties of those relations rather than simply contingent factors. Exploitation defines a structure of interdependent interests in which advancing the interests of exploiters depends on their capacity to impose deprivations on the exploited. This is a stronger antagonism of interests than simple competition, and it underwrites a strong prediction within Marxist class analysis that class systems will be conflict ridden.

3. *Power.* At the very core of the Marxist construction of class analysis is the claim not simply that class relations generate deeply antagonistic interests but that they also give people in subordinate class locations forms of power with which to struggle for their interests. As already noted, since exploitation rests on the extraction of labor effort and since people always retain some measure of control over their own effort, they always confront their exploiters with capacities to resist exploitation.[5] This is a crucial form of power reflected in the complex counterstrategies that exploiting classes are forced to adopt through the elaboration of instruments of supervision, surveillance, monitoring, and sanctioning. It is only by virtue of this inherent capacity for resistance—a form of social power rooted in the interdependencies of exploitation—that exploiting capacities are forced to devote some of their resources to ensure their ability to appropriate labor effort.

4. *Coercion and consent.* Marxist class analysis contains the rudiments of what might be termed an endogenous theory of the formation of consent. The argument is basically this: The extraction of labor effort in systems of exploitation is costly for exploiting classes because of the inherent capacity of people

to resist their own exploitation. Purely coercively backed systems of exploitation will often tend to be suboptimal since under many conditions it is too easy for workers to withhold diligent performance of labor effort. Exploiting classes will therefore have a tendency to seek ways of reducing those costs. One of the ways of reducing the overhead costs of extracting labor effort is to do things that elicit the active consent of the exploited. These range from the development of internal labor markets that strengthen the identification and loyalty of workers to the firms in which they work to the support for ideological positions that proclaim the practical and moral desirability of capitalist institutions. Such consent-producing practices, however, also have costs attached to them, and thus systems of exploitation can be seen as always involving trade-offs between coercion and consent as mechanisms for extracting labor effort.

This argument points to a crucial difference between systems of non-exploitative oppression and exploitative class relations. In nonexploitative oppression, there is no dependency of the oppressing group on the extraction of labor effort of the oppressed and thus much less need to elicit their active consent. Purely repressive reactions to resistance—including genocidal repression—are therefore feasible. This is embodied in the abhorrent nineteenth-century American folk expression that "the only good Indian is a dead Indian," an expression that reflects the fact that Native Americans were generally not exploited, although they were certainly oppressed. The comparable, if less catchy, expression for workers would be that "the only good worker is an obedient worker"; it would make no sense to say that "the only good worker is a dead worker." This contrast points to the ways in which an exploitation-centered class analysis suggests an endogenous understanding of the construction of consent.

5. *Historical/comparative analysis.* As originally conceived, Marxist class analysis was an integral part of a sweeping theory of the epochal structure and historical trajectory of social change. However,

even if one rejects historical materialism, the Marxist exploitation-centered strategy of class analysis still provides a rich menu of concepts for historical and comparative analysis. Different kinds of class relations are defined by the specific mechanisms through which exploitation is accomplished, and these differences in turn imply different problems faced by exploiting classes for the reproduction of their class advantage and different opportunities for exploited classes to resist. Variations in these mechanisms and in the specific ways in which they are combined in concrete societies provide an analytically powerful road map for comparative research.

These are all reasons why a concept of class rooted in the linkage between social relations of production on the one hand and exploitation and domination on the other should be of sociological interest. Still, the most fundamental payoff of these conceptual foundations is the way in which it infuses class analysis with moral critique. The characterization of the mechanisms underlying class relations in terms of exploitation and domination focuses attention on the moral implications of class analysis. Exploitation and domination identify ways in which these relations are oppressive and create harms, not simply inequalities. Class analysis can thus function as part not simply of a scientific theory of interests and conflicts but also of an emancipatory theory of alternatives and social justice. Even if socialism is off the historical agenda, the idea of countering the exploitative logic of capitalism is not.

## Discussion Questions

1. According to Wright, what is the primary "payoff" of the Marxist strategy of social class analysis in contrast to the Weberian model?
2. Discuss the primary concepts Wright analyzes to demonstrate that Marx's notion of social class allows for a discussion of the "moral implications" of a class analysis.

## Notes

1. This may not seem to be the standard definition of feudalism as a class structure. Typically, feudalism is defined as a class system within which extraeconomic coercion is used to force serfs to perform labor for lords, either in the form of direct labor dues or in the form of rents. Here I am treating "direct economic coercion" as an expression of a property right of the lord in the labor power of the serf. This is reflected in the fact that the serf is not free to leave the land of the lord. This is equivalent to the claim that the flight of a serf from the land is a form of theft—stealing labor power partially owned by the lord. For a discussion of this conceptualization of feudalism, see Wright (1985: chap. 3).

2. Class structures are thus complex for two reasons: The rights and powers within given forms of class relations can be redistributed in various ways, and a given class structure may combine a variety of different kinds of class relations.

3. For a more extensive discussion of these three principles, see Wright (1997:9–19).

4. While Weberians generally do not talk about exploitation, domination is an important theme within Weberian sociology. It is not, however, generally linked so directly with the problem of rights and powers over economic resources and thus is less closely tied to the problem of class as such. Weberian discussions of domination are thus typically found in general discussions of forms of authority and power rather than the specific issue of class.

5. For a discussion of class and exploitation specifically in terms of principal/agent issues, see Bowles and Gintis (1990).

# 10

# Is Capitalism Gendered and Racialized?

## Joan Acker

*This second reading in the section on theory builds on Erik Olin Wright's arguments concerning social class and Marxism. Here, Joan Acker, professor emerita of sociology at the University of Oregon, adds race and gender to our understanding of social class analysis. Acker argues that capitalism is an organization that is both racialized and gendered, and to fully comprehend this social system, we need always to take gender and race into account. This reading also compliments well Gerda Lerner's history of social class (Reading 5). This excerpt is from Acker's critically acclaimed 2006 book,* Class Questions: Feminist Answers.

The class practices, or practices of provisioning, ... are, of course, aspects of the ongoing functioning of capitalism.... I make the claim that capitalism as an organization of production and distribution is gendered and racialized. I argue, along with R. W. Connell (1987) that "gender divisions ... are a deep-seated feature of production itself.... They are not a hangover from pre-capitalist modes of production" (pp. 103–104). The same is true for race divisions. I explore the ways in which capitalism can be seen as gendered and racialized and what this analysis means for understanding the ongoing production of gendered and racialized class practices and outcomes such as continuing gender and race segregation and divisions of labor. This exploration builds upon the valuable insights in socialist feminist work of the 1970s and early 1980s.

Although talk about globalizing capitalism is common today, class relations are usually seen as situated within particular nation-states and are

---

*Source:* Acker, Joan. 2006. "Is Capitalism Gendered and Racialized?" in *Class Questions: Feminist Answers*. Reproduced with permission of Rowman & Littlefield Publishing Group, Inc. in the format Textbook via Copyright Clearance Center.

usually analyzed within national boundaries. Good reasons exist for doing this: Nation-states and their gendered and racialized class structures have differing national characteristics produced by different political, social, and economic histories. However, to see the historical relations through which capitalism emerged in different countries as gendered and racially structured, a broader view is helpful. Therefore, in the following discussion, which deals primarily with the United States, I give some attention to processes that span state boundaries, or are transnational from the beginning. Organizations are critical locations for many of the activities and practices that comprise capitalism and class. The development of large organizations shaped and still shapes changing class processes (Perrow 2002) that are at the same time gender and race processes. Therefore, looking at these processes requires paying attention to organizations and what people do within them to create, implement, or oppose the practices that constitute relations of power and exploitation. I discuss some actions taken in the name of organizations in this reading . . . .

Capitalism is racialized and gendered in two intersecting historical processes. First, industrial capitalism emerged in the United States dominated by white males, with a gender- and race-segregated labor force, laced with wage inequalities, and a society-wide gender division of caring labor. The processes of reproducing segregation and wage inequality changed over time, but segregation and inequality were not eliminated. A small group of white males still dominate the capitalist economy and its politics. The society-wide gendered division of caring labor still exists. Ideologies of white masculinity and related forms of consciousness help to justify capitalist practices. In short, conceptual and material practices that construct capitalist production and markets, as well as beliefs supporting those practices, are deeply shaped through gender and race divisions of labor and power and through constructions of white masculinity.

Second, these gendered and racialized practices are embedded in and replicated through the gendered substructures of capitalism. These gendered substructures exist in ongoing incompatible organizing

of paid production activities and unpaid domestic and caring activities. Domestic and caring activities are devalued and seen as outside the "main business" (Smith 1999) of capitalism. The commodification of labor, the capitalist wage form, is an integral part of this process, as family provisioning and caring become dependent upon wage labor. The abstract language of bureaucratic organizing obscures the ongoing impact on families and daily life. At the same time, paid work is organized on the assumption that reproduction is of no concern. The separations between paid production and unpaid life-sustaining activities are maintained by corporate claims that they have no responsibility for anything but returns to shareholders. Such claims are more successful in the United States, in particular, than in countries with stronger labor movements and welfare states. These often successful claims contribute to the corporate processes of establishing their interests as more important than those of ordinary people.

## THE GENDERED AND RACIALIZED DEVELOPMENT OF U.S. CAPITALISM

### Segregations and Wage Inequalities

Industrial capitalism is historically, and in the main continues to be, a white male project, in the sense that white men were and are the innovators, owners, and holders of power.[1] Capitalism developed in Britain and then in Europe and the United States in societies that were already dominated by white men and already contained a gender-based division of labor. The emerging waged labor force was sharply divided by gender, as well as by race and ethnicity, with many variations by nation and regions within nations. At the same time, the gendered division of labor in domestic tasks was reconfigured and incorporated in a gendered division between paid market labor and unpaid domestic labor. In the United States, certain white men, unburdened by caring for children and households and already the major wielders of gendered power, buttressed at least indirectly by the profits from slavery and the exploitation of other minorities, were, in the nineteenth century, those who built the U.S. factories and railroads, and owned and managed the developing capitalist enterprises.[2] As far as we know, they were also heterosexual and mostly of Northern European heritage. Their wives and daughters benefited from the wealth they amassed and contributed in symbolic and social ways to the perpetuation of their class, but they were not the architects of the new economy.[3]

Recruitment of the labor force for the colonies and then the United States had always been transnational and often coercive.[4] Slavery existed prior to the development of industrialism in the United States: Capitalism was built partly on profits from that source.[5] Michael Omi and Howard Winant (1994:265) contend that the United States was a racial dictatorship for 258 years, from 1607 to 1865. After the abolition of slavery in 1865, severe exploitation, exclusion, and domination of blacks by whites perpetuated racial divisions cutting across gender and some class divisions, consigning blacks to the most menial, low-paying work in agriculture, mining, and domestic service. Early industrial workers were immigrants. For example, except for the brief tenure (twenty-five years) of young, native-born white women workers in the Lowell, Massachusetts, mills, immigrant women and children were the workers in the first mass production industry in the United States, the textile mills of Massachusetts and Philadelphia, Pennsylvania (Perrow 2002). This was a gender and racial/ethnic division of labor that still exists, but now on a global basis. Waves of European immigrants continued to come to the United States to work in factories and on farms. Many of these European immigrants, such as impoverished Irish, Poles, and eastern European Jews, were seen as nonwhite or not-quite-white by white Americans and were used in capitalist production as low-wage workers, although some of them were actually skilled workers (Brodkin 1998). The experiences of racial oppression built into industrial capitalism varied by gender within these racial/ethnic groups.

Capitalist expansion across the American continent created additional groups of Americans who were segregated by race and gender into racial and ethnic enclaves and into low-paid and highly exploited work. This expansion included the extermination and expropriation of native peoples, the subordination of Mexicans in areas taken in the war with Mexico in 1845, and the recruitment of Chinese and other Asians as low-wage workers, mostly on the west coast (Amott and Matthaei 1996; Glenn 2002).[6]

Women from different racial and ethnic groups were incorporated differently than men and differently than each other into developing capitalism in the late nineteenth and early twentieth centuries. White Euro-American men moved from farms into factories or commercial, business, and administrative jobs. Women aspired to be housewives as the male breadwinner family became the ideal. Married white women, working class and middle class, were housewives unless unemployment, low wages, or death of their husbands made their paid work necessary (Goldin 1990:133). Young white women with some secondary education moved into the expanding clerical jobs and into elementary school teaching when white men with sufficient education were unavailable (Cohn 1985). African Americans, both women and men, continued to be confined to menial work, although some were becoming factory workers, and even teachers and professionals as black schools and colleges were formed (Collins 2000). Young women from first- and second-generation European immigrant families worked in factories and offices. This is a very sketchy outline of a complex process (Kessler-Harris 1982), but the overall point is that the capitalist labor force in the United States emerged as deeply segregated horizontally by occupation and stratified vertically by positions of power and control on the basis of both gender and race.

Unequal pay patterns went along with sex and race segregation, stratification, and exclusion. Differences in the earnings and wealth (Keister 2000) of women and men existed before the development of the capitalist wage (Padavic and Reskin 2002). Slaves, of course, had no wages and earned little after abolition. These patterns continued as capitalist wage labor became the dominant form and wages became the primary avenue of distribution to ordinary people. Unequal wages were justified by beliefs about virtue and entitlement. A living wage or a just wage for white men was higher than a living wage or a just wage for white women or for women and men from minority racial and ethnic groups (Figart, Mutari, and Power 2002). African American women were at the bottom of the wage hierarchy.

The earnings advantage that white men have had throughout the history of modern capitalism was created partly by their organization to increase their wages and improve their working conditions. They also sought to protect their wages against the competition of others, women and men from subordinate groups (for example, Cockburn 1983, 1991). This advantage also suggests a white male coalition across class lines (Connell 2000; Hartmann 1976), based at least partly in beliefs about gender and race differences and beliefs about the superior skills of white men. White masculine identity and self-respect were complexly involved in these divisions of labor and wages.[7] This is another way in which capitalism is a gendered and racialized accumulation process (Connell 2000). Wage differences between white men and all other groups, as well as divisions of labor between these groups, contributed to profit and flexibility, by helping to maintain growing occupational areas, such as clerical work, as segregated and low paid. Where women worked in manufacturing or food processing, gender divisions of labor kept the often larger female work force in low-wage routine jobs, white males worked in other more highly paid, less routine, positions (Acker and Van Houten 1974). While white men might be paid more, capitalist organizations could benefit from this "gender/racial dividend." Thus, by maintaining divisions, employers could pay less for certain levels of skill, responsibility, and experience when the worker was not a white male.

This is not to say that getting a living wage was easy for white men, or that most white men achieved it. Labor-management battles, employers' violent tactics to prevent unionization, massive unemployment during frequent economic depressions characterized the situation of white industrial workers as wage labor spread in the nineteenth and early twentieth centuries.[8] During the same period, new white-collar jobs were created to manage, plan, and control the expanding industrial economy. This rapidly increasing

middle class was also stratified by gender and race. The better-paid, more respected jobs went to white men; white women were secretaries and clerical workers; people of color were absent. Conditions and issues varied across industries and regions of the country. But, wherever you look, those variations contained underlying gendered and racialized divisions. Patterns of stratification and }segregation were written into employment contracts in work content, positions in work hierarchies, and wage differences, as well as other forms of distribution.

These patterns persisted, although with many alterations, through extraordinary changes in production and social life. After World War II, white women, except for a brief period immediately after the war, went to work for pay in the expanding service sector, professional, and managerial fields. African Americans moved to the North in large numbers, entering industrial and service sector jobs. These processes accelerated after the 1960s, with the civil rights and women's movements, new civil rights laws, and affirmative action. Hispanics and Asian Americans, as well as other racial/ethnic groups, became larger proportions of the population, on the whole finding work in low-paid, segregated jobs. Employers continued, and still continue, to select and promote workers based on gender and racial identifications, although the processes are more subtle, and possibly less visible, than in the past (for example, Brown et al. 2003; Royster 2003).[9] These processes continually recreate gender and racial inequities, not as cultural or ideological survivals from earlier times, but as essential elements in present capitalisms (Connell 1987:103–106).

Segregating practices are a part of the history of white, masculine-dominated capitalism that establishes class as gendered and racialized. Images of masculinity support these practices, as they produce a taken-for-granted world in which certain men legitimately make employment and other economic decisions that affect the lives of most other people. Even though some white women and people from other-than-white groups now hold leadership positions, their actions are shaped within networks of practices sustained by images of masculinity (Wacjman 1998).

## Masculinities and Capitalism

Masculinities are essential components of the ongoing male project, capitalism. While white men were and are the main publicly recognized actors in the history of capitalism, these are not just any white men. They have been, for example, aggressive entrepreneurs or strong leaders of industry and finance (Collinson and Hearn 1996). Some have been oppositional actors, such as self-respecting and tough workers earning a family wage, and militant labor leaders. They have been particular men whose locations within gendered and racialized social relations and practices can be partially captured by the concept of masculinity. "Masculinity" is a contested term. As Connell (1995, 2000), Hearn (1996), and others have pointed out, it should be pluralized as "masculinities," because in any society at any one time there are several ways of being a man. "Being a man" involves cultural images and practices. It always implies a contrast to an unidentified femininity.[10]

Hegemonic masculinity can be defined as the taken-for-granted, generally accepted form, attributed to leaders and other influential figures at particular historical times. Hegemonic masculinity legitimates the power of those who embody it. More than one type of hegemonic masculinity may exist simultaneously, although they may share characteristics, as do the business leader and the sports star at the present time. Adjectives describing hegemonic masculinities closely follow those describing characteristics of successful business organizations, as Rosabeth Moss Kanter (1977) pointed out in the 1970s. The successful CEO and the successful organization are aggressive, decisive, competitive, focused on winning and defeating the enemy, taking territory from others.[11] The ideology of capitalist markets is imbued with a masculine ethos. As R. W. Connell (2000:35) observes, "The market is often seen as the antithesis of gender (marked by achieved versus ascribed status, etc.). But the market operates through forms of rationality that are historically masculine and involve a sharp split between instrumental reason on the one hand, emotion and human responsibility on the other" (Seidler 1989). Masculinities embedded in collective practices are part of the context within which certain men made and still make the decisions that drive and shape the ongoing development of capitalism. We can speculate that how these men see themselves, what actions and choices they feel compelled to make and they think are legitimate, how they and the world around them define desirable masculinity, enter into that decision making (Reed 1996). Decisions made at the very top reaches of (masculine) corporate power have consequences that are experienced as inevitable economic forces or disembodied social trends. At the same time, these decisions symbolize and enact varying hegemonic masculinities (Connell 1995). However, the embeddedness of masculinity within the ideologies of business and the market may become invisible, seen as just part of the way business is done. The relatively few women who reach the highest positions probably think and act within these strictures.

Hegemonic masculinities and violence[12] are deeply connected within capitalist history: The violent acts of those who carried out the slave trade or organized colonial conquests are obvious examples. Of course, violence has been an essential component of power in many other socioeconomic systems, but it continues into the rational organization of capitalist economic activities. Violence is frequently a legitimate, if implicit, component of power exercised by bureaucrats as well as "robber barons." Metaphors of violence, frequently military violence, are often linked to notions of the masculinity of corporate leaders, as "defeating the enemy" suggests. In contemporary capitalism, violence and its links to masculinity are often masked by the seeming impersonality of objective conditions. For example, the masculinity of top managers, the ability to be tough, is involved in the implicit violence of many corporate decisions, such as those cutting jobs in order to raise profits and, as a result, producing unemployment. Armies and other organizations, such as the police, are specifically organized around violence. Some observers of recent history suggest that organized violence, such as the use of the military, is still mobilized at least partly to reach capitalist goals, such as controlling access to oil supplies. The masculinities of those making decisions to deploy violence in such a way are hegemonic, in the sense of powerful and exemplary. Nevertheless, the connections between masculinity, capitalism, and violence are complex and contradictory, as Jeff Hearn and Wendy Parkin (2001) make clear. Violence is always a possibility in mechanisms of control and domination, but it is not always evident, nor is it always used.

As corporate capitalism developed, Connell (1995) and others (for example, Burris 1996) argue that a hegemonic masculinity based on claims to expertise developed alongside masculinities organized around domination and control. Hegemonic masculinity relying on claims to expertise does not necessarily lead to economic organizations free of domination and violence, however (Hearn and Parkin 2001). Hearn and Parkin (2001) argue that controls relying on both explicit and implicit violence exist in a wide variety of organizations, including those devoted to developing new technology.

Different hegemonic masculinities in different countries may reflect different national histories, cultures, and change processes.[13] For example, in Sweden in the mid-1980s, corporations were changing the ways in which they did business toward a greater participation in the international economy, fewer controls on currency and trade, and greater emphasis on competition. Existing images of dominant masculinity were changing, reflecting new business practices. This seemed to be happening in the banking sector, where I was doing research on women and their jobs (Acker 1994). The old paternalistic leadership, in which primarily men entered as young clerks expecting to rise to managerial levels, was being replaced by young, aggressive men hired as experts and managers from outside the banks. These young, often technically trained, ambitious men pushed the idea that the staff was there to sell bank products to customers, not, in the first instance, to take care of the needs of clients. Productivity goals were put in place; nonprofitable customers, such as elderly pensioners, were to be encouraged not to come into the bank and occupy the staff's attention. The female clerks we interviewed were disturbed by these changes, seeing them as evidence that the men at the top were

changing from paternal guardians of the people's interests to manipulators who only wanted riches for themselves. The confirmation of this came in a scandal in which the CEO of the largest bank had to step down because he had illegally taken money from the bank to pay for his housing. The amount of money was small; the disillusion among employees was huge. He had been seen as a benign father; now he was no better than the callous young men on the way up who were dominating the daily work in the banks. The hegemonic masculinity in Swedish banks was changing as the economy and society were changing.

Hegemonic masculinities are defined in contrast to subordinate masculinities. White working class masculinity, although clearly subordinate, mirrors in some of its more heroic forms the images of strength and responsibility of certain successful business leaders. The construction of working class masculinity around the obligations to work hard, earn a family wage, and be a good provider can be seen as providing an identity that both served as a social control and secured male advantage in the home. That is, the good provider had to have a wife and probably children for whom to provide. Glenn (2002) describes in some detail how this image of the white male worker also defined him as superior to and different from black workers.

Masculinities are not stable images and ideals, but shifting with other societal changes. With the turn to neoliberal business thinking and globalization, there seem to be new forms. Connell (2000) identifies "global business masculinity," while Lourdes Beneria (1999) discusses the "Davos man," the global leader from business, politics, or academia who meets his peers once a year in the Swiss town of Davos to assess and plan the direction of globalization. Seeing masculinities as implicated in the ongoing production of global capitalism opens the possibility of seeing sexualities, bodies, pleasures, and identities as also implicated in economic relations.

In sum, gender and race are built into capitalism and its class processes through the long history of racial and gender segregation of paid labor and through the images and actions of white men who dominate and lead central capitalist endeavors.

Underlying these processes is the subordination to production and the market of nurturing and caring for human beings, and the assignment of these responsibilities to women as unpaid work. Gender segregation that differentially affects women in all racial groups rests at least partially on the ideology and actuality of women as carers. Images of dominant masculinity enshrine particular male bodies and ways of being as different from the female and distanced from caring.... I argue that industrial capitalism, including its present neoliberal form, is organized in ways that are, at the same time, antithetical and necessary to the organization of caring or reproduction and that the resulting tensions contribute to the perpetuation of gendered and racialized class inequalities. Large corporations are particularly important in this process as they increasingly control the resources for provisioning but deny responsibility for such social goals....

## Conclusion

I have tried to demonstrate in this discussion that "A capitalist economy that operates through a gender division of labour is, necessarily, a gendered accumulation process" (Connell 2000:25). I would add that an economy that operates through a racial division of labor is necessarily a racialized accumulation process. I have argued that the fundamental organization of capitalist production, including the transformation of human labor into a commodity, separates production and reproduction, creating tensions, even contradictions, between these two necessary social activities. These are gendered tensions, as women are historically assigned to caring work and subordinated in the world of paid work. This organization of production undergirds: 1) the devaluation of unpaid work and caring, 2) abstract conceptual practices that obscure unpaid work and caring, 3) a lack of fit between paid work and the rest of life, 4) corporate claims to nonresponsibility for human needs, and 5) efforts to create new forms of distribution to ordinary people. In the United States, this organization of production emerges within systems of slavery and racial/ethnic subordination,

building in racial exclusion and discrimination from the beginning.

This sets the stage for more detailed examination of gendered and racialized class practices and relations in future research. I intend to leave open the question of whether or not fundamental changes can occur without basically altering capitalist practices. Certainly, tremendous positive changes have occurred in United States' society in the last thirty to forty years in patterns of subordination and exclusion based on gender and race, while gendered and racialized class-linked increases in income and wealth inequality have soared. Gendered and racialized practices are not erased, and new configurations of exploitation, domination, and inequality seem to be continually produced in the ongoing processes of global corporate expansion and organizational restructuring.

## Discussion Questions

1. How do unequal pay, the separation of paid and unpaid work, and continually changing masculine ideologies racialize and gender capitalism?
2. How are masculinity and violence "deeply connected" within capitalist history?

## Notes

1. Omi and Winant (1994) develop the notion of *project* to discuss racial formation. This is a helpful notion that I borrow to assist in thinking about capitalism and class, but use in a somewhat different way. To think about the development of capitalism as a project or as many projects brings actors' bodies and activities, as well as the cultural representation of those bodies and activities of actors, into a central place in "processes."
2. The male identity of the leaders of industrialization is obvious in every history of the process. See, for example, Gutman (1976) or Perrow (2002).
3. Chris Middleton (1983) argued that, in Britain, male heads of households in the emerging capitalist class appropriated the labor of members of the household, including wives and daughters. In the process,

patriarchal power was reorganized and women in this class actually saw the range of their contributions to production shrink as they were excluded from various occupations and economic sectors.

4. There is a huge literature on the working lives of women, their history, and present configurations. See, for example, Kessler-Harris (1982), Amott and Matthaei (1996), Glenn (2002) for histories and Padavic and Reskin (2002) for a contemporary overview.

5. See Eric Williams (1944).

6. While race/ethnicity–based dominations of colonial peoples were built into capitalist development in Britain and European countries, these patterns of racial exploitation and oppression did not become integrated into gender and class processes within national boundaries until after World War II. Each country had a different history of colonialism, different labor force recruitment policies in the postwar period, and different policies in regard to immigration. All of these patterns result in different racial patterns, different problems today.

7. For example, Dolores Janiewski (1996) shows how preexisting race and gender ideologies, along with employers' commitments to maintaining the existing sexual and racial order, shaped Southern managerial strategies in the textile and tobacco industries.

8. Many histories of labor struggles exist. See, for example, Foner (1947), Taylor (1992), Milton (1982). For examples of women's participation in labor struggles, see Frankel (1984) and Kessler-Harris (1982).

9. For interpretations of the processes and policies resulting in hierarchical segregation, horizontal segregation between occupations, and manual and non-manual work and the pay gap, see Reskin, McBrier, and Kmec (1999) and Kilbourne, England, and Beron (1994).

10. Connell (2000) defines masculinities as "configurations of practice within gender relations, a structure that includes large-scale institutions and economic relations as well as face-to-face relationships and sexuality" (29). The referent of "masculinities" is often ambiguous (Connell 1995). "Configurations of practice within gender relations" could refer to ideologies, images, ideals, myths, or behaviors and emotions of actual men. Moreover, masculinities are often changing, reproduced through organizational and institutional practices, social interaction, and through images, ideals, myths, or representations of behaviors and emotions. Jeff Hearn (2004) reviews the problems with the concept of "hegemonic masculinity" and proposes that talking about "the hegemony of men" and dropping the notion of masculinity may solve some of these problems.

11. Although prescriptions for successful management have included in the last few years human relations skills and softer, more emotional, and supportive approaches to supervision usually identified with femininity, these have not, it seems to me, disturbed the images of hegemonic masculinities. See Wacjman (1998).

12. Violence is another ambiguous term. Jeff Hearn and Wendy Parkin (2001) in *Gender, Sexuality and Violence in Organizations,* include sexual harassment and bullying along with physical violence and expand the concept to include "violation," which denotes a wide variety of actions that demean, coerce, and intimidate within work organizations.

13. Linda McDowell's (1997) study of merchant bankers in London describes another embodied hegemonic masculinity, a manly, heterosexual, class-based masculinity that dominates and disempowers many "others."

# 11

# The Social Construction and Institutionalization of Gender and Race

## An Integrative Framework

Evelyn Nakano Glenn

*Evelyn Nakano Glenn, professor of gender and women's studies and ethnic studies at the University of California, Berkeley, has studied the intersections between race-ethnicity and gender for decades. A sociologist by training, Glenn has contributed greatly to both our theoretical understanding of race, social class, and gender and to our research knowledge of different racial-ethnic groups. This reading is excerpted from the 1999 book* Revisioning Gender, *edited by Myra Marx Ferree, Judith Lorber, and Beth B. Hess. In this theoretical piece, Glenn argues that there are important convergences between the concepts of racial formation and the social construction of gender that allow for the development of a more integrative framework in the study of race and gender.*

## Toward a Social Constructionist Approach to Gender and Race

Historically, gender and race have constituted separate fields of scholarly inquiry. By studying each in isolation, however, each field marginalized major segments of the communities it claimed to represent. In studies of "race," men of color stood as the universal racial subject, whereas in studies of "gender," White women were positioned as the universal

Source: Nakano Glenn, Evelyn. 1999. "The Social Construction and Institutionalization of Gender and Race: An Integrative Framework." In *Revisioning Gender*. Edited by Myra Marx Ferree, Judith Lorber, and Beth B. Hess. Reproduced with permission of Rowman & Littlefield Publishing Group, Inc. in the format Textbook via Copyright Clearance Center.

female subject. Women of color were left out of both narratives, rendered invisible both as racial and as gendered subjects.[1]

In the 1980s, women of color began to address this omission through detailed historical and ethnographic studies of Black, Latina, and Asian American women in relation to work, family, and community (e.g., Cheng 1984; Dill 1980; Gilkes 1985; Glenn 1986; Ruiz 1987; Zavella 1987). These studies not only uncovered overlooked dimensions of experience, they exposed flaws in theorizing from a narrow social base. For example, explanations for gender inequality based on middle-class White women's experience focused on women's encapsulation in the domestic sphere and economic dependence on men. These concepts did not apply to Black women and therefore could not account for their subordination.

Initial attempts to bring race into the same frame as gender treated the two as independent axes. The bracketing of gender was in some sense deliberate, because the concern of early feminism was to uncover what women had in common that would unite them politically. However, if we begin with gender separated out, we have to "add" race in order to account for the situation of women of color. This leads to an additive model in which women of color are described as suffering from "double" jeopardy (or "triple" oppression, if class is included). Women of color expressed dissatisfaction with this model, which they said did not correspond to the subjective experiences of African American, Latina, Asian American, and Native American women. These women did not experience race and gender as separate or additive, but as simultaneous and linked. They offered concepts such as "intersectionality," "multiple consciousness," "interlocking systems of oppression," and "racialized gender" to express this simultaneity (Crenshaw 1989, 1992; Harris 1990; Collins 1990; Glenn 1992).

Yet, despite increased recognition of the interconnectedness of gender and race, race remained undertheorized even in the writings of women of color. In the absence of a "theory" of race comparable to a "theory" of gender, building a comprehensive theory has proven elusive. Especially needed is a theory that

neither subordinates race and gender to some broader (presumably more primary) set of relations, such as class, nor substantially flattens the complexity of these concepts.[2] Lacking a comprehensive theory, can we do analyses that recognize and account for the simultaneity of gender and race? In this reading, following on the valuable work of such scholars as Liu (1991), Brooks Higginbotham (1992), Kaminsky (1994), and Stoler (1996), I argue that a synthesis of social constructionist streams within critical race and feminist studies offers a framework for integrated analysis. Social constructionism provides a useful "mid-level" framework, a common vocabulary and set of concepts for looking at how gender and race are mutually constituted—at the ways gender is racialized and race is gendered.

## Gender

Social constructionism has had a somewhat different trajectory with respect to gender and race. In both fields, social constructionism arose as an alternative to biological and essentialist conceptions that rendered gender and race static and ahistorical, but it achieved centrality earlier and has been elaborated in greater detail in feminist scholarship on women and gender than in race studies. This is so even though—or perhaps because—gender seems to be rooted more firmly than race in biology: in bodies, reproduction, and sexuality. Indeed, feminist scholars adopted the term *gender* precisely to free our thinking from the constrictions of naturalness and biological inevitability attached to the concept of sex. Rubin (1975) has proposed the term *sex-gender system* to capture the idea of societal arrangements by which biological sexuality is transformed into socially significant gender.

Since its introduction, gender has emerged as the closest thing we have to a unifying concept in feminist studies, cutting across the various disciplines and theoretical schools that make up the field. Many feminist historians and sociologists use gender as an analytic concept to refer to socially created meanings, relationships, and identities organized around reproductive differences

(Connell 1989; Laslett and Brenner 1989; Scott 1986). Others focus on gender as a social status and organizing principle of social institutions detached from and going far beyond reproductive differences (Acker 1990; Lorber 1994). Still others see gender as an ongoing product of everyday social practice (Thorne 1993; West and Zimmerman 1987). The concept of gender thus provides an overarching rubric for looking at historical, cultural, and situational variability in definitions of womanhood and manhood, in meanings of masculinity and femininity, in relationships between men and women, and in the extent of their relative power and political status. If one accepts gender as variable, then one must acknowledge that it is never fixed, but rather is continually constituted and reconstituted.

By loosening the connection to concrete bodies, the notion of socially constructed gender freed us from thinking of sex/gender as solely, or even primarily, a characteristic of individuals. By examining gender as a constitutive feature and organizing principle of collectivities, social institutions, historical processes, and social practices, feminist scholars have demonstrated that major areas of life—including sexuality, family, education, economy, and state—are organized according to gender principles and shot through with conflicting interests and hierarchies of power and privilege. As an organizing principle, gender involves both cultural meanings and material relations. That is, gender is constituted simultaneously through deployment of gendered rhetoric, symbols, and images and through allocation of resources and power along gender lines. Thus an adequate account of any particular gender phenomenon requires an examination of both structure and meaning. For example, an understanding of the persistent gender gap in wages involves an analysis of divisions of labor in the home, occupational segregation and other forms of labor market stratification, cultural evaluations of gendered work, such as caring, and gendered meanings of concepts such as "skill."

The most recent theoretical work is moving toward imploding the sex-gender distinction itself. The distinction assumes the prior existence of "something real" out of which social relationships

and cultural meanings are elaborated. A variety of poststructuralist feminist critics have problematized the distinction by pointing out that sex and sexual meanings are themselves culturally constructed (e.g., Butler 1990). Lorber (1994), a sociologist, carefully unpacks the concepts of biological sex (which refers to either genetic or morphological characteristics), sexuality (which refers to desire and orientation), and gender (which refers to social status and identity), and shows that they are all equally socially constructed concepts. One result of this kind of work is the undermining of the idea that there are "really" two sexes or two genders or two sexual orientations. At present, the conceptual distinctions among sex, sexuality, and gender are still being debated, and new work on the body is revealing the intertwining and complexity of these concepts (e.g., Butler 1993).

### Race

Scholars of race have been slower to abandon the idea of race as rooted in biological markers, even though they recognize that social attitudes and arrangements, not biology, maintain White dominance.[3] Fields (1982) notes the reluctance of historians to digest fully the conclusion reached by biologists early in the twentieth century that race does not correspond to any biological referent and that racial categories are so arbitrary as to be meaningless. Race had thus been exposed as a social creation—a fiction that divides and categorizes individuals by phenotypic markers, such as skin color, that supposedly signify underlying differences. Nonetheless, as Pascoe (1991) notes, historians continued well into the 1980s to study "races" as immutable categories, to speak of race as a force in history, and to view racism as a psychological product rather than a product of social history. Pascoe suggests that the lack of a separate term, like *gender*, to refer to "socially significant race" may have retarded full recognition of race as a social construct. In sociology, liberal scholarship took the form of the study of "race relations"—that is, the examination of relations among groups that were already constituted as distinct entities. Quantitative researchers treated race as a preexisting "fact" of social life, an independent variable to be correlated with or regressed against other variables. How categories such as Black and White were historically created and maintained was not interrogated.

Only in the late 1980s did historians and social scientists begin to study systematically variations and changes in the drawing of racial categories and boundaries. The greatest attention has been paid to the construction of Blackness. In an influential pair of essays, Fields (1982, 1990) examines how the definition and concept of Blackness shifted over the course of slavery, Reconstruction, and the Jim Crow era. Slave owners created the category "Black" from disparate African groups, and then maintained the category by incorporating growing numbers of those of "mixed" parentage. Concerned with maximizing the number of slaves, slave owners settled on the principle that a child's status followed that of the mother, in violation of the customary patriarchal principle of inheritance. Exploring the origins of the principle of hypodescent and the "one-drop rule" for defining Blackness in the United States, Davis (1991) has shown it to be peculiar in light of the wide range of variation among Latin American, Caribbean, and North American societies in the status of people of mixed ancestry. In her study of "Creole" identity in Louisiana, Dominguez (1986) found that competing understandings of racial categories may coexist in the same society. The Creole designation was claimed both by people of mixed Black-White ancestry (to distinguish themselves from darker "Blacks") and by White descendants of original French settlers (to distinguish themselves from later Anglo immigrants). By the 1970s, however, White "Creoles" had ceded the label to the mixed population and relabeled themselves:"French."

"Whiteness" has also been problematized. Historians have looked at the shift from an emphasis on "Anglo-Saxon" identity to a more inclusive "White" identity and the assimilation of groups that had been considered separate races in an earlier period, such as the Irish, Jews, and Mexicans, into the White category (Almaguer 1994; Ignatiev 1995; Roediger 1991; Sacks 1994). These groups achieved "Whiteness" through a combination of external circumstances and their own agency. State and social

policies organized along a Black-White binary required individuals and groups to be placed in one category or the other. Individuals and groups also actively claimed Whiteness in order to attain the rights and privileges enjoyed by already established White Americans. Because of the association of Whiteness with full legal rights, scholars in the field of critical legal studies have scrutinized the concept of Whiteness in the law (e.g., Haney Lopez 1996; Harris 1993). Harris (1993) argues that courts have protected racial privilege by interpreting Whiteness as property, including the right to exclude others.

Only a few studies have looked beyond the Black-White binary that dominates conceptions of race. For example, Espiritu (1992) examined the forging of a pan-Asian American identity in the late 1960s, when Chinese, Japanese, and Filipino student activists came together to organize in "Third World" solidarity with Black and Latino students. Activists asserted both essentialist grounds (similarities in culture and appearance) and instrumental grounds (a common history of discrimination and stereotyping) as the basis for the new identity. In contrast to the notion that Asian groups experience similar treatment that leads to pan-Asian identity, Ong (1996) argues that among new Asian immigrants, rich and poor groups are being differentially "racialized" within the Black-White binary in the United States. Well-educated professional and managerial Chinese immigrants are "Whitened" and assimilated into the American middle class, whereas poor Khmer, dependent on welfare, are "Blackened."

Many of the studies of shifting racial categories and meanings have been influenced by the pathbreaking theoretical work of Omi and Winant (1986, 1994). Their racial formation model is rooted in neo-Marxist conceptions of class formation, but they specifically position themselves against existing models that subsume race under some presumably broader category, such as class or nation. They firmly assert that "race is a fundamental axis of social organization in the U.S.," not an epiphenomenon of some other category (1994:13). At the same time, they see race not as fixed, but as "an unstable and 'decentered' complex of social meaning constantly being transformed by political struggle"

(1994:55). The terrain on which struggle is waged has varied historically. Just as social constructionism arose as an alternative to biologism or essentialism in the twentieth century, the concept of biological race arose in the eighteenth and nineteenth centuries to replace religious paradigms for viewing differences between Europeans (Christians) and (non-Christian) "others" encountered in the age of conquest. With the waning of religious beliefs in a God-given social order, race differences and the superiority of White Europeans to "others" came to be justified and legitimated by "science." As Omi and Winant (1994) note, the "invocation of scientific criteria to demonstrate the natural basis of racial hierarchy was both a logical consequence of the rise of [scientific] knowledge and an attempt to provide a subtle and more nuanced account of human complexity in the new 'enlightened' age" (p. 63).

After World War II, liberal politics emphasized equality under the law and an assumption of sameness in daily encounters. In the 1960s and 1970s, identity politics among civil rights activists emphasized differences, but valorized them in such ideas as Black power and la raza. The 1980s and 1990s saw a questioning of the essentialism and solidity of racial and sex/gender categories and a focus on structural concepts of racial and patriarchal social orders. Paralleling the structural approach to gender, Omi and Winant assert that race is a central organizing principle of social institutions, focusing especially on the "racial state" as a central arena for creating, maintaining, and contesting racial boundaries and meanings. Their concept of the racial state is akin to MacKinnon's (1989) concept of the patriarchal state.

## An Integrative Framework

There are important points of congruence between the concept of racial formation and the concept of socially constructed gender. These convergences point the way toward an integrative framework in which race and gender are defined as mutually constituted systems of relationships—including norms, symbols, and practices—organized around perceived differences. This definition focuses attention on the *processes* through which racialization and engendering take place, rather than on the elucidation of characteristics of fixed race-gender categories. These processes take place at multiple levels, including *representation,* or the deployment of symbols, language, and images to express and convey race/gender meanings; *micro-interaction,* or the application of race/gender norms, etiquette, and spatial rules to orchestrate interaction within and across race/gender boundaries; and *social structure,* or the allocation of power and material resources along race/gender lines.

Within this integrated framework, race and gender share three key features as analytic concepts: They are *relational* concepts whose construction involves *both representational and social structural processes* in which *power* is a constitutive element. Each of these features is important in terms of building a framework that both analyzes inequality and incorporates a politics of change.

### Relationality

By *relational* I mean that race-gender categories (e.g., Black/White, woman/man) are positioned and therefore gain meaning in relation to each other. According to poststructural analysis, meaning within Western epistemology is constructed in terms of dichotomous oppositions or contrasts. Oppositional categories require the suppression of variability within each category and the exaggeration of differences between categories. Moreover, because the dichotomy is imposed over a complex "reality," it is inherently unstable. Stability is achieved when the dichotomy is made hierarchical—that is, one term is accorded primacy over the other. In race and gender dichotomies, the dominant category is rendered "normal" and therefore "transparent," whereas the other is the variant and therefore "problematic." Thus White appears to be raceless (Dyer 1988) and man appears to be genderless. The opposition also disguises the extent to which the categories are actually interdependent.

One can accept the notion of meaning being constructed through contrast without assuming that such contrasts take the form of fixed dichotomies. In the United States "White" has been primarily constructed against "Black," but it has also been positioned in relation to varying "others," and therefore has varying meanings. The category "Anglo" in the Southwest, which is constructed in contrast to "Mexican," and the category "haole" in Hawaii, which is constructed in contrast to both Native Hawaiians and Asian plantation workers, both have meanings that are similar to and different from those of the category "White" in the South and Northeast. For example, haole was originally a simultaneous race-class designation for Europeans and Anglo-Americans of the planter-manager class; European groups, such as the Portuguese, who were plantation laborers and supervisors were not considered haole (Fuchs 1983). Similarly, the meanings of dominant masculinity have varied by time and place by way of contrast to historically and regionally differing subordinate masculinities and femininities.

The concept of relationality is important for several reasons. First, as in the above example, it helps to problematize the dominant categories of Whiteness and masculinity, which depend on contrast. The importance of contrast is illustrated by the formation of "linked identities" in the cases of housewives and their domestic employees (Palmer 1989), reformers and the targets of reform (Pascoe 1990), and colonizers and colonized peoples (Ware 1992). In each of these cases, the dominant group's self-identity (e.g., as moral, rational, and benevolent) depends on the casting of complementary qualities (e.g., immoral, irrational, and needy) onto the subordinate "other."

Second, relationality helps to point out the ways in which "differences" among groups are systematically related. Too often, "difference" is understood simply as experiential diversity, as in some versions of multiculturalism (Barrett 1987). The concept of relationality suggests that the lives of different groups are interconnected, even without face-to-face relations. Thus, for example, a White person in the United States enjoys privileges and a higher standard of living by virtue of the subordination and lower standard of living of people of color, even if she or he is not personally exploiting or taking advantage of any persons of color.

Third, relationality helps to address the critique that social constructionism, by rejecting the fixity of categories, fosters the postmodern notion that race and gender categories and meanings are free-floating and can mean anything we want them to mean. Viewing race and gender categories and meanings as relational partly addresses this critique by providing "anchor" points that are not, however, static.

### Structure and Representation

The social construction of race/gender is a matter of *both* social structure and cultural representation. This point is important because, by virtue of its eschewal of biology and essentialism, a social constructionist approach could be interpreted as concerned solely with representation. This is particularly tempting in the case of race, where it can be argued that there is no objective referent. Indeed, Fields (1990), an eminent historian, has argued that race is a category without content; having no rooting in material reality, race is pure ideology, a lens through which people view and make sense of their experiences. However, Fields seems to be conflating biology and material reality. It is one thing to say that race and gender are not biological givens, but quite another to say that they exist only in the realm of representation or signification. As noted above, race and gender are features of social structures. Social structural arrangements, such as labor market segmentation, residential segregation, and stratification of government benefits, produce race and gender "differences" in ways that cannot be understood purely in representational terms. For this reason, I find neoliberal attacks on affirmative action and other measures aimed at redressing race and gender disadvantage to be either perverse or disingenuous. Proponents of this view argue that these measures falsely reify race and gender and that therefore social policy ought to be race- and gender-blind. Unfortunately, not paying attention to race and gender does not make gender-race inequalities go away, precisely because these inequalities are institutionalized and not just ideas in people's heads.

Conversely, other theorists view meaning systems as epiphenomena and maintain that race and gender inequalities can be understood through structural analysis alone. However, historical evidence suggests that a structural approach alone is not sufficient either. As historians of working-class formation have pointed out, one cannot make a direct connection between particular structural conditions and specific forms of consciousness, identity, and political activity. Rather, they have found that race, gender, and class consciousness draw on the available rhetoric of race, gender, and class. In nineteenth-century England, skilled artisan men experiencing changes in their conditions due to industrialization were able to organize and articulate their class rights by drawing on available concepts of manhood—the dignity of skilled labor and family headship (Rose 1995). Symbols of masculinity were thus constitutive of class identity. Their counterparts in the United States drew on symbols of race, claiming rights on the basis of their status as "free" labor, in contrast to Black slaves, Chinese contract workers, and other figures symbolizing "unfree labor" (Roediger 1994). Class formation in the United States was then and continues to be infused with racial as well as gender meanings.

In the contemporary United States, the paucity of culturally available class discourse seems to play a role in damping down class consciousness. Breslow Rubin (1994) found that White working-class men and women, whose economic circumstances were becoming more perilous due to stagnating or declining income, were strikingly silent about class. Instead, they drew on a long tradition of racial rhetoric, blaming immigrants and Blacks, not corporations or capitalists, for their economic anxieties. By constructing immigrants and Blacks as unworthy beneficiaries of welfare and affirmative action, they articulated their own identities as Whites, rather than as members of an economic class.

The preceding examples suggest a dialectical relation between material and structural conditions and cultural representation. The language of race, gender, and class formation draws on historical legacy, but also grows out of political struggle. Omi and Winant's concept of rearticulation—the investment of already present ideas and knowledge with new meanings—is relevant here. For example, the Black civil rights and women's liberation movements in the 1960s and 1970s drew on existing symbols and language about human rights, but combined them in new ways and gave them new meanings (e.g., "The personal is political," "Black power") that fostered mass political organizing.

## Power

The organization and signification of power are central to the constructionist framework, despite the frequent charge that this approach elides issues of power and inequality. Yet power is a central element in the formulations of Scott (1986) and Connell (1989). For Scott, gender is a primary way of signifying relations of power; for Connell, gender is constituted by power, labor, and cathexis. Power and politics are also integral to Omi and Winant's (1994) definitions of race and racism, when they describe race as constantly being transformed by political struggle and racism as aimed at creating and maintaining structures of domination based on essentialist conceptions of race.

The concept of power as constitutive of race and gender draws on an expanded notion of politics coming from three sources. First has been the feminist movement, whose most widely publicized slogan was "The personal is political" (Echols 1989). Feminist activists and scholars have exposed the power and domination, conflict and struggle that saturate areas of social life thought to be private or personal: sexuality, family, love, dress, art. Second has been Gramsci's (1971) concept of hegemony, the taken-for-granted practices and assumptions that make domination seem natural and inevitable to both the dominant and the subordinate. Social relations outside the realm of formal politics establish and reinforce power—art, literature, ritual, custom, and everyday interaction; for this reason, oppositional struggle also takes place outside the formal realm of politics, in forms such as artistic and cultural production. Third has been Foucault's (1977, 1978) work on sexuality and scientific knowledge. Power in these loci is often not recognized because it is exercised not through formal domination but through disciplinary complexes and modes of knowledge.

In all of these formulations, power is seen as simultaneously pervasive and dispersed in social relations of all kinds, not just those conventionally thought of as political. This point is particularly relevant to an examination of race and gender, where power is lodged in taken-for-granted assumptions and practices, takes forms that do not involve force or threat of force, and occurs in dispersed locations. Thus, contestation of race and gender hierarchies may involve challenging everyday assumptions and practices, may take forms that do not involve direct confrontation, and may occur in locations not considered political.

## APPLICATION

The framework I have laid out above makes race and gender amenable to historical analysis, so that they can be seen as mutually constitutive. If race and gender are socially constructed, they must arise at specific moments under particular circumstances and will change as these circumstances change. One can examine how gender and race differences arise, change over time, and vary within different social and geographic locations and institutional domains. Race and gender are not predetermined, but are the products of men's and women's actions in specific historical contexts. An understanding of race and gender requires us to examine not only how dominant groups and institutions attempt to impose particular race/gender meanings, but also how subordinate groups contest dominant conceptions and construct alternative meanings.

All institutions in the contemporary United States are organized and permeated by race and gender. The most central of these are the economy, the state, the family, and cultural production. In each of these areas, racialized engendering and gendered racialization occur through processes taking place at the levels of representation, interaction, and social structure. In the following pages, I examine these processes in an institutional area that is particularly central to the formation of race and gender relations: the labor system (through the race and gender construction of reproductive labor).

## The Race and Gender Construction of Reproductive Labor

Feminist sociologists and historians have revolutionized labor studies by making gender a central part of the analysis of work.[4] One of their most significant contributions has been to expand the concept of labor to include activities that were not previously recognized as forms of work, especially unpaid work in the household. In this discussion I will focus on the analysis of nonmarket work, particularly the labor of social reproduction, which has been extensively explored as a form of gendered labor, but not as labor that is simultaneously racialized.

### Gender and Reproductive Labor

The term *social reproduction* was coined by feminist scholars to refer to the array of activities and relationships involved in maintaining people both on a daily basis and intergenerationally (Laslett and Brenner 1989). Reproductive labor includes such activities as purchasing household goods, preparing meals, washing and repairing clothing, maintaining furnishings and appliances, socializing children, providing emotional support for adults, and maintaining kin and community ties. Marxist feminists in the 1970s and 1980s placed the gendered construction of reproductive labor at the center of women's oppression (Barrett 1980; Bose, Feldberg, and Sokoloff 1987; Hartmann 1976). They pointed out that this labor is performed disproportionately by women and is essential to the industrial economy. Yet because it takes place mostly outside the market, it is invisible, not recognized as real work. Men benefit directly and indirectly from this arrangement—directly in that they contribute less labor in the home while enjoying the services that women provide as wives and mothers, and indirectly in that, freed of domestic labor, they can concentrate their efforts in paid employment and attain primacy in that area. Thus, the gender division of reproductive labor in the home interacts with and reinforces the gender division in paid work.

These analyses drew attention to the way the gender construction of reproductive labor helped to create and maintain inequality between men and women and, conversely, how unequal power has enabled men to avoid doing reproductive labor and hampered women's ability to shift the burden. When feminist scholars represent gender as the sole basis for assigning reproductive labor, they imply that all women have the same relationship to it and that it is therefore a universal female experience. And although feminists increasingly are aware of the interaction of race and gender in stratifying the labor market, they have rarely considered whether race might interact with gender in shaping reproductive labor; thus, they have failed to examine differences across racial, ethnic, and class groups in women's relationship to that labor.

### The Racial Construction of Labor

Because scholarship on race and labor has been, consciously or unconsciously, male-centered, it has focused exclusively on the paid labor market and especially on male-dominated areas of production. U.S. historians have documented the ways in which race has been integral to the structure of labor markets since the beginnings of the nation. In the 1970s, several writers seeking to explain the historic subordination of peoples of color pointed to dualism in the labor market—its division into distinct markets for White workers and for racial ethnic workers—as a major vehicle for maintaining White domination (e.g., Barrera 1979; Blauner 1972). According to these formulations, labor systems have been organized to ensure that racial ethnic workers are relegated to the low tier of low-wage, dead-end, marginal jobs; institutional barriers, including restrictions on legal and political rights, prevent workers from moving out of that tier.

Writers have differed in their views about the relative agency of capitalists and White workers in the creation and maintenance of color lines. Some have interpreted the color line as a divide-and-conquer strategy of capital to prevent workers from organizing (e.g., Reich 1981); others have depicted White workers as active agents in drawing color lines in order to secure a privileged position in the market (e.g., Bonacich 1972, 1976). Both camps see class conflict as generating race conflict. Whatever the ultimate cause of the conflict, labor struggles in the United States have often taken the form of racial exclusion movements. Forbath (1996) describes how European American men workers in the nineteenth century constructed their identities as Whites and claimed their rights in contrast to Blacks around racialized notions of work: "skilled" versus "unskilled," "free" versus "unfree," and "dirty" versus "clean" work. These studies draw attention to the material and ideological advantages Whites gain from the racial division of labor. However, these studies either take for granted or ignore women's paid and unpaid household labor and fail to consider whether this work might also be "racially divided."

In short, the analysis of the race construction of reproductive labor has been a missing piece of the picture in both literatures. The omission stems from a focus on race alone or gender alone. Only by viewing reproductive labor as simultaneously raced and gendered can we grasp the distinct exploitation of women of color. Using a race-gender lens reveals that reproductive labor is divided along racial as well as gender lines, with White and racial ethnic women having distinctly different responsibilities for social reproduction, not just in their own households but in other work settings. The specific characteristics of the division have varied regionally and changed over time as capitalist economic structures have reorganized reproductive labor, shifting parts of it from the household to the market. Before World War II, racial ethnic women were employed as servants to perform reproductive labor in White households, relieving White middle-class women of more onerous aspects of that work. Since that time, with the expansion of commodified services (services turned into commercial products or activities), racial ethnic women are disproportionately employed as service workers in institutional settings to carry out lower-level "public" reproductive labor, while cleaner white-collar supervisory, as well as lower professional, positions are filled by White women. In both periods, less desirable or more onerous aspects of reproductive labor have devolved on women of color, "freeing" White women for higher-level pursuits. Thus the organization of reproductive labor is as much a source of division and hierarchy as it is of unity and commonality among women.

## The Race and Gender
## Division of Private Reproductive Labor

From the late nineteenth century to the mid–twentieth century, poor and working-class women not only did reproductive labor in their own homes, they also performed it for middle-class families. The division between White women and women of color grew in the latter half of the nineteenth century, when the demand for household help and the number of women employed as servants expanded rapidly (Chaplin 1978). Rising standards of cleanliness, larger and more ornately furnished homes, the sentimentalization of the home as a "haven in a heartless world," and the new emphasis on childhood and the mother's role in nurturing children all served to enlarge middle-class women's responsibilities for reproduction at a time when technology had done little to reduce the sheer physical drudgery of housework (Cowan 1983; Degler 1980; Strasser 1982).

By all accounts, middle-class women did not challenge the gender-based division of labor or the enlargement of their reproductive responsibilities. To the contrary, as readers and writers of literature, and as members and leaders of clubs, charitable organizations, associations, reform movements, religious revivals, and the cause of abolition, they helped to elaborate and refine the domestic code (Epstein 1981; Ryan 1981). Instead of questioning the inequitable gender division of labor, they sought to slough off the burdensome tasks onto more oppressed groups of women (see Kaplan 1987).

In the United States, the particular groups hired for private reproductive work varied by region. In the Northeast, European immigrant women, especially Irish, were the primary servant class. In regions with a substantial racial minority population, the servant caste consisted almost exclusively of women of color. In the early years of the twentieth century, 90 percent of non-agriculturally employed Black women in the South were servants or laundresses, constituting more than 80 percent of female servants (Katzman 1978:55). In cities of the Southwest, such as El Paso and Denver, where the main division was between Anglos and Mexicans, approximately half of all employed Mexican women were domestic or laundry workers (Deutsch 1987; Garcia 1981). In the San Francisco Bay Area and in Honolulu, where there were substantial numbers of Asian immigrants, a quarter to half of all employed Japanese women were private household workers (Glenn 1986; Lind 1951, table 1:74).

Women of color shouldered not only the burdens of household maintenance, but also those of family nurturing for White middle-class women. They did both the dirty, heavy manual labor of cleaning and laundering and the emotional work of caring for children. By performing the dirty work and time-consuming tasks, they freed their mistresses for supervisory tasks, for leisure and cultural activities, or, more rarely during this period, for careers. Ironically, then, many White women were able to fulfill White society's expectation of feminine domesticity only through the domestic labor of women of color.

For the domestic worker, the other side of doing reproductive labor for White families was not being able to perform reproductive labor for their own families. Unlike European immigrant domestics, who were mainly single young women, racial ethnic servants were usually wives and mothers (Stigler 1946; Watson 1937). Yet the code that sanctified White women's domesticity did not extend to them. In many cases, servants had to leave their own children in the care of relatives in order to "mother" their employers' children. A 6 ½-day workweek was typical. A Black children's nurse reported in 1912 that she worked 14 to 16 hours a day caring for her mistress' four children. Describing her existence as a "treadmill life," she said she was allowed to go home

only once in every two weeks, every other Sunday afternoon—even then I'm not permitted to stay all night. I see my own children only when they happen to see me on the streets when I am out with the children [of her mistress], or when my children come to the "yard" to see me, which isn't often, because my white folks don't like to see their servants' children hanging around their premises. (quoted in Katzman 1982:179)

The dominant group ideology naturalized the mistress-servant relationship by portraying women of color as particularly suited for service. These racialized gender constructions ranged from the view of African American and Mexican American women as incapable of governing their own lives and requiring White supervision to the view of Asian women as naturally subservient and accustomed to a low standard of living. Although racial stereotypes undoubtedly preceded their entry into domestic work, household workers were also induced to enact the role of race-gender inferiors in daily interactions with employers. Domestic workers interviewed by Rollins (1985) and Romero (1992) described a variety of rituals that affirmed their subordination and dependence; for example, employers addressed the household workers by their first names and required them to enter by the back door, eat in the kitchen, wear uniforms, and accept with gratitude "gifts" of discarded clothing and leftover food.

The lack of respect for racial ethnic women's family roles stood in marked contrast to the situation of White middle-class women in the late nineteenth and early twentieth centuries, when the cult of domesticity defined White womanhood primarily in terms of wifehood and motherhood. While the domestic code constrained White women, it placed racial ethnic women in an untenable position. Forced to work outside the home, they were considered deviant according to the dominant gender ideology. On the one hand, they were denied the buffer of a protected private sphere; on the other, they were judged deficient as wives and mothers compared with White middle-class women who could devote themselves to domesticity fulltime (Pascoe 1990). Women of color had to construct their own definitions of self-worth and womanhood outside the standards of the dominant culture. Their efforts to maintain kin ties, organize family celebrations, cook traditional foods, and keep households together were crucial to the survival of ethnic communities.

## The Race and Gender Construction of Public Reproductive Labor

Due to the expansion of capital into new areas for profit making, the fragmentation of families and breakdown of extended kin and community ties, and the squeeze on women's time as they moved into the labor market, the post–World War II era saw the expansion of commodified services to replace the reproductive labor formerly performed in the home (Braverman 1974:276). Among the fastest-growing occupations in the economy in the 1980s and 1990s were lower-level service jobs in health care, food service, and personal services (U.S. Department of Labor 1993). Women constitute the main labor force in these occupations. Within this new realm of "public reproductive labor," we find a clear race-gender division of labor. Women of color are disproportionately assigned to do the dirty work, as nurse's aides in hospitals, kitchen workers in restaurants and cafeterias, maids in hotels, and cleaners in office buildings. In these same institutional settings, White women are disproportionately employed as supervisors, professionals, and administrative support staff. This division parallels the earlier division between the domestic servant and the housewife. And just as in the household, dirty work is considered menial and unskilled, and the women who do it are too; moreover, White women benefit by being able to do higher-level work.

With the shift of reproductive labor from the household to market, face-to-face race and gender hierarchies have been replaced by structural hierarchies. In institutional settings, race and gender stratification is built into organizational structures, including lines of authority, job descriptions, rules, and spatial and temporal segregation. Distance between higher and lower orders is ensured by structural segregation. Much routine service work is organized to be out of sight. It takes place behind institutional walls, where outsiders rarely penetrate (nursing homes, chronic care facilities), in back rooms (restaurant kitchens), or at night or other times when occupants are gone (office buildings and hotels). Although workers may appreciate this time and space segregation, which allows them some autonomy and freedom from demeaning interactions, it also makes them and their work invisible. In this situation, more privileged women do not have to acknowledge the workers or confront any contradiction between shared womanhood and inequality by race and class.

*Implications*

Both historically and in the contemporary United States, the racial construction of gendered labor has created divisions between White and racial ethnic women that go beyond differences in experience and standpoint. Their situations have been interdependent: The higher status and living standards of White women have depended on the subordination and lower standards of living of women of color. Moreover, White women have been able to meet more closely the hegemonic standards of womanhood because of the devaluation of the womanhood of racial ethnic women. This analysis suggests that if these special forms of exploitation were to cease, White women as well as men would give up certain privileges and benefits. Thus, social policies to improve the lot of racial ethnic women may entail loss of privilege or status for White women and may therefore engender resistance from them as well as from men . . . .

## Discussion Questions

1. According to Glenn, what are the three analytic concepts that race and gender share within an integrative analysis?
2. What is reproductive labor? How does Glenn use reproductive labor to demonstrate the convergences between the concepts of race and gender?

## Notes

1. The title of a collection on African American women edited by Hull, Scott, and Smith (1982) puts it this way: *All the Women Are White, All the Blacks Are Men, but Some of Us Are Brave.*
2. Some preliminary attempts, including those of West and Fenstermaker (1995), Bonacich (1994), and Brodkin Sacks (1989), have nonetheless been illuminating.
3. In this regard, see, for example, Jordan's (1968) "Note on the Concept of Race" at the end of his monumental study of the history of White American attitudes toward Blacks, in which he attempts to clarify the latest scientific understanding of race as directed toward the study of genetics and evolution.
4. Much of the material in this section is drawn from Glenn (1992).

# 12

# CRITICAL THINKING ABOUT INEQUALITY

## An Emerging Lens

BONNIE THORNTON DILL

RUTH ENID ZAMBRANA

*This fourth reading in the theory section is by Bonnie Thornton Dill and Ruth Enid Zambrana, both professors of women's studies at the University of Maryland. This excerpt is taken from the introduction to their 2009 edited volume,* Emerging Intersections: Race, Class, and Gender in Theory, Policy, and Practice. *This reading introduces the reader to both the concepts of social inequality and to intersectional theory and analysis. Intersectionality has provided scholars with a better tool to simultaneously comprehend multiple social categories and their relationships to power and privilege in society.*

Inequality and oppression are deeply woven into the tapestry of American life. As a result large disparities exist on measures of income, wealth, education, housing, occupation, and social benefits. These disparities are neither new nor randomly distributed throughout the population, but occur in patterns along such major social divisions as race, gender, class, sexuality, nationality, and physical ability. Social scientists have traditionally analyzed inequalities by isolating these factors and treating them as if they are independent of one another. Even when their interactions are discussed they are still

*Source:* Dill, Bonnie Thornton, and Ruth Enid Zambrana. *Emerging Intersections: Race, Class, and Gender in Theory, Policy, and Practice.* Copyright 2009 by Rutgers, the State University. Reprinted by permission of Rutgers University Press.

conceptualized as if they are largely independent forces that happen to overlap under specific conditions. For example, studies of race often focus upon contrasting Whites with Blacks and other racially identifiable groups without taking into account historical modes of incorporation of each group. Historical linkages and systematic interrelationships that reveal the underlying ways any one dimension of inequality is shaped by another are rarely fully examined. A problematic result is that the experiences of whole groups are ignored, misunderstood, or erased, particularly those of women of color.

This reading discusses intersectionality as an innovative and emerging field of study that provides a critical analytic lens to interrogate racial, ethnic, class, physical ability, age, sexuality, and gender disparities and to contest existing ways of looking at these structures of inequality. It identifies and discusses four theoretical interventions that we consider foundational to this interdisciplinary intellectual enterprise. We argue that intersectionality challenges traditional modes of knowledge production in the United States and illustrate how this theory provides an alternative model that combines advocacy, analysis, theorizing, and pedagogy—basic components essential to the production of knowledge as well as the pursuit of social justice and equality.

Research and teaching that focuses on the intersections of race, ethnicity, gender, and other dimensions of identity is a relatively new approach to studying inequality. (Inequality for these purposes is defined as institutionalized patterns of unequal control over and distribution of a society's valued goods and resources such as land, property, money, employment, education, healthcare, and housing.) Intersectionality has gained its greatest influence in the post–civil rights era and has been developed and utilized most prominently in the new scholarship created in the interdisciplinary fields of ethnic studies, women's studies, area studies, and, more recently, lesbian, gay, bisexual, and transgender studies, cultural studies, critical legal studies, labor studies, multicultural studies, American studies, and social justice education. Intersectional analysis begins with the experiences of groups that occupy multiple social locations and finds approaches and ideas that focus on the complexity rather than the singularity of human experience.

Traditional disciplinary boundaries and the compartmentalization and fixity of ideas are challenged by these emerging interdisciplinary fields. These fields seek not only to reexamine old issues in new ways, but also to shift the lens through which humanity and social life are viewed—identifying new issues, new forms, and new ways of viewing them. Thus intersectional scholarship reflects an ongoing intellectual and social justice mission that seeks to: (1) reformulate the world of ideas so that it incorporates the many contradictory and overlapping ways that human life is experienced; (2) convey this knowledge by rethinking curricula and promoting institutional change in higher education institutions; (3) apply the knowledge in an effort to create a society in which all voices are heard; and (4) advocate for public policies that are responsive to multiple voices . . . .

## THE INTERSECTIONAL LENS: AN EMERGING PERSPECTIVE

Discussion of the origins of intersectionality most often begins with the research, writings, and teaching by and about women of color in the United States (both native and migrant). Women of color scholars have used the idea of intersections to explain our own lives and to critique the exclusion of our experiences, needs, and perspective from both White, Eurocentric, middle-class conceptualizations of feminism and male-dominated models of ethnic studies. We have laid claim to a U.S. scholarly tradition that began in the nineteenth century with women like Maria Stewart and men like W. E. B. DuBois, whose work of "cultural social analysis," according to ethnic studies scholar Johnella Butler, claimed the right to articulate a sense of self and act on it.[1] Contemporary women of color have continued this legacy by locating ideas that explore the intersections of race, gender, ethnicity, and sexuality at the center of their thinking about their own lives and those of women,

men, and families of color (Baca Zinn & Dill 1994; Collins 1998, 2000; Crenshaw 1993a and b; Davis 1983; Anzaldua 1999; Dill 1983; hooks 1992; Moraga and Anzaldua 2002; Hull, Bell Scott, & Smith 2003). Intersectionality is a product of seeking to have our voices heard and lives acknowledged.

Although considerable ground work for this kind of scholarship was laid first in the fields of ethnic and women's studies—areas that perhaps have the longest published record of grappling with these issues—as this body of ideas and knowledge grew and developed, new ways of thinking, which were emerging in other fields, began to influence one another, broadening the intellectual appeal and practical applicability of intersectional approaches to questions of identity and social life.

In addition to its academic and intellectual concerns, intersectional scholarship matters outside the academy because day-to-day life and lived experience is the primary domain in which the conceptualization and understanding of these constructs is and has been grounded. Scholars emphasize that the work itself grew out of movements with a social justice agenda such as those focused on civil rights, women's rights, and the struggles to include ethnic studies within university curricula. Thus this work is not seen as emanating solely from a series of linked theoretical propositions but from an effort to improve society, in part, by understanding and explaining the lives and experiences of marginalized people and by examining the constraints and demands of the many social structures that influence their options and opportunities. For example, rather than think that one could understand the responses of young Black women to hip-hop music merely through an analysis that focuses on race, an intersectional framework would analyze the relationships among sexuality, gender, class, and popular culture, within an historical as well as a contemporary framework, in order to shed light on this phenomenon (Crenshaw 1993a; Rose 1994; Morgan 1999; Pough 2004).

One point of general agreement among intersectional scholars is that the experiences and texts of traditionally marginalized groups were not considered knowledge thirty years ago. Yet the writings,

ideas, experiences, and perspectives of people whose lives were once considered unimportant are increasingly influencing traditional disciplines. In the field of sociology, for example, intersectional analysis has extended and combined traditional subareas of stratification, race and ethnicity, and family by drawing on conflict theory, theories of racialization (Omi & Winant 1994; Oliver & Shapiro 1995; Massey & Denton 1993), and gender stratification (Lorber 1994, 1998; Gardiner 2002; Kimmel 2000; Myers, Anderson, & Risman 1998). These subareas, combined with ideas drawn from ethnic studies, critical legal theory, and postmodernism, explore the ways identity flows from and is entangled in those relationships and how systems of inequality (race, ethnicity, class, gender, physical ability, and sexuality) are embedded in and shape one another. Intersectionality is both a reflection of and influence upon some of the newer directions in fields such as history, sociology, legal studies, and anthropology to name a few. It does this by examining relationships and interactions between multiple axes of identity and multiple dimensions of social organization—at the same time.

Throughout this reading, we treat intersectionality as an analytical strategy—a systematic approach to understanding human life and behavior that is rooted in the experiences and struggles of marginalized people. The premises and assumptions that underlie this approach are: inequalities derived from race, ethnicity, class, gender, and their intersections place specific groups of the population in a privileged position with respect to other groups and offer individuals unearned benefits based solely on group membership; historical and systemic patterns of disinvestment in nonprivileged groups are major contributors to the low social and economic position of those groups; representations of groups and individuals in media, art, music, and other cultural forms create and sustain ideologies of group and individual inferiority/superiority and support the use of these factors to explain both individual and group behavior; and individual identity exists within and draws from a web of socially defined statuses some of which may be more salient than others in specific situations or at specific historical moments.

As Weber (2001) points out, intersectional analysis operates on two levels: at the individual level, it reveals the way the intermeshing of these systems creates a broad range of opportunities for the expression and performance of individual identities. At the societal/structural level, it reveals the ways systems of power are implicated in the development, organization, and maintenance of inequalities and social injustice. In both writing and teaching, scholars engaged in this work are challenged to think in complex and nuanced ways about identity and to look at both the points of cohesion and fracture within groups (Dill and Johnson 2002; Weber 2001) as they seek to capture and convey dynamic social processes in which individual identities and group formations grow and shift in continuous interaction with one another, within specific historical periods and geographic locations.

Additionally, intersectional analysis provides an important lens for reframing and creating new knowledge because it asserts new ways of studying power and inequality and challenges conventional understanding of oppressed and excluded groups and individuals. Collins (2000) in her discussion of Black feminist thought as critical social theory states:

> For African American women, the knowledge gained at intersecting oppressions of race, class and gender, provides the stimulus for crafting and passing on the subjugated knowledge of Black women's critical social theory. As a historically oppressed group, U.S. Black women have produced social thought designed to oppose oppression.

Thus, to use Collins's language, intersectional analysis is a tool that reveals the subjugated knowledges of people of color and produces social thought that can be considered critical social theory. One of the key ways this is accomplished is through the unveiling of power in interconnected structures of inequality. Intersectional analysis explores and unpacks relations of domination and subordination, privilege and agency, in the structural arrangements through which various services, resources, and other social rewards are delivered; in the interpersonal experiences of individuals and groups; in the practices that characterize and sustain bureaucratic hierarchies; and in the ideas, images, symbols, and ideologies that shape social consciousness (Collins 2000). It is characterized by the following four theoretical interventions: (1) Placing the lived experiences and struggles of people of color and other marginalized groups as a starting point for the development of theory; (2) Exploring the complexities not only of individual identities but also group identity, recognizing that variations within groups are often ignored and essentialized; (3) Unveiling the ways inter-connected domains of power organize and structure inequality and oppression; and (4) Promoting social justice and social change by linking research and practice to create a holistic approach to the eradication of disparities and to changing social and higher education institutions.

## INTERSECTIONALITY'S THEORETICAL INTERVENTIONS

### Centering the Experiences of People of Color

The intersectional approach to the study of inequality, as it has developed in U.S. social thought, is rooted in illuminating the complexities of race and ethnicity as it intersects with other dimensions of difference. In doing this, the multiple and intersectional influences of these characteristics become clear. For example, for African American men and women, if we begin with their own understandings of the ways race is used to limit their life choices and chances, we see that opportunity is not just structured by race, but by the confluence of race, class, gender, and other dimensions of difference. Similarly, the opportunity for a college preparatory K–12 education is influenced by one's race but also by class position in the society and within that racial group, as well as by gender and the perceptions and expectations of one's gender based on class, race, region, ability, and so on. (A low-income woman from Appalachia, who is White, faces a different set of opportunities and constraints on the path to a college degree than a middle-income woman who is White and living in New York City.)

As discussed earlier, intersectional knowledge is distinctive knowledge generated by the experiences of previously excluded communities and multiply oppressed groups. It tells, interprets, and analyzes the stories of Black, Latino/a,[2] Asian American, and Native American Indian women and/or of gay men, lesbians, and transgender people of all racial and ethnic groups in the United States.[3] It is knowledge based upon and derived from what intersectional scholars have called the "outsider-within," "subaltern," and "borderland"[4] voices of society, creating counterhistories and counternarratives to those based primarily on the experiences of social elites. Importantly, this approach focuses on the relationships of opportunity and constraint created by the dimensions of inequality so that racism, for example, is analyzed not only in terms of the constraints it produces in the lives of people of color but also in terms of the privileges it creates for Whites.

An example can be found in some of the earliest work in what has come to be termed "Whiteness studies." Other scholars (Frankenberg 1993; Waters 1990; Brodkin 1998; Lipsitz 1998; Roediger 1991) have extended the concept of race to Whites and revealed the unacknowledged privilege that is derived from White skin, a privilege that is taken for granted and remains invisible.

## Complicating Identity

Both individual and group identity are complex—influenced and shaped not simply by a person's race, class, ethnicity, gender, physical ability, sexuality, religion, or nationality—but by a combination of all of those characteristics. Nevertheless, in a hierarchically organized society, some statuses are more valued than others. Within groups, there is far greater diversity than appears when, for analytical purposes, people are classified with a single term.

For example, the term Latino/a—as a gendered, ethnic, and racial construct—is interconnected with multiple discourses on social stratification and political/national identity. Its meaning varies depending on the social context in which it is employed and the political meanings associated with its usage.

The term Latino/a challenges the privileging of Spanish or Hispanic lineage over the other indigenous and African lineages of Spanish-speaking individuals in the United States. Nevertheless Latino/a as a social construct needs to be problematized because its underlying political discourse seeks to disrupt "neat" categories of what is now perceived as the Latino or brown race. Thus, by homogenizing all Latino/as into one category, the discourse on national identity is dismissed and the effects of the intersection of race, ethnic sub-group, and socioeconomic status on Latinas are overlooked.

Identity for Latinos, African Americans, Asians, and Native Americans is complicated by differences in national origin or tribal group, citizenship, class (both within the sending and host countries—for recent migrants), gender, as well as race and ethnicity. A contemporary example is found in the controversy surrounding whether or not Black students who migrated from Africa or the West Indies to the United States should be permitted to take advantage of scholarships designed for historically underrepresented African Americans. In several articles it has been argued that in their pursuit of diversity, universities have redefined the original remedies of civil rights law to include immigrant Africans and Afro-Caribbeans as substitutes for native-born African American Blacks (Guinier 2004; Bell 2004). An intersectional approach necessitates acknowledging such intragroup differences in order to address them.

## Unveiling Power in Interconnected Structures of Inequality

Collins, in *Black Feminist Thought* (2000:275), conveys a complex understanding of power by describing it as *both* a force that some groups use to oppress others *and* "an intangible entity that operates throughout a society and is organized in particular domains." This complex notion of power provides tools for examining the ways that people experience inequalities are organized and maintained through four interrelated domains:

1. the structural domain, which consists of the institutional structures of the society including government, the legal system, housing patterns, economic traditions, and educational structure;

2. the disciplinary domain, which consists of the ideas and practices that characterize and sustain bureaucratic hierarchies;

3. the hegemonic domain, which consists of the images, symbols, ideas, and ideologies that shape social consciousness (Collins 2000);

4. the interpersonal domain, which consists of patterns of interaction between individuals and groups.

Intersectional analyses, as knowledge generated from and about oppressed groups, unveil these domains of power and reveal how oppression is constructed and maintained through multiple aspects of identity simultaneously. Understanding these aspects of power draws on knowledge of the historical legacies of people who have experienced inequality due to discriminatory practices and policies based on combinations of race, class, gender, ethnicity, and other dimensions of difference. Because arrangements of power shift and change over time and in different cultural contexts, individuals and groups experience oppression and inequalities differently according to their social, geographic, historical, and cultural location (Weber 2001).

*Structural Power*

Within the structural domain, we are particularly interested in the ways "institutions are organized to reproduce subordination over time" (Collins 2000:277). In U.S. history, people of color have been controlled by policies in every institution of the society. These included, but are not limited to, racial segregation, exclusion acts, internment, forced relocation, denial of the right to own property, and denial of the right to marry and form stable families. Within each of these forms of institutional subordination, the various categories intersect to provide distinctive experiences for groups of individuals.

For example, in a recent essay using an intersectional approach to Latina health, we argue that the location of health services in relationship to low-income Latino communities structures access to healthcare and is a major factor affecting the health of Latino women, children, and families. The distribution of governmental resources, ranging from funding for research to the provision of public health services, is examined in terms of historical patterns and political considerations, which have led to a concentration of health resources in middle- and upper-income communities and the prioritization of research on diseases and illnesses, which are more prevalent in those populations (Zambrana and Dill 2006).

Intersectional analysis also directs us to look at structural inequities by examining questions of social and economic justice, both to reveal the sources of these inequities and to begin to redress them. Poverty is primarily the result of the unequal distribution of society's goods and resources and the concentration of wealth in the hands of a few. When one examines the interaction of poverty with race/ethnicity and gender, it is apparent that these factors, taken together, have a disproportionately negative effect on people of color, especially women (Higginbotham and Romero 1997; Williams and Collins 1995), and result in an overconcentration of detrimental social, economic, and political outcomes for them and their families.

Race, ethnicity, and geography matter, as they are all determinants of access to social capital or social resources (Massey and Denton 1993).[5] Intersectional analysis draws attention to the policies, practices, and outcomes of institutional racism and discrimination, one result of which is the concentration of low-income people of color in resource-poor neighborhoods with poorly financed and underdeveloped public systems such as schools and public health services.

*Disciplinary Power*

In addition to formal policies or the location of resources away from some communities, intersectional analyses draw attention to the bureaucratic practices that perpetuate and maintain inequality.

Linda Gordon, in her book *Pitied but Not Entitled: Single Mothers and the History of Welfare, 1890–1935* (1994) provides an analysis that illustrates the intertwining of structural and disciplinary power. The book focuses upon the ways in which U.S. social welfare policies and their implementation have resulted in the impoverishment of single mothers. Gordon's history outlines the development during the New Deal of a two-tier welfare system: a nationally supported social insurance system of generous benefits for workers who were disproportionately White and male, and a poorly funded, state-supported system of "means-tested" morally evaluated benefits for those who were irregularly employed, a disproportionate number of whom were women and minorities. In her telling of this story, Gordon reveals the behind the scenes politics, rivalries, and values within the Children's Bureau in which "feminist" social workers of the progressive era became the advocates of a system of maternal and child health that gave primacy to women's role as mother and advocated for states to implement these policies. An unintended consequence was that the primary program for single mothers, Aid to Families with Dependent Children (AFDC), became subject to state politics and local bureaucratic practices. It was, therefore, more likely to be governed by state legislation that openly discriminated on the basis of race or immigrant status and to bureaucratic practices that gave or denied benefits on the basis of morality, political loyalty, and the value judgments of individual caseworkers.

In sum, Gordon's work shows how disciplinary power administered through case workers at the national and state levels combined with structural power organized in state and federal legislation shaped historical patterns of racial and gender relations within the U.S. system of social welfare. This example is repeated throughout the society not only in public welfare systems but across all public systems, including education, housing, and employment.

## Hegemonic Power

Hegemonic power refers to the cultural ideologies, images, and representations that shape group and individual consciousness and support or justify policies and practices in the structural and disciplinary domains. Through the manipulation of ideology it links social institutions—structural power, organizational practices—disciplinary power, and everyday experiences—interpersonal power (Collins 2000:284). These ideas influence the ways members of various social groups are viewed and depicted in the society at large and the expectations associated with these depictions (hooks 1992; Chin and Humikowski 2002; Zambrana, Mogel, and Scrimshaw 1987). Intersectional analyses challenge us to interrogate those ideologies and representations, to locate and uncover their origins and multiple meanings, and to examine the reasons for their existence and persistence.

For example, dominant representations of people of color build upon and elaborate ideas, images, and stereotypes that are deeply rooted in American history and become the rationale for the differential treatment of groups and individuals (Portes 2000). In the case of Latinas, scholars have argued that stereotypes of Latinas as aliens, hypersexual, exotic, and passive promote the myth that they need to be controlled by state institutions through such policies as those that deny prenatal care or force sterilization. These false representations affect not only the ways dominant culture healthcare providers treat their Latina patients but the. kinds of public policies that are designed to determine access to healthcare (Silliman et al. 2004: 216).

Welfare reform provides another example of the ways stereotypes and representations affect social policies, access to services, and the location of groups within the social structure. An essay written by Dill, Baca Zinn, and Patton examines this issue in depth. This essay demonstrates that representations of single motherhood as the cause of delinquency, crime, violence, abandonment, abuse, and gangs and depictions of single mothers as self-centered, free-loading, idle, and sexually promiscuous, have been nationally linked to Black women, Latinas—especially on the West Coast and in the Mexican border states—and Native American women in the West. These representations have been used to justify welfare reform strategies specifically designed to promote work and decrease childbirth among low-income women. In the essay we argue that a major source of the power and appeal of welfare reform was its effort to discipline and control the behavior of Black women, other women of color, and by example, White women (1999).

These stereotypes exist, are interpreted, understood, and reinscribed within larger social and historical narratives that have a long history in U.S. society. Another example discussed at length in the Dill, Baca Zinn, and Patton essay cited above, relies heavily on scholar Rickie Solinger's book, *Wake up Little Susie: Single Pregnancy and Race before* Roe v. Wade (1992).

According to Solinger, social services available to pregnant single women in the post–World War II era were strikingly dissimilar based on race. Young, White, middle-class women who got pregnant during this era were typically sent to homes for unwed mothers far away from their communities where they were heavily counseled that giving up their children for adoption and "forgetting" the experience was the only psychologically acceptable thing to do (Cole and Donley 1990; Solinger 1992). During this same time period, however, she shows that African American women were excluded from most homes for unwed mothers on the basis of race, and there were very few all-Black homes. In contrast to White women, African American women went virtually unserved in the child welfare system. Black women were frequently turned away from adoption agencies (Day 1979) and directed to public welfare departments. Thus the stereotype of the Black welfare mother was both drawn on and enforced by policies that limited African American women's access to social resources while maintaining the myth of White moral superiority (Dill, Baca Zinn, and Patton 1999).

*Interpersonal Power*

Interpersonal power refers to "routinized, day-to-day practices of how people treat one another. Such practices are systematic, recurrent and so familiar that they often go unnoticed." They have been referred to as everyday racism or everyday sexism, etc., and are powerful "in the production and reinforcement of the status quo" (Collins 2000:287; Bonilla Silva 2006:26; Essed 1991). Everyday racism is entwined with the

implementation of disciplinary and hegemonic power. It is exemplified in the simple acts of referring to White men as "men" and men of color with a racial modifier in news reports; or reports by White women of experiencing feelings of threat or fear when encountering a Black man on the street in the evening.

In her book, *Understanding Everyday Racism*, Essed analyzes interviews with fifty-five women of African descent in the Netherlands and the United States who recount experiences of everyday racism. She argues that these accounts are not ad hoc stories but have a specific structure with several recurring elements and reflect the fact that Whites in the Netherlands and the United States have very different and narrower definitions of racism than Blacks. For Whites, racism is seen as extreme beliefs or actions that endorse White supremacy. For Blacks, the emphasis is on a wide variety of actions including White supremacy as well as Eurocentrism, avoidance of contact with other ethnic groups, underestimating the abilities of minorities, and passive tolerance of racist behavior by others.

Within intersectional analyses, unveiling the workings of power, which is understood as both pervasive and oppressive, is vitally important. It reveals both the sources of inequality and its multiple and often conflicting manifestations. It provides a way to examine how different identity markers overlay or intersect with one another at all levels of social relations (structural/institutional/ideological/macro and interpersonal/everyday/micro) in different historical and geographical contexts (Collins 1998; Crenshaw 1993b; Weber 2001).

## PROMOTING SOCIAL JUSTICE AND SOCIAL CHANGE

Grounded in the everyday lives of people of diverse backgrounds, intersectional knowledge reveals the various impacts of the presence of racial and gender disparities, and is a critical first step toward eliminating inequality. The social justice agenda of the intersectional approach is inextricably linked to its utility in unveiling power. It also provides an analytical framework for combining the different kinds of work that need to be included in the pursuit of social justice: advocacy, analysis, policy development, theorizing, and education. Because intersectional work validates the lives and stories of previously ignored groups of people, it is seen as a tool that can be used to help empower communities and the people in them. Implicitly the production of this knowledge offers the potential for creating greater understanding among groups of people.

The Declaration of the NGO (nongovernmental) Forum of the UN Conference on Racism in 2001 included in its opening statement the following under the topic of gender:

> 119. An intersectional approach to discrimination acknowledges that every person be it man or woman exists in a framework of multiple identities, with factors such as race, class, ethnicity, religion, sexual orientation, gender identity, age, disability, citizenship, national identity, geopolitical context, health, including HIV/AIDS status and any other status, are all determinants in one's experiences of racism, racial discrimination, xenophobia and related intolerances. An intersectional approach highlights the way in which there is a simultaneous interaction of discrimination as a result of multiple identities. (Declaration and Programme of Action 2001)

This statement, in an international document that begins with an assessment of the contemporary circumstances of discrimination in a global context and continues by laying out a program of action that individual nation-states are encouraged to follow is an excellent example of the ways the ideas on intersectionality are linked to social action. In this case, the statement about gender immediately links gender issues to a variety of other issues for which specific action steps are delineated. In effect, it is argued that gender, as part of a complex set of relationships, must be also considered within each of the concerns delineated in the plan of action.

A second example of the link between intersectional thinking, social justice, and social change is the work of LatCrit. LatCrit, Latina and Latino Critical Legal Theory, Inc., describes itself as "an intellectual and social community of people engaged in critical 'outsider jurisprudence' that centers Latino/as in all of their diversity." One of its goals is "to develop a critical, activist, and interdisciplinary discourse on law and policy toward Latinas/os and to foster both the development of coalitional theory and practice as well as the accessibility of this knowledge to agents of social and legal transformation" (www.LatCrit.org). To accomplish these goals, LatCrit supports projects at a number of law schools around the country. One project that exemplifies the link between theory and activism is the Community Development Externship Network, "an experiential learning project designed to provide legal assistance to local communities or activists working on social justice efforts in rural and urban sites in the United States and the Americas. Central to this project is that students are engaged in the work of securing material remedies to social injustices suffered both by groups and individuals, including land reclamation projects and other kinds of reparations-oriented efforts."

In conclusion, transformation of knowledge and of individual lives is a fundamental aspect of intersectional work. Strong commitments and desires to create more equitable societies that recognize and validate differences drive the research of scholars and the practice of activists. Among these scholars, discussions of social change focus not just on changing the society at large but also on changing structures of knowledge within institutions of higher learning and the relationship of colleges and universities to the society. *Transformative* is perhaps one of the best words to characterize this scholarship because it is seen not only as transforming knowledge but using knowledge to transform society.

## DISCUSSION QUESTIONS

1. According to Dill and Zambrana, what is intersectionality? Why is this theoretical approach important for studying social inequality?
2. Provide examples of the way in which an intersectionalist approach to social inequality provides a basis for social action. Explain the

"intersectional lens" as an emerging perspective and how and why it grew out of movements with a social justice agenda.

## Notes

1. Johnella Butler, Spelman College, personal communication.
2. The term Latina/o is used interchangeably with Hispanics, consistent with federal standards. Under the category of Hispanic/Latino are included persons of Spanish-speaking origin from the Spanish-speaking Caribbean, Central America, Mexico, and Latin America. Hispanics/Latinos may be of any race and/or mixed race but have a preference for identifying with their national origin.
3. Examples include: E. N. Glenn, *Unequal Citizens*; R. Ferguson, *Aberrations in Black*; P. Hondagneau-Sotelo, *Domestica*; Audre Lorde, *Sister Outsider*; P. H. Collins, *Black Feminist Thought*, A. Hurtado, *The Color of Privilege*, among many others.
4. These terms are drawn from the work of Patricia Hill Collins, Gayatri Spivak, and Gloria Anzaldua, respectively.
5. Social capital broadly refers to access to resources that improve educational, economic, and social position in society (Bourdieu 1985; Ellen and Turner 1997).

# 13

# WHITENESS BY ANY OTHER COLOR IS STILL WHITENESS

## PEM DAVIDSON BUCK

*This fifth reading in the theory section is by Pem Davidson Buck, professor of sociology and anthropology at Elizabethtown Community and Technical College, Kentucky. This excerpt is taken from a revised 2009 paper Buck presented at the Midwest Meeting of the Committees of Correspondence for Democracy and Socialism. At her presentation and in this paper, Buck challenges her colleagues to understand how the modern nation-state relies on race, especially whiteness, to uphold systems of privilege. To make her case, Buck uses the history of Latino/a immigration as evidence.*

Eliminating racism, I argue, requires eliminating whiteness and race itself. Race is a fundamental stone in the foundation of modern capitalist states, and attempts to eliminate it will, I predict, be met by strategic manoevers which will *appear* to be an anti-racist relaxing of discrimination, a move toward inclusion and equality. In fact, these manoeuvers will reorganize race and whiteness in order to allow their persistence under new conditions. We need to recognize this tactic if we are to combat it. To make my argument, I need first to look at where we are in terms of the history of the relationship between race and state, focusing particularly on the reaction to Latino/a immigration.

We all remember W's reaction: "To defend this country, we have to enforce our borders . . . " (Bush 2005). Newspapers in the Southwest described immigration with phrases such as "There's a 'brown tide rising'" (Santa Ana 2002). What is the significance of such statements? Defend borders from what? Why does the rising tide metaphor invoke swamps awash in mud, rather than, say, a rising tide that raises all boats?

*Source:* Buck, Pem Davidson. 2007. "Whiteness by Any Other Color Is Still Whiteness." Paper presented at the Midwest meeting of the Committees of Correspondence for Democracy and Socialism, September 19, 2009. Louisville, KY. © Pem David Buck. Reprinted with permission of author.

What, in the militarily and economically most powerful nation, is so fragile, so vulnerable, so threatened, that it can be washed away in a brown tide coming over a border itself so fragile that it must be defended by a hightech version of the Great Wall of China?[1]

Answering these questions I think requires acknowledging that the modern nation state can't exist without race—and in the United States, without whiteness (cf. Mullings 2005:671; Goldberg 2002; Mills 1997). And it requires examining the re-ordering of whiteness occasioned by the construction of transnational corporate empire, particularly by the continuous warfare required in that construction (cf. Buck 2008; Kapferer 2004; Turner 2003:47–48). In this reordering I believe that race and whiteness will be redefined, and that whiteness will be expanded so that whites do not become a minority, as is often predicted (Warren and Twine 1997).

Whiteness is a juridical status established and maintained by the state for its own purposes—and too much is at stake to risk the loss of legitimacy that would result should whites lose the value of their proprietary interest in whiteness (Harris 1993). After all, whites' consent and participation is needed by transnational elites as they establish corporate empire. But at the same time, the United States, as the tool for enforcing corporate empire, needs more super-exploitable bodies for productive labor within the borders of the 'homeland,' and for military labor—people who can end up dead or maimed with minimal protest from the voting and potentially protesting public. The available new bodies are brown. But using them without arousing white folk, either in humanitarian protest or in nativist protest, is getting tricky. And it will get far more tricky as the realities of Operation Endgame begin to hit home—unless, of course, Obama actually rescinds Bush administration Homeland Security policies (cf. Vogel 2007; U.S. Department of Homeland Security 2003). Endgame is the codename for the policy of forced, and probably military, deportation of 12 million unauthorized immigrants. The Bush administration proposed that the deported, relatively uncontrolled, immigrant labor force would then be replaced through the importation of millions of state-controlled unfree "guest workers." Their restriction from citizenship

and from even ordinary human rights will be justified by race (Vogel 2007:1; Southern Poverty Law Center 2006:4; Hidden Slaves 2004)—reminiscent of the Black Codes' labor control after the Civil War. But this use of race is fairly standard behavior for modern states, having to do with both the need for cheap labor and the need to legitimize elite governance. States, generically, don't need race—inequalities can be ascribed in other ways—caste, slavery, the feudal system. Legitmacy also can come in other ways.[2] The *modern* nation state, however, does need race.

First, the legitimacy issue. Nation states base their legitimacy on a "presumption of homogeneity."[3] In a nation state, where people don't owe loyalty to a king or church (Anderson 1991:19 ff.), the myth of homogeneity—we are 'a people'—is important in getting people to be obedient patriots and workers. Nation states claim that the right of self-determination—their right to exist—is based on the existence of such a 'nation,' a 'people' who share the same values, culture, language, and history. But in fact most modern states are conquest states, containing sections of several so-called nations (Hill 1996) as well as immigrants. Since the claim to be one people therefore doesn't work, race, in our case whiteness, can serve as the unifying homogenizer. And since race has no physical reality, it can be extended and redefined as necessary to admit new members to the nation.

Second, the inequality issue. The modern state has none of the alternative systems for creating and justifying the inequality and super-exploitation which primes the pump of wealth creation. You can't have sweatshops or stoop labor harvesting lettuce or cutting tobacco on contracts that leave the worker deeper in debt without denying both the rights to legal recourse held by citizens and the human rights held by virtue of a common humanity[4]. The complication is that a modern state can't afford to challenge the ideology of equality before the law that is basic to the idea of a nation state and that justifies the loyalty of all its citizens. But super-exploitation *requires* the denial of the rights of equal citizenship. An apparently *natural* system is needed for providing that inequality.

Designating categories of people as *outside* the nation by "blood,"[5] by biology, and therefore as non-citizens, allows you do this without upsetting the ideology of equality *within* the nation. This ideology of equality within the nation that whiteness underwrites encourages an alliance between working class whites and the elites who exploit them.[6] But at least as important, race is needed so that people will go off to die or be mutilated for their elites, "defending our borders." As in the war on terror, race can both justify the deaths of "Others" and justify the requirement that "we" should die in the interests of the state that members of the race must die for the life of the race.

A state must be able to organize the use of force—against outsiders who challenge its elite's right to extract wealth from the territory it controls, and against insiders who challenge the extraction process itself (cf. Whitaker 2007:118; 157; Goldberg 2002: 101–102; 241). A modern state is a clearly bounded territory existing within a system of such states, jointly regulating each other and recognizing the right of each to defend its territory from incursion by other states (Giddens 1987:119–120; 281–282). The right of elites to extract wealth from within each state is thus dependent on their ability to participate in the game of regulation. Thus the ultimate obligation of both the state and its citizens is the obligation to maintain its integrity as a state; war and warriors are the *sine qua non* of a state—and of empire (Kapferer 2004:1; Shklar 1991:31; Trouillot 2001:132–133; Goldberg 2002:100). States within this international system thus have an enormous vested interest in regulating "blood"—in jointly regulating the processes that determine which state can claim allegiance and labor from which people, and who gets the rights and protections extended by which nation. People become what one analyst describes as "properties negotiated among state-nations" (Stevens 1999:207). Borders thus demarcate zones of differential exploitability, creating racialized "human resources" to be imported like other resources or used beyond the borders by imperial elites who can't as easily superexploit those in the imperial center who carry the blood of the nation.

When Bush, working to create consent to continuous war, talked about defending our borders he was using the panic of the nationalist/nativists who believe the continued existence of the United States as a nation state is in jeopardy.[7] In their eyes a permeable border is ultimately not a border; it does not separate and define the United States as a nation where whiteness is what makes us a 'people' with the rights of citizens and of self-determination—and where whites have a privileged grip on decent wages—a grip threatened by imperial use of unfree immigrant labor. The sovereign white state is what is so fragile, what could be overwhelmed by the rising brown tide.[8] And in fact, at least under Bush, perhaps under Obama, whiteness and white privilege as it has recently been known, U.S. sovereignty, self-determination, and the rights of citizens—all these really have been under siege. The threat has come with initiatives such as the North American Community–"Nafta on steroids,"[9] the proposed guest worker program, the gradual erosion of constitutional rights of citizens and the demolition of the constitutional separation of powers. But these threats do not exist because of a permeable border or because of a rising brown tide.

Instead these threats exist because we are being molded for our new role as transgressors against the system of joint state regulation, as enforcers of global corporate empire, and prepped to accept both continuous war and the neoliberal attack on the U.S. state, which may or may not have to ease off temporarily under Obama in response to citizen unrest. Because capitalism is being reorganized around the needs of the New World Order,[10] and capitalism is dependent on race, race also must be reorganized, and, under Bush, fascist ideology facilitated that process, carried on now more informally by right wing talk shows and the religious right.

Fascist ideology is designed to control an insecure, angry, and potentially conscience-stricken middle class during times like now, of capitalist crisis and re-organization. We have unauthorized immigrants bound in a form of debt peonage, and perhaps eventually in a form of indenture as guest workers. These workers must be managed by members of the middle class, people engaged in social control—police, factory supervisors, social workers, teachers, Homeland Security agents. Those involved need to believe the suffering they are supervising is good, just as they need to believe that they are patriots as officers supervising the military and mercenary killing of people of color. Meanwhile the middle class is itself undergoing increased exploitation.[11]

Membership in the social control segment of the middle class has always been basically white. One could argue, in fact, that the granting of unquestioned eligibility for admission to the social control class is the mark of whiteness. As new groups become a major source of labor, it may become eventually necessary to admit some to the social control class, thus buying off resistance, derailing claims of racism, and legitimizing their collaboration in controlling and managing exploitation. But how can not-white people be admitted to whiteness without threatening the security of the already existing social control class and without destroying the power of white privilege and the psychological wage of whiteness (DuBois 1995 [1935]: 700–701)—the belief that 'I may be poor, but at least I'm white'—to control the already existing white working class? This problem was solved before, as a then non-white immigrant eastern and southern European labor supply was incorporated into the blood of the nation; it was a two pronged process then, and I suspect it is playing itself out again today.

Incorporation then and now involves the state's need for force. Since wars and warriors are the sine qua non of the state, shedding blood is one prong. It is as exerters of violence, as soldiers shedding blood for the nation defending elite rights, as self-freed but formerly enslaved Africans did first during the Civil War and as their descendants did later during the World Wars, that people defined as outside the nation are often able to make progress toward second-class or full citizenship.[12] Shedding blood, sacrificing for the nation, can establish a claim, a 'blood-right,' to citizenship. And granting citizenship, if necessary, does not have to seriously disturb already existing power relations, since although citizenship confers status, and with it certain rights and obligations, unless it is accompanied by whiteness it does not convey privilege, and even for whites conveys little political power (cf. Olson 2004:77; Shklar 1991:28–30).

The second need of the state for force is in the internal enforcement of the extraction of wealth. As collaborators—the second prong—enforcing

extraction of wealth with violence if necessary, for instance as police, as the Irish did in the United States members of an exploited group help control their own category, and perhaps more important, they give the appearance of a race-free, "color-blind" level playing field. However, since access to the social control class has been a part of white privilege, and white privilege is critical to keeping all whites aligned with the interests of the elites, these new members of the social control class will have to become white to avoid alienating the already existing whites. Honorary whiteness of a few can be followed by a gradual whitening of the whole group, or segments of it.

Since there is nothing obvious, physically, about the blood claims on which race rests, race as a usable concept would cease to exist without the state's production of laws defining racial categories and regulating its reproduction (Haney-Lopez 2006). This process is infinitely malleable. Whiteness is actually about power, not about skin color or ancestry. Since there is no such thing as actual white skin, and since a tremendous range of off-tan is called white—just look around at the people who get identified as white—, and since humans are capable of seeing just about anything according to its definition, whiteness in the future could look very different from how it looks now. White will continue to be those with relative privilege, power, and access to resources.

Spending some time in a Los Angeles public swimming pool, where clothes, carriage, and language can't be used to interpret ancestry, clarifies how this might work. My daughter took me to her neighborhood pool a few summers back. While my daughter, like me, would be defined as white, my granddaughter, with a father from India, is racially ambiguous. She happily splashed in the toddler pool with other kids, most of whom were equally ambiguous, as were their bathing-suited parents. Taking off the present lens of race, and simply looking at bodies, it is easy to imagine a new lens, through which someone of fairly light skin who happens to have come from somewhere in Latin America doesn't look much different from someone from Eastern Europe who doesn't look much different from someone from Northern China or Japan, who doesn't look much different from lots of dark-haired people at present clearly defined as white. With a new definition that said these people were all white, and with the clothes and carriage of the middle class, present whites could eventually see them as white. The same shift in race happened with the Irish and Italians and Jews, who once were defined as not white (Brodkin 1998; Roediger 2005). But darker and working class people will still appear non-white—a different race.

So my guess is that what is at present perceived by whites as a single non-white category—say Latino/Latina—will eventually be split along more or less class lines.[13] The existence of continuous war and the need for bodies that the military is having trouble finding may provide the opportunity to shed blood for the nation; a green card army can replace the dependence on black soldiers, who are no longer so willing to sign up,[14] providing warriors without upsetting white privilege. Some in that category will eventually be white, members of the blood-defined nation. Many will join those who collaborate in the management of people being exploited, including the military and military families and the unfree guest workers. Those on the white side of the split will be seen by those who are presently white as indisputably members of the nation, just as Italians and Irish are now, part of the 'people,' part of the same 'blood.' White supremacy will be preserved, ensuring continued elite control of the state, with white privilege extended to the enlarged social control class, honorary whiteness extended to useful non-whites, and the psychological wage of whiteness still available for those whites for whom whiteness conveys minimal privilege.

The modern nation state cannot exist without race, so race there must be. But it does not have to be race as we know it. Race, but with a new racial order, will continue to be foundational to capitalism. Whiteness by any other color is still whiteness.

## DISCUSSION QUESTIONS

1. According to Buck, how do "whiteness" and other constructions of race uphold the nation-state?

2. Explain what Buck means by the assertion that "whiteness is actually about power, not about skin color or ancestry." How does Buck support this claim? How might the average American react to hearing it?

## NOTES

1. cf. Buchanan 2006:1–18 for a strongly stated version of the danger of the collapse of civilization under the weight of illegal (and legal) immigration. See Swain (2002) for interviews with white nationalists on the subject of immigration, and Santa Ana (2002) for analysis of media coverage of immigration.

2. Stratification can be based also on defined ascribed inequalities of religion, language. Mills points out, however, that religion was at first used by the colonial powers, but since people can convert, it was not dependable (1997:54). The same can be said of language. Race, once invented, is permanently inscribed on the body (or at least presumed to be). See also Goldberg (2002:119; 195).

3. Goldberg 2002:14–17; 120. For various discussions of the role of homogeneity see also Williams (1989:429–430); Trouillot (2001:126, 132); Mullings (2005:672), and Goldberg (2002:131, 154, 240)

4. Southern Poverty Law Center, 2006; also Hidden Slaves 2004. See Shklar 1991:28–29 on the tension between citizenship and exclusion.

5. See Williams 1989, esp. 431–432; Goldberg 2002: 240.

6. Olson 2004, esp. p. 68; Buck 2001. It also legitimates the wealth of the elite—it's a level playing field, and just watch, I may be the next Bill Gates.

7. cf. Olson on the history of the U.S. as a Herrenvolk democracy built on the distinction between citizen and non-citizen based on race (2004:31–63). He (2004:39) points out that in 1860 nearly twenty percent of the population of the northeast was foreign born. Thus massive immigration is not a new state of affairs, and in fact at present only 12% of the U.S. population is foreign born, according to the U.S. Census Bureau, with a plurality living in the West (Twelve Percent 2004).

8. Swain (2002:16–17) describes the fears of white nationalists, as does Buchanan (2006). Nordstrom (2004:52) maintains that the state's power is not the

only one, pointing to the largely invisible networks of illegal activity that control large segments of the world's economic and political activity. This could be another source of the sense of fragility of the state, especially combined with the far more visible but rarely discussed publicly power of corporations in threatening state sovereignty.

9. North American merger . . . (2006). See also "Building a North American Community" (2005); Bush sneaking . . . (2006). For the relationship between these initiatives and guest worker programs see Vogel (2007).

10. McMichael (1999), for instance, maintains that the state has been intimately involved in the formation of wage labor, that capitalism has always had non-wage labor forms tied into production of inputs for industrial production, and that "where labour is being disorganized, so is the nation-state as we know it. The state remains, often with strengthened powers, but with dwindling national legitimacy" (1999:36). He describes a global crisis of wage labor.

11. Fascist ideology plays on anger and racial insecurity to create consent to redefinition of the control class. See Buck (2008) for a more extended discussion of the role of the buffer social control class in the context of fascism.

12. Klinker with Smith (1999); see also Aihwa Ong's (2006:78–79) "graduated citizenship" and Shklar (1991:17–22). By the 1920s the majority of army draftees were not native born (Fleuhr-Lobban 2005:153).

13. Yancy (2003:127) and Tafoya (2007) present evidence that at least in terms of self-definition this is already happening.

14. Williams and Baron 2007. They also point out that the drop in Hispanic enlistment is the least, at 7%, with whites at 10%.

# 14

# My Body, My Closet

*Invisible Disability and the Limits of Coming-Out Discourse*

## Ellen Samuels

*This last reading in the theory section introduces us to theories of disability and sexuality. Ellen Samuels is an assistant professor of women's studies and English at the University of Wisconsin–Madison. In this excerpt from a 2003 journal article published in* GLQ: A Journal of Lesbian and Gay Studies, *Samuels compares the discourses of invisibility and of "coming out" to the social identities of sexuality and disability. Samuels finds the comparison to be useful but also limiting, and she suggests that we need new theories to help us understand these social categories.*

### The Limits of Analogy

A story: On a breezy afternoon one April I met with "Samantha," a student in an undergraduate course on literature and disability, to talk about her paper on cultural images of burn survivors. After showing me her draft, she remained, eager to talk about issues of disability and visibility, about her own experience as a person who appears "normal" until one looks closely enough to see the scars on her jaw and neck, the puckered skin that disappears under the neck of her T-shirt and reappears on her arm and wrist.

Since I almost always look "normal" despite my disabling chronic illness, I sympathized with her struggle over how and when to come out about her disability identity. "My parents don't understand why I would call myself disabled," Samantha said matter-of-factly; then she added with a mischievous grin, "In fact, there are two basic things my family just doesn't want to accept: that my cousin is gay and that I'm disabled. So we're going to take a picture of ourselves at a gay pride march next month and send it to them."

The moral: I admire Samantha's wit and intelligence. I am also struck by the convergence of many themes in her story: the shifting and contested meanings of disability; the uneasy, often self-destroying tension between appearance and identity; the social scrutiny that refuses to accept statements of identity without "proof"; and, finally, the discursive and practical connections between coming out—in all the meanings of the term—as queer and as disabled. Thus I begin with Samantha's story to frame a discussion not only of analogies between queerness and disability but of the specifics of coming out in each context as a person whose bodily appearance does not immediately signal one's own sense of identity. In the first section of this essay I consider the complicated dynamics inherent in the analogizing of social identities, with specific reference to feminist, queer, and disability studies. In the second section I turn to the politics of visibility and invisibility, drawing on autobiographical narratives as well as social theory to explore constructions of coming out or passing in a number of social contexts.[1] . . . Thus each section seeks to "queer" disability in order to develop new paradigms of identity, representation, and social interaction.

A number of disability theorists suggest that disability has more in common with sexual orientation than with race, ethnicity, or gender—other categories often invoked analogically to support the social model of disability.[2] One argument for this connection is that most people with disabilities, like most queers, do not share their identity with immediate family members and often have difficulty accessing

queer or crip culture.[3] The history of an oppressive medical model for homosexuality and the nature-nurture and assimilation- transformation debates in the modern LGBT civil rights movement offer additional areas of potential common ground with disability activism. Haunting such arguments, however, is the vexed issue of analogy itself, which cannot be extracted from the tangled history of the use and misuse of such identity analogies in past liberation movements.

In particular, most current analogies between oppressed social identities draw in some fashion on the sex-race analogy that emerged from the women's liberation movement of the 1970s. This analogy was used primarily by white women to claim legitimacy for feminist political struggle by analogizing it to the struggle of African Americans for civil rights. The sex-race analogy has been extensively critiqued, most importantly by feminists of color, and has by now been renounced by most white feminists. The gist of such a critique is suggested by the title of Tina Grillo and Stephanie M. Wildman's article "Obscuring the Importance of Race: The Implications of Making Comparisons between Racism and Sexism (or Other Isms)," and is summarized by Lisa Maria Hogeland:

> First, in its use of *race*, it represents a fantastic vision of African American identity, community, and politics—uncontested, uncontradictory, unproblematic—that is shaped by a simultaneous nostalgia for and forgetting of the Civil Rights Movement, as if identity, community, and politics had never been the subjects of struggle. Second, the analogy attempts to forge out of that nostalgia and forgetting an equally fantastic vision of a self-evident identity, community, and politics of *sex*, whether construed as gender or as sexuality. Third, implicit in the setting together of the two is a fantasy of coalition . . . [which] sidesteps the processes and practices that would make such coalition possible.[4]

Despite the validity of this critique, Hogeland observes that the sex-race analogy continues to function in feminist theory and has also emerged strongly in queer theory (45).

My own investigation of the analogies regarding disability, however, suggests that their use has transformed from a comparison between *similar* oppressions to a strategic *contrasting* of identities to elucidate a particular aspect of the primary identity under discussion. Such a transformation accords with the classic definition of analogy as based on "a similarity or resemblance of relations, in which the resemblance lies in the qualities of two or more objects that are essentially dissimilar."[5] In practice, such analogies often both create and rely on artificial dichotomies that not only produce inequality between the terms of comparison but exclude or elide anomalous experiences that do not fit easily within their terms.

For John Swain and Colin Cameron, strategic contrasting supports the claim that disability and sexual "preference" are both social labels that are "usually self-referent from only one side," so that, unlike dual or multiple labels such as male and female, and black, Asian, Latina, and white, the labels of nondisabled and heterosexuality are always already presumed "unless otherwise stated." Swain and Cameron conclude: "There is a coming out process for gay men and lesbian women, which has no real equivalent in gender and race categorizations," and "there is a similar coming out process for disabled people."[6] In this argument, the identities of gayness and disability are stabilized and opposed to those of gender and race. Such an analogy not only relies on an overly restrictive, unilateral view of gender and race but implies false equations between the two identities on each side of the opposition (gay = disabled; gender = race), thereby invoking the original sex-race analogy in a renewed form. While this analogy claims for sexual oppression the same legitimacy as that (supposedly) achieved for racial oppression—my experience is *like* your experience— contrasting analogies such as that employed by Swain and Cameron claim for gay or disabled oppression a different valence than that of gender or race: my experience is *different* from yours. Yet both analogies have the same goal—to persuade the listener of the validity and urgency of the speaker's original experience—and thus both implicitly devalue the other term of comparison.

An important difference between the analogies of sex-race and sexual orientation–disability is that the former relates to oppressions, while the latter describes processes of liberation and self-actualization, in this case, "coming out." Perhaps analogies between liberatory practices are less problematic than those between oppressions, since they claim a sameness not of experience but of resistance. This argument has a certain logic; however, it does not address the deeper issue of the presumption of sameness that produces oversimplified "mapping analogies." As Eve Tavor Bannet explains, the mapping analogy represents a historical mutation of analogy that, by "stressing resemblance over difference to make different entities more or less alike[,] transformed analogy into an equivalence—a rule of presumed resemblance, structural isomorphism, or homology between domains. The moment of essential difference which distinguishes analogy from identity, and different entities from each other, was flattened into a moment of proportional representation."[7] Clearly, the sex-race analogy suffers from the endemic flaws of the mapping analogy itself, yet all language functions in a sense through analogy, and so it remains an inescapable part of the communicative realm. Certainly, the tendency to make analogies between identities and liberation movements is pervasive and often persuasive, and so I suggest not that we attempt to escape from analogy but that we seek to employ it more critically than in the past.

Bannet examines a particular means of destabilizing and evolving mapping analogies through her discussion of Wittgenstein, for whom "analogy is not just an image, an extended simile, or the juxtaposition of objects of comparison ... analogy in Wittgenstein's sense is a traditional method of reasoning from the known to the unknown, and from the visible to the speculative, by carrying familiar terms, paradigms, and images across into unfamiliar territory."[8] I find this model of analogy especially useful, both because of its acknowledgement of the instability of its terms and because of its foregrounding of the issue of visibility as a key component of analogical language. Indeed, when we consider that "theories and practices of identity and subject formation in Western culture are largely structured around the logic of visibility, whether in the service of science (Victorian physiognomy), psychoanalysis (Lacan's mirror stage), or philosophy (Foucault's reading of the Panopticon)," it becomes apparent that the speculative or "invisible" has generally functioned as the subordinate term in analogical equations to this date.[9] Thus a central premise of this essay is that it behooves us to refocus our endeavors from the visible signs of these identities to their invisible manifestations. The focus on specularity and visible difference that permeates much disability theory creates a dilemma not only for nonvisibly disabled people who wish to enter the conversation but for the overarching concepts of disability and normalization themselves.[10] Passing, closeting, and coming out become vexed issues that strain at the limitations of the discourse meant to describe them.

## THE LIMITS OF VISIBILITY

*Coming out, then, for disabled people, is a process of redefinition of one's personal identity through rejecting the tyranny of the normate, positive recognition of impairment and embracing disability as a valid social identity. Having come out, the disabled person no longer regards disability as a reason for self-disgust, or as something to be denied or hidden, but rather as an imposed oppressive social category to be challenged and broken down . . . . Coming out, in our analysis, involves a political commitment. Acceptance of a medical model of disability and being categorized by others as disabled does not constitute coming out as disabled.*

—Swain and Cameron,
"Unless Otherwise Stated"

One of the limitations of Swain and Cameron's analogy between coming out as gay or lesbian and coming out as disabled is their one-sided definition of coming out itself. For these writers, coming out refers specifically to accepting one's "true" identity and must entail identification with the political analysis of the marginalized group. In both queer and disabled contexts, however, coming out can entail a variety of meanings, acts, and commitments. The dual meanings most crucial to my argument can be signified grammatically: to "come out *to*" a person or group usually refers to a specific revelatory event, while to "come out" (without an object) usually refers to the time that one first realized and came to terms with one's own identity. When *coming out* is considered as a self-contained phrase, as in Swain and Cameron's article, we may grant some validity to the observation that "people with hidden impairments are sometimes less likely to 'come out' as disabled, and move to a positive acceptance of difference and a political identity, because it is easier to maintain a 'normal' identity."[11] However, when we add the preposition *to* to the phrase, the above statement becomes almost an oxymoron: the narratives of people with "hidden impairments," like those of people with other nonvisible social identities, are suffused with themes of coming out, passing, and the imperatives of identity.

Nor is coming out a static and singular event, as Swain and Cameron imply, an over-the-rainbow shift that divides one's life before and after the event. Certainly, there must be some people who experience such momentous comings out, but I believe that the majority of us find that, even after our own internal shift, and even after a dozen gay pride marches, we must still make decisions about coming out on a daily basis, in personal, professional, and political contexts. In *Dress Codes*, Noelle Howey's memoir about her father's transition from male to female, she describes four separate moments of her father's coming out: when he told her mother, when her mother told her, when the family threw a party for Noelle's father to come out as female to friends and coworkers, and when Noelle's father came out to her years later as a lesbian.[12] Eli Clare writes of coming out as a complex convergence of identities and desires: "My coming out wasn't as much about discovering sexual desire and knowledge as it was about dealing with gender identity. Simply put, the disabled, mixed-class tomboy who asked her mother, 'am I feminine?' didn't discover a sexuality among dykes but rather a definition of woman large enough to be comfortable for many years."[13]

When we look at narratives of disabled people about their own coming-out processes, we see that the language of coming out is used liberally but often carries very different meanings. While many of these stories emphasize connections with a disability community, much as Swain and Cameron suggest, they also demonstrate the various methods and implications that coming out entails for different individuals. Rosemarie Garland-Thomson, who calls her book *Extraordinary Bodies* "the consequence of a coming-out process," describes how she had long thought of her congenital disability as a "private matter" and did not identify with disability culture or disabled people, although she did feel a special connection with disabled characters in the literature she studied.[14] Deciding to focus her scholarly work on disability was both a cause and a consequence of her coming to identify with the disability community. Similarly, Nomy Lamm, born with one leg, did not come out as disabled until late in her teens, when, through her involvement in queer and feminist activism, she met two other "freaky crip girls" and transitioned fairly quickly from "I'm not really disabled, and even if I am, nobody notices" to "I am a foxy one-legged dyke, and you will love it, or else."[15]

Not all coming-out processes are so straightforward. Carolyn Gage writes: "Did I come out? Not at first. I told my friends I had CFIDS [chronic fatigue immune dysfunction syndrome], but I did not really tell them what that meant . . . . When I did go places with friends, I passed for able-bodied as much as I could."[16] For Gage, coming out did not take place until nearly a decade after she first fell ill, and it took the form of a letter to her friends that explicitly spelled out her disability, her limitations, and what she needed in terms of accommodation and support. Perhaps because of the nonvisible, contingent, and fluctuating nature of chronic illness, as opposed to the disabilities of Garland-Thomson and Lamm, Gage's coming-out process was not primarily focused on claiming the label of "disability." Rather, it required her to construct a specific narrative explaining her body to a skeptical, ignorant, and somewhat hostile audience. Susan Wendell, who also has CFIDS, speaks of the difficulty of convincing people to take her word for it regarding her abilities: "Some

people offer such acceptance readily, others greet every statement of limitation with skepticism, and most need to be reminded from time to time."[17]

What is notable in Gage's and Wendell's accounts is that coming out is primarily portrayed as the process of revealing or explaining one's disability *to* others, rather than as an act of self-acceptance facilitated by a disability community. I would suggest that the nonvisible nature of Gage's and Wendell's disabilities means that, for them, the primary meaning of coming out includes the term *to* and connotes the daily challenge of negotiating assumptions about bodily appearance and function. This dynamic is not limited to those with chronic illnesses but can also be found in narratives by people with a range of nonvisible disabilities, especially sensory disabilities.[18] Megan Jones, a deaf-blind woman, writes of the response to the ubiquitous question, "So, how bad is your vision and hearing anyway? I mean, you seem to get around pretty good as far as I can tell."[19] Jones admits that she once felt obliged to respond with an extended narrative explaining exactly the permeability of her cornea and the sound frequencies she could detect. Georgina Kleege writes about her need "to identify [her] blindness in public," particularly in the classroom, so that her students will understand why she cannot see them raising their hands. Kleege also writes of situations in which she chooses *not* to mention her blindness, such as social settings and a previous job, largely to avoid patronizing reactions or the suspicion of fraud but also simply because her "blindness was an irrelevant fact that they did not need to know about me, like my religion or political affiliation."[20]

Kleege's account points to the flip side of having to come out to be recognized as disabled: the ability to pass. Like racial, gender, and queer passing, the option of passing as nondisabled provides both a certain level of privilege and a profound sense of misrecognition and internal dissonance. Kleege reflects ruefully on a circumstance in which, during a flight on which nondisabled passengers and flight attendants were ignoring or complaining about a wheelchair-using passenger, she did not come out: "Because my disability was invisible to them, it allowed them to assume I felt about the disabled as they did, that I would have behaved as they had."[21] Even though Kleege and her husband were the only passengers who assisted the wheelchair user, and Kleege came out to *her* as blind, she still expresses profound guilt that she failed to identify herself as a member of the woman's community to the airline staff and other passengers.

This dilemma can be even more complicated for those with a disability whose symptoms and severity fluctuate widely. Wendell writes:

> Because my disability is no longer readily apparent, and because it is an illness whose symptoms vary greatly from day to day, I live between the world of the disabled and the non-disabled. I am often very aware of my differences from healthy, non-disabled people, and I often feel a great need to have my differences acknowledged when they are ignored . . . . On the other hand, I am very aware of how my social, economic, and personal resources, and the fact that I can "pass" as non-disabled among strangers, allow me to live a highly assimilated life among the non-disabled.[22]

Wendell then emphasizes that, even when she herself passes as nondisabled, she makes a point of identifying herself with the disability community and working for disability rights. Thus she complicates the assumption of a direct relationship between visible impairment and political identification with disability rights, as well as crucially undermining the related claim that passing as "normal" is by definition a form of negative disability identity.[23]

Nevertheless, the perception persists that nonvisibly disabled people prefer to pass and the passing is a sign and product of assimilationist longings: "By passing as non-disabled, by minimizing the significance of their impairments within their own personal and social lives . . . people with hidden impairments often make an effort to avoid the perceived stigma attached to a disabled identity." Even when passing is acknowledged as a valid strategy for negotiating certain situations, it is portrayed as an undesirable response: "If . . . disabled people pursue normalization too much, they risk denying limitations and pain for the comfort of others and

may edge into the self-betrayal associated with 'passing.'"[24] I do not deny that some nonvisibly disabled people may wish to assimilate or choose to pass; however, I believe that such an overall negative perception of passing exceeds the reality and must be interpreted in the context of other forms of bodily passing in Euro-American culture. As Lisa Walker observes: "Traditionally, passing (for straight, for white) has been read as a conservative form of self-representation that the subject chooses in order to assume the privileges of the dominant identity. Passing is the sign of the sell out" and of the victim.[25]

Such condemnations of passing often conflate two dynamics: passing deliberately (as implied by the term *hidden*) and passing by default, as it were. I certainly do not make any effort to appear "heterosexual" or "nondisabled" when I leave the house in the morning; those are simply the identities usually derived from my appearance by onlookers. While there are a number of queer accoutrements, such as buttons, stickers, jewelry, and T-shirts, that I could (and often do) choose to wear to signal my lesbian identity, a very different cultural weight is placed on any attempt to signal a disabled identity, as suspicions of fraud attach to any visible sign of disability that is not functionally essential. The analogy between coming out as queer and coming out as disabled breaks down as the different meanings and consequences of such acts come into consideration.

My quandary is not unique, nor is my search for a nonverbal sign. Deborah Peifer observes that "I don't look blind, so strangers, sisters, don't realize that I'm not seeing them. After so many years of being defiantly out of the closet as a lesbian, I am, in some ways, passing as sighted. Other than wearing a 'Yes, I am legally blind' sign, I don't know of any way to provide that information to strangers." Jones became so frustrated with strangers not believing in her visual and hearing impairments, and so oppressed by their refusal to respect her assistance dog's status, that she began to use a white cane she did not need: "I find that when I use a cane people leave me alone . . . . people go right into their Blind-Person-With-A-Cane-And-Guide-Dog Red Alert mode." Kleege also mentions that "I now carry a white cane as a nonverbal sign that I don't see as much as I seem to. But like a lot of blind people who carry canes and employ guide dogs, these signs are not always understood, and the word still needs to be spoken."[26] These writers each contend with cultural assumptions that the identity they wish to signal exists only as visible physical difference. Since race, in Euro-American culture, is also assumed to be immediately visible and intelligible, Toi Derricotte, a light-skinned African American woman, writes of wishing for "a cross, a star, some sign of gold to wear so that, before they wonder or ask, I can present a dignified response to the world's interrogations."[27] In this case, coming out as disabled appears to have more in common with racial discourses of coming out or passing than with queer discourse, since the contingent (non)visibility of queer identity has produced a variety of nonverbal and/or spoken means to signal that identity, while the assumed visibility of race and disability has produced an absence of nonverbal signs and a distrust of spoken claims to those identities.

In the absence of recognized nonverbal signs, we often resort to the "less dignified" response of claiming identity through speech. The complex longing, fear of disbelief, and internal dissonance caused by coming out in this form resound through the narratives of all people who pass by default. Passing subjects must cope with a variety of external social contexts, few of which welcome or acknowledge spontaneous declarations of invisible identity. Derricotte writes that "for several years I wore my identity like a banner. 'Hello, I'm Toi Derricotte, I'm black.'" The awkwardness of such revelations is amplified in Peifer's account of how she chose to voice her lesbian identity after blindness prevented her from participating in the subtle visual signals with which queer people in public often acknowledge each other: "They now know at the grocery store ('As a lesbian, I wish to buy these peaches') and the drugstore ('As a lesbian, I wish to explain that the yeast infection for which I am purchasing this ointment was the result of taking antibiotics, not heterosexual intercourse')."[28] Clearly, simply voicing one's identity in any and all situations is a far-from-perfect solution to the dilemmas

presented by invisibility. In addition, the general cultural prejudice against such statements means that embarrassment may be the least disturbing negative response they evoke.

Suspicions of fraud often greet declarations of nonvisible identity. As Amanda Hamilton writes, people with nonvisible disabilities "are in a sense forced to pass, and the same time assumed to be liars." Adrian Piper, a light-skinned African American, also writes of the catch-22 of remaining silent versus speaking up: "For most of my life I did not understand that I needed to identify my racial identity publicly and that if I did not I would be inevitably mistaken for white. I simply didn't think about it. But since I also made no special effort to hide my racial identity, I often experienced the shocked and/or hostile reactions of whites who discovered it after the fact." Piper adds that "some whites simply can't take my avowed racial affiliation at face value, and react to what they see rather than what I say."[29] It takes tremendous chutzpah for nonvisibly disabled people to assert our disabilities in public settings or to ask for accommodation; denial, mockery, and silent disapproval are some of the cultural mechanisms used to inhibit us. While nonvisibly disabled people are usually required to produce medical documentation of our impairments, people who pass racially, like Derricotte and Piper, face semantic battles, interrogations about their ancestry, and challenges to their dedication to the African American community.[30]

Derricotte's memoir, *The Black Notebooks*, is an expanded mediation on race, passing, and the self. In the chapter "Diaries at an Artist's Colony" she describes hearing a racist comment on her first night at the colony and not confronting the speaker. Later, in a section of that chapter called "Coming Out," she concedes that "I [was] afraid to come out as a black person, to bear that solitude, that hatred, that invisibility."[31] Here Derricotte locates invisibility *not* as equivalent to passing but as the alienating consequence of coming out in a hostile context. When she does come out later to a white woman, the woman's resistance ironically foregrounds the white colonists' own anxiety about race:

She said, "There aren't any black people here. I haven't seen any."

"Yes there are," I said, smiling.

"Who?"

"You're looking at one."

"You're not really black. Just an eighth or something." . . .

A woman at the table said, "Did you read that article in *The New York Times* that said if they were strict about genetics, sixty percent of the people in the United States would be classified as black?"

I looked around the table; I was laughing. The others were not. They were worried about how black I was and they should have been worrying about how black *they* were. (1997: 145)

Derricotte's story can be read as a narrative enactment of Elaine Ginsberg's observation that "passing forces reconsideration of the cultural logic that the physical body is the site of identic intelligibility."[32] Derricotte reverses the terms of the racial dichotomy black/white to refocus racial anxiety onto whiteness as an artificial cultural construct, in a move that reflects Wittgenstein's reversal of analogy to lead us "from what we suppose *is* the case everywhere to what *might* happen otherwise in particular cases."[33] While Derricotte's coming out was necessary for the scene to unfold, her passing provided the foundational meaning of the exchange. Thus we see how passing can become a subversive practice and how the passing subject may be read not as an assimilationist victim but as a defiant figure who, by crossing the borders of identities, reveals their instability.[34]

## THE LIMITS OF SUBVERSION

A story: When a friend of mine read the story of Samantha with which this essay opens, she asked why Samantha would identify as disabled. I did not have a concrete answer for her. Faced with that question, many of us might point to our Social Security

status, our medical records, our neurological test results, or the signs of difference on our bodies. I cannot tell you where Samantha would point. I can only observe the pride with which she claims her identity, the eagerness with which she seeks to communicate it to others. I can only conclude that, for Samantha, "being disabled" means being not a victim, not a special case, but a member of a proud and fierce community.

Her attitude is refreshing. It demonstrates the usefulness of analogizing concepts of pride between queer and disability contexts.

## DISCUSSION QUESTIONS

1. What are the strengths and weaknesses of analogizing between the disabled and queer and between race and gender? How does the "coming out" analogy serve people who otherwise look "normal"?
2. How do the politics of visibility and invisibility affect how we understand categories of difference, especially sexuality and disability? How does visibility/invisibility affect the social categories of race, gender, and social class?

## NOTES

1. In current disability discourse, the terms *invisible disability* and *nonvisible disability* are often used interchangeably . . . . To minimize confusion in this essay, I employ *nonvisible* to indicate the condition of unmarked identity and *invisible* to indicate social oppression and marginality. However, I also seek to investigate how the two meanings and conditions intersect, since nonvisible disabilities remain largely invisible, both in disability discourse and in the culture at large.
2. For a prominent example of the disability/sexual orientation analogy see John Swain and Colin Cameron, "Unless Otherwise Stated: Discourses of Labelling and Identity in Coming Out," in *Disability Discourse,* ed. Mairian Corker and Sally French (Philadelphia: Open University Press, 1999), 68–78. Tom Shakespeare analogizes disability to gender,

sexual orientation, and race in "Disability, Identity, and Difference," in *Exploring the Divide: Illness and Disability,* ed. Colin Barnes and Geof Mercer (Leeds: Disability, 1996), 94–113. Rosemarie Garland-Thomson and Susan Wendell both make frequent analogies between disability and gender. See Garland-Thomson, *Extraordinary Bodies: Figuring Physical Disability in American Culture and Literature* (New York: Columbia University Press, 1997); and Wendell, *The Rejected Body: Feminist Philosophical Reflections on Disability* (New York: Routledge, 1996). Garland-Thomson also argues for a view of disability as ethnicity, but she invokes sexual orientation only with regard to nonvisible disability, which, "much like a homosexual identity, always presents the dilemma of whether or when to come out or to pass" (14). Lennard J. Davis, however, defines disability both in analogies to race, gender, and class and in contrast to them in *Enforcing Normalcy: Disability, Deafness, and the Body* (London: Verso, 1995), xvi, 2.

3. See Shakespeare, "Disability, Identity, and Difference," 105; and Wendell, *Rejected Body,* 82.

4. Tina Grillo and Stephanie M. Wildman, "Obscuring the Importance of Race: The Implications of Making Comparisons between Racism and Sexism (or Other Isms)," in *Critical White Studies: Looking behind the Mirror,* ed. Richard Delgado and Jean Stefancic (Philadelphia): Temple University Press, 1997), 619–26; Lisa Maria Hogeland, "*Invisible Man* and Invisible Women: The Sex/Race Analogy of the 1970s," *Women's History Review* 5 (1996):46.

5. Nilli Diengott, "Analogy As a Critical Term: A Survey and Some Comments," *Style* 19 (1985): 228.

6. Swain and Cameron, "Unless Otherwise Stated," 68. The example of "black, Asian, Latina, and white" is one that I have extrapolated from Swain and Cameron's article rather than one that they themselves offer.

7. Eve Tavor Bannet, "Analogy As Translation: Wittgenstein, Derrida, and the Law of Language," *New Literary History* 28 (1997):658.

8. Ibid., 655.

9. Linda Schlossberg, introduction to *Passing: Identity and Interpretation in Sexuality, Race, and Religion,* ed. María Carla Sánchez and Linda Schlossberg (New York: New York University Press, 2001), 1.

10. Davis writes that "disability is a specular moment" and argues that all disability, even mental illness, "shows up as a disruption in the visual field" (*Enforcing Normalcy,* xvi, 11–15, 129–42). Garland-Thomson also focuses on the "stare" that constructs the category of disability (*Extraordinary Bodies,* 26); Kenny Fries uses a similar focus (*Staring Back: The Disability Experience from the Inside Out* [New York: Plume, 1997], 1).

11. Tom Shakespeare, Kath Gillespie-Sells, and Dominic Davies, *The Sexual Politics of Disability: Untold Desires* (New York: Cassell, 1996), 55. These authors clearly share Swain and Cameron's definition of coming out, as seen in their summary on page 58.

12. From a private conversation with Noelle Howey, July 2001. Howey further discusses her experiences in *Dress Codes: Of Three Girlhoods—My Mother's, My Father's, and Mine* (New York: Picador, 2002).

13. Eli Clare, *Exile and Pride: Disability, Queerness, and Liberation* (Cambridge, Mass.: South End, 1999), 133.

14. Garland-Thomson, *Extraordinary Bodies,* ix.

15. Nomy Lamm, "Private Dancer: Evolution of a Freak," in *Restricted Access: Lesbians on Disability,* ed. Victoria A. Brownworth and Susan Raffo (Seattle: Seal, 1999), 160–61.

16. Carolyn Gage, "Hidden Disability: A Coming Out Story," in Brownworth and Russo, *Restricted Access,* 203. CFIDS is a debilitating systemic illness that primarily affects the neurological, immune, and muscular systems. It is also known as myalgic encephalomyelitis. For more detail see Peggy Munson, ed., *Stricken: Voices from the Hidden Epidemic of Chronic Fatigue Syndrome* (New York: Haworth, 2000).

17. Wendell, *Rejected Body,* 4.

18. This dynamic can be found as well in the writings of people with visible disabilities who ponder whether to "come out" textually, thus revealing their absent bodies much as nonvisibly disabled people who come out are revealing some aspect of their health or mental status. As Nancy Mairs reflects in *Waist-High in the World: A Life among the Nondisabled* (Boston: Beacon, 1996), "I might have chosen to write in such a way as to disregard or deny or disguise the fact that I have MS" (10).

19. Megan Jones, "'Gee, You Don't *Look* Handicapped . . . ': Why I use a White Cane to Tell People That I'm Deaf," *Electric Edge,* July–August 1997, accessed on 10 July 2002 at www.ragged-edge-mag.com/archive/look.htm.

20. Georgina Kleege, *Sight Unseen* (New Haven: Yale University Press, 1999), 11–12.

21. Ibid., 38–39.

22. Wendell, *Rejected Body*, 76.

23. See Shakespeare, "Disability, Identity, and Difference," 100.

24. Swain and Cameron, "Unless Otherwise Stated," 76; Garland-Thomson, *Extraordinary Bodies*, 13.

25. Lisa Walker, *Looking Like What You Are: Sexual Style, Race, and Lesbian Identity* (New York: New York University Press, 2001), 8.

26. Deborah Peifer, "Seeing Is Be(liev)ing," in Brownworth and Russo, *Restricted Access*, 34; Jones, "'Gee, You Don't *Look* Handicapped . . . '"; Kleege, *Sight Unseen*, 39.

27. Toi Derricotte, *The Black Notebooks: An Interior Journey* (New York: Norton, 1997), 112.

28. Ibid., 111; Peifer, "Seeing Is Be(live)ing," 34.

29. Amanda Hamilton, "Oh the Joys of Invisibility!" letter to the editor, *Electric Edge*, July–August 1997, accessed on 10 July 2002 at www.ragged-edge-mag.com/archive/look.htm; Adrian Piper, "Passing for White, Passing for Black," in *Passing and the Fictions of Identity*, ed. Elaine K. Ginsberg (Durham: Duke University Press, 1996), 256–57, 266.

30. Derricotte, *Black Notebooks*, 145, 160, 182; Piper, "Passing for White, Passing for Black," 234–38, 256–57, 262–64.

31. Derricotte, *Black Notebooks*, 142.

32. Ginsberg, *Passing*, 4.

33. Bannet, "Analogy as Translation," 663.

34. This dynamic may also be observed from the role of passing in transgender contexts, in which the ability to pass for a new or different gender, or to present an ambiguous gender, is often experienced as a validation of radical identity rather than as assimilation or misrecognition.

# PART II

# IDENTITIES MATTER

## The Social Construction and Experiences of Race, Gender, Sexuality, and Social Class

The readings in Part II focus on the micro level of identity. Formally defined, an identity is a person's position or social location in social relationships, social structures, and societal institutions. Our identities are influenced by the social categories of race, ethnicity, gender, sexuality, disability, and social class and by the ways they inform our sense of self. These readings show that these identities are not discrete categories but often intersect with others. Moreover, these personal and social identities often conflict with one another. Identity is not just a category that we assume from birth; identities evolve over time from the earliest ages when we become aware of and learn about gender, race, and other differences. Thus, our identities are fluid, contextual, and unique. Our worldviews are based on our identities, and our identities are also influenced by our worldviews.

Identities are about boundaries. Who we are, we demarcate for others. "I am X because I am not Y." We do identity work by giving off certain impressions, distinguishing our bodies, joining certain social groups, and trying to control how others perceive us. Our identities also are formed in relationship to others.

Others want to know our identities, and they read and interpret meaning in our race, social class, and gender identities. For example, if people do not know our gender, or our race, it can make them feel uncomfortable. A famous *Saturday Night Live* sketch from the 1990s featured a gender-ambiguous character named "Pat." No one knew whether Pat was male or female, so they did not know how to interact with her or him. People tried to read Pat's body, dress, speech, and body language for clues about her or his gender identity and judged what they saw. Being unable to read Pat's gender identity disrupted social interaction and often made people uncomfortable or angry. Gender, sexual, and/or racial ambiguity can be threatening to the social order. We look for markers of gender, sexuality, and race on people's bodies. We also look for markers of identity in consumption patterns, the way one dresses, one's language, social interaction, and other behaviors. Thus, while identities can predict behavior, they also are vulnerable to stereotypes.

Identities are the subject of study across several disciplines, including psychology, sociology, history, and human development. To better comprehend the power and influence of identities on the formulation of self and on social interaction, Part II is divided into three sections: "Identity Formation," "Identities and Social Interaction," and "Identity Construction and Stigma Management."

## IDENTITY FORMATION

The first subsection on identity formation highlights the different theories of identity formation and provides examples. Hazel Rose Markus, a psychologist, is the author of Reading 15, "Who Am I? Race, Ethnicity, and Identity." Markus defines identity and explains how it affects social behavior. She also defines and examines how race and ethnicity shape identity. Markus creates a valuable model that can be applied to a number of other readings in Part II. Identity consists of two parts: (1) the self or our self-definition and (2) the perception of how others see us. In this way, Markus illustrates where the self and society meet in framing social identity. Her model can be added to and further complicated, but it gives us a beginning point for understanding identity.

Reading 16, by Judith A. Howard and Ramira M. Alamilla, "Gender and Identity," also defines identity, but instead of a psychological approach, the authors argue for social and structural approaches to studying identity. Howard and Alamilla see a continuum of approaches to studying gender identity that includes four perspectives: essentialism, socialization, social construction, and structuralism. As in the Markus reading, Howard and Alamilla provide theoretical approaches that can be applied to other readings in this volume. Their work complements well the next three readings by Alex Wilson, Mia Tuan, and Katherine Franke. Wilson (Reading 17), for example, challenges traditional psychological models of identity development in her research on Native Americans and identity. She finds that Native Americans see their identities as more fluid than do individuals of Euro-American identity. This is especially true of gay and lesbian Native Americans, who construct their identities as having "two spirits." Similarly, Tuan also challenges psychological models of identity by studying the more interactive nature of identity in her piece "I'm an American With a Japanese Look"

(Reading 18). Sociological theories, like those found in Howard and Alamilla, prove to be more helpful in understanding Asian identity as it is constructed during social interaction. Mia Tuan's study also builds on Mary Waters's (1990) research regarding symbolic ethnicity, which also was discussed in Reading 7 by Michael Polgar. Tuan shows the flip side of symbolic ethnicity in her research on Asian Americans. Instead of being able to choose fully when to invoke their Asian ethnicity as an identity, as white ethnics do with their symbolic ethnicity, many Asian Americans are pressured by the majority to claim an ethnic identity. In fact, Tuan's respondents talk about feeling like they are foreigners more than white Americans, even though they have lived in the United States their entire lives. Moreover, while Waters's white ethnic respondents can self-select and interpret their ethnic identities, Tuan's Asian American respondents have more restrictions placed on their understandings of self and interpretations of identity.

Similar restrictions have been placed on identity by our legal system, as discussed in the final reading in this "Identities Formation" section by legal scholar Katherine M. Franke. Franke's analysis of the 1935 Supreme Court case *Suneri v. Cassagne* illustrates well how the two aspects of identity as defined by Markus (Reading 15) can conflict and power is given to the legal system to decide racial identity. One woman's definition of self as white is challenged by others' perceptions of her as black. The implications of this case and the use of legal authority reveal how social interaction and other social institutions can define one's identity, as well as the complex set of consequences that are attached to certain identities. This reading by Franke introduces a different frame for understanding identity, in general, and race-ethnicity, in particular. Franke, a professor of law at the University of Arizona College of Law, wrote this piece in 1996 to illustrate the complicated ways in which a legal case can produce a constructed social identity. In the Supreme Court case in question, the Court was trying to determine the racial identity of Cassagne to see whether her 1935 marriage to a white man was legal. Cassagne wanted the legal case to uphold her racial identity as white so she could legally divorce her husband and collect alimony. Sunseri, her husband, wanted the legal case to show that Cassagne's race was not white so that he could get the marriage annulled. The Court's deliberations about racial identity are telling, and they reveal that there are significant costs to these constructed identities, including the fact that a person who is defined as not White loses many privileges and benefits of society.

## IDENTITIES AND SOCIAL INTERACTION

The second section, "Identities and Social Interaction," shows how we construct identities through social interaction and how identities affect behavior. This subsection contains five readings that reveal how we learn and perform different identities and how our identities of race-ethnicity, gender, sexuality, and social class can intersect. Four of the five readings use ethnographic research to observe identities and social interaction, and Reading 22, by Amber Hollibaugh, is a narrative about intersectionality. Hollibaugh's narrative shows well how identities intersect in ways that can challenge the dominant culture's assumptions. Contrary to popular stereotypes, most gays are not wealthy. Hollibaugh argues against this stereotype by providing evidence of gays living on the economic margins of society. Similar to Reading 32 in the section on social institutions, where Nancy Mezey shows that coming out is a privilege among white and middle- and upper-class lesbians, this reading shows how queers in the lower classes face more obstacles than those in the middle and upper classes to obtaining resources in society. Hollibaugh's reading also ties nicely to the readings found in Part V of this book, on social change and empowerment, because she indicates how one's oppressed identities can influence social movements.

The other four readings in this subsection on identities and social interaction are sociological studies of different social locations and how they affect identity. Reading 20, "Using Racial and Ethnic Concepts: The Critical Case of Very Young Children," by Debra Van Ausdale and Joe R. Feagin, is a fascinating observational study of preschools. Contrary to

the commonsense notion that children do not identify race and ethnicity until they are much older, Van Ausdale and Feagin find that children as young as three to five years old are using racial and ethnic concepts to identify other children and to shape their social interactions with them. Reading 21 by Julie Bettie, "Women Without Class: *Chicas, Cholas,* Trash, and the Presence and Absence of Class Identity," takes Van Ausdale and Feagin's analysis further by studying the intersection of race-ethnicity, gender, and social class among working-class girls in their senior year of high school. This rich ethnography brings to light how different groups of girls understand and perform their social class identities and where that performance intersects with race-ethnicity and gender. Bettie reveals that the intersections of these identities create spaces of contradiction; for example, one group of Mexican American girls conflate social class norms with "acting white," although the white students attribute social class differences not to race but to clique membership.

Readings 23 and 24 both study how social spaces or places inform our understanding of social class and social interaction. When the social location changes from Bettie's high school to Carrie Yodanis's coffee shop to Jessica Holden Sherwood's country club, the performance of social class also changes greatly. Some social locations allow for more variability and more informality in the identity, performance, and hierarchy of social class; others do not. Carrie Yodanis's "A Place in Town: Doing Class in a Coffee Shop" is an ethnographic study of a group of women who meet regularly at a local coffee shop. Similar to Bettie, Yodanis finds that social class greatly informs the women's discourse and social interaction. Yodanis describes how the women perform and manage their social class identities in this fairly informal space. Jessica Holden Sherwood's "The View From the Country Club: Wealthy Whites and the Matrix of Privilege" is another ethnographic study of social class and social interaction, but in a more formal setting. Sherwood studies four different country clubs in the Northeast to see how gender and social class are performed. She finds that gender and sexism are incorporated into the elite culture and structure of country clubs, not in overt ways but in more subtle ways. Country club members enjoy a "matrix of privilege" in which wives make a gendered bargain in their marriages not to challenge the patriarchal power of their upper-class husbands. The men's privilege is invisible, and the country club members can only see discrimination existing in the workplace, not in their own families.

## IDENTITY CONSTRUCTION AND STIGMA MANAGEMENT

The third section in Part II concentrates on identity construction and stigma management. The five readings in this section show how larger social structures and institutions, such as the government, laws, schools, peer culture, and the media, affect identity construction. For example, Reading 25, by Eva Marie Garroutte, "The Racial Formation of American Indians: Negotiating Legitimate Identities Within Tribal and Federal Law," spotlights how legal definitions of racial-ethnic identity can vary and be problematic. Definitions vary at both the federal level and at the tribal level, creating gaps where non-Indians have been granted tribal citizenship. This reading emphasizes how citizenship is raced and socially constructed, similar to other blood definitions of race discussed in earlier readings (Readings 2, 6, and 19). The next three readings in this section indicate how we manage identities and social stigma. Stigma is defined as an attribute that devalues one's identity and "is a social construct that varies situationally; it is not an objective reality, nor a fixed characteristic of an individual" (Khanna and Johnson 2010:392). Stigma management is the attempt by persons with stigmatized social identities to approach interpersonal interactions in ways aimed at minimizing the social costs of carrying these identities (O'Brien 2011:292). Individuals with stigmatized identities attempt to manage the social stigma in a number of ways, as shown in Readings 18 and 19 by Mia Tuan on Asian Americans and by Katherine Franke on contested white identity, respectively.

Reading 26, by David Snow and Leon Anderson, complicates Markus's model (Reading 15) by studying homeless people and finding that the homeless construct identities preserve their self-worth and have more positive meanings than those identities that others try to place on them. Snow and Anderson find that the homeless actively manage the stigma surrounding their identities through a number of strategies. Nikki Khanna and Cathryn Johnson's reading, "Passing as Black: Racial Identity Work Among Biracial Americans" (Reading 27), shows a different strategy to manage racial stigma employed by black–white biracial Americans. Instead of trying to pass as white, these individuals find advantages to passing as black in certain contexts. Finally, Reading 28, by Amir Marvasti and Karyn D. McKinney, "The Stigma of Brown Skin and 'Foreign' Names," also demonstrates the work stigmatized individuals have to do in order to manage people's impressions. Muslim and Arab Americans are continually questioned about their brown skin and non-Anglo names. They manage the social stigma well through a number of strategies, including the use of humor, educating others, and confrontation. Marvasti and McKinney's piece reminds the reader of Mia Tuan's reading, which describes how the dominant group demands allegiance to an ethnic identity on the part of Asian Americans.

The final reading is this section, "'I Don't Like Passing as a Straight Woman': Queer Negotiations of Identity and Social Group Membership" by Carla Pfeffer, is an excerpt from a larger ethnographic study of women in relationships with transgender men in which she interviewed 50 cis women partners of trans men in the United States, Canada, and Australia. Instead of using the lens of race, Pfeffer analyzes stigma and identity work through the lenses of gender, sex, and sexuality. Her sample of women in relationships with transgender men or "cis women" challenge the essentialized identity binaries of male/female, man/woman, and heterosexual/homosexual. Pfeffer's study highlights how gender is often marked on the body, similar to arguments made by Crawley, Foley, and Shehan in Reading 3. Her research also shows the fluidity of identity and how often identity is negotiated and renegotiated depending upon the social interaction and social context. While some respondents strived for normativity, others resisted social norms. This last reading in the section on identity construction and stigma management examines how cis women who are partnered with trans men identify their gender and sexuality. In particular, Carla Pfeffer, a professor of sociology at the University of South Carolina, complicates our understanding of "passing" by challenging how sex, gender, and sexuality identities are based on social interaction and normative social privilege. She deliberates on the costs of misrecognition and passing as expressed by her respondents.

## SUMMARY

These three sections on identity formation, identities and social interaction, and identity construction and stigma management enable us to see the significance our race, ethnicity, gender, sexuality, and social class have for our identities. They not only inform and shape our sense of who we are, but they also influence social interaction. People will "read" our bodies for indicators of these social categories and then behave according to whether they read us as male or female, upper class or lower class, white or a person of color. How our identities are read could affect our access to opportunities and resources or result in acts of discrimination. So identity construction and interpretation have real consequences. Some identities are stigmatized by the larger society, and individuals with those identities may try to control others' impressions of them. These readings identify a number of techniques to manage social stigma. Our identities also influence our interactions with larger social structures and institutions, a topic that is explored more in depth in Part III.

## REFERENCES

Khanna, Nikki, and Cathryn Johnson. 2010. "Passing as Black: Racial Identity Work among Biracial Americans." *Social Psychological Quarterly* 73(4):380–97.

O'Brien, John. 2011. "Spoiled Group Identities and Backstage Work: A Theory of Stigma Management Rehearsals." *Social Psychological Quarterly* 74(3):291–309.

Waters, Mary C. 1990. *Ethnic Options: Choosing Identities in America*. Berkeley: University of California Press.

# 15

# WHO AM I?

## *Race, Ethnicity, and Identity*

HAZEL ROSE MARKUS

*This first reading in Part II, "Identities Matter," is the first of six readings that highlight theories of identity from different disciplinary perspectives. Hazel Rose Markus, a professor of psychology at Stanford University, is a social psychologist by training who introduced the concept of "self-schema." In this excerpt, taken from the 2010 edited volume* Doing Race: 21 Essays for the 21st Century, *Markus explains what identity is and how it affects social behavior. Markus models where the self (personal identity) meets society (social identities), and she argues that identity is a combination of how one sees oneself and how others perceive one. Thus, for Markus, identities are contextual, fluid, and subject to change.*

Who am I? After you read this first paragraph—but before you read the rest of the essay—jot down some answers to this deceptively simple question. You may have been asking yourself this question since kindergarten and feel that you have a good idea of what the answers might be. Perhaps you have spent years making T-shirts and posters that display your answers to the world and now have no trouble filling in your profile information on social networking sites. Alternatively, you may find the question a relatively novel one and somewhat difficult to answer—at least without some more guidance about what kind of information is being requested. Yet, whether or not you

*Source:* Markus, Hazel Rose. "Who Am I? Race, Ethnicity, and Identity." In *Doing Race: 21 Essays for the 21st Century.* Edited by Hazel Rose Markus and Paula M.L. Moya. Copyright © 2010 by W.W. Norton & Company, Inc.. Used by permission of W.W. Norton & Company, Inc.

have given much thought to this question, try to think about *what* you are thinking as you answer the question. Don't worry if your answers change as you read the chapter. This is not a test. There are no "right" answers—although some answers may make your life easier than others.

Every year, in a large introductory psychology class, I ask students to describe themselves. Stanford University has a very diverse undergraduate community; students come from throughout the United States and around the world. More than half of the students are non-white, and many Stanford students are not American. Consequently, when I do this exercise I get all sorts of answers to this question. Here is a sample of recent responses to the "Who am I?" question from some of the students who gave me permission to share them.

- I am motivated, responsible, caring, serious, intelligent with many diverse interests, like to play Halo, tired from studying, Asian American.

- I am 21 years old, African American, a woman, a student, a teacher, a daughter, a sister, a granddaughter, a best friend and a girl friend. I am a poet, a dancer. I am an optimist/realist who seeks to find love. I am a child of God.

- I am unique, a student, a musician and a singer, a huge nut for pop-culture, a protector for my friends, a giving individual, can be brilliant when motivated, a son and brother, a person with "good toys," somewhat lazy, overly emotional, worried about exams.

- I am friendly, generally outgoing, talkative, a little lazy, determined, stubborn, self-righteous, a woman, agnostic Mexican American, proud of cultural roots, very sensitive, a little crazy, someone who likes to wear cute clothes.

- Tall, male, biracial, motivated when I need to be, but certainly not all the time, a leader when I want to be but it is fun to follow. I am nice, carefree, a huge slob, and most importantly rarely serious. I am going to apply to law school.

- I am a student, son, sociology major, Japanese.

As you can see from these examples, the "Who am I?" question asks people to consider their selves, or their *identities*. Like these students, most people can quickly generate at least eight or ten characteristics with which to describe themselves, and, if given a bit more time, they can come up with another ten or so. This deceptively simple question opens a window into how people think about themselves—the stories they tell about themselves, who they would like to be, and who they are afraid of becoming. These answers, when combined with those of hundreds of other students in this class over many years, reveal some clear patterns. These patterns provide a set of interwoven insights into what identity is and why we have the ones we do. This essay is about why we answer the "Who am I?" question in the way we do and how this matters for behavior.

## DEVELOPING AN IDENTITY

In 1673, René Descartes, while attempting to establish a set of true principles that could not be doubted, made a declaration that has become a mainstay of Western philosophy. He famously wrote: "I think, therefore I am." Descartes was not wrong, but his statement captures only half of the truth. It is also the case that "*you* think, therefore I am." For a long time my own field, social psychology, has been preoccupied with and fascinated by the unavoidably social process that gives rise to the self or identity. In describing what he called the "looking glass self," psychologist Charles Horton Cooley (1922) suggested that other people are the mirror in which we see ourselves. And according to George Herbert Mead (1934), without other people to respond to our actions, we would not be aware that we "are" or that we exist. Taking all this together leads to two central insights about identity: A person's identity depends on *her own view* of herself, but it also depends on *others' view* of her. In the paragraphs that follow, I elaborate on these and other key features of the concept of identity. A good understanding of identity is fundamental to an accurate conception of the social categories of race and ethnicity.

## Identities Are Where the Self Meets Society

If you look back at the answers of the six students above, you can see that identities are complex, multifaceted, and dependent upon people's self-descriptions. Any one person's identity is a mix of personal characteristics (outgoing, optimistic, carefree, motivated); social roles (sister, friend, teacher); activities (dancer, musician); preferences (likes to wear cute clothes); and descriptions of past and future states, particularly hopes (going to law school) and fears (worries about exams). Many people have considerable freedom to compose their identities as they like, choosing what to emphasize and what to downplay. Certainly, the way you describe yourself—as outgoing, an optimist, serious, giving, anxious, or with one of a hundred other attributes—is pretty much up to you. Even though many of the things you think about yourself come from the reflections of others, you can decide whether to think of yourself or to describe yourself in these ways. You are free to say "I like to dance," or "I am a dancer," or "moving my body to music makes me happy," or to make no mention of dancing whatsoever. Developing an identity requires selectivity and allows for considerable creativity, and to a large extent this depends on you. Clearly, then, your identity depends on how you identify yourself—that i[s] . . . are, or how you would like t[o] . . . your way to law school, and . . .

The second insight about . . . vidual identities are, in part, given to us by *others*. A person's identity reflects her own list of who she is *but also* society's list of who she is, making it the meeting place between her and society. Many of the characteristics included in the students' responses above describe relationships and roles—I am a daughter, a brother, a student—and refer to many of the important categories that organize our communities and societies such as age, gender, race, and ethnicity. These aspects locate a person and give her a position in the world.

The realization that a person's identity necessarily involves others brings with it the realization that, with respect to her identity, she is not completely in control. Identities are only partly a matter of personal choice. The students in my examples can change their majors, their activities, and their preferences, but not all of their identity attributes are of this type. Unlike going to law school or being a dancer, most people have less freedom with respect to whether, when, and how to invoke or present identity characteristics involving our family relations or our ascribed race or ethnicity. To see what I mean, look back at the examples. Only one student gives her age. Five of the six say something that makes it evident that they are a male or a female. Five students mention either their ethnicity or race (Asian American, Mexican American, Japanese, African American, biracial), while one of the students mentions neither. In other words, some of the students mention their age, gender, race, or ethnicity and some do not—thus making it seem as though they have a choice regarding whether to identify themselves using these categories. Yet social psychological studies of identity reveal that whether people decide to emphasize age, gender, race, or ethnicity in their own story of who they are, these characteristics will necessarily influence their identity and experiences in the world.

This is why identities are individual but also collective projects. A person cannot really answer the "Who am I?" question without thinking about what [peo]ple think of her. Her identity is not just her [. . .] alone; what her identity ends up being [. . .] also on how other people identify her. [. . .] are, in fact, group projects, and as such, "you can't be a self by yourself." A person's identity depends on who she is in relation to others (a daughter, a girlfriend), as well as how others identify her (as a woman, as Mexican, as Japanese, or as African American).

Erik Erikson, one of the most important theorists of identity, described identity as what "the 'I' reflects on when contemplating the body, the personality, and the roles to which it is attached," and also as an implied constant conversation with the others with whom for better or for worse we are constantly comparing ourselves (1968:217). Erikson's own life story demonstrates the power of others in determining one's identity. Erikson's parents, his Jewish mother and stepfather, had adopted him and raised him, giving him the last name of Homburger. Yet Erikson's biological father was Danish, and Erikson was tall, blond, and blue-eyed; he did not know the details of his birth until later in his life. What he did know was that during the weekend, at the Temple School where all the students were Jewish, he was teased for looking "Nordic." What he also knew was that during the week, at grammar school, where there were relatively few Jews, he was taunted for being Jewish. What identity is and how it is sensitive to the social context became a lifelong concern for Erikson.

Some of you may have had experiences that give you an insight into Erikson's identity predicament. Consider, for example, Sarah, an African American student in my class whose father identifies as black and whose mother identifies as white. In her junior year, Sarah enrolled in an overseas study program in South Africa. Arriving in Capetown, she identified herself as black just as she always had growing up in the Bay Area. The South African students, who have a very different set of historical and sociopolitical understandings of race, would have none of it. From their perspective, Sarah was obviously colored or maybe white, but certainly not black. Or consider Kenji, another student in the same class with Sarah. Growing up in Japan, Kenji never thought much about his ethnicity except on trips with his parents to Taiwan and Hong Kong. He knew at Stanford that his ethnicity would matter, yet when he arrived, he was surprised to realize that he was regarded as "Asian"—not Japanese, not East Asian, just "Asian." As Sarah and Kenji discovered, the answer to a question that seems so personal and private—"Who am I?"—was not completely up to them. Other people are always involved. Sometimes others affirm a person's identity and see her the way she would like to be seen, sometimes they ignore or deny the ways she would like to be seen, and at other times they impose on her a set of categories or labels that she dislikes, resists, or finds irrelevant. The fact that a person's identity comes in part from her relationships to others leads to a third significant feature of identity: because identities depend on the contexts from which they emerge, they are dynamic and evolving.

## Identities Are Dynamic

As the examples of Sarah and Kenji show, the answers to the "Who am I?" question partly depend on the context—the "where" in the web of social relations a person is located at any particular time. There are, in other words, spatial as well as temporal dimensions to identity. As is the case with buying real estate, the three rules of understanding identity are "location, location, location." Who you are at any given moment depends on where you happen to be and who else is there in that place with you. Looking across the six self-descriptions quoted earlier, most include some mention of being a student. This is not accidental. The "Who am I?" question was posed in the classroom during exam week. Two students refer to exams and studying. Had we asked this question later in the day when the students were in the dorm or in their family homes, some different aspects of the students' identities would have surfaced.

To illustrate the effects of location on identity, consider a study my colleagues and I (Kanagawa, Cross, and Markus 2001) did in which we asked students in the United States and Japan the "Who am I?" question in one of four different locations—alone in the psychological laboratory, with a friend in the cafeteria, in their professor's office, or in a classroom with many other students. We found that their answers varied by location at the local as well as the national level. The students in the United States were most likely to describe themselves in terms of attributes (creative, athletic, friendly), while the Japanese students were most likely to describe themselves in terms of activities (working part-time, preparing for exams). This pattern reflects cultural differences between the two groups of students in the way they construct their identities, an issue to which I will return in more detail later on in this essay. For both sets of students, what they said and how much they said about themselves depended on the immediate situation. For example, when thinking about who they were while in the professor's office, the Japanese students seemed to become very aware of the high standards others might have for them and were more likely to make critical statements about themselves than were the students who described themselves while sitting alone in the laboratory.

It is important to note that the "Who am I?" question captures only the part of identity that a person is conscious of at a given moment in a given context, like a snapshot or a stop-action film clip of the whole identity. People move around from place to place, and even when they stay in one place, the context around them changes. Consequently, identities are always in flux. They are continually formed, expressed, changed, affirmed, and threatened in the course of everyday life. As a person moves from home, to the classroom, to the store, to the bank, to a university office, to the gym, or to the home of a friend, the different social worlds she is part of can all work to shuffle the various aspects of her identity.

### Identities Are Unique

Finally, we come to our last insight about identity: every identity is unique. Because a person's identity is a joint project between her and the others around her, and because it changes over time and according to her environment(s), it is her personal signature. Although we all share many contexts with others (families, neighborhoods, schools, workplaces) and may develop some aspects of our identities that are similar to theirs, in the end, our identities derive from our particular experiences in the world, which are unlikely to overlap completely with those others. So, for example, when two people attend the same school, how the school context influences their separate identities will depend on many other aspects of their lives—whether they are female or male, Hispanic or white, whether they get good grades, and whether they are attending college in 1990 or 2008. Even twins who have grown up in the same family, experienced many of the same events, and formed relations with many of the same people are unlikely to have completely overlapping identities.

In sum, identities are complex, dynamic, and unique. In addition, and most notably for a volume on "doing race," they are social and depend on the context. In other words, they are both private and public property—others have a say in who a person becomes. This is the case even if the person says, for example, "I don't think of myself as black," or "I don't think of myself as white," or "I am Filipino but I

don't think about it." If a social category matters in a given community, and if a person claims an association with this category, *or* if others associate her with this category, that category will have some impact on her behavior.

## THE BEHAVIORAL SIGNIFICANCE OF IDENTITY

"We don't see things as they are, we see them as we are" is a claim widely attributed to Anaïs Nin, a French-Cuban writer known for her diaries and journals. This statement summarizes one powerful role of identity: how a person sees the world depends on her identity, and her identity depends on her experiences in the world. For the sake of illustration, consider two students who attend the same university. As students at the same school, they will probably have some overlapping experiences. Yet a white female student from San Francisco majoring in biology is likely to have had a somewhat different social history and to have gained a different repertoire of experiences from those of a Latino student from Atlanta who is getting a degree in electrical engineering. As a result of having different histories and experiences, they are likely to develop different understandings about and perspectives on the world. Through our particular individual experiences we all begin to develop frameworks of meaning and of value—what psychologists call schemas—to help us make sense of the world and organize our experiences. These interpretive sch--- ...ey tell us what is _____ ...matter. Moreover, _____ ...d how we are po _____ ...is are deeply inte _____ ...ies. Since different identities indicate different locations in the various social networks and contexts of our lives, they will be associated with different perspectives and understandings. This is why paying attention to people's identities is an important part of understanding the social world.

In addition to telling us what to pay attention to and what to *see*, our identities also tell us how to think, feel, and act—what to do and what not to do

(Markus and Sentis 1982; Oyserman and Markus 1993). They help us determine what is good, what is bad, what should count, and what should not. Identities, then, are both frames of reference and sets of blueprints for action. Given this foundational role of identity, any situation or event that is relevant to an aspect of identity can have a powerful impact on your actions.

An easy way to see identities at work in organizing the world is to ask a number of people for directions to the same location and then track the reference points. The foodie/gourmet will tell you to go a block until the Left Bank restaurant, then go halfway down that street until you see Whole Foods Market, and slow down right before the driveway to Peet's Coffee store. The contractor will tell you to go a block and a half until Home Depot, turn right just past the big construction site, and look for the driveway by the office building with all the new solar panels. For the foodie/gourmet, food plays an important role for her identity, as construction does for the contractor. These important aspects of identity then become the point of orientation for the individual's behavior. In other words, "we see things as we are."

Figure 15.1 illustrates some elements of the dynamic and relational process through which our social experiences in the world have an influence on identity and behavior. Race and ethnicity, because they are the focus of this essay, are shown in bold. However, depending on the context and the details of our particular lives, many other social categories are also likely to be important in shaping our experiences. Moreover, the influences of these different social categories will intersect, depending on the particular social situation and which aspects of identity are salient. As the earlier student self-descriptions suggest, we see ourselves in terms of categories that blend race, gender, and age—"21-year-old African American woman." Specifically, however, in those spaces where race and ethnicity are salient, the social categories of race and ethnicity will influence identity. In Figure 15.1, identity is indicated as the meeting place described earlier—that is, as a combination of our *own* view of *ourselves* with *others' views* of us. Sometimes, in some situations, these views converge;

at other times or in other situations, they diverge. The Xs in the figure refer to those schemas about the self that derive from previous social experience and that provide the interpretive frameworks, the anchors, and the benchmarks for behavior. The role that race and ethnicity will play in identity depends on the details of our social experience both currently and as we were growing up. For some of us, the schemas related to race or ethnicity will be highly elaborated and chronically accessible for making sense of the world (indicated by the bold Xs); for others these schemas may be less dense and may become available only when something in a social situation makes them relevant. In general, however, our actions will reflect these schemas and will, in turn, reinforce them.

Nin's observation that "we see things as we are" suggests that identities can provide powerful clues for predicting behavior—our own and others. If we know something about a person's life experiences, we can make a reasonable guess about some features of her identity. From there, we can hypothesize about what her interpretive schemas are likely to be—that is, what she is likely to pay attention to, what she might care about, what might please her, what might make her sad, what might prepare her to fight, or even to die. Events that are consistent with a person's preferred identities (past, present, or future) or that affirm her in some way—put her in a good light, make her feel competent or proud—are likely to have consequences that she will regard as desirable. Events that are inconsistent with or that threaten a person's identity—make her feel anxious, incapable, humiliated, or ashamed—are likely to have undesirable consequences. If the rule of thumb for understanding political events is to "follow the money," surely the rule for understanding behavior is to "follow the identity."

## RACE AND ETHNICITY AS A SOURCE OF IDENTITY

Whenever someone participates in a group or community or society, the factors that are important in how the nation, states, cities, neighborhoods, families,

**FIGURE 15.1**    The Society-Identity-Behavior-Society Cycle.

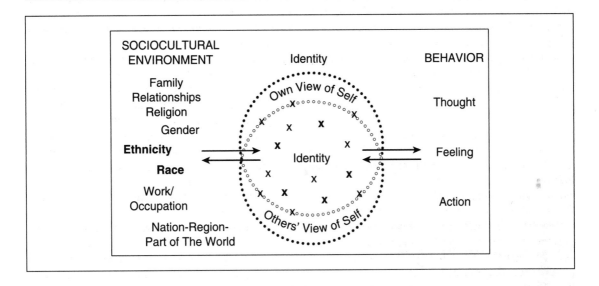

and schools are organized will have some influence on who she is, whether she notices them, and whether she thinks a particular factor is important to her. If a category—whether it is race, gender, ethnicity, or religion—is associated with the distribution of power, resources, status, respect, knowledge, or other cultural capital in a particular context, that category will matter for identity. For example, in the United States, everyday life is powerfully shaped by the categories of race and ethnicity. A person's race and ethnicity influences where she is likely to live and who her friends are likely to be. They also predict her health and wealth as well as the quality of schools, neighborhoods, workplaces, medical care, and other life outcomes she is likely to have access to (Krysan and Lewis 2005; Massey and Denton 1992). Of course, there are many other factors that matter for these outcomes as well, but the extent to which race and ethnicity are important to a person's life chances often remains unseen or even deliberately ignored. After all, as Americans, we want to believe in the hope expressed by the American Dream—that all that matters for success is the willingness to work hard, and that who you are or where you have come from should not matter. Certainly, as the election of Barack Obama

powerfully reveals, the American Dream can sometimes be realized. His election proves that an association with a non-mainstream racial and ethnic category does not, by itself, preclude inclusion and full success in our society.

Yet, in American society, the race or ethnicity you are associated with does still matter. It will continue to matter until the realities of American life—the policies, institutions, representations, and everyday social practices—reflect broadly the ideals of the American Dream. At present, race and ethnicity still afford some people a wide set of advantages and privileges that are systematically denied to others. However, not everyone is equally aware that this is the case; those in the minority ethnic or racial group are much more likely to understand this connection than those in the majority. Studies over several decades have documented the tendency of people in the majority not to be aware of their own race or ethnicity and so not to mention it as an answer to the "Who am I?" question (Tatum 2002; Oyserman 2008). This is the key to why some white people are perplexed about why people of color refer to or focus on their race or ethnicity. From the majority and/or dominant location, race and ethnicity are unremarkable and irrelevant. Like water to the fish, the racial or ethnic aspects of identity are invisible. In a now-classic piece on white privilege, Peggy McIntosh (1997) suggests that one of the hidden privileges of being white in the United States is that a white person can choose to ignore her racial identity and to imagine that she can be "beyond race." She can claim not to see race and to regard herself only as a human being.

### Defining Race and Ethnicity

One significant misconception about race and ethnicity is that they are products of the body or the blood—inherent qualities that are present and unchangeable inside a person from birth. Yet race and ethnicity are anything but natural. Rather than permanent, immutable characteristics of a person, specific races and ethnicities are organizational categories that have been created by humans over time as a way of orienting themselves in the world. As Paula Moya and I define the concepts . . . race and ethnicity are dynamic sets of ideas (e.g., meanings, values, goals, images, associations) and practices (e.g., meaningful actions, both formal and routine) that people use to distinguish groups of people from other groups and to organize their own communities. Throughout history, differences in the physical characteristics of people such as skin color, eye color, and hair texture have become associated—deliberately as well as inadvertently—with different meaningful behavioral outcomes, both positive and negative. Specific racial and ethnic categories (i.e., Asian, Black, Latina/o) are, in this way, human-made, as are the identities based on them.

The circumstance of dividing up the world according to visible physical and behavioral characteristics, while understandable, is not inevitable. It is not necessary for people to be divided by skin color, or according to the continent on which some of their ancestors might have lived several generations ago. The world could be arranged so that the physical characteristics now used to assign race and ethnicity do not matter for life outcomes. Of course, some people will argue that humans will always make some type of distinction to note who is "our kind" and who is not. Importantly, however, the basis of these distinctions can vary and, in fact, have varied throughout history. For example, in ancient Greece, distinctions were not made on skin color—this came with modernity and science—but in terms of language and belief. Most likely language and belief had as much of an impact on a person's identity and his life chances in ancient Greece as race and ethnicity do now in the United States of America.

Up to this point, I have been using the terms *race* and *ethnicity* simultaneously in a way that might give the impression that these two concepts are interchangeable. While they do overlap in meaning, and though they are similar in the way they are formed by others and have been reinforced throughout history to the present day, there is a very important difference between the two that must be addressed.

First, the term *race* specifically indexes a history in which group characteristics have been used to establish a hierarchy and to accord one group a higher status and the other group a lower status (Fredrickson 2002). Therefore, categorizing people as a racial group draws attention to the difference in the power relationships among this group and other groups. Race is important for identity because if a person is associated with a racial group, her race is likely to have affected the way she has been viewed and treated by others. Many of the ideas and practices associated with particular races have been constructed and imposed on the group by those not associated with the group and are unlikely to be claimed by those associated with the group. When people do claim association with a particular racial group, they are often acknowledging, as a part of their identities, the history of unequal relations between their group and a dominant group. Categorizing people as an *ethnicity*, on the other hand, focuses attention on differences in meanings, values, and ways of living (social practices) that are often regarded as equally viable and need not establish a status ranking among the groups. People in groups called ethnicities are often relatively willing to claim or elaborate on these differences between the groups they are associated with and other groups.

When a person identifies with an ethnic group, her focus is usually on how people in the in-group—those who identify with her group—think about their group. By contrast, when a person thinks about her group as a racial group, her focus is likely to be on how people in the out-group—those who do not identify with her group—think about her group. She is, moreover, likely to be highly aware of the nature of the power relations between her group and other groups.

Using the definitions of race and ethnicity presented above, most groups can be classified as ethnic, racial, or both. In practice in the United States, African Americans typically think of themselves as a racial group, Asian Americans more commonly identify themselves as an ethnic group, and Latino/as sometimes classify themselves as one or the other or both. Yet groups typically conceptualized as races can also be analyzed as ethnic groups, and ethnic groups can be analyzed as racial groups, a process that will certainly have consequences for identity. The case of Muslims with Middle Eastern heritage living in the United States is a good example. Before the attack on the World Trade Center and the Pentagon on September 11, 2001, in most instances, Muslims with Middle Eastern heritage were considered ethnic groups, and members of that group identified themselves as Muslim and Middle Eastern, because that was the way they saw themselves. New meanings and representations are now associated with being Muslim and Middle Eastern, and those identified with this group must now deal with these imposed representations as they negotiate their identities. To the extent that being Muslim is being broadly devalued and Muslims are facing increasing prejudice and discrimination, we can say that this ethnic group is being racialized.

## When and How Race and Ethnicity Matter

I have suggested here that if race and ethnicity are important in society, they will always have an impact on identity, and if they have an impact on identity, they will influence some aspect of behavior. Currently, in American society, one finds a great deal of anxiety around racial and ethnic identities.

Many imagine that these social distinctions can be only the basis of division and conflict, and that our individual and societal goal should be to get beyond these group boundaries. Yet while racial and ethnic identities can certainly be the basis of prejudice, discrimination, and inequality, they can also—and sometimes simultaneously—be the source of pride, meaning, motivation, and belongingness.

Specifying the type of influence race and ethnicity will have for identity and action and whether it will be personally or collectively beneficial or detrimental for behavior is currently the focus of a great deal of exciting research and scholarship in the social sciences and humanities (see Alcoff 2006; Alcoff and Mendieta 2003; Moya 2002; Prentice and Miller 1999). The evidence is now compelling. Race and ethnicity influence identity (1) whether or not people are aware of their race or ethnicity, and (2) whether or not they claim a racial or ethnic association (develop an elaborated self-schema) as an aspect of identity. When and how racial and ethnic associations and categorizations influence identity and behavior depends on a wide array of personal and social factors, including how others in a given context (e.g., nation, neighborhood, workplace, classroom) regard the ethnic or racial group with which a person is associated, and whether others regard that person as belonging to the group.

This research reveals that racial and ethnic associations can pattern behavior in ways that are surprising and not always immediately apparent. Very significantly, however, to say that race or ethnicity "influence" or "constitute" identity is not to say they *determine* identity. Race and ethnicity are among many influences that can shape identity. People are indeed intentional agents who, as I have noted, can be highly selective in what aspects of their experience they attend to and elaborate. Once a person becomes aware of her race and ethnicity and its potential role in shaping behavior, she can (1) *claim* this influence and emphasize its role in identity or (2) actively *resist* any influence of race and ethnicity. That said, given a society organized according to race and ethnicity, it would be impossible for her to escape *all* influence. Even if she actively tries to separate herself from these categories, the very fact of separating herself from them will affect her behavior and remind her that she has to contend with their effects.

## DISCUSSION QUESTIONS

1. How does Descartes' "I think, therefore I am," differ from Cooley and Mead's two different concepts of self here, and what does this difference mean for racial and ethnic identities?

2. "Identities are only partly a matter of personal choice," says Markus. With reference to Figure 15.1, discuss the ways in which identity is shaped by both personal and social factors. How does this construction of identity work with respect to racial and ethnic identity?

# 16

# GENDER AND IDENTITY

JUDITH A. HOWARD

RAMIRA M. ALAMILLA

*This second reading in this introduction to theories about identity is by Judith A. Howard and Ramira M. Alamilla. Howard, a professor of sociology at the University of Washington, is a well-known gender scholar, and her work here with Alamilla provides an overview of four sociological perspectives on gender identity. These four views of gender identity are essentialism, socialization, social construction, and structuralism. These perspectives complement well Markus's social psychological theories of identity, and they can be applied to many of the readings to follow in Part II. The reading was first published in* Gender Mosaics: Social Perspectives *(2001), edited by Dana Vannoy.*

## OVERVIEW

The difference between the sexes is, happily, one of great profundity. Clothes are but a symbol of something hid deep beneath. It was a change in Orlando herself that dictated her choice of a woman's dress and of a woman's sex (Woolf 1928:188).

"A pox on them!" she said, realizing for the first time, what, in other circumstances, she would have been taught as a child, that is to say, the sacred

responsibilities of womanhood. "And that's the last oath I shall ever be able to swear," she thought, "once I set foot on English soil . . . . All I can do once I set foot on English soil, is to pour out tea, and ask my lords how they like it" (Woolf 1928:157–158).

Her braces are gone. She has smoothed the frizzy mane of curls that once reached to such dazzling heights. Her makeup is now subtle and based on natural, not neon, hues. Her clothing is inspired by the board room instead of the secretarial pool. She

*Source:* Howard, Judith A and Ramira M. Alamilla. 2001. "Gender and Identity." Pp. 54–64 in *Gender Mosaics: Social Perspectives*, edited by Dana Vannoy. By permission of Oxford University Press, USA.

has embraced the markers of dignity, refinement, and power. "There's a haircut that belongs on Wall Street and a different one that belongs in Hollywood" (Givhan 1998:9A).

> When I started using AFDC, my mom was like, "People won't like it." I think that's why I'm so self-conscious about the food stamps. People judge it. It feels like everybody's respect is dependent on what you're doing and how much you're doing. It's hard to be part of a system that doesn't work. But when you're on welfare, you're part of that system, no matter how hard you try not to be (Duerr Berrick 1995:84).

These excerpts from literary, newspaper, and academic sources illustrate four distinct ways of thinking about gender identity. The first and second quotations are from Virginia Woolf's *Orlando* (1928), which illustrates the life of a person who was first biologically male, then became biologically female, and later alternated between being a woman or a man by changing clothes and modifying behavior. The first quotation casts gender identity as an *essential* set of qualities by focusing on biological foundations of sex differences that become associated with gender differences. The second quotation emphasizes *socialization*, the training and learning that occur primarily in childhood (although in some respects they continue throughout the life course) and tend to be consistent with and to reproduce culturally defined gender stereotypes. The third quotation refers to the makeover of Paula Jones, a litigant against President Bill Clinton. This quote illustrates *social construction*, the creation of gender through human actions, as well as the negotiation and interpretation of those actions in terms of social expectations and accountability to those expectations. The fourth quotation, from a welfare recipient, focuses on gender as a *social structure*, an organizing principle of society that, together with other stratification statuses, determines allocation of material resources and opportunities. This reading evaluates each of these four approaches to gender identity. It concludes that a synthesis that combines processes of social construction and social structure provides the fullest understanding of contemporary gender identities.

## DEFINITION OF TERMS

Identity is based not only on responses to the question, "Who am I?" but also on responses to the question, "Who am I in relation to others?" thus rooting the question in a person's external circumstances. *Identity* is a person's position, or space, in social relationships, social structures, and societal institutions. A 34-year-old middle-class mother, for example, has a particular position in society that carries with it certain perceived responsibilities and parameters. These may differ greatly from the responsibilities of a 20-year-old college student in a sorority. The relationship between individuals and social structures is expressed in the concept of identity.

There are at least two key approaches to identity: a *structural approach*, emphasizing the more stable, internalized aspects of identity, and a *processual approach*, emphasizing the less stable, socially constructed aspects of identity. Rather than setting the two approaches against each other, we propose a continuum of approaches that vary in their views of identity from more to less stable. Some approaches contain elements of both views and are found at midpoints along this continuum. We refer to this continuum throughout the reading as we discuss four theoretical perspectives on gender identity and how they contribute to the study of gender stratification.

At this point, it may be helpful to define a number of other terms used throughout this essay. Identity has been defined. *Gender identity* specifically is one's inner sense of oneself as female or male. This sense develops in early childhood and, once established, is resistant to change. Gender identity tends to be dichotomous—people see themselves as only male or only female—which reflects the societal expectation that there are two, and only two, sexes. *Sex* refers to biological characteristics such as reproductive organs, chromosomes, and secondary sex characteristics. *Gender* refers to culturally produced behaviors and personality characteristics that may be associated with, but are not determined by, biological sex. The term *gender role*, which has been used interchangeably with *sex role*, refers to the characteristics and behaviors believed to be appropriate for men or for women. We make further distinctions among these terms throughout the reading.

## FOUR PERSPECTIVES
## ON GENDER IDENTITIES

The quotations at the beginning of this chapter illustrate four general sociological perspectives on gender: essentialism, socialization, social construction, and structuralism. The views of identity located within these four perspectives can be conceptualized along a continuum of identity, from more structural and stable to more processual and active. The discussion of these perspectives is framed in terms of gender identities that also refer, often only implicitly, to race, class, sexuality, age, and other manifestations of social structures and institutions. The discussion stresses the links of these identities with the social structures to which they refer.

### Essentialism

Located at the more stable end of the continuum of identity are markedly essentialist perspectives on identity. Essentialist conceptions of gender identity assume everyone is born with a particular sex, this sex is associated with a corresponding gender, and both are fixed from birth. According to this perspective, there are innate, and therefore stable, differences between the two sexes. The differences between the sexes in turn shape sex differences in social behaviors. This idea follows from the functionalist analysis of sex, which casts women and men as serving different, and complementary, roles in society. Essentialist conceptions persist most likely because they are consistent with deeply held cultural beliefs about sex and the relationship between sex and gender.

Essentialist assumptions are evident in the common use of sex as a variable representing gender. In this "sex-as-variable" research, respondents are categorized as female or male, and any differences found between the two are labeled "gender differences." Sex and gender are treated as one and the same. One example of this type of research focuses on sex differences in mathematical ability. For years, study after study showed that boys outperformed girls on math tests, beginning in the seventh grade.

The studies were used to support the assertion that boys were superior to girls both in mathematical and general cognitive abilities. Parallel findings that girls had superior reading skills during the same developmental period were ignored. In the past twenty years studies have begun to consider the social contexts in which such differences occur. Gender differences in mathematical ability all but disappear when one takes into account social factors such as prevailing expectations about the math education of boys and girls. In considering how social context might produce apparent sex differences, this latter line of research distinguishes between sex and gender rather than treating them as identical, and innate, properties of individuals.

Early sociological research on race, echoing research on gender, was also marked by essentialist assumptions. Characteristics associated with racial categories were assumed to be innate and irreversible properties of the individual resulting from biological differences. These assumptions continue to shape some research even today. For example, although a number of responses to the book have argued persuasively against its key tenets, Richard Herrnstein and Charles Murray's *The Bell Curve* (1994) argues that racial differences in intelligence do exist and are based on genetic differences.

In contrast, social class has more often been treated as an achieved rather than an ascribed or innate social position. This treatment implies that class differences can be best understood through constructionist or structural processes. Close readings of both material and textual sources suggest, however, that class too is often treated as essential or at least deeply rooted in cultural traditions. In Woolf's novel, for example, Orlando comes from a wealthy, privileged background. Despite her awareness of the processes through which her family became privileged, she deals with her perceptions of the contrasting style of Gypsy life through essentialist attributions of barbarity.

It is now conventional among social scientists to distinguish between the terms *sex* and *gender* rather than to equate female or male with culturally based assumptions about women or men. The concept of sex, however, is so strongly shaped by cultural understandings of gender that in everyday use, the two terms are rarely distinguished. Because contemporary Western society assumes a close relationship between sex and gender, well-socialized members often do behave in ways that live up to societal expectations about gender. In many ways, this behavior obscures the structural constraints and inequalities of stratification that shape those expectations of behavior and appearance. A consideration of other theories of gender identity reveals them to look toward interactional, cultural, and structural factors, rather than innate, individual characteristics, as the source of human identities and behavior.

## Socialization

The concept of identity associated with the socialization perspective is only slightly less stable than that of essentialism. There are two variants of the socialization perspective on understanding gender identities: a social learning theory of the initial learning of identities in childhood and a social cognitive theory of the formation of cognitive schemas among adults. These theories assert that we learn what behavior is appropriate to our gender, race, class, age, and sexuality from our environment through various learning processes.

Social learning theories maintain that children are not innately gendered (or raced); rather, they model the behavior of others through observation, imitation, and interaction. Other people become agents of reinforcement, and children are rewarded or punished for the masculine or feminine behaviors they exhibit. As they learn these patterns, they acquire the capacity to reinforce themselves—this is the capacity of internalization. As children develop cognitive capacities and become adults, these social learning processes eventually shape the content of their cognitive schemas about themselves, including schemas organized around other significant categories in society such as gender, race, class, age, and sexuality.

Cognitive schemas are internal mental structures that allow us to organize social information about various concepts, objects, people, groups, and situations, as well as about ourselves. Human beings are assumed to form and rely upon these organizational cognitive structures because of our limited cognitive capacities. People can simplify reality through schemas; schemas act as filters of information, interpreting specific instances in light of a general category. These cognitive preconceptions about ourselves (self-schemas) and others (social or group schemas) and social situations (event schemas) shape what we pay attention to and how we think we are supposed to behave in various situations. Through socialization we learn the appropriate content of schemas and which schemas to use for different kinds of information. Schemas are assumed to be relatively stable, in part because the efficiency needs they serve imply that they should not be easily altered. Schemas thus contribute to perpetuating behaviors that sustain the social order.

Self-schemas represent identity, or our answers to the question, "Who am I?" The development of a self-schema based on gender reflects one's gender identity. From this perspective, gender identity is relatively fixed: it develops during early childhood and once established, is resistant to change. Paralleling essentialist perspectives on gender identity, this cognitive conception also tends to be dichotomous: people generally think of themselves as either female or male, not as something in between or as both. Gender identity is a subjective feeling rooted in how one perceives oneself and cannot be determined by external observation. A person's gender identity may or may not correspond with the person's sex or gender, and it is unrelated to sexual orientation. Transsexuals (people who have changed their biological sex), for example, generally feel their gender identity does not "fit" their biological sex.

Though located toward the stable end of the continuum of identity, these socialization perspectives cast gender differences as the result of social and cultural forces rather than innate biological properties. Through social learning, children internalize cultural prescriptions (what they should do) and cultural proscriptions (what they should not do) in order to behave in appropriately masculine or feminine ways according to the norms of their society. These processes result in gendered personalities and patterns of behavior . . . .

Social schemas also guide people's preconceptions of others, and indirectly themselves, through group schemas. Group schemas include organized information about social roles, such as student or teacher, and stratification statuses according to gender, race, age, and class. Much of the content of these schemas is learned during childhood socialization. Following the need for cognitive efficiency, the content of these schemas is often acquired through learning the most readily available information. Often gender, race, and age offer the most visible information, based on prevailing norms of dress, hairstyle, and body language. In leading people to rely on group characteristics rather than paying attention to individual differences, categorization contributes to the formation of stereotypes.

Stereotypes are primarily descriptive: they tell people what to believe about the characteristics of members of particular groups. Beliefs sometimes include prescriptions of how those groups should or should not behave. In addition to personality traits polarized into femininity and masculinity, gender stereotypes also include prescriptions for social behaviors, physical characteristics, occupations, types of dress and bodily adornment, and codes of sexual behavior . . . .

Stereotypes are clearly a significant force in shaping social behaviors. Socialization explains how people are taught and learn these stereotypes and behaviors. Socialization perspectives tend to emphasize the processes of learning, however, rather than the expectations to which children are socialized. This distinction is significant because the analysis of cultural and structural factors can inform us about how principles of stratification may be internalized (through the content of schemas), thus explaining to some extent how Western society's expectations about gender may form part of our own identities. Some researchers in this area have asked whether social systems such as gender, race, or class affect how people are socialized and the content of what is learned. They ask, for example, why certain behaviors are rewarded when performed by boys but punished when girls perform them. Or why the sorts of behaviors girls are encouraged to perform are often valued less than the sorts of behaviors boys are encouraged to perform.

As one example, Barrie Thorne's book *Gender Play* (1993) illustrates how girls and boys in school settings learn how to play together and apart. Children may initially learn from others how to separate into lines or into assigned seating, but Thorne observes that they continue to separate themselves through "borderwork." Gender boundaries are strengthened by contests between boys and girls; cross-gender rituals of chasing and pollution games (cooties); and invasions, mostly by boys of girls' public spaces. Thorne notes that inequalities of gender, as well as of race and social class, are often expressed in this borderwork. Girls can give cooties more often than boys; boys invade girls' groups and activities more often than the reverse; girls complain more often to adults when boys invade. Thorne maintains that these inequalities reflect dominant cultural images. As her work implies, the specific content of what results from the processes of socialization depends on the cultural context and the values of the community.

The cultural context is necessarily shaped by systems of social stratification. It should be noted, however, that social institutions such as families, education, religion, many occupations, and so forth, could not operate effectively without an available pool of well-socialized actors who know the accepted cultural conventions and perform appropriately. In other words, gender, class, age, race, nationality, sexuality, and other meaningful social systems serve as the "organizing principles" by which the content of socialization is defined.

Farther along the continuum of conceptualizing identity, the concept of *role identities* provides a conceptual bridge from the socialization perspectives to the social constructionist perspectives. This conceptual bridge retains an assumption of internal psychological structure but also emphasizes identity as a position in external social hierarchies. Sheldon Stryker asserts that role identities are "internalized role designations" in which the societal and cultural expectations for a particular role associated with a position in society are internalized by the individual (1987). The stable, structural aspect of this view of identity is these role designations; the more processual aspect is reflected in the emphasis on how interaction shapes commitment to these role designations. This commitment depends upon the quality of relationships formed by the individual through interaction in that role. Thus the concept of role identities includes a structural view of roles, but it also recognizes the significance of interaction and the creative agency of the individual.

Much sociological thought in the first half of the twentieth century relied heavily on the functionalist concept of social roles as positions in social structures. Roles provided a repertoire of expectations for appropriate behavior associated with particular social positions. In the second half of the century this traditional definition of roles has provoked considerable criticism for its lack of attention to the power and inequality associated with particular roles and its failure to ask: Functional for whom? The concept of *gender roles*, in particular, has been heavily criticized. This term refers to role schemas, or stereotypes for gender performance, which define the expectations about what women and men should or should not be or do. The very concept of role schemas legitimizes the perceived differences between women and men and ignores the differences within, and the overlap between, genders. Gender roles often are unrelated to how people actually behave, for many people resist or undermine the prescriptions of gender. Helena Lopata and Barrie Thorne (1978) maintain that gender is not a role in the sense that student, friend, and sister are roles but goes deeper and infuses the other roles individuals play. There are no parallel concepts of "class roles" or "race roles," presumably implying that it is unacceptable to suggest that the social order depends on class-based and race-based social inequalities. In contrast, the use of gender roles, prescribing the allocation of women and men to different types of tasks, implies that gender inequalities are an acceptable foundation for the social order. Although the concept of gender roles has thus received considerable criticism, this concept of role identities within the socialization perspective does recognize the significance of interaction. In doing so, it forms a bridge to the social construction perspective that emphasizes interactional processes.

## Social Construction

The third perspective on gender identity is markedly more processual, conceptualizing identities as more fluid and less stable, and thus is located at the opposite pole of the continuum of identity. Central to this perspective is the assumption that the meaning of objects and behaviors is not fixed or inherent. The symbolic value of a car, for example, may be quite different for an 18-year-old just learning to drive and a 9-year-old dependent on others to be chauffeured everywhere. Meanings and agreement about social reality are created in the process of negotiating a common interpretation of a situation through the interactions between and among people. Social constructionism sees interaction as crucial to the construction of identity, not only in childhood but beyond it in every interaction. Impression management, or the presentation of self in interaction, refers to those processes by which individuals present particular selves to particular others for particular reasons. According to their own goals for the definition of a particular situation, individuals attempt to manage the perceptions others have of them by intentionally shaping their own appearance and behavior. Students who wish to appear more knowledgeable than they are, for example, may answer a question only when they know the answer, or they may adopt a certain appearance, such as wearing glasses or assuming an attentive expression.

Actors engaged in mutual impression management develop a working consensus, or agreement, about the type of situation they are in and which roles or identities they are playing. When two strangers meet, for example, they rely both on visual cues and on questions related to their social positions: What do you do? Where do you work? Are you married? The identities they establish in this interaction then shape the definition of the situation. If a professor waits with a salesperson at a bus stop, for example, they may not even acknowledge each other. If the salesperson waits on the professor at a store, their agreed-upon identities are likely to be based on their jobs and their interaction is likely to be fairly formal. If they encounter each other as parents at their children's school, however, they may define each other as parents and their relationship as one of potential friendship. This publicly agreed-on, negotiated definition of the situation thus guides subsequent interaction, with the expectation that actors are obliged to behave in accordance with this working consensus and treat each other accordingly . . . .

Social constructionism maintains that gender identity is accomplished by individuals in everyday behavior and display, and that this is what sustains the social reality of gender. This perspective focuses on the performance of social identities. These identities are performed through negotiation in accordance with the expected behavior associated with those positions.

The strategies women and men employ are defined by certain cultural and essentialist assumptions regarding gender. Some of these assumptions are that there are two, and only two, genders; that genitals are the essential sign of gender; that everyone must be classified as one gender or another; and that the male/female dichotomy is "natural." In *Orlando* Woolf plays with these assumptions about sex and gender. The following example shows how gender display can elicit certain behaviors on the part of its witnesses:

> [C]lothes have, they say, more important offices
> than merely to keep us warm. They change our view
> of the world and the world's view of us. When
> Captain Bartolus saw Orlando's skirt, he had an
> awning stretched for her immediately, pressed her to
> take another slice of beef, and invited her to go
> ashore with him in the long boat. These
> compliments would certainly not have been paid her
> had her skirts, instead of flowing, been cut tight to
> her legs in the fashion of breeches . . . . The man has
> his hand free to seize his sword; the woman must
> use hers to keep the satins from slipping from her
> shoulders. Had they both worn the same clothes, it
> is possible that their outlook might have been the
> same too. (187–88)

Suzanne Kessler and Wendy McKenna (1978) challenge these cultural assumptions by arguing that the idea of two distinct sexes itself is socially constructed. They note that the assumed correspondence between genitals and gender is not total or "natural": some individuals are born with both female and male characteristics. There are also individuals who are physically assignable to one sex but who take on the social behaviors and characteristics of the other. These examples demonstrate, according to Kessler and McKenna, that even sex is not dichotomous, and that it is cultural assumptions that lead to the categorization of each individual from birth into one of only two sexes. Thus behavior appropriate for one's culturally assigned sex category becomes overdetermined, regardless of whether it "fits" one's gender identity. (That some individuals do choose to violate these expectations shows, however, that this system is not seamless.)

"Doing gender" means behaving so that whatever the situation, whoever the other actors, one's behavior is seen as gender-appropriate for that context . . . .

Candace West and Don Zimmerman (1987) maintain that women and men "choose" gender-appropriate behavior because in almost every activity they will be called to account for actions that may contradict norms for their gender . . . . Doing gender in accord with this responsibility to account for one's actions is one way social interaction sustains broader, macro-level systems of gender inequality.

Social constructionism emphasizes the processes of interaction and the characteristics of the situation as they shape interactional possibilities for individuals. In its emphasis on individual agency, however, this perspective tends to minimize social-structural constraints and relationships of power and inequality. Social construction contributes an explanation of how individual agents in situations perpetuate or resist institutional and interpersonal constraints. Further elaboration is necessary, however, of how social structures and institutions constrain interactional possibilities and also of how the accumulation of specific social interactions contributes to the maintenance and redefinition of various institutions and structures.

## Structuralism

The structuralist perspective on social identities, as noted, addresses macro-level patterns organized in terms of gender, race, age, class, sexuality, and other significant social positions. This perspective addresses questions of power and inequality in the institutions and structures of society that govern the allocation of resources. This chapter has considered how gender operates as a micro-level structure, shaping interactional possibilities and expectations. Gender is also the basis for macro-level allocation of material resources and opportunities. The structural perspective emphasizes how a pervasive system of male dominance affects these allocations for women as a category and for men as a category. As discussed in earlier research, the structural perspective focuses on the distribution of resources in social institutions such as the family, the workplace, or small groups, demonstrating how these resources shape gendered behaviors. The distribution of wages, for example, is inequality weighted in favor of men. More women may work today than 30 years ago—still for lower wages than men—but studies of household work reveal that women still spend more time on unpaid household labor than men. These patterns are strongly qualified by racial and class backgrounds as well and are a continuing reminder of the ways in which gender, race, class, age, and sexuality intersect at the macro level.

As a macro-level theory, the structural perspective does not refer directly to social identities. It should be noted explicitly, however, that social structures rely on and create the conditions within which identities are enacted. It is social structures that locate people within repeated situations, situations that become habitual and institutionalized—work situations, family situations, and so forth. As Philip Blumstein (1991) shows, the repeated performance of identities in habitual situations eventually leads to the ossification of those identities into what we recognize as self. For social institutions such as families to endure in their culturally recognized forms, the actors who perform within those institutions must have developed, and be competent to perform, identities suitable for those institutions and their cultural definitions.

An analysis incorporating both social constructionism and the structural emphasis on relationships of power and inequality provides a more complete understanding of how social stratification extends even to what has traditionally been considered intra-individual: social identity. We conclude with a final example that merges social construction with structuralism. In so doing, we demonstrate the central place identity occupies in analyses of stratification.

Julie Brines (1993, 1994) examines how the relative earnings of husband and wife affect the time each spends on housework. In households in which labor is divided traditionally, with the husband providing for the family and the wife dependent upon his support, women do more housework than men. Brines found, however, that even in nontraditional households, when the wife is the primary breadwinner with the husband dependent on her for support, the pattern remained the same and the woman did more housework than the man. In fact, the dependent men did *less* housework than men whose financial contributions were equal to or greater than those of their wives. Brines explains these unexpected findings by viewing the division of household labor as an opportunity for doing gender. In order to compensate for failing to live up to cultural expectations of primary breadwinners, dependent men reassert their masculinity by avoiding "feminine" housework. And women in the nontraditional role of primary breadwinner continue to do the bulk of the housework to affirm their femininity and to help their husbands affirm their own masculinity. Brines maintains that doing gender is so compelling that it leads husbands and wives to perpetuate inequalities associated with the allocation of labor.

Brines' research combines an emphasis on the social construction of gender with recognition of the structural circumstances within which those interactions occur. The women and men she studies are engaged in the very active production of gender identity, because structural circumstances have called those identities into question. This example, as well as others offered throughout this reading, clearly illustrate the centrality of gender identity to gender stratification. This line of research is an exemplar, then, of how gender identities, and social identities more generally, can be most fully comprehended: social identities are produced by active human beings but always within prevailing normative and structural circumstances.

## DISCUSSION QUESTIONS

1. Using the Howard and Alamilla reading, compare and contrast the four sociological perspectives on identity and gender.

2. Discuss the ways in which gender identity is socially constructed along the continuum from stable and essentialist to more negotiated and process oriented. Be sure to include in your analysis the degree to which structural constraints both determine and modify gender identity.

# 17

# HOW WE FIND OURSELVES

*Identity Development and Two-Spirit People*

ALEX WILSON

*In contrast to the theories of identity presented by Markus or by Howard and Alamilla, Alex Wilson presents a non-Euro-American perspective of identity. Wilson, a psychologist, published this article in 1996 in the* Harvard Educational Review *as a challenge to traditional psychological theories about identity development. Most of these theories see identities such as race and sexuality as developing independently of one another. Wilson argues that, instead, many Native Americans have an understanding of identity that combines many of these categories. For example, Wilson examines how several gay, lesbian, and bisexual Native Americans identify themselves as "two-spirit people." This multifaceted construction of gender and sexuality not only challenges traditional theories of identity but also lends itself to thinking about identity as being more contextual in terms of one's culture and community.*

The interconnectedness of sexual identity and ethnicity contributes to the complex nature of the process of identity development. As educators, we must acknowledge that fact in the supports and services we offer to our students. Although the research on lesbian, gay, and bisexual Indigenous Americans is extensive, these inquiries are typically from an anthropological perspective.[1] Much of this research is based on the rereading and reinterpretation of early field notes, testimony, and biographical sketches, twice removed from Indigenous American experiences, and twice filtered through non-Indigenous eyes (C. McHale, personal communication, March 21, 1996). Anthropologists and historians such as Evelyn Blackwood (1984), Beatrice Medicine (1983), Harriet Whitehead (1981), Walter Williams

Source: Alex Wilson, "How We Find Ourselves: Identity Development and Two-Spirit People," *Harvard Educational Review*, Volume 66:2 (Summer 1996), pp. 303–317. Copyright by the President and Fellows of Harvard College. All rights reserved. For more information, please visit www.harvardeducationalreview.org.

(1986), and Will Roscoe (1988, 1991) have contributed to a body of work that describes and documents the construction of sexuality and gender in Indigenous American communities. Their work provides a critique of Western assumptions about sexuality and gender, but generally fails to recognize the existence of and to acknowledge the contributions of "two-spirit" Indigenous Americans today.[2] From my perspective as a two-spirit Swampy Cree woman, I will critically assess current theory in identity development through reflection on my life and identity development.[3] This reassessment has implications for developmental theorists, counselors, and educators who engage with two-spirit people.

I have chosen the terms "two-spirit" and "Indigenous American" carefully. Until recently, anthropologists claimed authority to name two-spirit people by labeling them the *berdache* (Blackwood 1984; Jacobs and Cromwell 1992; Jacobs and Thomas 1994; Weston 1993). *Berdache* described anthropological subjects who did not fit neatly into European American gender and sex role categories, meaning a category of (gendered and sexual) "other." The term was imported to North America by Europeans who borrowed it from the Arabic language. Its use, to describe an "effeminate" (Blackwood 1984:27) or "morphological male who does not fill a society's standard man's role, who has a non-masculine character" (Williams 1986:2), spoke articulately about European assumptions about gender roles and sexuality (Weston 1993). The metaphoric power of the term grew over time; the role of *berdache* acquired, at least within gay history and storytelling, considerable spiritual power . . . .

Because of the historical and spiritual connotations that had been vested in the term, some members of Indigenous American communities embraced it as their self-descriptor (Roscoe 1988). More recently, in recognition of the poor fit of the term *berdache*, we have looked for language that more accurately describes our historic and present-day realities.

The growing acceptance of the term two-spirit as a self-descriptor among lesbian, gay, and bisexual Indigenous American peoples proclaims a sexuality deeply rooted in our own cultures (Brant 1995; Fife 1993). Two-spirit identity affirms the interrelatedness of all aspects of identity, including sexuality,

gender, culture, community, and spirituality. That is, the sexuality of two-spirit people cannot be considered as separate from the rest of an individual's identity (Jacobs and Thomas 1994). Two-spirit connects us to our past by offering a link that had previously been severed by government policies and actions.

Pueblo psychologist and educator Terry Tafoya (1990) states that there have been "direct attempts [by] the federal government to regulate, control, and destroy Native American behavior patterns . . . . There are more than 2,000 laws and regulations that only apply to American Indians and Alaskan Natives and not to other American Citizens" (p. 281). The religious freedom of Indigenous peoples in the United States was not legally supported until 1978 (Tafoya 1990). The Canadian federal government made a similar effort to separate Indigenous peoples from their cultural traditions (York 1990). Two-spirit reconstitutes an identity that, although misstated by anthropologists, had been based on the recognition of people with alternative genders and/or sexualities as contributing members of traditional communities. In contemporary European American culture, sexuality is perceived as a discrete aspect of identity, constructed on the basis of sexual object choice (Almaguer 1993; Whitehead 1981). This conception stands in sharp contrast to two-spirit identity.

There are over five hundred Nations (tribes) in the United States and Canada. In spite of the vast physical distances between the autoch thonous people of North America, few ideological barriers exist between these Nations (Sioui 1992). Each of our traditional worldviews recognizes the deep interdependency between humans and nature, that our origin is in the soil of the land, and that we are bound to each other in an intimately spiritual way. This shared understanding of the world shapes the life experiences of North America's Indigenous peoples and, in turn, their identity development.

The existence and value of two-spirit people's difference is recognized in most Indigenous American cultures, oral histories, and traditions. In some cultures, two-spirit people were thought to be born "in balance," which may be understood as androgyny, a balance of masculine and feminine qualities, of male and female spirits. In many

Indigenous American cultures, two-spirit people had (have) specific spiritual roles and responsibilities within their community. They are often seen as "bridge makers" between male and female, the spiritual and the material, between Indigenous American and non-Indigenous American. The term two-spirit encompasses the wide variety of social meanings that are attributed to sexuality and gender roles across Indigenous American cultures. Many gay historians, anthropologists, and other researchers have struggled with the "epistemological differences in Native American concepts of gender and sexual behaviors" (Tafoya 1990:287) and veered into dangerous generalizations about the specialness and spiritual power of two-spirit people. Today, academics argue over whether or not two-spirit people had a "special" role or were special people in Native societies. In my community, the act of declaring some people special threatens to separate them from their community and creates an imbalance. Traditionally, two-spirit people were simply a part of the entire community; as we reclaim our identity with this name, we are returning to our communities.

Since European contact with the Americas, many of these Indigenous American traditions have been misrepresented and misinterpreted. Within an imposed construct based on eighteenth-century European values, difference became deviance (D'Emilio and Freedman 1988; Jacobs and Cromwell 1992; Tafoya 1990; Williams 1986). It is difficult to understand the concept of two-spirit from these perspectives. Within the European American perspective, the male and female genders are the only two acknowledged. Transsexuals who surgically alter their bodies to become physically the "opposite" sex, individuals who choose to dress in clothing thought to be only appropriate for the "opposite" gender, or those who choose not to adhere to either of the dichotomous gender types are seen as abnormal and, therefore, as deviant.

Cartesian definitions of gender, which impose dual roles defining the respective "acceptable behaviors" for women and men, have procreation as their ultimate goal (Jacobs and Cromwell 1992). These notions of gender categorization have been misapplied to Indigenous Americans. For European explorers, philosophers, and anthropologists, too many Indigenous American people did not fit into the two categories found in Cartesian theories.

The anthropologist Sue-Ellen Jacobs has reconstructed her own notions about gender and sexual identity. In her ethnographic observations of Tewa Pueblo people, she observed a number of gender categories reflecting an individual's "sexuality, sexual identity and sociocultural roles" (Jacobs and Cromwell 1992:48). This conception of gender reflects a fluid understanding of sexual identity that has persisted for many present-day Indigenous Americans who consider themselves bisexual, rather than strictly lesbian or gay (Tafoya 1990).

Traditional teachings, however, have also been influenced by events that have altered the construction of sexual identity in contemporary Indigenous American communities. In an attempt to assimilate Indigenous Americans, government policy has been directly involved in the destruction of many aspects of Indigenous American life (Ross 1992; York 1990). For almost one hundred years it was illegal to practice traditional religion in both the United States (Deloria 1969) and Canada (Cardinal 1969; Miller 1989). Generations of children were forcibly removed from their families and placed in residential schools, where they were punished for speaking their own language, for practicing their own religion, or for any other expressions of their "Indian-ness" (Berkhofer 1978; Ing 1991; York 1990). In spite of these assaults on traditional values, they still shape the lives and communities of Indigenous American people. Today, most leaders in Indigenous communities express a commitment to traditional spirituality and an Indigenous worldview.

## INDIGENOUS ETHICS

Our worldviews are shaped by our values, our ideologies, theories, and assumptions about the world. They circumscribe our encounters with the world, creating and re-creating our cultures and our epistemologies, pedagogies, psychologies, and experiences. How are Indigenous American worldviews constructed?

The Mohawk psychiatrist Clare Brant, in his work with Iroquois, Ojibway, and Swampy Cree people, has identified five ethics that, he believes, underpin these Indigenous people's worldview (1990). These cultural ethics and rules of behavior include: an Ethic of Non-Interference, an Ethic That Anger Not Be Shown, an Ethic Respecting Praise and Gratitude, the Conservation-Withdrawal Tactic, and the Notion That Time Must Be Right. As Brant himself points out, these Ethics cannot be assumed to describe all Indigenous American people. At the same time, these Ethics resonate deeply with me and describe the emotional substance of much of my own experiences in the Cree community. Although Indigenous American cultures have changed since first contact with Europeans, and continue to change, it is important to realize that these traditionally based Ethics exist in some form today and will persist in some form into the future. Brant's Ethics are further developed by Rupert Ross (1992) in his book *Dancing with a Ghost: Exploring Indian Reality*, which includes an important reminder:

> Until we realize that Native people have a highly developed, formal, but radically different set of cultural imperatives, we are likely to continue misinterpreting their acts, misperceiving the real problems they face, and imposing, through government policies, potentially harmful "remedies" (p. 42).

These Ethics shape our worldview and direct our behavior. The Ethic of Non-Interference refers to the expectation that Indigenous Americans should not interfere in any way with another person. This has shaped culturally distinctive childrearing practices in Indigenous American communities. Generally, children are allowed to explore the world without the limitations of punishment and praise, or of privileges withheld and rewards promised by members of the community. Children are taught through the patient practice of modeling, by stories, and by example. There are unwritten rules against giving advice or telling someone what to do (Ross 1992; B. Wilson, personal communication).

The Ethic That Anger Not Be Shown is demonstrated by the absence of emphasis on or displays of emotions in speech and other forms of communication by Indigenous American people. Implicit in this ethic is a prohibition against showing grief and sorrow. Ross goes so far as to say that it is not acceptable even to *think* about one's own confusion and turmoil; in this way, one does not "burden" others with one's own personal emotional stress. The Ethic Respecting Praise and Gratitude may appear as a lack of affect to a non-Indigenous observer. Rather than vocally expressing gratitude to someone, a person might simply ask the other to continue their contribution, because voicing appreciation may be taken by an Indigenous American as creating an embarrassing scene. Because the idea of community is inherent in the Indigenous American philosophy and existence, an egalitarian notion of place within a society exists. To call attention to one person is to single them out and to imply that they have done better or are better in some way or at something than others are.

The Conservation-Withdrawal Tactic emphasizes the need to prepare mentally before choosing to act. Thinking things through before trying them or thinking thoughts through before voicing them is seen as a well-calculated preservation of physical and psychic energy. According to Ross (1992), the more unfamiliar the new context, the more pronounced a withdrawal into stillness, silence, and consideration may become. This concern that time should be taken to reflect on the possible outcomes of a particular action and to prepare emotionally and spiritually for a chosen course of action is reflected in the Notion That Time Must Be Right. Attention to the spiritual world gives a person the opportunity to examine her or his state of mind before initiating or participating in the task at hand (Ross 1992).

Additionally, an important part of Indigenous American traditional spirituality is paying respect to our ancestors, to those who died tens of thousands of years ago as well as those who have just recently entered the spirit world. The land that we live on today is made up of our ancestors; the food that we eat (for the most part) is grown from the soil that our ancestors went back to when they died; and the animals and plants in our world have also grown out of and been nourished by this soil. We thank the spirits of animals, minerals, and plants, and turn to them for strength and continuity. This gratitude helps to maintain or regain the balance that is necessary to be a healthy and complete person. We understand that the spiritual, physical, emotional, and intellectual parts of ourselves are equally important and interrelated. When one aspect of a person is unhealthy, the entire person is affected. This too is true for the entire community; when one aspect of the community is missing, the entire community will suffer in some way.

## SOME CURRENT MODELS OF SEXUAL IDENTITY AND DEVELOPMENT

Within the context of these basic principles, identity development can be examined. How do these ethics become incorporated into who we are or whom we identify as? What impact do they have on our responses to experiences? How do they shape our identities? For Indigenous American Nations now in contact with European American culture, racism and homophobia are inevitably present to some degree. Currently, the way some Indigenous Americans deal with homophobia and racism and the way that they construct their sexual and racial identity is framed by an Indigenous American spirituality and worldview.

This traditional Indigenous worldview can inform current theories of sexual and racial identity development for theorists and educators. I will examine three developmental theories, one of which addresses sexual identity, another racial identity, and a third sexual and/or racial identity. Sexual identity formation is typically presented in stage theory models. In her book *Psychotherapy with Lesbian Clients: Theory into Practice*, psychologist Kristine Falco (1991) presents a review of theory on lesbian identity formation.[4] Finding many similarities in the five models she examines, Falco sketches a generalized model for the sexual identity development of lesbians by combining and summarizing others' models. In the first stage, a person is aware of being different and begins to wonder why. In the

second phase, she begins to acknowledge her homosexual feelings and may tell others. Sexual experimentation marks the next stage, as the person explores relationships while seeking a supportive community. She then begins to learn to function in a same-sex relationship, establishing her place in the lesbian subculture while passing as heterosexual when needed. In the final stage, she integrates her private and social identities.

Racial identity development theory examines the psychological implications of membership in a racial group and the resultant ideologies. William Cross's Black Racial Identity Development model is often assumed to represent the racial identity formation experience of people of color in general (Tatum 1992, 1993). Cross's model representing the racial identity formation experience of people of color in general doesn't hold for Indigenous Americans. In the Preencounter stage, which is described in the model as the initial point, an individual is unaware or denies that race plays any part in the definition of who they are. Thereafter, they move through a predictable series of stages: Encounter, after a sequence of events forces them to realize that racism does affect their life; Immersion/Emmersion, as they respond by immersing themselves in their culture, and reject with anger the values of the dominant culture; Internalization, as they develop security in their identity as a person of color; and Internalization/Commitment, when they have acquired a positive sense of racial identity (Cross, Parham, and Helms 1991; Tatum 1992, 1993).

Susan Barrett (1990) offers a developmental theory that attempts to encompass the experiences of all "others," including those of us who have been "othered" because of racial and sexual identity. This is the five-stage Minority Identity Development Model, which Barrett suggests can be applied to anyone who is not part of the dominant European American male heterosexual culture. In the Conformity stage, a person is ashamed of her membership in a minority culture, and accepts the devaluing judgments of the dominant culture. In the Dissonance stage, she wants to express her membership in a minority culture, but is still restricted by discomfort with it. She then moves into a Resistance and Immersion stage, as she becomes aware of the positive value of her membership in a minority culture and rejects the dominant culture. Following immersion in her minority culture, she enters an Introspective period, as she realizes that she cannot express herself fully within the constraints of an isolated minority identity. Finally, in the stage Barrett calls Synergetic Articulation and Awareness, she finds self-fulfillment when she integrates her minority identity into all aspects of her life.

Each of the above identity development models was constructed in an attempt to fill some gaps in developmental psychology. They attempt to recognize the diversity of human experience by describing the developmental sequences that occur in response to the experience and context of homophobia or racism. They do not, however, describe the effects of the *simultaneous* experience of homophobia and racism. These models assume an availability of supportive experiences that provide the means for an individual to progress from one stage to the next. Although each of these models is claimed to be non-linear and nonhierarchic, each posits a final stage that represents a developmental peak of mental health. In this self-actualized stage, a person's sexual identity is no longer problematic and their bicultural adaptation (comfortably being the "other" within the dominant culture) has become a source of empowerment. Therefore, the underlying assumption is that a supportive bicultural experience is available to all "others." We (two-spirits) become self-actualized when we become what we've always been, empowered by our location in our communities (versus the micro-management of an individuated identity).

## INDIGENOUS AMERICAN PERSPECTIVES ON SEXUAL AND RACIAL IDENTITY

Despite the relationship between sexual and racial identity development presented in European American models, for Indigenous American lesbian, gay, or bisexual people, the effects of racism and homophobia cannot be separated from each other or from the rest of their experiences. The emphasis of the Indigenous American worldview on the interconnectedness of all aspects of an individual's life challenges the compartmentalized structure of developmental stage models. As Pueblo psychologist and educator Terry Tafoya states, "[D]etermination of an individual's identity on the basis of sexual behavior makes no conceptual sense to many American Indians" (1989:288). That is, any presentation of sexual and racial identity development as two distinct phenomena and any analysis proceeding from that assumption cannot adequately describe the experiences of Indigenous American people.

Furthermore, Indigenous Americans may respond to homophobia and racism in markedly different ways than people from other cultures. For example, if she respects the Ethic That Anger Not Be Shown, she may appear not to react to the "isms" that affect her. If she uses the Conservation-Withdrawal Tactic or the Notion That Time Must Be Right in her response, the strength of her resistance might not be recognized. Also, the Ethic of Non-Interference would require her friends and family to respect and trust the choices she makes . . . .

## RETURNING PRACTICE TO THEORY

Last summer, I was part of a gathering of two-spirit people. When I first arrived, I was cautious. Everyone seemed cautious, as though we were all unsure of how we should act. On the wall of the main cabin a sign was posted: it said, "pow-wow, Saturday night." When I read it, I felt dizzy, overwhelmed by my imagining what the dance might be. Two-spirit people dancing. I have lived with dreams of dancing, dreams where I spin around, picking up my feet. I have many feathers on my arms and my body and I know all the steps. I turn into an eagle. Arms extended, I lift off the ground and begin to fly around in big circles. Would this be my chance?

For the rest of the week I listened for tidbits about the pow-wow. I learned that a local drum group would be singing. I heard about a woman who was collecting her regalia—"Her regalia . . . "—and wondered, did that mean men's? I waited patiently for Saturday night to come. Listening.

When the drumming started, I was sitting still, listening and watching. The first people to dance were women. They had their shawls with them. Next, some men came in; they were from different Nations, but still danced in distinctively male styles. I watched with disappointment in my heart but said to myself that I would still enjoy the pow-wow. And then a blur flew by me and landed inside the circle of dancers that had formed. It was a man in a jingle dress. He was beautiful and he knew how to dance and he danced as a woman. It was a two-spirit dancing as it should be. After that, more two-spirits drifted into the circle. I sat and watched, my eyes edged with tears. I knew my ancestors were with me; I had invited them. We sat and watched all night, proud of our sisters and brothers, yet jealous of their bravery. The time for the last song came. Everybody had to dance. I entered the circle, feeling the drumbeat in my heart. The songs came back to me. I circled the dance area, in my most humble moment, with the permission of my ancestors, my eleven-year-old two-spirit steps returned to me.

The aspect of my own experience (and that of my two-spirit friends) that current sexual and racial identity development models cannot encompass is that my strength and identity, along with the strength and identity of my peers, is inseparable from our culture. Educators and school counselors need to acknowledge that this is the reality for our community. This means that we need to stop assuming that all lesbian and gay people can find support in mainstream gay culture, and that we make a point of creating opportunities for two-spirit indigenous people to find their place in their traditional communities. There has been little research done on the developmental experiences of Indigenous American people, and there is almost no research on the experiences of two-spirit people, despite grim statistics that reveal the urgency of addressing the needs of these groups. Gay and lesbian youth are two to six times more likely to attempt suicide than heterosexual teens (Kroll and Warneke 1995), and Indigenous Canadians have the highest suicide rate of any racial group in the world (York 1990).

Whenever possible, we need to ensure that two-spirit youth have access to the history and unwritten knowledge of their community, and that it is available to them in a culturally congruous way. Educators can also easily access written texts by important Indigenous American leaders, such as Beatrice Medicine (1983), Terry Tafoya (1989, 1990), Chrystos (1988, 1991, 1993), Connie Fife (1992, 1993), and Beth Brant (1985, 1988, 1991, 1993, 1995). These authors ground their work in their identities as Indigenous Americans, and they offer insight into the historic and present-day realities of two-spirit people. Tafoya's work as a psychologist and educator has made invaluable contributions to an effective approach to AIDS education for Indigenous American people. Two-spirit writers such as Chrystos, Connie Fife, and Beth Brant provide stories and narrative texts that record the contemporary life of two-spirit people. Their body of work is a rich resource for identity development theorists, and an invaluable affirmation for two-spirit youth.

Educators and developmental theorists need to study the resistance, strength, and liberation strategies two-spirit people employ as part of their development of an empowered identity. By examining the meaning of these strategies relative to an Indigenous American worldview, educators and theorists can increase their awareness in a way that will inevitably have a spill-over effect. They will learn to look beyond the limits inscribed by mainstream lesbian and gay culture and into the lives of the women, men, and children who are lesbian, gay, and two-spirit. We, whether educators, Indigenous Americans, or two-spirit people, must abandon the assumptions of a European American worldview in order to understand the identity development of two-spirit Native American and Canadian First Nations people, and to develop our theory and practice from within that understanding.

## DISCUSSION QUESTIONS

1. How does Wilson's reading challenge theories of identity development found in the Markus reading (Reading 15) or in the Howard and Alamilla reading (Reading 16)?

2. Explain why the Cree concept of two-spirit people neither fits Western concepts of homosexuality nor harmonizes with the contemporary gay and lesbian cultural movements. Provide examples from the reading to support your analysis.

## NOTES

1. The term "Indigenous American" in this article refers to Canadian First Nations and Native American peoples. I acknowledge that, in a sense, this term presents our diverse cultures and communities as monolithic. However, my use of the term here is an appeal to the commonality of our origins and colonial/post-colonial experiences.

2. The term "two-spirit" will be used in this article to describe lesbian, gay, and bisexual Indigenous Americans.

3. The Cree Nation spreads in a wide swath across central Canada, from Quebec in the east, west through Ontario and Manitoba along the James and Hudson Bays, across Saskatchewan to the plains of Alberta, and south from there into northern Montana. Most of these communities are located in remote areas. I am from the Opaskwayak Cree Nation, located five hundred miles north of the border between the United States and Canada. The Cree Nations form one of the largest groups of Indigenous people in North America. There are over twenty-three Cree dialects.

4. I choose Falco because lesbian identity formation theory is the most appropriate focus for the use of my own narrative as a critique of contemporary developmental theory. Theorists who describe the developmental stages of gay men's sexual identity use similarly structured models (e.g., Coleman, 1982).

# 18

# "I'M AN AMERICAN WITH A JAPANESE LOOK"

## Emerging Identities and Practices

MIA TUAN

*While the previous reading by Alex Wilson examines how Native Americans construct their racial and sexual identities, this reading by Mia Tuan examines how Asian Americans often are not given much choice in how they construct their ethnic identities. Tuan, a sociologist by training, is a professor in the education studies department and the director of the Center on Diversity and Community at the University of Oregon. Her research focuses on racial and ethnic identity development, Asian transracial adoption, and multicultural organizational development. This excerpt is taken from Tuan's 1998 book,* Forever Foreigners or Honorary Whites? The Asian Ethnic Experience Today, *for which Tuan interviewed a number of Asian Americans about their experiences with ethnicity. Her respondents often equate whiteness with being American, while white Americans perceive Asian Americans as foreigners.*

In this chapter I discuss the ways ethnicity has retained meaning in the lives of our respondents. The cultural values and practices that are salient to them, however, are more Chinese American, Japanese American, and increasingly Asian American in orientation than traditionally Chinese or Japanese. They were raised within emergent and hyphenated cultural environments, and it is to these that our respondents show genuine allegiance.

But there are also involuntary reasons why they continue to identify in ethnic and, increasingly, racial terms. Our respondents do not believe they have the option of doing away with ethnic or racial labels since these remain salient markers to others, influencing how they are defined, responded to, and treated. Furthermore, they believe the unhyphenated label, *American*, is reserved for describing white ethnics and would not be accepted by others if used to describe themselves. This belief is based on personal experiences with intentional prejudice, stereotyping, and a general perception that Asian Americans are seen as a population composed of recent immigrants. This, in turn, has implications for their own attitudes and feelings toward Asian immigrants . . . .

## "IT DOESN'T MAKE ME ANY LESS OF AN ASIAN PERSON BECAUSE I CAN'T SPEAK THE LANGUAGE": EVOLVING CULTURAL VALUES AND PRACTICES

Despite all of the ways ethnicity has ceased to influence their daily lives, our respondents do consider ethnicity a salient aspect of their identity. What matters to them, however, has increasingly little to do with cultural traditions as practiced by Chinese and Japanese nationals. Instead, their focus rests squarely on the evolving cultural patterns being generated in this society by Japanese American, Chinese American, and other Asian American groups. The cultural elements they feel are worth retaining are the emergent as well as reinterpreted values and practices they grew up with that weave together strands of Japanese, Chinese, and American mainstream cultures. Lisa Lowe (1996) speaks to this theme when she writes: "The making of Asian American culture includes practices that are partly inherited, partly modified, as well as partly invented" (p. 65).

Greg Okinaka, a Sansei in his twenties, was particularly insightful about the dynamic character of culture. He describes his philosophy here:

*I mean, I think it is very important for the next generation, the younger, the next bunch of people to realize . . . I think there's such a specific Japanese, no,*

*not Japanese, well, Asian American [pause] culture that has evolved and that is in the process of evolving [and] that it's more important to learn about that than it is to learn about . . . I mean because the Asia, the Japan that my parents knew when they were my age was a completely different Japan than I know at my current age. And it's gonna be a different Japan that any other generations learn fifteen or twenty years from now.*

Greg is speaking of a "homegrown" culture and identity that reflect the cultural frames of reference influencing his life, and his pride as well as defensiveness about that developing identity are important features. It is more important, he thinks, to be well versed in the culture that is evolving here in the United States (which is increasingly panethnic in orientation) than in Japan's culture, a value he acquired from his parents and continues to uphold in his own life.

Greg's interpretation of culture as a dynamic medium was shared by many others. Gary Hong, for instance, was only interested in maintaining cultural practices that held meaning for him:

*In culture I basically [pause] it's important. But the traditions, I'm not into doing customs just for the sake of doing customs. That's sort of silly. Just because they've been around for a long time that people do it. Like lighting incense and bowing three times. Just because they do it for the hell of it doesn't mean a damn thing to me. I could really care less. I think it's important to be educated, to know why people do it and to know that people do it.*

Similarly, while Jan Muramoto acknowledged she would like to know more about Japanese cultural traditions, it did not make her any "less Asian" simply because she did not:

*I took three years of Spanish to qualify for college because it was easier, and you know, people say to me all the time, don't you feel guilty? And I say, you know, you can't live your life feeling guilty. It doesn't make me any less of an Asian person because I can't speak the language. It doesn't make me any less of a person because I don't make sushi. There are other things that*

*I teach my children. I mean my parents didn't speak Japanese at home. They spoke English to us . . . . We speak English at home. We live in this country. We speak English.*

Jan is clearly defensive about her authenticity as an "Asian person" because she has been challenged on this issue before. She is rebelling against a static definition that stipulates that unless she is fluent in Japanese and can make sushi, she is not "really Japanese." She prefers a more fluid interpretation of culture since that is how she was brought up to understand it herself.

### "When I'm With My Caucasian Friends It Seems Like There's Less in Common": A Preference for Asian American and Coethnic Friends

One cultural value modified to reflect the boundary shifts taking place among different Asian ethnic groups includes their preference for ethnic friendships. While clearly not a new cultural value, our respondents have put their own twist on it by expanding the category panethnically to include Asian Americans more generally. Less than a fifth described their friends as consisting exclusively of coethnics, but more than a third have friendship circles consisting primarily of other Asian Americans; the remainder describe their friends as racially diverse or primarily white.

Those with predominantly Asian American friends claim to share a special bond or sense of kinship with them that they do not necessarily experience with non-Asians. Barry Sato:

*It was easier to hang out with Asians. Thing is, when you talk about things, your experiences and values seem to mesh a little bit more.*

References were repeatedly made to perceived similarities between themselves and their Asian American friends based on similar up-bringing, parental expectations, values, and even experiences with stereotyping and intentional prejudice, discrimination, and marginalization. These shared experiences, as Laura Nee remarked, result in comfortable interactions: "There's less explaining because we were brought up pretty much the same." Whereas in the past this sentiment would have extended only to coethnics, today it increasingly applies to other Asian Americans irrespective of ethnicity, a finding that concurs with their attitudes toward inter-ethnic dating and marriage. This sense of camaraderie does not extend to Asian immigrants, however, unless they are far along in their acculturation process, as will be discussed below.

Since most live in racially diverse or predominantly white communities, the question of where these friendships develop naturally arises. Some were forged during their youth in school, sports leagues, church, and the neighborhood. It seems the efforts of their parents years earlier did not go to waste since close friendships were formed in the very places their families hoped they would. As adults, they meet other Asian Americans in a variety of settings. Because of their concentration in the San Francisco and Los Angeles areas, they do not need to look very far to find Asian Americans.

As often happened during their childhood, the activities they engage in with their Asian American friends are not ethnically centered in any traditional sense. As later-generation Americans, they are highly acculturated and participate in many of the same activities as other Californians despite race or ethnicity. About a third are members of one or more organized ethnic activities. Especially popular among younger respondents are Asian American sports leagues from which there are myriad to choose: J.A.V.A. (Japanese American Volleyball Association), the Westside Volleyball League, and the L.A. Asian Ski Club, to name only a few. Some have also joined college fraternities and sororities and other campus groups geared toward Asian American students. For professionals, a wide range of business networks and employee associations where members share both classes and ethnic resources (e.g., Asian Professional Exchange [A.P.E.X.], Asian Business League [A.B.L.O], Asian American Journalist Association, Young Generation Asian Professionals [Y.G.A.P.], Asian Business Association [A.B.A.], M Society, and Orange County Chinese American Chamber of Commerce are available. Vo's (1996) research, for example, on the San Diego branch of the A.B.A. explains how members develop business opportunities and deal with issues such as glass ceilings in the workplace and trade with the Pacific Rim. And, of course, membership in long-standing political interest groups such as the Japanese American Citizens League (J.A.C.L.) and the Organization of Chinese Americans (O.C.A.) is common, as is church attendance in predominantly Asian congregations.

In this sense, our respondents are carrying on a tradition dating back to an earlier period of racism and social exclusion. Because native-born Asian Americans were barred from participating in mainstream clubs and activities with white children, community leaders took it upon themselves to sponsor their own chapters and clubs to meet their children's needs (Chan 1991). Many of these clubs have survived to the present day and, while no longer forced to participate in ethnically specific leagues, many choose to do so out of family tradition or sense of comfort.

### Wiener Teriyaki, the Culinary Future?

Another cultural value that has been maintained yet also altered is an appreciation for ethnic food. Despite some drop-off, a surprisingly resilient number continue to eat some version of Chinese or Japanese food on a regular or semiregular basis. While a few still put in the effort to cook "authentic" meals, most simply go to restaurants. Carol Wong prepares Chinese food more regularly than others, but acknowledged that the abundant availability of Chinese restaurants in the Bay Area was a real bonus:

*I cook Chinese food around three times a week. But we go out to eat. I mean, around here you can go out. So we have to choose like what do we want. Do we want Little Hong Kong? Do we want Sun Hong Kong? Do we want Little Golden Dynasty for down-home Cantonese cooking?*

Not only are they free to sample different regional cuisines within one ethnicity (in Carol's case, Chinese), they can easily explore the foods of different Asian groups (Thai, Korean, Filipino, Lao,

Hmong, Vietnamese, Malaysian, Singaporean, Cambodian). The gastronomic possibilities are endless. By virtue of living in the San Francisco Bay Area and southern California, areas with the largest and most diverse Asian populations in the United States and, thus, best selection of restaurants, they have the good fortune to be able to sample from a wide range of authentic cuisines.

More commonly, however, they prepare quick and novel versions of ethnic dishes or use Asian ingredients to make what would otherwise be American dishes. The most common complaint for not cooking traditional dishes is the time and difficulty involved in preparing quality Chinese or Japanese food. Nevertheless, preferences for certain Chinese and Japanese spices, sauces, and condiments they grew up eating are hard to quell. This is why during a last-minute rush to prepare a meal, they are more inclined to grab a bottle of soy sauce rather than steak sauce to pour over some hamburger. They are continuing a practice started by their parents and kin of modifying ethnic dishes to fit their lifestyles and food tastes.

Rice continues to be a staple food for many, although even here there is evidence of change. Laura Hong, a fifth-generation Chinese American, provides an example: "We always have Chinese rice at [my parents'] home, but I have a lot of Japanese friends who eat sticky rice, and I like sticky rice, so I make that more." As our respondents are moving toward embracing a panethnic identity and befriending other Asian Americans, they are also sampling other cuisines and expanding their taste preferences. Arnie Kumamoto and his Japanese American wife, for example, are just as likely to prepare stir-fry meals in a wok, traditionally considered a Chinese practice, as they are to prepare Japanese food:

*My wife and I eat [Japanese] about twice a week. But see, it's not considered real Japanese food like people you expect from Japan to eat. I think we kind of eat, we mix things around. We throw on the Chinese food and the Japanese food and throw on a steak or something. We do a lot of stir-fry. The steaks are always stir-fry. We cook things out of a wok. Most of the time we eat steamed rice instead of bread. We have that for breakfast with eggs, etc. But it's a little hard to say what's Japanese . . . . Sometimes we get some sushi and have it, eat out late and have some [pause] soup that would be Japanese [pause] but a lot we just mix things.*

This passage nicely captures the mixing and melding taking place for this young couple as they carve out a lifestyle of their own. Arnie and his wife feel at ease in reinterpreting, combining, and borrowing from a variety of culinary sources. Some Japanese elements have been retained, some Chinese elements added, and some American influences (steak) modified to suit their individual preferences.

### "I'm Not Your Typical American When People Think American": Identity Options and Constraints

A third cultural value our respondents adhere to . . . is they believe that having pride in their emerging identities is more important than to be knowledgeable of cultural traditions, a theme that has also surfaced in studies of white ethnicity (Alba 1990; Gans 1979; Kellogg 1990; Waters 1990).

Whereas whites can capriciously base identity choices on nothing more than "a sense that it is nicer to be an X, rather than a Y" (Alba 1990: 62), the choices available to Asian ethnics are markedly more circumscribed. Most identify in hyphenated terms as Chinese American, Japanese American, and, increasingly, Asian American. Cathy Leong, who identifies as an Asian American, explained her choice:

*For myself I have more Japanese, Korean, Filipino friends, just through work and the people we associate with, you know, my co-workers and stuff like that. So I think there's more of an emphasis on Asian American.*

As more individuals come to think of themselves as members of a general family of Asian Americans and associate accordingly, they are more likely to embrace the panethnic label to describe themselves. Since the bulk of her friends are other Asians, Cathy feels more comfortable reinforcing the bond between them all, their common race, and thus downplaying ethnic differences.

Emily Woo, who also identifies as an Asian American, does so because it encompasses both her Chinese and Japanese roots:

**Q:**   *How do you identify yourself?*

**A:**   *That's a really hard question actually. I guess as an Asian American. I don't consider myself just Japanese, just Chinese. I don't consider myself just American. I don't know. I kinda like terminology like Asian American and African American because it's kinda messy . . . . By blood, I'm Chinese and Japanese. By culture, I don't know if I am so much of either. I don't know . . . . Mom would always tell me I used to get confused growing up. "How can I be Japanese and Chinese and American?" "Well, you are half Japanese, half Chinese, and all American."*

For Emily, identifying along racial lines as an Asian American eliminates the cumbersome task of acknowledging both components of her ancestry. Her rationale allows a glimpse into how future generations of mixed-ancestry Asians may possibly identify.

Tony Lam, also of Chinese and Japanese ancestry, prefers to call himself an American Asian. As the son of a career soldier and a veteran himself, he chooses to emphasize his patriotism to this country by asserting his American identity first. Yet, Tony also expressed great frustration over what could be characterized as a societal "blind spot" to the role Asian Americans have played in this country:

**Q:**   *How do you identify yourself?*

**A:**   *American Asian . . . . I saw that parade in '92 on Hollywood Boulevard and they had veterans marching down [pause]. I tell you which group was missing. Asian. There was not one Chinese, Japanese, Filipino, Korean, Pacific Islander in uniform. Now I know they served [pause]. It's either the fault of those people who plan that parade or the fault due to a lack of vigilance for an Asian veterans organization by not insisting on it [pause] through all hard times. I still persist that I'm an American, but*

*I'm not going to deny that I'm Asian because first thing they're not going to let me do it. I still got to [pause] about Asian culture whether I like it or not . . . . You see, Caucasians must understand that they [pause] put that on us, and we must learn to confront people who say those kinds of things so we should say things like, "No I don't know that, I hope you know your French food. Or, he's Scottish [pause] look, look, what are you? Okay, Armenian. Tell me about Armenian stuff. We should put that on them. I think it's fair, they got to get a taste of what they did or how dumb they sound or who's truly American. Yeah, I am American and then Asian.*

Tony considers himself to be a loyal American who risked his life to defend his country. The irony, however, is that there are others who do not consider the United States to be his country. Even if he chose to identify solely as an American, he believes "they," presumably white Americans, would not legitimate his choice—"they're not going to let me do it."

Others also spoke about the pressures they experienced to identify in ethnic or racial terms. Ted Uyematsu:

**Q:** *How about identifying as just a plain old American?*

**A:** *Yeah I would, but you know [pause] there's [pause] but then again you have to realize that I'm not your typical American when people think American. In your mind you don't see a whole-blooded Japanese guy you know. They conjure up some blond-headed dude that [pause] but I would have no problem seeing myself but I think it would confuse certain people if I were to say that.*

Ted shows a clear understanding of what the typical American male presumably looks like—and he does not even come close. Subsequently, while he had no qualms calling himself an American, Ted believed others might take issue with him since he feels white ethnics feel a sense of proprietary claim

to the term. As such, he was unsure how his usage of the term would be received.

As a compromise, most have chosen a hyphenated identity to honor their American as well as ethnic roots. Victor Ong spoke insightfully about his decision to call himself a Chinese American:

*Usually I say Chinese American because I realize I'm not Chinese. People from China come over here and like, whoa, they're like a foreign species. And I'm not American because just one look and I'm apart. I used to struggle with this question a lot and to make a long story short, Chinese American is a hybrid of its own. It's kind of like Afro Americans. Boy, they're not African and they're not American, and it's just its own species, and that's the way it is.*

Victor did not feel comfortable describing himself in strictly ethnic terms as Chinese because he does not identify with Chinese immigrants. But he also sensed that identifying solely as an American was problematic—he did not believe that others would accept his choice since "just one look and I'm apart." In other words, he believed his physical features did not conform to commonly accepted notions of what a "real" American looked like.

Others were even more direct in stating how inappropriate *in other people's eyes* it would be if they were to identify as Americans without any hyphenation. Rick Wubara and Kevin Fong explain why they identify as Japanese American and Chinese American, respectively:

**[Rick]:** *I don't think I can be just American just for the fact that I look different from the typical American, white. [Why not just Japanese then?] Because I definitely am Americanized, an American raised in America. And I don't always agree with what Japanese, Japan stands for.*

**[Kevin]:** *First and foremost I was born Chinese, and this goes back to what my brother told me one time. He said, and I totally related with that, "You're born Chinese, but when you're around Chinese people,*

*like when I'm around real Chinese
people, they don't think I'm Chinese
because I was born here, and I'm kind of
Americanized. And if I call myself an
American, I hang around with American
guys, they don't consider me American
because I don't look American, I'm
Chinese. So I would say that I'm Chinese
American first and foremost. I was born
Chinese, and I'm proud of that but I'm
also proud that I'm an American of the
United States.*

"I don't look American." "I'm not your typical American." "I'm not Chinese . . . and I'm not American." These statements vividly convey the dilemma our respondents, as racialized ethnics, face. They have learned by watching how others respond to them that this society views them as outsiders. Despite being longtime Americans, they are not perceived as such since they do not fit the image of what a "real" American looks like (Espiritu 1992; Jiobu 1988; Lowe 1996; Nagel 1994). This, I believe, is the key difference separating the white ethnic from the Asian ethnic experience. While white ethnics must actively assert their ethnic uniqueness if they wish this to feature prominently in their interactions with others, Asian ethnics are assumed to be foreign unless proven otherwise.

## "That's When I Knew I Was Chinese": The Realization of Difference

*No one ever asks a Polish American after the first
generation why they don't speak Polish or are they
ashamed of being Polish because they don't speak
Polish. But [they will say] that you're ashamed of
being Chinese, or you don't understand Chinese
culture because you don't speak Chinese. But no one
ever asks that of anybody else. I mean if your
grandparents speak French, and you still cook coq au
vin, but no one ever demands that you also know how
to speak French. And no one ever asks you, where did
you come from.*

The frustration Carol Wong experiences is hard to miss in this passage. She believes a double standard is operating. While white ethnics are free to discard their ethnic links and merge with the American mainstream after the first generation, Asian ethnics do not have this option; an assumption of foreignness stubbornly clings to them despite generational status.

Carol was not alone in her way of thinking. Others concurred with her assessment of the status difference between Asians and whites. Based on their experiences with prejudice, discrimination, and stereotyping, they understand that the public is unable or unwilling to distinguish between Asian ethnics and immigrants. That our respondents, residents of such diverse and cosmopolitan areas as Los Angeles and San Francisco, still feel this way is telling. Subsequently, our respondents believe their status in this society is vulnerable to changing social, political, and economic conditions beyond their personal control (Nishi 1989). For instance, the majority agree their lives would be affected not only if the United States was to go to war with their country of origin but if war was declared on *any* Asian country since "whites or blacks can't tell the difference between Asian Americans and Asians." Carol Wong again:

*When there was all the whoop-de-do about Japan and
all the businesses that Japan owns and all the property
that Japan owns in this country, [while] England,
Canada, and the Netherlands own a whole lot more
individually than Japan ever did. But it was this thing
of the Pacific horde. And of course American car
companies screwed up, and they had to blame it on
someone else.*

Respondents frequently made references to Japan and Middle Eastern "bashing" as well as the wartime internment of Japanese Americans to substantiate their views. And while not everybody believed that a mass internment sanctioned by the federal government could happen again, most agreed that hostilities from the general citizenry were likely. Friends and co-workers who knew them as individuals probably would not act differently, but strangers and nativists certainly would. As Jonathan Tse put it, "They'd see us as being evil, and they'd start, it's just like what they do with the Middle East and the Soviet Union. They would all look down on us."

Would the lives of white ethnics be affected if war was declared on their country or countries of origin? Most answered no. Morrison Hum, who was required to wear a badge identifying himself as Chinese during World War II, looked to the past to substantiate his opinion:

**Q:** *If [the] U.S. were to go to war with Europe . . . .*

**A:** *Probably not, because they are considered white. I don't believe so. Like the Germans [pause] but you stand out because you are colored. It would make you feel bad too. Feel ashamed of your native country.*

Whiteness, once again, is equated with being American; Asianness is not. And because Asianness is not, questions regarding their loyalty to this country are raised. This was the case during World War II, and many of our respondents believe this is still the case today. Daphne Kitano:

**Q:** *If [the] U.S. were to go to war with Europe . . . .*

**A:** *No, because it didn't really happen to Germans in World War II, and they were our enemies, and the Italians were our enemy, and it didn't happen to them, you know, which leads me to believe the obvious, that it was just on the basis of the color of your skin. If you weren't white, and you were Japanese, and even though you were American, you were still the enemy . . . . I still feel there's some trend that the media is generating about how Japanese are taking over the United States or buying out everything, which is totally not the real case. They're not looking at the investments that England has in the United States, or the Canadians or Australians, the Dutch, the Germans. And I was like, you know, the media say all these things about Japanese taking over and it [pause] it's*

*going to affect me here, a Japanese American, because the ignorant white person isn't going to [pause] it's going to be like, "Oh you're just one of those Japanese who are trying to take over." So they don't realize the effect, the effect on how people view Asians in this country.*

As for the possibility of another mass internment, opinions were mixed. About one third did not believe it could happen again. Some felt the country had learned its lesson and would not repeat the mistakes made with Japanese Americans. References were made to how "times have changed," as indicated by interest in multicultural issues and greater respect for human rights. Others referred to the growing political power of Asian American organizations that would fight against such actions. Still a third response, captured by Greg Okinaka's comments, suggests that the imprisonment of the spirit may be more damaging than that of the flesh:

*I don't think they'd be sending mass people to prison, but if something like a war came up with the Japanese, you would be getting a lot more widespread discrimination. It's more like a mental internment than an actual physical internment, understand?*

The rest either conceded internment was possible but unlikely or adamantly agreed that mass incarceration was not only possible but probable if the political situation became volatile enough.

In response to the question, "Does it mean something different to say you are an American of Irish (or any European ethnicity) descent compared to saying you are an American of Chinese or Japanese descent?" Morrison Hum had this to say:

*Yeah, there is a difference. They still look at the Chinese as a foreigner. For an Irish American, they don't see him as a foreigner. I don't know how long it is going to take, but you are still looked upon as a foreigner. I think so.*

Diane Okihiro chose to personalize the question by applying it to her Irish American girlfriend and herself. Her response is revealing:

*Like my girlfriend, it's kinda funny because she's of Irish descent, but people would never think that or ask where are you from because they see her as being Caucasian. And if they look at me they would say, "Oh, where are you from," because I'm perceived as being Asian first. It's like girl, an Asian girl, and anything that follows after that. For my girlfriend it would be like, she's white, she's of Irish descent but it doesn't really matter. It's like way down the list of whatever.*

Here Diane refers to her racial distinctiveness as featuring prominently in her interactions with strangers; she believes it is the first aspect of her identity to register with others. This, in turn, triggers an assumption of being from somewhere else, since being Asian is not equated with being from the United States. No one ever thinks to ask her girlfriend of Irish ancestry where she is from, however, because of her white racial background combined with a high degree of acculturation.

## "Where Are You Really From?": Playing the Ethnic Game

Most of our respondents have been asked the question, "Where are you from?" at some point in their lives. All have learned that the question really being asked is, "What is your ancestral homeland?" since answering "San Jose" or "Los Angeles" usually fails to satisfy whoever is asking. Such a localized answer typically results in the response, "No. Where are you *really* from?" While some answer straightforwardly, others choose to play an "ethnic game" with their interrogator. This involves mischievously bantering with whomever is asking the questions until the that person gives up or refines their query. Dani Murayama's and Greg Okinaka's experiences provide excellent examples:

[Dani]:     *A lot of times people will come up to me, and ask me where I'm from, and I'll answer Los Angeles, and they'll look at me really strange [laugh]. But that's where I'm from, and then they'll say, "No, no, no. Where were you born?" And I'll say Los Angeles. And then they'll ask*

*me where my parents were born, and I'll tell them the United States. And then they'll ask me where my grandparents were born, and I'll tell them the United States [laugh].*

[Greg]:     *I get it all the time. I think it's kind of funny because I always say, "I'm from so and so." And then they say, "No. Where are you from?" And then you say, "Well, actually I'm from Oakland." "No. Where are you from?" And then it's like, "Well, I'm from North Dakota, if you want to go there." Then it's like, "No, no, no . . ." [laugh].*

What strikes me about these passages is the insistence on the part of their interrogators to get to the *truth*, to find out where Dani and Greg are *really* from. They were not satisfied with the responses provided because they believed these two had to come from some place other than this country. Dani and Greg, for their parts, were only willing to provide opaque answers as a gesture of defiance.

Tony Lam, who also plays the ethnic game, refuses to give others the satisfaction of pigeonholing him as a foreigner to this country:

*Yeah, I get that all the time. You know what I tell them? I use this tactic now. This guy [was] asking me and I could tell he's really excited [and] he's anticipating the answer. "Will it be Thailand? Will it be Japan?" He's all excited. Maybe he went to the Orient. And I tell him with a perfect look, "San Jose." And all of a sudden he has all his enthusiasm, flustered, and goes, "Oh, San Jose." I'm answering honestly where I came from.*

Some might think Tony, Dani, and Greg are being unnecessarily cheeky and too sensitive to a seemingly innocuous question. After repeatedly facing this line of questioning, however, they have grown impatient with others' needs to categorize them. After all, the answers they provide are truthful given what is being asked. Where are they from? They are from this country, as are their parents, and, in some cases, their grandparents and great-grandparents . . . .

## SUMMARY

As racialized ethnics, our respondents maneuver between a maze of choices and constraints in constructing an identity for themselves. On one hand, they feel constrained to identify in ethnic or racial terms because others continue to define, respond to, and treat them as separate from the American mainstream. Despite their long-standing roots in this country, they understand that others still view them as foreigners and therefore may approach them with curiosity ("I've been to China before" "Where did you learn to speak English so well?" "Tell me about Chinese culture") or hostility ("Go back to your country!" "Stop stealing our jobs!"). As such, identifying solely as an American, they believe, is not an option available to them as yet.

On the other hand, there are signs of resistance and reappropriation as they struggle to work within imposed limitations and fashion an identity that resonates for them. As such, many insist on a hyphenated identity in order to honor their American as well as ethnic roots. The sentiment, "I may be Chinese, but I'm an American too," captures this spirit. Furthermore, as ethnic distinctions matter less and less in the face of an emerging racial consciousness, they are increasingly embracing an Asian American identity (Espiritu 1992; Onishi 1996).

## DISCUSSION QUESTIONS

1. According to Tuan, what is the "maze of choices and constraints" Asian Americans negotiate in crafting a hyphenated identity?
2. To what degree is Espiritu's concept of "pan-Asian" identity applicable to the "emerging identity" practices of Asian Americans?

# 19

# WHAT DOES A WHITE WOMAN LOOK LIKE?

*Racing and Erasing in Law*

KATHERINE M. FRANKE

*This reading by Katherine M. Franke introduces a different frame for understanding identity, in general, and race-ethnicity, in particular. Franke, a professor of law at the University of Arizona College of Law, wrote this piece in 1996 to illustrate the complicated ways in which a legal case can produce a constructed social identity. The Supreme Court case in question is* Sunseri v. Cassagne, *in which the Court was trying to determine the racial identity of Cassagne to see if her 1935 marriage to a white man was legal or not. Cassagne wanted the legal case to uphold her racial identity as white so she could legally divorce her husband and collect alimony. Sunseri, her husband, wanted the legal case to show that Cassagne's race was not white so that he could get the marriage annulled. The Court's deliberations about racial identity are telling, and they reveal that there are significant costs to these constructed identities, including the fact that a person who is defined as not white loses many privileges and benefits of society.*

In significant ways, legal texts produce a narrative of national identity. They weave stories about who we are, what we are committed to, and what we expect of one another, individually and collectively. The concept of justiciability can be understood as a set of rules determining what stories courts are allowed to tell about who we are and who we can be. In this sense, Ronald Dworkin's account of judging as

*Source:* Franke, Katherine. M. 1996. "What Does a White Woman Look Like? Racing and Erasing in Law." *Texas Law Review* 74:1231 (May). Reproduced with permission of Texas Law Review in the format Textbook via Copyright Clearance Center.

writing ongoing chapters in a chain novel provides a compelling conception of law as both describing where we have been and directing where we are going.[1] If the salience of national identity is derived, in significant part, from our membership in an imagined community,[2] then the production of a national symbolic through legal storytelling is an appropriate and legitimate role for courts—particularly in a nation as large as ours. In this process, certain foundational fictions, like "We the People," provide the glue that over time binds a people to its past and to one another as a nation.

But should law play the same role with respect to other aspects of human identity? I think not. Current debates surrounding affirmative action, congressional redistricting, the Million Man March, and the appointment of Clarence Thomas to the Supreme Court all represent cultural flashpoints in an ongoing national discussion about two fundamental questions: what does it mean to have a race or be a member of a particular race, and who has the authority to decide?

In the service of enslaving, segregating, and subordinating African Americans, law has claimed for itself the authoritative license to tell the story of racial meaning in this country—whether by declaring a certain race of people the status of property,[3] by defining as negro any person who has one drop of negro blood,[4] or by determining that race is a factor that may not be taken into account in the distribution of social goods or political rights because our Constitution is color-blind.[5]

Therefore, I have selected *Sunseri v. Cassagne*[6] as my favorite judicial opinion. It represents an absolutely fascinating judicial confrontation with the problems of proof that arise when racial identity is litigated in a manner similar to that of, say, quieting title.[7] In *Sunseri* the Louisiana Supreme Court considered an appeal from a trial court order granting the request of Cyril Sunseri, a white man, that his marriage be annulled because, he maintained, his wife was legally negro. Verna Cassagne, the woman Sunseri married and who all agreed was phenotypically white, sought a divorce and alimony because, she insisted, she was white. In 1935, when the couple was married, the state of Louisiana prohibited and rendered void the marriage of any white person to any person having a trace of negro blood.[8]

The court was thus faced with adjudicating Verna Cassagne's racial identity. It was presented with this problem only because it took it as given that looking like and identifying as a white person did not mean that one was a white person. Several interesting consequences flow from this conception of racial identity: if a person could look white, but not be white, then what does it mean to be white? Could one be white but not look white? Perhaps looking white is a necessary yet not sufficient condition of being white. What does a white woman look like anyway? If phenotype is not what racial identity means, then is how you look a representation of racial identity? If so, a representation of what? Finally, who should decide the answers to any of these questions?

In determining whether Cassagne possessed a trace of negro blood, the court rejected the reliability of Cassagne's white looks and denied her the authority to declare her own race. Thus, the court had to look to other evidence to prove her "true race"—statutorily defined in sanguinary terms. Because there is no scientific test to determine either the racial makeup of particular blood samples or the percentage of a particular kind of racialized blood that a person has in her veins, racial identity quickly reveals itself to be a metaphor, essentialized through the sign of blood. But how does one go about proving a metaphor? By resort to anecdote, of course—anecdote masquerading as objective fact. Given the statute at issue, Cassagne's racial identity was to be resolved atavistically, that is, by focusing upon the racial identity of Verna Cassagne's relatives, particularly her great-great grandmother Fanny Ducre, a slave. Sunseri maintained she was "a full-blooded negress," while Cassagne swore she was an Indian.

Both parties relied heavily on anecdotal testimony to show the race of Cassagne's relatives. Cassagne showed that her mother was christened and confirmed as a white person in a white church, educated as a white girl in a white school, registered as a white democratic voter, patronized hotels as a white woman, and traveled as a white person in buses, railroad cars, and streetcars. When Verna was born, her mother was assigned to the white maternity ward. And, if that weren't enough, the court noted that all of Verna's parents' friends and associates were white. The court thus observed that "the overwhelming testimony [is] that [Verna] and her immediate associates have always been regarded as members of the white race and have associated with persons of that race."[9]

Yet, proof of this nature demonstrates the social, not legal, race of Cassagne and her relatives. Given the impossibility of proving legal race according to the sanguinary formula set forth in the statute, what else could she look to? One might wonder how evidence of this sort survived a relevance objection from Sunseri. While the court did not address the issue, proof of social race was relevant to a determination of legal race on two primary grounds: First, one might believe that social race bears a "stands for" relationship to legal or true race. In this sense, social race was indirect proof of the thing itself. Second, one might argue that notwithstanding her actual sanguinary pedigree or lack thereof, the community or an intimate associate such as a husband, or both, were estopped from denying Cassagne's whiteness where she and her relatives had relied, over generations, on the community's and her husband's acquiescence in and acceptance of her identity as white. Given the great social significance of and investment in rigid racial boundaries, the court was not prepared to allow the conduct of some members of the community to bind the larger culture by permitting a kind of racial amnesty for people like Cassagne who could pass. Passing was not and could not be the same thing as being white.

Ultimately, the court determined that the question of Cassagne's true race turned on the contents of three legal documents: Cassagne's birth certificate, which registered her as colored, and the marriage license applications of her mother's sisters, which had been stamped "colored." The court then proceeded to cite approvingly the testimony of two white men who had stated that they "knew" that many of Cassagne's relatives were negro and that they had always been so regarded in the community. Based upon this, the court concluded that it had no alternative but to affirm the annulment of the marriage of Sunseri and Cassagne because there was "no room for doubt" that Cassagne was legally negro.

This case shows the authority of law to race bodies through what Eva Saks calls an autonomous miscegenous discourse[10]—autonomous in the sense that the legal meaning of race stands independent of and often in opposition to the social meaning of race. As such, in cases like Sunseri a person who is socially white can be declared legally black. Verna Cassagne told a story about her racial identity that was authentic—for her. The court and Cyril Sunseri, however, had another story of what it meant to be a white woman in Louisiana in 1940. Many may agree that racial identity is not something that we can take literally at face value, but rather is something that needs interpretation. What then emerges is a struggle over whose interpretation counts—law's "official" story or the story of the party to be raced?

At stake in the current debates about affirmative action, racial redistricting, Justice Thomas's ascension to the Supreme Court, and the Million Man March are fundamental questions about what it means to be African American and who gets to decide. There are many who claim that Justice Thomas is not really black. Or that he has betrayed his black identity. Many have criticized the vision of African American masculinity that was promoted by the leaders of the Million Man March in Washington last year.[11] What was powerful about the event, however, was the wresting of control of the instruments of identity away from government and the assertion of a degree of agency by some African Americans with respect to what it means to be an African American man, at this time, in this culture.

The power to name oneself is fundamentally critical to any individual and to any civil rights movement. One of the negative consequences of affirmative action has been the degree to which control over the meaning of racial difference and identity has been ceded to government for the purpose of achieving remedial redistribution of resources. The government now has interpreted the goal of our constitutional and statutory equality principles to be the creation of a color-blind society. The call for children to be judged by the content of their characters and not by the color of their skin has been taken to mean that we should aspire to a world in which racial differences are understood as normatively equivalent to differences in hair color—that is, meaningless. The radical individualism of this normative vision of the Fourteenth Amendment has frustrated the empowerment of peoples of color in this country. A politics of empowerment, as contrasted with an ethic of formal equality, requires a thick conception of racial identity produced through a fluid cultural, nonlegal process of self-definition engaged in by the communities to be empowered. Law is ill-suited to this task because racial meanings are always local and partial—they are always in media res.

Whether the state invokes its power to reinforce the salience of race, as it did in *Sunseri,* or to erase the salience of race, as it has with contemporary equality jurisprudence, the state renders legally static that which must remain contested and fluid. The cultural contestation of racial meaning and identity must be reclaimed from government as a significant foundation of our struggles for racial empowerment. Empowerment requires not only that we demand what we want, but also that we define who "we" are.

## DISCUSSION QUESTIONS

1. Identify all the different ways in which *race* is defined or constructed in this reading. What does the multiplicity of understandings of this term illustrate about the concept of race in the United States?
2. Why is the law involved in adjudicating Verna Cassagne's racial identity? What are the implications of having the legal system involved in defining race?

## NOTES

1. See Ronald Dworkin, *Law's Empire* 229, 228–38 (1986) (comparing the judge to a novelist who "interprets the chapters he has been given in order to write a new chapter, which is then added to what the next novelist receives, and so on").
2. Benedict Anderson, *Imagined Communities: Reflections on the Origin and Spread of Nationalism* 14–16 (1983).
3. E.g., *Dred Scott v. Sandford,* 60 U.S. (19 How.) 393, 410 (1857) ("The unhappy black race were separated from the white by indelible marks, and laws long before established, and were never thought of or spoken of except as property. . . .").
4. See, e.g., *Loving v. Virginia,* 388 U.S. 1, 5 (1967) (striking down a Virginia miscegenation statute that in part stated, "Every person in whom there is ascertainable any Negro blood shall be deemed and taken to be a colored person. . . ." (quoting Va. Code Ann. 1–14 (1960 Repl. Vol.)); *Morgan v. Virginia,* 328 U.S. 373, 382 (1946) (citing the state codes of Alabama, Arkansas, Georgia, Oklahoma, and Virginia as defining a person with "any ascertainable Negro Blood" as a colored person for the purposes of separation).
5. See, e.g., *Holder v. Hall,* 114 S. Ct. 2581, 2598 (1994) (Thomas, J., concurring) ("The assumptions upon which our vote dilution decisions have been based should be repugnant to any nation that strives for the ideal of a color-blind Constitution.").
6. 196 So. 7 (La. 1940) [hereinafter Sunseri II].
7. See generally Cheryl I. Harris, "Whiteness as Property," 106 *Harvard Law Review* 1709, 1725–45 (1993) (arguing that "whiteness" is theoretically, expectationally, functionally, and legally akin to a property right). Sunseri II, 196 So. at 7. See id. at 9 ("The defendant and her mother have always been considered as being of the white race by their acquaintances in the City of New Orleans.").
8. La. Civ. Code art. 94 (Bobs-Merrill 1932) (repealed 1972). *Sunseri v. Cassagne,* 185 So. 1, 2 (La. 1938) [hereinafter Sunseri 1]. Id. Id. at 4–5. Id. at 4.
9. Sunseri II, 196 So. 7, 9 (La. 1940). Id. at 7–8. Id.at 8–9. Id. at 7.
10. See Eva Saks, "Representing Miscegenation Law," *Raritan,* Fall 1988, at 39, 40 ("Miscegenation cases have a relative autonomy from other social definitions of miscegenation. This autonomy, along with their internal cohesiveness and cross-references, allow them to be analyzed as a genre: miscegenation discourse.").
11. See, e.g., Marlene Cimons, "Unity' March Exclusion Divides Women," *Los Angeles Times,* Oct. 17, 1995, at A14 ("Listen carefully to what the leaders of this event are saying: 'We've been bad masters; now we're going to be good ones.'" (quoting Marcia Gillespie)).

# 20

# Using Racial and Ethnic Concepts

## The Critical Case of Very Young Children

Debra Van Ausdale

Joe R. Feagin

*This second section, on identities and social interaction, contains five readings that illustrate how we construct social identities through social interaction and how identities affect behavior. Many of the readings use ethnographic fieldwork, which involves scholars spending time observing or interviewing the research population, like Mia Tuan did in her study of Asian Americans (Reading 18). The first reading excerpted here, from a 1996 article in the* American Sociological Review, *is by Debra Van Ausdale and Joe R. Feagin. Van Ausdale and Feagin, both sociologists, observe preschool children and their conceptualizations of race and ethnicity. Contrary to what most people think, Van Ausdale and Feagin find that children as young as three to five years old already are using racial and ethnic concepts to define others and to shape their social interactions with other children.*

Since the 1930s social science has examined children's attitudes toward race. Research has focused on situations in which race has meaning for children and on how children form racial identities (Clark and Clark 1939; Spencer, Brookins, and Allen 1985), create in-group racial and ethnic orientations (Aboud 1977; Cross 1987; Spencer 1987), form attitudes toward others (Williams and

*Source:* Van Ausdale, Debra, and Joe R. Feagin. 1996. "Using Racial and Ethnic Concepts: The Critical Case of Very Young Children." *American Sociological Review* 61(5): 779, 781, 783–786, 788–793. Reprinted with permission from the American Sociological Association and the authors.

Morland 1976), and use race in friend selection (Schofield and Francis 1982). The literature clearly demonstrates that racial identification and group orientation are salient issues for children (Ramsey 1987).

Cognitive development theories propose stage models to explain children's acquisition of racial and ethnic knowledge (Aboud 1977; Porter 1971). These models assume an age-related progression in children's ability to interpret racial and ethnic information, usually depicting children as proceeding in linear fashion toward cognitively mature adulthood. Most research focuses on children over five years of age; very young children are rarely studied . . . .

Researchers have rarely sought children's views directly, beyond recording brief responses to tests. Few have interviewed children or made in-depth, long-term observations to assess social attitudes, limiting the ability to investigate more fully the nature of children's lives. Children's abilities have been seriously underestimated by reliance on techniques that do not make real-life sense to children (Donaldson 1978). Investigations often have assumed that young children are incapable of using abstract concepts (Holmes 1995). An emphasis on psychological testing is often coupled with the notion that children have limited understandings of race and ethnicity (Goodman 1964; Katz 1976; Porter 1971). Children are typically assumed to have temporary or naive views about social concepts until at least age seven. Prior to that age, children's use of concepts differs from that of adults in form and content.

Little attention has been devoted to how children create and assign meaning for racial and ethnic concepts . . . .

We provide data indicating that racial concepts are employed with ease by children as young as age three. Research based on the conception of children as incapable of understanding race (Menter 1989) presents an incorrect image of children's use of abstractions. Drawing on Willis (1990) and Thorne (1993), we suggest that notions of race and ethnicity are employed by young children as integrative and symbolically creative tools in the daily construction of social life.

## THE RESEARCH APPROACH

We gathered experiential data on how children use racial and ethnic understandings in everyday relationships. Influenced by Dunn's (1991) approach, we made unstructured field observations and recorded everyday behaviors. Our data come from extensive observations of 58 three-, four-, and five-year-old children in a large preschool in a southern city. The school employed a popular antibias curriculum (Derman-Sparks 1989). Over an 11-month period in 1993, we systematically observed everyday interactions in one large classroom containing a very diverse group of children. The center's official data on the racial and ethnic backgrounds of children in the classroom are: White = 24, Asian = 19, Black = 4, biracial = 3, Middle Eastern = 3, Latino = 2, and other = 3 . . . .

Like the children and teachers, the senior author (hereafter Debi), a White woman, was usually in the classroom all day for five days a week. As observer and playmate, Debi watched the children and listened to them in their free play and teacher-directed activities. Over 11 months Debi observed 370 significant episodes involving a racial or ethnic dimension, about 1 to 3 episodes per day. When children mentioned racial or ethnic matters, Debi noted what they said, to whom they spoke, and the context of the incident. Extensive field notes were entered immediately on a computer in another room when the children were otherwise occupied. This was done to preserve the details of any conversations and the accuracy of the data . . . .

We began with the assumption that very young children would display no knowledge of racial or ethnic concepts and that any use of these concepts would be superficial or naive. Our data contradicted these expectations.

## USING RACIAL AND ETHNIC CONCEPTS TO EXCLUDE

Using the playhouse to bake pretend muffins, Rita (3.5: White/Latina) and Sarah (4: White) have all the muffin tins. Elizabeth (3.5: Asian/Chinese), attempting to join them, stands at the playhouse door and asks if she can play. Rita shakes her head vigorously, saying, "No, only people who can speak Spanish can come in." Elizabeth frowns and says, "I can come in." Rita counters, "Can you speak Spanish?" Elizabeth shakes her head no, and Rita repeats, "Well, then you aren't allowed in."

Elizabeth frowns deeply and asks Debi to intercede by telling her: "Rita is being mean to me." Acting within the child-initiated framework, Debi asks Rita, "If only people who speak Spanish are allowed, then how come Sarah can play? Can you speak Spanish, Sarah?" Sarah shakes her head no. "Sarah can't speak Spanish and she is playing," Debi says to Rita, without suggesting she allow Elizabeth in. Rita frowns, amending her statement: "OK, only people who speak either Spanish or English." "That's great!" Debi responds, "because Elizabeth speaks English and she wants to play with you guys." Rita's frown deepens. "No," she says. Debi queries, "But you just said people who speak English can play. Can't you decide?" Rita gazes at Debi, thinking hard. "Well," Rita says triumphantly, "only people who speak two languages."

Elizabeth is waiting patiently for Debi to make Rita let her play, which Debi has no intention of doing. Debi then asks Rita: "Well, Elizabeth speaks two languages, don't you Elizabeth?" Debi looks at Elizabeth, who now is smiling for the first time. Rita is stumped for a moment, then retorts, "She does not. She speaks only English." Debi smiles at Rita: "She does speak two languages—English and Chinese. Don't you?" Debi invites Elizabeth into the conversation. Elizabeth nods vigorously. However, Rita turns away and says to Sarah, "Let's go to the store and get more stuff."

Language was the ethnic marker here. Rita defined rules for entering play on the basis of language—she was aware that each child not only did not look like the others but also spoke a different language. From a traditional Piagetian perspective, Rita might be seen as egocentric and strongly resistant to alternative views. However, here we see the crucial importance of the social-cultural context, in particular the development of racial and ethnic concepts in a collaborative and interpersonal context. Defending her rules, Rita realized her attempts to exclude Elizabeth by requiring two languages had failed. This three-year-old child had created a social rule based on a significant understanding of ethnic markers. The final "two languages" rule did not acknowledge the fact that Sarah only spoke English. Rita's choice of language as an exclusionary device was directed at preventing Elizabeth from entering, not at maintaining a bilingual play space . . . .

## USING RACIAL AND ETHNIC CONCEPTS TO INCLUDE

The children also used racial and ethnic understandings and concepts to include others—to engage them in play or teach them about racial and ethnic identities.

Ling (5: Asian/Chinese) has a book that teaches the Chinese language. She announces to Debi that her grandmother has given her the book and that she is learning Chinese. Debi asks if she is making progress. "Oh yes," Ling says happily, "I have already learned many characters. They're called characters, you know." She points out several. "What does that say?" Debi asks, pointing to one. "Cat!" Ling beams. Debi and Ling spend some time reading from Ling's book, then Ling leaves to show off her reading prowess to another child.

Over several weeks, Ling's behavior underscores for the observer how racial and ethnic understandings develop in social contexts. Ling engages numerous others in reading Chinese with her. Carrying the book everywhere, she earnestly tries to teach others to read and write Chinese characters. Chinese characters appear on other children's drawings and on the playground. Other children actively embrace these new characters and concepts and incorporate them into their activities, a clear indication of how children learn ethnic ideas from each other. Ling's efforts demonstrate that she is aware that non-Chinese, including adults, do not know how to read Chinese. Clearly she is aware that Chinese is distinct from the experience of most people around her, and she recognizes this even though she herself is just learning to read Chinese . . . .

## USING RACIAL AND ETHNIC CONCEPTS TO DEFINE ONESELF

The use of racial and ethnic concepts to include or exclude others is often coupled with the use of these concepts to describe and define oneself. For most children, racial and/or ethnic identity is an important aspect of themselves, and they demonstrate this in insightful ways in important social contexts.

Renee (4.5: White), a very pale little girl, has been to the beach over the weekend and comes to school noticeably tanned. Linda (4: White) and Erinne (5: biracial) engage her in an intense conversation. They discuss whether her skin would stay that color or get darker until she became, as Linda says, "an African American, like Charles" (another child). Renee denies she could become Black, but this new idea, planted in her head by interaction with the other children, distresses her. On her own initiative, she discusses the possibility with Debi and her mother, both of whom tell her the darker color is temporary.

Renee was unconvinced and commented on her racial identity for weeks. She brought up the issue with other children in many contexts. This linking of skin color with racial identity is found in much traditional literature on children's racial understandings (Clark and Clark 1940). But this racial marking was more than a fleeting interest, unlike the interest mainstream cognitive theorists might predict for such a young child. Renee reframed the meaning of skin color by questioning others on their thoughts and comparing her skin to others'.

Corinne (4: African/White) displays an ability to create meaning by drawing from her personal world. Corinne's mother is Black and is from an African country; her father is a White American. Corinne speaks French and English and is curious about everything at the center. She is a leader and often initiates activities with other children. Most children defer to her. One day Corinne is examining a rabbit cage on the playground. A teacher is cleaning out the cage and six baby bunnies are temporarily housed in an aluminum bucket that Corinne is holding. Three bunnies are white, two are black, and one is spotted black and white.

As Corinne is sitting at a table, Sarah (4: White) stuck her head into the bucket. "Stop that!" Corinne orders. Sarah complies and asks, "Why do you have the babies?" "I'm helping Marie [teacher]," says Corinne. "How many babies are there?" Sarah asks Corinne. "Six!" Corinne announces. "Three boys and three girls." "How can you tell if they're boys or girls?" Sarah questions. "Well," Corinne begins, "my daddy is White, so the white ones are boys. My mommy is Black, so the black ones are girls." Sarah counts: "That's only five." The remaining bunny is black and white. "Well, that one is like me, so it's a girl," Corinne explains gently. She picks up the bunny and says, "See, this one is both, like me!" Sarah then loses interest, and Corinne returns to cooing over the bunnies.

This four-year-old's explanation incorporates an interesting combination of color, race, and gender. While her causal reasoning was faulty, she constructed what for her was a sophisticated and reasonable view of the bunnies' sexes. She displayed an understanding of the idea that an offspring's color reflects the colors of its parents, a knowledge grounded in her experience as a biracial child. Strayer (1986) underscores how children develop appropriate attributions regarding situational determinants. Corinne's use of parental gender to explain the unknown gender of the bunnies was an appropriate explanation of how bunnies got certain colors. Skin color was a salient part of her identity, and it was reasonable in her social world to assume that it would be salient for the identity of others, even animals . . . .

In another setting, Corinne (4: African/White) provides an example of the complexity of young children's racial understandings: She refines the nature of racial identity during a handpainting activity. The children have taken a field trip and are asked to make a thank-you poster for their host, a poster constructed of a large sheet of paper featuring handprints of the children. Children are asked by the teacher to choose a color that "looks just like you do." The paints are known as "People Colors," and are common at daycare centers concerned with diversity issues. The activity was designed to increase appreciation of differences in color among the children (Derman-Sparks 1989).

The six paints ranged from dark brown to pale pink. The handprint poster activity is familiar to the children, and the teacher asks Debi to help. Debi accepts but keeps her involvement to a minimum. Several children wait in line to participate in this desirable activity. Each chooses paint according to the teacher's criterion, has Debi apply the paint to the palm of one hand, and then presses the painted hand onto the poster. Debi then writes the child's name next to the handprint. Some children point out how closely the paint matches their skin color or ask Debi if she thought the choice was "right."

Corinne approaches the table, and Debi says, "OK, which color is the most like you? Which color matches your skin?" Corinne looks over the bottles carefully and chooses pale brown. "This one for one hand," she replies, continuing to scan the bottles, "and this one for the other hand," she concludes, choosing a second, dark brown color. When Debi asks if that color matches her skin, Corinne calmly replies, "I have two colors in my skin." Debi smiles and paints one of her palms pale brown and the other dark brown. Corinne places both hands on the poster, making two prints. Debi then writes Corinne's name between the two handprints. "Perfect!" Corinne says.

This four-year-old chose appropriately for her understanding of the situation. That the paints she picked did not exactly match her skin color was not important to her because she was thinking in terms of her parents' different racial identities. Corinne insisted that she be allowed to choose two colors to reflect her biracial origin. For her, choosing two colors is not an example of cognitive confusion or inconsistency (as a mainstream analysis might see it), but rather her innovative way of recognizing that her mother is dark brown ("Black") and her father is pale brown ("White"). These examples show that children's abilities exceed what would be predicted from the mainstream research perspective.

## USING RACIAL AND ETHNIC CONCEPTS TO DEFINE OTHERS

We observed many examples of children exploring the complex notions of skin color, hair differences, and facial characteristics. They often explore what these things mean and make racial and/or ethnic interpretations of these perceived differences. Mindy (4: White) insists that Debi is Indian. When queried, Mindy replies that it is because Debi is wearing her long dark hair in a braid. When Debi explains that she is not Indian, the child remarks that maybe Debi's mother is Indian.

These statements show not only awareness of the visible characteristics of race and ethnicity but also insight into how visible markers are passed from generation to generation. They demonstrate a child's ability to grasp salient characteristics of a racial and/or ethnic category not her own and apply them to others in a collaborative and evolving way.

In another episode, Taleshia (3: Black) approaches the handpainting table. Asked if she wants to make a handprint, she nods shyly. A child with dark brown skin, Taleshia scans the paint bottles and points to pale pink. Curious about her preference, Debi asks, "Taleshia, is this the color that looks like you?" Taleshia nods and holds out her hand. Behind her, Cathie (3.5: White) objects to Taleshia's decision. "No, no," Cathie interjects, "She's not that color. She's brown." Cathie moves to the table. "You're this color," Cathie says and picks out the bottle of dark brown paint. Cathie is interested in helping Taleshia correct her apparent mistake about skin color. "Do you want this color?" Debi asks Taleshia. "No," she replies, "I want this one," touching the pink bottle. Regarding Taleshia with amazement, Cathie exclaims, "For goodness sake, can't you see that you aren't pink?" "Debi," Cathie continues to insist, "you have to make her see that she's brown." Cathie is exasperated and takes Taleshia by the arm. "Look," she instructs, "you are brown! See?" Cathie holds Taleshia's arm next to her own. "I am pink, right?" Cathie looks to Debi for confirmation. "Sure enough," Debi answers, "you are pink." "Now," Cathie continues, looking relieved, "Taleshia needs to be brown." Debi looks at Taleshia, who is now frowning, and asks her, "Do you want to be brown?" She shakes her head vigorously and points to pale pink, "I want that color."

Cathie is frustrated, and trying to be supportive, Debi explains that "Taleshia can choose any color she thinks is right." Cathie again objects, but Taleshia smiles, and Debi paints her palm pink. Then Taleshia makes her handprint. Cathie stares, apparently convinced that Taleshia and Debi have lost touch with reality. As Taleshia leaves, Cathie takes her place, remarking to Debi, "I just don't know what's the matter with you. Couldn't you see that *she is brown!*" Cathie gives up and chooses pale pink for herself, a close match. Cathie makes her handprint and says to Debi, "See, I am *not* brown."

Taleshia stuck to her choice despite Cathie's insistence. Both three-year-olds demonstrate a strong awareness of the importance of skin color, and their views are strongly held. This example underscores the importance of child-centered research. A traditional conceptualization of this Black child's choice of skin color paint might suggest that the child is confused about racial identity. If she chose pink in the usual experimental setting (Clark and Clark 1940; Porter 1971), she would probably be evaluated as rejecting herself for a preferred whiteness. Debi had several other interactions with Taleshia. The three-year-old had, on other occasions, pointed out how pale Debi was and how dark her own skin was. She had explained to Debi that she was Black, that she thought she was pretty, and that pink was her favorite color. One possible explanation for her choice of pink for her skin color in the handpainting activity relies on Debi's knowledge of Taleshia's personality, family background, and previous interactions with others. Taleshia may have chosen pink because it is her favorite color, but this does not mean that she is unaware that most of her skin is dark. Another explanation for Taleshia's choice of skin color representation is that, like other African Americans, Taleshia's palms are *pink* while most of her skin is very dark. Perhaps she was choosing a color to match the color of her palms, a reasonable choice because the task was to paint the palms for handprints. The validity of this interpretation is reinforced by another episode at the center. One day Taleshia sat down and held Debi's hands in hers, turning them from top to bottom. Without uttering a word, she repeated this activity with her own hands, drawing Debi's attention to this act. The three-year-old was contrasting the pink-brown variations in her skin color with Debi's pinkish hand color. This explanation for the child's paint

choice might not occur to a researcher who did not pay careful attention to the context and the child's personal perspective. Taleshia's ideas, centered in observations of herself and others, were more important to her than another child's notions of appropriate color. Far from being confused about skin color, she was creating meaning for color based on her own evaluations.

## USING RACIAL CONCEPTS TO CONTROL

The complex nature of children's group interactions and their solo behaviors demonstrates that race and ethnicity are salient, substantial aspects of their lives. They understand racial nuances that seem surprisingly sophisticated, including the power of race. How children use this power in their relationships is demonstrated in further episodes . . . .

In another encounter, this time among three children, a White child demonstrates her knowledge of broader race relations, demonstrating her grasp of race-based power inequalities. During play time Debi watches Renee (4: White) pull Ling-mai (3: Asian) and Jocelyn (4.5: White) across the playground in a wagon. Renee tugs away enthusiastically. Suddenly, Renee drops the handle, which falls to the ground, and she stands still, breathing heavily. Ling-mai, eager to continue this game, jumps from the wagon and picks up the handle. As Ling-mai begins to pull, Renee admonishes her, "No, no. You can't pull this wagon. Only *White Americans* can pull this wagon." Renee has her hands on her hips and frowns at Ling-mai. Ling-mai tries again, and Renee again insists that only "White Americans" are permitted to do this task.

Ling-mai sobs loudly and runs to a teacher, complaining that "Renee hurt my feelings." "Did you hurt Ling-mai's feelings?" the teacher asks Renee, who nods, not saying a word. "I think you should apologize," the teacher continues, "because we are all friends here and friends don't hurt each others feelings." "Sorry," mutters Renee, not looking at Ling-mai, "I didn't do it on purpose." "OK," the teacher finishes, "can you guys be good friends now?" Both girls nod without looking at each other and quickly move away.

This interaction reveals several layers of meaning. Both children recognized the implications of Renee's harsh words and demands. Renee accurately underscored the point that Ling-mai, the child of Asian international students, was neither White nor American. Her failure to be included in these two groups, according to Renee's pronouncement, precluded her from being in charge of the wagon. Ling-mai responded, not by openly denying Renee's statements, but by complaining to the teacher that Renee had hurt her feelings. Both children seem knowledgeable about the structure of the U.S. and global racial hierarchy and accept the superior position accorded to Whites. The four-year-old child exercised authority as a White American and controlled the play with comments and with her stance and facial expressions. Our findings extend previous research on young children's knowledge of status and power (Corsaro 1979; Damon 1977) by showing that children are aware of the power and authority granted to Whites. The children were not confused about the meanings of these harsh racial words and actions.

## ADULT MISPERCEPTIONS

Children's use of racial and ethnic concepts often goes unnoticed, even by adults in daily contact with them. This is illustrated by the responses of classroom teachers and the center director to preliminary reports on our research. Debi wrote two research reports, one for the classroom teachers and one for the director. After reading the reports, the teachers insisted to Debi that she must have been observing "some other children" and that "these are not our kids." The director seemed determined to "guess" the identity of children whose incidents Debi described at a meeting. Throughout the episodes Debi described, he interrupted with remarks like "I'll bet that's Sarah you're talking about, isn't it?" His determination to attach names to the children revealed his investment in "curing" racism. He seemed determined to discover the culprits so unlearning might begin.

Adults' strong need to deny that children can use racial and ethnic concepts is also revealed in the next account. Here two children are engaged in a discussion of "what" they are. Debi is sitting with all the children on the steps to the deck playing "Simon Says." "Simon," a child selected by teachers to lead the game, directs the main action, while Debi observes that Rita (3.5: White/Latina) and Louis (4: Black) are engaged in their own private side activity. While the game continues, Rita and Louis discuss what they are. "What are you?" Louis asks Rita, and without waiting for her reply announces. "I'm Black and you're White." "No," she retorts, correcting him, "I'm not White, I'm mixed." Louis regards her curiously, but at this moment Joanne, the lone Black teacher in the classroom, intervenes. "You're not mixed, Rita, you're Spanish," she informs the child. "What race am I?" Joanne continues, trying to get the children to change the subject and glancing over at me anxiously. Rita replies, "Mixed." "Mixed!?" Joanne, laughing, responds, "Mixed with what?" "Blue," Rita says, looking only at her hands. Joanne is wearing a solid blue outfit. "Oh no, honey," Joanne says, "I'm Black too, like Louis, not mixed. What an interesting conversation you guys are having." Rita says nothing in response, and Louis remains silent throughout Joanne's attempt at dialogue. Suddenly, "Simon Says" ends and the kids run to the playground, escaping Joanne's questions. Joanne smiles and remarks to Debi, "Boy, it's really amazing what they pick up, isn't it?"

When Joanne intervened, Rita and Louis had to refocus their attention from a discussion between themselves about what they "are" to responding to Joanne's questioning. The adult interruption silenced Louis completely and made Rita defensive and wary. As other research has demonstrated, adult involvement in children's discourse can result in changes in the nature of the children's relations (Danielewicz, Rogers, and Noblit 1996). Rita realized that she must avoid sanctions when Joanne introduced her own racial identity into the game, attempting to distract the children from what Joanne perceived as an argument based on racial differences. However, the children were engaged in an appropriate discussion about their origins. Rita is indeed a "mixed" Latina, for her mother is from one Latin American country and her father is from another Latin American country. Rita understood this and had on other occasions described trips to visit her father's home. Louis is indeed Black and views Rita as White. Rita seemed to be trying to extend the concept beyond skin color and thus to educate Louis, until the teacher interrupted. Joanne's assumption seemed to be twofold: that Rita was confused and that as a teacher Joanne must act preventively. Here the teacher focused on quashing prejudice rather than seizing an opportunity to listen to the children and discuss their racial and ethnic perspectives. Adults tend to control children's use of racial and ethnic concepts and interpret children's use of these concepts along prejudice-defined lines. Clearly, the social context of children's learning, emphasized in the interpretive approach, includes other children and adults, but our accounts also demonstrate the way in which children's sophisticated understandings are developed without adult collaboration and supervision . . . .

## CONCLUSION

Through extensive observation, this study has captured the richness of children's racial and ethnic experiences. The racial nature of children's interactions becomes fully apparent only when their interactions are viewed over time and in context. Close scrutiny of children's lives reveals that they are as intricate and convoluted as those of adults.

Blumer (1969:138) suggests that any sociological variable is, on examination, "an intricate and inner-moving complex." Dunn (1993) notes that children's relationships are complex and multidimensional, even within their own families . . . . By exploring the use of racial concepts in the child's natural world, instead of trying to remove the child or the concepts from that world, we glean a more complete picture of how children view and manipulate racial and ethnic concepts and understandings.

For most children, racial and ethnic issues arise forcefully within the context of their interaction with others. Most of the children that we observed had little or no experience with people from other racial or ethnic groups outside of the center. For these very young children, who are having their first extensive

social experiences outside the family, racial and ethnic differences became powerful identifiers of self and other. Whether this is also true for children who do not experience such a diverse range of exposure to racial and ethnic concepts is beyond the scope of this project. However, over the 11 months we observed dozens of slowly evolving transformations in these children's racial and ethnic explorations and understandings. For many children, racial and ethnic awareness increased. Some, like Taleshia, regularly explored racial identities by comparing their skin color with that of others. Others, like Renee, faced crises over identity. For still others, racial and/or ethnic matters arose intermittently, but these matters did not seem to be central to the children's explorations. Children varied in how often they expressed or indicated racial or ethnic understandings, but we were unable to observe each child constantly and cannot make a more detailed judgment on this issue.

To fully understand the importance of children's racial and/or ethnic understandings, the nuanced complexity and interconnected nature of their thinking and behavior must be accepted and recognized. Measures of racial and ethnic awareness should consider not only children's cognitive abilities but also the relationships that children develop in social situations . . . .

Regarding the racial and ethnic hierarchy, young children understand that in U.S. society higher status is awarded to White people. Many understand that simply by virtue of their skin color, Whites are accorded more power, control, and prestige. Very young children carry out interactions in which race is salient. Racial knowledge is situational, and children can interact in a race-based or race-neutral manner, according to their evaluations of appropriateness. In children's worlds race emerges early as a tool for social interaction and quickly becomes a complex and fluid component of everyday interaction.

The behaviors of the children in this preschool setting are likely to be repeated in other diverse settings. The traditional literature accepts that children display prejudice by the time they arrive at school, but offers no explanation about the acquisition of this prejudice beyond it being an imitation of parental behavior. We expect continuity of children's racial and ethnic categories across settings, for children reveal a readiness to use their knowledge of race and ethnicity.

The observed episodes underscore problems in traditional theories of child development. When children fail cognitive tasks framed in terms of principles such as conservation and reciprocity, researchers often conclude that children lack the cognitive capability to understand race. However, surveys and observations of children in natural settings demonstrate that three-year-old children have constant, well-defined, and negative biases toward racial and ethnic others (Ramsey 1987). Rather than insisting that young children do not understand racial or ethnic ideas because they do not reproduce these concepts on adult-centered cognitive tests, researchers should determine the extent to which racial and ethnic concepts—as used in daily interaction—are salient definers of children's

social reality. Research on young children's use of racial and gender concepts demonstrates that the more carefully a research design explores the real life of children, the more likely that research can answer questions about the nature of race and ethnicity in children's everyday lives.

## DISCUSSION QUESTIONS

1. What is the principal flaw of researchers in assessing racial and ethnic awareness in children? What have Van Ausdale and Feagin learned to do instead?

2. Describe the ways in which "race emerges early as a tool for . . . social interaction" within the social contexts in the daily lives of very young children.

# 21

# WOMEN WITHOUT CLASS

## Chicas, Cholas, *Trash, and the Presence or Absence of Class Identity*

JULIE BETTIE

*This second reading in the section on identities and social interaction also involves fieldwork to study identity at school. Instead of studying preschools like Van Ausdale and Feagin did, Julie Bettie, in a reading first published in* Signs: Journal of Women in Culture and Society *(2000), examines working-class white and Mexican American female students in high school. Bettie, a sociology professor at the University of California, Santa Cruz, argues that social class is often underexamined in studies of gender, and she utilizes her ethnographic research to explore how race, gender, and social class intersect. In particular, Bettie is interested in how young women "perform" their gender and social class.*

A cover story in the San Francisco *Examiner Magazine* (Wagner 1996) on the topic of "wiggas" (which, the article explains, is shorthand for "white niggas") reads, "suburban kidz hip-hop across the color line." The story is about white youth who appropriate hip-hop culture and perform "black" identity. The cover picture is a collage of magazine cutouts showing white kids with blue eyes and blond hair (functioning as a code for racial purity) wearing hip-hop fashion and standing in front of a white picket fence behind which sits a charming two-story house and an apple tree. Although there is a girl pictured on the front cover, girls are absent from the story itself.

*Source:* Bettie, Julie. 2000. "Women with Class: Chicas, Cholas, Trash and the Presence /Absence of Class Identity." In Signs: *Journal of Women in Culture and Society.* Reproduced with permission of University of Chicago Press—Journals in the format Textbook via Copyright Clearance Center.

In a 1993 episode of the TV talk show *Oprah* on the same topic, several groups of boys, white and black, sat on the stage. The audience was confounded by the white boys in hip-hop style who "grew up in 'the 'hood'" and by the young black man who, as one guest explained, "looks like he walked out of Eddie Bauer," as participants debated what it meant to dress black or dress white. During the course of the hour-long program all parties failed to note that, race and ethnicity aside, these were different versions of *masculinity* and that girls were missing again from this story about "youth." The "urban romanticism" and "masculinist overtones" (McRobbie 1991:20) of subculture studies, where the supposedly gender-neutral term *youth* actually stands for male, are equally often present in popular culture and news media portrayals of youth. In order to envision themselves as class or racial/ethnic subjects in either site, girls must read themselves as boys.

But beyond the invisibility of gender, there is also a failure to "think class" with much clarity. On the *Oprah* show, as with the magazine cover, the same sets of binaries surface repeatedly: white is middle class is suburban; black is lower class is urban. But a slippage occurs where the class references are dropped out and white stands in for middle, where black stands in for lower, or where suburban stands in for white and urban for black. Class and race signifiers are melded together in such a way that "authentic" black, and sometimes brown, identity is imagined as lower class, urban, and often violent and male as well. These are the overly simplified identity categories offered, but they do not reflect the complexity of life. Middle-class youth of color are missing, for example, as are multiracial/multiethnic identity and small-town or rural poverty. The racial/ethnic and class subject positions offered by the "identity formation material" (McRobbie 1994:192) of popular culture often do not allow for more nuanced social locations . . . .

The observations I make in this article are based on my ethnographic study of working-class white and Mexican American girls in their senior year of high school in a small town in California's central valley. Where Pipher sees girls derailed by romance and mass culture, I see "changing modes

of femininity" (McRobbie 1994:157): a generation of young women, most of whom at no point expect or hope to be economically supported by a man. These were girls who knew from experience in their own families of origin that male wages cannot support families alone and that men cannot be counted on to meet their ideals of intimacy and egalitarianism in relationships. These were girls who saw that the men in their working-class community were often unemployed or underemployed and too often dealt with this hardship by abandoning their obligation and responsibilities to the women in their lives and to the children they helped create. These girls were not holding out for princes.

My title, "Women without Class," has multiple meanings. Most simply, it reflects my interest in young women from families of modest means and low educational attainment who therefore have little "cultural capital" (Bourdieu 1984) to enable class mobility.[1] The other meanings of the title speak to the theory debates I engage and to which I already have alluded: a second meaning refers to the fact that class analysis and social theory have, until recently perhaps, remained insufficiently transformed by feminist theory, unable to conceptualize women as class subjects. Ignoring women's experience of class results in a profound androcentric bias such that women are routinely invisible as class subjects. In much leftist analysis women are assumed to be without class, as these theorists often seem unable to see the category "working class" unless it is marked white and male. Such biases promote the invisibility of both white women and women of color as class subjects.

The failure to perceive women as class subjects, or as racial/ethnic subjects, has been part of the "youth and social class couplet" (McRobbie 1994) of subculture studies and the school ethnographies of cultural Marxists. This bias is a consequence of two separate but related problems:

(*a*) the focus on male (white and/or nonwhite) subjects and (*b*) the employment of conceptual schemes that fail to adequately explain the way women experience class and, further, render gender and race epiphenomenal to class formation.

With regard to subculture studies, these biases can be seen not only in the focus primarily on male youth in public places but also in the use of normative conceptions of "class consciousness" that are defined by relations of production, by the focus on youth's transition to work identity, and by the failure to consider gender, family futures and pasts, and racial/ethnic identity as shapers of class subjectivity . . . .

It was with these theory debates and empirical gaps in mind that I set off to explore if and how young women understand class difference. I intended to foreground, while not privileging, class as I examined how gender, color, and ethnicity intersect with and shape class as a lived culture and a subjective identity. The context of the lives of these young women includes a deindustrializing economy, the growth of service-sector occupations held largely by women and men of color and by white women, the related family revolutions of the twentieth century, the elimination of affirmative action, a rise in anti-immigrant sentiment, and changing cultural representations and iconographies of class, race, and gender meanings. These are social forces that render the term *working class* anachronistic even as many of these girls move toward low-wage, low-prestige jobs in their community. My goal was to explore the relationship between class symbolism and the formation of subjective class identity to understand "the complex and contradictory ways" (Long 1989:428) in which class subjectivity is constructed in relationship to gender and racial/ethnic identity under late capitalism.

I examined girls' experience of class difference and identity by documenting and analyzing the "commonsense" categories they used and created to describe and explain class-based differences among themselves. I documented the unspoken boundary work that was a part of everyday interaction among students—the kinds of interaction that reveal symbolic class distinctions and differences in "cultural capital" between working- and middle-class girls. Most important, I investigated the ways these commonsense class categories are infused with gender and racial/ethnic meanings.

## NOTES TOWARD CLASS AS "PERFORMANCE" AND "PERFORMATIVE"

My study was done in a small town of approximately forty thousand people. The high school reflects the town demographically, being about 60 percent white and 40 percent Mexican American, with other people of color composing less than 2 percent each of the population. Located in California's central valley, the town was built on agriculture and the industries that support it. Approximately 16 percent of the Mexican American students were Mexican-born, while the remainder were second and third generation. The majority of students at the school, both white and Mexican American, were from working-class families, but the children of middle-class professionals were a present minority. Most of the latter were white, but a handful were Mexican American. Working-class students ranged from "hard-living" to "settled-living" (Howell 1973) in experience. The former term describes lives that are chaotic and unpredictable, characterized by low-paying, unstable occupations, lack of health care benefits, and no home ownership. The latter describes lives that are orderly and predictable, characterized by relatively secure, higher-paying jobs, sometimes health benefits, and sometimes ownership of a modest home.

I "hung out" with girls in classrooms and hallways, during lunch hours, at school dances, sports events, Future Homemakers of America meetings, at a Future Farmers of America hay-bucking contest and similar events, at MEChA meetings (Movimiento Estudiantil Chicano de Aztlán; the Chicano student movement organization), in coffee shops, restaurants, the shopping mall, and the school parking lot, near the bleachers behind the school, at birthday parties, and sometimes sitting cross-legged on the floor of a girl's bedroom, "just talkin.'" I spent almost every day at the school during the school year, often returning in the evening to attend an extracurricular event and sometimes on weekends to meet and "kick it" with the girls. I came to know more than sixty girls well (approximately half were white and half Mexican American) and many more as acquaintances. I talked with them about such details of their lives as friendships, dating, partying, clothes, makeup, popular culture, school, family, work, and their hopes and expectations for the future.

Over the course of the school year, I came to know the clique structure, or informal peer hierarchy, at the school, as it was the primary way students understood class and racial/ethnic differences among themselves. Labels and descriptions of each group varied, of course, depending on the social location of the student providing the description. Nonetheless, there was a general mapping that almost all students agreed on and provided easily when asked. Although there were exceptions, the groups were largely race/ethnic and class segregated. Among whites they included "preps" (middle class), "skaters/alternatives" (settled-living), "hicks" (settled- and hard-living), and "smokers/rockers/trash" (hard-living); among Mexican American students there were "Mexican preps" (middle class and settled-and hard-living), "*las chicas*" (settled-living), and "*cholas/os*" or "hard cores" (hard-living).

Group membership was linked to social roles, including curriculum choices (college prep or vocational track) and extracurricular activities (whether a student was involved in what are considered either college-prep or nonprep activities). These courses and activities combined to shape class futures leading some girls to four-year colleges, some to vocational programs at junior colleges, and some to low-wage jobs directly out of high school. While there is a strong correlation between a girl's class of "origin" (by which I mean her parents' socioeconomic status) and her class performance at school (which includes academic achievement, prep or nonprep activities, and membership in friendship groups and their corresponding style), it is an imperfect one, and there are exceptions in which middle-class girls perform working-class identity and vice versa. In other words, some students were engaged in class "passing" as they chose to perform class identities that were not their "own."

Although clique membership was not entirely determined by class, there was certainly "a polarization of attitudes toward class characteristics," and group categories (such as preps, smokers, *cholas,* etc.) were "embodiment[s] of the middle and

working-class[es]" (Eckert 1989:4–5). On the one hand, embracing and publicly performing a particular class culture mattered more than origins in terms of a student's aspirations, her treatment by teachers and other students, and her class future. On the other hand, class origins did matter significantly, of course, as girls' life chances were shaped by the economic and cultural resources provided at home.[2] Because of the imperfect correlation, I came to define students not only as working or middle class in origin but also as working- or middle-class *performers* (and, synonymously, as prep and nonprep students). Girls who were passing, or metaphorically cross-dressing, had to negotiate their "inherited" identity from home with their "chosen" public identity at school. There was a disparity for them between how their and their friends' families looked and talked at home and their own class performances at school. As I came to understand these negotiations of class as cultural (not political) identities, it became useful to conceptualize class as not only a material location but also a performance.

The work on performativity that has come out of cultural studies and poststructuralist feminism, with their radical constructionist analyses of gender, race, and sexuality, has much in common with the constructionism of symbolic interactionist sociology and, in particular, ethnomethodology. But little attention has been paid by either to thinking about *class* as a performance, as something that is accomplished, instead of, or not only, as a material location. To think about class as a performance is not to ignore its materiality. The materiality of class includes both economic and cultural resources about which we make meaning, and power lies in the naturalization and sanctioning of kinds of class subjects and class relations . . . .

The normalization and institutionalization of class inequality regulates class performances. For example, class-specific styles, such as standard or nonstandard grammar usage, accents, mannerisms, and dress (all of which are also specific to race/ethnicity and region), are learned sets of expressive cultural practices that express class membership. Group categories at school require different class performances, and students engage in practices of exclusion contingent on authentic class performances (Foley 1990). Cultural differences in class (linked to both education and income) are key to the middle-class practices of exclusion that make school "success" difficult for working-class students across color and ethnicity. Class can be conceptualized as performative in that there is no *interior* difference (innate and inferior "intelligence" or "taste," e.g.) that is being expressed; rather, institutionalized class inequality creates class subjects who *perform*, or display, differences in cultural capital.

Consequently, I ask: What are the cultural gestures involved in the performance of class? How is class "authenticity" accomplished? And how is it imbued with racial/ethnic and gender meaning? Little attention has been paid to the ways class subjectivity, as a cultural identity, is experienced in relation to the cultural meanings of race/ethnicity, gender, and sexuality . . . .

## DISSIDENT FEMININITIES

Because I spent my first few days at the school in a college-preparatory class (one that fulfills a requirement for admission to state universities), the first girls I met were college bound. Later I came to know these girls through the eyes of non-college-prep students as "the preps." They were mostly white but included a handful of Mexican American girls. Some of the white girls were also known as "the 90210s" after the television show *Beverly Hills 90210* about wealthy high schoolers in Beverly Hills. The preps related easily to what they saw as my "school project." They eagerly volunteered to help me out and were ready and willing to talk at length about themselves and others. Displaying both social and academic skills, they were, in short, "teacher's pets" (Luttrell 1993) or "the rich and populars" (Lesko 1988) . . . .

Pipher's (1994) account of the "well-adjusted" girl, who exists before the alleged moment of poisoning or gender-subordinate indoctrination by mass culture, sounds suspiciously like a "prep," one of those girls who tended to be heavily involved in athletics or some other school-sanctioned extracurricular activity, who

were high academic achievers, who usually wore looser, more unisex clothing and little or no makeup, and who were favored by teachers. Applauding girls with these characteristics, Pipher tells us that "androgynous adults are the most well adjusted . . . since they are free to act without worrying if their behavior is feminine or masculine" (18).

But the girls I came to know, both white and Mexican American, were not only worrying about whether their actions were masculine or feminine, they were equally concerned with the race/ethnic and, in a more convoluted way, the class meanings of their performances. Accounts of boys that suggest that the expressive cultural styles of youth subcultures often have their source in and reflect class and race/ethnic inequalities regardless of whether they are articulated as such apply to girls as well. I could not see Lorena and her friends, who called themselves "*las chicas*," as mere victims of a mass culture that promotes their subordination based on gender. One thing white and Mexican American working-class girls had in common, in spite of their many differences, was that they were, by their own naming, not "preps," the primarily white middle-class college-preparatory girls they so despised. In centering gender, Pipher (1994) does not adequately explore the ways that girls' practices, especially the ones that disturb her (such as heavy makeup, tattoos, piercing, drugs, school refusal), often mark hierarchical class and race/ethnic relations among girls themselves and are not solely the consequence of gender inequality. Girls do not define themselves only in relation to boys; "one can become a woman in relationship to other women" (Alarcón 1990).

The expression of self through one's relationship to and creative use of commodities (both artifacts and the discourses of popular culture) is a central practice in capitalist society. The girls' alternative versions of gender performance were shaped by a nascent knowledge of race and class hierarchies. They were very able to communicate a sense of unfairness, a "structure of feeling" (Williams 1965), where inequalities were felt but not politically articulated. Their struggles were often waged less over explicit political ideologies than over modes of identity expression. In short, among students there existed a symbolic economy of style that was the ground on which class and race relations were played out. A whole array of gender-specific commodities were used as markers of distinction among different groups of girls who performed race/ethnic- and class-specific versions of femininity. Hairstyles, clothes, shoes, and the colors of lip liner, lipstick, and nail polish were key markers used to express group membership as the body became a resource and a site on which difference was inscribed. For example, Lorena and her friends preferred darker colors for lips and nails, in comparison to the preps who either went without or wore clear lip gloss, pastel lip and nail color, or French manicures (the natural look). Each group knew the others' stylistic preferences and was aware that their own style was in opposition. Girls created and maintained symbolic oppositions in which, as Penelope Eckert puts it, "elements of behavior that come to represent one category [are] rejected by the other, and . . . may be exploited by the other category through the development of a clearly opposed element" (1989:50) . . . .

It is too simple to treat the meaning of the expression of what appears as a sexualized version of femininity for working-class girls, and girls of color in particular, as a consequence of competitive heterosexuality and gender-subordinate learning. This fails to explain why girls made the choices they did from a variety of gender performances available to them. Rather, girls were negotiating meanings in a race- and class-stratified society, using commodities targeted at them as girls. They performed different versions of femininity that were integrally linked and inseparable from their class and race performances.

*Las chicas*, having "chosen" and/or been tracked into non-college-prep courses, were bored with their vocational schooling and often brought heterosexual romance and girl culture into the classroom as a favorite form of distraction, demonstrated in their repeated attempts to "set me up" with subs (which became almost a hazing ritual). But their gender performance and girl culture were not necessarily designed to culminate in a heterosexual relationship. Despite what appeared to be an obsession with heterosexual romance, a "men are dogs" theme was prevalent among them. Some said they

didn't want to marry until their thirties if at all, and they resented their boyfriends' infidelities and attempts to police their sexuality by telling them what they should and should not wear. They knew that men should not be counted on to support them and any children they might have, and they desired economic independence. Their girl culture was less about boys than about sharing rituals of traditional femininity as a kind of friendship bonding among girls. Although the overt concern in girl culture may be with boys and romance, girls often set themselves physically apart from boys (McRobbie 1991) . . . .

In short, *las chicas* had no more or less interest in heterosexual romance than did girls who performed prep or school-sanctioned femininity. Nonetheless, teachers and preps often confused the expression of class and race differences in style and activities among working-class girls as evidence of heterosexual interest. They often failed to perceive girls' class and race performances and unknowingly reproduced the commonsense belief that what is most important about girls, working-class performers in particular, is their girlness. *Las chicas'* style was not taken as a marker of race/ethnic and class distinction but was reduced to gender and sexuality.

In spite of the meanings that working-class girls themselves gave to their gender-specific cultural markers, their performances were always overdetermined by broader cultural meanings that code women in heavy makeup and tight clothes as oversexed—in short, cheap. In other words, class differences are often understood as sexual differences, where "the working class is cast as the bearer of an exaggerated sexuality, against which middle-class respectability is defined" (Ortner 1991:177). Among women, "clothing and cosmetic differences are taken to be indexes of the differences in sexual morals" between classes (178). Indeed, this is what I observed: middle-class performing prep girls (both white and Mexican American) perceived *las chicas,* as well as working-class performing white girls, as overly sexually active.

But Mexican American nonprep girls were perceived as even more sexually active than their white counterparts because, although there was no evidence that they were more sexually active, they were more likely to keep their babies if they became pregnant, so there was more often a visible indicator of their sexual activity. And while school personnel at times explained working-class Mexican American girls' gender performances as a consequence of "their" culture—an assumed real ethnic cultural difference in which women are expected to fulfill traditional roles and/or are victims of machismo and a patriarchal culture—the girls' generational status (according to two meanings) was not taken into account. On the one hand, *las chicas* were a generation of girls located in a historical context of dual-wage families, and they did not describe parents who had traditional roles in mind for their daughters. Moreover, they were second-generation Mexican Americans, young women with no intention of submitting to traditional gender ideologies.

Class was thus a present social force in the versions of femininity that the girls performed, but it was unarticulated and rendered invisible because it was interpreted (by school personnel, by preps, and at times by working-class girls themselves) as primarily about gender and a difference of sexual morality between good girls and bad girls. Likewise, class is rendered invisible in feminist theory when girls' poor school performance is seen primarily as a consequence of the fact that as girls they are "educated in romance" (Holland and Eisenhart 1990), rather than as a consequence of race and class tracking . . . .

## MIDDLE-CLASS *CHOLAS*

A handful of the girls were third-generation Mexican Americans from professional middle-class families. They had struggled to find their place in this race-class system. They had grown up in white neighborhoods and gone to elementary school with primarily white kids, where, as Rosa explained, "I knew I was different, because I was brown." In junior high, which was less segregated, some of them became *cholas* and were "jumped in" to a gang. When I asked why, Ana explained that she hated her family:

**Ana:**    *My mom wanted this picture-perfect family, you know. And I just hated it.*

**Julie:**    *What do you mean by a perfect family?*

**Ana:**    *You know, we had dinner at night together, and everything was just, okay. She was so happy. And I hated that. My life was sad, my friends' lives were sad.*

**Julie:**    *Why were they sad?*

**Ana:**    *One friend's mom was on welfare, the other didn't know who her dad was. Everything was wrong in their families.*

As she described class differences between herself and her friends, she struggled for the right words to describe it. And as Lorena sought to describe the difference between herself and her friend Ana, she too searched for words: "Well, in junior high she was way down kinda low, she got in with the bad crowd. But in high school she is higher up kinda. I mean not as high as Patricia is (another middle-class performer) but she's not as low as she used to be." Lorena's perception of Ana as high but low was shaped by Ana's crossover style and the sense that she had "earned" her "low" status by performing *chola* identity and gang-banging. In Ana's attempt to understand her place in a social order where color and poverty correlate more often than not, the salience of color was integral to her identity formation. She felt compelled to perform working-class identity at school as a marker of racial/ethnic belonging. As she explained, "the Mexican Mexicans, they aren't worried about whether they're Mexican or not."

Although Ana, Rosa, and Patricia eventually had accepted the cultural capital their parents had to give them and were now college prep and headed to four-year colleges, they were friendly with *las chicas* and still dressed and performed the kind of race-class femininity that *las chicas* did. In this way, they distanced themselves from preps and countered potential accusations of "acting white." In short, their style confounded the race-class equation and was an intentional strategy. By design, they had middle-class aspirations without assimilation to prep, which for them meant white, style. It went beyond image to a set of race politics as they tried to recruit *las chicas* to be a part of MEChA. In fact, when I went along on a bus ride to tour a nearby business school with *las chicas,* I was surprised to find that Ana, Rosa, and Patricia came along. I asked why they had come along since they had already been accepted to four-year schools. Rosa responded, "Because we're with the girls, you know, we have to be supportive, do these things together."

Mexican American girls' friendships crossed class performance boundaries more often than white girls' did because of a sense of racial alliance that drew them together in relation to white students at school and because the Mexican American community brought them together in activities outside school. They were also far more pained about divisions among themselves than white girls ever were (an aspect of whiteness that can seem invisible). They felt the need to present a united front, and this was particularly acute among girls who were politicized about their racial/ethnic identity and participated in MEChA. For white girls, competition among them did not threaten them as a racial/ethnic minority community.

In spite of their cross-class friendships, class differences were still salient among Mexican American girls, as evidenced in Lorena's description of Ana and in working-class performers' descriptions of MEChA, if they knew what it was at all, as "for brainy types," since MEChA was understood as a college-prep activity. Some of *las chicas* did join MEChA, but they typically played inactive roles. When I asked Yolanda about it, she replied, "Well, we joined, but it's not the same for me as it is for Patricia 'cause her mom is educated and all. She's real enthusiastic about it. You know, she's going to go to college and will do it there. But like Lorena and me, we can't always make it to the meetings. They're at lunch time and I have to go to work then, or I want to at least get some lunch before I go to work." Yolanda and Lorena both had vocational, work-experience "classes" for the last two periods of school, which allowed them to receive school credit for working. Patricia expressed some frustration with *las chicas'* failure to be very involved, as she and the other college-prep MEChA members struggled to find ways to reach *la raza* and get the people to come to the functions they organized.

The politicized racial identity offered by MEChA allowed Ana, Rosa, Patricia, and their friends to be middle-class performers and not deracinate. Ironically, although it embraced a working-class, community-based agenda, MEChA served middle-class performers who were already tracked upward more than it did a working-class base. It appealed less to working-class performers whose racial/ethnic identity was more secure, who were less vulnerable to accusations of acting white, and who understood it as a college-prep activity (it comes from the university, promotes schooling, and is therefore intimidating to working-class performers who experience class injury in relation to it). Class performance stood in the way of the racial alliance that MEChA students desired. Class differences were salient among Mexican American students, but they were not often articulated as such.

## WHITE TRASH *CHOLA*

Not surprisingly, white students generally did not explain class differences among themselves in racial terms. Rather, class difference was articulated as individual difference (she's "popular" or she's a "loser") and as differences in group membership and corresponding style (hicks, smokers, preps, etc.). But class meaning was at times bound to racial signifiers in the logic of white students, as it was among Mexican American students. This was apparent in the way the most marginalized white working-class students, who were at times described by other white students as "white trash," worked hard interactionally to clarify that they were not Mexican. In our very first conversation, Tara explained, without any solicitation, "I'm kinda dark, but I'm not Mexican." In our conversation about her boyfriend's middle-class parents, she explained that his mom had "accused me of being Mexican." She explained to me that she was Italian American, and her color and features did match this self-description (although it is also possible that there may be family secrets she does not know). Her father, a poor man, had worked in the fields for a time and drove what she called "a tex-mex truck," which was "one of those old beaters like the Mexicans in the fields drive." I couldn't help but think that her defensiveness about her racial status was linked to her class location and, further, that her class location assisted her boyfriend's mother's assessment of Tara as much as her coloring did. In short, Tara seemed to experience herself as "too close for comfort," so to speak, and she took every opportunity to make it clear that she was not Mexican.

Similarly, Starr, a white girl who grew up in a Mexican American neighborhood and went to the largely Mexican American elementary school in town, also had the sense that some whites, those at the bottom of the heap like herself, were almost brown. We were talking in the lunchroom one day about girls and fights when she told me this story:

**Starr:**   *Well the worst one was back in junior high. All of my friends were Mexican, 'cause I went to Landon. So I was too.*

**Julie:**   *You were what?*

**Starr:**   *Mexican. Well I acted like it, and they thought I was. I wore my hair up high in front you know. And I had an accent. Was in a gang. I banged [gang-banged] red [gang color affiliation].*

**Julie:**   *Were you the only white girl?*

**Starr:**   *Yeah.*

**Julie:**   *What happened? Why aren't you friends with them now?*

**Starr:**   *We got into a fight. I was in the bowling alley one day with my boyfriend. They came in and called him a piece of white trash. That made me mad and I smacked her. Lucky for her someone called the cops. They came pretty fast.*

**Julie:**   *What did she mean by white trash?*

**Starr:**   *Welfare people. He was a rocker. Had long hair, smoked.*

This episode ended her *chola* performance, and she was part of the white smoker crowd when I met her.

Like most other girls, Starr had told me that girls fight primarily about "guys." But her actual story reveals something different. A boy was central to the story, but the girls were not fighting *over* him. Rather, Starr's *chola* friends were bothered by her association with him, which pointed to her violation of the race-class identity she had been performing as a *chola*. Her friends forced her to make a choice.

Starr's race-class performance was a consequence of the neighborhood in which she grew up, and, like Tara, she had absorbed the commonsense notions that white is middle, that brown is low, and, most interesting, that low may become brown in certain contexts. Not unlike the experience of middle-class *cholas* for whom being middle-class Mexican American felt too close to being white, Starr's working-class version of whiteness felt too close to being Mexican American in this geographic context. Girls reported that cross-race friendships were more common in grade school, but in junior high a clear sorting out along racial lines emerged (and along class lines too, although with less awareness). Starr's story is about junior-high girls working to sort out class and color and ethnicity, about the social policing of racial boundaries, and about her move from a brown to a white racial performance (where both remained working class). Not insignificantly, her white performance included a racist discourse by which she distanced herself from Mexican Americans via derogatory statements about them.

Understanding Starr's *chola* performance as a cultural appropriation would be overly simplistic. This is what is implied by the discourse on "wiggas," whereby white (and, by some accounts, middle-class) youth appropriate what is marketed in popular culture as black style. Blackness is currently ubiquitous in pop culture, present more than it ever has been historically, and it has become synonymous with hip-hop (Gray 1995). Indeed, in spite of the near absence of black students at this school, "blackness" was ever present in their youth culture. Importantly, Mexican American signifiers do not carry the same currency in an economy of "cool" that "black" (read hip-hop) ones do, at least not among white students. Starr says that she did not understand her *chola* performance as a choice, an attempt to be cool. Social geography and the ways self is shaped by the degree of class and race homogeneity or diversity in one's community seem salient to Starr's identity options: "I didn't really think about it. Those were just who my friends were. Who I grew up with. There wasn't really anyone else around."

## CONCLUSION

"Class" is largely missing as a category of identity offered by popular culture and political discourse in the late twentieth-century United States. Working-class subjects are present among the imagery of popular culture, but they are not often articulated as "working class." Likewise, in political discourse a "working-class" constituency goes unrecognized as class difference is downplayed and Americans are constructed as all a part of a great "middle." Moreover, a liberal version of multicultural education too often provides attention to race/ethnic and gender inequalities only as a consequence of "discrimination," failing to explore both as linked to institutionalized class inequality. In short, class subjectivity is not discursively present even though the social force of class continues, of course, to shape political and cultural life.

Recognizing that identity and experience are always discursively mediated, I take girls' common-sense understandings of self-identity and experience (in particular, the presence/absence of class as an articulated identity) less as truths than as windows into "the complicated working of ideology," the webs of power and meaning that make such experiences and subjectivities possible (Fuss 1989:118). Experience is mediated by the frameworks for understanding ourselves that are made available to us. When we look to the multiple discursive sites (popular culture, politics, social science, schooling) and ways in which women are and are not constructed as, and do and do not experience themselves as, class subjects, we can see that there are "classifying projects" (Skeggs 1997) at work, but they are rarely named as such. Class remains obscure and often absent from the repertoire of possible cultural and political subjectivities.

The class futures of the girls I came to know are secured by the historical context in which they live, where race and gender projects in unison with a deindustrializing U.S. economy offer them only low-wage service-sector jobs, largely without labor union protection, and where a middle-income, blue-collar "family wage" job after high school is still not an option for women, no longer a real possibility for men, and still less likely for workers of color than white workers. Moreover, the shift from industrial to service work, where the latter is often coded feminine and middle class, poses a challenge to the (re)creation of a U.S. working-class identity and to the anachronistic language of class itself. It is ironic that, even under these conditions, class remains invisible in public discourse and, too often, in critical social theory. But these changes give good cause to renew an interest in "class" and imagine antireductionist ways of retheorizing class as we work to understand the ways in which class subjectivity might be constructed in relation to gender and racial/ethnic identity in late-twentieth-century global capitalism.

I have tried to model one way of thinking about class in relation to other axes of identity by exploring what utility might come of thinking through class as a performance and as performative and by exploring how the various gestures of class performance and performativity never exist outside of race and gender meanings. In the end, inequality along multiple axes was reproduced at the school, but the invisibility of class was also reproduced, in that race and gender often took its place in girls' own understandings and "the school's" perception of who they were. This is not to say that race and gender were understood accurately while class was left obscure. In fact, it was the essentialized conceptualizations of race and gender that helped to keep the difference of class invisible. Race and gender were more readily perceived as natural and inevitable causal social forces, while class left unnamed altogether, invisible as a category of belonging or causality.

It was left unnamed because of the lack of a fully articulated political or cultural discourse on class as such. The difference that economic and cultural resources make did structure girls' lives, but class meaning was routinely articulated through other categories of difference. Understanding group differences as differences of "style" was a way of simultaneously displacing and recognizing class difference. Accusations of "acting white" obscured class at the same time that they provided a way of talking about class difference between white middle-class preps and working-class Mexican Americans, as well as among Mexican American students themselves. Likewise, the distinction between "good girls" and "bad girls" was wrongly perceived as about sexual morality, yet at the same time school-sanctioned femininity and dissident femininity were read as symbolic markers of class and race difference.

Thinking through class as a performance enables us to acknowledge exceptions to the rule that class origin equals class future and to understand that economic and cultural resources often, but not inevitably, determine class futures. It allows us to explore the experience of negotiating inherited and chosen identities, as, for example, when middle-class students of color felt compelled to perform working-class identities as a marker of racial/ethnic belonging. It helps demonstrate, too, how other axes of identity intersect with and inform class identity and consequently shape class futures. Thinking through class as a performance is useful for understanding exceptions, those who are consciously "passing" (whether it be up or down).

But it is also useful to think of class as performative in the sense that class as cultural identity is an *effect* of social structure. Social actors largely perform the cultural capital that is a consequence of the material and cultural resources to which they have had access. Cultural performances most often reflect one's habits or unconscious learned dispositions, which are not natural or inherent or prior to the social organization of class inequality but are in fact produced by it. Considering class as performative is consistent with regarding it more as a cultural than a political identity and more as a "sense of place" than as class consciousness in a political, Marxist sense. It helps explain why class struggle is often waged more over modes of identity expression than over explicit political ideologies.

In anti-essentialist fashion, class as a cultural identity cannot be uncoupled from one's gendered and racialized self or from how these categories are historically reconstructed and changing. Highlighting this points to how and why other axes of identity might inform and motivate political action more than class. In short, directing our attention to class culture and identity (rather than to class as a political consciousness or to class-for-itself) "is a way of focusing class analysis on the *cultural politics* of how economic classes are culturally reproduced and resisted" (Foley 1990; emphasis added). It is not the case that race and gender are mere ideologies that mask the reproduction of class inequality; they are organizing principles in their own right, processes that are co-created with class. In our attempts to explore the ways these processes are and are not parallel, contemporary feminist and cultural studies theorists often suggest the need to think of these multiple social formations *evenly*. But we might consider that social actors do not experience them this way and explore the meanings people actually give to these categories, in ways that render class invisible.

## DISCUSSION QUESTIONS

1. How does Bettie's research illustrate intersectionality? What is missing from her analysis?
2. Within sociology, social class is traditionally treated as a masculine objective economic category. Bettie argues instead that social class can be seen as a feminine subjective cultural category that engages "cultural meanings of race/ethnicity, gender, and sexuality." Provide examples in which Bettie demonstrates how and why this happens among the young women she studied in one high school in central California.

## NOTES

1. Cultural capital refers to class-based knowledge, skills, linguistic and cultural competencies, and a worldview that is passed on via family; it is related more to educational attainment than to occupation. See Bourdieu and Passeron 1977 and Bourdieu 1984. Also

see Lamont and Lareau 1988 for an overview of the multiple and contradictory uses of the concept, especially as applied to the United States.

2. Defining class "origin" is problematic in itself since the fluidity of economic and cultural capital within any given family often makes its "class" hard to name. Frequently, the class status of women, their husbands or partners, and their children differs. Given divorce and the coming and going of parents and stepparents (usually fathers and stepfathers) from children's lives, women's economic resources are often quite fluid (even in the lives of middle-class women). But women still are not likely to pair with men outside of their social class, so parents are usually not too disparate from one another in educational achievement. Moreover, women and men of color and white women often experience a disparity between educational attainment and economic reward. Thus, it is useful to think of economic and cultural capital as somewhat independent of each other.

# 22

# QUEERS WITHOUT MONEY

*They Are Everywhere. But We*
*Refuse to See Them.*

AMBER HOLLIBAUGH

*Amber Hollibaugh identifies as an ex-hooker, incest survivor, biracial radical feminist, high-femme lesbian, working-class, white-trash organizer, and AIDS activist. Not an academic, Hollibaugh writes to raise awareness in the queer community and beyond. This article, published in* The Village Voice *online in 2001, challenges the reader to look beyond the stereotypes that most gays are wealthy. Hollibaugh argues there are no images of poor gays in the media, and that in reality, many queer youth are homeless. Moreover, we are lacking social services that can serve these double- or triple-oppressed populations who are poor, queer, and possibly homeless.*

*I mean, homosexuals have high incomes, they have high levels of education; they're owners of major credit cards. There was a survey done. So you're not talking about poor people, homeless people living under a bridge.*

—Reverend Lou Sheldon,
a conservative Christian leader

I lived the first year of my life in a converted chicken coop in back of my grandmother's trailer. The coop was hardly tall enough for my 6'4" father and 5'8" mother to stand up in. My dad, a carpenter, tore out the chickens' egg-laying ledges and rebuilt the tiny inside space to fit a bed, a table, two chairs, a basin they used as a sink (there was no running water), a shelf with a hot plate for cooking,

---

*Source:* "Queers Without Money: They Are Everywhere. But We Refuse to See Them," by Amber Hollibaugh, *Village Voice*, June 20, 2001. Reprinted with permission.

and a small dresser. They used the hose outside to wash with, and ran extension cords in from my grandmother's trailer for light and heat. My bed, a dresser drawer, sat on top of the table during the day. At night it was placed next to where they slept.

I was sick the entire first year of my life. So was my mother, recovering from a nasty C-section and a series of ensuing medical crises. By the time she and I were discharged, three months later, whatever money my parents had managed to save was used up, and they were deeply in debt. They had been poor before my birth, and poor all of their lives growing up, but this was the sinker.

After my first year, we moved from the chicken coop into a trailer. My father worked three jobs simultaneously, rarely sleeping. My mother took whatever work she could find: mending, washing, and ironing other people's clothes. But we never really recovered. We were impoverished. Growing up, I was always poor. I am also a lesbian.

This, then, is my queer identity: I am a high-femme, mixed-race, white-trash lesbian. And even after all these years of living in a middle-class gay community, I often feel left outside when people speak about their backgrounds, their families. And if you listen to the current telling of "our" queer tale, people like me would seem an anomaly. Because, we are told—and we tell ourselves—queerness can't be poor.

Yet this seeming anomaly is the tip of the proverbial iceberg. It represents hundreds of thousands of us who come from poor backgrounds, or are living them still—and are very, very queer.

That would seem obvious when you combine the proportion of the population reputed to be queer (between 4 and 10 percent) with the 37 million poor people in America. Yet the early surveys done on gay and lesbian economic status in this country told a different tale: that queers had more disposable income than straights, lived more luxurious lives, and were all DINKs (Dual Income No Kids). "My book begins as a critique of those early surveys, which were done largely to serve the interests of gay and lesbian publications and a few marketing companies," says economist M. V. Lee Badgett in her new book, *Money, Myths, and Change: The Economic Lives of Lesbians and Gay Men.* "Those surveys are deeply flawed."

Badgett notes that "opposition to gay people is often based on the perception that queers are better off than everybody else; that we're really asking for 'special rights'—and that breeds resentment." Badgett's research shows something else. It constitutes the first true picture of queer economic reality. Among other things, Badgett found that:

Gays, lesbians, and bisexuals do *not* earn more than heterosexuals, or live in more affluent households.

Gay men earn 13 to 32 percent less than similarly qualified straight men (depending on the study).

Though lesbians and bisexual women have incomes comparable to straight women—earning 21 percent less than men—lesbian couples earn significantly less than heterosexual ones.

But . . . try finding representations of poor or working-class gay people on *Will & Grace*. See how hard you have to search for media images of queers who are part of the vast working poor in this country. Find the homeless transgendered folks. Find stories of gay immigrants, lesbian moms working three jobs, bisexual truckers falling asleep from too many hours on the road, gay men in the unemployment line. Try finding an image of queer people who are balancing on the edge—or have fallen off.

The myth of our wealth goes deep, so deep that even other gay people seem to believe it. We have tried to protect ourselves from the hard truths of our economic diversity by perpetuating the illusion of material wealth, within the confines of male/female whiteness. This is a critical aspect of how we present ourselves in this country at this point in time. We treat the poverty that exists among us—as well as the differences of class—as a dirty secret to be hidden, denied, repelled. We treat economic struggle as something that functions outside the pull of queer desires, removed from our queerly lived lives.

As Badgett notes, by celebrating the myth of queer affluence, we have "drawn attention to exactly the kind of picture that Lou Sheldon is drawing of gay and lesbian people." There is a richer—and ultimately more sympathetic—queer reality: "We are everywhere—but we're all different."

Why is it so hard to acknowledge this? Why is poverty treated as a queer secret? And why does it produce a particular kind of homosexual shame? Bear with me. Imagine what you've never allowed yourself to see before.

When I directed the Lesbian AIDS Project at Gay Men's Health Crisis, stories of the hundreds of HIV-positive lesbians who were a part of that project literally came roaring out of those women's mouths. These were lesbians who had almost never participated in queer politics or visited any of New York City's queer institutions. On those rare occasions when they had tried, they quickly departed, unseen and unwelcomed.

Andrew Spieldenner, a young gay organizer of color who has worked for years with men who have sex with men, has a name for this phenomenon. He calls it "a queer and invisible body count." It is made up of poor lesbians and gay men, queer people of color, the transgendered, people with HIV and AIDS and—always and in large numbers—the queer young and the queer elderly.

The Metropolitan Community Church, a largely gay denomination, reports that the demand for food at its New York pantry has doubled since the beginning of welfare reform in 1996. The Lesbian and Gay Community Services Center says that homeless people in their addiction programs have tripled since then. The Hetrick-Martin Institute, which serves "gay and questioning youth," estimates that 50 percent of homeless kids in New York City are queer.

"We are entering a time when the economy is going into a slump," says Joseph De Filippis, who coordinates the Queer Economic Justice Network. "This isn't going to be like the '90s, when it was easy for employers to give things like domestic-partner benefits. There are going to be more and more of us who are affected by joblessness and economic crisis. And the welfare reform law expires in 2002. It's our issue, damn it. It has always been our issue."

Ingrid Rivera, director of the Racial and Economic Justice Initiative of the National Gay and Lesbian Task Force, has lived this issue. "I was on welfare, I was homeless, I thought I'd be lucky if I finished high school. I am a woman of color, I am a mother, and I am queer. I've worked and lived in a poor world and I've worked in queer organizations that are primarily white. I've seen it from both perspectives, and there's a kind of disconnect. In the gay, mostly white world, race and economic justice isn't talked about as a queer issue. And because of that split, queerness becomes a white thing."

Poverty and outright destitution can happen to anyone—and the queerer you are, the fewer safety nets exist to hold you up or bounce you back from the abyss. Queerness intensifies poverty and compounds the difficulty of dealing with the social service system. The nightmares—even in this city, with its gay rights law—include:

Being separated from your partner if you go into the shelter system. Straight couples can remain together by qualifying for the family system.

Being mandated into homophobic treatment programs for drug or drinking problems and having the program decide to treat your queerness instead of your addiction. If you leave the program, you lose any right to benefits—including Medicaid.

Being unable to apply as a family for public housing.

Ending up a queer couple in the only old-age home you can afford and being separated when you try to share a room.

Barbara Cassis came from a wealthy Long Island family. But when he began to understand and acknowledge his transgendered nature, his parents kicked him out. He was homeless, young, and broke. "Thank God for drag queens," she says, looking back. "A drag queen found me crying in Times Square and took me home. She talked to me about what I was going through, let me stay with her in her apartment, taught me how to support myself, how to get clients as a prostitute or in the gay bars where I could work as I transitioned. But then she died of AIDS and I was homeless again."

The homeless shelters were the worst experience of all for Barbara as a trans woman. Often, it felt easier to just stay on the streets. If you're homeless, and you haven't transitioned—which costs a fortune—you're forced to go to a shelter based on birth gender. The risk of violence and danger is always high for everyone; the shelters are crowded, short of staff, and the staff that is there has no training in how to deal with trans or gay issues. So if you are a trans person, just taking a shower means that you're taking your life in your hands.

"It took me years to get on my feet," says Cassis, now an administrative assistant at the Positive Health Project, "to start dealing with being HIV-positive, and get the training and education I needed to find a decent job. It has also taken years for me to reconcile with my family, which I have. If it hadn't been for the kind of people the gay community often discounts and despises, I wouldn't be here today."

Like my mother said, the only difference between a poor drunk and a rich one is which drunk can hide it. The shame of being poor is an acutely public shame, difficult to hide. And *queer* homosexuality—the kind of queerness that makes gender differences and radical sexual desires crystal clear—this queerness triggers similar ruinous social perils.

We punish people in this country for being poor and we punish homosexuality. When both are combined, it does more than double the effect: It twists and deepens it, gives it sharper edges, and heightens our inability to duck and cover or slide through to a safer place. It forces you to live more permanently outside than either condition dictates.

The problem intensifies when you realize what queers are in the mind of America. We stand for the culture's obsession with the erotic. It is we who are portrayed as always doing it or trying to, we who quickly become the sexual criminals at the heart of any story. We are the ones who are dangerous; our sexuality is more explosive, more explicit, more demanding, more predatory.

And so it goes for poor people: part stereotype (read trailer trash or welfare queen), part object of blame for being too stupid not to have done better. The underlying assumption is that the only appropriate desires are those that rest comfortably atop plenty of money. The desires and needs afforded by wealth—and plenty of it, earned or not—are appropriate, acceptable, good. But messy desires? Desires that combine with class and color? Desires and needs that ricochet around the erotic? These needs are not acceptable. They are condemned.

No wonder the gay movement can't see the poverty in its midst. The one thing this culture longs for and seems to value in queer life is the image of wealth. It appears to be the only thing we do right. And it is the only piece of our queerness that we can use when our citizenship is at stake. We learned this at the beginning of the AIDS crisis, when we activated that wealth to do what the government wouldn't: We built institutions to care and protect and serve our own. It is a riveting example of how we have claimed our own and valued what the mainstream culture despised about our lives. We could do the same with queer poverty.

"If the community got involved in the issues of being queer and poor," says Jay Toole, a lesbian in the LGBT caucus of the Coalition for the Homeless, "it would be like the community saying, 'I'm here, and here's my hand. You can go further, I'm here.'

Toole is finishing school now. She plans to work as a substance abuse counselor, to go back into the shelters and bring gay people into the community, "so that they don't have to be so alone as I was. Because when Ann Duggan [from the Coalition] brought me back down to the Lesbian and Gay Center from the shelter, it was finally like coming home."

## Discussion Questions

1. How does Hollibaugh refute the myth that all gay people are well-off?
2. Why is Hollibaugh's argument about the stereotyping of gays as wealthy important?

# 23

# A PLACE IN TOWN

*Doing Class in a Coffee Shop*

CARRIE YODANIS

*Carrie Yodanis, an associate professor of sociology at the University of British Columbia, studies marriages and families. This reading is an excerpt from an ethnographic study Yodanis did of a small-town coffee shop and the social interactions that occur there as shaped by gender and social class. The study, published in 2006 in the* Journal of Contemporary Ethnography, *illustrates well how individuals manage and perform their social class identities. Yodanis argues that the process of doing social class is so entrenched in our social interactions that classed behaviors seem to be innate. To challenge this notion, Yodanis examines the discourse women use to discuss their work lives, leisure time, and families.*

## THEORY

Twenty-five years ago, Elijah Anderson (1976) wrote *A Place on the Corner*, an ethnographic study of the men who frequent an urban bar and liquor store. By hanging out with, observing, and listening to the men in a public place, Anderson uncovered the localized aspects of stratification systems. Through interaction, including how "people defer to one another, are deferred to, ally themselves with certain others, and help prop up the identity of valued members of the respective crowds," individuals collectively create systems of social status and rank (Anderson 1976:216).

*Source:* "A Place in Town: Doing Class in a Coffee Shop," by Carrie Yodanis, 2006, *Journal of Contemporary Ethnography, 35*, pp. 341–344, 346–366. Copyright 2006 by Sage Publications. Reprinted with permission.

Thirty-five years before that, Warner and Lunt (1941) conducted their classic community study of Yankee City, in which they also argue that social classes are rooted in social interaction. In the community, Warner and Lunt found six social classes. At first, following most research and theories of class, they believed the basis of the classes to be economic. Yet as they spent more time in the community, they concluded that membership to one of the six classes emerged from behaviors and interactions . . . .

Differential access to wealth, income, and education unquestionably provides uneven opportunities in life. However, as Randall Collins (2000) emphasizes, considering macrolevel socioeconomic differences is not enough. It is important for sociologists to consider how macro differences in material positions play out in micro situations. He writes,

> Microsituational encounters are the ground zero of all social action and all sociological evidence. Nothing has reality unless it is manifest in a situation somewhere . . . . We need to undertake a series of studies looking at the conversion of abstract macrodistributions, which we have constructed by taking survey aggregations as if they were real things with fixed transsituational values, into the actual distribution of advantages in situational practice. (Collins 2000:18)

Thus, it is in micro situations that the consequences of class are felt in our daily lives. From a "doing class" perspective, the micro situation is where class comes to exist . . . .

The process of doing class is so entrenched in our interactions that classed behaviors seem nearly innate to socioeconomic positions. Bourdieu (1984) implies this innateness when he uses his concept of habitus to argue that individuals develop unconscious worldviews based on their structural, socioeconomic positions that determine their tastes and behaviors. Individuals of a given socioeconomic position are held accountable for acting according to roles defined as associated with that position. In this paper, however, I argue that tastes and behaviors do not merely emerge from structural positions; instead,

individuals ascribe different tastes, values, and behaviors to socioeconomic positions and then act according to these tastes, values, and behaviors during interaction to group themselves with people who are similar and to distance themselves from those who are different. Class categories are created and continually reinforced during these ongoing interactions . . . .

## THE COFFEE SHOP

The Coffee Shop sits in the middle of an interesting town. Situated on a remote coast, most of the full-time, year-round residents work in the fishing or small tourist industry. A number of residents also work for summer residents on the exclusive colony of mansions to the south of the town. Since the 1800s the summer residents have had a striking influence over the local residents, providing not only employment but also financial support to the town, including funding for the town library and medical center and individual families (paying for houses and cars). There are also a number of other "people from away," who have moved to the area. Some of these people are affiliated with the military base, sitting to the north of the town. Others are back-to-the-landers who moved to the town over the past decades to enjoy the slower pace of rural life and work on their art or farms. The symbolic meaning of these diverse populations for the year-round residents of the town comes into play as they do class in the Coffee Shop.

Each weekday morning from 8:00 until 10:30, nine women and I came to the Coffee Shop. Although these women have known each other for years and some for their whole lives, they segregated themselves into groups. Nancy, Sharon, and Holly sat at the counter. They were the first to arrive when the Coffee Shop opened at 8:00 and sat at their "regular stools" at the counter, rarely turning around to even acknowledge the other women in the Coffee Shop. Around 9:15, Gigi, Jean, and Helen arrived and sat together at a table toward the front of the Coffee Shop. Guests visited their table only when invited, and invitations were infrequent. Amy, Dorothy, and

Tricia formed a third group. They sat at the far back table. They got together less regularly than the other women, but were in the Coffee Shop at least a few days each week.

These seating arrangements, which were rarely if ever violated, were the most obvious way in which women created boundaries and distinctions among themselves . . . .

While there are similarities across the groups and important exceptions within each group, the groups tended to be somewhat differentiated by levels of education, occupation, and income and wealth. The women at the counter tend to have lower socioeconomic positions. Nancy and her husband have high school degrees. She worked for years as a cook, at local factories and fish dealers, as a housekeeper, and as a clerk at local stores. Recently, she got a job as a teacher's aide. While school was out for the summer, she was not working for pay. Her husband works on fishing boats and as a maintenance worker. Sharon did not graduate from high school, but her husband did. During the summer of 1996, she worked at the fish plant in the neighboring town and has worked at a number of factories and as a housekeeper throughout the years. Her husband works for a local construction company. Holly graduated from technical school and has some college education. She worked at the Coffee Shop, as a nurse's aide, and as a housekeeper. Her partner has a high school degree and works as a fisherman.

In comparison, the women at the front table are generally wealthier. Gigi is from the elite summer colony. Her husband is a lawyer, and she is president of the women's board of a hospital in her home city. During the summer, she had no work to do. Helen is also of a higher socioeconomic status. She has a college degree and her husband has a Ph.D. She has worked intermittently for pay throughout her life. During the summer, she was in the Women's Club, works in the library, and volunteers for retirement homes. Jean is an interesting exception, because compared to the other women she is not wealthy. She has technical school training and is a home-duty nurse's aide. She is also active in many community organizations. She was not married, but her former husband was in the military.

Among the final group of women at the back table, Tricia managed the Coffee Shop during the summer season and worked for pay sporadically during winter, making wreaths or assisting at a day care. She has a college degree, but her husband did not go to school beyond high school. He works as a gardener for the summer colony. Dorothy has technical school training and works part-time as a secretary. Her husband also has technical training and owns a small retail store. Amy went to college for a while but did not complete her degree. She works sporadically for pay throughout the year as a substitute teacher, in retail stores, and making crafts to sell. Her husband has some technical school training and is a fisherman.

So there are socioeconomic differences between the women. Nonetheless, differences in income, occupational prestige, and education in and of themselves were not sufficient for creating class categorization. Within the seating arrangements that physically created the groups, the women continually use or reject behaviors, tastes, and values during interaction to categorize themselves and the other women into three classes. As a result, Nancy, Sharon, and Holly became working-class women, with a strong work ethic. Gigi, Helen, and Jean became upper-class women, enjoying high culture and fine dining and dedicated to their volunteer work. Tricia, Dorothy, and Amy became new middle-class women, dedicated to intellectual and liberal, politically active pursuits. In the rest of the paper, I describe these interactions, based in different orientations to work, leisure, and family, which I observed during my time in the Coffee Shop.

## WORK

In the Coffee Shop, different orientations toward work were continually acted out. While in the Coffee Shop, the working-class women worked and talked about work. Even when hanging out in a restaurant, a supposed leisure activity, they managed to work. Among Nancy, Sharon, and Holly, the overwhelming topic of conversation was work. While at the Coffee Shop, they often commented on how they are being lazy or a "slug" by sitting around. Yet their actions and conversations always contradicted this. They came into the Coffee Shop the earliest and left the soonest. While sitting having coffee, they discussed the paid or household work they did before or would do after leaving the shop. Nancy, who was not employed for the summer, emphasized work by talking about the housework she did . . . . Describing the amount of work they did became almost competitive between the working class women.

The most obvious behavior was the work that Nancy and Holly did while at the Coffee Shop. Holly was employed at the Coffee Shop and rarely sat to talk. Instead, she held conversations from behind the counter while she washed dishes, prepared food, and cleaned up. When Holly was in the Coffee Shop and not working, She was always stopping on her way to her other nursing or housekeeping work. Although not employed at the Coffee Shop, Nancy frequently worked while there. She got up from her stool and did the dishes, made egg salad or coffee, or changed the displays. She started doing this without pay, but later in the summer was asked to fill in on the weekends for pay. Yet, she continued to help out during the week even if she was not on the payroll.

At times, Sharon did not come to the Coffee Shop for a few days. When she did return, she would report that she had been working double shifts at the fish plant, and she talked about the hours she put in this week and how she only got one day off a week. She also showed her hands and the cuts, dirty nails, and stained fingers as a sign of her work at the factory.

The working-class women used these values to distinguish themselves from others. In addition to acting out their work ethic, the working-class women talked about how lazy others are. Holly, who cleans houses for the summer colony, was telling me about how the job varies depending on the family. She told the story about one family who never puts the new roll of toilet paper on the holder. They always just put it on top, and she has to put it on the holder. She said she really doesn't understand—they have nothing else to do while they are just sitting there, so can't they just do that one simple job? . . .

At the same time, however, the other women in the Coffee Shop treated the working-class women as inferior based on these values. They were treated by the other women as being lazy, although they were the only women working while at the Coffee Shop. Although they were there far fewer hours than the other women, the other women and customers would comment on how often they were in the Coffee Shop. It was not uncommon to hear someone say to Nancy, "You should have your name engraved in that stool." They were often asked if they were "working hard" and were praised when they started a new job. For example, Sharon had been working double shifts for most of the summer at the fish-processing plant. The work is hard, hot, and dirty. She had only one day off a week. Yet, the following excerpts from my field notes show how the other women view her:

> Jean [an upper-class woman] came into the Coffee Shop. Sharon was sitting at the counter and said that she had worked 13 days in a row. Jean asked in a very condescending way, "So you got a job? Where are you working?" and then after Sharon answers, she said, "Now you finally have work and now you are working too hard . . . . You jumped right into it. You went from nothing to overtime."

So while the working-class women acted out a strong work ethic, the other women acted to undermine and downgrade their orientations and values. This created bounded categories between the women and began the struggle for hierarchies between the groups.

In sharp contrast, the upper-class women acted according to a volunteer rather than a paid work ethic. In the Coffee Shop, Gigi, Jean, and Helen were all highly involved in community organizations and presented this work as their primary concern whether or not they also worked for pay. When they said, "I have to work," they were referring to their community activities. They frequently talked about the unpaid community work that they were doing and often left stating that they had some community work to conduct. Gigi had to return to the city because September was going to be a busy month for the women's board at the hospital. Helen had to go to dance practice for a retirement home. Jean had to sell tickets to raise money for a new roof for a historic hall in town.

Jean does not have the socioeconomic class standing of Gigi or even Helen and thus was most active in creating her class category through interaction in the Coffee Shop. She is a good example of how class categorization does not necessarily correspond to one's socioeconomic position. Nearly everyday, Jean talked about the unpaid work she was conducting in the town, noting how important this work is to the social foundation of the town. Jean talked about the many hours she puts into running the plays and described the plays as providing worthwhile leisure activities and cultural experiences for the young people in town. She discussed the scholarships and charity work which were conducted by the Women's Club. She mentioned the "anonymous" charity work that she did on her own. She distributed and posted fliers advertising the plays or fundraisers which she organized. She sold tickets for community events from the card table that she set up on the sidewalk right outside of the Coffee Shop. She would laugh and call the Coffee Shop her "office" for her community work.

Describing their time in the Coffee Shop, Jean, Gigi, and Helen explained "that is what we do here, we form a community." They sat near the door and watched and greeted everyone who came into the Coffee Shop. They saw these actions as important for building community and presented themselves as community-minded residents. As compared to the working-class women, they stayed the longest at the Coffee Shop.

While acting as volunteers, the upper-class women never acted as paid workers. Helen and Gigi did not work for pay. Jean, on the other hand, financially needed to work for pay. She worked as a private home nurse's aide, cleaned the summer cottage that her sister owns and rents, and filled in for her friend at his art shop. She worked anywhere from 3 to 6 days a week, but never discussed her paid work in the Coffee Shop. When listing her day's activities, her paid work was never mentioned. On days when she was unable to come to the Coffee Shop because she had to work, she did not provide an explanation unless she was asked directly and

then only gave a brief answer. When she did talk about her work as a nurse's aide, she discussed it in terms of volunteer work. She was "taking care of an older woman in town" or "giving a massage to a woman who had an injury."

The upper-class women also used their work values in an effort to gain status in the class hierarchy of the Coffee Shop. The upper-class women distinguished themselves from others by talking about the apathy in town, referring to the lack of interest in joining community organizations or volunteering for tasks or positions within the organizations. Jean frequently talked about the frustration she felt when others were not willing to help and often criticized the projects that she sees as so essential to the community. Gigi and Helen agreed and saw it within their own community work . . .

The middle-class women acted according to yet another orientation toward work—a commitment to progressive, political work—in the process of doing class and being categorized as members of the new middle class of intellectual, liberal professionals. In complete contrast to the working-class women, they lacked a paid work ethic and openly share it. Like the upper-class women, they kept later hours at the Coffee Shop, often hanging out until the middle of the afternoon. While Holly and Nancy, working-class women, worked in the Coffee Shop, Tricia, who also worked at the Coffee Shop, left her work and joined Amy and Dorothy at their table in the back. In my first conversation with Amy at the Coffee Shop, she presented her lack of a paid work ethic to me when she told me, "The two most important things about the Protestant work ethic is that religion should be first and the work should be second in importance, and neither are very important to me."

Tricia, Amy, and Dorothy are political. They are all involved in local politics, serving on the school board and other committees, and this work was a near daily topic of conversation at the Coffee Shop. Who was at the town meeting? When will the teachers' contract be settled? If the military leaves, how will that impact the town? Will the town buy the water company? They also talked about national and state politics—public policies, the presidential campaigns, and the candidates for state government.

Tricia closed the Coffee Shop or had someone fill in for her so that she could do work for the school board in the state capital.

Their political orientation was very specific, however. They defined themselves as "liberal" and presented themselves as such. They distinguished themselves from the people in the town who have sexist, homophobic, and racist ideas and acted as social change agents trying to enlighten people to change their backward ideas . . . .

Actions of the middle-class women confirmed their values. Amy parked her van, with a bumper sticker supporting gay and lesbian rights, outside of the Coffee Shop. During a referendum regarding a gay rights bill, Tricia wore a button to work which revealed her support for gay and lesbian rights. She listened to National Public Radio while working.

The Coffee Shop is a public place where women "do class." The women could have just done different jobs and work outside of their time at the Coffee Shop, but that would not necessarily translate into categorization into particular social classes. Without acting according to class-associated work values and orientations, they would not be identified as members of a particular social class based on their work. By doing hard work, Nancy, Sharon, and Holly acted to be categorized as working class; while emphasizing volunteer work, Gigi, Helen, and Jean sought categorization as upper class; and through their political work, Amy, Tricia, and Dorothy did class as intellectual, liberals of the new middle class. I argue here that these repeated, patterned actions were not random but rather involved the women acting according to behaviors and values associated with a particular social class. These behaviors categorized women into social classes in their daily interactions in the Coffee Shop.

## LEISURE

As with work values and orientations, the women in the Coffee Shop also used leisure in the process of doing class. In this section, I show how their tastes for leisure activities were used in interaction for class categorization. In other words, preferences in leisure do not just emerge from socioeconomic positions but are in fact used to place meaning on and categorize people according to these differences.

The working-class women downplayed leisure as they emphasized their work ethic. Nonwork activities were rarely a topic of conversation. When I would ask Nancy or Sharon, "How was your weekend?" or "Did you get to enjoy this beautiful day?" they answered according to how productive the day or weekend was, such as "I got a lot done" or "Didn't get enough done."

The working-class women shunned any orientation toward high culture. They do not travel, even to nearby places . . . .

When Holly criticized a local cultural event as something she did not want to participate in, Sharon held her accountable for acting working class by being quick to remind her that she was violating her working-class category by being like the summer residents.

Among the upper-class women, Gigi, a member of the elite summer colony, was the clearest symbol used by Jean and Helen in their leisure. By sitting and being seen with Gigi, leisure time was very important for acting out affiliation with the summer colony, and Gigi's friendship continued to be used in interaction even when she was not there. For example, after Gigi had returned to her permanent residence in the fall, she wrote a note to Jean. In the setting of the Coffee Shop, Jean shared the letter with the women in the Coffee Shop, demonstrating her personal ties and knowledge of Gigi:

> *Jean announced that she got a card from Gigi. She said that "She said to say Hi to everyone, Helen, Carrie, Tricia and someone else . . . . Oh, Sharon" (and laughed). "She will be back at the end of October. She said that she is back into her routine which she enjoys although she 'whines' about it a lot. She is such a real person."*

In contrast to the working-class women, the upper-class women frequently discussed their leisure activities, in particular those related to high culture. Indeed, discussion of high culture dominated their daily conversations. They discussed experiences in Europe and tropical vacation spots. Almost 20 years ago, Jean lived in Germany, Hawaii, and the Philippines as a result of her former husband's military career. Yet, she used these experiences in her interactions to display orientations toward high travel. Everyday, even when quite irrelevant, Jean reminded women in the Coffee Shop that she had lived in these exotic locations . . . .

One day, she brought me a stack of *Condé Nast Traveler* magazines. The vacation spots covered in the magazines range from "55 Islands of Desire" to Rome, Thailand, and Latin America. Although she had not been outside of the country since her divorce and her travel was a result of military assignments rather than exotic vacations, both her subscription to this magazine and bringing them to the Coffee Shop were important actions in her display and creation of class category. In contrast, although Amy, another woman in the Coffee Shop, also lived in Europe as a result of her husband's work in the military, she never discussed her experiences as engaging in high culture.

Tastes for high culture pervade their actions. One day, Jean explained that during the afternoon she and a friend who was visiting were planning to have tea at 4:00 on the rocky shore of the summer colony. Her friend's sister-in-law, a concert flutist who teaches at a private school, was going to play the flute. Helen, nearly every day, talked about listening to classical music and attending musical performances. She shared her knowledge about high culture by listing performers and evaluating the technical quality of performances. Jean kept everyone updated on the progress of the local plays she was organizing. She brought in a tape of classical music to share with Helen. The upper-class women openly made plans to attend the opera and the local plays together, excluding the other women in the Coffee Shop.

At the same time, the upper-class women showed disdain for the local working-class culture of the town. In doing so, they continued to categorize themselves as upper class and strove to gain a superior position relative to the working class. They talked openly about avoiding the Diner, a casual seafood restaurant in town where many of the fishermen and other local families hang out. Their criticism centered on the atmosphere, which they did not see as on their level. Jean said she doesn't like the Diner: "I am going to sound snobby, but [pause] it is the level of conversation that goes on." . . .

In comparison, upper-class women often discussed dinner at the Dining Room, a more formal, expensive seafood restaurant, where residents of the summer colony often ate. They talked about the excellent meals they had and the good service they received. They invited me to meet them at the Dining Room for dinner. As Jean explained one day, she and a friend wanted to go to dinner, but she was getting sick of the Dining Room because they went so frequently.

Related to this, Jean had very high standards for service at the Coffee Shop, which other women approached as very casual. Everyday when she came in, she demanded that her service be prompt and that her tea and popcorn were prepared just right. She got visibly upset and annoyed if she did not receive the service she expected . . . .

Like the upper class and unlike the working class, the middle-class women engaged in conspicuous leisure during their interactions in the Coffee Shop. For example, Tricia did not work on the weekends in the Coffee Shop. Rather, she had younger women fill the Saturday and Sunday shifts. In addition, she often took an additional day off to make the weekend longer and provide more time for leisure activities. Amy came into the Coffee Shop to socialize on days when she had turned down substitute teaching jobs because she was feeling ill.

What was unique about their leisure was the focus on new age, liberal, intellectual interests and hobbies. For example, Tricia, who manages the Coffee Shop, did the purchasing for the small gift shop in the back of the store. She included aromatherapy and environmentally friendly and Native American print greeting cards in the stock. By selecting these items for the store, Tricia displayed her class-associated values and interests. Similarly, Amy one day asked me, while ignoring the upper-class women I was sitting with, if I would like to visit an herb shop with her in a neighboring town. I agreed, and we visited two herb shops and an organic farm along the way. Throughout the trip, Amy shared her knowledge of herbs for both artistic and medicinal purposes.

The middle-class women also often discussed films and books. For example, one day they were talking about an author whose books they have all read. The author writes about Hasidic Jews. None of them are Jewish, and they all loved the books. Tricia said that she was "thrown off" by the author's last book because it was about African Americans. She quickly explained that there was "nothing wrong" with a book about African American culture, but that she was "just really in a mood for a book about Hasidic Jews." Another day, I referred to the movie *Bound*. Tricia, who hadn't seen it, asked what it was about. I described it as a "lesbian Mafia movie," to which Sharon, a working-class woman, joked, "Maybe we shouldn't talk to Carrie anymore," and Tricia replied, "That sounds really interesting." Nancy and Sharon laughed with each other when Amy and Tricia talked about how much they enjoy visiting bookstores.

These values ran through all of the leisure activities they discussed in the Coffee Shop. Amy talked about the interesting guests who were on *Oprah* the day before, especially the lesbian congressperson. Tricia talked about an article she read in *Ms.* magazine. Amy talked about how she wants to visit the Holocaust Museum while visiting her children in Washington, D.C . . . .

While it first appeared when entering the Coffee Shop that all of the women were there to enjoy some leisure time, upon closer observation it became apparent that the three groups of women acted out different values and tastes toward leisure. Leisure was then used by the women to associate themselves with others seeking the same class category and to distance themselves from the other women.

## FAMILY

In the process of doing class in the Coffee Shop, women brought their family members into the action. The women in the Coffee Shop selectively used expectations and accomplishments of children as they "did" class.

The working-class women deemphasized socioeconomic mobility among their children. Instead, they encouraged them to stay and work in the town, for which a university education is not necessary and instead usually results in children moving away.

Nancy's discussion of the future plans of her 17-year-old daughter, who was soon graduating from high school, provides a good example. Nancy said her daughter's friend left to go to school in Florida and that her daughter was dead set on going to a college outside of the state—something she discouraged. Instead, Nancy showed her preference that her daughter stays in town. A few months later, her daughter decided to enlist in the military. Nancy was afraid of her daughter traveling and being so far away from the town. One day at the Coffee Shop, Nancy said that she thought that her daughter was changing her mind and no longer wanted to leave. When pushed by other women to explain further, she admitted that her daughter never actually said that she did not want to go, but that she just sensed it. In the presentation of her daughter's future plans, Nancy stressed the importance of maintaining her relationship with a local young man. She told other women at the Coffee Shop that she asked her daughter about her plans for her new relationship after she leaves town: "Are you going to break up and just be friends, or are you going to try to make it work?" Nancy described their relationship to the other women as "very serious," although her daughter is only 17 and they have only been dating 2 months. Thus, within the public setting of the Coffee Shop, Nancy demonstrated how she discouraged her daughter from social mobility. Instead she presented her desire for her daughter to stay in the area and maintain a local relationship rather than travel in the military. Nancy's daughter later took steps to retract her commitment to the military and remain in town in order to maintain her relationship with the young man. Nancy supported her decision.

What Nancy did not say in the public setting is just as important as what she did. There were aspects of her daughters' lives, especially those based in educational attainment, which Nancy did not talk about. For example, her older daughter was taking, very interested in, and doing well in Advanced Placement English classes in her high school. Yet, Nancy never mentioned this among the other women. Furthermore, her younger daughter was the only student in the local grammar school class who got straight A's consistently every semester. Yet I learned this only from reading the local newspaper. Nancy did not talk about this. She could have easily presented this information in the Coffee Shop. But in the process of "doing" class, Nancy buried her daughters' socioeconomic mobility.

In comparison, the upper-class women bragged about educational and financial success in their families. Helen, whose children have acquired the greatest educational and financial success, most frequently talked about the accomplishments of her children. She talked about her son's success in college, where he applied and was accepted to graduate school for engineering, and where he works. As the following field note shows,

> Helen said that her daughter got straight "A's" because she was an over-achiever. Gigi said that her daughter, too, was an overachiever. Helen talked about her son and how he was very smart, was told to do liberal arts, but wanted to do sciences and that he was very good at science. He went to Stanford. Gigi added, "Like your husband?"

As stated before, however, what women hid is just as important as what they showed in the process of doing class. Jean rarely mentioned her two daughters who had not attained educational and occupational mobility. Her daughters had not graduated from college, do not hold prestigious jobs, and are married to men who perform physical work. Because they do not fulfill the expectations for children which correspond with her desired class category, she never mentioned her daughters in the Coffee Shop.

The middle-class women used a third set of expectations of their children during the process of class categorization in interaction. Amy, Dorothy, and Tricia neither encouraged nor discouraged socioeconomic mobility. Rather, they emphasized knowledge and worldly experiences. During our interview, Amy described her daughter as follows:

> My daughter went to school in Pennsylvania and she actually remarked several times about how she felt that she was more aware of things going on in the world, like independence and getting along and that kind of stuff, than a roommate she had one year who was from New York City . . . . She is the curious kind of a person that would be more aware . . . . Of course, everybody has

their own interpretation of what success is, but Barbara is one of those kids that will definitely be a success in her eyes and in other people's eyes. It's just because she really loves life, enjoys life, is curious and wants to know. She doesn't sit down and read novels very often, but she always is reading something that non-fiction kind of things . . . . Even though she came from a small town, she's pretty with what's going on in the world and everything. And very liberal social ideas.

Here she emphasized that her daughter is not "small town" but is knowledgeable of the ways of the world, even in comparison to young women from New York City. Her knowledge came from her intellectual curiosity and being well-read. In the end, she connected her daughter's knowledge to liberal social ideas . . .

Like Amy, Tricia wanted her children to gain knowledge and become worldly. The thing Tricia would not tolerate would be her children doing what Nancy, a working-class woman, wanted for her daughter:

> I would be real upset if [my daughter] got married when she was 18 or 19. I mean very upset. And the same with [my son] . . . . I don't what him graduating from high school, then just marrying the first girl that he dated and stay living here for the rest of his life.

Thus, the women used expectations for their children in the process of doing class. Upper-class women presented socioeconomic mobility, while the working-class women did not. The middle-class women pushed for knowledge of and experience with diverse cultures and people outside of the small town . . . .

## CONCLUSION

The Coffee Shop provides a setting for observing how class is "done" in microlevel interactions of everyday life. Each morning, women were continually creating and re-creating local social class distinctions and working to categorize themselves into social classes. They did this by acting against or according to behaviors and tastes which are associated with a particular socioeconomic position. They also selectively associated with or distinguished themselves from other women and acted to gain status relative to other women based on their behaviors, values, and tastes.

As many researchers have documented over the decades, there is no question that socioeconomic differences matter. But these structural differences in and of themselves are not sufficient for creating class categorizations, identities, and ranking. Rather, it is through interactions that given socio-economic positions take on meaning in the daily lives and encounters with other people. Without these actions, involving the taking and acting out of class symbols, there would not be class categories in the Coffee Shop.

There are similarities in what occurs in the Coffee Shop and previous literature on class. For example, the value of a physical work ethic has been found in studies of working classes (Halle 1984; Ferree 1987; Rosen 1987; Rubin 1976, 1995), the significance of volunteer work has been found among upper-class women (Ostrander 1984; Daniels 1987), and the new middle classes, comprised of highly educated professionals such as academics and artists, tend to value liberal political and social orientations in their work (Brint 1985; Lamont 1987; Brooks and Manza 1997). Bourdieu (1984) outlines the preferences for music, food, reading material, sports, travel, and entertainment that demarcate socioeconomic positions, some of which correspond to what I found in the Coffee Shop.

Yet these studies assume two things that I did not find in the Coffee Shop. First, these studies define class membership based on occupation, income, and wealth. In the Coffee Shop, these objective criteria were neither necessary nor sufficient for class categorization. For example, while the new middle class is usually believed to be comprised of highly educated professionals, within the Coffee Shop and town, Amy sought a similar class category although she had not graduated from college, works as a substitute teacher, and makes crafts to sell locally rather than working as a professor or professional artist. Similarly, Jean was able to be categorized with Gigi, a wealthy summer resident, and distanced from the working-class women at the counter. Thus, class categories are not merely about wealth, education, and occupational prestige. Rather, they are outcomes of performances and interaction. This is similar to what Anderson (1976) and Warner and Lunt (1941)

find—stratification systems are systems of patterned and selective, symbolic action and interaction.

What I observed in the Coffee Shop, however, is also different from what Anderson (1976) and Warner and Lunt (1941) found. In the Coffee Shop, there was a class system but no set stratification system. Unlike Anderson's study, no one group deferred to another. Instead, there was an ongoing struggle between the groups to gain status relative to each other with no one accepting a lower rank. What emerges from the Coffee Shop is that the process of doing class does not necessarily result in a set system of inequality but rather involves efforts to situate one's own class higher, not lower, than the others in any resulting system of inequality.

This is something often missed in research on social class. It is assumed that differences in income, formal education, and occupation rank people into a fixed, predetermined hierarchy. While it is unquestionably important that people have sufficient access to resources to live a healthy and full life, other important aspects of class are overlooked when the focus is solely on socioeconomic differences. When the micro situations of classed interactions are observed, it is not so clear that individuals of different class categories agree on or experience a predetermined ranking (Collins 2000). For example, while those categorized as upper class may define themselves as superior in ways to those categorized as working class, it is also likely that those categorized as working class do not define themselves as inferior, but rather likely superior in ways, to those categorized as upper class. Doing class involves an ongoing struggle for class status.

## DISCUSSION QUESTIONS

1. What evidence does Yodanis provide to validate her claim that social class categories within the context of a coffee shop are outcomes of performances and interactions rather than based on education, social class background, or the occupations of the diners?
2. How does this analysis of social class differ from the traditional sociological approach to social class analysis?

# 24

# THE VIEW FROM
# THE COUNTRY CLUB

*Wealthy Whites and the Matrix of Privilege*

JESSICA HOLDEN SHERWOOD

*The last reading in this section on identities and social interaction is an ethnographic study of elite country clubs by Jessica Holden Sherwood. Sherwood, an adjunct assistant professor of sociology at the University of Rhode Island, researches gender and social class inequality. The reading, a chapter in the 2009 anthology* The Intersectional Approach, *edited by Michele Tracy Berger and Kathleen Guidroz, focuses on Sherwood's study of race, class, and gender in wealthy country clubs, where she finds that membership requires assimilation into the dominant white culture. Moreover, this elitism also is gendered, with traditional gender roles and asymmetric power dynamics expected between husbands and wives of the elite.*

Exclusive country clubs are an important context for research, for two reasons. The first is that the people there are unusually privileged. Scholars of inequalities have paid much good attention to the poor, women, and people of color; but no matter the approach, there are insurmountable limits to a scholarship of inequality that only looks "down." Some social scientists issue reminders to look up, emphasizing "the ruling capitalist class, for it is the major initiator of action" (Domhoff 1979:xiv). Michelle Fine decries the tendency to always study the Other, or the "marked" side of every categorical distinction, calling it collusion in the othering done by the elite. She charges that the collective neglect to study dominant groups contributes to the sanitization of their lives, keeping their

*Source:* Sherwood, Jessica Holden. 2009. "The View from the Country Club: Wealthy Whites and the Matrix of Privilege." In *The Intersectional Approach: Transforming the Academy Through Race, Class, and Gender*, edited by Michele Tracy Berger and Kathleen Guidroz. Copyright 2009 by the University of North Carolina Press. Used by permission of the publisher. www.uncpress.unc.edu.

dysfunctions hidden (Fine 1994). Similarly, Susan Ostrander encourages people to study up because "a lack of knowledge about elite contributes to obscuring and therefore maintaining their position in society" (Ostrander 1993:7).

The second reason clubs are important to examine is that, while they do not autonomously reproduce inequalities, they *are* cogs in a more complex machinery. Along with private schools, exclusive neighborhoods, and other voluntary and professional organizations, country clubs provide important opportunities for face-to-face interaction and solidarity building among wealthy people. These experiences foster a consciousness that transcends one's family or firm, a consciousness that inspires classwide coordinated actions. At the same time, clubs provide a context in which to know the important people with whom to coordinate (Mills 1956; Domhoff 2002). Clubs like those in this study serve important purposes. Club members' talk about inequalities is equally important, given their influential and privileged positions in class and race hierarchies.

While scholars of inequality recommend "studying up" (Nader 1969), they acknowledge that it can be more difficult than studying members of subordinated groups. Especially when it comes to social class, the privileged are thought of as elusive subjects of study. I thought that my own social locations—being white, knowing some people who are rich or powerful, and having the cultural capital to interact with them effectively and comfortably—might enable me to overcome that elusiveness.

Seeking a setting characterized by the concentration of privilege, I decided to study the most exclusive and prestigious social clubs in my area. I used personal contacts to start a snowball sample of club members and asked each subject for referrals. This technique relies on club members' social networks, precisely the same tool used to determine club membership. I had no trouble securing interviews, probably because I always introduced myself using one or more names of previous subjects. I conducted interviews with a total of thirty-eight club members; all interviews were recorded and transcribed, and all interviewees were given pseudonyms.

I focus on a club that I call "Oldfamily." Subjects describe its character as "the white-shoe WASPY[1] club," and say that its reputation was of a "typical old Yankee blue blood, sort of . . . sodgy, nose-in-the-air kind of place." With its hundred-year history, Oldfamily traditionally topped the area's prestige hierarchy. Subjects disagree on whether that hierarchy is obsolete or persists today. If nothing else, there are senior Oldfamily members known informally as the "old guard," who embody the conservative traditions of an earlier time.

I interviewed twenty-one members of Oldfamily, and eleven members of two comparable local clubs. One is "Rosary," whose members' pseudonyms begin with "R." Though it began a hundred years ago as another WASP club, it developed into the club for Irish Catholics. The other club is "Suburban," whose members' pseudonyms begin with "S." In contrast to Oldfamily, Suburban's reputation among other clubs' members is one of "new money" and an attendant lack of refinement. Still, its history is of WASP exclusiveness. But like Oldfamily and Rosary, this exclusiveness has softened in recent years to include some members of other ethnic groups.

In addition to Oldfamily, Rosary, and Suburban, I also interviewed six members of a slightly different club. "Northern" is in a different geographical area, and less prestigious, so it is not included in the "Class" and "Race" sections below. But I sought it out because Northern is a battleground of women's status: some women there (names starting with "N") chafed at limitations on their golfing times. They agitated for change and eventually sued the club for gender discrimination.

# Privileged Perspectives on Inequalities

## Class Accounts and Intersections

Given the American ideals of open access and equal opportunity, club members must account for the fact that their clubs only admit new members by selective invitation. They account for their exclusion in either of two ways: by arguing that there is really no meaningful exclusion taking place, or, if exclusion is acknowledged, by excusing and justifying it.

Variants of the first theme range from simply denying that there is any screening to saying that the only filter is social ties, or residence, or affordability, to saying that virtually anyone could afford to belong. The affordability filter will be discussed below, since it is prominent in accounts of the clubs' racial-ethnic compositions.

Accounts that justify or excuse the exclusion are more common. There are several ways in which club members can claim to be innocent of performing exclusion. They can pawn it off on club leaders, as in Rosary member Regina's comment, "There's a bunch of old guys apparently that run the place."

Club members can claim that they belong only for the golf course and don't personally care about the composition of the club. In an account that simultaneously provides a pat on the back, they can claim to participate in clubs only as part of their identity as good parents.

> **KEN** (Oldfamily member): *One of the major benefits of being a member there is as much for [my son] as it's been for me, because . . . he has just been exposed to a lot of successful people as role models that he may otherwise not have been exposed to.*

Club members use these and other discursive tools to de-problematize country clubs' policies and their own membership. Whether or not it's intended, this helps to keep strong both socioeconomic solidarity and the legitimation of inequality.

The class hierarchy in America is sustained by the system of capitalism. Capitalism, and the government that supports it, are the reasons why Americans have such a pronounced class hierarchy. And yet, subjects in this study are not merely "classed actors," neutral and unified. There is internal variation just as there is among all persons; and as in any group, people's gender and race influence some of this variation.

The upper classes are gendered in the following ways. Perhaps most importantly, it has traditionally been overwhelmingly men whose income and assets qualify them for the top economic stratum. Women generally qualify as wives or inheriting daughters;

many wealthy heiresses even turn their own fortunes over to their husbands' control (Ostrander 1993). This is a sign that wealth is not a direct road to power. It's also a reminder that compulsory heterosexuality (Rich 1983) is an important influence on how men and women relate. Gender relations in the upper classes remain male dominant. As shown below, the norms of masculinity and femininity influence the identities, behaviors, and relationships of people in the upper classes.

The upper classes are mostly culturally and demographically white.[2] Club traditions of homogeneous membership and intergenerational continuity hint at the racial segregation historically accompanying class segregation. Whiteness has been, until recently, a definite requirement for belonging in exclusive clubs and other elite contexts. Today, nonwhites are granted admission; but the contexts remain culturally white. Those nonwhites—indeed, any non-WASPS—who belong to the clubs in this study are assimilated enough so that they do not disturb the "comfort zone" that dominates members' conception of who does and does not belong. Also, the persistent overlap between the categories of white and affluent subtly strengthens class and race inequalities, because each dimension of inequality is lent legitimacy by its alignment with the other.

## Racial-Ethnic Accounts and Intersections

Interviewees offer two groups of accounts for the racial-ethnic composition of their clubs, which is somewhat more diverse today than what it was traditionally.[3] The first account justifies the homogeneity that still largely characterizes the clubs, and the second emphasizes what heterogeneity there is.

Interviewees *justify homogeneity* mainly by asserting that affordability is the one hurdle to belonging. When members must account for the racial-ethnic homogeneity of their clubs, sometimes they do refer to the racialized character of class stratification—without ever acknowledging the racism responsible. Interviewees simply point out that nonwhites are, on the whole, less likely to be able to afford to belong.

EVAN (Oldfamily member): *You have to think that any country club, by virtue of membership and dollars, limits who belongs there. And so I think to that end, you don't get the broader spectrum of people who can belong, because you're dealing with people who have enough disposable income to belong to the club, or play the games or whatever, so it does limit somewhat the people who belong, and I think . . . so it's not a cross section of the world we're looking at, that belong there.*

Affordability provides an impersonal account for the overwhelmingly white character of the clubs. This account reflects, and relies on, the presumption that economic stratification (of the acuteness found in America) is correct and natural. The club's exclusiveness is framed not as something that members are doing but simply as the outcome of impartial market forces. As for the potentially awkward fact that affordability varies by racial-ethnic group, there are ways to explain it. The dominant stratification ideology (Huber and Form 1973) of American culture presumes meritocracy and equal opportunities for all individuals. This color-blind assessment of affordability neglects the history of institutionalized discrimination that has prevented racial-ethnic minorities from accumulating wealth at the rate of their white counterparts (Oliver and Shapiro 1995). In other words, the institutionalization of white privilege is unacknowledged and remains unchallenged.

On the other hand, interviewees *emphasize* how much *heterogeneity* there is in their clubs. Four out of every five subjects point to the presence of non-WASPS in their clubs. In an overstatement, one Suburban members says, "Now we've got United Nations over there."

Additionally, to emphasize their heterogeneity, interviewees note that their club is more diverse than in the past. Another account is that, while one's own club may not be terribly diverse, it's at least better than others. Of the three clubs, accusations of homogeneity are leveled at *each of the other* clubs. For example, one Oldfamily member says that his club has the most African Americans of any club in the area; but a Rosary member calls his club "more diverse" than Oldfamily. Another Oldfamily member calls Suburban "less diverse than Oldfamily"; but

a Suburban member counters that "we probably have a broader spectrum of people," and so on.

This circularity suggests that the accusations of homogeneity do not reflect real knowledge about differences in club composition. The finger-pointing represents a strategy to improve the image of one's own club, given the new cultural value placed on diversity.

Country club members are proud of the recent diversification of their membership. Where possible, they portray themselves as heroes of a new, color-blind era of racial harmony. They do deserve some credit for the changes, but exclusion remains. Only wealthy minorities gain admission, and as exclusive club members make clear, the proper cultural capital is needed, whatever one's racial-ethnic status. Even if admissions decisions are color-blind, they remain conscious of culture. One white interviewee mused that, when blacks joined Oldfamily, they must have thought, "Okay, yeah, I'll be the well-behaved WASP with dark skin." The cultural conformity—assimilation—required for country club membership points to the shallowness of the diversity that is currently valued. By admitting a couple of affluent, prominent black men who like to play golf—minorities with gender and class privilege—these clubs are only complying with the "letter of the law" in the current cultural climate. They have achieved racial-ethnic diversity without becoming at all multicultural—never mind the "strong multiculturalism" that seeks to redress inequalities (Gordon and Lubiano 1992).

The dominant diversity discourse ignores racism and can distract attention from power differences and inequalities that remain to exclude most Americans from "the good life." As such, contemporary efforts to create diversity at exclusive clubs, schools, and so on are superficial measures that fail to address the original reasons why the remedies are necessary. Worse, the legitimacy lent by token diversity can help to preserve intact the social structures that reproduce inequalities.

The upper class remains culturally white today, though a few nonwhites now belong. Research shows that those nonwhites who have gained entry into the power elite have done so by assimilating into white culture (Zweigenhaft and Domhoff 2006). The few nonwhites in this study bear this out.

Race is gendered here, too, because of the truism that the upper classes are more open to men than women arrivistes. Though blacks are closer than whites to gender parity in earnings, this disappears at the top of the economic scale: for nonwhites as well as whites, the very top earners are more likely to be men than women (Morris and Western 1999:623). The nonwhite club members in this study are all men, which may also reflect that the dominance required to arrive at the door of the club appears more fitting, to existing members, as part of a man's rather than a woman's identity.

### Gender Accounts and Intersections

Women—white women, at least—have always been a part of country clubs. This section covers not women's exclusion but the explanations for the status of women within their clubs. Given the situation of the country clubs within the larger societal gender order, and systems of class and race privilege, they are more alike than different. This is not a sample with tremendous internal diversity, but there are the following distinctions: Oldfamily's founding history is gender neutral. At Rosary, Suburban, and Northern, by contrast, tradition dictated that the "man of the house" holds a family membership, and only he may vote and serve in leadership positions. Northern has struggled with sex discrimination lawsuits. Rosary and Suburban recently changed their restrictions to remove gendered language: now it's something like "principal members" having more privileges than "restricted members." But de facto, women's status remains lower than men's.

Gender discourse stands in contrast to positive talk about racial diversification. By and large, both men and women shrug off the gender inequality in country clubs as sensible and unproblematic. From this, three themes emerge: marriage, femininity, and masculinity, each as peculiar to this affluent context.

***Marriage and Money.*** Interviewees' accounts about women at country clubs rest on an important principle that is at once obvious and terribly consequential. The talk presumes that nearly everyone involved is part of a heterosexual, procreative marriage where the woman assumes the majority of the domestic duties. This is compulsory heterosexuality: people are automatically thought of within this framework. This is especially true in the context of the club. Members think of their clubs as "family places"; so it follows that women in clubs are viewed in terms of their domestic identities. The existence of nontraditional women—without children, without husbands, with high-powered careers—barely registers in subjects' minds.

In the clubs in this sample, the majority of members are not only married couples, but—as I was consistently told—the majority are breadwinner-homemaker marriages. This is an inversion of the national pattern, where wives are more likely than not to be in the paid labor force.

Homemakers are considered to be lower-status adults, both by these interviewees and in mainstream culture (Hays 1996). This sentiment is reflected in the restrictions on women at many clubs and also in interviewees' comments. Disparagement of homemaker wives can be "self-serving othering," which by contrast reflects well on one's own group.

| | |
|---|---|
| **Jessica:** | *Why do you think the women at these other clubs haven't made an issue out of their limitations?* |
| **Olivia (Oldfamily member):** | *Because I think it's the makeup of the women also. They're happy to be stay-at-home wives. They're happy for that. They're happy to stand in the reflected lights of their husbands, so to speak, where I don't think the Oldfamily women are.* |

The litigants at Northern indulge in some of this talk, when discussing the more traditional women in their club.

| | |
|---|---|
| **Nell:** | *He makes the real money, he's the breadwinner, and you're just this sub— and they grew up like that. I've heard the women talking how lucky they are. It's sad.* |

Nina:    *They currently, I think, have five women on the board. They're all bought and paid for in different ways.*

Perhaps men are too savvy today to so bluntly disparage homemakers. But their talk—and club policies—show that they consider them subordinate.

Ralph:    *Most of all the women in this club are nonworking females.*

Jessica:    *The majority?*

Ralph:    *The vast majority are women who are married to men who are successful men, and the women don't work. And they play golf all the time. I can tell you right now there isn't a woman at that table who (gestures across the club veranda) doesn't play a lot more golf than I do. And I can also tell you that there probably isn't a woman at that table that gives a damn about playing Saturday or Sunday morning either. They play with their husbands Saturday or Sunday afternoon and they play all week, all week.*

The implication is that the homemaker is, or at least should be, grateful and uncomplaining. This popular sentiment contributes to the persistence of gender inequality in marriages and, thus, in country clubs, too.

Gender equality is especially unlikely to spring from the breadwinner-homemaker marriages that populate these clubs. Much research documents the elusiveness of marital equality and the material and ideological reasons why most husbands retain the upper hand. Among other factors, "it seems to be easier to create an egalitarian relationship . . . if both partners make similar amounts of money" (Schwartz 1994:6). This is because money is a well-documented source of marital power. Given that the men of these country clubs earn incomes in the very top tier nationally, their wives are especially unlikely to approach matching them in income. In this way, country club wives with jobs are still much like their homemaker counterparts and are, on this criterion, further from gender equality than wives in most dual-earner marriages. Wives in such asymmetrical marriages are unlikely to have the power to decide which club the family will join, or to call for resigning if conditions are unsatisfactory.

*Feminine Civility.* Femininity—acting appropriately like a woman—means different things in different contexts. Country club members' expectations are influenced by the most culturally valued form, emphasized femininity: "femininity organized as an adaptation to men's power, and emphasizing compliance, nurturance, and empathy as womanly virtues" (Connell 1987:88).

A sociologist studying an upper-class women's organization found its members more concerned with preserving their status as "ladies" than with the organization's stated social mission. Following the expectations for emphasized femininity, the members excused their limited activity by saying that "they did not want to offend people in the community by being controversial" (Myers 2004:23). Elsewhere, women at an elite college paid a price for displaying such disagreeability. Wellesley students protested the choice of Barbara Bush as commencement speaker, and hundreds of letters to the school reprimanding the young women followed, many chiding them as lacking in the "manners" suitable to "real (upper-class) women" (Hertz and Reverby 1995:594).

Similarly, interviewees here consider the struggle for women's equality at clubs in terms of manners. Marian, an Oldfamily woman who did lobby for improvements in the women's locker room, insisted, "I'm not a strident person, and I'm not, I'm really not, a Bella Abzug type or whoever they were afraid I was gonna be." She may have been trying to frame herself as not disagreeable, but she and her husband still felt punished by the club leadership.

Marian is exceptional in her assertiveness. I spoke to Suburban women and asked them how they felt about the restrictions on their golfing. Suzanne, a serious golfer, expressed dissatisfaction about the weekend restrictions and said she mentioned it repeatedly to club leaders.

**Jessica:** *You keep bringing it up, but have you organized other women members?*

**Suzanne:** *Oh, no. I wouldn't do it because I've been a member since the day I've been born.*

Though her standing as a legacy might add to her clout at the club, Suzanne sees it instead as entrenching her in mannerly social obligations.

Sabrina is an athletic career woman, younger than Suzanne and never married. I expected her to be a candidate for lobbying for change at Suburban. When she noted that she didn't get to golf much, I asked:

**Jessica:** *Did you speak up about the tee-time restrictions?*

**Sabrina:** *Oh, yeah. I mean all the women did, but it was not like they're going to do much about it, so I just ended up quitting.* (later)

**Jessica:** *So when you resigned, did you let them know, "I'm resigning because I'm unhappy about these things"?*

**Sabrina:** *No. Basically I told them that I was going to be working in [another city] and that since there were no times that I was going to be able to play, what was the use? So I don't think I was particularly belligerent about it or anything. It's been so long I can't remember. No, I don't think so. I don't think I was obnoxious or anything.*

Note how Sabrina equates this simple truth telling—a far cry from circulating a petition or bringing a lawsuit—with being "belligerent" and "obnoxious." Given the constraints of emphasized femininity, there is very little cultural space for women to speak up on their own behalf.

Like Suzanne, Sophia grew up at Suburban. She admits, "I just wasn't a person that stood up for women's rights," and attributes her complacency to growing up amidst sexism. Familiar with the case at Northern, she blames the litigants for their agitation:

**Sophia:** *They have a terrible reputation at the course. And they've ruined it for themselves . . . Terrible. Even their husbands are blackballed. That's the awful thing. (emphasis added)*

Instead of a lawsuit, Sophia advocates adjustment and patience in the face of club sexism. Even with her career, she notes that she simply doesn't mind waiting until afternoon to play on weekends. Sophia is adhering to "the genteel code that expects women, especially elite women, to suffer in silence when they disagree or are offended" (Hertz and Reverby 1995:602).

Olivia, in considering women's predicament, notes, "So you bring a lawsuit. Who's gonna play [golf] with you?" Women at sexist country clubs are indeed in a bind. I argue that their bind is tightened both by the expectations of femininity and also by the implicit deals they have in marriages to wealthy men.

***Genteel Masculine Dominance.*** Traditionally, the men at Oldfamily have been some of the most powerful in the state. Their privilege has been so unshakable that they have not needed to make a display of superiority over their wives. Research on gender relations usually supports this rule via its converse: that men who *lack* social/economic/institutional power are more prone to making exaggerated masculine displays of dominance. These masculine displays are seen both in public settings of "the street" and the workplace, and in domestic arenas of housework and violence.[4] In the case of elite clubs, the dramatic displays are absent because the men's power is so certain. Hondagneu-Sotelo and Messner use the term "quiet control" to convey how men with race and class privilege rule their families (1994:214). Conversely, overt sexism is part of the culture at other clubs: because the men elsewhere are less elite, they may be more motivated to enforce masculine privileges at their clubs.

Oldfamily members are proud of their egalitarianism, and both men and women in the club give the men rhetorical pats on the back for their progressiveness. It works well for Oldfamily members to attribute women's status at clubs to the enlightenment of Oldfamily men and the backwardness of men elsewhere. (Though to be fair, some Oldfamily members supplement this account with other ones, too.) One Oldfamily member attributed the difference to "new money" at Suburban. But more often, the reason given for the difference is ethnicity. (In fact, "new money" is sometimes a veiled reference to Jewish or other non-WASP people.)

| Ursula (Oldfamily member): | *I also think that WASPS are, I never sat around and talked about WASPS the way I am today, but I think WASPS are better about giving women equality than some other ethnic groups are, who like to assert their masculine right. I truly think that's the case.* |
|---|---|

Many interviewees, when considering sexism at country clubs, invoke Italians as the prime example.

| Harold (Oldfamily member): | *I don't want to really stereotype people, but if you look at the club here in [this state] that's the most notorious in terms of the treatment of women, it's Venetian. And it's all Italian. And I think it's cultural.* |
|---|---|
| Gloria: | *Venetian, that was a big one, because I remember it being in the paper. I don't know how it was resolved, but I remember thinking, "I'm glad I belong to the Oldfamily, where we're so progressive, I can play golf when I want."* |

The masculinity at the elite clubs of this sample is sanitized in comparison to the "others," which are backward. Interviewees are extolling masculinity of a certain culturally ethnic sort. This is also a class-specific masculinity: as noted, men with the most power have the least need for overtly sexist displays.

Some scholars critique the apparent gender liberalism of powerful men as shallow. Messner writes that the sensitive displays of the (usually white and affluent) "New Man" deserve more skepticism than praise (2003:293). Rather than heralding real change, "these gender displays may serve as signs that, in

fact, serve to divert the feminist critique of masculinity on to less powerful groups of men, who supposedly embody the atavistic traits of 'traditional masculinity.'"[5] A structural analysis of power reveals how a focus on men's personal styles and gender displays shifts attention away from a critical scrutiny of men's institutional power, thus helping to restabilize hegemonic masculinity, and the positions of power held by upper-class, white, heterosexual men. Interviewees' veneration of elite, WASP masculinity is an example of this very phenomenon. Their talk shows how racism can be used in the service of male dominance. Also, Messner's argument serves to remind observers that the apparent liberalism at Oldfamily and similar sites should not be confused with a real antisexist social movement.

It is no surprise that Oldfamily members proudly report their progressivism. However, it is notable that members at *all four* clubs use the strategy of pointing out how another club is worse than their own.

| Jessica: | *Well, that sort of brings me to tee times for men and women, because isn't it true that women's tee times are restricted?* |
|---|---|
| Sophia: | *Right. I think less and less, however. You could find some clubs, I can mention a couple to you. Rosary is the prime one where women don't have much say in the doings of the club. Suburban is more family oriented and I think women have a lot more say.* |
| Richard (*about the Northern leaders*): | *The idiots running the joint didn't he first time. I mean that to me is learn tindustrial-strength stupidity. But you can't protect stupid people from themselves. They're gonna do that; it's mind-boggling why they did what they did, but they're paying for it now.* |

These put-downs are similar to finger pointing about racial-ethnic exclusivity. They are best interpreted not as gauges of the gender regimes at different clubs but as examples of a useful account that serves speakers and their own clubs well. Putting down another group is a common way to make a status distinction while simultaneously minimizing or excusing the flaws in one's own group.

In their complacency about gender inequality, club members are reflecting the state of contemporary mainstream culture. As in the case of race, most people think of "discrimination" as a workplace issue; outside the workplace, women as a whole are not widely considered to be an oppressed group.

Interviewees' talk also reflects the state of their marriages, or at least of the average marriage among club members. Women are presumed to be homemaker wives, whose duty it is to support their husbands. One small piece of this support is to stay off the golf course so men may use it at certain prime times. Note that in many clubs, these prime times are reserved for "men," not for "people with careers," a designation that would include working women and exclude retired men. Such a lack of clarity shows that the account about careers is, at least partly, a smoke screen for sexism.

Country club women in general have made a deal in marriage of "trading power for patronage," which is one option for adapting to subordinate status (Schwalbe et al. 2000:419). This deal restricts their opportunity to advocate on their own behalf, as does the related set of expectations for upper-class femininity. The women in this population are thus in a bind, which makes their seeming complacency more understandable.

Conversely, the men in this population are cultivating a discourse that sanitizes their class- and race-specific brand of masculinity. Their moderate displays are contrasted with those of men who are not WASPS, who are denigrated in racial-ethnic terms as less progressive and more chauvinistic. Thus, gender here is race-specific as well as class-specific. By replacing displays of male dominance with gender-equal displays, such men hope to escape feminist critique. But these privileged men in fact possess and use the power to keep themselves at the top of gender, class, and race hierarchies.

The hegemony of asymmetrical marriage and the images of dominant femininity and masculinity are some of the components of the societal gender order. This order is reproduced at multiple sites, and the country club should be viewed as one of many interlocking contexts, rather than as the single causal agent in its own right. As long as the broader gender order has legitimacy, little real change will take place at exclusive clubs.

## DISCUSSION

Club members contend, using several kinds of accounts, that the exclusion they practice is inoffensive. This is despite the fact that the financial and cultural requirements for membership bar people from most ethnic groups and economic strata from belonging.

However, subjects' accounts concerning gender are necessarily different from the ones addressing class and race exclusivity. White women have always been part of country clubs. While not (in most cases) kept off the club property, women have typically been kept off the golf course at certain prime times, off the board of governors, and out of the men's grill room. Gender is different from the other two main axes of domination in that, while class and race depend on various distancing mechanisms, gender hierarchy depends on a close symbiosis between men and women (Collins 1990:210). Gender segregation is more culturally accepted than explicit racial segregation. Some club members speak approvingly of separating the sexes, in a way that they would not, today, of separating "the races." This may be, ironically, because gender subordinates are in many ways closer to their dominators than class and race subordinates.

Class, race, and gender hierarchies are all important organizing principles of American society, with some uniqueness and some overlap. Ideologies justifying economic stratification and racial stratification are related, since class is raced and race is classed. According to the dominant ideology about inequality, the American Dream of meritocratic, color-blind equal opportunity is a reality. The talk of club members reflects complete support for this ideology. Their color blindness includes ignoring white privilege institutionalized in America and so, ironically, can be deemed racist.

The dominant ideology is individualistic about class and race more than gender. The dominant, though not unanimous, position is that men and women are "just different." Club members seem to think of the women in terms of their domestic identities, in keeping with their view of the club as a family place. But the notion that men and women are just different extends beyond home and family, helping to maintain male privilege.

We have seen some examples of the intersections of male privilege with class privilege and race privilege: men in this population dominate in their marriages, thanks to their wealth. At the same time, their security allows them gender displays that seem superior to the more blatantly patriarchal nonwhite men.

The rich white men profiled here are triply privileged by class, race, and gender. We might suppose that any subordinate status would take some time and energy away. The drag of one subordinate status amid privilege affects both the affluent white women studied by Susan Ostrander (1984) and also the affluent black men studied by Ellis Cose (1995). The men here, by contrast, are especially able to coordinate self-interested action; the weight of wealth, culture, and social structure are generally on their side.

This overdetermination of privilege poses a challenge for activist interventions such as regulating social activities like country club membership. That would require radical change; however, radical success would be evident in neighborhoods, classrooms, and social lives that are no longer bounded by class, race, or gender. The problem of exclusive private social clubs would have disappeared.

In the meantime, what do we learn by studying this phenomenon? These country club members enjoy a "matrix of privilege"[6] more than most. But their talk is very mainstream, reflecting the assumption that inequalities occur naturally and unproblematically. In the interviews, club members use tools of the dominant culture to give accounts. In recirculating these beliefs about class, race, and gender, country club members contribute to reproducing the inequalities and maintaining their privileges.

My goal was to expose and critique the cultural accounts that support inequalities. The analysis presented here shows how much of elite discourse—discourse that is taken for granted in America—actually serves to reproduce inequalities. This analysis might contribute to the articulation of both a counterdiscourse challenging the transmission of privilege and to an activism interrupting it.

## DISCUSSION QUESTIONS

1. Provide examples of the ways in which discussions by elites in an exclusive country club both justify and reproduce social class and racial inequality.
2. How do country club elites reproduce patriarchy and male privilege?

## NOTES

1. "WASP" stands for "White Anglo-Saxon Protestants," a term commonly used by my interviewees, including when they characterize their own country clubs.
2. On the "culturally white" concept, see Feagin and O'Brien, *White Men on Race*, chapter 2.
3. All three clubs claim that membership is open to people from every religious, racial, and ethnic group. Each has a few members who personify "diversity," but all the clubs remain prominently "WASPy" (Oldfamily and Suburban) or Irish Catholic (Rosary). Exact numbers are unavailable: as Domhoff notes, "The carefulness with which new members are selected extends to a guarding of club membership lists, which are usually available only to club members." Domhoff, *Who Rules America Now*, 51. A journalist reports, "Although few managers will speak publicly on the subject, most agree that clubs that would not or did not admit people from certain racial or ethnic groups in the past now probably do, although not in large enough numbers to affect their profile." Schumer, "Peek Inside the Country Club."
4. On masculine displays in public settings, see Zinn, "Chicano Men and Masculinity," 29; Bourgois, *In Search of Respect*. For domestic settings, see Brines, "Economic Dependency," 652; Hochschild, *Second Shift*; Anderson,

"Gender, Status, and Domestic Violence," 655; Hondagneu-Sotelo and Messner, "Gender Displays," 214; Messner, "Men as Superordinates," 293.

5. Similar critiques of the display of powerful men come from Hondagneu-Sotelo and Messner 1994 (quoted in Messner 2003), and also from Pyke, "Class-Based Masculinities," 527.

6. See Collins, *Black Feminist Thought*, for "matrix of oppression"; for matrix of privilege," see Disch, "General Introduction."

# 25

# THE RACIAL FORMATION OF AMERICAN INDIANS

## Negotiating Legitimate Identities Within Tribal and Federal Law

EVA MARIE GARROUTTE

*This reading begins the third section of Part II, "Identity Construction and Stigma Management." The previous readings show how larger social structures (that is, government, laws, schools, and the family) affect identity construction. The readings also illustrate how individuals manage identities and social stigma. This first reading is by Eva Marie Garroutte, a professor at Boston University and a citizen of the Cherokee Nation. Garroutte argues that there is much difficulty defining who is and who is not American Indian due to the varying legal definitions at both the federal and tribal levels. This excerpt, taken from a 2001 article in the* <u>American Indian Quarterly</u>, *illustrates well the social construction and institutionalization of race and citizenship.*

## TRIBAL LEGAL DEFINITIONS

There are a large number of legal rules defining American Indian identity, and they are formulated and applied by different actors for different purposes. I will begin with the ones that tribes use to determine their citizenship. Many people are surprised to discover that each tribe sets its own legal criteria for citizenship. They imagine that the U.S. government controls such aspects of tribal lives. In reality, tribes typically have the right to create their own legal definitions of identity and to do so in any way they choose. Indeed, this prerogative is commonly viewed legislatively as one of the most fundamental powers of an Indian tribe.[1]

The most common tribal requirement for determining citizenship revolves around "blood quantum" or degree of Indian ancestry. About two-thirds of all federally recognized tribes of the coterminous United States specify a minimum blood quantum in their legal citizenship criteria, with one-quarter blood degree being the most frequent minimum requirement.[2]

Degree of blood is calculated on the basis of the immediacy of one's genetic relationship to ancestors whose bloodlines were (supposedly) unmixed. The initial calculation often begins with a "base roll," a listing of tribal membership and blood quanta in some particular year.[3] These base rolls make possible very elaborate definitions of identity. They allow one to reckon that the offspring of, say, a full-blood Navajo mother and a white father is one-half Navajo. If that half Navajo child in turn produced progeny with a Hopi person of one-quarter blood degree, those progeny would be judged to be one-quarter Navajo and one-eighth Hopi. Alternatively, they could also be said to have "three-eighths general Indian blood." Certain tribes require not only that citizens possess tribal ancestry but also that this ancestry come from a particular parent. Thus, the Santa Clara Pueblo (New Mexico) will not enroll children in the tribe without paternal descent, and the Seneca Tribe (New York) requires maternal descent.

Such modern definitions of identity based on blood quantum closely reflect nineteenth- and early-twentieth-century theories of race introduced into indigenous cultures by Euro-Americans. These understood blood as quite literally the vehicle for the transmission of cultural characteristics: "Half-breeds" by this logic could be expected to behave in "half-civilized," i.e., partially assimilated, ways while retaining one half of their traditional culture, accounting for their marginal status in both societies.[4] Given this standard of identification, full bloods tended to be seen as the "really real," the quintessential Indians, while others were (and often continue to be) viewed as Indians in diminishing degrees.[5]

These theories of race articulated closely with political goals characteristic of the dominant American society. The original stated intention of blood quantum distinctions was to determine the point at which the various responsibilities of that dominant society to Indian peoples ended. The ultimate and explicit federal intention was to use the blood quantum standard as a means to liquidate tribal lands and to eliminate government trust responsibility to tribes along with entitlement programs, treaty rights, and reservations.[6] Indians would eventually, through intermarriage combined with the mechanism of blood quantum calculations, become citizens indistinguishable from all other citizens.

A significant number of tribes—almost one-third of those populating the lower forty-eight states—have rejected specific blood quantum requirements for determining tribal citizenship. They often require, instead, that any new enrollee be simply a lineal (direct) descendant of another tribal member. They may also invoke additional or alternative criteria. For instance, the Tohono O'Odham (Arizona) consider residency definitive, automatically admitting to citizenship all children born to parents living on the reservation. The Swinomish (Washington) take careful stock of various indicators of community participation, ignoring blood quantum, while the Lower Sioux Indian Community (Minnesota) requires a vote of the tribal council. In still other tribes, community recognition or parental enrollment may also be a means to or a prerequisite for enrollment, and a few tribes only accept applicants whose parents submit the necessary paperwork within a limited time after their child's birth. Some tribes also require members to fulfill certain minimal duties, such as maintaining annual contact with the tribal council, in order to maintain their citizenship in good standing.[7]

## TRIBAL IDENTITY
## NEGOTIATIONS: CONSEQUENCES

Tribes, in short, possess the power to define their citizenship through self-generated legal definitions, and they do so in many different ways. Legal definitions regulate the right to vote in tribal elections, to hold tribal office, and generally to participate in the political, and sometimes the cultural, life of the tribe. One's ability to satisfy legal definitions of identification may also determine one's right to share in certain tribal revenues (such as income generated by tribally controlled businesses). Perhaps most significantly, it may determine the right to live on a reservation or to inherit land interests thereon.

As this list suggests, failure to negotiate an identity as a "real" Indian within the legal definition of one's tribe can lead to some dire outcomes for individual people. For instance, legal criteria can tear apart families by pushing certain members off the reservation while allowing others to stay. Thus, in 1997 an article in *Indian Country Today* described the following family scenario: "Mr. Montoya has lived at Santa Clara Pueblo, his mother's home, his whole life. He raised his four children at the pueblo, and now has grandchildren there."[8] But Mr. Montoya cannot be enrolled at Santa Clara (New Mexico) because, since 1939, the pueblo has operated by a tribal law that allows for enrollment only on the basis of paternal descent—and his father was not from Santa Clara but, rather, from the nearby Isleta Pueblo. Montoya has inherited rights to his mother's property in Santa Clara, but his ability to enforce those rights remains uncertain.

Families in Montoya's situation sometimes cannot tolerate the tenuousness of their position and choose to abandon the pueblo, their relatives, and their intimate participation in the traditional tribal culture wherein they were born and raised. But family dissolution "by legal definition" has elsewhere occurred by force. It has occurred to the extent that mixed-race children have been actively expelled from the reservation, even in cases in which the children had been living there under the care of an enrolled relative.

Such an event occurred on the Onondaga Reservation in the recent past. The Onondaga, by a law that reverses the practice of the Santa Clara Pueblo, are matrilineal, enrolling children only if their mothers are tribal citizens. In 1974, the tribal council ordered all noncitizens to leave the reservation or face ejection. This order included even non-citizen spouses, who were mostly women, and the children born to Onondaga men by such women. The Onondaga men could stay—but only if they chose to live apart from their wives and children. The national journal of Native news and issues, *Akwesasne Notes*, reported that the rationale behind the expulsion was that, over a period of years, a large number of non-Indians had moved onto Onondaga land and the council feared that the federal government might consequently dissolve the reservation.[9] Most individuals affected by the ruling left peaceably; others had to be forcibly removed. One family burned down its home before leaving.

Legal definitions, then, allow tribes to determine their citizenship as they choose. This determination allows them to delimit the distribution of certain important resources, such as reservation land, tribal monies, political privileges, and the like. But this is hardly the end of the story of legal definitions of identity.

## FEDERAL LEGAL DEFINITIONS

Although tribes possess the right to formulate legal definitions for the purpose of delimiting their citizenship, the federal government has many purposes for which it, too, must distinguish Indians from non-Indians, and it uses its own, separate legal definition for doing so. More precisely, it uses a whole array of legal definitions. Because the U.S. Constitution uses the word *Indian* in two places but defines it nowhere, Congress has made its own definitions on an ad hoc basis.[10] A 1978 congressional survey discovered no less than thirty-three separate definitions of "Indians" in use in different pieces of federal legislation.[11] These may or may not correspond with those any given tribe uses to determine its citizenship.

Thus, most federal legal definitions of Indian identity specify a particular minimum blood quantum—frequently one-quarter but sometimes one half—and others do not. Some require or accept tribal citizenship as a criterion of federal identification, and others do not. Some require reservation residency or ownership of land held in trust by the government, and others do not. Many other laws affecting Indians specify no definition of identity, such that the courts must determine to whom the laws apply. Because of the wide variation in federal legal identity definitions, and their frequent departure from the various tribal ones, many individuals who are recognized by their tribes as tribal citizens are nevertheless considered non-Indian for some or all governmental purposes. The converse can be true as well.

There are a variety of contexts in which federal legal definitions of identity become important. The matter of economic resource distribution—involving access to various social services, monetary awards, and opportunities—will probably come immediately to the minds of many readers. The particular legal situation of Indian people and its attendant opportunities and responsibilities are the result of historic negotiations between tribes and the federal government, in which the latter agreed to compensate tribes in various ways for the large amounts of land tribes surrendered, often by force. Benefits available to those who can satisfy federal definitions of Indian identity are administered through a variety of agencies, including the Bureau of Indian Affairs, the Indian Health Service, the Department of Agriculture, the Office of Elementary and Secondary Education, and the Department of Labor, to name a few.[12]

Legal definitions also affect specific economic rights deriving from treaties or agreements that some (not all) tribes made with the federal government. These may include such rights as the use of particular geographic areas for hunting, harvesting, fishing, or trapping, as well as certain water use rights.[13] Those legally defined as Indians are also sometimes exempted from certain requirements related to state licensure and state (but not federal) income and property taxation.[14]

Legal definitions also determine the applicability of a number of protections available to individual Indians from the federal government. Notable among these are an Indian parent's rights under the Indian Child Welfare Act of 1978 (25 U.S.C. 1901 et seq.). Before the passage of this act, as many as 25–35 percent of Indian children in some states were being removed from their homes and placed in the care of non-Indians through such means as adoption and foster care. Many commentators have suggested that a number of Indian families lost their children less because they were genuinely unsuitable parents and more because they refused to abandon traditional cultural values in favor of those enforced by the essentially white, middle-class, social service bureaucracy.[15] For instance, it is a rather common custom in many Indian cultures to share child-rearing responsibilities among various members of the extended family, with the outcome that children do not necessarily live with their biological parents. It has been a common complaint among Indian families that Social Services representatives have automatically assumed, in such cases, that a child suffers parental "neglect" and have used this reasoning as an excuse to initiate foster care placement.

The Indian Child Welfare Act was passed in order to stem the wholesale transfer of children out of their families, tribes, and cultures. It requires that, when Indian children must be removed from their homes, efforts be made to place them with another family member or at least with another Indian family rather than a non-Indian one. The law allows Indian people a means to protect the integrity of their family units and to ensure some cultural continuity for children.

Just as important, federally specified legal definitions provide for certain religious freedoms. For one thing, they allow Indian people to seek protection from prosecution for the possession of specific ceremonial objects, otherwise restricted by law. (For instance, many Indian people own eagle feathers that they use in prayer and ceremonies, although non-Indians are not permitted to possess any part of this endangered species. Similarly, Indian members of the Native American Church ingest peyote, legally classified as a hallucinogen, as a sacramental substance in closely controlled worship settings. Non-Indians are forbidden to possess it.) Since the passage of the Native American Graves Protection and Repatriation Act of 1990, federal legal definitions also allow Indian people to claim sacred ceremonial objects, as well as to receive and rebury the remains of their ancestral dead, if these are being held in federally funded museums for display or study (as they very frequently are).

Federal legal definitions of Indian identity can even affect some individuals' ability to pursue their livelihood. A particularly controversial protection that has recently become available to those legally defined as Indians revolves around the Indian Arts and Crafts Act of 1990. Arguments for this legislation started from the recognition that many buyers consider artwork more desirable and valuable if it is created by an Indian person. They proceeded to the observation that a great deal of art was therefore being falsely labeled as Indian-made. The same arguments then concluded that such misrepresentations were seriously reducing the revenues of artists who were, in fact, Indian.[16]

The Indian Arts and Crafts Act forbids any artist who is not a citizen of a federally or state-acknowledged tribe from marketing work as "Indian produced." Penalties for violation of the act include large fines and imprisonment. Certain galleries and organizations have also voluntarily chosen to restrict exhibitions and art commissions to people who can demonstrate that they are Indians by reference to formal, legal criteria.[17]

## IDENTITY AND LEGITIMACY

All the legal rights and protections sketched above offer their significant advantages only to those who are able to make claims to Indianness that are formally judged as legitimate within tribal or federal definitions of identity. However, many people cannot manage to pass successfully through one or the other of these definitions. (As noted before, there is no guarantee that those definitions correspond.) By what process is the legitimacy of claims to Indian identity asserted and evaluated within definitions of law? Who is able to negotiate a legal identity, and who is not? How is it that people with seemingly

identical characteristics may meet with very different outcomes within the process of racial formation set out in legal definitions? The answers to such questions are frequently quite astonishing.

Let us begin with a consideration of the criterion of blood quantum. Some people of American Indian ancestry find their identity claims challenged because their blood quanta are judged too low, by one standard or another. The question of how much "blood" is "enough" for an individual to call him- or herself Indian is hotly contested in Indian country—and well beyond. As sociologist Eugeen Roosens writes,

> There is . . . [a] principle about which the whites and the Indians are in agreement . . . [P]eople with more Indian blood . . . also have more rights to inherit what their ancestors, the former Indians, have left behind. In addition, full blood Indians are more authentic than half-breeds. By being pure, they have more right to respect. They are, in all aspects of their being, more integral.[18]

Degree of biological ancestry can take on such a tremendous significance in tribal contexts that it literally overwhelms all other considerations of identity (especially when it is constructed as "pure"). As Cherokee legal scholar G. William Rice points out, "Most [people] would recognize the full-blood Indian who was enrolled in a federally recognized tribe as an Indian, even if the individual was adopted at birth by a non-Indian family and had never set foot in Indian country nor met another Indian."[19]

In this, American Indian claims to identity are judged very differently under the law than the claims of other racial groups have been, even into the present day. We see this most clearly if we consider the striking difference in the way that the American popular and legal imaginations work to assign individuals to the racial category of "Indian" as opposed to the racial category "black." As a variety of researchers have observed, social and legal attributions of black identity have often focused on the "one-drop rule" or rule of "hypodescent."[20] . . .

Although people must show only the slightest trace of "black blood" to be forced (with or without their consent) into the category "African American," modern American Indians must formally produce strong evidence of often rather substantial amounts of "Indian blood" to be allowed entry into the corresponding racial category. The regnant racial definitions applied to Indians are simply quite different than those that have applied (and continue to apply) to blacks. Modern Americans, as Native American studies professor Jack Forbes puts the matter, "are always finding 'blacks' (even if they look rather un-African), and . . . are always losing 'Indians.'"[21]

Another group of people who may find the legitimacy of their racial identities challenged or denied comprises individuals of tribally mixed ancestry. This can be true even for those whose total American Indian blood quanta are relatively high. The reader will remember that the majority of tribes make documentation of a minimum blood quantum—often one-fourth degree Indian blood—part of their legal definitions of identity and that the federal government does the same for at least some of its various purposes. In light of this requirement, consider the hypothetical case of a child possessing one-half Indian ancestry and one-half white ancestry, meaning that he or she has one parent who is exclusively white and one parent who is exclusively Indian. This child's identity claim is likely to get a green light from both the federal government and the tribe—so long as his or her Indian ancestry comes from a single tribe. But compare these potential fortunes with those of another child whose half-Indian heritage derives from several different tribes. Let us say that this second child, in addition to his or her one-half white ancestry, is also one-eighth Sisseton Dakota, one-eighth Cheyenne, one-eighth Assiniboine, and one-eighth Sicangu Lakota. This child is, like the first child, one-half Indian. But each tribe of his or her ancestry requires its citizens to document a one-quarter blood degree, from that tribe only. From the perspective of each individual tribe, this child possesses only one-eighth tribal blood and is therefore ineligible for citizenship. As far as the several tribes are concerned, he or she is simply non-Indian within their legal definitions of identity.

Some people of Indian ancestry fall afoul, in legal definitions of identity, of still another potential

snare. This entanglement has to do with one's ability to establish relationship to a historic Indian community in the way that many legal definitions require. As previously noted, individuals seeking tribal or federal identification as Indian must typically establish that one, or more, of their ancestors appears on one of the tribe's base rolls. Unfortunately, many people who clearly conform to any other definition of Indian identity do not have ancestors who appear on the base rolls, for a multitude of reasons. Historians agree that the process by which many tribal rolls were initially compiled was almost unbelievably complicated. In the compilation of some tribal rolls, including the Dawes Rolls (1899–1906), from which all of today's enrolled Oklahoma Cherokees (and various other tribes) must show descent, the process that registrants endured took so long that a significant number of them died before the paperwork was completed. This meant that their descendants would be forever barred from becoming tribal citizens.

Even when applicants did manage to live long enough to complete the entire process of enrollment, they frequently found themselves denied. Dawes commissioners enrolled only a small fraction of all those who applied, and they readily agreed that they had denied many people of indubitably tribal ancestry.[22]

Other Indian people of the period actively resisted their registration on the Dawes Rolls, either individually or collectively. For instance, among Oklahoma Creeks, Cherokees, Chickasaws, and Choctaws in the late nineteenth and early twentieth centuries, conservative traditionalists or "irreconcilables" fought a hard fight against registration with the Dawes Commission. The reason was that the Dawes Roll was the explicit first step in what President Theodore Roosevelt had rapturously declared (in his first annual address to Congress in 1901) would be "a mighty, pulverizing engine to break up the tribal mass."[23] The effort, in a nutshell, was to destroy indigenous cultures by destroying their foundation— their collective ownership of land—and to integrate the Indians thus "liberated" into the dominant American culture. It was to allow for Indians to be remade into individual private owners of small farms who would quickly become independent of government attention and expenditures.

Probably no one could have foreseen all of the specific, catastrophic results that would befall tribes with the destruction of the old, traditional system of land tenure. The irreconcilables, however, at least intuited the outlines of the coming disaster. In the words of historian Angie Debo, they "clung to the old order with the stubbornness of despair."[24] In many tribes opposition to allotment ran high. In some, leaders arose who used all their resources, from cunning to force, to discourage their fellows' enrollment and subsequent allotment.[25]

Government patience with such conservative obduracy soon wore thin, and the more influential and uncooperative leaders and their families were hunted out and forcibly enrolled. (Cherokee leader Redbird Smith consented to his own enrollment only after he was finally jailed for his refusal.) However, others who shared his sentiments did manage to elude capture altogether and were never entered onto the census documents used today as the base rolls for many tribes.

The stories of Redbird Smith, and others like him, are narratives of a determined and principled resistance to a monumental step in the process of the Indians' forced acculturation to the dominant American culture. Yet the descendants of those traditionalists who succeeded in escaping census enumeration find themselves worse off, in the modern legal context, for their forebears' success in the fight to maintain cultural integrity. By the criteria their tribes have now established, they can never become enrolled citizens. This fact frequently affects, in turn, their ability to satisfy federal definitions.[26]

All of the foregoing demonstrates that there are great numbers of peculiarities of exclusion spawned by legal definitions of identity. The reverse side of this observation, however, is that a number of people who may have no ancestral connections to tribes have been and are defined as Indian in the legal sense alone. In some places and times, for instance, non-Indian spouses of Indian people have been allowed to become legal citizens of Indian nations. Among several Oklahoma tribes, certain African American slaves, formerly owned by Indian people, were likewise made, by due legal process following the Civil War, into tribal citizens even in the absence of any Indian ancestry.[27] And, where census registration implied eligibility for distribution of tribal lands, as it did in Oklahoma, it was not uncommon for individuals with no Indian ancestry, but with active homesteading ambitions and perhaps unscrupulous lawyers in tow, to seek to acquire places on the rolls through dishonest means. Thousands of them succeeded.[28] In so doing, they earned for themselves the name of "five-dollar Indians," presumably in reference to the amount required to bribe the census enumerator.

Finally, this discussion of the oddities that legal definitions of identity have created would not be complete without the acknowledgement that it is not only non-Indian people who have made their way onto the tribal census lists and thus "become" Indian, in the legal sense. Nonexistent people sometimes did, as well. An amusing example comes from the 1885 census of the Sicangu Lakota (South Dakota). As historian Thomas Biolsi records, census takers at the Rosebud Agency "recorded some remarkable English translations of Lakota names."[29] Nestled in among the common and dignified appellations—Black Elk, Walking Bull, Dull Knife, and others—are personal names of a more colorful class: Bad Cunt, Dirty Prick, Shit Head. "What happened," Biolsi notes, "is not difficult to unravel: Lakota people were filing past the census enumerator, and then getting back in line—or lending their babies to people in line—to be enumerated a second time using fictitious and rather imaginative names."[30] Because this particular census was being taken for the purpose of distributing rations, the ploy was one aimed at the very practical goal of enhancing survival—but the Lakota apparently felt that even such serious work need not be undertaken without humor.

For the purposes of the present discussion, I should note that at least some of the historic oddities of Indian census rolls have continued to create more of the same—forever. That is, while the nonexistent Indians of Rosebud clearly could not have produced children, the living, breathing, "five-dollar Indians" who bought their way onto the census rolls in Oklahoma and other states certainly could.

It is impossible to estimate the number of modern-day descendants of those numerous non-Indian "Indians," but one might suppose that it could be fairly large. It seems probable that at least some descendants have maintained tribal enrollment and the privileges attendant on a legally legitimated identity, even while many people of actual Indian descent were and are unable to acquire the same.

In conclusion, the example of Indian identity illustrates the complex and often mystifying nature of racial formation processes as they apply to American Indians. "Indianness" emerges out of complex negotiations that occur within the context of specifiable legal definitions of identity. There are many ways to gain and to lose it that may have little to do with the qualities that most people assume to be of central importance in determining racial identity. At the same time, achieving an Indian identity that satisfies various legal criteria (or failing to do so) has serious consequences. The specific elements of the racial formation process for Indian people make Native Americans' experience unique among those of modern-day U.S. racial groups.

## ADDED MATERIAL

From *Real Indian: Identity of the Survival of Native American.* © 2002 The Regents of the University of California. Used with the permission of the University of California Press.

## DISCUSSION QUESTIONS

1. Discuss some of the negative consequences of both tribal and federal legal definitions upon the lives of Native Americans and their children.
2. How does the federal definition for tribal membership based on blood quantum levels reinforce the Eurocentric view of indigenous people? When tribes reject blood quantum levels as criteria, what alternative criteria do they choose for deciding who belongs to a particular tribe?

## NOTES

1. This tribal right was determined in the 1905 court case *Waldron v. United States* (143 F. 413, C.C.D.S.D., 1905) and later clarified in a celebrated lawsuit, *Martinez v. Santa Clara Pueblo* (540 F.2d 1039, 10th Cir. 1976). However, as with nearly every other rule in Indian country, there are exceptions. A handful of tribes are federally required to hold to specific criteria in defining tribal membership—for instance, by maintaining a specific blood quantum standard for citizenship. In most legal discussions, the right to determine citizenship is closely tied to the concept of tribal sovereignty. See Sharon O'Brien, *American Indian Tribal Governments* (Norman: University of Oklahoma Press, 1989); Charles F. Wilkinson. *American Indians, Time and the Law: Native Societies in a Modern Constitutional Democracy* (New Haven: Yale University Press, 1987).

2. Russell Thornton surveyed 302 of the 317 tribes in the lower forty-eight states that enjoyed federal acknowledgment in 1997. He found that 204 tribes had some minimum blood quantum requirement, while the remaining ninety-eight had none; see Thornton, "Tribal Membership Requirements and the Demography of 'Old' and 'New' Native Americans," *Population Research and Policy Review* 16 (1997):37.

3. Although a few tribes have no written records of citizenship even today—some of the Pueblos, for instance, depend on their oral traditions—the majority of tribes maintain written membership documents, which are called "tribal rolls"; see Russell Thornton. *American Indian Holocaust and Survival: A Population History* (Norman: University of Oklahoma Press, 1987), 190. The roll chosen as definitive for later citizenship determinations is known as the "base roll." The General Allotment Act of 1887 provided for the creation of some base rolls, but most were compiled in response to the Indian Reorganization Act of 1934. Tribes continued to create membership listings that they use as base rolls after 1934 as well. In some cases, tribes created their base rolls only a few years ago. This is true, for instance, with the Passamoquoddy (Maine), who (having only enjoyed federal acknowledgment as a tribe for two decades) use a 1990 census for their base roll.

4. C. Matthew Snipp, "Who Are American Indians? Some Observations about the Perils and Pitfalls of

Data for Race and Ethnicity," *Population Research and Policy Review* 5 (1986):249.

5. For an excellent discussion of the evolution, over several centuries, of ideas about blood relationship among European and Euro-American peoples and transference of these ideas into American Indian tribal populations, see Melissa L. Myer, "American Indian Blood Quantum Requirements: Blood Is Thicker Than Family," in *Over the Edge: Remapping the American West*, ed. Valerie J. Matsumoto and Blake Allmendiger (Berkeley: University of California Press, 1999).

6. Thomas Biolsi, "The Birth of the Reservation; Making the Modern Individual among the Lakota," American Ethnologist 22, no. 1 (February 1995):28–9; Patricia Limerick, The Legacy of Conquest: The Unbroken Past of the American West (New York: W. W. Norton, 1988).

7. To view a variety of tribal constitutions and their citizenship requirements, see http://thorpe.ou.edu/.

8. "Mixed Marriages Present Some Property Problems," *Indian Country Today* (26 May–2 June 1997):D10.

9. Akwesasne Notes 6 (Autumn 1974):32.

10. The two mentions of "Indians" in the Constitution appear in passages regarding the regulation of commerce and the taking of a federal census. The word tribe also appears once in the Constitution, in the Commerce Clause.

11. Sharon O'Brien, "Tribes and Indians: With Whom Does the United States Maintain a Relationship?" *Notre Dame Law Review* 66 (1991):1481.

12. These agencies administer resources and programs in areas such as education, health, social services, tribal governance and administration, law enforcement, nutrition, resource management, tribal economic development, employment, and the like. The most recently published source describing various programs and the requirements for participation is Roger Walk, *Federal Assistance to Native Americans: A Report Prepared for the Senate Select Committee on Indian Affairs of the U.S. Senate* (Washington, DC: Government Printing Office, 1991).

13. For a discussion of the history of American Indian hunting, fishing, and water rights, see Wilcomb E. Washburn, *Red Man's Land/White Man's Law: A Study of the Past and Present Status of the American Indian* (New York: Charles Scribner's Sons, 1971).

14. Non-Indian students in my classes sometimes tell me that Indians also regularly receive such windfalls as free cars and monthly checks from the government strictly because of their race. It is my sad duty to puncture this fantasy. The common belief that Indians receive "free money" probably stems from the fact that the government holds land in trust for certain tribes. As part of its trust responsibility, it may then lease that land, collect the revenue, and distribute it to the tribal members . . . . For details on the special, political-economic relationship of Indians to the federal government in relation to taxation and licensure, see Gary D. Sandefur, "Economic Development and Employment Opportunities for American Indians," in *American Indians: Social Justice and Public Policy, Ethnicity and Public Policy Series*, vol. 9, ed. Donald E. Green and Thomas V. Tonneson (Milwaukee: University of Wisconsin System Institute on Race and Ethnicity, 1991).

15. Suzan Shown Harjo, "The American Indian Experience," in *Family Ethnicity: Strength in Diversity*, ed Harriet Pipes McAdoo (Newbury Park, CA: Sage, 1993); R. B. Jones, "The Indian Child Welfare Act: The Need for a Separate Law," available at http://www.abanet.org/genpractice/compleat/f95child.html, accessed 1995.

16. To be specific, the Commerce Department estimated in 1985 that specious "Indian art" imported from foreign countries created $40–80 million in lost income, or 10–20 percent of annual Indian art sales, for genuine Indian artists every year (H.R. 101–400, 101st Cong., 1st Sess., *Congressional Record* [1990]: 4–5).

17. An excellent, detailed discussion of this legislation appears in Gail K. Sheffield, *The Arbitrary Indian: The Indian Arts and Crafts Act of 1990* (Norman: University of Oklahoma Press, 1997), 30–31.

18. Eugeen E. Roosens, *Creating Ethnicity: The Process of Ethnogenesis* (Newbury Park, CA: Sage, 1989), 41–42. Roosens is discussing the situation of Canadian Indians, but the same remarks apply to American Indians.

19. G. William Rice, "There and Back Again—An Indian Hobbit's Holiday: Indians Teaching Indian Law," *New Mexico Law Review* 26, no. 2 (Spring 1996):176.

20. Naomi Zack, "Mixed Black and White Race and Public Policy," *Hypatia* 10, no. 1 (Winter 1995):120–32.

21. Jack D. Forbes, "The Manipulation of Race, Caste, and Identity: Classifying Afroamericans, Native Americans and Red-Black People," *Journal of Ethnic Studies* 17, no. 4 (1990):24.

22. Kent Carter, "Deciding Who Can Be Cherokee: Enrollment Records of the Dawes Commission," *Chronicles of Oklahoma* 69, no. 2 (Summer 1991):174–205.

23. Theodore Roosevelt, *The Works of Theodore Roosevelt*, vol 15: *State Papers as Governor and President, 1899–1909* (New York: Scribner's Sons, 1926), 129. Contrast Roosevelt's optimism about allotment with the opinion of U.S. Commissioner of Indian Affairs John Collier, who would later call it "the greatest single practical evil" ever perpetrated on American Indians (quoted in Fergus Bordewich, *Killing the White Man's Indian* [New York: Doubleday, 1996], 124).

24. Angie Debo, *And Still the Waters Run: The Betrayal of the Five Civilized Tribes* (Princeton: Princeton University Press, 1972), 53.

25. In Oklahoma, the Creeks were especially resistant . . . Cherokees used their own strategies, often under the guidance of traditionalist leader Redbird Smith. For further discussion of tribal resistance to allotment, see D. S. Otis, *The Dawes Act and the Allotment of Indian Lands* (Norman: University of Oklahoma Press, 1973), 40–46.

26. Modern tribes do realize that some of their proper members are being excluded from legal citizenship, and most have created a mechanism for dealing with this reality. Many tribal constitutions allow for legally "adopting" individuals who do not meet formally specified identity criteria.

27. Modern descendants of such individuals—referred to then and now as "freedmen"—often continue to maintain documentation of tribal affiliation. Presently, they do not qualify for social service benefits, mineral rights, and other benefits that sometimes accrue to those who are tribal citizens by blood.

28. Debo, *And Still the Waters Run*, 38.

29. Biolsi, "The Birth of the Reservation."

30. Biolsi, "The Birth of the Reservation," 28.

# 26

# SALVAGING THE SELF

DAVID SNOW

LEON ANDERSON

*The second reading in this section on identity construction and stigma management is an excerpt from the classic 1992 book* Down on Their Luck: A Study of Homeless People. *David Snow, a professor of sociology at the University of California, Irvine, and Leon Anderson, a professor of sociology at Ohio University, spent several years doing fieldwork to understand the lives and identities of the homeless. Using the theoretical perspective of symbolic interactionism, Snow and Anderson find that the homeless employ a number of strategies to construct meaningful identities and senses of self-worth. The reading illustrates well and also complicates Markus's model of personal versus social identities (Reading 15) and how the homeless manage social stigma related to their identities. Howard and Alamilla's four perspectives of identity (Reading 16) also could be applied to this case.*

To be homeless in America is not only to have fallen to the bottom of the status system; it is also to be confronted with gnawing doubts about self-worth and the meaning of existence. Such vexing concerns are not just the psychic fallout of having descended onto the streets, but are also stoked by encounters with the domiciled that constantly remind the homeless of where they stand in relation to others.

One such encounter occurred early in the course of our fieldwork. It was late afternoon, and the homeless were congregating in front of the Sally [the Salvation Army building] for dinner. A school bus approached that was packed with Anglo junior high school students being bused from an eastside barrio school to their upper-middle- and upper-class homes in the city's northwest neighborhoods. As the bus rolled by, a fusillade of coins came flying out the

*Source:* Snow, David and Leon Anderson. 1994. "Salvaging the Self" in *Down on Their Luck: A Study of Homeless People.* Reproduced with permission of University of California Press–Books in the format Textbook via Copyright Clearance Center.

windows, as the students made obscene gestures and shouted, "Get a job." Some of the homeless gestured back, some scrambled for the scattered coins— mostly pennies—others angrily threw the coins at the bus, and a few seemed oblivious to the encounter. For the passing junior high schoolers, the exchange was harmless fun, a way to work off the restless energy built up in school; but for the homeless it was a stark reminder of their stigmatized status and of the extent to which they are the objects of negative attention.

Initially, we did not give much thought to this encounter. We were more interested in other issues and were neither fully aware of the frequency of such occurrences nor appreciative of their psychological consequences. We quickly came to learn, however, that this was hardly an isolated incident. The buses passed by the Sally every weekday afternoon during the school year; other domiciled citizens occasionally found pleasure in driving by and similarly hurling insults at the homeless and pennies at their feet; and, as we have seen, the hippie tramps and other homeless in the university area were derisively called "Drag worms," the police often harassed the homeless, and a number of neighborhoods took turns vilifying and derogating them.

Not all encounters with the domiciled are so stridently and intentionally demeaning, of course, but they are no less piercingly stigmatizing. One Saturday morning, for instance, as we walked with Willie Hastings and Ron Whitaker along a downtown street, a woman with a station wagon full of children drove by. As they passed, several of the children pointed at us and shouted, "Hey, Mama, look at the street people!" Ron responded angrily:

*"Mama, look at the street people!" You know, it pisses me off the way fucking thieves steal shit and they can still hold their heads high 'cause they got money. Sure, they have to go to prison sometimes, but when they're out, nobody looks down on them. But I wouldn't steal from nobody, and look how those kids stare at us!*

The pain of being objects of curiosity and negative attention are experienced fairly regularly by the homeless, but they suffer just as frequently from what has been called "attention deprivation." In *The Pursuit of Attention*, Charles Derber commented that "members of the subordinate classes are regarded as less worthy of attention in relations with members of dominant classes and so are subjected to subtle yet systematic face-to-face deprivation" (1979:42). For no one is Derber's observation more true than for the homeless, who are routinely ignored or avoided by the domiciled . . . ., pedestrians frequently avert their eyes when passing the homeless on the sidewalk, and they often hasten their pace and increase the distance between themselves and the homeless when they sense they may be targeted by a panhandler. Pedestrians sometimes go so far as to cross the street in order to avoid anticipated interaction with the homeless. Because of the fear and anxiety presumably engendered in the domiciled by actual or threatened contact with the homeless, efforts are often made at the community level, as we saw earlier, to regulate and segregate the homeless both spatially and institutionally. Although these avoidance rituals and segregative measures are not as overtly demeaning as the more active and immediate kinds of negative attention the homeless receive, they can be equally stigmatizing, for they also cast the homeless as objects of contamination. This, too, constitutes an assault upon the self, albeit a more subtle and perhaps more insidious one.

Occurring alongside the negative attention and attention deprivation the homeless experience are an array of gestures and acts that are frequently altruistic and clearly indicative of goodwill. People do on occasion give to panhandlers and beggars out of sincere concern rather than merely to get them off their backs. Domiciled citizens sometimes even provide assistance without being asked. One evening, for instance, we found Pat Manchester sitting on a bench near the university eating pizza. "Man, I was just sitting here," he told us, "and this dude walked up and gave me half a pizza and two dollar bills." Several of the students who worked at restaurants in the university area occasionally brought leftovers to Rhyming Mike and other hippie tramps. Other community members occasionally took street people to their home for a shower, dinner, and a good night's sleep. Even Jorge Herrera, who was nearly incoherent, appeared never to wash or bathe, and was covered with rashes and open sores, was the recipient of such assistance. Twice during our field research he appeared on the streets after a brief absence in clean clothes, shaved, and with a new haircut. When we asked about the changes in his appearance, he told us that someone had taken him home, cleaned him up, and let him spend the night. These kinds of unorganized, sporadic gestures of goodwill clearly facilitate the survival of some of the homeless, but the numbers they touch in comparison to those in need are miniscule. Nor do they occur in sufficient quantity or consistently enough to neutralize the stigmatizing and demeaning consequences of not only being on the streets but being objects of negative attention or little attention at all.

In addition to those who make sporadic gestures of goodwill, thousands of domiciled citizens devote occasional time and energy to serving the homeless in an organized fashion in churches, soup kitchens, and shelters. Angels House kitchen was staffed in part by such volunteers, and their support was essential to the operation of the kitchen. Yet the relationship between these well-meaning volunteers and the homeless is highly structured and sanitized. The volunteers typically prepare sandwiches and other foods in a separate area from the homeless or encounter them only across the divide of a serving counter that underscores the distance between the servers and the served. Thus, however sincere and helpful the efforts of domiciled volunteers, the structure of their encounters with the homeless often underscores the immense status differences and thereby reminds the homeless again of where they stand in relation to others.

Gestures of goodwill toward the homeless and the kinds of attention they receive are not constant over time. Instead, they tend to follow an annual cycle, with sympathetic interest increasing with the first cold snap in the fall and reaching its zenith during the Christmas holiday season . . . . Based on a frequency count of newspaper stories on the homeless across the country, the figure reveals a dramatic increase in the number of stories as the Thanksgiving/Christmas holiday season approaches. Moreover, once Christmas passes, coverage declines precipitously. This same pattern was seen in Austin in the activities both of the media and of many community residents. At times this expression of holiday concern reached almost comical dimensions. One Thanksgiving Day, for instance, the homeless were inundated with food. In the morning several domiciled citizens came to the Labor Corner to hand out sandwiches, and a few gave away whole turkeys, assuming they would be devoured on the spot. The Assembly of God Church served a large meal around noon, and the Salvation Army served its traditional Thanksgiving meal in midafternoon. At one point in the early afternoon the Sally officials appeared to be worried that only a few people would show up for the meal. Newspaper and television reporters lingered around the Sally much of the afternoon, taking pictures and interviewing both officials and street people for stories that would be aired that evening or would appear in the morning newspaper.

After Christmas, charitable interest in the homeless declined dramatically. The public span of sympathy seemed to have run its course. Thus, except for a two- to three-month period, the homeless tend to be recipients only of negative attention, ignored altogether, or dealt with in a segregated and sanitized fashion that underscores their stigmatized status.

The task the homeless face of salvaging the self is not easy, especially since wherever they turn they are reminded that they are at the very bottom of the status system. As Sonny McCallister lamented shortly after he became homeless, "The hardest thing's been getting used to the way people look down on street people. It's real hard to feel good about yourself when almost everyone you see is looking down on you." Tom Fisk, who had been on the streets longer, agreed. But he said that he had become more calloused over time:

*I used to let it bother me when people stared at me while I was trying to sleep on the roof of my car or change clothes out of my trunk, but I don't let it get to me anymore. I mean, they don't know who I am, so what gives them the right to judge me? I know I'm okay.*

But there was equivocation and uncertainty in his voice. Moreover, even if he no longer felt the stares and comments of others, he still had to make sense of the distance between himself and them.

How, then, do the homeless deal with the negative attention they receive or the indifference they encounter as they struggle to survive materially? How do they salvage their selves? And to what extent do the webs of meaning they spin and the personal identities they construct vary with patterns of adaptation? We address these questions . . . by considering two kinds of meaning: existential and identity-oriented. The former term refers to the kinds of accounts the homeless invoke in order to make sense of their plight; the latter refers to the kinds of meaning they attach to self in interactions with others . . . .

How do the homeless carve out a sense of meaning in the seemingly insane and meaningless situation in which they find themselves? Are they able to make sense of their plight in a fashion that helps to salvage the self?

Some are able to do so and others are not. Many of the homeless invoke causal accounts of their situation that infuse it with meaning and rescue the self; others abandon both concerns by drifting into the world of alcoholism or into an alternative reality that is in this world but not of it and that is often treated as symptomatic of insanity by those not privy to it. Of the two lines of response, the first is clearly the most pronounced.

## Invoking Causal Accounts

By causal accounts we refer to the reasons people give to render understandable their behavior or the situations in which they find themselves. Such accounts are essentially commonsense attributions that are invoked in order to explain some problematic action or situation. Whether such accounts seem reasonable to an observer is irrelevant; what is at issue is their meaningfulness to the actor.

These explanatory accounts are seldom new constructions. Rather, they are likely to be variants of folk understandings or aphorisms that are invoked from time to time by many citizens and thus constitute part of a larger cultural vocabulary. This view

of causal accounts accords with the contention that culture can best be thought of as a repertoire or "'tool kit' of symbols, stories, rituals, and world views which people use in varying configurations to solve different kinds of problems" (Swidler 1986:273) These stories, symbols, or accounts are not pulled out of that cultural tool kit at random, however. Instead, the appropriation and articulation process is driven by some pressing problem or imperative. In the case of the homeless, that predicament is the existential need to infuse their situation with a sense of meaning that helps to salvage the self. In the service of that imperative, three folk adages or accounts surfaced rather widely and frequently among the homeless in Austin in their conversations with us and each other. One says, "I'm down on my luck." Another reminds us, "What goes around, comes around." And the third says, "I've paid my dues."

*"I'm down on my luck."* The term *luck*, which most citizens invoke from time to time to account for unanticipated happenings in their lives, is generally reserved for events that influence the individual's life but are thought to be beyond his or her control. To assert that "I'm down on my luck," then, is to attribute my plight to misfortune, to chance. For the homeless, such an attribution not only helps to make sense of their situation, but it does so in a manner that is psychologically functional in two ways: it exempts the homeless from responsibility for their plight, and it leaves open the possibility of a better future.

Exemption from personal responsibility was a consistent theme in the causal accounts we overheard. As Willie Hastings asserted aggressively in discussing with Ron Whitaker and us the negative attention heaped on all of us just a few minutes earlier by the children in the passing car:

*Shit, it ain't my fault I'm on the streets. I didn't choose to become homeless. I just had a lot of bad luck. And that ain't my fault. Hell, who knows? Those kids and their old lady might get unlucky and wake up on the streets someday. It can happen to anyone, you know!*

Ron chipped in:

*Yeah, a lot of people think we're lazy, that we don't give
a shit, that this is what we want. But that sure in hell
ain't so—at least not for me. It wasn't my fault I lost my
job in Denver. If I'd been working down the street,
maybe I'd still be there. I was just at the wrong place at
the wrong time. Like Willie said, some people just ain't
got no luck!*

Sonny McCallister, Tom Fisk, Tony Jones, Tanner
Sutton, and Hoyt Page would all have agreed, in large
part because their recently dislocated or straddler
status makes them take street life less for granted than
the outsiders do and therefore prompts them to try to
explain their situation. But why invoke luck? Why not
fix the blame for their plight on more direct, tangible
factors, such as family discord, low wages, or being
laid off? Not only are such biographic and structural
factors clearly operative in their lives, . . . but reference to them can also exempt people from personal
responsibility for their plight. After all, it was not
Tony Jones's fault that he lost his job as a security
guard at a Chicago steel mill when the plant cut back.
Yet, although he referred to this event as the one that
triggered his descent onto the streets, he still maintained that he was primarily the victim of "bad luck"
rather than less mysterious structural forces that
clearly intruded into his life. Apparently, he felt that
had he chanced to work at a different job or in a different factory, his fate would have been different.

The same logic is evident in Hoyt's efforts to
make sense of his situation. His biography is strewn
with a host of factors not of his own doing, such as
having been orphaned and not having received
proper attention for a learning disorder, which could
have been woven into a responsibility-free account
for being homeless. Yet, he too often said that he was
simply "down on my luck."

This tendency to cling to the luck factor in lieu of
structural or biographic accounts of homelessness
does not stem from ignorance about these other
factors or from false consciousness regarding their
causal influence . . . . The homeless often name
structural and biographic factors when discussing
the reasons for their homelessness. But the bad-luck
account more readily allows for the possibility of a
better day down the road. The victim of bad luck can
become the recipient of good luck. "Luck changes,"
as we were frequently reminded. So, too, do structural trends and biographic experiences, but perhaps
not so readily or positively from the standpoint of
the homeless. Luck is also more fickle and mysterious, and its effects are supposedly distributed more
randomly across the social order than are the effects
of most structural trends. For good reason, then,
some of the homeless cling to the luck factor.

Yet, the lives of most homeless are devoid of
much good fortune, as is clear from the biographies
of virtually all of our key informants. Why, then, do
some of the homeless talk as if good luck is about to
come their way? The answer resides in two other
frequently invoked causal accounts that are intertwined with the luck factor: "What goes around,
comes around," and "I've paid my dues."

*"What goes around, comes around."* . . . Insofar as
there is a moral code affecting interpersonal relations on the streets, it is manifested in the phrase,
"What goes around, comes around." But the relevance of this phrase is not confined solely to the
interpersonal domain. It is also brought into service
with respect to the issue of meaning in general and
the luck factor in particular.

Regarding the former, the contention that "what
goes around, comes around" suggests a cyclical
rather than linear conception of the process by
which events unfold. This circularity implies, among
other things, a transposition of opposites at some
point in the life course. Biblical examples of such
transpositions abound, as in the New Testament declarations that "The last shall be first and the first last"
and "The meek shall inherit the earth." Although few
homeless harbor realistic thoughts of such dramatic
transpositions, many do assume that things will get
better because "what goes around, comes around."

This logic also holds for luck. Thus, if a person
has been down on his or her luck, it follows that the
person's luck is subject to change. Hoyt, among others, talked as though he believed this proposition.
"Look," he told us one evening over dinner and a few
beers at a local steak house:

*I've been down on my luck for so damn long, it's got to
change . . . . Like I said before, I believe what goes*

*around, comes around, so I'm due a run of good luck, don't you think?*

We nodded in agreement, but not without wondering how strongly Hoyt and others actually believed in the presumed link between luck and the cyclical principle of "what goes around, comes around." Whatever the answer, there is certainly good reason for harboring such a belief, for it introduces a ray of hope into a dismal situation and thereby infuses it with meaning of the kind that helps keep the self afloat.

"*I've paid my dues.*" This linkage is buttressed further by the third frequently articulated causal account: "I've paid my dues." To invoke this saying is to assert, as Marilyn Fisch often did in her more sober moments, that "I deserve better" after "what I've been through" or "what I've done." The phrase implies that if there are preconditions for a run of good luck, then those conditions have been met. Thus, Gypsy Bill told us one afternoon that he felt his luck was about to change as he was fantasizing about coming into some money. "You may think I'm crazy," he said, "but it's this feeling I've got. Besides, I deserve it 'cause I've paid my dues." A street acquaintance of Gypsy's, a man who fancied himself as "a great blues harmonica player," broke in:

*Yeah, man, I know what you mean. I was playing the blues on Bleeker Street once when Jeff Beck comes by and tells me I'm the best blues harmonica player he's ever heard. "Where do you live?" he asks me. And I tell him, "Here on this sidewalk, and I sleep in the subways." And he asks me, "What do you want from me?" And I tell him, "Nothing, man. A handshake." And he reaches into his pocket and pulls out a hundred-dollar bill and gives it to me 'cause I had it coming! I know the blues, man. I live them. I sleep on the fucking street, paying my dues. That's why no one plays the blues like me!*

He then pointed to the knapsack on his back and asked if we knew what was in it. We shook our heads, and he said, "My jeans, man. I fucking pissed in 'em last night, I was so drunk. That's what I'm saying: I know the blues, man! I've paid my dues."

So a streak of good luck, however fleeting, or anticipation of such a streak, albeit a more sustained one, is rationalized in terms of the hardships endured. The more a person has suffered, the greater the dues that have been paid and the more, therefore, a run of good luck is deserved. Perhaps this is why some of those with the longest stretches of time on the streets, namely, outsiders, were heard to assert more often than others that "I've paid my dues." As Shotgun explained in one of his moments of sobriety, "I been on the streets for about fifteen years . . . . I've rode the boxcars and slept out in the wintertime. That's how you pay your dues." Yet, many outsiders do not often invoke this phrase. The reason, we suspect, is that they have been down on their luck for so long that their current fate seems impervious to change and they have therefore resigned themselves to life on the streets. Those who assert that they've paid their dues, however, invoke the phrase in service of the luck factor and the corollary principle of what goes around, comes around. And for good reason. Together, these accounts both exempt the homeless from responsibility for their plight and hold the door ajar for a change in luck . . . .

## CONSTRUCTING IDENTITY-ORIENTED MEANING

However the homeless deal with the issue of existential meaning, whether by stringing together causal accounts borrowed from conventional cultural vocabularies or by seeking refuge in alcohol, drugs, or alternative realities, they are still confronted with establishing who they are in the course of interaction with others, for interaction between two or more individuals minimally requires that they be situated or placed as social objects. In other words, situationally specific identities must be established. Such identities can be established in two ways: they can be attributed or imputed by others, or they can be claimed or asserted by the actor. The former can be thought of as social or role identities in that they are imputations based primarily on information gleaned from the appearance or behavior of others and from the time and location of their action, as when children in a passing car look out the window and yell, "Hey, Mama, look at the street people!" or when junior high school students yell out the windows of their school bus to the homeless lining up for dinner in front of the Sally, "Get a job, you bums!" In each case, the homeless in question have been situated as social objects and thus assigned social identities.

When individuals claim or assert an identity, by contrast, they attribute meaning to themselves. Such self-attributions can be thought of as personal identities rather than social identities, in that they are self-designations brought into play or avowed during the course of actual or anticipated interaction with others. Personal identities may be consistent with imputed social identities, as when Shotgun claims to be "a tramp," or inconsistent, as when Tony Jones yells back to you passing junior high schoolers, "Fuck you, I ain't no lazy bum!" The presented personal identities of individuals who are frequent objects of negative attention or attention deprivation, as are the homeless, can be especially revealing, because they offer a glimpse of how those people deal interactionally with their pariah-like status and the demeaning social identities into which they are frequently cast. Personal identities thus provide further insight into the ways the homeless attempt to salvage the self.

What, then, are the personal identities that the homeless construct and negotiate when in interaction with others? Are they merely a reflection of the highly stereotypic and stigmatized identities attributed to them, or do they reflect a more positive sense of self or at least an attempt to carve out and sustain a less demeaning self-conception?

The construction of personal identity typically involves a number of complementary activities: (a) procurement and arrangement of physical settings and props; (b) cosmetic face work or the arrangement of personal appearance; (c) selective association with other individuals and groups; and (d) verbal construction and assertion of personal identity. Although some of the homeless engage in conscious manipulation of props and appearance—for example, Pushcart, with his fully loaded shopping cart, and Shotgun, who fancies himself a con

artist—most do not resort to such measures. Instead, the primary means by which the homeless announce their personal identities is verbal. They engage, in other words, in a good bit of identity talk. This is understandable, since the homeless seldom have the financial or social resources to pursue the other identity construction activities. Additionally, since the structure of their daily routines ensures that they spend a great deal of time waiting here and there, they have ample opportunity to converse with each other.

Sprinkled throughout these conversations with each other, as well as those with agency personnel and, occasionally, with the domiciled, are numerous examples of identity talk. Inspection of the instances of the identity talk to which we were privy yielded three generic patterns: (1) distancing; (2) embracement; and (3) fictive storytelling. Each pattern was found to contain several subtypes that tend to vary in use according to whether the speaker is recently dislocated, a straddler, or an outsider. We elaborate in turn each of the generic patterns, their varieties, and how they vary in use among the different types of homeless.

## Distancing

When individuals have to enact roles, associate with others, or utilize institutions that imply social identities inconsistent with their actual or desired self-conceptions, they often attempt to distance themselves from those roles, associations, or institutions. A substantial proportion of the identity talk we recorded was consciously focused on distancing from other homeless individuals, from street and occupational roles, and from the caretaker agencies servicing the homeless. Nearly a third of the identity statements were of this variety.

### Associational Distancing

Since a claim to a particular self is partly contingent on the imputed social identities of the person's associates, one way people can substantiate that claim when their associates are negatively evaluated is to distance themselves from those associates. This distancing technique manifested itself in two ways among the homeless: disassociation from the homeless as a general social category, and disassociation from specific groupings of homeless individuals.

Categoric associational distancing was particularly evident among the recently dislocated. Illustrative is Tony Jones's comment in response to our initial query about life on the streets:

> I'm not like the other guys who hang out down at the Sally. If you want to know about street people, I can tell you about them; but you can't really learn about street people from studying me, because I'm different.

Such categorical distancing also occurred among those individuals who saw themselves as on the verge of getting off the street. After securing two jobs in the hope of raising enough money to rent an apartment, Ron Whitaker indicated, for example, that he was different from other street people. "They've gotten used to living on the streets and they're satisfied with it, but not me!" he told us. "Next to my salvation, getting off the streets is the most important thing in my life." This variety of categorical distancing was particularly pronounced among homeless individuals who had taken jobs at the Sally and thus had one foot off the streets. These individuals were frequently criticized by other homeless for their condescending attitude. As Marilyn put it, "As soon as these guys get inside, they're better than the rest of us. They've been out on the streets for years, and as soon as they're inside, they forget it."

Among the outsiders, who had been on the streets for some time and who appeared firmly rooted in that life-style, there were few examples of categorical distancing. Instead, these individuals frequently distinguished themselves from other groups of homeless. This form of associational distancing was most conspicuous among those, such as the hippie tramps and redneck bums, who were not regular social-service or shelter users and who saw themselves as especially independent and resourceful. These individuals not only wasted little time in pointing out that they were "not like those Sally users," but were also given to derogating the more

institutionally dependent. Indeed, although they are among the furthest removed from a middle-class life-style, they sound at times much like middle-class citizens berating welfare recipients. As Marilyn explained, "A lot of these people staying at the Sally, they're reruns. Every day they're wanting something. People get tired of giving. All you hear is gimme, gimme. And we transients are getting sick of it."

### Role Distancing

Role distancing, the second form of distancing employed by the homeless, involves a self-conscious attempt to foster the impression of a lack of commitment or attachment to a particular role in order to deny the self implied. Thus, when individuals find themselves cast into roles in which the social identities implied are inconsistent with desired or actual self-conceptions, role distancing is likely to occur. Since the homeless routinely find themselves being cast into or enacting low-status, negatively evaluated roles, it should not be surprising that many of them attempt to disassociate themselves from those roles.

As did associational distancing, role distancing manifested itself in two ways: distancing from the general role of street person, and distancing from specific occupational roles. The former, which is also a type of categorical distancing, was particularly evident among the recently dislocated. It was not uncommon for these individuals to state explicitly that they should "not be mistaken as a typical street person." Role distancing of the less categoric and more situationally specific type was most evident among those who performed day labor, such as painters' helpers, hod carriers, warehouse and van unloaders, and those in unskilled service occupations such as dishwashing and janitorial work. As we saw earlier, the majority of the homeless we encountered would avail themselves of such job opportunities, but they seldom did so enthusiastically, since the jobs offered low status and low wages. This was especially true of the straddlers and some of the outsiders, who frequently reminded others of their disdain for such jobs and of the belief that they deserved better, as exemplified by the remarks of a drunk young man who had worked the previous day as a painter's helper: "I made $36.00 off the Labor Corner, but it was just nigger work. I'm twenty-four years old, man. I deserve better than that." . . .

### Institutional Distancing

An equally prevalent distancing technique involved the derogation of the caretaker agencies that attended to the needs of the homeless. The agency that was the most frequent object of these harangues was the Sally. Many of the homeless who used it described it as a greedy corporation run by inhumane personnel more interested in lining their own pockets than in serving the needy. Willie Hastings claimed, for example, that "the major is money-hungry and feeds people the cheapest way he can. He never talks to people except to gripe at them." He then added that the "Sally is supposed to be a Christian organization, but it doesn't have a Christian spirit. It looks down on people . . . . The Salvation Army is a national business that is more worried about making money than helping people." Ron Whitaker concurred, noting on another occasion that the "Sally here doesn't nearly do as much as it could for people. The people who work there take bags of groceries and put them in their cars. People donate to the Sally, and then the workers there cream off the best." Another straddler told us after he had spent several nights at the winter shelter, "If you spend a week here, you'll see how come people lose hope. You're treated just like an animal."

Because the Salvation Army is the only local facility that provides free shelter, breakfast, and dinner, attention is understandably focused on it. But that the Sally would be frequently derogated by the people whose survival it facilitates may appear puzzling at first glance, especially given its highly accommodative orientation. The answer lies in part in the organization and dissemination of its services. Clients are processed in an impersonal, highly structured assembly line–like fashion. The result is a leveling of individual differences and a decline in personal autonomy. Bitching and complaining about such settings create psychic distance from the self implied and secure a modicum of personal autonomy. This variety of

distancing, though observable among all of the homeless, was most prevalent among the straddlers and outsiders. Since these individuals have used street agencies over a longer period of time, their self-concepts are more deeply implicated in them, thus necessitating distancing from those institutions and the self implied. Criticizing the Sally, then, provides some users with a means of dealing with the implications of their dependency on it. It is, in short, a way of presenting and sustaining a somewhat contrary personal identity . . . .

### Embracement

Embracement connotes a person's verbal and expressive confirmation of acceptance of and attachment to the social identity associated with a general or specific role, a set of social relationships, or a particular ideology. So defined, embracement implies that social identity is congruent with personal identity. Thus, embracement involves the avowal of implied social identities rather than their disavowal, as in the case of distancing. Thirty-four percent of the identity statements were of this variety . . . .

## SUMMARY

All animals are confronted with the challenge of material subsistence, but only humans are saddled with the vexing question of its meaning. We must not only sustain ourselves physically to survive, but we are also impelled to make sense of our mode of subsistence, to place it in some meaningful context, to develop an account of our situation that does not destroy our sense of self-worth. Otherwise, the will to persist falters and interest in tomorrow wanes. The biblical prophets understood this well when they told us that "man does not live by bread alone." The homeless appear to understand this existential dilemma, too, at least experientially; for while they struggle to subsist materially, they confront the meaning of their predicament and its implications for the self. These concerns weigh particularly heavily on the recently dislocated, but they gnaw at the other homeless as well— sometimes when they drift off at night, sometimes when they are jarred from sleep by their own dreams or the cries of others, and often throughout the day when their encounters with other homeless and with the domiciled remind them in myriad subtle and not-so-subtle ways of their descent into the lowest reaches of the social system and of their resultant stigmatized status.

In this reading we have explored the ways the homeless deal with their plight, both existentially and interactionally, by attempting to construct and maintain a sense of meaning and self-worth that helps them stay afloat. Not all of the homeless succeed, of course. The selves of some have been so brutalized that they are abandoned in favor of alcohol, drugs, or out-of-this-world fantasies. And many would probably not score high on a questionnaire evaluating self-esteem. But the issue for us has not

been how well the homeless fare in comparison to others on measures of self-esteem, but that they do, in fact, attempt to salvage the self, and that this struggle is an ongoing feature of the experience of living on the streets . . . .

## DISCUSSION QUESTIONS

1. Discuss the ways in which the homeless "construct and maintain a sense of meaning and self-worth" even as they struggle on the material level. To what degree do these strategies of emotional survival succeed in giving homeless people some dignity?

2. How can Snow and Anderson's arguments about identity maintenance and accounting be applied to other social identities, such as race-ethnicity, gender, or sexuality?

# 27

# Passing as Black

## *Racial Identity Work Among Biracial Americans*

Nikki Khanna

Cathryn Johnson

*This reading is the first of three to examine passing and stigma management in this section on identity construction and stigma management. Nikki Khanna, a professor of sociology at the University of Vermont, and Cathryn Johnson, a sociology professor at Emory University, both specialize in social psychology. This excerpt, taken from their 2010 article in the* Social Psychology Quarterly, *introduces the reader to the concept of racial passing, where an individual identifies and presents her- or himself as another race. Their research focuses on forty biracial (black and white) adults who use racial passing to primarily pass as black for various reasons. Khanna and Johnson build on the theories of "identity work" presented in Snow and Anderson's work on the homeless (Reading 26).*

My father has sixteen brothers and sisters and . . . a lot of them used to pass as white . . . I mean it's easier if you can go to any movie theater you want. [A] few of my aunts told me about a place they used to go to and eat all the time that was "whites only" . . . they did it as a joke . . . they did it because they wanted to show how stupid [segregation] was.

Olivia, age 45

Until relatively recently, few racial options have been available to multiracial people—especially those with black ancestry. The one-drop rule, rooted in slavery and Jim Crow segregation, defined multiracial people with any drop of black blood as *black* (Davis 1991). Just like their monoracial black counterparts, they had few, if any, rights (e.g., they were enslaved, they could not vote, they were restricted from many public facilities). According to Daniel (1992), "Multiracial individuals for the most part have accepted the racial status quo, and have identified themselves as Black. A significant number of individuals, however, have chosen the path of resistance . . . Individual resistance has taken the form primarily of 'passing'" as white (91). Like Olivia's aunts (described above), many Americans passed as white to resist the racially restrictive one-drop rule and the racial status quo of the Jim Crow era (Daniel 2002; Williamson 1980).

Racial passing has generally been understood as a phenomenon in which a person of one race identifies and presents himself or herself as another (usually white). According to Ramona Douglass, a multiracial activist and cofounder of the Association of Multiethnic Americans, however, the *concept* of passing (not the act itself) is racist in origin (Russell, Wilson, and Hall 1992; see also Williamson 1980) because it is entwined with the racist one-drop rule. Even if a person has white ancestry and looks white, he is considered "really" black because of his black ancestry (no matter how distant); white identity is perceived as somehow "fraudulent" (Daniel 2002:83). Kennedy (2003) provides a more precise definition and defines passing as "a deception that enables a person to adopt specific roles or identities from which he or she would otherwise be barred by *prevailing social standards*" (p. 283; emphasis added). Thus, if one were "really" black, as defined by the social standards of the Jim Crow era (e.g., the one-drop rule) and presented himself or herself as white, he or she was perceived as deceiving the public with a false identity.

Passing as white was especially attractive during the Jim Crow era, when blacks had few rights and opportunities, yet little is known about racial passing today. Some scholars argue that given the increase in opportunities to black Americans, passing is a relic of the past. For instance, Russell et al. (1992) claim that "Today . . . while some African Americans pass 'part time' for economic reasons, the vast majority of those who could pass don't—and would never dream of doing so" (73). Similarly, Daniel (1992) says, "It would be difficult to say whether passing has actually decreased with the dismantling of segregation and the implementation of civil rights legislation . . . [but] it would be safe to conclude . . . that the most immediate impetus behind passing has been removed" (93). While the driving force behind passing may have faded, we ask: Are biracial people still passing today? If yes, how so and why?

Further, Brunsma and Rockquemore (2001) argue that racial identities are subject to some degree of constraint, especially for those with black ancestry. They claim, however, that "It remains to be seen how much negotiation and strategy [of race] is involved" (244). Focusing on this gap in the literature, this study also investigates the ways in which black-white people manage their racial identities in day-to-day interactions. Passing is one strategy of racial presentation, but there are likely other ways in which people manage their identities. Thus, we also ask: How much individual strategy is involved in racial identity today? And what types of strategies, other than passing, are used?

To address these questions, we first . . . review the identity literature. Symbolic interactionists suggest that identity is process—society influences identities, yet individuals are also active agents in shaping their identities (Cooley 1902; Gecas and Schwalbe 1983). Certainly this is true among those who actively passed as white during the Jim Crow era. Much remains to be learned, however, about how biracial people may act as active agents today; more general research on "identity work" (Snow and Anderson 1987), however, provides some clues. Third, we describe the research methodology, the sample characteristics, and limitations of the sample. The first author interviewed 40 black-white biracial adults, and based on these results we describe the key findings of the study . . . .

## IDENTITY AS A PROCESS: INDIVIDUAL AGENCY AND "IDENTITY WORK"

Much of the work that examines identity among biracial/multiracial people draws on the symbolic interactionist framework (Blumer 1969; Mead 1934; see Rockquemore and Brunsma 2002). The key aspect of this framework is *social interaction*—race and identity arise out of a social process in which meanings are created and modified through social interaction with others. Society shapes an individual's identity, while at the same time, the individual plays an active role in shaping his/her own racial identity.

While much of the research on biracial people draws on the symbolic interactionist perspective, a majority of studies on biracial people focus on factors (e.g., one-drop rule, social networks, social class) and processes (e.g., reflected appraisals) that act on individuals to shape their racial identities. Khanna (2004, 2010), for instance, looks at how reflected appraisals (i.e., how people think others see them) and the one-drop rule influences racial identity among biracial adults. Scholars, however, argue that people are not merely passive objects shaped by society, but are also active and creative agents of identity (Cooley 1902; Gecas and Schwalbe 1983). Williams (1996) suggests that biracial individuals are "active participants in shaping their racial identities... Not only do biracial individuals 'get race done unto them,' but they also do race as well" (208). Jim Crow–era passing is a clear example of people who were active agents in shaping their identities, yet little is known about the ways in which biracial people "do race" today. Racial passing is one type of racial performance, but likely there are additional ways in which people perform race (e.g., by highlighting and/or downplaying particular identities, but not necessarily concealing an aspect of their ancestry to pass as monoracial).

Further, little work examines racial strategies, yet research on stigma and identity suggest some strategies which may be applicable to biracial people. Goffman (1963), for instance, describes ways in which people cope with a stigmatized identity; strategies include "passing" (concealing the stigma), but also "covering" (managing the intrusiveness of the stigma). For instance, ethnic minorities might conceal their stigmatized ethnicity to pass as white, or they may cover their ethnicity by anglicizing their name. According to Goffman (1963), they cover the ethnicity, not to pass, but rather to "restrict the way a known-about attribute obtrudes itself into the center of attention" (103).

Extending this work, scholars further examine how stigmatized groups manage stigma, and much of this work looks at strategies of stigma management (see Kaufman and Johnson 2004). Many of these strategies comprise what Snow and Anderson (1987) call "identity work." In their study of the homeless, for example, they find that individuals "engage in a range of activities to create, present, or sustain identities" (1348), and these activities include: (1) procuring or arranging physical settings/props, (2) cosmetic face work/arrangement of personal appearance, (3) selective association with other individuals/groups, and (4) assertion of personal identity through verbal construction or identity talk . . . .

## DATA AND METHODS

This paper is part of a larger study examining racial identity among black-white biracial adults. In 2005 and 2006, the first author conducted semi-structured interviews with 40 black-white biracial adults living in a large urban area in the South. To participate in the study, respondents must have had one black and one white parent (as identified by respondents). Respondents were asked open-ended questions on a range of topics such as their racial identities, how others have influenced their identities, how their identities have changed over time and situation, and if and how they assert particular identities to others. Interviews were audio-taped and respondents' names were replaced with pseudonyms.

Because locating biracial individuals within the general population is often difficult, we primarily relied on convenience sampling. The first author began recruiting respondents by placing flyers in a variety of places, including local colleges, universities, and places of worship. Flyers read, "Do you have one black parent and one white parent?" We omitted terms such as "biracial" or "multiracial" from the flyers, aware that individuals who did not consider themselves biracial or multiracial may not have responded. The first author also asked interviewees to pass along her information to others with similar backgrounds.

## Characteristics of Respondents

Our data collection efforts resulted in a sample of 40 black-white biracial individuals. The ages ranged from 18 to 45, with the average age a little over 24 years of age. More than half of the respondents, 57.5 percent, fell between the ages of 18 and 22, which is typical college age; this is not surprising considering that our recruitment efforts began at local colleges and universities. Of the remaining respondents, 27.5 percent fell between the ages of 23 and 30, and 15 percent were over the age of 30. Regarding gender, 22.5 percent are men and 77.5 percent are women.

In terms of socioeconomic background, the majority of respondents have a middle- to upper-middle class background as measured by their educational backgrounds and that of their parents. All respondents are currently enrolled in college or are college-educated—67.5 percent are current college students and 32.5 percent had completed a bachelor's degree; 15 percent of respondents are pursuing advanced degrees. While respondents often had limited information about their parents' incomes, they frequently described parents who were highly educated. Most had at least one parent with a bachelor's degree (75 percent) or some college (87.5 percent), and 47.5 percent had at least one parent who held an advanced degree. The middle- to upper-middle class social status of the sample is further evidenced by the professional occupations of many of the parents (e.g., doctors, entrepreneurs, college professors, teachers, lawyers, nurses, as well as a dentist, scientist, college dean, accountant, airline pilot, judge, and minister).

Finally, regarding racial identification, the majority of respondents (33 of 40) label themselves using multiracial descriptors (e.g., as biracial, multiracial, mixed-race). In comparison, only six respondents

labeled themselves as black, and one respondent as white. The fact that so few respondents labeled themselves as black mirrors recent studies, which similarly show a weakening of the one-drop rule and widening of racial options (Brunsma and Rockquemore 2001; Korgen 1998). Furthermore, respondents' identifications are situational; they generally identified themselves to others as biracial, but in some contexts, passed as black or white . . . .

## Racial Identity Work: Strateties and Motivations

We find that respondents regularly do racial "identity work" (Snow and Anderson 1987) and employ a variety of strategies to present their preferred racial identities to others. In this section, we first explore the strategies that respondents use to manage their identities, and we identify factors which influence the accessibility and efficacy of these strategies. After outlining the various identity strategies and limitations, we then examine the motivations of identity work—with a focus on passing as black. Of those presenting monoracial identities to others, we find that they more often pass as black, rather than white—31 respondents describe situations in which they pass as black as compared to only three respondents who situationally pass as white.

### Strategies of Identity Work

Respondents use a variety of strategies to pass or, when passing is not desirable or feasible, to cover an identity (i.e., downplay its obtrusiveness [Goffman 1963]). Further, identity work is not just about concealing or covering a stigmatized identity, but highlighting a non-stigmatized or preferred identity, or what we term *accenting*. While covering involves downplaying an attribute, accenting involves emphasizing or accentuating it. Further, accenting differs from passing; not everyone can pass as black or white (e.g., one's ancestry may be well-known; one's phenotype may prevent it), but they may be able to accent their black or white ancestry as a form of identity work. To conceal (i.e., pass), cover, or accent particular aspects of their racial ancestries, respondents use five strategies: (1) verbal identification/disidentification, (2) selective disclosure, (3) manipulation of phenotype, (4) highlighting/downplaying cultural symbols, and (5) selective association.

First, respondents do "identity talk" (Snow and Anderson 1987) via *verbal identification/disidentification*. In short, they claim or disclaim identities by verbally saying, "I'm this" or "I'm not that." Anthony presents himself as black through verbal identification, and says, "I guess I just always make sure people know I'm black. Like even when I went to an all-white school, I used to say, 'I'm black'... Even though they knew I had a white father, if they ask, 'I'm black. That's it.'" By saying "I'm black," Anthony invokes a "me" identity (McCall 2003).

According to McCall (2003), identity processes must be studied in terms of the "Me" (identifications), but also the "Not-Me" (disidentifications). Caroline, for example, verbally resists being classified as black and says:

*In my [graduate] program, I think we maybe have like four black people, not including myself. And the other day, one of the [black] guys said to me, "Oh, in our class, there are only three of us." And I said, "Three of who?" And I didn't know what he was talking about and he looked at me. And I was like, "Don't do that. Don't lump me in [with being black] because I don't see myself that way and I don't like it when you just assume that." And then one time, I was taking an African Cultural Studies class and our teacher was black and she made reference to the black students in the class and lumped me in there with them. And I raised my hand and I was like, "I'm not black." And she almost wanted to argue with me like, "Yes you are." And no, no I'm not.*

As a reactive form of identity work, she creates a "Not-Me" identity by saying, "Don't lump me in" with being black and "I'm not black."

A second, and related, identity strategy is *selective disclosure*—selectively revealing and/or concealing particular racial identities to others. Unlike Anthony and Caroline (above), where peers were aware of their biracial backgrounds, some respondents manage the racial information they give to others to pass as monoracial (often as black). Storrs (1999), in her study of multiracial women, similarly finds that her respondents used selective disclosure to maintain their non-white identities by neglecting to reveal their white ancestry unless directly asked or challenged. In school, Samantha intentionally conceals her biracial background and says, "There was a time in middle school [that] I never told anyone what I was. A lot of times they never asked. They just kind of assumed, Well she's black. They just assumed... I [was] like, Okay, what's the reason for bringing it up?" Similarly, Natasha, who currently attends an HBCU (an Historically Black College/University), selectively reveals only her black background to her black peers. She says, "Since I've been at college, I don't even mention [that I'm biracial]. I don't bring it up unless it's brought up to me.... I would just rather say 'I'm black' and that be the end of it. It's definitely not something that I advertise." Both Samantha and Natasha conceal their white/biracial ancestry to pass as black.

In addition to selectively disclosing particular identities in face-to-face social interactions, respondents strategically reveal and conceal particular ancestries when filling out race questions commonly found on school, job, and scholarship applications. While Natasha (above) reveals only her black identity to black peers, she consciously manipulates her identity in different ways on forms. Highlighting the situational nature of her identity, she says, "[W]hen I fill out the little question things, I used to always check 'other.' Now I just check 'black'.... I've also learned to manipulate the situation that I'm in. I know that if I say I'm 'biracial,' I will get certain things, and if I say I'm 'black' I will get certain things. So I know I probably play with that a little bit." Like Natasha, the majority of respondents use selective disclosure on applications (more on their motivations in the next section).

Third, respondents manipulate their phenotypes (e.g., hair, skin) to manage their identities; this parallels Snow and Anderson's (1987) "cosmetic facework or arrangement of personal appearance" in their study of the homeless. Most respondents cannot alter their phenotypes in ways to present themselves as white, but they often describe modifying their phenotypes to pass as black or to accent their black ancestry. Others alter their phenotypes to cover or downplay their white ancestry. When growing up, Olivia's peers knew she was biracial, yet she manipulated her hair to downplay her white ancestry and says:

*When I was younger... I had very long hair and I identified more with African Americans... So I usually kept my hair pulled black or kept it up or tried to do different things to blend in more... [Other black girls] used to call me "white girl" because my hair was very long and it would blow in the wind... Back then I used to get up in the morning for school and leave my hair down and run out. And then when they started saying I was a white girl... I would never leave my hair down.*

Likewise, Anthony modifies his hair to pass as black and says, "I used to have really long hair and sometimes I would pick it up into a "fro." Michelle, who claims that she looks white, covers her white background by manipulating her skin color (e.g., tanning) because she does not "want to be seen as a white person."

Fourth, respondents manage their identities by highlighting and/or downplaying cultural symbols they perceive associated with whiteness and blackness (e.g., clothing/dress, food, language). While altering phenotype is not an option for everyone (e.g., not everyone can pick their hair into an afro), invoking cultural symbols is frequently employed in racial identity work. For example, to pass as black, Anthony draws on cultural symbols of clothing and language. Describing how he presented himself as black in school, he says, "You know, pants sagging... I used to kind of slur my speech a little bit because I used to talk very properly and I used to force myself to sound different. Sound like I was more black." Denise, too, describes passing as black especially when "trying to get into a step team or... choir... or... something where people in the organization are black, like a fraternity or sorority." When asked how she presents herself as black, she responds, "Probably the way I style my clothes... looking like I dress like I'm a black person... I have to change how I appear."

While Anthony and Denise highlight black cultural symbols (via clothing and language) to manage their black identities, Stephanie managed her black identity in school by distancing herself from cultural symbols of whiteness:

*[I attended] an all-black school and so all my friends were black then... I remember NSync being out... and my friends listened to them and I hated that. I hated any music that wasn't black. I hated any clothes that black people didn't wear... I felt like I had to stress to people that I was black... So I felt like "I hate NSync. I hate this white music."*

By distancing herself from these so-called white symbols (e.g., white music, clothing), Stephanie works to downplay or cover her white ancestry.

A final identity strategy is selective association. Respondents selectively associate with a particular racial group (via peers, friends, and romantic partners) and organizations/institutions (e.g., clubs, colleges, churches), which mirrors Snow and Anderson's (1987) strategy of "selective association with other individuals or groups." This strategy is often used by respondents to pass as black or to accent their black identity. For example, Stephanie says, "When I got to high school, all the white people were so nice... And I hated them. I didn't want to be friends with them. I didn't want to sit with them. I didn't want them to talk to me. I wanted to sit at the black table. I felt like I had to stress to people that I was black." While Stephanie associated only with black peers, Olivia dated only dark black men as a strategy to emphasize her black identity: "*I used to only date very dark-skinned black men because I didn't want people to think I was trying to be white... So I stayed with dark-skinned men because it's like I want to prove that I was black. Yeah, that I'm this black woman. 'See, I've got this very dark man.' It sounds stupid now, but back then it was important.*"

Other respondents manage black identities by joining organizations that reflect their preferred black identities. Alicia limits her peer network to black people and dates only black men, but she also describes being drawn to black organizations:

*I'm pretty black . . . Maybe I'm just more concerned about being black right now . . . And I want to have kids that are part of Jack and Jill and I'm infatuated with my [black] boyfriend. I want to marry him and have children with him. I can't imagine a life where I wasn't part of Jack and Jill and I wasn't in AKA . . . things that are exclusively black . . . I feel like I'm pretty segregated. I kind of segregate myself and I pretty much just hang out with black people.*

Alicia, who is "concerned about being black," consciously controls the racial makeup of her social circles and purposefully participates in organizations (Jack and Jill of America, Alpha Kappa Alpha[1]) that reflect her preferred black identity.

***Factors limiting the accessibility/usefulness of identity strategies.*** Respondents draw on various identity strategies, and clearly these findings indicate that biracial people have considerable agency with regard to how they identify themselves. We find, however, that these options are not without limits. Extending previous research on identity work (Snow and Anderson 1987; see also Killian and Johnson 2006; McCall 2003; Storrs 1999), we discover several factors that limit the accessibility and/or effectiveness of these strategies—one's phenotype, social class background, and racial networks.

For instance, race in American society is intertwined with phenotype (i.e., we are often raced by how we look); depending upon which identity one is presenting, manipulation of one's phenotype may or may not be an option. The majority of respondents cannot modify their phenotypes to pass as white, and some respondents have difficulty in altering their physical characteristics to pass as black. However, given the phenotypic variation among blacks (due to centuries of mixing with whites), passing as black is arguably less complicated than passing as white. Having light skin or straight hair, for instance, is not unique to those defined as biracial today; many individuals classified as black also share these traits. In contrast, those wanting to pass as white may face more challenges (e.g., hair cannot always be styled straight, skin tones are not easily lightened) . . . .

In addition to phenotype, social class and social networks influence the accessibility and effectiveness of certain identity strategies. For instance, many respondents perform identity work by highlighting or downplaying cultural symbols they associate with whiteness and blackness, yet access to and knowledge of cultural symbols is arguably tied to these larger structural factors. For example, respondents frequently describe using language as an identity strategy (i.e., "talking black"/Ebonics or "talking white"/ standard English), yet these different forms of speech are often linked with social class background and racial networks growing up. Some respondents describe having a difficult time doing this type of identity work simply because they do not know how.

Stephanie, for instance, tried to "talk black" to accent her black identity. Recalling an experience in school, she says, "I just remember my [black] friends . . . always telling me that I'm acting white. I need to act more black . . . But like my mom's very businesslike, so it's very proper. So I got it from her. I wasn't very slangish . . . . And I went through a period where if someone heard me, they'd say, 'Why do you talk like that?'" At first, Stephanie had considerable difficulty accenting her black identity primarily because she did not know how to "talk black." To remedy the situation, however, she literally worked to learn "black slang" from her black peers . . . .

Harris (2004) similarly finds in her study of the black middle-class that they, too, have considerable difficulty in accessing stereotypically black cultural symbols such as language. Often raised in middle-class neighborhoods surrounded by whites, they do not know how to speak in ways that they perceive as "authentically" black. What is considered "authentically" black is merely a social construction . . . .

Furthermore, one's racial networks will also influence, to some extent, one's ability to selectively associate with a particular racial group. Anthony grew up around black people and currently attends an HBCU, but describes a desire to "know more about white people" and a desire to assert that part of his identity. While he wants to broaden his racial networks, he says, "I want to know more white people, but I don't know how to go about it. I mean you can't just go into the grocery store and say, 'Hey, will you be my friend?' I just don't know how to meet [white] people. I pretty much just know black people."

Anthony's current racial networks, which are predominantly black, make it difficult for him to selectively associate with other whites in an effort to assert that part of his identity.

In sum, these respondents draw on various identity strategies to conceal, cover, or accent identities, although some strategies are more accessible than others and depend on several individual-level and structural-level factors. Here we identify phenotype, social class, and racial networks as important factors, yet this list is in no way exhaustive. Moreover, we find that identity is contextual. Most identify as biracial or multiracial, but in some contexts, they pass as monoracial—sometimes they pass as white, but most often they pass as black. In the next section, we examine motivations for identity work, with a focus on passing as black.

### Motivations for Passing as Black

Motivations for passing as white, especially during the Jim Crow era, are well-documented (see Conyers and Kennedy 1963; Daniel 1992, 2002; Kennedy 2003; Williams 2004). Less is known, however, about the motivations for passing as black. While we find a few respondents have passed as white in rare situations, the majority of respondents have, at one time or another, passed as black and they do this for several reasons—to fit in with black peers, to avoid a (white) stigmatized identity, and/or for some perceived advantage or benefit.

***To fit in.*** Not wanting to stand out, especially in adolescence, respondents often describe working to "blend in" to feel accepted by peers. In some cases, they try to fit in with both black and white peers. Kristen grew up attending a predominantly white school and a predominantly black gymnastics program, and says,*"Going to school and going to the gym were just two totally different things for me. So it's like I had to switch. I was like Superman. I was kind of like Clark Kent—take off my glasses going to the gym and then put them back on when I was in school . . . I would just kind of change. I would just do little things that I very well knew what I was doing."* The "little things" included changing her clothing and speech depending upon the race of her audience (i.e., drawing on black

and white cultural symbols). When asked why she altered her appearance and behavior between friends, she says, "To fit in probably. Because I wanted friends in both areas."

While some respondents employ identity strategies to "fit in" with their black *and* white peers, the majority claim that their black characteristics (e.g., dark skin) prevent their full acceptance by whites (unlike Kristen, above, who claims she looks white). Feeling thwarted by whites, many respondents pass as black to find a place with their black peers. Stephanie describes her experiences in school and says, "First grade through eighth grade I was in the same school and it was an all black private school. So everybody there was black . . . . And all the kids . . . basically told me I was white . . . . And I got so frustrated because I wanted to fit in and they kind of made me feel like I wasn't going to fit in if I didn't go along with being totally black." As described earlier, Stephanie uses several strategies (e.g., downplaying white cultural symbols, selective association with black peers) to present a black identity. Michaela similarly managed a black identity for her black peers, and describes how she modified her speech. When asked why, she responds, "Trying to fit in with [my black peers], you try to pick up the lingo they say. I will say 'crunk this' . . . 'that's the bomb.'"

Kendra, too, passed as black in high school. Using selective disclosure, she says, "In high school, I was trying to fit in . . . I didn't want people to know that I was half white. That I was mixed. I just wanted to be black because there was a majority of black kids there . . . Like if [black peers] asked, I would just say I was black." Trying to fit in with black peers was a frequent theme among the majority of respondents when describing middle school and high school (and to some extent elementary school), yet this motivation appears less important beyond the high school years.

Fitting in with black peers also appeared more important for women than men in the sample; they more often described situations in which they were discredited as black if their biracial background was revealed. Rockquemore and Brunsma (2002) find that biracial women often encounter negative experiences with black women because of their looks and/or biracial ancestry, and we also find that they, at times, find their blackness challenged. Describing her experiences with black women, Natasha says:

*For some [black] people, [a biracial background] is a strike against you . . . with girls, I can't escape [my white] side. It's constantly being brought up . . . they always seem to make sure to tell me I'm not really black. If I would tell someone I'm black, they would say, "No, you're mixed" . . . when people are always reminding you, "You're mixed" . . . trying to discredit you, it's hard.*

Natasha is constantly reminded that she is biracial and "not really black." Olivia, too, describes how some black women do not see her as black: "I think when I was growing up, [black girls] just did not accept me as being a black girl . . . with [black] women, I still think there are some instances where they don't see me as an authentic black woman . . ." Thus, wanting to fit in, not have their blackness discredited, nor feel contention with black peers, some respondents consciously concealed their white/biracial ancestries.

***To avoid a stigmatized identity.*** In the Jim Crow era, blackness was stigmatized (e.g., as inferior, backward) and is arguably stigmatized today. In describing an experience as an undergraduate, Caroline notes the stigma and says:

*I can remember when I was an undergrad, one time I got braids in my hair . . . that were down my back. And it wasn't anything dramatic and I thought it looked really nice and I liked it. And as soon as I went back to school in the city . . . I was immediately on guard when I was walking down the street. And I was like, "Oh gosh, I don't want people to think I'm black because I have these braids in my hair." . . . I was so nervous . . . that was all that went through my mind, "I don't want people to think that I'm black." . . . I know it sounds awful, but I don't want people to think that I'm stupid or that I'm bitchy or anything like that. So I didn't keep them in for very long.*

Conscious about how her braids raced her as black, Caroline manipulates her phenotype (removes her braids) to avoid negative stereotypes she associates with blackness (e.g., stupidity, bitchiness).

While Caroline describes covering her black background because of stigma associated with blackness (her phenotype prevents her from passing as white), others pass as black because of stigma associated with whiteness. Storrs (1999) finds that multiracial women "manage their potentially discreditable non-white identities through identity work, including reversing the stigma associated with the non-whiteness" (188). In short, they stigmatized whiteness by equating it with oppression, prejudice, and discrimination, and we find that some respondents in the present study similarly stigmatize whiteness or find it stigmatized by others. Stephanie describes the negativity associated with whiteness among her black peers, and says:

*[My black friends] had never been around white people before. So they only knew what their parents told them. And they were told certain things . . . . So their parents might have said something about a white coworker and [my friends] would have thought all white people were bad . . . . I'd change myself around and then I was black, so it didn't matter anymore . . . .*

Likewise, Olivia (as described earlier), covered her white ancestry in high school to avoid stigma associated with whiteness (because her multiracial family was known in the community, passing as black was not an option). She downplayed her white background by tying her straight hair back as a way of distancing herself from whites whom she perceived as "oppressive." Jackie passes as black with her black coworkers to avoid the stigma that she associates with whiteness. She says, "Well at work, I'm black. That's it. No one knows that I'm half white. I don't want to be associated with all that. [What's 'all that'?] You know, white people think they're better. They can sometimes be ignorant. And that's not me. You can't trust them either. I don't want anyone to think they can't trust me." By passing as black, she distances herself from the associated stigma of superiority, ignorance, and untrustworthiness.

For Goffman (1963), stigma is an attribute that devalues one's identity and, most important here, it is a social construct that varies situationally; it is not an objective reality, nor a fixed characteristic of an individual. According to Marvasti (2005), an ascribed status such as race or ethnicity is not inherently stigmatizing, but can become so under certain social conditions. Clearly whiteness in most contexts is a privileged identity and does not hold the same stigma as blackness, yet in some contexts having white ancestry arguably carries at least some degree of stigma. In these situations, respondents perform identity work (e.g., covering their white ancestry or passing as black) to manage what they perceive as a situationally stigmatized identity.

***For advantage.*** Finally, whiteness in the slave and Jim Crow eras conferred many advantages and privileges, and three respondents describe occasionally passing as white, even today, for some perceived benefit. Beth describes a context when she passed as white via selective disclosure: "I used to be a caseworker. Some of [my white co-workers] assumed I was white and I just rolled with it . . . yeah, you're just sitting there like, 'You really don't have a clue. I'll just continue to be white, if that's what you're going to insist on.' . . . I just left it as 'I'm going to let you assume [I'm white]. And I'll go along with it.'" When asked why she allowed others to assume she is white, she describes this as a protective strategy to avoid prejudice from coworkers. Similarly, Michelle uses selective disclosure to pass as white at work, and says:

> I [identify as white] more so when it's convenient to me in corporate America. I've witnessed where white people get further than the black people . . . . And I just think in my whole experience, not just with this job but other jobs, I have to . . . put forth that I'm white. Then they're more likely to trust me . . . I think I use it to my advantage when I need to. [In the work setting?] Yes, because I'm trying to get ahead.

While these respondents pass as white for some perceived workplace advantage, the majority (29 respondents) pass as black in other contexts for perceived advantage—in particular, on college, scholarship, financial aid, and job applications. Frequently unaware that being biracial is often sufficient for affirmative action purposes, they presented themselves exclusively as black. While Michelle describes

passing as white at work to "get ahead," she also describes passing as black on college applications. Explaining why she checks the "black box," she says, "I thought maybe if I chose black, especially in college, I'd get more financial aid. I'd get more opportunities, and so I kind of thought it was to my best advantage to just say I was black." Rockquemore and Arend (2002) find that a minority of their biracial respondents identify as white, but they argue that some "mixed-race individuals, who understand themselves as White, *pass for Black* in order to receive social, economic, and educational opportunities" (emphasis in original; 60). We find that the majority of respondents in this sample, who generally identify themselves to others as biracial or mixed, occasionally pass as black when they perceive some advantage in doing so.

Denise passes as black when filling out various forms and says, "[S]ometimes there are more opportunities if you're black . . . . Some are nicer to you. There are some job opportunities where you have more weight if you're a minority. And there are more scholarships." Stephanie expresses similar sentiments and says, "The funny thing is like when I applied to [college], like for affirmative action, I checked 'black.' I do not check 'other.' . . . if I'm applying for a scholarship or something, I am 'black.'" When asked how she identifies herself to others, Julie says, "I put 'other.' Or when you can check both, I put 'African American' and 'Caucasian.' But also, I would have to say that it depends on what I'm trying to do. If I'm trying to get more money from the government, I am 'African American.' There is no white aspect to me." Concealing their white backgrounds, Julie and others selectively disclose only their black backgrounds on these forms and in doing so pass as black in order to obtain education and/or employment opportunities, scholarships, and financial aid.

## Discussion and Conclusion

This study adds to the literature on biracial identity by examining, not the external factors that act upon individuals, but rather the considerable *agency* most have in asserting their preferred racial identities to others. Brunsma and Rockquemore (2001:244) claimed that it remained to be seen just "how much negotiation and strategy is involved" in racial identity for biracial people, and we find considerable strategy and conscious effort. Drawing on Snow and Anderson's (1987) concept of "identity work," we find that biracial people use a variety of strategies to "do race"—verbal identification/disidentification, selective disclosure, manipulation of phenotype, use of cultural symbols, and selective association. At times, they use these strategies to conceal an identity in order to pass as monoracial or, when passing is not possible or desired, they use them to cover or accent particular aspects of their racial ancestry. Adding to research on identity work, we identify several individual and structural-level factors which affect the accessibility and/or effectiveness of certain identity strategies; they include (but are not limited to) phenotype, social class, and racial networks.

Further, that people perform race is not new; during the Jim Crow era some "blacks" passed as white. With the implementation of civil rights legislation, however, many argue that the strategy of passing is a relic of the past. We surprisingly find, however, that passing still occurs today and quite frequently, although it looks different today. While passing during the Jim Crow era involved passing as white, we find a reverse pattern with regard to passing today—a few respondents occasionally pass as white, but the majority of respondents describe situations in which they pass as black.

That so few respondents passed as white is not surprising given that this option is unavailable to most (unless they have white skin and appearance) and because passing as white is often "viewed with disdain by other blacks" today (Russell et al. 1992:73). Also not surprising were the motivations for the few individuals who did pass as white—in all three cases, respondents passed as white to avoid prejudice/discrimination and/or for advantage in the workplace. Further, we find that passing as white today is temporary and situational, not the continuous type of passing that marked the Jim Crow era.

Most interesting, however, are not the few respondents who passed as white, but the many that passed as black. Scholars understand the motivations of passing as white in a society dominated by whites, but less is known about motivations for passing as black. We find that biracial people pass as black for several reasons. Most notably, we argue, because they can. While passing as white is difficult for most, passing as black is less difficult given the wide range of phenotypes in the black community regarding skin color and other physical features. With generations of interracial mixing between blacks and whites and the broad definition of blackness as defined by the one-drop rule, Khanna (2010) argues that most Americans cannot tell the difference between biracial and black. Hence, there is little difficulty when many biracial people conceal their biracial background; this is because many "blacks" also have white phenotypic characteristics (because they, too, often have white ancestry). Further, we find that biracial respondents pass as black for additional reasons—to fit in with black peers in adolescence (especially since many claim that whites reject them), to avoid a white stigmatized identity, and, in the post–civil rights era of affirmative action, to obtain advantages and opportunities sometimes available to them if they are black (e.g., educational and employment opportunities, college financial aid/scholarships).

The phenomenon of passing as black is a particularly important finding because it underscores the changing terrain of race relations and racial politics in the United States. The practice of passing as black, rather than white, suggests that blackness is arguably less stigmatized today than in earlier eras of American history—at least in certain contexts. Most respondents express pride in their blackness and embrace (and often highlight through identity work) this part of their background. In fact, in some contexts, whiteness is stigmatized, which suggests a shift in how some attribute meaning to the categories of black and white (see also Storrs 1999) . . . .

## DISCUSSION QUESTIONS

1. How are biracial people active in shaping their racial identity—that is, what strategies do they use in doing racial identity work?
2. What evidence do Khanna and Johnson present to demonstrate a weakening of the "one-drop rule" for blackness, even as we see a widening of racial identity options? What are the motivations for passing as black today?

## NOTES

1. Jack and Jill of America is one of oldest black social organizations in the United States; Alpha Kappa Alpha was the first sorority established by black women.

# 28

# THE STIGMA OF BROWN SKIN AND "FOREIGN" NAMES

AMIR MARVASTI

KARYN D. MCKINNEY

*This fourth reading in the section on identity construction and stigma management builds on the previous two readings (26 and 27) to illustrate further how individuals manage their racial-ethnic identities. Amir Marvasti and Karyn D. McKinney are both professors of sociology at Pennsylvania State University and study race and identity. This excerpt, taken from Marvasti and McKinney's 2008 book, Middle Eastern Lives in America, investigates how individuals of Middle Eastern descent must manage other Americans' impressions of their identity. Similar to Mia Tuan's reading (Reading 18), ethnically different individuals are often asked to account for their racial-ethnic identity to the dominant group (white Americans). Marvasti and McKinney document the number of strategies individuals use to manage their identities and the stigma associated with being assumed to be foreign or from having brown skin.*

Much of what is known about Middle Eastern Americans is based on media stereotypes that feed public anxieties about terrorism. As discussed in earlier research, a general preoccupation with the terrorist threat posed by Middle Eastern Americans, particularly those of Islamic faith, existed long before September 11, 2001. However, for some laymen, commentators, and policy makers, the tragic events of this date provided the rationale for scrutinizing every aspect of the lives of members of this ethnic

*Source:* Marvasti, Amir and Karyn D. McKinney. 2004. "The Stigma of Brown Skin and 'Foreign' Names" in *Middle Eastern Lives in America*. Reproduced with permission of Rowman & Littlefield Publishing Group, Inc. in the format Textbook via Copyright Clearance Center.

minority. In this reading we describe the strategies that Middle Eastern Americans use to cope with situations in which they are asked to explain themselves. We specifically look at how they use humor, education, or direct confrontation as a way of responding to those who call into question their sense of dignity or personhood.

## ACCOUNTING FOR ONE'S IDENTITY

Receiving and wanting attention from others is a natural part of human existence. We interact with other people and would like to be noticed by them. We especially want to be recognized for our achievements (e.g., when we excel in academics or sports). It is not, however, natural to be the focus of others' scorn or suspicion, especially when you have not done anything to evoke the negative attention. For example, it is not natural to be repeatedly subjected to so-called random searches at airports under the eyes of menacing men with hands on their guns simply because of one's appearance, as the first author, Amir, has. That kind of attention is neither desired nor deserved.

Sadly, this is an all too common experience for Middle Eastern Americans. Frequently, they find themselves in social encounters in which they are asked to essentially explain themselves, or to produce an account of their identity. We borrow the term "account" from Stanford Lyman and Marvin Scott to refer to encounters in which a person is called to "explain unanticipated or untoward behavior—whether that behavior is his or her own or that of others, and whether the approximate cause of the statement arises from the actor himself or someone else.[1] Thus accounts are given when an unusual situation or something or someone out of the ordinary is presented . . . .

In many ways, the case of Middle Eastern Americans is similar to that of Japanese Americans in the first half of the twentieth century. Turmoil in the Middle East and acts of terrorism committed in the United States by Middle Easterners have created an identity crisis for those who were either born or have ancestry from that part of the world. The issue

of accountability has become an everyday reality for Middle Eastern people in light of official policies that systematically demand that they explain their every action. This state of heightened awareness is exemplified by a public address by Attorney General John Ashcroft, in which he suggested that if suspected terrorists as much as spit on the sidewalk, they would be arrested.[2] Of course, the term "suspected terrorists" has become so broadly defined that thousands of Middle Eastern men were arrested for minor immigration violations, thousands more were systematically interviewed by FBI agents, and many were deported in the months following the terrorist attacks. It could be said that in a very concrete sense, thousands of Middle Eastern people were officially required to provide accounts . . . .

For the purpose of data analysis, our interviews and Amir's personal experiences were coded broadly into styles of accounting, or ways in which the respondents and Amir accounted for being Middle Eastern when either implicitly or explicitly required to do so. This approach is similar to Joe Feagin and Karyn McKinney's "resistance strategies" in their analysis of how blacks cope with racist incidents or racist situations.[3] Feagin and McKinney found that African Americans have learned a repertoire of coping mechanisms, both through personal experience and through collective memory.[4] Despite the fact that many white Americans believe that people of color react quickly or always with anger to discrimination, Feagin and McKinney's research showed that African Americans choose carefully from this complex set of responses each time they face a discriminatory incident. The repertoire includes two main types of responses: attitudinal coping mechanisms and action-oriented resistance strategies.[5] Attitudinal coping mechanisms reported by the African American respondents included being always prepared for discrimination, avoiding internalization of the discrimination or of feelings of anger and bitterness, knowing oneself, and using spirituality and mental withdrawal. The respondents also discussed more active resistance strategies. Some of these included verbal confrontation, educating whites, protesting through formal channels, using humor, and physical withdrawal.[6]

Several of these resistance strategies described by Feagin and McKinney are similar to the accounting practices of our Middle Eastern American respondents. In the following sections, excerpts from our interviews are presented in the form of encounter stories from the respondents' and Amir's everyday experiences. Several styles of accounting emerge from the analysis: humorous accounting, educational accounting, confrontational accounting, and passing.

### Humorous Accounting

When faced with questions about their ethnic identity, sometimes respondents use humor to present themselves. Consider, for example, the following cases that involve accounting for Middle Eastern–sounding names. A contractor named Ali[7] explains how he uses humor when questions about his name are raised:

**Amir:**    *Do you get any reactions about your name? Like people asking you what kind of name is that?*

**Ali:**    *Sometimes they do; sometimes they don't. Sometimes, if they haven't met me or if they are sending me correspondence, they think it's a lady's name and a lot of correspondence comes in Ms. Ali. They think I'm either Alison or something like that. Nowadays, when my name comes up [in face-to-face contacts with clients], I use my sense of humor. For example, when they can't spell my name or ask questions about it, I say, "I'm the brother of Muhammad Ali, the boxer."*

Another respondent, whose first name "Ladan" (the name of a flower in Persian) brings up unwelcome and troubling associations with the notorious terrorist Osama bin Laden, tells this story about how she used humor with an inquisitive customer:

**Amir:**    *With the name Ladan, do you run into any problems?*

**Ladan:**    *Where I work [at a department store] we all wear nametags, with the name Ladan*

*very clearly spelled out L A D A N. And this old couple, they approached me and I was very friendly with them—I usually chitchat with my customers. And he started asking me all these questions like, "You're so pretty, where're you from?" [I respond,] "I'm from Iran." [He says,] "What?" [I repeat,] "I'm from Iran." So he asks, "What's your name?" And I say, "Ladan." So he bent down to read my nametag and he just looked at me with a funny face and asked, "Are you related to bin Laden?"*

**Amir:**    *Was he joking?*

**Ladan:**    *No, he was not. But I did joke back to him and I said, "Yes, he's my cousin and actually he's coming over for dinner tonight." [She chuckles.]*

**Amir:**    *So, when this sort of thing happens, you use humor to deal with it?*

**Ladan:**    *Yeah, I do, because otherwise, if I don't turn it into a joke or a laughing mood, I get upset. I get really, really offended.*

**Amir:**    *So what was this guy's reaction? Did he laugh with you?*

**Ladan:**    *When this guy realized my name is Ladan and I'm from Iran, he changed his attitude. He became reserved and he even went one step backward. When I noticed he was uncomfortable, I completed the transaction with his wife and let them leave as soon as they wanted.*

Note that in this case her use of humor does not necessarily result in the proverbial "happy ending," or any kind of clearly discernible resolution. The customer turned away and ended the interaction. Clearly, an account was called for and one was given in a way that allowed Ladan to highlight the ludicrousness of the account-taker's assumptions and his right to solicit an account.

The following is the story of how Amir accounted for his name using humor. This encounter took place at a voting precinct in a small town in Pennsylvania on Election Day, November 14, 2002. He was there to vote in the midterm elections. The encounter begins with the examination of his photo identification.

| | |
|---|---|
| **The election supervisor:** | *Okay . . . this is a hard one! [squinting at my driver's license] You're ready? [alerting her coworker] It says "AMAR." . . . It's "A" . . .* |
| | *I wait, silent and motionless, as the three old women probe my ID. I fear that any sudden movement might send people running out of the building screaming for help. "Say something!" I scream in my head. The words finally roll out of my mouth:* |
| **Amir:** | *You know, my dad gave me a long name, hoping that it would guarantee my success in life. [They laugh.]* |
| **Election Supervisor:** | *Well, you must be a doctor because you sure sign your name like one.* |
| **Amir:** | *[I can't resist] Actually, I am a doctor . . . maybe my dad had the right idea after all.* |

Here humor is a method of introduction. It was not clear to Amir what the election supervisors thought about him, but he did sense that there were unanswered questions, an account had to be given for who he was. Note that the immediate substance of Amir's identity was not in question—they had his photo identification in front of them and most likely could tell from his swarthy appearance that he was not a native Pennsylvanian. Humorous accounting allowed Amir to communicate something more important about himself than simply his name, namely, that he is from a "normal" family that aspires to the universal notion of "success in life"; and that he is aware that there are concerns about his identity and is capable of responding to them in a mutually sensible way. In humorous accounting the substance of the account is incidental, as it is deliberately trivialized.

Middle Eastern Americans use this way of accounting as a way of acknowledging the need to explain themselves while at the same time subtly mocking the necessity of the encounter.

## Educational Accounting

Sometimes accounting takes on a deliberate pedagogical form. In such cases Middle Eastern Americans assume the role of educators, informing and instructing their fellow citizens about relevant topics. For example, in response to suspicion and antagonism from his neighbors, a Pakistani Muslim, Hassan, did a sort of door-to-door educational accounting:

*After September 11, I walked the street the whole week and talked to every single one of my neighbors for at least 3 hours. And one of my neighbors—his brother was in Tower Two and he got out, and his mother was there and she was furious with Muslims and me. And we were there for three hours, my wife, my kids, her [the neighbor], her son and her other son that came out of the World Trade Center—he had come down by the time the buildings came down. And I was like, "Look, that's not Islam. That's not who Muslims are. Ask your son, what type of person am I? What type of person is my wife? Do I oppress my wife? Do I beat my wife? Have you ever heard me say anything extreme before?" . . . They all know I don't drink, they all know that I pray five times a day, they all know I fast during the month of Ramadan. At the end of Ramadan, we have a big party and invite everyone over to help celebrate the end of fast. This year, they'll all probably fast one day with me so they can feel what it's like.*

Hassan's approach is proactive, addressing potential questions before they are explicitly opened for accounting. In some ways, this case of educational accounting is similar to what John P. Hewitt and Randall Stokes call "disclaimers or a "prospective construction of meaning" in an attempt to avoid being categorized in an undesirable way.[8] In the above excerpt, Hassan tries to transform the relationship between him, as an account-giver, and the account-takers who suspect him of being an "evildoer."

Middle Eastern Americans have to be selective about which inquiries are worthy of an educational account. For example, an Iranian respondent, Mitra, speaks of how she filters the inquiries about her culture and identity before answering them:

*If they ask about the government or the senate over there [Iran], I don't know anything about it. I know who the president is, but they ask me about the senate or the name of the senator over there, I don't know. Since I don't know I'm not going to get involved. I'll say I don't know or I'm not interested. If they say, "Oh, you are from that country!" or "You are from the Middle East and you are a terrorist," those kinds of comments I'm not going to get into. I'll just say, "No, I'm not." But if they ask me about the culture I'll tell them, "Alright," and inform them about it—as much as I know.*

Mitra, while inclined to assume the role of an educator, is not willing or prepared to respond to every question. Part of her educational accounting strategy involves evaluating the degree of her expertise on the subject and the tone of the questions. As she says, if the account-taker begins with accusations, such as "you are a terrorist," the only reasonable reply might be to deny the accusation and end the interaction.

Educational accounting is a common strategy for Middle Eastern Muslim women who wear the hijab.[9] Many of them are approached by strangers who ask questions like: "Isn't it hot under there?" "Does that come in many colors?" or simply "Why do you wear that?" or "Are you going to make *them* [referring to the ten- and twelve-year-old girls who were standing in a grocery store line with their mother] wear it too?" Our respondents reported that whenever time and circumstances allowed, they provide detailed accounts based on their religious teachings. Some of these answers include: "I wear it because it is my culture," "I wear it so that you won't stare at my body when you are talking to me," or "It's cooler under my scarf than you think." It should be noted that some of these women did report being verbally harassed or physically attacked (one was pelted with spitballs when she was in high school, another reported that her friend's scarf was pulled off by a teenage boy at a grocery store, and another was repeatedly yelled at "Go home!" by people in passing cars as she walked to her office on campus). However, such overt acts of discrimination were fairly isolated. The pattern for these women was that of perfect strangers literally stopping them on the street and asking questions about the hijab, sometimes so directly as to be rude.

Similarly, as a Middle Eastern sociology professor, Amir is often asked by his students to explain a wide range of topics about the region and Islam, from customs and culture to the mind-set of terrorists. Like Mitra, he evaluates each question before providing an account. For example, a student in his undergraduate criminology seminar began every session with a trivial question about Iran, such as "Do they have trees over there?" At first, Amir provided a detailed educational account whenever asked to do so, even for seemingly inane items. Given the limited time he had to cover the assigned readings, later in the semester it became necessary for Amir to remind his students that he was not paid to educate them about the Middle East; the topic of the course was crime, specifically, the criminogenic aspects of American culture. For those interested in the topic, Amir recommended a trip to the library for references on the Middle East and Iran. In this case, the educational accounting became unfeasible simply because it was consuming too much time and diverting attention from the subject matter at hand.

Indeed, a recurring problem with being Middle Eastern in a professional context is that the process of accounting for oneself (be it educational, humorous, or otherwise) could hinder one's job performance. With rare exceptions, when professional duties and the accounting demands coincide (such as the writing of this research, for example), the work of answering for one's ethnic background and religion could become a considerable chore. Another problem with becoming a "cultural ambassador" is that it tests the limits of the account-giver's knowledge about the topic.[10] Middle East is a vast and diverse cultural entity representing many people and religions. Unstructured attempts at educating others in everyday encounters inevitably translate into sketchy overgeneralizations. Therefore, while educational accounting may be the most intelligible and productive accounting strategy for one's identity, it is also the most time- consuming and potentially misleading approach.

## Confrontational Accounting

When prompted to provide an account, some Middle Eastern Americans make their anger and frustrations with the encounter explicitly known. We refer to this as confrontational accounting. This strategy involves providing information while at the same time directly challenging the other's right and rationale to request it. For example, consider how a young Iranian woman speaks of her experiences with a coworker:

> She [the coworker] would tell me, "I don't know which country you come from but in America we do it like this or that." I let it go because I was older than her and we had to work together . . . . But one day I pulled her aside and I told her, "For your information, where I come from has a much older culture. And what I know, you can't even imagine. So why don't you go get some more education. And if you mention this thing again—'my country is this your country is that'—I'm going to take it to management and they're going to fire you or they're going to fire me." And that was it.

Here the accounting is not intended to repair the interaction or to restore it to a state of equilibrium. On the contrary, the goal is to explicitly challenge the conventional format of the encounter. Instead of aiming for consensus, confrontational accounting foregrounds divergent and conflicting viewpoints as it signals the account-giver's objection to the entire affair.

Confrontational strategies are used especially in times when the accounting, while seemingly a rational concern for everyone involved, crosses the boundary of basic fairness in the eyes of the account-giver. Specifically, Middle Eastern Americans who are subjected to profiling may become confrontational in response to the practice. For example, when Amir learned that unlike himself, his white colleagues were not asked to show ID cards upon entering the campus gym, he felt justified in becoming

confrontational. In one instance, while pulling out his ID card from his wallet, he asked the woman at the front counter why his white faculty friend, who had just walked in ahead of him, was not asked to present an ID. She explained that she had not noticed the other person entering or she would have asked that person to do the same.

This encounter highlights the risky nature of confrontational accounting for both parties involved in the interaction. At its core, this strategy counters an account request with another: They ask for his ID and Amir asks why he should be the only one subjected to this rule. In turn, the other side presents their account and so on. What follows is a chain of accounts and counteraccounts possibly escalating into a formal dispute. Though it is possible that in some cases, when confronted, the account-takers simply back down and cease their efforts, it is just as likely that they intensify their demands, especially when they are backed by policies or other public mandates.

Since September 11, when flying, Amir has been very conscious of this fact. While Amir is certain that he has been singled out for security checks, he fears that objecting and confronting these practices would lead to additional hardships (i.e., a direct confrontation with law enforcement agents in which they have the greater authority and likelihood to win). Even after boarding the plane, he is often questioned by those seated next to him. Their inquiries typically begin with the ordinary (i.e., What is your name?) and proceed to the very personal and official matters (i.e., Are you a U.S. citizen? Do you have a green card?). In these encounters, Amir feels that to refuse to answer or to confront the other's right to ask about personal and private details of his life will lead to other more serious accounting demands.

So for Middle Eastern Americans confrontational accounting is a risky approach that could, on the one hand, rid them of a potentially humiliating process, or, on the other hand, generate additional requests and demands. Of course, confrontational accounting, when used by large numbers, can become a type of mass rebellion, as with African Americans and the passive resistance component of the Civil Rights Movement of the 1960s.

## Passing or Avoiding Accounts

Sometimes, the best accounting strategy is to put oneself in a position not to have to give an account at all.[11] One way of conceptualizing such strategies is to think of them as attempts at "passing."[12] We view passing as a strategy for eliminating the need for accounting for one's identity. For many Middle Eastern Americans, passing is accomplished by manipulating their appearance. The stereotypical image of a Middle Eastern person roughly translates into someone with dark hair, large facial features, swarthy skin, non-European foreign accent, and beards in the case of men and veils and scarves in the case of women. Faced with these stereotypes, some respondents consciously altered their looks to avoid anything that might associate them with being Middle Eastern. Ironically the ultimate dubious achievement in this game of passing is hearing something like the following: "I know you are from Iran, but you don't *really* look or sound Middle Eastern . . . . You could be Hispanic for all I know."

In fact, some Middle Eastern Americans try to pass by trading their own ethnic identity with a less controversial one. The simplest way to do this is to move to an ethnically diverse region. Some of the respondents from South Florida stated that one reason they don't experience negative episodes of ethnic accounting is because they are thought to be Hispanic. For example, an Iranian woman was asked what kind of Spanish she was speaking when she was at a shopping mall having a conversation in Farsi with her teenage daughter. Another Iranian man tried to pass as Italian by placing an Italian flag vanity license plate on his car. As a general rule, displaying Western or patriotic symbols (e.g., an American flag) at work, in front of one's house, or on one's car are ways of avoiding ethnic accounting for Middle Eastern Americans. After September 11, Amir's neighbors gave him an American flag to place outside his apartment for his own safety. In a sense, the symbols of patriotism become accounting statements in their own right; they become declarations of loyalty to "the American culture."

Another strategy for passing is to give an ambiguous account in response to ethnic identity questions. For example, an Egyptian man in response to questions about his country of origin states that he is Coptic (the designation of people from pre-Islamic Egypt). He noted that in many cases the account-takers find it too embarrassing to ask follow-up questions and therefore pretend to know what "Coptic" means and drop the subject altogether. Iranians create this kind of ambiguity by stating that they are Persians (the designation of ancient Iranians).

Accounts are also circumvented by stating the name of the city of one's ancestral origin rather than one's country of birth. Amir once told a college classmate that he was from Tehran. To his astonishment, his classmate asked, "Is that near Paris?" Changing one's name is another way to pass. Some respondents change their Muslim names (e.g., Hossein) to typical American names (e.g., Michael). When asked why he changed his name, one person explained that he was tired of people slamming down the phone when he made inquiries about jobs. Some change from widely known ethnic-sounding names to lesser-known ones as in the change from Hossein to Sina. Finally, attention to clothes and grooming are equally important considerations for those who want to pass. For example, wearing jeans and having a clean shave draw less attention and lead to fewer occasions to have to account for oneself.

Passing strategies for Middle Eastern Americans are not without complications. To start with, for some, passing is tantamount to "selling out" (i.e., giving up one's native culture in favor of another). More important, for Middle Eastern Americans, passing has been construed by the media as an extension of an evil terrorist plot. After September 11, numerous media reports referred to how the hijackers were specifically instructed to wear jeans and shave their faces. Therefore, rather than being viewed as a sign of cultural assimilation, Middle Eastern Americans' conspicuous attempts at passing are sometimes considered part of a diabolical plan to deceive and destroy Americans.

Finally, especially where passing for Hispanic is concerned, Middle Eastern Americans face direct opposition and disavowals from some members of the Hispanic community. On the one hand, according to some of our respondents in South Florida,

Middle Eastern Americans have been "outed" by Hispanics who point them out in public and announce to everyone that they are really Middle Eastern and not to be confused with Hispanics. On the other hand, Hispanics are self-consciously changing their self-presentation as to not be mistaken for Middle Eastern. For example, a Mexican man was warned by his wife not to wear a certain hat for fear that it made him look "Middle Eastern."

## Not a Knee-Jerk Reaction

Our respondents did not go off half-cocked, as it were. In dealing with the situations they faced, they tried to select the most reasonable reaction. It is important to note that these respondents are not passive. Their strategies are about fighting back, about speaking in a way that preserves their dignity in the face of intimidation, scrutiny, and insults. Having said that, for ethnic minorities there are situations when there is no opportunity for giving an account or talking back. For example, when a man driving by in his truck yelled at Amir, "Ragheads go home!" he had no opportunity to choose an accounting strategy or offer an account. In the same way, when the respondents in this study report being assaulted, the concept of accounting does not apply. Clearly, such aggressive or violent actions cannot be classified as requests for accounts. These are statements, declarations, or actions that by definition exclude any kind of dialogue.

The accounting strategies of Middle Eastern Americans discussed earlier also underline an important dimension of belonging to a stigmatized group. At its core, being an outcast is about having to explain oneself above and beyond what "normal" members of society are required to do. The relationship between an account-giver and an account-receiver is a relationship between a dominant and a subordinate. One party is entitled to ask questions like, "Where are you from and why are you here?" whereas the other party is expected to obediently provide legitimate replies.

This is not a mere exercise in social roles, but particularly in the context of the War on Terror, this relationship has very practical consequences for Middle Eastern Americans. Their lives have to be transparent. They have to be mindful of the fact that their attempts to protect their privacy could be misread as a clandestine plan. Furthermore, legislation, such as the PATRIOT Act, can reinforce the lower status of this minority group in relation to the white majority. In essence, the roles are becoming more institutionalized, slowly expanding beyond informal encounters and entering the realm of official policy.

## Discussion Questions

1. Why do Muslim and Arab Americans feel a need to be proactive about managing their racial-ethnic identities when interacting with other Americans? Does this need reflect a form of discrimination?
2. Explain the survival strategies Marvasti and McKinney found that Middle Eastern people use to challenge the stigma they face. How do educational accounting, confrontational accounting, and passing enable them to neutralize a stigma based upon ignorance and false information?

## Notes

1. Stanford Lyman and Marvin Scott, *A Sociology of the Absurd* (Dix Hills, N.Y.: General Hall, 1989), p. 112
2. Siobhan Gorman, "National Security: The Ashcroft Doctrine," *National Journal* 34 (2002): 3712–19.
3. Joe Feagin and Karyn McKinney, *The Many Costs of Racism* (Lanham, Md.: Rowman & Littlefield, 2003): 147–79.
4. Feagin and McKinney, *The Many Costs of Racism*, p. 119.
5. Feagin and McKinney, *The Many Costs of Racism*, p. 123
6. Feagin and McKinney, *The Many Costs of Racism*, pp. 124–67.
7. Most names have been fictionalized to protect the identity of respondents. In cases where it is necessary to use an actual first name, every effort is made to disguise other personal identifying information about a respondent.

8. John P. Hewitt and Randall Stokes. "Disclaimers," *American Sociological Review* 40 (1975):1–11, specifically pp. 1–3.

9. Islamic word for modesty in dress that applies to both men and women. In the case of many Muslim women living in the United States, this means wearing a scarf that covers the hair and the neck, as well as wearing loose-fitting garments so that the outlines of the body are not exaggerated.

10. Bruce Jacobs, *Race Manners: Navigating the Minefield between Black and White Americans* (New York: Arcade Publishing, 1999), pp. 144–48.

11. See Lyman and Scott, *A Sociology of the Absurd*, pp. 126–27.

12. Erving Goffman, *Stigma: Notes on the Management of Spoiled Identity* (Englewood Cliffs, N.J.: Prentice Hall, 1963).

# 29

# "I Don't Like Passing as a Straight Woman"

## Queer Negotiations of Identity and Social Group Membership

Carla Pfeffer

*This last reading in this section on identity construction and stigma management examines how cis women who are partnered with trans men identify their gender and sexuality. In particular, Carla Pfeffer, a professor of sociology at the University of South Carolina, complicates our understanding of "passing" by challenging how sex, gender, and sexuality identities are based on social interaction and normative social privilege. She deliberates on the costs of misrecognition and passing as expressed by her respondents. This research article is a piece of Pfeffer's larger research project, in which she interviewed 50 cis women partners of trans men in the United States, Canada, and Australia.*

Social recognition and affirmation of gay and lesbian identities and rights have increased alongside claims advancing the biological etiology of sexual orientation. Despite broader social acknowledgment of gender and sexual diversity, transgender individuals and their significant others remain relatively unrecognized in both mainstream and academic discourse and are often subsumed under the limited theoretical frame of social "passing" when they do appear. Building a sociological critique against overly simplified biological frameworks for understanding complex gender and sexual identities, I analyze in-depth interviews with non-transgender women partners of transgender men.

*Source:* Pfeffer, Carla. 2014. "'I Don't Like Passing as a Straight Woman': Queer Negotiations of Identity and Social Group Membership." *American Journal of Sociology* 120(1):1–44. Used by permission of the University of Chicago Press.

The personal identifications and experiences of this group of "queer" social actors are proposed as sociopolitically distinguishable from those of other more commonly recognized sexual minority groups. Data reveal the interactive social processes that often determine "rightful" social inclusion and exclusion across gender and sexual identity categories as well as their capacities to generate and limit possibilities for social movements and political solidarity. . . .

My purpose in this article is not to make broad claims resolutely negating potential biological origins or contributions to sex, gender, and sexuality. Rather, it is to propose two expressly sociological questions: (1) What is at stake when we foreclose opportunities for considering the myriad ways in which sex, gender, and sexual identities are formed in and through processes of social interaction? (2) In what ways might a focus on "passing" curtail opportunities to critically examine the efforts of those with normative social privilege to maintain and naturalize such privilege? For example, white racial anxieties about black people "passing"—both in the past and present—are generally understood as symptomatic of the desire to maintain white social privilege and a sense of inherent (supposedly biological) superiority (Harris 1993; Renfrow 2004). Might a similar lens for understanding social anxieties about gender "passing" and beliefs about the fixity and naturalness of sexual identities be both sociologically illuminating and increasingly necessary today?

I suggest here that it is time for sociology to push beyond both "passing" and "born this way" approaches to sex, gender, and sexuality to consider alternative frameworks for theorizing the experiences of social actors. In this article, I draw upon Connell's (2009) notion of "recognition" (in lieu of "passing") to argue that social rights, privileges, and group membership connected to categories of sex, gender, and sexuality depend largely upon social interpellation. More specifically, I will demonstrate how gender and sexual identities are interactional accomplishments that often reveal more about the workings of normative social privilege than they reveal about the social actors whose gender and sexual identities are being (mis)recognized. This study considers queer social actors' often strategic and

pragmatic management of these (mis)recognition processes to gain access to particular social and material benefits of social group membership, offering theoretical and empirical insights on identity negotiations, and moments of "trouble" in these negotiations, across contested and regulated social categories and groups more broadly. As such, this work provides insights that actively respond to Irvine's (1994:245) still-relevant call to sociologists nearly two decades earlier: "Sociological theory must . . . [place] social categories such as sexuality and race in the foreground in the context of power and difference." Finally, this work proposes a sociological queer analytic framework that compels solidarity-based approaches to social movement organizing around identity-based rights. . . .

## STUDY DESIGN, SAMPLE, AND ANALYSIS

### Participant Recruitment and Sample

This work represents the largest and most comprehensive study conducted, to date, with cis women partners of trans men . . . Research participants were recruited using online and paper-flyer postings targeting the significant others, friends, families, and allies of trans men. Most study participants were recruited via Internet-facilitated social network ("snowball") sampling, the primary method of purposeful sampling when targeting sexual minorities and their partners (Patton 1990; Mustanski 2001; Shapiro 2004; Rosser et al, 2007). I also enlisted key informants across the United States and Canada to distribute materials to potential participants in their local regions.

I conducted interviews with 50 cis women partners of trans men for this study. Participants discussed their experiences in 61 individual relationships with trans men (several participants reported multiple relationships with trans men). Participants resided across 13 states in the United States, three Canadian provinces, and one Australian state, expanding existing work on sex and gender minorities that focuses almost exclusively on one or two states, with large urban centers, in the United States . . . The most frequent sexual orientation self-identification label, used by 50% of participants in this sample, was "queer." Participants' trans partners (according to participant reports) were also most likely to identify as "queer" (48%), with "heterosexual" as second most common (33%). When asked to describe how they would define or label their relationship(s) with their trans partner(s), study participants described their relationships as "queer" 65% of the time among those providing information for this question.

Despite aiming for racial and age diversity, only variation on age was successfully achieved. Interviewees' ages ranged from 18 to 51 years, with an average age of 29 years, and, on average, cis women's trans partners were slightly younger. Participants largely self-identified as white. When considering the race/ethnicity of the trans partners of participants, the sample begins to reflect somewhat greater racial/ethnic variation, with 18% identified as "multiracial." Participants and their partners were highly educated (with 24% and 11%, respectively, holding postgraduate degrees) yet reported household incomes that were quite low among participants providing these data. Trans men partners of participants were at various stages of sex or gender transition—with most being just a bit over two years into the process. Most were taking testosterone, a considerable minority had had "top" surgery, while a very slim minority had had "bottom" surgery of any kind . . . Likely due in large part to the powerful masculinizing effects of testosterone, according to evidence provided in the accounts of cis women in the sample, the majority of their trans men partners were "always or almost always" perceived in social contexts as male (these accounts will be discussed further in the section on findings). . . .

# Findings and Discussion: Doing Gender and Sexuality Through (Mis)Recognition Processes

Just as trans men have their own transition experiences to manage on multiple levels, so, too, do their cis women partners (see Nyamora 2004; Pfeffer 2008;

Brown 2009; Joslin-Roher and Wheeler 2009; Ward 2010). Study participants relayed, in great detail, the various struggles they experienced as they sought to maintain, transform, understand, proclaim, and refute various personal and social identities in the context of their lives. The following sections present narrative data, using pseudonyms to protect participant confidentiality, illustrating the ways in which queer social actors negotiate intersecting and sometimes conflicting social identities, relationships, politics, and social groups. These narratives prompt consideration of the ways in which gender and sexual identity are interactive social accomplishments involving boundary negotiations and (mis)recognition processes that carry tangible personal and social consequences.

## Language and Social "Reading"

*"Queer"* as a distinct social identity category.— Cis women partners of trans men frequently wondered aloud, when I asked them about their own shifting and contingent sexual identities in relation to their trans partners, "What does that make me?" Martha (25 years old, Massachusetts) described the challenge of personally struggling with issues connected to identity in the context of her relationship with her trans partner:

> I thought of myself as a dyke and then now I'm with someone who identifies as a man and I'm thinking— how do I identify now? I'm not a lesbian. . . . I'm not really perceived as queer by many other people right now. And it really messed with me for awhile—what am I? Who am I? Not that I didn't know who I was, but what identity should I give to people? A lot of times I'd try to adopt my identity as my own and it doesn't matter what other people think. But it's hard not to judge myself by other people's judgments.

Having difficulty figuring out how to self-identify was described often by participants in my sample as not only an internal struggle, but one that emerges from various social and cultural imperatives and in social interactions with others. As Tiffany (20 years old, Massachusetts) told me,

"People are wondering what your sexuality is. . . . I get asked on surveys and things like that and I really don't know what to put." . . .

Cis women partners of trans men described facing persistent challenges in actively negotiating their own (and their partner's) shifting identities across a variety of personal, interpersonal, and social contexts. One of the ways in which this negotiation manifested for many participants was through language and determining how they would self-identify, with regard to sexuality, in the context of their unique relationships.

Just over half of the cis women participants in this study self-identified their sexual orientation as "queer" at the point of interview and about 65% described their relationship with their trans partner as "queer." According to these cis women's accounts, over 60% of their trans men partners were perceived as men in social spaces "always" or "almost always." When in public together, therefore, many cis women in this sample reported being frequently (mis)recognized as part of a heterosexual couple. Verbal evidence participants provided in their accounts of these social encounters included social others using the words "sir," "bro," "boyfriend," "husband," "dad," and "father," as well as pronouns such as "he" and "him" when referring to participants' trans partners, and use of words/pronouns such as "Miss," "Mrs.," "Ms.," "ma'am," "girl," "girlfriend," "wife," "mom," "mother," "she," and "her" when referring to the participants themselves. . . .

Nonverbal indicators that trans partners were being socially "read" as men or that the couple was being "read" as heterosexual included the check being consistently handed to one's trans partner at restaurants and other service establishments, other men giving a head "nod" when passing one's trans partner on the street, being smiled at by older persons when holding hands with one's trans partner in public,[1] and not being scrutinized when in sex-segregated public spaces (such as restrooms). In these instances, (mis)recognition processes often conferred social advantage, privilege, and mainstream acceptance. Yet being (mis)recognized as heterosexual was described as personally and socially problematic by many participants—particularly

insofar as they feared being (mis)recognized as "heteronormative" by social others. Participants described their understandings of heteronormativity as fulfilling stereotypically gendered "roles" in their relationships, endorsing majoritarian politics, and not being seen as queer or politically radical.[2] . . .

Cis women and their trans partners must often work to (re)define their identities—as individuals and in relationship to one another—in ways that both challenge and extend existing linguistic and social categories. Furthermore, the rising visibility and media presence of partnerships between cis women and trans men, particularly via the medium of the Internet, contributes to the emergence of queer cultural communities through which language and support may be continuously developed, challenged, and shared (see Shapiro 2004). The Internet emergence of a new linguistic identity term, "queer-straight" (which two participants in this study used to describe their relationship with their trans partner), may be one way in which sociolinguistic innovation is developing out of existing frustrations over lack of specificity and meaning with "queer."

In addition to negotiating language and identity-classificatory systems, study participants reported marked and sometimes painful discrepancies between how they see and understand themselves and how they are seen and understood (or not) by others in their social communities and contexts. Two themes that frequently emerged for cis women partners of trans men were actually flip sides of the same "(mis)recognition coin"—being (mis)recognized (or "passing") as unremarkably straight in both queer and nonqueer social spaces and becoming invisibly queer (i.e., no longer being recognized as a rightful member of the queer community) within queer social spaces. Clearly, (mis)recognition—or being "seen" and "not seen"—by various communities is a powerful social process that critically informs, validates, and invalidates personal identities and group memberships. The following sections detail these flip sides of this same coin of social group (mis)recognition and membership processes as well as describe how the cis women in this study negotiated these processes.

## Identity and Social
## Norm Resisting and Affiliating

*"I don't want to be a housewife!"*—Participants often spoke explicitly about not wanting to fall into relational patterns with their partner that might be interpreted as normative. Some cis women voiced this intention directly to their trans partner—as in the case of Emma (22 years old, Ontario), who spoke of a conversation during which she reportedly told him: "I am a feminist and I don't want to be a housewife. . . . That's not who I am and that's not who you're going to be in a relationship with." Some cis women and their trans partners shared in the desire to reject and resist normativity. According to Sage (21 years old, Ontario): "It sort of is a little disturbing to both of us—as individuals and together—to think that we might fall into sort of a heterosexuality, a heteronormative pattern. Being queer, interacting as queer, presenting as queer, and being queer in the world is something that's really important to both of us." In a similar vein, Belinda (24 years old, Ontario) explained: "We both say that it's a queer relationship. Neither of us are interested in passing as a straight couple or having people believe that we're a straight couple."

Recall that the majority of cis women's accounts include discussion of being (mis)recognized as heterosexual by social others. As such, these cis women's vocal and instrumental resistance to being socially (mis)recognized as anything but "queer" offers possibilities for destabilizing normativity insofar as it challenges social others' notions of what a "heterosexual couple" is like. Further, it reveals the ways in which participants position themselves explicitly against habituated, iterative enactments of normativity—which they explicitly counterpose to feminist and queer identities. Of course, their resistance may be limited given that opportunities to correct the social (mis)recognition of others do not always readily present themselves, may be unsuccessful, may be resisted by one's partner, or may be unsafe in certain social contexts. Similar to McFarland's (2004) analysis of resistance as a "social drama," I interpret resistance in the lives of cis women partners of trans men as structurally

embedded relational processes that are both transformative and fraught—pushing against and disrupting the contours of normativity from within powerful interlocking social systems that push back and resist in dynamic response (see Pfeffer 2012). . . .

Cis women participants also articulated their experiences enacting what some may interpret as habituated and stereotypically gendered relational structures in ways they explicitly linked to conscious gender performativity and normative resistance (Pfeffer 2012). According to Rachel (27 years old, Ohio): "I think he had this fantasy . . . which I don't think exists for anybody anymore. But, in his head, part of becoming a man was becoming a *Leave It to Beaver* dad—like coming home and mom has dinner on the table and whatever else is happening. But it turns out he cleans house more than I do and he cooks more than I do. So I think, at this point, our relationship is undefinable by present terms; so I would just say, 'queer.' It's just different. It's different than anything available." Eliza (24 years old, Nova Scotia) offered another example that paralleled Rachel's but also explicitly considered the importance of others' social perceptions of her relationship structure:

*We're both very sort of intrigued by 50s decor and roles and all that sort of stuff. . . . I will take on the role of housewife and, a lot of the time, it's this tongue-in-cheek sort of thing. He'll be like, "Get me a beer!" and I'll put on an apron and run off into the other room, "Here ya go, dear!" It's very sort of playful. Again, it's the performance of gender instead of really taking it all that seriously. But, at the same time . . . the kitchen is my kitchen and all this sort of stuff that's very gendered. . . . Sometimes I'm concerned that other people might not quite get it and that they might think that we're really espousing these very traditional roles. . . . I don't want to be the passive wife. . . . I'd much rather be the tough wife.*

For these participants, performing normativity is a reportedly conscious dynamic that holds the potential to be simultaneously nostalgic, flexible, ironic, and difficult to define. Cis women and their trans men partners clearly engage in dynamic, relational processes that produce and validate enactments of gender in ways that may be simultaneously normative and counternormative, despite the commonly voiced concern to not be (mis)recognized as traditional or unremarkably heterosexual (for more on this, see Brown 2009; Ward 2010; Pfeffer 2010, 2012).

A sociological queer analysis might also usefully trouble assertions that those in relationships with trans people must have relationships that are somehow more transgressive or counternormative than other types of relationships. As Kessler and McKenna (2003) note, the prefix "trans" in "transgender" does not necessarily refer to the "transcendence" or "transformation" of gender or gender normativity, and to assume that it does is to minimize decades of sociological work testifying to the rigidity and recalcitrance of the socially structuring gender binary in our society. These assertions also fail to consider the ways in which identity choices are socially embedded, strategic, and constrained. From a queer sociological analytic perspective, we might approach questions about whether the relationships between cis women and trans men reflect a radical subversion of cultural normativity or merely mirror and repackage cultural normativity with some degree of critical suspicion. Such questions implicitly suggest that the onus of responsibility for radically reconfiguring gendered power relations ultimately lies with a numerical and marginalized social minority. Indeed, we might usefully redirect such questions toward whether or not relationships between cis women and cis men—the numerical majority in our culture—currently reflect radical subversion of cultural normativity. Doing so reminds us of the powerful structuring forces of inequality for all social actors and also points to potentially fruitful alliances between social actors working toward equality aims. Building these communities of political and social alliance and resistance was described as an area of particular struggle for the cis women in this study. . . .

These narratives reveal the extent to which queer visibility remains culturally synonymous with social perceptions of female masculinity and male femininity (Hutson 2010), often rendering those who embody cis femininity within queer communities invisible as queer. These narratives also echo earlier writings on lesbian butch and femme genders as socially intelligible identities around which communities materialized and organized (cf. Ponse 1978; Krieger 1983; Taylor and Whittier 1992; Kennedy and Davis 1993). Queer invisibility was of particular concern and consideration to many of the femme-identified cis women I interviewed. This articulated invisibility serves as a marked empirical contrast to theorizing around femme identity (e.g., Hollibaugh 1997; Munt 1998; Levitt, Gerrish, and Hiestand 2003), which marks it as politically transgressive (and even "transgender") in its own right. Such fissures between personal experience and political potential further highlight the need to examine the processes by which gender and sexual identities are produced through social interaction. . . .

While some trans men and their cis women partners described being (mis)recognized as heterosexual and becoming invisible as queer within LGBTQ communities, other participants reported that their partners were (mis)recognized as trans men or as cis women, rather than cis men, more often in gay and lesbian social spaces than in mainstream or non-LGBTQ social spaces. The tensions between these (mis)recognition processes carried striking social consequences. One set of trends that emerged in participants' accounts involved (1) explicit exclusion of trans people and their partners from primarily gay and lesbian social spaces and (2) intimidating and even violent interactions aimed toward "finding out" the "real" sex of those who are trans as they interact within primarily gay and lesbian social spaces. Seventeen (34%) participants described instances of being told by leaders of gay and lesbian organizations (or hearing through the grapevine) that their or their partner's presence was no longer welcome since their partner's transition. Martha (25 years, Massachusetts) described making reservations at a lesbian bed and breakfast only to be told that she and her partner were no longer welcome upon the innkeeper's learning of her partner's transition. Lynne (35 years old, California) described the exclusion of trans men from the yearly "dyke march" in her town. . . .

These narratives attest to the permeability and instability of membership and recognition within various identity-based communities. In a social context that continues to affirm fixed and naturalized binaries (male/female, man/woman, heterosexual/homosexual) despite increasing evidence documenting the fluidity and diversity of sex, gender, and sexual identifications, we find herein evidence for these identities as interactive social accomplishments. Perhaps even more important, we are urged to reconsider just who should be held accountable when it comes to recognizing the sex, gender, and sexual identities of others.

## CONCLUSION: POSSIBILITIES FOR SOCIAL SOLIDARITY AND BROADER APPLICATION

In this study, I draw from Connell's (2009) notion of "recognition" to demonstrate the myriad ways in which we "do" not only gender, but sexuality as well, revealing sexual identities as interactional social accomplishments through which status, rights, and group membership may be stripped or conveyed. By challenging the essentialist notion that sexual identities are largely fixed and natural/biological, we are better poised to consider what is at stake when social actors recognize and misrecognize their peers' sexual self-identifications. The cis women I interviewed often vocally asserted their self-identification as queer. Yet in many instances, these cis women's accounts focused on being (mis)recognized by both queer and nonqueer social others as unremarkably heterosexual. Which of these accounts of their sexual identity is "true"? These findings prompt consideration of how the social effects of (mis)recognition processes (e.g., being able to access regulated social institutions and social membership within particular groups) are powerfully structuring—perhaps even largely determinant—of social group membership.

This study is a step toward theorization of queer social (mis)recognition processes to consider how seeing and not seeing/recognizing and not recognizing one another's social identities and embodiments

matters.[3] More specifically, this study outlines strategies deployed by queer social actors to strategically manage these (mis)recognition processes and to gain access to particular social and material benefits of social group membership. Extending Connell's (2009) "recognition" framework, this study highlights what is at stake in social (mis)recognition processes not only for queer social actors but also for everyone, as these processes reveal the ways in which access to regulated social groups and institutions is often mediated largely through interactional and perceptual social processes rather than static or essential aspects of individuals. . . .

## DISCUSSION QUESTIONS

1. How does this reading on transgendered men and their cis women partners complicate our understanding of sex, gender, and sexual identity? Does this research on cis women and trans men challenge the gender binary?
2. Why might some queer couples choose to perform gender normativity instead of resisting traditional gender roles?
3. Why does Pfeffer want us to use the concept of "recognition" instead of "passing" to understand identities and social interaction?

## NOTES

1. Some participants, who had been with the same partner prior to his transition, found this form of social exchange particularly salient as they noticed very different reactions from older persons when engaging in public hand-holding with the very same partner. Prior to transition, when their partner was reportedly "read" as female and the couple was "read" as lesbian, they recalled older individuals staring at them while not smiling, whispering, avoiding eye contact, and not returning smiles.
2. Participants themselves used the term "roles" (e.g., "1950s housewife role") to describe the enactments of traditional wife/husband, and mother/father family dynamics as they understood them.

3. Here, I nod to Judith Butler's (1993) germinal text, "Bodies That Matter: On the Discursive Limits of 'Sex,'" in which she revisits the social change potential of "gender performativity" by considering the social constructedness of sex and the material body. In this article, I work to provide a more empirically grounded consideration of the ways in which sex, gender, and sexuality are social processes than Butler's (in many ways problematic—see Namaste 2000) textual reading of the documentary film *Paris Is Burning*. In other words, I argue here not only that social identities and their (mis)recognition are sociologically important but also that it is sociologically useful to consider how embodiments and identities presumed natural or biological may be produced by and through social processes.

# PART III

# SOCIAL INSTITUTIONS AND THE PERPETUATION OF INEQUALITY

Part II of this anthology explored the micro level of identities and social interaction. Race, gender, sexuality, and social class inform how we see ourselves and how others perceive and behave toward us. This third part of the book turns our attention from the micro level of the individual to the macro level of society by investigating social institutions. Social institutions contain established patterns of norms and values that organize social life to fulfill certain functions or needs. For example, the institution of government fulfills a variety of functions, including maintaining order, protecting citizens from external threats, collecting taxes and revenues, and so on. As such, social institutions are larger social structures that profoundly affect our lives because they organize social life and dictate expected behavior. Since all social institutions provide norms or rules for individual behavior (for example, the eight-hour workday, paying taxes, who takes care of children), they are seen as mechanisms of social control, and their norms often conflict with one another. Moreover, social institutions vary in strength: they can be strong or weak depending on the confidence people have in them in a given society and how well they adapt to change.

Since social institutions reflect the norms and values of those who have power in society, they also perpetuate oppression and privilege. They maintain and reproduce social stratification and social inequalities found in society. Beliefs about race, gender, sexuality, and social class are woven into the functions and ideologies of these institutions. For example, President Barack Obama's administration challenged the "Don't Ask, Don't Tell" policy of the military, which asked gays to be closeted while serving in uniform. This policy was heterosexist and encouraged homophobia. Other examples of institutional inequalities are U.S. tax regulations that favor the wealthy and enable them to preserve more of their income and assets. The institution of education reproduces social class and racial inequality through the myth of meritocracy and the value it places on the cultural capital of the middle and upper classes. The institution of the family reproduces gender inequality and heterosexism through privileging traditional heterosexual marriage over other family forms. And the institution of the media can distort reality by framing race, social class, gender, and sexuality in negative ways or by objectifying or stereotyping certain groups of people. Many scholars study the institutionalization of racism, sexism, classism, or homophobia in organizations or social institutions.

## THE FAMILY

The first section of Part III considers the institution of the family. The institution of the family replicates and upholds other social hierarchies in society. The family helps to preserve social class positions of power and privilege through the maintenance and transfer of wealth via marriage and inheritance. Reading 30 by Patricia Hill Collins, "It's All in the Family: Intersections of Gender, Race, and Nation," analyzes the traditional family ideal to demonstrate how this ideological construction also is a fundamental principle in social organization. Our schools, legal system, property and tax laws, religious institutions, and even the economy have all been organized around the traditional family ideal. Collins also argues that, contrary to popular sentiment, families are not mutual or equal. They are hierarchical arrangements of power and resources that are distributed based on age, gender, and sexuality. Collins also examines how families maintain privilege through intergenerational transfers of wealth and property, through the tax code, and through family planning.

Another aspect of family that Collins discusses is how the social construction of family is often influenced by racial constructions. For instance, definitions of family often have relied on a notion of "blood ties" and concerns over miscegenation or the racial mixing of blood in families. Thus, another way the institution of the family upholds privilege for some and oppresses others is by laws that allow some groups to marry and others not to marry. For example, U.S. antimiscegenation laws were put into place to ensure that marriage upheld the color line. Recall Reading 19 by Katherine Franke that discussed the famous case of *Suneri v. Cassagne*, which upheld antimiscegenation. The U.S. Supreme Court decision in the case of *Loving v. Virginia* (1967) overturned antimiscegenation laws, and now interracial couples can cross that color line. Reading 31, by Karen Pyke, investigates the interracial relationships

between Asian American women and white men. Pyke interviews 128 second-generation Korean American and Vietnamese American women to find out how these women see Asian men compared with white men as romantic partners. Even though these women have crossed the color line by dating white men, they glorify white masculinity as more egalitarian and denigrate Asian masculinity as more oppressive. Ironically, these Asian American women internalize racial oppression and end up reproducing white male heterosexual privilege.

Reading 32, the last reading in this section on the institution of the family, also examines race and social class privilege in the family. In "The Privilege of Coming Out: Race, Class, and Lesbians' Mothering Decisions," Nancy Mezey studies different races and classes of lesbian mothers and child-free lesbians to see which groups have an easier time coming out about their sexual identity as compared to others. She finds that white, middle-class lesbians have an easier time coming out to their families and friends than do women of color or working-class women. Moreover, because of their race and social class privilege, white, middle-class lesbians also have an easier time making decisions about becoming mothers and tend to have more familial support.

## EDUCATION

The second institution investigated is education. There are a number of structural inequalities in education in terms of race, social class, gender, and sexuality.

The Supreme Court decision in *Brown v. Board of Education of Topeka* (1954) outlawed racial segregation in schools, but other types of segregation by social class or gender increased after this decision. Roslyn Arlin Mickelson, in Reading 33, "How Tracking Undermines Race Equity in Desegregated Schools," argues that, while formal racial segregation ended after the *Brown* decision, other types of racial segregation (such as tracking), which she calls "second-generation segregation," occur in schools. Students of color tend to be tracked to lower-level academic classes, which also have lower-credentialed teachers and fewer resources than do the higher-tracked classes, which tend to contain more white students. Mickelson's case study of one school district on the East Coast highlights the harm of segregation, in general, and how second-generation segregation occurs, in particular. Mickelson argues that desegregation has failed to close the racial gap in education and thus needs to be reevaluated and reimplemented at all levels of education.

Reading 34, "The Schooling of Latino Children," is by Luis Moll and Richard Ruiz. Moll and Ruiz use a case study of one school district, the Los Angeles Unified School District (LAUSD), to summarize some of the major issues related to the schooling of Latino children in the United States. In addition to identifying the problems, Moll and Ruiz end their reading with some suggestions to improve the educational outcomes of Latino students.

In Reading 35, "Class Matters," Peter Sacks elucidates how education is structurally disadvantaging the poor. Sacks studies educational attainment differences based on social class and compares them to differences by gender and race. The critical lynchpin according to Sacks is how hierarchical higher education is structured at community colleges, larger state schools, and elite colleges and universities, all of which reproduce the existing class structure.

## THE ECONOMY AND EMPLOYMENT

The third social institution discussed in Part III is the economy and employment. The three readings in this section examine how employment structurally re-creates social inequality. Reading 36 by Joan Acker, "Inequality Regimes: Gender, Class, and Race in Organizations," provides an analytical framework for understanding how organizations create and maintain hierarchies of race and gender. All social institutions use social control to get people to conform to expected behaviors. Acker argues that employment organizations also use social control to maintain social class, race, and gender hierarchies in the workplace. In particular, Acker analyzes the various control mechanisms, such as direct controls of hiring and firing, to indirect controls, such as using

certain technologies and telephone monitoring. She finds multiple levels on which discrimination can occur in employment organizations. Some of this inequality is invisible or is taken for granted by the workers.

Reading 37 by Marianne Bertrand and Sendhil Mullainathan, "Are Emily and Greg More Employable Than Lakisha and Jamal? A Field Experiment on Labor Market Discrimination," illustrates how inequality regimes appear in the hiring decisions of employers. Their field experiment is evidence for employer-level discrimination because employers make racial distinctions based on the names of applicants on job résumés and call back and interview fewer people perceived to be of color.

Similarly, Reading 38 on the economy and employment by Pierrette Hondagneu-Sotelo, "Families on the Frontier: From *Braceros* in the Fields to *Braceras* in the Home," demonstrates other layers of institutional discrimination reflected in the fact that immigrants have been historically recruited to take jobs in the United States and in the way that some labor—the reproductive labor done in homes—is very influenced by gender, race, and social class.

## HEALTH CARE AND MEDICINE

The U.S. health care system is often referred to as a "nonsystem" because there are so many gaps in medical coverage and care. More than 49 million people did not have health insurance in 2011, and many more Americans were underinsured and could not afford the out-of-pocket costs of medical care. Medical inflation is out of control, and political efforts to reform our health care system, including the recent Affordable Care Act by President Obama, meet major resistance from the ruling elite, big business, and lobbying groups. The three readings on the social institution of medicine and health care show some of the grave inequalities in the U.S. health care system. Taken together, the three readings demonstrate that inequality exists on the individual level, on the institutional level, and even in the research that is done on health issues. Janet R. Grochowski's Reading 39 illustrates how an individual's race, social class, or gender affect one's health. The cases Grochowski spotlights illustrate well how health care fails at an individual level in this country.

Reading 40 by Ryan Blitstein examines racial bias in medical and public health research. White assumptions about teenage pregnancy, female sexuality, and African Americans in general can distort how scholars view health outcomes in a given population.

The final reading in this section, Reading 41 by Keith Wailoo, "A Slow, Toxic Decline: Dialysis Patients, Technological Failure, and the Unfulfilled Promise of Health in America," also shows how the race and social class inequality in our health care system has set up certain groups to get inadequate care, especially in times of crisis such as during Hurricane Katrina.

# Media

The mass media is the fifth social institution we examine in Part III. *Mass media* refers to the communication that is disseminated to large audiences, typically without direct feedback. There are at least four kinds of media: (1) broadcast media such as television and radio; (2) print media such as books and newspapers; (3) digital or electronic media such as websites, blogs, and other online sources; and (4) visual media such as film and photography. We need to ask, What are the purposes or functions of the media as a social institution? How do the media create and maintain social hierarchies? Who owns and controls the media?

Diana Kendall, the author of Reading 42, "Framing Class, Vicarious Living, and Conspicuous Consumption," addresses these three questions in her reading. Kendall analyzes how broadcast media, in particular, portray different social classes in the United States. Kendall is concerned about how the way in which the media frame stories about social class makes a difference in how people spend money and consume products.

Instead of analyzing social class as does Kendall, Reading 43 analyzes racial-ethnic portrayals in broadcast and print media around the crisis of September 11, 2001. Brigitte L. Nacos and Oscar

Torres-Reyna are concerned about the stereotyping of Muslim and Arab Americans.

Some scholars have been concerned about how the media negatively affect behavior, such as with gendered advertisements that show extremely thin women or violence on television that children might see. Reading 44 by Amanda Hess, "Why Women Aren't Welcome on the Internet," looks at the excessively high amounts of cyberstalking and sexual harrassment that women experience online.

# Politics and Government

The last social institution covered is politics and government. Race, class, and gender scholars want to understand how the government, like the other social institutions discussed, creates and maintains social hierarchies and how the government can challenge them. The two U.S. Supreme Court cases discussed above, *Brown v. Board of Education* (1954) and *Loving v. Virginia* (1967), are examples of government attempts to change the structure of inequality in the United States by changing the laws and making racial discrimination illegal.

Policies can have unintended consequences that create more social inequality. Such is the case of the Community Mental Health Centers Act of 1963, which was intended to get more people out of institutions but ended up putting many mentally ill people into the homeless population and on the streets instead of into appropriate care facilities. Lillian B. Rubin talks about this policy in Reading 45, "Sand Castles and Snake Pits."

Problematic law enforcement policies and mass incarceration are examined in Reading 46 by Michelle Alexander, an associate professor of law at Ohio State University. As Rubin does in her argument, Alexander believes that governmental policies such as the War on Drugs have greatly contributed to this growing problem. The excerpt here is based on Alexander's 2010 best-selling book, *The New Jim Crow: Mass Incarceration in the Age of Colorblindness.* In it, Alexander outlines how she came to see the U.S. legal system acting as a system of racialized social control. She argues that mass incarceration is a type of a racial caste system, similar to Jim Crow, which has led to continuous and virulent forms of discrimination. This situation is an example of structural oppression, as discussed by Young (Reading 51), and it also signifies a failure of our legal and political system.

The final reading in Part III, Reading 47 by Richard Lachmann, examines the causes of the weakening economic and political power of the United States. In "The Roots of American Decline," taken from a 2011 article of the same name in the journal *Contexts,* Lachmann uses a comparative and historical frame to analyze how military expenditures and domestic spending affect the current global status of the United States and our ability to invest in the future. He begins by reviewing common arguments from both the left and right of the political spectrum about why the United States is in decline. After analyzing those claims, Lachmann argues that instead, the source of American decline is located in how elites have gained greater control over fiscal and civilian policies and blocked all attempts at reform. Lachmann, a professor of sociology at the State University of New York at Albany, is a historical and comparative sociologist who has studied government and political power for more than 32 years, and his nationally acclaimed book, *Capitalists in Spite of Themselves: Elite Conflict and Economic Transitions in Early Modern Europe* (2000), received the 2003 Distinguished Scholarly Publication Award from the American Sociological Association. As we turn to examine social stratification and social inequality more specifically in the next section, keep Lachmann's insightful arguments in mind.

# 30

# IT'S ALL IN THE FAMILY

*Intersections of Gender, Race, and Nation*

## PATRICIA HILL COLLINS

*This reading is the first of three readings that explore the social institution of the family and how it affects both individual identities and social inequality. Patricia Hill Collins, Distinguished University Professor of Sociology at the University of Maryland, examines how the traditional family ideal in the United States upholds systems of privilege in terms of gender, race, and nationality. This reading, taken from the 1998 journal* Hypatia, *begins with an analysis of public concerns around "family values" and then provides an overview of intersectionality and how it can be applied to the institution of the family. Collins argues that while the family seems to be a social organization that promotes equality, in reality, it replicates and maintains other power hierarchies found in society.*

When former vice president Dan Quayle used the term *family values* near the end of a speech at a political fundraiser in 1992, he apparently touched a national nerve. Following Quayle's speech, close to three hundred articles using the term *family values* in their titles appeared in the popular press. Despite the range of political perspectives expressed on "family values," one thing remained clear—"family values," however defined, seemed central to national well-being. The term *family values* constituted a touchstone, a phrase that apparently tapped much deeper feelings about the significance of ideas of family, if not actual families themselves, in the United States.

Situated in the center of "family values" debates is an imagined traditional family ideal. Formed

*Source:* Collins, Patricia Hill. 1998. "It's All in the Family: Intersections of Gender, Race, and Nation." *Hypatia* 13(3):62–82. Used by permission of Wiley Blackwell.

through a combination of marital and blood ties, ideal families consist of heterosexual couples that produce their own biological children. Such families have a specific authority structure; namely, a father-head earning an adequate family wage, a stay-at-home wife, and children. Those who idealize the traditional family as a private haven from a public world see family as held together by primary emotional bonds of love and caring. Assuming a relatively fixed sexual division of labor, wherein women's roles are defined as primarily in the home and men's in the public world of work, the traditional family ideal also assumes the separation of work and family. Defined as a natural or biological arrangement based on heterosexual attraction, this monolithic family type articulates with governmental structures. It is organized not around a biological core, but a state-sanctioned, heterosexual marriage that confers legitimacy not only on the family structure itself but on children born into it (Andersen 1991).[1]

The power of this traditional family ideal lies in its dual function as an ideological construction and as a fundamental principle of social organization. As ideology, rhetoric associated with the traditional family ideal provides an interpretive framework that accommodates a range of meanings. Just as reworking the rhetoric of family for their own political agendas is a common strategy for conservative movements of all types, the alleged unity and solidarity attributed to family is often invoked to symbolize the aspirations of oppressed groups. For example, the conservative right and Black nationalists alike both rely on family language to advance their political agendas.

Moreover, because family constitutes a fundamental principle of social organization, the significance of the traditional family ideal transcends ideology. In the United States, understandings of social institutions and social policies are often constructed through family rhetoric. Families constitute primary sites of belonging to various groups: to the family as an assumed biological entity; to geographically identifiable, racially segregated neighborhoods conceptualized as imagined families; to so-called racial families codified in science and law; and to the U.S. nation-state conceptualized as a national family.

The importance of family also overlaps with the emerging paradigm of intersectionality. Building on a tradition from Black Women's Studies, intersectionality has attracted substantial scholarly attention in the 1990s.[2] As opposed to examining gender, race, class, and nation as separate systems of oppression, intersectionality explores how these systems mutually construct one another, or, in the words of Black British sociologist Stuart Hall, how they "articulate" with one another (Slack 1996). Current scholarship deploying intersectional analyses suggests that certain ideas and practices surface repeatedly across multiple systems of oppression and serve as focal points or privileged social locations for these intersecting systems.[3]

The use of the traditional family ideal in the United States may function as one such privileged exemplar of intersectionality.[4] In this reading, I explore how six dimensions of the traditional family ideal construct intersections of gender, race, and nation. Each dimension demonstrates specific connections between family as a gendered system of social organization, race as ideology and practice in the United States, and constructions of U.S. national identity. Collectively, these six dimensions illuminate specific ways that ideological constructions of family, as well as the significance of family in shaping social practices, constitute an especially rich site for intersectional analysis . . . .

## Manufacturing Naturalized Hierarchy

One dimension of family as a privileged exemplar of intersectionality lies in how it reconciles the contradictory relationship between equality and hierarchy. The traditional family ideal projects a model of equality. A well-functioning family protects and balances the interests of all its members—the strong care for the weak, and everyone contributes to and benefits from family membership in proportion to his or her capacities. In contrast to this idealized version, actual families remain organized around varying patterns of hierarchy. As Ann McClintock observes, "the family image came to figure *hierarchy within unity* [emphasis in original] as an organic element of historical progress, and thus became indispensable for legitimating exclusion and hierarchy within nonfamilial social forms such as nationalism, liberal individualism and imperialism" (McClintock 1995:45). Families are expected to socialize their members into an appropriate set of "family values" that simultaneously reinforce the hierarchy within the assumed unity of interests symbolized by the family and lay the foundation for many social hierarchies. In particular, hierarchies of gender, wealth, age, and sexuality within actual family units correlate with comparable hierarchies in U.S. society. Individuals typically learn their assigned place in hierarchies of race, gender, ethnicity, sexuality, nation, and social class in their families of origin. At the same time, they learn to view such hierarchies as natural social arrangements, as compared to socially constructed ones. Hierarchy in this sense becomes "naturalized" because it is associated with seemingly "natural" processes of the family.

The "family values" that underlie the traditional family ideal work to naturalize U.S. hierarchies of gender, age, and sexuality. For example, the traditional family ideal assumes a male headship that privileges and naturalizes masculinity as a source of authority. Similarly, parental control over dependent children reproduces age and seniority as fundamental principles of social organization. Moreover, gender and age mutually construct one another; mothers comply with fathers, sisters defer to brothers, all with the understanding that boys submit to maternal authority until they become men. Working in tandem with these mutually constructing age and gender hierarchies are comparable ideas concerning sexuality. Predicated on assumptions of heterosexism, the invisibility of gay, lesbian, and bisexual sexualities in the traditional family ideal obscures these sexualities and keeps them hidden. Regardless of how individual families grapple with these hierarchical notions, they remain the received wisdom to be confronted.

In the United States, naturalized hierarchies of gender and age are interwoven with corresponding racial hierarchies, regardless of whether racial hierarchies are justified with reference to biological, genetic differences or to immutable cultural differences (Goldberg 1993). The logic of the traditional family ideal can be used to explain race relations. One way that this occurs is when racial inequality becomes explained using family roles. For example, racial ideologies that portray people of color as intellectually underdeveloped, uncivilized children require parallel ideas that construct Whites as intellectually mature, civilized adults. When applied to race, family rhetoric that deems adults more developed than children, and thus entitled to greater power, uses naturalized ideas about age and authority to legitimate racial hierarchy. Combining age and gender hierarchies adds additional complexity. Whereas White men and White women enjoy shared racial privileges provided by Whiteness, within the racial boundary of Whiteness, women are expected to defer to men. People of color have not been immune from this same logic. Within the frame of race as family, women of subordinated racial groups defer to men of their groups, often to support men's struggles in dealing with racism . . . .

This notion of naturalized hierarchy learned in family units frames issues of U.S. national identity in particular ways. If the nation-state is conceptualized as a national family with the traditional family ideal providing ideas about family, then the standards used to assess the contributions of family members in heterosexual, married-couple households with children become foundational for assessing group contributions to overall national well-being. Naturalized hierarchies of the traditional family ideal influence understandings of constructions of first- and second-class citizenship. For example, using a logic of birth order elevates the importance of time of arrival in the country for citizenship entitlements. Claims that early-migrating, White Anglo-Saxon Protestants are entitled to more benefits than more recent arrivals resemble beliefs that "last hired, first fired" rules fairly discriminate among workers. Similarly, notions of naturalized gender hierarchies promulgated by the traditional family ideal—the differential treatment of girls and boys regarding economic autonomy and free-access to public space— parallel practices such as the sex-typing of occupations in the paid labor market and male domination in government, professional sports, the streets, and other public spaces.

As is the case with all situations of hierarchy, actual or implicit use of force, sanctions, and violence may be needed to maintain unequal power relations. However, the very pervasiveness of violence can lead to its invisibility. For example, feminist efforts to have violence against women in the home taken seriously as a bona fide form of violence and not just a private family matter have long met with resistance. In a similar fashion, the extent of the violence against Native American, Puerto Rican, Mexican American, African American, and other groups who were incorporated into the United States not through voluntary migration but via conquest and slavery remains routinely overlooked. Even current violence against such groups remains underreported unless captured in a dramatic fashion, such as the videotaped beating of motorist Rodney King by Los Angeles police officers. Despite their severity and recent increase, hate crimes against gays, lesbians, and bisexuals also remain largely invisible. Through these silences, these forms of violence not only are neglected, they become legitimated . . . .

Subordinated groups often face difficult contradictions in responding to such violence (Crenshaw 1991). One response consists of analyzing one or more hierarchies as being socially constructed while continuing to see others as naturalized. In African American civil society, for example, the question of maintaining racial solidarity comes face-to-face with the question of how naturalized hierarchies construct one another. Maintaining racial solidarity at all costs often requires replicating hierarchies of gender, social class, sexuality, and nation in Black civil society . . . .

## LOOKING FOR A HOME: PLACE, SPACE, AND TERRITORY

The multiple meanings attached to the concept of "home"—home as family household, home as neighborhood, home as native country—speak to its significance within family as a privileged exemplar of intersectionality. In the United States, the traditional family ideal's ideas about place, space, and territory suggest that families, racial groups, and nation-states require their own unique places of "homes." Because "homes" provide spaces of privacy and security for families, races, and nation-states, they serve as sanctuaries for group members. Surrounded by individuals who seemingly share similar objectives, these homes represent idealized, privatized spaces where members can feel at ease.

This view of home requires certain gendered ideas about private and public space. Because women are so often associated with family, home space becomes seen as a private, feminized space that is distinct from the public, masculinized space that lies outside its borders. Family space is for members only—outsiders can be invited in only by family members or else they are intruders. Within these gendered spheres of private and public space, women and men again assume distinctive roles. Women are expected to remain in their home "place." Avoiding the dangerous space of public streets allows women to care for children, the sick, and the elderly, and other dependent family members. Men are expected to support and defend the private, feminized space that houses their families. Actual U.S. families rarely meet this ideal. For example, despite feminist analyses that discredit the home as a safe place for women, this myth seems deeply entrenched in U.S. culture (Coontz 1992).

A similar logic concerning place, space, and territory constructs racialized space in the United States. Just as the value attached to families reflects their placement in racial and social class hierarchies, the neighborhoods housing these families demonstrate comparable inequalities. Assumptions of race- and class-segregated space mandate that U.S. families and the neighborhoods where they reside be kept separate. Just as crafting a family from individuals from diverse racial, ethnic, religious or class backgrounds is discouraged, mixing different races within one neighborhood is frowned upon. As mininations-states, neighborhoods allegedly operate best when racial and/or class homogeneity prevails. Assigning Whites, Blacks, and Latinos their own separate spaces reflects efforts to maintain a geographic, racial purity. As the dominant group, Whites continue to support legal and extra-legal measures that segregate African Americans, Native Americans, Mexican Americans, Puerto Ricans, and other similar groups, thereby perpetuating cultural norms about desirability of racial purity in schools, neighborhoods, and public facilities . . . .

Overall, by relying on the belief that families have assigned places where they truly belong, images of place, space, and territory link gendered notions of family with constructs of race and nation (Jackson and Penrose 1993). In this logic that everything has its place, maintaining borders of all sorts becomes vitally important. Preserving the logic of segregated home spaces requires strict rules that distinguish insiders from outsiders. Unfortunately, far too often, these boundaries continue to be drawn along the color line.

## On "Blood Ties": Family, Race, and Nation

Presumptions of "blood ties" that permeate the traditional family ideal reflect another dimension of how family operates as a privileged exemplar of intersectionality. In the United States, concepts of family and kinship draw strength from the flow of blood as a substance that regulates the spread of rights (Williams 1995). While the legal system continues to privilege heterosexual married couples as the preferred family organization, the importance given to bonds between mothers and children, brothers and sisters, grandmothers and grandchildren, illustrates the significance of biology in definitions of family. Representing the genetic links among related individuals, the belief in blood ties naturalizes the bonds among members of kinship networks. Blood, family, and kin are so closely connected that the absence of such ties can be cause for concern. As the search of adoptees for their "real" families or blood relatives suggests, blood ties remain highly significant for definitions of family.

Given the significance attached to biology, women of different racial groups have varying responsibilities in maintaining blood ties. For example, White women play a special role in keeping family bloodlines pure. Historically, creating White families required controlling White women's sexuality, largely through social norms that advocated pre-marital virginity. By marrying White men and engaging in sexual relations only with their husbands, White women ensured the racial purity of White families. Thus, through social taboos that eschewed pre-marital sexuality and interracial marriage for White women, White families could thereby avoid racial degeneration (Young 1995). When reinserted into naturalized hierarchies of gender, race, class, and nation, and institutionally enforced via mechanisms such as segregated space and state-sanctioned violence, efforts to regulate sexuality and marriage reinforced beliefs in the sanctity of "blood ties." . . .

Definitions of race as family in the United States traditionally rested on biological classifications legitimated by science and legally sanctioned by law. By grouping people through notions of physical similarity, such as skin color, facial features, or hair texture, and supported by law and custom, scientific racism defined Whites and Blacks as distinctive social groups (Gould 1981). Just as members of "real" families linked by blood were expected to resemble one another, so were members of racial groups descended from a common bloodline seen as sharing similar physical, intellectual, and moral attributes. Within this logic, those lacking biological similarities became defined as family outsiders, while racially different groups became strangers to one another.

A similar logic can be applied to understandings of nation. One definition views a nation as a group of people who share a common ethnicity grounded in blood ties. Cultural expressions of their peoplehood—their music, art, language, and customs—constitute their unique national identity . . . .

U.S. national identity may be grounded more in ethnic nationalism than is typically realized. Notions of U.S. national identity that take both family and race into account result in a view of the United States as a large national family with racial families hierarchically arranged within it. Representing the epitome of racial purity that is also associated with U.S.

national interests, Whites constitute the most valuable citizens. In this racialized nation-state, Native Americans, African Americans, Mexican Americans, and Puerto Ricans become second-class citizens, whereas people of color from the Caribbean, Asia, Latin America, and Africa encounter more difficulty becoming naturalized citizens than immigrants from European nations. Because all of these groups are not White and thereby lack appropriate blood ties, they are deemed to be less-worthy actual and potential U.S. citizens . . . .

## MEMBERSHIP HAS ITS PRIVILEGES: RIGHTS, OBLIGATIONS, AND RULES

By suggesting an ideal relationship between the rights and responsibilities of family membership, the traditional family ideal operates as a privileged exemplar of intersectionality in yet another way. In a situation in which notions of belonging to a family remain important to issues of responsibility and accountability, individuals feel that they "owe" something to, and are responsible for, members of their families. For example, people within family units routinely help their family members by babysitting, lending money, helping relatives find employment and housing, or caring for the elderly. Family members linked by blood are entitled to these benefits merely by belonging. Even when family members lack merit, they are entitled to benefits simply because they belong. Beyond this issue of access to entitlements, individuals incur differential responsibilities that depend on their placement in family hierarchies. For example, women are expected to perform much of the domestic labor that keeps the family going, whereas men's duties lie in providing financial support.

In a similar fashion, U.S. citizens by birth or naturalization acquire certain rights and responsibilities that accrue from membership. Citizens are promised entitlements such as equal protection under the law, access to unemployment insurance, old age pensions, free public education, and other social welfare benefits. Citizens are also expected to fulfill certain

obligations to one another. U.S. citizens are expected to pay taxes, observe the law, and engage in military service when required. In contrast to the rights and responsibilities provided insiders, outsiders lack both the entitlements provided group members and the obligations attached to belonging. Similar to non-family members, non-U.S. citizens are neither entitled to citizenship benefits nor responsible for national duties . . . .

In a situation of naturalized hierarchy, conceptualizing U.S. national identity as composed of racial groups that collectively comprise a U.S. national family fosters differential patterns of enforcement of the rights and obligations of citizenship. Members of some racial families receive full benefits of membership while others encounter inferior treatment. Gender hierarchies add additional complexity. African American women's experiences with entitlement criteria for 1930s Social Security programs, for example, illustrate how institutionalized racism and gender-specific ideology public policies shaped national public policy. Race was a factor in deciding which occupations would be covered by Social Security. Two occupational categories were expressly excluded from coverage: agricultural and domestic workers, the two categories that included most African American women. Also, by providing differential benefits to men and women through worker's compensation (for which Black women did not qualify) and mothers's aid, from its inception, Social Security encompassed ideas about gender. Eligibility rules rewarded women who remained in marriages and were supported by their husbands but penalized women who became separated or divorced or who remained single and earned their own way. Black women who were not in stable marriages lacked access to spousal and widows benefits that routinely subsidized White women. In this case, the combination of race-targeted polices concerning occupational category and gender-targeted policies concerning applicants' marital status worked to exclude Black women from benefits (Gordon 1994). On paper, Black women may have been first-class U.S. citizens, but their experiences reveal their second-class treatment.

## Family Genealogy:
## Inheritance and the Family Wage

Naturalized hierarchies embedded in the traditional family ideal articulate not only with hierarchies of race and nation but also with hierarchies of economic or social class (Collins 1998, chapter 6). The traditional family ideal may be more heavily implicated in social class organization in the United States than previously imagined. Using the individual as the unit of analysis, social class analyses have traditionally examined men's incomes as central to family organization. However, moving from individuals to families as the basic unit of social class analysis, and from income to wealth as a measure of class, illustrate yet another way that family serves as a privileged exemplar for intersectionality. Shifting to wealth as a measure of social class status suggests that families serve as important social units for wealth's intergenerational transmission. As Oliver and Shapiro observe, "private wealth thus captures inequality that is the product of the past, often passed down from generation to generation" (Oliver and Shapiro 1995:2).

Focusing on wealth not only references contemporary economic inequality but also incorporates the historical origins and reproduction of class differences over time. Despite ideas that social mobility is widespread, U.S. children routinely enjoy or suffer the economic status of their parents. Families constitute important sites for inheritance, not solely of cultural values, but of property. Families use wealth to create opportunities, secure a desired standard of living, and pass their social class status to their children. In this process, the family home becomes more than a private respite from the demands of the public sphere. When "family values" and "property values" become intertwined, homes in racially segregated neighborhoods become important investments. The traditional family ideal shows the family not only occupying a home, but owning it. Ensconced in tax policies that provide lucrative benefits for homeowners, for many Americans, the single-family home as a tangible symbol of wealth remains central to the American dream (Coontz 1992). Wealth matters because, if one adheres to rules of marriage and childbearing, it is directly transferable from generation to generation . . . .

Despite the historical concentration of wealth among a small percentage of families, the intergenerational transmission of wealth through family also operates among working-class families. Traditional analyses view working-class families in purely wage-earning terms. Such families are thought to have no property to pass on to their children, and are seen as mere employees of other more wealthy families. However, the notion of working-class men being entitled to a "family wage" emerges at the intersection of expectations of family inheritance and a naturalized gender hierarchy. In this situation, working-class men inherit opportunities to earn a wage and are expected to use that wage to support their families. According to this logic, women's and children's social class status derives from that of men.

When these relationships regulating intergenerational property transmission are racialized, as they are in the United States, another level of complexity emerges. In her analysis of how racism undermined the War on Poverty program, Jill Quadagno describes the resistance that craft unions put forth when pressured to change entrenched patterns of racial discrimination. As Quadagno points out, the right of unions to select their own members was seen as a "property right of the working class. This was a most compelling argument for nepotism—the tradition of passing on the craft from fathers to sons" (Quadagno 1994:65). Among Philadelphia plumbers, 40 percent of the apprentices were sons of members. Fathers wanted their sons to be trained as plumbers and to continue in the business. Practices such as these virtually ensured that African Americans and other groups were excluded from lucrative positions. Quadagno quotes one construction worker who explains the concept of property rights and property transmission in White working-class families:

> Some men leave their sons money, some large
> investments, some business connections and some a
> profession. I have none of these to bequeath to my

sons. I have only one worthwhile thing to give: my trade . . . . For this simple father's wish it is said that I discriminate against Negroes. Don't all of us discriminate? Which of us when it comes to choice will not choose a son over all others? (1994:65)

In effect, racial discrimination in education, employment, and housing historically reflected White working-class understandings of these social locations as "private property" to be disposed of as inherited wealth. While such attitudes certainly may reflect personal prejudice, racial discrimination thus may be more closely attached to property rights and concerns about the value of inheritable property than actual attitudes toward African Americans.

## FAMILY PLANNING

The significance of the family as an exemplar of intersectionality can also be seen in one final dimension of family rhetoric. Family planning comprises a constellation of options, ranging from coercion to choice, from permanence to reversibility regarding reproduction of actual populations. In the case of individual families, decision-making lies with family members; they decide whether to have children, how many children to have, and how those children will be spaced. Feminist scholars in particular have identified how male control over women's sexual and reproductive capacities has been central to women's oppression (see, for example, Raymond 1993). However, just as women's bodies produce children who are part of a socially constructed family grounded in notions of biological kinship, women's bodies produce the population for the national "family" or nation-state, conceptualized as having some sort of biological oneness. In this sense, family planning becomes important in regulating population groups identified by race, social class, and national status (Heng and Devan 1992; Kuumba 1993).

Social policies designed to foster the health of the United States conceptualized as a national family follow a family planning logic, as demonstrated via eugenic thinking. Early twentieth century "racial

hygiene" or eugenic movements compellingly illustrate the thinking that underlies population policies designed to control the motherhood of different groups of women for reasons of nationality and race (Haller 1984; Proctor 1988). Eugenic philosophies and the population policies they supported emerged in political economies with distinctive needs, and in societies with particular social class relations. Common to eugenic movements throughout the world was the view that biology was central to solving social problems. Societies that embraced eugenic philosophies typically aimed to transform social problems into technical problems amenable to biological solutions affected via social engineering. Eugenic approaches thus combined a "philosophy of biological determinism with a belief that science might provide a technical fix for social problems" (Proctor 1988:286).

Three elements of eugenic thinking seem remarkably similar to themes in American public policy. Those embracing eugenic thinking saw "race and heredity—the birth rates of the fit and the unfit—as the forces that shape[d] . . . political and social developments" (Haller 1984:78). First, eugenic thinking racializes segments of a given population by classifying people into mutually exclusive racial groups. Because the United States has operated as a racialized state since its inception, race remains a fundamental principle of U.S. social organization. While racial meanings change in response to political and economic conditions, the fundamental belief in race as a guiding principle of U.S. society remains remarkably hardy. Associating diverse racial groups with perceived national interests, a second element of eugenic thinking, also has a long history in the United States. The third feature of eugenic thinking, the direct control of different racial groups through various measures also is present in U.S. politics. So-called positive eugenic—efforts to increase reproduction among the better groups who allegedly carried the outstanding qualities of their group in their genes—and negative eugenic—efforts to prevent the propagation by less desirable groups—also have affected U.S. public policy . . . .

In periods of profound social change, such as the massive European migration that preceded the

*Buck vs. Bell* decision, eugenic philosophies can reemerge. With the civil rights, women's, anti-war, and other social movements of the 1950s and 1960s, as well as the growing nonwhite immigrant population of the 1970s and 1980s, the United States experienced profound change. Omi and Winant (1994) interpret the expanding conservative social projects that emerged during this period as a direct response to the perceived gains of Blacks and women. One core feature characterizing the rhetoric of social projects of the Right was a return to the family values of the traditional U.S. family. By associating the ideal family with U.S. national interests, these movements linked those interests to their own political agendas concerning race and gender. Returning to "family values" not only invoked racial and gendered meanings, it set the stage for reviving a logic of eugenics that could be applied to adolescent pregnancy, women's poverty, street crime, and other social issues.

In this context, contemporary American social policies from the 1960s through the "family values" debate of the 1990s become more comprehensible. When attached to state policy in a racialized nation-state, questions of controlling the sexuality and fertility of women from diverse race, social class, and citizenship groups become highly politicized. For example, White women, especially those of the middle class, are encouraged to reproduce. In contrast, women of color, especially those lacking economic resources or not in state-sanctioned marriages, are routinely discouraged from having children (Raymond 1993). Population policies such as providing lavish services to combat infertility for White, middle class women, while offering a limited range of Norplant, Depo Provera, and sterilization to poor African American women constitute contemporary reflections of the logic of eugenic thinking (Davis 1981; Nsiah-Jefferson 1989) . . . .

## RECLAIMING FAMILY

Family occupies such a prominent place in the language of public discourse in the United States that rejecting it outright might be counterproductive for groups aiming to challenge hierarchies. Because the family functions as a privileged exemplar of intersectionality in structuring hierarchy, it potentially can serve a similar function in challenging that hierarchy. Just as the traditional family ideal provides a rich site for understanding intersectional inequalities, reclaiming notions of family that reject hierarchical thinking may provide an intriguing and important site of resistance . . . .

Given the power of family as ideological construction and principle of social organization, Black nationalist, feminist, and other political movements in the United States dedicated to challenging social inequality might consider recasting intersectional understandings of family in ways that do not reproduce inequality. Instead of engaging in endless criticism, reclaiming the language of family for democratic ends and transforming the very conception of family itself might provide a more useful approach.

## DISCUSSION QUESTIONS

1. Why does Collins argue that the traditional family ideal is problematic and creates social inequality?
2. What are some of the dimensions of Collins's intersectional analysis of the family as a gendered and racial system of national identity? How does the institution of the family serve both ideologically and structurally as a "principle" of social organization?

## NOTES

1. By dislodging beliefs in the naturalness or normality of any one family form, feminist scholarship analyzes the significance of specific notions of family to gender oppression (Thorne 1992). As Stephanie Coontz (1992) reports, this traditional family ideal never existed, even during the 1950s, a decade that is often assumed to be the era of its realization. Feminist anthropologists also challenge the traditional family ideal by demonstrating that the heterosexual, married couple form in the United States is neither "natural," universal, nor cross-culturally normative (Collier et al. 1992). Recent family

scholarship suggests that large numbers of U.S. families never experienced the traditional family ideal, and those who may have once achieved this form are now abandoning it (Coontz 1992; Stacey 1992).

2. In the early 1980s, several African American women scholar-activists called for a new approach to analyzing Black women's lives. They claimed that African American women's experiences were shaped not just by race but also by gender, social class, and sexuality. In this tradition, works such as *Women, Race, and Class* by Angela Davis (1981), "A Black Feminist Statement" drafted by the Combahee River Collective (1982), and Audre Lorde's (1984) classic volume *Sister Outsider* stand as groundbreaking works that explore interconnections among systems of oppression. Subsequent work aimed to name this interconnected relationship with terms such as *matrix of domination* (Collins 1990) and *intersectionality* (Crenshaw 1991) . . . .

3. A wide range of topics, such as the significance of primatology in framing gendered, raced views of nature in modern science (Haraway 1989); the social construction of Whiteness among White women in the United States (Frankenberg 1993); race, gender, and sexuality in the colonial conquest (McClintock 1995); and the interplay of race, class, and gender in welfare state policies in the United States (Quadagno 1994) have all received an intersectional treatment. Moreover, the initial emphasis on race, social class, and gender has expanded to include intersections involving sexuality, ethnicity, and nationalism (Anthias and Yuval-Davis 1992; Parker et al. 1992; Daniels 1997).

4. Theoretical and empirical work on women of color's location in work and family not only challenges the traditional family ideal, but paves the way for the more general question of family as a privileged site of intersectionality. For work in this tradition, see Dill 1988, Zinn 1989, and Glenn 1992.

# 31

# AN INTERSECTIONAL APPROACH TO RESISTANCE AND COMPLICITY

## The Case of Racialized Desire Among Asian American Women

KAREN PYKE

*This second reading in the section on the social institution of the family is by Karen Pyke, associate professor of sociology at the University of California, Riverside, where she conducts research on the intersection of gender and race, with a special emphasis on Asian Americans. In this excerpt, taken from a 2010 article in the* Journal of Intercultural Studies, *Pyke delves into the social constructions of race and gender among Asian American women who prefer white men as romantic partners. Pyke's study is an excellent example of both intersectionality and how the family creates and maintains racial hierarchies similar to what Collins discussed in the previous reading. Pyke's interviews of 128 second-generation Asian American women reveal fascinating insights into these women's contradictory beliefs about men and masculinity based on racial assumptions.*

A romantic preference for white men among Asian American women is a perennial topic of controversy, anger and pain among Asian Americans. In 1993, the U.S. magazine *Asian Week* posed the question "Are Asian American Men Wimps?" While the question is disturbing enough,

*Source:* Pyke, Karen. "An Intersectional Approach to Resistance and Complicity: The Case of Racialized Desire among Asian American Women." In *Journal of Intercultural Studies* 31(1):81–94. Reproduced with permission of Taylor & Francis Ltd. in the format journal via Copyright Clearance center

the response from readers was even more so. One Asian American man described a dinner discussion prompted by the question:

*The Asian American women in the room proceeded, one after another, to describe how Asian American men were too passive, too weak, too uncertain, too boring, too traditional, too abusive, too domineering, too ugly, too greasy, too short, too . . . Asian. Several described how they preferred white men, and how they never had and never would date an Asian man.*

This study explores the power of racialised gender discourses and controlling images of Asian American masculinity in shaping the racialised romantic desires of heterosexual Asian American women. Based on interviews with unmarried, heterosexual second-generation Korean and Vietnamese American women, I find widely circulating discourses that glorify white masculinity and denigrate Asian masculinity inform many respondents' romantic preference for white men. Relying on the concepts of resistance and complicity, I pose the following questions: Should we interpret Asian American women's romantic preference for white men as compliance with white (male) superiority and the reproduction of a hierarchy of racialised masculinities? Or, since the belief that white men are more gender egalitarian than Asian ethnic men often motivates this racial preference, should we interpret it as resistance to gender oppression? Or are both resistance and complicity at play? My inquiry focuses on the limits of resistance given recent feminist work that interprets women's cross-racial desires for white Western men as resistance.

## RESISTANCE AND COMPLICITY

Discussion in the social sciences and humanities of gender, racial, class and colonial oppressions, including their intersections, is rife with reference to resistance. Resistance has much intuitive appeal to liberation scholars as it accords agency to the subjugated, inspires oppositional politics and is a powerful resource in identity politics (Pyke 2007). Attention to resistance also corrects for Western feminism's depiction of Third World women as the epitome of the passive, oppressed, gendered subject (Narayan 1998; Ong 1994). Indeed, the current fixation with Resistance reflects a shift from an earlier view of the oppressed as *passive victims*, which many scholars attacked for portraying the subordinated as helpless dupes. As Chappell (2000:210–211) observes, *victim* was inseparable "from its hitchhiking adjective, *passive*," which, by implying the inadequacy and pathology of the oppressed, easily expanded to blaming the victim. In correcting this tendency, liberation scholars bestowed "the gift of agency" upon the oppressed (Chappell 2000:207). The resulting conflation of agency and resistance transformed the subordinated from passive victims to active resistors. Hence, for the oppressed, to act *is* to resist: "I am, therefore I resist" (Mohanty 2002:208). The result is what I call the *model resistor* stereotype—the oppressed are now treated as *super resistors* "able to leap tall" structures of inequality "in a single bound" (Preamble to *Superman*, US radio show 1940; Pyke 2007). This is not a benign stereotype, however. Take, for example, the case of black women who comply with controlling images that cast them as strong and ever-resilient by denying their hardships and depression, thus their oppression. As a result, they are more likely to suffer alone in silence and less likely to seek help and retribution (Beauboeuf-Lafontant 2007). The shift from an emphasis on women's victimisation to "agency in contemporary feminist scholarship underestimates the role of power in shaping social relations. This error discounts the significance of class and race (and other social structural forms of inequality) in shaping the experiences of different groups of women" (Andersen 2005:443). Particularly disconcerting is how this fixation on resistance normalises domination (Bordo 1993). Even worse is how the glorification and celebration of resistance can inadvertently pay tribute to the oppressive conditions that make resistance necessary (Pyke 2007).

By criticising the current emphasis on resistance, I am not recommending a return to the *passive victim* approach. Rather, we need to shift from the Western penchant for either/or thinking (Collins 1990), as in seeing either resistance or complicity. Further, when we interpret individual action as resistance and agency, we must be careful not to forget larger power structures or "what people *do to women*" (Andersen 2005:443). When we define as resistance any individual act designed to increase the mobility of the oppressed, we risk overlooking how such actions can rely on and reproduce larger structures of domination. We need to consider how structures of power can direct and co-opt resistance, rendering it ineffective, or worse, obscuring how it reproduces the very structures it intends to oppose. Given the simultaneity of systems of domination, like gender, race, class, colonialism and sexuality (Collins 1990; Crenshaw 1993), liberation scholars must reflect on how actions that resist one form of oppression (e.g., gender) can be complicit with domination on intersecting fields of oppression (e.g., race and/or class), and how resistance can be compromised by the complex relations of power it confronts.

For these reasons, I approach actions and ideologies characterised as resistance with circumspection. I do so by adapting Matsuda's method for understanding the intersectionality or "interconnection of subordination" by "asking the other question" (1996:64). Matsuda explains: "When I see something that looks racist, I ask, 'Where is the patriarchy in this?' When I see something that looks sexist, I ask, 'Where is the heterosexism in this?'" (64–65). And so on with other forms of oppression. I adapt Matsuda's method for examining the limits of resistance by asking: Where is the complicity with racial oppression in this resistance to gender oppression? Where is the resistance or challenge to gender inequality in this complicity with racial domination? Asking the other question(s) to uncover the simultaneity of oppression takes us beyond ill-fitting either/or models of resistance and accommodation (agency and structure). Applying this method to the intersectional study of cross-racial and international romantic and sexual relationships can enhance that literature which, as I discuss next, has often relied on binary models of resistance and complicity.

## FEMINIST RESEARCH ON GLOBAL CROSS-RACIAL ROMANCE

Feminist scholars have long studied the effects of global inequalities on relationships and sexual exchanges between Western males and non-Western women. This research initially framed Western men's romantic and sexual liaisons with (putatively impoverished) non-Western women through tourism, the "mail-order bride industry" and international matchmaking services as exploitation (Glodava and Onizuka 1994; Narayan 1995). Globally circulating imaginaries that cast Asian, Latin American, Caribbean and East European women as more subservient than their allegedly liberated white counterparts in the USA and Western Europe drives Western men's demand for non-Western women. Fed up with the independence, career-orientation, materialism, assertiveness and egalitarian expectations associated with white Western women, Western men pursue traditional, subservient wives from abroad, or immigrant populations in their own country (Constable 2003; Schaeffer-Grabiel 2004, 2005).

Early feminist work focused on the motivations of the men and the stereotypes shaping their desires while ignoring the women's subjective experiences and racialised desires, treating them simply as passive victims. More recent scholarship considers how idealised images of white Western masculinity influence the romantic desires and strategic liaisons of women in non-Western countries (Brenann 2001; Kelsky 2001; Schaeffer-Grabiel 2004, 2005; Yuh 2002), and among immigrant groups in the West (Kim 2006; Nemoto 2009). Women who pursue white Western romantic partners through travel, immigration, the Internet, matchmaking services and sex tourism are now cast as strategically engaging with white hegemonic masculinity to resist the "patriarchy" of their homeland or co-ethnic men in the immigrant communities of the West, at the same time that they are re-generating discourses that support white Western men's global dominance. These women view Western men as romantic, gender egalitarian "white knights in shining armour" who can rescue them from a so-called "ethnic patriarchy"

(Nemoto 2009:5) and provide economic security, access to careers, cosmopolitanism and an elevated status (Brennan 2001; Kelsky 2001; Kim 2006; Nemoto 2009; Schaeffer-Grabiel 2004, 2005; Yuh 2002). While this research focuses on cross-border imagining, Nemoto also finds Asian American women who have married or dated white American men invoke this imagery in describing white men as offering greater mobility and gender egalitarianism than Asian American men.

The argument that non-Western and/or women of colour deploy discourses glorifying white Western masculinity to resist co-ethnic male dominance is largely without empirical examination of the local patriarchies and gender arrangements being resisted. Indeed, the presumption of "ethnic patriarchy" is troublesome given its origin in the very same Western ideological notions that cast Western men as egalitarian Prince Charmings who will save women of non-Western origins from the ensconced patriarchy of co-ethnic men. Another problem in casting this as a resistance strategy of mobility is the implication that it is successful. Many women who pursue Western partners in search of a better life never succeed in finding a partner, or, if they do, do not receive the expected rewards (Brennan 2001; Narayan 1995). The over-emphasis on individual resistance in this literature gives too little attention to the project of collective uplift. These concerns inform my analysis of Asian American women's interview accounts of their romantic preference for white American men or for men who display characteristics associated with white men. I suggest this is a limited resistance strategy as it complies with oppressive ideologies that maintain the racialised hierarchy of masculinities.

## METHODS

This study consists of intensive interviews with 61 Korean American women and 67 Vietnamese American women, all of whom identify as heterosexual. These data are from a larger study of adaptation, family and racial and gender experiences among 429 male and female Korean and Vietnamese American children of immigrant parents. The interview guide

for the current analysis included open-ended questions about respondents' ideal partner, dating experiences, racial preferences for dating and marriage, and their parents' racial preferences for their future spouse. Additional probes about the reasons for their preferences were asked to uncover respondents' racial assumptions. The author, who is white, trained student assistants, a majority of whom are second-generation Asian Americans, to conduct the face-to-face interviews, which were tape-recorded, transcribed and coded into thematic categories for ease of analysis. The analysis focused on interviews in which respondents describe a romantic preference for white males and/or the traits they associate with white and Asian American men. Most interviews lasted from 45 to 60 minutes, and a smaller number from two to three hours.

Respondents range in age from 18 to 34, and average 22 years. All respondents were either born in the USA to immigrant parents or immigrated at an average age of five years. When designing the larger study of adaptation, I chose second-generation Vietnamese and Korean Americans, as they constitute relatively new ethnic groups in the USA and have very different pathways of immigration. In 1996, when this study began, most in-depth studies of immigrant adaptation examined only one ethnic group, contributing to a tendency to generalise the experience of one ethnicity to all Asian ethnics. So as not to reiterate this shortcoming, I included two ethnic groups in this sample (for more on methods, see Pyke 2000).

Koreans and Vietnamese constitute a large proportion of recent Asian immigrants to southern California, the site of the study. More ethnic Vietnamese live in southern California than anywhere outside of Vietnam (Collet 2005), and Los Angeles is home to the largest population of Korean Americans in the USA (Yu 2002). The majority of respondents are students at two southern California universities where Asian Americans compose the largest racial group (over 40 percent). Additional respondents were referred by students at these universities. Given the large local Asian American population, respondents who state a preference for white males are not responding to a lack of available heterosexual Asian American partners.

The analysis revealed a recurring and unprompted tendency to glorify white masculinity and denigrate Asian masculinity in explaining a romantic preference for white men, or to describe difficulties in finding a compatible Asian American partner. The repeated use of this discourse suggests its centrality as an interpretive frame in understanding racialised romance. While many respondents did *not* invoke stereotypes of racialised masculinities, I focus on those who did, as the goal of the current analysis is not to gauge the frequency of this phenomenon or make ethnic comparisons but, rather, to examine how this discourse is invoked and what its use suggests about resistance and complicity. Thus my findings should not be misunderstood to suggest that this discourse informs the romantic desires of *most* respondents.

The stereotypes of Asian masculinity apply to both Asian and Asian American men, and respondents often refer to Asian American men simply as "Asian." Rather than repeatedly referring to both Asian and Asian American men, I switch back and forth, as do the respondents. In the findings, I present quotes that reflect broader patterns and identify respondents with pseudonyms.

## Findings

### Discourse of Racialised Masculinities

Respondents, including many who do not prefer to date white men, regularly invoke stereotypes in constructing Asian American men as the inferior inverse of white men. They describe Asian American men as "dominant," "mean," "dictators," "not liking a girl who has too many opinions," "treating women like property" and "wife beaters." They depict white men, on the other hand, as attractive, romantic, loving, sensitive, communicative and gender egalitarian—traits they claim are lacking in Asian American men. Inah, a Korean American, observes, "Korean American men are very unaffectionate to their wives from what I see, and *American* [meaning white] men are more caring and they tend to love their wife a lot more than Korean American guys would."

Respondents commonly juxtaposed images of despotic, unloving Asian men against those of white men as romantic liberators in constructing two different forms of racialised masculinity. As Mimi, a Korean American, states:

*Most Asian guys have this expectation that Asian women belong at home and they shouldn't go out at night, whereas I think a white person feels that a woman has a more equal status with the man, and she can do whatever she wants.*

Similarly Jennifer, also Korean American, says:

*Let me go ahead and make one comparison. I know I'm judging all the white guys from this one white guy [I dated], but white guys are very chivalrous. Maybe they don't open doors and stuff like that, but they do what you would expect to only happen in fairy tales. Asian guys don't do that. They don't really give a shit.*

Even though Jennifer acknowledges drawing on her experience with only one white man, she nonetheless uses him as confirmatory evidence of white and Asian men as polar opposites. Such over-generalisation is common in these narratives. Some respondents who have not dated or interacted much with Asian American or white men admit their racialised assumptions are not based on actual contact. Mimi, who has never dated a white man, says:

*So I was thinking maybe I should go for a Caucasian to marry because I'll be happier, you know? [Interviewer asks: Why do you think marrying a Caucasian would make you happier?] Well, I've never really dated a Caucasian before, but I hear that most of them don't treat their women like a possession. Like they want communication instead of the woman always doing what the man wants. Like in Korea, or actually many Asian cultures, the girl is expected to be like submissive and real quiet, not talk back to the husband, be the husband's slave. I don't think a white guy would be like that. If I married a white guy, then of course he would be nontraditional. But with a Korean guy, well, you do anything the guy says pretty much. It's like they have this power over you that you can't do anything about because it is not our place to*

What Mimi "hears" and believes about racialised masculinities is based on the widely circulating imagery perpetuated by the white dominated society, shaping her expectations of white and Asian American men, rather than actual contact. As I describe next, these beliefs also shape respondents' interactions with men, affecting how they "see" Asian and white American men.

## Internalised Racial Oppression in Constructions of Asian Masculinity

Several women refer to domineering fathers as epitomising the despotism they associate with Asian American males, and to explain why they will not date co-ethnic males. In so doing, they assume Asian American men's gender attitudes do not differ across generations, between men raised in Asia and the USA, nor among Asian American male peers. They view co-ethnic males as bound to the gender dictates of their upbringing in immigrant families, which they presume to be entirely male-dominated. This is another site where respondents construct Asian masculinity as monolithic and invariable. As Star, a Korean American, says:

*I think my dad turned me off to Korean men. I don't find them attractive and, like with my Korean friends, there is no way I could picture myself with someone like that. Because they are still into that old Korean thing where they want their women to be submissive and stuff. I mean, they won't say it but you can tell.*

Similarly, Jen, who is Vietnamese, states:

*I am not attracted [to Vietnamese males] because I am thinking of the way my dad is. I love my dad but I would never marry someone like him. So that is probably why I tend to not look that way [toward Vietnamese males]. [ . . . ] My dad doesn't understand why I am so outspoken, which is why someone like him would be very incompatible because we would always be arguing. You think that a Vietnamese guy was raised by [Vietnamese] parents so they must have given him their values. That is the way I think of it and that is why I don't look that way.*

In these examples, the attributes of one Asian man (their father) are generalised to all Asian men, expanding a negative trait to the entire group. It is difficult to imagine white heterosexual women referring to their father's dominance as a reason they prefer to date or marry a man who is *not* white. White male domination and privilege means that white men are not subjected to stereotypes based on the "bad" behaviour of a few white males. Racial oppression, on the other hand, including that which has been internalised by the oppressed, encourages the over-generalisation of the "bad" behaviour of a few men of colour to the entire group. In fact, respondents do not generalise the male dominance of their fathers to *all* males, but only to Asian males. Male dominance is not regarded as part of a cross-racial system of gender inequality but a racialised feature of Asian masculinity. Meanwhile, in the case of white men, the positive traits of egalitarianism and chivalry associated with one white boyfriend are generalised to the entire group. This illustrates the power of white racial domination in winning the consent of the oppressed through the perpetuation and inculcation of racist images. It is not a matter of "seeing is believing", but rather, the racialised assumptions the dominant society teaches the oppressed shape how and what they see (Pyke and Johnson 2003).

Latina scholar Laura Padilla observes that critical race theorists have yet to explore the sensitive topic of internalised oppression and white privilege in the selection of white spouses by people of colour. She admits her choice of a white husband may be due to associating infidelity with Latinos, even though she knows male infidelity has no racial boundaries.

*I never believed that all Latino males were unfaithful, but my family history made me nervous. [ . . . ] When I experience this unease, am I unconsciously succumbing to internalized racism by believing negative stereotypes about Latino men? My need to ask this question reveals one of the dangers of internalized oppression—we frequently do not even realize when or how we are prejudiced against ourselves. (Padilla 2001)*

Some respondents say they avoid interacting with co-ethnic males precisely because they believe the stereotype of Asian male dominance. They thus have fewer opportunities to meet males who violate their assumptions. As Jen comments:

*I have never met a Vietnamese guy that I have ever been attracted to. I don't know why. I think I look at one race more than the other. I look at white guys more. I think they are really cute. But then I haven't seen very many Vietnamese men either. Like I told you I don't interact with very many so that might be why.*

By juxtaposing images of controlling Asian American men with those of egalitarian white men, respondents re-construct a racialised hierarchy of masculinities that privileges whiteness. This discourse is grounded in the presumption of essential differences between racial groups of men. These accounts draw on and reproduce two fundamental components of an ideology of white racial domination: (1) a belief that race is an essential human feature that determines behaviour; and (2) the belief in white supremacy. I am not suggesting that these respondents are creating or causing racism. Rather, white racial domination is so pervasive and insidious that it shapes our common-sense understandings of everyday life and is thus easily internalised by the racially subordinated. Indeed, all systems of inequality not maintained by overt repression depend upon some degree of complicity from the oppressed (Pyke 2007). This is an important point, as discussion of internalised racial oppression has sometimes given way to blaming the victims rather than the system of racism.

## Internalised Orientalism and Pro-assimilationism in Constructions of Asian Masculinity

Not all who engage a discourse of racialised masculinity overlook variation within racial categories. Some consider acculturative differences among Asian American men and regard the more ethnically identified as the most domineering of co-ethnic males. Some respondents refuse to date men with a strong ethnic identity. As Sandra, a Vietnamese American, remarks:

*I won't date [someone who is not assimilated] because I think they'd expect me to be like the traditional Vietnamese girl, like cook for the husband. That's not me. That's a role I could never fulfil. And in some ways, I think they'd probably look down on me because maybe they'd think, "Oh she's bad because she goes out. She's outspoken. She talks back." That's one of the reasons why I wouldn't date someone who's not assimilated.*

Similarly some respondents associate ethnic pride with male dominance. Angela, a Korean American says, "Simply put, [Korean American men are] short-tempered, controlling, dominant, hard-headed and lacking in communication skills. You know they've got this like Korean pride." Angela suggests that Asian American men who embrace and uphold their ethnicity are unable to engage in any gender practice other than male dominance. One cannot be strongly identified as Korean or Vietnamese *and* gender egalitarian. Thus ethnic culture and patriarchy are conflated and assimilation to US society is the *only* path to gender egalitarianism (see Pyke and Johnson 2003). These assumptions reveal two additional ways that some respondents have internalised a discourse of white domination: (1) They reiterate Orientalist assumptions of the West that dichotomise the East as monolithically backward, gender traditional and impervious to change, and the West as modern and gender progressive (Said 1978). (2) By presenting ethnic pride and a strong identity as inherently detrimental, respondents fashion an implicitly pro-assimilation narrative. They thus echo the disdain of the white-dominated society toward immigrants who do not cast off their foreign ways and eagerly adopt white American values and traits.

## Internalised Stereotypes and Self-Fulfilling Prophecies

The racialisation of Asian masculinity as solidly gender traditional can create self-fulfilling prophecies when respondents expect white and Asian American men to comply with the stereotypes in their interactions. For example, Mimi offers as evidence of Asian American men's traditionalism the domestic tasks that she and a girlfriend performed in the home of a male Korean friend:

> I remember once when we were in my guy friend's house, and we started doing the dishes and doing the laundry. We were like, "What the heck are we doing?" So it's weird because I see how I'm acting now, and that is not even my husband. So I know that with my husband, he would probably expect that from me, and I don't want to do that. Although I guess I was doing it at this guy's house, but it wasn't like I was pressured this time. Whereas I know it would be like that if I were married to someone with more traditional beliefs.

Admitting her friend did not pressure her to do household chores, Mimi nonetheless performs them, assuming that as a Korean American he expects that of her. She thus complies with a generalised expectation she has of what constitutes appropriate gender arrangements when in the presence of Korean American males. Mimi poignantly reveals how racial stereotypes that drive certain social expectations can encourage a romantic preference for white men. Because male dominance and female submission are so tightly bound with notions of traditional ethnic society, some females engage a form of femininity that they *believe* is expected when interacting with co-ethnic males, even when such behaviour is not overtly demanded or expected, and may actually be unwanted. They place blame for this behaviour on the gender traditionalism they associate with co-ethnic males and thus underestimate the feasibility of successfully resisting male power and privilege in ethnic settings (see Pyke and Johnson 2003).

Meanwhile, those who expect white males to be gender progressive are likely to behave in egalitarian ways when interacting with them, and credit this to an egalitarianism they project onto white men. Racialised expectations that white males are egalitarian while co-ethnic males are not could prompt a gross misreading of the gender arrangements individual men actually prefer. Women might engage in an egalitarian, assertive femininity with white males, including those who prefer traditional gender hierarchies, and a submissive femininity with co-ethnic males, including those who prefer gender egalitarianism (Pyke and Johnson 2003). By engaging in gendered behaviour that conforms to racialised notions of white and Asian American men, these women might be participating in a self-fulfilling prophecy. Further, by behaving in a more servile manner with co-ethnic males, they re-construct the stereotype of Asian American women as submissive, including in the eyes of co-ethnic males.

Such dynamics reproduce white male heterosexual privilege. The racial myths that glorify white masculinity and denigrate Asian masculinity can dissuade Asian American women, and women of all racial groups, from regarding Asian American men as desirable romantic partners, and encourage them to turn their gaze toward white men. This makes heterosexual Asian American women more available to white men; as well, heterosexual white women are less inclined to view Asian American men as romantically appealing (Pyke and Nemoto 2009). These dynamics help to explain gender differentials in racial out-marriage rates. Asian American women out-marry at nearly double the rate of Asian American men, and, when they do, are most likely to partner with white men (Lee and Fernandez 1998; Nemoto 2009). Hence the reiteration of ideologies of racialised masculinities bolsters the power and privilege of white men over Asian American men on the marriage market.

## Conclusion

When respondents mimic the racialised gender stereotypes perpetuated in the larger racist society, Asian masculinity is constructed as the opposite of white masculinity—it is the "other" against which white masculinity is defined as superior. This juxtaposition locates the subordination of Asian masculinity in its racialness; suggesting it is an essentialised racial component of one's blood, body and culture. As such, Asian masculinity is unalterable and invariable. This objectification of Asian masculinity is part of the larger racial project that accords superiority to white males over Asian males, as well as over women in general.

By framing their lack of attraction to Asian males as a matter of personal preference, respondents present as normal and acceptable the anti-Asian racism and glorified imagery of white masculinity they have internalised. In a real sense, many are unaware of the underlying reasons behind their lack of attraction to Asian males. While they provide lists of derogated stereotypical traits as reasons, few offer critique these stereotypes or suggest white gendered racism informs their desires. When racism is so fully woven into the fabric of society that it informs common-sense thought, it becomes normalised and more difficult to resist, resulting in phrases like "I'm not attracted to Vietnamese males for some reason" and "I don't know what it is."

Through the re-generation of racialised discourses of masculinity, male dominance is configured as uniquely Asian rather than a pan-racial problem. Respondents focus their resistance of gender inequality on that form linked with Asian males, whom they construct as monolithically male domineering, overlooking those committed to gender egalitarianism. This racialised construction of Asian masculinity obscures the patriarchal practices of white men. I have suggested that by "asking the other question," we can see how the resistance of male dominance in these accounts reproduces white (male) racial and gender dominance. Respondents' reiteration of racial discourses of masculinity reproduces the racial and gendered power of white men, including over Asian males, and challenges the interpretation of Asian American women's preference for white men as a way of resisting "ethnic patriarchy." Nonetheless, there are components of resistance here worth mentioning. When respondents denigrate Asian American men as domineering, they implicitly denigrate its counterpart, the stereotype of the Asian

American women as submissive, slavishly dutiful and gender traditional (see Pyke and Johnson). By deriding traditional gender attitudes associated with Asian American men, these respondents can distance themselves from stereotypes of Asian femininity and forge a gender egalitarian identity. That they do so by reiterating rather than challenging the stereotypes, however, points to the limits of such resistance (see Pyke 2007). While it is understandable that scholars who study the oppressed are eager to emphasise resistance, this study cautions that by failing to consider the simultaneity of various forms of domination, what might look like resistance and result in some individual gains for the oppressed can, when examined through the prism of intersectionality, reveal dynamics of complicity at play as well. That is, we need to consider the larger reproductive aspects of situated forms of resistance by deploying an intersectional frame of analysis which requires "asking the other question" so as to uncover the interconnections and limits of resistance and complicity within the matrix of oppression.

## DISCUSSION QUESTIONS

1. How does Pyke's research on interracial relationships illustrate how masculinities are racialized? Are Asian American women challenging social inequality by crossing the color line in their interracial relationships? Or are they upholding forms of oppression?
2. How might social class be a key variable to add to this analysis of interracial relationships between Asian American women and white American men?

# 32

# THE PRIVILEGE OF COMING OUT

*Race, Class, and Lesbians' Mothering Decisions*

NANCY MEZEY

*Similar to the ethnographic research used by Karen Pyke in the previous reading on Asian American women's perceptions of men, Nancy Mezey uses interviews to understand better how lesbian mothers make decisions about whether to come out or not. Mezey, an associate professor of sociology at Monmouth University, in West Long Branch, New Jersey, published the following reading in 2008 in the* International Journal of Sociology of the Family. *In it, Mezey investigates how social class and race affect the coming-out process for childfree lesbians and lesbian mothers. Her findings suggest that both race and social class privilege some women to come out more readily and to be accepted more by their families of origin than other women. This reading illustrates well Patricia Hill Collins's arguments in Reading 30 about how the institution of the family upholds heterosexual privilege, but that this privilege is very much influenced by the intersections of race and social class.*

Deciding to come out, or reveal one's sexual identity, is an ongoing process. Lesbians don't just have to decide to come out once. Rather, they are continually faced with the decision of who to come out to and when to do it. Sometimes lesbians carefully plan how and when they will come out, particularly when it involves parents, close friends, or co-workers. But sometimes it just happens. For example, you're at a party and someone asks about your husband, and you respond with, "my partner . . . ." Deciding when and to whom to come out is a constant decision: Do I tell my family? Do I tell my friends? What about my neighbors? Do I come out to the new person at work? Do I come out

*Source:* Mezey, Nancy. 2008. "The Privilege of Coming Out: Race, Class, and Lesbian's Mothering Decisions." *International Journal of Sociology of the Family* 34(2):257–276. Used with permission.

to the man at the hardware store who asks what project my husband and I are working on? What are the risks of coming out? Are there any benefits to coming out at this moment? The list goes on.

Coming out is difficult for many lesbians because it means going against dominant beliefs that heterosexuality is the only good, healthy, and natural way to be (Rubin 1993). We live in a society influenced by compulsory heterosexuality where we assume that everyone is, and ought to be, heterosexual. People enforce their heterosexual biases through institutionalized privilege and subordination (Cabaj 1998; Rubin 1993; Silvera 1995; Stacey 1996). One form of this subordination is through homophobia, in which people fear and dislike people with diverse sexual identities.

Compulsory heterosexism and homophobia exist both within secular and religious institutions. Within secular institutions, political policies focus on a narrow heterosexual definition of family, thus denying lesbians, gays, bisexuals, and transgendered people (LGBT) the right to legally marry, the right to adopt children, and the right to access national and state-level domestic partnership benefits. Secular institutions also exclude sexual identity from hate crimes, deny equal protection clauses for LGBTs in work and housing, ban LGBT materials from school curricula, and limit government funding on HIV/AIDS research. Similarly, religious institutions throughout most of the U.S. describe homosexual behavior as sinful, largely because they limit sexual relations to married men and women (Hartman 1999). This is particularly true in White fundamentalist, Black, and Latino churches where a strict religious foundation denounces homosexuality (Espín 1997; Greene 1994; hooks 1989; Roberts 2004). While some religious groups are beginning to accept same-sex relationships and identities, others stand firmly against diverse sexualities (Hartman 1999).

Heterosexism and homophobia in both secular and religious institutions makes coming out, even to oneself, a difficult and scary process because it involves sifting through beliefs about "good" and "bad" sexuality and creating and understanding a personal identity. Personal identities form through a process that is situated within a particular social, cultural, and political setting (Stein 1997). Therefore, lesbians' willingness and ability to come out, as well as their experiences with coming out, are shaped by the social conditions around them. However, because structures of race and class intersect with structures of sexuality and gender to create varying conditions for different groups of lesbians, coming out for lesbians is easier, or more restrictive, depending on their race and class positions.

In 1999 I set out to study lesbians' mothering decisions (i.e., how lesbians decide to become mothers or remain childfree), how their decisions are embedded in larger social and cultural processes, and how those processes are shaped by race and class. I was particularly interested in this topic because no research to date had focused on lesbians' decisions to remain childfree and nearly all the literature on lesbian mothers drew on the experiences of middle-class White lesbians (Lewin 1993; Sullivan 2004). In addition, current literature on lesbian mothers focuses primarily on lesbians' experiences once they become mothers, and does not discuss the coming-out processes prior to them being mothers. The literature on coming out, on the other hand, has greatly documented struggles that lesbians of color face in coming out (Clarke 1983; Espín 1997; Silvera 1995; Smith 1998), but almost completely ignores the struggles of White lesbians, lesbians who are not in the middle-class, and lesbian mothers. In discussing their mothering decisions, lesbians in my study talked about coming out to their families and communities of origin, not only as lesbians, but also as lesbian mothers. This article begins to fill the research gap, therefore, by examining how structures of race and class shape the coming-out process for childfree lesbians and lesbian mothers of diverse race and class backgrounds . . . .

## GATHERING VOICES

My research is based on a series of focus groups conducted in 2000 with lesbians from diverse class and racial-ethnic backgrounds who had either decided to become mothers or to remain childfree.

Prior to starting my study, I defined several terms including lesbians in general, lesbian mothers, child-free lesbians, race, and class. In keeping with practice from previous studies, I defined lesbians as women who identify themselves as lesbian (Weston 1991). I defined lesbian mothers as lesbians who, within their identities as lesbians, had become or were actively seeking (i.e., in the process of adopting or inseminating) to become mothers. I specifically excluded lesbians who had become mothers through previous heterosexual marriages because the processes they went through to become mothers differ from "out" lesbians who decide to become mothers. For example, lesbians in heterosexual relationships may become mothers through accidental pregnancies. Because a primary component of my study was to understand how sexuality shapes the decision-making process, I only wanted to include women who made mothering decisions within their identities as lesbians.

For childfree lesbians, I selected lesbians who did not want to enter into motherhood and who did not already have children (Bartlett 1994). I chose the term "childfree" because it does not center "mother" as the norm (as does "non-mother" or "not-mother") and does not suggest a lack of something (as does "childless" and "non-mother").

I asked potential participants to define their own racial-ethnic identities (Luttrell 2000). For my focus groups and later my analysis, I collapsed participants into two racial categories: "lesbians of color" and "White" lesbians. Lesbians of color referred to lesbians who identified as Black and/or Latina. White lesbians were those who identified as Euro-American (i.e., from European descent). I was able to group race into two racial categories without compromising the integrity of the study because my research looked specifically at how racial privilege and discrimination shape mothering decisions. Therefore, I divided my participants into those who have access to racial privilege (i.e., Whites) and those who do not (i.e., Blacks and Latinas).

The two categories of class that I used were middle- and working-class, categories initially grouped loosely on education and occupation. Definitions of class also often include income and wealth, but I did not try to determine either of these at the time of recruitment for fear of offending potential participants. I classified working-class participants as those with an associate's degree or less and who worked at "blue collar" jobs. I classified middle-class participants as those holding a bachelor's degree or higher and who worked at managerial or professional jobs. In cases where education and occupation did not neatly fit into either category, I used any additional information I had about the participants, such as their partners' occupation, to help determine their class position . . . .

My next step was to recruit lesbians into the study. I chose an area of five counties in a Midwest state because I was familiar with, and had contacts in, those counties, and because they offered me access to a large population of lesbians from which to draw a diversified sample . . . .

After four months, I had recruited 35 willing participants. Although I faced some constraints in recruiting a diverse sample, by using a combination of sampling strategies, and by hustling around five counties, I was able to recruit a fairly diverse sample. In my study there was almost an even division between lesbian mothers (17) and childfree lesbians (18). Participants fell between the ages of 22 and 46 years. Thirteen (37.1%) of the participants were either Black or Latina. The remaining 22 (62.9%) were White. Similarly, I recruited 13 (37.1%) working-class lesbians and 22 (62.9%) middle-class lesbians. During the focus groups, several participants in the middle-class focus group identified themselves as working-class and came from working-class backgrounds. Therefore, the breakdown of participants by class is not neatly discernable . . . .

## COMING OUT TO FAMILY AND COMMUNITY

No matter how difficult, in making mothering decisions lesbians in my study had to weigh whether or not to come out to their families and communities of origin. To elicit responses about coming out, during the focus groups, I asked lesbians the following questions: "Have you come out to your family of origin? Has your coming out or staying closeted influenced your decision to parent/remain childfree?" In their responses, lesbians discussed coming out as being integral to their mothering decisions because their relationships with their families and communities of origin were important to them. Many questions loomed large, such as what the responses of their families and community members would be, if coming out would jeopardize relationships with those people, and whether or not they themselves cared about jeopardizing those relationships. The answer to such questions varied greatly by race and class.

Lesbians of color, and particularly those from the middle-class, greatly feared that coming out would endanger family and community relationships. Most middle-class lesbians of color discussed how families and communities of origin were supportive in many ways, but not necessarily supportive of being a lesbian. As previous literature has documented, a combination of the historical and current racialized view that Whites have held regarding Black sexuality, cultural norms concerning sexuality and gender among communities of color, and the tight connections between communities of color and organized religion create social conditions in which lesbians of color often clash with the sexual norms of, and face denunciation from, their families and communities of origin.

Such denunciation is scary because it means being alienated from family and loved ones who protect each other from racism in larger society, including racism within lesbian communities. It is not surprising, therefore, that lesbians of color in my study did not want to risk rejection by family and community of origin. Amy, a middle-class Black lesbian, explained how the importance of family and community created both support and anxiety for her:

*One of the reasons to stay in the closet is you don't have to go through that drama. And I'll have to tell you from my perspective, and this will be from being an African American woman: Home is what I can depend on. Home is always there. It's unconditional, and when you live in a society where you have to have some place you can go, you can't [risk losing that]. I mean it floors me when I hear about parents disowning their children because they're gay or lesbian, and I've heard those [stories] for years. But I can't even imagine what that's like . . . .*

Similar to other lesbians of color, Amy needed her family of origin and was unwilling to jeopardize that support by coming out to family members. Like others, Amy also knew that coming out to her family meant coming out to her church. Her discussion of homophobia in her church shows how racism, sexism, and heterosexism intersect to shape the discrimination lesbians of color experience within the very social institutions that in many ways support them. In discussing coming out, Amy explained:

*My church is probably the hardest thing of all things for me. It is very difficult to be, I just have to say I'm a . . . Southern Baptist. Black. This is very different from the White Southern Baptist. And I want everybody to know that there are two different groups. Southern Baptists are a really fun group. We're pretty tolerant of just about everything. We tend to see gays and lesbians as an invisible amongst us, but we know they exist. We're not particularly comfortable, and that's the way I'm treated. The church is . . . a large community. So not only do I have to deal with my extended family, but the church extends forever, and they don't like that I'm a lesbian. They don't like that I like women . . . . And see, for me, my mother was my introduction to my church. So it's very difficult, because she made it seem so appealing. You know the fact that I choose to be closeted, and I used to be concerned about being closeted, but it's my choice. Who knows who I am? What I am? I don't need the extra headache 'cause being an African American, being a woman, being a lesbian . . . .*

Amy's experiences illustrate how discrimination particularly in the church affects her decision not to reveal her sexual identity. Because of homophobia that she experienced in the church, she very clearly chose not to come out in that setting or any setting connected with church, such as her family. As with families of origin, church acts as a strong social network in general, but also as a source of stress for lesbians. Diane, a working-class Black lesbian, echoed

Amy's concern about the clash between her sexual identity and religious community when she stated:

> I've always been out [of the closet]. There's no other choice. If you know me, you know me as out. There's no other choice. I've never been in. That's not an option. Except for church. I'm dealing with that.

Diane's reluctance to come out at church echoes Amy's response, as well as the response of other lesbians of color I interviewed, that connections between church and communities of color make coming out a hard choice for lesbians of color.

Although many lesbians of color did not want to directly come out to family and communities of origin, they managed to negotiate their sexual identities by following a "silent tolerance," or "don't ask, don't tell" practice. Most lesbians of color said that if they presented their partners in subtle ways to their families, if they did not openly discuss their sexual identities, then they could maintain stability and harmony within their families and communities of origin. Desiree, a middle-class Latina, exemplified this position when she described how she was told by her community of origin not to discuss her lesbian relationship:

> The Mexican community, I remember very much being a part of it, coming out as Mexican and feeling very much a part of it and then people kind of telling me when I met Miriam, they were like, "You know as long as you don't say it. As long as you're just still a part of the community. As long as you don't make an issue of it, you're in. You're still in." And people were still cool with me and stuff.

Desiree and other lesbians of color understood that they would not be alienated from their communities of origin as long as they did not explicitly come out as lesbians.

In contrast with lesbians of color, many White lesbians, regardless of class, seemed willing to risk their family relationships by coming out. This was partly because the risk they felt they were taking did not seem as great as that of lesbians of color. Most White lesbians were not coming out to extended families or communities of origin. But even though most White lesbians were willing to come out, their responses suggest that how their families responded to their coming out varied by class. Middle-class White lesbians reported that their families were far more accepting that those of working-class White lesbians. During the interview, Kristy and Tammy, middle-class White lesbians, discussed coming out and the positive responses from their families:

**Kristy:**    *I came out to my parents when I was in my 20s and the knowledge then kind of spread through my family. I was pretty such much told not to tell my grandmother. And then once she passed it was sort of like, "Okay, now we can talk about it." So I'm out to my family, to my siblings. I make jokes about good-looking women with my brothers-in-law. You know, it's all very friendly . . . .*

**Tammy:**    *I'm very out to my family. My mom loves my friends. She came to watch my dog, probably it was a year ago, maybe two, and I called from vacation to see how everything was going and she was having a poker party with all my lesbian friends. So she is totally part of the group.*

As a result of having positive experiences, families of many middle-class White lesbians remained a large source of support throughout their lives. However, some middle-class White lesbians were more hesitant about directly coming out than others. Instead, similar to lesbians of color, they followed a "don't ask, don't tell" practice. Andrea explained:

> I've never said the word to my family, but they clearly know. My partner right now is facing a life-threatening illness, and my family is really rallying around her. And they consider her my partner, so, yes, I'm sure that they know.

Barb also engaged in a "don't ask, don't tell" practice with her family. During the interview, Barb initially said that she was out to her family. But after Andrea's statement, she explained:

*I have to qualify. I mean like Andrea I never walked in the room and said, "Hey Mom and Dad and the rest of my family, I'm gay," or anything like that. It was an unspoken assumption. And then eventually some of them started approaching me, were asking me, and I would answer them. I mean my niece did it very early on and they all have come to realize the relationship, though I've never made some proclamation.*

Barb's experience began as a "don't ask, don't tell" practice but ended up where she was open with her family, or at least some family members who probed her for information. Regardless of whether or not middle-class White lesbians directly or indirectly came out to their families, most resulted in positive outcomes leaving supportive relationships intact.

Working-class White lesbians did not have the same experiences. They found that coming out to their families at worst severed relationships and, at best, remained neutral. Kerry and Amanda, two working-class White lesbians, discussed how coming out damaged their relationships with their families:

**Amanda:**   *Out of a family of 7 kids, my brother's deceased. I have not spoken to my parents or five other siblings in five years. The one thing that my mother said to me when I came out, she was saying, "Well don't count on those friends being a part of your life forever. Your family's the one who'll be around forever." Excuse me?! I have a very low opinion of how cohesive families really are, I don't believe that they are any different [than friends]. I mean, they come and go.*

**Kerry:**   *Before I figured out that I was gay and Trish and I got together, I could go to my parents for anything. And at that point there was a 6-month period [when] I lived with my parents. There was 6 months where I was not even spoken to. And after that and all of the problems since then. No, I don't go home.*

Kerry's situation was particularly strained because of a messy custody case involving her younger brother's children. But the above discussion shows a class difference between the responses regarding working- and middle-class White lesbians coming out to their families: a difference most likely due to working-class families developing strong beliefs about gender and sexuality based on an understanding of the "traditional family" in which there is a clear gender division of labor (Connell et al. 1993).

## COMING OUT AS A MOTHER

Lesbians in my study who wanted to remain childfree had some flexibility in whether or not they came out to people in their families and communities. Although never easy to hide an identity, childfree lesbians could choose whether or not they wanted to come out in any given situation. To better understand how coming out as a mother affected lesbians' mothering decisions, I asked lesbians the following questions: "Does your family of origin know that you are planning on having/not having children? If so, what has been their reaction? Has that reaction affected your decision to remain childfree?"

Many lesbians who wanted to become mothers felt that if they were to have children and wanted to maintain support from their families and communities, as well as not instill their children with a sense of shame, they needed to come out to their families. Some lesbians found, however, that there was a difference between coming out as a lesbian and telling family members that they wanted to become mothers. Particularly within communities of color, families that were comfortable with lesbian *identities* were often not fully comfortable with lesbian *motherhood*. Leslie, a middle-class Black lesbian, made this position clear. She said that for lesbians who do not feel able to come out to their parents, the thought of bringing children into their families is often too difficult:

*I think having a child would change the dynamics . . . . I think they'd come around after a while, but I think that initial thing would be really difficult 'cause it would push the issue. It would put [my sexuality] so much in their face that they would have to deal with it. At the present time, you don't really have to think about [my sexual identity].*

Leslie said that her family's potential reaction did not affect her decision to remain childfree because she had made that decision much earlier in her life. However, her story suggests that other lesbians in similar situations may take family responses into consideration in making their mothering decisions. Interestingly, lesbians' lack of coming out as mothers perpetuates the belief within Black communities that childbearing is a purely heterosexual endeavor. In fact, the perception of lesbians as "not mothers" exists despite the presence of Black lesbian mothers within their communities (Clarke 1983; Silvera 1995). By not coming out, lesbians leave intact heterosexist beliefs about motherhood, which in turn make it harder for them to come out. In other words, Black lesbians' fears about coming out as mothers, and Black families' heterosexist understanding about motherhood, keep each other intact.

While lesbians who wanted to remain childfree could avoid coming out to their families of origin, those who wanted to become mothers were often forced to have risky conversations. Anita, a middle-class Latina, not only found it difficult to tell her family that she was a lesbian, but particularly that she wanted to become a mother. Anita's story shows how the connections between families and communities of color, and the homophobia that infuses both, not only made it hard for her to come out publicly as a lesbian, but also to herself. In addition, it made her decision to become a mother a difficult one:

> *The communities that I belonged to were, their view of mother and everything was more traditional, and I grew up with my step-dad being a minister and the whole church thing. It was really, really difficult for me to get past, accepting my being a lesbian; then getting to the point of telling anybody in my family. They could be accepting of me adopting a child as a single mother, but for me adopting a child with a*

> *partner or having a child co-parenting with another woman was taboo. It took a long time for me to be willing to take the risk of being put out of that community: nuclear family and church. The church was a little bit easier, but not really because I had always belonged to the same church as my parents and it was really difficult knowing their view of motherhood. I knew that I had to make that decision [to leave the church] if I was going to be a mother. And so basically that's what I ended up doing, but it took a long time, several years.*

When I interviewed Anita, she said that her family of origin had learned to tolerate her immediate family and now comes to events such as her children's birthday parties. But her family of origin does not view her immediate family as having the same status as a heterosexual family. Anita's experience shows the personal energy and courage some lesbians of color need to challenge the beliefs of both family of origin and church community in order to become mothers. In Anita's case, she found support among friends and lesbian networks that helped her take a risk other lesbians may not be willing to take.

Working-class lesbians of color shared similar concerns about telling their families that they wanted to become mothers. Like other lesbians in the study, Kizzy and Joy, both working-class Blacks, discussed their families of origins' practice of silent tolerance. They said certain members of their families knew they were lesbians, but no one discussed it. But if coming out as a lesbian was not difficult enough, Kizzy said she was not sure how her mother would respond to her wanting to have children because her mother did not approve of donor insemination.

Similar to lesbians of color, working-class White lesbians, and those from working-class backgrounds, discussed their concerns with coming out as lesbian mothers to their families. The same class differences that appeared when middle- and working-class White lesbians came out to their families *in general* existed when they wanted to come out *as mothers*. Lilly, a middle-class White lesbian from a working-class background, explained these differences when talking about the reaction of her own family, as opposed to the reaction of her middle-class White partner's family:

> My partner and I are both Euro-Americans but we're from real different cultural backgrounds. And, her family much more, um, educated class, and my family is working-class folks. And I think more than anything, we shared a lot more in the process with her family. But we didn't tell my parents until the kids [we adopted] were at the house. It works out better in my family just to spring things on them. You know, all the anticipatory stuff is not helpful—let's just deal with it. (Laughter). Really. I've learned that. But with her family, they've been really involved in the process and she has a brother . . . . He and his wife adopted five kids and have three others, so they were really part of the process too. So I think more than anything, her family was really involved, where with my family, no, if they would have gotten involved it would have been a bigger mess. I guess that's the best way to look at it.

Lilly's experience of class differences in coming out as a mother to her and her partner's families of origin was similar to that of other White lesbians. Working-class White lesbians found their families of origin to be difficult to tell, but ultimately somewhat neutral to both coming out and becoming mothers. For example, in discussing coming out, Martha, a working-class White lesbian who wanted to become a mother, said:

> I have (come out). It went pretty good. I only had one family member say, "I'll go to counseling with you when you're ready to change."

Martha kept a sense of humor regarding her family member's comment, which shows her level of comfort with her own sexual identity. Similarly, in telling her family that she wanted to become a mother, Janet, a working-class White lesbian, stated,

> People always ask about my family. It's not necessarily supportive, as they don't seem to care one way or the other. They're just, "Everybody has a family and this is yours." I'm fairly fortunate in that respect.

While the responses of Martha and Janet's families are not fully supportive of their sexual identities or decisions to mother, they did not pose real barriers to becoming mothers.

Middle-class White lesbians, on the other hand, worried about telling their families that they wanted to become mothers, but ultimately found that their families supported their decisions. For example, Grace, a middle-class White lesbian, decided to come out to her parents when she decided to have children:

> I felt like I needed to come out to my family and friends. I'd been in a relationship for 2, 2 ½ years, my partner and I. She had tried to have children. She was [thinking about having children] on her own as a single parent. And I went through the struggle of, "Can I do this? Can I live like this?" I decided, yes I could, but I needed to come out in order to do it. And I was ready to have children right then. But first I felt like I had to come out to my family and my friends and that was difficult for me to [do]. It's gone fine and I still have the same friends and same family. It's gone great, actually, but it was a scary thing.

Grace's comment demonstrates how important it was for her to have her family's support. White lesbians who wanted children seemed willing to risk their families' adverse reactions. But they also found that their families' responses, particularly those of middle-class White lesbians, were positive. Unlike lesbians of color, because White families and communities were less intertwined with one another, the White lesbians I interviewed did not risk losing as much as lesbians of color in telling their families that they wanted to become mothers. Having strong family support facilitated White lesbians' decisions to become mothers. In fact, while lesbians of color feared that coming out to their families and communities would jeopardize their support networks, coming out to families of origin was a strategy White lesbians, particularly those from the middle-class, used to increase their support networks.

## THE RISKS AND
## BENEFITS OF COMING OUT

Being able to come out to family of origin gives lesbians greater access to an important support system. When lesbians feel they cannot come out to their families, or they actually come out and are shunned, they find themselves with limited support. My findings strongly suggest that the greater a lesbian's privilege by race and class, the easier it is for her to come out to her family.

In my study, accessing family and community networks depended on how lesbians weighed the benefits of coming out with the risk of alienating key support systems. This was particularly true for lesbians of color for whom family and community were hard to separate. Lesbians of color, regardless of class, followed a practice of silent tolerance and spoke of how difficult it would be to tell their families that they wanted to become mothers. Those who decided to tell their families found the coming-out process, as well as the acceptance by their families, to be difficult because while the silent tolerance left a racial support network intact, it offered little if any support for lesbians and the families they wanted to create.

Beyond this one overarching finding about how race shapes the coming-out process, the relationships that lesbians of color had with family support networks varied both by class and by mothering decision. Many working-class lesbians of color found that their families did not think that lesbians should be mothers. Those lesbians who wanted to become mothers and who had strong commitments to raising their children with community support found it hard to come out to their families. The lack of family and community support made the decision to mother a difficult one, one that delayed and sometimes deterred their decisions to become mothers.

In contrast to lesbians of color, my data on White lesbians point to how race and class privilege facilitated this group's ability to come out to, and be accepted by, their families of origin. Similar to lesbians of color, some White lesbians, particularly those from working-class backgrounds, also adhered to a practice of silent tolerance within their families of origin. Those who did choose to tell and come out found that their families were often neutral, not fully embracing their lesbian identities, but not rejecting them either. However, because they were privileged by race, White lesbians did not fear alienating communities of origin by coming out. Furthermore, they did not rely on communities of origin in the same way that lesbians of color did because White lesbians did not need those communities to protect them from racism.

Among the middle-class White lesbians I interviewed, coming out to family was perhaps stressful, but did not deter or delay mothering decisions. Although some of these lesbians followed a similar practice of silent tolerance to lesbians of color and working-class White lesbians, most middle-class White lesbians had positive experiences coming out to their families of origin, and therefore a supportive family network.

## DISCUSSION QUESTIONS

1. How do race and social class influence lesbians' decisions about coming out and about becoming mothers?
2. What does Mezey's reading imply about who has the privilege or right to become a parent in the United States? How could this situation be changed?

# 33

# How Tracking Undermines Race Equity in Desegregated Schools

## Roslyn Arlin Mickelson

*This reading is the first of three to focus on the social institution of education. Rosyln Arlin Mickelson, professor of sociology at the University of North Carolina–Charlotte, is one of the leading scholars in the sociology of education. This reading, "How Tracking Undermines Race Equity in Desegregated Schools," is an excerpt from Mickelson's chapter of the same title in the 2005 book* Bringing Equity Back: Research for a New Era in American Educational Policy, *edited by Janice Petrovich and Amy Stuart Wells. Mickelson uses a case study of schools in Charlotte, North Carolina, to survey the effects of racial desegregation in schools since* Brown v. Board of Education *in 1954. Mickelson reports on the history of desegregation in this school district before turning her attention to contemporary data. She finds structural inequalities in education based on race, including the presence of second-generation segregation that occurs in many schools through racial tracking.*

Beginning with the Supreme Court's declaration in *Brown* v. *Board of Education* (1954) that public schools separated by race are inherently unequal, school desegregation has played a central role in efforts to provide the equality of educational opportunity that is essential to the American dream. The rationale for school desegregation rests largely on claims that it improves minority students' access to the higher-quality education more often provided to Whites. For this reason, desegregation has been expected to improve both minorities' educational outcomes as well as their longer-term life chances. Consequently, since 1954, desegregation has been considered an essential tool in the struggle for race equity in education.

This chapter advances our understanding of the persistent barriers to equality of educational opportunity by presenting findings from a detailed case study of the relationship of school segregation and tracking to race equity in the Charlotte-Mecklenburg Schools (CMS)—a district that, prior to the end of its federal court order in 2002, was considered to be one of the nation's most successfully desegregated school systems. In this reading I raise questions about the extent to which CMS actually deserved that reputation. I demonstrate that curriculum tracking resegregated students within the district's high school classrooms, thereby subverting much of the potential academic gains from school desegregation at the school level. At the same time, this study compares achievement outcomes of students who attended segregated and desegregated schools, and demonstrates that racially diverse learning environments are clearly better than segregated ones. In other words, this chapter offers empirical support for the use of desegregation at both the school and classroom levels to close the racial gap and provide more equal educational opportunities . . . .

## WHY RACE EQUITY IN EDUCATION REQUIRES DESEGREGATED SCHOOLS AND CLASSROOMS

The relationship between school desegregation and classroom tracking often is discussed in terms of first- and second-generation segregation. First-generation segregation generally refers to the racial segregation among schools in the same district, and it has been the focus of national desegregation efforts since *Brown*. Second-generation segregation refers to the relationship between race and the allocation of educational opportunities within schools, typically brought about through curricular tracking of core academic classes in English, math, social

studies, and science. Black and Latino students are far more likely to be in the low-track classes, where their opportunities to learn are limited relative to high-track classes.

Any serious discussion of desegregation must include the topic of tracking. In theory, tracking is designed to enhance teaching and learning through targeting instruction and course content to the student's ability and prior knowledge. However, there is no consistent evidence that, as implemented, tracking is the best form of classroom organization for maximizing opportunities to learn for the majority of students. On the contrary, ample evidence suggests that tracking hinders mid- and low-ability students' opportunities to learn, while there is a growing body of evidence that diverse learning environments maximize opportunities to learn for all students. Moreover, as I noted above, track placements are strongly correlated with students' race/ethnicity and social class. In racially diverse schools White students typically are disproportionately found in the top tracks, while children of color are disproportionately found in the lower ones. In this way, tracking limits Blacks' access to higher-quality education. The federal courts recognized that tracking has the ability to undermine the potential benefits of policies, such as busing, designed to eliminate racial segregation among schools (*Hobson v. Hansen* 1967).

The fact that tracking can subvert potential gains from desegregation is very important for understanding the relationship between school desegregation policy and racial equity in education. There is considerable unambiguous evidence that desegregation positively affects minority students' long-term outcomes such as educational and occupational attainment (see Wells and Crain 1994, for a review). Yet the evidence with respect to desegregation's effects on short-term educational outcomes like achievement is more ambiguous and contested (see Crain and Mahard 1972). Design flaws in desegregation programs, their implementation, and many of the studies that evaluate them contribute to this ambiguity (see Crain and Mahard 1983). Another reason for the ambiguity is that much prior school desegregation research did not examine the ways in which segregated academic programs or tracks *within* desegregated schools affect race equity in academic outcomes.

The complicated relationships among race equity in education, desegregation, and tracking lie at the heart of this chapter in which I investigate their effects on the academic outcomes of students in the Charlotte-Mecklenburg Schools. CMS is an especially interesting district in which to study the effects of desegregation on the academic outcomes of students because of its pivotal role in school desegregation history. CMS's historical significance rests on its use of mandatory busing to desegregate its schools. This practice was upheld by the U.S. Supreme Court its 1971 decision, *Swann v. Charlotte-Mecklenburg Schools*. Since the mid-1970s, CMS has been considered one of the nation's premier desegregated school systems. For many years, CMS served as a model for other school systems of how to provide seemingly equitable, high-quality, desegregated public education using busing and other tools (Douglas 1995).

As of Spring 2002, however, the Charlotte-Mecklenberg Schools were no longer under federal court orders to desegregate. In 2001, the 4th Circuit Court of Appeals declared the district "unitary," or legally desegregated, and in 2002 the U.S. Supreme Court refused to hear the case, thereby leaving the Appeals Court's ruling in place. In Fall 2002, CMS began a student assignment policy based on neighborhood schools and parental choice. As a consequence of the new student assignment plan, levels of desegregation have decreased markedly since I collected the data for this study (see Mickelson 2003; Walsh 2002).

The return to a neighborhood school-based assignment plan makes this study highly relevant because it provides an assessment of the significance of the district's 3-decade-old effort to desegregate its schools. Indeed, what this study reveals is that despite CMS's laudable attempts to racially balance enrollment in its schools, the race gap in achievement persisted (Smith and Mickelson 2000). A central component of that gap is racially correlated curricular tracking. In 1997, when the survey data used in this study were collected, anyone familiar with the historical relationship between tracking and race who observed a math, science, social studies, or English classroom in any of CMS's regular high

schools or middle schools could accurately guess the academic level of the course simply by observing the racial composition of the students in it. Other key findings are:

- On a positive note, those Black (and White) students who experience desegregated education achieve more, have higher test scores, and hold higher future aspirations than their counterparts who experience segregated schooling.

- Yet 30 years after *Swann*, even though CMS was under a court order to eliminate all segregation from 1971 through 2002, both first-and second-generation segregation continued in the Charlotte-Mecklenburg Schools.

- Both forms of segregation harm academic achievement.

- The more time Black (and White) students spend in segregated Black elementary schools (first-generation segregation), the lower their high school track placements, grades, test stores, and future aspirations are compared with their comparably able peers who are educated in desegregated learning environments.

- Track placement (second-generation segregation) is influenced by a student's race as well as by degree of exposure to segregated Black elementary education. Black students are more likely to be in lower tracks than White students with comparable prior achievement, family background, and other individual characteristics, including self-reported effort.

- Track placement, in turn, has an extremely powerful effect on high school grades and scores on standardized tests, including the SAT.

- Resource differences between racially segregated and desegregated learning environments suggest some reasons why separate is not equal.

- The pattern of continuous segregation in spite of the 1971 Supreme Court *Swann* decision ordering the district to desegregate is important because CMS is considered by many to be one of the nation's most successfully integrated school systems. Thus, Charlotte's failure to *implement* desegregation and to provide equitable education for all children is reflective of our nation's inability to seriously address the roots of the race gap in academic achievement.

Using the Charlotte-Mecklenburg Schools as a case study, my research shows why racially segregated schooling is inimical to race equity in education. It demonstrates how the full desegregation mandated by the *Swann* decision was subverted by the continued existence of school segregation and the pervasive resegregation of secondary students into racially identifiable tracked math, science, English, and social studies classes.

Because of the persistence of the race gap in academic achievement, and the many questions raised about the efficacy of desegregation to improve the academic outcomes of Black students, the findings from Charlotte offer important insights for understanding why so many desegregation programs seem to offer minority students such limited redress from the inequality in educational opportunities mandated by *Brown*. At the same time, the chapter also demonstrates why desegregation is an essential element of educational equity. The more that CMS students—both Black and White—were exposed to truly desegregated education, the better were their academic outcomes . . . .

## A SURVEY OF HIGH SCHOOL STUDENTS

The research reported in this chapter is part of a 14-year-long case study of school reform in the Charlotte-Mecklenburg Schools. The results come from a survey of high school seniors I conducted in 1997. A random sample of about 50% of the 1997 graduating class answered questions about their family background, school experiences, attitudes toward education, and plans for the future. Their answers were combined with information provided by CMS on their grades, test scores, and educational histories . . . .

This study's design offers a number of advantages over previous research on the effects of desegregation.

Most important, my measure of the effects of segregation is unique in the history of desegregation research. It is an individualized longitudinal measure of the effects of segregation (from kindergarten through grade 6) on each student's academic outcomes. In contrast, cross-sectional studies of the effects of segregation examine the relationship of attending a segregated school to student achievement at the time when the student's achievement was measured. Also, the study utilizes an entire school system rather than a selection of schools isolated from the context of their larger societal and educational environments. Finally, the fact that CMS was under a mandatory desegregation order means there is minimal selection bias in either schools or students.

## LESSONS LEARNED

The findings can be grouped conveniently into five categories: (1) trends in first-generation segregation; (2) direct effects of first-generation segregation on academic outcomes; (3) indirect effects of first-generation segregation on outcomes; (4) effects of second-generation segregation on academic outcomes; and (5) why segregated schooling negatively affects academic outcomes and undermines educational equity and why desegregated education has positive effects.

### First-Generation Segregation

Although first-generation segregation in CMS was never fully eliminated, during the early 1980s, the district came very close to fulfilling the court's order to eliminate the dual system. By the late 1980s, however, the number of racially identifiable schools began to grow so that by the 1998–99 school year, about one-fourth of schools were racially imbalanced, Black or White, at the building level (Armor 1998; CMS 1970–1999; Mickelson 1998; Peterkin 1998; Smith 1998; Trent 1998).

In the early 1980s when CMS was approximately 38% Black, fewer than 5% of Black students attended schools whose Black enrollment exceeded court-mandated ceilings; in the mid- and late 1990s when

CMS was approximately 40% Black, the corresponding figure attending racially imbalanced Black schools was approximately 27% (Smith 1998). Ironically, this increase in school segregation at the building level occurred while Mecklenburg County became less residentially segregated than it was in 1971 (Lord 1999).

Until 2001, CMS was a majority-White school district. Court desegregation guidelines defined a school as racially imbalanced if it has fewer than 44% White students. Of the 1997 CMS seniors who participated in this study, 15% of Whites and 37% of Blacks had had some experience in segregated or racially imbalanced elementary schools that had Black student enrollments higher than the balanced schools . . . . )

### Direct Effects of School-Level Segregation

Attending a segregated Black elementary school has direct negative effects on achievement and track placement. Even after I hold constant a number of individual and family background characteristics, the statistical analyses (multilevel regression) indicate that the more time students—both Blacks and Whites—spend in segregated Black elementary schools, the lower are their 6th-grade California Achievement Test (CAT) and 12th-grade End of Course (EOC) scores. Segregated elementary school experiences also lower their high school track placement. Given that CAT scores, the measure of prior achievement I used, and high school track placement are the most powerful predictors of grades and high school test scores, elementary school segregation's negative impact on students' academic trajectories is noteworthy. These findings are summarized in Figure 33.1. The arrows from each factor in the model to the next indicate the causal paths, and the positive or negative signs above the path indicate the direction of the relationship. For example, the arrow with a negative sign from segregated elementary schooling to CAT scores indicates that the greater the proportion of a person's elementary education that took place in segregated schools, the lower were his or her CAT scores, controlling for the student's race, gender, family background, peer groups, attitudes toward education, effort, and so on.[1] Similarly, the arrows with negative signs from

segregated elementary education to high-track placement and grades, EOC, and SAT scores indicate that as time in the former increases, values of the latter decrease.

To be sure, the magnitude of the direct effects of elementary segregation on achievement is relatively small in comparison with the effects of track placement and prior achievement, the two most powerful influences on academic outcomes. What is relevant to our understanding of the effects of segregation, though, is that even after controlling for student and family background factors, elementary segregation still has a significant direct negative effect on both Black and White students' North Carolina EOC scores, the influential high-stakes standardized measure of what they have learned in high school.

### Indirect Effects of School-Level Segregation

In addition to the direct effects of segregated elementary education on test scores and track placement, it also has an indirect effect on academic outcomes. As noted earlier, CAT scores and track placement are the most powerful forces underlying EOC scores, high school grade point averages, and SAT scores. If one traces the pathways in Figure 33.1 from segregated elementary education to achievement outcomes, one must pass through track placement and CAT scores. This is the reason school-level segregation has an indirect negative effect on high school seniors' academic outcomes.

Taken together, the results presented in Figure 33.1 indicate the consistent pattern of direct and indirect negative effects of segregated Black elementary education on student achievement and track placement. Whether the measure of achievement is local (grade point average), statewide (North Carolina EOC), or national (CAT and SAT scores), the greater the proportion of a 12th grader's elementary education that took place in a segregated Black school, the lower are his or her grades, test scores, and high school track placement compared with otherwise similar students whose elementary education took place in desegregated environments. These findings are true for both Black and White students alike, but because Blacks are more likely to have learned in a segregated environment, the results have a particular salience for Black students' opportunities for educational equity.

FIGURE 33.1    Schematic Model of the Effects of Segregation on Academic Outcomes.

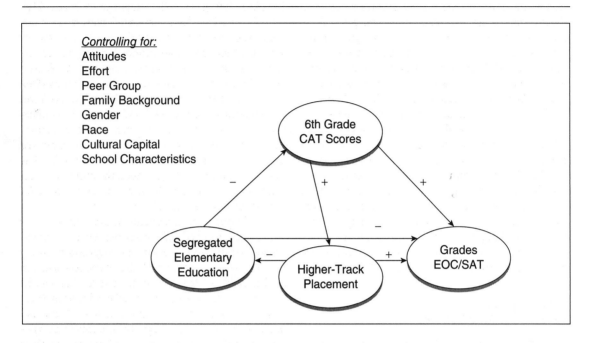

## Tracking, or Second-Generation Segregation

Tracking, or grouping that resegregates students within desegregated schools, is known as second-generation segregation. My analysis of the racial composition of all math, science, English, and social studies courses taken by the entire 1997 student high school population reveals that, within CMS high schools, courses were tracked.[2] In all CMS high schools, not only are core academic classes tracked, but irrespective of the racial composition of the schools— even within schools considered to be racially balanced—tracking resegregates students such that the lowest tracks (special education) are largely Black and the highest tracks (advanced placement and international baccalaureate) are overwhelmingly White. Thus, a majority of CMS high school students learned social studies, math, science, and English in racially imbalanced classrooms . . . . The most racially balanced discipline was English, with 46% of classes racially balanced, and the least was social studies, with only 37% racially balanced.[3] Given that track placement is a

powerful influence on high school grades, EOC scores, and SAT scores, the presence of racially imbalanced tracks is relevant to questions regarding the efficacy of school desegregation policies to enhance students' equality of educational opportunities.

One might argue that track assignments merely reflect technical decisions to allocate opportunities to learn commensurate with student merit, and that any correlations with student race are coincidental. But students' track assignments *are* related to their race: . . . Black students are disproportionately found in lower tracks while Whites are disproportionately found in higher tracks.

The relationship of a student's race to his or her likely track placement is also clear when I conducted a decile analysis comparing the 12th-grade English track placements of Blacks with those of academically similar Whites. For this comparison, I used CAT scores as a measure of prior achievement. I first divided students' 6th-grade CAT English battery scores into deciles. Next, I compared 12th-grade English track placements of Blacks and Whites whose 6th-grade CAT scores fell within the same decile range. If race does not affect track placement, Blacks and Whites within a given 6th-grade CAT score decile should have similar 12th-grade track placements. Yet I found that among students whose 6th-grade CAT English scores ranged from the 40th to 49th percentile, 56% of Whites compared with 74% of Blacks were placed in regular English. Among the best students—those with 6th-grade CAT scores between the 90th and 99th percentiles—52% of Whites but only 20% of Blacks were in advanced placement or international baccalaureate English.

The findings from the decile analysis, taken together with the regression analyses I described earlier, indicate that achievement or merit alone cannot explain track placement. They suggest that subjective judgments—influenced by students' ascribed characteristics of race, gender, and family background—affect track placements.[4]

## Why Segregation Undermines Educational Equity

There are specific reasons why segregated Black elementary schools and racially correlated lower tracks offer students fewer opportunities to learn. In Charlotte, as is true across the nation, segregated Black learning environments offer fewer material and teacher resources compared with desegregated ones. Both racially identifiable tracks and segregated Black schools suffer from similar teacher resource inequities. For example, Table 33.1 presents the correlations between percentage of Black students and various characteristics associated with teacher quality. Table 33.1 shows that the higher the percentage of Blacks in a school, the lower the percentage of the school's teachers who are fully credentialed, are experienced, and possess master's degrees (Mickelson 1998; Peterkin 1998; Smith 1998; Trent 1998).

Qualified, certified teachers are the most important resource available to children. Starkly different levels of material resources (up-to-date media centers, ample access to current technology, and newer buildings) are also related to the racial composition of a school, with fewer resources associated with

higher percentages of Black students (Gardner 1998; Peterkin 1998). In 1997, segregated Black high schools also had fewer advanced placement offerings, and racially identifiable Black elementary schools at all levels had proportionately fewer services for gifted and talented students (Mickelson 1998, Exhibit 1A-1H; Peterkin 1998). As late as 1999, racially identifiable Black high schools had far fewer formal classes and informal SAT preparation opportunities (after school, weekend, or at a Stanley Kaplan review course) than did either desegregated or racially identifiable White high schools. The fewer the Blacks in a high school, the more opportunities, both formal and informal, there are for SAT preparation (Mickelson 2003).

In addition to this, students in the highest tracks (academically gifted, advanced placement, international baccalaureate)—which are disproportionately White—are the most likely to have teachers who are credentialed and teaching in their field. Conversely, students in the lowest non-special education track (regular)—who are disproportionately Black—are much more likely to be taught by unlicensed, inexperienced instructors who are teaching out of their field. The consensus among the CMS high school

**TABLE 33.1**  Correlation Between Selected High School Characteristics and Percent African American in Student Population, Charlotte-Mecklenburg Schools, 1996–1998.

| Selected Characteristics of High Schools (N = 11) | Correlation with % African American in Student Population |
|---|---|
| % Gifted in Student Population | −.60 |
| % Teachers with Full Licensure | −.72 |
| % Teachers with MA Degree | −.43 |
| % Students on Free/Reduced Lunch | .95 |
| % ESL Students | .64 |

*Source*: Charlotte-Mecklenburg Schools, electronic data files, 1996–1998.

principals who were interviewed about tracking, race, and opportunities to learn is that while students in the lower tracks may have fully licensed and experienced teachers with advanced degrees, those in the highest tracks always do (Mickelson 1998–1999).

In CMS, then, access to the greatest number of opportunities to learn is strongly related to the racial composition of the elementary school a child attends and the level of the secondary track in which the student learns. For these reasons, and others I do not discuss here because of space considerations, it is not surprising that segregated Black educational settings offer fewer opportunities to learn, and that those who learn in these environments are less likely to succeed academically compared with peers educated in desegregated settings . . . .

## CONCLUSION

For more than 50 years, communities across the United States have grappled with *Brown*'s mandate to provide equality of educational opportunities to Black children—to all children—by ending segregated schooling. Yet despite significant narrowing in the past quarter-century, the Black-White gap in achievement that existed in 1954 continues today. And today, even thoughtful observers question the efficacy of school desegregation for closing that gap. Other critics lament the social, educational, and political fallout from it. They point to a host of adverse consequences to the Black community, including job losses, removal of cultural integrity in the curriculum, and destruction of extended caring communities that were integral to the well-being of Black children and their education during Jim Crow (Anderson 1998; Walker 2000). Although it is important to acknowledge these losses, it is also important to avoid romanticizing segregated Black schools. To do otherwise is to substitute an idealized conception of segregated education for the brutal realities of grossly inferior opportunities to learn that characterized segregated Black schools in Charlotte and elsewhere (Anderson 1988; Douglas 1995; Walker 2000).

As I pointed out earlier, while there is considerable unambiguous evidence that desegregation positively affects students' long-term outcomes, such as enhancing educational and occupational attainment, the situation with respect to short-term educational outcomes has been more ambiguous and contested. Contributing to the ambiguity are design flaws in many desegregation programs, in their implementation, and in the studies that evaluate them. Based on my findings, I suggest that one reason for previous studies' ambiguous conclusions regarding the academic benefits of desegregated schooling is that the studies typically did not examine whether second-generation segregation undermines the benefits of first- generation desegregation. My research does precisely this, and I find that second-generation segregation, in the form of tracking, undermines or subverts much of the potential of first-generation desegregation to close the racial gap in equity in educational opportunities and outcomes.

This study's distinctive design addresses many of the shortcomings found in previous research on the effects of desegregation. The unique design includes a longitudinal measure of exposure to segregated Black elementary education, multiple indicators of educational outcomes, measures of track location, numerous control variables, and a large representative sample of 12th graders from an entire school system. The fact that even with this conservative methodology the study demonstrates both direct and indirect effects from segregated education, indicates, to paraphrase Cornel West, that with respect to educational equity—race matters. This chapter, then, moves us toward a greater understanding of the contributions of segregated schooling to maintaining the racial gap in academic achievement, by demonstrating how first- and second-generation segregation jointly affect academic outcomes for all students, and how—even in an ostensibly desegregated school system—Whites retain privileged access to greater opportunities to learn.

At the same time, the findings offer hope. The results of the analyses also show clearly that for all those students who experienced it, desegregated education had a positive effect on their academic outcomes. Effectively implemented desegregation, then, is a prime example of a successful equity-minded reform. This is an especially important finding with regard to Black students. Both the scholarly and popular literature is replete with claims that desegregation fails to improve the academic achievement of Black students. The findings presented in this chapter demonstrate otherwise. They show that Black students educated in desegregated learning environments do better than their comparable peers schooled in segregated ones. This is true even when holding constant school- and individual-level factors such as family background, individual effort, peer group influence, attitudes toward education and the future, and prior achievement—social forces that typically confound the effects of desegregation.

The findings also suggest the importance, once again, of attending to educational policy implementation issues. The policy of desegregation—no matter how well crafted and designed—is of little value if it is unevenly implemented and if it coexists with other initiatives, policies, and practices—like tracking—that counteract or subvert desegregation's intent.

## DISCUSSION QUESTIONS

1. What does Mickelson mean by the term *second-generation segregation*? Why is this term significant in studying the institution of education in the United States?

2. How does Mickelson's study of Charlotte-Mecklenburg Schools (CMS) point out the major flaws of previous studies of the use of desegregation as a means of achieving racial equality? What is the role of tracking in subverting the gains of first-generation desegregation?

## NOTES

1. The effects of segregated Black elementary education on CAT scores are still important even though their level of significance is only slightly larger than that of conventional standards (p <.06). It is worth noting that the sample does not include a sizable portion of the CMS student population that is most likely to have had extended exposure to segregated Black elementary education—those who dropped out of school before reaching 12th grade and those who, as 12th graders, were enrolled in special education classes, special programs, and special high schools. Consequently, this regression model likely underestimates the effects of elementary segregation on CAT scores.

2. A CMS document showing the course name, track level, student count by race, period, and teacher name for every course offered in each of the 11 high schools provides the data for this analysis (CMS 1996–1999).

3. I considered a high school classroom to be racially balanced if its percentage of Black students lay within plus or minus 15% of the specific school's percentage of Black enrollment. This standard reflects an extrapolation to the classroom of the standard used to determine whether a school was racially balanced. The 38-page table that presents this analysis is available from the author upon request. It appeared as Exhibit A1-H1 in my expert report in the *Capacchione* case (Mickelson 1998).

4. Four years after I collected the survey data discussed in this chapter, CMS was still engaging in course selection and placement processes that resulted in comparably able Blacks and Whites being assigned to different tracks, with Blacks more likely than Whites to be in the lower ones . . . .

# 34

# THE SCHOOLING OF LATINO CHILDREN

LUIS C. MOLL

RICHARD RUIZ

*This reading by Luis C. Moll and Richard Ruiz, both education scholars, introduces us to the educational issues facing many Latino students in the United States. Similar to Mickelson in the previous reading, Moll and Ruiz use a case study approach when analyzing the structure and issues in contemporary education. While Mickelson investigated schools in Charlotte, North Carolina, Moll and Ruiz look at the Los Angeles Unified School District in California. After reviewing the history of educational issues facing the Latino population, Moll and Ruiz argue that education must be understood in relation to social class. This excerpt, taken from the 2009 collection* Latinos: Remaking America, *edited by Marcelo M. Suarez-Orozco and Mariela M. Paez, concludes with Moll and Ruiz arguing for "educational sovereignty" for Latino students, and they propose five strategies to help create positive social change in the institution of education.*

In perhaps no other domain of society is the growth of the Latino population in the United States more marked than in education. Latino students, along with African Americans, now constitute the majority in the principal urban school districts, and their growing presence is also becoming noticeable in rural schools (Young 1999). The purpose of this chapter is to summarize some major issues related to the schooling of Latino students in the United States, a challenging task given

*Source:* Moll, Luis C. and Richard Ruiz. 2009. "The Schooling of Latino Children." In *Latinos: Remaking America*, edited by Marcelo M. Suarez-Orozco and Mariela M. Paez. Reproduced with permission of University of California Press in the format textbook via Copyright Clearance Center.

the variability of this population, its wide geographic dispersal, and the complexity of the topic.[1] We start by providing an overview of the sociohistorical context of the education of Latino students, for it reveals issues of coercion and control that are still very much a part of the contemporary scene. This education must also be understood in relation to the social class characteristics of the population, because it is this factor, more than any other that determines the nature of their schooling.

In order to illustrate briefly the most pressing educational issues, we will develop a "case example" of one school district, the Los Angeles Unified School District (LAUSD), the second largest in the country. We claim that the issues revealed through this example arise in other regions of the country as well, although with much diversity in how they are manifested and addressed. We then propose the concept of "educational sovereignty" as a means of challenging the legacy of control and imposition that characterizes the education of Latino students in this country.[2] Educational sovereignty means that communities create their own infrastructures for development, including mechanisms for the education of their children that capitalize on rather than devalue their cultural resources. It will be their prerogative to invite others, including those in the academic community, to participate in such a creation. These forms of education must address Latino self-interest or self-determination, while limiting the influence of the Anglocentric whims of the majority that historically have shaped their schooling. We conclude this chapter by presenting some themes that may help shape any future educational-research agenda for Latino students.

## SOCIOHISTORICAL CONTEXT

Latinos have a varied history in the United States, and that variation has been used to explain their schooling achievement. Relatively recent immigrant groups from Central and South America and the Caribbean exhibit some of the characteristics posited by Ogbu and his colleagues (Gibson and Ogbu 1991) for immigrant groups historically: a sense of appreciation for their host country, a need to acculturate to a new set of norms and values, and allegiance to a political system that may require great adjustments on their part. Such groups may be expected to acquiesce to the expectation that they "become Americans" as quickly as possible, with the school as primary agent of the transformation. Although school achievement levels for these groups have in general been low, studies suggest variations depending on such factors as age on arrival, previous schooling experiences, the existence of social support networks within the receiving community, effort expended on studies, and social class (see, for example, Rumbaut 1999).

Other immigrant Latinos have higher achievement levels, both in school and in social mobility. This is especially true for Cubans, whose arrival in large numbers in this country (principally south Florida) coincided with the Cuban Revolution of the late 1950s. Although there was little in the way of a support infrastructure for them in place, their relatively high economic standing and (therefore) extensive schooling experience helped them create networks of support for themselves.[3] Moreover, and perhaps most important, their strong anticommunist sentiments fitted well with the emerging U.S. ideological phobias of that era. The U.S. interest in demonstrating the superiority of democratic capitalism over the socialist system compelled the government to promote and sustain (through the infusion of billions of dollars) social supports, including school programs that would ensure the new arrivals' success. It is not accidental that the first—and in some ways still the best—bilingual programs for Spanish speakers in public schools were developed in Dade County with the full blessing of the government and with support from local, state, and national agencies and foundations.

The situation is very different for two other major Latino groups, who have a much longer history in this country and by and large do not consider themselves "immigrants." Puerto Rico became a possession of the United States at the turn of the twentieth century (1898). The major migration to the mainland, primarily to New York City, commenced in the 1950s and extended, with considerable fluctuations, through the 1960s and beyond; thus Puerto Ricans became the dominant Latino population of the northeastern coast of the United States (Carrasquillo and Sánchez-Korrol 1996; Rodríguez 1995). The status of Puerto Ricans as citizens has been tenuous from the beginning and remains contentious today, given the continuing U.S. colonial domination and ongoing discussions of statehood or independence for the island. In general, Puerto Ricans in the United States have had low school achievement and socioeconomic mobility (Nieto 1999).

Similarly, Mexican Americans (or Chicanos) also exhibit low achievement and mobility (García 1995). Their history in North America predates that of any other Latino group, a fact that is not lost on many within the community (Gutierrez 1995). Upon the signing of the Treaty of Guadalupe-Hidalgo in 1848, Mexicans became Mexican Americans with the stroke of a pen. The treaty gave this country nearly half of Mexico's territory, what are now the states (or parts thereof) of Texas, New Mexico, Arizona, Colorado, Utah, Nevada, and California. As Anglo Americans occupied the new territories, motivated by the mining for gold in California and the rapid spread of railroad lines and commerce, the ideology of white supremacy followed, under the philosophical guise of "manifest destiny," providing justification for the displacement not only of lands and property but also of language and culture (Vélez-Ibáñez 1997).

The schools played an important role in facilitating the Anglo American dominance of new territories, in both the occupation of the Southwest and the colonization of Puerto Rico. In the Southwest, the schools used two primary methods of social control, both intended to preserve the status quo by denying the Mexican population the knowledge necessary to protect its political and economic rights and to advance economically in society (see Spring 1997:82–89). One method was exclusion from schooling, which entailed not enforcing the compulsory school laws. The second method (more relevant for our present purposes) was to control the content and purpose of schooling. Public officials wanted Mexican children in schools but segregated so that they could be controlled and indoctrinated—so that they could be "Americanized," learn English, and rid

themselves of their native language and customs, which the officials deemed detrimental to assimilation and to the maintenance of a unified nation. This strategy springs from the same ideology used to justify the separate schooling of Indian and African American children. And it is the same strategy pursued today in California and other states through initiatives designed to eliminate bilingual education, to impose a highly controlled English monolingual education, and to make it illegal to use languages other than English in school.

This dual strategy of exclusion and condemnation, divesting Latino students of their primary resources—their language and culture—is what Valenzuela (1999) has called "subtractive schooling." This form of schooling has become a major feature of the education of poor and working-class Latino students all over the country. It results in disdain for what one knows and what one is, influences children's attitudes toward knowledge, and undermines their personal competence. That is, subtractive schooling creates a social distance between the students and the world of school knowledge. It creates the impression that someone else possesses great knowledge and expertise, whereas, in contrast, one is unskilled and incompetent—that one's language and knowledge are inadequate because they are not privileged (formalized and accorded special status) by the school. This mind-set (the superiority of the other and the inferiority of one's own) is accepted as "natural," as just the way things are. It is considered "common sense," and it easily becomes self-imposed (cf. Banks 1994).

Consequently, some students even appropriate the ideology that learning English at all costs is the way to guarantee success in life. The result is the great illusion of American education: that to learn English (and have academic success), it is necessary to shed Spanish and the intimate social relations created through that language. The logical extension of this ideology is the overwhelming obsession, as manifested in the schools and in the current laws in various states, with teaching the children English "as quickly as possible," *to the detriment of critical subject matter learning*. As a consequence, we are left with the impression that these children are either unable or unwilling to learn English, although all recent studies suggest otherwise (López 1999; Rumbaut 1999).

Our claim, then, is that the control and coercion exemplified by subtractive forms of schooling are a major feature of the schooling of Latino students, especially given their working-class status. Further, the pervasiveness of this form of schooling is reinforced by both current educational policies and language ideologies about English and Spanish. We now turn to an example from LAUSD to illustrate these issues in a contemporary urban context.

## LOS ANGELES: A PROTOTYPE OF ISSUES

The Los Angeles metropolitan area has undergone major demographic shifts during the last two decades, most prominently the increase of the Latino population, both immigrant and U.S.-born, and of other immigrant populations. Rumbaut (1998) has estimated that 62 percent of the population of Los Angeles County, or approximately 6 million people, are of "immigrant stock," most of them Latinos. A current estimate is that the Latino population of the city and county of Los Angeles ranges from 40 to 45 percent of the total population. In the county this percentage represents a total of about 4,240,000 people, the majority population of Los Angeles, and about 40 percent of them are of school age (from birth to ages seventeen); moreover, about 63 percent of young children (from birth to age five) in the county are Latinos (Children Now 1999).

The great majority of this population, be they recent immigrants or of second-generation or other vintage, is working-class or poor (Ong and Blumenberg 1996). In fact, Ortíz (1996) has suggested that because of broader social and economic factors, the Mexican-origin population of Los Angeles, which is approximately 80 percent of the overall Latino population, may be mired in a "permanent" low working-class status (cf. Myers 1998). This low socioeconomic standing has major implications for the schooling of children, an issue to which we shall return.

The Latino student population of the Los Angeles Unified School District (LAUSD), according to state data (1998–1999), numbers approximately half a million students (480,655), or 69 percent of the total student population; the Anglo student population is 10.5 percent (73,321).[4] Therefore, this school district is approximately 90 percent "minority," if such a term is still applicable. Furthermore, 74 percent of students in the district are eligible for free or reduced-cost lunch services, an index of poverty. In addition, of the total number of students in the district (695,885), approximately half (45.9 percent) are designated as limited-English-proficient (LEP), about 300,000 of these students being Spanish speakers. Nearly all of these LEP students (95 percent) are in the free or reduced-cost lunch program; hence they are among the poorest students in the district.

The teaching corps, however, remains largely white (49.4 percent), with 23.6 percent Latino and 14.7 percent African American members. Statewide, we should point out, the discrepancies are larger: the Latino student population is at 41 percent (37.8 percent are white), whereas 76.2 percent of teachers are white and only 12.1 percent are Latinos. Thus Latinos constitute the majority of students at LAUSD and statewide, and they are largely working-class and poor, but the teaching corps is primarily white and middle-class—and English monolingual as well.[5]

The academic performance of the Latino students is generally low. The dropout rate (grades 9–12) for Latinos, and for African Americans, exceeds 20 percent, a figure that also reflects the national trend. In addition, the national percentile rank of test scores for all Latino students (collectively) is considerably below the national average, even when the LEP scores are excluded. These high dropout rates and low achievement rates are a consistent finding in all school districts nationally that have comparable socioeconomic profiles. However, within LAUSD, even taking this profile into account, about 41 percent of the Latino students (46 percent for all students in the district; 30 percent countywide) who graduate are eligible for entrance into the University of California or California State University system. This percentage is clearly a positive development, although the white graduates' percentage of eligibility is much higher at 57 percent, a significant difference.

In addition to these general characteristics of the district, there are other interrelated issues that help capture the Gestalt of the educational situation of Latino students in this district and, by implication, elsewhere in the country as well.[6] We will mention only two of them for illustration purposes. The most recent is the passage (on June 2, 1998) of Proposition 227 banning bilingual education. This proposition is part of an insidious pattern of oppressive actions aimed at Latinos—maneuvers that have successfully circumvented legislative channels where Latinos may hold some leverage, especially in California (Santoro 1999). The extent to which this proposition represents a quasicolonial imposition on the Latino population of Los Angeles is made clear by the following figures: 68 percent of Latinos in Los Angeles favor bilingual education; this figure increases to 88 percent when respondents are limited to those parents with children in the classrooms of the city (Crawford 1999). Consider the coercive ideological context that such a law perpetuates, establishing Spanish as a pariah language in the schools, privileging English exclusively, and demonstrating clearly how only the interests that an elite Anglo monolingual community deems worthwhile can be represented in the schools.

A second issue is the prominence of reductionist pedagogies as illustrated by the phonics reading mandates. These mandates require, under penalty of law, employing English-language phonic drills as the *only* way to teach beginning reading, usually as part of a highly rigid and prescriptive packaged curriculum imposed on teachers and students. The intent is to reduce or eliminate teacher autonomy by dictating what and how they teach. This includes reducing any flexibility teachers might otherwise have to develop meaning-based literacy innovations to help the students. This reading agenda, which excludes all but certain forms of positivist research from funding and marginalizes all those who do not toe the ideological line of a particular model of reductionist reading research (Allington and Haley 1999; Taylor 1998), also removes the possibility of biliteracy approaches that have great promise for bilingual children.

The key point is that these are not just isolated issues that coincide. It is vital to recognize the organized political forces that guide these activities as part of a broader ideological coalition and an urgent agenda to control schools. Our claim is that this situation, whatever varied form it takes, represents several steps backward for Latino students in the United States—a population that is overwhelmingly working-class and poor, is growing demographically, and is daily suffering the consequences of increasing numbers and its low position in the social order.

## EDUCATIONAL SOVEREIGNTY

In what follows we present two promising responses to the encapsulation of schooling by dominant policies, practices, and ideologies. We use the term *educational sovereignty* to capture the need to challenge the arbitrary authority of the white power structure to determine the essence of education for Latino students. In particular, we emphasize the type of agency that considers the schooling of Latino children within a larger education ecology and that respects and responds to the values of education possessed by Latino families (see Goldenberg and Gallimore 1995; Ruiz 1997). This larger ecology includes not only the schools but also the social relationships and cultural resources found in local households and other community settings.

The emphasis is on challenging the ideological and structural constraints that are so dominant in the schooling of Latino children through a strategic and vigorous agency that builds on the culturally grounded resources of children, families, and communities.

### Mediating Institutional Arrangements

One line of study is the reorganization of the schooling experience itself to mediate ingrained structural constraints. An important example is provided by the work of Mehan and colleagues (Mehan et al. 1996) on a teacher-initiated innovation, a three-year "untracking" program known as AVID (Advancement via Individual Determination). This work featured two key elements. One was the placement of students within a regular academic track, requiring that they take courses that lead to college admission. A second element was providing the "social scaffolds" necessary to ensure that the students would succeed within these courses (cf. Lee and Smith 1999). In particular, this social support included rigorous, weekly academic tutoring, with explicit instruction on note taking, test taking, and study strategies. It also included teacher advocacy on the students' behalf, the creation of social networks that facilitated acquiring the knowledge and wherewithal necessary to deal with the school culture, and acquaintance of the students with the procedural knowledge they needed to deal with college applications and admission.

Another central factor in the success of the Latino (and African American) low-income students was the development of an "academic identity." This identity featured the formation of academically oriented associations among students, while dealing with potentially incompatible social identities and relationships. Just as important, both students and teachers developed a "critical consciousness" about race, class, and school politics and about resistance to the innovation as manifested either in or out of school (see Hubbard and Mehan, in press). In all, of the sample ($n = 248$) studied by Mehan and his colleagues in San Diego, 88 percent graduated to a college education (48 percent in four-year colleges, 40 percent in two-year colleges), with the highest proportion of college attendance among the students from low-income and working-class families.

Other examples of school-based changes to provide additive forms of schooling for Latino students include "maintenance" bilingual education and dual-language programs (Brisk 1998), the school reorganization research of Goldenberg and Sullivan (1994), and the dual-language school in Tucson documented by Smith (2000).

### Activating Cultural Resources

There are forms of schooling that deliberately attempt to build upon the resources of the students and their communities in doing academic work. One example is our collaborative research on "funds of knowledge," those bodies of knowledge developed socially and historically by households. This work, which was conducted mostly in working-class, Latino neighborhoods and schools in Tucson, Arizona, has been particularly successful in helping teachers approach, understand, and define their school's community in terms of these funds of knowledge (Moll and González 1997; Mercado and Moll 1997). The teachers in these studies visit their students' households to learn from the families; they are convinced that it is of great value to understand the ways in which people generate knowledge as they engage in life. This work by implication debunks the preconception that working-class Latino households lack worthwhile knowledge and experiences, replacing it with the assumption that the knowledge and experiences of the children and their families can be identified, documented, and accessed for teaching. This view of households as possessing valuable resources for learning changes radically how the students are perceived, talked about, and taught.

Other work features schools with curricula that critically engage community needs and realities (Rivera and Pedraza 2000) and the creation of alliances between teachers and families in support of schooling (Delgado-Gaitán 1990) Still other innovations feature community-based alliances among social and educational institutions to create nonschool settings for the learning and development of children and adults. Outstanding efforts include those of Vásquez (1994) and Gutiérrez, Baquedano-López, and Alvarez (in press). There are also community-based settings especially created for the personal and intellectual development of women . . . .

## ANTICIPATING RESEARCH THEMES

In this final section we project three themes that might help shape a future educational agenda for Latino students. These themes emphasize the need to create strategic alliances in enhancing the educational landscape of these students, especially in the changing demographic context of the United States, and the need to stimulate new theoretical thinking about educational issues.

## Interethnic Coalitions

The character and dimension of the schooling of Latinos should be analyzed not independently, as is usually the case, but rather in relation to the situation of African American children, for they share similar political environments and colonial forms of education. Clearly, the degree of similarity may vary considerably with the urban area, the political and economic history and arrangements, and the specific social issues that arise. Just as clearly, however, education is an issue that lends itself to intergroup analysis and action, because schools remain crucial institutions for both Latino and African American communities.

## Transnational Dynamics

This issue reflects one of the most important developments in Latino communities across the country. It refers to the proliferation of social networks that facilitate more or less continuous links between the society of origin and the society where the immigrants have settled. Although they are not a new phenomenon, these transnational communities may have a new character given the large number of people involved and, especially, the new modes of communication.

The social, economic, or political activities that these international social networks facilitate may have implications for the formation of identities and for education. One such effect may be the creation of a strong "linguistic marketplace" where language proficiency is seen as real capital in the global economy, thus establishing the desirability of bilingualism and biliteracy for all populations, but especially for Latinos (Fradd 1999; Skutnabb-Kangas 1999). In a sense, these transnational activities extend the borders of the countries in question, and in this context, Latinos in the United States are hardly a minority. Instead, they are part of a much larger and international community.

## Linguistic Human Rights

The last few years of the twentieth century saw a virtual explosion in scholarly interest in the issue of how to extend rights to language-minority communities, especially those in large, multinational states (Kontra et al. 1999). Although this interest emerged most dramatically out of concern for saving the world's dying indigenous languages (Krauss 1992), it has been broadened to portray the language rights of immigrant and other minority communities as essential civil rights, regardless of the status of the languages (Hernández-Chávez 1995). This will surely be a matter of great concern with respect to Latinos in the United States as the Spanish-speaking population grows to be the largest minority group in the country.

## CONCLUSION

The discussion of the schooling of Latino students that is presented in this chapter is designed to provide an overview of the sociohistorical context of this schooling, and a summary of the most important contemporary issues that help perpetuate disabling pedagogical conditions. In response, we proposed the concept of educational sovereignty as the mediating agency needed to challenge such conditions. This educational sovereignty must (1) attend to the larger historical structures and ideologies of schooling, with the goal of making educational constraints, especially those related to social class, visible and unstable, (2) teaching and learning as part of a broader education ecology, and (3) tap into existing social and cultural resources in schools, households, and communities in promoting change.

We are well aware of the difficulty of the task for those who want to change the fortunes of schooling for Latino children. Concerted efforts, combined with the disposition to challenge the constraining ideologies and practices that characterize the educational status quo for Latino children, are the minimal requirements to produce such change.

## DISCUSSION QUESTIONS

1. According to Moll and Ruiz, what are some of the problems with the schooling of Latinos in the United States? Are these structural-level or individual-level problems?

2. What are the solutions that Moll and Ruiz suggest to reduce racial-ethnic inequalities in schools? Can you think of other solutions?

## Notes

1. For present purposes, we limit our comments to K–12 schooling in public schools.
2. Our use of the term *educational sovereignty* was inspired by the work of colleagues doing research in and with indigenous communities (such as Warner 1999).
3. There has been considerable variation, especially in terms of social class, in the different waves of Cuban immigration (Pedraza 1996); we are referring here to the dominant, first wave of wealthy and highly educated refugees.
4. Unless otherwise indicated, all LAUSD figures are from the California State Department of Education Web site. See goldmine.cade.gov and ed-data.k12.ca.us /dev/ District.asp.
5. The middle-class status of the teachers is an estimate based on their reported salaries and levels of education. LAUSD teachers must be college graduates, and they earn between $32,569 (entry level) and $61,169. Source: certificated.lausd.k12.ca.us/cert/info/Teaching_in_L.A./ teaching_in_l.a..html.
6. There are several important issues that we do not discuss for lack of space, such as differential school financial resources by social class, school segregation, tracking, disproportionate special-education referrals, bias in high-stakes testing, violence, and harassment by immigration officials. All of these issues form part of the daily reality of the schooling of Latino children.

# 35

# CLASS MATTERS

PETER SACKS

*This final reading in the section on the institution of education is by Peter Sacks, an author, economist, essayist, and social critic. This excerpt, taken from Sacks's 2007 book,* Tearing Down the Gates: Confronting the Class Divide in American Education, *challenges societal notions that the institution of education is a meritocracy in which anyone can succeed. Using statistical data as evidence, Sacks considers educational attainment differences by social class and compares them to gender and race inequalities in education. Sacks makes the case that college educational inequality is mostly social class–based: the race gap and gender gap are not as pronounced. In particular, Sacks also examines two contemporary educational debates about whether community colleges are making a difference for lower socioeconomic classes and whether elite colleges base their admissions more on merit or on family background.*

In the past few decades, the controversies over affirmative action in higher education have preoccupied America's debates about equal educational opportunity. This battle led to feverish public and media attention in the summer of 2003, when the U.S. Supreme Court finally entered the affirmative action fray for the first time in a quarter century. In *Grutter v. Bollinger*, a case involving the University of Michigan's law school, the Court in a 5–4 vote upheld the use of affirmative action in the school's admissions policy. Justice Sandra Day O'Connor's majority opinion largely turned on the question of the educational benefits of having a diverse student body at the law school. That was an important educational goal, O'Connor argued, because the University of Michigan law school, like similar elite programs across the country, served as a training ground for the nation's future leaders.[1]

*Source:* Sacks, Peter. 2007. "Class Matters" Ch. 6 in *Tearing Down the Gates: Confronting the Class Divide in American Education.* Reproduced with permission of University of California Press in the format textbook via Copyright Clearance Center, and the author.

But in a separate opinion involving the University of Michigan's undergraduate college, *Gratz v. Bollinger*, the Court in a 6–3 vote struck down that institution's admissions system, arguing that its affirmative action plan placed too much emphasis on race. In a subsequent interview with the *Chronicle of Higher Education*, the University of Michigan president, Mary Sue Coleman, announced that the university would create a new undergraduate admissions system in response to the *Gratz* ruling that "continues our commitment to a richly diverse student body."[2] But even as Coleman was talking expansively about diversity, the university's commitment to diversity was, in practice, rather narrow. In fact, around the time Coleman made that statement, only 12.6 percent of Michigan's undergraduate students were eligible for Pell Grants, the federal aid program for students from families with low and modest incomes. In contrast, about 31 percent of undergraduates at all public universities were eligible for the low-income grants. Although Michigan is one of the nation's most prestigious public universities, its limited commitment to social class diversity put it on a par with highly selective private universities.[3]

The virtual silence of educational leaders on the question of social class inequities at their institutions has been particularly curious in light of the critical trends in higher education over the past thirty or forty years. During that time, not only has social class been a generally more intractable problem of equal educational opportunity than gender or race, but America's higher education system has also become more dangerously stratified by social class.

After the Second World War, the higher education system expanded rapidly, fueled first by the GI Bill, then later by the Baby Boom generation, and, perhaps most important, by the political will among national leaders to open up educational opportunities to segments of American society which had been excluded in the past. Given the growing political strength of previously disenfranchised groups, particularly women and minorities, and their demands to level the educational playing field, national leaders had little choice. Since 1970, the nation has experienced a staggering transformation in the opportunity structure for women and, to a lesser extent, for minorities as well.

But the opportunity gaps between advantaged and disadvantaged social classes in the United States have *not* lessened over the past thirty years. In fact—though one might not know it, given the nation's focus on the affirmative action remedy—disparities between social classes have significantly worsened on several dimensions of educational opportunity. From reading achievement in high school to enrollment in graduate and professional schools, educational inequalities along gender, racial, and ethnic lines have significantly diminished. At the same time, educational gaps have widened between students of affluent backgrounds and those of low and modest economic means.

To the extent that educational inequities remain between American minority groups and Caucasians, many—though certainly not all—of these disparities are rooted in persistent inequalities of social class: family income; parental education level; and other social, cultural, and economic circumstances that shape children's lives. All these we may sum up as features of one's social class background.[4]

For example, in terms of high school achievement, social class disparities continue to surpass those of gender and race, according to national statistics compiled by the U.S. Department of Education. In 1972, young women achieved slightly less than males in reading. That gap was eliminated by 1982. By 1992, girls' reading achievement surpassed that of boys. Over the same two decades, though reading and math achievement gaps hardly disappeared, both African Americans and Hispanics steadily improved relative to whites.[5]

Despite these improvements along gender and racial lines, school achievement gaps between rich students and poor ones—already sizable—worsened between 1972 and 1992. Even among those high school seniors who tested at the highest levels of academic achievement, the gaps by social class are far more pronounced than those by gender and race. If we look at students who scored in the highest quartile of academic achievement, for instance, equal percentages of girls and boys were performing at this level. Whites tested in the highest quartile at about four times the rate of blacks (32 percent versus 8 percent). But students from the highest socioeconomic group scored in the highest quartile at almost eight times the rate of students from the lowest socioeconomic group (50 percent versus 6.5 percent).[6]

A similar pattern holds when we look at the number of high school seniors enrolled in an academic track curriculum that prepared them for college. In 1972, fewer girls than boys were on the academic track; but by 1992, the percentage of girls surpassed that of boys. Blacks and Hispanics also showed significant improvement during the twenty-year period. But while the lower socioeconomic groups improved slightly on this measure, their disadvantage compared to their more affluent peers far exceeded the gender and racial gaps. In fact, in 1992, fully 63 percent of students in the highest socioeconomic group were enrolled in the academic track—35 percentage points more than the lowest socioeconomic group. In contrast, whites and blacks, who had been 16 percentage points apart in 1972, differed by only 7 percentage points in academic track enrollment by 1992.[7]

For all the fury over former Harvard president Lawrence Summers's off-the-cuff conjectures in early 2005 regarding the supposed inferior performance of women in the upper reaches of academic science,[8] it may be only a matter of time before Summers is simply proved wrong by the sheer force of history. Among the most significant changes in the landscape of educational opportunity over the past thirty years has been the democratization of a "college-going culture" for previously underrepresented groups, particularly women.

In the 1970s, Mary Tyler Moore was a novelty on the television screen, playing a young professional woman trying to bust into the world of male-dominated broadcasting. A decade later, Candice Bergen's Murphy Brown ran the newsroom. By the close of the twentieth century, the same Candice Bergen was playing the power broker, a senior partner in a powerful Boston law firm, calling the shots from behind the scenes in *Boston Legal*. And that's just TV, though the cultural symbolism remains profound. In real life, women were managing Fortune 500 companies, running the U.S. State Department, and legitimately contending for the office of president of the United States. All of which required, at a minimum, a bachelor's degree—and by

the 1990s, women were significantly more likely than men to expect to earn a bachelor's degree and to take the necessary steps to do so.

What's more, in terms of who expected to go to college and who actually applied to college, the differences between whites and most minorities declined to negligible quantities. For example, when high school seniors in 1992 were asked about their expectation of graduating from college, the white-black gap had shrunk to just 3 percentage points, and the white-Hispanic difference had declined to 9 percentage points. However, the expectations gap along class lines dwarfed these modest differences by race. Indeed, a 50-point expectations gap existed between seniors from the highest and lowest socioeconomic groups, and a 26-point difference remained between the highest and the middle social classes.[9]

If one doesn't apply to college, one naturally can't go to college. In 1992, 45 percent of high school seniors from the lowest social class group submitted at least one college application. That compared to 58 percent from the middle socioeconomic group and 79 percent from the highest group. On average, 60 percent of seniors submitted at least one college application. Even among seniors who scored in the highest quartile on achievement tests, who would presumably be college-bound, the differences among the social classes are astonishing. Indeed, 34 percent of students from the lowest social class with high test scores filed no college applications, compared with just 8 percent of seniors from the highest social class. In contrast, the difference between whites and blacks on this dimension had become almost trivial.[10]

Furthermore, the social class inequities in educational attainment have largely proven much more difficult to remedy than the gender or racial gaps (see Figure 35.1). For example, on average, 26 percent of students surveyed as eighth graders in 1988 had earned a bachelor's degree by the year 2000. Males earned BAs at slightly less than the average rate, and females at slightly more than average. The gaps between whites and blacks and between whites and Hispanics in the attainment of bachelor's degrees were significant, at 14 percentage points and 16 percentage points, respectively. But consider the social class differences. Fifty percent of eighth graders whose parents had gone to college earned BAs, compared to only 11 percent of those whose parents were not college-educated—a gap of 39 points. The chasm between eighth graders from the highest social class and the lowest was a staggering 44 percentage points.[11]

Even once students begin college, the racial and gender gaps in attaining bachelor's degrees are far less than the differences along class lines. According to the National Center on Education Statistics, which surveyed beginning college students in 1989–1990 and followed up four years later, about 27 percent of white students completed their BA degrees within four years, compared to about 17 percent and 18 percent of black and Hispanic students, respectively. However, 41 percent of affluent college students completed their degrees in four years, compared to just 6 percent of low-income students.[12]

The unfortunate fact of the matter is this: a wealthy low-achiever in America has a significantly greater chance of attending a four-year university than a highly accomplished student from a lower-income family. According to U.S. Department of Education data, for instance, 77 percent of students from the highest socioeconomic quartile who score in the lowest quartile on high school achievement tests go to college. In contrast, 63 percent of students from the lowest socioeconomic quartile who score in the highest quartile on achievement tests attend college.[13]

None of this is to suggest, however, that class and race can be separated or that racial equality of educational opportunity is a done deal in American higher education. The fact is that class and race continue to overlap to an astonishing degree in American society, a fact that bears heavily on who gets a college education in this country. According to the U.S. Census Bureau, the median income of white families with college-age children in 2003, at $62,900, was approaching twice the $36,700 income of a black family.[14]

. . . Such differences in income and wealth, reinforced by differences in cultural and social capital between rich and poor families, produce staggering inequalities in children's educational aspirations and achievement. Because too many minority children grow up in families that bear the brunt of low-paying jobs and high levels of unemployment, the odds are stacked heavily against their graduating from high school, being admitted to a university, finding the money to pay for college, and then, finally, graduating with a bachelor's degree. Indeed, underrepresented minorities made up 26 percent of high school graduates in 2001, and yet they constituted just 10.8 percent of the enrollments at the fifty flagship state universities.[15]

Consider, for example, the persistently slow progress of black males in American higher education. The glacial pace of their progress is especially pronounced at the nation's flagship public universities, according to a 2006 report by the Joint Center for Political and Economic Studies, a Washington, D.C., think tank. In its analysis of federal education data, the center found that, while college-age black males made up almost 8 percent of the U.S. population, they constituted just 2.8 percent of undergraduate enrollments at the fifty flagship state universities. Shaun R. Harper, a researcher at Pennsylvania State University's Center for the Study of Higher Education and author of the report, told the *Chronicle of Higher Education*, "Given all of the institutional rhetoric regarding access to equity, multiculturalism, and social justice, I just see next to no evidence of those espoused values being enacted on behalf of black male undergraduates."[16]

I had a conversation with an independent college counselor who advises students from elite private high schools who are working on their college applications. When I mentioned the word "stratification" to describe the opportunity structure of American higher education, he responded with what I have found to be a common objection: "Well, when you say 'stratified,' people complain about something being elitist, and everything in our society has an element of elitism to it," he told me. "It is very easy for anyone in the United States who wants to get a college education to get one—and to get one at a reasonably inexpensive price. Community colleges are open to anyone for the first two years. They are open admission, and they are relatively cheap. And there are state universities, and there are local private schools that pretty much accept almost

FIGURE 35.1    1988 Eighth Graders Who Earned BAs by 2000, by Demographic Group.

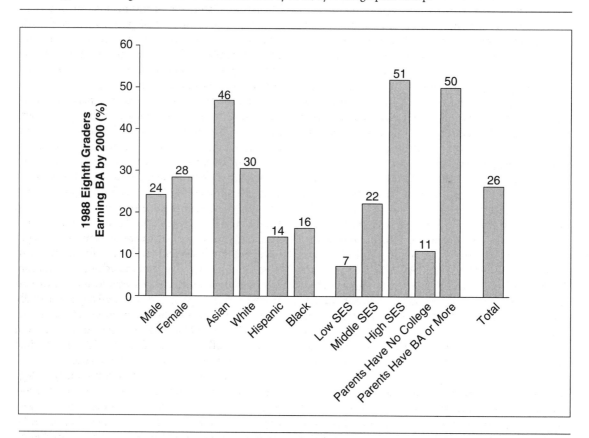

*Source:* U.S. Department of Education, National Center for Education Statistics, *Coming of Age in the 1990s: The Eighth-Grade Class of 1988, 12 Years Later,* by Steven J. Ingels, T. R. Curtin, Phillip Kaufman, Martha Naomi Alt, Xianglei Chen, and Jeffrey A. Owings, NCES 2002–321 (Washington, D.C.: U.S. Government Printing Office, 2002).

everyone who applies. We have an enormous spectrum from which to choose, which doesn't exist in any other country."[17]

Indeed, America's vaunted system of higher education is an institution worthy of immense pride for many people. Between 1965 and 2003, the number of colleges and universities grew by 92 percent. Public community colleges alone ballooned 171 percent during that period. These open-access institutions enrolled 17 percent of all college and university students in 1965; four decades later, they enrolled almost 40 percent of all students in higher education. The number of four-year colleges and universities

also increased, growing 51 percent for private institutions, and 55 percent for public ones.[18]

The American higher education system resembles a pyramid, consisting of a relatively few highly desirable and selective institutions at the top, a sizable number of moderately selective institutions in the middle, and a far larger number of nonselective community colleges at the base. It's the sheer size and variety of colleges and universities that observers often point to when they suggest that American higher education is a relatively free, open, and egalitarian enterprise. But the massive expansion of the system, especially at the bottom of the pyramid, along with America's apparently flexible system of individual consumer choice among a myriad of public and private institutions, has masked the tightening rigidity of the system as a whole along class lines.

It seems hard to fathom, given our generally optimistic views of educational opportunity, but the chance of getting a bachelor's degree by age twenty-four has improved *only for those who come from families in the upper half of the nation's income distribution.* In 1970, about 6 percent of high school graduates from families in the lowest income quartile obtained a bachelor's degree by their twenty-fourth birthday. This statistic essentially flatlined in subsequent decades: in 2002, it remained at just 6 percent. The number of students from lower-middle-class families (in the lower middle income quartile) who attained their BAs also stagnated during this period. In contrast, students from upper-middle-income families (in the upper middle income quartile) saw their prospects for earning a BA nearly double, from 14.9 percent to 26.8 percent. Prospects for those from the highest-income families improved from 40 percent to more than 50 percent.[19]

Perhaps the most glaring aspect of this stratification is the growing concentration of poor and working-class people at the bottom of the educational pyramid, in community colleges and, increasingly, in proprietary schools (colleges that primarily serve older students who return to college later in life, such as the University of Phoenix). In 2002, community colleges, which at that time enrolled more than 43 percent of all undergraduates in the country, also housed almost 40 percent of all recipients of Pell Grants.[20] In contrast, four-year colleges and universities have become more exclusive domains for America's middle and upper-middle classes. In the early 1970s, public four-year institutions enrolled 40 percent of all Pell Grant students; but by 2001, this figure had dropped to 31 percent. Private four-year institutions enrolled 22 percent of Pell Grant students in the early 1970s but only about 13 percent a quarter century later. By 2002, proprietary institutions served a larger share of low-income students than private four-year colleges and universities.

"What is emerging is a postsecondary education opportunity system based on economic class in the United States," says education policy analyst Thomas Mortenson. "Students born into low-income families face a narrowing set of postsecondary choices. They are increasingly concentrated in community colleges, while students from more affluent family backgrounds are concentrated in four-year public and private colleges and universities."[21]

Community colleges represent a particular contradiction, in terms of creating meaningful educational opportunity for disadvantaged groups. Admirably, such two-year colleges have, by definition, greatly expanded access at the bottom of the pyramid; and those students who do obtain associate degrees or transfer to four-year institutions to earn bachelor's degrees are better off than they would be without community colleges. What remains controversial, however, is whether community colleges have made a sufficient difference for a sufficient number of people. The vast majority of community college students, some 63 percent, would *like* to earn at least a bachelor's degree. But relatively few actually do so. In fact, of students who started at a community college in 1995, who expected to transfer to a four-year college eventually, just 23 percent had earned a bachelor's degree six years later.[22]

What's more, the chances of community college students transferring to a four-year university—often their ticket into the middle class—largely depend on the social class from which they come. Of students who expected to earn at least a bachelor's degree in 1995, just 21 percent from both the bottom and the lower-middle socioeconomic classes actually transferred to a four-year institution. In contrast, 36 percent of the upper-middle-class quartile and 49 percent of the top socioeconomic quartile transferred to a four-year college or university.[23]

The contradictions of the community college movement are hardly new concerns. In fact, the democratization of American higher education after the Second World War, as it changed from an institution exclusive to elites to one nominally open to the masses, has appeared to follow a familiar pattern. Consider the public high school as an American institution. Prior to the period when education was expanded to the masses, as Martin Trow has observed, a high school diploma was an elite educational credential. But even as the American high school opened its doors early in the last century, it also became more stratified and segmented, as separate curricular tracks were created to differentiate the college-bound from the vocationally bound.[24] Similarly, educational opportunities expanded with the massive growth of community colleges. But so did stratification of the entire higher education system. The growing rigidity of the dividing lines between sectors within the system raises serious doubt that simply enlarging the system of higher education has fundamentally diminished social class inequalities.

Indeed, an increasingly vivid line is dividing American higher education. On one side are those trained at intellectually elite academic centers, professional schools, and selective undergraduate programs, who are part and parcel of the fabric of the American leadership establishment that Justice O'Connor envisioned. On the other side are individuals trained to serve the interests of a leadership class. Which side of this growing divide a young person inhabits can mean that he or she is exposed to quite disparate notions about what it means to be educated, how knowledge is defined, and whose knowledge even matters. For all the hopes and dreams of the community college movement, its existence may ultimately be counterproductive in terms of a genuine attack on inequality. The institutions, in effect, permit the creation of a separate system of postsecondary education for the poor, recent immigrants, and children of the working class, who receive training and credentials for jobs that serve the dominant leadership class. Separate and unequal systems of higher education—one for the rich, the other for the not-rich—would not exist but for the deeply stratified nature of the social and economic structure in the larger society.

As Jerome Karabel, a UC Berkeley sociologist, writes in an article that first appeared in the *Harvard Educational Review*:

> Despite the idealism and vigor of the community college movement, there has been a sharp contradiction between official rhetoric and social

reality. Hailed as the "democratizers of higher education," community colleges are, in reality, a vital component of the class-based tracking system. The modal junior college student, though aspiring to a four-year diploma upon entrance, receives neither an associate nor a bachelor's degree. The likelihood of his persisting in higher education is negatively influenced by attending a community college. Since a disproportionate number of community-college students are of working-class origins, low-status students are most likely to attend those institutions, which increases the likelihood that they will drop out of college. Having increased access to higher education, community colleges are notably unsuccessful in retaining their students and in reducing class differentials in educational opportunity.[25]

It hardly takes a Supreme Court opinion to note that a great deal of America's cultural and intellectual attention is given not to community colleges but rather to the opposite end of the educational pyramid: the relatively few elite colleges and universities that close their doors to the vast majority of those who seek admission. It is primarily at such highly selective institutions that questions of racial preferences come into play, because most other American colleges and universities continue to admit most students who apply.

Because highly selective institutions are so few in number, observers sometimes wonder why, as a society, we should be so preoccupied with them as a policy matter . . . .

But Justice O'Connor was exactly right. America's elite institutions do represent the training grounds for the nation's future leaders—and thus for any nation that purports to uphold egalitarian and democratic values, it matters who is educated at these institutions. It matters that the University of Michigan law school and schools like it be diverse in many ways, not only racially and ethnically diverse. To the extent that these colleges and universities educate the individuals who will lead in government, education, and commerce, it matters fundamentally that access to these schools is guided by the principles of equal opportunity, open to individuals from all walks of life. It matters that these training grounds are not merely playgrounds for the children of privilege.

Notwithstanding the importance of these principles, America's record of upholding them is indeed bleak. Despite the overall growth of the higher education sector—indeed, perhaps because of that expansion—American higher education by the 1990s had become even more rigidly divided by social class than it had been thirty years earlier. By the last decade of the twentieth century, a mere 3 percent of the freshmen enrolled at the nation's 146 most selective institutions came from the lowest socioeconomic quartile, according to a 2004 study by the Century Foundation. But almost 75 percent of the freshmen at these widely respected and influential universities came from the highest socioeconomic quartile.[26]

To be sure, access to the best universities in the United States has also been highly skewed by race and ethnicity, as blacks and Hispanics each accounted for only 6 percent of the freshmen at the same universities. But access to such colleges and universities remains even more distorted by one's social class. Consider the seminal defense of affirmative action in college admissions, *The Shape of the River*, by William Bowen and Derek Bok. The authors report that students from affluent families, both white and black, dominated enrollments at twenty-eight highly selective colleges and universities. Fully 98 percent of the white students at these colleges came from social class backgrounds that ranged from middle class to upper class, as did 86 percent of the black students.[27]

What's more, evidence suggests that access to the nation's most desirable colleges and universities has over time become more powerfully influenced by family background factors and relatively less so by the meritocratic factors that these institutions have long labored under the illusion of upholding.

The advantages that accrue to students who attend selective colleges are not merely symbolic. "The economic benefits of attending a selective college are clear," write Anthony P. Carnevale and Stephen J. Rose in the Century Foundation's 2004 book *America's Untapped Resource: Low-Income Students in Higher Education*. Compared to those who attend less selective institutions, students who go to selective colleges graduate at significantly higher rates, have a greater chance of attending graduate or professional schools, and are likely to earn significantly more money. Indeed, Carnevale and Rose cite several recent studies suggesting that attending a top university compared to a middling one boosts one's earnings roughly 10 to 20 percent. The economic payoffs are also evident when one considers the differing amounts that colleges spend on students in the form of student subsidies, which can show up vividly in the quality and quantity of resources devoted to teaching and learning, as well as in cultural and recreational activities. In fact, annual student subsidies at wealthy private institutions can be several times greater than those at less selective public institutions, ranging as high as $24,000 per student and as low as $2,000, according to Carnevale and Rose.[28]

What accounts for the growing class stratification of American higher education? One possibility is that differences in educational attainment among social classes or any demographic group are largely the impartial result of the American "meritocracy" working as it should. Is the meritocracy machine, then, simply grinding away, impervious to the winners and losers?

Astin and Osegueva suggest otherwise. They examined the changing relationship over time between academic factors such as test scores, a student's family background, and the student's chances of enrolling in a highly selective college. Between 1990 and 2000, they found that the correlation between the SAT or ACT admissions tests and the chances of enrollment remained stable, that high school grades declined in importance, and that both parental income and parental education increased in importance.[29] Their results suggest that academic factors became relatively less important in the 1990s and that nonacademic factors associated with social class—parental income, educational levels, and the cultural capital that students inherit from birth— became relatively more powerful influences on one's chances of going to an elite university . . . .

This isn't to suggest that academic merit, at least as determined by test scores and grades, makes little difference. Ellwood and Kane's research suggests that merit so defined remains central to a student's chances of going to college. Indeed, the chances of attending a four-year institution increase from 29 percent to 74 percent when we compare a student with modest grades and test scores to one with high grades and scores. "The single most powerful determinant of college-going remains high school achievement," Ellwood and Kane write. "Anything we do to reduce the achievement gaps that are present by high school will do a great deal to equalize the enrollments of students from various backgrounds. But that effort is gargantuan indeed, and major successes remain rare."[30]

In a nation in which 40 percent of adults believe that they currently are at the top of the social and economic pyramid, or will someday rise to that position, regardless of their circumstances of birth or how they grew up, the notion that a student's social class origins remain important to his or her educational prospects can be hard to collectively rationalize. So we invent various stories that we like to tell ourselves, to make us feel that the world is working as it should.

## DISCUSSION QUESTIONS

1. How would Sacks and other researchers of higher education and social class respond to this question: Does social class matter in gaining access to a college education? Does their research negate any myths Americans hold dear about education in the United States?

2. Why does Sacks argue that students at elite colleges are unaware of their privilege? Do you agree or disagree?

## NOTES

1. *Grutter v. Bollinger* et al., 02–241, Sup. Ct. 20 (2003).

2. *Gratz v. Bollinger* et al., 02–516, Sup. Ct. 3 (2003); Peter Schmidt, "Affirmative Action Survives, and So Does the Debate," *Chronicle of Higher Education*, July 4, 2003, http://chronicle.com/weekly/v49/i43/43S00101.htm (accessed February 13, 2006).

3. Thomas Mortenson, "Pell Grant Share of Undergraduate Enrollment at the 50 Best National Universities, 1992–93 and 2001–02," *Postsecondary Education Opportunity* 141 (March 2004): 18; Thomas Mortenson, "Economic Segregation of Higher Education Opportunity, 1973 to 2001," *Postsecondary Education Opportunity* 136 (October 2003):3.

4. In the figures that accompany this discussion, families designated as low SES are typically those in which neither parent has attended college and family income is in the lowest quartile. The highest SES category typically means that both parents have at least a bachelor's degree and that the family's income is in the highest quartile. Middle SES typically means that one parent has a bachelor's degree or higher and family income is in the middle two quartiles of the income distribution.

5. U.S. Department of Education, National Center for Education Statistics, *National Educational Longitudinal Study 1988: Trends among High School Seniors, 1972–1992*, NCES 95–380 (Washington, D.C.: U.S. Government Printing Office, 1995), http://nces.ed.gov/pubsearch/pubsinfo.asp?pubid=95380 (accessed September 2006).

6. Ibid.

7. Ibid.

8. Piper Fogg, "Harvard's President Wonders Aloud about Women in Science and Math," *Chronicle of Higher Education*, January 28, 2005, http://chronicle.com/weekly/v51/i21/21a01201.htm (accessed September 29, 2006).

9. U.S. Department of Education, National Center for Education Statistics, *National Educational Longitudinal Study 1988–1994: Descriptive Summary Report*, by Allen Sanderson, Bernard Dugoni, Kenneth Rasinski, John Taylor, and C. Dennis Carroll, NCES 96–175 (Washington, D.C.: U.S. Government Printing Office, 1996).

10. Ibid.

11. U.S. Department of Education, National Center for Education Statistics, *Coming of Age in the 1990s: The Eighth-Grade Class of 1988, 12 Years Later*, NCES 2002-231 (Washington, D.C.: U.S. Government Printing Office, 2002).

12. U.S. Department of Education, National Center for Education Statistics, *Descriptive Summary of 1989–90 Beginning Postsecondary Students: Five Years Later—Statistical Analysis Report, March 1996*, by Lutz K.

Berkner, Stephanie Cuccaro-Alamin, and Alexander C. McCormick, NCES 96–155 (Washington, D.C.: U.S. Government Printing Office, 1996), Table 1.3, p. 34, http://nces.ed.gov/pubs/96155all.pdf (accessed February 14, 2006).

13. Lawrence E. Gladieux, "Low-Income Students and the Affordability of Higher Education," in *America's Untapped Resource: Low-Income Students in Higher Education,* ed. Richard D. Kahlenberg (New York: Century Foundation Press, 2004), p. 25.

14. Thomas Mortenson, "Segregation of Higher Education Enrollment by Family Income and Race/Ethnicity, 1980 to 2004," *Postsecondary Education Opportunity* 160 (October 2005):8.

15. Thomas Mortenson, "Underrepresented Minorities' Share of Undergraduate Enrollments at State Flagship Universities, 1992 and 2001," *Postsecondary Education Opportunity* 146 (August 2004):10.

16. Jane R. Porter, "State Flagship Universities Do Poorly in Enrolling and Graduating Black Men, Report Says," *Chronicle of Higher Education,* September 29, 2006, http://chronicle.com/daily/2006/09/ 200609290 1n.htm (accessed September 2006).

17. Bill Ruben, telephone interview with author, December 18, 2004.

18. U.S. Department of Education, National Center for Education Statistics, *Digest of Education Statistics 2003,* by Thomas D. Snyder, Alexandra G. Tan, and Charlene M. Hoffman, NCES 2005–02 (Washington, D.C.: U.S. Government Printing Office, 2004), Table 246, "Degree-Granting Institutions by Control and Type of Institution, 1949–50 to 2002–03," http://nces .ed.gov/programs/digest/do3_tf.asp (accessed February 14, 2006).

19. Thomas Mortenson, "Bachelor's Degree Attainment by Age 24 by Income Quartile, 1970-2002," *Postsecondary Education Opportunity* 143 (May 2004):I.

20. Mortenson, "Economic Segregation of Higher Education Opportunity," p. 1.

21. Ibid.

22. U.S. Department of Education, National Center for Education Statistics, *Community College Students: Goals, Academic Preparation, and Outcomes— Postsecondary Education, Descriptive Analysis Reports,* by Gary Hoachlander, Anna C. Sikora, and Laura Horn, NCES 2003-164 (Washington, D.C.: U.S. Government Printing Office, 2003).

23. U.S. Department of Education, National Center of Education Statistics, *Community College Transfer Rates to 4-year Institutions Using Alternative Definitions of Transfer,* by Ellen M. Bradburn and David G. Hurst, NCES 2001-197 (Washington, D.C.: U.S. Government Printing Office, 2001).

24. Martin Trow, "The Second Transformation of American Secondary Education," in *Class, Status, and Power,* ed. Reinhard Bendix and Seymour Martin Lipset, 2nd ed. (New York: Free Press, 1966); quoted in Jerome Karabel, "Community Colleges and Social Stratification: Submerged Class Conflict in American Higher Education," *Power and Ideology in Education,* ed. Jerome Karabel and A. H. Halsey (New York: Oxford University Press, 1977), p. 234.

25. Karabel, "Community Colleges and Social Stratification," p. 248.

26. Anthony P. Carnevale and Stephen J. Rose, "Socioeconomic Status, Race/Ethnicity, and Selective College Admissions," in Kahlenberg, *America's Untapped Resource,* p. 106.

27. William Bowen and Derek Bok, *The Shape of the River: Long-Term Consequences of Considering Race in College and University Admissions* (Princeton, N.J.: Princeton University Press, 1998), p. 49.

28. Carnevale and Rose, "Socioeconomic Status," pp. 107–114.

29. Astin and Osegueva, "Declining Equity."

30. David T. Ellwood and Thomas J. Kane, "Who Is Getting a College Education? Family Background and the Growing Gaps in Enrollment," in *Securing the Future: Investing in Children from Birth to College,* ed. Sheldon Danzinger and Jane Waldfogel (New York: Russell Sage Foundation, 2000), pp. 283–313.

# 36

# INEQUALITY REGIMES

## Gender, Class, and Race in Organizations

### JOAN ACKER

*Joan Acker, a well-known sociologist and feminist scholar, provided an overview of capitalism from a gender and race lens in Reading 10 in Part I. In this reading, excerpted from a 2006 article in the academic journal* Gender & Society, *Acker provides a thorough examination of how social organizations create and maintain hierarchies of power. Acker, a professor emerita of sociology at the University of Oregon, has studied gender, women and work, and families since the early 1960s, and is the founding director of the Center for the Study of Women in Society at the University of Oregon. This rich reading provides an introduction to the concept of "inequality regimes," which Acker uses to describe the "interrelated practices, processes, actions, and meanings that result in and maintain social class, gender, and racial inequalities." This concept is useful in illustrating how social structures and organizations create and maintain social inequality.*

Much of the social and economic inequality in the United States and other industrial countries is created in organizations, in the daily activities of working and organizing the work. Union activists have grounded their demands in this understanding, as have feminist and civil rights reformers. Class analyses, at least since Harry Braverman's 1974 dissection of *Labor and Monopoly Capital,* have often examined the doing of work, the labor process, to understand how class inequalities are produced and perpetuated (Burawoy 1979). Feminists have looked at the gendering of organizations

*Source:* "Inequality Regimes: Gender, Class, and Race in Organizations," by Joan Acker, 2006. *Gender and Society, 20,* pp. 441–464. Copyright 2006 by Sociologists for Women in Society. Reprinted with permission.

and organizational practices to comprehend how inequalities between women and men continue in the face of numerous attempts to erase such inequalities (Acker 1990; Ferguson 1984; Kanter 1977). Scholars working on race inequality have examined the production in work organizations of racial disparities that contribute to society-wide racial discrimination and disadvantage (Royster 2003).

Most studies of the production of class, gender, and racial inequalities in organizations have focused on one or another of these categories, rarely attempting to study them as complex, mutually reinforcing or contradicting processes. But focusing on one category almost inevitably obscures and oversimplifies other interpenetrating realities. Feminist scholars of color have argued for 30 years, with the agreement of most white feminist scholars, that much feminist scholarship was actually about white middle-class women, ignoring the reality that the category gender is fundamentally complicated by class, race/ethnicity, and other differences (Davis 1981; hooks 1984; Joseph 1981). Similar criticisms can be made of much theory and research on race and class questions: "race," even when paired with "ethnicity," encapsulates multiple social realities always inflected through gender and class differences. "Class" is also complicated by multiple gendered and racialized differences. The conclusion to this line of thinking—theory and research on inequality, dominance, and oppression must pay attention to the intersections of, at least, race/ethnicity, gender, and class.

The need for intersectional analyses has been, for the past 15 years at least, widely accepted among feminist scholars (Collins 1995; Crenshaw 1995; Weber 2001). How to develop this insight into clear conceptions of how dimensions of difference or simultaneous inequality-producing processes actually work has been difficult and is an ongoing project; (McCall 2005; Weber 2001). Different approaches provide complementary views of these complex processes. For example, Leslie McCall (2005), using large data sets, shows how patterns of gender, race, and class inequality vary with the composition of economic activity in various areas of the United States. The analysis I suggest contrasts with McCall's approach, as

I propose looking at specific organizations and the local, ongoing, practical activities of organizing work that, at the same time, reproduce complex inequalities. The organizing processes that constitute inequality regimes are, of course, related to the economic decision making that results in dramatically different local and regional configurations of inequality across the United States. Exploring the connections between specific inequality regimes and the various economic decisions that affect local economies would be still another approach to these complex interrelations. Here, my goal is limited—to develop the analysis of organizational inequality regimes.

## INEQUALITY REGIMES

All organizations have inequality regimes, defined as loosely interrelated practices, processes, actions, and meanings that result in and maintain class, gender, and racial inequalities within particular organizations. The ubiquity of inequality is obvious: Managers, executives, leaders, and department heads have much more power and higher pay than secretaries, production workers, students, or even professors. Even organizations that have explicit egalitarian goals develop inequality regimes over time, as considerable research on egalitarian feminist organizations has shown (Ferree and Martin 1995; Scott 2000).

I define inequality in organizations as systematic disparities between participants in power and control over goals, resources, and outcomes; workplace decisions such as how to organize work; opportunities for promotion and interesting work; security in employment and benefits; pay and other monetary rewards; respect; and pleasures in work and work relations. Organizations vary in the degree to which these disparities are present and in how severe they are. Equality rarely exists in control over goals and resources, while pay and other monetary rewards are usually unequal. Other disparities may be less evident, or a high degree of equality might exist in particular areas, such as employment security and benefits.

Inequality regimes are highly various in other ways; they also tend to be fluid and changing. These regimes are linked to inequality in the surrounding society, its politics, history, and culture. Particular practices and interpretations develop in different organizations and subunits . . . .

In the following sections, I discuss in some detail the varying characteristics of inequality regimes, including the bases of inequality, the shape and degree of inequality, organizing processes that create and recreate inequalities, the invisibility of inequalities, the legitimacy of inequalities, and the controls that prevent protest against inequalities. I also discuss efforts to reduce inequality in organizations, including consideration of what elements in inequality regimes impede and/or further change . . . .

## WHAT VARIES? THE COMPONENTS OF INEQUALITY REGIMES

### The Bases of Inequality

The bases for inequality in organizations vary, although class, gender, and race processes are usually present. "Class," as I use the term, refers to enduring and systematic differences in access to and control over resources for provisioning and survival (Acker 2006; Nelson 1993). Those resources are primarily monetary in wealthy industrial societies. Some class practices take place as employment occurs and wages are paid. Thus, class is intrinsic to employment and to most organizations. In large organizations, hierarchical positions are congruent with class processes in the wider society. The CEO of the large corporation operates at the top of the national and often global society. In smaller organizations, the class structure may not be so congruent with society-wide class relations, but the owner or the boss still has class power in relations with employees. "Class" is defined by inequality; thus, "class equality" is an oxymoron (Ferguson 1984).

Gender, as socially constructed differences between men and women and the beliefs and identities that support difference and inequality, is also present in all organizations. Gender was, in the not too distant past, almost completely integrated with class in many organizations. That is, managers

were almost always men; the lower-level white-collar workers were always women. Class relations in the workplace, such as supervisory practices or wage-setting processes, were shaped by gendered and sexualized attitudes and assumptions. The managerial ranks now contain women in many organizations, but secretaries, clerks, servers, and care providers are still primarily women. Women are beginning to be distributed in organizational class structures in ways that are similar to the distribution of men. Gender and class are no longer so perfectly integrated, but gendered and sexualized assumptions still shape the class situations of women and men in different ways.[1]

"Race" refers to socially defined differences based on physical characteristics, culture, and historical domination and oppression, justified by entrenched beliefs. Ethnicity may accompany race, or stand alone, as a basis for inequality. Race, too, has often been integrated into class hierarchies, but in different patterns than gender. Historically, in the United States, women and men of color were confined to the lowest-level jobs or excluded from all but certain organizations. People of color were totally excluded from the most powerful (white, male) organizations that were central in shaping the racialized and gendered class structure of the larger society. For example, the twentieth-century U.S. military was, until after World War II, a racially segregated organization dominated by white men. Other examples are the elite universities such as Harvard and Yale.

Other differences are sometimes bases for inequality in organizations. The most important, I believe, is sexuality. Heterosexuality is assumed in many organizing processes and in the interactions necessary to these processes. The secretary is or was the "office wife" (Kanter 1977). Homosexuality is disruptive of organizing processes because it flouts the assumptions of heterosexuality. It still carries a stigma that produces disadvantages for lesbians and gays. Other bases of inequality are religion, age, and physical disability. Again, in the not too distant past, having the wrong religion such as being a Jew or a Catholic could activate discriminatory practices. Today, having a Middle Eastern origin or being a Muslim may have similar consequences. Currently, age seems to be a significant basis for inequality, as are certain physical inabilities. I believe that although these other differences are important, they are not, at this time, as thoroughly embedded in organizing processes as are gender, race, and class.

## Shape and Degree of Inequality

The steepness of hierarchy is variation in the shape and degree of inequality. The steepest hierarchies are found in traditional bureaucracies in contrast to the idealized flat organizations with team structures, in which most, or at least some, responsibilities and decision-making authority are distributed among participants. Between these polar types are organizations with varying degrees of hierarchy and shared decision making. Hierarchies are usually gendered and racialized, especially at the top. Top hierarchical class positions are almost always occupied by white men in the United States and European countries. This is particularly true in large and influential organizations.[2] The image of the successful organization and the image of the successful leader share many of the same characteristics, such as strength, aggressiveness, and competitiveness. Some research shows that flat team structures provide professional women more equality and opportunity than hierarchical bureaucracies, but only if the women function like men . . . .

In a study of high-level professional women in a computer development firm, Joanne Martin and Debra Meyerson (1998) found that the women saw the culture of their work group as highly masculine, aggressive, competitive, and self-promoting. The women had invented ways to cope with this work culture, but they felt that they were partly outsiders who did not belong.

Other research (Barker 1993) suggests that team-organized work may not reduce gender inequality. Racial inequality may also be maintained as teams are introduced in the workplace (Vallas 2003). While the organization of teams is often accompanied by drastic reductions of supervisors' roles, the power of higher managerial levels is usually not changed: Class inequalities are only slightly reduced.

The degree and pattern of segregation by race and gender is another aspect of inequality that varies considerably between organizations. Gender and race segregation of jobs is complex because segregation [is hierarc]hical across jobs at different class levels [occupa]tion, across jobs at the same level, and [(C]harles and Grusky 2004). Occupations [disti]nguished from jobs: An occupation is [a t]ype of work; a job is a particular cluster of tasks in a particular work organization. For example, emergency room nurse is an occupation; an emergency room nurse at San Francisco General Hospital is a job . . . . Research indicates that "sex segregation at the job level is more extensive than sex segregation at the level of occupations" (Wharton 2005:97). In addition, even when women and men "are members of the same occupation, they are likely to work in different jobs and firms" (Wharton 2005:97). Racial segregation also persists, is also complex, and varies by gender.

Jobs and occupations may be internally segregated by both gender and race: What appears to be a reduction in segregation may only be its reconfiguration. Reconfiguration and differentiation have occurred as women have entered previously male-dominated occupations. For example, women doctors are likely to specialize in pediatrics, not surgery, which is still largely a male domain . . . .

The size of wage differences in organizations also varies. Wage differences often vary with the height of the hierarchy: It is the CEOs of the largest corporations whose salaries far outstrip those of everyone else. In the United States in 2003, the average CEO earned 185 times the earnings of the average worker; the average earnings of CEOs of big corporations were more than 300 times the earnings of the average worker (Mishel, Bernstein, and Boushey 2003). White men tend to earn more than any other gender/race category, although even for white men, the wages of the bottom 60 percent are stagnant. Within most service-sector organizations, both white women and women of color are at the bottom of the wage hierarchy.

The severity of power differences varies. Power differences are fundamental to class, of course, and are linked to hierarchy. Labor unions and professional associations can act to reduce power differences across class hierarchies. However, these organizations have historically been dominated by white men with the consequence that white women and people of color have not had increases in organizational power equal to those of white men. Gender and race are important in determining power differences within organizational class levels. For example, managers are not always equal. In some organizations, women managers work quietly to do the organizational housekeeping, to keep things running, while men managers rise to heroic heights to solve spectacular problems (Ely and M........ zations, women and (Wacjman 1998) . . . .

## Organizing Processes That Produce Inequality

Organizations vary in the practices and processes that are used to achieve their goals; these practices and processes also produce class, gender, and racial inequalities. Considerable research exists exploring how class or gender inequalities are produced, both formally and informally, as work processes are carried out (Acker 1989, 1990; Burawoy 1979; Cockburn 1985; Willis 1977). Some research also examines the processes that result in continuing racial inequalities. These practices are often guided by textual materials supplied by consultants or developed by managers influenced by information and/or demands from outside the organization. To understand exactly how inequalities are reproduced, it is necessary to examine the details of these textually informed practices.

### Organizing the General Requirements of Work

The general requirements of work in organizations vary among organizations and among organizational levels. In general, work is organized on the image of a white man who is totally dedicated to the work and who has no responsibilities for children or family demands other than earning a living. Eight hours of continuous work away from the living space, arrival on time, total attention to the work, and long hours if requested are all expectations that incorporate the image of the unencumbered worker. Flexibility to bend these expectations is more available to high-level managers, predominantly men, than to lower-level managers (Jacobs and Gerson 2004). Some professionals, such as college professors, seem to have considerable flexibility, although they also work long hours. Lower-level jobs have, on the whole, little flexibility. Some work is organized as part-time, which may help women to combine work and family obligations, but in the United States, such work usually has no benefits such as health care and often has lower pay than full-time work (Mishel, Bernstein, and Boushey 2003). Because women have more obligations outside work than do men, this gendered organization of work is important in maintaining gender inequality in organizations and, thus, the unequal distribution of women and men in organizational class hierarchies. Thus, gender, race, and class inequalities are simultaneously created in the fundamental construction of the working day and of work obligations.

### Organizing Class Hierarchies

Techniques also vary for organizing class hierarchies inside work organizations. Bureaucratic, textual techniques for ordering positions and people are constructed to reproduce existing class, gender, and racial inequalities (Acker 1989). Job classification systems describe job tasks and responsibilities and rank jobs hierarchically. Jobs are then assigned to wage categories with jobs of similar rank in the same wage category. Our study found that the bulk of sex-typed women's jobs, which were in the clerical/secretarial area and included thousands of women workers, were described less clearly and with less specificity than the bulk of sex-typed men's jobs, which were spread over a wide range of areas and levels in the organization . . . . The result was, we argued, an unjustified gender wage gap: Although women's wages were in general lower than those of men, women's skilled jobs were paid much less than men's skilled jobs, reducing even further the average pay for women when compared with the average pay for men . . . .

Often, we observed, managers were credited with responsibility for tasks done by their assistants. The assistants did not get credit for these tasks in the job evaluation system, and this contributed to their relatively low wages. But if managers' and assistants' jobs could never be compared, no adjustments for inequities could ever be made. The hierarchy was inviolate in this system . . . .

In sum, class hierarchies in organizations, with their embedded gender and racial patterns, are constantly created and renewed through organizing practices. Gender and sometimes race, in the form of restricted opportunities and particular expectations for behavior, are reproduced as different degrees of organizational class hierarchy and are also reproduced in everyday interactions and bureaucratic decision making.

### Recruitment and Hiring

Recruitment and hiring is a process of finding the worker most suited for a particular position. From the perspectives of employers, the gender and race of existing jobholders at least partially define who is suitable, although prospective coworkers may also do such defining (Enarson 1984). Images of appropriate gendered and racialized bodies influence perceptions and hiring. White bodies are often preferred, as a great deal of research shows (Royster 2003). Female bodies are appropriate for some jobs; male bodies for other jobs.

A distinction should be made between the gendered organization of work and the gender and racial characteristics of the ideal worker. Although work is organized on the model of the unencumbered (white) man, and both women and men are expected to perform according to this model, men are not necessarily the ideal workers for all jobs. The ideal worker for many jobs is a woman, particularly a woman who, employers believe, is compliant, who will accept orders and low wages (Salzinger 2003). This is often a woman of color; immigrant women are sometimes even more desirable (Hossfeld 1994).

Hiring through social networks is one of the ways in which gender and racial inequalities are maintained in organizations. Affirmative action programs altered hiring practices in many organizations, requiring open advertising for positions and

selection based on gender- and race-neutral criteria of competence, rather than selection based on an old boy (white) network. These changes in hiring practices contributed to the increasing proportions of white women and people of color in a variety of occupations. However, criteria of competence do not automatically translate into gender- and race-neutral selection decisions. "Competence" involves judgment: The race and gender of both the applicant and the decision makers can affect that judgment, resulting in decisions that white males are the more competent, more suited to the job than are others. Thus, gender and race as a basis for hiring or a basis for exclusion have not been eliminated in many organizations, as continuing patterns of segregation attest.

### Wage Setting and Supervisory Practices

Wage setting and supervision are class practices. They determine the division of surplus between workers and management and control the work process and workers. Gender and race affect assumptions about skill, responsibility, and a fair wage for jobs and workers, helping to produce wage differences (Figart, Mutari, and Power 2002).

Wage setting is often a bureaucratic organizational process, integrated into the processes of creating hierarchy, as I described above. Many different wage-setting systems exist, many of them producing gender and race differences in pay. Differential gender-based evaluations may be embedded in even the most egalitarian-appearing systems . . . .

Supervisory practices also vary across organizations. Supervisory relations may be affected by the gender and race of both supervisor and subordinate, in some cases preserving or reproducing gender or race inequalities. For example, above I described how women and men in the same aspiranter job classification in Swedish banks were assigned to different duties by their supervisors. Supervisors probably shape their behaviors with subordinates in terms of race and gender in many other work situations, influencing in subtle ways the existing patterns of inequality. Much of this can be observed in the informal interactions of workplaces.

*Informal Interactions While "Doing the Work"*

A large literature exists on the reproduction of gender in interactions in organizations (Reskin 2003; Ridgeway 1997). The production of racial inequalities in workplace interactions has not been studied so frequently (Vallas 2003), while the reproduction of class relations in the daily life of organizations has been studied in the labor process tradition, as I noted above. The informal interactions and practices in which class, race, and gender inequalities are created in mutually reinforcing processes have not so often been documented, although class processes are usually implicit in studies of gendered or racialized inequalities.

As women and men go about their everyday work, they routinely use gender- , race- , and class-based assumptions about those with whom they interact . . . . Body differences provide clues to the appropriate assumptions, followed by appropriate behaviors. What is appropriate varies, of course, in relation to the situation, the organizational culture and history, and the standpoints of the people judging appropriateness. For example, managers may expect a certain class deference or respect for authority that varies with the race and gender of the subordinate; subordinates may assume that their positions require deference and respect but also find these demands demeaning or oppressive. Jennifer Pierce (1995), in a study of two law firms, showed how both gendered and racialized interactions shaped the organizations' class relations: Women paralegals were put in the role of supportive, mothering aides, while men paralegals were cast as junior partners in the firms' business . . . .

## The Visibility of Inequalities

Visibility of inequality, defined as the degree of awareness of inequalities, varies in different organizations. Lack of awareness may be intentional or unintentional. Managers may intentionally hide some forms of inequality, as in the Swedish banks I studied (Acker 1991). Bank workers said that they had been told not to discuss their wages with their coworkers. Most seem to have complied, partly because they had strong feelings that their pay was part of their identity, reflecting their essential worth. Some said they would rather talk about the details of their sex lives than talk about their pay.

Visibility varies with the position of the beholder: "One privilege of the privileged is not to see their privilege." Men tend not to see their gender privilege; whites tend not to see their race privilege; ruling class members tend not to see their class privilege (McIntosh 1995). People in dominant groups generally see inequality as existing somewhere else, not where they are. However, patterns of invisibility/visibility in organizations vary with the basis for the inequality. Gender and gender inequality tend to disappear in organizations or are seen as something that is beside the point of the organization . . . .

Class also tends to be invisible. It is hidden by talk of management, leadership, or supervision among managers and those who write and teach about organizations from a management perspective. Workers in lower-level, nonmanagement positions may be very conscious of inequalities, although they might not identify these inequities as related to class. Race is usually evident, visible, but segregated, denied, and avoided. In two of my organization studies, we have asked questions about race issues in the workplace (Morgen, Acker, and Weigt n.d.). In both of these studies, white workers on the whole could see no problems with race or racism, while workers of color had very different views. The one exception was in an office with a very diverse workforce, located in an area with many minority residents and high poverty rates. Here, jobs were segregated by race, tensions were high, and both white and Black workers were well aware of racial incidents. Another basis of inequality, sexuality, is almost always invisible to the majority who are heterosexual. Heterosexuality is simply assumed, not questioned.

## The Legitimacy of Inequalities

The legitimacy of inequalities also varies between organizations. Some organizations, such as cooperatives, professional organizations, or voluntary organizations with democratic goals, may find inequality illegitimate and try to minimize it. In other organizations, such as rigid bureaucracies, inequalities are highly legitimate. Legitimacy of inequality also varies with political and economic conditions . . . .

High visibility and low legitimacy of inequalities may enhance the possibilities for change. Social movements may contribute to both high visibility and low legitimacy while agitating for change toward greater equality, as I argued above. Labor unions may also be more successful when visibility is high and legitimacy of inequalities is low.

### Control and Compliance

Organizational controls are, in the first instance, class controls, directed at maintaining the power of managers, ensuring that employees act to further the organization's goals, and getting workers to accept the system of inequality. Gendered and racialized assumptions and expectations are embedded in the form and content of controls and in the ways in which they are implemented. Controls are made possible by hierarchical organizational power, but they also draw on power derived from hierarchical gender and race relations. They are diverse and complex, and they impede changes in inequality regimes.

Mechanisms for exerting control and achieving compliance with inequality vary. Organization theorists have identified many types of control, including direct controls, unobtrusive or indirect controls, and internalized controls. Direct controls include bureaucratic rules and various punishments for breaking the rules. Rewards are also direct controls. Wages, because they are essential for survival in completely monetized economies, are a powerful form of control (Perrow 2002). Coercion and physical and verbal violence are also direct controls often used in organizations (Hearn and Parkin 2001). Unobstrusive and indirect controls include control through technologies, such as monitoring telephone calls or time spent online or restricting information flows. Selective recruitment of relatively powerless workers can be a form of control (Acker and Van Houten 1974). Recruitment of illegal immigrants who are vulnerable to discovery and deportation and recruitment of women of color who have few

employment opportunities and thus will accept low wages are examples of this kind of control, which preserves inequality.

Internalized controls include belief in the legitimacy of bureaucratic structures and rules as well as belief in the legitimacy of male and white privilege. Organizing relations, such as those between a manager and subordinates, may be legitimate, taken for granted as the way things naturally and normally are. Similarly, a belief that there is no point in challenging the fundamental gender, race, and class nature of things is a form of control. These are internalized, often invisible controls.[3] Pleasure in the work is another internalized control, as are fear and self-interest. Interests can be categorized as economic, status, and identity interests, all of which may be produced as organizing takes place. Identities, constituted through gendered and racialized images and experiences, are mutually reproduced along with differences in status and economic advantage. Those with the most powerful and affluent combination of interests are apt to be able to control others with the aim of preserving these interests. But their self-interest becomes a control on their own behavior.

## CAN INEQUALITY REGIMES CHANGE?

Inequality regimes can be challenged and changed. However, change is difficult and change efforts often fail. One reason is that owner and managerial class interests and the power those interests can mobilize usually outweigh the class, gender, and race interests of those who suffer inequality. Even where no obvious economic interests are threatened by changes, men managers and lower-level employees often insist on maintaining ongoing organizing patterns that perpetuate inequalities. For example, white masculine identity may be tied to small relative advantages in workplace power and income. Advantage is hard to give up: Increasing equality with devalued groups can be seen and felt as an assault on dignity and masculinity. Several studies have shown that these complicated motives on the part of white men, in particular, can scuttle efforts at organizational change, even when top management is supporting such change . . . .

Successful change projects seem to have had a number of common characteristics. First, change efforts that target a limited set of inequality- producing mechanisms seem to be the most successful. In addition, successful efforts appear to have combined social movement and legislative support outside the organization with active support from insiders. In addition, successful efforts often involve coercion or threat of loss. Both affirmative action and pay equity campaigns had these characteristics. Affirmative action programs sought to increase the employment opportunities for women of all races and men of color in organizations and jobs in which they had very low representation. The federal legislation required such programs, and similar equality efforts, in organizations that received government funds. Employers who did not follow the law were vulnerable to loss of funds. Pay equity projects, intended to erase wage inequality between women-predominant jobs and men-predominant jobs of equal value, were authorized primarily by state and local legislation and took place primarily in public-sector organizations. In both types of efforts, the mobilization of civil rights and women's movement groups was essential to success . . . .

The history of pay equity projects reveals a fundamental contradiction facing many efforts to reform inequality regimes: The goals of inequality reduction or elimination are the opposite of some of the goals of employing organizations, particularly in the United States at the beginning of the twenty-first century. In the private sector, management wants to reduce costs, increase profit, and distribute as much as possible of the profit to top management and shareholders. In the public sector, management wants to reduce costs and minimize taxes. Reducing costs involves reducing wages, not raising them, as pay equity would require. While wage inequality is not the only form of inequality, eliminating that inequality may be basic to dealing with other forms as well.

Another lesson of this history is that a focus on delimited areas of inequality, such as gender and racial imbalance in job categories or pay gaps between female and male jobs of equal value, do nothing to address underlying organizationl class inequality. Both of these models of intervention work within the organizational class structure: Affirmative action intends to remove racial and gender barriers to entry into existing hierarchical positions; pay equity efforts compare male and female jobs and sometimes white predominant jobs and other-than-white predominant jobs within organizational class levels, not across those levels.[4]

These interventions also fail to address other underlying processes of inequality regimes: the male model of organizing or the persistent gendering and racialization of interactions in the workplace. Family-friendly policies provide only temporary relief for some people from the male model of organizing. The use of family-friendly policies, primarily by women when they have young children, or the use of part-time work, again primarily involving women, may increase gender inequalities in organizations (Glass 2004). Such measures may reinforce, not undermine, the male model of organizing by defining those who conform to it as serious, committed workers and those who do not as rather peripheral and probably unworthy of promotions and pay increases (Hochschild 1997).

Diversity programs and policies seem to be often aimed at some of the more subtle discriminatory processes dividing organizational participants along lines of race/ethnicity and sometimes gender through education and consciousness raising. Diversity programs replaced, in many organizations, the affirmative action programs that came under attack. As Kelly and Dobbin (1998) point out, diversity programs lack the timetables, goals, and other proactive measures of affirmative action and may be more acceptable to management for that reason. But that may also be a reason that diversity training will not basically alter assumptions and actions that are rooted in the legitimation of systems of organizational power and reward that favor whites, particularly white men. The legitimacy of inequality, fear of retaliation, and cynicism limit support for change. The invisibility of inequality to those with privilege does not give way easily to entreaties to see what is going on. The intimate entwining of privilege with gendered and racialized identity makes privilege particularly difficult to unsettle.

Change projects focused on gendered behaviors that are dysfunctional for the organization provide examples of the almost unshakable fusion of gendered identities and workplace organizing practices. For example, Robin Ely and Debra Meyerson (2000) describe a change project aimed at discovering why a company had difficulty retaining high-level women managers and difficulty increasing the proportion of women in upper management.... Although members of the management group could see that these ways of behaving were dysfunctional for the organization, they did not make the links between these organizing practices, gender, and the underrepresentation of women. In their eyes, the low representation of women in top jobs was still due to the failure of individual women, not to system processes.

## CONCLUSION

I had two goals in writing this article. The first was to develop a conceptual strategy for analyzing the mutual production of gender, race, and class inequalities in work organizations. I have suggested the idea of inequality regimes, interlinked organizing processes that produce patterns of complex inequalities. These processes and patterns vary in different organizations; the severity of inequalities, their visibility and legitimacy, and the possibilities for change toward less inequality also vary from organization to organization. In the United States at the present time, almost all organizations have two characteristics that rarely vary: Class inequality, inflected through gendered and racialized beliefs and practices, is the normal and natural bedrock of organizing, and white men are the normal and natural top leaders.

My second goal was to better understand why so many organizational equality projects have had only modest success or have failed altogether. Looking at organizations as inequality regimes may give some clues about why change projects designed to increase equality are so often less than successful. Change toward greater equality is possible, but difficult, because of entrenched economic (class) interests, the legitimacy of class interests, and allegiances to gendered and racialized identities and advantages. When class identities and interests are integrated with gender and racial identities and interests, opposition may be most virulent to any moves to alter the combined advantages. However, top male executives who are secure in their multiple advantages and privileges may be more supportive of reducing inequalities than male middle managers who may lose proportionately more through equality organizing.

Greater equality inside organizations is difficult to achieve during a period, such as the early years of the twenty-first century, in which employers are pushing for more inequality in pay, medical care, and retirement benefits and are using various tactics, such as downsizing and outsourcing, to reduce labor costs. Another major impediment to change within inequality regimes is the absence of broad social movements outside organizations agitating for such changes. In spite of all these difficulties, efforts at reducing inequality continue. Government regulatory agencies, the Equal Employment Opportunity Commission in particular, are still enforcing antidiscrimination laws that prohibit discrimination against specific individuals (see www.eeoc.gov/stats/). Resolutions of complaints through the courts may mandate some organizational policy changes, but these seem to be minimal. Campaigns to alter some inequality regimes are under way. For example, a class action lawsuit on behalf of Wal-Mart's 1.3 million women workers is making its way through the courts (Featherstone 2004). The visibility of inequality seems to be increasing, and its legitimacy decreasing. Perhaps this is the opening move in a much larger, energetic attack on inequality regimes.

## DISCUSSION QUESTIONS

1. Discuss some of the principal features of inequality regimes in organizations and how they continue to foster inequality by gender, race, and social class.
2. How much do you think identity is affected by invisible organizational factors? How can these factors be made more visible?

## NOTES

1. See Rosabeth Moss Kanter's (1977) *Men and Women of the Corporation* for an early analysis of the gendered realities faced by managerial women, realities of the workplace that made top jobs more difficult for women than for men. These gendered class realities still exist 30 years later, although they may not be as widespread as in 1977.

2. Women have never been more than a tiny fraction of the CEOs of *Fortune* 500 companies. In 2004, eight women were 1.6 percent of the CEOs of these companies (see http://www.catalyst.org/files/fact/COTE%20Factsheet%202002updated.pdf).

3. Charles Perrow (1986) calls these "premise controls," the underlying assumptions about the way things are.

4. Cynthia Cockburn (1991) also makes this point.

# 37

# Are Emily and Greg More Employable Than Lakisha and Jamal?

## A Field Experiment on Labor Market Discrimination

Marianne Bertrand

Sendhil Mullainathan

*This second reading on the social institution of the economy and employment provides evidence for the structural inequalities Joan Acker describes in the previous reading. Marianne Bertrand, professor of economics at the University of Chicago, and Sendhil Mullainathan, professor of economics at Harvard University, study how race-ethnicity and racism affect employment hiring decisions. This reading, taken from their 2004 article in the journal* American Economic Review, *reports on the field experiment that Bertrand and Mullainathan conducted to test whether or not potential employers discriminate based on the perceived ethnicity of names on fictitious job applications. Their experimental design randomly assigned names and quality of resumes that were sent to more than 1,300 employment ads. Their results reveal statistically significant differences in the number of callbacks each resume received based on whether the name sounded white or African American.*

*Source:* Bertrand, Marianne, and Sendhil Mullainathan, 2004. "Are Emily and Greg More Employable than Lakisha and Jamal? A Field Experiment on Labor Market Discrimination." *The American Economic Review* 99:991–1011. Used by permission of Vanderbilt University Press and the author.

Every measure of economic success reveals significant racial inequality in the U.S. labor market. Compared to Whites, African Americans are twice as likely to be unemployed and earn nearly 25 percent less when they are employed (Council of Economic Advisers 1998). This inequality has sparked a debate as to whether employers treat members of different races differentially. When faced with observably similar African American and White applicants, do they favor the White one? Some argue yes, citing either employer prejudice or employer perception that race signals lower productivity. Others argue that differential treatment by race is a relic of the past, eliminated by some combination of employer enlightenment, affirmative action programs and the profit-maximization motive. In fact, many in this latter camp even feel that stringent enforcement of affirmative action programs has produced an environment of reverse discrimination. They would argue that faced with identical candidates, employers might favor the African American one.[1] Data limitations make it difficult to empirically test these views. Since researchers possess far less data than employers do, White and African American workers that appear similar to researchers may look very different to employers. So any racial difference in labor market outcomes could just as easily be attributed to differences that are observable to employers but unobservable to researchers.

To circumvent this difficulty, we conduct a field experiment that builds on the correspondence testing methodology that has been primarily used in the past to study minority outcomes in the United Kingdom. We send resumes in response to help-wanted ads in Chicago and Boston newspapers and measure callback for interview for each sent resume. We experimentally manipulate perception of race via the name of the fictitious job applicant. We randomly assign very White-sounding names (such as Emily Walsh or Greg Baker) to half the resumes and very African American-sounding names (such as Lakisha Washington or Jamal Jones) to the other half. Because we are also interested in how credentials affect the racial gap in callback, we experimentally vary the quality of the resumes used in response

to a given ad. Higher-quality applicants have on average a little more labor market experience and fewer holes in their employment history; they are also more likely to have an e-mail address, have completed some certification degree, possess foreign language skills, or have been awarded some honors. In practice, we typically send four resumes in response to each ad: two higher-quality and two lower-quality ones. We randomly assign to one of the higher- and one of the lower-quality resumes an African American-sounding name. In total, we respond to over 1,300 employment ads in the sales, administrative support, clerical, and customer services job categories and send nearly 5,000 resumes. The ads we respond to cover a large spectrum of job quality, from cashier work at retail establishments and clerical work in a mail room, to office and sales management positions . . . .

## I. Experimental Design

### A. Creating a Bank of Resumes

The first step of the experimental design is to generate templates for the resumes to be sent. The challenge is to produce a set of realistic and representative resumes without using resumes that belong to actual job seekers. To achieve this goal, we start with resumes of actual job searchers but alter them sufficiently to create distinct resumes. The alterations maintain the structure and realism of the initial resumes without compromising their owners.

We begin with resumes posted on two job search Web sites as the basis for our artificial resumes.[2] While the resumes posted on these Web sites may not be completely representative of the average job seeker, they provide a practical approximation.[3] We restrict ourselves to people seeking employment in our experimental cities (Boston and Chicago). We also restrict ourselves to four occupational categories: sales, administrative support, clerical services, and customer services. Finally, we further restrict ourselves to resumes posted more than six months prior to the start of the experiment. We purge the selected resumes of the person's name and contact information.

During this process, we classify the resumes within each detailed occupational category into two groups: high and low quality. In judging resume quality, we use criteria such as labor market experience, career profile, existence of gaps in employment, and skills listed. Such a classification is admittedly subjective, but it is made independently of any race assignment on the resumes (which occurs later in the experimental design). To further reinforce the quality gap between the two sets of resumes, we add to each high-quality resume a subset of the following features: summer or while-at-school employment experience, volunteering experience, extra computer skills, certification degrees, foreign language skills, honors, or some military experience. This resume quality manipulation needs to be somewhat subtle to avoid making a higher-quality job applicant over-qualified for a given job. We try to avoid this problem by making sure that the features listed above are not all added at once to a given resume. This leaves us with a high-quality and a low-quality pool of resumes . . . .

This produces distinct but realistic-looking resumes, similar in their education and career profiles to this subpopulation of job searchers.[4]

### B. Identities of Fictitious Applicants

The next step is to generate identities for the fictitious job applicants: names, telephone numbers, postal addresses, and (possibly) e-mail addresses. The choice of names is crucial to our experiment.[5] To decide on which names are uniquely African American and which are uniquely White, we use name frequency data calculated from birth certificates of all babies born in Massachusetts between 1974 and 1979. We tabulate these data by race to determine which names are distinctively White and which are distinctively African American. Distinctive names are those that have the highest ratio of frequency in one racial group to frequency in the other racial group.

As a check of distinctiveness, we conducted a survey in various public areas in Chicago. Each respondent was asked to assess features of a person with a particular name, one of which is race. For each name, 30 respondents were asked to identify the name as either "White," "African American," "Other," or "Cannot Tell." In general, the names led respondents to readily attribute the expected race for the person but there were a few exceptions and these names were disregarded.[6] . . .

Applicants in each race/sex/city/resume quality cell are allocated the same phone number. This guarantees that we can precisely track employer callbacks in each of these cells. The phone lines we use are virtual ones with only a voice mailbox, attached to them. A similar outgoing message is recorded on each of the voice mailboxes, but each message is recorded by someone of the appropriate race and gender. Since we allocate the same phone number for applicants with different names, we cannot use a person name in the outgoing message.

While we do not expect positive feedback from an employer to take place via postal mail, resumes still need postal addresses. We therefore construct fictitious addresses based on real streets in Boston and Chicago using the White Pages. We select up to three addresses in each 5-digit zip code in Boston and Chicago. Within cities, we randomly assign addresses across all resumes. We also create eight e-mail addresses, four for Chicago and four for Boston. These e-mail addresses are neutral with respect to both race and sex. Not all applicants are given an e-mail address. The e-mail addresses are used almost exclusively for the higher-quality resumes. This procedure leaves us with a bank of names, phone numbers, addresses, and e-mail addresses that we can assign to the template resumes when responding to the employment ads . . . .

### C. Measuring Responses

We measure whether a given resume elicits a callback or e-mail back for an interview. For each phone or e-mail response, we use the content of the message left by the employer (name of the applicant, company name, telephone number for contact) to match the response to the corresponding resume-ad pair.[7] Any attempt by employers to contact applicants via postal mail cannot be measured in our experiment since the addresses are fictitious. Several human resource managers confirmed to us that employers rarely, if ever, contact applicants via postal mail to set up interviews.

## III. RESULTS

### A. Is There a Racial Gap in Callback?

Resumes with White names have a 9.65 percent chance of receiving a callback. Equivalent resumes with African American names have a 6.45 percent chance of being called back. This represents a difference in callback rates of 3.20 percentage points, or 50 percent that can solely be attributed to the name manipulation . . . . Put in other words, these results imply that a White applicant should expect on average one callback for every 10 ads she or he applies to; on the other hand, an African American applicant would need to apply to about 15 different ads to achieve the same result.[8]

How large are these effects? While the cost of sending additional resumes might not be large per se, this 50-percent gap could be quite substantial when compared to the rate of arrival of new job openings. In our own study, the biggest constraining factor in sending more resumes was the limited number of new job openings each week. Another way to benchmark the measured return to a White name is to compare it to the returns to other resume characteristics. For example, we [found] show that, at the average number of years of experience in our sample, an extra year of experience increases the likelihood of a callback by a 0.4 percentage point. Based on this point estimate, the return to a White name is equivalent to about eight additional years of experience . . . .

About 20 percent more resumes were sent in Chicago than in Boston. The average callback rate (across races) is lower in Chicago than in Boston. This might reflect differences in labor market conditions across the two cities over the experimental period or maybe differences in the ability of the MIT and Chicago teams of research assistants in selecting resumes that were good matches for a given help-wanted ad. The percentage difference in callback rates is, however, strikingly similar across both cities.

White applicants are 49 percent more likely than African American applicants to receive a callback in Chicago and 50 percent more likely in Boston. These racial differences are statistically significant in both cities . . . .

Looking across occupations, we find a significant racial gap in callbacks for both males (52 percent) and females (49 percent). Comparing males to females in sales occupations, we find a larger racial gap among males (52 percent versus 22 percent). Interestingly, females in sales jobs appear to receive more callbacks than males; however, this (reverse) gender gap is statistically insignificant and economically much smaller than any of the racial gaps discussed above . . . .

### B. Do African Americans Receive Different Returns to Resume Quality?

Our results so far demonstrate a substantial gap in callback based on applicants' names. Next, we would like to learn more about the factors that may influence this gap. More specifically, we ask how employers respond to improvements in African American applicants' credentials. To answer this question, we examine how the racial gap in callback varies by resume quality.

As we explained in Section I, for most of the employment ads we respond to, we send four different resumes: two higher-quality and two lower-quality ones . . . . Higher-quality applicants have on average close to an extra year of labor market experience, fewer employment holes (where an employment hole is defined as a period of at least six months without a reported job), are more likely to have worked while at school, and to report some military experience. Also, higher-quality applicants are more likely to have an e-mail address, to have received some honors, and to list some computer skills and other special skills (such as a certification degree or foreign language skills) on their resume. Note that the higher- and lower-quality resumes do not differ on average with regard to applicants' education level. This reflects the fact that all sent resumes, whether high or low quality, are chosen to be good matches for a given job opening. About 70 percent of the sent resumes report a college degree.[9] . . .

The differences in callback rates between high- and low-quality resumes . . . show that the resume quality manipulation works: higher-quality resumes receive more callbacks . . . . Most strikingly, African Americans experience much less of an increase in callback rate for similar improvements in their credentials. African Americans with higher-quality resumes receive a callback 6.7 percent of the time, compared to 6.2 percent for African Americans with lower-quality resumes. This is only a 0.51-percentage-point, or 8-percent, difference, and this difference is not statistically significant ($p = 0.6084$).

. . . Many of the resume characteristics have the expected effect on the likelihood of a callback. The addition of an e-mail address, honors, and special skills all have a positive and significant effect on the likelihood of a callback. Also, more experienced applicants are more likely to get called back: at the average number of years of experience in our sample (eight years), each extra year of experience increases the likelihood of a callback by about a 0.4 percentage point. The most counterintuitive effects come from computer skills, which appear to negatively predict callback, and employment holes, which appear to positively predict callback.

The same qualitative patterns hold . . . where we focus on White applicants. More importantly, the estimated returns to an e-mail address, additional work experience, honors, and special skills appear economically stronger for that racial group. For example, at the average number of years of experience in our sample, each extra year of experience increases the likelihood of a callback by about a 0.7 percentage point.

As might have been expected from the two previous columns, we find that the estimated returns on these resume characteristics are all economically and statistically weaker for African American applicants. In fact, all the estimated effects for African Americans are statistically insignificant, except for the return to special skills. Resume characteristics thus appear less predictive of callback rates for African Americans than they are for Whites . . . . In summary, employers simply seem to pay less attention or discount more the characteristics listed on the resumes with African American-sounding names. Taken at face value, these results suggest that African Americans may face relatively lower individual incentives to invest in higher skills.

## IV. INTERPRETATION

Three main sets of questions arise when interpreting the results above. First, does a higher callback rate for White applicants imply that employers are discriminating against African Americans? Second, does our design only isolate the effect of race or is the name manipulation conveying some other factors than race? Third, how do our results relate to different models of racial discrimination?

### A. Interpreting Callback Rates

Our results indicate that for two identical individuals engaging in an identical job search, the one with an African American name would receive fewer interviews. Does differential treatment within our experiment imply that employers are discriminating against African Americans (whether it is rational, prejudice-based, or other form of discrimination)? In other words, could the lower callback rate we record for African American resumes *within our experiment* be consistent with a racially neutral review of the *entire pool* of resumes the surveyed employers receive?

In a racially neutral review process, employers would rank order resumes based on their quality and call back all applicants that are above a certain threshold. Because names are randomized, the White and African American resumes we send should rank similarly on average. So, irrespective of the skill and racial composition of the applicant pool, a race-blind selection rule would generate equal treatment of Whites and African Americans. So our results must imply that employers use race as a factor when reviewing resumes, which matches the legal definition of discrimination . . . .

### C. Relation to Existing Theories

What do these results imply for existing models of discrimination? Economic theories of discrimination can be classified into two main categories: taste-based and statistical discrimination models.[10] Both sets of models can obviously "explain" our average racial gap in callbacks. But can these models explain our other findings? More specifically, we discuss the relevance of these models with a focus on two of the facts that have been uncovered in this paper: (i) the lower returns to credentials for African Americans; (ii) the relative uniformity of the race gap across occupations, job requirements and, to a lesser extent, employer characteristics and industries.

Taste-based models (Gary S. Becker 1961) differ in whose prejudiced "tastes" they emphasize: customers, coworkers, or employers. Customer and co-worker discrimination models seem at odds with the lack of significant variation of the racial gap by occupation and industry categories, as the amount of customer contact and the fraction of White employees vary quite a lot across these categories. We do not find a larger racial gap among jobs that explicitly require "communication skills" and jobs for which we expect either customer or coworker contacts to be higher (retail sales for example).

Because we do not know what drives employer tastes, employer discrimination models could be consistent with the lack of occupation and industry variation. Employer discrimination also matches the finding that employers located in more African American neighborhoods appear to discriminate somewhat less. However, employer discrimination models would struggle to explain why African Americans get relatively lower returns to their credentials. Indeed, the cost of indulging the discrimination taste should increase as the minority applicants' credential increase.[11] . . .

Perhaps the skills of African Americans are discounted because affirmative action makes it easier for African Americans to get these skills. While this is plausible for credentials such as an employee-of-the-month honor, it is unclear why this would apply to more verifiable and harder skills. It is equally unclear why work experience would be less rewarded since our study suggests that getting a job is more, not less, difficult for African Americans.

The uniformity of the racial gap across occupations is also troubling for a statistical discrimination interpretation. Numerous factors that should affect the level of statistical discrimination, such as the importance of unobservable skills, the observability of qualifications, the precision of observable skills and the ease of performance measurement, may vary quite a lot across occupations.

This discussion suggests that perhaps other models may do a better job at explaining our findings. One simple alternative model is lexicographic search by employers. Employers receive so many resumes that they may use quick heuristics in reading these resumes. One such heuristic could be to simply read no further when they see an African American name. Thus they may never see the skills of African American candidates and this could explain why these skills are not rewarded. This might also to some extent explain the uniformity of the race gap since the screening process (i.e., looking through a large set of resumes) may be quite similar across the variety of jobs we study.[12]

## V. Conclusion

This paper suggests that African Americans face differential treatment when searching for jobs and this may still be a factor in why they do poorly in the labor market. Job applicants with African American names get far fewer callbacks for each resume they send out. Equally importantly, applicants with African American names find it hard to overcome this hurdle in callbacks by improving their observable skills or credentials.

Taken at face value, our results on differential returns to skill have possibly important policy implications. They suggest that training programs alone may not be enough to alleviate the racial gap in labor market outcomes. For training to work, some general-equilibrium force outside the context of our experiment would have to be at play. In fact, if African Americans recognize how employers reward their skills, they may rationally be less willing than Whites to even participate in these programs.

## DISCUSSION QUESTIONS

1. Describe Bertrand and Mullainathan's research question, methodology, and results, as well as their analysis of this particular "field experiment on labor market discrimination."
2. For those who say that race is not an impediment to being successful in America anymore, what is your response based on this study? What are some solutions to employer-based discrimination of the types found in this study?

## NOTES

1. This camp often explains the poor performance of African Americans in terms of supply factors. If African Americans lack many basic skills entering the labor market, then they will perform worse, even with parity or favoritism in hiring.
2. The sites are www.careerbuilder.com and www.americasjobbank.com.
3. In practice, we found large variation in skill levels among people posting their resumes on these sites.
4. We also generate a set of different fonts, layouts, and cover letters to further differentiate the resumes. These are applied at the time resumes are sent out.
5. We chose name over other potential manipulations of race, such as affiliation with a minority group, because we felt such affiliations may especially convey more than race.
6. For example, Maurice and Jerome are distinctively African American names in a frequency sense yet are not perceived as such by many people.
7. Very few employers used e-mail to contact an applicant back.
8. This obviously assumes that African American applicants cannot assess a priori which firms are more likely to treat them more or less favorably.
9. This varies from about 50 percent for the clerical and administrative support positions to more than 80 percent for the executive, managerial, and sales representatives positions.
10. Darity and Mason (1998) provide a more thorough review of a variety of economic theories of discrimination.
11. One could, however, assume that employer tastes differ not just by race but also by race and skill, so that employers have greater prejudice against minority workers with better credentials. But the opposite preferences, employers having a particular distaste for low-skilled African Americans, also seem reasonable.
12. Another explanation could be based on employer stereotyping or categorizing. If employers have coarser stereotypes for African Americans, many of our results would follow. See Melinda Jones (2002) for the relevant psychology and Mullainathan (2003) for a formalization of the categorization concept.

# 38

# FAMILIES ON THE FRONTIER

*From* Braceros *in the Fields to* Braceras *in the Home*

PIERRETTE HONDAGNEU-SOTELO

*This last reading on the social institution of the economy and employment is by Pierrette Hondagneu-Sotelo, professor of sociology at the University of Southern California. Hondagneu-Sotelo has studied gender, migration, and transnational families for a number of years, and this reading, taken from the 2009 anthology* Latinos: Remaking America*, examines the gendered nature of Mexican immigrant work. Hondagneu-Sotelo explores the history of the American Bracero Program that brought many male Mexican immigrants to the United States to do agricultural labor; more recently, it has changed to the Bracera Program, which recruits female Mexican workers to do domestic labor in American homes. This need to hire others to perform the reproductive labor in homes has enabled many white, middle-, and upper-class women to complete their educations and pursue careers. Ironically, at the same time, this reproductive labor keeps Mexican and Central American immigrant women from raising their own families.*

Why are thousands of Central American and Mexican immigrant women living and working in California and other parts of the United States while their children and other family members remain in their countries of origin? In this chapter, I argue that U.S. labor demand, immigration restrictions, and cultural transformations have encouraged the emergence of new transnational family forms among Central American and Mexican immigrant women. Postindustrial economies bring with them a labor demand for immigrant workers that is differently gendered

*Source:* Hondagneu-Sotelo, Pierrette. 2009. "Families on the Frontier: From Braceros in the Fields to Braceras in the Home." In *Latinos: Remaking America*, edited by Marcelo M. Suarez-Orozco and Mariela M. Paez. Reproduced with permission of University of California Press in the format textbook via Copyright Clearance Center.

from that typical of industrial or industrializing societies. In all postindustrial nations, we see an increase in demand for jobs dedicated to social reproduction, jobs typically coded as "women's jobs." In many of these countries, such jobs are filled by immigrant women from developing nations. Many of these women, because of occupational constraints—and, in some cases, specific restrictionist contract labor policies—must live and work apart from their families.

My discussion focuses on private paid domestic work, a job that in California is nearly always performed by Central American and Mexican immigrant women. Not formally negotiated labor contracts, but rather informal occupational constraints, as well as legal status, mandate the long-term spatial and temporal separation of these women from their families and children. For many Central American and Mexican women who work in the United States, new international divisions of social reproductive labor have brought about transnational family forms and new meanings of family and motherhood. In this respect, the United States has entered a new era of dependency on braceras. Consequently, many Mexican, Salvadoran, and Guatemalan immigrant families look quite different from the images suggested by Latino familism.

This chapter is informed by an occupational study I conducted of over two hundred Mexican and Central American women who do paid domestic work in private homes in Los Angeles (Hondagneu-Sotelo 2001). Here, I focus not on the work but on the migration and family arrangements conditioned by the way paid domestic work is organized today in the United States. I begin by noting the ways in which demand for Mexican—and increasingly Central American—immigrant labor shifted in the twentieth century from a gendered labor demand favoring men to one characterized by robust labor demand for women in a diversity of jobs, including those devoted to commodified social reproduction. Commodified social reproduction refers to the purchase of all kinds of services needed for daily human upkeep, such as cleaning and caring work. The way these jobs are organized often mandates transnational family forms, and in the subsequent section, I

(1) draw on a modest-size survey to suggest the prevalence of this pattern and (2) sketch trajectories leading to these outcomes.

I then note the parallels between family migration patterns prompted by the Bracero Program and long-term male sojourning, when many women sought to follow their husbands to the United States, and the situation today, when many children and youth are apparently traveling north unaccompanied by adults, in hopes of being reunited with their mothers. In the earlier era, men were recruited and wives struggled to migrate; in a minority of cases, Mexican immigrant husbands working in the United States brought their wives against the latters' will. Today, women are recruited for work, and increasingly, their children migrate north some ten to fifteen years after their mothers. Just as Mexican immigrant husbands and wives did not necessarily agree on migration strategies in the earlier era, we see conflicts among today's immigrant mothers in the United States and the children with whom they are being reunited. In this regard, we might suggest that the contention of family power in migration has shifted from gender to generation. I conclude with some questions for a twenty-first-century research agenda.

## GENDERED LABOR DEMAND AND SOCIAL REPRODUCTION

Throughout the United States, a plethora of occupations today increasingly rely on the work performed by Latina and Asian immigrant women. Among these are jobs in downgraded manufacturing, jobs in retail, and a broad spectrum of service jobs in hotels, restaurants, hospitals, convalescent homes, office buildings, and private residences. In some cases, such as in the janitorial industry and in light manufacturing, jobs have been re-gendered and re-racialized so that jobs previously held by U.S.-born white or black men are now increasingly held by Latina immigrant women (Cranford, forthcoming). Jobs in nursing and paid domestic work have long been regarded as "women's jobs," seen as natural outgrowths of essential notions of women as care providers. In the late-twentieth-century United States, however, these jobs have entered the global marketplace, and immigrant women from developing nations around the globe are increasingly represented in them. In major metropolitan centers around the country, Filipina and Indian immigrant women make up a sizable proportion of HMO nursing staffs—a result due in no small part to deliberate recruitment efforts. Caribbean, Mexican, and Central American women increasingly predominate in low-wage service jobs, including paid domestic work.

This diverse gendered labor demand is quite a departure from patterns that prevailed in the western region of the United States only a few decades ago. The relatively dramatic transition from the explicit demand for Mexican and Asian immigrant *male* workers to demand that today includes women has its roots in a changing political economy. From the late nineteenth century until 1964, the period during which various contract labor programs were in place, the economies of the Southwest and the West relied on primary extractive industries. As is well known, Mexican, Chinese, Japanese, and Filipino immigrant workers, primarily men, were recruited for jobs in agriculture, mining, and railroads. These migrant workers were recruited and incorporated in ways that mandated their long-term separation from their families of origin.

As the twentieth century turned into the twenty-first, the United States was once again a nation of immigration. This time, however, immigrant labor is not involved in primary, extractive industry. Agribusiness continues to be a financial leader in the state of California, relying primarily on Mexican immigrant labor and increasingly on indigenous workers from Mexico, but only a fraction of Mexican immigrant workers are employed in agriculture. Labor demand is now extremely heterogeneous and is structurally embedded in the economy of California (Cornelius 1998). In the current period, which some commentators have termed "postindustrial," business and financial services, computer and other high-technology firms, and trade and retail prevail alongside manufacturing, construction, hotels, restaurants, and agriculture as the principal sources of demand for immigrant labor in the western region of the United States.

As the demand for immigrant women's labor has increased, more and more Mexican and (especially) Central American women have left their families and young children behind to seek employment in the United States. Women who work in the United States in order to maintain their families in their countries of origin constitute members of new transnational families, and because these arrangements are choices that the women make in the context of very limited options, they resemble apartheid-like exclusions. These women work in one nation-state but raise their children in another. Strikingly, no formalized temporary contract labor program mandates these separations. Rather, this pattern is related to the contemporary arrangements of social reproduction in the United States.

## WHY THE EXPANSION IN PAID DOMESTIC WORK?

Who could have foreseen that as the twentieth century turned into the twenty-first, paid domestic work would become a growth occupation? Only a few decades ago, observers confidently predicted that this job would soon become obsolete, replaced by such labor-saving household devices as automatic dishwashers, disposable diapers, and microwave ovens, and by consumer goods and services purchased outside the home, such as fast food and dry cleaning (Coser 1974). Instead, paid domestic work has expanded. Why?

The exponential growth in paid domestic work is due in large part to the increased employment of women, especially married women with children, to the underdeveloped nature of child care centers in the United States, and to patterns of U.S. income inequality and global inequalities. National and global trends have fueled this growing demand for paid domestic services. Increasing global competition and new communications technologies have led to work speedups in all sorts of jobs, and the much-bemoaned "time bind" has hit professionals and managers particularly hard (Hochschild 1997). Meanwhile, normative middle-class ideals of child rearing have been elaborated (consider the proliferation of soccer, music lessons, and tutors). At the other end of the age spectrum, greater longevity among the elderly has prompted new demands for care work.

Several commentators, most notably Saskia Sassen, have commented on the expansion of jobs in personal services in the late twentieth century. Sassen located this trend in the rise of new "global cities," cities that serve as business and managerial command points in a new system of intricately connected nodes of global corporations. Unlike New York City, Los Angeles is not home to a slew of Fortune 500 companies, but in the 1990s it exhibited remarkable economic dynamism. Entrepreneurial endeavors proliferated and continued to drive the creation of jobs in business services, such as insurance, real estate, public relations, and so on. These industries, together with the high-tech and entertainment industries in Los Angeles, spawned many high-income managerial and professional jobs, and the occupants of these high-income positions require many personal services that are performed by low-wage immigrant workers. Sassen provides the quintessentially "New York" examples of dog walkers and cooks who prepare gourmet take-out food for penthouse dwellers. The Los Angeles counterparts might include gardeners and car valets, jobs filled primarily by Mexican and Central American immigrant men, and nannies and house cleaners, jobs filled by Mexican and Central American immigrant women. In fact, the numbers of domestic workers in private homes counted by the Bureau of the Census doubled from 1980 to 1990 (Waldinger 1996).

I favor an analysis that does not speak in terms of "personal services," which seems to imply services that are somehow private, individual rather than social, and are superfluous to the way society is organized. A feminist concept that was originally introduced to valorize the nonremunerated household work of women, *social reproduction* or alternately, *reproductive labor*, might be more usefully employed. Replacing *personal services* with *social reproduction* shifts the focus by underlining the objective of the work, the societal functions, and the impact on immigrant workers and their own families.

Social reproduction consists of those activities that are necessary to maintain human life, daily and intergenerationally. This includes how we take care of ourselves, our children and elderly, and our homes. Social reproduction encompasses the purchasing and preparation of food, shelter, and clothing; the routine daily upkeep of these, such as cooking, cleaning, and laundering; the emotional care and support of children and adults; and the maintenance of family and community ties. The way a society organizes social reproduction has far-reaching consequences not only for individuals and families but also for macrohistorical processes (Laslett and Brenner 1989).

Many components of social reproduction have become commodified and outsourced in all kinds of new ways. Today, for example, not only can you purchase fast-food meals, but you can also purchase, through the Internet, the home delivery of customized lists of grocery items. Whereas mothers were once available to buy and wrap Christmas presents, pick up dry cleaning, shop for groceries and wait around for the plumber, today new businesses have sprung up to meet these demands—for a fee.

In this new milieu, private paid domestic work is just one example of the commodification of social reproduction. Of course, domestic workers and servants of all kinds have been cleaning and cooking for others and caring for other people's children for centuries, but there is today an increasing proliferation of these services among various class sectors and a new flexibility in how these services are purchased.

## GLOBAL TRENDS IN PAID DOMESTIC WORK

Just as paid domestic work has expanded in the United States, so too it appears to have grown in many other postindustrial societies, in the "newly industrialized countries" (NICs) of Asia, in the oil-rich nations of the Middle East, in Canada, and in parts of Europe. In paid domestic work around the globe, Caribbean, Mexican, Central American, Peruvian, Sri Lankan, Indonesian, Eastern European, and Filipina women—the latter in disproportionately large numbers— predominate. Worldwide, paid domestic work continues its long legacy as a racialized and gendered occupation, but today, divisions of nation and citizenship are increasingly salient.

The inequality of nations is a key factor in the globalization of contemporary paid domestic work. This has led to three outcomes: (1) Around the globe, paid domestic work is increasingly performed by women who leave their own nations, their communities, and often their families of origin to do the work. (2) The occupation draws not only women from the poor socioeconomic classes, but also women who hail from nations that colonialism has made much poorer than those countries where they go to do domestic work. This explains why it is not unusual to find college-educated women from the middle class working in other countries as private domestic workers. (3) Largely because of the long, uninterrupted schedules of service required, domestic workers are not allowed to migrate as members of families.

Nations that "import" domestic workers from other countries do so using vastly different methods. Some countries have developed highly regulated, government-operated, contract labor programs that have institutionalized both the recruitment and the bonded servitude of migrant domestic workers. Canada and Hong Kong provide paradigmatic examples of this approach. Since 1981 the Canadian federal government has formally recruited thousands of women to work as live-in nannies/housekeepers for Canadian families. Most of these women came from Third World countries in the 1990s (the majority came from the Philippines, in the 1980s from the Caribbean), and once in Canada, they must remain in live-in domestic service for two years, until they obtain their landed immigrant status, the equivalent of the U.S. "green card." This reflects, as Bakan and Stasiulis (1997) have noted, a type of indentured servitude and a decline in the citizenship rights of foreign domestic workers, one that coincides with the racialization of the occupation. When Canadians recruited white British women for domestic work in the 1940s, they did so under far less controlling mechanisms than those applied to Caribbean and Filipina domestic workers. Today, foreign domestic workers in Canada may not quit their jobs or collectively organize to improve the conditions under which they work.

Similarly, since 1973 Hong Kong has relied on the formal recruitment of domestic workers, mostly Filipinas, to work on a full-time, live-in basis for Chinese families. Of the 150,000 foreign domestic workers in Hong Kong in 1995, 130,000 hailed from the Philippines, and smaller numbers were drawn from Thailand, Indonesia, India, Sri Lanka, and Nepal (Constable 1997:3). Just as it is now rare to find African American women employed in private domestic work in Los Angeles, so too have Chinese women vanished from the occupation in Hong Kong. As Nicole Constable reveals in her detailed study, Filipina domestic workers in Hong Kong are controlled and disciplined by official employment agencies, employers, and strict government policies. Filipinas and other foreign domestic workers recruited to Hong Kong find themselves working primarily in live-in jobs and bound by two-year contracts that stipulate lists of job rules, regulations for bodily display and discipline (no lipstick, nail polish, or long hair, submission to pregnancy tests, etc.), task timetables, and the policing of personal privacy. Taiwan has adopted a similarly formal and restrictive government policy to regulate the incorporation of Filipina domestic workers (Lan 2000).

In this global context, the United States remains distinctive, because it takes more of a *laissez-faire* approach to the incorporation of immigrant women into paid domestic work. No formal government system or policy exists to legally contract foreign domestic workers in the United States. Although in the past, private employers in the United States were able to "sponsor" individual immigrant women who were working as domestics for their "green cards" using labor certification (sometimes these employers personally recruited them while vacationing or working in foreign countries), this route is unusual in Los Angeles today. Obtaining legal status through labor certification requires documentation that there is a shortage of labor to perform a particular, specialized occupation. In Los Angeles and in many parts of the country today, a shortage of domestic workers is increasingly difficult to prove. And it is apparently unnecessary, because the significant demand for domestic workers in the United States is largely filled not through formal channels of foreign recruitment but through informal recruitment from the growing number of Caribbean and Latina immigrant women who are *already* legally or illigally living in the United States. The Immigration and Naturalization Service, the federal agency charged with enforcement of illegal-migration laws, has historically served the interests of domestic employers and winked at the employment of undocumented immigrant women in private homes.

As we compare the hyperregulated employment systems in Hong Kong and Canada with the more *laissez-faire* system for domestic work in the United States, we find that although the methods of recruitment and hiring and the roles of the state in these processes are quite different, the consequences are similar. Both systems require the incorporation as workers of migrant women who can be separated from their families.

The requirements of live-in domestic jobs, in particular, virtually mandate this. Many immigrant women who work in live-in jobs find that they must be "on call" during all waking hours and often throughout the night, so there is no clear line between working and nonworking hours. The line between job space and private space is similarly blurred, and rules and regulations may extend around the clock. Some employers restrict the ability of their live-in employees to receive phone calls, entertain friends, attend evening ESL classes, or see boyfriends during the workweek. Other employers do not impose these sorts of restrictions, but because their homes are located in remote hillsides, suburban enclaves, or gated communities, live-in nannies/housekeepers are effectively restricted from participating in anything resembling social life, family life of their own, or public culture.

These domestic workers—the Filipinas working in Hong Kong or Taiwan, the Caribbean women working on the East Coast, and the Central American and Mexican immigrant women working in California constitute the new "braceras." They are literally "pairs of arms," disembodied and dislocated from their families and communities of origin, and yet they are not temporary sojourners. In the section that follows, I suggest some of the dimensions of this phenomenon and present several illustrative career trajectories.

## THE NEW BRACERAS AND TRANSNATIONAL MOTHERHOOD

What are the dimensions of this phenomeon which I refer to as the new braceras and the new forms of transnational motherhood? Precise figures are not available; no one has counted the universe of everyone working in private paid domestic work, which continues to be an informal sector—an "under the table" occupation—and accurately estimating the numbers in immigrant groups that include those who are poor and lack legal work authorization is always difficult. Several indicators, however, suggest that the dimensions are quite significant. My nonrandom survey of 153 Latina immigrant domestic workers, which I conducted at bus stops, at ESL evening classes, and in public parks where Latina nannies take their young charges, revealed the following. Approximately 75 percent of the Latina domestic workers had children of their own, and a startling 40 percent of the women with children had at least one of their children "back home" in their country of origin.

The survey finding that 40 percent of Latina domestic workers with children of their own had at least one child living in their country of origin is substantiated by other anectodal indicators. In a study of immigrant children in the Pico-Union area of Los Angeles, a largely Central American and Mexican immigrant neighborhood, sociologists Barrie Thorne and Marjorie Faulstich-Orellana found that half of the children in a first-grade class had siblings in El Salvador. Investigative journalist Sonia Nazarrio (personal communication), who has researched immigration in Mexico, in El Salvador, and in newcomer schools in Los Angeles, reports that a high percentage of Central American children remain "back home" for lengthy periods while their parents are working in the United States. Similarly, sociologist Cecilia Menjivar (2000), in her study of Salvadorans in San Francisco, finds that many Salvadoran immigrant workers are supporting their children in El Salvador.

Given these various indicators, an estimated 40 to 50 percent of Central American and Mexican women leave their children in their countries of origin when they migrate to the United States. They believe the separation from their children will be temporary, but physical separation may endure for long, and sometimes undetermined, periods of time. Job constraints, legal-status barriers, and perceptions of the United States as a dangerous place to raise children explain these long-term separations. In the remainder of this section, I discuss how job constraints in live-in paid domestic work encourage this pattern, but first, I briefly discuss how legal status and perceptions of the United States play a role.

Private domestic workers who hail primarily from Mexico, Central America, and the Caribbean hold various legal statuses. Some, for example, are legal permanent residents or naturalized U.S. citizens, many of them beneficiaries of the Immigration Reform and Control Act's amnesty-legalization program, enacted in 1986. Most Central American women, who prevail in the occupation, entered the United States after the 1982 cutoff date for amnesty-legalization, so they did not qualify for legalization. Throughout the 1990s, a substantial proportion of Central Americans either remained undocumented or held a series of temporary work permits, granted to delay their return to war-ravaged countries.

Their precarious legal status as an "illegal" or "undocumented immigrant" discouraged many immigrant mothers from migrating with their children or bringing them to the United States. The ability of undocumented immigrant parents to bring children north was also complicated in the late 1990s by the militarization of the U.S.–Mexico border through the implementation of various border control programs (Operation Gate-keeper, etc) . . . . The U.S.–Mexico border has become a zone of danger, violence, and death. This not only made it difficult to migrate with children, it also made it difficult to travel back and forth to visit family members "back home." Bound by precarious legal status in the United States, which might expose them to the risk of deportation and denial of all kinds of benefits, and by the greater danger and expense in bringing children to the United States, many immigrant mothers opted not to travel with their children or send for them. Instead, they endure long separations.

Many immigrant parents of various nationalities also view the United States as a highly undesirable place to raise children. Immigrant parents fear the dangers of gangs, violence, drugs, and second-rate schools to which their children are likely to be exposed in poor, inner-city neighborhoods. They are also appalled by the way immigration often weakens generational authority. As one Salvadoran youth put it, "Here I do what I please, and no one can control me" (Menjivar 2000:213).

Even mothers who enjoyed legal status and had successfully raised and educated their children through adolescence hesitated to bring them to this country. They saw the United States as a place where their children would suffer job discrimination and economic marginalization. As one Salvadoran domestic worker, who had raised her children on earnings predicated on her separation from them, exclaimed when I spoke with her at an employment agency, "I've been here for 19 years. I've got my legal papers and everything, but I'd have to be crazy to bring my children here. All of them have studied for a career, so why would I bring them here? To bus tables and earn minimum wage? So they won't have enough money for bus fare or food?" (Hondagneu-Sotelo and Avial 1997).

Although precarious legal status and perceptions of the United States as an undesirable place in which to raise children are important in shaping transnational family forms, the constraints of paid domestic work, particularly those that are typical in live-in work, virtually mandate family separations.

Live-in jobs serve as a port of entry for many Latina immigrant women, especially for those who lack access to rich social networks. According to the survey I conducted in Los Angeles, live-in domestic workers work, on average, sixty-four hours per week. Work schedules typically consist of six very long workdays and may include overnight responsibilities with sleepless or sick children. This makes it virtually impossible for live-in workers to sustain daily contact with their own family members. As a consequence of the sub-minimum wages typical of live-in work, and the blurred line around hourly parameters in their jobs, some women remain separated from their families and children while working as "braceras" for more years than they had originally anticipated. Two cases will illustrate some of these trajectories.

When I met her, Carmen Velasquez, a thirty-nine-year-old Mexicana, was working as a live-in nanny-housekeeper, in charge of general housekeeping and the daily care of one toddler, in the hillside suburban home of an attorney and schoolteacher. Carmen, a single mother, had migrated to California alone ten years before, leaving behind her three children when they were four, five, and seven years old. Since then, she had seen them only in photographs. The children were now in their teens. She regularly sent money to the children and communicated by letters and phone calls with them and her three *comadres* (co-godmothers), who cared for one of the children each in Mexico.

Carmen had initially thought that it would be possible for her to maintain these arrangements for only a short while. She knew she could work hard and thought that working as a live-in domestic worker would enable her to save her earnings by not paying rent or room and board. But, as she somberly noted, "Sometimes your desires just aren't possible."

A series of traumatic events that included incest and domestic violence prompted her migration and had left her completely estranged from the father of her children, from her parents, and from her siblings. With the support only of her female comadres in Mexico, and assisted by the friend of a friend, she had come north "without papers," determined to pioneer a new life for herself and her children.

Her first two live-in jobs, in which she stayed for a total of seven years, included some of the worst arrangements I have had described to me. In both cases, she worked round-the-clock schedules in the homes of Mexican immigrant families, slept on living room couches or in hallways, and earned only $50 a week. Isolated, discouraged, and depressed, she stayed in those jobs out of desperation and lack of opportunity.

By comparison with what she had endured, she expressed relative satisfaction with her current live-in job. Her employers treated her with respect, paid $170 a week, gave her a separate bedroom and bathroom, and were not, she said, too demanding in terms of what they expected of her. Unlike the workdays of many other live-in nannies/housekeepers, her workday ended when the *señora* arrived home at 5 P.M. Still, when I asked whether she now had plans to bring her children to Los Angeles, she equivocated.

She remained vexed by the problem of how she could raise her children in Los Angeles and maintain a job at the same time. "The *señora* is kind and understanding," she said, "but she needs me here with the baby. And then how could I pay the rent, the bus fare to transport myself? And my children [voice quivering] are so big now. They can't have the same affection they once had, because they no longer know me . . . ." As psychologist Celia Falacov underscores, there are many losses incurred with migration and family reunification. Women such as Carmen sacrifice to provide a better life for their children, but in the process, they may lose family life with their children.

Some women *do* successfully bring and reintegrate their children with them in the United States, but there are often unforeseen costs and risks associated with this strategy. Erlinda Castro, a Guatemalan mother of five children, came to the United States in 1992. She left all five children behind in Guatemala, under the care of the eldest, supervised by a close neighbor, and joined her husband in Los Angeles. She initially endured live-in domestic jobs. These jobs were easy to acquire quickly, and they enabled her to save on rent. After two years, she moved into an apartment with her husband and her sister, and she moved out of live-in domestic work into house cleaning. By cleaning different houses on different days, she gained a more flexible work schedule, earning more with fewer hours of work. Eventually, she was able to send money for two of the children to come north.

The key to Erlinda's ability to bring two of her children to the United States was her shift in domestic employment from live-in work to house cleaning. According to my survey results, Latina immigrant mothers who work in live-in nanny/housekeeping jobs are the most likely to have their children back home (82 percent) than are women who work cleaning houses. And mothers who clean different houses on different days are the least likely to have their children in their countries of origin (24 percent).

Bringing children north after long periods of separation may entail unforeseen "costs of transnationalism," as Susan Gonzalez-Baker suggests. Just as migration often rearranges gender relations between spouses, so too, does migration prompt challenges to familiar generational relations between parents and offspring . . . .

## Conclusion

The trajectories described here pose an enormous challenge to those who would celebrate any and all instances of transnationalism. These migration patterns alert us to the fact that the continued privatization of social reproduction among the American professional and managerial class has broad repercussions for the social relations among new Latina immigrants and their families. Similarly, strong emotional ties between mothers and children, which

we might dismiss as personal subjectivities, are fueling massive remittances to countries such as El Salvador and the Philippines. Our most fundamental question remains unanswered: Who will continue to pick up the cost of raising the next generation? Surely, we can hope for a society wherein Latina immigrant women and children are not the first to bear those costs.

## Discussion Questions

1. What is reproductive labor, and why is it an important concept to study when examining social inequality in employment and the economy? How do we reconcile the fact that social mobility of some women comes at a large cost for others?

2. What are some of the historically unprecedented findings Hondagneu-Sotelo presents about transnational Latina laborers, the *braceras,* and their parenting of children in Mexico and Central America? What are the implications of this postindustrial situation for the future of the family?

# 39

# SOCIAL DETERMINANTS AND FAMILY HEALTH

## JANET R. GROCHOWSKI

*Janet R. Grochowski, chair of the education department at College of St. Benedict/St. John's University, has studied families and health for a long time. This reading, the first of three on the institution of health care and medicine, is taken from Grochowski's 2010 book, Families and Health. Grochowski begins the reading by illustrating four cases of how social determinants such as race-ethnicity, gender, income, occupation, and others can affect health. According to Grochowski, these social factors are as important as biological and psychological factors in determining health status and access to care. After documenting ways that race, gender, and education can affect illness outcomes, Grochowski argues that these social determinants create health disparities and social inequality that need to be addressed by the U.S. health care system.*

## HEALTH DISPARITIES AMONG FAMILIES

### Case 1: The Injustice of Health Inequities

Ted worked hard to reach his current position of a chief executive officer (CEO) at a major American insurance company. At age 59, he takes pride in his success as well as in his health and that of his family. Ten years earlier he and his wife, Terry, quit smoking with the support of their medical plan. They and their three children strive to maintain healthful diet and exercise behaviors. They live in a lovely, quiet neighborhood with ample biking and walking trails surrounded by a safe and beautiful environment. As college graduates, Ted and Terry

*Source:* Grochowski, Janet R. 2010. "Social Determinants and Family Health." Pp.71–98 in *Families and Health,* edited by Janet R. Grochowski. 2nd ed. Thousand Oaks, CA: Sage.

*are keen that their children attend the best schools and experience a life rich in travel, activities, and health care.*

*Juanita works as a claims adjustor for the same company where Ted works. She is 37 years old and recently completed her college degree while working full time. She and her partner, Glenda, purchased a house last year, so college debt and mortgage payments are major concerns for Juanita. She enjoys her job and considers herself to be middle class. Her position demands significant responsibility, but she struggles with pressure from her division boss, whose management style is harsh and often disrespectful of Glenda's sex and sexual orientation. Yet, with the job market so tight, Juanita does not want to cause any trouble. She is finally making a decent salary, has health care coverage, and can live away from the Latino projects she grew up in.*

*Jonathan works as a custodian for this insurance company. At the age 45, he is glad to have a job, but frustrated that his family cannot seem to get ahead. He and his wife, Tiffany, finished high school, but are unprepared for a job market that demands higher skills. Jonathan has a heart condition and Tiffany suffers from type 2 diabetes. They cannot afford the increasing out-of-pocket costs of regular health exams or dental coverage. Their African American neighborhood is plagued with violence and underfunded schools. They and their two sons (aged 12 and 10 years, respectively) are overweight.*

*Morning Dew, 51 years of age, is unemployed and is living in an American Indian reservation 50 miles from the urban area where Ted, Juanita, and Jonathan live. Her husband is physically disabled and has been out of work for the past 15 years. They live below the poverty line in a crowded two-bedroom apartment in an impoverished rural area with their three teenage children. Morning Dew suffers from depression and both she and her husband have type 2 diabetes. Their children are overweight, smoke, and two of them have dropped out of high school.*

Case 1 illustrates some of the health disparities found within the American culture . . . health disparities are disproportionate burdens on or risks of disease, illness, disability, or death found among specific segments of the population. Health disparities fall under the social determinants of health that include features of and channels by which families' social-cultural circumstances impact health and well-being. Social determinants often include income, social status, occupation, housing, geographic location, education, social support, community structure, availability of health services, cultural beliefs and attitudes, discrimination, prejudice, and inequality. If you had to guess from the brief descriptions in Case 1 which of these four individuals (Ted, Juanita, Jonathan, and Morning Dew) has the best and worst health circumstances, who would you pick? If you identified Ted and Morning Dew respectively, you are correct. Would you also say that Juanita and Jonathan enjoy the same level of health opportunity as Ted? If you said yes, you would be incorrect. While Juanita and Jonathan may be healthier than Morning Dew, neither enjoys the full level of health or longevity as that of Ted. Why? Statistically, based on Ted's race and ethnicity (non-Hispanic white), socioeconomic status (SES), education, housing, and geographic location, he will not only live approximately five years or more longer than Morning Dew, but also will have a longer life span than either Juanita and Jonathan. From 1980 to 1982, the life expectancy for the most affluent Americans was 2.8 years longer than that of the most deprived, but by 1990 to 2000 this gap increased to 4.5 years and continues to increase (Singh and Siahpush 2006:975). Consider that, in 2000, the difference in life expectancy between poor black men and wealthy white women was 14 years (2006:975). The quantity and quality of these additional years are important measures of family and population health.

While overall health and life expectancy continues to improve for many Americans, a disturbing number of Americans are not benefiting equally. African Americans, Latinos, American Indians and Alaskan Natives, and Native Hawaiian and other Pacific Islanders suffer greater prevalence of illness and experience higher death rates than the remainder of the U.S. population. Minorities and others living in poverty, therefore, have earlier mortality rates, are in poorer health, often are uninsured, and experience more difficulties accessing quality, effective health care (Mead et al. 2008). According to Sarah Gehlert and colleagues:

> Health disparities occur by race, ethnicity, sex, socioeconomic status, education, geographic location, and sexual orientation, with inequalities in screening, incidence, treatment, and mortality across a number of diseases and conditions, including cancer, diabetes, cardiovascular disease, infant mortality, and HIV/AIDS. (2008:339)

The link between wealth and health has long recognized as a cause of health disparities in the United States as revealed in Case 1. As the SES gap widens, health disparities increase. Even when data are adjusted for income, education, and health care coverage, however, health disparities continue to persist and even increase (Mead et al. 2008). What is less understood, therefore, is the interactive nature of social determinants resulting in health disparities. David Mechanic and Jennifer Tanner (2007) argue that vulnerability to health disparities result from a "social stress process," during which stressors, such as financial downturns, illness, and discrimination, are balanced against resources, such as income and wealth, education, cognitive ability, social networking, and community resources. These authors emphasize that the primary sources of vulnerability are poverty, race, and the "related issues of stigma and discrimination" (2007:1223).

For example, consider the factor of geographic location in Case 1. Ted's family lives in a safer neighborhood that provides more healthful opportunities (e.g., recreation and more healthful food options) as compared to Jonathan's or Morning Dew's families. According to scholars (Acevedo-Garcia et al. 2008), even with policy initiatives to reduce poverty and enhance access to medical care, health disparities continue to plague segments of the population along racial and ethnic lines. What is new is their identification of "residential segregation" between minority and white populations as a major determinant of health disparity. They further argue that the SES and affordable housing issues alone do not account for the continued high levels of segregation and note that residential segregation plays a major role. A documentary, *Unnatural Causes: Is Inequality Making Us Sick?* (California Newsreel and National Minority Consortia of Public Television, 2008) supports a position that discrimination and residential segregation interlinked with issues of poverty, poor education, limited health care access, and lower quality of health services is creating a complex challenge to improving the health of American families. While genetics, health behaviors, environmental exposures, and health care policy and services remain crucial influences on family health, social determinants take center stage in understanding and addressing health disparities among families. Scholars urge professionals in medical, social, and related sciences to focus on the impact of this reality (Sankar et al. 2004).

Delores Acevedo-Garcia and her colleagues (2008) report that opportunities for better health are tied to geographical location with disadvantaged neighborhoods struggling with barriers of geography (i.e., limited transportation, poor housing, unemployment, unsafe neighborhoods, limited recreation, and unhealthy food options). Linked to these geographic location issues is the impact of education. Ellen Meara, Seth Richards, and David Cutler (2008) explain that the majority of gains in life expectancy made during the 1981 to 2000 period occurred primarily among highly educated groups with any college education, thus exposing an educational gap in life expectancy. From 1990 to 2000, life expectancy increased 1.6 years for the highly educated group, but did not change for the less-educated group. Thus, in 2000, a 25-year-old with some college education had a life expectancy almost seven years longer than a peer with a high school diploma or less education (2008:353). Hence, being educationally disadvantaged, such as Morning Dew's children in Case 1, raises the risk of poorer health and earlier death rates. While recognizing education as a powerful factor in health status, however, Rachel Tolbert Kimbro and her colleagues (2008) note that the education gradient appears to vary in its impact with some racial, ethnic, and nativity groups, with foreign-born immigrants enjoying better health and mortality rates than their American-born peers even at lower education levels. There are several rationales for this paradox found within certain racial and ethnic groups. The main point, however, is that in order to better understand and address health disparities, researchers and practitioners need to recognize the important impact of education in conjunction with culture on family health.

Such an eclectic approach is represented by longitudinal studies that provide a solid basis for the vital role of social determinants and their impact on health disparities. One of the premiere studies is the Whitehall I Study that began in 1967 examining the social circumstances of 18,000 British Civil Service men and how these determinants impacted their well-being and health. This initial study was followed by nine waves of data with the latest one occurring in 2007. Whitehall II includes a cohort of over 10,000 women and men employees of the British Civil Service. While this rich study provides extensive data on the important influence of the "social gradient" on health, it also dispelled two myths. The first is that those with the highest status positions have the highest risk of heart disease. In fact, those individuals in jobs with high demand and little control (e.g., office managers, custodians) have a much higher risk of heart disease, as noted with Jonathan in Case 1. The second myth is the belief that in developed, industrialized societies, health "is simply a matter of poor health for the disadvantaged and good health for everyone else" (Turnbull and Serwotka 2008:4). The Whitehall and other studies emphasize that health disparities are not solely a matter of poverty, but rather a complex web of social determinants. The social circumstances at home, in the community, and at work all significantly influence family health in general and health disparities in particular.

*Healthy People 2010*, a nationwide, comprehensive health promotion and disease prevention agenda of the Department of Health and Human Services, serves as a framework for improving the health of the American people. The two primary goals include: (1) an increase in quality and number of years of healthy life, and (2) the elimination of health disparities (U.S. Department of Health and Human Services 2008). Consistent evidence reveals that "race and ethnicity correlate with persistent and often increasing, health disparities among U.S. populations ..." and minorities suffer higher rates of mortality and prevalence of most illnesses and diseases (Office of Minority Health and Health Disparities 2007:1). In 2005, minorities composed over one-third of the U.S. population, with Hispanics making up the largest segment of minorities. By 2050, it is estimated that minority groups will make up almost 50 percent of the population ....

Anticipated demographic shifts during the next few decades raise both ethical and practical concerns over these health disparities. In light of these concerns, six areas have been targeted by *Healthy People 2010*. The following provides a glimpse at the scope of health disparities in these areas.

### Infant Mortality

Infant mortality is defined as the proportion of babies who die before they reach their first birthday, and it is often used to compare the health and well-being status across and within countries. In 2008, the United States ranked only 27th among 30 developed nations at 6.9 deaths in 1,000 live births, while the average was only 5.2. Within the nations of the European Union the rate is less than five in 1,000 babies, and in Japan, Singapore, Sweden, and Norway the proportion of babies who die is less than half that of the United States (Organization for Economic Co-Operation and Development 2008:2). When viewed through a minority health lens, the rate of infant mortality more than doubles (13.7) for non-Hispanic African American families. The mission of the Office of Minority Health and Health Disparities (2007:1) is to "improve and protect the health of racial and ethnic minority populations through the development of health policies and programs that will eliminate health disparities."

This wide variation in infant mortality rates by race and Hispanic origin continues with the highest rate (13.7) for infants of non-Hispanic African

American mothers, more than three times higher than the lowest rate of 4.3 for infants of Cuban mothers. Rates of infant mortality for infants of American Indian (8.6) and Puerto Rican (8.1) mothers were also significantly higher than the national rating (National Center for Health Statistics 2007:177). The causes of this higher prevalence of infant mortality remains unclear, but looking at any of a wide variety of risk factors related to infant mortality reveals that non-Hispanic African American, American Indian, and Puerto Rican mothers did not receive adequate prenatal care, often were unmarried or were teenagers, were having a fourth or higher order birth, or had not completed high school. Again, there appears to be a complex web of social determinants such as SES, geographic location, and education level intertwined with poverty (Acevedo-Garcia, Soobader, and Berkman 2005).

## Cardiovascular Disease

Cardiovascular disease (CVD) (i.e., heart disease and stroke) is the leading cause of death in Americans across all racial and ethnic groups and for both sexes. Yet, low-income and minority segments have a disproportional higher level of death and disability rates due to CVD, with African Americans developing high blood pressure earlier and at the highest rate of all groups (Office of Minority Health and Health Disparities 2007). Black men and women have the highest rates of cardiovascular disease mortality among all races and ethnic groups . . . .

The burden of disease borne by minority groups is considerable, "with the greatest evidence of a disproportionate disease burden and disproportionate distribution of risk factors [endured] by the African American population" (Yancy 2008:276). Medical professionals increasingly recognize that while biological factors are important in this imbalance, "psychosocial and socioeconomic factors" also must be considered and addressed in CVD treatment and preventive care practices (Yancy 2008:283). For example, as the rates of obesity among non-Hispanic African Americans and Hispanic adults climb, so does the prevalence of CVD within these populations.

## Diabetes

The Centers for Disease Control and Prevention (2009:1) state that 23.6 million Americans have diabetes. The prevalence rates of diagnosed diabetes, however, show disparities in terms of age, sex, race, and ethnicity with African Americans or blacks, Hispanics or Latinos, American Indian, and Alaska Native adults diagnosed at twice the rate than non-Hispanic whites. From 1980 to 2006, the rate doubled for black men and increased by 69 percent for black women, the highest rate of all racial groups. (Centers for Disease Control and Prevention 2008a:1). The rate of prevalence of diabetes per 100 persons, when measured by age, sex, race, and ethnicity, revealed significant disparities with aged 65- to 75+-year-old black females and 65- to 74-year-old Asian and Pacific Islander males with the highest prevalence rates.

## Cancers

In addition, racial and ethnic disparities exist for many cancers (e.g., breast, cervical, colorectal, and prostate) that are amenable to early diagnosis and treatment. Non-Hispanic white women continue to have a higher incidence of breast cancer than minorities, yet non-Hispanic black women have much higher rates of breast cancer mortality. Hispanic women have twice the risk of having cervical cancer than whites, but black women are twice as likely to die from this disease. While poverty and limited access to health care are significant factors in these health disparities, it is vital to note that while black women were just as likely to have had a mammogram as white women, the follow-up communication and treatment regarding their screening results were not as adequate as that provided to white women. Hence, when considering health disparities, the probe needs to flesh out the complex interactions of social determinants. Similar statistics are found for males in that black men are 50 percent more likely to have prostate cancer than whites, but are twice as likely to die from it (Mead et al. 2008:37–38). Overall, African Americans of both sexes suffer more malignant tumors and have a lower survivor rate than the general population (American Cancer Society 2003). Both Hispanic women and men have higher rates of infection-related cancers such as liver (related to Hepatitis C infections) and cervical (related to human papilloma virus [HPV] infection) than other racial and ethnic groups. American Indians and Alaskan Natives were more than twice as likely to be diagnosed with stomach and liver cancers than non-Hispanic whites (Office of Minority Health and Health Disparities 2008:1).

### HIV Infection and AIDS

.... Human immunodeficiency virus/acquired immunodeficiency syndrome (HIV/AIDS) is noted here to illustrate the dramatic health disparity found within this disease. In 2006, African Americans and Hispanics represented only 27 percent (12 percent and 15 percent, respectively) of the U.S. population, yet they accounted for 68 percent of the HIV/AIDS diagnoses and face more barriers in accessing health care (Kaiser Family Foundation 2008). The disparity grows even more troublesome when the demographic of sex is considered. While African American men represent 43 percent of all new AIDS diagnoses compared to whites (35 percent) and Hispanics (20 percent), African American women suffered 66 percent compared to whites (17 percent) and Hispanics (16 percent) (Kaiser Family Foundation 2008:1). African Americans, therefore, are disproportionately affected at all stages of the HIV/AIDS epidemic as compared to other races and ethnicities. The disparity of the epidemic continues to grow, with African Americans having the highest rates of those living with AIDS- and HIV-related deaths than any other racial and ethnic group in the United States (Centers for Disease Control and Prevention 2008) ....

### Immunizations

The issue of neglecting childhood vaccinations ... illustrates the influence of health behavior patterns in family health. While refusing immunizations cuts cross SES lines, troubling race and ethnic disparities exist that are linked to social determinants

over family behavior patterns. Racial and ethnic disparities in completion of vaccinations persist, with non-Hispanic African American and Hispanic children significantly undervaccinated as compared to non-Hispanic white children (Smith and Stevenson 2008). A similar trend is found among adults. Michael Link and colleagues (2006) reported that influenza and pneumococcal vaccination coverage (completion) disparities by race and ethnicity persisted for non-Hispanic black and Hispanic adults aged 65 years and older during the period from 2000 to 2005. Vaccination disparities also exist for those less than 65 years old ....

In addition to these six diseases and conditions, other serious health concerns, such as mental illness, also reveal disparities based on race, ethnicity, gender, age, income, marital status, education, and the very nature of the illness itself.

### Mental Illness

In the United States alone, mental illnesses are the second leading cause of disability, with mental disorders affecting one in four Americans aged 15 to 44 (National Institute of Mental Health 2008:1). According to the Surgeon General, mental illness reflects a group of diagnosable disorders ranging from "alterations in thinking, mood, or behavior (or combination thereof) associated with distress and/ or impaired functioning" (U.S. Department of Health and Human Services 1999:vii). [Earlier], Alzheimer's disease was presented as a mental disorder marked by impaired thinking, in other words, lost memory. Depression represents alternation in mood, while attention-deficit disorder is an example of altered behavior (e.g., inability to concentrate). Impairments in thinking, mood, or behavior contribute to a range of health problems including increased risk of death, disability, pain, distress, impaired functioning, or reduced freedom (American Psychiatric Association 1994).

According to Stephanie Riolo and colleagues (2005), non-Hispanic whites had the highest prevalence of depression (which is clinically termed *major depressive disorder*) as compared to African Americans and Mexican Americans, but minorities who suffered depression were less likely to receive medical care, which may contribute to their higher rates of "lingering depression," "dysthyma disorder."[1] This difference was partially explained by poverty and lower education; however, not speaking English may also play a key role. Violent neighborhoods, such as Jonathan's in Case 1, has a direct (e.g., victims of violence) and indirect (e.g., fear and perceptions of neighbor as disordered) connection to distress and depression of their residents (Curry, Latkin, and Davey-Rothwell 2008).

Gender reveals significant disparity in mental illness. While the overall rates of psychiatric disorders are somewhat similar for men and women, there are striking differences in the patterns of mental illness with women experiencing depression twice than that of men. On a global scale, depression is the most common mental health problem for women, and it remains more persistent in females than males. It is estimated that 20 percent of women seeking primary health care in developed countries suffer from anxiety and/or depressive disorders. According to the World Health Organization (2008:2):

> Pressures created by [women's] multiple roles, gender discrimination and associated factors of poverty, hunger, malnutrition, overwork, domestic violence and sexual abuse, combine to account for women's poor mental health. There is a positive relationship between the frequency and severity of such social factors and the frequency and severity of mental health problems in women.

While the diagnostic criteria for depression are similar for both sexes, women with depression more frequently experience higher levels of anxiety and guilt, along with increased appetite and sleep, weight gain, and eating disorders (Bhatia and Bhatia 1999). According to Phyllis Moen and Kelly Chermack, gender and health are both biological, yet are dependent on social determinants, for while women tend to live longer than men, females often endure poorer health, greater stress, and more disabilities (2005). Gender imposes critical influence on mental health and mental illness since gender is related to power and control over the social determinants of individuals' lives including social status, treatments, and exposure to specific mental risks. Gender risk factors for common mental disorders include lower SES, gender-based violence, genetic (family health history), and persistent psychosocial stressors (e.g., loss of job, discrimination) (Bhatia and Bhatia 1999).

Many women, sometime during their lives, develop depression at a rate almost twice that of men. According to Mayo Clinic's researchers "[a] woman's unique biological, psychological, and cultural factors may increase her risk of depression" (2008:1). In addition to hormonal shifts and physical changes, social and cultural determinants play a role in female depression. The stressors of balancing work and family responsibilities along with increased rates of female sexual abuse and domestic violence increase the depression gender gap. American women, as with most women globally, often earn less than men and enjoy lower SES. Stressors include, but are not limited to, an uncertainty about the future, community support, economic downturns, and limited access to health care that all increase women's vulnerability. Single, divorced, or widowed women living alone in rural areas also report greater instances of depression than their married peers, which may be due to isolation, lower SES, and general fears about the future (Mayo Clinic 2008). Some minority women also face the additional stressor of discrimination. When depression prevalence for women is examined by race and ethnicity, Hispanic-Latina women have the highest lifetime rate of depression (24 percent) among women. While the rate of depression among women for non-Hispanic white women (22 percent) is higher than that for non-Hispanic African American women (16 percent), almost half (47 percent) of non-Hispanic African American women suffer with severe depression. Finally, 14 percent of American Indians and Alaskan Native female adolescents report feeling extremely sad and hopeless (Women's Health 2003). In Case 1, Morning Dew's depression may have a genetic component, but when combined with SES, educational and geographic location disparities a risk of mental illness significantly increases among her children.

While race, ethnicity, age, and gender offer greater insight to the health disparities surrounding mental illness, the concept of "healthy immigrant effect" raises a core issue of social relationships. Healthy immigrant effect occurs when foreign-born populations enjoy better mental and physical health than their native-born peers as revealed in the literature (Kennedy, McDonald, and Biddle 2006; Lincoln et al. 2007). This advantage erodes after 10 years of living in their adopted country, which focuses attention on the potential harm of discrimination, prejudice, and isolation. Karen Lincoln and her colleagues (2007) report that SES alone did not account for the variation between Caribbean-born blacks living in the United States for 10 or fewer years who had lower levels of depression, when compared with U.S.-born blacks and Caribbean-born blacks living in America for more than 10 years. The factor of nativity is linked to social networking and relationships within families as well as within the larger community. Perceived discrimination may be "one of the most endemic and enduring stressors facing minority groups in the US [United States]" (Lincoln et al. 2007:202). The issue of the negative impact of perceived discrimination also is documented in international studies in which black participants reported much higher levels of psychological distress and depressive symptoms than whites even after adjustments were made for SES (Williams et al. 2008).

### Discrimination, Stigmatization, and Health

Overt and recently more covert forms of discrimination and prejudice, therefore, remain factors in health disparities (Institute of Medicine 2003). Discrimination tends to focus on disparities related to race, ethnicity, gender, age, and social class as discussed earlier (Phelan, Link, and Dovidio 2008). Yet, stigmatization of health conditions, such as mental illness and HIV/AIDS, also marginalizes individuals and their families, thus negatively impacting prevention and treatment efforts (U.S. Department of Health and Human Services 2003; Stuber, Meyer, and Link 2008). Stigma labels a person as different from his or her peers and leads to a

devaluation of the individual. In Erving Goffman's classic work, stigma is defined as "an attribute that links a person to an undesirable stereotype, leading other people to reduce the bearer from a whole and usual person to a tainted, discounted one" (1963:3). Building on Goffman's efforts, Bruce Link and Jo Phelan (2001) identified five specific aspects of stigmatization that help hone the concept to better understand its presence with medical conditions such as mental illness and HIV/AIDS. Stigmatizing a person due to an illness means:

- labeling the medical difference as less important than other, more acceptable conditions, such as cancer or diabetes;

- linking those afflicted with the undesirable illness to negative stereotypes;

- separating "them" from "us";

- perpetuating a loss of status for those with this trait (illness) through discrimination (employment, health insurance coverage, etc.);

- societal elements (social, economic, and political) that allow this stigma and prejudice to exist and continue.

One who suffers stigmatization not only suffers from the "[n]egative social attitudes [stereotypes] and even enacted discrimination [prejudice]," but often engages in "self-discrimination, concealment, withdrawal and other forms of stigma management" due to the overriding societal stigma (Burris 2008:474). The issue of mental illness stigma remains a serious personal, familial, and population health concern with families playing a crucial role in providing support to members with mental illness or disorders. Scholars currently are reaching across disciplines and various levels of society to better understand the causes of stigmatization, prejudice, and discrimination, arguing "that stigma is defined in and enacted through social interaction . . . [that] takes place in a context where organizations and institutions structure norms that create the possibility of marking [labeling] and sharing notions of 'difference'" (Pescosolido et al. 2008:432).

While the battle for parity between mental and physical health continues at local, state, national, and international levels, families remain at the forefront. Consistent and positive family support in the face of persistent stigmatization provides vital elements in both mental health promotion and particularly mental illness treatment and recovery . . . .

## CONCLUSION

While health disparities are not new, current studies regarding social and political attitudes, practices, and policies define a culture by continuing to impact and "get under the skin" of individual, family, and population health (Aronowitz 2008). Social determinants, therefore, play pivotal roles in family health. Recognizing this reality allows individuals, families, communities, societies, and nations to understand that health is not a static state dictated solely by genetics, behaviors, environmental exposures, and political policy, but rather a dynamic process in which social determinants (i.e., the heart, soul, and will of society) can foster or hinder health disparities, which in turn intertwine with genetics, behaviors, environments, and health policy and services.

There is no shame in being ill. The only shame falls on those who deny full respect, care, and coverage based on race, ethnicity, gender, age, SES, education, geographic location, or type of illness. The goals of the *Healthy People 2010* initiative include: (1) increase length and quality of healthy life, and (2) eliminate health disparities. Health disparities on national and global levels, however, provide formidable obstacles. The disproportionate toll on racial and ethnic minorities, women, the urban and rural poor, and other medically underserved individuals and their families result in poorer health status not only for the afflicted individual, but also for their families, communities, and nations . . . . The United States spends more on health care than any other nation and yet is ranked only 24th out of 33 developed nations in life expectancy (Organization of Economic Co-Operation and Development 2008). This low ranking was due in large part to health disparities. These disparities reveal themselves in unequal and unfair rates of infant mortality, cardiovascular diseases, cancers, diabetes, HIV/AIDS, and immunizations, thus serving as rallying points. Yet, areas related to stigma toward classes of diseases and illnesses, such as mental illness and HIV/AIDS, remain relatively underrecognized and undertreated. Here the illness itself suffers from stigmatization, discrimination, disregard, and disrespect . . . . Promoting healthful living and eliminating health disparities are everyone's concerns and in the best social and economic interests of all. Awareness of social determinants and their impacts along with proactively engaging in reducing social inequities that lead to poorer and unequal health care and treatment form a foundation of resilient family health and well-being.

## DISCUSSION QUESTIONS

1. What health disparities does Grochowski cite to show how social categories affect health?
2. Based on Grochowski's data, what changes could the U.S. health care system enact immediately to improve the health care of subordinate groups?

## NOTES

1. Dysthymic disorder is a type of mild or moderate depression that lasts at least two years, causing difficulty in functioning at home, school, or work. This "lingering depression" includes symptoms of over, or undereating, difficulty in sleeping or over sleeping, low energy, frequent fatigue, and feelings of hopelessness [(American Academy of Family Physicians. 2008. "Dysthymic Disorder: When Depression Lingers." Retrieved May 3, 2008. http://familydoctor.org/online/famdocen/home/common/mentalhealth/depression/054.html)].

# 40

# RACISM'S HIDDEN TOLL

## RYAN BLITSTEIN

*The second reading in this section on health care and medicine is by Ryan Blitstein, a freelance journalist for* Miller-McCune. *Similar to Grochowski's argument in the previous reading, Blitstein investigates how race and racism may affect the understanding and incidence of illness. Using a case study of the work of Arline Geronimus, a former graduate student at Princeton University and currently professor of health behavior and health education in the School of Public Health at the University of Michigan, Blitstein shows how medical and public health researchers have made false assumptions about the health and illness rates among African Americans. Blitstein looks specifically at how Geronimus's research challenged the 1970s assumption that teen pregnancy had only negative health outcomes, while in fact, teen pregnancy had different outcomes for girls based on their race and socioeconomic status. Since the late 1970s, Gernonimus has continued to investigate how race and racism can affect illness rates among African Americans.*

I n the fall of 1976, Arline Geronimus began living in two separate, unequal worlds. At Princeton University, the political theory major became a research assistant to Charles Westoff, a professor who studied teen pregnancy among the urban poor. Down the road at Planned Parenthood in Trenton, New Jersey, she spent time with real-life, impoverished pregnant teens.

A self-assured, middle-class Jewish girl from Brookline, Massachusetts, Geronimus shuttled between the extremes of haves and have-nots, eventually spotting a chasm between the theories of Princeton researchers and the experiences of the women she taught.

Geronimus would sit in on the professors' meetings, listening to them discuss how young girls, ignorant of family planning, were ruining their lives with accidental pregnancies. Bearing children at an early age would rewrite these mothers' life scripts, with terrible consequences. The funders behind the academic studies— including those in charge of Planned Parenthood's own research arm—supported the consensus opinion that teen pregnancy was a crucial cause of ghetto poverty and ill health among America's urban blacks. The only question was how to get these girls to stop having babies before they'd come of age.

The girls Geronimus met at Planned Parenthood's alternative school for expectant teens, however, seemed to know exactly what they were doing. When she tried to teach them about contraception— something they supposedly knew nothing about— they laughed at her. The girls in the program told Geronimus they were overjoyed to have children. Far from blundering into motherhood, many were experienced with child rearing, having helped raise siblings or cousins. Some talked about how long they'd been trying to have a baby.

As the months wore on, the professor's belief— that poor childhood health and ghetto joblessness would disappear, if only these girls would stop getting themselves pregnant— started to seem absurd. "What I was hearing in the halls of Princeton was inaccurate," she remembers. "It just didn't fit in, in any way, with what I was seeing."

Though Geronimus didn't understand the discrepancy, she noticed that these girls, even at 15 or 16, had been worn down by tough lives. Compared with her classmates in Princeton's dorms—many of them hailing from America's WASP elite—the poor black girls at the clinic seemed to lack the energy and health of youth. Geronimus couldn't quite put her finger on it, except to say these girls seemed older— and not in a good way.

Somebody, Geronimus thought, had to put the facts together and change things for the better for these girls and others like them. In a fit of youthful arrogance, she took it upon herself to become that person. Now a professor at the University of Michigan, Geronimus has spent the last 30 years challenging the received wisdom of researchers about a pressing social question: Why are some racial minority groups less healthy than others?

A multitude of figures illustrate the stark health differences between African Americans and whites. Black residents of high-poverty areas, for instance,

are as likely to die by the age of 45 as American whites are to die by 65. The disability rates of black 55-year-olds approach the rates of 75-year-old whites. Traditional theories, which blame the phenomenon on factors like genetics or income differences, fail to fully explain these huge disparities. Geronimus has devoted her career to finding the real reasons. Her own complex explanation for what's happening—the weathering framework—rests on two unexpected, controversial causes: racism and stress, in the broadest senses of both terms. American minorities face a bevy of chronic obstacles that whites and the socioeconomically advantaged cope with far less often: environmental pollution, high crime, poor health care, overt racism, concentrated poverty. Over the course of a person's life, the psychological and physiological response to this kind of stress leads to dire health problems, advanced aging and early death.

Geronimus' papers, published in top-flight economics, medicine, sociology and public health journals, have attracted criticism from major foundations and led some colleagues to virtually blacklist her; early in her career, her findings even provoked death threats. Yet public health scholars are beginning to accept unconventional ideas from Geronimus and her allies about why blacks and other minorities generally aren't as healthy as whites. As she's gathered more evidence and refined her theory, Geronimus has become increasingly vocal about how weathering-inspired public policies might save and improve lives. Instead of brief interventions based on conjecture, she favors radical change in health care, welfare and other social policies based on thorough research and cultural understanding.

But Geronimus' idea of structural economic and social change has never been an easy sell to the wider American public, to government officials or even to some of the liberal academics and activists one would think might be on her side.

The existence of health disparities between racial and ethnic groups is common knowledge among public health wonks. But the average American may find the numbers shocking: In impoverished urban areas like Harlem, one-third of black girls and two-thirds of boys who reach their 15th birthdays don't reach their 65th. That's almost triple the rate of early death among average Americans.

While the inner-city ghetto is an extreme case, a broad national trend ranges across a variety of health problems, from prostate cancer to hypertension. Since World War II, Americans' health outcomes have generally improved. For minorities, though, progress has come slowly. Blacks now die at a rate comparable to the death rate for whites of 30 years ago. Every year, 100,000 more African Americans die than would be the case if black and white death rates were the same. For many diseases, the situation is worsening: In 1950, blacks had a slightly lower cancer death rate than whites. By 2000, the rate was 30 percent higher among blacks.

Experts have offered three approaches to closing the gap: behavioral (if we could only get them to eat better and exercise more), medical (if we could only give them better health care), and socioeconomic (if we could only get them better education and jobs). After a panoply of interventions, the numbers have barely budged.

Long before she'd heard the phrase "health disparities," Geronimus was primed to view the issue through the prism of civil rights. As a young girl, she would visit the tiny Brooklyn apartment where her father and six siblings had grown up, listening to her grandmother's harrowing tales of escape from brutal Russian pogroms. In high school, Geronimus, then managing editor of the student newspaper, thought the school's black population didn't have enough say in student affairs, so she created "Black Voices," a column for African American classmates. The other editors were furious. After college, during a Fulbright Scholarship to Sweden, she befriended Iranian refugees in her Swedish class and became involved in protests related to Iran. The Fulbright Commission asked her to stop. "I always somehow felt these compulsions or noticed these things and got in trouble over and over," she says.

After an unsuccessful attempt at studying Sweden's minuscule teenage pregnancy rate, Geronimus returned to Princeton as a research assistant and then served a short stint as an admissions officer. But the question of the Trenton girls nagged at her, so she went home to Massachusetts to attend the Harvard School of Public Health.

While she was learning to conduct empirical research, Geronimus mulled the puzzle: The girls understood family planning and birth control, and many were consciously making the decision to become pregnant. At the same time, then-current research showed that teenage pregnancy led to socio-economic difficulties for the young mothers, along with pre-term birth, low-birth-weight babies and high infant mortality rates. To Geronimus, it didn't make sense that the vast majority of a millions-strong population was having kids at the "wrong" time.

A professor recommended she read *All Our Kin*, anthropologist Carol Stack's early '70s ethnographic account of three years in a low-income black community. Inspired, Geronimus attacked the quandary the way Stack might have, guessing that something in their families or communities must have influenced the teens toward having babies early. She thought through the cultural differences between her life and theirs. If Geronimus had come home pregnant as a high schooler, her father would've thrown her out of the house. But most of the Trenton girls' families embraced their expectant daughters. Geronimus' grandmother, like many in her generation, had given birth as a teen, and nobody had criticized her.

The concept of teenage motherhood as a problem *per se* seemed to be a societal construct. Maybe, Geronimus thought, researchers were just viewing the minority community through cultural blinders.

Geronimus hypothesized that the black infants' poor health wasn't because their mothers were too young; it was due to their mothers' social disadvantages. If she could take into account factors like income and race, she might show that teen mothers were no worse off than moms in their 20s. Unlike most studies, which separated mothers into the broad categories of teen and not-teen, Geronimus broke down maternal ages by year. The results among white women were expected: higher infant mortality rates among teen mothers. Yet the numbers for blacks astounded even Geronimus. Black teenage mothers had lower infant death rates than black mothers in their 20s. Because infant health is a decent predictor of maternal health, Geronimus' data meant the average black woman might be less healthy at 25 than she was at 15. Perhaps the population of pregnant teens in Trenton was onto something. Consciously or not, the black teen mothers might be doing what was best for their infants' health.

Geronimus' advisers were enthralled, though a few faculty members were "pretty allergic" to her theories. But she was only a lowly grad student, so no one paid much attention. She taught at Harvard for a few years, then moved on to Michigan without event . . . .

After 15 years, the people whose careers depended on the scientific status quo had finally taken notice of Geronimus' work. They were angry.

Together with earlier studies, Geronimus was presenting new data showing that teen mothers' socioeconomic outcomes were as good as or better than those of older moms. In many cases, pregnancy made the teens eligible for social programs like Medicaid, or they formed alliances with the families of the fathers of their children, improving their economic positions. Geronimus hoped to explain why these girls were making these choices and to show that efforts to prevent teen pregnancy wouldn't solve anything. Her goal was to convince people to focus on larger underlying causes of poverty and poor health. After all, even the young mothers who were slightly better off still had it very rough.

Amid a climate of culture-war controversies over family planning and abortion rights, many didn't hear the nuanced version of Geronimus' work. It didn't help that her conclusions undercut the mission of a major Children's Defense Fund campaign against teen pregnancy, along with the work of prominent researchers nationwide.

"Her facts are misrepresentative, her premise is wrong and the policy implications of her arguments are perverse," Karen Pittman told *The New York Times.* Many news stories published in subsequent months were horrendously critical, with liberals painting Geronimus as racist and conservatives dismissing her as dangerous. One nationally syndicated columnist accused her of "prescribing pregnancy for poor teenage girls."

Geronimus now blames the anger on a lack of empathy. "Most of us can take for granted that we could have healthy babies any time between 18 and 40. The concept that if you're 25, you're not going to have healthy kids? That just doesn't compute," she says.

Michigan's public relations staff received more calls about Geronimus than any professor in the history of the press office. People sent letters to the university president demanding she be fired. Others called her at work and home, telling her she should be shot. One said there were people around the corner with Uzis, coming to kill her family.

"I found out the hard way just how controversial what I was saying was," she says. "It was very sudden, and I wasn't in any way prepared for it."

Though the storm soon abated, clouds lingered for years. Michigan faculty members would tell students not to take her courses; some no longer wanted to collaborate with her on research projects. The National Institutes of Health, which funded much of her work, held a days-long forum on teen-childbearing research that left Geronimus feeling at times like she was being interrogated. Neighbors wouldn't let their kids sit next to her daughter at Dairy Queen . . . .

Geronimus retreated to health research, which seemed safer territory. Scholars had criticized teens' mothering skills, so she studied intelligence among the children of pairs of sisters. Geronimus showed that when a woman gave birth as a teen and her sister did so during her 20s, the younger mother's children were no less intelligent than their cousins. She also examined antisocial behavior among children of teen mothers. They differed little from average American children.

Harsh criticism also drove Geronimus to concentrate on teaching, hoping to cultivate her brand of skepticism in a rising generation of scholars. As chair of the admissions committee at Michigan's Department of Health Behavior and Health Education, she boosted the number of students from underrepresented racial and socioeconomic groups.

Slowly, she and the graduate students she advised built up evidence of accelerating, lifelong decline in health among minorities—first among mothers, then across a variety of illnesses and unhealthy behaviors like smoking. While it was well known that blacks are more likely than whites to be hypertensive, no one had looked at the age patterns of that risk. Geronimus found that black and white hypertension rates are virtually identical for people in their 20s, but the differences increase sharply during middle age. Similar patterns appeared in almost every health condition.

Those disparities don't subside on the way up the income ladder. Geronimus and then-graduate student Cynthia Colen, now a professor at Ohio State University, led a study showing that upwardly mobile white women who grew up poor improved their birth outcomes, but similar income increases didn't help black mothers much at all. Other researchers have established that the health of Latino immigrants declines as they stay in America longer and improve their lots in life, and that South Asian Indian mothers, who have socioeconomic profiles comparable to whites, suffer from birth outcomes as poor as those of low-income blacks.

As Geronimus built a theory to explain her findings, the work of her one-time colleague Sherman James, now at Duke University, was particularly influential. James described a phenomenon called "John Henryism," named for the powerful black steel-driver of American folklore who dropped dead after winning a contest with a mechanical drill. James claimed that African Americans' high levels of circulatory diseases were caused by exposure to psychosocial stressors, including chronic financial strain and subtly racist insults. He drew on research into high-effort coping, in which people exposed to long-term stress expend cognitive and emotional effort on those problems and then develop stress-induced health conditions.

The more results Geronimus produced, and the more she read, the more she began to agree with the radical notion that it wasn't anything inherent to their race that made black people sick—it was being black in a racist society. The phrase "racism kills" would be a vast oversimplification of Geronimus' ideas, but the way she describes it, racism is a fundamental cause of health disparities. The intolerance may be overt—several studies document high blood pressure and preterm labor among victims of discrimination. It might also be structural or societal, keeping even middle-class blacks in crime-ridden, environmentally poisonous neighborhoods.

Geronimus believes white Americans are too culturally removed from the minority experience to grasp the crisis. They take for granted that they'll be healthy through middle age and essentially ignore those who aren't so lucky. "We haven't lived it, haven't seen it close up. We have a different narrative . . . and we all grew up knowing that narrative, seeing everything through that prism. In all these different ways, different life experiences get marginalized and ignored," she says. "That's not for individual, conscious racist reasons, but because we have a highly segregated society and such entrenched inequality that dates back to when racism was in neon lights."

In the early 1990s, Geronimus unified her ideas into a notion she calls "weathering." At the time, scholars tended to view the course of life through developmental theory, which depicts humans as moving through stages of maturation, adulthood and senescence. Weathering takes the opposite approach: During a person's life, Geronimus hypothesized, stressors ranging from pollution to racism-induced anger can weather the systems of the human body, fueling the progression of disease. The stressors accumulate and feed on each other, altering the culture and behavior of a community—leading, for instance, to earlier pregnancies or high smoking rates. Minorities suffer from weathering more often than whites because they're more likely to experience socioeconomic and political exclusion. In the worst cases, as in the inner-city part of Trenton where Geronimus had worked, weathering accelerates the aging process at an alarming rate.

Geronimus' early weathering papers generated a limited, though positive, response. For some researchers, the concepts jibed with their own conclusions and intuitions. "It's such a compelling theory, many of us who work in this area almost take it for granted that it's true," says Chris Dunkel Schetter, director of UCLA's health psychology program.

Weathering's sociological slant was part of a broad move among public health experts toward social epidemiology, which analyzes communities and societies to understand disease. A throwback to the early 20th-century focus on person-to-person infection, the approach received a major boost from

Clinton administration Surgeon General David Satcher, among others. Since then, Geronimus' weathering framework, based on concepts that had once been attacked as dead wrong, has become part of the *lingua franca* of health research.

"She was willing to say things that people don't want to hear," says Marianne Hillemeier, who worked with Geronimus as a graduate student and is now a health policy professor at Pennsylvania State University. "It takes a toll on a person. It's difficult to do that. But she did it, and she changed the field."

Even Pittman, who now directs the Forum for Youth Investment and calls Geronimus' thinking "backward," notes that The National Campaign to Prevent Teen Pregnancy now concentrates on preventing unplanned pregnancies among adults.

It wasn't a large logical jump from weathering to the idea that health disparities are a social justice issue. Geronimus returned to her politico-activist roots, authoring papers with titles like, "To Denigrate, Ignore, or Disrupt: Racial Inequality in Health and the Impact of a Policy-Induced Breakdown of African American Communities." She argues that doctors and academics should address the health disparities by fighting for structural economic and social change . . . .

For all its descriptive power and intuitive reasonableness, the weathering framework has a significant weakness: It was created as a metaphor for social and cultural disadvantage. To be sure, minorities deal with chronic stressors, and they often get sick. But until recently, Geronimus couldn't explain how stress leads to illness.

Academics have studied the issue for years, though rarely with a focus on race. The most prominent is Rockefeller University's Bruce McEwen, who during the 1990s devised a concept known as "allostatic load," which measures the levels of hormones—including cortisol and 15 other chemicals—the body creates in response to stress. Several studies have shown correlations between allostatic load and illness, and Geronimus has long been aware of them. Yet she once felt a biological explanation of weathering would be too reductionist.

Her opinion changed as she watched her two sons, monozygotic twins, grow up. Most people would call them "identical twins," but Geronimus doesn't. Despite sharing the same genomes and looks, from infancy the boys had completely different personalities. In the mornings, one would wake up happy, the other in a foul mood. In adolescence, one had his growth spurt well before his brother. As she saw nature and nurture interact within her children, Geronimus thought about how biology and environment intermingle at the cellular level in ways scholars don't understand. She began to think of allostatic load as a mechanism to explain the black box she called weathering converting the stressors of the social world into physiological disease.

In stressful situations, the body activates hormones that help us, for example, think efficiently or improve memorization. When the threat or challenge recedes, the stress system shuts down production. But during periods of acute or near-constant stress, the body undergoes hormone overexposure, and with time, a high allostatic load causes wear and tear leading to cardiovascular disease, diabetes and accelerated aging. McEwen now calls allostatic load the "biological conceptualization" of the weathering framework. As Geronimus describes it, the results among African Americans are disease and death, the physiological manifestations of social inequality.

Geronimus knew if she could show the biology of allostatic load and the social conditions of weathering in action, she'd silence many critics. So she and Jay Pearson, a research fellow at Michigan, led the creation of a first-of-its-kind study of both phenomena in the same group of people. The data will come from Detroit, where the University of Michigan already partners with community organizations and health agencies to gather information.

With the help of researchers at the University of California, San Francisco, Geronimus and Pearson's team will use blood samples taken from participants to measure allostatic load, comparing it to information they collect on psychosocial and environmental stressors, as well as disease rates. They'll also look at telomeres, the repetitive DNA structures that cap the ends of cell chromosomes. Telomeres shorten when cells divide, so they're known as a "mitotic clock" that may provide a better measure of age than the number of years a person has been alive. A few small studies have shown that socioeconomic stressors may induce telomere shortening. Geronimus hopes to track racial discrimination and stress as they get underneath the skin, producing hormonal responses and accelerating cellular aging. She expects the new experiment to show that many blacks are, biologically speaking, older than whites of the same chronological age.

The government has long been aware of racial health disparities. In 1984, the Department of Health and Human Services established a Task Force on Black and Minority Health, and in 2000, its once-per-decade Healthy People plan was refocused to concentrate on the subject. That same year, Congress elevated the National Institutes of Health Office of Minority Health, making it into the higher-profile National Center on Minority Health and Health Disparities.

Yet no major legislation on the problem was signed under George W. Bush. Now, data show the vast majority of health disparity measures are stagnant, with many getting worse. "Whatever is being done is the wrong thing," Geronimus says.

While traditional interventions, like increased heart disease screening for black males, are often helpful, they barely impact overall outcomes. A weathering-inspired public policy, on the other hand, would aim to address the stressors that boost allostatic load—though not in the way one might think. Geronimus' plan isn't about managing stress on an individual level: Sending armies of yogis and therapists to America's ghettos wouldn't address the larger crisis. Simplistic paeans to racial harmony won't work, either. The issues are too systemic.

Geronimus doesn't offer an all-encompassing solution, just a better method for creating policies that might produce results. One potential idea might address some unintended consequences of Clinton-era welfare reform. By most accounts, the policy was a roaring success, with hundreds of thousands of African Americans leaving the dole for full-time work, or trading up for higher-paying jobs. The changes even reduced poverty rates in many urban areas.

While black women shared the income benefits of economic expansion, though, their health, on average, declined. Geronimus says stress and changed behavior are the best explanation: Black women took jobs that required hours-long bus rides to reach far-away employers, leading to sleep deprivation and little time for medical visits. Others worked the night shift, a practice the World Health Organization recently linked to increased cancer risk. Many faced difficulties finding and paying for child care for their kids. Despite working hard and playing by the rules, stress levels for many shot up. Because of the social interdependence within impoverished African American communities, it may have set in motion problems for friends and family members.

"It wasn't on the policy radar screen to think about these health issues," Geronimus says. "Is it a big surprise that in stress-related diseases you'd see their lives got worse? Probably not."

More enlightened policymakers might also have predicted that tearing down public housing and relocating residents—a common practice in many cities from the 1990s through the present—would disrupt the social networks and community support that deflect the stress of weathering.

With a better understanding of minority cultures, even small policy changes might make a difference. For example, many health-promotion programs are aimed at teens who smoke, but in some minority communities, people take up tobacco in their 20s. The same can be said for prenatal risk screening, which currently sees 20-something women (no matter their race) as low-risk, when, in fact, blacks in that age demographic face greater health dangers than teenagers . . . .

For now, though, President Obama's health care and civil rights agendas describe vague plans to address health disparities, largely through the types of interventions that have failed in the past. (The White House did not respond to questions on Geronimus' research and conclusions.) And sometimes, when she's holed up in her book-filled office in the latte town of Ann Arbor, it's easy for Geronimus to forget why she's devoted her life to a grand effort that has created few signs of progress. She often doubts her work will lead to real change. If she were a betting woman, she'd bet against that prospect.

Some days, she asks herself why she's even doing the research at all, and lets her thoughts drift toward retirement.

But when she visits her community research partners in Detroit, the humbling, heartrending American city that's become a sort of urban reservation for black Americans, she chats with the people who show up as numbers in her data sets. She listens to them talk of their struggles to find meaning in life or just to make it through the day. Compared to what they're dealing with, the cushy existence of reading journals and running statistical analyses seems like nothing.

Visiting Detroit reminds her of the girls she knew in Trenton, back when she was younger and less jaded, when she had more faith that she could make a difference. "There's just no way to think about doing anything else once I'm there and seeing real people," Geronimus says. "It feels like something has to get done. You know, something."

## DISCUSSION QUESTIONS

1. What did Geronimus reveal about attitudes toward teen pregnancy in the African American community that other researchers found problematic?
2. What does Geronimus's research add to our knowledge of the effects of poverty and race upon health and longevity?

# 41

# A Slow, Toxic Decline

## Dialysis Patients, Technological Failure, and the Unfulfilled Promise of Health in America

### Keith Wailoo

*This last reading in the section on health care and medicine utilizes the tragic case of Hurricane Katrina to highlight some of the race and social class inequalities in the U.S. health care system. Keith Wailoo, a medical historian, is the Townsend Martin Professor of History and Public Affairs at Princeton University, and is jointly appointed in the department of history and the Woodrow Wilson School of Public and International Affairs. Wailoo's research examines a wide array of issues in public health, innovation in medical care, and the role of identity, especially gender, race, and ethnicity, in health and disease. This reading, taken from the 2010 book* Katrina's Imprint: Race and Vulnerability in America, *edited by Keith Wailoo, Karen M. O'Neill, Jeffrey Dowd, and Roland Anglin, examines how U.S. government and medical officials responded to the critical needs of dialysis patients before, during, and after the massive storm and power outage caused by Hurricane Katrina. Wailoo argues pervasively that this health crisis did not begin with the hurricane but has deeper social roots in the high rates of kidney failure and other health problems among New Orleans's poor and minority populations.*

Hurricane Katrina made private illness experiences and health vulnerabilities shockingly public, and nothing more graphically captures this fact than the drama surrounding dialysis patients in the days after the storm. Their commonplace and everyday problems

---

were thrown open to deeper scrutiny, framed as a metaphor for the tragic moment and, as I shall argue, a metaphor for the nation's unfulfilled political and economic commitments. Many commentators rightly connected the story of these patients to the uneven and endemic health vulnerabilities that long predated the storm. "How many of the dead will turn out to be dialysis patients?" asked one expert. One July 2007 study answered that "the best guess is that of over 5,800 Gulf Coast dialysis patients affected by Katrina, 2.5 percent died in the month after the storm—although given the high mortality rate among dialysis patients, it is difficult to determine how many deaths were storm-related."[1] Commentaries placed dialysis squarely in the center of political analysis. In one ironic letter in the *San Diego Union Tribune,* the writer voiced deep disdain for the delayed and incompetent federal response: "And across the ocean in his supposed cave, I can picture Osama bin Laden, who can manage to get dialysis while, on Thursday, Charity Hospital in New Orleans had only fruit punch to offer its patients."[2] In this telling, the story epitomized government's broken promise to its most needy citizens.

This chapter examines what the appearance of dialysis patients in the story of Katrina reveals about race, health, region, and the nation's commitments. In the hours and days following the storm, diabetics and patients whose kidneys had failed and who depended on dialysis technology figured prominently in news coverage. They were unable to move themselves out of harm's way for want of transportation and further immobilized because of their health challenges. "Thousands of victims of Hurricane Katrina face homelessness and devastation," announced the National Kidney Foundation, "but kidney patients without access to dialysis treatment face life-threatening danger."[3] They needed what had become over the previous two decades a standard medical treatment to cleanse their blood, but the instrument itself depended on clean water, running electricity, and medical staff and facilities. Many of these patients were diabetics whose kidneys had failed. Requiring regular dialysis treatments, such people found themselves stranded in airports, in homes, in the Superdome—tethered to a city without

electricity and lacking medical services—suffering from a slow, toxic demise as impurities built up in their bodies. This small subset of victims symbolized a peculiarly American kind of vulnerability arising from poor access in a technology-rich environment. Among the most vulnerable of the vulnerable, they became—along with the elderly in nursing homes, the residents of Charity Hospital, the cancer patients, and other infirm citizens of the region—a graphic symbol of Katrina's toll. One Washington, D.C.–based kidney specialist predicted in the *Washington Post* on September 13, 2005, "It's going to take months, if not years, to actually find out what proportion of the dead were actually dialysis patients."[4]

As one physician in the Tulane University Department of Nephrology later stated, the dialysis machines were part of a more extensive technological system that failed: "I had a group of about seven or eight patients that we needed to take care of, then we got ten additional patients from the Superdome brought by the police, and a few people walked into the ER needing dialysis, . . . [but in the immediate wake of the storm] we didn't have enough water pressure." At first, only two machines could be run, but then "about six or seven hours later we lost the pressure completely."[5] The other problem for such patients was that, even if the pressure returned, the water was not potable. And clean water was also essential for running these machines that do the essential work of the kidneys—removing toxins from the blood that build up slowly in the course of normal life. As another New Orleans specialist later noted, "People didn't understand the extent to which they were a special needs population."[6] In these stranded patients, even those who were evacuated "were very worse off for the trip they had to make under the conditions . . . . People were lined up [for example] waiting for machines up in Baton Rogue."[7]

These people's predicaments were powerful reminders of health promises unfulfilled in America. They were a subset of Louisiana's many health problems, which included low immunization rates; high rates of stroke, diabetes, and heart disease; and deteriorating public health infrastructure.[8] All of these problems had social origins. Susceptibility to kidney failure, for example, had grown over the decades, making the population more and more dependent on dialysis. And since the early 1970s, the federal government had sanctioned a special relationship between patients and dialysis through a law granting universal access to the technology. It was, then, a technology with a unique place in the health-care system—a federally mandated entitlement for citizens if their kidneys failed. Thus the dialysis story in Katrina was not merely a local crisis; it was in some sense a national one. But the federal guarantee of dialysis meant little if water, electricity, equipment, and cooperation in the social delivery of care did not exist.

Dialysis patients turned up as a recurring leitmotif in the media's efforts to convey the gravity of the Katrina story.[9] The failure of dialysis technology—like failed levees, canals, and pumps—revealed the weakness inherent in a technologically reliant society. And just as proximity to the levees and residence in low-lying homes had a distinctly racial cast, so too did the story of dialysis.

## THE STROKE BELT, THE DIABETES BURDEN, AND DEPENDENCE ON DIALYSIS

New Orleans and Louisiana are part of the so-called stroke belt—a stretch of states across the American Southeast associated with high rates of stroke and an array of hypertension-related disorders.[10] Since the 1940s, experts have pondered the reasons, speculating that high-fat diets and obesity, smoking, genetic predisposition, or other unknown factors are responsible for these elevated rates.[11] The "belt" remains an enigma, but many experts believe that diet and higher rates of hypertension among African Americans put them at increased risk of stroke. The high rate of hypertension was also linked to other ailments. "In the Southeast," noted one researcher in 1994, "hypertension is the most common cause of ESRD [kidney failure], followed by diabetes mellitus, occurring most frequently in older minority patients, particularly blacks." Kidney failure—the endpoint in a cascade of other ailments—was, he concluded, "a Southern epidemic."[12]

The correlation between end-stage renal disease (ESRD), diabetes, and being black cut in many directions—and these links were also associated with income. Diabetes is believed to be caused by "a complex interplay of genetic, cultural, social and environmental influences, as well as healthcare inequities."[13] In Louisiana as elsewhere, the correlation between poverty and diabetes is also well established. Some 11 percent of black people in the state and 7.2 percent of white people were diabetic in the years before Katrina, among the highest occurrences in the nation. These rates rise in the population as incomes falls, and as a 2004 report noted, nearly 16 percent of people in Louisiana with incomes under $15,000 per year were diabetic. Conversely, the income correlation with diabetes showed that for people with incomes over $50,000 per year, the percentage dropped to 4.8 percent. Only a few months before Katrina, in March 2005, one physician cautioned that given this complex array of factors—from diet to obesity to poverty and diabetes—the vulnerability of black Americans in the region to kidney failure was disturbingly high.[14]

By 2005, Louisiana was second only to Washington, D.C., in the per capita rate of kidney failure, much of which resulted from diabetes. New Orleans was not exactly "ground zero" for American diabetes, but it was a close second—a major player in a national epidemic of kidney disease.[15] But, as one commentator noted a week before Katrina struck, these ailments were not high-profile disorders like AIDS, breast cancer, and prostate cancer—and the regional health challenges, although known to health experts, did not receive sustained or widespread public attention. "Where," he wondered, "are the lapel ribbons and the walkathons [for diabetes]?"[16]

Kidney failure is a less glamorous form of debility—a less prominent force in the identity-based struggles of patients' advocates for public attention and resources. It was this often- concealed, private reality that came starkly into view in the days after Katrina struck, propelling dialysis patients into the public eye as they battled for health services. Media coverage of Katrina—by spotlighting dialysis—made momentarily visible a form of debility, dependence, and death that is widespread and intimately linked to the region's culture and geography. But the sudden appearance of dialysis also draws our attention to a deeper story of a region and the nation: the story of kidney failure and dialysis intersects, as we shall see, with other stories about how technology-based dependence came about in the first place and feeds vulnerability, and how the promise of government and the federal entitlement to health services had brought these sufferers to a new political crossroads.

## WHO LIVES AND WHO DIES: VULNERABILITY AND TECHNOLOGICAL DEPENDENCE IN HISTORICAL PERSPECTIVE

To look more deeply into the story of diabetics and dialysis is to uncover a complex historical relationship between human beings, disease, technology, and the role of government in health care—a history that illuminates the irony of technology in the making of vulnerability. Indeed, this was not the first time dialysis made national headlines. Several decades before Katrina struck, dialysis patients had figured as an important touchstone in the national debate about vulnerability, government, and citizenship.

As the historian Steven Peitzman notes, a profound racial disparity exists in cities across the nation in the rate of kidney failure, which is three or four times higher for blacks than whites.[17] The disproportion, "apparent to all by the 1980s," he writes, has numerous origins, but principal among them is diabetes and less access to early kidney care, leading to organ failure in end-stage renal disease (ESRD). "Whatever the reasons for so much ESRD among blacks in the United States and elsewhere," Peitzman observes, a convergence has emerged between the dialysis experience and the broader African American experience: "'[G]oing on dialysis' is nearly as familiar a part of African American life in the cities as is going to church."[18]

But there is also a deeper backstory, for type 2 diabetes—in which the body does not produce enough insulin or becomes resistant to insulin—is often linked to diet and obesity. Thus, the economic geography of the region and the history of the southern diet, particularly New Orleans cuisine, also have become implicated in the question of dialysis reliance. The Big Easy, after all, has long been associated with good eating— carrying one set of meanings for tourists and another for residents. So, many people dependent on dialysis in New Orleans were brought to this fateful juncture with Hurricane Katrina through particular historical and social processes; yet their stories cannot be seperated from additional social factors that are important in explaining how, and why, peoples' kidneys can fail—from urinary tract infection (severe, untreated) to lead poisoning and HIV. Thus were race, diet, and a host of urban factors, along with poverty, implicated in higher rates of diabetes.

Dialysis in this country—a technology to allay the effects of slow, toxic death—has always been intimately tied to the logic of American government and to the debate over government's relationship to vulnerable citizens. The ability to artificially cleanse the blood of harmful waste products via hemodialysis emerged as a technical possibility after World War II, but access to the life-saving technology became an entitlement through federal law in the early 1970s— at a crucial moment in U.S. history. With passage of Public Law 92-603 in October 1972, a "dialysis entitlement" within a Social Security amendment committed the nation to paying the cost of dialysis for all patients (wealthy or poor) whose kidneys had failed. These people with end-stage renal disease were beneficiaries of a liberal era of still-expanding government services.[19] The driving force behind the ESRD legislation was the glaring inequalities of the era— with the shocking role played by income and economic privilege in private access to dialysis, thus determining who lived and who died. "In the earliest years of chronic dialysis," observes Steven Peitzman, "the number of people who might benefit from the procedure exceeded its availability."[20] In the 1960s, hospitals with the still-scarce dialysis machines found that it was necessary to choose worthy recipients from among the many who sought to benefit. In a few well-known cases, hospitals with few dialysis facilities formed panels (criticized as "God committees") to decide on the criteria for distributing access to this rare, life-extending commodity. Precisely because the vagaries of class played such a powerful and unfortunate role in who did and did not get dialysis, pressure for equity grew. ESRD legislation thus sought to remedy these flaws, while building on the unprecedented passage only a few years earlier of Medicare, which ensured federal health coverage for the elderly. The argument for covering ESRD at the time was compelling: American technological prowess was well demonstrated. We could, after all, send men to the moon; surely, the nation could ensure access to lifesaving kidney dialysis. But as one of the Senate staffers involved in the legislation later recalled, "ironically, rather than serving as a demonstration or pilot, the ESRD legislation proved to be the last train out of the station for national health insurance. No other group has had a chance to get on board."[21]

For more than the past three decades, then, the story of dialysis and the government's commitment to extending life has been a political one—tied closely to the growth of the national health-care system and its underlying political and economic commitments. But the growth of dialysis has also spawned a large and growing sector of private, commercial dialysis centers, many of them in the South (where diabetes is more prevalent). And as the incidence of ESRD has increased year by year—"growing about 3 percent a year, fueled by the rise of diabetes"—and the number of dialysis patients has expanded, the cost and profit associated with this unique entitlement has grown too, along with the debate over whether the U.S. as a nation could afford to live up to its commitment to care for these patients.[22]

The story of dialysis and diabetes in Katrina is, in some ways, one of the latest chapters in this unfolding political debate over government's priorities, its citizens, and how the state responds to those in need. The disease and its treatment are also part of the story of growing dependence on a technology that is tied to the ideals of a liberal society. Thus, the emergence of dialysis patients into the national spotlight during Katrina was not dramatically new. Long before the storm struck New Orleans, they had been identified as a particularly vulnerable group, warranting special protection and safeguards. Only a

year earlier, New Orleans's Mayor Ray Nagin had acknowledged as much. Looking out into the Gulf at the looming threat of Hurricane Ivan, he observed that the city's "priorities are first to secure the ongoing treatment of seriously ill patients in hospitals and for people on dialysis machines."[23] From the era of the "God committees" into the age of ESRD and Katrina, the history of dialysis showed how society wavers in its commitment to these citizens.[24] Against this political backdrop, it should not surprise us that the plight of dialysis/diabetes patients was one prominent story within the broader Katrina narrative and that it carried powerful technological and historical resonance. These resonances hung in the air as one Florida medic commented when the waters remained high, "people have been without medicine and in some cases without dialysis for coming up on a week," and he reminded listeners about the deadly consequences of the buildup of toxins in the blood if these conditions were to continue.[25]

Dialysis patients were not the only ones made vulnerable by disability, of course; the health effects were widespread, yet technologically dependent dialysis patients often epitomized the crisis. The chairman of the Touro Infirmary Hospital, Stephen Kupperman, observed on September 3 that "the government was totally unprepared for something of this size . . . . We could not get any assistance . . . at first." The hospital ultimately turned to private buses and private air ambulances, with a little assistance from government helicopters, to evacuate patients and staff.[26] Many hospitalized patients could not be moved at all, notes one subsequent study, because "for patients who were disoriented or on respirators or in traction, for example, evacuation posed enormous logistical challenges."[27] But in the news coverage, the diabetics and dialysis patients often stood out. As one New Orleans citizen wrote at the time, "On Tuesday evening, my skeletal neighbor Kip, a kidney-transplant patient, waded home alone by flashlight from the convention center, where there were neither dialysis machines nor buses to get him to one. His last treatment had been four days earlier, and he was bloating. We had to get him out."[28] Another article early in the aftermath reported that a nurse at the United Medical Rehab Hospital in the city worried that "several diabetic patients had been without dialysis for nearly a week" and "after the fruit cocktail and peanut butter ran out, the staff broke into the candy and drink machines for sugary items to keep patients from going into shock."[29] Her voice cracking, she complained, "these are people who are not going to make it." Reports on September 5 from a hospital in Atlanta found that of those who fled, "many survivors are shell-shocked, unable to eat or sleep. Some need intravenous hydration; others suffer from not receiving regular dialysis treatment."[30] And nine days later, the *Wall Street Journal* bemoaned that "health officials are searching for hundreds of dialysis patients"—about half of the 3,000 or 3,500 patients whose dialysis centers were destroyed were unaccounted for.[31] And a year later, dialysis continued to frame the storm's effects. One reassessment of life and death at the Houston Astrodome (where many New Orleans residents had been taken) commented that "doctors, administrators and staff from the Harris County Hospital District created a 'virtual hospital without beds' at the Astrodome. Among the seventeen thousand cases handled at the clinic were kidney patients in desperate need of dialysis and diabetics suffering from lack of insulin."[32]

Coverage of the human drama of patients dying while waiting for dialysis inevitably blurred the more complex issues of region, class, race, technology, history, disease, and government that had created this crisis. The story of dialysis provoked some to see New Orleans as a city outside the narrative of American technological progress, a city left behind. For some observers, dialysis became a vehicle for talking about profound failures to progress. In the midst of the wreckage, one observer described a "frail fellow, a diabetic whose limbs are too swollen to walk . . . unable to obtain dialysis treatment for a week, being pushed along in a wheelchair by an elderly friend."[33] Seeing the sad picture, one disgusted resident spat out, "We are a third world city in a first world country."[34] Frequently using the word "primitive," CNN's Sanjay Gupta reported from the airport that "the utter lack of coordination" combined with the devastating impact of the water throughout the city meant that "it was more primitive than what we saw in Iraq. In some ways, it was more primitive than what we saw in Sri Lanka during the tsunami as well."[35] And reflecting on the story of dialysis patients, another Tulane-based nephrologist recalled, "conditions were pretty primitive for the period of time from Monday when the storm hit until Friday when the complete evacuation went on."[36]

Understanding diabetes and dialysis (with its unique national history and regional profile) considerably expands our understanding of the failure that was Katrina. The notion that a privileged society with its complex systems of technological care had so obviously failed its most defenseless citizens provoked outrage at the time. But as we now approach the fifth anniversary of the 2005 storm, the story of dialysis and Katrina has largely subsided from the headlines, reemerging from time to time in subtle ways. It is now mostly left to specialists in health and nephrology to ask crucial questions. Where have the dialysis patients of New Orleans gone? How many have died? Will the survivors return? Will the dialysis centers of the city be rebuilt? These questions are, even now, unanswerable because of the massive dispersion of population. Nearly a year after the story, one physician at Tulane noted, "Prior to Hurricane Katrina there were about eight thousand [dialysis] patients in the state of Louisiana. About four thousand of those . . . resided in the New Orleans metropolitan area . . . . And since the storm I think it's only half the level."[37] Another Tulane physician noted that two of the three university dialysis units were not functioning: "Both of those flooded; neither is open right now. One . . . received such structural damage that it will have to be rebuilt." Would it be rebuilt? "You can't open a dialysis unit in a way unless you have patients, and the patients can't come back unless there is a dialysis unit . . . . You can't do one without the other."[38] And a study done two years after Katrina found that "before the 2005 hurricane season, there were 2,011 and 362 dialysis patients residing in the [two] parishes (the Louisiana equivalent to counties) most affected by hurricanes Katrina and Rita, respectively. Each of these parishes had experienced increases in dialysis patient populations over the past 5 years. However, following the storms, there were 1,014 and 316 dialysis patients residing in the affected parishes."[39] Where those patients went remains something of a public health mystery.

The questions embedded in the story of dialysis are microcosms of a large question about the nation's commitment to its people most at risk. In the storm itself, health policy researchers Bradford Gray and Kathy Hebert noted, "the situation was particularly urgent for hospitals that lost power, communications, and water/sewer service, and that couldn't re-supply such essentials as drugs, blood, linen, and food."[40] Many dialysis centers and diabetes care clinics, hard hit that month, disappeared in the months after the storm.[41] "According to figures assembled by the Louisiana Hospital Association (LHA) during the storm," Gray and Hebert continued, "1,749 patients occupied the 11 hospitals surrounded by the floodwaters."[42] In this context, what happened to dialysis patients became a microcosm of the broader social drama. Their dispersion from New Orleans still raises fundamental questions about what kind of new city will emerge in the wake of the storm and whether its medical infrastructure will ever be the same. In the end, the story of the dialysis patients reveals particular faces in the human geography of vulnerability and suffering. But in its broadest features, the story remains a tale about the limits of American technological capacity; the intersecting economic, cultural, and historical dynamics of disease; the changing nature of the government's fragile promises to its vulnerable citizens; and the nation's inability to maintain a steady spotlight on, let alone care for, its people in need.

## DISCUSSION QUESTIONS

1. Why does Wailoo contend that the fate of dialysis patients in the Katrina Hurricane disaster epitomizes the intersecting problems of health and race in America?
2. Why is end-stage renal disease higher in African American populations than in white populations? What health policies could be put into place to lower these rates?

## NOTES

1. "Kidney Specialists Review Plans for Disaster Response," *Science Daily*, June 22, 2007, http://www.sciencedaily.com/releases/2007/06/070620121247.htm. The report summarizes a new finding published in the *Clinical Journal of the American Society of Nephropology*.
2. Lynn Macey, "Letters to the Editor: Hurricane Katrina," *San Diego Union Tribune*, September 7, 2005, B9.
3. "National Kidney Foundation Offers Information, Resources to Kidney Patients Affected by Hurricane Katrina," *PR Newswire*, September 2, 2005, http://www.highbeam.com/doc/1P2-13202169.thm.
4. January W. Payne, "At Risk before the Storm Struck: Prior Health Disparities Due to Race, Poverty Multiply Death, Disease," *Washington Post*, September 13, 2005.
5. Vecihi Batuman (Department of Nephrology, Tulane University Medical Center), interviewed by Richard Mizelle Jr. (graduate assistant, Rutgers University), July 20, 2006.
6. Paul Muntner (Department of Epidemiology, Tulane University Medical Center), interviewed by Richard Mizelle Jr. (graduate assistant, Rutgers University), July 20, 2006.
7. Ibid.
8. National Center for Health Statistics (NCHS), *Health, United States, 2004–with Chartbook on the Trends in Health of Americans* (Hyattsville, Md.: NCHS, 2004), http://www.ncbi.nlm.gov/books/bookres.fcgi/healthus04/healthus04.pdf. Cited in Bailus Walker and Rueben Warren, "Katrina Perspectives," *Journal of Health Care for the Poor and Underserved* 18 (2007):233–240.
9. An earlier book of mine, *Dying in the City of the Blues* (Chapel Hill: University of North Carolina Press, 2001), provided the starting point for my analysis. In the story of one disease—sickle cell anemia—one can see the intersection of disease, race, and politics in the South, and the ways that we can use the study of particular maladies, pains, and health experiences to offer a lens on a broader discourse of race, health, and American society.
10. David Warnock et al., "Prevalence of Chronic Kidney Disease and Anemia among Participants in the Reasons for Geographic and Racial Differences in Stroke (REGARDS) Cohort Study: Baseline Results," *Kidney International* 68 (2005):1427–1431.

11. Douglas J. Lanska and Lewis H. Kuller, "The Geography of Stroke Mortality in the United States and the Concept of a Stroke Belt," *Stroke* 26 (1995):1145–1149; Daniel T. Lackland and Michael A. Moore, "Hypertension-Related Mortality and Morbidity in the Southeast," *Southern Medical Journal* 90 (February 1997):191–198.

12. Michael A. Moore, "End-Stage Renal Disease: A Southern Epidemic," *Southern Medical Journal* 87 (October 1994):1013–1017.

13. Janice P. Lea and Susanne B. Nicholas, "Diabetes Mellitus and Hypertension: Key Risk Factors for Kidney Disease," *Journal of the American Medical Association* 94 (suppl.) (August 2002):7S–15S, quote on 7S.

14. Moore, "End-Stage Renal Disease."

15. There are more than four hundred thousand people on dialysis nationwide. A disproportionate percentage of dialysis centers and patients are in the South.

16. Ranit Mishori, "A Dubious Distinction: The District Is at the Front of a National Surge in Kidney Disease," *Washington Post*, August 23, 2005, F1.

17. Steven J. Peitzman, *Dropsy, Dialysis, Transplant: A Short History of Failing Kidneys* (Baltimore: Johns Hopkins University Press, 2007), 128.

18. Ibid., 129.

19. Richard Rettig, "Origins of the Medicare Kidney Disease Entitlement: The Social Security Amendments of 1972," in *Biomedical Politics*, ed. Kathi E. Hanna (Washington, D.C.: Institute of Medicine and National Academy Press, 1982).

20. Peitzman, *Dropsy, Dialysis, Transplant*, 112.

21. James Mongan quoted in Charles Plante, "Reflections on the Passage of the End-Stage Renal Disease Medicare Program," *American Journal of Kidney Disease* 35 (2000):48. For a broader discussion of Medicare politics and the place of kidney dialysis within it, see Jonathan Oberlander, *The Political Life of Medicare* (Chicago: University of Chicago Press, 2003).

22. Andrew Pollack, "The Dialysis Business: Fair Treatment?" *New York Times*, September 16, 2007, 1.

23. Nagin quoted in "New Orleans Battens Down Hatches for Hurricane Ivan," *Irish Times*, September 15, 2004, 15.

24. David Sanders and Jesse Durkheimer, "Medical Advance and Legal Lag: Hemodialysis and Kidney Transplantation," *UCLA Law Review* 15 (1968):357–413; see also Committee on Chronic Kidney Disease, *Report of the Committee on Chronic Kidney Dialysis* (Washington, D.C.: U.S. Bureau of the Budget, 1967); and Rettig, "Origins of the Medicare Kidney Disease Entitlement."

25. M.A.J. McKenna, "Katrina Aftermath: Medical: CDC Flies in to Deal with Health Crisis," *Atlanta Journal-Constitution*, September 4, 2005, 5A.

26. Quoted in Felicity Barringer and Donald McNeil Jr., "Grim Triage for Ailing and Dying at a Makeshift Airport Hospital," *New York Times*, September 3, 2005, A4.

27. Bradford Gray and Kathy Hebert, "Hospitals in Hurricane Katrina: Challenges Facing Custodial Institutions in a Disaster," *Journal of Health Care for the Poor and Underserved* 18 (2007):283, 298, quote on 286.

28. Quoted in James Nolan, "Our Hell in High Water," *Washington Post*, September 4, 2005, B1.

29. Quoted in Allen G. Breed, "Katrina Survivors Face Tragedy, Triumph," Associated Press Online, August 31, 2005, http://www.ewoss.com/articles/D8CBE5182.aspx.

30. Patricia Guthrie, "Metro Facilities Face Long-Term Health Burden," *Atlanta Journal-Constitution*, September 5, 2005, 1A.

31. Michael J. McCarthy, "The Katrina Cleanup: Health Officials Seek Missing Dialysis Patients," *Wall Street Journal*, September 14, 2005, AIO; "Hurricane: Health Officials Search for Missing Dialysis Patients," *American Health Line,* September 14, 2005.

32. Allan Turner, "Katrina: One Year Later," *Houston Chronicle*, August 28, 2006, A1.

33. Rosie DiManno, "Tales of Woe Shame a Nation," *Toronto Star,* September 2, 2005, A1.

34. Quoted in ibid.

35. Tom Foreman, Adora Udoji, Sanjay Gupta, Jamie McIntyre, Jeff Koinange, Barbara Starr, Miles O'Brien, and Soledad O'Brien, "Hurricane Katrina's Aftermath," *American Morning: CNN* (transcript), September 3, 2005.

36. Lee Hamm (nephrologist, chair of the Department of Medical Education, Tulane University), interviewed by Richard Mizelle Jr. (graduate assistant, Rutgers University), July 20, 2006.

37. Myra Kleinpeter (Department of Medicine, Tulane University), interviewed by Richard Mizelle Jr. (graduate assistant, Rutgers University), July 20, 2006.

38. Hamm, interview.

39. M[yra] A. Kleinpeter, "Shifts in Dialysis Patients from Natural Disasters in 2005." *Hemodialysis International* II, suppl. 3 (October 2007):33. As another study by a Baton Rouge nephrologist notes, "No matter how quickly a dialysis unit may reopen after some local or regional disaster, there exists the real possibility that the facility may experience economic consequences that may threaten the very survival of the unit." These challenges include loss of patients and staff, problems in obtaining property or flood insurance, replacement of destroyed dialysis machines, and difficulties in receiving government assistance such as Small Business Administration loans. Robert J. Kenney, "Emergency Preparedness Concepts for Dialysis Facilities: Reawakening after Hurricane Katrina," *Clinical Journal of the American Society of Nephrology* 2 (2007):812–813.

40. Gray and Hebert, "Hospitals in Hurricane Katrina."

41. Adrienne Allen, Wayne Harris, and Kathleen Kennedy, "A Diabetes Pharmaceutical Care Clinic in an Underserved Community," *Journal of Health Care for the Poor and Underserved* 18 (2007):255–261.

42. Gray and Hebert, "Hospitals in Hurricane Katrina," 284.

# 42

# FRAMING CLASS, VICARIOUS LIVING, AND CONSPICUOUS CONSUMPTION

DIANA KENDALL

*This is the first of three readings to examine the social institution of the mass media. Mass media are communications that are disseminated to large audiences, typically without direct feedback. There are at least four kinds of media, including broadcast media (television, radio, and so on), print media (books, newspapers, and so on), digital or electronic media (online), and visual media (film, photography). Diana Kendall, professor of sociology at Baylor University, examines how the media frame stories about social class. This reading, taken from Kendall's 2005 book* Framing Class: Media Representations of Wealth and Poverty in America, *illustrates well how television shows construct a reality of social class that is not an accurate reflection of American society.*

## MEDIA FRAMING AND THE PERFORMANCE OF CLASS IN EVERYDAY LIFE

In a mass-mediated culture such as ours, the media do not simply mirror society; rather, they help to shape it and to create cultural perceptions (Delaney and Wilcox 2002). The blurring between what is real and what is not real encourages people to emulate the upper classes and shun the working class and the poor. Television shows, magazines, and newspapers sell the idea that the only way to get ahead is to identify with the rich and powerful and to live vicariously

*Source:* Kendall, Diana. 2005. "Framing Class, Vicarious Living, and Conspicuous Consumption." In *Framing Class: Media Representations of Wealth and Poverty in America.* Reproduced with permission of Rowman & Littlefield Publishing Group, Inc. in the format Textbook via Copyright Clearance Center.

through them. From sitcoms to reality shows, the media encourage ordinary people to believe that they may rise to fame and fortune; they too can be the next *American Idol*. Constantly bombarded by stories about the lifestyles of the rich and famous, viewers feel a sense of intimacy with elites, with whom they have little or no contact in their daily lives (hooks 2000:73). According to the social critic bell hooks, we overidentify with the wealthy, because the media socialize us to believe that people in the upper classes are better than we are. The media also suggest that we need have no allegiance to people in our own class or to those who are less fortunate (hooks 2000:77).

Vicarious living—watching how other individuals live rather than experiencing life for ourselves—through media representations of wealth and success is reflected in many people's reading and viewing habits and in their patterns of consumption. According to hooks, television promotes hedonistic consumerism:

> Largely through marketing and advertising, television promoted the myth of the classless society, offering on one hand images of an American dream fulfilled wherein any and everyone can become rich and on the other suggesting that the lived experience of this lack of class hierarchy was expressed by our *equal right to purchase anything we could afford* (2000:71).

As hooks suggests, equality does not exist in contemporary society, but media audiences are encouraged to view themselves as having an "equal right" to purchase items that somehow will make them equal to people above them in the social class hierarchy. However, the catch is that we must actually be able to afford these purchases. Manufacturers and the media have dealt with this problem by offering relatively cheap products marketed by wealthy celebrities. Paris Hilton, an heir to the Hilton Hotel fortune, has made millions of dollars by marketing products that give her fans a small "slice" of the good life she enjoys. Middle- and working-class people can purchase jewelry from

the Paris Hilton Collection—sterling silver and Swarovski crystal jewelry ranging in price from fifteen to a hundred dollars—and have something that is "like Paris wears." For less than twenty dollars per item, admirers can purchase the Paris Hilton Wall Calendar; a "Paris the Heiress" Paper Doll Book; Hilton's autobiography, *Confessions of an Heiress;* and even her dog's story, *The Tinkerbell Hilton Diaries: My Life Tailing Paris Hilton*. But Hilton is only one of thousands of celebrities who make money by encouraging unnecessary consumerism among people who are inspired by media portrayals of the luxurious and supposedly happy lives of rich celebrities. The title of Hilton's television show, *The Simple Life*, appropriates the image of simple people, such as the working class and poor, who might live happy, meaningful lives, and transfers this image to women whose lives are anything but simple as they flaunt designer clothing and spend collectively millions of dollars on entertainment, travel, and luxuries that can be afforded only by the very wealthy (hooks 2000:72).

How the media frame stories about class *does* make a difference in what we think about other people and how we spend our money. Media frames constitute a mental shortcut (schema) that helps us formulate our thoughts.

## THE UPPER CLASSES: AFFLUENCE AND CONSUMERISM FOR ALL

Although some media frames show the rich and famous in a negative manner, they still glorify the material possessions and lifestyles of the upper classes. Research has found that people who extensively watch television have exaggerated views of how wealthy most Americans are and what material possessions they own. Studies have also found that extensive television viewing leads to higher rates of spending and to lower savings, presumably because television stimulates consumer desires (Schor 2004).

For many years, most media framing of stories about the upper classes has been positive, ranging from *consensus framing* that depicts members of the upper class as being like everyone else, to *admiration framing* that portrays them as generous, caring individuals. The frame most closely associated with rampant consumerism is *emulation framing*, which suggests that people in all classes should reward themselves with a few of the perks of the wealthy, such as buying a piece of Paris's line of jewelry. The writers of television shows such as ABC's *Life of Luxury*, E!'s *It's Good to Be . . .* [a wealthy celebrity, such as Nicole Kidman], and VH1's *The Fabulous Life* rely heavily on admiration and price-tag framing, by which the worth of a person is measured by what he or she owns and how many assistants constantly cater to that person's whims. On programs like FOX's *The O.C.* and *North Shore* and NBC's *Las Vegas*, the people with the most expensive limousines, yachts, and jet aircraft are declared the winners in life. Reality shows like *American Idol, The Billionaire, For Love or Money*, and *The Apprentice* suggest that anyone can move up the class ladder and live like the rich if he or she displays the best looks, greatest talent, or sharpest entrepreneurial skills. It is no wonder that the economist Juliet B. Schor (2004) finds that the overriding goal of children age ten to thirteen is to get rich. In response to the statement "I want to make a lot of money when I grow up," 63 percent of the children in Schor's study agreed, whereas only 7 percent disagreed.

Many adults who hope to live the good life simply plunge farther into debt. Many reports show that middle- and working-class American consumers are incurring massive consumer debts as they purchase larger houses, more expensive vehicles, and many other items that are beyond their means. According to one analyst, media portrayals of excessive consumer spending and a bombardment of advertisements by credit-card companies encourage people to load up on debt (Nocera 1994). With the average U.S. household now spending 13 percent of its after-tax income to *service* debts (not pay off the principal!), people with average incomes who continue to aspire to lives of luxury like those of the upper classes instead may find themselves spending their way into the "poor house" with members of the poverty class.

## THE POOR AND HOMELESS: "NOT ME!"— NEGATIVE ROLE MODELS IN THE MEDIA

The sharpest contrasts in media portrayals are between depictions of people in the upper classes and depictions of people at the bottom of the class structure. At best, the poor and homeless are portrayed as deserving of our sympathy on holidays or when disaster strikes. In these situations, those in the bottom classes are depicted as being temporarily down on their luck or as working hard to get out of their current situation but in need of public assistance. At worst, however, the poor are blamed for their own problems; stereotypes of the homeless as bums, alcoholics, and drug addicts, caught in a hopeless downward spiral because of their *individual* pathological behavior, are omnipresent in the media.

For the most part, people at the bottom of the class structure remain out of sight and out of mind for most media audiences. *Thematic framing* depicts the poor and homeless as "faceless" statistics in reports on poverty. *Episodic framing* highlights some problems of the poor but typically does not link their personal . . . concerns to such larger societal problems as limited educational opportunities, high rates of unemployment, and jobs that pay depressingly low wages.

The poor do not fare well on television entertainment shows, where writers typically represent them with one-dimensional, bedraggled characters standing on a street corner holding cardboard signs that read "Need money for food." When television writers tackle the issue of homelessness, they often portray the lead characters (who usually are white and relatively affluent) as helpful people, while the poor and homeless are depicted as deviants who might harm themselves or others. Hospital and crime dramas like *E.R., C.S.I.,* and *Law & Order* frequently portray the poor and homeless as "crazy," inebriated in public, or incompetent to provide key information to officials. Television reality shows like *Cops* go so far as to advertise that they provide "footage of debris from the bottom tiers of the urban social order" (De Coster and Edmonds 2001). Statements such as this say a lot about the extent to which television producers, directors, and writers view (or would have us view) the lower classes.

From a sociological perspective, framing of stories about the poor and homeless stands in stark contrast to framing of stories about those in the upper classes, and it suggests that we should distance ourselves from "those people." We are encouraged to view the poor and homeless as the *Other*, the outsider; in the media we find little commonality between our lives and the experiences of people at the bottom of the class hierarchy. As a result, it is easy for us to buy into the dominant ideological construction that views poverty as a problem of individuals, not of the society as a whole, and we may feel justified in our rejection of such people.[1]

## THE WORKING CLASS:
## HISTORICAL RELICS AND JOKES

As we have seen, the working class and the working poor do not fare much better than the poor and homeless in media representations. The working class is described as "labor," and people in this class are usually nothing more than faces in a crowd on television shows. The media portray people who *produce* goods and services as much less interesting than those who *excessively consume* them, and this problem can only grow worse as more of the workers who produce the products are thousands of miles away from us, in nations like China, very remote from the typical American consumer.[2]

Contemporary media coverage carries little information about the working class or its problems. Low wages, lack of benefits, and hazardous working conditions are considered boring and uninteresting topics, except on the public broadcasting networks or an occasional television "news show" such as *60 Minutes* or *20/20* when some major case of worker abuse has recently been revealed. The most popular portrayal of the working class is *caricature framing*, which depicts people in negative ways, such as being dumb, white trash, buffoons, bigots, or slobs. Many television shows featuring working-class characters play on the idea that the clothing, manners, and speech patterns of the working class are not as good as those of the middle or upper classes. For example, working-class

characters (such as Roseanne, the animated Homer Simpson, and *The King of Queens'* Doug) may compare themselves to the middle and upper classes by saying that they are not as "fancy as the rich people." Situation comedy writers have perpetuated working-class stereotypes, and now a number of reality shows, such as *The Swan* and *Extreme Makeover*, try to take "ordinary" working-class people and "improve" them through cosmetic surgery, new clothing, and different hairstyles.

Like their upper-class celebrity counterparts, so-called working-class comedians like Jeff Foxworthy have ridiculed the blue-collar lifestyle. They also have marketed products that make fun of the working class. Foxworthy's website, for example, includes figurines ("little statues for *inside* the house"), redneck cookbooks, Games Rednecks Play, and calendars that make fun of the working class generally. Although some people see these items as humorous ("where's yore sense of humor?"), the real message is that people in the lower classes lack good taste, socially acceptable manners, and above all, middle-class values. If you purchase "redneck" merchandise, you too can make fun of the working class and clearly distance yourself from it.

## MIDDLE-CLASS FRAMING
## AND KIDDY-CONSUMERISM

Media framing of stories about the middle class tells us that this economic group is the value center and backbone of the nation. *Middle-class values framing* focuses on the values of this class and suggests that they hold the nation together. Early television writers were aware that their shows needed to appeal to middle-class audiences, who were the targeted consumers for the advertisers' products, and middle-class values of honesty, integrity, and hard work were integral ingredients of early sitcoms. However, some contemporary television writers spoof the middle class and poke fun at values supposedly associated with people in this category. The writers of FOX's *Malcolm in the Middle* and *Arrested Development*, for example, focus on the dysfunctions in a fictional middle-class family, including conflicts between husband and wife, between parents and children, and between members of the family and outsiders.

Why do these shows make fun of the middle class? Because corporations that pay for the advertisements want to capture the attention of males between ages eighteen and thirty-nine, and individuals in this category are believed to enjoy laughing at the uptight customs of conventional middle-class families. In other shows, as well, advertisers realize the influence that their programs have on families. That is why they are happy to spend billions of dollars on product placements (such as a Diet Coke can sitting on a person's desk) in the shows and on ads during commercial breaks. In recent research, Schor examined why very young children buy into the consumerism culture and concluded that extensive media exposure to products was a key reason. According to Schor, "More children [in the United States] than anywhere else believe that their clothes and brands describe who they are and define their social status. American kids display more brand affinity than their counterparts anywhere else in the world; indeed, experts describe them as increasingly 'bonded to brands'" (2004:13).

Part of this bonding occurs through constant television watching and Internet use, as a steady stream of ads targets children and young people. Schor concludes that we face a greater problem than just excessive consumerism. A child's well-being is undermined by the consumer culture: "High consumer involvement is a significant cause of depression, anxiety, low self-esteem, and psychosomatic complaints" (2004:167). Although no similar studies have been conducted to determine the effects of the media's emphasis on wealth and excessive consumerism among adults, it is likely that today's children will take these values with them into adulthood if our society does not first reach the breaking point with respect to consumer debt.

The issue of class in the United States is portrayed in the media not through a realistic assessment of wealth, poverty, or inequality but instead through its patterns of rampant consumerism. The general message remains, one article stated, "We pledge allegiance to the mall" (Uchitelle 2004).

## MEDIA FRAMING AND OUR DISTORTED VIEW OF INEQUALITY

Class clearly permeates media culture and influences our thinking on social inequality. How the media frame stories involving class constitutes a *socially constructed reality* that is not necessarily an accurate reflection of the United States. Because of their pervasive nature, the media have the symbolic capacity to define the world for other people. In turn, readers and viewers gain information from the media that they use to construct a picture of class and inequality—a picture that becomes, at least to them, a realistic representation of where they stand in the class structure, what they should (or should not) aspire to achieve, and whether and why they should view other people as superior, equal, or inferior to themselves.

Because of the media's power to socially construct reality, we must make an effort to find out about the objective nature of class and evaluate social inequality on our own terms. Although postmodern thinkers believe that it is impossible to distinguish between real life and the fictionalized version of reality that is presented by the media, some sociologists argue that we can learn the difference between media images of reality and the actual facts pertaining to wealth, poverty, and inequality. The more we become aware that we are not receiving "raw" information or "just" entertainment from the media, the more we are capable of rationally thinking about how we are represented in media portrayals and what we are being encouraged to do (engage in hedonistic consumerism, for example) by these depictions. The print and electronic media have become extremely adept at framing issues of class in a certain manner, but we still have the ability to develop alternative frames that better explain who we are and what our nation is truly like in regard to class divisions.

## THE REALITIES OF CLASS

What are the realities of inequality? The truth is that the rich are getting richer and that the gulf between the rich and the poor continues to widen in the

United States. Since the 1990s, the poor have been more likely to stay poor, and the affluent have been more likely to stay affluent. How do we know this? Between 1991 and 2001, the income of the top one-fifth of U.S. families increased by 31 percent; during the same period, the income of the bottom one-fifth of families increased by only 10 percent (DeNavas-Walt and Cleveland 2003). The chasm is even wider across racial and ethnic categories; African Americans and Latinos/Latinas are overrepresented among those in the bottom income levels. Over one-half of African American and Latino/Latina households fall within the lowest income categories.

Wealth inequality is even more pronounced. The super-rich (the top 0.5 percent of U.S. households) own 35 percent of the nation's wealth, with net assets averaging almost nine million dollars. The very rich (the next 0.5 percent of households) own about 7 percent of the nation's wealth, with net assets ranging from $1.4 million to $2.5 million. The rich (9 percent of households) own 30 percent of the wealth, with net assets of a little over four hundred thousand dollars. Meanwhile, everybody else (the bottom 90 percent of households) owns only 28 percent of the nation's wealth. Like income, wealth disparities are greatest across racial and ethnic categories. According to the Census Bureau, the net worth of the average white household in 2000 was more than ten times that of the average African American household and more than eight times that of the average Latino/Latina household. Moreover, in 2002, almost thirty-five million people lived below the official government poverty level of $18,556 for a family of four, an increase of more than one million people in poverty since 2001 (Proctor and Dalaker 2003).

## THE REALITIES OF HEDONISTIC CONSUMERISM

Consumerism is a normal part of life; we purchase the things that we need to live. However, hedonistic consumerism goes beyond all necessary and meaningful boundaries. As the word *hedonism* suggests, some people are so caught up in consumerism that this becomes the main reason for their existence, the primary thing that brings them happiness. Such people engage in the self-indulgent pursuit of happiness through what they buy. An example of this extreme was recently reported in the media. When Antoinette Millard was sued by American Express for an allegedly past-due account, she filed a counterclaim against American Express for having provided her with a big-spender's credit card that allowed her to run up bills of nearly a million dollars in luxury stores in New York.[3] Using the "victim defense," Millard claimed that, based on her income, the company should not have solicited her to sign up for the card. Although this appears to be a far-fetched defense (especially in light of some of the facts), it may be characteristic of the lopsided thinking of many people who spend much more money than they can hope to earn. Recent studies have shown that the average American household is carrying more than eight thousand dollars in credit-card debt and that (statistically speaking) every fifteen seconds a person in the United States goes bankrupt (Lohr 2004). Although fixed costs (such as housing, food, and gasoline) have gone up for most families over the past thirty years, these debt-and-bankruptcy statistics in fact result from more people buying items that are beyond their means and cannot properly use anyway. Our consumer expectations for ourselves and our children have risen as the media have continued to attractively portray the "good life" and to bombard us with ads for something else that we *must* have.

Are we Americans actually interested in learning about class and inequality? Do we want to know where we really stand in the U.S. class structure? Although some people may prefer to operate in a climate of denial, media critics believe that more people are finally awakening to biases in the media, particularly when they see vast inconsistencies between media portrayals of class and their everyday lives. According to the sociologists Robert Perrucci and Earl Wysong, "It is apparent that increasing experiences with and knowledge about class-based inequalities among the nonprivileged is fostering a growing awareness of and concerns about the nature and extent of superclass interests, motives, and power in the economic and political arenas" (Perucci and Wysong 2003:199). Some individuals are becoming aware of the effect that media biases can have on what they read, see, and hear. A recent Pew Research Center poll, for example, reflects that people in the working class do not unquestioningly accept media information and commentary that preponderantly support the status quo (Perucci and Wysong 2003).

Similarly, Perucci and Wysong note that television can have a paradoxical effect on viewers: It can serve both as a pacifier and as a source of heightened class consciousness. Programs that focus on how much money the very wealthy have may be a source of entertainment for non-elites, but they may also produce antagonism among people who work hard and earn comparatively little, when they see people being paid so much for doing so little work (e.g., the actress who earns seventeen million dollars per film or the sports star who signs a hundred-million-dollar multiyear contract). Even more egregious are individuals who do not work at all but are born into the "right family" and inherit billions of dollars.

Although affluent audiences might prefer that the media industry work to "reinforce and disguise privileged-class interests" (Perucci and Wysong 2003:284), there is a good chance that the United States will become more class conscious and that people will demand more accurate assessments of the problems we face if more middle- and working-class families see their lifestyles continue to deteriorate in the twenty-first century.

## Is Change Likely? Media Realities Support the Status Quo

Will journalists and entertainment writers become more cognizant of class-related issues in news and in television shows? Will they more accurately portray those issues in the future? It is possible that the media will become more aware of class as an important subject to address, but several trends do not bode well for more accurate stories and portrayals of class. Among these are the issues of media ownership and control.

## Media Ownership and Senior Management

Media ownership has become increasingly concentrated in recent decades. Massive mergers and acquisitions involving the three major television networks (ABC, CBS, and NBC) have created three media "behemoths"—Viacom, Disney, and General Electric—and the news and entertainment divisions of these networks now constitute only small elements of much larger, more highly diversified corporate structures. Today, these media giants control most of that industry, and a television network is viewed as "just another contributor to the bottom line."[4] As the media scholar Shirley Biagi states, "The central force driving the media business in America is the desire to make money. American media are businesses, vast businesses. The products of these businesses are information and entertainment . . . . But American media are, above all, profit-centered" (2003:21).

Concentration of media ownership through chains, broadcast networks, cross-media ownership, conglomerates, and vertical integration (when one company controls several related aspects of the same business) are major limitations to change in how class is represented in the news and entertainment industry. Social analysts like Greg Mantsios are pessimistic about the prospects for change, because of the upper-class-based loyalties of media corporate elites:

It is no wonder Americans cannot think straight about class. The mass media is neither objective, balanced, independent, nor neutral. Those who own and direct the mass media are themselves part of the upper class, and neither they nor the ruling class in general have to conspire to manipulate public opinion. Their interest is in preserving the status quo, and their view of society as fair and equitable comes naturally to them. But their ideology dominates our society and justifies what is in reality a perverse social order—one that perpetuates unprecedented elite privilege and power on the one hand and widespread deprivation on the other (Mantsios 2003:108).

According to Mantsios, wealthy media share-holders, corporate executives, and political leaders have a vested interest in obscuring class relations not only because these elites are primarily concerned about profits but because—being among the "haves" themselves—they do not see any reason to stir up class-related animosities. Why should they call attention to the real causes of poverty and inequality and risk the possibility of causing friction among the classes?

Media executives do not particularly care if the general public criticizes the *content* of popular culture as long as audiences do not begin to question the superstructure of media ownership and the benefits these corporations derive from corporate-friendly public policies. According to the sociologist Karen Sternheimer,

> Media conglomerates have a lot to gain by keeping us focused on the popular culture "problem," lest we decide to close some of the corporate tax loopholes to fund more social programs . . . . In short, the news media promote media phobia because it doesn't threaten the bottom line. Calling for social programs to reduce inequality and poverty would (Sternheimer 2003:211).

Although the corporate culture of the media industry may be set by shareholders and individuals in the top corporate ranks, day-to-day decisions often rest in the hands of the editor-in-chief (or a person in a similar role) at a newspaper or a television executive at a local station. Typically, the goals of these individuals reflect the profit-driven missions of their parent companies and the continual need to generate the right audiences (often young males between eighteen and thirty-five years of age) for advertisers. Television commentator Jeff Greenfield acknowledges this reality: "The most common misconception most people have about television concerns its product. To the viewer, the product is the programming. To the television executive, the product is the audience" (Biagi 2003:170). The profits of television networks and stations come from selling advertising, not from producing programs that are accurate reflections of social life.

Recent trends in the media industry—including concentration of ownership, a focus on increasing profits, and a move toward less regulation of the media by the federal government—do not offer reassurance that media representations of class (along with race, gender, age, and sexual orientation) will be of much concern to corporate shareholders or executives at the top media giants—unless, of course, this issue becomes related to the bottom line or there is public demand for change, neither of which seems likely.

## DISCUSSION QUESTIONS

1. What does Diana Kendall argue about how the media frame social class in the United States?
2. To what degree are the media's framing and misrepresentation of social class differences—for example, the glamorization of the wealthy and the denigration of the poor and working class—responsible for unhealthy behaviors such as excessive consumerism and a vicarious life?

## NOTES

1. Judith Butler ("Performative Acts and Gender Constitution: An Essay in Phenomenology and Feminist Theory," in *Performing Feminisms: Feminist Critical Theory and Theatre*, ed. Sue-Ellen Case [Baltimore: Johns Hopkins University Press. 1990], 270) has described gender identity as performative, noting that social reality is not a given but is continually created as an illusion "through language, gesture, and all manner of symbolic social sign." In this sense, class might also be seen as performative, in that people act out their perceived class location not only in terms of their own class-related identity but in regard to how they treat other people, based on their perceived class position.
2. See Thomas Ginsberg, "Union Hopes to Win Over Starbucks Shop Workers," *Austin American-Statesman*, July 2, 2004, D6.
3. Antoinette Millard, also known as Lisa Walker, allegedly was so caught up in hedonistic consumerism that she created a series of false identities (ranging from

being a Saudi princess to being a lawyer, a model, and a wealthy divorcée) and engaged in illegal behavior (such as trying to steal $250,000 from an insurance company by reporting that certain jewelry had been stolen, when she actually had sold it). See Vanessa Grigoriadis, "Her Royal Lie-ness: The So-Called Saudi Princess Was Only One of the Many Identities Lisa Walker Tried on Like Jewelry," *New York Metro*, www.newyorkmetro.com/ nymetro/news/people/columns/intelligencer/n_10418 (accessed December 18, 2004); Samuel Maull, "Antoinette Millard Countersues American Express for $2 Million for Allowing Her to Charge $951,000," credit suit.org/credit.php/blog/comments/antoinette_millard_ coun tersues_american_express_for_2_million_for_ allow ing (accessed December 18, 2004).

4. Committee of Concerned Journalists, "The State of the News Media 2004," www.journalism.org (accessed June 17, 2004).

# 43

# MUSLIM AMERICANS IN THE NEWS BEFORE AND AFTER 9/11

BRIGITTE L. NACOS

OSCAR TORRES-REYNA

*Brigitte L. Nacos, professor of political science at Columbia University, has written extensively on the news media, the politics of Germany, and terrorism. As the title of this reading implies, Nacos and her former graduate student, Oscar Torres-Reyna, examine how American media treated Muslim Americans before and after the terrorist attacks on New York City and Washington, D.C., on September 11, 2001. This reading is excerpted from their 2007 book,* Fueling Our Fears: Stereotyping, Media Coverage, and Public Opinion of Muslim Americans. *Nacos and Torres-Reyna describe the changes in the news reporting of Muslim and Arab Americans, and, surprisingly, not all of their findings are negative.*

When a powerful bomb destroyed the Alfred P. Murrah Federal Building in Oklahoma City on April 19, 1995, news organizations were quick to identify Middle Easterners as suspects and reported that the FBI was specifically looking for two men with dark hair and beards. Within hours, Arab and Muslim Americans became the targets of physical and verbal assaults. As it turned out, an American with European ancestors, Timothy McVeigh, committed what was said at the time to be the most deadly terrorist deed on American soil. When the twin towers of the World Trade Center crumbled into a nuclear-winter-like cityscape and part of the Pentagon outside of Washington, DC, went up in flames on September 11, 2001, news organizations reported soon thereafter, this time correctly, that the perpetrators were Arabs and Muslims. And once again, perfectly peaceful Arab and Muslim Americans as well as persons "looking like them" became the victims of hate crimes and of the stereotypical image of Muslims and Arabs as perpetrators of violence and terrorists.

The preponderant use of clichés to characterize and demonize Muslims and Arabs has been perceived for a long time by some observers and documented well by others.[1] "The reason why many Arab and Muslim Americans are discriminated [against]," wrote one Amazon.com customer-reviewer shortly after the events of 9/11, "is because many people probably think of the 'TV-Arab' image (i.e., suicide bomber, fanatics, lazy, etc.)."[2] Although Hollywood movies, television shows, and popular fiction have long dwelled on stereotypical portrayals of Arabs and Muslims, one would not necessarily expect similar typecasting and clichés in the news. However, popular culture and news reporting do not operate in a vacuum but seem to feed on each other. Discussing the depiction of Middle Easterners in crime fiction, Reeva Simon concluded that "authors know that today, after watching the evening news and reports of bombed American embassies, kidnapped or killed diplomats, and the latest exploits of religious fanatics, the public will readily read about Middle Eastern conspirators and that books about the area will sell" (1989:140) . . . .

According to the American Muslim Poll that questioned Muslims in the United States in October and November 2001, more than two in three (68 percent) respondents said that the news media were not fair in their portrayal of Muslims and Islam (better than three of four or 77 percent thought that Hollywood was not fair in this respect).[3] This chapter examines how major American news organizations have reported on Muslim Americans. We were particularly interested in answering the following questions:

1. Was the portrayal of Muslim Americans in the news mostly negative and stereotypical?

2. Did the events of 9/11 alter the coverage of the Muslim American minority, and if so, how did these changes manifest themselves?

3. Did the pertinent news coverage of New York City and neighboring counties with rather large Muslim populations differ from the national coverage?

## The News and the "Pictures in Our Heads"

Some eighty years ago, before the advent of radio and television, Walter Lippmann observed that what people know about the world around them is mostly the result of secondhand knowledge received through the press and that the "pictures in our heads" are the result of a pseudoreality reflected in the news. In modern-day mass societies people are even more dependent on the news because they have "nowhere else to turn for information about public affairs and for cues on how to frame and interpret that information" (Neumann et al. 1992:11).

The media tend to report the news along explanatory frames that cue the reader, listener, and viewer to put events, issues, and political actors into contextual frameworks of reference. Framing can and does affect the news in many ways, for example, in the choice of topics, sources, language, and photographs. According to Robert Entman, "a frame operates to select and highlight some features of reality and obscure others in a way that tells a consistent story about problems, their causes, moral implications, and remedies" (1996:77–78). Accordingly, reporters, editors, producers, and others in the news media constantly make decisions as to what and whom to present in the news and how . . . .

Some framing patterns seem especially important in terrorism news and the perceptions and reactions of news consumers. Shanto Iyengar found that TV network coverage of terrorism in the 1980s was overwhelmingly episodic or narrowly focused rather than thematic or contextual. His research demonstrated that narrowly focused coverage influenced audiences to hold the individual perpetrators responsible, while thematic reporting was more likely to assign responsibility to societal conditions and public policies. Moreover, when exposed to episodic framing of terrorism, people were more inclined to support punitive measures against individuals; when watching thematically framed terrorism news, audience members tended to be more in favor of policies that deal with and even remove the root causes of terror.

## OF STEREOTYPES
## AND "SYMBOL HANDLERS"

We know more of the portrayal of African Americans in the news than about the coverage patterns with respect to other minorities. Research has pointed to one persistent problem in the way the news reports about black Americans, namely the tendency to highlight the extraordinary at the expense of what is the routine of everyday life in black communities. As a result, non-black Americans—especially whites— think of black America in terms of stereotypes— positive in regard to African American superstars in sports and entertainment and negative as to black males as criminals and black females as welfare queens.[4] Researchers found that few whites are aware of this hero-or-villain syndrome that seems especially prevalent in TV news.[5]

It seems that reporting on other minorities is equally spotty and stereotypical . . . .

By framing the news along the lines of the traditional attitudes and prejudices of society's predominant groups, the news media convey stereotypes that affect a broad range of public perceptions, among them how people think about race, ethnicity, and religion. According to Todd Gitlin media frames are "persistent patterns . . . , by which symbol handlers routinely organize discourse, whether verbal or visual" (1980:7). "Symbol handlers" are still most and foremost members of the white majority and their news judgments are increasingly affected by the profit imperatives of the large media corporations, but day-to-day decisions in the newsrooms are also influenced by deep-seated prejudices in the dominant white Western culture. A generation ago, Herbert Gans found that "the news reflects the white

male social order" (1979:61). While contemporary newsrooms are more diverse than twenty-five years ago, entrenched prejudices and stereotypical perceptions have not disappeared . . . . It seems equally true that the media affect how religiously diverse people view each other. Referring to the predominant visual images of black Americans in the media's depiction of poverty in America, Martin Gilens concluded that "subconscious stereotypes" guide newsroom decisions (1999:150). Similarly, overtly rejected stereotypes may nevertheless affect subconsciously the judgments concerning the news about American Muslims and Arabs.

Given the persistent complaints about media bias by American Muslims and their organizations and the growth of this minority, our research aimed at shedding light on the way the news media report on Muslim Americans in New York City and across the United States. Since the U.S. government is prohibited from collecting census data on people's religious affiliations, there are no official data on the total number of Muslims in the United States. Estimates range from one to seven million—with the real number somewhere in the middle—and, according to Muslim organizations, closer to the higher end of these assumptions.[6] According to a recent religious survey, the proportion of Muslims in the U.S. population may be 1 percent, but experts among American Muslims believe 2 percent to be more realistic.[7] As for New York City, researchers at Columbia University, who canvassed the city's five boroughs to locate Muslims and their communities, have estimated that a total of about six hundred thousand Muslims live in these areas.[8] Assuming that this is a sound number and considering that New York City has a total population of just over eight million according to the 2000 census, Muslims represent about 7.5 percent of the city's population and thus a sizable religious minority.

We are aware that not all Arabs in the United States (or abroad) are Muslims and that probably only about one in four Arab Americans are Muslims. We have nevertheless included Arab Americans in this study because as the news media report on Muslims and Arabs at home and abroad, they frequently seem to use the terms as if they were interchangeable.

The stereotypes that depict Muslims and Arabs as perpetrators of violence and terrorism were magnified by a long series of spectacular anti-American acts of terror that extended from the long-lasting Iranian hostage crisis (1979–81) to the suicide attack on the USS *Cole* in 2000. All of these incidents in the 1980s and 1990s (including the first World Trade Center bombing in 1993) were widely reported, indeed over-reported, as the news media dwelt on shocking images of death, destruction, and the victims of this sort of political violence.[9] But because none of the previous strikes came even close to what happened on September 11, 2001, there was reason to investigate whether this unprecedented event triggered changes in the news with respect to American Muslims.

## SELECTION OF LOCAL AND NATIONAL NEWS MEDIA

For our newspaper analysis we selected the three largest daily newspapers that are published in New York City, the *New York Times, New York Post*, and *Daily News*. While the *Times* has a sizable national circulation besides its local and regional readership and a reputation as an influential local, regional, and national news organ (and a leading international news source as well), the *Post* and the *Daily News* are mostly read in the New York metropolitan area. Additionally, we chose *USA Today* because of its national focus and readership. We also examined the transcripts of pertinent stories televised by CBS News on *The Early Show* and the *Evening News with Dan Rather*. Since earlier research has demonstrated that the news broadcasts of the major TV networks have very similar content, we restricted our analysis to only one of the TV networks.[10]

## 9/11 AND THE NEWS ABOUT AMERICAN MUSLIMS

It came hardly as a surprise that we found significantly more news that reported about or mentioned Muslim Americans and Arab Americans in the post-9/11 period than in the months preceding the attacks. We did not, however, expect to find that the four newspapers combined published nearly eleven times as many relevant stories in the six months after 9/11 as in the six months before and three times as many as in the twelve months before the terror attacks. (See Table 43.1)

Just as news organizations paid far more attention to American Muslims and Arabs following the terror of 9/11, they covered Muslims, Arabs, and Islam in general far more frequently as well (see Table 43.2). One comprehensive content analysis of religious news in ten American daily newspapers, nine newsmagazines, and one wire service (the Associated Press) found that stories on Islam and Muslims dominated this coverage in the weeks following the events of 9/11. Indeed, 70 percent of the stories fully devoted to religion concerned Islam and Muslims and the remaining 30 percent dealt with Christianity and Christians, multifaith and nondenominational persons, Judaism and Jews, and Buddhism and Buddhists.[11] This surge was a natural reaction to the attacks that killed almost three thousand Americans and were perpetrated by Muslim and Arab followers of America's most wanted terrorist leader, Osama bin Laden. In the process, Americans learned a great deal about the Muslims in their midst and their religion. On the other hand, the sudden media attention to the Muslim and Arab world and the religion of Islam also happened to satisfy terrorists' perennial need for publicity[12] . . . .

While in all four newspapers the number of articles that covered, mentioned, or quoted American Muslims and American Arabs increased after 9/11, there was otherwise no uniformity: The *Times* and *Daily News* presented their readers with significantly more news analyses, the *Post* and *USA Today* carried a larger proportion of opinion columns that addressed one or the other aspect of American Muslims and Arabs, and *USA Today* published more pertinent letters-to-the-editor and more editorials. Taken together, the newspapers devoted a significantly larger proportion of their total news about American Muslims to analytical perspectives, elite opinion, and the sentiments of readers at a time when the American public needed to be informed and educated about fellow Americans who happened to be Muslims . . . .

**TABLE 43.1**    Muslim and Arab Americans in the News Before and After 9/11.

|  | Sept. 11, 2000, to March 11, 2001 (6 months) | March 12, 2001, to Sept. 11, 2001 (6 months) | Sept. 12, 2001, to March 11, 2002 (6 months) |
|---|---|---|---|
|  | (N) | (N) | (N) |
| New York Times | 37 | 17 | 376 |
| New York Post | 58 | 15 | 50 |
| Daily News (NY) | 52 | 21 | 99 |
| USA Today | 8 | 6 | 128 |
| Total | 155 | 59 | 653 |

N = Number of stories.

Source: Muslims in New York City Project

## FROM PARTISAN CONTROVERSIES TO CIVIL LIBERTIES AND CIVIL RIGHTS ISSUES

Before September 11, 2001, the predominant news themes that related to American Muslims and American Arabs were taken from local, domestic, and international politics. Typically, this sort of news focused on partisan controversies, especially during election campaigns, and concerned one or the other candidate's relationships with American Muslim and/or Arab individuals or groups with alleged sympathies for or ties to terrorists and terrorist organizations in the Middle East. This became a prominent issue in the fall of 2000, when published reports revealed that the Republican presidential candidate, George W. Bush, had received $1,000 and the Democratic candidate in the New York race for the U.S. Senate, Hillary Clinton, $50,000 for their respective campaigns from American Muslim groups. Because of New York City's large bloc of Jewish voters, these revelations became hot issues in the city. In the last stage of the race, the *Daily News* reported that the First Lady's campaign had benefited from a

**TABLE 43.2**    Muslims, Arabs, and Islam in the News Before and After 9/11.

|  | Muslim Period I | Muslim Period II | Arab Period I | Arab Period II | Islam Period I | Islam Period II |
|---|---|---|---|---|---|---|
|  | (N) | (N) | (N) | (N) | (N) | (N) |
| ABC News | 31 | 163 | 11 | 99 | 1 | 31 |
| CBS News | 32 | 144 | 27 | 117 | 1 | 27 |
| NBC News | 9 | 98 | 5 | 90 | — | 18 |
| CNN | 23 | 203 | 43 | 200 | 1 | 31 |
| Fox News | 1 | 100 | 2 | 64 | 1 | 46 |
| NY Times | 345 | 1,468 | 345 | 1,272 | 216 | 1,190 |
| NPR | 54 | 217 | 53 | 182 | 10 | 84 |

N = Number of news segments/articles mentioning the search words Muslim, Arab, and/or Islam; Period I = 6 months before the terrorist attacks of September 11, 2011; Period II = 6 months after the attacks of 9/11.

Source: Muslims in New York City Project.

fundraiser thrown by an American Muslim organization and thereby provided Clinton's opponent Rick Lazio and the New York State Republican Party with ammunition to attack her as proterrorist and anti-Israel. While literally all news organizations in New York City (as well as the media elsewhere) reported on what became the central campaign issue, the *New York Post* was especially relentless in bashing Mrs. Clinton for her alleged ties to alleged terrorist-friendly organizations and individuals. The following lines were quite typical for the *Post*'s tirades:

Do you believe that Israel has a right to exist?

Do you believe that America needs a dependable, democratic ally in the strategically vital, oil-rich Middle East?

Then Hillary's record should really give you pause.

* Before becoming First Lady, Hillary chaired the New World Foundation—an organization that funded groups controlled by the Palestinian Liberation Organization. And this was back when even liberals considered the PLO a terrorist group.

* Over the years, she's befriended Arab and Muslim American organizations that refuse to denounce—and often defend—terrorist groups . . . .

* And just last month, frequent White House guest Nihad Awad, of the Council on American-Islamic Relations, railed against the notion of Arab coexistence with Israel, preaching instead the virtues of violence—and of Arab plans to reclaim "all Palestine."

Hillary's response?

None to speak of[13] . . . .

The dominance of news about Muslim and Arab Americans' involvement in the American body politic and the frequently mentioned allegations that these minorities had ties to or sympathized with terrorists in the Middle East diminished in the months after 9/11. There was also less news about the American Muslims' religious observances, holidays, or customs. Instead, the news media paid a great deal of attention to the government's curbs on civil liberties and civil rights as they affected Muslims and Arabs in the United States. Before the attacks on the World Trade Center and the Pentagon, these topics were not particularly prominent, comprising only 6 percent of the total themes in the four newspapers' combined coverage. After 9/11 there was a drastic change in this respect in that the four newspapers combined devoted about one-third of their total coverage of Muslims and Arabs in the United States on civil rights/civil liberties issues and the violation of those rights—including physical attacks on members of these groups.

Not surprisingly, 9/11 often took center stage in stories about American Muslims and Arabs, but perhaps surprisingly, it did so in mostly positive ways. For example, a wave of reports highlighted the patriotism of American Muslims and Arabs and downplayed the stereotype that members of these groups support terrorism. Headlines such as "Muslims in B'klyn call for peace" (*NY Post*, September 17, 2001); "City Arabs & Muslims back U.S." (*NY Daily News*, October 8, 2001); "Public Lives: A daughter of Islam, and an enemy of terror" (*NY Times*, October 25, 2001) were quite common in the weeks and months after 9/11. In all, 9 percent of all discernible themes in this sort of news dealt directly with the terror of 9/11 as it affected the Muslim or Arab minorities.

There was also a surge in topics that dealt with the difficult life circumstances and identity problems of some American Muslims. The *New York Times*, for example, devoted several articles to this topic and, in some cases, managed to educate non-Muslim Americans about their Muslim fellow citizens. Thus, a twenty-one-year-old woman in Bridgeview, Illinois, told the *Times*, "I love Islam and I love anything in this country." But because her apparel identified her as a Muslim," she also admitted that she is sad and fearful in the wake of 9/11."[14] But these stories also intensified the uneasy feelings in some non-Muslim Americans. Reporting on high school students in a private Islamic academy in Brooklyn, Susan Sachs wrote: "They are Americans who feel duty-bound by Islam to obey American laws. But some of them say that if their country called them to war against a Muslim army, they might refuse to fight . . . . Some of the students, for example, said they would support any leader who they decided was fighting for Islam."[15] Another story in the *Times* contained a quote by a female college student who said:

"In high school I was asking myself, am I more Pakistani or more American? Being Muslim answers that question." Her friend was even more specific when she said: "I am Muslim first, not even American Muslim. Because so much of the American culture is directly in conflict with my values as a Muslim, I can't identify solely as an American, or even as an American Muslim."[16] The question of whether the views of some of these teenagers were representative among young American Muslims was not discussed in these kinds of articles that typically reflected an understanding for the plight of American Muslims but raised troubling questions in the minds of some, perhaps many, readers. Thus, the *Times* published a letter-to-the-editor that described one of these stories as "one of the more frightening you have published in memory" and continued, "Though raised in our free society, some might not fight for America against fellow Muslims. Imagine what we would think of Christian students who refused to fight Germany in World War II because Germans were Christians." The letter closed with this sentence: "If the views of these young Muslim Americans are at all typical, we are in trouble."[17]

## SUPPORT FOR THE CIVIL LIBERTIES OF AMERICAN MUSLIMS AND ARABS

After 9/11, voices that defended the civil liberties and civil rights of American Muslims and Arabs were more numerous in the mass-mediated debate than were those who advocated curbing those freedoms: Of all positions mentioned in the news about Muslim and Arab citizens and residents, 15 percent expressed their support for unfettered civil liberties and civil rights for these minorities, while 5 percent were against protecting these fundamental freedoms for Muslim and Arab Americans. Before 9/11, these issues were not frequently discussed in the news media, counting for only 2 percent of all pertinent positions—1 percent each for and against protecting these rights for the Muslim and Arab minorities. While differing in degree, the post-9/11 debate on civil liberties and civil rights of American Muslims

and Arabs was in all four newspapers substantially tilted in favor of those who supported American Muslims' and Arabs' fundamental freedoms.

When the issue of American Muslims' and Arabs' alleged support of terrorism came up in the news before 9/11, twice as many voices made this allegation expressly or implicitly than rejected this proposition. But after 9/11, there was a complete turnaround in the newspapers mentioned: twice as many voices opposed the notion that Muslim and Arab Americans support terrorists than made this accusation.

Before 9/11, when positions on Israel were expressed in stories that also mentioned or were exclusively about Muslim or Arab Americans, more revealed anti-Israel rather than pro-Israel views. There were far fewer references to the Jewish state in pertinent post-9/11 articles, but when this issue was addressed by sources, the reported viewpoints were equally divided between anti- and pro-Israel sentiments.

## MORE POSITIVE DESCRIPTIONS OF MUSLIM AMERICANS AFTER 9/11

Surprisingly, the textual depiction of American Muslims and Arabs in the news was more positive and less negative in the wake of the terrorist events of 9/11 than before the event. Whereas one-fourth of the pertinent articles in the four newspapers were categorized by our coders as positive or supportive before 9/11, better than four in ten described these minorities in a sympathetic light after the attacks. Similarly, the stories that painted American Muslims and Arabs in a negative light decreased from nearly one-third before 9/11 to less than one-fourth afterwards. In the *Times* and *Post* the share of positive stories grew significantly after 9/11, in the *Daily News* only modestly. And while negative depictions of American Muslims and Arabs decreased after "Black Tuesday" in the *Times* and *Post*, the share of negative stories went up in the *Daily News* and *USA Today*. These differences are best explained by the negligible percentage of negative stories and the high share of positive articles in *USA Today* before the terror strikes. In the *Daily News*, too, the proportion of stories that our coders perceived as negative was significantly lower before 9/11 than in the *Times* and *Post*. Regardless of these differences, three of the newspapers (*Times*, *Post*, and *USA Today*) depicted American Muslims and Arabs more favorably than unfavorably after 9/11, and the fourth newspaper (*Daily News*) carried an equal share of positive and negative articles . . . .

## MUSLIM AND ARAB AMERICANS IN TELEVISION NEWS

In the twelve months before 9/11 CBS-TV's *Early Show* and the *Evening News with Dan Rather* aired only seven stories mentioning Muslim and/or Arab Americans, compared to fifty-one such stories in the six months after the terror in New York and Washington, DC. Thus, a comparison between the pre-9/11 and post-9/11 coverage seems to be not very meaningful. Yet, our analysis demonstrated that television news changed mostly in the same directions as newspaper reporting did. One of the exceptions was the dominance of journalistic sources before and after 9/11 that was far more pronounced than in the print press—a tendency observed with respect to television coverage in general.[18] But the share of media-based sources shrank in CBS's news from more than half of all sources before 9/11 to more than one-third after 9/11. In the sparse *CBS News* coverage of Muslim Americans before 9/11, about 10 percent of all interviewees or sources were identified as local or national politicians, while no Muslim American was interviewed or mentioned as a source at all. After 9/11, however, nearly one-fourth of all interviewees and sources in pertinent stories were members of these minorities, while the share of politicians remained constant. While American Muslims' religious customs and holidays were the topics of the pre-9/11 coverage, afterward *CBS News*, just like the print press, reported extensively on civil liberties issues as they affected Muslims and Arabs in the United States. Indeed, nearly two of five pertinent stories were devoted to this particular

topic. However, contrary to the newspaper coverage, which was strongly tilted in favor of voices that rejected curbs on Muslim and Arab Americans' civil liberties and rights, television coverage showed a less pronounced advantage in favor of these positions.

Television news tends to be significantly more episodic than reporting in the print media. Yet, just as we found in the reporting of newspapers, there was a decline of episodic stories in CBS newscasts after 9/11 and an increase in thematic segments, so that about the same number of overwhelmingly episodic and thematic stories were aired.

## DISCUSSION OF FINDINGS

The terrorist attacks of 9/11 changed the ways in which newspapers and television news reported about Muslim and Arab Americans. We found that there was a distinct shift from a limited and stereotypical coverage in the pre-9/11 period to a more comprehensive, inclusive, and less stereotypical news presentation thereafter. Besides covering and referring to Muslim and Arab Americans more frequently and featuring pertinent stories more prominently in the post-9/11 period, reporters and editors selected American Muslims and Arabs far more frequently as interviewees and sources after the catastrophic attacks on New York and Washington than in the months before. Or, to put it differently, the preferential news treatment of officialdom and authoritative sources weakened as a result of the 9/11 disaster in stories that reported on the Muslim and Arab minorities. Moreover, in the wake of the terrorist nightmare, the print media were more inclined to publish news analyses, columns, and letters-to-the-editor concerning Muslim and Arab Americans and thereby contributed to or even initiated mass-mediated debates concerning these minorities in their pages.

Probably the most important change occurred in the choice of news topics and how they were reported. Before 9/11 by far the most prominent news theme concerned Muslim and Arab Americans who participated in the political process, or tried to do so, especially during election campaigns, but were accused of sympathizing with or supporting terrorists in the Middle East. We are not suggesting that the press should have ignored these political controversies, but we do note that the news media failed to cover other aspects of American Muslim life as frequently and extensively . . . .

After 9/11, the predominant themes, especially the status of the civil liberties and civil rights of American Muslims and Arabs, arose from the reactions to an unprecedented terrorist attack that was perpetrated by Arabs and Muslims. But in spite of the context in which these issues arose, there was no jump in stereotypical coverage. Perhaps that was the consequence of news items reporting on public figures' pleas for a better understanding between Muslims and non-Muslims in the United States, and their assurances that most Muslims here and abroad have absolutely nothing to do with terrorism and that the religion of Islam does not preach violence. Just as important, there was significantly more support in the mass-mediated discourse for protecting the civil liberties and rights of American Muslims and Arabs than for curbing their freedoms. Large parts of the post-9/11 news topics that concerned or touched on the interests of Muslim and Arab Americans were framed by domestic rather than foreign story lines.

Another positive change was the increase in thematic and the decrease of episodic news frames in the months after September 11. When stories provide readers with more than bare-boned facts and explain news events in a larger context, news consumers get more comprehensive information and are able to make their evaluation of individuals and groups on a more informed and educated basis. Taken together, these changes added up to a significantly more positive and less negative media coverage of American Muslims and Arabs.

Since most Americans' knowledge about Muslim Americans is to a large extent based on media reports, not personal encounters, we wondered whether the changes in the pertinent news content affected the ways in which the American public viewed the Muslim minority in the months after September 11, 2001. Opinion surveys revealed that two months after the attacks on New York and

Washington the American public viewed Muslim Americans significantly more favorably than before. Moreover, after a huge increase in the volume of coverage after 9/11, fewer survey respondents said that they had never heard of Muslim Americans or that they could not rate their attitude towards them. While they were still more favorably inclined toward the Muslim minority than before 9/11, this spike in positive attitudes already showed signs of decline by February 2002 . . . .

To sum up, then, the events of 9/11 forced the media to cover the Muslim and Arab minorities more frequently. In a strange way, this caused the press to present news consumers with a more comprehensive picture of these groups. One result was that the news media granted Muslim Americans in particular more access after 9/11 and that members of this minority made themselves available to the media. The limited news about Muslim and Arab Americans, the prevalent topics, and the more episodic than thematic framing patterns before 9/11 added up to more negative and stereotypical associations than the more frequent reporting, the different topics, and the dominance of thematic frames in the post-9/11 months. As one expert in the field has pointed out, the cultures and peoples of the Middle East "are not easily explained in quick two-minute network news stories." The same holds true for episodically framed stories in the print media.

## DISCUSSION QUESTIONS

1. What were the results of the study concerning attitudes toward Muslim Americans after the attacks of 9/11, and what is Nacos and Torres-Reyna's analysis of those results?
2. How can you explain why most Americans rely on the media to understand Muslim and Arab Americans? Why is the stereotyping so strong?

## NOTES

1. See, for example, Jack Shaheen, *Arab and Muslim Stereotypes in American Popular Culture* (Washington,

DC: Center for Muslim-Christian Understanding, 1997) *Reel Bad Arabs: How Hollywood Vilifies a People* (Northampton, MA: Interlink Publishing Group, 2001); and Reeva Simon, *The Middle East in Crime Fiction* (New York: Lilian Barber Press, 1989).

2. The reviewer was Adil Sohail Qureshi, and the comment concerned Jack Shaheen's book *Reel Bad Arabs: How Hollywood Vilifies a People*. See www.amazon.com/exdec/obidos/ASIN/1566563887/ref=pd_sim . . . /002-929853-184886 (accessed October 22, 2001).

3. The first ever systematic pool of American Muslims was conducted for Project MAPS: Muslims in American Public Square by Zogby International. See www.projectmap.com/PMReport.htm.

4. For more on these stereotypes see Christopher P. Campbell, *Race, Myth, and the News* (Thousand Oaks, CA: Sage, 1995); Robert M. Entman and Andrew Rojecki, *The Black Image in the White Mind* (Chicago: University of Chicago Press, 2000); and Brigitte L. Nacos and Nastasha Hritzuk, "The Portrayal of Black America in the Mass Media," in *Black and Multicultural Politics in America*, ed. M. Alex Assensoh and Lawrence Hanks (New York: New York University Press, 2000), 165–95.

5. Entman and Rojecki, *Black Image in the White Mind*, 207.

6. See, for example, Dr. Barry A. Kosmin and Dr. Egon Mayer, "Profile of the U.S. Muslim Population," ARIS Report No. 2, October 2001, The Graduate Center of the City University of New York.

7. Interview with Louis Abdellatif Cristillo, Columbia University, July 25, 2002.

8. The research was part of the ongoing Muslims in New York City project at Columbia University. The canvassing was conducted between 1998 and 1999.

9. For the coverage of anti-American terrorism in the 1980s and the early 1990s, see Brigitte L. Nacos, *Terrorism and the Media: From the Iran Hostage Crisis to the World Trade Center Bombing* (New York: Columbia University Press, 1996).

10. For the uniformity of TV news broadcasts see David L. Altheide, "Three-in-One News: Network Coverage of Iran," *Journalism Quarterly* 59 (1982):482–86.

11. "A Spiritual Awakening: Religion in the Media, Dec. 2000-Nov. 2001," study prepared by Douglas Gould & Co. for the Ford Foundation.

12. For the publicity imperative of terrorists see Brigitte L. Nacos, *Mass-Mediated Terrorism: The Central Role of the Media in Terrorism and Counterterrorism* (Lanham, MD: Rowman & Littlefield, 2002).

13. "Hillary's World," *New York Post*, October 26, 2000, 44.

14. John W. Fountain, "Sadness and Fear as They Feel Doubly Vulnerable," *New York Times*, October 5, 2001, 10.

15. Susan Sachs, "The 2 Worlds of Muslim American Teenagers," *New York Times*, Oct. 7, 2001.

16. Laurie Goldstein, "A Nation Challenged: Islamic Traditions; Muslims Nurture Sense of Self on Campus," *New York Times*, November 3, 2001, B1.

17. "America at War: Voices in a Nation on Edge. Roles of Religion," *New York Times*, October 9, 2001, A24.

18. During the 2000 presidential election campaign, for example, reporters received 74 percent of the pertinent airtime on the three broadcast networks ABC, CBS, and NBC, while the candidates themselves were granted 12 percent only, according to the Center for Media and Public Policy. See "Campaign 2000 Final," *Media Monitor* XIV, no. 6 (November/December 2000):1–5.

# 44

# WHY WOMEN AREN'T WELCOME ON THE INTERNET

## AMANDA HESS

*This third and final reading on the institution of the media is by Amanda Hess, a journalist and feminist blog-ger, who writes for <u>Slate Magazine</u> online and also is a contributor to the <u>New York Times Magazine</u>. This reading, published in 2014 on <u>Pacific Standard</u>, a print and online journal, documents a growing problem facing many women online, cyberstalking and sexual harassment on the Internet. As Hess argues, instead of telling women just to ignore the violent threats and harassing messages they receive online, we need to recognize the negative impacts this harassment has on women's careers and psychological health. This harassment leads to "digital inequality," or how certain populations do not have equal access and opportunity to online resources. It also is a type of hate crime that is difficult to monitor and to prosecute.*

I was 12 hours into a summer vacation in Palm Springs when my phone hummed to life, buzzing twice next to me in the dark of my hotel room. I squinted at the screen. It was 5:30 a.m., and a friend was texting me from the opposite coast. "Amanda, this twitter account. Freaking out over here," she wrote. "There is a twitter account that seems to have been set up for the purpose of making death threats to you."

I dragged myself out of bed and opened my lap-top. A few hours earlier, someone going by the user-name "headlessfemalepig" had sent me seven tweets. "I see you are physically not very attractive. Figured," the first said. Then: "You suck a lot of drunk and drug fucked guys cocks." As a female journalist who writes about sex (among other things), none of this feedback was particularly out of the ordinary. But this guy took it to another level: "I am 36 years old,

*Source:* Hess, Amanda. "Why Women Aren't Welcome on the Internet." *Pacific Standard Magazine,* January 6, 2014. Reprinted with permission of Miller-McCune Center for Research, Media, and Public Policy.

I did 12 years for 'manslaughter', I killed a woman, like you, who decided to make fun of guys cocks." And then: "Happy to say we live in the same state. Im looking you up, and when I find you, im going to rape you and remove your head." There was more, but the final tweet summed it up: "You are going to die and I am the one who is going to kill you. I promise you this."

My fingers paused over the keyboard. I felt disoriented and terrified. Then embarrassed for being scared, and, finally, pissed. On the one hand, it seemed unlikely that I'd soon be defiled and decapitated at the hands of a serial rapist-murderer. On the other hand, headlessfemalepig was clearly a deranged individual with a bizarre fixation on me. I picked up my phone and dialed 911.

Two hours later, a Palm Springs police officer lumbered up the steps to my hotel room, paused on the outdoor threshold, and began questioning me in a steady clip. I wheeled through the relevant background information: I am a journalist; I live in Los Angeles; sometimes, people don't like what I write about women, relationships, or sexuality; this was not the first time that someone had responded to my work by threatening to rape and kill me. The cop anchored his hands on his belt, looked me in the eye, and said, "What is Twitter?"

Staring up at him in the blazing sun, the best answer I could come up with was, "It's like an e-mail, but it's public." What I didn't articulate is that Twitter is the place where I laugh, whine, work, schmooze, procrastinate, and flirt. It sits in my back pocket wherever I go and lies next to me when I fall asleep. And since I first started writing in 2007, it's become just one of the many online spaces where men come to tell me to get out.

The examples are too numerous to recount, but like any good journalist, I keep a running file documenting the most deranged cases. There was the local cable viewer who hunted down my email address after a television appearance to tell me I was "the ugliest woman he had ever seen." And the group of visitors to a "men's rights" site who pored over photographs of me and a prominent feminist activist, then discussed how they'd "spend the night with" us. ("Put em both in a gimp mask and tied to

each other 69 so the bitches can't talk or move and go round the world, any old port in a storm, any old hole," one decided.) And the anonymous commenter who weighed in on one of my articles: "Amanda, I'll fucking rape you. How does that feel?"

None of this makes me exceptional. It just makes me a woman with an Internet connection. Here's just a sampling of the noxious online commentary directed at other women in recent years. To Alyssa Royse, a sex and relationships blogger, for saying that she hated *The Dark Knight*: "you are clearly retarded, i hope someone shoots then rapes you." To Kathy Sierra, a technology writer, for blogging about software, coding, and design: "i hope someone slits your throat and cums down your gob." To Lindy West, a writer at the women's website Jezebel, for critiquing a comedian's rape joke: "I just want to rape her with a traffic cone." To Rebecca Watson, an atheist commentator, for blogging about sexism in the skeptic community: "If I lived in Boston I'd put a bullet in your brain." To Catherine Mayer, a journalist at *Time* magazine, for no particular reason: "A BOMB HAS BEEN PLACED OUTSIDE YOUR HOME. IT WILL GO OFF AT EXACTLY 10:47 PM ON A TIMER AND TRIGGER DESTROYING EVERYTHING."

A woman doesn't even need to occupy a professional writing perch at a prominent platform to become a target. According to a 2005 report by the Pew Research Center, which has been tracking the online lives of Americans for more than a decade, women and men have been logging on in equal numbers since 2000, but the vilest communications are still disproportionately lobbed at women. We are more likely to report being stalked and harassed on the Internet—of the 3,787 people who reported harassing incidents from 2000 to 2012 to the volunteer organization Working to Halt Online Abuse, 72.5 percent were female. Sometimes, the abuse can get physical: A Pew survey reported that five percent of women who used the Internet said "something happened online" that led them into "physical danger." And it starts young: Teenage girls are significantly more likely to be cyberbullied than boys. Just appearing as a woman online, it seems, can be enough to inspire abuse. In 2006, researchers from the University of Maryland set up a bunch of fake online accounts and then dispatched them into chat rooms. Accounts with feminine usernames incurred an average of 100 sexually explicit or threatening messages a day. Masculine names received 3.7.

There are three federal laws that apply to cyber-stalking cases; the first was passed in 1934 to address harassment through the mail, via telegram, and over the telephone, six decades after Alexander Graham Bell's invention. Since the initial passage of the Violence Against Women Act, in 1994, amendments to the law have gradually updated it to apply to new technologies and to stiffen penalties against those who use them to abuse. Thirty-four states have cyberstalking laws on the books; most have expanded long-standing laws against stalking and criminal threats to prosecute crimes carried out online.

But making quick and sick threats has become so easy that many say the abuse has proliferated to the point of meaninglessness, and that expressing alarm is foolish. Reporters who take death threats seriously "often give the impression that this is some kind of shocking event for which we should pity the 'victims,'" my colleague Jim Pagels wrote in *Slate* this fall, "but anyone who's spent 10 minutes online knows that these assertions are entirely toothless." On Twitter, he added, "When there's no precedent for physical harm, it's only baseless fear mongering." My friend Jen Doll wrote, at *The Atlantic Wire*, "It seems like that old 'ignoring' tactic your mom taught you could work out to everyone's benefit. . . . These people are bullying, or hope to bully. Which means we shouldn't take the bait." In the epilogue to her book *The End of Men*, Hanna Rosin—an editor at *Slate*—argued that harass-ment of women online could be seen as a cause for celebration. It shows just how far we've come. Many women on the Internet "are in positions of influence, widely published and widely read; if they sniff out misogyny, I have no doubt they will gleefully skewer the responsible sexist in one of many available online outlets, and get results."

So women who are harassed online are expected to either get over ourselves or feel flattered in response to the threats made against us. We have the choice to keep quiet or respond "gleefully."

But no matter how hard we attempt to ignore it, this type of gendered harassment—and the sheer volume of it—has severe implications for women's status on the Internet. Threats of rape, death, and stalking can overpower our emotional bandwidth, take up our time, and cost us money through legal fees, online protection services, and missed wages. I've spent countless hours over the past four years logging the online activity of one particularly com-mitted cyberstalker, just in case. And as the Internet becomes increasingly central to the human experi-ence, the ability of women to live and work freely online will be shaped, and too often limited, by the technology companies that host these threats, the constellation of local and federal law enforcement officers who investigate them, and the popular com-mentators who dismiss them—all arenas that remain dominated by men, many of whom have little per-sonal understanding of what women face online every day.

★　★　★

This summer, Caroline Criado-Perez became the English-speaking Internet's most famous recip-ient of online threats after she petitioned the British government to put more female faces on its bank notes. (When the Bank of England announced its intentions to replace social reformer Elizabeth Fry with Winston Churchill on the £5 note, Criado-Perez made the modest suggestion that the bank make an effort to feature at least one woman who is not the Queen on any of its currency.) Rape and death threats amassed on her Twitter feed too quickly to count, bearing messages like "I will rape you tomorrow at 9 p.m . . . Shall we meet near your house?"

Then, something interesting happened. Instead of logging off, Criado-Perez retweeted the threats, blasting them out to her Twitter followers. She called up police and hounded Twitter for a response. Journalists around the world started writing about the threats. As more and more people heard the story, Criado-Perez's follower count skyrocketed to near 25,000. Her supporters joined in urging British police and Twitter executives to respond.

Under the glare of international criticism, the police and the company spent the next few weeks passing the buck back and forth. Andy Trotter, a communications adviser for the British police, announced that it was Twitter's responsibility to crack down on the messages. Though Britain criminalizes a broader category of offensive speech than the U.S. does, the sheer volume of threats would be too difficult for "a hard-pressed police service" to investigate, Trotter said. Police "don't want to be in this arena." It diverts their attention from "dealing with something else."

Meanwhile, Twitter issued a blanket statement saying that victims like Criado-Perez could fill out an online form for each abusive tweet; when Criado-Perez supporters hounded Mark Luckie, the company's manager of journalism and news, for a response, he briefly shielded his account, saying that the attention had become "abusive." Twitter's official recommendation to victims of abuse puts the ball squarely in law enforcement's court: "If an interaction has gone beyond the point of name calling and you feel as though you may be in danger," it says, "contact your local authorities so they can accurately assess the validity of the threat and help you resolve the issue offline."

In the weeks after the flare-up, Scotland Yard confirmed the arrest of three men. Twitter—in response to several online petitions calling for action—hastened the rollout of a "report abuse" button that allows users to flag offensive material. And Criado-Perez went on receiving threats. Some real person out there—or rather, hundreds of them—still liked the idea of seeing her raped and killed.

★   ★   ★

The Internet is a global network, but when you pick up the phone to report an online threat, whether you are in London or Palm Springs, you end up face-to-face with a cop who patrols a comparatively puny jurisdiction. And your cop will probably be a man: According to the U.S. Bureau of Justice Statistics, in 2008, only 6.5 percent of state police officers and 19 percent of FBI agents were women. The numbers get smaller in smaller agencies. And in many locales, police work is still a largely analog affair: 911 calls are immediately routed to the local police force; the closest officer is dispatched to respond; he takes notes with pen and paper.

After Criado-Perez received her hundreds of threats, she says she got conflicting instructions from police on how to report the crimes, and was forced to repeatedly "trawl" through the vile messages to preserve the evidence. "I can just about cope with threats," she wrote on Twitter. "What I can't cope with after that is the victim-blaming, the patronising, and the police record-keeping." Last year, the American atheist blogger Rebecca Watson wrote about her experience calling a series of local and national law enforcement agencies after a man launched a website threatening to kill her. "Because I knew what town [he] lived in, I called his local police department. They told me there was nothing they could do and that I'd have to make a report with my local police department," Watson wrote later. "[I] finally got through to someone who told me that there was nothing they could do but take a report in case one day [he] followed through on his threats, at which point they'd have a pretty good lead."

The first time I reported an online rape threat to police, in 2009, the officer dispatched to my home asked, "Why would anyone bother to do something like that?" and declined to file a report. In Palm Springs, the officer who came to my room said, "This guy could be sitting in a basement in Nebraska for all we know." That my stalker had said that he lived in my state, and had plans to seek me out at home, was dismissed as just another online ruse.

Of course, some people are investigated and prosecuted for cyberstalking. In 2009, a Florida college student named Patrick Macchione met a girl at school, then threatened to kill her on Twitter, terrorized her with lewd videos posted to YouTube, and made hundreds of calls to her phone. Though his victim filed a restraining order, cops only sprung into action after a county sheriff stopped him for loitering, then reportedly found a video camera in his backpack containing disturbing recordings about his victim. The sheriff's department later worked with the state attorney's office to convict Macchione on 19 counts, one of which was cyberstalking (he successfully appealed that count on grounds that the law hadn't been enacted when he was arrested); Macchione was sentenced to four years in prison. Consider also a recent high-profile case of cyberstalking investigated by the FBI. In the midst of her affair with General David Petraeus, biographer Paula Broadwell allegedly created an anonymous email account for the purpose of sending harassing notes to Florida socialite Jill Kelley. Kelley reported them to the FBI, which sniffed out Broadwell's identity via the account's location-based metadata and obtained a warrant to monitor her email activity.

In theory, appealing to a higher jurisdiction can yield better results. "Local law enforcement will often look the other way," says Dr. Sameer Hinduja, a criminology professor at Florida Atlantic University and co-director of the Cyberbullying Research Center. "They don't have the resources or the personnel to investigate those crimes." County, state, or federal agencies at least have the support to be more responsive: "Usually they have a computer crimes unit, savvy personnel who are familiar with these cases, and established relationships with social media companies so they can quickly send a subpoena to help with the investigation," Hinduja says.

But in my experience and those of my colleagues, these larger law enforcement agencies have little capacity or drive to investigate threats as well. Despite his pattern of abusive online behavior, Macchione was ultimately arrested for an unrelated physical crime. When I called the FBI over headless-femalepig's threats, a representative told me an agent would get in touch if the Bureau was interested in pursuing the case; nobody did. And when Rebecca Watson reported the threats targeted at her to the FBI, she initially connected with a sympathetic agent—but the agent later expressed trouble opening Watson's file of screenshots of the threats, and soon stopped replying to her emails. The Broadwell investigation was an uncommon, and possibly unprecedented, exercise for the agency. As University of Wisconsin-Eau Claire criminal justice professor Justin Patchin told *Wired* at the time: "I'm not aware of any case when the FBI has gotten involved in a case of online harassment."

After I received my most recent round of threats, I asked Jessica Valenti, a prominent feminist writer (and the founder of the blog Feministing) who's been repeatedly targeted with online threats, for her advice, and then I asked her to share her story. "It's not really one story. This has happened a number of times over the past seven years," she told me. When rape and death threats first started pouring into her inbox, she vacated her apartment for a week, changed her bank accounts, and got a new cell number. When the next wave of threats came, she got in touch with law enforcement officials, who warned her that though the men emailing her were unlikely to follow through on their threats, the level of vitriol indicated that she should be vigilant for a far less identifiable threat: silent "hunters" who lurk behind the tweeting "hollerers." The FBI advised Valenti to leave her home until the threats blew over, to never walk outside of her apartment alone, and to keep aware of any cars or men who might show up repeatedly outside her door. "It was totally impossible advice," she says. "You have to be paranoid about everything. You can't just not be in a public place."

And we can't simply be offline either. When *Time* journalist Catherine Mayer reported the bomb threat lodged against her, the officers she spoke to—who thought usernames were secret codes and didn't seem to know what an IP address was—advised her to unplug. "Not one of the officers I've encountered uses Twitter or understands why anyone would wish to do so," she later wrote. "The officers were unanimous in advising me to take a break from Twitter, assuming, as many people do, that Twitter is at best a time-wasting narcotic."

All of these online offenses are enough to make a woman *want* to click away from Twitter, shut her laptop, and power down her phone. Sometimes, we do withdraw: Pew found that from 2000 to 2005, the percentage of Internet users who participate in online chats and discussion groups dropped from 28 percent to 17 percent, "entirely because of women's fall off in participation." But for many women, steering clear of the Internet isn't an option. We use our devices to find supportive communities, make a living, and construct safety nets. For a woman like me, who lives alone, the Internet isn't a fun diversion—it is a necessary resource for work and interfacing with friends, family, and, sometimes, law enforcement officers in an effort to feel safer from both online and offline violence.

The Polish sociologist Zygmunt Bauman draws a distinction between "tourists" and "vagabonds" in the modern economy. Privileged tourists move about the world "on purpose," to seek "new experience" as "the joys of the familiar wear off." Disempowered vagabonds relocate because they have to, pushed and pulled through mean streets where they could never hope to settle down. On the Internet, men are tourists and women are vagabonds. "Telling a woman to shut her laptop is like saying, 'Eh! Just stop seeing your family,'" says Nathan Jurgenson, a social media sociologist (and a friend) at the University of Maryland.

What does a tourist look like? In 2012, *Gawker* unmasked "Violentacrez," an anonymous member of the online community Reddit who was infamous for posting creepy photographs of underage women and creating or moderating subcommunities on the site with names like "chokeabitch" and "rapebait." Violentacrez turned out to be a Texas computer programmer named Michael Brusch, who displayed an exceedingly casual attitude toward his online hobbies. "I do my job, go home, watch TV, and go on the Internet. I just like riling people up in my spare time," he told Adrian Chen, the *Gawker* reporter who outed him. "People take things way too seriously around here."

Abusers tend to operate anonymously, or under pseudonyms. But the women they target often write on professional platforms, under their given names, and in the context of their real lives. Victims don't have the luxury of separating themselves from the crime. When it comes to online threats, "one person is feeling the reality of the Internet very viscerally: the person who is being threatened," says Jurgenson. "It's a lot easier for the person who made the threat—and the person who is investigating the threat—to believe that what's happening on the Internet isn't real."

★　★　★

When authorities treat the Internet as a fantasyland, it has profound effects on the investigation and prosecution of online threats. Criminal threat laws largely require that victims feel tangible, immediate, and sustained fear. In my home state of California, a threat must be "unequivocal, unconditional, immediate, and specific" and convey a "gravity of purpose and an immediate prospect of execution of the threat" to be considered a crime. If police don't know whether the harasser lives next door or out in Nebraska, it's easier for them to categorize the threat as non-immediate. When they treat a threat as a boyish hoax, the implication is that the threat ceases to be a criminal offense.

So the victim faces a psychological dilemma: How should she understand her own fear? Should she, as many advise, dismiss an online threat as a silly game, and not bother to inform the cops that someone may want to—ha, ha—rape and kill her? Or should she dutifully report every threat to police, who may well dismiss her concerns? When I received my most recent rape and death threats, one friend told me that I should rest assured that the anonymous tweeter was unlikely to take any physical action against me in real life; another noted that my stalker seemed like the type of person who would fashion a coat from my skin, and urged me to take any action necessary to land the stalker in jail.

Danielle Citron, a University of Maryland law professor who focuses on Internet threats, charted the popular response to Internet death and rape threats in a 2009 paper published in the *Michigan Law Review*. She found that Internet harassment is routinely dismissed as "harmless locker-room talk," perpetrators as "juvenile pranksters," and victims as "overly sensitive complainers." Weighing in on one online harassment case, in an interview on National Public Radio, journalist David Margolick called the threats "juvenile, immature, and obnoxious, but that is all they are ... frivolous frat-boy rants."

Of course, the frat house has never been a particularly safe space for women. I've been threatened online, but I have also been harassed on the street, groped on the subway, followed home from the 7-Eleven, pinned down on a bed by a drunk boyfriend, and raped on a date. Even if I sign off Twitter, a threat could still be waiting on my stoop.

Today, a legion of anonymous harassers are free to play their "games" and "pranks" under pseudonymous screen names, but for the women they target, the attacks only compound the real fear, discomfort, and stress we experience in our daily lives.

★　★　★

If American police forces are overwhelmingly male, the technology companies that have created the architecture of the online world are, famously, even more so. In 2010, according to the information services firm CB Insights, 92 percent of the founders of fledgling Internet companies were male; 86 percent of their founding teams were exclusively male. While the number of women working across the sciences is generally increasing, the percentage of women working in computer sciences peaked in 2000 and is now on the decline. In 2012, the Bureau of Labor Statistics found, women made up just 22.5 percent of American computer programmers and 19.7 percent of software developers. In a 2012 study of 400 California companies, researchers at the University of California-Davis, found that just seven percent of the highest-paid executives at Silicon Valley companies were women.

When Twitter announced its initial public offering in October, its filings listed an all-male board. Vijaya Gadde, Twitter's general counsel, was the only woman among its executive officers. When Vivek Wadhwa, a fellow at Stanford's Rock Center for Corporate Governance, suggested that the gender imbalance on Twitter's board was an issue of "elite arrogance" and "male chauvinistic thinking," Twitter CEO Dick Costolo responded with a joking tweet, calling Wadhwa "the Carrot Top of academic sources."

Most executives aren't intentionally boxing women out. But the decisions these men make have serious implications for billions of people. The gender imbalance in their companies compromises their ability to understand the lives of half their users.

Twitter "has a history of saying 'too bad, so sad'" when confronted with concerns about harassment on its platform, says Citron, the University of Maryland law professor who studies the emerging legal implications of online abuse against women. The culture of the platform has typically prioritized freewheeling discussion over zealous speech policing. Unlike Facebook, Twitter doesn't require people to register accounts under their real names. Users are free to enjoy the frivolity—and the protection—that anonymous speech provides. If a user runs afoul of Twitter's terms of service, he's free to create a new account under a fresh handle. And the Communications Decency Act of 1996 protects platforms like Twitter from being held legally responsible for what individuals say on the site.

The advent of the "report abuse" button is a development Citron finds "very heartening." Allowing people to block an abuser's account helps women avoid having to be faced with vile and abusive tweets. But our problems can't all be solved with the click of a button. In some cases, the report-abuse button is just a virtual Band-Aid for a potentially dangerous real-world problem. It can undermine women by erasing the trail of digital evidence. And it does nothing to prevent these same abusers from opening a new account and continuing their crimes.

When I received those seven tweets in Palm Springs, a well-meaning friend reported them as abusive through Twitter's system, hoping that action on the platform's end would help further my case. A few hours later, the tweets were erased from the site without comment (or communication with me). Headlessfemalepig's Twitter feed was replaced with a page noting that the account had been suspended. Luckily, I had taken screenshots of the tweets, but to the cops working with a limited understanding of the platform, their sudden disappearance only confused the issue. The detective assigned to my case asked me to send him links pointing to where the messages lived online—but absent a subpoena of Twitter's records, they were gone from law enforcement's view. If someone had reported the threats before I got a chance to see them, I might not even have been able to indicate their existence at all. Without a proper investigation, I am incapable of knowing whether headlessfemalepig is a one-time offender or the serial stalker who has followed me for many years. Meanwhile, nothing's stopping headlessfemalepig from continuing to tweet away under a new name.

It shouldn't be Twitter's responsibility to hunt down and sanction criminals who use its service—that's what cops are (supposedly) for. Twitter has to balance its interests in addressing abusive behavior with its interests in protecting our private information (or that of, say, political dissidents), which means keeping a tight lid on users' IP addresses and refusing to offer up deleted material to civilians. When I asked how Twitter balances those demands, Nu Wexler, who leads public policy communications for the company, pointed me to a chart published by the Electronic Frontier Foundation—an advocacy group dedicated to defending the free speech and privacy rights of Internet users—that illustrates the platform's "commitment to user privacy." The chart, titled "Who Has Your Back: Which Companies Help Protect Your Data From the Government?," awards Twitter high marks for fighting for users' privacy rights in court and publishing a transparency report about government data requests.

A high score awarded by the Electronic Frontier Foundation communicates to users that their Internet activity will be safe from overreaching government snoops—and post–Edward Snowden, that concern is more justified than ever. But in some cases, the impulse to protect our privacy can interfere with the law's ability to protect us when we're harassed. Last year, the Electronic Frontier Foundation came out against an amendment to the Violence Against Women Act. Until recently, the law criminalized abusive, threatening, and harassing speech conveyed over a telephone line, provided the abuser placed the call; the new law, passed in March, applies to any electronic harassment targeted at a specific person, whether it's made over the telephone or by another means. Critics of the legislation pulled out the trope that the Internet is less real than other means of communication. As the Foundation put it, "a person is free to disregard something said on Twitter in a way far different than a person who is held in constant fear of the persistent ringing of a telephone intruding in their home."

The Electronic Frontier Foundation—and the tech companies that benefit from its ratings—are undoubtedly committed to fighting government First Amendment abuses. But when they focus their efforts on stemming the spread of anti-harassment laws from outdated media, like landline telephones, to modern means like Twitter, their efforts act like a thumb on the scale, favoring some democratic values at the expense of others. "Silicon Valley has the power to shape society to conform to its values, which prioritize openness and connectivity," Jurgenson says. "But why are engineers in California getting to decide what constitutes harassment for people all around the world?"

Tech companies are, of course, fully aware that they need a broad base of users to flourish as billion-dollar businesses. Today women have the bargaining power to draft successful petitions calling for "report abuse" buttons, but our corporate influence is limited, and alternative venues for action are few. Local police departments "have no money," Jurgenson says, and "it feels unlikely that the government is going to do more anytime soon, so we're forced to put more pressure on Twitter." And while an organized user base can influence the decisions of a public, image-conscious company like Twitter, many platforms—like the dedicated "revenge porn" sites that have proliferated on the Web—don't need to appease women to stay popular. "I call this the myth of the market," Citron says. "There's definitely a desire for anti-social behavior. There are eyeballs. And there are users who are providing the content. The market isn't self-correcting, and it's not going to make this go away."

★   ★   ★

In a 2009 paper in the *Boston University Law Review*, Citron proposed a new way of framing the legal problem of harassment on the Internet: She argued that online abuse constitutes "discrimination in women's employment opportunities" that ought to be better addressed by the U.S. government itself. Title VII of the Civil Rights Act of 1964, which outlawed discrimination based on race, religion, or gender, was swiftly applied to members of the Ku Klux Klan, who hid behind hoods to harass and intimidate black Louisianans from voting and pursuing work. Anonymous online harassment, Citron argued, similarly discourages women from "writing and earning a living online" on the basis of their gender. "It interferes with their professional lives. It raises their vulnerability to offline sexual violence. It brands them as incompetent workers and inferior sexual objects. The harassment causes considerable emotional distress."

On the Internet, women are overpowered and devalued. We don't always think about our online lives in those terms—after all, our days are filled with work to do, friends to keep up with, Netflix to watch. But when anonymous harassers come along—saying they would like to rape us, or cut off our heads, or scrutinize our bodies in public, or shame us for our sexual habits—they serve to remind us in ways both big and small that we can't be at ease online. It is precisely the banality of Internet harassment, University of Miami law professor Mary Anne Franks has argued, that makes it "both so effective and so harmful, especially as a form of discrimination."

The personal and professional costs of that discrimination manifest themselves in very real ways. Jessica Valenti says she has stopped promoting her speaking events publicly, enlisted security for her public appearances, signed up for a service to periodically scrub the Web of her private information, invested in a post-office box, and begun periodically culling her Facebook friend list in an attempt to filter out readers with ulterior motives. Those efforts require a clear investment of money and time, but the emotional fallout is less directly quantifiable. "When people say you should be raped and killed for years on end, it takes a toll on your soul," she says. Whenever a male stranger approaches her at a public event, "the hairs on the back of my neck stand up." Every time we call the police, head to court to file a civil protection order, or get sucked into a mental hole by the threats that have been made against us, zeroes drop from our annual incomes. Says Jurgenson, "It's a monetary penalty for being a woman."

Citron has planted the seed of an emerging debate over the possibility of applying civil rights laws to ensure equal opportunities for women on the Internet. "There's no silver bullet for addressing this problem," Citron says. But existing legislation has laid the groundwork for potential future reforms. Federal civil rights law can punish "force or threat[s]

of force" that interfere with a person's employment on the basis of race, religion, or national origin. That protection, though, doesn't currently extend to threats targeted at a person's gender. However, other parts of the Civil Rights Act frame workplace sexual harassment as discriminatory, and requires employers to implement policies to both prevent and remedy discrimination in the office. And Title IX of the Education Amendments of 1972 puts the onus on educational institutions to take action against discrimination toward women. Because Internet harassment affects the employment and educational opportunities of women, laws could conceivably be amended to allow women to bring claims against individuals.

But it's hard to get there from here. As Citron notes, the Internet is not a school or a workplace, but a vast and diffuse universe that often lacks any clear locus of accountability. Even if online threats are considered a civil rights violation, who would we sue? Anonymous tweeters lack the institutional affiliation to make monetary claims worthwhile. And there is the mobbing problem: One person can send just one horrible tweet, but then many others may pile on. A single vicious tweet may not clear the hurdle of discriminatory harassment (or repetitive abuse). And while a mob of individuals each lobbing a few attacks clearly looks and feels like harassment, there is no organized group to take legal action against. Bringing separate claims against individual abusers would be laborious, expensive, and unlikely to reap financial benefits. At the same time, amending the Communications Decency Act to put the onus on Internet platforms to police themselves could have a serious chilling effect on all types of speech, discriminatory or otherwise.

Citron admits that passing new civil rights legislation that applies to a new venue—the Internet—is a potentially Sisyphean task. But she says that by expanding existing civil rights laws to recognize the gendered nature of Internet threats, lawmakers could put more pressure on law enforcement agencies to take those crimes seriously. "We have the tools already," Citron says. "Do we use them? Not really." Prosecuting online threats as bias-motivated crimes would mean that offenders would face stronger penalties, law enforcement agencies would be better incentivized to investigate these higher-level crimes—and hopefully, the Internet's legions of anonymous abusers would begin to see the downside of mouthing off.

Our laws have always found a way to address new harms while balancing long-standing rights, even if they do it very slowly. Opponents of the Civil Rights Act of 1964 characterized its workplace protections as unconstitutional and bad for business. Before workplace sexual harassment was reframed as discriminatory under Title VII, it was written off as harmless flirting. When Title IX was first proposed to address gender discrimination in education, a Senate discussion on the issue ended in laughter when one senator cracked a co-ed football joke. Until domestic violence became a national policy priority, abuse was dismissed as a lovers' quarrel. Today's harmless jokes and undue burdens are tomorrow's civil rights agenda.

★  ★  ★

My serial cyberstalker began following me in 2009. I was on the staff of an alt-weekly when a mini-controversy flared up on a blog. One of the blog's writers had developed a pattern of airing his rape fantasies on the site; I interviewed him and the site's other contributors and published a story. Then I started receiving rape threats of my own. Their author posted a photo of me on his blog and wrote, "Oh, sure, you might say she's pretty. Or you might say she looks sweet or innocent. But don't let looks fool you. This woman is pure evil." (To some harassers, you're physically not very attractive; to others, you're beautiful.) "I thought I'd describe her on my blog as 'rape-worthy,' but ultimately decided against it," he added. "Oops! I've committed another thought crime!"

In the comments section below the article, threats popped up under a dozen fake names and several phony IP addresses—which usually point to a device's precise location, but can be easily faked if you have the right software. "Amanda, I'll fucking rape you," one said. "How's that feel? Like that? What's my IP address, bitch?" On his Twitter

account, my stalker wrote that he planned to buy a gun—apparently intending to defend his First Amendment rights by exercising the Second.

Then, one night when my boyfriend and I were in our apartment, my cell phone started ringing incessantly. I received a series of voicemails, escalating in tone from a stern "You cut the shit right fucking now" to a slurred "You fucking dyke . . . I will fuck you up." For the first time ever, I called the police. When an officer arrived at my house, I described the pattern of abuse. He expressed befuddlement at the "virtual" crime, handed me his card, and told me to call if anyone came to my house—but he declined to take a report.

Without police support, I opted to file a civil protection order in family court. I posted a photograph of my stalker at my office's front desk. When the local sheriff's department failed to serve him court papers, I paid $100 for a private investigator to get the job done. It took me five visits to court, waiting for my case to be called up while sitting quietly across the aisle from him in the gallery as dozens of other local citizens told a domestic violence judge about the boyfriends and fathers and ex-wives who had threatened and abused them. These people were seeking protection from crowbar-wielding exes and gun-flashing acquaintances—more real crimes the justice system had failed to prosecute. By the time the judge finally called up my protection order for review, I had missed a half-dozen days of work pursuing the case. I was lucky to have a full-time job and an understanding boss—even if he didn't understand the threats on the same level I did. And because my case was filed under new anti-stalking protections—protections designed for cases like mine, in which I was harassed by someone I didn't have a personal relationship with—I was lucky to get a court-appointed lawyer, too. Most victims don't.

My harasser finally acquiesced to the protection order when my lawyer showed him that we knew the blog comments were coming from his computer—he had made a valiant attempt to obscure his comments, but he'd slipped up in a couple of instances, and we could prove the rape threats were his. When the judge approved the order, she instructed my harasser that he was not allowed to contact me in any way—not by email, Twitter, phone, blog comment, or by hiring a hot air balloon to float over my house with a message, she said. And he had to stay at least 100 feet away from me at all times. The restraining order would last one year.

Soon after the order expired, he sent an email to my new workplace. Every once in a while, he re-establishes contact. Last summer, he waded into the comments section of an article I wrote about sex website creator Cindy Gallop, to say, "I would not sacrifice the physiological pleasure of ejaculating inside the woman for a lesser psychological pleasure.... There is a reason it feels better to do it the right way and you don't see others in the ape world practicing this behavior." A few months later, he reached out via LinkedIn. ("Your stalker would like to add you to his professional network.") A few days before I received the threats in Palm Springs, he sent me a link via Twitter to a story he wrote about another woman who had been abused online. Occasionally, he sends his tweets directly my way—a little reminder that his "game" is back on.

It's been four years, but I still carry the case files with me. I record every tweet he sends me in a Word document, forward his emails to a dedicated account, then print them out to ensure I'll have them ready for police in analog form if he ever threatens me again (or worse). Whenever I have business travel to the city where he lives, I cart my old protection order along, even though the words are beginning to blur after a dozen photocopies. The stacks of paper are filed neatly in my apartment. My anxieties are harder to organize.

## DISCUSSION QUESTIONS

1. According to Hess, what are the specific facts we know to date about the amount and types of cyberharassment that are occurring in the United States? Why is this issue a problem?
2. What are some potential solutions to online stalking and sexual harassment?

# 45

# SAND CASTLES AND SNAKE PITS

LILLIAN B. RUBIN

*This reading is the first of three to examine the institution of politics and government. Lillian B. Rubin, who had a Ph.D. in sociology, was an internationally known sociologist and writer who had published twelve books over the past thirty years. This excerpt from a 2007 issue of* Dissent, *a quarterly magazine of politics and culture, illustrates some of the unintended consequences of social policies. Similar to Keith Wailoo's research in Reading 42, Rubin argues argues that our government has failed to create effective social policies to help disadvantaged populations such as the mentally ill and the homeless. Rubin's research also raises questions about how social class is connected to mental health (see Grochowski in Reading 40) and how the homeless, in particular, have special social and health needs. A prolific and well-respected scholar, Rubin died in 2014 at the age of 90 years old.*

The walk from my home on top of San Francisco's Nob Hill down to my studio at its bottom is a lesson in class and status in America. As each few blocks take me down another rung on the socioeconomic ladder, I move from the clean, well-tended streets at the summit through increasingly littered, ill-kept neighborhoods where property values decrease as the numbers of pot-holes and homeless people increase. At the bottom of the hill sits the notorious "Tenderloin," a district that houses what the Victorians called "the lower orders," where the desperate and the dangerous hang on every street corner waiting for the local food kitchen to open its doors.

Three blocks later, I'm downtown looking at the visible signs of gentrification—an upscale shopping mall featuring the recently opened Bloomingdale's

*Source:* Lillian B. Rubin, "Sand Castles and Snake Pits." *Dissent*, 54(4), pages 51–56. Reprinted with permission of the University of Pennsylvania Press.

West Coast flagship store and an Intercontinental Hotel under construction next door. From there I pass into the more industrial parts of the city, where my studio sits in an old warehouse building, an entrance to the freeway on one corner and St. Vincent de Paul's homeless shelter—the biggest in the city—on the other.

How did this, the richest nation in the world, give birth to an enormous population of people who live on the streets or in shelters—men, women, and children, impoverished, desperate, and very often mentally ill? Three-quarters of a million Americans in 2005, the most recent national estimate, without a place to call home—a reckoning that most experts agree is far too low because it includes only those they could find to count. How did homelessness become so pervasive that a college student in the class on poverty in America I taught a few years ago couldn't conceive of a world without "the homeless"?

"Are you saying there didn't used to be homeless?" he asked, bewildered. "They've always been there, all my life," he continued, as other students nodded assent. How is it that even those of us who remember a time when homelessness was something that happened in India, not here in these United States, have become so inured to the sight of people living on the street that we walk past and around them without really seeing them?

Maybe it takes a few years of working next door to people without homes to see them, not as an undifferentiated mass—"the homeless"—but as men and women (mostly men) with whom I share a greeting when I arrive in the morning, people with names and faces and hard-luck stories. They're unclean, unkempt, and with a bone-deep weariness that seems to seep out of their pores, yet someone offers help when he sees me struggling to manage more than I can comfortably carry up the stairs. And once, when I tripped and fell, another picked me up off the sidewalk, wiped the blood off my face (Never mind that he pulled a filthy rag of a handkerchief out of his pocket to do the job), and despite my protests, refused to leave until he saw me safely to my destination.

Homelessness in America isn't new, but it had a distinctly different flavor and meaning in earlier times. Then, homelessness was a transient phenomenon, generally tied to a sudden seismic event or the cycles of the economy. The Great Depression, for example, spawned a "hobo" population, mostly men from rural and urban communities who wandered from one part of the country to another in a fruitless search for work that didn't exist. But when the depression lifted and the economy brightened, they found jobs and homes. American cities, too, have always had pockets of homelessness, the skid row "bums" in neighborhoods like the Bowery in New York, "West Madison" in Chicago, the Tenderloin in San Francisco where the poor, the transient, the sick sought escape, and where alcoholics, still clutching the bottle, could be seen sleeping on the streets. But modern homelessness isn't just about "bums" or "hobos," nor is it confined to some small, out-of-sight corner of the city. Instead, it's on our streets and in our face and, for those of us who live in any major city in the country, it's an inescapable fact of life.

They're black and brown and less often white; they're usually single and mostly men. For some being without a home is episodic, the result of an illness, an injury, a layoff, or for some of the women, domestic violence. The problem clears, and they're back on their feet—at least until the next time. But for hundreds of thousands of Americans, homelessness is a near-permanent, chronic condition from which there is currently no real escape.

The large structural forces that have changed the face of homelessness are no mystery: an increasingly stratified society with little opportunity for the unschooled and unskilled, a minimum wage that doesn't approach a living wage, unemployment and underemployment, cuts in public assistance, and urban rents that continue to rise well beyond what an unskilled worker can afford. But all of these together would not have created the scale of the problem we now face without the aid of two major public policy initiatives: the Housing Act, passed by Congress in 1949, and the Community Mental Health Centers Act, signed into law by President John F. Kennedy in 1963—good ideas with lofty goals, whose unintended consequences we see in the legions of homeless on the streets of our cities today.

In the landmark Housing Act of 1949, Congress declared that every American deserves a "decent home and a suitable living environment" and instituted a complex set of provisions to achieve that goal. For the growing post–World War II middle class, the increased authorization for the Federal Housing Administration (FHA) mortgage insurance (known as Title II) was a bonanza that helped millions realize the dream of homeownership. But for the poor, Title I, which called for an urban redevelopment program, became a disaster when its stated intent—to provide federal funds to upgrade decaying inner cities—fell victim to greedy local governments and the developers in their employ. Urban renewal, as it was known, soon became little more than an excuse for "poor removal" as bulldozers and wrecking balls demolished entire neighborhoods, some of them home to poor but vital communities, others featuring the shabby tenements, boardinghouses, and dilapidated hotels that offered single-room occupancy (SRO) housing to the poor, the lonely, the debilitated, the ill, and the drug addicts. And despite a provision (Title III) that committed the federal government to building 810,000 new public housing units—another policy that experience has shown created at least as many problems as it solved—local, state, and federal governments looked the other way as urban renewal, with its promise of increased land values, quickly came to replace concerns for housing, and far more living units were destroyed than were built.

This isn't to say that urban renewal was a failure for everyone. Not by a long shot. Parts of many inner cities did, indeed, become more attractive, as blighted neighborhoods were cleared for such amenities as hotels, shops, cultural centers, and even small patches of green. But in the game of winners and losers, it's no surprise that only the poor lost. The developers lined their pockets. Local governments reaped the reward of increased land values as the new steel, concrete, and glass towers attracted business that brought jobs and revenue to the city. The glossy high-rise condominium buildings that rose in place of rundown homes, tenements, and SROs brought the affluent, who had fled to the suburbs decades earlier, back to the city where they could now live in style and comfort while enjoying the convenience of having Macy's, Neiman Marcus, a bank branch, and the city's cultural offerings at their doorstep. Only the poor and the sick were left with no place to go, except into the streets or the public housing projects that now look and are more like prisons for the poor than the "decent home and suitable living environment" Congress declared as every American's right.

Lest anyone think urban renewal is a thing of the past, I'll be happy to take them on a tour of the projects under way in my hometown of San Francisco or, if that's too far to go, to direct them to a *New York Times* article of June 16, 2007, whose opening words tell the story: "For nearly three decades, Charlotte Johnson witnessed the drug dealing and violence on the streets in front of her modest row house in East Baltimore. She rode it out only to face a new challenge today—the community's transformation under the largest planned urban renewal in the country, which could soon drive her out of the neighborhood."

Step back to the past again, to 1963 and the Community Mental Health Centers Act, a historic piece of legislation whose good intentions would set the stage for yet another social debacle. The American mental health reform movement has a long and not very successful history. In 1868, after Elizabeth Packard was released from an asylum to which her husband had committed her some years earlier, she founded the Anti–Insane Asylum Society and published a series of pamphlets describing her experiences. Shocking as her tale was, her entreaties for public attention fell on deaf ears, because most people then still believed that madness was the result of demonic possession.

Forty years later, Clifford W. Beers's *A Mind That Found Itself* was somewhat more successful in stimulating public interest, but it would be several more decades before *The Snake Pit*, a film starring Olivia de Havilland, opened in 1948 to a stunned American audience. Everyone knew, of course, that there were insane asylums, places where crazy people were locked up so the rest of us could sleep easily at night. But it is testimony to the power of film that the visual images woke the American conscience in ways that hundreds of thousands of written words had not. Suddenly, the "insane" were not just some undifferentiated mass, they were women and men hidden from view in human warehouses, held in the care of sadistic guards, shackled to walls in dungeon-like cells, and subjected to torturous "treatments"—immersed in tanks of ice water, spun in chairs for hours, secluded naked in isolation rooms, restrained in straitjackets or cuffed hand and foot to a bed in spread-eagled position, force-fed medications, shocked with high volts of electricity to the brain, and lobotomized—all by psychiatrists who knew little about the cause or relief of their symptoms.

Still, the mental health reform movements didn't gain any real traction until the mid-1950s, when the development of psychotropic medications gave promise of symptom relief, if not a cure, for some of the worst of the mental ailments. Although the new drugs were not without significant, and often dangerous, side effects, thousands of patients were taking them and, by the end of the decade, people who would once have been committed to asylums for life were managing to live outside them and tell their stories.

The hope the new medications brought, coupled with the various rights movements that were roiling society in the 1960s, set the stage for the emergence of a vigorous patients' rights movement, led largely by former hospital patients and their families. They offered a stinging critique of institutional psychiatry that was instrumental in discrediting the practices and treatments that had turned hospitals into snake pits, called for an end to involuntary commitment, and demanded that patients have a voice in their treatment.

The presidency of John F. Kennedy gave the reform movement a big lift when his family made their private pain public with the announcement that a family member had been mentally ill and institutionalized for years. With increasing pressure from the reformers and the backing of a sympathetic president, Congress passed the Community Mental Health Centers Act in 1963, which sought to create an alternative to institutionalization in state mental hospitals by developing a system of mental health centers that would focus on preventive, community-based outpatient care.

What happened? It's always easier for the federal government to spell out good ideas than it is to put up the hard cash necessary to make them work. So perhaps the simplest explanation is that the road to hell is paved with unfunded and underfunded government programs. Still, there's rarely a single cause to explain either the success or failure of a policy initiative.

As the social and political background changed in the decades following the passage of the Community Mental Health Centers Act, the good intentions that brought it into being faded away. The Vietnam War was a continuing drain on the public purse. Tax revolts and antigovernment ideologies of both the right and the left blossomed in the 1970s, which, together with the recession of the early 1980s, further weakened both the government's coffers and its resolve. Ronald Reagan's election to the presidency in 1980 turned a budding conservative movement into a full-scale revolution that changed the American social and political landscape for decades to come. All these played a part in restricting federal funding for social programs, including mental health, so that by the mid-1980s the regional funding model the 1963 law promised—never enough even at the beginning—was scaled back, and mental health services shifted once again to state and local levels until now, when federal funds support only about 2 percent of total state mental health budgets.

But long before federal funds dried up, the states played their part in turning a good idea into a fiasco. Until the new law, mental health care was the province and the burden of the states. When the federal government entered the picture with a plan for community care and the promise of funds to support it, it was a gift that offered states relief from the enormous financial costs of supporting a large hospitalized patient population. Not surprisingly, therefore, state and local officials spoke the language of mental health advocacy and community care, but they acted on their concern for fiscal policy. Without waiting for the promise of the law to become a reality, they jumped on the deinstitutionalization bandwagon and transferred tens of thousands of mentally ill women and men, many who had spent years in confinement, to communities that had no way to support their care.

Before long, the few Community Mental Health Centers (CMHCs) that existed were overwhelmed by demands they simply couldn't meet. It was a devastating experience for both the patients and the professionals. "We had no choice but to turn people out into the street," one veteran of the time recalls. "The state hospital, the place of last resort, was gone; there were no halfway homes, no treatment programs, nothing." Yet deinstitutionalization continued, ultimately closing nearly half the hospitals in the country and dramatically reducing bed capacity in those that are left, leaving uncounted tens of thousands of people to fend for themselves.

Although thousands of deinstitutionalized patients made a more or less successful transition to life outside the hospital, living with families or in adult group homes where they existed, many others fell through the cracks—and are still falling. For serious mental illnesses such as schizophrenia and bipolar disorder are not a one-time problem that can be cured with a pill. Even patients who seem to be doing well need regular monitoring and counseling if they're not to slip and fall. Moreover, welcome as each new generation of psychotropic drugs has been, they are no free lunch for the men and women who must live on them to maintain their sanity. For along with the gift of gaining some control over the delusions of schizophrenia or the excessive mood swings of bipolar disorder, come side effects that can range from such discomfiting problems as weight gain and blurred vision, to serious and sometimes irreversible neuromotor difficulties with Parkinsonian symptoms that can disfigure a life.

In addition to physical side effects that can be almost as disabling as the disease itself, drugs that alter the mind also alter consciousness in ways that challenge a person's experience of self. Patients often complain that they "feel different," that, as one person said to me some years ago, "I feel like a stranger to myself"—feelings that drive a very large proportion of the mentally ill to stop taking the drugs, which inevitably throws them into crisis.

Ask any family with a schizophrenic or bipolar member, and you'll hear stories about the weird and sometimes dangerous behavior that suddenly appears when the patient secretly stops taking medication.

Listen to them speak of the difficulty of finding their way through the chaotic maze of uncoordinated public agencies that is now our mental health system, only to fail because there are no beds or community services available. Hear their agony as they describe what it's like to find a loved one living on the street and be helpless to do anything about it.

In the recent uproar about the Virginia Tech shootings, the executive director of the Virginia Commission on Mental Health Reform was asked why a young man who had been diagnosed as "mentally ill and in need of hospitalization" wasn't either hospitalized or closely monitored in an outpatient setting before he walked onto the campus and killed thirty-two-people. His reply? "The system doesn't work very well." An understatement of breathtaking proportions.

Whether homelessness or crazed killing sprees, they don't happen because "the system doesn't work very well," but because it's broken, not just in Virginia but throughout the land. The Virginia Tech shooter wasn't closely monitored by mental health professionals because, whatever the services his community may say it offers, there simply are never enough resources or staff to provide them. Homelessness isn't an accident or an artifact of some strange modern urban disease, but a product of failed social policy. It got its first big push when urban renewal destroyed poor neighborhoods without offering adequate housing alternatives. Deinstitutionalization shoved it even harder when the plan to provide community-based mental health services turned out to be an empty promise, starved of funds even before the first patients were sent off to find their unsteady way into communities that had no services or facilities for them. And while all this was happening, the patients' rights movement won victories in the legislatures and the courts (including the United States Supreme Court in 1999 in *Olmstead v. L.C.*) that make it virtually impossible to hold someone with serious and sometimes dangerous mental problems involuntarily for more than a few days without proof, certified by a court, that the person is an immediate threat to society and/or to self—a test that isn't easy to meet absent violence or proof of intent to commit it.

"You think it's a problem, just try living with it," sighed the director of a clinic with whom I spoke recently about the mental health problems of the homeless. "We try, but we don't have the staff or the resources. And even if I could find a bed for some of the worst of them—which, frankly, I usually can't—if they don't want to go, the law won't let me hold them for more than seventy-two hours no matter how crazy they are. So what's the point? You knock yourself out to find a place where maybe, just maybe, they can get help, and a couple of days later, they're back out on the street."

True, but even for those who are amenable to treatment, the best any mentally ill homeless person is likely to get these days is a bed to rest in just long enough for the doctors to find the right drug regimen to stabilize a crisis. After that he or she is back out into the community with no services, no follow-up, and no place to live—a revolving door that never stops turning.

The result? About 500,000 of the 750,000 homeless Americans, men and women who are sick, desperate, and without hope, presently live in shelters or on the streets because of some form of mental illness. Yes, there are other social and economic forces that have contributed to the rise of homelessness. But the virtual epidemic we know today wouldn't exist without the fallout from two historic public policy initiatives: the Housing Act of 1949 that set urban renewal in motion and the Community Mental Health Centers Act of 1963 that sought to reform the mental health system—both well-intentioned, if flawed, good ideas that fell victim to the law of unintended consequences.

Do we conclude, then, that good intentions don't matter, that, as conservatives would have it, it's the nature of government to make a mess of even the best ideas, and that, therefore, we need less and less government intervention, no matter what the intent? I don't think so. True, government is not always as efficient as we'd like it to be. It's too cumbersome, too often unprepared for the unforeseen consequences of its actions, too slow to correct its mistakes, and our legislators are too often more beholden to special interests than to the common good. But even in a pluralist democracy like ours, where legislation is

the product of compromise and negotiation that can subvert the framers' good intentions, it doesn't always happen that way, as the Social Security and Medicare programs aptly demonstrate. Not that they're perfect, not that the compromises made to ensure their passage haven't left their mark. But compare the successes of the original single-payer Medicare program to the recent Medicare Prescription Drug Benefit—a complicated bureaucratic nightmare that relies on the private sector to provide insurance. Despite the fact that our costs exceed anything government-insured programs spend in countries that offer better, cheaper, and more complete drug coverage, Medicare Part D, as the drug benefit is known here, has brought far more benefit to the insurance companies and their pharmaceutical allies than to the old and the sick.

How, then, do we avoid the unintended consequences that can cause the kind of social dislocation and personal pain I've described here? Perhaps we can't; perhaps it's in the nature of the system—any system—that we can't always foresee the pitfalls until we tumble into them. But the problems of legislation such as the Medicare Prescription Drug Benefit should remind us that it isn't government's attempts at reform that need to be curbed but the influence of corporate America on the legislative process. Indeed, recent experience—the turn to the private sector for what earlier had been part of the public trust, the many revelations of corporate malfeasance, greed, and incompetence—suggests that only the willfully blind can continue to insist that the government has no place in reform and that the private sector will always do it better and cheaper.

## DISCUSSION QUESTIONS

1. Discuss the historical context and good intentions that explain to a large degree why so many of the homeless have mental problems and why the government still does not provide for them. How is social class linked to mental health issues?
2. What would mental health policy that addresses the needs of the homeless look like?

# 46

# THE NEW JIM CROW

## MICHELLE ALEXANDER

*This second reading on the institution of politics and government is by Michelle Alexander, an associate professor of law at Ohio State University. This excerpt is based on Alexander's 2010 best-selling book,* The New Jim Crow: Mass Incarceration in the Age of Colorblindness. *In it, Alexander outlines her argument for how she came to see the U.S. legal system as a system of racialized social control. She argues that mass incarceration is a type of a racial caste system, similar to Jim Crow, which has led to continuous and virulent forms of discrimination. This situation is an example of structural oppression, as discussed by Young (Reading 51), and it also signifies a failure of our legal and political system.*

The first time I encountered the idea that our criminal-justice system functions much like a racial caste system, I dismissed the notion. It was more than 10 years ago in Oakland when I was rushing to catch the bus and spotted a bright orange sign stapled to a telephone pole. It screamed in large, bold print: "The Drug War is the New Jim Crow." I scanned the text of the flyer and then muttered something like, "Yeah, the criminal-justice system is racist in many ways, but making such an absurd comparison doesn't help. People will just think you're crazy." I then hopped on the bus and headed to my new job as director of the Racial Justice Project for the American Civil Liberties Union of Northern California.

What a difference a decade makes. After years of working on issues of racial profiling, police brutality, and drug-law enforcement in poor communities of color as well as working with former inmates struggling to "re-enter" a society that never seemed to have much use for them, I began to suspect that I was wrong about the criminal-justice system. It was not just another institution infected with racial bias but a different beast entirely. The activists who posted the sign on the telephone pole were not crazy, nor were the smattering of lawyers and advocates around the country who were beginning to connect the dots between our current system of mass incarceration and earlier forms of racial control. Quite belatedly, I came to see that mass incarceration in the United States has, in fact, emerged as a comprehensive and well-disguised system of racialized social control that functions in a manner strikingly similar to Jim Crow.

What has changed since the collapse of Jim Crow has less to do with the basic structure of our society than with the language we use to justify severe inequality. In the era of colorblindness, it is no longer socially permissible to use race, explicitly, as justification for discrimination, exclusion, or social contempt. Rather, we use our criminal-justice system to associate criminality with people of color and then engage in the prejudiced practices we supposedly left behind. Today, it is legal to discriminate against ex-offenders in ways it was once legal to discriminate against African Americans. Once you're labeled a felon, depending on the state you're in, the old forms of discrimination—employment discrimination, housing discrimination, denial of the right to vote, and exclusion from jury service—are suddenly legal. As a criminal, you have scarcely more rights and arguably less respect than a black man living in Alabama at the height of Jim Crow. We have not ended racial caste in America; we have merely redesigned it.

More than two million African Americans are currently under the control of the criminal-justice system—in prison or jail, on probation or parole. During the past few decades, millions more have cycled in and out of the system; indeed, nearly 70 percent of people released from prison are re-arrested within three years. Most people appreciate that millions of African Americans were locked into a second-class status during slavery and Jim Crow, and that these earlier systems of racial control created a legacy of political, social, and economic inequality that our nation is still struggling to overcome. Relatively few, however, seem to appreciate that millions of African Americans are subject to a new system of control—mass incarceration—which also has a devastating effect on families and

communities. The harm is greatly intensified when prisoners are released. As criminologist Jeremy Travis has observed, "In this brave new world, punishment for the original offense is no longer enough; one's debt to society is never paid."

The scale of incarceration-related discrimination is astonishing. Ex-offenders are routinely stripped of essential rights. Current felon-disenfranchisement laws bar 13 percent of African American men from casting a vote, thus making mass incarceration an effective tool of voter suppression—one reminiscent of the poll taxes and literacy tests of the Jim Crow era. Employers routinely discriminate against an applicant based on criminal history, as do landlords. In most states, it is also legal to make ex-drug offenders ineligible for food stamps. In some major urban areas, if you take into account prisoners—who are excluded from poverty and unemployment statistics, thus masking the severity of black disadvantage—more than half of working-age African American men have criminal records and are thus subject to legalized discrimination for the rest of their lives. In Chicago, for instance, nearly 80 percent of working-age African American men had criminal records in 2002. These men are permanently locked into an inferior, second-class status, or caste, bylaw and custom.

The official explanation for this is crime rates. Our prison population increased sevenfold in less than 30 years, going from about 300,000 to more than 2 million, supposedly due to rising crime in poor communities of color.

Crime rates, however, actually have little to do with incarceration rates. Crime rates have fluctuated during the past 30 years and today are at historical lows, but incarceration rates have consistently soared. Most sociologists and criminologists today will acknowledge that crime rates and incarceration rates have moved independently of each other; incarceration rates have skyrocketed regardless of whether crime has gone up or down in any particular community or in the nation as a whole.

What caused the unprecedented explosion in our prison population? It turns out that the activists who posted the sign on the telephone pole were right:

The "war on drugs" is the single greatest contributor to mass incarceration in the United States. Drug convictions accounted for about two-thirds of the increase in the federal prison system and more than half of the increase in the state prison system between 1985 and 2000—the period of the U.S. penal system's most dramatic expansion.

Contrary to popular belief, the goal of this war is not to root out violent offenders or drug kingpins. In 2005, for example, for example, four out of five drug arrests were for possession, while only one out five were for sales. A 2007 report from Sentencing Project found that most people in state prison for drug offenses had no history of violence or significant selling activity. Nearly 80 percent of the increase in drug arrests in the 1990s, when the drug war peaked, could be attributed to possession of marijuana, a substance less harmful than alcohol or tobacco and at least as prevalent in middle-class white communities and on college campuses as in poor communities of color.

The drug war, though, has been waged almost exclusively in poor communities of color, despite the fact that studies consistently indicate that people of all races use and sell illegal drugs at remarkably similar rates. This is not what one would guess by peeking inside our nation's prisons and jails, which are overflowing with black and brown drug offenders. In 2000, African Americans made up 80 percent to 90 percent of imprisoned drug offenders in some states.

The extraordinary racial disparities in our criminal-justice system would not exist today but for the complicity of the United States Supreme Court. In the failed war on drugs, our Fourth Amendment protections against unreasonable searches and seizures have been eviscerated. Stop-and-frisk operations in poor communities of color are now routine; the arbitrary and discriminatory police practices the framers aimed to prevent are now commonplace. Justice Thurgood Marshall, in a strident dissent in the 1989 case of *Skinner v. Railway Labor Executive Association*, felt compelled to remind the Court that there is "no drug exception" to the Fourth Amendment. His reminder was in vain. The Supreme Court had

begun steadily unraveling Fourth Amendment protections against stops, interrogations, and seizures in bus stops, train stations, schools, workplaces, airports, and on sidewalks in a series of cases starting in the early 1980s. These aggressive sweep tactics in poor communities of color are now as accepted as separate water fountains were several decades ago.

If the system is as rife with conscious and unconscious bias, many people often ask, why aren't more lawsuits filed? Why not file class-action lawsuits challenging bias by the police or prosecutors? Doesn't the 14th Amendment guarantee equal protection of the law?

What many don't realize is that the Supreme Court has ruled that in the absence of conscious, intentional bias—tantamount to an admission or a racial slur—you can't present allegations of race discrimination in the criminal-justice system. These rulings have created a nearly insurmountable hurdle, as law-enforcement officials know better than to admit racial bias out loud, and much of the discrimination that pervades this system is rooted in unconscious racial stereotypes, or "hunches" about certain types of people that come down to race. Because these biases operate unconsciously, the only proof of bias is in the outcomes: how people of different races are treated. The Supreme Court, however, has ruled that no matter how severe the racial disparities, and no matter how overwhelming or compelling the statistical evidence may be, you must have proof of conscious, intentional bias to present a credible case of discrimination. In this way, the system of mass incarceration is now immunized from judicial scrutiny for racial bias, much as slavery and Jim Crow laws were once protected from constitutional challenge.

As a nation, we have managed to create a massive system of control that locks a significant percentage of our population—a group defined largely by race—into a permanent, second-class status. This is not the fault of one political party. It is not merely the fault of biased police, prosecutors, or judges. We have all been complicit in the emergence of mass incarceration in the United States. In the so-called era of colorblindness, we have become blind not so much to race as to the re-emergence of caste in America. We have turned away from those labeled "criminals," viewing them as "others" unworthy of our concern. Some of us have been complicit by remaining silent, even as we have a sneaking suspicion that something has gone horribly wrong. We must break that silence and awaken to the human-rights nightmare that is occurring on our watch.

We, as a nation, can do better than this.

## DISCUSSION QUESTIONS

1. According to Alexander, how has the U.S. prison system changed in the last 30 years?
2. Why does Alexander call the U.S. prison system the "New Jim Crow"? What does that statement signify?

# 47

# THE ROOTS OF AMERICAN DECLINE

R ICHARD L ACHMANN

*This final reading on the institution of politics and government is by Richard Lachmann, professor of sociology at the State University of New York at Albany. Lachmann, a historical and comparative sociologist who has studied government and political power for more than 32 years, examines why the American political and economic systems are failing. His nationally acclaimed book,* <u>Capitalists in Spite of Themselves: Elite Conflict and Economic Transitions in Early Modern Europe</u> *(2000), received the 2003 Distinguished Scholarly Publication Award from the American Sociological Association. This excerpt, "The Roots of American Decline," is taken from a 2011 article of the same name in the journal* <u>Contexts</u>. *Lachmann begins by reviewing common arguments from both the left and right of the political spectrum about why the United States is in decline. After analyzing those claims, Lachmann argues instead that the source of American decline is located in how elites have gained greater control over fiscal and civilian policies.*

The United States, we are told ever more frequently and emphatically, is heading toward fiscal disaster, unable to simultaneously pay for its extensive military involvements around the world, its current commitments to social programs, and the investments in education, infrastructure, and research needed to compete with China and other rivals.

If current trends continue, American economic and military dominance will be lost, the era of American empire over. Whether the United States will be succeeded by a new hegemon or the world will enter an era of multiple power centers is as yet uncertain.

What is the cause of the fiscal crisis at the root of American decline and how can it be solved?

The dominant view, shared by almost all those on the right and many "centrists," is that fiscal crisis is due to rising spending on social programs. (An alternative version of this theory points to increases in military spending for the Iraq and Afghanistan

*Source:* Lachmann, Richard. 2011. "The Roots of American Decline." *Contexts*, Winter 2011.

wars.) From this perspective, excessive spending produces fiscal crisis which, in turn, causes decline. The solution, then, is to cut back social benefits (or military commitments) in order to head off a run on the U.S. dollar and drastic increases in interest rates that would fatally weaken the U.S. economy.

This approach doesn't square with basic facts about American state spending. The federal budget in the United States. has held steady as a share of GDP since 1968 (see below). That lack of growth is possible in part because social benefits in the United States are among the skimpiest of any industrialized country, according to the Organization for Economic Co-operation and Development (OECD), a group of the thirty-three richest countries. The OECD also reports that poverty rates are higher in the U.S. than most other rich countries. The last expansion of Federal social programs occured with the Great Society of the 1960s. And military spending, again as a percentage of GDP, has actually declined drastically since the Cold War (see below).

If neither military nor overall spending are increasing burdens on the U.S. economy, then they cannot account for U.S. decline. Instead, I hope to show that the real problem is the misallocation of government revenue and expenditure, resulting in resources being diverted from the tasks vital to maintain economic or geo-political dominance.

To understand American economic and geopolitical decline we must identify the elites who determine much of the federal spending and then explain how the transformation of U.S. politics in recent decades has allowed those elites to exert control over governmental resources and agencies. Sociologists, beginning with C. Wright Mills, have found that elites—the heads of large corporate and governmental organizations—exercise disproportionate power in the United States. I have found that conflicts among elites and with non-elites shaped the emergence of capitalism in early modern Europe and, as we will see in the next section, the decline of dominant powers in that era.

Our understanding can be clarified if we compare U.S. dominance and decline with the histories of two previous great powers.

**FIGURE 47.1** Federal Spending Since 1948.

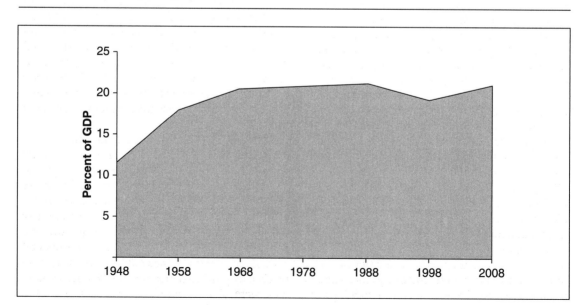

FIGURE 47.2   Military Spending by Presidency.

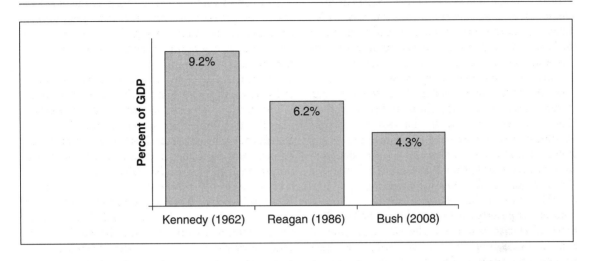

## GREAT POWERS, WAR, AND DECLINE

Just as social spending is incorrectly blamed for the United States' current budgetary woes, military expenses are viewed as the cause of past great powers' fiscal crises and decline. In his 1987 book, *The Rise and Fall of the Great Powers,* British historian Paul Kennedy argued that for the most powerful nations, whose interests span the globe, the costs of their military commitments outweigh the benefits of empire. Eventually, "imperial overstretch" saps economic growth as resources are diverted to the costs of empire, and the dominant power's economy declines until it's no longer able to afford the military needed to sustain its position. That, in Kennedy's view, was the cause of each previous great power's decline—and, he predicted, so it would be for the United States.

In fact, as I've previously found, the temporal sequence was the *opposite* of what Kennedy describes: military defeats and the loss of colonies *preceded* each hegemon's fiscal crisis. The Netherlands won its independence and took colonies from Spain when its budget was a fifth of its former ruler's. The Dutch, in turn lost most of their colonies to Britain while their budget was three times greater. The problem wasn't the availability of resources: colonies yielded enough revenues to pay for the general costs of fighting wars against other European nations and controlling empires. Rather, European powers lost wars and colonies because they were unable to gain central control over the troops and weapons their budgets bought, or to ensure that colonial profits and domestic taxes actually arrived in the central treasury.

The Netherlands was a coalition of provinces, cities, and chartered companies that defeated Spain when they fought together. The Dutch grabbed colonies on three continents, because Amsterdam and the companies were able to send their own ships and men around the world without getting approval or resources from the provinces that did not share their interests or daring. In so doing, the Dutch became the dominant economic and naval power of the seventeenth century.

However, when the Netherlands needed to mobilize greater resources against the rising British, their fragmentation ensured defeat. Even though the Dutch were richer than the British and had more ships, they were divided into separate navies (seven of them!) that did not fight in unison because they didn't share the same commercial or geo-strategic interests. Proposals to centralize governmental authority or create a unified military command were blocked by provincial interests, and colonial companies were able to withhold revenues from the national government. While these problems were apparent to Dutch state officials and to outside commentators who formulated reform proposals, their proposals were blocked by provincial elites who retained the capacity to protect their particular interests even at the expense of their nation's geopolitical and economic dominance.

Britain was alone among the European great powers in creating a government able to prevent particular families or elites from appropriating tax revenues or claiming hereditary rights to offices and military commands. The national parliamentary system forged in the Civil War and institutionalized after the Glorious Revolution allowed the gentry and big London merchants to block each other's unilateral grabs for office and resources, and it forced those elites to build party coalitions spanning counties and interests. Unable to exit those coalitions by appropriating private privileges, British elites forged agreements that controlled policy and operated the state's fiscal levers in their collective self-interest. While nobles and gentry dominated the highest ranks in the navy and army, there was promotion from below and incompetent highborn officers were not entrusted with key commands. Britain's military was reformed in time for the decisive showdown with Napoleon.

The corrupt East India Company and its army had been nationalized in the eighteenth century when self-dealing by corrupt company officials threatened Britain's economic and military hegemony in Asia. The nineteenth century reform of the civil service maintained Britain's advantage in state capacity, guaranteeing the nation's continued fiscal and military dominance over its European rivals. Britain was able to finance its imperial and military costs out of the profits of empire until World War 1.

## The Military Now

The contemporary American military faces the same problem of divided commands and misallocation of resources that plagued the seventeenth century Dutch (and all the other European powers except Britain). Even as U.S. military spending has fallen as

a share of GDP, its advantage over other powers has increased. In 2009, according to data compiled by the Stockholm International Peace Research Institute, the U.S. accounted for 43 percent of total world military spending—more than the next fifteen biggest spenders combined. This margin is far greater than that enjoyed by any of the dominant powers in the past 500 years, and probably ever in world history. At present, though fighting just two wars that by historical standards are small (as seen in the chart, the number of U.S. troops in Iraq and Afghanistan combined peaked in 2009 at 190,000, far less than the maximums of 550,000 in Vietnam and 480,000 in Korea) and not particularly bloody (U.S. deaths in the two current wars totaled 5,316 at the end of 2009, less than a tenth of the Vietnam fatalities and a seventh of Korea's), the American military describes itself as "overextended" and its forces as "tapped out." How can that be?

Much of America's military budget is still spent on weapons systems designed to counter the Soviet Union but now worthless for fighting in Afghanistan, Iraq, or any other area the country might plausibly become involved in. Despite having twice run on a platform of military restructuring (to fight precisely the sorts of wars he initiated), President George W. Bush succeeded in only canceling the Army's Crusader Artillery system. President Obama cancelled the F-22 fighter jet in his first year. If he attempts to further reorient military spending, the President will meet resistance from all who benefit from current priorities.

The misallocation of American military budgets is not mainly caused by the self-dealing of oligarchs who control military spending, as was the case in early modern Europe, although the recent privatization of some military functions is diverting an increasing fraction of the military budget. Rather, I have found that consolidation of the defense industry has allowed interlocking elites (defense contractors, military service heads, and bankers) who have financed industry consolidation to resist the reallocation of spending away from highly profitable though strategically worthless weapons systems. New weapons systems and types of forces proposed by military reformers as appropriate for the actual wars

FIGURE 47.3    Scale of American Wars by Number of Troops and War Deaths.

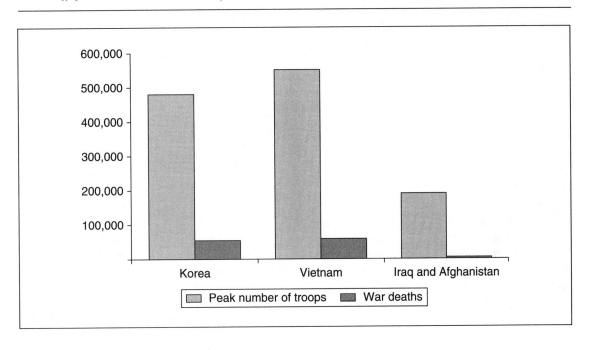

fought by the U.S. today aren't expensive enough to generate sufficient profits to justify the capital invested in the merged defense firms.

Such institutional interests are embodied in and reinforced by the structure of careers within the U.S. military. Officers are assigned to units that man and deploy specific weapons systems. A naval officer, for example, commands submarines designed to fire nuclear missiles or aircraft carriers built to allow fighter planes to shoot down enemy air forces. A decision to invest in mine sweepers to counter the sort of low-cost and low-tech challenge most likely to be posed by today's actual enemies would stymie the careers of officers attempting to rise in the resultantly stagnant submarine or carrier corps. And since officers almost never receive further promotions and often have to leave the military if they transfer from one weapons system to another, they're naturally reluctant to take command of forces devoted to counterinsurgency, civilian administration, or low-tech weapons designed for actual combat.

## BUDGET PRIORITIES

These days, competition among putative hegemons is mainly economic rather than military—a marked change from at least the past 500 years. Investment in infrastructure, scientific research, and education are paramount, and this is the realm in which China has focused almost all its efforts. In fact, Johns Hopkins sociologist Giovanni Arrighi has argued that China hasn't even attempted to compete with the U.S. militarily. Unlike previous challenges to dominant powers (like those mounted by Germany and Japan to Britain and the U.S. in the first half of the twentieth century), the Chinese threat comes from economic growth, not military might.

America's economic and military competitiveness have been hobbled as elites have gained greater control over civilian spending and taxes to the detriment of the kinds of investment fundamental to long-term economic growth. Federal outlays for "general science, space, and technology" are by far the largest source of the basic scientific research that

FIGURE 47.4    Share of Federal Revenues by Tax Type.

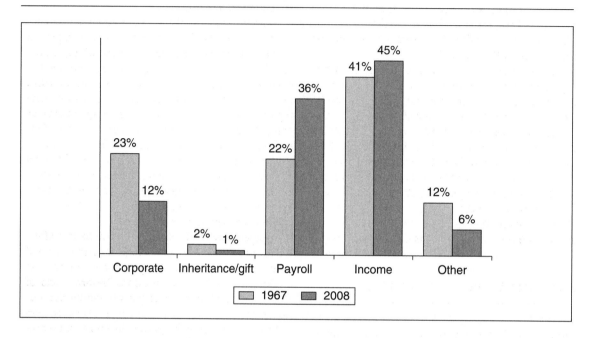

is essential to compete with rival economic powers, but they fell from 4 percent of the budget and 0.786 percent of GDP in 1967 to 0.93 percent of the budget and 0.21 percent of GDP in 2009. Spending on infrastructure has stagnated as bridges collapse, air and road traffic snarl, and a shrinking network of passenger trains struggle to reach early twentieth-century speeds. From arrival at the airport to the high-speed train or subway trip into town, a visit to most countries in Europe and East Asia can seem to an American like a journey to Tomorrowland, never to be realized in the U.S. outside of Disney World.

Instead of addressing these needs, our budget is languishing in terms of GDP, and, as documented by nonpartisan organizations like the Center on Budget and Policy Priorities, increasing portions are spent on unproductive subsidies to well-connected firms and elites. Current examples include: subsidies, water rights and access to federal lands for the overproduction of certain agricultural commodities; a commitment to a Medicare drug plan that pays prices significantly higher than anywhere else in the

world for drugs developed mainly in federal or university labs (or for copycat drugs designed to extend patents with no medical advantage over older generic drugs); free access to federal lands for mining, ranching, and logging with no obligation to pay for environmental effects which are then borne by public funds and health; and federal tax benefits and direct subsidies for the export of technology and capital to foreign subsidiaries and customers.

The 40-year stability of the federal budget masks a dramatic reallocation of the taxes that support it (see above). Corporate, inheritance, and gift taxes have declined as a share of revenue (from 25 percent in 1967 to 13 percent in 2008). That decline has been made up entirely by increases in Social Security and Medicare payroll taxes. The top income tax rate, which was 75 percent in 1968, is now 35 percent, and President Obama has faced resistance to his modest proposal to return it to the 39.6 percent level of the Clinton years. The top estate tax rate dropped from 77 percent in the 1960s to 45 percent by 2008, and (at least temporarily) to 0 percent in 2010 (and every twenty-first century Republican presidential candidate and virtually every GOP member of Congress has pledged to permanently abolish that tax, which falls only on the wealthiest 2 percent of Americans, and mainly on the richest 0.1 percent).

In this context, it is not surprising that many taxpayers resist further increases to make up for tax cuts for those at the top and instead support politicians who advocate tax cuts for all. Nor is it surprising that the wealthiest seek to maintain the political structures and politicians who have delivered tax cuts and subsidies to them that dwarf those in every other developed nation. What needs explanation is the absence of any significant effort by the state to force elites to coordinate spending in a way that would provide the infrastructure, research, and trained workers needed to compete internationally.

## POLITICAL SOURCES OF DECLINE

The shift in spending from programs that further national productivity and competitiveness toward ones that don't is a consequence of the restructuring of elite relations in the United States over the past four decades. This process has been traced most clearly by sociologist Mark Mizruchi, who writes that the United States was characterized, until the 1980s, by a dual elite structure. Like the similar structure in imperial Britain, this setup ensured that local and national elites could limit each other's attempts to appropriate state powers and offices. That, in turn, gave federal officials a high degree of autonomy to appropriate revenues and to implement policies that furthered national military and economic dominance, even at the expense of individual elites.

National banks, linked together by directors who serve on multiple corporate boards, coexisted with regional and local banks and firms that were shielded from competition with bigger rivals thanks to federal and state regulations. Local elites had the political muscle to sustain these through influence on their Congressional delegations and in their state governments. Both national and local firms in most industries, then, had enough political power to prevent each other from fully capturing state

agencies and from monopolizing markets or governmental resources.

But this structure of elite relations has been transformed in recent decades by waves of mergers in sectors such as banking, telecommunications, media, utilities, retail sales, and agriculture and by the declining capacity of national banks to control firms. Once-dominant banks face competition from new regional behemoths created by the merger of smaller competitors and from non-bank firms freed by federal deregulation to issue their own financial instruments. Competition and the relaxation of federal regulations have led national banks to focus their resources on more lucrative investment banking, further removing them from active involvement in the management of industrial firms.

Mergers have also reduced intra-industry differences over government policy, creating unified voices push legislative changes to enactment. The banking and telecommunications "reform" acts of the 1990s failed to pass Congress in earlier decades due to counter-lobbying by (mainly regional) sectors of those industries with opposed interests. But mergers resolved those disagreements as secondary sectors were brought into larger firms (or merged themselves to form new large firms) and so came to share the most general interest of their industries. Deregulation opened the way to further waves of mergers and acquisitions, intensifying elite consolidation within major industries.

Consolidation within sectors facilitates the capture of government agencies and their powers and budgets by firms: the bigger the firms, and especially the less competition they face within their sectors, the greater the slice of the federal budget they control. The drastic fall in the share of workers in unions and the decline of national membership organizations have weakened the main sources of popular challenges to elite control over government resources and policies.

## FUTURE PROSPECTS

As previous great powers faced decline, there were voices in each polity that correctly diagnosed the problem and proposed solutions, which, in retrospect, would have made significant differences. Each had schemes to eliminate tax privileges, end elite control over offices and governmental powers, and reform the military. Voices called for measures to invest in infrastructure and to hold or attract skilled craftsmen and businessmen and their enterprises from foreign competitors. Almost all of those reforms were stillborn. Only in Britain, where single elites or families were limited in their ability to seize and hold pieces of the state, were significant reforms enacted, and that's why British dominance lasted so much longer than previous hegemons or, it now appears, the United States.

All of President Obama's proposed (and enacted) reforms—in health care, energy, research funding, infrastructure investment, and financial regulation—are premised on winning support by accommodating elites and firms through continued subsidies and privileges. But such offers have the double effect of deepening the federal government's fiscal crisis and fostering popular cynicism about the possibilities of genuine reform within the American political system.

Scenarios for significant change are based on hopes that the financial or other crises will foster a sprit of sacrifice among the public at large. However, decline and fiscal crisis are reversed only when elites are forced to surrender privileges. Ralph Nader's most recent book, *Only the Super-Rich Can Save Us!* (2009), a utopian novel that imagines billionaires undermining corporate power and revitalizing citizen action, shows how much current progressive plans are based on hopes for elite generosity rather than realistic efforts at political mobilization. It is especially revealing, and depressing, that this book is the latest word from the American who has been the most successful at building citizen organizations over the past forty years. Claims that the Internet might foster effective political movements that can replace defunct or shrunken unions and mass organizations have yet to be realized.

Good ideas and high hopes did not save previous imperiums. There is no historical or social scientific basis for expecting they will do so for the United States—unfortunately, if we examine the contemporary United States as cold-eyed sociologists, rather than as hopeful citizens, our elites seem to match the capacities of their Dutch (and Habsburg Spanish, czarist Russian, and imperial Roman) predecessors to block reforms and withhold resources, thus remaining first class passengers on a sinking ship.

## Discussion Questions

1. According to Lachmann, what is the root cause of American decline and the current fiscal crisis?
2. How does Lachmann's analysis of military and government policies help us to better understand social inequality in the United States? What about global inequality?

# PART IV

# POWER AND PRIVILEGE UNMASKED

Part IV, "Power and Privilege Unmasked," contains eight readings that focus on power, privilege, and oppression. Instead of examining the individual effects of social inequality, as we did in Part II of this anthology, the readings in Part IV emphasize institutional or systemic levels of discrimination. As a collection, they show both the blatant and hidden costs of racism, sexism, and classism. Moreover, because of their institutional-level focus, many of them could be added to the readings in Part III on social institutions. For example, Mary Romero's piece, "Racial Profiling and Immigration Law Enforcement: Rounding Up of Usual Suspects in the Latino Community" (Reading 53), could be added to the readings on the social institution of politics and government. Romero's reading studies the 1997 immigration raid in Chandler, Arizona, that targeted Latinos. Beth A. Quinn's piece, "Sexual Harassment and Masculinity: The Power and Meaning of 'Girl Watching'" (Reading 55), could be added to the section in Part III on the social institution of employment and the economy. Quinn's reading provides another example of discrimination in the workplace.

The first four readings in Part IV provide a framework for understanding social stratification and the scholarship on social inequality. All four also adopt an intersectional framework—that is, they look at more than one social category at a time. Reading 48 by Douglas S. Massey, "America Unequal," explains how social stratification happens, how privilege is maintained, and how social stratification maintains power and privilege over time. Massey argues that social stratification does not occur in a vacuum; on the contrary, the social structure of any given society continuously divides people into social categories and labels some of those categories as "out-groups." Social mechanisms, then, such as laws, discrimination, and violence, are deployed to reserve certain resources for the in-groups (higher social categories in the social stratification system) while excluding others. For example, U.S. racial stratification has been upheld by slavery, Jim Crow, and discrimination in all social institutions. Similarly, social class stratification has been maintained by changes in labor laws, anti-union activities, offshore production, and cuts in taxes for the wealthy. Finally, gender stratification is upheld by gender segregation in the workplace, the traditional family ideology, and gender discrimination. Massey concludes that, compared to other developed countries, the United States is the most unequal of all; other countries do a better job of redistributing income after taxes than does the United States.

Reading 49 by Sonia Hanson, Peter Kivisto, and Elizabeth Hartung, expands on Massey's arguments in the previous reading by identifying many of the ideologies that reinforce systems of social stratification. Some of these ideologies are religious in origin; others are economic theories; and still others are essentialist or biologically determinist views of people, such as Social Darwinism. All have been used as arguments to subordinate and maintain lower social categories. Similar to Massey in Reading 48, Hanson, Kivisto, and Hartung not only argue that the United States has the highest level of income inequality among developed nations, but they also identify a number of indices measuring social inequality, like income distribution, wealth, and home ownership. While Massey found that income varies across educational attainment levels and gender, Hanson and colleagues analyze the consequences of social inequality across seven areas of data: physical and mental health, food and nutrition, housing and neighborhood quality, crime and punishment, environmental risk, schooling and the development of human capital, and social capital. At the end of their reading, Hanson, Kivisto, and Hartung provide some suggestions for social change.

Reading 50 by Abby L. Ferber is titled "The Culture of Privilege: Color-Blindness, Postfeminism, and Christonormativity" and was originally published in the *Journal of Social Issues*. Ferber utilizes and builds on both Massey's and Hanson et al.'s arguments about social stratification and social inequality but draws more on feminist theories of intersectionality and on critical race theory. This reading also ties in nicely with Patricia Hill Collins's arguments concerning the matrix of oppression and the study of social inequality in Reading 56. Written twenty-three years after Collins's work, Ferber's reading reviews some of the most critical scholars in whiteness studies, privilege, contemporary racial discourse, and intersectionality, and it pushes our thinking about white privilege by using an intersectional framework to compare the ideology of color-blind racism to the ideologies of postfeminism and christonormativity. According to Ferber, all three of these discourses reinforce a culture of privilege. She demonstrates the continuing need to critically examine these discourses within the larger social context of social change and the backlash against progressive social movements. Ferber, a professor of sociology and women's and ethnic studies at the University of Colorado, Colorado Springs, is also the director of The Matrix, a Center for the Advancement of Social Equity and Inclusion. A sociologist by training, Ferber has published widely on race, gender, and privilege in both academic books and as a regular blogger for The *Huffington Post*.

The fourth reading in Part IV, titled "The Five Faces of Oppression," is a classic work by Iris Marion Young, who was a professor of political science at the University of Chicago. It is excerpted from *Justice and the Politics of Difference* (1990), which won the 1991 Victoria Schuck Award of the American Political Science Association and transformed academic discourse about social inequality and oppression. In this excerpt, Young defines and expands the concept of oppression to include many acts that are often overlooked in society, arguing that scholars concerned with social justice must reconceptualize oppression beyond the individual level. As Young argues, "oppression also refers to systemic constraints on groups that are not necessarily the result of the intentions of a tyrant. Oppression in this sense is structural, rather that the result of a few people's choices or policies" (1990:41). Thus, well-intentioned individuals and social groups can be participating in oppression because oppression is systemic, beyond the realm of individual choice. That is to say, problematic individuals are not the only source of oppressive behavior and discrimination. Instead, we need to rethink oppression and see it as something structural. This reading summarizes Young's view of oppression as multidimensional in nature. Young describes her five faces of oppression as Exploitation, Marginalization, Powerlessness, Cultural Imperialism, and Violence. Reflect on Young's model of the five faces of oppression as you read other examples in this section and other parts of the anthology.

The last four readings in Part IV exemplify different types of discrimination oppressed groups might face, including racial profiling, immigration raids, and sexual harassment. The abuse of power by those who wield authority in social organizations and institutions is widespread. Every day there are news stories about oppressive social control tactics used by law enforcement, employers, schools, and other social institutions. And, as Iris Marion Young illustrated in the previous reading, "The Five Faces of Oppression," sometimes this abuse of power is systemic, beyond the control of well-intentioned individuals. Nonetheless, regardless of source or intention, oppression greatly affects individuals. Reading 52 by Ellis Cose, "Rage of the Privileged" excerpted from his 1993 book *The Rage of a Privileged Class*, delineates the ways in which racial discrimination affects people on a daily basis. Cose's classic "dozen demons," or twelve factors that continually remind people they are not quite good enough, personify the effects of discrimination on one's identity. While Cose's line of reasoning focuses on black professionals, his claims can be applied to any racial-ethnic or minority group.

One group that has been an increasing target of discrimination is Latinos and Hispanics, especially with concern growing in the United States over illegal immigration. For example, a recent news report in the *New York Times* addresses a case in East Haven, Connecticut, in which members of the police department were charged with "terrorizing the town's Hispanic neighborhoods, stopping and detaining people, searching businesses without a cause, beating people in handcuffs, smashing a man's head into a wall" (*New York Times,* January 26, 2012). Police brutality and racial profiling are nothing new, as the reading by Mary Romero, "Racial Profiling and Immigration Law Enforcement: Rounding Up of Usual Suspects in the Latino Community" (Reading 53), demonstrates. Her case study of an immigration raid in 1997, in Chandler, Arizona, illustrates well the discriminatory and oppressive tactics used by some in law enforcement against Latino communities.

Reading 54, by Rosalind S. Chou and Joe R. Feagin, turns our attention toward Asian Americans and the discrimination they face. Chou and Feagin's interviews confirm how systematic the experiences of anti-Asian discrimination are because of the "model minority" myth. Asian Americans experience high rates of pressure to succeed by their families and by others in society, with high personal costs. However, many of them do not see the model minority myth as a form of discrimination and racism. Also, as with the Latinos in Romero's research, the citizenship of Asian Americans is often questioned by others. In contrast, as part of their white privilege, white Americans do not have to think about their citizenship or have to respond to continual questions about their citizenship status by legal authorities or others in society.

The final reading in Part IV examines another common form of discrimination in the United States: sexual harassment. Beth A. Quinn's reading, "Sexual Harassment and Masculinity: The Power and Meaning of 'Girl Watching'" (Reading 55), examines gender discrimination in the workplace. As this analysis of male privilege explains, many men do not see this behavior as problematic but instead discount it as insignificant. Quinn analyzes these statements and others in her interviews of male and female employees and finds that men and women view these gendered behaviors differently. Sexual harassment also leads to other types of social inequality, including having less access to health care, jobs, and schools. Many women report that they have left employment positions because of harassment. Thus, this reading and the others in Part IV demonstrate that the effect of one type of discriminatory behavior or policy can ripple outward, creating additional barriers for both individuals and groups in society.

## References

Young, Iris Marion. 1990. *Justice and the Politics of Difference.* Princeton, NJ: Princeton University Press.

# 48

# AMERICA UNEQUAL

## DOUGLAS S. MASSEY

*This first reading in Part IV, on power and privilege, is by Douglas S. Massey, the Henry G. Bryant Professor of Sociology and Public Affairs at Princeton University. Massey, a prolific scholar of social stratification, studies how power and privilege persist over time. This reading, excerpted from Massey's 2007 book,* Categorically Unequal: The American Stratification System, *explains how stratification happens, how privilege is maintained, and how the history of stratification in the United States occurred and persists in terms of race, social class, and gender. Using education as a proxy for social class, Massey illustrates the intersections among education, race, income, and gender.*

Stratification does not just happen. It is produced by specific arrangements in human societies that allow exploitation and opportunity hoarding to occur along categorical lines.

An effective system of social stratification requires three basic things: a social structure that divides people into categories on the basis of some combination of achieved and ascribed traits; the labeling of certain of these categories as social out-groups composed of people who are perceived as lacking on two fundamental dimensions of human social evaluation; and the existence of one or more social mechanisms to reserve certain resources for in-group members while extracting other resources from out-group members without full remuneration.

Human beings are cognitively programmed to form conceptual categories and use them to classify the people they encounter. The definition of categorical boundaries and the content of conceptual categories are not, however, automatic. They are learned through instruction and modified by experience. As social beings, people constantly test, extend, and refine the social schemas they carry in their heads, typically through interactions and

*Source:* Massey, Douglas S. Chapter 7, "America Unequal." In *Categorically Unequal: The American Stratification System.* © 2007 Russell Sage Foundation, 112 East 64th Street, New York, NY 10065. Reprinted with permission.

discussions with other people. Whenever a person works to convince others in society to accept a particular categorization of social reality, the process is called framing.

People are naturally prone to favor frames that give them advantages and privilege their own access to material, symbolic, and emotional resources. Although everyone may prefer a framing of social reality that serves their interests, people with power and resources have more influence than others, and their frames are more likely to be accepted and used in society. Within any social setting, the definition of boundaries and the content of social categories are disproportionately influenced by people at the top of the socioeconomic hierarchy. Although people at the bottom may challenge and resist categorical frames that work against their interests, their ability to control the definition of social reality is constrained by the fact that they have little to offer others to accept their preferred framing.

Any set of socially constructed categories yields a set of social identities that encompass many different attributes and characteristics. Despite this complexity, social groups can be classified along two fundamental dimensions that define the conceptual space of social cognition: warmth and competence. People naturally frame themselves and others like them as both warm (likable, approachable, trustworthy) and competent (efficacious, capable, astute). People perceived in this way are seen as in-group members, or at least as members of groups that are very similar to the in-group. People who are framed as lacking either warmth or competence are socially defined as members of out-groups—as others who are not perceived as "people like us."

Social actors who are seen as warm but not competent fall into the category of pitied out-groups, common examples of which are the sick, the disabled, and the aged. In contrast, people perceived as competent but not warm fall into the category of envied out-groups, the classic examples of which are middleman minorities such as the Chinese in Malaysia, Indians in East Africa, or Jews in medieval Europe. Under normal circumstances, neither of these two kinds of out-groups makes a good candidate for exploitation. Pitied out-groups are not readily exploited because people feel sorry for them, and envied out-groups are not exploited because they usually occupy positions of power and authority by virtue of their competence.

For exploitation to occur smoothly and seamlessly, people in out-groups must be framed as neither competent nor warm—as people who are not likable, approachable, or trustworthy and not efficacious, capable, or astute. The relevant emotion toward out-groups lacking warmth and competence is contempt. People in such groups are despised and perceived as less than fully human at the most fundamental neural level. As a result, they lend themselves to exploitation with relative impunity. Because they are socially despised, they encounter few defenders in society, and because they are perceived as despicable, victimizing them is unlikely to trigger countervailing emotions such as pity or fear.

Paralleling the work of framing in the conceptual realm is the work of boundary definition in the social realm. Boundary work involves actions and behaviors undertaken to differentiate people socially; they are publicly labeled as members of an in- or out-group who thus embody the social traits associated with that category of people. Labeling may occur through informal mechanisms such as gossip, ridicule, shaming, ostracism, praise, or harassment that serves to "put people in their place," or it may be effected formally through regulations and laws such as the one-drop rule and the antimiscegenation laws enacted throughout the South before the civil rights era. Boundary work distinguishes people from one another socially by highlighting interpersonal differences across categorical lines.

Once social groups are created conceptually through framing and reified socially through boundary work, then stratification—the unequal allocation of material, symbolic, and emotional resources among social categories—is accomplished by establishing social mechanisms that operate according to one of two templates: exploitation or opportunity hoarding. Exploitation is the expropriation of resources from an out-group by members of an in-group such that out-group members receive less than full value for the resources they give up. Opportunity hoarding is the monopolization by in-group members of access to a resource so as to keep it for themselves or charge rents to out-group members in return for access. In contemporary American society, the most common form of exploitation is discrimination within markets, and the most common form of opportunity hoarding is exclusion from markets and resource-rich social settings.

Once established, and in the absence of any countervailing social force, mechanisms of discrimination and exclusion tend to persist over time because of two ancillary social processes: emulation, the transfer of stratifying mechanisms from one social setting to another; and adaptation, the structuring of individual actions and expectations in ways that assume the continued operation of a particular stratification system. Together emulation and adaptation institutionalize a system of categorical stratification and make it quite durable over time and across space.

## STRATIFICATION AMERICAN-STYLE

Although, in theory, any socially defined group may be subject to discrimination and exclusion, in the United States categorical inequalities historically have been produced and reproduced along three principal lines: race, class, and gender. African Americans have traditionally been stereotyped as shiftless, dumb, and strong; the poor have been stereotyped as lazy, self-indulgent, and unmotivated; and women have been stereotyped as warm and caring yet lacking in judgment and resolve. Consistent with these prejudicial stereotypes, throughout most of U.S. history minorities, women, and the poor have been denied full social, political, and economic rights. Formal legal rights were not accorded to African Americans until 1869; women were not politically enfranchised until 1920; and poll taxes routinely excluded the poor from political life until the 1960s. Discrimination against women and minorities was not fully outlawed in U.S. markets until the 1970s.

[My research has] . . . described the framing techniques and boundary-reinforcing mechanisms that function in the United States to enable exploitation and exclusion along categorical lines. African Americans offer by far the clearest historical example of categorical stratification. Slavery institutionalized exploitation and opportunity hoarding to the extreme, of course, and the system of Jim Crow segregation that replaced it was little better. Most white Americans are aware of the history of slavery and legal segregation, but they are less aware of the de facto system of discrimination and exclusion that prevailed in the United States until the 1960s, or the degree to which the U.S. welfare state was itself racialized to exclude African Americans from the wealth-producing engines of postwar America. Whites also remain oblivious to the power of unconscious racism, and most deny the reality of explicit prejudice and discrimination. As a result, they are unwilling to bear the social, economic, and political costs required to end racial stratification.

The dismantling of Jim Crow in the South, the outlawing of discrimination nationwide, and the recognition of black civil rights have failed to produce anything approaching racial equality. After the civil rights era, racial discrimination did not cease—it simply went underground and occurred in more surreptitious ways. Although less observable, clandestine discrimination proved no less effective in undermining the status and welfare of African Americans, yielding high levels of residential segregation and large, persistent black-white gaps in health, education, income, wealth, and occupational achievement.

During the 1970s, new mechanisms of racial exclusion and exploitation arose through the criminal justice system. Crimes likely to be committed by African Americans were singled out for longer sentences, judicial discretion was limited, parole authority was curtailed, and harsher sentencing rules were imposed. Rates of black male incarceration skyrocketed and contributed to a decisive reduction in black earnings and employment, the removal of fathers and husbands from black families, and the spread of family violence and HIV-AIDS throughout the black community.

Although African Americans have historically borne the brunt of America's racial animus, Latinos came in for much harsher treatment in the 1980s.

Although Latinos historically have occupied a middle position in the socioeconomic hierarchy between blacks and whites, their status deteriorated markedly during the 1980s and 1990s and now approximates that of African Americans. Latinos from the Caribbean region are often of African ancestry and thus experience the same color prejudice and discrimination as African Americans. By far the most Latinos originate in Mexico, however, and increasingly these people have been framed as a "racialized other" who constitute a serious threat to America's economy, security, and culture. Since the 1980s, categorical stratification against Mexicans has been effected through an increasingly repressive system of immigration and border control.

The militarization of the Mexico–U.S. border after 1986 dramatically lowered the rate of return migration by illegal immigrants, which increased the number of people living north of the border without social, economic, or political rights. Geographically selective border enforcement, meanwhile, deflected migrant flows away from traditional destination areas and helped transform Mexican immigration from a regional into a national phenomenon. As a result, there are now more exploitable Latinos living in more places under more vulnerable circumstances than at any point in American history.

As America's border policies increased the number of residents living in exploitable social circumstances, immigration policies penalized the same people in ever-harsher ways. The criminalization of undocumented hiring increased discrimination against people who "look Hispanic" and "sound foreign" and fomented a broader shift to labor subcontracting that undermined wages and working conditions for all low-skill workers. Avenues for documented entry were systematically reduced by Congress, and social programs were curtailed for legal as well as illegal immigrants. Hispanic children were pushed out of school and into the labor force to raise family incomes enough to sponsor the entry of family members still abroad, and after September 11, police actions against immigrants were extended from the border to the interior of the United States. Not surprisingly, given these trends, during the 1990s Latino incomes fell and poverty rates rose, reaching levels comparable to those historically observed among African Americans.

The foregoing transformations occurred against a backdrop of rising class stratification in the United States. Modifications to U.S. labor law in 1947 and 1959 put the American labor movement on a path of sustained decline compared to other industrial nations, and aggressive anti-union actions undertaken by federal authorities in the 1980s brought unionization levels to record lows. Sharp reductions in the real value of the minimum wage and income transfers, when combined with reduced spending on unemployment and food supplements, sharp cutbacks in access to federal employment, and the imposition of new time limits on welfare receipt, put new economic pressure on middle- and lower-class families and led to rising rates of consumer borrowing despite higher real interest rates and more punitive bankruptcy laws.

As the situation deteriorated for most Americans in the middle and lower reaches of the U.S. socioeconomic hierarchy, things improved markedly for those at the upper end. Progressivity in the American tax structure was largely eliminated as top tax rates were scaled back, taxes on capital gains were reduced, and enforcement efforts were redirected away from the rich and toward the poor. At the same time, regressive payroll taxes were increased, and the tax burden was shifted from the upper to the middle and lower portions of the income distribution. By 2005, levels of inequality with respect to income and wealth had returned to values not seen since the laissez-faire days of the 1920s.

The 1920s were the period in which the foundations for twentieth-century gender inequality were laid. Prior to this era, gender stratification occurred largely outside the market, since few women worked, but as women flooded into the expanding white-collar workforce during the 1920s, a new system of occupational segregation was imposed to confine women to a "pink-collar" ghetto of jobs characterized by low wages and few mobility prospects. In the nonmanual sector, women were excluded from positions of power, authority, and prestige, whereas in the manual sector they were banned from the skilled and unionized job categories reserved for people presumed to be "breadwinners."

Gender segregation was institutionalized throughout the American occupational structure by the 1940s, and given the limitations of their earning power and career prospects, women had few incentives to invest in education, training, or work experience. During the baby boom of the 1950s and 1960s, women put time and effort into family labor rather than the labor market, but resentments and dissatisfactions festered and burst forth in a feminist movement during the 1970s that was successful in outlawing most forms of gender discrimination.

The validation of female employment combined with the stagnation of male wages after 1975 combined to raise the rate of female labor force participation to the point where most women now hold paying jobs, even those with young children. The consequences of this gender revolution have played out in very different ways, however, at the lower and upper ends of the socioeconomic distribution. Jobs in management and the professions have opened up, and women have gained new access to careers in law, medicine, business, and higher education. In an era of lagging male income and rising inequality, the high salaries earned by women in professional and managerial jobs make them attractive as marital partners. Rates of within-class marriage have increased, rates of divorce have fallen, unwed childbearing has fallen, and within families the drudgery of housework has been relieved by the hiring of outside workers and greater sharing with well-educated men who conform more readily than their lower-class counterparts to the ideal of egalitarian marriage. Although a glass ceiling still persists to prevent upper-class women from reaching the top of America's administrative, corporate, and educational hierarchies, in material terms upper-class women and their children are much better off than before.

At the lower end of the socioeconomic distribution, the situation is entirely different. Occupational segregation has remained rigid in the blue-collar workforce, and women without education are confined mostly to unskilled manual and service jobs that offer few chances for mobility and very low pay. Given low earnings and the decoupling of sex from marriage enabled by effective contraception, lower-class women have became less attractive as marriage partners, and as male wages and employment fell, the supply of "marriageable males" was reduced. The end result was a decline in marriage rates, a rise in divorce rates, and an increase in unwed childbearing among lower-class women. In addition, men whose traditional role of breadwinner was increasingly being called into question by stagnant wages and diminishing employment did not so readily adapt to more egalitarian relationships; working-class women continued to do the lion's share of the housework, and their children received smaller investments of paternal time and money.

## STRATIFICATION AT HOME AND ABROAD

Processes of categorical stratification occurring along the lines of race, class, and gender have combined to make the United States the most unequal among advanced industrial nations.

A common way of measuring inequality is by forming the ratio of the ninetieth to the tenth percentile of the income distribution. Figure 48.1 uses data from Smeeding (2005) to show this ratio for selected nations in the Organization for Economic Cooperation and Development (OECD), essentially the "club" for developed nations around the world. These ratios reveal the exceptional nature of American inequality. The American income ratio of 5.45 is well above the average level of 4.0 for OECD nations as a whole and much greater than the ratios that prevail in most European countries. Although not shown in the figure, the only countries that exceed the United States with respect to income inequality are Russia, with a ratio of 8.4, and Mexico, with a ratio of 9.4, both of which are much less developed and characterized by much lower levels of income generally (Smeeding 2005). The United States thus stands out among developed nations for the severity of its inequality.

Rising inequality over the past thirty years has been attributed to a variety of factors, including globalization, technological change, and the segmentation of markets (Danziger and Gottschalk 1995; Levy 1998; Massey 1996). Nonetheless, all

FIGURE 48.1    Ratio of 90th to 20th Percentile of Income Distribution in Selected OECD Nations.

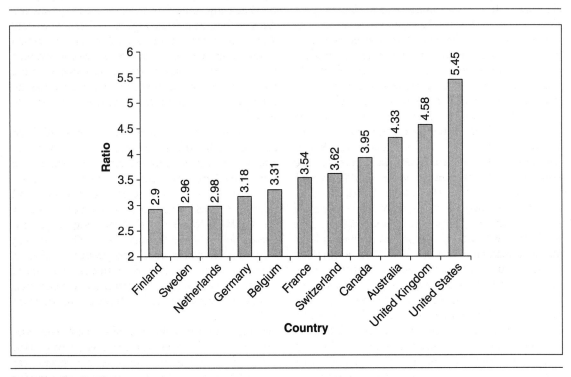

*Source:* Smeeding (2005).

countries compete in the same global economy and face the same technological and market conditions, yet the United States is unique among advanced nations in the degree to which it allows these large, macrolevel forces to generate inequality. The end of Jim Crow segregation in the South, the prohibition of open discrimination in the North, and the deracialization of the welfare state paradoxically led to the reinstitution of categorical mechanisms of class stratification that had largely been eliminated during the New Deal. At the same time, older mechanisms of racial and gender stratification did not disappear but evolved to become more subtle and less observable. As discrimination moved underground, new mechanisms for exclusion were built into the criminal justice system for African Americans and into the immigration system for Mexican Americans.

American society can be conceptualized as a three-dimensional social space defined by the axes of race, class, and gender. Gender is easy to define, of course, since the vast majority of people are clearly identifiable as either males or females and statistical data are routinely broken down by sex. Race is more of a social construction, though owing to America's racist legacy, persons of African ancestry have always been well identified in government statistics. The arrival of Asians in the late nineteenth century led to their separate identification as well, and the more recent upsurge in Latin American migration produced a new classification of Latinos, first as "Spanish-surnamed" individuals and after 1970 as "Hispanics." The cross classification of race and Hispanic origin yields five categories: non-Hispanic whites, non-Hispanic blacks, non-Hispanic Asians, Hispanics, and a residual "other" category.

Class is even more of a social construction and difficult to define from available data. Drawing on Marxist and Weberian conceptualizations of class, Erik Wright (1997) distinguished between people on the basis of their relation to the means of production, their relation to authority, their relation to scarce skills, and, among owners, the number of employees. He applied this scheme to classify people using detailed occupational codes. He identified twelve mutually exclusive class categories, which for purposes of parsimony may be collapsed into seven: capitalists and small employers (8 percent of the workforce), the petty bourgeoisie (7 percent), experts and skilled employees with authority (18 percent), nonskilled employees with authority (9 percent), experts without authority (3 percent), skilled employees without authority (14 percent), and unskilled workers without authority (42 percent).

Ideally an assessment of the role played by race, class, and gender would make use of a similar conceptualization of class to analyze changes over time, but such a task is beyond the scope of what can be accomplished here. Instead, for purposes of illustration class is defined by access to human capital—or more specifically, education, the most important resource in today's knowledge-based economy.

Figure 48.2 thus proxies the U.S. class structure by dividing people into four groups—college graduates, those with some college, high school graduates, and those with less than a high school education—which when combined with the other categorizations yields a four-by-five-by-two social space of class, race, and gender within which we can examine the distribution of income to assess the basis for U.S. stratification.

Data on personal income were obtained from the 1950 to 2000 censuses and the 2005 Current Population Survey using the Integrated Public Use Microdata Sample (IPUMS). Income was then classified according to the scheme of Figure 48.2, and a three-way analysis of variance was performed on the resulting income distribution using the general linear model available from SAS.[1] The resulting main effects of race, class, and gender are plotted by year in Figure 48.3. Specifically, this figure shows the percentage of variance in personal income explained by each categorical factor from 1950 to 2005.

As can been, in 1950 most of the explained variance in personal income was accounted for by gender. The predominant cleavage in American society was thus between male and female workers, with gender

**FIGURE 48.2**    Four-by-Five-by-Two Factorial Design for Analysis of Variance in U.S. Income Inequality, 1950 to 2005.

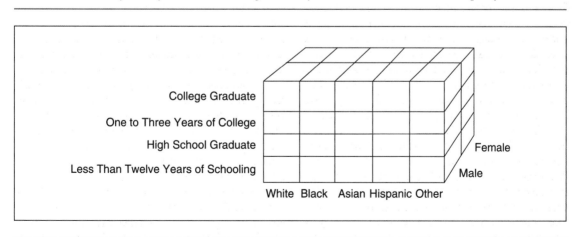

*Source:* Author's compilation.

FIGURE 48.3    Variance in Personal Income Explained by Race, Education, and Gender, 1950 to 2005.

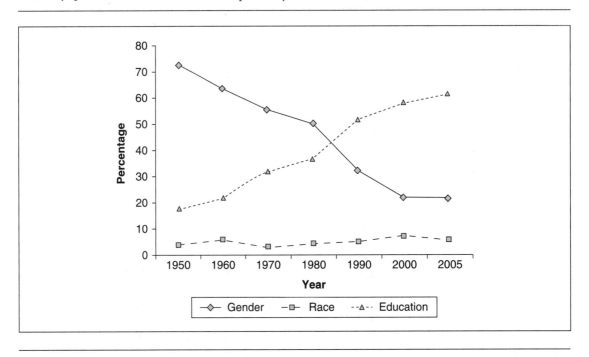

*Source:* IPUMS.

explaining 74 percent of the variance compared with only 18 percent for class (as measured by education) and 4 percent for race. Over the next fifty-five years, however, gender steadily declined as a significant factor in the American stratification system, with the share of variance explaining stratification dropping at a rate of 0.8 percent per year from 1950 to 1980, then accelerating to 1.4 percent per year between 1950 and 1980 before leveling off in 2000 and 2005. Over the entire period, the share of income stratification explained by gender fell from nearly three-quarters in 1950 to less than one-quarter in 2005.

What replaced gender in terms of explanatory power was class: the share of income explained by education went from 18 percent in 1950 to 62 percent in 2005. The percentage of variance explained by race fluctuated somewhat over the period but changed little overall, bottoming out in 1970 when it reached 3 percent and then rising to 8 percent in 2000 before falling back to 7 percent in 2005.

Consistent with . . . other research, the interaction between class and gender also increased in importance over the period, as shown in Figure 48.4, which plots the percentage of variance captured by the various interactions between race, class, and gender from 1950 to 2005. Although the percentage of variance explained by the class-gender interaction is small compared to the main effects, its relative importance nonetheless rose steadily and significantly from 1950 through 2000, going from 3 percent to 7.5 percent before dropping to 5.5 percent in 2005. . .

## THE FUTURE OF CATEGORICAL INEQUALITY

American income inequality has thus shifted from stark divisions on the basis of gender to new

FIGURE 48.4    Variance in Personal Income Explained by Race-Education-Gender Interactions.

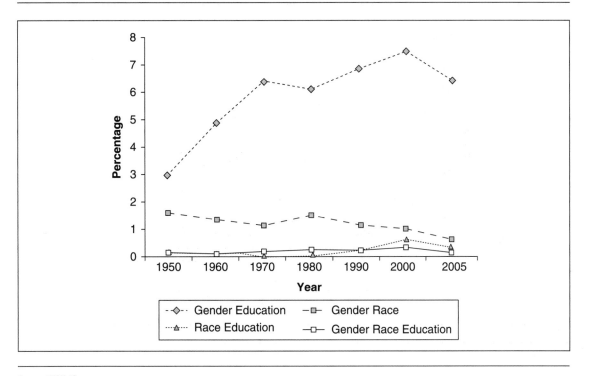

*Source:* IPUMS.

foundations based on class. That class-based categorical mechanisms have risen to undergird America's new system of inequality is also suggested by Figure 48.5, which shows Gini indices of income inequality for selected OECD nations computed before and after the deduction of taxes. The before-tax Gini coefficients indicate the amount of raw inequality generated by capitalist markets in each country, whereas the after-tax Gini indicates the degree of inequality that remains after transfers have been made to fund the social welfare system in each country. As the gray bars show, before taxes the United States is no more or no less equal than any other country. Its pre-tax Gini is.45, only slightly above the value of.44 in Sweden,.43 in Germany, and.42 in the Netherlands, but well below the values of.50 and.49 in Belgium and France and the same as those prevailing in Australia and Britain.

Taxation works in a redistributive direction for all countries, as indicated by the universally lower values for the after-tax Ginis, but the extent of the redistribution is much less in the United States. Its coefficient drops much less as a result of taxation than happens in other countries. The Gini coefficient for income inequality in Belgium, for example, falls from.50 before taxes to just.26 after taxes. The after-tax Gini coefficient is at.30 or below for all countries except Australia, the United Kingdom, and the United States, and in the former two nations the respective figures are.31 and.34, compared with.37 in the United States. Thus, whereas the economy of Belgium produces a distribution of income that is 11 percent more unequal than in the United States before taxes, afterward the institutionalized mechanisms of redistribution yield a distribution that is 22 percent less unequal.

FIGURE 48.5    Gini Index of Income Inequality Before and After Taxes in Selected OECD Nations.

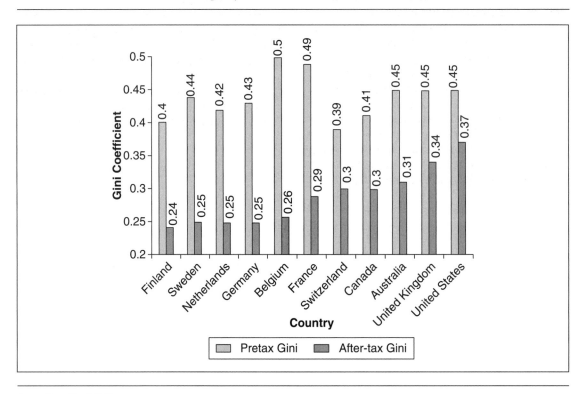

*Source:* Smeeding (2005).

By almost any measure, the United States is unambiguously a more class-stratified place than it was before 1975. The clear increase in class stratification over the past thirty years and the rising share of the variance in income distribution that is explained by education do not mean, however, that race and gender have receded in significance. Indeed, ... these cleavages continue to function in powerful ways to generate categorical inequalities in the United States. What Figures 48.2 to 48.5 indicate is that mechanisms of race and gender stratification increasingly operate through education, the ultimate scarce resource in a knowledge-based economy. Were it possible to define a class variable in the manner of Erik Wright (1997) rather than using education as a proxy, the share of income variance explained by race and gender might well have been larger.

To the extent that education itself is unevenly allocated across categorical boundaries, race and gender are not likely to disappear as salient bases for American stratification. Categorical inequalities in access to quality education are not hard to observe. In terms of race, black males are now more likely to go to prison than to college (Western 2006); the racial segregation of American schools has increased (Orfield and Eaton 1996); and racial differentials in the quality of education have widened (Kozol 2005). Likewise, changes in immigration policy have pushed the children of legal immigrants out of school (Massey 2003) and discouraged school attendance by the children of illegal migrants (Donato, Massey, and Wagner 2006). In terms of class, shifts in welfare policy have made it more difficult for poor people to continue in school (Shaw et al. 2006), while special recruitment programs for athletes and alumni children give the affluent preferential access to elite colleges and universities (Bowen, Kurzweil, and Tobin 2005; Golden 2006; Karabel 2005; Massey and Mooney, forthcoming). In terms of gender, although females now outnumber males in higher education, majors remain quite segregated, with females generally concentrating in lower-earning fields (Jacobs 1996). As long as the quantity and quality of education are so strongly linked to race, class, and gender, categorical mechanisms of stratification will continue to operate with considerable force in the political economy of the United States of America.

## DISCUSSION QUESTIONS

1. What does Massey mean by "categorical inequality," and what evidence does he provide of social stratification and social inequality in this reading?
2. How would you use Massey's analysis to answer the question: Is America still the beacon of equality and opportunity for the world?

# 49

# CONFRONTING INTERSECTING INEQUALITIES

SONIA HANSON

PETER KIVISTO

ELIZABETH HARTUNG

*The second reading on power and privilege is from Peter Kivisto and Elizabeth Hartung's 2007 book,* Intersecting Inequalities: Class, Race, Sex, and Sexualities. *Kivisto, the Richard Swanson Professor of Social Thought at Augustana College, and Hartung, professor of sociology at California State University, Channel Islands, have both studied and taught social inequality for a number of years. This reading, written with Sonia Hanson, explores the effects of power and inequality in the United States. In addition to illustrating various types of inequalities by race, social class, and gender, a key emphasis of this reading is an examination of the effects these inequalities have on life chances and on human and social capital.*

## INEQUALITY IN THE UNITED STATES IN THE EARLY TWENTY-FIRST CENTURY

That the United States is the advanced industrial nation with the highest level of inequality in the world is virtually undisputed by scholars today.

There are a variety of ways that social scientists attempt to understand the extent and the scope of inequality. One of the most commonly used measuring sticks is income distribution. Employing this measure, we find a highly skewed distribution pattern. In 2003, the bottom fifth of all households with

*Source:* Hanson, Sonia, Peter Kivisto, and Elizabeth Hartung. 2007. "Confronting Intersecting Inequalities." In *Intersecting Inequalities: Class, Race, Sex, and Sexualities,* edited by Peter Kivisto and Elizabeth Hartung. Reproduced by permission of Pearson Education, Inc., New York, New York.

the lowest incomes received only 3.4 percent of the total income earned that year, while the second quintile earned 8.7 percent, the middle quintile 14.8 percent, the next to the top quintile 23.4 percent, and the top quintile earned 49.8 percent. In other words, the top 20 percent of the population possessed nearly half of all earned income (DeNavas-Walt, Proctor, and Mills 2004:8). These distribution figures are the most recent in a significant trend that began in the 1970s. During the past thirty years, beginning in 1974, the percentages earned by the lowest quintile fell 2.1 percent, the second quintile lost 3.3 percent, and the third quintile lost 2.7 percent. The fourth quintile has shown small up and down fluctuations, currently down 0.6 percent, and the percent of total income of the top quintile has increased 8.8 percent (Danziger and Gottschalk 1995:42; Jones and Weinberg 2000:4).

A similar trend is demonstrated by evaluating income inequality over time. During the 1980s, the entire income structure expanded dramatically, with the top stretching upward away from the center and the center moving up away from the bottom. In the 1990s, the gap between the 90th and 50th percentile continued to grow, increasing inequality between the top tenth and the rest of the population, while at the same time the difference between the 50th and 10th percentiles shrank. Since 1999, however, it appears that the decreasing inequality in the bottom half of the income structure has stopped and has shown signs of increasing while the widening disparity between the top and the middle persists (Mishel, Bernstein, and Boushey 2003:152). In fact, the highest incomes have continuously increased at rather rapid rates. In 1979, about 13,500 U.S. taxpayers claimed incomes equivalent to $1 million or more. By 1994, the number earning this much had exceeded 68,000 (Kingston 2000:159–160). The disparities between the salaries of executives and their employees have widened considerably as CEO and other executive-level salaries have soared, particularly since the 1990s. The use of stock options as a key component of many executive pay packages has led to much higher levels of income inequality (Frydman and Saks 2004).

Frank and Cook (1995) have explored the runaway incomes at the top of the distribution, which are fed by "winner-take-all" markets. The most popular musicians, athletes, actors, artists, authors, car manufacturers, and even producers of food and ordinary household items increasingly tend to receive a disproportionate amount of the monetary benefits in their respective markets, pushing those of only slightly lesser quality (and sometimes of equal quality) far down the income scale if not out of the market entirely. Indeed, the mean income of the top 5 percent of earners in the United States nearly doubled in a decade, from $138,000 in 1991 to $260,000 in 2001, while earners further down the distribution ladder made comparatively meager gains (U.S. Census 2003).

However, while the income and wage distributions do provide a glimpse of the extent of inequality in the United States, a factor that even more profoundly gets at the heart of inequality is wealth. Wealth, determined by a household's assets minus debts, is distributed even more unevenly than income. Wealth is an especially important consideration shaping economic security in changing times. The wealthiest people in the society have in their wealth a buffer from downward economic trends for family and other crises that is not always available to the middle class, and when it is, it is far more limited—and is largely absent from the working class and the poor. If a household experiences financial hardship—the loss of a job, illness, and so forth—wealth is the cushion that breaks a fall. Given this reality, a significant portion of the U.S. population live in very vulnerable circumstances. Only one third of households has any (or has negative) financial assets, and the average family in 1988 held $3,700 in net financial assets, enough to sustain them at the poverty line for a mere three months (Oliver and Shapiro 1997:69). The economic precariousness of the entire bottom half of the population is in stark contrast to their more affluent counterparts. In 1992, the wealthiest quintile possessed a whopping 84 percent of the wealth in the United States (Mishel, Bernstein, and Boushey 2003:281) and was the beneficiary of 99 percent of the wealth gain between 1983 and 1989. The bottom 80 percent of households received a mere 1 percent of the increase (Marshall 2000:5).

Much of this social class inequality tracks along lines defined by race and gender. First considering race, in 2003 the median income was about $55,000 for Asian households; $48,000 for non-Hispanic white households; $33,000 for Hispanic, American Indian, and Alaska Native households; and $30,000 for African American households (DeNavas-Walt, Proctor, and Mills 2004:4–10). Likewise, whereas only 8.2 percent of non-Hispanic whites were living at or below the poverty line in 2003, 11.8 percent of Asians, 22.5 percent of Hispanics, 23.9 percent of American Indians and Alaska Natives (2002–2003 average), and 24.3 percent of blacks lived in poverty. Even when they are found in the same occupations and work full-time and year-round, Asian men earn 94 percent of the income of white men, Hispanic men only 86 percent, and black men only 84 percent (Xu and Leffler 1996:119).

Wealth is similarly divided along racial lines. While a quarter of white households possess no wealth or negative wealth, 61 percent of black and 54 percent of Hispanic households fit into this category. While 38 percent of white households lack the financial assets to survive for three months at the poverty line, as many as 73 percent of Hispanic households and 80 percent of black households live in this precarious financial position (Oliver and Shapiro 1997: 86–87). Viewed another way, the median white household possesses $7,000 in net financial assets in contrast to the zero assets held by the median black household. The median white household has over eight times the net worth of the median black household (Mishel, Bernstein, and Boushey 2003:284).

Even considering only middle-class households, whether defined by income ($25,000 to $50,000, calculated with 1988 dollars), college education, or white-collar occupation, black households possess only 35 percent of the net worth of white households by the first definition, 23 percent by the second, and 15 percent by the third. In terms of financial assets—that which can help prevent financial disaster in extenuating circumstances—black households have 1 to 4 percent that of whites, with white-collar black households having no net financial assets whatsoever, a figure that excludes equity in a home or vehicle (Oliver and Shapiro 1997:94). This means that the average black middle-class family has to rely almost entirely on income alone for its middle-class

standard of living and cannot withstand a single financial obstacle without it becoming a potential financial catastrophe.

The disparity in earnings by gender has significantly decreased in recent decades; however, the gap between women and men remains, and it is not an insignificant gap. In 1984, full-time, year-round working women of privileged racial groups—white and Asian—made 68 to 77 percent that of white men *in the same occupations;* men of the least privileged racial groups—Hispanic and black—earned 84 to 86 percent that of white men (Xu and Leffler 1996:119). However, since 1984, women of all races combined (irrespective of occupation) have jumped from an average $0.64 per men's dollar to $0.76 per men's dollar. Whereas men's incomes have made little progress since 1973 (then $27,802, and $29,101 in 2001), women's incomes have increased 72 percent—up from $9,649 in 1973 to $16,614 in 2001 (U.S. Census 2001).

This can be construed as welcome change in the right direction. However, substantial inequalities still exist for women. While the median earnings gap between women and men may be decreasing, this does not reveal the fact that most of women's pay increase is occurring in the lower and middle rungs of the income distribution and to a far lesser degree at the top (Blau and Kahn 1997); this is particularly the case for black women (Bernhardt, Morris, and Handcock 1995). Since 1983, the greatest income distribution change for men occurred in the category of those earning $75,000 and above—an increase of 5.7 percentage points. For women, the most progress was made in the lowest income group—those with negative earnings to making $2,499, a drop of 7.3 points (U.S. Census 2001). The phrase "glass ceiling" used in reference to women's low rates of advancement in upper-level income brackets is affirmed by these figures.

Motherhood is one major factor that stunts financial compensation for women, especially if they are unmarried. Budig and England (2001) found that women pay a "wage penalty" of about 7 percent per child, only a third of which is explained by differences in work experience or interrupted employment. Three fifths of the impoverished population in the United States is composed of women (Rank 2004:32). The "feminization of poverty" is especially evident among unmarried mothers (including divorcees, widows, and the never married) and their children. For the 10.5 percent of people living in female-headed households in 2002, 35.2 percent were at or below the poverty line, nearly three times the rate for all people, 12.1 percent (Rank 2004:31). McLanahan and Booth (1989) contend that most single mothers become poor as a result of divorce. Post-divorce women earn a mere 67 percent of the prior family income, while their ex-husbands garner about 90 percent of what they had brought in before the marital breakup. Making matters worse, although most women have custody of their children, 60 percent receive no child support at all (Furstenberg, Morgan, and Allison 1987), and the payments are meager for many of those who do.

## THE CONSEQUENCES OF INEQUALITY: CONSTRAINTS ON EQUAL OPPORTUNITY

What are the implications of these existing levels of inequality on life chances? This is the topic we turn to in the following section. While a vast majority of Americans claim to embrace the idea of equal opportunity (but not equality of outcomes), the issue becomes one of sorting out the various ways that existing levels of inequality impede the realization of creating an equal opportunity society. In this section, we explore the following issues: (1) quality of life issues associated with physical and mental health; (2) food and nutrition; (3) housing and neighborhood quality; (4) crime; (5) environmental risk; (6) schooling and the development of human capital; and (7) social capital.

It should be stressed at the outset that this is only a snapshot of aspects of the consequences of inequality. What is clear is that inequality is a complex and multidimensional phenomenon. What follows is by no means intended to be comprehensive. Rather, its purpose is to illustrate some of the key multifaceted elements involved in determining the varied impacts of inequality on different sectors of the disadvantaged population.

## Physical and Mental Health

Inequality in the United States is in no way limited simply to economics. The "losers" in this unequal society endure a number of consequences deriving from their lower socioeconomic status (SES), consequences that pervade virtually all aspects of life. One of these is a generic term called "quality of life." While this term can be used to account for a number of factors, we concentrate here on only two: mental and physical health.

Numerous studies have demonstrated that low SES is correlated with a wide range of psychological disorders (Merva and Fowles 2000). Although the direction of causality is still debated, Marva and Fowles's study of the mental health of laid-off workers suggests that financial privation, at least in some cases, precedes psychiatric distress. Furthermore, it appears that not only is absolute economic deprivation strongly associated with mental health but so too is relative deprivation. Increasing inequality causes those in the lower rungs of the wage scale to feel alienated from the rest of society and to increasingly view themselves as inadequate.

Mental health problems frequently result from the negative impacts of poverty and inequality, and once individuals are suffering from a mental illness, they become less likely to find or keep gainful employment. Add to this that the mentally ill are often left untreated, particularly if they do not have insurance to pay for counseling or medication. More of the poor with treatable mental illnesses go untreated than is the case with the general population.

Pressure to "keep up with the Joneses" is strong throughout the society, but for those at the bottom it is especially stressful because success seems to be out of reach. Indeed, the lower class is no less influenced than the middle class by the values of a consumer culture, despite that there are so many goods and services that they cannot possibly afford to purchase (Caplovitz 1967:12). If all members of a consumption-oriented society confront the problem of seeing their desires always unmet because there is always something more that one might possess, the frustrations are more intense for those who have access to so much less than others. The result is stress. These stressors often result in not only mental health problems but also violence; indeed, wage inequality is positively associated with accident mortality, homicide, and aggravated assault. Single, low-income mothers are among the most likely to develop stress-related disorders (Merva and Fowles 2000). Hughes and Thomas (1998) demonstrate that African Americans experience a lower quality of life (measurements include life satisfaction, marital happiness, degree of trust, happiness, anomie, and health) than whites, even when classified as middle or upper class. The authors suggest that this is because of a "racial tax"—the harmful psychological effects of a long historical legacy of racism.

The physical health consequences of inequality are no less serious. Regardless of the exact measurement used, low-income level and poor health are strongly linked. For example, impoverished African Americans have disproportionately high incidences of high blood pressure, heart problems, diabetes and its complications, and sudden infant death syndrome (Mullahy and Wolfe 2001:284). Cancer (among males), sickle-cell anemia, tuberculosis, hypertension, arteriosclerosis, and AIDS also affect significantly higher percentages of blacks than whites (Pearson 1994). Because of the high concentration of blacks among the poor, it is likely that these are related to poverty and not only to racism. Life expectancy is another factor that varies considerably by race, gender, SES, and also location. Geronimus and her colleagues (2001) found that the life expectancy at age 16 of a black man living in urban poverty is 42 years. Likewise, black women have shorter life expectancies, and spend more time disabled by poor health, than white women.

This difference may be because those in poverty tend to exhibit more unhealthy behaviors than the rest of the population (Mullahy and Wolfe 2001:285). Smoking, in particular, appears to be concentrated among those of low SES and among racial minorities (Williams and Collins 1995). The disparity in health is also in large part due to an underuse of health care. One third of the African American deaths above the white death rate are the result of treatable conditions (Williams and Collins 1995). Much of this is certainly because access to health care is severely limited for low SES Americans, and the number of

people without health insurance has recently increased. In 2003, 15.6 percent of the population was without coverage, amounting to 45 million people, 1.4 million more than in 2002 (DeNavas-Walt, Proctor, and Mills 2004:14). Employer-provided health insurance is decreasing as health care costs increase, and those who still have insurance via an employer are expected to pay larger portions of the premiums even as quality of care is decreasing because of the increasing adoption of managed care plans (Davis 2000). These recent trends most sharply affect the lower classes—as income level decreases, so does access to quality health insurance—and racial minorities, particularly Hispanics, of whom nearly a third have no health coverage (DeNavas-Walt, Proctor, and Mills 2004:15).

Living in hazardous neighborhoods and being exposed to injurious work conditions further endangers the physical health of the disadvantaged. Individuals at the bottom of the social structure are more likely to hold jobs that involve heavy lifting; awkward body postures; exposure to toxic substances, dust, fumes, explosives, acids, and other harmful substances; as well as long hours of mechanical, routinized actions (William and Collins 1995). These hazards are also correlated with race. For example, steelworkers occupying the most dangerous positions in the production process are three times more likely to be black than white (Evans and Kantrowitz 2002). All of these take a toll on the bodies and on the life expectancies of the most disadvantaged sectors of the society.

## Food and Nutrition

Hunger is another problem that disproportionately affects racial minorities, low-income households, and female-headed households. Alaimo, Briefel, Frongillo, Jr., and Olson (1998) estimate that 4.1 percent of the overall U.S. population—between 9 and 12 million people—does not have enough food to eat either occasionally or frequently. However, in their study of Minneapolis–St. Paul, 15.2 percent of Mexican Americans fell into this category; even when controlling for other economic and demographic factors, twice as many Mexican Americans as whites claimed to experience food deficiency. Nearly 8 percent of African Americans reported food deficiency compared to 2.5 percent of non-Hispanic whites, which at least in part is attributable to disparities in SES. Obviously, SES plays an enormous role in food sufficiency; 14 percent of the low-income population[1] does not have enough food at times. Other studies report even higher percentages of hunger levels. Forty-five percent of children living under the poverty line in 2002 suffered food insecurity. America's Second Harvest, the nation's largest food relief distributor, came to the assistance of 23.3 million people in 2001; the median income for those helped was well below the poverty line (Rank 2004:38). Getting enough food to eat can be especially problematic for the poor during the winter months. Bhattacharya, Deleire, Haider, and Currie (2002) found that while both the rich and poor increase heating expenditures in very cold times, the poor compensate for this increase by reducing their food expenditures by about the same cost. While the rich tend to increase their food intake, the poor eat about 200 fewer calories per day than in warmer months. This "heat or eat" dilemma significantly impacts the nutrition and the health of the poor.

Making matters worse, Chung and Myers (1999) demonstrate that food actually costs more for the urban poor. They found a $16.62 difference in market-basket prices, or the cost for a week's worth of food that meets minimum nutritional requirements, between chain and non-chain grocery stores. Because many chain stores are not located in or near urban poor neighborhoods, and many poor people do not have cars or adequate public transportation, residents have little choice but to shop at closer but more expensive non-chain stores. Furthermore, these non-chain stores carry a far smaller selection of certain types of foods, particularly fresh produce, meat, and dairy products (Barnes 2005:67–93).

But food insufficiency also affects households in the lower-middle income range,[2] particularly those with children headed by employed females; when other factors are controlled, these households are 5.5 times more likely to suffer food deficiency than other households. In part, this deficiency appears to be the result of difficulties associated with affording childcare during work hours while not being eligible for federal assistance, such as food stamps. This situation is particularly acute for female-headed households. The adverse effects of hunger are obvious: malnutrition not only affects an individual's health in various ways but also impedes children's physical and cognitive development (Alaimo, Briefel, Frongillo, Jr., and Olson 1998).

Inequality does not only impact food in terms of insufficiency and hunger. Many people conceive of eating disorders as being primarily white, middle- to upper-class female phenomena, resulting from social pressures to conform to our culture's thin ideal of beauty. However, Thompson (1992) asserts that these disorders have class, race, and sexual orientation dimensions as well. She claims that some women develop bulimia, anorexia, unhealthy dieting, and binging as a means of coping with such "traumas" as discrimination and high levels of stress based on the factors just mentioned. For example, many women living in poverty respond to the stress of their lives by using food as a drug. Excessive eating can produce effects similar to alcohol consumption, is far cheaper, and does not result in hangovers that would hinder productivity. This phenomenon can explain one of the paradoxes of contemporary poverty. While there is hunger, it is also true that poor people are more likely to be overweight than the general population. Obesity and its related problems, such as hypertension and diabetes, result not only from overeating but from eating cheaper but unhealthy foods, particularly those high in saturated fat.

## Housing and Neighborhood Quality

Inequality also profoundly affects housing and neighborhood quality. Housing discrimination based primarily on race remains an endemic problem in the United States, which, combined with a shortage of decent affordable housing, is responsible for the concentration of poverty in select geographic areas (Massey, Gross, and Shibuya 1994). While some of the most overt forms of housing discrimination are far less obvious since the civil rights era, new and more subtle modes of discrimination persist, many of them difficult to detect. For example,

Yinger (1986) has demonstrated that housing agents show blacks 36 percent fewer apartments than they show whites; more to the point, they purposefully do not introduce them to apartments located in predominantly white neighborhoods. To make matters worse, even when SES is controlled, blacks looking to procure housing in black neighborhoods are significantly less likely to be approved for a loan than are their white counterparts (Massey and Fong 1990). This anomaly is caused in part by redlining practices and in part by discriminatory lending policies. And when blacks do move into predominantly white areas, they often must endure the antagonisms directed at them by white residents. Whites searching for new homes tend to avoid these neighborhoods, and as a result, minority households will eventually dominate them. The above is true for Hispanics as well, though to a lesser extent.

What is the result of this geographic segregation? Massey and Fong (1990) show that while highly educated black communities can truly uphold a "separate but equal" status with socioeconomically similar white communities, poorer and less-educated blacks experience neighborhood conditions inferior to other impoverished populations because of their relative concentration in urban inner city settings. These are neighborhoods characterized by what Massey and Denton (1993) call "hypersegregation." Police protection, firefighting, sanitation services, and similar municipal services tend to be of poorer quality in low SES areas, and children have fewer places to play and an even smaller numbers of *safe* recreation areas (Evans and Kantrowitz 2002). More youth in these neighborhoods drop out of high school, have decreased childhood IQ, and become pregnant as teenagers (Brooks-Gunn, Duncan, Klebanov, and Sealand 1993; Crane 1991). Those who live in impoverished and racially segregated (especially African American, but to a lesser degree Mexican American) neighborhoods suffer significantly higher mortality rates, even when variance in individual characteristics is controlled (LeClere, Rogers, and Peters 1997). Wilson (2000) is particularly concerned about "jobless ghettoes" that continue to grow in inner cities, which are plagued with crime, prostitution, drug trafficking, and gang activity. Often, potential employers do not welcome individuals raised in these locales, in part because of discrimination but also because of the underdevelopment of skills in these communities; unfortunately, this inability to find work only reinforces and thus perpetuates disadvantage.

## Crime and Punishment

Socioeconomic and racial inequality also negatively affect crime and violence. In terms of racial inequality, in 2002, 49 percent of all murder victims were black and 49 percent were white, while only 13 percent of Americans are black and 80 percent are white (Bureau of Justice 2002; Rasmussen 2003). Blacks are seven times more likely than whites to commit murder and six times more likely to be murdered (Bureau of Justice 2002). Turning to another type of crime, households earning less than $7,500 were victims of burglary and assault at significantly higher rates than higher earning households (Bureau of Justice 2003). Why blacks and those of low SES are so much more likely to be exposed to crime is the object of much speculation. Of interest to this discussion, Harer and Steffensmeier (1992) have shown that for whites, low SES is strongly correlated with violent crime. For blacks, on the other hand, this is not the case.

A possible explanation is put forward by Alba, Logan, and Bellair (1994). In their study, which focused on suburbs, they also found that black SES, and additionally family structure and other personal traits, do not explain the race's disproportionately large exposure to crime. Rather than these factors, they suggest that the culprit is the residential segregation process that locates blacks—even if affluent—in crime-prone areas. Sampson, Raudenbush, and Earls (1997) show that neighborhoods characterized by a high percentage of disadvantaged households (including high levels of lower class families, minority households, and female-headed households), immigrants, and residential instability are less likely to have strong ties to one another and to uphold informal social control, such as watching over neighbors' property, keeping track of neighbors' kids, and so forth. Thus, they experience much higher rates of crime and violence because they lack the control necessary to prevent these things from happening.

In general, insofar as high levels of inequality are associated with high crime levels, and socioeconomic inequality and racial inequality are intertwined, it is not surprising that disadvantaged racial minorities are involved in crime at a greater rate than the general population, both as offenders and victims. Evidence suggests that this is particularly the case in instances of violent crime (Blau and Blau 1982).

The significance of class location and racial identity is reflected in the state's punishment practices for criminal violations. The United States imprisons far more of its citizens per capita than any other advanced industrial nation. It incarcerates approximately 600 individuals per 100,000. The average for other advanced industrial nations ranges from around 55 to 120 per 100,000. The rate in Scandinavian countries, for example, is one tenth the U.S. rate (Currie 1998). Moreover, the United States sends people to prison for much longer periods of time than is the case in other economically comparable nations. The typical prisoner in both state and federal prisons is relatively young and relatively poor. It is also the case that blacks disproportionately constitute the largest plurality of the current prison population. At the beginning at this century the United States imprisoned almost 1.5 million individuals, 44 percent of whom were black, compared to 35 percent white, 19 percent Latino, and 2 percent other (Human Rights Watch 2002).

A similar scenario can be seen in the use of the death penalty—a practice that has been abolished in virtually all other advanced industrial nations. Costanzo (1997:84) summarizes the nature of the racial disparities in capital punishment cases in the following way:

> Those who are accused of murdering a white victim are more likely to be charged with a capital crime; those convicted of killing a white victim are more likely to receive a death sentence; black defendants who are convicted of killing a white person are the group most likely to receive the death penalty; [and] white defendants who murder black victims are the group least likely to receive a death sentence.

While 58 percent of the defendants executed between 1976 and 2004 were white, at 34 percent, blacks are overrepresented. Moreover, as of 2004, blacks and whites had nearly reached parity in terms of their respective percentages of the death row population, with blacks registering at 42 percent and whites at 46 percent (NAACP Legal Defense and Fund 2004).

The capacity of the state to punish its citizenry is a reflection of its monopoly on the power to do so. The need to punish large numbers of citizens is related to levels of inequality. It is not fortuitous that the United States has the highest level of inequality among the advanced industrial nations and it also has, by far, the highest level of incarceration and is the only one routinely using the death penalty. Social control, in short, is more problematic and difficult to achieve in highly unequal societies.

### Environmental Risk

Those at the bottom of the social class system and the racial hierarchy are endangered not only by greater violence and crime but also by environmental hazards. Because minimizing pollution and toxic wastes is costly, plants that produce these by-products tend to carefully locate themselves in areas where land is less expensive, where residents are not likely to protest their presence, and where challenges to their mishandling of wastes is least likely. These locations are found in low-SES and minority communities (Krieg 1998). In the Southeast, 26 percent to 42 percent of households proximal to (within the same census tract as) a hazardous waste landfill live in poverty. Other sources of environmental dangers plague the disadvantaged as well. As many as 68 percent of urban African American children living in households earning less than $6,000 yearly suffer dangerous levels of lead in their blood. On the other hand, white children in families above $15,000 experience unsafe lead levels at a rate of only 12 percent. Likewise, impoverished children are nearly 40 percent more likely to be exposed to cigarette smoke in the home than are those above the poverty line. Air pollution (CO and $NO_2$) from stoves and heating systems is also far more prevalent in low-income homes. Water pollution affects primarily rural, low-SES populations, including poor Mexican Americans residing near the nation's southern border. As noted earlier, a variety of environmental risks are associated with various low-income occupations (Evans and Kantrowitz 2002).

While these and related environmental risks have profound effects on their victims' health, often due to daily exposure year after year, other less apparent environmental factors also deeply influence the lives of the urban poor. First, exposure to high levels of noise pollution is also linked with low SES. Not only does constant clamor often result in hearing damage but also it has been shown to elevate stress, to impede the execution of complex tasks, to hinder children's mastery of reading, and to undermine the development of certain crucial "interpersonal processes" related to the emergence of altruism and the control of aggression. Furthermore, it may also spur feelings of helplessness and inhibit motivation—apparently from the individual's inability to control the noise.

Overcrowding (less than one room per resident) is yet another environmental risk factor associated with SES. Living in crowded conditions has virtually the same result as noise exposure and also contributes to the spread of infectious diseases. Overcrowding is not limited to the home. This also translates to outdoor space, both in the yard as well as in park areas: children in low-income New York City neighborhoods average about 17 square yards of park space per child, whereas the rest of the city's children each have 40 square yards (Evans and Kantrowitz 2002).

While many environmental risks, such as air pollution, are shared by all sectors of the population, it is clearly the case that environmental risks in general disproportionately impact lower income people and disadvantaged racial minorities.

## Schooling and the Development of Human Capital

Race and social class inequality, more than gender inequality, result in vast educational disadvantages for lower class and minority children. These inequities appear to be rooted in three main factors: unequal funding for schools, family structure and parental involvement in their child's education, and discrimination. First, school funding is based largely on local property taxes. This means that schools located in areas populated primarily with lower class households are going to have significantly smaller budgets than schools in wealthier middle- to upper-class districts. However, this inequality is exacerbated in the inner cities, where lower class youth and racial minorities are likely to be concentrated. Operating inner-city schools tends to be more expensive than running suburban schools. The school properties themselves tend to cost more, and the upkeep and insurance of the buildings, which are often old and subject to frequent vandalism, demands a larger portion of the educational budget than elsewhere. Furthermore, other needs of inner cities, such as large police forces and fire departments, compete with the neighborhood schools for limited local tax revenues (Spratlen 1973).

Despite *Brown v. Board of Education of Topeka*, the 1954 landmark Supreme Court decision that found that segregated schools led to racially unequal educational opportunities, a half century after the decision, American schools are undergoing a process of resegregation. In a recent study conducted by Harvard's Civil Rights Project, the researchers determined that the gains made in the 1960s and 1970s have eroded and, particularly in the 1990s, the rate of resegregation has increased dramatically. At present, 70 percent of black students attend schools that contain predominantly minority student populations, while Latinos have also witnessed increasing levels of educational segregation (Orfield 2004). Thus, minority students, particularly poorer ones, increasingly attend public schools that are inferior to those of their white counterparts.

In general, less money is spent per capita on the education of low-SES and minority youth than on higher social class whites. Somewhat more debated is the effect of this inequity on disadvantaged students. The frequently cited Coleman Report, which appeared in 1966, convinced many that school characteristics, most of which can be linked directly to the school's economic resources, have very little bearing on student achievement. The report argued that the single most important factor was the role played by parents. However, more recent research has contradicted this finding. School resources and class size both appear to affect students' test scores, and going to underprivileged schools has been demonstrated to be as strong a predictor as intelligence of low future SES (Walters 2001; Pong 1998). It is not surprising that youth who attend schools that use dated textbooks, that have inadequate or no science labs, inadequate library materials, underpaid teachers, and large classrooms, and that lack access to computer technologies are at a significant disadvantage compared to youth who attend schools with well-paid instructors, who are provided individualized attention, and who have access to up-to-date educational materials

Coleman was not entirely wrong: family characteristics and parental involvement do affect education by race and SES as well. Roscigno and Ainsworth-Darnell (1999) have shown that high-SES parents tend to provide their children with more household educational resources (periodicals, reference materials, computers, books, calculators); enroll their children in more nonschool classes involving art, music, or dance; and take their children on more cultural trips to museums, historical sites, concerts, and so forth. Interestingly, while white students who receive these household benefits appear to benefit from them (as measured by higher grades and test scores), black students do not receive the same educational return.

Parental interaction with their children also facilitates educational success. Hence, children in single-parent households tend to operate at an educational disadvantage; single parents supervise their children's homework less often and generally have less contact with their children. Pong (1998) provides evidence that a high level of parental involvement in a school boosts student achievement. However, since single working parents generally have little time available to attend PTA meetings and other such activities, their students do not receive this benefit to their education to the same extent as more privileged students in two-parent households. Finally, female-headed households are disproportionately characteristic of minority families and lower class families, reflecting the interactive impact of race, class, and gender.

Finally, simple discrimination appears to explain much of the leftover disparity in educational achievement between blacks and whites. The racial difference in academic success is profound. African Americans on average are as many as four years behind white students in reading, math, science, and writing. They are more likely to be held back a grade. They are less likely to attend and complete college. They are vastly underrepresented at the top of national test distributions. Although black students at higher SES schools score higher on the SAT than do those at lower SES schools, they do not perform as well as their white classmates (Hallinan 2001). While many of these differences can be explained by the aforementioned economic and family factors, these do not fully account for the differences. Although discrimination is far less easy to operationalize, it seems highly likely that racial discrimination also plays a part in educational inequality (Hedges and Nowell 1999).

Although women do not experience significant educational differences from men before graduating from high school, there are gender disparities in higher education. In many ways, of the many inequalities discussed in this essay, education may be the arena in which women and men are nearly equal, with women sometimes even surpassing men. A slightly higher percentage of women (among whites and in virtually all minority groups; see Hoffman, Llagas, and Snyder 2003:95) enroll in college and graduate with two-year, bachelors, master's, and professional degrees compared to men. However, only 37.3 percent of PhD degrees were earned by women in 1992, and they remain a minority among college and university faculty. Additionally, women tend to be disproportionately enrolled in less selective schools; men still enroll in and receive degrees from choice institutions at higher rates than women (Jacobs 1996).

Many of these factors related to higher education provide evidence for the perpetuation of racial disparities. A smaller percentage of African Americans and Hispanics enroll in colleges and universities than do whites; in 2000, 39 percent of

18- to 24-year-old whites were enrolled, 31 percent of blacks, and 22 percent of Hispanics (Hoffman, Llagas, and Snyder 2003:93). Additionally, the percentage of degrees earned by blacks decreases as the level of the degree increases, earning 11 percent of associate's degrees, 9 percent of bachelor's, 8 percent of master's, 7 percent of professional, and 5 percent of doctorate degrees. For Hispanics, the respective percentages are 9 percent, 6 percent, 4 percent, 5 percent, and 3 percent (Hoffman, Llagas, and Snyder 2003:96–97).

Education has a direct effect on the development of human capital, or one's skill, education, and experience that can be used to secure a quality position or to advance in the job market. As mentioned earlier, lower class students and racial minorities do not receive educations equivalent to their more advantaged counterparts and therefore are often at a human capital disadvantage that starts early in childhood. Insofar as the school system in the nation fails to provide genuinely equal educational opportunities, it serves to reinforce existing inequalities rather than contribute to overcoming them.

Women's human capital has made great gains in recent decades; women are completing undergraduate and some graduate degrees at higher rates than men. However, these high levels of education often do not translate into financial benefits comparable with men's. Partly as a function of earning degrees in female-dominated fields, women earn less money than men (Jacobs 1996:169). Additionally, while not lacking in educational achievement, women may on average lag somewhat behind men in experience. Since the responsibilities of childrearing fall primarily upon women, many married women put their careers on hold or work part time, both of which decrease experience and depress earning potential (Budig and England 2001). These effects of household labor persist across class lines, although nonworking-class women experience a more significant drop in wages (Coverman 1983). However, this does *not* fully account for the difference between women's and men's earnings. Discrimination continues to play a role in persisting gender-based earnings differentials.

## Social Capital

Inequality not only leads to vast discrepancies in social capital but also perpetuates it by deterring upward mobility for those at the bottom of the social structure and by facilitating it for those already near the top. Lin (2000:786) describes social capital as "the quantity and/or quality of resources that an actor (be it an individual or group or community) can access or use through its location in a social network." Access to these resources, then, enables people to attain higher paying and more prestigious jobs as well as other quality of life benefits.

While social capital is important to the attainment of SES, its benefits are distributed highly inequitably by initial SES location, gender, and race. Since individuals tend to maintain social networks with others of similar characteristics, the networks of members of the lower class tend to consist primarily of other low-SES contacts. These connections tend to be lacking not only in the number of beneficial resources for socioeconomic advancement but also in the diversity of resources that are available to those of higher SES (Lin 2000). In his review of the literature, Portes (1998) explains that all too frequently for inner-city residents, social networks do not reach outside of the inner city, and their knowledge of and ability to obtain good jobs is therefore severely limited. Furthermore, since inner-city communities tend to be more transitory, even the social ties within these poor locales are likely to be less extensive and more tenuous as a result.

Clearly, these factors have implications for race as well. African Americans have less extensive networks than Hispanics and whites, with whites having the largest networks. Since blacks are often segregated in certain neighborhoods, their social networks consist largely of other African Americans, which is not advantageous in an economy more or less dominated by whites. Even in the middle and upper classes, blacks often have relatively few weak ties to white networks, instead forming strong social ties among themselves (Lin 2000). These differences play out in explicit ways, for example, when a person seeking a job begins to turn to people he or she knows who might be of assistance. Blacks tend not to have the social capital that will work to their advantage. But social capital also works in more implicit ways, as well. The example of IQ scores, which are the product of the social forces that shape one's background, is revealing. Black children adopted by white families tend to demonstrate higher IQ scores than those adopted by black families, but black children adopted by black families that have ties to racially diverse networks or predominantly white networks have higher IQs than those in black families that do not have these social network characteristics (Moore 1987). It appears that disparities in social capital between blacks and whites contribute to the lower socioeconomic attainment of blacks.

Social capital also varies greatly by gender. McPherson and Smith-Lovin (1982) have shown that although women and men on average have the same number of memberships in organizations, women are members of much smaller organizations than are men. Thus, men have more social contacts (men average 600 contacts via these groups, women 185). Furthermore, the type of organization differs between men and women. Women predominantly take part in organizations concerned with domestic matters, whereas men are far more involved in work-related organizations.

This disparity is exaggerated during childrearing years. Munch, McPherson, and Smith-Lovin (1997) suggest that especially when children are around 3 years old, childcare responsibilities tend to restrict mothers' social contacts significantly in terms of both network size and contact frequency. They further suggest that these social ties, while lessening somewhat as children grow older, may never reach their pre-parenting extent, strength, and richness. Men, on the other hand, do not experience any of these significant, lasting effects on social networks as a result of having young children. In sum, women's social capital provides fewer socioeconomic benefits than that of men, because women's smaller networks provide them primarily domestic information, and their focus on childrearing severely limits beneficial social contacts for a number of years.

## Durable Inequalities

Although this survey of the extent of inequality in the contemporary United States and its implications in such varied areas of social life as physical and mental health, food and nutrition, housing and neighborhood quality, crime and punishment, environmental risk, schooling and human capital development, and social capital only manages to skim the surface, it does reveal the depth of the levels of inequality and the deleterious consequences they have on the life chances of the more disadvantaged sectors of the population. It also indicates the complexity of inequality, a complexity that contributes to its durability (McCall 2001; Tilly 1998) . . . .

## DISCUSSION QUESTIONS

1. According to Hanson and colleagues, what are the implications of social inequality for one's life chances? Why should we care?
2. Hanson and colleagues discuss seven areas in which income inequality is a "constraint on equal opportunity." Take two of those areas and explain how income inequality constrains the life chances of those at the bottom rung of the economic ladder.

## NOTES

1. Low income is defined in this study as households having a "poverty index ratio (PIR; ratio of family income to the federal poverty line times 100) less than or equal to 130 percent of the poverty line" (422).
2. Low middle income includes "PIR 131% to 185% of the poverty line" (422).

# 50

# THE CULTURE OF PRIVILEGE

## Color-Blindness, Postfeminism, and Christonormativity

### ABBY L. FERBER

*Abby L. Ferber is a professor of sociology and women's and ethnic studies at the University of Colorado, Colorado Springs. She also is the director of The Matrix, a Center for the Advancement of Social Equity and Inclusion. A sociologist by training, Ferber has published widely on race, gender, and privilege in both academic books and as a regular blogger for* <u>The Huffington Post.</u> *Ferber's work in intersectionality builds directly on the previous two readings, but it draws more on feminist theories of intersectionality (see Reading 56 by Patricia Hill Collins) and on critical race theory. In this reading, published in the* <u>Journal of Social Issues</u>, *Ferber uses intersectionality to examine the interconnections among discourses on color-blindness, postfeminism, and christonormativity. According to Ferber, all three of these discourses reinforce a culture of privilege.*

I argue in this article that the ideology of color-blind racism, the contemporary framework for understanding and defending white privilege, is part of a broader, overarching ideology of "oppression blindness." This article begins with an explication of intersectionality, and then examines the concept of privilege from an intersectional perspective. I then apply this framework to examine the phenomena of color-blind racism, not as a distinct ideology, but as one which overlaps with and reinforces other systems of inequality in the United States. I focus on two specific examples

*Source:* Ferber, Abby L. 2012. "The Culture of Privilege: Color-Blindness, Postfeminism, and Christonormativity." *Journal of Social Issues* 68(1):63–77. Used by permission of Wiley.

here, comparing the contours of color-blind racism with the ideologies of postfeminism and christonormativity. Examining their similarities, I argue that we approach each discourse as one strand in a larger tapestry that intertwine and work together to reinforce and defend the culture of privilege.

Kimberle Crenshaw coined the term intersectionality to direct attention to the interaction of multiple social identities in shaping the reality of oppression and privilege (African American Policy Forum 2009). She argues that we must embrace an intersectional approach to analyze social problems and develop more effective social movement responses. An intersectional framework can be employed at every level of analysis. Traditionally, analysts of racial inequality and racism have identified three levels for analysis: the individual level, the cultural level, and the structural level (Blumenfeld 2006; Hardiman and Jackson 1997). . . .

Intersectional analyses focus most often on those who are multiply disadvantaged by numerous systems of inequality. There is less research, however, examining systems of privilege intersectionally (Coston and Kimmel 2012). In this article, I examine privilege from an intersectional perspective, and focus specifically on the level of culture. Culture gives meaning to our experiences, and shapes the ways we make sense of the world. Race itself is a cultural construct, and it is through culture that we learn to "see" and "read" race (Ferber 1998; Hartigan 2010). Culture is key in socializing people into a system of racial inequality, and cultural constructions of race shape our own individual identities, as well as our participation in institutions and systems that reproduce inequality (Blumenfeld 2006; Hardiman and Jackson 1997).

Researchers from many disciplines identify racial ideology as one of the most important factors contributing to ongoing racial inequality (Blumenfeld 2006; Bonilla-Silva 2010; Feagin 2001; Ferber 1998; Hartigan 2010). Ideology is a central feature of culture, that "consists of broad mental and moral frameworks, or 'grids,' that social groups use to make sense of the world, to decide what is right and wrong, true or false, important or unimportant" (Bonilla-Silva 2010:62). Racial ideology mediates individuals and institutions, providing the rationalization for the nature of current race relations. It provides a system of assumptions and rules that inform the decisions, behaviors, and interactions of individuals. Racial ideology is an interpretive repertoire that provides storylines, narratives, and common frames for making sense of race relations.

## WHITE PRIVILEGE

Whiteness is a privileged status. To be White is to have greater access to rewards and valued resources simply because of one's group membership. Our failure to interrogate white privilege has serious consequences. The invisibility of whiteness serves to "reinforce the existing racial understandings and racial order of society" (Doane 2003:11.) Making whiteness visible allows us to examine the ways in which all White people gain benefits from their race, expanding the discussion of racism and racial inequality beyond the actions of individual "racists" to examine institutionalized, systemic racism and the racist culture which nourishes it (Case 2012; Feagin 2001; Hartigan 2010).

One of the most significant features of white privilege is that those who experience it do not have to think about it. People of color are confronted with the reality of inequality and oppression on a daily basis, but those who experience privilege are often unaware of it and do not see how it impacts their own lives. Their social location becomes both invisible, and assumed as the norm (Kendall 2006; Kimmel and Ferber 2009). Consequently, those with white privilege, or any form of privilege, often become angry when confronted by the fact of their privilege, having been taught to see their own accomplishments as based on their own efforts and hard work alone (Ferber 2003; Stewart, Latu, and Denney 2012).

## THE DEFENSE OF WHITE PRIVILEGE: COLOR-BLIND IDEOLOGY

Sociologists, psychologists, social workers, and economists continue to research the ways in which racial oppression remains entrenched in the United States (Feagin 2001; Plaut 2010). Centuries of what Feagin (2001) calls "undeserved impoverishment and undeserved enrichment," provide some people a huge head start and plenty of help along the way.

Yet many White people believe that discrimination against people of color is a thing of the past (Plaut 2010). For example, despite all evidence to the contrary, White people generally believe that Whites are actually more likely to face job discrimination than people of color (Pincus 2003). As Collins (2004) argues,

> recognizing that racism even exists remains a challenge for most White Americans, and increasingly for African-Americans as well. They believe that the passage of civil rights legislation eliminated racially discriminatory practices and that any problems that Blacks may experience now are of their own doing. (p. 5)

To understand this gap between reality and the stories we tell, we need to examine the cultural framework informing our stories. Plaut (2010) argues that we must

> [examine] the cultural ideas and beliefs that are prevalent in people's social worlds. These socially, culturally, and historically constituted ideas and beliefs, or cultural models, get inscribed in institutions and practices (e.g., language, law, organizational policies), and daily experiences (e.g., reading the newspaper, watching television, taking a test) such that they organize and coordinate individual understandings and psychological processes (e.g., categorization, attitudes, anxiety, motivation) and behavior. (p. 82)

Work in numerous disciplines highlights the importance of cultural stories and narratives. The rise of narrative therapy affirms this approach, recognizing that humans use sociocultural frameworks to make sense of the world. Meanings "are thus never singular, individual, or simply subjective, never outside the social, but have shared or intersubjective meaning within a cultural nexus of power and knowledge" (Brown and Augusta-Scott 2007:ix).

Over time, our hegemonic stories and narratives about race change, connected to the changing social and economic organization of race relations. Just when the blatantly discriminatory policies and practices of Jim Crow racism were finally crumbling under attack, the early foundations of a "new racism" were taking form (Irons 2010). This new racism is much less overt, its predominant operating narrative characterized as an ideology of color-blind racism which avoids the use of blatantly racist terminology (Bonilla-Silva 2010; Irons 2010; Plaut 2010).

A color-blind perspective assumes that discrimination is a thing of the past, and denies the reality of race and racial inequality today. This approach argues that we should treat people as simply human beings, rather than as racialized beings (Plaut 2010).

According to Bonilla-Silva (2010), color-blind ideology consists of four key frames that organize our understandings of racial inequality:

1. *Abstract liberalism:* relies upon the language of political liberalism, referring to abstract concepts of equal opportunity, rationality, free choice, individualism, etc. (i.e., discrimination is no longer a problem, and any individual who works hard can succeed).

2. *Naturalization:* reframes ongoing inequality as the result of natural processes, rather than social relations (i.e., segregation today is the result of the natural inclination of people to live near others of the same race).

3. *Cultural racism:* reframes ongoing inequality as the result of inherent cultural differences between racialized groups.

4. *Minimization of racism:* assumes that we now have a fairly level playing field, everyone has equal opportunities to succeed, and racism is no longer a real problem.

Color-blind racism assumes racial discrimination has ended, people are being treated in a color-blind fashion, and any differences we see in the success of racial groups is therefore due to inherent differences in the groups themselves.

Color-blind ideology leads to the conclusion that we have done all we can. For many Whites, the election of Obama has been evoked to confirm their assumptions of a color-blind nation (Bonilla-Silva 2010; Cunnigen and Bruce 2010). Although many people naively embrace this view as non-racist, it reinforces and reproduces contemporary systemic racial inequality by denying its reality. These storylines "become part of the racial folklore and thus are shared, used, and believed by members of the dominant race. They are storylines because the words, phrases, and ideas used in these stories are very similar and seem scripted" (Bonilla-Silva 2010:70).

These scripts are so ubiquitous that they are drawn upon to explain other forms of inequality as well. Color-blind racism needs to be examined from an intersectional perspective, making visible the ways it is connected and mutually constitutive of others ideologies of privilege. In the remainder of this article, I will examine discourses of oppression and privilege that rationalize male and Christian privilege, and argue that we must examine the ways in which these ideologies mirror color-blind racism, and reinforce one another. Postfeminism has emerged to justify and rationalize gender inequality, just as Christonormativity works to naturalize and protect Christian privilege. As Plaut argues, these cultural ideologies work together, therefore each one must be dismantled to advance the cause of social justice.

## FROM NEW RACISM TO POSTFEMINISM

Intersectional analyses of both the Civil Rights and women's movements of the 1960s era have revealed the ways in which their failures to address the concerns, needs, and demands of women of color limited their success. Exclusion of women from leadership in the civil rights movement, and the women's movement's failure to fully engage issues of race and sexuality (both the first and second waves), led to divisions in both movements.

There are also striking similarities among the predominant narratives of backlash to both of these movements, yet efforts to respond and attack these narratives still proceed from separate silos, with little collaboration. On the one hand, scholars of race focus on color-blind racism, with little discussion of gender, whereas feminist scholars tackle postfeminism, with almost no discussion of race.

I argue that the same four frames of color-blindness identified by Bonilla-Silva, operate to defend and normalize gender inequality (Ferber 2007). It is common today for journalists and conservative commentators to argue that we have moved beyond the need for feminism, and have entered a "postfeminist" phase. Like the Civil Rights Movement, the Women's Movement did much to advance formal, legal equality for women. Nevertheless, gender inequality also remains widespread, and feminist scholars have observed the rise of a new discourse around gender, remarkably similar to new racism's color-blind framework.

The ideology of postfeminism assumes that the law and society are now "gender-blind" in their treatment of men and women, reflecting the utilization of a "minimization of racism/discrimination" frame. Mainstream media promotes the assumption that the women's movement has accomplished its goals, and barriers facing women have been removed. According to the advocates of postfeminism, men and women now have equal opportunities: women now have the right to vote, legal protection from discrimination, and the same legal rights as men (Douglas 2010; McRobbie 2004).

Some commentators argue that the push for equality has gone too far, arguing that men are now victims of feminist frenzy. Just as the advocates of color-blind racism believe that racial inequality is a thing of the past, and that further attempts to remedy inequality lead to "reverse discrimination" against Whites, we see similar arguments about gender. This rearticulation of the minimization of discrimination frame leads to reifying the values of "abstract liberalism," where feminism is attacked for violating the values of individualism and equal opportunity. After all, if everyone is already equal, then interventions aimed at women violate the principle of equal opportunity and hurt men. Faludi (1991) examines the "steady stream of indictments" of feminism that began in the 1980s in the mainstream media. Problems facing women are often framed as now the result of feminism, and women's push for equality, rather than the product of inequality itself. In this way, feminism is discredited, and claims of ongoing inequality dismissed. According to McRobbie (2004), postfeminist culture is undermining the gains of the women's movement and feminism, arguing that "equality is achieved, to install a whole repertoire of new meanings which emphasize that it is no longer needed" (p. 255).

Consistent with the "abstract liberalism" frame, women's status today is depicted as a product of their own individual choices. According to the logic of the postfeminist storyline, women legally have the same opportunities and rights as men, therefore, if women are more likely to be found in low paying, part-time jobs, it must be because of their own choosing, because "women are now free to choose for themselves" (McRobbie 2004:259). Job segregation and the persistent wage gap are often dismissed with the "prevailing ideological constructions of women as carers," which is also used to explain why women are more likely to be found in the home, responsible for childcare, eldercare, and housework. Further, as an extension of women's care giving "natures," they are assumed to be more likely to choose careers in nursing, teaching, day care, or social work than men, knowing that these jobs pay significantly less compared to male careers requiring similar skills and education levels (Glenn 2010). Here we have moved into the frames of "naturalization" and "cultural racism/sexism." Both natural, biological differences between men and women, as well as gender-based cultural differences, are invoked to rationalize gender inequality (Cole, Avery, Dodson, and Goodman 2012). In *Forced to Care*, Glenn (2010) examines the ways in which this gender ideology of caring, in conjunction with ideologies of race, relegate women of color to the lowest paying, least valued caregiving jobs, such as working in nursing homes. She strikingly reveals the coercion at the heart of this enterprise, examining the role of the state in enforcing women's obligation to provide "care," including the training of Native American women in boarding schools and the formal "Americanization" programs for immigrant women. A tremendous amount of effort and force has been extended to make women acquiesce with the ideology of women as natural caregivers.

Yet postfeminism makes this history and enforcement invisible; "there is little trace . . . of the enduring inequities which still mark out the relations between men and women" (McRobbie 2004:260). Any inequality between men and women, therefore, is seen as a result of men and women's different natures, and the choices men and women make. Both color-blind racism and postfeminism ignore the vast body of literature which examines the ways in which the social institutions of education, work, health care, criminal justice, and the family shape and constrain all of our choices and opportunities (Crittenden 2001; Faludi 1999; Feagin 2001; Glenn 2010; Lewis 2003; Van Ausdale and Feagin 2001).

Given the ideological similarities of color-blind racism and postfeminism, we need to examine both discourses within a broader framework of political backlash against the social movements of the 1960s and 1970s. According to Coppock, Haydon, and Richter (1995) "the proclamation of 'postfeminism' has occurred at precisely the same moment as acclaimed feminist studies demonstrate that not only have women's real advancements been limited, but also that there has been a backlash against feminism of international significance" (p. 3). The concept of "postfeminism" itself is part of this backlash, an "attempt to retract the handful of small and hard-won victories that the feminist movement did manage to win for women" (Faludi 1999:12).

Similarly, Bonilla-Silva (2003) argues that color-blind racism "has become a formidable political tool for the maintenance of the racial order [serving] as the ideological armor for a covert and institutionalized system [of racial oppression] in the post-Civil Rights era" (p. 3). Both postfeminism and color-blind racism are part of an ideology of "oppression-blindness" that operates to defend the culture of privilege against perceived attacks (Ferber 2003, 2007; Ferber and Samuels 2010; Pratto and Stewart 2012). As Steinberg (1995) observes, the Civil Rights movement "assaulted the structure of oppression. . . . It was only a matter of time before non-victims—the powerful and privileged majority—would reclaim lost status and restore victims to their socially assigned place" (p. 156).

Kincheloe (2009) builds upon this argument. Detailing the widespread backlash to the various social justice movements of the 1960s and 1970s, he argues that the "politics, cultural wars, and educational and psychological debates, policies, and practices of the last three decades cannot be understood outside of the efforts of conservative forces to 'recover' White supremacy, patriarchy, class privilege, colonialism, heterosexual 'normality,' Christian dominance and the European intellectual canon" (p. 24). Kincheloe describes this cultural backlash as imbued with an "ideology of recovery," focusing on recovering what has been supposedly lost with the limited gains of these social movements. McRobbie (2004), however, argues that what we are witnessing is more than simply a backlash, but a "double entanglement," which to some degree confirms the successes of feminism, but suggests we can now move beyond it. In other words, this new ideology does not promote a return to the past, but instead persuades us that feminism and the Civil Rights movement have done what they set out to do. Structural barriers are removed, and all individuals now benefit from free choice, so "the individual is compelled to be the kind of subject who can make the right choices" (McRobbie 2004:255). This broad oppression-blind narrative relies upon the "tropes of freedom and choice" (McRobbie 2004:255).

This discourse results in blaming the victim for their own oppression. William Ryan first described the contours of "Blaming the Victim" in 1971 (Ryan 1971). Ryan saw this ideology as widespread, indeed, he claimed that "the generic process of Blaming the Victim is applied to almost every American problem." He observed that this new ideology is "very different from the open prejudice and reactionary tactics of the old days." Instead, this new ideology is "often very subtle. Victim-blaming is cloaked in kindness and concern" (p. 576). Ryan emphasizes that blaming the victim is essentially a defense of privilege: "those who buy this solution with a sigh of relief are inevitably blinding themselves to the basic causes of the problems being addressed. They are, most crucially, rejecting the possibility of blaming, not the victims, but themselves" (p. 583). In this way, blaming the victim allows privilege to remain intact

and unexamined, not simply rationalizing, but reproducing, privilege.

## CHRISTONORMATIVITY

I now turn to a third category, Christian privilege. Christonormativity refers to the normalization and privileging of Christianity as the dominant religious and spiritual culture in the United States (Steinberg and Kincheloe 2009). Christian privilege has been well documented by numerous scholars (Blumenfeld 2006; Blumenfeld and Jaekel 2012; Blumenfeld, Joshi, and Fairchild 2009; Todd 2010). Todd (2010) argues that Christianity "not only dominates other religious and atheistic traditions in this country, but is implicated in virtually every other category of oppression: racism, sexism, heterosexism, ableism, classism . . . every one of these categories has been undergirded by Christian theological justifications" (p. 142). Indeed, Christianity played a central role historically in constructing racial categories, and continues to impact decisions over who counts as "White." Tehranian's (2009) recent work on Middle-Eastern Americans demonstrates that when the majority of Arab immigrants to the United States were Christian, they were more likely to be defined legally as White, yet as the percentage of Arab immigrants that are Muslim has grown, that is changing. "As it has grown less Christian, the Middle Eastern population in the United States is thought of as less assimilable and, consequently, less White" (p. 70).

Blumenfeld describes a system of Christian hegemony, which normalizes Christianity, bestows privilege and advantages on those who embrace Christianity, and marginalizes everyone else. Christian privilege is embedded in our laws, policies, schools and workplaces (Cole, Avery, Dodson, and Goodman 2012). In schools, for example, the curriculum, dress codes, cafeteria food, and even the calendar reinforce Christian values and practices as universal norms, where their underlying Christian foundation is often invisible to all except those who are marginalized and excluded by such practices (Blumenfeld et al. 2009; Nelson 2009).

In 2009, I published a blog examining the pervasive atmosphere of Christian privilege I was observing (Ferber 2009). In the blog, I argue that Christonormativity is a system of privilege that marginalizes and excludes those who are not Christian, especially during the winter holiday season. In the blog, I described a typical December day:

> I woke up and turned on my favorite morning show. I learned new recipes for the favorite holiday drink—egg nog; tips on how to decorate for the holidays on a budget by trimming the mantel and staircase with wreaths, green swags, and small lights; followed by the best toys to buy for kids this holiday season. I then read my local newspaper, which featured a big story about how the Colorado governor's mansion has been decorated for the holidays, accompanied by a large photo of the Christmas tree. . . . I entered my office building, where a large Christmas tree sat in the lobby. Due to concerns raised a few years back about the heavy focus on Christmas, the tree has now been renamed 'The Giving Tree.' It is decorated by ornaments made by children at the campus day care center, with requests for donations as a part of our annual Holiday Service Project. I wonder how Jewish, Muslim, and other non-Christian students feel each time they enter the building.

> On my way home, I stop off on a few errands. In the grocery store, I am greeted by another large Christmas tree. As I wander the aisles I hum along to "Jingle Bells," "All I want for Christmas," "Blue Christmas," "Feliz Navidad," and "Here Comes Santa Claus". . . . So you see, although it may not seem like a big deal that someone wishes me a "Merry Christmas," and I genuinely appreciate the good will and cheer being offered, for non-Christians like myself, this time of year can be anything but merry (24% of the U.S. population of about 304 million do not define themselves as Christian). . . . Not only is it all-pervasive, all day long, when I do the math, I discover that it adds up to about ten years of my life that I live in this exclusionary Christian culture. (If I live to be eighty, one and a half months per year of that time adds up to ten years over a lifetime!) . . . the question is <u>not</u> how do we stop the celebrations, but instead, how do we create a more inclusive culture, a climate where everybody feels included? . . . (full text of blog can be found at: http://www.huffingtonpost.com/abby-ferber/please-dont-wish-me-a-mer_b_389824.html, as accessed on January 10, 2012).

My arguments here are threefold. First, I introduce the concept of Christonormativity, documenting the manner in which Christian culture has become the normative, dominant culture in the United States at this time of year. Like other forms of privilege, it is often invisible and unexamined. Second, I highlight the way in which attempts to make Christian privilege visible are rearticulated as an attack on Christianity. This is another example of blaming the victim. Finally, I ask that we think about what it means to be inclusive.

## DEFENDING CHRISTIAN PRIVILEGE

I received a flood of negative responses to this blog. The blog appeared on *The Huffington Post*, a news/blog site generally characterized as liberal. I have a regular blog there, and in previous blogs I have received a maximum of 21 comments, whereas this post received 79 comments. I often focus on issues of race and gender. I wrote an entry entitled "I am racist" and have often written about white privilege, yet received very few negative responses. I was therefore shocked by the number of negative responses to this post. Of the 79, 40 were explicitly negative or sarcastic, and contained elements of an oppression-blind ideology. The remaining responses consisted of short replies to other posts, were neutral, or were positive. In examining the responses, there is a clear pattern that can be discerned. Like the discourses of color-blind racism and postfeminism, these oppression-blind ideologies minimize Christian privilege and reframe the issue in the abstract liberal terms of free choice and individualism.

One of the most common themes I found was the "minimization of discrimination" and the concomitant attempt to preserve the culture of privilege:

- "The only thing Christian about Christmas is the name 'Christ'mas... about 95% of all Christmas traditions are non-christian... growing up I never really noticed the Christ in Christmas.... To me it's like Thanksgiving."

- "Christ was born in September, the holiday that you are so offended by is a secular holiday, there are no real Christian holidays.... The American Christmas is a family celebration of giving and love... everyone can join in, it's really not Christian in any real sense."

- "May I suggest you go to 'Blintzes and Bling' and get a Star of David necklace the size of a hub cap so that I know you are Jewish. Then I promise to wish you a Happy Hanukkah... People of all faiths are dying across the globe for their religious beliefs. December is a month of hope and light and joy for most faiths—and also for those of no particular faith-who can enjoy the secular spirit of giving and cheer."

These quotes and many others argue that there is no evidence of privilege or exclusion. Christmas is reframed in universal terms, depicted as good fun that everyone can be a part of. These responses also provide evidence of the "naturalization" of Christianity. Christian values are naturalized as simply human values that are inherent in all people. As one respondent put it, "These are universal beliefs, that for this time of year, just happen to be wrapped in green and red bows."

Not only do the respondents minimize and trivialize Christian discrimination and privilege, they draw upon the "abstract liberalism" frame by emphasizing the abstract principles of individualism, rationality and free choice:

- "What an awful whiner... The vast majority of this country is Christian, and even many secular people celebrate Christmas; is it any wonder that the average person is assumed to celebrate it? Anybody who is 'offended' or 'uncomfortable' really needs to find something new to complain about."

- "You have two choices. You can either be terribly offended and act pissy when someone smiles and wishes you a Merry Christmas or you can embrace the friendly, positive sentiment as it was intended and smile back. How you react say's much about who you are..."

- "We can choose to continue to live in a world where we seek out an offense where none is intended and continue down this dangerous path of perpetuating the 'us vs. them' mentality that serves to divide us more than we are already. Or we can decide to be participants in a world where we look beyond our differences."

- "As an atheist, I am constantly bombarded with God from the government, from friends and strangers alike. However, I am not offended by anyone wishing me Merry Christmas, Happy Hanukkah, Happy Kwanzaa, etc.... I would be in a constant state of irritation if I let these things bother me."

- "I am not a Christian. I could choose to feel excluded and marginalized because a lot of people are celebrating a holiday important to their religion, or I can choose my own interpretation of a winter holiday with rituals and traditions that I select and enjoy the lights and colors and giving and general goodwill. It's of no relevance to me what the holiday means to anyone else, and mine is of no matter to them. If I choose to forgo Christmas completely (and I've done that in previous years), I certainly don't resent others continuing to celebrate nor do I take offense that they assume that I share in their celebration. . ."

These arguments are the very same arguments used to justify color-blind racism and postfeminism. They erase from view Christian privilege, reinscribing Christianity as normative. They blame the victim for choosing to focus on differences. Like advocates of affirmative action or those "frenzied feminists," anyone who argues that race, gender, and religious differences still matter in shaping people's daily lives is attacked. The reality of institutional inequality is ignored, and the issue is reduced to simply one of individual choice.

According to Plaut (2010), our cultural ideologies of race "impart to people the meanings they use to live their everyday lives while reinforcing social and cultural systems. Cultural ideas and beliefs are widely shared and instantiated in everyday practices, yet they may often go unnoticed and thus remain invisible or at least uninterrogated—especially if they serve the interests of powerful groups" (p. 82). Clearly, contemporary discourses that are relied upon to justify and rationalize White, masculine, and Christian privilege in the United States share much in common. The findings of this analysis have implications, however, for understanding systems of inequality across the globe. Sutton (2010) argues that a central "premise of the intersectional approach is that systems of inequality . . . mutually constitute and reinforce each other" (p. 10). Our failure to examine their interconnections carries consequences and undermines our efforts to advance social justice. When we only interrogate this cultural storyline of privilege and oppression in terms of its implications for racial inequality, we leave the broader storyline in place. Focusing only on race is like trying to pull one strand out of a tapestry. Even if we are successful, the tapestry remains intact, and thus that strand can always be picked up and woven back in. It is the entire tapestry we must unravel. We need to analyze these as strands in a broader, comprehensive ideological tapestry explaining away inequality and trying to naturalize and justify oppression and privilege.

Although the goals of most research on white privilege are to contribute to antiracist activism, approaches which focus only on race have limited potential. For example, the belief that legal obstacles to equality have been removed and everyone has equal opportunities to succeed, is used to justify not only race, but gender and religious inequality, which is rearticulated as the product of the poor choices of individuals, rather than a systemic issue. When we hear the very same arguments offered to explain each one of these systems of inequality, it gives them more legitimacy. The more familiar the arguments are, the more they feel intuitively right to people. The frames are more likely to resonate, and to feel like "common sense."

Analysis of color-blindness has proceeded as a "single-axis analysis" which the African American Policy Forum (2009) argues corresponds to the "silo-oriented structure of social justice mobilization" (p. 2). Wherever we are situated, we will have greater potential for success if we attack the entire ideology of oppression-blindness and victim blaming—in all of its forms, rather than only one of its manifestations. We must work to shift the entire discussion from this individualist approach to a sociocultural perspective, which examines the institutionalized culture of privilege and oppression. It is only by adopting an intersectional approach, which examines the ways in which race, gender, and other systems of inequality interact and intersect as part of a matrix of privilege and oppression, that we can fully comprehend and work to develop successful strategies for combating any and all forms of oppression (Collins 2000; Ferber et al. 2008).

## DISCUSSION QUESTIONS

1. What is postfeminism, and how is it similar to color-blindness?
2. According to Ferber, what is christonormativity, and why is it problematic?
3. How do ideologies of color-blindness, postfeminism, and christonormativity reinforce each other? Can you think of specific examples where this occurs in U.S. society?

# 51

# FIVE FACES OF OPPRESSION

## IRIS MARION YOUNG

*Iris Marion Young was a professor of Political Science at the University of Chicago. Her book,* Justice and the Politics of Difference *(1990), won the 1991 Victoria Schuck Award of the American Political Science Association. This reading, "The Five Faces of Oppression," is excerpted from this award-winning book that transformed academic discourse about social inequality and oppression. In it, Young argues that scholars concerned with social justice must reconceptualize oppression beyond an understanding of it at the individual level. That is to say, problematic individuals are not the only source of oppressive behavior and discrimination. Instead, we need to rethink oppression and see it more as something that is structural and systemic. This reading summarizes Young's view of oppression as multidimensional in nature.*

I have proposed an enabling conception of justice. Justice should refer not only to distribution, but also to the institutional conditions necessary for the development and exercise of individual capacities and collective communication and cooperation. Under this conception of justice, injustice refers primarily to two forms of disabling constraints, oppression and domination. While these constraints include distributive patterns, they also involve matters which cannot easily be assimilated to the logic of distribution: decisionmaking procedures, division of labor, and culture.

Many people in the United States would not choose the term "oppression" to name injustice in our society. For contemporary emancipatory social movements, on the other hand—socialists, radical feminists, American Indian activists, Black activists, gay and lesbian activists—oppression is a central category of political discourse. Entering the political discourse in which oppression is a central category involves adopting a general mode of analyzing and evaluating social structures and practices which is incommensurate with the language of liberal individualism that dominates political discourse in the United States.

*Source:* Young, Iris Marion. 1990. "Five Faces of Oppression." Pp. 39–65 in *Justice and the Politics of Difference*. Princeton, NJ: Princeton University Press. Used by permission of Princeton University Press.

The concept of oppression has been current among radicals since the 1960s partly in reaction to Marxist attempts to reduce the injustices of racism and sexism, for example, to the effects of class domination or bourgeois ideology. Racism, sexism, ageism, homophobia, some social movements asserted, are distinct forms of oppression with their own dynamics apart from the dynamics of class, even though they may interact with class oppression. From often heated discussions among socialists, feminists, and antiracism activists in the last ten years a consensus is emerging that many different groups must be said to be oppressed in our society, and that no single form of oppression can be assigned causal or moral primacy (see Gottlieb, 1987). The same discussion has also led to the recognition that group differences cut across individual lives in a multiplicity of ways that can entail privilege and oppression for the same person in different respects. Only a plural explication of the concept of oppression can adequately capture these insights.

Accordingly, I offer below an explication of five faces of oppression as a useful set of categories and distinctions which I believe is comprehensive, in the sense that it covers all the groups said by new left social movements to be oppressed and all the ways they are oppressed. I derive the five faces of oppression from reflection on the condition of these groups. Because different factors, or combinations of factors, constitute the oppression of different groups, making their oppression irreducible, I believe it is not possible to give one essential definition of oppression. The five categories articulated in this chapter, however, are adequate to describe the oppression of any group, as well as its similarities with and differences from the oppression of other groups. . . .

## The Faces of Oppression

### Exploitation

The central function of Marx's theory of exploitation is to explain how class structure can exist in the absence of legally and normatively sanctioned class distinctions. In precapitalist societies domination is overt and accomplished through directly political means. In both slave society and feudal society the right to appropriate the product of the labor of others partly defines class privilege, and these societies legitimate class distinctions with ideologies of natural superiority and inferiority.

Capitalist society, on the other hand, removes traditional juridically enforced class distinctions and promotes a belief in the legal freedom of persons. Workers freely contract with employers and receive a wage; no formal mechanisms of law or custom force them to work for that employer or any employer. Thus the mystery of capitalism arises: when everyone is formally free, how can there be class domination? Why do class distinctions persist between the wealthy, who own the means of production, and the mass of people, who work for them? The theory of exploitation answers this question. . . .

The central insight expressed in the concept of exploitation, then, is that this oppression occurs through a steady process of the transfer of the results of the labor of one social group to benefit another. The injustice of class division does not consist only in the distributive fact that some people have great wealth while most people have little (cf. Buchanan 1982:44–49; Holmstrom 1977). Exploitation enacts a structural relation between social groups. Social rules about what work is, who does what for whom, how work is compensated, and the social process by which the results of work are appropriated operate to enact relations of power and inequality. These relations are produced and reproduced through a systematic process in which the energies of the have-nots are continuously expended to maintain and augment the power, status, and wealth of the haves.

Many writers have cogently argued that the Marxist concept of exploitation is too narrow to encompass all forms of domination and oppression (Giddens 1981:242; Brittan and Maynard 1984:93; Murphy 1985; Bowles and Gintis 1986:20–24). In particular, the Marxist concept of class leaves important phenomena of sexual and racial oppression unexplained. Does this mean that sexual and racial oppression are nonexploitative, and that we should reserve wholly distinct categories for these oppressions? Or can the concept of exploitation be broadened to include other ways in which the labor and energy expenditure of one group benefits another, and reproduces a relation of domination between them?

Feminists have had little difficulty showing that women's oppression consists partly in a systematic and unreciprocated transfer of powers from women to men. Women's oppression consists not merely in an inequality of status, power, and wealth resulting fom men's excluding them from privileged activities. The freedom, power, status, and self-realization of men is possible precisely because women work for them. Gender exploitation has two aspects, transfer of the fruits of material labor to men and transfer of nurturing and sexual energies to men.

Christine Delphy (1984), for example, describes marriage as a class relation in which women's labor benefits men without comparable remuneration. She makes it clear that the exploitation consists not in the sort of work that women do in the home, for this might include various kinds of tasks, but in the fact that they perform tasks for someone on whom they are dependent. Thus, for example, in most systems of agricultural production in the world, men take to market the goods women have produced, and more often than not men receive the status and often the entire income from this labor. . . .

Most feminist theories of gender exploitation have concentrated on the institutional structure of the patriarchal family. Recently, however, feminists have begun to explore relations of gender exploitation enacted in the contemporary workplace and through the state. Carol Brown argues that as men have removed themselves from responsibility for children, many women have become dependent on the state for subsistence as they continue to bear nearly total responsibility for childrearing (Brown 1981; cf. Boris and Bardaglio 1983; A. Ferguson 1984). This creates a new system of the exploitation of women's domestic labor mediated by state institutions, which she calls public patriarchy.

In twentieth-century capitalist economies the workplaces that women have been entering in increasing numbers serve as another important site of gender exploitation. David Alexander (1987) argues that typically feminine jobs involve gender-based tasks requiring sexual labor, nurturing, caring for others' bodies, or smoothing over workplace tensions. In these ways women's energies are expended in jobs that enhance the status of, please, or comfort others, usually men; and these gender-based labors of waitresses, clerical workers, nurses, and other caretakers often go unnoticed and undercompensated.

To summarize, women are exploited in the Marxist sense to the degree that they are wage workers. Some have argued that women's domestic labor also represents a form of capitalist class exploitation insofar as it is labor covered by the wages a family receives. As a group, however, women undergo specific forms of gender exploitation in which their energies and power are expended, often unnoticed and unacknowledged, usually to benefit men by releasing them for more important and creative work, enhancing their status or the environment around them, or providing them with sexual or emotional service.

Race is a structure of oppression at least as basic as class or gender. Are there, then, racially specific forms of exploitation? There is no doubt that racialized groups in the United States, especially Blacks and Latinos, are oppressed through capitalist superexploitation resulting from a segmented labor market that tends to reserve skilled, high-paying, unionized jobs for whites. There is wide disagreement about whether such superexploitation benefits whites as a group or only benefits the capitalist class (see Reich 1981), and I do not intend to enter into that dispute here.

However one answers the question about capitalist superexploitation of racialized groups, is it possible to conceptualize a form of exploitation that is racially specific on analogy with the gender-specific forms just discussed? I suggest that the category of *menial* labor might supply a means for such conceptualization. In its derivation "menial" designates the labor of servants. Wherever there is racism, there is the assumption more or less enforced, that members of the oppressed racial groups are or ought to be servants of those, or some of those, in the privileged group. In most white racist societies this means that many white people have dark- or yellow-skinned domestic servants, and in the United States today there remains significant racial structuring of private household service. But in the United States today much service labor has gone public: anyone who goes to a good hotel or a good restaurant can have servants. Servants often attend the daily—and nightly—activities of business executives, government officials, and other high-status professionals. In our society there remains strong cultural pressure to fill servant jobs—bellhop, porter, chambermaid, busboy, and so on—with Black and Latino workers. These jobs entail a transfer of energies whereby the servers enhance the status of the served. . . .

## Marginalization

Increasingly in the United States racial oppression occurs in the form of marginalization rather than exploitation. Marginals are people the system of labor cannot or will not use. Not only in Third World capitalist countries, but also in most Western capitalist societies, there is a growing underclass of people permanently confined to lives of social marginality, most of whom are racially marked—Blacks or Indians in Latin America, and Blacks, East Indians, Eastern Europeans, or North Africans in Europe.

Marginalization is by no means the fate only of racially marked groups, however. In the United States a shamefully large proportion of the population is marginal: old people, and increasingly people who are not very old but get laid off from their jobs and cannot find new work; young people, especially Black or Latino, who cannot find first or second jobs; many single mothers and their children; other people involuntarily unemployed; many mentally and physically disabled people; American Indians, especially those on reservations.

Marginalization is perhaps the most dangerous form of oppression. A whole category of people is expelled from useful participation in social life and thus potentially subjected to severe material deprivation and even extermination. The material deprivation marginalization often causes is certainly unjust, especially in a society where others have plenty. Contemporary advanced capitalist societies have in principle acknowledged the injustice of material deprivation caused by marginalization, and have taken some steps to address it by providing welfare payments and services. The continuance of this welfare state is by no means assured, and in most welfare state societies, especially the United States, welfare redistributions do not eliminate large-scale suffering and deprivation.

Material deprivation, which can be addressed by redistributive social policies, is not, however, the extent of the harm caused by marginalization. Two categories of injustice beyond distribution are associated with marginality in advanced capitalist societies. First, the provision of welfare itself produces new injustice by depriving those dependent on it of rights and freedoms that others have. Second, even when material deprivation is somewhat mitigated by the welfare state, marginalization is unjust because it blocks the opportunity to exercise capacities in socially defined and recognized ways. . . .

Today the exclusion of dependent persons from equal citizenship rights is only barely hidden beneath the surface. Because they depend on bureaucratic institutions for support or services, the old, the poor, and the mentally or physically disabled are subject to patronizing, punitive, demeaning, and arbitrary treatment by the policies and people associated with welfare bureaucracies. Being a dependent in our society implies being legitimately subject to the often arbitrary and invasive authority of social service providers and other public and private administrators, who enforce rules with which the marginal must comply, and otherwise exercise power over the conditions of then lives. In meeting needs of the marginalized, often with the aid of social scientific disciplines, welfare agencies also construct the needs themselves. Medical and social service professionals know what is good for those they serve, and the marginals and dependents themselves do not have the right to claim to know what is good for them (Fraser 1987a; K. Ferguson 1984, chap. 4). Dependency in our society thus implies, as it has in all liberal societies, a sufficient warrant to suspend basic rights to privacy, respect, and individual choice.

Although dependency produces conditions of injustice in our society, dependency in itself need not be oppressive. One cannot imagine a society in which some people would not need to be dependent on others at least some of the time: children, sick people, women recovering from childbirth, old people who have become frail, depressed or otherwise emotionally needy persons, have the moral right to depend on others for subsistence and support. . . .

Marginalization does not cease to be oppressive when one has shelter and food. Many old people, for example, have sufficient means to live comfortably but remain oppressed in their marginal status. Even if marginals were provided a comfortable material life within institutions that respected their freedom and dignity, injustices of marginality would remain in the form of uselessness, boredom, and lack of self-respect. Most of our society's productive and recognized activities take place in contexts of organized social cooperation, and social structures and processes that close persons out of participation in such social cooperation are unjust. Thus while marginalization definitely entails serious issues of distributive justice, it also involves the deprivation of cultural, practical, and institutionalized conditions for exercising capacities in a context of recognition and interaction.

The fact of marginalization raises basic structural issues of justice, in particular concerning the appropriateness of a connection between participation in productive activities of social cooperation, on the one hand, and access to the means of consumption, on the other. As marginalization is increasing, with no sign of abatement, some social policy analysts have introduced the idea of a "social wage" as a guaranteed socially provided income not tied to the wage system. Restructuring of productive activity to address a right of participation, however, implies organizing some socially productive activity outside of the wage system (see Offe 1985:95–100), through public works or self-employed collectives.

## Powerlessness

As I have indicated, the Marxist idea of class is important because it helps reveal the structure of exploitation: that some people have their power and wealth because they profit from the labor of others. For this reason I reject the claim some make that a traditional class exploitation model fails to capture the structure of contemporary society. It remains the case that the labor of most people in the society augments the power of relatively few. Despite their differences from nonprofessional workers, most professional workers are still not members of the capitalist class. Professional labor either involves exploitative transfers to capitalists or supplies important conditions for such transfers. Professional workers are in an ambiguous class position, it is true, because they also benefit from the exploitation of nonprofessional workers.

While it is false to claim that a division between capitalist and working classes no longer describes our society, it is also false to say that class relations have remained unaltered since the nineteenth century. An adequate conception of oppression cannot ignore the experience of social division reflected in the colloquial distinction between the "middle class" and the "working class," a division structured by the social division of labor between professionals and nonprofessionals. Professionals are privileged in relation to nonprofessionals, by virtue of their position in the division of labor and the status it carries. Nonprofessionals suffer a form of oppression in addition to exploitation, which I call powerlessness.

In the United States, as in other advanced capitalist countries, most workplaces are not organized democratically, direct participation in public policy decisions is rare, and policy implementation is for the most part hierarchical, imposing rules on bureaucrats and citizens. Thus most people in these societies do not regularly participate in making decisions that affect the conditions of their lives and actions, and in this sense most people lack significant power. At the same time, domination in modern society is enacted through the widely dispersed powers of many agents mediating the decisions of others. To that extent many people have some power in relation to others, even though they lack the power to decide policies or results. The powerless are those who lack authority or power even in this mediated sense, those over whom power is exercised without their exercising it; the powerless are situated so that they must take orders and rarely have the right to give them. Powerlessness also designates a position in the division of labor and the concomitant social position that allows persons little opportunity to develop and exercise skills. The powerless have little or no work autonomy, exercise little creativity or judgment in their work, have no technical expertise or authority, express themselves awkwardly, especially in public or bureaucratic settings, and do not command respect. Powerlessness names the oppressive situations Sennett and Cobb (1972) describe in their famous study of working-class men.

This powerless status is perhaps best described negatively: the powerless lack the authority, status, and sense of self that professionals tend to have. The status privilege of professionals has three aspects, the lack of which produces oppression for nonprofessionals.

First, acquiring and practicing a profession has an expansive, progressive character. Being professional usually requires a college education and the acquisition of a specialized knowledge that entails working with symbols and concepts. Professionals experience progress first in acquiring the expertise, and then in the course of professional advancement and rise in status. The life of the nonprofessional by comparison is powerless in the sense that it lacks this orientation toward the progressive development of capacities and avenues for recognition.

Second, while many professionals have supervisors and cannot directly influence many decisions or the actions of many people, most nevertheless have considerable day-to-day work autonomy. Professionals usually have some authority over others, moreover—either over workers they supervise, or over auxiliaries, or over clients. Nonprofessionals, on the other hand, lack autonomy, and in both their working and their consumer-client lives often stand under the authority of professionals. . . .

Thus, third, the privileges of the professional extend beyond the workplace to a whole way of life. I call this way of life "respectability." To treat people with respect is to be prepared to listen to what they have to say or to do what they request because they have some authority, expertise, or influence. The norms of respectability in our society are associated specifically with professional culture. Professional dress, speech, tastes, demeanor, all connote respectability. Generally professionals expect and receive respect from others. In restaurants, banks, hotels, real estate offices, and many other such public places, as well as in the media, professionals typically receive more respectful treatment than nonprofessionals. For this reason nonprofessionals seeking a loan or a job, or to buy a house or a car, will often try to look "professional" and "respectable" in those settings.

The privilege of this professional respectability appears starkly in the dynamics of racism and sexism. In daily interchange women and men of color must prove their respectability. At first they are often not treated by strangers with respectful distance or deference. Once people discover that this woman or that Puerto Rican man is a college teacher or a business executive, however, they often behave more respectfully toward her or him. Working-class white men, on the other hand, are often treated with respect until their working-class status is revealed. . . .

## Cultural Imperialism

Exploitation, marginalization, and powerlessness all refer to relations of power and oppression that occur by virtue of the social division of labor—who works for whom, who does not work, and how the content of work defines one institutional position relative to others. These three categories refer to structural and institutional relations that delimit people's material lives, including but not restricted to the resources they have access to and the concrete opportunities they have or do not have to develop and exercise their capacities. These kinds of oppression are a matter of concrete power in relation to others—of who benefits from whom, and who is dispensable.

Recent theorists of movements of group liberation, notably feminist and Black liberation theorists, have also given prominence to a rather different form of oppression, which following Lugones and Spelman (1983) I shall call cultural imperialism. To experience cultural imperialism means to experience how the dominant meanings of a society render the particular perspective of one's own group invisible at the same time as they stereotype one's group and mark it out as the Other.

Cultural imperialism involves the universalization of a dominant group's experience and culture, and its establishment as the norm. Some groups have exclusive or primary access to what Nancy Fraser (1987b) calls the means of interpretation and communication in a society. As a consequence, the dominant cultural products of the society, that is, those most widely disseminated, express the experience, values, goals, and achievements of these groups. Often without noticing they do so, the dominant groups project their own experience as representative of humanity as such. Cultural products also express the dominant group's perspective on and interpretation of events and elements in the society, including other groups in the society, insofar as they attain cultural status at all.

An encounter with other groups, however, can challenge the dominant group's claim to universality. The dominant group reinforces its position by bringing the other groups under the measure of its dominant norms. Consequently, the difference of women from men, American Indians or Africans from Europeans, Jews from Christians, homosexuals from heterosexuals, workers from professionals, becomes reconstructed largely as deviance and inferiority. Since only the dominant group's cultural expressions receive wide dissemination, their cultural expressions become the normal, or the universal, and thereby the unremarkable. Given the normality of its own cultural expressions and identity, the dominant group constructs the differences which some groups exhibit as lack and negation. These groups become marked as Other.

The culturally dominated undergo a paradoxical oppression, in that they are both marked out by stereotypes and at the same time rendered invisible. As remarkable, deviant beings, the culturally imperialized are stamped with an essence. The stereotypes confine them to a nature which is often attached in some way to their bodies, and which thus cannot easily be denied. These stereotypes so permeate the society that they are not noticed as contestable. Just as everyone knows that the earth goes around the sun, so everyone knows that gay people are promiscuous, that Indians are alcoholics, and that women are good with children. White males, on the other hand, insofar as they escape group marking, can be individuals.

Those living under cultural imperialism find themselves defined from the outside, positioned, placed, by a network of dominant meanings they experience as arising from elsewhere, from those with whom they do not identify and who do not identify with them. Consequently, the dominant culture's stereotyped and inferiorized images of the group must be internalized by group members at least to the extent that they are forced to react to behavior of others influenced by those images. This creates for the culturally oppressed the experience that W.E.B. Du Bois called "double consciousness"—"this sense of always looking at one's self through the eyes of others, of measuring one's soul by the tape of a world that looks on in amused contempt and pity" (Du Bois 1969 [1903]:45). Double consciousness arises when the oppressed subject refuses to coincide with these devalued, objectified, stereotyped visions of herself or himself. While the subject desires recognition as human, capable of activity, full of hope and possibility, she receives from the dominant culture only the judgment that she is different, marked, or inferior.

The group defined by the dominant culture as deviant, as a stereotyped Other, is culturally different from the dominant group, because the status of Otherness creates specific experiences not shared by the dominant group, and because culturally oppressed groups also are often socially segregated and occupy specific positions in the social division of labor. Members of such groups express their specific group experiences and interpretations of the world to one another, developing and perpetuating their own culture. Double consciousness, then, occurs because one finds one's being defined by two cultures; a dominant and a subordinate culture. Because they can affirm and recognize one another as sharing similar experiences and perspectives on social life, people in culturally imperialized groups can often maintain a sense of positive subjectivity.

Cultural imperialism involves the paradox of experiencing oneself as invisible at the same time that one is marked out as different. The invisibility comes about when dominant groups fail to recognize the perspective embodied in their cultural expressions as a perspective. These dominant cultural expressions often simply have little place for the experience of other groups, at most only mentioning or referring to them in stereotyped or marginalized ways. This, then, is the injustice of cultural imperialism: that the oppressed group's own experience and interpretation of social life finds little expression that touches the dominant culture, while that same culture imposes on the oppressed group its experience and interpretation of social life. . . .

## Violence

Finally, many groups suffer the oppression of systematic violence. Members of some groups live with the knowledge that they must fear random, unprovoked attacks on their persons or property, which have no motive but to damage, humiliate, or destroy the person. In American society women, Blacks, Asians, Arabs, gay men, and lesbians live under such threats of violence, and in at least some regions Jews, Puerto Ricans, Chicanos, and other Spanish-speaking Americans must fear such violence as well. Physical violence against these groups is shockingly frequent. Rape Crisis Center networks estimate that more than one-third of all American women experience an attempted or successful sexual assault in their lifetimes. Manning Marable (1984:238–41) catalogues a large number of incidents of racist violence and terror against blacks in the United States between 1980 and 1982. He cites dozens of incidents of the severe beating, killing, or rape of Blacks by police officers on duty, in which the police involved were acquitted of any wrongdoing. In 1981, moreover, there were at least five hundred documented cases of random white teenage violence against Blacks. Violence against gay men and lesbians is not only common, but has been increasing in the last five years. While the frequency of physical attack on members of these and other racially or sexually marked groups is very disturbing, I also include in this category less severe incidents of harrassment, intimidation, or ridicule simply for the purpose of degrading, humiliating, or stigmatizing group members.

Given the frequency of such violence in our society, why are theories of justice usually silent about it? I think the reason is that theorists do not typically take such incidents of violence and harassment as matters of social injustice. No moral theorist would deny that such acts are very wrong. But unless all immoralities are injustices, they might wonder, why should such acts be interpreted as symptoms of social injustice? Acts of violence or petty harrassment are committed by particular individuals, often extremists, deviants, or the mentally unsound. How then can they be said to involve the sorts of institutional issues I have said are properly the subject of justice?

What makes violence a face of oppression is less the particular acts themselves, though these are often utterly horrible, than the social context surrounding them, which makes them possible and even acceptable. What makes violence a phenomenon of social injustice, and not merely an individual moral wrong, is its systemic character, its existence as a social practice.

Violence is systemic because it is directed at members of a group simply because they are members of that group. Any woman, for example, has a reason to fear rape. Regardless of what a Black man has done to escape the oppressions of marginality or powerlessness, he lives knowing he is subject to attack or harrassment. The oppression of violence consists not only in direct victimization, but in the daily knowledge shared by all members of oppressed groups that they are *liable* to violation, solely on account of their group identity. Just living under such a threat of attack on oneself or family or friends deprives the oppressed of freedom and dignity, and needlessly expends their energy.

Violence is a social practice. It is a social given that everyone knows happens and will happen again. It is always at the horizon of social imagination, even for those who do not perpetrate it. According to the prevailing social logic, some circumstances make such violence more "called for" than others. The idea of rape will occur to many men who pick up a hitch-hiking woman; the idea of hounding or teasing a gay man on their dorm floor will occur to many straight male college students. Often several persons inflict the violence together, especially in all-male groupings. Sometimes violators set out looking for people to beat up, rape, or taunt. This rule-bound, social, and often premeditated character makes violence against groups a social practice.

Group violence approaches legitimacy, moreover, in the sense that it is tolerated. Often third parties find it unsurprising because it happens frequently and lies as a constant possibility at the horizon of the social imagination. Even when they are caught, those who perpetrate acts of group-directed violence or harrassment often receive light or no punishment. To that extent society renders their acts acceptable.

An important aspect of random, systemic violence is its irrationality. Xenophobic violence differs from the violence of states or ruling-class repression. Repressive violence has a rational, albeit evil, motive: rulers use it as a coercive tool to maintain their power. Many accounts of racist, sexist, or homophobic violence attempt to explain its motivation as a desire to maintain group privilege or domination. I do not doubt that fear of violence often functions to keep oppressed groups subordinate, but I do not think xenophobic violence is rationally motivated in the way that, for example, violence against strikers is.

On the contrary, the violation of rape, beating, killing, and harrassment of women, people of color, gays, and other marked groups is motivated by fear or hatred of those groups. Sometimes the motive may be a simple will to power, to victimize those marked as vulnerable by the very social fact that they are subject to violence. If so, this motive is secondary in the sense that it depends on a social practice of group violence. Violence-causing fear or hatred of the other at least partly involves insecurities on the part of the violators; its irrationality suggests that unconscious processes are at work. . . .

Cultural imperialism, moreover, itself intersects with violence. The culturally imperialized may reject the dominant meanings and attempt to assert their own subjectivity, or the fact of their cultural difference may put the lie to the dominant culture's implicit claim to universality. The dissonance generated by such a challenge to the hegemonic cultural meanings can also be a source of irrational violence.

Violence is a form of injustice that a distributive understanding of justice seems ill equipped to capture. This may be why contemporary discussions of justice rarely mention it. I have argued that group-directed violence is institutionalized and systemic. To the degree that institutions and social practices encourage, tolerate, or enable the perpetration of violence against members of specific groups, those institutions and practices are unjust and should be reformed. Such reform may require the redistribution of resources or positions, but in large part can come only through a change in cultural images, stereotypes, and the mundane reproduction of relations of dominance and aversion in the gestures of everyday life.

## APPLYING THE CRITERIA

Social theories that construct oppression as a unified phenomenon usually either leave out groups that even the theorists think are oppressed, or leave out important ways in which groups are oppressed. Black liberation theorists and feminist theorists have argued persuasively, for example, that Marxism's reduction of all oppressions to class oppression leaves out much about the specific oppression of Blacks and women. By pluralizing the category of oppression in the way explained in this chapter, social theory can avoid the exclusive and oversimplifying effects of such reductionism.

I have avoided pluralizing the category in the way some others have done, by constructing an account of separate systems of oppression for each oppressed group: racism, sexism, classism, heterosexism, ageism, and so on. There is a double problem with considering each group's oppression a unified and distinct structure or system. On the one hand, this way of conceiving oppression fails to accommodate the similarities and overlaps in the oppressions of different groups. On the other hand, it falsely represents the situation of all group members as the same.

I have arrived at the five faces of oppression— exploitation, marginalization, powerlessness, cultural imperialism, and violence—as the best way to avoid such exclusions and reductions. They function as criteria for determining whether individuals and groups are oppressed, rather than as a full theory of oppression. I believe that these criteria are objective. They provide a means of refuting some people's belief that their group is oppressed when it is not, as well as a means of persuading others that a group is oppressed when they doubt it. Each criterion can be operationalized; each can be applied through the assessment of observable behavior, status relationships, distributions, texts and other cultural artifacts. I have no illusions that such assessments can be value-neutral. But these criteria can nevertheless serve as means of evaluating claims that a group is oppressed, or adjudicating disputes about whether or how a group is oppressed.

The presence of any of these five conditions is sufficient for calling a group oppressed. But different group oppressions exhibit different combinations of these forms, as do different individuals in the groups. Nearly all, if not all, groups said by contemporary social movements to be oppressed suffer cultural imperialism. The other oppressions they experience vary. Working-class people are exploited and powerless, for example, but if employed and white do not experience marginalization and violence. Gay men, on the other hand, are not qua gay exploited or powerless, but they experience severe cultural imperialism and violence. Similarly, Jews and Arabs as groups are victims of cultural imperialism and violence, though many members of these groups also suffer exploitation or powerlessness. Old people are oppressed by marginalization and cultural imperialism, and this is also true of physically and mentally disabled people. As a group women are subject to gender-based exploitation, powerlessness, cultural imperialism, and violence. Racism in the United States condemns many Blacks and Latinos to marginalization, and puts many more at risk, even though many members of these groups escape that condition; members of these groups often suffer all five forms of oppression.

Applying these five criteria to the situation of groups makes it possible to compare oppressions without reducing them to a common essence or claiming that one is more fundamental than another. One can compare the ways in which a particular form of oppression appears in different groups. For example, while the operations of cultural imperialism are often experienced in similar fashion by different groups, there are also important differences. One can compare the combinations of oppressions groups experience, or the intensity of those oppressions.

## DISCUSSION QUESTIONS

1. Why does Young argue that a simple definition of *oppression* is not enough? Why are particular groups oppressed in the way they are?
2. List the five faces of oppression and provide unique examples of each one from any of the earlier readings in this volume. Are there any causal connections among the five forms of oppression?

# 52

# RAGE OF THE PRIVILEGED

ELLIS COSE

*In the previous reading by Iris Marion Young, "The Five Faces of Oppression," Young illustrates a multidimensional view of oppression that enhances our understanding of how power and privilege are manifested in social structures. This classic reading by Ellis Cose elucidates another aspect of oppression: the impact it has on individuals and their daily lives. This excerpt, "Rage of the Privileged," is based on his book* <u>The Rage of a Privileged Class</u> *(1993). Cose argues that raced individuals face "a dozen demons," or twelve factors that continually remind them that they are not quite good enough. While Cose's line of reasoning focuses on black professionals, his claims can be applied to any racial-ethnic or minority group.*

*Though they struggle to hold their anger in check, even the most successful blacks find themselves haunted by racial demons. . . .*

I was studying rage, I told my host, an eminently successful corporate lawyer. Specifically, I was looking into the anger of middle-class blacks—into why people who seemingly had so much to celebrate were filled with resentment and rage. "Well, I can tell you why I'm angry," he began, launching into a long tale about his compensation package. Despite the millions he had brought into

the firm the year before, his partners were balking at giving him his due. "They want you to do well, but not that well," he grumbled. The more he talked, the more agitated he became. What I had originally thought would be a five-minute conversation stretched on for nearly an hour as this normally restrained and unfailingly gracious man vented long-buried feelings.

Much more was on his mind than the fact that his partners were still "fumbling with my compensation." One source of immense resentment was an encounter of a few days previous, when he had arrived at the office earlier than usual and entered the

*Source:* Cose, Ellis. "Rage of the Privileged." *Newsweek.* November 15, 1993. Copyright © 1993 by Ellis Cose. Reprinted by permission of Don Congdon Associates, Inc.

elevator along with a young white man. They got off at the same floor. No secretaries or receptionists were yet in place. As my friend turned toward the locked outer office doors, his elevator mate blocked his way and asked. "May I help you?" My friend shook his head and attempted to circle around his would-be helper, but the young man stepped in front of him and demanded in a loud and decidedly colder tone, "May I help you?" At this, the older man fixed him with a stare, spat out his name, and identified himself as a partner, whereupon his inquisitor quickly stepped aside.

My friend's initial impulse was to put the incident behind him. Yet he had found himself growing angrier and angrier at the young associate's temerity. After all, he had been dressed much better than the associate. His clients paid the younger man's salary. The only thing that could have conceivably stirred the associate's suspicions was race: "Because of his color, he felt he had the right to check me out."

He paused in his narration and shook his head. "Here I am, a black man who has done all the things I was supposed to do," he said, and proceeded to tick off precisely what he had done: gone to Harvard, labored for years to make his mark in an elite law firm, married a highly motivated woman who herself had an advanced degree and a lucrative career. He and his wife were in the process of raising three exemplary children. Yet he was far from fulfilled.

"Had I been given a fair shot, who knows where I would be?" he sighed. Moreover, despite his own clear achievements, he was concerned for his children. With so many black men in jail or beaten down by society, whom would his daughters marry? With prejudice still such a force, who could ensure their success? As for himself, he said, he had come to terms with reality. He no longer expected praise, honor, or acceptance from his white colleagues, or from the white world at large. "Just make sure my money is at the top of the line. I can go to my own people for acceptance."

I was certain he did not mean what he said. If acceptance was not important to him, the perceived lack of it would not have caused him such pain. I was certain as well that his distress was not atypical. Again and again, as I spoke with blacks who have

every accouterment of success, I heard a plaintive declaration—always followed by various versions of an unchanging and urgently put question. "I have done everything I was supposed to do. I have stayed out of trouble with the law, gone to the right schools, and worked myself nearly to death. What more do they want? Why in God's name won't they accept me as a full human being? Why am I pigeonholed in a 'black job'? Why am I constantly treated as if I were a drug addict, a thief, or a thug? Why am I still not allowed to aspire to the same things every white person in America takes as a birthright? Why, when I most want to be seen, am I suddenly rendered invisible?"

That well-to-do blacks should have any gripes at all undoubtedly strikes many as strange. The Civil Rights revolution, after all, not only killed Jim Crow but brought blacks more money, more latitude, and more access to power than enjoyed by any previous generation of African Americans. Some blacks in this new era of opportunity have amassed fortunes that would put Croesus to shame. If ever there was a time to celebrate the achievements of the color-blind society, now should be that time.

Yet, instead of celebrating, much of America's black privileged class claims to be in excruciating pain. Donald McHenry, former U.S. permanent representative to the United Nations, told me that though he felt no sense of estrangement himself, he witnessed it often in other blacks who had done exceptionally well: "It's sort of the in talk, the in joke, within the club, an acknowledgment of and not an acceptance . . . of the effect of race on one's life, on where one lives, on the kinds of jobs that one has available." Dorothy Gilliam, a columnist for *The Washington Post*, expressed a similar thought in much stronger terms. "You feel the rage people [of] your group . . . just being the dogs of society."

Ulric Haynes, dean of the Hofstra University School of Business and a former corporate executive who served as President Carter's ambassador to Algeria, has given up hope that racial parity will arrive this—or even in the next—millennium. "During our lifetimes, my children's lifetimes, my grandchildren's lifetimes, I expect that race will . . . matter. And perhaps race will always matter, given the historical circumstances under which we came to this country." That makes Haynes angry. "Not for myself. I'm over the hill," he says, "I'm angry for the deception that this [racial prejudice] has perpetrated on my children and grandchildren." Though his children have traveled the world and received an elite education, they "in a very real sense are not the children of privilege. They are dysfunctional, because I didn't prepare them, in all the years we lived overseas, to deal with the climate of racism they are encountering right now."

Even many Americans who acknowledge Haynes' distress will be disinclined to care. For one thing, few Americans of any color are as well-fixed as Haynes. For another, the problems of the black middle class pale by comparison with those of the underclass. Yet, formidable as the difficulties of the so-called underclass are, the nation cannot afford to use the plight of the poor as an excuse for blinding itself to the difficulties of the black upwardly mobile. For though the problems of the two classes are not altogether the same, they are in some respects linked. And one must at least consider the possibility that a nation which embitters those struggling hardest to believe in it and work within its established systems is seriously undermining any effort to provide would-be hustlers and dope dealers with an attractive alternative to the streets.

Why would people who have enjoyed all the fruits of the civil rights revolution—who have Ivy League educations, high-paying jobs, and comfortable homes—be consumed with angers? To answer that question is to go a long way toward explaining why quotas and affirmative action remain such polarizing issues; why black and white Americans continue to see race in such starkly different terms; and why solving America's racial problems is infinitely more complicated than cleaning up the nation's urban ghettos and educating the inhabitants—even assuming the will, wisdom, and resources to accomplish such a task.

It is to understand, among other things, what a black financial manager feels upon being told that a client is uncomfortable with his handling an account, or what a black professor goes through upon being asked whether she is really qualified to teach. For many black professionals, these are not so much isolated incidents as insistent and galling reminders that whatever they may accomplish in life, race remains their most salient feature as far as much of America is concerned.

## The Dozen Demons

What is it exactly that blacks spend so much time coping with? For lack of a better phrase, let's call them the dozen demons. This is not to say that they affect blacks only, or that there are only twelve, or that all black Americans encounter every one. Still, you're not likely to find a bet more certain than this: that any random gathering of black American professionals, asked what ails them, will eventually end up describing, in one guise or another, the following items.

1. *Inability to fit in*: During the mid 1980s, I had lunch in the Harvard Club in Manhattan with a newsroom recruiter from *The New York Times*. The lunch was primarily social, but my companion was also seeking help in identifying black, Hispanic, and Asian American journalists he could lure to the *Times*.

As we talked, it became clear that he was focusing on such things as speech, manners, dress, and educational pedigree. He had in mind, apparently, a certain button-down sort, an intellectual, nonthreatening, quiet-spoken type—something of a cross between William F. Buckley Jr. and Bill Cosby. Someone who might be expected to have his own membership at the Harvard or Yale Club. That most Whites at the *Times* fit no such stereotype seemed not to have occurred to him. I suggested, rather gingerly, that perhaps he needed to expand his definition of a "*Times* person."

Even as I made the argument. I knew that it was unpersuasive. Not because he disagreed—he did not offer much of a rebuttal—but because he and many similarly placed executives almost instinctively screened minority candidates according to criteria they did not apply to whites. The practice has nothing to do with malice. It stems more from an unexamined assumption that whites, purely because they are white, are likely to fit in, while blacks and other minority group members are not.

2. *Lack of respect*: Ron Brown, a psychologist and specialist in interracial relations, notes that black professionals—like the corporate lawyer cited above—constantly have to prove they are worthy of respect. He recalls being in a car with a black general and several other blacks near a military base in Biloxi, Mississippi. As they approached the gates to the base, the general said. "Don't worry," and flashed his two-star badge. The guard replied, "No sir," and demanded to see some identification. "And you could just tell from the back he [the general] was rocking with rage . . . These little incidents boil over [into fury] where you should feel . . . pride."

Knowing that race can undermine status, African Americans frequently take aggressive countermeasures in order to avoid embarrassment. One woman, a Harvard-educated lawyer, carries a Bally bag when going to certain exclusive shops. Like a sorceress warding off evil with a wand, she holds the bag in front of her to rebuff racial assumptions, in the hope that the clerk will take it as proof that she is fit to enter.

3. *Low expectations*: Shortly after I was appointed editorial board chairman of the *New York Daily News*, I was visited by a black employee who had worked at the paper for some time. More was on his mind than a simple desire to make my acquaintance. He had also come to talk about how his career was blocked, how the deck was stacked against him—how, in fact, it was stacked against any black person who worked there. His frustration and anger I easily understood. But what struck me as well was that his expectations left him absolutely no room to grow. He believed so strongly that the white men at the *Daily News* were out to stymie black achievement that he had no option but failure, whatever the reality of the situation.

Even those who refuse to internalize the expectation of failure are often left with nagging doubts, with a feeling, as journalist Joseph Boyce puts it, "that no matter what you do in life, there are very few venues in which you can really be sure that you've exhausted your potential. Your achievement is defined by your color and its limitation. And even if in reality you've met your fullest potential, there's an aggravating, lingering doubt . . . because you're never sure. And that makes you angry."

4. *Shattered hopes*: Of the executives sociologist Sharon Collins met while doing her research, one black senior manager stood out. He was such a corporate politician, she recalls that he could "hardly say anything without putting it in terms of what's good for the company." Yet, as he neared the end of an illustrious career, he had noticed that colleagues were passing him by; and he had reluctantly concluded that racial discrimination was the only explanation that made sense. That realization left him profoundly disillusioned. "He knows the final threshold is there, and he's losing hope that he can cross it," says Collins.

An associate in a prominent law firm experienced a similar disappointment after two years of trying desperately to succeed. The lawyer is Mexican American, but insists his experience was also typical of the firm's black associates—none of whom ever got a shot at any big assignments. This discontent, he makes plain, was felt by all the nonwhite lawyers. He remembers one in particular, a black woman who graduated with honors from Yale. All her peers thought she was headed for the stars. Yet when associates were ranked by the firm, she was never included in the first tier but at the top of the second.

If he had been alone in his frustration, he says, one could reject his complaint as no more than a case of sour grapes. "But the fact that all of us were having the same kinds of feelings" means something more systemic was at work. He acknowledges that many whites had similar feelings. That in the intensely competitive environment of a top law firm, no one is guaranteed an easy time. But the sense of abandonment, he contends, was exacerbated for nonwhites. He finally quit in disgust and became a public defender. By his count, every minority group member who entered the firm with him ended up leaving, having concluded that nonwhites—barring the spectacularly odd exception—were not destined to make it in that world.

5. *Faint praise*: For a year and a half during the early 1980s, I was a resident fellow at the National Research Council—National Academy of Sciences, an august Washington institution that evaluates scientific research. One afternoon, I mentioned to a white colleague who was also a close friend that it was a shame the NRC had so few blacks on staff. She replied, "Yes, it's too bad there aren't more blacks like you."

I was stunned enough by her comment to ask her what she meant. She answered, in effect, that there were so few really intelligent blacks around who could meet the standards of the NRC. I, of course, was a wonderful exception. Her words, I'm sure, were meant as a compliment, but they angered me, for I took her meaning to be that blacks (present company excluded) simply didn't have the intellect to hang out with the likes of her.

6. *Coping fatigue*: When Armetta Parker took a job as a public relations professional at a large manufacturing company, she assumed that she was on her way to big-time corporate success. A bright, energetic woman then in her early thirties, Parker had left a good position at a public utility in Detroit to get on the Fortune 100 fast track.

Corporate headquarters was in a town of nearly forty thousand people, but only a few hundred black families lived there, and she met virtually no black singles her own age. Though she expected a certain amount of social isolation, "I didn't expect to get the opportunity to take a really hard look at me, at what was important to me and what wasn't." She had to face the fact that success, in that kind of corporate environment, meant a great deal of work and no social life, and that it also required a great deal of faith in people who found it difficult to recognize competence in blacks.

Nonetheless, Parker did extremely well, at least initially. Her first year at the company, she made it into "The Book"—the firm's roster of those who had been identified as people on the fast track. But eventually she realized that "I was never going to be vice president of public affairs [at that company]." Moreover, "even if they gave it to me, I didn't want it. The price was too high." Part of that

price would have been accepting the fact that her race was not seen as an asset but as something she had to overcome.

After six years she left. A large portion of her ambition for a corporate career had vanished. She had realized that "good corporate jobs can be corporate handcuffs. You have to decide how high of a price you're willing to pay." Dave Johnson, a former IBM executive who retired last year after 29 years of service, agrees. "Corporate America's culture will force you to retire real quick," he says. Johnson now runs his own consulting business in Baltimore and spends much of his time helping younger black managers cope with corporate frustrations.

7. *Pigeonholing*: Once upon a time one would never have thought of appointing a black city editor, a big-city newspaper executive told me. Now one could not think of not seriously considering and even favoring a black person for the job.

The executive was making several points. One was about himself and his fellow editors, about how they had matured to the extent that they valued all managerial talent—even in blacks. He was also acknowledging that blacks had become so central to the city's political, economic, and social life that a black city editor had definite advantages, strictly as a function of race. His third point, I'm sure, was wholly unintended but clearly implied: that it was still possible, even for the most enlightened management, to classify jobs by color. And logic dictates that if certain managerial tasks are best handled by blacks, others are best left to whites.

What this logic has meant in terms of the larger corporate world is that black executives have landed, out of all proportion to their numbers, in community relations and public affairs, or in slots where their only relevant expertise concerns blacks and other minorities.

8. *Identity troubles*: The man was on the verge of retiring from his position as personnel vice president for one of America's largest companies. He had acquired the requisite symbols of success: a huge office, a generous compensation package, a summer home away from home. But he had paid a price. He

had decided along the way, he said matter-of-factly, that he could no longer afford to be black.

I was so surprised by the man's statement that I sat silent for several seconds before asking him to explain. Clearly he had done nothing to alter his dark brown complexion. What he had altered, he told me, was the way he allowed himself to be perceived. Early in his career, he had been moderately outspoken about what he saw as racism within and outside his former corporation. He had learned, however, that his modest attempts at advocacy got him typecast as an undesirable. So when he changed jobs, he decided to disassociate himself from any hint of a racial agenda. The strategy had clearly furthered his career, even though other blacks in the company labeled him an Uncle Tom. He was aware of his reputation, and pained by what the others thought, but he had seen no other way to thrive. He noted as well, with evident pride, that he had not abandoned his race. He had quietly made it his business to cultivate a few young blacks in the corporation and bring their careers along; and he could point to some who were doing very well and would have been doing considerably worse without his intervention. His achievements brought him enough pleasure to balance out the distress of not being "black."

**9. *Self-censorship and silence*:** Many blacks find their voices stilled when sensitive racial issues are raised. They are painfully aware, as New York politician Basil Paterson puts it, that "whites don't want you to be angry."

A big-city police officer once shared with me his frustration at waiting nineteen years to make detective. In those days before affirmative action, he had watched, one year after another, as less qualified whites were promoted over him. Each year he had swallowed his disappointment, twisted his face into a smile, and congratulated his white friends as he hid his rage—so determined was he to avoid being categorized as a race-obsessed troublemaker.

He had endured other affronts in silence, including a vicious beating by a group of white cops while carrying out a plainclothes assignment. As an undercover officer working within a militant black organization, he had been given a code word to whisper to a fellow officer if the need arose. When he was being brutalized, he had screamed out the word and discovered it to be worthless. His injuries required surgery and more than thirty stitches. When he was asked by his superior to identify those who had beat him, he feigned ignorance; it seems a fellow officer had preceded his commander and bluntly passed along the message that it was safer to keep quiet.

Even though he made detective years ago, and even though, on the side (and on his own time), he managed to become a successful businessman and an exemplary member of the upwardly striving middle class, he says the anger still simmers within him. He worries that someday it will come pouring out, that some luckless white person will tick him off and he will explode, with tragic results. Knowing him, I don't believe he will ever reach that point. But I accept his fear that he could blow up as a measure of the intensity of his feelings, and of the terrible cost of having to hold them in.

**10. *Mendacity*:** Even more damaging than self-imposed silence are the lies that seem an integral part of America's approach to race. Many of the lies are simple self-deception, as when corporate executives claim their companies are utterly color-blind. Some stem from unwillingness to acknowledge racial bias, as when people who have no intention of voting for a candidate of another race tell pollsters that they will. And many are lies of business, social, or political convenience, as was the case with Massachusetts Senator Edward Brooke in the early 1970s.

At the time, Brooke was the highest-ranking black politician in America. His name was routinely trotted out as a vice presidential possibility, though everyone involved knew the exercise was a farce. According to received wisdom, America was not ready to accept a black on the ticket, but Brooke's name seemed to appear on virtually everyone's list. During one such period of vice presidential hype, I interviewed Brooke for a newspaper profile. After asking the standard questions, I could no longer contain my curiosity. Wasn't he tired, I asked, of the charade of having his name bandied about when no one intended to select him? He nodded wearily and said yes, he was.

To me, his response spoke volumes, probably much more than he'd intended. But I took it as his agreement that lies of political convenience are not merely a nuisance for those interested in the truth but a source of profound disgust and cynicism for those on whose behalf the lies are supposedly told.

11. *Collective guilt*: Political scientist James Q. Wilson has argued that the "best way to reduce racism . . . is to reduce the black crime rate." There is much wrong with that way of thinking, but probably the most pernicious is that it makes hard-working, honest black people responsible for the acts of unregenerate crooks—which is not very different from defining the entire race by the behavior of its criminal class.

Law-abiding blacks generally find such presumptions galling and point out that well-behaved whites rarely have to answer for the sins of white criminals. Until white middle-class people accept responsibility for "poor white trash," says Ulric Haynes, "I'm not willing to accept the burden of my black brethren who behave outrageously . . . although I am concerned. And I will demonstrate my concern." Yet, rejecting the "burden" of (or blame for) misbehaving blacks is not always an option.

In the mid 1980s, I was unceremoniously tossed out of Cafe Royale, a restaurant that catered to yuppies in San Francisco, on the orders of a maitre d' who apparently took me for someone who had caused trouble on a previous occasion. I sued the restaurant and eventually collected a few thousand dollars from its insurance company. But that seemed cold consolation for the humiliation of being dismissed by an exalted waiter who would not suffer the inconvenience of distinguishing one black person from another.

12. *Exclusion from the Club*: Many African Americans who have made huge efforts to get the right education, master the right accent, and dress in the proper clothes still find that certain doors never seem to open, that there are private clubs—in both a real and a symbolic sense—they cannot join.

In 1990, in testimony before the U.S. Senate Judiciary Committee, Darwin Davis, senior vice president of the Equitable Life Assurance Society, told of the frustrations he and some of his black friends had experienced in trying to join a country club. "I have openly approached fellow executives about memberships. Several times, they have said, 'My club has openings: it should be no problem. I'll get back to you.' Generally one of two things happens. They are too embarrassed to talk to me or they come right out and tell me they were shocked when they made inquiries about bringing in a black. Some have even said they were told to get out of the club if they didn't like the situation as it is."

Two years after his testimony, Davis told me his obsession with private clubs sprang in part from concerns about his children. Several years before, he had visited a club as a guest and happened to chance upon a white executive he knew. As they were talking, he noticed the man wave at someone on the practice range. It turned out that he had brought his son down to take a lesson from the club pro. Davis was suddenly struck by a depressing thought. "Damn!" he said to himself. "This is being perpetrated all over again . . . I have a son the same age as his. And when my son grows up he's going to go through the same crap I'm going through if I don't do something about this. His son is learning how to . . . socialize, get lessons, and do business at a country club." His own son (who is now an Equitable agent), Davis concluded, would "never ever be able to have the same advantages or even an equal footing."

## THE ROAD FROM HERE

When the lawyer fuming over his compensation package declares that he will "go to my own people for acceptance," he is not only expressing solidarity with other members of his race, he is also conceding defeat. He is saying that he is giving up hope that many of his white colleagues will ever see him as one of them. His white peers would, of course, be shocked to discover that he finds his workplace a hostile environment and that he feels a need to protect himself from them emotionally. What, they would wonder, can be his problem?

Administrators watching black students huddled together on many college campuses often ask essentially the same question: Why can't they join "the mainstream"? Whites often take such behavior as a manifestation of irrational antiwhite prejudice. But in most cases, it is perhaps better understood as a retreat from a "mainstream" many blacks have come to feel is an irredeemably unwelcoming place. Some people would say that blacks who feel that way are flat-out wrong, that for African Americans who are willing to meet whites halfway, race no longer has to matter, at least not all that much.

Yet pretending (or convincing ourselves) that race no longer matters (or wouldn't if minorities stopped demanding special treatment) is not quite the same as making it not matter. Creating a color-blind society on a foundation saturated with racism requires something more than simply proclaiming that the age of brotherhood has arrived. Somehow, as America went from a country concerned about denial of civil rights to one obsessed with "reverse racism" and "quotas" that discriminate against white males, some important steps were missed. Among other things, we neglected as a nation to make any serious attempt to understand why, if racial conditions were improving so much, legions of those who should be celebrating were instead singing the blues.

In many respects, that is not at all remarkable. For the United States clearly has more pressing problems than the complaints of affluent blacks unwilling to accept a few race-related inconveniences. And don't whites have problems too? Don't struggling whites—even if they are male—deserve a little sympathy? Isn't there an inequality of compassion here? Life is rough for a lot of people, not all of whom are black. So why, given the advantages at least some African Americans conspicuously enjoy, should whites feel any consternation (much less, guilt) whatsoever?

To an increasing number of whites, that question seems less and less outrageous. And that may not be entirely bad. It would probably be healthier for all concerned if the current dialogue about racial justice focused much less on issues of guilt and victimization. Making someone feel sorry for you, after all, is somewhat different from getting them to recognize you as an equal—or even as a human being. At best, pity provides a foundation for charity, or for what is perceived as charity—for which one is expected to be appropriately grateful, even if what is offered is not what one needs or feels one deserves.

It may very well be that the civil rights debate has been so distorted by strategies designed to engender guilt that many whites, as a form of self-defense, have come to define any act of decency toward blacks as an act of expiation. If an end to such strategies—and indeed an end to white guilt—would result in a more intelligent dialogue, I, for one, am all for wiping the slate clean. Let us decide, from here on out, that no one need feel guilty about the sins of the past. The problem is certainly not that people do not feel guilty enough; it is that so many are in denial. And though denial may be a great way to avoid an unpleasant reality, avoidance is not a good substitute for changing that reality. Nor, more to the point, will it do much to narrow the huge chasm that separates so many blacks and whites.

The racial gap will never be completely closed—not as long as blacks and whites in America live fundamentally different lives. But we can nonetheless take our hands away from our eyes and recognize, at the very least, that exhorting blacks to escape the ghetto then psychologically battering those who succeed is a sure prescription for bitterness. Honest dialogue may not be a solution. But it is certainly preferable to censorship that passes for civility.

## DISCUSSION QUESTIONS

1. According to Cose, how are we to understand the anger of middle-class African Americans? That is to say, how can intersectionality and other theories of oppression help us understand the contradictory positionality of being both privileged and oppressed simultaneously?
2. Cose's "dozen demons" are critical lenses through which to understand the effects of oppression and discrimination in the United States. Given the diversity of readings we have encountered in the anthology so far, apply some of the "demons" to others' experiences.

# 53

# RACIAL PROFILING AND IMMIGRATION LAW ENFORCEMENT

## Rounding Up of Usual Suspects in the Latino Community

MARY ROMERO

*In this reading on power and privilege, sociologist Mary Romero encourages us to examine another type of abuse of power in the racial profiling and civil rights violations of Mexicans and Mexican Americans. Similar to Michelle Alexander's analysis of mass incarceration in Reading 46, Romero analyzes structural policies practiced within law enforcement that discriminate. Romero, professor of sociology in the School of Justice and Social Inquiry at Arizona State University, utilizes a case study approach of an immigration raid in 1997 to investigate what functions immigration raids serve to maintain and reinforce subordinated status among working-class Latino citizens and immigrants. This reading was originally published in the journal* Critical Sociology *in 2006.*

*"Where are you from?"*

*I didn't answer. I wasn't sure who the agent, a woman, was addressing.*

*She repeated the question in Spanish, "¿De dónde eres?"*

*Without thinking, I almost answered her question—in Spanish. A reflex. I caught myself in midsentence and stuttered in a non-language. "¿Dónde naciste?" she asked again . . . .*

*Source:* "Racial Profiling and Immigration Law Enforcement: Rounding Up of Usual Suspects in the Latino Community," by Mary Romero, 2006. *Critical Sociology, 32*, pp. 447–473. Copyright 2006 by Sage Publications, UK. Reprinted with permission.

*She was browner than I was. I might have asked her the same question . . . . "Are you sure you were born in Las Cruces?" she asked again.*

*I turned around and smiled, "Yes, I'm sure." She didn't smile back. She and her driver sat there for a while and watched me as I continued walking . . . .*

*"Sons of bitches," I whispered, "pretty soon I'll have to carry a passport in my own neighborhood." . . . .It was like a video I played over and over—memorizing the images . . . . "Are you sure you were born in Las Cruces?" ringing in my ears. (Sáenz 1992:xii)*

The personal and community cost of racial profiling to Mexican Americans who are treated as outside the law does not appear in official criminal justice statistics. Benjamin Alire Sáenz captured the racial-affront experience when Immigration and Naturalization Service (INS) agents use racial profiling; he emphasized the irony when Mexican American INS agents interrogate other Mexican Americans about their citizenship. Citizenship appears embodied in skin color (that is, brown skin absent a police or border patrol uniform) serving as an indicator of illegal status. Carrying a bodily "figurative border" (Chang 1999), "Mexican-ness" becomes the basis for suspecting criminality under immigration law. Mexican Americans and other racialized Latino citizens[1] and legal residents are subjected to insults, questions, unnecessary stops, and searches. Surveillance of citizenship, relentless in low-income and racialized neighborhoods along the border and in urban barrios, increases the likelihood of discrimination in employment, housing, and education. Latinos (particularly dark complected, poor, and working class) are at risk before the law. The following article uses a case study approach to identify the use of racial profiling in immigration law enforcement; and to document the impact on US citizens and legal residents . . . .

## THE CASE OF THE CHANDLER ROUNDUP

INS data provide statistics on the number of individuals apprehended but the agency does not collect data on the number of individuals stopped and searched who were citizens or legal residents. Consequently, the impact of racialized immigration law enforcement on communities of color is rarely visible in legal reporting procedures. However, every once in a while, community protests against raids gain sufficient media attention to require public officials to respond by conducting investigations into allegations of law-enforcement wrongdoings. In these rare instances it becomes possible to uncover "more covert, hidden forms of discrimination" (Georges-Abeyie 2001:xiv) in the documentation by law-enforcement and public officials responding to allegations of civil-rights or human rights violations. Formal investigations reveal the groups and communities targeted and the ways that public and private space is regulated under the auspices of immigration law enforcement. These institutional practices are "relations of ruling" and unravel the everyday management of social control and domination (Smith 1990, 1999).

In order to identify micro- and macro- aggressions and petit apartheid accomplished by immigration raids, I analyzed data from two official investigations into a five-day immigration raid in Chandler, Arizona. The raid was the third of its kind conducted by the Chandler Police during the summer of 1997 (Fletcher 1997). The immigration sweep came to be known as the "Chandler Roundup," reinforcing both the cowboy legacy of law enforcement in Mexican American communities and the notion that Mexicans are "strays." On July 27, 1997, the Chandler Police Department and Border Patrol agents from Casa Grande Station and the Tucson area began a five-day immigration raid as a joint operation in the most highly populated Latino section of the city. Over the five days, 432 suspected undocumented Mexicans were arrested . . . .

Immigrant advocates and Mexican American residents in Chandler began organizing and held several community meetings with the police chief, Chandler City Council members, and the State Attorney General's staff. As a consequence of the public outcry, the investigations and lawsuits that followed produced government documentation of law-enforcement practices that detail the use of micro- and macro-aggressions toward Mexican Americans and other Latinos racially profiled as criminal, unauthorized, or extralegal. The primary focus of the investigations was police misconduct and violation of civil rights. A secondary issue concerned the role of local police departments participating in joint operations with the INS.

The State Attorney General's office immediately responded to complaints and began collecting eyewitness accounts from individuals willing to be interviewed. The Office of the Attorney General Grant Woods issued a report, *Results of the Chandler Survey*, in December 1997. Data collected and analyzed in the report included: minutes of meetings with the Latino community in Chandler, interviews with citizens and legal residents stopped during the five-day operation, minutes of City Council Meetings with community members, newspaper articles, memoranda between city officials, review of Chandler Police radio dispatch audio tapes, police field notes, and witness testimonies. The Attorney General's report is organized into the following sections: background information,[2] summary of the survey,[3] summary of the Commission on Civil Rights Report, and an evaluation of claims of civil-rights violation and recommendations.

The following summer, the City of Chandler paid for an independent investigation (Breen et al. 1998). The final product was the three-volume report. Volume I, *Report of Independent Investigation Into July 1997 Joint Operation Between Border Patrol and Chandler Police Department*, includes a mission statement, narrative,[4] and summaries of interviews conducted with public officials.[5] . . .

This study is an analysis of the official reports. While these data were obtained from legal documents constructed within a specific political, social, and economic context, the variety of documents produced presents diverse perspectives, including interested community members, citizens and legal residents stopped and searched, police officers participating in the raid, and City Council members. Clearly, the data analyzed do not include a complete profile of all the stops that were made during the five-day operation. However, the two reports provide a rare insight into strategically planned immigration law enforcement targeting low-income areas highly populated by Mexican Americans.

*Complainants* (Volume II of the *Report of Independent Investigation*) contained the following data: a profile of the type of individuals stopped and searched, activities by these individuals that warranted "reasonable suspicion," the type of documents these individuals are expected to carry, and the outcomes of stops . . . .

Narratives are also an important source of data for identifying micro- and macro-aggressions and petit apartheid restricting citizenship rights, freedom of movement, and use of public and private urban space. Two types of narratives were coded. First, the narrative of the reports itself. This included setting up the story of the Chandler Roundup (what is the context selected as background information to the raid?), an explanation of Mexican immigration requiring a joint operation between the Chandler Police Department and the INS (how is the problem defined?), and the justification for using racial profiling (why were low-income Mexican Americans stopped and searched?). The second type of narrative appears in the Attorney General's Report. These are summaries of witness accounts and detailed descriptions of incidents documented by the police in their radio-dispatch reports . . . .

My analysis focuses first on identifying the distinct differences in each report for explaining the occurrence of a Joint Operation between the Chandler Police and the INS. I begin with the *Report of Independent Investigation's* narration of Mexican immigration as a problem requiring the immediate attention of the Chandler Police. Next, I contrast this with the community's depiction of Mexican immigration as a problem constructed by the Chandler City Council's urban-renewal project, Operation Restoration. I then turn to a quantitative analysis of data from the complaints complied in Volume II of the *Report of Independent Investigation*. A qualitative analysis of witness accounts from the Attorney General's Report follows. Here, I analyze the ways that citizenship is policed and the impact this form of policing has on freedom of movement and use of urban space.

## NARRATING MEXICAN IMMIGRATION AS A PROBLEM

Considering that the USA acquired Arizona as a result of the Mexican-American War, and that the Chandler area is the homeland of the Tohono O'Odham Nation, the version of history narrated in the *Report of Independent Investigation*'s (Breen et al. 1998:1) is clearly biased and self serving: "Chandler, Arizona is a city of about 160,000 that has blossomed in slightly more than a century from a seed planted by Alexander Chandler, who came to Arizona in 1887 as territorial veterinary surgeon." The first mention of Mexicans in the narrative describes their presence as workers and Anglos as employers:

> In the first years after the town's founding, cotton became the crop of choice for central Arizona farmers. These were the years of the Mexican Revolution, and thousands of Mexicans streamed northward to escape the violence spawned by it. Labor-intensive cotton farming provided a way for those fleeing the revolution to earn a living. Thus began a marriage between Chandler and those of Hispanic heritage that has lasted till the present day. (Breen et al. 1998:1)

This seeming "marriage" involved Mexicans providing the labor and Americans (read whites) providing the land from which the cotton was to be harvested. Mexican presence is also noted during WWII in reference to the Bracero Program: "the Arizona Farm Bureau approved the importation of Mexican workers, who found themselves harvesting cotton alongside German prisoners of war in the labor-starved market" (Breen et al. 1998:2).

The narrative continues by describing the "streams" that turn into the present "hordes" of Mexican immigrants entering the area. "Ron Sanders, chief patrol agent for the Border Patrol's Tucson sector, calls Chandler 'the most notorious hub for alien smuggling in the United States of America'"... until "literally thousands" of illegal aliens were in Chandler (Breen et al. 1998:2). INS intelligence in Dallas is the source for citing Chandler "as a major smuggling area as far south as Honduras and El Salvador" (Breen et al. 1998:2). The narrative continues with a litany from a handful of growers who complained about garbage, use of water, stolen fruit, and violence. To reinforce immigration as a social problem, the report lists six "homicides allegedly committed by illegal aliens" dating back to 1982 (Breen et al. 1998:10). In 1997, the Casa Grande Border Patrol station began targeting operations in groves. According to the Chandler Police, complaints about harassment of citizens and an increase in crime led to a series of joint actions in the summer of 1997. No doubt the federal government's Operations Gatekeeper, Hold-the-Line, and other steps in militarizing the USA–Mexico border, gave local authorities in Chandler tacit approval to engage in the Joint Operation.

However, the Attorney General's *Survey* argues that another chain of events led up to the Joint Operation. Based on community protests voiced at meetings and interviews given to the media, the beginning of the "immigration problem" is not dated to the founding of the city but rather to the City of Chandler's 1995 urban-renewal project, Operation Restoration. City Council members began Operation Restoration by creating a task force to study issues affecting residents. The Neighborhood Empowerment Team conducted several mail-in surveys and held neighborhood meetings. Their final report found that residents were concerned about broken streetlights, uncollected garbage, trash in the streets, and unkempt alleys. From its inception, Operation Restoration targeted four older neighborhoods in the city located next to the newly developed downtown area. The targeted areas had the highest percentage of Latinos and low-income residents in the City. Claiming the Joint Operation was about redevelopment, City

Council member Martin Sepulveda argued that the Mayor's dream of transforming Chandler into "'The jewel of the East Valley' would push out poor Hispanics" (Office of the Attorney General 1997:5). Operation Restoration was perceived by the Mexican American community as urban renewal to create high-income real estate and zoning for strip malls, which would dislocate residents and raise land value beyond the reaches of local businesses.

In response to the community's accusation that the immigration sweep was a Mexican American removal program, the *Report* stated that the Chandler Police involvement was merely "to undertake intensive zoning code enforcement and . . . step up patrol of the area" (Breen et al. 1998:14). Although the independent investigators acknowledged that the Neighborhood Empowerment Team's report was limited to repairing and cleaning the surrounding area, they accepted the police department's claim that the Joint Operation with the INS was conducted as their part in implementing Operation Restoration. Since Operation Restoration had already targeted "the downtown redevelopment zone, ranging from an eight-block to a four square mile area," using similar parameters for the roundup was justified and did not discriminate against Latinos . . . .

## POLICING CITIZENSHIP, MOVEMENT, AND THE USE OF URBAN SPACE

The policing of citizenship by the Chandler Roundup exemplifies procedures used to determine status and urban spaces that require regulation. The focus on policing was the redevelopment area targeted under Operation Restoration: that is, the cultural space inhabited by the large Latino population, low-income residents, and a commercial area serving a Spanish-speaking clientele. However, the image of citizenship visible in the discretionary stops suggests that beyond geography, the landscape of suspicion was embodied in particular behavior and appearance. Complaints made against the Chandler Police make visible the type of persons suspected as unauthorized and thus requiring surveillance. Requests for various types of identification reveal surveillance and restraint of

movement in public areas. Embedded in witness accounts are the aesthetics of authority that enforce exclusionary use of public urban space, remaking the Mexican cultural space into white space. The material consequences of policing reinforce the vulnerability of undocumented workers in the local economy; place low-income, racialized citizens at risk before the law; and legitimate discriminatory behavior toward persons under surveillance.

### Complainants Analysis

Analysis of the data in the 91 complaints indicates specific patterns of racial and ethnic typing used in the Joint Operation. Data show that cultural and class behavior or activity was only monitored in targeted locations. The dominant feature of identifiable complainants was their racial ethnic background; all were of Mexican ancestry or Latino.[6] Fourteen of the complainants were stopped more than once during the five-day raid. Complainants ranged in age from 16 to 75; 49 were male and 22 were female. The majority of males were between 18 and 39 years old and the majority of females were between the ages of 30 and 49. Complaints for 42 complainants contained the following information: 11 were US citizens of Mexican ancestry, 15 were Latino legal residents, 1 was a permanent resident, 3 had work permits, 1 had a green card, and 11 were undocumented. There is no documentation in the reports or in the newspaper coverage of a white person stopped during the raid. Ironically, one newspaper quoted a blond, blue-eyed, undocumented Irish immigrant employed at a local law firm as stating that she had never been asked to show proof of her citizenship status: "I don't have to worry. I blend in very well" (Amparano 1997:A1).

The phrase "driving while black" became familiar in debates over racial profiling, similarly the experience of "walking/driving/biking/standing while brown" is common for Mexican Americans in the vicinity of an immigration raid or during national sweeps, such as Operation Wetback in 1954 (Calavita 1992) or Operation Jobs in 1995 (US Attorney General Report 1995). The activities recorded in the complaints are accurately captured in the media's initial reporting of Mexican Americans' experience during the five-day immigration raid: "As they walked down sidewalks, drove cars or walked outside their homes" they are stopped by the police (Amparano 1997). Based primarily on interviews with police officers assigned to the target area during the operation (few Border Patrol agents agreed to be interviewed), the independent investigators found that illegal aliens were arrested in residential areas, in front of stores (especially the local Circle K), in trailer courts, and driving between 4:00 and 6:00 AM (the time many workers are traveling to construction sites during the summer).

The wide net that was cast made it inevitable that citizens and legal residents would be stopped by the police. The complaints indicate that, when proof of citizenship status was requested by law-enforcement agents, 33 of the 91 were driving, 24 were walking in their neighborhood or to a nearby store, 17 were at home, 10 were shopping (most were approached in the parking lot or in front of stores), 3 were riding bikes, and 2 were using public telephones. Significantly, only 2 were approached at their place of employment, suggesting the tacit desire to protect employers from possible sanctions. Specific activities are significant when class-based racial profiling is occurring. As in most urban areas, being a pedestrian is a sign of poverty. Middle and upper classes rarely walk or bike in Arizona heat unless they are engaged in exercise and dressed in special "work-out" clothes. They might be observed walking if a leashed dog is attached to their bodies. Using a public telephone is a similar sign of poverty when most homes in the US have several phones as well as cell phones.

After the stops were made, investigators documented only 33 outcomes for the 91 incidents. Of the 33 outcomes documented in the complaints, 23 were detained. Three of the people detained were illegal and twenty were legal. Four of those detained were handcuffed, including one US citizen. The period that the 23 were detained ranged from five minutes to four hours. Some of those detained for long periods of time reported that they stood in the 100+ degree weather common in July. After they showed proof of legal status, three complainants were issued citations for minor traffic violations (e.g., a rolling stop at a stop sign, a broken windshield, a missing headlamp, or a turn into the wrong lane).

Eighty-six claims involved law enforcement agents requesting proof of citizenship status. However, the kinds of documents requested were inconsistent, at times vague, and confusing to US citizens who had never been stopped before— 51 incidents involved officers requesting to see the person's "papers" or *papeles,*" 2 incidents involved request for immigration papers, 13 incidents requested drivers' licenses, 9 were asked to show "an identification," 10 were asked specifically for their green cards, and 1 officer requested to see "a card." Birth certificates, Social Security cards, green cards, or drivers' licenses were produced by the claimants before the police allowed them to leave. In some cases, particularly for children and adolescents, family members assisted in obtaining documents.

## Witness Accounts Analysis

Based on the writings of immigration-critical race legal scholars (i.e., Benitiez 1994; Chang and Aoki 1997; Johnson 2000, 2004; Vargas 2001), I identified five patterns of immigration law enforcement that placed Mexican Americans at risk: (1) discretionary stops based on ethnicity and class; (2) use of intimidation to demean and subordinate persons stopped; (3) restricting the freedom of movement of Mexicans but not others in the same vicinity; (4) reinforced stereotypes of Mexican, as "alien," "foreign," inferiors and criminal; and (5) limited access to fair and impartial treatment before the law. Recurring expressions that witnesses used to describe stops and searches were pain and humiliation, frightened, fearful, nervous, scared, embarrassed, violated, and mortified. Witness accounts offer descriptive narratives of the micro- and macro-aggressions occurring in immigration law enforcement.

Embedded in all the accounts is the recognition that they were stopped, questioned, and inspected by the police because their physical appearance was classified by law enforcement agents as "Mexican" and, thus, they were assumed to be unauthorized to be in the US. Skin color is used in the everyday immigration law-enforcement practice of operationalizing "reasonable suspicion":

> T was stopped and questioned by Chandler police and INS/Border Patrol when he stopped at a Circle K.... The Chandler Police were stopping every "Mexican-looking" person as they entered or exited the store. "Non-Mexican-looking" people entered and exited without being stopped. (Office of Attorney General Wood 1997:22)

An excerpt from witness account "D" demonstrates community members' recognition of INS and police officers' "discretion," as well as their power to violate civil rights:

> All the people shopping at this shopping center appeared to be Hispanic and many were being stopped and questioned by the officers. D and his uncle were conversing in Spanish and leaving the store with a package when they were approached by a Chandler police officer and an INS/Border Patrol agent on bicycles. The INS/Border Patrol agent asked them in Spanish for their papers. The uncle, who had just become a United States citizen, had his citizenship papers with him and showed those to the officer. D had only a Social Security card and a driver's license . . . D took his wallet from his pocket to get his identification; the INS/Border Patrol officer then asked him for the wallet and examined everything in it. D feared that if he did not give the officers his wallet he would be arrested. Neither officer wrote any information down or kept anything from the wallet. No explanation was given for the stop (Office of Attorney General Wood 1997:21).

Although "D" is a US citizen, he understood that he does not have the same rights as whites and has limited access to fair dealings before the law. He was intimidated by the INS officer extending the citizenship inspection beyond his driver's license and Social Security card and into his personal belongings without a search warrant or a basis for probable cause.

"U" provided a description of an incident involving a person who questioned stops without probable cause and police discretion.

> U has a permit to work in the United States and is here legally . . . he and his cousin stopped at a Circle K . . . While they were parking their car, they were approached by a Chandler police officer on a bicycle who asked, in Spanish, for their papers. The cousin said that the police had no right to ask for papers and the Chandler police officer asked if they wanted him to call Immigration. They said yes and INS/Border patrol agents soon appeared. The cousin showed the agents his papers but U did not have his on him and when he showed them his Social Security card, there was a discrepancy in the computer and they were told the number had been canceled. The INS/Border Patrol agent said "I'm tired of this, everybody lies and says they have papers when they don't." The officers put U in handcuffs, searched him and took him to the Chandler Police Station where he was detained. He asked them to give him a chance to call his home and have his wife bring his papers but they refused. He was held until about 11:30 (from 7 p.m.) until his cousin and his wife brought his papers to the police station. U was afraid that the Chandler police were going to take his green card away, or that he was going to be separated from his family (Office of Attorney General Wood 1997:23).

"U" assumed protection and rights that his work permit grants and distinguished between city police officers and the INS. However, his attempt to assert his rights resulted in the use of excessive force and he was treated like a violent criminal requiring physical restraint. His account points to extensive discretionary power given to immigration law enforcement; the incident exemplifies intimidation, excessive force, and the lack of probable cause in the police stop.

Since the downtown redevelopment zone targeted in the roundup was not completely racially segregated, discretionary stops of persons of Mexican ancestry who appear to be poor or working class became visible. Public areas like stores, phone booths, and gas stations produced a spectacle for white gaze and allowed the immigration inspectors to employ stereotypes of Mexicans as foreign, alien, and criminal. However, appearances of class and citizenship can be deceiving, as the following witness testimony reveals.

C is the highest-ranked left-handed golfer in Arizona. C is a large, dark complected, Hispanic, and native-born Arizonan . . . Returning from a golf match in July, he stopped . . . for a cold drink and saw Chandler police officers talking to different people of apparent Mexican descent. At the time he was wearing an old tee shirt and a baseball cap. As he tried to exit the market, he was barred exit by a Chandler Police officer who asked if he was a local, if he had papers, and whether he was a citizen. C told the officer that he was a citizen and was leaving and the officer told him, "No, you are not." C then walked around the officer and went over to his car, which was a 1997 Acura. The officer followed him but when he saw what car he was driving, permitted him to drive off . . . . (Office of Attorney General Wood 1997:21)

Clearly "C" assumed "class privilege," challenging the officer's attempt to stop and search without probable cause. This account demonstrates the significance of class in immigration law enforcement. Once middle- and upper- middle-class status is identified by officers, police are less likely to violate civil rights.

In response to the extraordinary policing, community members avoided public areas. Witnesses reported that elderly neighbors feared the police, asking for assistance in obtaining food and medication so they could remain home, behind closed doors. Law enforcement agents' treatment of Mexicans thus deterred civic participation and shaped the field of action that Latinos perceived as available to them (Davis et al. 2001; Nelson 2001). By the fifth day of the operation, the community avoided local grocery stores and gas stations that had been heavily patrolled by the police and INS. Mexican shop owners complained that they lost revenue during the raid because their customers feared shopping in the area. In the absence of people in the streets and shopping areas, the police developed alternative strategies that included homes and construction sites.

Alongside stores with the largest number of Latino customers, the second major target areas were apartment complexes and trailer courts occupied by low-income Mexican Americans and Mexican immigrants. In a newspaper interview with a Chandler police officer, the claim was made that they did not bust "down doors in search of illegal immigrants." Witness accounts provide a counter narrative. Not only were neighborhoods in the targeted area searched house by house, but apartment and trailer court managers assisted Chandler Police by identifying residents of Mexican descent. The following testimony describes the intimidation and demeaning actions used by law enforcement agents.

On July 28, 1997, at approximately 11 P.M., B and his family were sound asleep in a trailer owned by his brother-in-law . . . The family was wakened by a loud banging on the front door and bright lights shining through the windows. When B looked around, he saw two Chandler police officers, with an INS/Border Patrol agent behind them. All officers were bicycle officers. The officers demanded to be allowed into the trailer and when B asked if they had the right to come in, he was told "We can do whatever we want, we are the Chandler Police Department. You have people who are here illegally." . . .

Home searches conducted in the presence of children serve as powerful socialization, teaching them about their lack of rights, inferior status, and unequal access to protection under the law. For many children, the house searches were probably their first encounter with a police officer, and they witnessed their parents, grandparents, and other family elders humiliated and treated as criminals. Witnessing stops and searches serves as an important lesson for children that the law distinguishes between family and neighbors on the basis of immigration status rather than criminal activity that harms others. Unlike stops made at shopping centers, house-to-house searches conducted on private property concealed civil and human rights violations from public view.

In addition to the house-to-house searches conducted, apartment complexes and trailer courts were also targeted for traffic enforcement. Several officers' interview summaries acknowledged that, outside of special D.U.I. enforcement, the Chandler Roundup was the first time they used traffic enforcement with a spotter. Vehicles leaving specific housing units that appeared to contain "migrant workers" were followed. Several officers reported that they "were to follow them and if probable cause was established" the vehicle was stopped. Officers were "instructed to issue a citation for the probable cause in case there was a question in reference to the stop." A summary of radio-dispatch transcripts for July 29, 1997, demonstrated that laborers driving to work were targeted as vehicles left apartment complexes housing low-income Mexican Americans and Mexican immigrants . . . .

## CONCLUSION

While legal scholars, civil rights advocates, and the general public denounced federal law enforcement practices toward Muslims and persons of Middle-Eastern descent under the Patriot Act, racialized immigration stops and searches, abuse, and harassment are ongoing processes honed over a century of citizenship inspections of Mexicans. Immigration policing is based on determining that citizenship is visibly inscribed on bodies in specific urban spaces rather than "probable cause." In the Chandler Roundup, official investigations found no evidence that stops and searches were based on probable cause of criminal activity. The conclusion drawn by the Attorney General's investigation underscores the harms of micro- and macro-aggressions and the use of petit apartheid:

> . . . there were no other warrants, charges, or holds for these individuals that in any way indicated other criminal activity or that required extraordinary security or physical force. The issue raised by this type of treatment is not whether the arrest and deportation is legal, but whether human beings are entitled to some measure of dignity and safety even when they are suspected of being in the United States illegally. (1997:28–9)

The Chandler Roundup fits into a larger pattern of immigration law-enforcement practices that produce harms of reduction and repression and place Mexican Americans at risk before the law and designate them as second-class citizens with inferior rights. Latino residents in Chandler experienced racial affronts targeted at their "Mexicanness" indicated by skin color, bilingual speaking abilities, or shopping in neighborhoods highly populated by Latinos. During immigration inspections, individuals stopped were demeaned, humiliated, and embarrassed. Stops and searches conducted without cause were intimidating and frightening, particularly when conducted with discretionary use of power and force by law enforcement agents.

Like other metropolitan areas surrounding Phoenix, Chandler depends heavily upon low-wage, non-union, undocumented Mexican workers for their tourism and construction industries. These powerful business interests are influential at the state level, and cooperative efforts are made to assure seasonal labor needs are met. Both official investigations into the Chandler Roundup demonstrate complete disregard for enforcing sanctions of employers under IRCA. Yet the ability to clearly identify the everyday work patterns of immigrants and to use these circumstances to arrest immigrants as undocumented workers indicate that employers operate with complete immunity to IRCA provisions. The case of the Chandler Roundup demonstrates how INS enforcement practices not only favor and protect employers' access to an exploitable labor force, but remove or relocate workers as specific industries' needs warrant. Enforcement is structured specifically at eliminating and relocating undocumented workers from areas no longer relevant to the local economy or redevelopment plans. The Chandler Roundup was intended to remove a low-income population to allow for urban renewal, by creating a hostile environment for citizens, violating their civil rights through immigration law enforcement employing micro- and macro-aggressions. Racialized immigration stops establish, maintain, and reinforce second-class citizenship and limit civil, political, economic, and cultural rights and opportunities. In urban barrios, the costly enterprise of selected stops and searches, race-related police abuse, and harassment results in deterring political participation, in identifying urban space racially, in classifying immigrants as deserving and undeserving by nationalities, and serves to drive a wedge dividing Latino neighborhoods on the basis of citizenship status.

## Discussion Questions

1. Why does Romero argue that police immigration raids such as the "Chandler Roundup" constitute racial profiling? What are the consequences to the community and the mundane activities of its inhabitants of such raids?
2. What are the conclusions Romero draws from data in the Chandler Survey about the Chandler Roundup by local police and Immigration and Naturalization Service (INS) agents about racial profiling and violations of basic citizen rights?

## Notes

1. Unlike the census categories, which make a distinction between race and ethnicity for the category "Hispanic," and restricting race to black and white, law enforcement clearly uses the ethnic descriptors of Mexican and Hispanic to identify an individual's physical characteristics. Therefore, this study makes a distinction between Latinos who can racially pass as white and those who are socially constructed (but nevertheless have real consequences) as racially distinct from whites or blacks (Romero 2001).

2. Background information is based on media coverage from local newspapers, community meetings, and the minutes from the Chandler City Council meeting.

3. The summary of the survey includes a detailed description of the Chandler Redevelopment Initiative developed by the City Council. The survey describes the Initiative's efforts and its connection to the joint operation carried out in areas with the highest concentration of Latino residents; INS protocols for joint operation; description of day-to-day activities based on Border Patrol documents; summary of witness accounts regarding children and schools, home contacts, and contacts around businesses, because these were areas that the police and public officials claimed were not included in the raid; and descriptions of the types of requests made for proof of citizenship.

4. The narrative offers a history of the City of Chandler and describes the development of immigration issues as a social problem that led to the joint operation. A description of the operation and the aftermath of community meetings, complaints, and lawsuits is also included.

5. Interviews were conducted with the police who participated in the joint operation, supervisors and officers involved with processing illegal aliens, Border Patrol agents, City Council members, and Chandler city officials.

6. Citizenship status is not recorded for 29 complainants (involved in 41 stops).

# 54

# THE MANY COSTS OF ANTI-ASIAN DISCRIMINATION

ROSALIND S. CHOU

JOE R. FEAGIN

*While Mary Romero's reading focused on discrimination against Latinos, this reading by Rosalind S. Chou and Joe R. Feagin analyzes discrimination against Asian Americans. Chou, a professor of sociology at Texas A&M University and the Samuel DuBois Cook Postdoctoral Fellow at Duke University, and Feagin, a graduate research professor of sociology at the University of Florida, conduct interviews with Asian Americans to determine some of the social and psychological costs of white hostility and discrimination. This reading, taken from their 2008 book, The Myth of the Model Minority: Asian Americans Facing Racism, challenges many arguments about assimilation and the achievement orientation of Asian Americans. The reality is that many Asian Americans report experiencing pressure from families and from the larger society to succeed, while at the same time experiencing internalized racial oppression.*

## RESPONDING TO EVERYDAY RACISM

In this society, model minority imagery is omnipresent and dangerous, especially because it forces unrealistic and unobtainable expectations on Asian Americans. As noted previously, in the 1960s white social scientists and journalists began to use the stereotyped concept and phrase "model minority" to accent the substantial educational and other achievements of Japanese Americans. Japanese Americans had been on the West Coast for two generations when during World War II white

*Source:* Chou, Rosalind S., and Joe R. Feagin. 2008. "The Many Costs of Anti-Asian Discrimination." Pp. 100–137 in *The Myth of the Model Minority: Asian Americans Facing Racism.* Boulder, CO: Paradigm Publishers. Used by permission of the publisher.

authorities forced them into U.S. concentration camps because of their racial characteristics. After that war, educational and job achievement became a major survival response to continuing discrimination. Young parents decided and hoped to protect their children from future discrimination by having them become model and conforming students and citizens who would not question white-imposed folkways . . . .

### Accenting Achievements and the "Back Story"

Indeed, a major Asian American collective memory exists in regard to identity construction and encompasses the "model minority" imagery. Because this imagery is stereotypical and relentless, it is highly stress-provoking and does not assist Asian Americans in dealing directly and effectively with persistent racial discrimination. Such model imagery serves mainly as spoken and unspoken behavior guidelines for how Asian Americans are supposed to think and act so as to please, or not displease, white Americans. It also provides a stereotype-riddled script for white Americans to follow in imaging, and interacting with, Asian Americans . . . .

Throughout their interviews our respondents reveal the great internal and external pressures associated with conformity to the model minority expectations and to related expectations in usually white-normed institutions. The internal forces include the specific roles that Asian Americans are expected to fill. Asian Americans growing up with these expectations usually work, at least in part, to fit the mold. For example, Asian American students struggle with not meeting these high expectations; they somehow feel inadequate if they are not outperforming most other students. Asians and non-Asians alike buy into this model framing and perpetuate racialized stereotypes, thereby creating external pressures. Family, friends, teachers, and strangers are named by respondents as those who expect the latter to think, act, and become a model minority person. Researchers have shown that such a strong stereotype will often influence a person to try to meet the expectation, whether that expectation is positive or negative.[1] All respondents noted at some point how model stereotypes have affected their daily lives . . . .

For example, Alice grew up as a Japanese American during and after World War II. She made a film about her family history, which began as a class project that exposed the suicide, substance abuse, and psychological damage resulting from internment during World War II. Like Tanaka, Alice discovered that not only were interned Nisei affected, but their children, the Sansei, were as well. Alice explains:

> I really was aware of this drug problem that was happening with all of these suicides, with all of these drugs that came out, and I happened to go to school with this [Japanese American] girl that became really well known for sending out a lot of messages that she's going to commit suicide. Because she tried like four or five times, and nobody paid attention to her. And then all of a sudden she became successful at it. So, that's what started the thought about, we talk about internment in terms of what it did to the Issei and Nisei. But what did that particular incident in history do as a legacy for generations? You know, you study psychology in college, and the way the Nisei operated after the war had a huge impact on how we operated in the world. Meaning okay, we were interned because we lacked the education, or there was something wrong with us. So we are going to make sure that our next generation has a perfect world that they go into. So expectations were really high. It was really high and it was really hard for Japanese Americans to live up to the standards.

Like other Japanese Americans, Alice accents the protective strategy that the Nisei used. Academic achievement was a shield protecting the next generation from mistreatment, but her research found that the pressures were great. The use of drugs and committing suicide were tragic mechanisms some used to deal with the impact of white oppression.

Such responses are not new for Asian Americans. Much earlier, from the mid-1800s to the early 1900s, some Chinese American workers became very depressed, turned to drugs, or committed suicide because of extreme discrimination and poor living conditions in California, where they had been brought in as contract workers to do hard labor for white employers.[2] Today, Chinese Americans still face much racial stereotyping and discrimination. Many white and other non-Asian Americans have extended the model minority image to anyone with an Asian face. Thereby, outside forces create substantial internalized pressures.

Charlene's family, which is Taiwanese American, has put great pressure on her to succeed. Charlene's parents have pushed her and her siblings hard to excel academically, with the hope that they will be able to secure the proverbial American dream:

> When my brother was five, there was this child psychologist that came to school and gave everyone an IQ test. And they discovered that my five-year-old brother was this genius, and then my mother was like, "Oh my gosh, I must train him in math and science." From that, it just opened up the doors to evils. And when my brother was in seventh grade, he was allowed to take the SAT . . . . So, I was in fourth grade at that time, and my mom was just like, "Well, you'll be [in] seventh grade in three years, you might as well study." And so, I was in fourth grade studying for the SATs until I was in seventh grade . . . .

The pressure for Charlene to excel was extreme even at this young age. Her family viewed her performance as affecting the whole family, and even the thought of disappointing them was very painful. In his career her father, . . . has faced job discrimination even though he is often more talented and educated than white coworkers who are better treated. Nonetheless, he has pressed his children to excel in the hope that somehow they will be treated better than he has been.

## Achievement Orientation:
## Adaptation to Racism or Asian Cultures?

In explaining this type of situation, scholarly and media commentators have frequently made the argument that Asian cultures are mainly responsible for these pressures to excel, because they supposedly value education more than U.S. culture does. There are numerous problems with this argument. First, it groups all Asian national cultures together. Yet these cultures vary significantly. Some of our respondents note that they come from agrarian Asian cultures where children are rarely pushed to excel in higher levels of education. Indeed, excelling academically in the United States has often alienated them from their agrarian family and cultural background. Second, assuming that people of Asian descent are culturally inclined to value education tends to be linked by whites to the argument that certain other racial or ethnic groups are culturally devoid of such a value. This argument is frequently used by commentators in assessing the educational attainment of African Americans, which is often less on average than that of white or certain Asian American groups. This lesser attainment is then attributed to a cultural deficiency, such as an alleged lack of respect for education, even though numerous surveys and research studies have shown that African American adults generally place a high priority on education for themselves and their children.[3]

Major structural and historical factors shaping family and individual resources must be taken into account . . . .

A third weakness of the typical "Asian culture" argument is that it ignores the very substantial and continuing negative impacts that white hostility and discrimination have had on Asian Americans. As we show here, accentuated educational achievement is substantially a protective and survival strategy against anti-Asian discrimination . . . .

Many Asian Americans believe that education serves as a great equalizer in their competition with white Americans. John, a Chinese American computer scientist, has this to say about academic achievement:

> Academia is important because, if they don't like you because of the color of your skin, you're never going to have the social networks. At some level there are some people who are never going to like you. But, in academia, right, okay, I get a 100 on this test, you get a

*95, I mean the rules are clear. In order to achieve in academia, or in order to get good grades, you study these things. You pass the test. Once you pass the test, then good stuff [happens]—people say nice things about you. And the fact [is] that in order to advance that way, there are clear rules. They're fairly objective, there's very little room—okay you spell this right, you spell this wrong. There is not very much argument.*

John accents a meritocratic rationale in arguing why it is so important for Asian Americans like him to do well in higher education. In John's and many other Asian Americans' eyes, academic excellence helps to improve, if not level, the playing field. Admitting that he appears to be a model minority, John hopes to overcome discrimination with achievement, while conceding that even with such achievement whites will still discriminate and "are never going to like you." He asserts, thus, that in college settings skin color is a characteristic used to exclude or include people by those in control of the most important social networks, who are usually white. He realizes what our respondents demonstrate . . . . there is, in fact, *no* protection from racial hostility and discrimination regardless of one's record of achievement . . . .

## FAMILY PRESSURES TO SUCCEED

In numerous interview accounts of these pressures to achieve, we see the central role of parents, most of whom are trying to protect their children from direct or indirect discrimination in a racist society. For example, Indira notes the immense pressure that Asian Americans often face as they try to succeed in higher education:

*Understand that we aren't coming to schools as [just seeking] "you and your success." Yes, that's a part of it. But what [more] you carry, like for me . . . the day that I left for college, my mother said to me, "I know that I will be able to die in peace, my daughter is going to become a doctor now." Can you imagine every time I tried to tell my mother that I didn't want to be a doctor, those were the words that haunted me. My mother will*

*not be able to die. My mother will die because I am a failure. When she dies, she will carry that, that disappointment with her, to her grave. That is huge, you know.*

Notice again that pressure to succeed in a rather proscribed and stereotyped way is often heavy, and typically comes from loved ones. Alex, a Korean American, sheds more light on these intense family pressures on Asian American youth: "I think that families, the older members of the families, that's what they preach when they are growing up, 'Do well in school so you let our family be proud. And then, don't, whatever you do, don't bring shame to our family regardless of your happiness.' That's what they're preaching, 'Don't bring shame to our family, regardless of your happiness.'" For many Asian Americans, he suggests in his interview, a family feels shamed if a young person fails to conform to aspects of the model stereotype, which serves in the Asian American collective memory as an important guide as to what it is to be successful in society. This socially constructed idea of "Asian American" success increases pressures on them.

Why do so many hopes and dreams seem to be riding on the successes of younger generations? As we have already seen, one answer lies in the overt and subtle racial barriers routinely placed by whites in the way of their parents. To take just one example from our interviews, Min, a first-generation Taiwanese American, discusses why she has pushed her own children so hard to achieve in school:

*It's hard to separate from the old world, and that's why I push, push my children so hard. I want my children to be better than me, to do better than I did. My life here, it wasn't supposed to be like this. I wasn't supposed to come here and work so hard for this long. My husband came to get his Ph.D., not have a restaurant. I worked; I worked in that hot kitchen three days before [my daughter] was born and had to go back, had to work three days after. I was still bleeding! [She cries.] I am a failure here. I have a bachelor's degree in math, I was a teacher before I came here, now, now I am nothing. I did the best I could, but it wasn't supposed to be like this.*

Min hopes for her children to be educationally and materially successful because she and her husband were unsuccessful in their bid to achieve their American dream. Her husband struggled with graduate school for some years but, like many Asian Americans in his generation, did not finish his dissertation because his English was not adequate. His Anglocentric university likely did not provide the necessary support to deal with his language and other adaptive problems, as is often the case for Asian immigrant students. Whites at colleges and universities often stereotype Asian international students as speaking English with accents that make understanding them too difficult; and, thus, those in authority may force some to drop classes, or revise or abandon their educational programs, when this is unnecessary . . . .

Instead of a prestigious career as a professor, Min's husband ran a modest restaurant. Now they are of retirement age with no end of work in sight. A college graduate, she sees herself as a "failure" and wants much more for her children. Clearly, in such families second- and third- generation Asian Americans have the great hopes of their parents and grandparents riding heavily on their shoulders, and this strong reality adds substantially to the stress that they already feel as Asian Americans caught in the white-generated model minority straightjacket . . . .

## The Absence of Help

Many Asian Americans attempt to achieve academic and economic success whatever the personal and psychological cost. Yet, when they need psychological help for accumulating stress and pain, they frequently have a difficult time obtaining the necessary services. Indira, an Asian Indian professor, describes an incident with one of her Asian American students: "I had a student who was trying to seek phone counseling, she was struggling with the pressure, you know she's like sixteen years old and an undergrad, so she's really [the age of] a junior in high school but is a junior in college . . . . A [counselor] on the phone started asking, 'How'd you manage that [getting in college]?' She's called to say that

she's suicidal, and this person is asking her, "How'd that happen?'" This stress and anxiety over educational performance can be overwhelming, and white and other counselors who do not understand that intense pressure may fail, often significantly, in helping a young Asian American in dire need.

Indira worked closely with school administrators to hire an Asian American counselor at the student health center, but to no avail. As of early 2008, the university still has not hired an Asian American counselor, but Indira has been holding training sessions for members of her academic community. She continues with this assessment of that effort:

*To me it's shocking. I did a training [of] college of liberal arts faculty because 20 percent of the incoming class was to be Asian. How do you deal with a student who has this mental breakdown in front of you, and they are suicidal because they want to change majors from chemistry to English? And you are looking at them like it's gonna be OK. I am not a counselor, but I believe this. Any time someone tells you that they are suicidal, you believe them, number one. Number two, just because you don't understand the pressure doesn't mean that it doesn't exist. Just because it's as simple as a [college] major thing for you, doesn't mean that's what it is to them.*

Judging from commentaries of several respondents, few administrators or policy-makers in these institutions of higher education seem to care enough about the serious psychological problems often faced by these students to take significant action to deal with them.

This neglect of Asian and Asian American health problems extends well beyond higher education. Those seeking help from public servants often face callous disregard. Recall the case of Ethan, a high-achieving student targeted by an overt act of racist violence. This event dramatically changed his life. Ethan got no assistance from the police or the district attorney's office in dealing with the vicious attack. After unsuccessful attempts to get the attacker punished by the "justice" system, he chose to deal with the trauma privately, leaning only on his parents:

*Part of it, as a victim, is finding a balance between seeking justice versus the amount of exposure that you want. It's difficult to say you've been a victim of a hate crime, but I didn't feel comfortable going public. I talked about it with my family. I could have gone to the papers or the television stations, but I wanted to move on with my life. I was still in school and I wanted to move past it; I didn't want it to hold me back in any ways . . . . It would be a distraction. I want to be Ethan, not Ethan the victim of a hate crime. You are perceived differently when something like this happens, and I didn't want to be treated any differently. I was not seeking sympathy. I think it might be that way because of my race. Particularly, my parents were not as willing and did not want me to pursue talking with the D.A. They wanted me to move on from this.*

Ethan's account indicates yet another Asian American dealing with discrimination mostly by himself, in this case with a little support from parents. Like the Japanese American internees during and after World War II, Ethan's parents seemed fearful and wanted him to move on and forget about the violent attack.

Until the white violence, Ethan reports, he had not really thought much about being Asian American. Now that reality is at the front of his mind. Physically he is healing, but serious psychological and related problems persist: "Not a day goes by that I don't have to make sure that my tooth is still in. It's a constant reminder every day about what happened to me. Not a day goes by that I don't think about it. It was senseless, stupid, and unprovoked, and he [the assailant] is still out there." Ethan is forced to think daily about the incident and its implications, including the fact that his assailant remains unpunished. Ethan has experienced a paradigm shift in how he views and operates in his community and in society generally:

*I am more cautious now when I am out at night. I am much more vigilant, and I am always looking at the environment . . . . I am lucky that this was not more serious. I am definitely more aware, watching and avoiding situations . . . . Also, I am definitely more aware of race. I now know that discrimination is more prevalent than I noticed before. I didn't assume it happened, but now I do. My mindset has swung the other way. I realize now that racism is a lot more prevalent than most people think, and I am more aware of that. Sometimes I worry that I see things when they are not there, thinking it has to do with race. I never thought that way before. I always thought those kind of things would never happen to me, at least not to an Asian American.*

Reportedly, over his first two decades, Ethan had not paid much attention to racial issues and believed that he was fully accepted by whites in a just society. He apparently thought being Asian American would protect him from difficulties experienced by other people of color. Yet, in an instant he found out that he has no control over the racial order. Now he carefully assesses interactions with others, especially whites, and wonders if he is being treated differently because of his Asian ancestry.

Asian Americans frequently deal with whites' discrimination internally and privately rather than collectively and organizationally. Many Asians immigrated to the United States after the civil rights movement and have not yet learned the necessary strategies of resistance, especially to subtle and covert forms of discrimination. Often lacking a collective memory of resistance strategies, a great many have not developed the strong community and organizational responses that they really need to contend with contemporary racism.

## GENDERED RACISM: BODY IMAGE AND SELF-ESTEEM

Long-term discrimination has had serious consequences on the self-images and self-esteem of Americans of color, including women, men, and children of Asian ancestry. Social science research shows that women of color in particular face the double burden of racism and sexism, as well as blended combinations of the two. In research on black women, Grier and Cobbs found that they "have a nearly bottomless well of self-depreciation into which they can drop when depressed. The well is prepared by society and stands waiting, a prefabricated pit which they have had no hand in fashioning."[4]

Some of our female respondents are very clear in describing how the dominant physical image for women has affected them. Fareena, a Bangladeshi American, recalls a painful time in her youth: "I had the lowest self-esteem issues . . . and so did my brother. I remember *hating* myself. I remember *hating* my features . . . and I remember being really excited the one day they had multicultural day [at school], and I got to dress up. But everyone else was dressing up in things that weren't even part of their ethnic identity, so . . . I still didn't feel recognized then."

In contrast, when Fareena describes growing up in Bangladesh before her family emigrated, she reports no problem with self-esteem. The timing of her self-hatred coincided with her move to an all-white school in the United States. She is not alone in this, for her brother also has felt the pain of being in a hostile all-white environment. Fareena continues:

> I remember I hated myself in the sixth grade. Hated myself. And that was the time I went to [an] all-white, all very rich white [school]. I remember that the type of girls that all the boys started liking didn't look like me, you know, being a brown woman. Issues of body hair came in to play. I have body hair that other girls don't have. I have to pluck my eyebrows, and other girls don't have to. It looks dirty on me. And there is this concept of dirt. I had real issues of just wanting to purge, physically purge things out of me. You know, my elbows are darker, my knees are darker, when I scar I leave a brown mark instead of a pink mark that fades. And all that is looked at as dirty or ugly or scarred, and not simply like a part of life. So, I felt very dirty . . . .

In the United States the white-controlled media and other sources accent a racialized standard of female beauty, one that is typically blond, white-skinned, and relatively thin.[5] Women of color obviously cannot fit much of this image, yet it is pressed on them from many sources, as in this school situation. Fareena's troubled self-concept encompassed concerns with "fatness" and "puniness" at the same time. Her early sexual development differentiated her from her white peers, as did her color, hair, and muscle mass. White students clearly perceived these differences as negative.

Jessica, a second-generation Vietnamese American, had a similar difficulty with being a young woman who does not meet the conventional white standard of beauty, as she makes clear:

> You know what people think is beautiful, and you don't know how to be that. I didn't know how to put on eye shadow right, because they only teach you how to put on eye shadow if you only have a certain shape of eye in a magazine. And if you don't have that eye, how do you put on eye shadow? And you try to look for models in the magazine that have your eyes so you can do it like them, and none of them have your eyes. It was like, great! And none of the makeup looks right on your skin, and so it's nothing that one student does. It's that you know how different you are from them, and it's hard to reconcile it . . . . I guess, like, for a long time I didn't see myself as a person of color, because I didn't know what it meant to be a person of color. I knew that I wasn't white. I knew that it would be nice to be white, it's so much simpler.

Jessica's poignant and probing comments reveal awareness of the ways that numerous privileges are routinely awarded to whites that people of color do not receive. White privilege leaves people of color wishing they were white so that they would not have to deal with the stigma and pain of being racially othered by many societal sources.

## DISCUSSION QUESTIONS

1. On the one hand, how does the model minority image serve as a survival strategy for Asian Americans in a white-dominated culture, and on the other hand, what kind of internal and external pressures does it exert upon them?
2. How can you explain Chou's and Feagin's findings that many Asian Americans do not see discrimination as racism?

## NOTES

1. Peter J. Burke, "Identity Processes and Social Stress," *American Sociological Review* 56 (1991):836–849.
2. Ronald Takaki, *Iron Cages: Race and Culture in the 19th-Century U.S.* (New York: Oxford University Press, 1994).
3. Joe R. Feagin and Melvin P. Sikes, *Living with Racism: The Black Middle Class Experience* (Boston: Beacon, 1994); Joe R. Feagin, Hernan Vera, and Nikitah Imani, *The Agony of Education: Black Students in White Colleges and Universities* (New York: Routledge, 1996).
4. Grier and Cobbs, *Black Rage*, p. 19.
5. Ibid., p. 40.

# 55

# SEXUAL HARASSMENT AND MASCULINITY

## The Power and Meaning of "Girl Watching"

BETH A. QUINN

*The previous readings by Mary Romero and by Rosalind S. Chou and Joe R. Feagin examined racial discrimination. This reading by Beth A. Quinn, the eighth on power and privilege, turns our attention to sexual discrimination. Quinn, a professor of sociology at Montana State University, uses in-depth interviews of both men and women to investigate how they understand the practice of "girl watching," a form of sexual harassment in many workplaces. This reading, taken from a 2002 article in the journal <u>Gender & Society</u>, describes why some men take part in or condone sexual harassment at work. Similar to what Chou and Feagin found among their Asian American respondents who have suppressed memories of racism or have other forms of denial regarding discriminatory practices, Quinn finds her male respondents are not ignorant about what they are doing, but rather they choose to ignore the consequences. This study reveals how those with power have the privilege to see or not to see how they abuse their power.*

Confronted with complaints about sexual harassment accounts in the media, some men claim that women are too sensitive or that they too often misinterpret men's intentions (Bernstein 1994; Buckwald 1993). In contrast, some women note with frustration that men just "don't get it" and lament the seeming inadequacy of sexual harassment policies (Conley 1991; Guccione 1992). Indeed, this ambiguity in defining acts of sexual harassment might be, as Cleveland and

*Source:* Quinn, Beth A. 2002. "Sexual Harassment and Masculinity: The Power and Meaning of 'Girl Watching.'" *Gender & Society* 16(3):386–402.

Kerst (1993) suggested, the most robust finding in sexual harassment research.

Using in-depth interviews with 43 employed men and women, this article examines a particular social practice—"girl watching"—as a means to understanding one way that these gender differences are produced. This analysis does not address the size or prevalence of these differences, nor does it present a direct comparison of men and women; this information is essential but well covered in the literature.[1] Instead, I follow Cleveland and Kerst's (1993) and Wood's (1998) suggestion that the question may best be unraveled by exploring how the "subject(ivities) of perpetrators, victims, and resistors of sexual harassment" are "discursively produced, reproduced, and altered" (Wood 1998:28).

This article focuses on the subjectivities of the perpetrators of a disputable form of sexual harassment, "girl watching." The term refers to the act of men's sexually evaluating women, often in the company of other men. It may take the form of a verbal or gestural message of "check it out," boasts of sexual prowess, or explicit comments about a woman's body or imagined sexual acts. The target may be an individual woman or group of women or simply a photograph or other representation. The woman may be a stranger, coworker, supervisor, employee, or client. For the present analysis, girl watching within the workplace is centered.

The analysis is grounded in the work of masculinity scholars such as Connell (1987, 1995) in that it attempts to explain the subject positions of the interviewed men—not the abstract and genderless subjects of patriarchy but the gendered and privileged subjects embedded in this system. Since I am attempting to delineate the gendered worldviews of the interviewed men, I employ the term "girl watching," a phrase that reflects their language ("they watch girls").

I have chosen to center the analysis on girl watching within the workplace for two reasons. First, it appears to be fairly prevalent. For example, a survey of federal civil employees (U.S. Merit Systems Protection Board 1988) found that in the previous 24 months, 28 percent of the women surveyed had experienced "unwanted sexual looks or gestures," and 35 percent had experienced "unwanted sexual teasing, jokes, remarks, or questions." Second, girl watching is still often normalized and trivialized as only play, or "boys will be boys." A man watching girls—even in his workplace—is frequently accepted as a natural and commonplace activity, especially if he is in the presence of other men.[2] Indeed, it may be required (Hearn 1985). Thus, girl watching sits on the blurry edge between fun and harm, joking and harassment. An understanding of the process of identifying behavior as sexual harassment, or of rejecting this label, may be built on this ambiguity.

Girl watching has various forms and functions, depending on the context and the men involved. For example, it may be used by men as a directed act of power against a particular woman or women. In this, girl watching—at least in the workplace—is most clearly identified as harassing by both men and women. I am most interested, however, in the form where it is characterized as only play. This type is more obliquely motivated and, as I will argue, functions as a game men play to build shared masculine identities and social relations.

Multiple and contradictory subject positions are also evidenced in girl watching, most notably that between the gazing man and the woman he watches. Drawing on Michael Schwalbe's (1992) analysis of empathy and the formation of masculine identities, I argue that girl watching is premised on the obfuscation of this multiplicity through the objectification of the woman watched and a suppression of empathy for her. In conclusion, the ways these elements operate to produce gender differences in interpreting sexual harassment and the implications for developing effective policies are discussed.

## PREVIOUS RESEARCH

The question of how behavior is or is not labeled as sexual harassment has been studied primarily through experimental vignettes and surveys.[3] In both methods, participants evaluate either hypothetical scenarios or lists of behaviors, considering whether, for example, the behavior constitutes sexual harassment, which party is most at fault, and what consequences the act might engender. Researchers manipulate factors such as the level of "welcomeness" the target exhibits and the relationship of the actors (supervisor-employee, coworker-coworker).

Both methods consistently show that women are willing to define more acts as sexual harassment ... and are more likely to see situations as coercive. When asked who is more to blame in a particular scenario, men are more likely to blame, and less likely to empathize with, the victim. In terms of actual behaviors like girl watching, the U.S. Merit Systems Protection Board (1988) survey found that 81 percent of the women surveyed considered "uninvited sexually suggestive looks or gestures" from a supervisor to be sexual harassment. While the majority of men (68 percent) also defined it as such, significantly more men were willing to dismiss such behavior. Similarly, while 40 percent of the men would not consider the same behavior from a coworker to be harassing, more than three-quarters of the women would.

The most common explanation offered for these differences is gender role socialization. This conclusion is supported by the consistent finding that the more men and women adhere to traditional gender roles, the more likely they are to deny the harm in sexual harassment and to consider the behavior acceptable or at least normal (Gutek and Koss 1993; Malovich and Stake 1990; Murrell and Dietz-Uhler 1993; Popovich et al. 1992; Pryor 1987; Tagri and Hayes 1997). Men who hold predatory ideas about sexuality, who are more likely to believe rape myths, and who are more likely to self-report that they would rape under certain circumstances are less likely to see behaviors as harassing (Murrell and Dietz-Uhler 1993; Pryor 1987; Reilly et al. 1992).

These findings do not, however, adequately address the between-group differences. The more one is socialized into traditional notions of sex roles, the more likely it is for both men and women to view the behaviors as acceptable or at least unchangeable. The processes by which gender roles operate to produce these differences remain underexamined.

Some theorists argue that men are more likely to discount the harassing aspects of their behavior because of a culturally conditioned tendency to misperceive women's intentions. For example, Stockdale (1993:96) argued that "patriarchal norms create a sexually aggressive belief system in some people more than others, and this belief system can lead to the propensity to misperceive." Gender differences in interpreting sexual harassment, then, may be the outcome of the acceptance of normative ideas about women's inscrutability and indirectness and men's role as sexual aggressors. Men see harmless flirtation or sexual interest rather than harassment because they misperceive women's intent and responses.

Stockdale's (1993) theory is promising but limited. First, while it may apply to actions such as repeatedly asking for dates and quid pro quo harassment,[4] it does not effectively explain motivations for more indirect actions, such as displaying pornography and girl watching. Second, it does not explain why some men are more likely to operate from these discourses of sexual aggression contributing to a propensity to misperceive.

Theoretical explanations that take into account the complexity and diversity of sexual harassing behaviors and their potentially multifaceted social etiologies are needed. An account of the processes by which these behaviors are produced and the active construction of their social meanings is necessary to unravel both between- and within-gender variations in behavior and interpretation. A fruitful framework from which to begin is an examination of masculine identities and the role of sexually harassing behaviors as a means to their production.

## METHOD

I conducted 43 semistructured interviews with currently employed men and women between June 1994 and March 1995 . . . . The interviews ranged in length from one to three hours. With one exception, interviews were audiotaped and transcribed in full.

Participants were contacted in two primary ways. Twenty-five participants were recruited from "Acme Electronics," a Southern California electronic design and manufacturing company. An additional 18 individuals were recruited from an evening class at a community college and a university summer school class, both in Southern California. These participants referred 3 more individuals. In addition to the interviews, I conducted participant observation for approximately one month while on site at Acme. This involved observations of the public and common spaces of the company.

At Acme, a human resources administrator drew four independent samples (salaried and hourly women and men) from the company's approximately 300 employees. Letters of invitation were sent to 40 individuals, and from this group, 13 women and 12 men agreed to be interviewed.[5]

The interviews began with general questions about friendships and work relationships and progressed to specific questions about gender relations, sexual harassment, and the policies that seek to address it.[6] Since the main aim of the project was to explore how workplace events are framed as sexual harassment (and as legally bounded or not), the term "sexual harassment" was not introduced by the interviewer until late in the interview.

While the question of the relationship between masculinity and sexual harassment was central, I did not come to the research looking expressly for girl watching. Rather, it surfaced as a theme across several men's interviews in the context of a gender reversal question:

> It's the end of an average day. You get ready for bed and fall to sleep. In what seems only a moment, the alarm goes off. As you awake, you find your body to be oddly out of sorts . . . . To your surprise, you find that you have been transformed into the "opposite sex." Even stranger, no one in your life seems to remember that you were ever any different.

Participants were asked to consider what it would be like to conduct their everyday work life in this transformed state. I was particularly interested in their estimation of the impact it would have on their interactions with coworkers and supervisors. Imagining themselves as the opposite sex, participants were forced to make explicit the operation of

gender in their workplace, something they did not do in their initial discussions of a typical workday.

Interestingly, no man discussed girl watching in initial accounts of his workplace. I suspect that they did not consider it to be relevant to a discussion of their average *work* day, even though it became apparent that it was an integral daily activity for some groups of men. It emerged only when men were forced to consider themselves as explicitly gendered workers through the hypothetical question, something they were able initially to elide.[7]

Taking guidance from Glaser and Strauss's (1967) grounded theory and the methodological insights of Dorothy Smith (1990), transcripts were analyzed iteratively and inductively, with the goal of identifying the ideological tropes the speaker used to understand his or her identities, behaviors, and relationships. Theoretical concepts drawn from previous work on the etiology of sexual harassment (Bowman 1993; Cleveland and Kerst 1993), the construction of masculine identities (Connell 1995, 1987), and sociolegal theories of disputing and legal consciousness (Bumiller 1988; Conley and O'Barr 1998) guided the analysis.

Several related themes emerged and are discussed in the subsequent analysis. First, girl watching appears to function as a form of gendered play among men. This play is productive of masculine identities and premised on a studied lack of empathy with the feminine other. Second, men understand the targeted woman to be an object rather than a player in the game, and she is most often not the intended audience. This obfuscation of a woman's subjectivity, and men's refusal to consider the effects of their behavior, means men are likely to be confused when a woman complains. Thus, the production of masculinity though girl watching, and its compulsory disempathy, may be one factor in gender differences in the labeling of harassment.

## FINDINGS: GIRL WATCHING AS "HOMMO-SEXUALITY"

> [They] had a button on the computer that you pushed if there was a girl who came to the front

*counter . . . . It was a code and it said "BAFC"— Babe at Front Counter . . . . If the guy in the back looked up and saw a cute girl come in the station, he would hit this button for the other dispatcher to [come] see the cute girl.*

Paula, police officer

In its most serious form, girl watching operates as a targeted tactic of power. The men seem to want everyone—the targeted woman as well as coworkers, clients, and superiors—to know they are looking. The gaze demonstrates their right, as men, to sexually evaluate women. Through the gaze, the targeted woman is reduced to a sexual object, contradicting her other identities, such as that of competent worker or leader. This employment of the discourse of asymmetrical heterosexuality (i.e., the double standard) may trump a woman's formal organizational power, claims to professionalism, and organizational discourses of rationality (Collinson and Collinson 1989; Gardner 1995; Yount 1991).[8] As research on rape has demonstrated (Estrich 1987), calling attention to a woman's gendered sexuality can function to exclude recognition of her competence, rationality, trustworthiness, and even humanity. In contrast, the overt recognition of a man's (hetero) sexuality is normally compatible with other aspects of his identity; indeed, it is often required (Connell 1995; Hearn 1985). Thus, the power of sexuality is asymmetrical, in part, because being seen as sexual has different consequences for women and men.

But when they ogle, gawk, whistle and point, are men always so directly motivated to disempower their women colleagues? Is the target of the gaze also the intended audience? Consider, for example, this account told by Ed, a white, 29-year-old instrument technician.

*When a group of guys goes to a bar or a nightclub and they try to be manly . . . . A few of us always found [it] funny [when] a woman would walk by and a guy would be like, "I can have her." [pause] "Yeah, OK, we want to see it!" [laugh]*

In his account—a fairly common one in men's discussions—the passing woman is simply a visual cue for their play. It seems clear that it is a game played by men for men; the woman's participation and awareness of her role seem fairly unimportant.

As Thorne (1993) reminded us, we should not be too quick to dismiss games as "only play." In her study of gender relations in elementary schools, Thorne found play to be a powerful form of gendered social action. One of its "clusters of meaning" most relevant here is that of "dramatic performance." In this, play functions as both a source of fun and a mechanism by which gendered identities, group boundaries, and power relations are (re)produced.

The metaphor of play was strong in Karl's comments. Karl, a white man in his early thirties who worked in a technical support role in the Acme engineering department, hoped to earn a degree in engineering. His frustration with his slow progress—which he attributed to the burdens of marriage and fatherhood—was evident throughout the interview. Karl saw himself as an undeserved outsider in his department and he seemed to delight in telling on the engineers.

Girl watching came up as Karl considered the gender reversal question. Like many of the men I interviewed, his first reaction was to muse about premenstrual syndrome and clothes. When I inquired about the potential social effects of the transformation (by asking him, Would it "be easier dealing with the engineers or would it be harder?") he haltingly introduced the engineers' "game."

**Karl:** *Some of the engineers here are very [pause] they're not very, how shall we say? [pause] What's the way I want to put this? They're not very, uh [pause] what's the word? Um. It escapes me.*

**Researcher:** Give me a hint?

**Karl:** *They watch women but they're not very careful about getting caught.*

**Researcher:** Oh! Like they ogle?

**Karl:** *Ogle or gaze or [pause] stare even, or [pause] generate a commotion of an unusual nature.*

His initial discomfort in discussing the issue (with me, I presume) is evident in his excruciatingly formal and hesitant language. The aspect of play, however, came through clearly when I pushed him to describe what generating a commotion looked like: "'Oh! There goes so-and-so. Come and take a look! She's wearing this great outfit today!' Just like a schoolboy. They'll rush out of their offices and [cranes his neck] and check things out." That this is a form of play was evident in Karl's boisterous tone and in his reference to schoolboys. This is not a case of an aggressive sexual appraising of a woman coworker but a commotion created for the benefit of other men.

At Acme, several spatial factors facilitated this form of girl watching. First, the engineering department is designed as an open-plan office with partitions at shoulder height, offering a maze-like geography that encourages group play. As Karl explained, the partitions offer both the opportunity for sight and cover from being seen. Although its significance escaped me at the time, I was directly introduced to the spatial aspects of the engineers' game of girl watching during my first day on site at Acme. That day, John, the current human resources director, gave me a tour of the facilities, walking me through the departments and offering informal introductions. As we entered the design engineering section, a rhythm of heads emerged from its landscape of partitions, and movement started in our direction. I was definitely aware of being on display as several men gave me obvious once-overs.

Second, Acme's building features a grand stairway that connects the second floor—where the engineering department is located—with the lobby. The stairway is enclosed by glass walls, offering a bird's eye view to the main lobby and the movements of visitors and the receptionists (all women). Robert, a senior design engineer, specifically noted the importance of the glass walls in his discussion of the engineers' girl watching.

*There's glass walls around the upstairs right here by the lobby. So when there's an attractive young female . . . someone will see the girl in the area and they will go back and inform all the men in the area.*

*"Go check it out." [laugh] So we'll walk over to the glass window, you know, and we'll see who's down there.*

One day near the end of my stay at Acme, I was reminded of his story as I ventured into the first-floor reception area. Looking up, I saw Robert and another man standing at the top of the stairs watching and commenting on the women gathered around the receptionist's desk. When he saw me, Robert gave me a sheepish grin and disappeared from sight.

## Producing Masculinity

I suggest that girl watching in this form functions simultaneously as a form of play and as a potentially powerful site of gendered social action. Its social significance lies in its power to form identities and relationships based on these common practices for, as Cockburn (1983:123) has noted, "patriarchy is as much about relations between man and man as it is about relations between men and women." Girl watching works similarly to the sexual joking that Johnson (1988) suggested is a common way for heterosexual men to establish intimacy among themselves.

In particular, girl watching works as a dramatic performance played to other men, a means by which a certain type of masculinity is produced and heterosexual desire displayed. It is a means by which men assert a masculine identity to other men, in an ironic "hommo-sexual" practice of heterosexuality (Butler 1990).[9] As Connell (1995) and others (Butler 1990; West and Zimmerman 1987) have aptly noted, masculinity is not a static identity but rather one that must constantly be reclaimed. The content of any performance—and there are multiple forms—is influenced by a hegemonic notion of masculinity. When asked what "being a man" entailed, many of the men and women I interviewed triangulated toward notions of strength (if not in muscle, then in character and job performance), dominance, and a marked sexuality, overflowing and uncontrollable to some degree and natural to the male "species." Heterosexuality is required, for just as the label "girl" questions a man's claim to masculine power, so does the label "fag" (Hopkins 1992; Pronger 1992). I asked

Karl, for example, if he would consider his sons "good men" if they were gay. His response was laced with ambivalence; he noted only that the question was "a tough one."

The practice of girl watching is just that—a practice—one rehearsed and performed in everyday settings. This aspect of rehearsal was evident in my interview with Mike, a self-employed house painter who used to work construction. In locating himself as a born-again Christian, Mike recounted the girl watching of his fellow construction workers with contempt. Mike was particularly disturbed by a man who brought his young son to the job site one day. The boy was explicitly taught to catcall, a practice that included identifying the proper targets: women and effeminate men.

Girl watching, however, can be somewhat tenuous as a masculine practice. In their acknowledgment (to other men) of their supposed desire lies the possibility that in being too interested in women the players will be seen as mere schoolboys giggling in the playground. Taken too far, the practice undermines rather than supports a masculine performance. In Karl's discussion of girl watching, for example, he continually came back to the problem of men's not being careful about getting caught. He referred to a particular group of men who, though "their wives are [pause] very attractive—very much so," still "gawk like schoolboys." Likewise, Stephan explained that men who are obvious, who "undress [women] with their eyes" probably do so "because they don't get enough women in their lives. Supposedly." A man must be interested in women, but not too interested; they must show their (hetero) sexual interest, but not overly so, for this would be to admit that women have power over them.

## The Role of Objectification and (Dis)Empathy

As a performance of heterosexuality among men, the targeted woman is primarily an object onto which men's homosocial sexuality is projected. The presence of a woman in any form—embodied, pictorial, or as an image conjured from words—is required, but her subjectivity and active participation is not. To be sure, given the ways the discourse of asymmetrical sexuality works, men's actions may result in similarly negative effects on the targeted woman as that of a more direct form of sexualization. The crucial difference is that the men's understanding of their actions differs. This difference is one key to understanding the ambiguity around interpreting harassing behavior.

When asked about the engineers' practice of neck craning, Robert grinned, saying nothing at first. After some initial discussion, I started to ask him if he thought women were aware of their game ("Do you think that the women who are walking by . . . ?"). He interrupted, misreading my question. What resulted was a telling description of the core of the game:

> It depends. No. I don't know if they enjoy it. When I do it, if I do it, I'm not saying that I do. [big laugh] . . . If they do enjoy it, they don't say it. If they don't enjoy it— wait a minute, that didn't come out right. I don't know if they enjoy it or not [pause]; that's not the purpose of us popping our heads out.

Robert did not want to admit that women might not enjoy it ("that didn't come out right") but acknowledged that their feelings were irrelevant. Only subjects, not objects, take pleasure or are annoyed. If a woman did complain, Robert thought "the guys wouldn't know what to say." In her analysis of street harassment, Gardner (1995:187) found a similar absence, in that "men's interpretations seldom mentioned a woman's reaction, either guessed at or observed."

The centrality of objectification was also apparent in comments made by José, a Hispanic man in his late 40s who worked in manufacturing. For José, the issue came up when he considered the topic of compliments. He initially claimed that women enjoy compliments more than men do. In reconsidering, he remembered girl watching and the importance of intent.

> There is [pause] a point where [pause] a woman can be admired by [pause] a pair of eyes, but we're talking about "that look." Where, you know, you're admiring her because she's dressed nice, she's got a nice figure, she's got nice legs. But then you also have the other side.

*You have an animal who just seems to undress you with his eyes and he's just [pause], there's those kind of people out there too.*

What is most interesting about this statement is that in making the distinction between merely admiring and an animal look that ravages, José switched subject position. He spoke in the second person when describing both forms of looking, but his consistency in grammar belies a switch in subjectivity: you (as a man) admire, and you (as a woman) are undressed with his eyes. When considering an appropriate, complimentary gaze, José described it from a man's point of view; the subject who experiences the inappropriate, violating look, however, is a woman. Thus, as in Robert's account, José acknowledged that there are potentially different meanings in the act for men and women. In particular, to be admired in a certain way is potentially demeaning for a woman through its objectification.

The switch in subject position was also evident in Karl's remarks. Karl mentioned girl watching while imagining himself as a woman in the gender reversal question. As he took the subject position of the woman watched rather than the man watching, his understanding of the act as a harmless game was destabilized. Rather than taking pleasure in being the object of such attention, Karl would take pains to avoid it.

*So with these guys [if I were a woman], I would probably have to be very concerned about my attire in the lab. Because in a lot of cases, I'm working at a bench and I'm hunched over, in which case your shirt, for example, would open at the neckline, and I would just have to be concerned about that.*

Thus, because the engineers girl watch, Karl feels that he would have to regulate his appearance if he were a woman, keeping the men from using him in their game of girl watching. When he considered the act from the point of view of a man, girl watching was simply a harmless antic and an act of appreciation. When he was forced to consider the subject position of a woman, however, girl watching was something to be avoided or at least carefully managed.

When asked to envision himself as a woman in his workplace, like many of the individuals I interviewed, Karl believed that he did not "know how to be a woman." Nonetheless, he produced an account that mirrored the stories of some of the women I interviewed. He knew the experience of girl watching could be quite different—in fact, threatening and potentially disempowering—for the woman who is its object. As such, the game was something to be avoided. In imagining themselves as women, the men remembered the practice of girl watching. None, however, were able to comfortably describe the game of girl watching from the perspective of a woman and maintain its (masculine) meaning as play.

In attempting to take up the subject position of a woman, these men are necessarily drawing on knowledge they already hold. If men simply "don't get it"—truly failing to see the harm in girl watching or other more serious acts of sexual harassment—then they should not be able to see this harm when envisioning themselves as women. What the interviews reveal is that many men—most of whom failed to see the harm of many acts that would constitute the hostile work environment form of sexual harrassment—did in fact understand the harm of these acts when forced to consider the position of the targeted woman.

I suggest that the gender reversal scenario produced, in some men at least, a moment of empathy. Empathy, Schwalbe (1992) argued, requires two things. First, one must have some knowledge of the other's situation and feelings. Second, one must be motivated to take the position of the other. What the present research suggests is that gender differences in interpreting sexual harassment stem not so much from men's not getting it (a failure of the first element) but from a studied, often compulsory, lack of motivation to identify with women's experiences.

In his analysis of masculinity and empathy, Schwalbe (1992) argued that the requirements of masculinity necessitate a "narrowing of the moral self." Men learn that to effectively perform masculinity and to protect a masculine identity, they must, in many instances, ignore a woman's pain and obscure her viewpoint. Men fail to exhibit empathy with women because masculinity precludes them from taking the position of the feminine other, and men's moral stance vis-à-vis women is attenuated by this lack of empathy.

As a case study, Schwalbe (1992) considered the Thomas-Hill hearings, concluding that the examining senators maintained a masculinist stance that precluded them from giving serious consideration to Professor Hill's claims. A consequence of this masculine moral narrowing is that "charges of sexual harassment . . . are often seen as exaggerated or as fabricated out of misunderstanding or spite" (Schwalbe 1992:46). Thus, gender differences in interpreting sexually harassing behaviors may stem more from acts of ignoring than states of ignorance.

## The Problem with Getting Caught

But are women really the untroubled objects that girl watching—viewed through the eyes of men— suggests? Obviously not; the game may be premised on a denial of a woman's subjectivity, but an actual erasure is beyond men's power! It is in this multiplicity of subjectivities, as Butler (1990:ix) noted, where "trouble" lurks, provoked by "the unanticipated agency of a female 'object' who inexplicably returns the glance, reverses the gaze, an contests the place and authority of the masculine position." To face a returned gaze is to get caught, an act that has the power to undermine the logic of girl watching as simply a game among men. Karl, for example, noted that when caught, men are often flustered, a reaction suggesting that the boundaries of usual play have been disturbed.[10]

When a woman looks back, when she asks, "What are you looking at?" she speaks as a subject, and her status as mere object is disturbed. When the game is played as a form of hommo-sexuality, the confronted man may be baffled by her response. When she catches them looking, when she complains, the targeted woman speaks as a subject. The men, however, understand her primarily as an object, and objects do not object.

The radical potential of sexual harassment law is that it centers on women's subjectivity, an aspect prompting Catharine MacKinnon's (1979) unusual hope for the law's potential as a remedy. For men

engaged in girl watching, however, this subjectivity may be inconceivable. From their viewpoint, acts such as girl watching are simply games played with objects: women's bodies. Similar to Schwalbe's (1992) insight into the senators' reaction to Professor Hill, the harm of sexual harassment may seem more the result of a woman's complaint (and law's "illegitimate" encroachment into the everyday work world) than men's acts of objectification. For example, in reflecting on the impact of sexual harassment policies in the workplace, José lamented that "back in the '70s, [it was] all peace and love then. Now as things turn around, men can't get away with as much as what they used to." Just whose peace and love are we talking about?

## Reactions to Anti–Sexual Harassment Training Programs

The role that objectification and disempathy play in men's girl watching has important implications for sexual harassment training. Consider the following account of a sexual harassment training session given in Cindy's workplace. Cindy, an Italian American woman in her early 20s, worked as a recruiter for a small telemarketing company in Southern California.

*[The trainer] just really laid down the ground rules, um, she had some scenarios. Saying, "OK, would you consider this sexual harassment?" "Would you . . . " this, this, this? "What level?" Da-da-da. So, um, they just gave us some real numbers as to lawsuits and cases. Just that "you guys better be careful" type of a thing.*

From Cindy's description, this training is fairly typical in that it focuses on teaching participants definitions of sexual harassment and the legal ramifications of accusations. The trainer used the common strategy of presenting videos of potentially harassing situations and asking the participants how they would judge them. Cindy's description of the men's responses to these videos reveals the limitation of this approach.

*We were watching [the TV] and it was [like] a studio audience. And [men] were getting up in the studio audience making comments like "Oh well, look at her! I wouldn't want to do that to her either!" "Well, you're darn straight, look at her!"*

Interestingly, the men successfully used the training session videos as an opportunity for girl watching through their public sexual evaluations of the women depicted. In this, the intent of the training session was doubly subverted. The men interpreted scenarios that Cindy found plainly harassing into mere instances of girl watching and sexual (dis)interest. The antiharassment video was ironically transformed into a forum for girl watching, effecting male bonding and the assertion of masculine identities to the exclusion of women coworkers. Also, by judging the complaining women to be inferior as women, the men sent the message that women who complain are those who fail at femininity.

Cindy conceded that relations between men and women in her workplace were considerably strained after the training. ("That day, you definitely saw the men bond, you definitely saw the women bond, and there was a definite separation.") The effect of the training session, rather than curtailing the rampant sexual harassment in Cindy's workplace, operated as a site of masculine performance, evoking manly camaraderie and reestablishing gender boundaries.

To be effective, sexual harassment training programs must be grounded in a complex understanding of the ways acts such as girl watching operate in the workplace and the seeming necessity of a culled empathy to some forms of masculinity. Sexually harassing behaviors are produced from more than a lack of knowledge, simple sexist attitudes, or misplaced sexual desire. Some forms of sexually harassing behaviors—such as girl watching—are mechanisms through which gendered boundaries are patrolled and evoked and by which deeply held identities are established. This complexity requires complex interventions and leads to difficult questions about the possible efficacy of any workplace training program mandated in part by legal requirements.

## CONCLUSIONS

In this analysis, I have sought to unravel the social logic of girl watching and its relationship to the question of gender differences in the interpretation of sexual harassment. In the form analyzed here, girl watching functions simultaneously as only play and as a potent site where power is played. Through the objectification on which it is premised and in the non-empathetic masculinity it supports, this form of girl watching simultaneously produces both the harassment and the barriers to men's acknowledgment of its potential harm.

The implications these findings have for anti–sexual harassment training are profound. If we understand harassment to be the result of a simple lack of knowledge (of ignorance), then straightforward informational sexual harassment training may be effective. The present analysis suggests, however, that the etiology of some harassment lies elsewhere. While they might have quarreled with it, most of the men I interviewed had fairly good abstract understandings of the behaviors their companies' sexual harassment policies prohibited. At the same time, in relating stories of social relations in their workplaces, most failed to identify specific behaviors as sexual harassment when they matched the abstract definition. As I have argued, the source of this contradiction lies not so much in ignorance but in acts of ignoring. Traditional sexual harassment training programs address the former rather than the later. As such, their effectiveness against sexually harassing behaviors born out of social practices of masculinity like girl watching is questionable.

Ultimately, the project of challenging sexual harassment will be frustrated and our understanding distorted unless we interrogate hegemonic, patriarchal forms of masculinity and the practices by which they are (re)produced. We must continue to research the processes by which sexual harassment is produced and the gendered identities and subjectivities on which it poaches (Wood 1998). My study provides a first step toward a more process-oriented understanding of sexual harassment, the ways the social meanings of harassment are constructed, and ultimately, the potential success of antiharassment training programs.

## DISCUSSION QUESTIONS

1. What does Quinn's study of "girl watching" within a workplace tell us about masculinity at work, targeted power, and sexual harassment?

2. Why is it difficult for men to see this behavior as problematic? What can workplaces do to change this and other types of gender discrimination?

## NOTES

1. See Welsh (1999) for a review of this literature.

2. For example, Maria, an administrative assistant I interviewed, simultaneously echoed and critiqued this understanding when she complained about her boss's girl watching in her presence: "If he wants to do that in front of other men . . . you know, that's what men do."

3. Recently, more researchers have turned to qualitative studies as a means to understand the process of labeling behavior as harassment. Of note are Collinson and Collinson (1996), Giuffre and Williams (1994), Quinn (2000), and Rogers and Henson (1997).

4. Quid pro quo ("this for that") sexual harassment occurs when a person with organizational power attempts to coerce an individual into sexual behavior by threatening adverse job actions.

5. This sample was not fully representative of the company's employees; male managers (mostly white) and minority manufacturing employees were underrepresented. Thus, the data presented here best represent the attitudes and workplace tactics of white men working in white-collar, technical positions and white and minority men in blue-collar jobs.

6. Acme employees were interviewed at work in an office off the main lobby. Students and referred participants were interviewed at sites convenient to them (e.g., an office, the library).

7. Not all the interviewed men discussed girl watching. When asked directly, they tended to grin knowingly, refusing to elaborate. This silence in the face of direct questioning—by a female researcher—is also perhaps an instance of getting caught.

8. I prefer the term "asymmetrical heterosexuality" over "double standard" because it directly references the dominance of heterosexuality and more accurately reflects the interconnected but different forms of acceptable sexuality for men and women. As Estrich (1987) argued, it is not simply that we hold men and women to different standards of sexuality but that these standards are (re)productive of women's disempowerment.

9. "Hommo" is a play on the French word for man, *homme*.

10. Men are not always concerned with getting caught, as the behavior of catcalling construction workers amply illustrates; that a woman hears it is part of the thrill (Gardner 1995). The difference between the workplace and the street is the level of anonymity the men have vis-à-vis the woman and the complexity of social rules and the diversity of power sources an individual has at his or her disposal.

# PART V

# EMPOWERMENT AND SOCIAL CHANGE

In this last part of the anthology, we turn our attention to empowerment and social change. As argued in Part I of this volume, "Introduction to Race, Gender, Sexuality, and Social Class," if social inequality and the social categories of race, social class, and gender are socially created—that is, produced by people—then they also can be modified. Moreover, since societies and social structures are created by people, and are not innate or static objects, people are responsible for assessing and improving these social structures. We have choices about how we want to live and how we want societies to structure social relationships.

The first part of this book also showed how constructions of race, for example, have changed over time as needed by the ruling elites. The construction of race also changes as we look across different countries and cultures. This dynamic nature of social categories is what social constructionism theoretically implies, and it also means that we can alter the construction of race yet again. Looking at the historical evidence, as we did in Part I, helps us to understand the historical roots of social inequality and empowers us to take social action. By understanding these roots, we have better knowledge about how we can change the present and the future. With each

social problem we have identified in the readings throughout this anthology, we need to ask: Who are the critical change makers? What are the potential solutions to gender, racial, and social class inequality? The readings in Part V on empowerment and social change reveal how people are taking action to challenge or lessen the impacts of social inequality.

Some of the readings discuss social change on the individual or interactional (micro) level of society, while others examine the organizational or community (meso) level, and still others look at the societal (macro) level of social change. The macro level includes changing larger social institutions, the dominant culture, language, laws, and ideologies. Many scholars argue that social change at the individual level may be easier than at the other levels. Changing one person at a time, however, is not enough when social inequality and discrimination are embedded in the social structure of organizations and institutions and large numbers of people are being affected by the disparity. However, these inequalities in the social structures of society are harder to change. Social change can range on a continuum from reform (making changes within an organization or social institution) to revolution, which advocates changing the entire society.

Whether the emphasis is on reform or on revolution, sometimes you need a larger group of people or a social movement to convince an organization to make alterations.

Some social movements are dedicated to one issue, while others are multifaceted. Our readings on intersectionality demonstrate that, since social categories intersect, in order to be effective, movements for social change need to address more than one social group. For example, the U.S. feminist movement became much stronger once the issues of men and masculinity and the needs of women of color, lesbians, and working-class women were addressed.

Several of the readings in this anthology, including those in Part V, address social change from an academic perspective—that is, how we can study, create new theories, and disseminate information about social inequality and the need for social change. Other readings address social change from an activist perspective. These individuals are using their knowledge to educate and empower others to make changes. Not surprisingly, many of the academics also are activists, such as Patricia Hill Collins, who authored Reading 56. This work calls for individuals to have more empathy with people who are different from them and to find ways to build bridges across differences to effect social change. Another example of academics who are also activists is the group of economists and social scientists who formed the Coalition for a New Economy and authored Reading 60.

Reading 56, a seminal work written in 1989 by Collins titled "Toward a New Vision: Race, Class, and Gender as Categories of Analysis and Connection," is considered a classic because Collins is one of the first scholars to argue for the necessity of an intersectional framework to better address systems of social inequality. Collins's work is both academic and activist in orientation. Collins frames this reading around two questions: (1) How can we reconceptualize race, social class, and gender as categories of analysis? (2) How can we transcend the barriers created by our own experiences with race, social class, and gender oppression in order to build the types of coalitions essential for social change? Collins argues, first, for the need for new theories of

race, social class, and gender, and second, for making connections among our personal lives, our scholarship, our teaching, and our relationships with our colleagues and students. Like the scholars from Part I, "Introduction to Race, Gender, Sexuality, and Social Class," Collins argues that dichotomous social categories are problematic, as are additive analyses of oppression in which, for instance, scholars studying gender decide to add race-ethnicity to their analysis instead of addressing both variables simultaneously. Instead, Collins maintains that we need to understand how oppression operates at various levels in society—the individual, the institutional, and the symbolic levels—in what she describes as a matrix of oppression. Once we understand what we are studying, we can turn our attention to social change.

The second reading on empowerment and social change looks at how individuals can effect social change by becoming more aware and educated about their own privileges and experiences of oppression in society. Reading 57 by Paul Kivel, "How White People Can Serve as Allies to People of Color in the Struggle to End Racism," comes from a workshop Kivel leads to educate whites on the privilege of their whiteness and how they can become allies of people of color. When whites become allies, we can work together in the struggle to lessen and, we hope, to end racial discrimination. Kivel concludes his short reading with a practical list of strategies whites can use to help minimize racism.

Reading 58 turns our attention to larger questions of social transformation by asking, What does a world with racial equality look like? Jacqueline Johnson, Sharon Rush, and Joe Feagin in "Doing Anti-racism: Toward an Egalitarian American Society," provide a utopian vision of how racial inequality could be lessened in the United States. They address primarily macro-level social changes in institutions and in the larger political and cultural values of the society. However, Johnson and colleagues also advocate social change at the micro level of individuals and social interaction. Specifically, the authors talk about how individuals first need to have sympathy for or care about a group that is different from them. For example, whites need to care about issues of racism that people of color may be experiencing, and wealthy people need to be concerned about homeless individuals in their communities. But sympathy is not enough. Individuals also need to feel empathy for others to really enact social change. (Patricia Hill Collins also calls for more empathy when she advocates for social change in Reading 56.) To feel empathy for someone who is different from you means not only that you care about them but also that you can feel their pain. Thus, a deeper emotional connection motivates you to act on their behalf. Finally, Johnson and colleagues argue that after individuals feel sympathy and empathy for people who are different from them, the final stage is transformative knowledge. Individuals are then able to educate themselves and act toward changing the situations that are creating the oppression or unfair privilege.

Judith Lorber authored Reading 59, "Dismantling Noah's Ark." Like Johnson and colleagues, Lorber primarily articulates a vision for eradicating gender inequality on a macro level of society—that is, "dismantling Noah's ark." Clearly, individuals and relationships between men and women need to change, but Lorber's attention is more on the social structures of employment and the family, where much gender discrimination occurs. Lorber asks the reader to envision what gender equality would look like. Is it having equality of opportunity, such that both women and men have equal access to education, jobs, assets, and prestigious positions in society? Or, is it having equality of outcome, such that women and men have equal incomes, leisure time, and access to power? Or, do we need some combination of both? These questions apply to any area of social inequality we have studied.

The final reading in Part V on empowerment and social change, and in this anthology, is by a group of scholars who formed the Coalition for a New Economy. Meizhu Lui, Barbara J. Robles, Betsy Leondar-Wright, Rose Brewer, and Rebecca Adamson are a group of progressive academics who wanted to educate their students about social inequality and teach workshops about economic disparities in the United States. Their book, *The Color of Wealth: The Story Behind the U.S. Racial Wealth Divide*, is being taught in economics classes across the nation, and we include as Reading 60 an excerpt from the conclusion, "Policy Steps Toward Closing the Gap."

This book's website (www.sagepub.com/ferguson) lists resources and websites for activism so that you may further educate yourself about needed social change. You must ask yourself, What would a society with racial equality look like? What would a society of gender equality look like? Social class equality? Do not be afraid to dream big. More important, what can you do to become an agent of social change in your relationships, on your campus, in your community, and in other social structures? What strategies can you use to build coalitions and bridge differences between social groups? We all gain something significant when social inequality is lessened; we all become more fully human.

# 56

# TOWARD A NEW VISION

*Race, Class, and Gender as*
*Categories of Analysis and Connection*

PATRICIA HILL COLLINS

*Most people focus on how they are oppressed but often have a more difficult time seeing how they are at the same time oppressors. In this reading by Patricia Hill Collins, Distinguished University Professor of Sociology at the University of Maryland, the author challenges the reader to think about how victims of oppression are part of systems of oppression. This classic piece was written in 1989 as a speech in which Collins presented to an audience of academics her thinking about a cornerstone of new theorizing and scholarship in social inequality and intersectionality. To push scholars' thinking at the time, Collins frames this work around two key questions: (1) How can race, class, and gender, as categories of analysis, be reconceptualized beyond dichotomous, additive, or ranked categories?; and (2) How can we transcend the barriers created by our raced, classed, and gendered experiences to build coalitions? Thus, this work is both theoretical and activist in intent.*

*The true focus of revolutionary change is never merely the oppressive situations which we seek to escape, but that piece of the oppressor which is planted deep within each of us.[1]*

Audre Lorde

Audre Lorde's statement raises a troublesome issue for scholars and activists working for social change. While many of us have little difficulty assessing our own victimization within some major system of oppression, whether it be by race, social class, religion, sexual orientation,

*Source:* Hill Collins, Patricia. 1989. "Toward a New Vision: Race, Class, and Gender as Categories of Analysis and Connection." Research paper published by the Center for Research on Women at the University of Memphis. Memphis, Tennessee. Reprinted by permission of the author.

ethnicity, age or gender, we typically fail to see how our thoughts and actions uphold someone else's subordination. Thus, White feminists routinely point with confidence to their oppression as women but resist seeing how much their white skin privileges them. African Americans who possess eloquent analyses of racism often persist in viewing poor White women as symbols of white power. The radical left fares little better. "If only people of color and women could see their true class interests," they argue, "class solidarity would eliminate racism and sexism." In essence, each group identifies the type of oppression with which it feels most comfortable as being fundamental and classifies all other types as being of lesser importance.

Oppression is full of such contradictions. Errors in political judgment that we make concerning how we teach our courses, what we tell our children, and which organizations are worthy of our time, talents and financial support flow smoothly from errors in theoretical analysis about the nature of oppression and activism. Once we realize that there are few pure victims or oppressors, and that each one of us derives varying amounts of penalty and privilege from the multiple systems of oppression that frame our lives, then we will be in a position to see the need for new ways of thought and action.

To get at that "piece of the oppressor which is planted deep within each of us," we need at least two things. First, we need new visions of what oppression is, new categories of analysis that are inclusive of race, class, and gender as distinctive yet interlocking structures of oppression. Adhering to a stance of comparing and ranking oppressions—the proverbial "I'm more oppressed than you"—locks us all into a dangerous dance of competing for attention, resources, and theoretical supremacy. Instead, I suggest that we examine our different experiences within the more fundamental relationship of domination and subordination. To focus on the particular arrangements that race or class or gender take in our time and place without seeing these structures as sometimes parallel and sometimes interlocking dimensions of the more fundamental relationship of domination and subordination may temporarily

ease our consciences. But while such thinking may lead to short-term social reforms, it is simply inadequate for the task of bringing about long-term social transformation.[2]

While race, class, and gender as categories of analysis are essential in helping us understand the structural bases of domination and subordination, new ways of thinking that are not accompanied by new ways of acting offer incomplete prospects for change. To get at that "piece of the oppressor which is planted deep within each of us," we also need to change our daily behavior. Currently, we are all enmeshed in a complex web of problematic relationships that grant our mirror images full human subjectivity while stereotyping and objectifying those most different than ourselves. We often assume that the people we work with, teach, send our children to school with, and sit next to in conferences such as this, will act and feel in prescribed ways because they belong to given race, social class or gender categories. These judgments by category must be replaced with fully human relationships that transcend the legitimate differences created by race, class and gender as categories of analysis. We require new categories of connection, new visions of what our relationships with one another can be.

Our task is immense. We must first recognize race, class and gender as interlocking categories of analysis that together cultivate profound differences in our personal biographies. But then we must transcend those very differences by reconceptualizing race, class and gender in order to create new categories of connection.

My presentation today addresses this need for new patterns of thought and action. I focus on two basic questions. First, how can we reconceptualize race, class and gender as categories of analysis? Second, how can we transcend the barriers created by our experiences with race, class and gender oppression in order to build the types of coalitions essential for social change? To address these questions, I contend that we must acquire both new theories of how race, class and gender have shaped the experiences not just of women of color, but of all groups. Moreover, we must see the connections between these categories of analysis and the personal issues in our everyday lives, particularly our scholarship, our teaching and our relationships with our colleagues and students. As Audre Lorde points out, change starts with self, and relationships that we have with those around us must always be the primary site for social change.

## How Can We Reconceptualize Race, Class and Gender as Categories of Analysis?

To me, we must shift our discourse away from additive analyses of oppression.[3] Such approaches are typically based on two key premises. First, they depend on either/or, dichotomous thinking. Persons, things and ideas are conceptualized in terms of their opposites. For example, Black/White, man/woman, thought/feeling, and fact/opinion are defined in oppositional terms. Thought and feeling are not seen as two different and interconnected ways of approaching truth that can coexist in scholarship and teaching. Instead, feeling is defined as antithetical to reason, as its opposite. In spite of the fact that we all have "both/and" identities (I am both a college professor and a mother—I don't stop being a mother when I drop my child off at school, or forget everything I learned while scrubbing the toilet), we persist in trying to classify each other in either/or categories. I live each day as an African American woman, a race/gender specific experience. And I am not alone. Everyone in this room has a race/gender/class specific identity. Either/or, dichotomous thinking is especially troublesome when applied to theories of oppression because every individual must be classified as being either oppressed or not oppressed. The both/and position of simultaneously being oppressed and oppressor becomes conceptually impossible.

A second premise of additive analyses of oppression is that these dichotomous differences must be ranked. One side of the dichotomy is typically labeled dominant and the other subordinate. Thus, Whites rule Blacks, men are deemed superior to women, and reason is seen as being preferable to emotion. Applying this premise to discussions of oppression leads to the assumption that oppression can be quantified, and that some groups are oppressed more than others. I am frequently asked, "Which has been most oppressive to you, your status as a Black person or your status as a woman?" What I am really being asked to do is divide myself into little boxes and rank my various statuses. If I experience oppression as a both/and phenomenon, why should I analyze it any differently?

Additive analyses of oppression rest squarely on the twin pillars of either/or thinking and the necessity to quantify and rank all relationships in order to know where one stands. Such approaches typically see African American women as being more oppressed than everyone else because the majority of Black women experience the negative effects of race, class and gender oppression simultaneously. In essence, if you add together separate oppressions, you are left with a grand oppression greater than the sum of its parts.[4]

I am not denying that specific groups experience oppression more harshly than others—lynching is certainly objectively worse than being held up as a sex object. But we must be careful not to confuse this issue of the saliency of one type of oppression in people's lives with a theoretical stance positing the interlocking nature of oppression. Race, class and gender may all structure a situation but may not be equally visible and/or important in people's self-definitions. In certain contexts, such as the antebellum American South and contemporary South Africa, racial oppression is more visibly salient, while in other contexts, such as Haiti, El Salvador and Nicaragua, social class oppression may be more apparent. For middle class White women, gender may assume experiential primacy unavailable to poor Hispanic women struggling with the ongoing issues of low paid jobs and the frustrations of the welfare bureaucracy. This recognition that one category may have salience over another for a given time and place does not minimize the theoretical importance of assuming that race, class and gender as categories of analysis structure all relationships.

In order to move toward new visions of what oppression is, I think that we need to ask new questions. How are relationships of domination and subordination structured and maintained in the American political economy? How do race, class and gender function as parallel and interlocking systems that shape this basic relationship of domination and subordination? Questions such as these promise to move us away from futile theoretical struggles concerned with ranking oppressions and toward analyses that assume race, class and gender are all present in any given setting, even if one appears more visible and salient than the others. Our task becomes redefined as one of reconceptualizing oppression by uncovering the connections among race, class and gender as categories of analysis.

## 1. Institutional Dimension of Oppression

Sandra Harding's contention that gender oppression is structured along three main dimensions—the institutional, the symbolic, and the individual—offers a useful model for a more comprehensive analysis encompassing race, class and gender oppression.[5] Systemic relationships of domination and subordination structured through social institutions such as schools, businesses, hospitals, the workplace, and government agencies represent the institutional dimension of oppression. Racism, sexism and elitism all have concrete institutional locations. Even though the workings of the institutional dimension of oppression are often obscured with ideologies claiming equality of opportunity, in actuality, race, class and gender place Asian American women, Native American men, White men, African American women, and other groups in distinct institutional niches with varying degrees of penalty and privilege.

Even though I realize that many in the current administration would not share this assumption, let us assume that the institutions of American society discriminate, whether by design or by accident. While many of us are familiar with how race, gender and class operate separately to structure inequality, I want to focus on how these three systems interlock in structuring the institutional dimension of oppression.

To get at the interlocking nature of race, class and gender, I want you to think about the antebellum plantation as a guiding metaphor for a variety of American social institutions. Even though slavery is typically analyzed as a racist institution, and occasionally as a class institution, I suggest that slavery was a race, class, gender-specific institution. Removing any one piece from our analysis diminishes our understanding of the true nature of relations of domination and subordination under slavery.

Slavery was a profoundly patriarchal institution. It rested on the dual tenets of White male authority and White male property, a joining of the political and the economic within the institution of the family. Heterosexism was assumed and all Whites were expected to marry. Control over affluent White women's sexuality remained key to slavery's survival because property was to be passed on to the legitimate heirs of the slaveowner. Ensuring affluent White women's virginity and chastity was deeply intertwined with maintenance of property relations.

Under slavery, we see varying levels of institutional protection given to affluent White women, working class and poor White women, and enslaved African women. Poor White women enjoyed few of the protections held out to their upper class sisters. Moreover, the devalued status of Black women was key in keeping all White women in their assigned places. Controlling Black women's fertility was also key to the continuation of slavery, for children born to slave mothers themselves were slaves.

African American women shared the devalued status of chattel with their husbands, fathers and sons. Racism stripped Blacks as a group of legal rights, education, and control over their own persons. African Americans could be whipped, branded, sold, or killed, not because they were poor, or because they were women, but because they were Black. Racism ensured that Blacks would continue to serve Whites and suffer economic exploitation at the hands of all Whites.

So we have a very interesting chain of command on the plantation—the affluent White master as the reigning patriarch, his White wife helpmate to serve him, help him manage his property and bring up his heirs, his faithful servants whose production and reproduction were tied to the requirements of the capitalist political economy, and largely propertyless, working class White men and women watching from afar. In essence, the foundations for the contemporary roles of elite White women, poor Black women, working class White men, and a series of other groups can be seen in stark relief in this fundamental American social institution. While Blacks experienced the most harsh treatment under slavery, and thus made slavery clearly visible as a racist institution, race, class and gender interlocked in structuring slavery's systemic organization of domination and subordination.

Even today, the plantation remains a compelling metaphor for institutional oppression. Certainly the actual conditions of oppression are not as severe now as they were then. To argue, as some do, that things have not changed all that much denigrates the achievements of those who struggled for social change before us. But the basic relationships among Black men, Black women, elite White women, elite White men, working class White men and working class White women as groups remain essentially intact . . . .

## 2. The Symbolic Dimension of Oppression

Widespread, societally sanctioned ideologies used to justify relations of domination and subordination comprise the symbolic dimension of oppression. Central to this process is the use of stereotypical or controlling images of diverse race, class and gender groups. In order to assess the power of this dimension of oppression, I want you to make a list, either on paper or in your head, of "masculine" and "feminine" characteristics. If your list is anything like that compiled by most people, it reflects some variation of the following:

| Masculine | Feminine |
| --- | --- |
| Aggressive | Passive |
| Leader | Follower |
| Rational | Emotional |
| Strong | Weak |
| Intellectual | Physical |

Not only does this list reflect either/or dichotomous thinking and the need to rank both sides of the dichotomy, but ask yourself exactly which men and women you had in mind when compiling these characteristics. This list applies almost exclusively to middle class White men and women. The allegedly "masculine" qualities that you probably listed are only acceptable when exhibited by elite White men, or when used by Black and Hispanic men against each other or against women of color. Aggressive Black and Hispanic men are seen as dangerous, not powerful, and are often penalized when they exhibit any of the allegedly "masculine" characteristics. Working class and poor White men fare slightly better and are also denied the allegedly "masculine" symbols of leadership, intellectual competence, and human rationality. Women of color and working class and poor White women are also not represented on this list, for they have never had the luxury of being "ladies." What appear to be universal categories representing all men and women instead are unmasked as being applicable to only a small group.

It is important to see how the symbolic images applied to different race, class and gender groups interact in maintaining systems of domination and subordination. If I were to ask you to repeat the same assignment, only this time, by making separate lists for Black men, Black women, Hispanic women and Hispanic men, I suspect that your gender symbolism would be quite different. In comparing all of the lists, you might begin to see the interdependence of symbols applied to all groups. For example, the elevated images of White womanhood need devalued images of Black womanhood in order to maintain credibility.

While the above exercise reveals the interlocking nature of race, class and gender in structuring the symbolic dimension of oppression, part of its importance lies in demonstrating how race, class and gender pervade a wide range of what appears to be universal language. Attending to diversity in our scholarship, in our teaching, and in our daily lives provides a new angle of vision on interpretations of reality thought to be natural, normal and "true." Moreover, viewing images of masculinity and femininity as universal gender symbolism, rather than as symbolic images that are race, class and gender specific, renders the experiences of people of color and of nonprivileged White women and men invisible. One way to dehumanize an individual or a group is to deny the reality of their experiences. So when we refuse to deal with race or class because they do not appear to be directly relevant to gender, we are actually becoming part of someone else's problem.

Assuming that everyone is affected differently by the same interlocking set of symbolic images allows us to move forward toward new analyses. Women of color and White women have different relationships to White male authority and this difference explains the distinct gender symbolism applied to both groups . . . .

Each of us lives with an allotted portion of institutional privilege and penalty, and with varying levels of rejection and seduction inherent in the symbolic images applied to us. This is the context in which we make our choices. Taken together, the institutional and symbolic dimensions of oppression create a structural backdrop against which all of us live our lives.

### 3. The Individual Dimension of Oppression

Whether we benefit or not, we all live within institutions that reproduce race, class and gender oppression. Even if we never have any contact with members of other race, class and gender groups, we all encounter images of these groups and are exposed to the symbolic meanings attached to those images. On this dimension of oppression, our individual biographies vary tremendously. As a result of our institutional and symbolic statuses, all of our choices become political acts.

Each of us must come to terms with the multiple ways in which race, class and gender as categories of analysis frame our individual biographies. I have lived my entire life as an African American woman from a working class family and this basic fact has had a profound impact on my personal biography. Imagine how different your life might be if you had been born Black, or White, or poor, or of a different race/class/gender group than the one with which you are most familiar. The institutional treatment you would have received and the symbolic meanings attached to your very existence might differ dramatically from what you now consider to be natural, normal and part of

everyday life. You might be the same, but your personal biography might have been quite different.

I believe that each of us carries around the cumulative effect of our lives within multiple structures of oppression. If you want to see how much you have been affected by this whole thing, I ask you one simple question—who are your close friends? Who are the people with whom you can share your hopes, dreams, vulnerabilities, fears and victories? Do they look like you? If they are all the same, circumstance may be the cause. For the first seven years of my life I saw only low income Black people. My friends from those years reflected the composition of my community. But now that I am an adult, can the defense of circumstance explain the patterns of people that I trust as my friends and colleagues? When given other alternatives, if my friends and colleagues reflect the homogeneity of one race, class and gender group, then these categories of analysis have indeed become barriers to connection.[6]

I am not suggesting that people are doomed to follow the paths laid out for them by race, class and gender as categories of analysis. While these three structures certainly frame my opportunity structure, I as an individual always have the choice of accepting things as they are, or trying to change them. As Nikki Giovanni points out, "We've got to live in the real world. If we don't like the world we're living in, change it. And if we can't change it, we change ourselves. We can do something."[7] While a piece of the oppressor may be planted deep within each of us, we each have the choice of accepting that piece or challenging it as part of the "true focus of revolutionary change."

## How Can We Transcend the Barriers Created by Our Experiences With Race, Class and Gender Oppression in Order to Build the Types of Coalitions Essential for Social Change?

Reconceptualizing oppression and seeing the barriers created by race, class and gender as interlocking categories of analysis is a vital first step. But we must transcend these barriers by moving toward race, class and gender as categories of connection, by building relationships and coalitions that will bring about social change. What are some of the issues involved in doing this?

## 1. Differences in Power and Privilege

First, we must recognize that our differing experiences with oppression create problems in the relationships among us. Each of us lives within a system that vests us with varying levels of power and privilege. These differences in power, whether structured along axes of race, class, gender, age or sexual orientation, frame our relationships. African American writer June Jordan describes her discomfort on a Caribbean vacation with Olive, the Black woman who cleaned her room:

> Even though both "Olive" and "I" live inside a
> conflict neither one of us created, and even though
> both of us therefore hurt inside that conflict, I may be
> one of the monsters she needs to eliminate from her
> universe and, in a sense, she may be one of the
> monsters in mine.[8]

Differences in power constrain our ability to connect with one another even when we think we are engaged in dialogue across differences. Let me give you an example. One year, the students in my course "Sociology of the Black Community" got into a heated discussion about the reasons for the upsurge of racial incidents on college campuses. Black students complained vehemently about the apathy and resistance they felt most White students expressed about examining their own racism. Mark, a White male student, found their comments particularly unsettling. After claiming that all the Black people he had ever known had expressed no such beliefs to him, he questioned how representative the viewpoints of his fellow students actually were. When pushed further, Mark revealed that he had participated in conversations over the years with the Black domestic worker employed by his family. Since she had never expressed such strong feelings about White racism, Mark was genuinely shocked by class

discussions. Ask yourselves whether that domestic worker was in a position to speak freely.[9] Would it have been wise for her to do so in a situation where the power between the two parties was so unequal? . . .

Coming from a tradition where most relationships across difference are squarely rooted in relations of domination and subordination, we have much less experience relating to people as different but equal. The classroom is potentially one powerful and safe space where dialogues among individuals of unequal power relationships can occur. The relationship between Mark, the student in my class, and the domestic worker is typical of a whole series of relationships that people have when they relate across differences in power and privilege. The relationship among Mark and his classmates represents the power of the classroom to minimize those differences so that people of different levels of power can use race, class and gender as categories of analysis in order to generate meaningful dialogues. In this case, the classroom equalized racial difference so that Black students who normally felt silenced spoke out. White students like Mark, generally unaware of how they had been privileged by their whiteness, lost that privilege in the classroom and thus became open to genuine dialogue.

Reconceptualizing course syllabi represents a comparable process of determining which groups are privileged by our current research and pedagogical techniques and which groups are penalized. Reforming these existing techniques can be a critical first step in moving toward a transformed curriculum reflecting race, class and gender as interlocking categories of analysis. But while reform may be effective as a short-term strategy, it is unlikely to bring about fundamental transformation in the long term. To me, social transformations, whether of college curricula or of the communities in which we live and work, require moving outside our areas of specialization and groups of interest in order to build coalitions across differences.

## 2. Coalitions Around Common Causes

A second issue in building relationships and coalitions essential for social change concerns knowing the real reasons for coalition. Just what brings people together? One powerful catalyst fostering group solidarity is the presence of a common enemy. African American, Hispanic, Asian American, and women's studies all share the common intellectual heritage of challenging what passes for certified knowledge in the academy. But politically expedient relationships and coalitions like these are fragile because, as June Jordan points out:

> It occurs to me that much organizational grief could be avoided if people understood that partnership in misery does not necessarily provide for partnership for change: When we get the monsters off our backs all of us may want to run in very different directions.[10]

Sharing a common cause assists individuals and groups in maintaining relationships that transcend their differences. Building effective coalitions involves struggling to hear one another and developing empathy for each other's points of view. The coalitions that I have been involved in that lasted and that worked have been those where commitment to a specific issue mandated collaboration as the best strategy for addressing the issue at hand.

Several years ago, master's degree in hand, I chose to teach in an inner city, parochial school in danger of closing. The money was awful, the conditions were poor, but the need was great. In my job, I had to work with a range of individuals who, on the surface, had very little in common. We had White nuns, Black middle class graduate students, Blacks from the "community," some of whom had been incarcerated and/or were affiliated with a range of federal anti-poverty programs. Parents formed another part of this community, Harvard faculty another, and a few well-meaning White liberals from Colorado were sprinkled in for good measure.

As you might imagine, tension was high. Initially, our differences seemed insurmountable. But as time passed, we found a common bond that we each brought to the school. In spite of profound differences in our personal biographies, differences that in other settings would have hampered our ability to relate to one another, we found that we were all deeply committed to the education of Black children. By learning to value each other's commitment and by recognizing that we each had different skills that were essential to actualizing that commitment we built an effective coalition around a common cause. Our school was successful, and the children we taught benefited from the diversity we offered them.

I think that the process of curriculum transformation will require a process comparable to that of political organizing around common causes. None of us alone has a comprehensive vision of how race, class and gender operate as categories of analysis or how they might be used as categories of connection. Our personal biographies offer us partial views. Few of us can manage to study race, class and gender simultaneously. Instead, we each know more about some dimensions of this larger story and less about others. While we each may be committed to an inclusive, transformed curriculum, the task of building one is necessarily a collective effort. Just as the members of the school had special skills to offer to the task of building the school, we have areas of specialization and expertise, whether scholarly, theoretical, pedagogical or within areas of race, class or gender. We do not all have to do the same thing in the same way. Instead, we must support each other's efforts, realizing that they are all part of the larger enterprise of bringing about social change.[11]

### 3. Building Empathy

A third issue involved in building the types of relationships and coalitions essential for social change concerns the issue of individual accountability. Race, class and gender oppression form the structural backdrop against which we frame our relationships—these are the forces that encourage us to substitute voyeurism and academic colonialism for fully human relationships. But while we may not have created this situation, we are each responsible for making individual, personal choices concerning which elements race, class and gender oppression we will accept and which we will work to change.

One essential component of this accountability involves developing empathy for the experiences of individuals and groups different than ourselves.

Empathy begins with taking an interest in the facts of other people's lives, both as individuals and as groups. If you care about me, you should want to know not only the details of my personal biography but a sense of how race, class and gender as categories of analysis created the institutional and symbolic backdrop for my personal biography. How can you hope to assess my character without knowing the details of the circumstances I face?

Moreover, by taking a theoretical stance that we have all been affected by race, class and gender as categories of analysis that have structured our treatment, we open up possibilities for using those same constructs as categories of connection in building empathy. For example, I have a good White woman friend with whom I share common interests and beliefs. But we know that our racial differences have provided us with different experiences. So we talk about them. We do not assume that because I am Black, race has only affected me and not her or that because I am a Black woman, race neutralizes the effect of gender in my life while accenting it in hers. We take those same categories of analysis that have created cleavages in our lives, in this case, categories of race and gender, and use them as categories of connection in building empathy for each other's experiences.

Finding common causes and building empathy is difficult, no matter which side of privilege we inhabit. Building empathy from the dominant side of privilege is difficult, simply because individuals from privileged backgrounds are not encouraged to do so. For example, in order for those of you who are White to develop empathy for the experiences of people of color, you must grapple with how your white skin has privileged you. This is difficult to do, because it not only entails the intellectual process of seeing how whiteness is elevated in institutions and symbols, but it also involves the often painful process of seeing how your whiteness has shaped your personal biography. Intellectual stances against the institutional and symbolic dimensions of racism are generally easier to maintain than sustained self-reflection about how racism has shaped all of our individual biographies. Were and are your fathers, uncles, and grandfathers really more capable than

mine, or can their accomplishments be explained in part by the racism members of my family experienced? Did your mothers stand silently by and watch all this happen? More importantly, how have they passed on the benefits of their whiteness to you?

These are difficult questions, and I have tremendous respect for my colleagues and students who are trying to answer them. Since there is no compelling reason to examine the source and meaning of one's own privilege, I know that those who do so have freely chosen this stance. They are making conscious efforts to root out the piece of the oppressor planted within them. To me, they are entitled to the support of people of color in their efforts. Men who declare themselves feminists, members of the middle class who ally themselves with anti-poverty struggles, heterosexuals who support gays and lesbians, are all trying to grow, and their efforts place them far ahead of the majority who never think of engaging in such important struggles.

Building empathy from the subordinate side of privilege is also difficult, but for different reasons. Members of subordinate groups are understandably reluctant to abandon a basic mistrust of members of powerful groups because this basic mistrust has traditionally been central to their survival. As a Black woman, it would be foolish for me to assume that White women, or Black men, or White men or any other group with a history of exploiting African American women has my best interests at heart. These groups enjoy varying amounts of privilege over me and therefore I must carefully watch them and be prepared for a relation of domination and subordination.

Like the privileged, members of subordinate groups must also work toward replacing judgments by category with new ways of thinking and acting. Refusing to do so stifles prospects for effective coalition and social change. Let me use another example from my own experiences. When I was an undergraduate, I had little time or patience for the theorizing of the privileged. My initial years at a private, elite institution were difficult, not because the coursework was challenging (it was, but that wasn't what distracted me) or because I had to work while my classmates lived on family allowances (I was used to work). The adjustment was difficult because I was surrounded by so many people who took their privilege for granted. Most of them felt entitled to their wealth. That astounded me.

I remember one incident of watching a White woman down the hall in my dormitory try to pick out which sweater to wear. The sweaters were piled up on her bed in all the colors of the rainbow, sweater after sweater. She asked my advice in a way that let me know that choosing a sweater was one of the most important decisions she had to make on a daily basis. Standing knee-deep in her sweaters, I realized how different our lives were. She did not have to worry about maintaining a solid academic average so that she could receive financial aid. Because she was in the majority, she was not treated as a representative of her race. She did not have to consider how her classroom comments or basic existence on campus contributed to the treatment her group would receive. Her allowance protected her from having to work, so she was free to spend her time studying, partying, or in her case, worrying about which sweater to wear. The degree of inequality in our lives and her unquestioned sense of entitlement concerning that inequality offended me. For a while, I categorized all affluent White women as being superficial, arrogant, overly concerned with material possessions, and part of my problem. But had I continued to classify people in this way, I would have missed out on making some very good friends whose discomfort with their inherited or acquired social class privileges pushed them to examine their position.

Since I opened with the words of Audre Lorde, it seems appropriate to close with another of her ideas. As we go forth to the remaining activities of this workshop, and beyond this workshop, we might do well to consider Lorde's perspective:

> Each of us is called upon to take a stand. So in these days ahead, as we examine ourselves and each other, our works, our fears, our differences, our sisterhood and survivals, I urge you to tackle what is most difficult for us all, self-scrutiny of our complacencies, the idea that since each of us believes she is on the side of right, she need not examine her position.[12]

I urge you to examine your position.

## DISCUSSION QUESTIONS

1. How are the two quotes by Audre Lorde at the beginning and the end of this reading relevant to Collins's thesis that we need new forms of thought and actions to deal with the intersecting categories of race, social class, and gender?
2. What are the three dimensions of oppression Collins uses to foster a new understanding of the connections among race, gender, and social class as categories of analysis?
3. What are Collins's suggestions for social change? How can you apply them to other issues we have studied in this volume?

## NOTES

1. Audre Lorde, *Sister Outsider*. (Trumansberg, NY: The Crossing Press, 1984), p. 123.
2. For a discussion of the difference between reform and transformation, see Johnnella Butler, "Difficult Dialogues," *The Women's Review of Books* 6, no. 5 (1989):16.
3. For a critique of additive analyses of oppression, see Elizabeth V. Spelman, "Theories of Race and Gender: The Erasure of Black Women," *Quest* 5 (1982):36–62. For a more comprehensive discussion of the epistemological underpinnings of additive analyses, see Patricia Hill Collins, "The Social Construction of Black Feminist Thought," *SIGNS: Journal of Women and Culture in Society,* Summer 1989.
4. I think that an adherence to the additive nature of oppression is one weakness in the work of standpoint theorists. For a summary and critique of standpoint epistemologies, see Sandra Harding, *The Science Question in Feminism* (Ithaca, NY: Cornell University Press, 1986). In my earlier essay, "Learning From the Outsider Within: The Sociological Significance of Black Feminist Thought," *Social Problems* 33, no. 6 (1986):14–32, I implied that Black women were more oppressed than other groups. I have since come to believe that Black women are differently oppressed.
5. Ibid.
6. I am indebted to Silvio Cancio for this point.
7. Claudia Tate, ed., *Black Women Writers at Work* (New York: Continuum, 1983), p. 68.

8. June Jordan, *On Call: Political Essays* (Boston: South End Press, 1985), p. 47.

9. For work on how power inequalities shape relationships between Black domestic workers and their employers, see Judith Rollins, *Between Women: Domestics and Their Employers* (Philadelphia: Temple University Press, 1985).

10. Jordan (note 11), p. 47.

11. For a more theoretical discussion of issues of curriculum transformation, see Margaret Andersen, "Changing the Curriculum in Higher Education," *SIGNS: Journal of Women and Culture in Society* 12, no. 2 (1987):222–254.

12. Audre Lorde, Keynote Address, "Sisterhood and Survival," Conference on the Black Woman Writer and the Diaspora, Michigan State University, 1985.

## 57

# How White People Can Serve as Allies to People of Color in the Struggle to End Racism

## Paul Kivel

*This second reading in Part V on social change and empowerment is by Paul Kivel. Kivel, a social justice educator, writer, and social activist, works as a speaker and trainer on men's issues, racism, and diversity. He often teaches workshops to help youth and adults become more involved in social justice work and community struggles to end oppression. Kivel also is the cofounder of the Oakland Men's Project, a nationally recognized multicultural organization dedicated to helping people understand the roots of violence in our society and to seek positive solutions. This reading, taken from Kivel's critically acclaimed 1996 book* Uprooting Racism: How White People Can Work for Racial Justice, *builds on Patricia Hill Collins' arguments for social change in the previous reading and is a brief discussion of strategies for individual-level social change. In this excerpt, Kivel reviews how individual whites can work for racial equality by serving as allies to people of color.*

## What Does an Ally Do?

Being allies to people of color in the struggle to end racism is one of the most important things that white people can do. There is no one correct way to be an ally. Each of us is different. We have different relationships to social organizations, political processes and economic structures. We are more or less powerful because of such factors as our gender, class, work situation, family and

*Source:* Kivel, Paul. 1996. "How White People Can Serve as Allies to People of Color in the Struggle to End Racism." In *Uprooting Racism: How White People Can Work for Racial Justice.* British Columbia, Canada: New Society Publishers. Reprinted by permission of the publisher.

community participation. Being an ally to people of color is an ongoing strategic process in which we look at our personal and social resources, evaluate the environment we have helped to create and decide what needs to be done.

Times change and circumstances vary. What is a priority today may not be tomorrow. What is effective or strategic right now may not be next year. We need to be thinking with others and noticing what is going on around us so we will know how to put our attention, energy, time and money toward strategic priorities in the struggle to end racism and other injustices.

This includes listening to people of color so that we can support the actions they take, the risks they bear in defending their lives and challenging white hegemony. It includes watching the struggle of white people to maintain dominance and the struggle of people of color to gain equal opportunity, justice, safety and respect.

We don't need to believe or accept as true everything people of color say. There is no one voice in any community, much less in the complex and diverse communities of color spanning our country. We do need to listen carefully to the voices of people of color so that we understand and give credence to their experience. We can then evaluate the content of what they are saying by what we know about how racism works and by our own critical thinking and progressive political analysis.

It is important to emphasize this point because often we become paralyzed when people of color talk about racism. We are afraid to challenge what they say. We will be ineffective as allies if we give up our ability to analyze and think critically, if we simply accept everything that a person of color states as truth.

Listening to people of color and giving critical credence to their experience is not easy for us because of the training we have received. Nevertheless, it is an important first step. When we hear statements that make us want to react defensively, we can instead keep some specific things in mind as we try to understand what is happening and determine how best to be allies.

We have seen how racism is a pervasive part of our culture. Therefore we should always assume that racism is at least part of the picture. In light of this assumption, we should look for the patterns involved rather than treating most events as isolated occurrences.

Since we know that racism is involved, we know our whiteness is also a factor. We should look for ways we are acting from assumptions of white power or privilege. This will help us acknowledge any fear or confusion we may feel. It will allow us to see our tendencies to defend ourselves or our tendencies to assume we should be in control. Then we will be able to talk with other white people so these tendencies don't get in the way of our being effective allies.

We have many opportunities to practice these critical listening and thinking skills because we are all involved in a complex web of interpersonal and institutional relationships. Every day we are presented with opportunities to analyze what is going on around us and to practice taking direct action as allies to people of color.

People of color will always be on the front lines fighting racism because their lives are at stake. How do we act and support them effectively, both when they are in the room with us, and when they are not?

It can be difficult for those of us who are white to know how to be strong allies for people of color when discrimination occurs. In the following interaction, imagine that Roberto is a young Latino student just coming out of a job interview with a white recruiter from a computer company. Let's see how one white person might respond.

Roberto is angry, not sure what to do next. He walks down the hall and meets a white teacher who wants to help.*

**R** = Roberto, **T** = teacher

*T:*    *Hey, Roberto, how's it going?*

*R:*    *That son of a bitch! He wasn't going to give me no job. That was really messed up.*

*T:*    *Hold on there, don't be so angry. It was probably a mistake or something.*

R:     *There was no mistake. The racist bastard. He wants to keep me from getting a good job, rather have us all on welfare or doing maintenance work.*

T:     *Calm down now or you'll get yourself in more trouble. Don't go digging a hole for yourself. Maybe I could help you if you weren't so angry.*

R:     *That's easy for you to say. This man was discriminating against me. White folks are all the same. They talk about equal opportunity, but it's the same old shit.*

T:     *Wait a minute, I didn't have anything to do with this. Don't blame me, I'm not responsible. If you wouldn't be so angry maybe I could help you. You probably took what he said the wrong way. Maybe you were too sensitive.*

R:     *I could tell. He was racist. That's all. (He storms off.)*

---

*Adapted from *Men's Work: How to Stop the Violence That Tears Our Lives Apart* (Hazelden/Ballantine, 1992).

What did you notice about this scene? On the one hand, the teacher is concerned and is trying to help. On the other hand, his intervention is not very effective. He immediately downplays the incident, discounting Roberto's feelings and underestimating the possibility of racism. He seems to be saying that racism is unlikely—it was probably just a misunderstanding, or Roberto was being too sensitive.

The teacher is clearly uncomfortable with Roberto's anger. He begins to defend himself, the job recruiter and white people. He ends up feeling attacked for being white. Rather than talking about what happened, he focuses on Roberto's anger and his generalizations about white people. By the end of the interaction he is threatening to get Roberto in trouble himself if he doesn't calm down. As he walks away he may be thinking it's no wonder Roberto didn't get hired for the job.

You probably recognize some of the tactics described. The teacher denies or minimizes the likelihood of racism, blames Roberto, and eventually counterattacks, claiming to be a victim of Roberto's anger and racial generalizations.

This interaction illustrates some of our common feelings that get in the way of intervening effectively where discrimination is occurring. First is the feeling that we are being personally attacked. It is difficult to hear the phrase "all white people," or "you white people." We want to defend ourselves and other whites. We don't want to believe that white people could intentionally hurt others. Or we may want to say, "Not me, I'm different."

There are some things we should remember when we feel attacked. First, this is a question of injustice. We need to focus on what happened and what we can do about it, not on our feelings of being attacked.

Second, someone who has been the victim of injustice is legitimately angry and they may or may not express that anger in ways we like. Criticizing the way people express their anger deflects attention and action away from the injustice that was committed. After the injustice has been dealt with, if you still think it's worthwhile and not an attempt to control the situation yourself, you can go back and discuss ways of expressing anger.

Often, because we are frequently complacent about injustice that doesn't affect us directly, it takes a lot of anger and aggressive action to bring attention to a problem. If we were more pro-active in identifying and intervening in situations of injustice, people would not have to be so "loud" to get our attention in the first place.

Finally, part of the harm that racism does is that it forces people of color to be wary and mistrustful of all white people, just as sexism forces women to mistrust all men. People of color face racism every day, often from unexpected quarters. They never know when a white friend, co-worker, teacher, police officer, doctor or passer-by may discriminate, act hostile or say something offensive. They have to be wary of *all* white people, even though they know that not all white people will mistreat them. They have likely been hurt in the past by white people they thought they could trust, and therefore they may make statements about all white people. We must remember that although we want to be trustworthy, trust is not the issue. We are not fighting racism so that people of color will trust us. Trust builds over time through our visible efforts to be allies and fight racism. Rather than trying to be safe and trustworthy, we need to be more active, less defensive, and put issues of trust aside.

When people are discriminated against they may feel unseen, stereotyped, attacked or as if a door has been slammed in their face. They may feel confused, frustrated, helpless or angry. They are probably reminded of other similar experiences. They may want to hurt someone in return, or hide their pain, or simply forget about the whole experience. Whatever the response, the experience is deeply wounding and painful. It is an act of emotional violence.

It's also an act of economic violence to be denied access to a job, housing, educational program, pay raise or promotion that one deserves. It is a practice which keeps economic resources in the hands of one group and denies them to another.

When a person is discriminated against it is a serious event and we need to treat it seriously. It is also a common event. For instance, the government estimates that there are over two million acts of race-based housing discrimination every year—twenty million every decade (Ezorsky 1991:13). We know that during their lifetimes people of color have to face many such discriminatory experiences in school, work, housing and community settings.

People of color do not protest discrimination lightly. They know that when they do white people routinely deny or minimize it, blame them for causing trouble and then counterattack. . .

People of color are experts in discrimination resulting from racism. Most experience it regularly and see its effects on their communities. Not every complaint of discrimination is valid, but most have some truth in them. It would be a tremendous step forward if we assumed that there was some truth in every complaint of racial discrimination even when other factors may also be involved. At least then we would take it seriously enough to fully investigate.

How could the teacher in the above scenario be a better ally to Roberto? We can go back to the guidelines suggested earlier for help. First, he needs to listen much more carefully to what Roberto is saying. He should assume that Roberto is intelligent, and if he says there was racism involved then there probably was. The teacher should be aware of his own power and position, his tendency to be defensive and his desire to defend other white people or presume their innocence. It would also be worthwhile to look for similar occurrences because racism is usually not an isolated instance, but a pattern within an organization or institution.

Let's see how these suggestions might operate in a replay of this scene.

**T:** *Hey, Roberto, what's happening?*

**R:** *That son of a bitch! He wasn't going to give me no job. He was messin' with me.*

**T:** *You're really upset, tell me what happened.*

**R:** *He was discriminating against me. Wasn't going to hire me cause I'm Latino. White folks are all alike. Always playing games.*

**T:** *This is serious. Why don't you come into my office and tell me exactly what happened?*

**R:** *Okay. This company is advertising for computer programmers and I'm qualified for the job. But this man tells me there aren't any computer jobs, and then he tries to steer me toward a janitor job. He was a racist bastard.*

**T:** *That's tough. I know you would be good in that job. This sounds like a case of job discrimination. Let's write down exactly what happened, and then you can decide what you want to do about it.*

**R:** *I want to get that job.*

**T:** *If you want to challenge it, I'll help you. Maybe there's something we can do.*

This time the teacher was being a strong, supportive ally to Roberto.

## I Would Be a Perfect Ally If . . .

We learn many excuses and justifications for racism in this society. We also learn many tactics for avoiding responsibility for it. We have developed a coded language to help us avoid even talking about it directly. Our training makes it easy find reasons for not being allies to people of color. In order to maintain our commitment to being allies, we must reject the constant temptation to find excuses for being inactive.

What reasons have you used for not taking a stronger stand against racism, or for backing away from supporting a person of color?

Following are some of the reasons I've recently heard white people use. I call them "if only" statements because that's the phrase they usually begin with. Our real meaning is just the reverse. We are often setting conditions on our commitment to racial justice. We are saying that "only if" people of color do this or that will we do our part. These conditions let us blame people of color for our not being reliable allies.

I would be a committed and effective ally:

- If only people of color weren't so angry, sensitive, impatient or demanding;

- If only people of color realized that I am different from other white people, I didn't own slaves, I treat everyone the same, I don't see color, I'm not a member of the KKK and I've even been to an unlearning racism workshop;

- If only people of color would give white people a chance, hear our side of things and realize that we have it hard too;

- If only people of color didn't use phrases like "all white people";

- If only people of color didn't expect the government to do everything for them and wouldn't ask for special treatment.

Being a white ally to people of color means to be there all the time, for the long term, committed and active. Because this is hard, challenging work, we often look for ways to justify not doing it. Rather than finding ways to avoid being allies, we need to look at what gets in our way. Where does it get hard? Where do we get stuck? Many of the reasons listed above are ways to justify withdrawal from the struggle against racism.

Another way we justify our withdrawal is to find a person of color who represents, in our minds, the reason why people of color don't really deserve our support. Often these examples have to do with people of color not spending money or time the way we think they should. "I know a person who spends all her money on . . . ."

We often set standards for their conduct that we haven't previously applied to white people in the same position. "Look what happened when so-and-so got into office." In most instances we are criticizing a person of color for not being perfect (by our standards), and then using that person as an example of an entire group of people.

People of color are not perfect. Within each community of color people are as diverse as white people, with all the human strengths and failings. The question is one of justice. No one should have to earn justice. We don't talk about taking away rights or opportunities from white people because we don't like them, or because they don't make the decisions we think they should. Even when white people break the law, are obviously incompetent for the position they hold, are mean, cruel or inept, it is often difficult to hold them accountable for their actions. Our laws call for equal treatment of everyone. We should apply the same standards and treatments to people of color as we do to white people.

Not only are people of color not perfect, neither are they representatives of their race. Yet how many times have we said,

- "But I know a person of color who . . . "

- "A person of color told me that . . . "

- "So and so is a credit to her race . . . "

- (Turning to an individual) "What do people of color think about that . . . ?"

- "Let's ask so and so, he's a person of color."

We would never say that a white person was representative of that race, even if that person were Babe Ruth, Mother Teresa, Hitler, John Lennon or Margaret Thatcher, much less the only white person in the room. When was the last time you spoke as a representative for white people?

Imagine yourself in a room of fifty people where you are the only white person. At one point in the middle of a discussion about a major issue, the facilitator turns to you and says, "Could you please tell us what white people think about this issue?" How would you feel? What would you say? Would it make any difference if the facilitator said, "I know you can't speak for other white people, but could you tell us what the white perspective is on this issue?" What support would you want from other people around you in the room?

In that situation would you want a person of color to be your ally by interrupting the racial dynamic and pointing out that there isn't just one white perspective, and you couldn't represent white people? Would you want them to challenge the other people present and stand up for you? Being a white ally to people of color calls for the same kind of intervention—stepping in to support people of color when we see any kind of racism being played out.

## BASIC TACTICS

Every situation is different and calls for critical thinking about how to make a difference. Taking the statements above into account, I have compiled some general guidelines.

### 1. Assume racism is everywhere, everyday.

Just as economics influences everything we do, just as our gender and gender politics influence everything we do, assume that racism is affecting whatever is going on. We assume this because it's true, and because one of the privileges of being white is not having to see or deal with racism all the time. We have to learn to see the effect that racism has. Notice who speaks, what is said, how things are done and described. Notice who isn't present. Notice code words for race, and the implications of the policies, patterns and comments that are being expressed. You already notice the skin color of everyone you meet and interact with—now notice what difference it makes.

### 2. Notice who is the center of attention and who is the center of power.

Racism works by directing violence and blame toward people of color and consolidating power and privilege for white people.

### 3. Notice how racism is denied, minimized, and justified.

### 4. Understand and learn from the history of whiteness and racism.

Notice how racism has changed over time and how it has subverted or resisted challenges. Study the tactics that have worked effectively against it.

### 5. Understand the connections between racism, economic issues, sexism and other forms of injustice.

### 6. Take a stand against injustice.

Take risks. It is scary, difficult, risky and may bring up many feelings, but ultimately it is the only healthy and moral human thing to do. Intervene in situations where racism is being passed on.

### 7. Be strategic.

Decide what is important to challenge and what's not. Think about strategy in particular situations. Attack the source of power.

### 8. Don't confuse a battle with the war.

Behind particular incidents and interactions are larger patterns. Racism is flexible and adaptable. There will be gains and losses in the struggle for justice and equality.

**9.  Don't call names or be personally abusive.**

Since power is often defined as power over others—the ability to abuse or control people—it is easy to become abusive ourselves. However, we usually end up abusing people who have less power than we do because it is less dangerous. Attacking people doesn't address the systemic nature of racism and inequality.

**10.  Support the leadership of people of color.**

Do this consistently, but not uncritically.

**11.  Don't do it alone.**

You will not end racism by yourself. We can do it if we work together. Build support, establish networks, work with already established groups.

**12.  Talk with your children and other young people about racism.**

## DISCUSSION QUESTIONS

1.  Discuss and evaluate some of the reasons Kivel gives for claiming that whites must become allies of people of color if we are ever to end racism in America.
2.  According to Kivel, what are some strategies whites can use to become better allies of people of color? What suggestions can you add to his list? What strategies do you currently practice in your own life?

# 58

# DOING ANTI-RACISM

## Toward an Egalitarian American Society

JACQUELINE JOHNSON

SHARON RUSH

JOE FEAGIN

*This third reading on social change and empowerment moves us beyond the individual level of social change. Jacqueline Johnson, Sharon Rush, and Joe Feagin, all sociologists, provide us with societal-level suggestions for reducing racism. This essay was originally published in 2000 in the journal* Contemporary Sociology. *Scholars were asked to create utopian visions of social change in terms of reducing gender, race, and social class inequalities. Johnson, Rush, and Feagin give the reader much food for thought in this reading. In particular, they propose radical changes to achieve a utopian, nonracist society in the United States, including a new sociopolitical structure; resocialization and education; and active, individual reconciliation of race-based prejudices.*

## ELIMINATING RACISM: UTOPIAN VISIONS OF A NONRACIST SOCIETY

We view both structural and individual change as crucial for creating a new society without racism. Prior efforts to destroy structures and institutions that reinforce a system of racism have generally not cut to the heart of the racist prejudice and discrimination still implemented in the lives of most whites. Serious desegregation efforts by U.S. governmental agencies lasted barely a decade, and weak enforcement of most civil rights laws in states and at the federal level is now a national scandal (see Bendick, Egan, and Lofhjelm 1998). Recurring white backlashes against affirmative

*Source:* Johnson, Jacqueline, Sharon Rush, and Joe Feagin. 2000. "Doing Anti-Racism: Toward an Egalitarian American Society." *Contemporary Sociology Vol. 29, No. 1, Utopian Visions: Engaged Sociologies for the 21st Century* (Jan., 2000), *pp. 95–109.* Reprinted by permission of the American Sociological Association and the authors.

action programs, such as Proposition 209 in California, and the ongoing struggle for meaningful school desegregation still convulse communities across the country. By passing Proposition 209 and similar laws in various state legislatures and in the U.S. Congress, white leaders and citizens consciously resist structural change in the entrenched racial hierarchy. Likewise, efforts that solely target individual racism do not root out the structural embeddedness of racism. Many programs, for example, that stress a liberal ideology of tolerance or color-blindness encourage people to accept individuals, opinions, and cultures that are different from their own, but require little or no work from those in dominant groups to critique and confront systematically their own privileges and power (see Carr 1997). These liberal programs tend to reinforce the separate-but-equal ideology that fueled the Jim and Jane Crow era of the past. In many multicultural programs, whites become just one more "ethnic group" like all the others, rather than the dominant group with great privileges associated with its racial classification (see Van Ausdale and Feagin, forthcoming). Thus, whites can be "liberal" and still be comfortable within the inegalitarian structure of economic, political, and social arrangements.

A nonracist society cannot be achieved if whites continue to deny the reality of the racist society and of racism within themselves. The painful emotional work of actually undoing individual racism must be accomplished in combination with collective efforts for structural change. Since this essay calls for a middle-range utopian vision, a useful place to begin undoing racism is to address the social, economic, and political embeddedness of white racism within the foundation of the U.S. political system.

The openly professed democratic ideals of the "founding fathers"—no "founding mothers" were immortalized in building the political institutions— were, by intention, never realized. The white men who created the political foundation of what became the United States intended that men like themselves would hold the reins of power for the foreseeable future. Thus, our first suggestion for beginning to eliminate institutionalized racism is to call for a new Constitutional Convention, one that will represent fairly and equally, for the first time, all major groups of U.S. citizens. What might the social, political, and economic landscape of the United States look like if we started with a social system constructed to actually meet the ideals of democracy and humanity rather than the goals of privilege-maintenance and racial hierarchy?

## Laying a New Sociopolitical Foundation

Our vision of an anti-racist future begins with a critique of the constitutional framework that limits the full participation and equality of all citizens. That over 90 percent of the American population, including all white women, African Americans, and Native Americans, lacked representation in the creation of the original Constitution is an omission that must be rectified if the principles of representative government and democracy are to be taken seriously. The original writers and interpreters of the Constitution for the United States were an elite group of white men. Yet, over 200 years later, women and people of color are woefully under-represented in the judicial, executive, and legislative branches of government.

Moreover, the original framers of the Constitution introduced at least two aspects of constitutional interpretation that still perpetuate the inequalities they had built into the document. First, the notion that the Constitution should be interpreted in an "originalist" framework—that is, according to the framers' intent—continues to be a viable, if not the most popular, theory of the proper method of interpretation. But central to the framers' intent in creating the Constitution was protection of *their own* interests. Second, the concept of *stare decisis*—that is, prior interpretations are binding on future ones— significantly increases the probability that inequalities will determine future cases.

Another issue involves the process of constitutional amendment. Although the Constitution can be and has been amended, it requires a super majority vote by Americans. Unless the issue that is the subject of an amendment is supported by the political majority who already receive the most constitutional protection, it has little chance of receiving protection in the written Constitution. The failure of the Equal Rights Amendment (the ERA) poignantly illustrates this. The ERA did not pass because many men, having little incentive to alter the balance of power, did not support it. Following the originalist framework, women's voices were not heard at the Convention, and the Supreme Court historically interpreted the Constitution to mean that women are less equal than men.

In short, a combination of barriers to receiving full equality under the Constitution for women and people of color—their lack of representation in the original drafting of the Constitution, their lack of representation in interpreting the Constitution, the continuing adherence to originalism, and the arduous process of constitutional amendment—all speak to the urgency of a new Constitutional Convention. The central goals of this convention are to assert the basic human rights of those previously excluded and oppressed, and to ensure that the governing document of the new multiracial, and soon-to-be nonracist democracy is produced by representatives of all the people.

As a starting point, this new convention might make use of the UN's Universal Declaration of Human Rights in beginning debates on an egalitarian democracy (Department of Public Information, United Nations 1995). The Declaration, now supported by most nations, indicates a growing consensus across the globe that human rights are essential to a healthy society. Since 1948, this Declaration has been used frequently in crafting many international treaties and agreements. As we see it, the official call for such a Constitutional Convention should include a prior acceptance of the democratic ideals of liberty and justice such as those expressed in the Universal Declaration of Human Rights. This call for the convention would indicate a grounding of discussions in a mutual respect for the plurality of U.S. cultures, heritages, and values. Given the bedrock of present human rights, a Constitutional Convention is not only possible but has a chance to create a just and democratic society.

A truly democratic constitution would be the political basis on which to build an array of new democratic institutions. The form that a new democratic government would take in a utopian society, if

it had one at all, is difficult to imagine because all current government models function with some type of hierarchical power. Whatever form the new governing bodies might take, however, their members would need to be elected democratically by an electorate that has reason to participate actively in the new political system. The representatives could be drawn from the general public, with strict term limits and guaranteed participation by all major groups. The new government's citizens would have to be raised to be committed to supporting the human dignity of its people.

There are many necessary steps to this political utopia. A new democratic government will need to take determined action to redress past oppression if it is to create a truly nonracist, egalitarian society. It must aggressively pursue desegregation—or, better, meaningful reciprocal racial, class, and gender integration—in schooling, housing, health care, employment, politics, and public accommodations. Private efforts will also need to be made to desegregate voluntary associations, including the now highly segregated churches, synagogues, and mosques of the nation.

Moreover, the new democratic governments will need to go far beyond conventional desegregation solutions. For more than a century now, black leaders have called for reparations for the racist oppression that African Americans have suffered for 15 generations (Bittker 1973; Brooks 1999). White oppression of African Americans has been more extensive and has lasted longer than that imposed on other Americans of color. For that reason, substantial compensation is just. The new democratic government would also need to take action to compensate Native Americans for the land stolen from them and to compensate other Americans of color for the land and labor taken from them. Interestingly, this idea is already accepted by the U.S. government. The recognition, albeit often grudging, that reparations for racist oppression are sometimes morally justified and necessary can be seen in the modest governmental reparations provided by the U.S. Congress in the early 1990s for the Japanese Americans incarcerated during World War II in U.S. detention and concentration camps, and by means of court decisions for some Native American groups whose land was stolen in violation of treaties with the U.S. government.

## Education and
## Re-education for a Nonracist Society

Another major step in our vision of a nonracist, egalitarian society is the re-education of white and other Americans to address the previous and current miseducation about racial differences and racial history. The new education cannot be launched in schools alone, but must also involve all structures that actively communicate and reinforce information about racial matters and racial ideology. This includes structures of mass communication (media), structures that facilitate the intergenerational transference of knowledge (families), and other social structures that have been used to reinforce racist dogma and white notions of privilege (American religion).

Eliminating institutional oppressions like racism is essential to achieve an egalitarian society, but institutions are sustained and administered by individuals. Therefore, it is important to emphasize that institutional and individual racism are co-dependent. Racist systems construct as "natural" the tendency of individuals to use skin color as a basis for assigning others to in-groups and out-groups (Tajfel 1982). But seeing and treating other human beings in such oppositional terms is "natural" only because such belief systems reflect racist, sexist, and classist societies. If these anti-human impulses were not overtly and covertly taught to children, a society would not embed them in its realities.

The integrationist intent of many civil rights activists of the 1950s and 1960s was noble; their goal was to bring all Americans together to foster collective understanding and to reduce the negative social meanings attached to racial categorization. Educational systems, such as public schools, were seen as primary sites where racial misconceptions could be refuted, resulting in greater racial accord in all social arenas. However, because most attempts at actual desegregation have been controlled by whites, the attempts to deal with institutional racism or reeducation were mostly tentative baby steps. Most white desegregationists did not seem to understand, or perhaps did not wish to understand, that racism was deeply embedded in white minds and institutions, including the educational institutions at hand. White policy makers in towns, cities, and states, as well as at the federal level, have not come close to achieving the idealistic goals of justice and equality often stated for school and other societal desegregation.

Changing the way that the public schools are supported is one way to attack segregation. The current system, where public schools are funded largely by local taxes, guarantees social inequality, segregation, and continued racism across large areas of cities and states. This system reinforces white notions of entitlement and privilege by linking wealth routinely to educational quality. What was once considered overtly racist "white flight" to avoid desegregated schools and neighborhoods has now been reconceptualized, as the socially conscious attempts of white parents to build a "better" life for their children. But, often what makes this life "better" is their limited contact with people of color.

We argue that racial segregation was then, and still is, harmful to white and black children, as well as to other children of color. It teaches them that separation is "natural" and conventional. These children, especially the white children, then have to rely on folk knowledge and mainstream media sources to gain information about people of color. Consequently, racist stereotypes and misconceptions will continue to flourish in minds of new generations as they work to construct a perception of reality that includes an analysis of self in relationship to others. Also, a declining tax base in central cities accompanies the movement of affluent families to the suburbs. This in turn affects the funding of schools and the quality of education—and also governmental support for inner-city businesses and job creation. Hence, the cycle of structural inequality is reproduced . . . .

Re-education must also involve all social structures that reinforce and support essentialist notions of racial hierarchy. One such structure, Western religion, historically has been used to support the idea of a "natural" or "divine" hierarchy of racial and class privilege. Indeed, long before the development of biological racism, Christianity was used to rationalize the enslavement of Africans (Ani 1994). Consequently, it is no accident that most modern-day white supremacist groups use a religious framework to support their racist dogma. Most Western religions divide the world into those who are divinely privileged and those who are divinely oppressed. As long as this stratifying and dividing exists, as we know from the history of Christianity in the West, there will always be outcasts. As long as some people are defined as outcasts in religious settings, then color, gender, and sexuality will likely be factored into demarcations of ostracism. Changes in religious attitudes do not mean that spirituality or religious ideology will disappear. Religious beliefs also provide hope and comfort. Slave accounts and narratives, for instance, provide many accounts of how spirituality was often the only source of comfort to people who were being brutalized— despite the simultaneous use of religious ideology to justify their oppressed condition (Lincoln and Mamiya 1990). Members of a nonracist utopian society would enjoy a common human spirituality grounded in universal tenets of humanity. Perhaps the most important tenets are assertions of the rights of every human being to be as free as possible from suffering and to enjoy a life of freedom and happiness. International agreements like the Universal Declaration of Human Rights speak of respect for the inherent dignity of human beings as a central aspect of human freedom and happiness. Personal suffering that arises from natural disasters may be inevitable, but suffering caused by institutional degradation of human beings would not exist in this nonracist utopia. Institutional racism and sexism violate these tenets, and the absence of these cruel oppressions would contribute significantly to community and individual happiness.

Furthermore, many churches, synagogues, mosques, and other houses of worship have been important gathering places for people to engage actively in anti-racist work. Southern black churches, for example, have long been important in the nation's civil rights movements (Lincoln and Mamiya 1990). Early in institutional history, thousands of runaway slaves found refuge in Quaker and other liberal churches throughout the South and Midwest. Still, churches remain one of the most racially segregated public arenas in modern societies. For our nonracist utopia we envision a return to the basic principles of humanity found in all major religions— principles that gave rise to the abolitionist and anti-racist activities of the past. As a result, racial segregation within houses of worship would be exposed as inconsistent with humanistic religious ideologies.

While moves can be made toward the egalitarian society, a fully egalitarian society cannot be reached without the simultaneous destruction of major axes of institutional domination brought about largely by collective and individual efforts. All those striving for this utopia have a large responsibility to enhance the egalitarian quality of the current societal environment and to model individually the basic human rights tenets.

## "Doing" Antiracism: Social and Personal Activism

Finally, we envision all pro-utopian individuals actively "doing" anti-racism. To some degree, most Americans of color are forced routinely to engage in anti-racism work, at least in regard to their own group. These Americans of color may need to expand their activities to include the discrimination faced by other groups of color. But the most challenging task is to move significant numbers of whites into anti-racist actions and activism. This means that whites must move out of their present comfort zones to confront personally the painful and usually emotional work of doing anti-racism every day. We also envision the widespread formation of cross-racial coalitions with others who are devoted to doing antiracism. Overall, we visualize many white individuals actively, consciously, and consistently working to eliminate racism by rejecting systems of privilege-maintenance in favor of human dignity, mutual respect, and liberty.

### Organizational Efforts

African Americans and other Americans of color have long led the struggles against racism in the United States. They continue to lead that struggle. As we see it, the goal must be to continue that struggle and to recruit more whites to the nonracist cause.

Some members of the dominant group, albeit a very small percentage, are moving already toward the ideal nonracist society. Over the last several decades nonracist whites, with other nonracist Americans, have participated in a number of grassroots organizations working against racial oppression. For example, the Institutes for the Healing of Racism, created in the early 1990s, hold seminars and dialogues on racism in more than 150 cities (Rutstein 1993). Numerous other multiracial groups are pursuing nonracist strategies; these include the People's Institute for Survival and Beyond (PI) and Anti-Racist Action (ARA). PI works in a variety of communities to establish Undoing Racism workshops. The mostly white ARA groups are working aggressively to counter local racist activities and organizations, such as neo-Nazi groups, in dozens of Canadian and U.S. cities (O'Brien 1999).

These nonracist organizations deal with individual prejudice and stereotyping and with the reality of institutional racism. A next step in a broad nonracist strategy for the United States would be to expand the number of these nonracist organizations and to connect them into a national and international network of all peoples working against systemic racism in this and other societies across the globe.

Whites in these organizations have gone well beyond the liberal position where one might spout some nonracist rhetoric but still engage in racist activities when encountering people of color in daily life. Many well-intentioned whites who would never consider themselves racist, who are active in civil rights organizations, who are aware of racism at the interpersonal and institutional levels as it affects the black poor "out there in the inner cities," still are threatened in their own organizational bailiwick. That is, they are pro–civil rights until there is a reversal of power—power as control over resources, such as knowledge, the construction of reality, and media imagery. To effect a genuine move away from racism and toward the nonracist egalitarian utopia, these well-intentioned whites must understand their own racism and that of the society. They must combat institutional racism—the racism built into every facet of American life. Although they may be opposed to discrimination, too many liberal whites

are unaware of the demon of white privilege in their own lives. The next step is for them to acknowledge that their own white privilege contributes to the persistence of racism.

### Individuals Undoing Racism

The inner views and attitudes of Americans, including white Americans, are not genetically ordained but are social and culturally constructed through hundreds of interactive influences and experiences. Whiteness and white racism must be carefully learned and maintained over lifetimes. Individual selves and psychologies are shaped by structural realities. Thus, the question arises: What would the nonracist individual in the nonracist society be like? If we can begin to construct such a person, then perhaps we can take real steps toward the utopian society. The emerging nonracist person, like all human beings, is not without faults. Many Americans of color have already moved well down the road to nonracist or nonracist attitudes and actions. It appears that a pressing need today is to create a multitude of whites who can be started along that road. Unlike most whites today, however, a white person committed to the nonracist utopia would be filled with a very deep and lasting *respect* for all human beings as equals, including those who are physically or culturally different.

Respect, not just tolerance, is the necessary emotional orientation. Because the primary goals of the nonracist utopian society are to eliminate unnecessary suffering and to create the rights to life, liberty, and human happiness so eloquently asserted in the U.S. Declaration of Independence, people therein would be motivated to treat each other equally with dignity and respect. Within this positive energy cycle, everyone will enjoy the equal rights to be free from unnaturally imposed suffering and to be happy. A skeptic might suggest that this sounds good, but ask whether individual Americans, especially individual whites, are up to this difficult task. How do we bring changes in those centrally responsible for racist oppression?

Clearly, being willing to talk candidly about individual and societal racism is one essential step for whites to take in moving toward the nonracist society. Honestly discussing with Americans of color the realities of racism increases the possibility that whites will move beyond their misunderstandings and fears and begin to put good intentions into the hard work of dismantling racism. This effort requires whites to actively join the struggle by working with African Americans and other people of color side by side, day in and day out. With this effort may come not only the loss of fearful emotions, but also a growth of caring and even loving relations. As skeptical as we are that the United States can achieve racial justice and equality in the near term, we are not without hope that some whites can begin to transcend their racism.

Moving to the ideal nonracist society will require much work on the cognitive and emotional aspects of contemporary racism. This is perhaps the most difficult task for white Americans. However, whites' identification with oppression on the other side of the color line can develop through at least three different stages: sympathy, empathy, and what might be called transformative insight. The initial stage, sympathy, is important but limited. It usually involves the willingness to set aside some of the racist stereotyping and hostility taught in white communities and the development of a friendly interest in what is happening to the racial other. Empathy is a much more advanced stage, in that it requires the ability to reject distancing stereotypes and a heightened and sustained capacity to see and feel the pain of the racial others. Empathy involves the capacity to sense deeply the character of another's pain and to act on that sensitivity.

Empathizing with victims of racial discrimination is an important and valuable but limited emotional skill. Such empathic feelings are limited because they stem largely from perceiving the reality of anti-black discrimination. The empathic person's energy may be directed mainly at ending those practices. However, this outward focus on blacks' pain may incline empathic whites to avoid the inward reflection necessary to understand the role that their own white privilege plays in maintaining patterns of racism.

Actually crossing the color line provides an opportunity for a more informed understanding of the dynamics of racism that even very liberal whites have not gained from academic studies, civil rights activities, or limited social contacts with black Americans. This third stage of white development we call transformative insight. Transformative insight is more likely to develop in loving and caring interracial relationships. Interpersonal love characterizes most relationships in which people care deeply about each other: parent/child, husband/wife, friend/friend, and so forth. Typical love can be powerful: Loving parents would not hesitate to die if it meant saving their child's life. Transformative insight, or transformative love, is most likely to develop in people who are in loving relationships that challenge institutional norms about power distribution. As a result, whites in such a position come to understand much more about the way in which the racialized hierarchy bequeaths power and privilege. The transformative insight includes a clear understanding of the broad range of privileges that comes from being white in a racist society, privileges a person has whether she or he wants them or not.

As we see it, people who are in loving relationships that do not challenge these norms are unlikely to develop transformative insight. For example, every loving relationship between a man and a woman in a patriarchal society reflects the institutional power imbalance between the sexes. The individual man who believes in gender equality empathizes with women living in a patriarchal society and strives to treat women equally to the way he treats men. Despite his good intentions, however, he will continue to support patriarchal values, albeit often unconsciously, if he lacks transformative insight. A man develops transformative insight when he personally and deeply feels both the injustice of patriarchy's subordinating women and the injustice of patriarchy's privileging men, including himself. It is the awareness that he is part of the problem that moves such a man beyond empathy.

There is even less likelihood that whites will develop transformative insight with respect to their racial hegemony. One reason is that there are far fewer interracial loving relationships than there are loving relationships between men and women. Moreover, even within many interracial loving relationships, well-intentioned whites have a difficult time understanding the pervasiveness of institutional racism. They do not directly experience it. It often takes many years of a loving relationship before a white person develops a strong, growing awareness of white privilege. However, once there, a white person starts on the path to transformative insight, a long journey because white privilege is so pervasive. A well-intentioned white person has to dig deep to uncover knowledge of this privilege, even though it is obvious to black Americans and other Americans of color. Unfortunately, most whites do not have a caring or loving relationship with even one black person. For that reason, increasing real respectful relations across the color line is essential to the long-term battle against white racism . . . .

Unlearning racism and the essential emotional work to eliminate individual racism are essential steps in becoming an effective nonracist activist. Nonracist activists cannot interact merely within limited social circles. They must actively work to break down existing structures that maintain and reproduce inequality. It is not enough to acknowledge difference or to be tolerant of others. The new anti-racists must acknowledge the real pain and the white privilege embedded in the existing system, must be willing to give up much privilege, and must work actively to create more egalitarian structures. This is tough work—emotionally, spiritually, and physically—but it is ultimately crucial for the construction of a nonracist utopia.

## CONCLUSION

There is only one race, the human race, and most human beings are shades of one color, brown. Racist hierarchies were created to do away with the oneness of the human race. Archaeological research indicates that the earliest members of *homo sapiens* evolved in Africa. All people now living have African ancestry and are thus at least distant cousins of one another. Yet this point about African ancestry is rarely made among white and other non-black Americans; Africa remains a distant and "dark" place in the minds of most non-black Americans. Sadly, by hating and attacking African Americans and other people of color, those who see themselves as white are in effect hating and attacking themselves, their own kin, and their own family tree . . . .

The realization that racism is so deep and persistent can be overwhelming. What hope is there for . . . all children of color to have joyful lives with the heaviness of racism constantly on their shoulders and weighing them down? The answer lies in a radical restructuring of the nation, the creation of a nonracist utopia where it is safe, perhaps even fun, to be dark, medium, or light in color. While a satisfactory set of solutions to end racism continues to elude us, all Americans must find ways to fight this racism, lest it drive us all mad, rob us of the joy life can bring, and end this society in bloodshed . . . . In the meantime, we must spend much time creating these utopian spaces, places of respite from a racist world that we are trying to change but which can no longer strip us of life's joy.

We call on social scientists and other intellectuals to lead the way in realizing this nonracist, utopian vision. We can begin by casting a mirror on ourselves, at the racist ideology that provides the framework for much of our intellectual history and academic knowledge. All Americans should participate in building a new democracy, perhaps with the first step of a new and democratic Constitutional Convention. We should reconstruct governing systems, mainstream sources of knowledge and institutions of higher learning in ways that reflect the full representation of all people.

We should heavily critique our educational systems, both in regard to curriculum and to real diversity of people within them. This is as important for Ph.D.-granting institutions as for undergraduate institutions, high schools and grammar schools, and pre-schools. A nonracist future is impossible to realize if those who achieve advanced degrees continue to be disproportionately white. A nonracist future is also out of reach if whites continue to live in worlds—personal, work, and educational worlds—where they are socially isolated from African Americans and other people of color. Most of us are at some level educating others, whether that teaching occurs within families, classrooms, or workplaces. We all share the responsibility for nonracist education.

To this end, we must critique ourselves and the way our social institutions, including our academic disciplines and careers, are structured in ways that reinforce existing systems of domination and privilege. We envision social scientists, other academics, and grassroots intellectuals providing some leadership in working toward personal transformative insight, as well as conscious, active work toward change in institutional racism. Moreover, we see this as much more than a task for "leaders." Often the best moral leadership has come from those in the trenches of everyday oppression, from the so-called "ordinary" citizens. Thus, we visualize all Americans, from all walks of life, working for change, for the nonracist utopian society. This anti-racist activism will affect all Americans and have a major impact on the ways that this society is structured.

Dr. Martin Luther King, Jr., often encouraged us to keep the utopian dream of a nonracist alive:

I have a dream that one day this nation will rise up and live out the true meaning of its creed: "We hold these truths to be self-evident; that all men are created equal." I have a dream that one day on the red hills of Georgia the sons of former slaves and the sons of former slave owners will be able to sit down together at the table of brotherhood. I have a dream that my four little children will one day live in a nation where they will not be judged by the color of their skin but by the content of their character. (1971: 349–50)

Dr. King's vision still remains a viable model. It awaits implementation.

## DISCUSSION QUESTIONS

1. What do Johnson and colleagues argue needs to be done at the individual level to reduce racial inequality? How can you explain their arguments about sympathy, empathy, and transformative knowledge?
2. What do Johnson and colleagues argue needs to be done at the macro level of society to reduce racial inequality? What do you think about their argument that we need to rewrite the U.S. Constitution? Could this happen?

# 59

# DISMANTLING NOAH'S ARK

## JUDITH LORBER

*In the fourth reading on social change and empowerment, we turn our attention to social change and gender. Judith Lorber is professor emerita of sociology and women's studies at the Graduate Center and Brooklyn College of the City University of New York. Lorber is the founding editor of the journal* Gender & Society, *and she has spent her career studying gender, theory, and social structure. This reading, excerpted from Lorber's comprehensive 1994 book,* Paradoxes of Gender, *informs the reader on how we should begin to "dismantle Noah's ark," or dismantle gender inequality in society. Lorber argues that women are doubly exploited in the home and in the workplace. To change this situation, gender equality would mean giving women some of men's privilege in society and also giving men some of women's responsibilities.*

*A feminist theory of the state has barely been imagined; systematically, it has never been tried.*

—Catharine A. MacKinnon (1989:249)

The defeated Equal Rights Amendment to the United States Constitution read simply, "Equality of rights under the law shall not be denied or abridged by the United States or any state on account of sex." Equal rights for women is a goal that resonates with individualism and freedom of choice. Yet that goal failed because, legally, in order to be treated alike, people have to *be* alike, and the prevailing belief in Western societies is that women and men are intrinsically different. Biological rationales for gender inequality not only are still part of the taken-for-granted assumptions of everyday reality in Western countries; they are built into public policy and law.[1] As a result, the liberal feminist goal of equality for women in Western societies will probably, as Robert Connell sardonically points out, have as little effect in countering men's domination of women as the rallying cries of liberal philosophers

*Source:* Judith Lorber, "Dismantling Noah's Ark," in *Paradoxes of Gender.* New Haven: Yale University Press. Pp. 282–285; 292–302. © 1994 Yale University Press. Reprinted with permission from Yale University Press.

that all *men* were equal had in countering rich men's domination of poor men: "Liberal feminism took the doctrine of 'rights' seriously and turned it against the patriarchal model of citizenship. 'Equal rights' is more than a slogan; it is a wholly logical doctrine that is as effective against the 'aristocracy of sex' as the doctrine of the 'rights of man' was against the aristocracy of property" (Connell 1990:512).

If women and men are alike, unlike treatment is inequality, but if they are not alike, dissimilar treatment is appropriate. As Catharine MacKinnon says:

> Gender is socially constructed as *difference* epistemologically, and sex discrimination law bounds gender equality *by difference* doctrinally. Socially one tells a woman from a man by their difference from each other, but a woman is discriminated against on the basis of sex only when she can first be said to be the same as man. A built-in tension exists between this concept of equality, which presupposes sameness, and this concept of sex, which presupposes difference. Sex equality becomes a contradiction in terms, something of an oxymoron. (1990:215)

Less emphasis on masculinity and femininity in bringing up children, depiction of diverse behavior by women and men in the mass media, and encouraging men's access to jobs traditionally filled by women and women's access to jobs traditionally filled by men are familiar ways feminists have recommended to avoid creating *unnecessary* differences— that is, differences that go beyond the biological. The alternative goal—equity— recognizes differences but tries to compensate for them by giving women benefits or protections, such as maternity leave or assignment to nonhazardous work. The goal of equality and of equity are actually the same: "for women to be in some way the same as men, whether this sameness be interpreted as identical treatment or as access to the same opportunities" (Jaggar 1990:250).

Much of the debate over gender equality revolves around procreation and sexuality (Kay 1985). The subjects of the debate seem to be females and males, not women and men. Females and males are physiologically different, so if they are treated differently, it is supposedly not an equal-rights problem. But a closer look at the way women are treated in Western

societies clearly indicates that although the rationale is biological, the differential treatment is political. In bureaucratic organizations, the workers and, more crucially, the people in the top positions, are expected to be *male*:

> It is the man's body, its sexuality, minimal responsibility in procreation, and conventional control of emotions that pervades work and organizational processes. Women's bodies—female sexuality, their ability to procreate and their pregnancy, breastfeeding, and child care, menstruation, and mythic "emotionality"—are suspect, stigmatized, and used as grounds for control and exclusion . . . . To function at the top of male hierarchies requires that women render irrelevant everything that makes them women. (Acker 1990:152, 153)

In order for female workers to be treated the same as male workers, their biological differences are considered disabilities that are not their fault. For example, in order to give females time off while pregnant and immediately after childbirth without discriminating against males, pregnancy in the United States is treated the way a male disability like a prostate infection would be, as an illness. The problem is that *women* are still discriminated against because their time off for pregnancy and childbirth is held against them as workers, whereas men's time off from work because of illness is not. Responsible women workers (especially the career-oriented) are supposed to use efficient contraception to time their pregnancies and childbirths, just as they are supposed to work out efficient child-care arrangements. But their ability to do so is heavily influenced by government policies on access to contraception and abortion, by employers' policies on maternity leave, and by the availability of affordable child care in their community.

Procreative and parenting statuses are rooted in social policies, not biological differences. Another example is fetal protection regulations, which usually concern potentially fertile women and developing fetuses, but not men, even though the same toxic substances affect sperm and can result in fetal malformation. Furthermore, as Elaine Draper points out, "Women have usually not been barred from all jobs entailing toxic risks, but only from the relatively high-paying production jobs traditionally held by men . . . . Significantly, the question of exclusion has not come up in jobs where the industry is heavily dependent on women workers. Those jobs may involve serious health risks, but where women are a majority, no one advocates removing all fertile women" (1993:94). Women hospital workers are exposed to radiation and powerful anesthetics and assemblers in electronics factories are exposed to potentially harmful solvents, but no one suggests barring them from these jobs.

The status of women and men is as much an issue of power and privilege as is the status of people of different races and social classes. To *not* ask why a social category called "men" has power over a social category called "women" is to accept the assumption that men's domination is natural and to seek for natural causes. In theories of race, it is the very categories themselves that are problematic, that are questions for theoretical analysis: Are they cultural divisions, structural divisions, or deliberate social constructions by the dominant group whose purpose is to justify the continuation of its dominance? Either way, "as myth and as a global sign, . . . it superimposes a 'natural' unity over a plethora of . . . differences" (E. B. Higginbotham 1992: 270).[2] Once pulled apart, the discourse of race reveals the social structural underpinnings that maintain racial inequality.

In *Capital*, Karl Marx provided the theory of class as relations to the means of production—that is, classes are social groupings with a material base, personal consequences, and ideological justification. The two classes (capitalists, or owners of the means of production, and the proletariat, or exploited workers) are inherently unequal not because of some intrinsic characteristics, although that was long the prevailing belief, but because of the different relations of each to the means of production and their conflictual interdependence. For race and class, then, the relational and political aspects of the categories are clear. The dominant groups define themselves and the subordinate groups as they construct and justify the boundaries of exclusion and power.

The concept of gender, however, has been theoretically grounded in sexuality and procreation. This conceptualization undermines the feminist focus on the relational aspects of women's and men's social status and the political aspects of gender inequality. I am arguing that gender inequality is located solely in the structure of gendered social practices and institutions. Procreation and sexuality are constructed as conditions of subordination within the social institution of gender; the social institution of gender is not built on procreation and sexuality. Human sexual reproduction is universal, but gender inequality is not. The gender status of women affects the social construction of sexuality, fertility, pregnancy, childbirth, and parenting, not the other way around. Responsibility for the work in the domestic sphere is an outcome of women's gender status, not its cause . . . .

Women's lives serve their families and the economy. Men's lives serve not only their families and the economy but also themselves. If women work hard for their families, they get vicarious gratification as wives and mothers; if men work hard for their families, the power, prestige, and income they earn is their own.[3] Among African Americans, even women who are upwardly mobile remain linked to their families, who are often the people who helped them get an education and prepare for a career (Higginbotham and Weber 1992). In contrast, for African American men, "self-determination and accountability . . . are at the core of the self and of manhood" (Hunter and Davis 1992:475).

The fault lines in this gendered social order are single parenthood for women and unemployment for men; both circumstances upset the complementary role expectations that tie women to individual men in order to have a family of their own and give individual men the resources for their dominant status. Bringing up children on the poor salary of a woman's job or on assistance from a government that questions their moral status can radicalize women, just as long-term unemployment has led men to question the legitimacy of an economy that deprives them of work. Rebellious men, once they have jobs, are likely to want a secure and even traditional family life; rebellious women have the potential to challenge the whole gendered social structure that makes it so difficult for them to live both comfortably and independently.

## CAN YOU HAVE
## GENDER AND EQUALITY, TOO?

I have argued throughout my research that gender is a social creation, a product of human inventiveness adopted for its usefulness in allocating reciprocal rights and responsibilities, work tasks, and the physical and social reproduction of new members of any society. The gendered division of work in early societies did not separate subsistence labor and child care—women did both—and many of these societies were egalitarian or possibly even woman-dominated, given women's important contribution to the food supply and their evident role in the procreation of valued children. Accidentally or deliberately, but in any case probably quite gradually, gender got inextricably built into stratification and inequality, producing a subordinate group, "women," whose labor, sexuality, and childbearing could be exploited.

The unequal distribution of power, property, and prestige between women and men is now part of the structure of modern societies. Gender statuses today are inherently unequal, and the whole point of gendering is to produce structured gender inequality. Subordination of women is an intrinsic part of the modern social order not because men are naturally superior or dominant (if they were, there would be no subordinate men) or because women bear children (if that were true, no mother would ever be a leader in her society). The subordination of women persists because it produces a group that can be exploited as workers, sexual partners, childbearers, and emotional nurturers in the marketplace and in the household. Policies that could establish true gender equality are not seriously implemented because they would erode the exploitation of women's labor, sexuality, and emotions. Societies and communities that have tried to establish egalitarianism rarely give as much attention to gender inequality as they do to economic inequity, the main concern of men.

Given a concept of natural differences between females and males that mystifies the pervasive and continual social construction of differentiated gender categories, to make all women and men equal would need perfect and scrupulously maintained equivalence between women's and men's rights, responsibilities, and rewards to compensate for these supposed immutable sex differences. Since gender is at present a system of power and dominance mostly favoring men, redressing the imbalance would mean giving women some of men's privileges, such as freedom from housework, and men some of women's responsibilities, such as taking care of infants. Instead, men have gotten women's privileges, such as limits on the number of hours a day paid workers can be required to work, and women have gotten men's responsibilities, such as economic support of their families (Stacey 1991:259). Lesbians and homosexual men are able to break the microsystem of domination and subordination, since personal power differentials are not gendered in their families and their communities, but they participate in the gendered macrosystem, especially in the world of work, as women and men.[4]

A truly radical goal for feminism would be not just gender equality but "a society in which maleness and femaleness are socially irrelevant, in which men and women, as we know them, will no longer exist" (Jaggar 1983:330), a society without gender.[5] A more pragmatic goal (but ultimately equally radical) would be a society without economic inequities, racial distinctions, or sexual exploitation, since they are all implicated in the social production of gender inequality. These goals are not really different. If gender inequality is the *raison d'être* for the social institution of gender today, making women and men equal in every sphere of life would undermine the need for the construction and maintenance of gender distinctions. The resultant degendered social order would not be a society of indistinguishable clones—individuality and cross-cutting groupings would produce much more variety than two genders.

## STRUCTURED EQUALITY

How can we restructure the institutionalized arrangements that subordinate and exploit women and build a society that is potentially egalitarian for women and men? Since race and class are intertwined with gender in the social arrangements that reproduce inequality, it is highly unlikely that gender inequality alone could (or should) be redressed without considering racial and economic exploitation. For example, capitalism currently exploits women as a reserve army of cheap labor, but it also exploits disadvantaged men. Socialism accumulates more surplus if some workers are paid less than others, but these lesser-paid workers are not necessarily women. These systems do not need gendered job segregation or gendered occupational stratification to survive in their current forms; they need only low-cost workers and hierarchies of management. If the low-paid and high-paid workers were a random mix of women and men, and the owners and managers were also mixed on gender, equality of women and men in each stratum could be accomplished without altering income inequalities or managerial hierarchies.

People with different social characteristics, however, are rarely randomly sorted into a stratification system because their characteristics are used to create or justify the contingencies of inequality—the structure of the education system, the rewards for different kinds of work, the allocation of responsibility for the care of dependents. Any socially constructed categories can be so used as long as structures of inequality organize a society. If we want to eliminate the exploitation of any social group by any other social group, a society has to be structured for equality. That means that all individuals within a group and all social groups within a society have to be guaranteed equal access to the valued resources of the society—education; work; sufficient income for a comfortable standard of living; satisfying emotional, sexual, and familial relationships; freedom from violence and exploitation; help in times of dependence; and the opportunity to produce knowledge, create culture, and lead in small and large ways. In order for individuals to be equal, the social groups that order their lives—their families, work organizations, schools, religions, ethnicities, sexual communities—have to be structurally equal, and within those groups, all the members have to be social equals. Equality does not mean sameness or even similarity; it means that different talents and contributions are equally valued and rewarded.

The meta-rule in a social order structured for equality is that no individual within a group and no group within the society monopolizes the economic, educational, and cultural resources or the positions of power.

In order to make all workers equal, everyone who does any kind of socially useful work, including the caretakers of dependents, must receive a wage that sustains a comfortable standard of living. Job segregation on the basis of gender and race would then be superfluous. Shared or rotated management would flatten hierarchies, and so there would be no point for the members of any group to monopolize positions of authority. But if some people, or some groups of people, disproportionately continued to be the caretakers of dependents, and production work continued to be more highly valued than social reproduction, inequality would persist. As Cynthia Cockburn says: "Until the symbolic man-as-citizen has his mind on the cooker, his eye on a toddler and a hand on grandad's wheelchair, no constitution would guarantee social equality" (1991:97). For true quality, care of children and the elderly would have to be made every able-bodied adult's responsibility equally, perhaps in a vertical kinship system, with each competent adult responsible for a child and an elderly parent or grandparent (Lorber 1975).

Pregnancy and childbirth are not insurmountable barriers to structures of equality. Childbearing is not most modern women's main role in life. As Connell suggests, in postindustrial societies,

> childbearing can be made a fairly short episode in any woman's life, and can be made socially equivalent to conception, pregnancy-support and infant care in men's lives. We have the knowledge and resources to share childcare and domestic work among adults to any extent desired in a balance between efficiency and privacy. Large numbers of men and women can choose to be childless without any danger of depopulation; a free choice of forms of cathexis becomes a general possibility. (1987:280)

That is, if parenting is seen as many adults' responsibility, then social, emotional, and economic support during pregnancy and childbirth could certainly be given by the nonpregnant and the nonbirthers to the woman who gestates and delivers a child for the household. Structuring for equality would do away not with procreative differences but with social roles and patterns of behavior that assign responsibilities that have nothing to do with pregnancy and childbirth to all females, many of whom are not and never will be birth mothers. Egalitarian child care and child support are already structured into some dual-career and two-income families, joint custody arrangements, and gay and lesbian households.

If every adult in a household is to be equal, household income has to be shared equally; otherwise the one with more economic resources has greater bargaining power. Even a household of unequal earners can be structured for equality. All household income could be pooled and allocated first to food, clothing, shelter, transportation, medical care, school fees, and other household expenses (perhaps including paid child care, house cleaning, laundry), donations, gifts, entertainment, vacations, retirement, and savings for emergencies. After that, to ensure equal resources, the remainder could be split evenly among the adult members of the household for their individual use (cf. Hertz 1986:84–113).[6] Each adult in a household should be able to claim the same amount of discretionary income, regardless of earnings, since that surplus buys the freedom to travel, donate, entertain, give gifts, save, work on private projects, and so on. Any earnings from this discretionary income should belong to the investor who is risking her or his own money. Individuals should also be able to leave what they have accumulated to whomever they want.

Any family work not done through paid services, as well as responsibility for hiring, overseeing, and transportation, would have to be evenly split or allocated by desirability, competence, convenience, and time. If all adults shared responsibility for domestic work, each would have equivalent time for educational and occupational advancement and political work. Any grouping of adults could share both the income from paid work and their domestic labor and thus provide economic support and nurturing care for the children, elderly, and sick in a household. If

the economic system and the political system were also structured for equality (by equitable income distribution and rotated positions of authority), the egalitarian structure of domestic life would support and be supported by the egalitarian structure of work and government.

Freed of exploitive economic, kinship, and procreative relationships, sexuality could indeed be the result of individual desires. But all kinds of sexual behavior would not be acceptable in an egalitarian society. Relations between adults and children and those imbued with acts of violence would erase the structural conditions of equality—that no one be exploited or subordinated in any way or by any means by anyone or any social institution. Children's equality depends on the protection of adults, protection that is violated by sexual exploitation. Violence creates the ultimate condition of inequality—unequal power—and so any use or threat of physical harm of one person by another must be absolutely forbidden legally and tabooed culturally as well. But for socially competent adults, all consenting sexual relationships, including those with *fantasies* of violence, would have equal value in a society structured for equality.

A structure of cultural equality would mean that all symbolic and ideological representations would have equal worth. The forms and content of culture might not even be that different from much that is produced throughout the world today, but the meanings would be different: "In a world in which the power structure was such that both men and women equally could be represented clothed or unclothed in a variety of poses and positions without any implications of dominance or submission—in a world of total and, so to speak, unconscious equality, the female nude would not be problematic" (Nochlin 1988:30).[7] What about pornography? In a utopian social order, such as true communism, says Alan Soble, "the making of pornography . . . will surely be libidinally satisfying, but that is not why it or any other work is meaningful and satisfying. It is nonalienated labor because it would be freely chosen, the project would be collectively planned without a hierarchy of authority, its completion would involve a playful creativity, and the product would be appreciated and admired by others" (1986:127).

Currently, the subordination, exploitation, and even extermination of some social groups by others as well as the inequality of individuals within all social groups is part of the laws, governments, and criminal justice systems of most countries, even those supposedly organized for equality. If societies are to reverse this pattern and build on their traditional or constitutional structures of equality, at a minimum every proposed law, court order, or state policy must be examined first for its effect on all the structural conditions of equality—the distribution of economic resources; production of knowledge and culture; shares of political power; help for children, the elderly, the sick, the less physically and mentally competent; valuation of ethnic traditions and religious beliefs; and acceptance of consenting adults' sexual practices.

Does a social world structured for equality mean people will be a varied, motley crew, or a version of middle-class, white, Anglo-Saxon Protestant men? It would probably take as deliberate an effort to counteract hegemonic masculine values in workplaces and other organizations as it would be to structure them for equality. That is, conscious reorganization along the lines suggested by Patricia Yancey Martin would be necessary to construct a social order based on qualities of "inclusion, participation and diversity" (1993:290).[8] These are the necessary conditions for gender equality.

## Into and Out of Noah's Ark

Human beings have constructed and used gender—human beings can deconstruct and stop using gender. The most obvious way would be to deliberately and self-consciously *not* use gender to organize social life. Gender-neutrality resonates with Western concepts of achievement, in which individual talents, ambitions, strengths, and weaknesses constitute the only basis for work roles and leadership positions. Gender-neutrality assumes that women and men who are similarly educated and trained are interchangeable and that gender equality will come when more women get the equivalent of prestigious men's jobs and positions of authority and more men participate in housework and child care.

Women and men at present are rarely interchangeable because the social order is structured to advantage men and disadvantage women. In the micropolitics of everyday life and the macropolitics of laws and state policies, dominant men are so privileged that they continue to dominate without much conscious effort. Women and subordinate men have to show that they are as good as dominant men to succeed economically, politically, or artistically—the burden of proof is on them. Social policies that ignore this structure of gender inequality and assume that remedies can take place on the individual level are doomed to failure, and the failure will be attributed to the attitudes, competencies, and motivations of the individuals concerned, both dominant and subordinate, not to the social structure.

Whether without a revolution it is possible to structure gender equality in social orders that are organized to guarantee the privileges of dominant men is questionable. To see how deeply gender inequality organizes work, parenting, leadership, politics, and culture in modern societies, consider what a world would be like where women and men equally worked in every occupation and profession, equally took care of children, governed equally, equally produced culture.

In a world of scrupulous gender equality, equal numbers of girls and boys would be educated and trained for the liberal arts and for the sciences, for clerical and manual labor, and for all the professions. Among those with equal credentials, women and men would be hired in an alternating fashion for the same type of job—or only men would be hired to do women's types of jobs and only women would be hired to do men's types of jobs until half of every workforce was made up of men and half, women.

If men did women's work, would the pay increase, autonomy be encouraged, and the work gain in prestige? If women were not seen as taking over men's work, but performing it interchangeably with men, would the work be devalued, deskilled, and paid less? Would upward mobility be restricted in order to encourage rapid turnover and low wages if half of all lower-level workers were men? If a work process was degraded, all workers would suffer, and they might resist employers as a group, instead of men competing against women for the best jobs or for any jobs at all.

If men as well as women cared for children, many ways might be found to equalize responsibility for parenting: crèches at work for breast-feeding and bottle-feeding parents, men taking as much time off as women to care for sick children, "daddy tracks" if "mommy tracks" persisted (in which case, there would probably be no separate tracks for parents). Please note that in no way am I suggesting that *females* and *males* could be interchanged, only women and men. Males do not get pregnant, but they can take care of infants; females gestate and lactate, but that does not mean that only they must take parental leave. Equal child care would involve staffing community child-care centers and schools with equal numbers of men and women doing every kind of task. How would primary parents who were interchangeably women and men alter children's gendered psychological development? How would children be socialized if their caretakers and teachers were equally women and men?

What would happen if positions of responsibility were alternated between women and men? In elected positions, two women then two men could run against each other alternately to ensure that neither men nor women predominated.[9] In appointed positions, women and men of equal qualifications would be alternated. What would be the effect on concepts of authority and leadership? On training and grooming for advancement? On gendered patterns of deference? On sexual harassment?

Although some modern countries have a high percentage of doctors and lawyers who are women, professional work has been stratified by gender, with men in the more prestigious sectors and in the policy-making positions. The same is true of education; women mostly occupy the lower grades of teaching and the lower levels of administration. Scientific research in all modern countries is dominated by men. These are the arenas where knowledge is produced in response to theoretical questions and pragmatic problems. If half of all medical specialists, medical school faculties, and researchers were women; if half the police and lawyers and judges at all levels were women; if half the university professors,

deans, provosts, presidents, and chancellors were women; if half the scientists in the world were women, what changes are predictable in medical practice and research priorities, in the criminal justice system and the interpretation of laws, in the knowledge produced and the knowledge taught, in the scientific problems considered important enough to command enormous resources?[10]

Suppose women had equal time with men in all cultural productions. In art museums, an equal number of acquisitions by women and men would be the rule. In concerts, an equal number of pieces composed by women and by men would be played by an equal number of women and men musicians.[11] An equal number of books by women and by men would appear on every publisher's list. An equal number of movies produced, directed, and written by women and by men would feature, in any year, an equal number of women and men heroes. The same principles would be used for every television channel's programming. How would canons of taste be affected? How would prestigious prizes be awarded? Would symbolic language change if women's experiences were as privileged as men's experiences?

In sports, every competition would have an equal number of women's and men's teams and players, the rules of competition would be the same for women and for men, and women's and men's events would receive equal time, pay, and prize money. The featured main event would alternate between women and men. The media would cover women's and men's sports and sports heroes equally. Would men begin to identify with women sports stars? Would women turn out to be physiologically similar to men in ways that are now hidden by the rules of the games?[12] Would some sports competitions become unisex?

Perhaps the most drastic upset of current ways of thinking would occur if all the armed forces were half women and half men, including combat units. In many wars and revolutions, women have fought side by side with men, both openly and disguised as men.[13] Frenchwomen played such an important part in the resistance to Nazism, running escape lines, sabotaging, spying, and printing clandestine newspapers, that they finally could no longer be denied the right to vote (M. L. Rossiter 1986:223). According to the *New York Times* of May 2, 1993, during World War II, Russian women were machine gunners and snipers, served on artillery and tank crews, and flew in three all-woman air force fighter and bomber units. In Israel, women fought in the underground for nationhood and in the War of Independence, reaching levels as high as 20 percent of all soldiers. On April 30, 1993, the *Jerusalem Post* published the following fifty-year-old news story:

> Malka Epstein, a 22-year-old girl, is now a legendary figure in Central Poland where she leads a guerilla unit with headquarters in old quarry caves in the Kielce district. From these headquarters this girl has been conducting sabotage raids on Nazi units in the last 18 months. She is credited with having destroyed many German munition stores and with derailing trains carrying German soldiers to the Russian front.

As long as battles and wars are fought, women must be able to fight if they are to be equal with men. Otherwise, men will continue to feel that since they put their lives on the line and women do not, they are entitled to privileges and powers unavailable to women (W. Brown 1990:25–26). Moreover, the idea of aggressive masculinity as protective of women lets men define which women are deserving of their protection. In World War II, women civilians were tortured, executed, bombed, and gassed; in all wars, they have been raped and murdered. Women should compose half of the peacemakers, but as long as there are wars, to be equal, they should be half of the fighters, too.

The other side of this exchange of expectations of men and women is that the nurturance and service to others that defines the "good woman" in Western cultures should apply to the "good man" as well. As Kay Ann Johnson points out, the Maoist utopian vision of the complete person (*to-mien-shou*) broke down the distinction between the intellectual and the manual laborer, the philosopher and the peasant, the artist and the artisan, but was never applied to women and men: "Never was it suggested, even in the most utopian movements, that men should learn from women . . . the value of, and how to perform, the nurturant human services" (1983:167).

Other radical changes in concepts of femininity and masculinity would occur in a scrupulously equal world. All forms of sexuality would have to be recognized as equally valid. There would, therefore, have to be equal numbers of pornographic magazines, movies, strip shows, erotic dancers, and any other sexual productions for heterosexual, homosexual, bisexual, transvestite, and sadomasochistic women as for the same groups of men. Movies, television, books, and popular songs can be expected to show women as sexual pursuers equally with men, and homosexuality and heterosexuality as producing equally happy and tragic relationships. You might see plots revolving around heterosexual women sexually harassing and abusing heterosexual men, and gay men and lesbians sexually harassing each other and heterosexuals.

Suppose all the major religions allowed women to become priests, to rise in the religious hierarchy, and to interpret the Old and New Testaments, the Qur'an, the Bhaghavad Gita. Since the practices of the world's major religions were originally based on social orders that separated women and men and assigned them different roles in life, fundamentalists could not allow women and men the same religious roles. But what would happen if religions that now profess gender equality really gave women and men an equal chance to be leaders?[14] If liturgies were completely gender-neutral? If "God" were not "the Lord," "our Father," or "King of the universe" but "the Leader," "our Parent," "Creator of the universe"?

The very radicalness of the effects of scrupulous gender equality throughout a whole social society, the cries of outrage you would predict if absolutely equal numbers of women and men had to be constantly maintained in all areas of life, the sense of unreality about a completely gender-balanced world, all make clear how very far the most progressive, most industrialized, most postmodern, most egalitarian society today would have to go to become truly gender-neutral. What government would organize a system of complete gender balance? Not only do we still want to know immediately whether an infant is a boy or girl, that information, that categorization, combined with race and other social characteristics, tells us and the infants just where in their social order they are going to be placed, and whether they are going to be encouraged to live their lives as dominant, self-confident, and central to society or as subordinate, subverted, and peripheral to the main action. When we no longer ask "boy or girl?" in order to start gendering an infant, when the information about genitalia is as irrelevant as the color of the child's eyes (but not yet the color of skin), then and only then will women and men be socially interchangeable and really equal. And when that happens, there will no longer be any need for gender at all.

Does all this equality mean that no one will criticize, satirize, parody, oppose, challenge, resist, rebel, start new groups, or live alone? I doubt it. Free of gender, race, and class inequality, what might we all be? Perhaps culturally identified women, men, heterosexuals, homosexuals, citizens of different countries, adherents of different religions, members of different occupations and professions, of different birth and social parents, and so on.[15] Perhaps people free to experience *jouissance*—the erotic passions expressed in human bodies, human identities, deeply held beliefs, work, love, spirituality.[16] Perhaps what Donna Haraway predicts—cyborgs who understand and can control the interface of humans and technology, who belong now to one group, now to another, identified with many or with none at all:

> The cyborg is a creature in a post-gender world; it has no truck with bisexuality, pre-Oedipal symbiosis, unalienated labor, or other seductions to organic wholeness through a final appropriation of all the powers of the parts into a higher unity . . . . The cyborg is resolutely committed to partiality, irony, intimacy, and perversity. It is oppositional, utopian, and completely without innocence . . . . I would rather be a cyborg than a goddess. (1985:67, 101)

So would I.

## DISCUSSION QUESTIONS

1. How does the act of imagining what complete gender neutrality would look like enable us to see the extent of gender inequality we still have today in this mostly industrial, postmodern country?

2. What does Lorber argue we need to do to lessen gender inequality in the United States? Do you agree with her arguments? Why or why not?

## NOTES

1. MacKinnon 1989.
2. Also see F. J. Davis 1991.
3. Acker 1988; Holcombe 1983; Weitzman 1985.
4. On class differences in a lesbian workplace, see Weston and Rofel 1984. On lesbian and gay families, see Bozett 1987; Weston 1991.
5. Badinter (1989:147–190) argues that women and men in Western societies are already coming to resemble each other and that gender differences are blurring considerably.
6. For examples of egalitarian marriage contracts for different types of couples, see Weitzman 1974:1278–88, and for a description of one couple's scrupulously equal financial arrangements, see Millman 1991:165–70.
7. Also see Ecker 1985.
8. Also see Cockburn 1991:227–36; Ferguson 1984:154–212. Without the separatism, these are similar to the values of lesbian feminism—egalitarianism, collectivism, an ethic of care, respect for experiential knowledge, pacifism, and cooperation (Taylor and Rupp 1993).
9. In some organizations I belong to, such an arrangement is used to ensure the sometime election of *white men*.
10. Feminists have raised these epistemological questions particularly with regard to science, which is supposed to be objective but actually reflects the values of dominant men. See Haraway 1988; Harding 1986, 1991; Keller 1985; Longino 1990. For an African American feminist perspective on law, see P. J. Williams 1991, and on social thought, see P. H. Collins 1990 . . . .
11. Block and Neuls-Bates (1979) found three thousand compositions by American women published from colonial times to 1920.
12. Remember that the Olympics had no marathon competition for women until fairly recently; that women's endurance is ignored in long-distance swimming and in tennis; and that in general, the rules for women's competition are based more on what the men who make the rules think women can or should do in sports than on women's actual capabilities.

13. Durova 1989; Freeman and Bond 1992; Graham 1977; Wheelwright 1989. In a review of "above-the-counter sex fiction," Kendrick (1992: 36) calls Ann Rice's novels "omnisexual."

14. Jesus Christ included women as founders and leaders of congregations, but within two hundred years the established church excluded women from the priesthood, just as the Jews did, and gave husbands authority over their wives, just as the Romans did (Farrell 1992; Fiorenza 1979). Judith Plaskow (1990: 36–48) argues that Judaic history has written women leaders out as well, and that there is evidence of their leadership roles in the synagogue through the sixth century c.e.

15. See Marge Piercy's communities in *Woman on the Edge of Time* (1976).

16. On the power of the erotic, see Lorde 1984; on sexuality and spiritual passion, see Plaskow 1990, 191–97; on the definition of *jouissance* as "total access, total participation, as well as total ecstasy," see Cixous and Clément [1975] 1986:165–66.

# 60

# POLICY STEPS TOWARD CLOSING THE GAP

MEIZHU LUI

BARBARA J. ROBLES

BETSY LEONDAR-WRIGHT

ROSE BREWER

REBECCA ADAMSON

*This final reading in Part V, on empowerment and social change, examines economic inequality in the United States. The authors, Meizhu Lui, Barbara J. Robles, Betsy Leondar-Wright, Rose Brewer, and Rebecca Adamson, are a group of concerned social scientists and activists who have formed the organization United for a Fair Economy, which gives workshops and provides educational and public policy materials to create economic social change. Similar to Johnson and colleagues, who in Reading 58 argue for larger macro changes in the structure of U.S. society to create social change, Lui and her colleagues also argue for macro changes in our economy and government policies. This reading, excerpted from a 2006 book by Lui and her colleagues,* The Color of Wealth: The Story Behind the U.S. Racial Wealth Divide, *suggests a number of progressive strategies the United States can take to lessen asset and wealth inequality.*

*Source*: Lui, Meizhu, Robles, Barbara J., Leondar-Wright, Betsy, Brewer, Rose, and Rebecca Adamson. "Policy Steps toward Closing the Gap." Excerpt from *The Color of Wealth: The Story Behind the U.S. Racial Wealth Divide*. Copyright © 2006 by United for a Fair Economy. Reprinted by permission of The New Press. www.thenewpress.com.

The following section highlights some ideas old and new, and lifts up some examples of useful and innovative work being done to close the wealth gap. This list is by no means comprehensive, but perhaps it can spark more energy to tackle the issue of wealth building for communities of color, and for all those currently without economic security.

## First Steps: Human Assets

Education has been an important tool in creating white advantage. It was a crime to teach African slaves to read and write; Latinos have been disadvantaged by English-only classrooms; Native Americans were forced into assimilationist school settings; and Asians had to sue to go to school with whites.

In today's economy, more than ever, you need an education to get ahead. Even for a menial job, a high school diploma is often required. Current mechanisms for public school funding—largely local property taxes—enable wealthier families in white suburbs who pay more property taxes to have more dollars invested in their public schools. Disparity in funding produces disparities in educational outcomes, and perpetuates a class and race divide. The infusion of federal dollars to invest more in communities that are poor could help close the gap.

As unionized jobs in manufacturing have shrunk, higher education has become an even more important ticket to a job at a decent wage with benefits. Professor Hubie Jones, former dean of the Boston University School of Social Work and a longtime community activist, grew up with his single mom in Harlem, New York. Without the possibility and promise of free higher education at the City College, he says, he would not have had the motivation to work hard in school in order to get that ticket up and out. Gangs and drugs would have been the only option.

Free public universities came about in 1862, the same year as the Homestead Act, when the Morrill Act established land-grant colleges in every state. Their purpose was to provide knowledge and skills to the newly landed masses.[1] Public institutions of higher education were the ticket out of poverty for many people of color who could not afford tuition at private colleges. Today, affordable higher education is moving out of reach for many of our children.

The federal government spends $55 billion on student aid, but the mix has been changing. Seventy-seven percent of that aid is in loans, not grants, a reversal of past policies. With tax cuts mostly for the wealthy, and the resulting budget shortfalls, states have been spending less on their public colleges, and tuitions have been growing at a faster rate than family income. The new welfare policies set in 1996 have led to a decline in enrollment of low-income women in college. Before the Temporary Assistance for Needy Families (TANF) program, forty-two states allowed women to count college attendance as employment in order to qualify for benefits: after TANF, only twenty-six states still allowed this option.[2] We can change the mix back again, and raise new taxes to invest in public colleges. A well-educated populace is the cornerstone of democracy, and the cornerstone is crumbling.

For those who don't speak English as their first language, English classes are the first stepping-stones to success. It is not possible to get a decent job without English skills. Some immigrants are not literate in their native language and need extended classes. Some come with degrees from other countries, and can learn English quickly. For all of them, long waiting lists for free or affordable classes prevent them from obtaining this skill so essential for entry of limited English speakers into the U.S. workforce. On the other hand, so that non-English speakers do not get cheated out of their assets, or miss out on the benefits of programs for which they qualify, English-only policies must be rejected.

One big health problem can wipe out a lifetime of savings. The cost of care for a premature baby in a neonatal intensive care unit can be $500,000. In 1999, one quarter of the families that filed for bankruptcy cited health problems and the related costs as the reason.[3]

A 2000 study found that people of color are more likely to be uninsured than non-Hispanic whites, and are less likely to have job-based health insurance.[4] Thirty percent of Latinos, 25 percent of African Americans, 20 percent of Asian Americans and Pacific Islanders, and 17 percent of Native Americans are uninsured.[5] (The relatively low percentage rate of uninsured Native Americans is mostly due to their access to Indian Health Services as opposed to private or Medicaid coverage.)[6] Medicaid, which cares for the poor in inner cities and rural areas, is increasingly underfunded, as states face budget crises.

Universal coverage is possible. In 1983, Hawaii received permission from the federal government to require all employers to provide insurance to employees. In 1993, they were able to pool all their public dollars to create one big statewide insurance system. Not only were they able to provide health, dental, and mental health coverage for all, but the system was also able to save public dollars through a competitive bidding system.[7]

## Hitting a Stride: Income Assets

One of the main reasons that nonwhite people were shut out of asset building was because they were restricted to no-wage or low-wage jobs. From African slaves in the South to Latino day laborers on the street corners of Los Angeles, people of color have been denied fair compensation for their labor power. They have been limited to jobs that whites did not and do not want, were excluded from unions, paid taxes to work, and have always been the last hired and the first fired.

Jobs are needed that provide the cash income to cover day-to-day needs, *with something left over to build savings*, the basis for financial wealth. Today, income disparity lays the groundwork for future wealth disparities. Thomas Shapiro, in *The Hidden Cost of Being African American: How Wealth Perpetuates Inequality*, analyzed the impact of income on wealth. Once basic living expenses are met, each additional dollar of annual income generates $3.26 in net worth over a person's lifetime. Wealth disparity grows because of differences in income. For example, the difference in net worth between someone making $30,000 a year and someone making $60,000 a year is nearly $100,000.[8] Income includes not just wages and salaries based on

working, but cash supports for those who are unemployed, retired, or parents of small children.

In Barbara Robles's class at the LBJ School at the University of Texas in Austin, students simply did not believe her when she told them that the minimum wage means a family must live on $10,000 a year. Over 27 million workers make less than $8 dollars an hour; of these workers, 16.8 million are adults twenty-five and over; more than 16 million are women; 22 million are white; 4.2 million are black; and more than 17.5 million work full-time.[9] The present federal minimum wage of $5.15 an hour translates into an annual income of $10,712. The Economic Policy Institute has done several studies that reveal that an increase in the minimum wage would primarily benefit full- and part-time workers of low-income families,[10] which are disproportionately headed by single women of color. It would require raising the minimum wage to at least $8.10 an hour as of 2004 for a family of four to move above the official poverty line.[11] Around the country, people are organizing for more than the minimum wage: they are demanding a living wage. Since the cost of living varies across the country, communities are calculating costs particular to their cities. For example, in San Francisco voters approved a city living wage of $8.50 an hour in 2003; this will put over $100 million per year into the pockets of roughly fifty-four thousand workers.

And what about a maximum wage? In most countries, the ratio of CEO pay to worker pay has been around 40 to one. In the United States in 2004, the ratio of CEO pay to the average worker's pay was 431 to 1.[12] Rep. Martin Sabo of Minnesota wants to curb that excess. His Proposed Income Equity Act would prevent corporations from claiming tax deductions on any executive pay that totals over 25 times what a company's lowest paid workers are earning.

The poorest group in the United States is women of color and their children. As Miami resident Thelma Brown puts it, "[C]ertified nursing assistants in Miami start at $5.75 an hour with no benefits. Day care costs ninety to one hundred dollars every two weeks per kid; then you have to pay rent, electricity, food, and everything else. A single mom can't live on one job at that rate."[13] They require government help to survive. For many years, it was mainly white women who received welfare payments. Attieno Davis, a longtime African American activist, remembers how empowering it was for black women in the 1960s to realize that they were *entitled* to these benefits, too. Latinos also were underenrolled, since no outreach was conducted in Spanish, nor were there Spanish-speaking workers in welfare offices. However, President Reagan's caricature of "welfare queens," stereotyped as a woman of color, created backlash. In 1996, the program changed to Temporary Assistance to Needy Families. To qualify for the meager payments, women cannot have assets of more than $1,000 in some states.

One positive tax provision for the poor is the Earned Income Tax Credit (EITC). It was born out of the welfare debates in the late 1960s and early 1970s. At the time, President Nixon was proposing a guaranteed income to all families with children, regardless of whether the parent(s) worked. It is amazing today to remember that Nixon was proposing such a progressive policy. But Democratic senator Russell Long of Louisiana felt that the Nixon proposal would discourage people from working. His alternate proposal provided tax relief to low-income workers, rather than guaranteed income for all. The EITC was passed in 1975. Its annual budget rose from $2 billion to $12 billion between 1980 and 1992.[14] According to the 2001 Census, forty-three million people were living in low-income working families with children, and two out of every three poor families with children had at least one parent working. The EITC has lifted more families with children out of poverty than any other government program.[15]

Low-wage workers use the money they receive from the EITC for investments in education and savings, as well as to help them pay daily living expenses. In order to encourage savings, Ray Boshara from the New America Foundation suggests that a portion of EITC refunds could be channeled directly into a basic savings account.[16] The Center on Budget and Policy Priorities found that EITC funds are often spent locally, serving as an economic development tool for low-income neighborhoods.

Decent pay and accumulation of assets is hard to come by if you are not allowed citizenship. As we have seen, immigrant status has been a major barrier to economic equality for people of color. Jeannette Huezo, a political refugee from El Salvador, has lived and worked in Boston for fifteen years. However, she had to leave four of her children behind when she fled, and they are not allowed to reunite; she has been sending money home to support them. Salvadorans in the United States send remittances back home that now amount to half of the Salvadoran economy. Being forced into low-paid jobs because of their tenuous legal status, coupled with the need to send money home, makes it difficult to build assets in either country. The National Coalition for Dignity and Amnesty developed a proposal for a federal Freedom Act. It would legalize undocumented immigrants currently living in the United States and create a status of "temporary residency" for future migrants, who would be eligible for permanent residency after three years.

People of color should be hired into jobs for which they are qualified and to rise to the level of their capabilities. Affirmative action, won through the Civil Rights Movement, did bring many more people of color into middle-income jobs where they could begin to save, buy homes, and build wealth. However, the gap is still not closed. Over their working lifetime, African Americans with a college degree can expect to earn $500,000 less than equally qualified white people.[17] Asians do fine getting in on the ground floor and moving up, but then encounter glass ceilings: an Asian with a college degree had median annual earnings in 1993 of $36,844; comparably qualified whites made $41,094.[18] The need for affirmative action and government enforcement of nondiscrimination laws is far from over.

# Going the Distance: Financial Assets

Over the course of history, the federal government has used public resources to create wealth-building starter kits as well as continuing subsidies for whites, and has removed assets from people of color and denied them the benefits given to whites. In recent years, the white middle class has taken a hit: overall, it's shrinking, and general economic inequality has reached the levels of the Gilded Age at the turn of the last century. As a result, more and more academics, advocates, foundations, and public officials are recognizing that income alone is not enough to lift a family out of poverty. While this attention is not mainly because of wide recognition of the racial wealth gap, there is an opportunity to bring race into the conversation.

It's not that there aren't federal asset policies currently in place. The government spends approximately $355 billion a year in direct outlays and tax expenditures (allowing tax breaks for certain kinds of income). However, they are not named as asset policies, and they disproportionately benefit those who already have assets.[19] As we have seen, the net worth of people of color is far below that of whites.

While there are many ways to group asset-building opportunities, the Asset Policy Initiative of California has designed a framework that is simple and user-friendly. They see that strategies in four areas are needed. *Asset accumulation* is about policy strategies that encourage families to save; *asset leveraging* policies help low-wealth families use their limited savings to get loans for larger assets such as home and business ownership. Unfortunately, if there are not *asset preservation* assistance programs, often low-wealth people lose everything they have to predatory lenders. And finally, "*asset creation*" goes beyond individual strategies; communities can gain control over development in their own neighborhoods and rural communities.

## ASSET ACCUMULATION

New thinking on how to help low-income people save money has been inspired by Michael Sherradan's ground-breaking book *Assets and the Poor: A New American Welfare Policy*. Sherradan and others recognize that income-support programs do not foster asset accumulation.[20]

Individual Development Accounts (IDAs) are nontaxable matching funds savings accounts that can be used—and used *only*—toward purchasing a home, retirement, education, starting a business, or other asset-accumulating endeavors. The outside matching source comes either from the public or private sector. Generally, the program has been targeted to the working poor, those who have a low but stable income in which some money can be set aside. Foundations and local banks have both provided funding to augment savings on the part of the poor. There are about 250 neighborhoods participating in IDA programs across the country, many in communities of color. The National Council of La Raza and the First Nations Development Institute have developed projects for Latinos and Native peoples.

Pilot IDA programs funded privately have encouraged policy change. According to the Corporation for Enterprise Development (CFED), since 1993, twenty-nine states and the District of Columbia have passed laws in support of IDAs. Thirty-two states have included IDA initiatives in their welfare reform programs and seven states have instituted state-funded IDA programs. In 1998, a federal pilot program of savings incentives for the poor was enacted, with $125 million over five years set aside for matching individual savings. While on the one hand this legislation helps to make the IDA idea more visible, it is not on a scale to be truly transformative.[21]

Another promising idea involves investing in our future: our nation's children. It is every parent's dream to leave their child a nest egg. And wouldn't it be great if everyone could be born with a trust fund! An impossible dream? Just such a program was instituted in England, sponsored by Prime Minister Tony Blair's Labor Party. In 2003, the British Parliament established what has become known as "baby bonds," a small child trust fund for each newborn in the country. Modest amounts of public funds will be deposited and invested for each newborn infant, and made available for withdrawal at the age of eighteen. If a child is given an initial deposit of $1,000, and then the parent makes a yearly contribution of $500, matched by another $500 from an outside source, this would translate into $40,000 available to eighteen-year-olds to use toward education, starting a business, or putting a down payment on a home.[22]

In 2005, a bill to create a similar program was introduced in Congress by an unusual alliance of conservative Republicans and progressive Democrats. The America Saving for Personal Investment, Retirement, and Education Act (the ASPIRE Act of 2005) proposed that a $500 KIDS Account be established for every newborn child. Children in households earning below the national median income would be eligible for a supplemental government contribution of up to $500. Additional benefits would include tax-free earnings, matched savings for lower income families, and financial education. Here is a program that provides a double incentive for lower-income people to save: no taxes on the savings account, and matched government contributions for the poor.

Whether such new asset subsidiary programs should be universal or targeted to people of color is a strategic question. In any case, additional resources for outreach, translation, and other mechanisms to ensure inclusion must be part of the program.

## ASSET LEVERAGING

When you have some savings, you can either keep them, or use them to leverage more assets through making bigger investments.

Rotating savings and credit associations (ROSCA) have been an important strategy utilized by immigrant households in order to start a small business, purchase a home, or pay for a child's education. This strategy has origins in many different ethnic groups from East Asia, Latin America, the Caribbean, the Near East, and Africa. The Vietnamese ROSCA is called a *hui*, the Ethiopian is *ekub*, Jamaican is *partners*, Dominican, *san*, Korean, *keh*, and Cambodian *tong-tine*.[23]

A ROSCA is formed among family members, friends, and kin groups. They require participants (usually five or more people) to pay in a monthly sum agreed upon by the group. A participant can make a request to borrow the month's pool of money, or there may be an agreed-upon sequence for withdrawal—tax- and interest-free, since these transactions take place outside of the mainstream economic structure. This continues until all members have had access to the funds. The system is based on trust and social pressure. Thus, if members do not return the money at some point, their reputation in the community is tainted, something they are usually not willing to risk.

A *Philadelphia Inquirer* reporter sat in on a ROSCA meeting. "A Vietnamese *hui* group listened as one member asked to break the payout schedule and let her have that month's collection . . . . [T]he group sat in judgment on her needs, then let her take the tax-free, no-interest pot of $14,000." But because ROSCAs are part of an unregulated, unprotected financing system, they have no recourse in case of theft. While sometimes immigrants do not trust banks, banks also do not make it easy to deposit ROSCA dollars. They treat deposits as belonging to an individual or household, and have no category to accommodate this unique form of savings. They report any deposit of more than $10,000 to the Internal Revenue Service. Without a financial institution to hold the money, one member has to keep the mounting dollars under his or her bed. A policy that recognized ROSCAs as a micro lending system, and allowed the money to be banked and borrowed tax-free, would build on existing community customs and help rather than hinder these activities.

Another way to use your small savings to leverage larger loans without worrying about a financial institution charging excessive fees and interest is to join a community credit union. The credit union movement was essentially a response to mainstream financial institutions' neglect of marginalized groups. Community Development Credit Unions (CDCU) provide basic financial services such as check cashing and small loans at fair rates to their members within a restricted area or community.[24] They are member based and member governed; some are based in churches or community organizations. One of the problems plaguing poor communities is that the meager resources present in poor communities tend to flow out of them. In response to this problem, CDCUs keep local money in the community, as well as draw in outside money.[25] The resources accrued from CDCUs are then channeled back into the community and are used to respond to its various needs.

Usually, the first asset leveraged from savings is a home to live in. Expanding opportunities for home ownership are critical in closing the racial wealth divide. Home equity is one of the first building blocks for wealth, and is the most significant source of assets for people of color. For blacks, 62 percent of their net worth is held in homes; for Latinos, 51 percent. For white families, housing accounts for only 32 percent of their net worth. Given the history of federal subsidies for home ownership for whites, targeted funding for people and communities of color is now needed.

The Community Reinvestment Act of 1977 (CRA) came out of community struggles demanding access to banks and mortgage companies. Evidence was compiled showing that financial institutions engaged in discriminatory lending practices based on race, age, and location, instead of on an applicant's creditworthiness. These discriminatory practices had contributed to the decline of low-income and minority neighborhoods. The CRA required banks to lend in low-income communities, and federal banking regulators were mandated to maintain a close watch on financial institutions to ensure that they were meeting the needs of local communities. Communities of color were successful in getting the federal government to use its powers to stop private industry from providing affirmative action in lending to whites.

Through the CRA, significant strides were made during the 1990s as major banking institutions, increase lending toward affordable housing and economic development to assist low-income people. Over $20 billion has been invested in low-income neighborhoods and communities of color thanks to the CRA.[26]

## ASSET PRESERVATION

Home ownership has been a double-edged sword for many home owners of color. It is a struggle first to gain access to fair loan terms, and another to try and keep the home. If we were to dig beneath the home ownership figures, which provide only a snapshot in time, we would find a lot more turnovers of home ownership among people of color than among whites. Lending predators target the weak—those unfamiliar with the rules of the game.

ACORN's Mary Gaspar described her ordeal: "Here's how my nightmare started: I got a check in the mail from Household Finance with an offer to refinance our home . . . . Household was misleading and dishonest. I received my first bill and it was $13,000 more than I thought it was going to be! I have seen how Household preys on people who are economically desperate as well as middle-class people like us." ACORN (Association of Community Organizations for Reform Now) responded by putting the public pressure on Household Finance by holding demonstrations at their annual shareholder meetings. They were joined in their efforts by members of the United for a Fair Economy's Responsible Wealth project. Proxy votes given to ACORN members by Responsible Wealth members who owned shares allowed Mary to tell her story—*inside* the halls of wealth, usually barred to the people of color whose hard-earned homes were being stolen from them. Having shareholders and ACORN members speaking with one voice brought Household to the table to discuss changing its behavior.[27]

Mortgage foreclosure has been another impediment to maintaining home ownership. A report done by the Family Housing Fund in Minneapolis found that the major reason home owners default on mortgage payments is job loss or a significant reduction in income; other causes include health emergencies and separation or divorce. While home ownership rates have increased, so have instances of foreclosure.

Foreclosure prevention is an important tool in stabilizing home owners at risk of losing their homes and neighborhoods by preventing houses from becoming vacant and boarded up. Between 1991 and 1997, the Mortgage Foreclosure Program (MFP) carried out by the Family Housing Fund assisted close to seventeen hundred home owners and helped to reinstate the mortgages of over half of them within the St. Paul and Minneapolis area.[28] Foreclosure prevention counseling provides a more affordable way for home owners to stabilize their home ownership, compared to going through a mortgage insurer. It costs an average of $2,800 to help a home owner reinstate a mortgage, while with a mortgage insurer it could cost $10,000 to $28,000, depending on the insurer and the location of the home.[29] Ana Moreno, a housing consultant who conducted the study, contends that "[p]rograms that promote home ownership for households with very low incomes need to be linked to the full continuum of homeownership support services—pre-purchase education and counseling, financial assistance, post-purchase support, and delinquency and foreclosure prevention."[30]

Even with a home, you can spend your final years in poverty, if you have no retirement account from which to draw. Social Security was invented to protect U.S. workers from this risk: it is the country's most successful insurance program. While 10 percent of those over age sixty-five live in poverty today, without social security that rate would be almost 50 percent.[31] Occupations held mostly by African Americans and Latinos were excluded initially, but all employment sectors were included beginning in 1950. Social Security was also expanded to include not only retirement benefits, but also benefits to disabled workers and the families of workers who have died.

Because people of color have less income from stock holdings or capital gains than whites, Social Security is especially important to them: it is the sole source of income for 40 percent of elderly African Americans. The shorter life span of African American men means that both survivor and disability benefits go disproportionately to African Americans. While African Americans make up 12 percent of the U.S. population, 23 percent of children receiving Social Security survivor benefits are African American, as are about 17 percent of disability beneficiaries.[32]

Private pension plans are also an important asset. They provide retirement income, often as an employment benefit. The loss of unionized manufacturing jobs in the 1990s led to the loss of this asset for many. Laid off from auto and steel jobs which opened up to them during World War II, African Americans in particular have had to shift to jobs in the low-wage service sector, which do not provide employer-sponsored pension plans. In 2001, the

mean value of the retirement account of a black family was $12,247, compared to $10,206 for a Latino family and $65,411 for a white family.[33]

For those who are fortunate to have jobs with pensions, there has been a change from defined benefit plans, in which workers receive a defined percentage of their wages, based on age and years of service, to defined contribution plans, in which employers and/or employees contribute a defined amount of money into a plan, but they do not guarantee that the money will still be there when you retire. The risk has been shifted to the worker. The AFL-CIO news related the story of Wanda Chalk, an African American employee at Enron. She had worked at Enron for fifteen years and had stock options worth $150,000, which was to generate income for her retirement. But due to Enron's fraudulent dealings, when Enron crashed, so did she. She lost her job, her stock value dropped to zero, and her retirement security went up in smoke.

Privatizing Social Security could produce the same effect. Preservation of assets, not risky schemes that could fail when you need the money most, needs to remain the cornerstone of retirement plans. As a society, we should not revert to a pre-Depression system, where our elders are at risk of dying in poverty.

## ASSET CREATION

Even if a few individuals of color hold greater assets that will not be enough to close the racial wealth divide. Just because in 2004 Bill Cosby was worth $540 million in assets, and just because the Unanues, owners of Goya Foods, were worth $700 million, it doesn't help those members of their racial groups who are stuck at the bottom. Assets need to be utilized to expand wealth for the community as a whole.

For example, Native land was given away to railroad owners and, in 1887 tribal land was broken into individual plots. Over the years, more and more Native owners lost their plots, resulting in a checkerboard pattern of landownership in what should have been tribally owned territory. In 2002, the Northwest Area Foundation, funded by heirs of James J. Hill, head of the Great Northern Railroad, who grew rich from the displacement of Ojibwes in Minnesota, made voluntary reparations. They gave $20 million in seed money for a buyback. Now millions of acres are back under tribal control.

In the 1970s, the inner city of Battle Creek, Michigan, became an economically depressed area, due to the closing of a military base nearby; by 1990, there were fifty recognized crack houses within a mile of downtown. Battle Creek Neighborhoods Incorporated, a community development financial institution, stepped in. Their approach has been to focus on lending to people who are willing to buy particular community blocks rather than to buyers of housing units scattered throughout the city. Their loans come with a requirement to improve the property and to participate in improving the quality of life on the block. For example, they sponsor "best of neighborhood" contests—Best Front Porch, Best Back Yard, Best Group Effort—that encourage home maintenance and improvement. Brenda Sue Woods wasn't going to participate in the Porch contest at first, but then decided to try. When she took first place, "I was just screaming like I won something on *The Price is Right*." The emphasis on neighborhoods will enable housing values to rise in the area.

The Hawai'i Alliance for Community-Based Economic Development, a statewide nonprofit organization, provides loans not to individuals, but to groups. For example, a group of young people put in a proposal with the goal of "reconnection with their elders." One of the ways they used the loan was for a community van to transport those elders to needed services.

In a variety of locations, nonprofit organizations and government entities are experimenting with wealth-creation frameworks that are "inclusive, community-driven, and action oriented, protecting community, cultural, and environmental concerns while shielding individual private rights."[34] These efforts are road signs to the future.

## DISCUSSION QUESTIONS

1. According to Lui and colleagues, what have been the most successful federal programs enabling

people of color to improve their economic situations?

2. Based upon Lui and colleagues' analysis, what types of programs do the authors recommend for minorities to gain wealth and to begin to share in the prosperity of America? Can you think of other policies and strategies to better distribute wealth in the United States?

## NOTES

1. Brown, et al., 9.
2. Price, 2003.
3. Sklar, et al., 122.
4. Henry J. Kaiser Family Foundation, 2004, 1.
5. Ibid., 2.
6. Ibid., 4.
7. Department of Health and Human Services, 1993.
8. Shapiro, *Hidden Costs*, 2004, 52.
9. Sklar, et al., 2001, 90.
10. Collins and Yeskel, 2000, 182.
11. Ibid.
12. Anderson et al., 2005, 1.
13. Root Cause, 2003.
14. Christopher, introduction and under "Humble Origins."
15. Sklar, et al., 2001, 118.
16. Boshara, et al., 2004, 1.
17. Muhammad, et al., 2004, 7.
18. Woo, 1997, 104.
19. Shapiro, Thomas, power point presentation, 2004.
20. Sherradan, 1991, 3–7.
21. Brown et al., 17.
22. Shapiro, *Hidden Costs*, 2004, 185.
23. Ginsberg and Ochoa, 2003, B1.
24. Isbister, 1994, 2.
25. Ibid., 5.
26. *Policy Link*, 2003.
27. United for a Fair Economy, 2002.
28. Moreno, 1998, 6–7.
29. Ibid., 1.
30. Ibid., 17.
31. Orr, 2004, 14.
32. Spriggs, 2004, 18.
33. Muhammad, et al., 17.
34. Agres, 2005, 37.

# REFERENCES

## READING 1

Arthur Levitt Public Affairs Center. 2006. "The Hamilton College Youth Hot Button Issues Poll: Guns, Gays and Abortion." Available from http://www.hamilton.edu/news/polls/HotButtonIssues/index.html, accessed January 4, 2009.

Badgett, M., V. Lee, Christopher Ramos, and Brad Sears. 2008. "Evidence of Employment Discrimination on the Basis of Sexual Orientation and Gender Identity: Complaints Filed with State Enforcement Agencies 1999–2007." Los Angeles, CA: Williams Institute, UCLA School of Law. Available from http://www.law.ucla.edu/williamsinstitute, accessed January 5, 2009.

Bonilla-Silva, E. 2003. "'New Racism,' Color-Blind Racism and the Future of Whiteness in America." In *White Out: The Continuing Significance of Racism*, ed. A. W. Doane and E. Bonilla-Silva, New York: Routledge.

Brodkin, Karen. 2004. "How Jews Became White Folks and What That Says about Race in America." In *Race, Class and Gender in the United States*, ed. Paula S. Rothenberg, New York: Worth.

Crosby, Faye J. and Margaret Sockdale, eds. 2007. *Sex Discrimination in the Workplace: Multidisciplinary Perspectives*. Boston, MA: Blackwell.

Gay and Lesbian Alliance Against Defamation. 2009. Available from http://glaad.org/eye/ontv/2008/index.php, accessed February 4, 2009.

Goodbyeminimallyadequate.com. 2009. Available from http://goodbyeminimallyadequate.com, accessed January 31, 2009.

Guinier, Lani, and Gerald Torres. 2002. *The Miner's Canary: Enlisting Race; Resisting Power, Transforming Democracy*. Cambridge, MA: Harvard University Press.

HarrisInteractive. 2009. "Gay, Lesbian, Bisexual & Transgender." Available from http://www.harrisinteractive.com/services/glbt.asp, accessed January 5, 2009.

Hartmann, Heidi. 1997. "The Unhappy Marriage of Marxism and Feminism." In *The Second Wave: A Reader in Feminist Theory*, ed. Linda Nicholson. New York: Routledge.

Human Rights Watch. 2008. "China: Olympic Sponsors Ignore Human Rights Abuses." Available from http://hrw.org/enlish/docts/2008/18/china1946_txt.htm, accessed January 6, 2009.

Ignatiev, N. 1995. *How The Irish Became White*. New York: Routledge.

Karabel, Jerome. 2005. *The Chosen: The Hidden History of Admissions and Exclusion at Harvard, Yale and Princeton*. Boston: Houghton Mifflin.

McDermott, Monica, and Frank L. Samson. 2005. "White Racial Iidentity in the United States." *Annual Review of Sociology* 31: 245–61.

Messner, Michael. 1992. *Power at Play: Sports and the Problem of Masculinity*. Boston: Beacon.

Morgen, Sandra, and Ann Bookman. 1988. "Rethinking Women and Politics: An Introductory Essay." In *Women and the Politics of Empowerment*, eds. Sandra Morgen and Ann Bookman. Philadelphia: Temple University Press.

Mullings, Leith. 1994. "Images, Ideology and Women of Color." In *Women of Color in the U.S. Society*, ed. Maxine Baca Zinn and Bonnie Thornton Dill. Philadelphia: Temple University Press.

Navarette, Ruben, Jr. 1997. "A Darker Shade of Crimson: Odyssey of a Harvard Chicano." In *Race, Class and Gender in a Diverse Society*. Diana Kendall, ed. Boston: Allyn and Bacon.

Perlman, Joel. 2005. *Italians Then, Mexicans Now: Immigrant Origins and Second-Generation Progress 1890–2000*. New York: Russell Sage Foundation.

Sturm, Susan, and Lani Guinier. 1996. "The Future of Affirmative Action: Reclaiming the Innovative Idea." *California Law Review* 84(4): 953–1036.

Vanneman, Reeve, and Lynn Weber Cannon. 1987. *The American Perception of Class*. Philadelphia: Temple University Press.

Wilke, Mike, and Michael Applebaum. 2001. "Peering Out of the Closet." *Brandweek* 42(41): 26–32.

Wright, Erik Olin. 2008. "Logics of Class Analysis." In *Social Class: How Does it Work?* Eds. Annette Lareau and Dalton Conley. New York: Russell Sage Foundation.

# READING 2

Alba, Richard, Rubén Rumbaut, and Karen Marotz. 2005. "A Distorted Nation: Perceptions of Racial/Ethnic Group Sizes and Attitudes Toward Immigrants and Other Minorities." *Social Forces*, 84: 901–919.

Alexander, Jeffrey. 2006. *The Civil Sphere*. New York: Oxford University Press.

Bloch, Marc. 1953. *The Historian's Craft*. Translated by Peter Putnam. New York: Vintage.

Bloemraad, Irene. 2006. *Becoming a Citizen: Incorporating Immigrants and Refugees in the United States and Canada*. Berkeley, CA: University of California Press.

Blumer, Herbert. 1958. "Race Prejudice as a Sense of Group Position." *The Pacific Sociological Review*, 1: 3–7.

Bobo, Lawrence. 2001. "Racial Attitudes and Relations at the Close of the Twentieth Century." Pp. 262–299 in Neil Smelser, William Julius Wilson, and Faith Mitchell (Eds.), *America Becoming: Racial Trends and their Consequences*. Washington, DC: National Academy Press.

Bonilla-Silva, Eduardo. 1997. "Rethinking Racism: Toward a Structural Interpretation." *American Sociological Review*, 62: 465–480.

Bourdieu, Pierre. 2003. *Language and Symbolic Power*. Translated by Gino Raymond and Matthew Adamson. Cambridge, MA: Harvard University Press.

Bourdieu, Pierre. 1998 [1994]. "Rethinking the State: Genesis and Structure of the Bureaucratic Field." Translated by Loïc Wacquant and Samar Farage.

Pp. 35–63 in Pierre Bourdieu (Ed.), *Practical Reason*. Stanford, CA: Stanford University Press.

Bourdieu, Pierre. 1996 [1992]. *The Rules of Art: Genesis and Structure of the Literary Field*. Translated by Susan Emanuel. Stanford, CA: Stanford University Press.

Bourdieu, Pierre, and Loïc Wacquant. 1992. *An Invitation to Reflexive Sociology*. Chicago, IL: University of Chicago Press.

Brown, Michael, Martin Carnoy, Elliott Currie, Troy Duster, David Oppenheimer, Marjorie Shultz, and David Wellman. 2003. *White-Washing Race: The Myth of a Color Blind Society*. Berkeley, CA: University of California Press.

Brubaker, Rogers, Mara Loveman, and Peter Stamatov. 2004. "Ethnicity as Cognition." *Theory and Society*, 33: 31–64.

Collins, Patricia Hill. 2000. *Black Feminist Thought: Knowledge, Consciousness, and the Politics of Empowerment*, Second Edition. New York: Routledge.

Conley, Dalton. 2001. "Universal Freckle, or How I Learned to Be White." Pp. 25–42 in Birgit Brander Rasmussen, Eric Klinenberg, Irene Nexica, and Matt Wray (Eds.), *The Making and Unmaking of Whiteness.*. Durham, NC: Duke University Press.

Cox, Oliver Cromwell. 1948. *Caste, Class, and Race: A Study in Social Dynamics*. Garden City, NY: Doubleday.

Crenshaw, Kimberlé. 1989. "Demarginalizing the Intersection of Race and Sex: A Black Feminist Critique of Antidiscrimination Doctrine, Feminist Theory and Antiracist Politics." *University of Chicago Legal Forum*, 1989:139–167.

Crenshaw, Kimberlé. 1990. "Mapping the Margins: Intersectionality, Identity Politics, and Violence against Women of Color." *Stanford Law Review*, 42: 1241–1299.

DaCosta, Kimberly. 2007. *Making Multiracials: State, Family, and Market in the Redrawing of the Color Line*. Stanford, CA: Stanford University Press.

Davis, F. James. 1991. *Who Is Black? One Nation's Definition*. University Park, PA: Pennsylvania State University Press.

Dikötter, Frank. 1992. *The Discourse of Race in Modern China*. Stanford, CA: Stanford University Press.

Duster, Troy. 2003. "Buried Alive: The Concept of Race in Science." Pp. 258–277 in Alan Goodman, Deborah Heath, and Susan Lindee (Eds.), *Genetic Nature/Culture: Anthropology and Science beyond* the Two-Culture Divide. Berkeley, CA: University of California Press.

Duster, Troy. 2001. "The "Morphing" Properties of Whiteness." Pp.113-137 in Birgit Brander Rasmussen, Eric Klinenberg, Irene Nexica, and Matt Wray (Eds.), The Making and Unmaking of Whiteness. Durham, NC: Duke University Press.

Eisenstadt, S. N. 1998. Japanese Civilization: A Comparative View. Chicago, IL: University of Chicago Press.

Emirbayer, Mustafa. 1997. "Manifesto for Relational Sociology." American Journal of Sociology, 103: 281–317.

Essed, Philomena. 1991 [1984]. Everyday Racism. Claremont, CA: Hunter House.

Feagin, Joe. 1991. "The Continuing Significance of Race: Antiblack Discrimination in Public Places." American Sociological Review, 56: 101–116.

Feagin, Joe, Hernan Vera, and Pinar Batur. 2001. White Racism: The Basics, Second Edition. New York: Routledge.

Ferree, Myra Marx. 2009. "Inequality, Intersectionality and the Politics of Discourse: Framing Feminist Alliances." Pp. 84–101 in Emanuela Lombardo, Petra Meier, and Mieke Verloo (Eds.), The Discursive Politics of Gender Equality: Stretching, Bending, and Policy-Making. New York: Routledge.

Gossett, Thomas. 1965. Race: The History of an Idea in America. New York: Schocken.

Graves, Joseph, Jr. 2001. The Emperor's New Clothes: Biological Theories of Race at the Millennium. New Brunswick, NJ: Rutgers University Press.

Hall, Stuart. 1980. "Race Articulation and Societies Structured in Dominance." Pp. 305–345 in UNESCO (Ed.), Sociological Theories: Race and Colonialism. Paris, FR: UNESCO.

Haney-López, Ian. 1996. White by Law: The Legal Construction of Race. New York: New York University Press.

Hannaford, Ivan. 1996. Race: The History of an Idea in the West. Baltimore, MD: The Johns Hopkins Press.

Harris, Angela. 2000. "Race and Essentialism in Feminist Legal Theory." Pp.261–274 in Richard Delgado and Jean Stefancic (Eds.), Critical Race Theory: The Cutting Edge, Second Edition. Philadelphia, PA: Temple University Press.

Holt, Thomas. 2000. The Problem of Race in the 21st Century. Cambridge, MA: Harvard University Press.

Jackson, John, Jr. 2001. Harlemworld: Doing Race and Class in Contemporary Black America. Chicago, IL: University of Chicago Press.

Loury, Glenn. 2001. The Anatomy of Racial Inequality. Cambridge, MA: Harvard University Press.

Loveman, Mara. 1999. "Is "Race" Essential?" American Sociological Review, 64: 891–898.

Marx, Anthony. 1998. Making Race and Nation: A Comparison of the United States, South Africa, and Brazil. New York: Cambridge University Press.

Massey, Douglas. 2007. Categorically Unequal: The American Stratification System. New York: Russell Sage Foundation.

Neckerman, Kathryn. 2007. Schools Betrayed: Roots of Failure in Inner-City Education. Chicago, IL: University of Chicago Press.

Ngai, Mae. 2004. Impossible Subjects: Illegal Aliens and the Making of Modern America. Princeton, NJ: Princeton University Press.

Oaks, Jeannie. 2005. Keeping Track: How Schools Structure Inequality, Second Edition. New Haven, CT: Yale University Press.

Oliver, Melvin and Thomas Shapiro. 1997. Black Wealth/ White Wealth. New York: Routledge.

Prins, Baukje. 2006. "Narrative Accounts of Origins: A Blind Spot in the Intersectional Approach?" European Journal of Women's Studies, 13: 277–290.

Quillian, Lincoln. 2006. "New Approaches to Understanding Racial Prejudice and Discrimination." Annual Review of Sociology, 32: 299–328.

Reich, Michael. 1981. Racial Inequality: A Political-Economic Analysis. Princeton, NJ: Princeton University Press.

Schuman, Howard, Charlotte Steeh, Lawrence Bobo, and Maria Krysan. 1997. Racial Attitudes in America: Trends and Interpretation, revised edition. Cambridge, MA: Harvard University Press.

Searle-Chatterjee, Mary, and Ursula Sharma. 1994. Contextualising Caste: Post-Dumontian Approaches. Oxford, U.K.: Blackwell.

Shklar, Judith. 1991. American Citizenship: The Quest for Inclusion. Cambridge, MA: Harvard University Press.

Smedley, Audrey. 1999. Race in North America: Origin and Evolution of a Worldview, Second Edition. Boulder, CO: Westview.

Smith, Lillian. 1994 [1949]. Killers of the Dream, 1994 edition. New York: Norton.

Southern Poverty Law Center Intelligence Project. 2005. Active U.S. Hate Groups in 2005. Montgomery, AL: Southern Poverty Law Center.

Sparks, Allister. 2006. *The Mind of South Africa: The Story of the Rise and Fall of Apartheid*. Johannesburg, ZA: Jonathan Ball.

Stephens, Thomas. 1999. *Dictionary of Latin American Racial and Ethnic Terminology*. Gainesville, FL: University of Florida Press.

Telles, Edward. 2004. *Race in Another America: The Significance of Skin Color in Brazil*. Princeton, NJ: Princeton University Press.

Wacquant, Loic. 1997. "For an Analytic of Racial Domination." *Political Power and Social Theory*, 11: 221–234.

Walby, Sylvia. 2007. "Complexity Theory, Systems Theory, and Multiple Intersecting Social Inequalities." *Philosophy of the Social Sciences*, 37: 449–470.

Waters, Mary. 1990. *Ethnic Options: Choosing Identities in America*. Berkeley, CA: University of California Press.

Waters, Mary. 1999. *Black Identities: West Indian Immigrant Dreams and American Realities*. New York, Cambridge, MA: Russell Sage Foundation, Harvard University Press.

Weber, Max. 1946. "Class, Status, Party." Pp.180-195 in H. H. Gerth and C. Wright Mills (Eds.), *From Max Weber: Essays in Sociology*. New York: Oxford University Press.

Western, Bruce. 2006. *Punishment and Inequality in America*. New York: Russell Sage Foundation.

Winant, Howard. 2001. *The World Is a Ghetto: Race and Democracy since World War II*. New York: Basic Books.

Yuval-Davis, Nira. 2006. "Intersectionality and Feminist Politics." *European Journal of Women's Studies*, 13: 193–209.

# Reading 3

Almaguer, Thomas. 1993. "Chicano Men: A Cartography of Homosexual Identity and Behavior." Pp. 255–273 in *The Lesbian and Gay Studies Reader*, edited by H. Abelove, M. A. Barale and D. M. Halperin. New York: Routledge.

Beauvoir, Simone de. 1952. *The Second Sex*. New York: Alfred A. Knopf, Inc.

Bem, Sandra Lipsitz. 1993. *The Lenses of Gender*. New Haven, CT: Yale University Press.

Blackless, Melanie, Anthony Charuvastra, Amanda Derryck, Anne Fausto-Sterling, Karl Lauzanne, and Ellen Lee. 2000. "How Sexually Dimorphic Are We? Review and Synthesis." *American Journal of Human Biology* 12:151–266.

Bordo, Susan. 1986. "The Cartesian Masculinization of Thought." *Signs* 11:439–56.

Bornstein, Kate. 1994. *Gender Outlaw: On Men, Women, and the Rest of Us*. New York: Routledge.

Bromley, Dorothy D., and Florence H. Britten. 1938. *Youth and Sex: A Study of 1300 College Students*. 3rd Ed. New York: Harper and Brothers.

Brown, Lester. 1997. *Two Spirit People: American Indian Lesbian Women and Gay Men*. New York: Haworth Press.

Butler, Judith. 1990. *Gender Trouble: Feminism and the Subversion of Identity*. New York: Routledge.

Cashmore, Ellis. 2005. *Making Sense of Sports*. 4th ed. London, England: Routledge.

Connell, R. W. 2002. *Gender: Short Introductions*. Cambridge, MA: Polity.

Coontz, Stephanie. 1992. *The Way We Never Were: American Families and the Nostalgia Trap*. New York: Basic Books.

Crawley, Sara L., and K. L. Broad. 2004. "'Be Your [Real Lesbian] Self': Mobilizing Sexual Formula Stories through Personal (and Political) Storytelling." *Journal of Contemporary Ethnography* 33:39–71.

Fausto-Sterling, Anne. 1986. *Myths of Gender: Biological Theories about Women and Men*. New York: Basic Books.

Fausto-Sterling, Anne. 2000. *Sexing the Body: Gender Politics and the Construction of Sexuality*. New York: Basic Books.

Feinberg, Leslie. 1996. *Transgender Warriors: Making History from Joan of Arc to Dennis Rodman*. Boston, MA: Beacon Press.

Garfinkel, Harold. 1967. *Studies in Ethnomethodology*. Englewood Cliffs, NJ: Prentice Hall.

Green, Jamison. 2004. *Becoming a Visible Man*. Nashville, TN: Vanderbilt University Press.

Halperin, David M. 1989. "Is There a History of Sexuality?" *History and Theory* 28: 257–74.

Homan, Leslie B. and Bertram Schaffner. 1947. "The Sex Lives of Unmarried Men." *The American Journal of Sociology* 52:501–7.

Humphreys, Laud. 1970. *Tearoom Trade: Impersonal Sex in Public Places*. Chicago, IL: Aldine Publishing Company.

Ingraham, Chrya. 1996. "The Heterosexual Imaginary: Feminist Sociology and Theories of Gender."

Pp. 168–193 in *QueerTheory/Sociology*, edited by S. Seidman. Malden, MA: Blackwell.

Jay, Nancy. 1981. "Gender and Dichotomy." *Feminist Studies* 7:38–56.

Katz, Jonathan Ned. 1995. *The Invention of Heterosexuality*. New York: Dutton.

Kessler, Suzanne J. 1998. *Lessons from the Intersexed*. New Brunswick, NJ: Rutgers University Press.

Kessler, Suzanne J. and Wendy McKenna. 1978. *Gender: An Ethnomethodological Approach*. Chicago, IL: University of Chicago Press.

King, J. L. 2005. *On the Down Low: A Journey into the Lives of "Straight" Black Men Who Sleep With Men*. New York: Harlem Moon.

Kinsey, Alfred C., Wardell B. Pomeroy, and Clyde E. Martin. 1948. *Sexual Behavior in the Human Male*. Philadelphia, PA: W. B. Saunders.

Kinsey, Alfred C., Wardell B. Pomeroy, Clyde E. Martin and Paul Gebhard. 1953. *Sexual Behavior in the Human Female*. Philadelphia, PA: W. B. Saunders.

Lorber, Judith. 1994. *Paradoxes of Gender*. New Haven, CT: Yale University Press.

Lorber, Judith. 1996. "Beyond the Binaries: Depolarizing the Categories of Sex, Sexuality and Gender." *Sociological Inquiry* 66:143–59.

Loseke, Donileen R. 1999. *Thinking about Social Problems: An Introduction to Constructionist Perspectives*. New York: Aldine de Gruyter.

Paechter, Carrie. 2003. "Masculinities and Femininities as Communities of Practice." *Women's Studies International Forum* 26:69–77.

Paechter, Carrie. 2006. "Power, Knowledge and Embodiment in Communities of Sex/Gender Practice." *Women's Studies International Forum* 29:13–26.

Rubin, Harry. 2003. *Self Made Men: Identity and Embodiment among Transsexual Men*. Nashville, TN: Vanderbilt University Press.

Rust, Paula C. 1995. *Bisexuality and the Challenge to Lesbian Politics: Sex, Loyalty and Revolution*. New York: New York University Press.

Schultz, Alfred. 1970. *On Phenomenology and Social Relations: Selected Writings*. Chicago, IL: University of Chicago Press.

Schwartz, Pepper, and Virginia Rutter. 1998. *The Gender of Sexuality*. Thousand Oaks, CA: Pine Forge Press.

Shilling, Chris. 1993. *The Body in Social Theory*. London, England: Sage.

Sprague, Joey. 1997. "Holy Men and Big Guns: The Can[n] on in Social Theory." *Gender and Society* 11:88–107.

Stone, Sandy. 1991. "The Empire Strikes Back: A Posttranssexual Manifesto." Pp. 280–302 in *Body Guards*, edited by J. Epstein and K. Straub. New York: Routledge.

Turner, Bryan S. 1996. *The Body and Society*. 2nd ed. London, England: Sage.

Weeks, Jeffrey. 2003. *Sexuality*. 2nd ed. London, England: Routledge.

Welter, Barbara. 1978. "The Cult of True Womanhood, 1820–1860." Pp. 313–333 in *The American Family in Social Historical Perspective*, 2nd edition, edited by M. Gordon New York: St. Martin's Press.

West, Candace and Don Zimmerman. 1987. "Doing Gender." *Gender and Society* 1:125–51.

Young, Antonia. 2000. *Women Who Became Men: Albanian Sworn Virgins*. Oxford: Berg.

Zerubavel, Eviatar. 1996. "Lumping and Splitting: Notes on Social Classification." *Sociological Forum* 11:421–33.

## READING 7

Alba, R. 2014. "The Twilight of Ethnicity: What Relevance for Today?" *Ethnic and Racial Studies* 37:781–785.

Alba, Richard. 2006. "On the Sociological Significance of the American Jewish Experience: Boundary Blurring, Assimilation, and Pluralism." *Sociology of Religion* 67:347–358.

Alba, Richard and Victor Nee. 1997. "Rethinking Assimilation Theory for a New Era of Immigration." *International Migration Review* 31:826–874.

Anderson, Elijah. 2011. The Cosmopolitan Canopy: Race and Civility in Everyday Life. New York, NY: W.W. Norton & Co.

Bonilla-Silva, Eduardo. 1997. "Rethinking Racism: Toward a Structural Interpretation." *American Sociological Review* 62:465–480.

Bonilla-Silva, Eduardo. 2014. *Racism without Racists: Color-blind Racism and the Persistence of Racial Inequality in America*. Lanham: Rowman & Littlefield Publishers.

Boyarin, Jonathan and Daniel Boyarin. 1997. *Jews and Other Differences: The New Jewish Cultural Studies*. Minneapolis: University of Minnesota Press.

Brodkin, Karen. 1998. *How Jews Became White Folks and What that Says about Race in America*. New Brunswick, N.J.: Rutgers University Press.

Chelsea, E. Schafer and M. Shaw Greg. 2009. "Tolerance in the United States." *Public Opinion Quarterly* 73:404.

Collins, Patricia Hill. 2013. "Toward a New Vision: Race, Class, and Gender as Categories of Analysis and Connection." in *Race, Gender, Sexuality, Social Class: Dimensions of Inequality*, edited by S. Ferguson. Thousand Oaks, CA: Sage.

DellaPergola, Sergio. 2014. "World Jewish Population, 2013." Pp. 279–358 in American Jewish Year Book 2013, vol. 113, *American Jewish Year Book*, edited by A. Dashefsky and I. Sheskin: Springer International Publishing.

Dodd, Christopher J. and Lary Bloom. 2007. *Letters from Nuremberg: My Father's Narrative of a Quest for Justice*. New York: Crown Publishers.

Fein, Helen. 1979. "Is Sociology Aware of Genocide? Recognition of Genocide in Introductory Sociology Texts in the United States, 1947-1977." *Humanity & Society* 3:177–193.

Fein, Helen. 1987. *The Persisting Question: Sociological Perspectives and Social Contexts of Modern Antisemitism*, vol. 1. New York: De Gruyter.

Fein, Helen. 2007. *Human Rights and Wrongs: Slavery, Terror, Genocide*. Boulder: Paradigm Publishers.

Gans, H. J. 1994. "Symbolic Ethnicity and Symbolic Religiosity—Towards a Comparison of Ethnic and Religious Acculturation." *Ethnic and Racial Studies* 17:577–592.

Gans, Herbert J. 1979. "Symbolic Ethnicity: The Future of Ethnic Groups and Cultures in America." *Ethnic and Racial Studies* 2:1–20.

Gerber, David A. 1986. *Anti-Semitism in American History*. Urbana: University of Illinois Press.

Gilbert, Martin. 2000. *Never Again: A History of the Holocaust*. New York, NY: Universe.

Gilbert, Martin. 2001. *The Jews in the Twentieth Century United States*. New York, NY: Schocken Books.

Goldscheider, Calvin. 1987. "Theoretical Issues in the Sociology of Contemporary Jewries: Comments on "What Is Conceptually Special about a Sociology of Jewry"." *Contemporary Jewry* 8:91–100.

Goldscheider, Calvin. 2002. "The Marshall Sklare Memorial Lecture. Social Science and the Jews: A Research Agenda for the Next Generation." *Contemporary Jewry* 23:196–219.

Goren, Arthur A. 1999. *The Politics and Public Culture of American Jews*. Bloomington: Indiana University Press.

Hochschild, Jennifer L. 1995. *Facing up to the American Dream: Race, Class, and the Soul of the Nation*. Princeton, N.J: Princeton University Press.

Kaplan, Mordecai Menaham. 1967. *Judaism as a Civilization: Toward a Reconstruction of American-Jewish Life*. New York: Schocken Books.

Klausner, Samuel Z. 1987. "What Is Conceptually Special about a Sociology of Jewry." *Contemporary Jewry* 8:71–89.

Konner, Melvin. 2003. *Unsettled: An Anthropology of the Jews*. New York: Viking Compass.

Kotler-Berkowitz, Laurence. 2005. "Ethnicity and political behavior among American Jews: Findings from the National Jewish population survey 2000–01." *Contemporary Jewry* 25:132–157.

Krysan, Maria. 2000. "Prejudice, Politics, and Public Opinion: Understanding the Sources of Racial Policy Attitudes." *Annual Review of Sociology* 26:135–168.

Krysan, Maria. 2012a. "From Color Castè to Color Blind, Part 1: Racial Attitudes in the United States During World War II, 1939-1945." Pp. 178–194 in *The Oxford Handbook of African American Citizenship*, edited by J. Henry L. Gates, C. Steele, and L. D. Bobo. New York: Oxford University Press.

Krysan, Maria. 2012b. "From Color Caste to Color Blind, Part II: 1946–75." Pp. 195–234 in *The Oxford Handbook of African American Citizenship*, edited by J. Henry L. Gates, C. Steele, and L. D. Bobo. New York: Oxford University Press.

Krysan, Maria. 2012c. "From Color Caste to Color Blind, Part IIi: 1976-2004." Pp. 235–275 in *The Oxford Handbook of African American Citizenship*, edited by J. Henry L. Gates, C. Steele, and L. D. Bobo. New York: Oxford University Press.

Krysan, Maria and Amanda E. Lewis. 2004. *The Changing Terrain of Race and Ethnicity*. New York: Russell Sage Foundation.

Lazerwitz, Bernard. 1995. "Jewish-Christian Marriages and Conversions, 1971 and 1990." *Sociology of Religion* 56:433.

Lazerwitz, Bernard Melvin. 1998. *Jewish Choices: American Jewish Denominationalism*. Albany: State University of New York Press.

Lee, Taeku. 2002. *Mobilizing Public Opinion: Black Insurgency and Racial Attitudes in the Civil Rights Era*. Chicago: University of Chicago Press.

Martin, Daniela. 2014. "Good Education for All? Student Race and Identity Development in the Multicultural

Classroom." *International Journal of Intercultural Relations* 39:110–123.

Michels, Tony. 2010. "Is America "Different?" A Critique of American Jewish Exceptionalism." *American Jewish History* 96:201-IV.

Michman, Dan. 1995. ""The Holocaust" in the Eyes of Historians: The Problem of Conceptualization, Periodization, and Explanation." *Modern Judaism* 15:233–264.

Myrdal, Gunnar, Richard Mauritz Edvard Sterner, and Arnold Marshall Rose. 1944. *An American Dilemma: The Negro Problem and Modern Democracy.* New York, London: Harper & Brothers.

National Foreign Assessment Center, United States Central Intelligence Agency, 1981. The World Factbook. Washington, D.C: Central Intelligence Agency.

Patterson, Orlando. 2013. "Making Sense of Culture." *Annual Review of Sociology* 40:1–30.

Rosenfeld, Alvin H. 1988. "Holocaust Fictions and the Transformation of Historical Memory." *Holocaust and Genocide Studies* 3:323-336.

Rosenfeld, Alvin H. 2001. "The Assault on Holocaust Memory." Pp. 3–20 in *American Jewish Yearbook*. New York: Jewish Publication Society of America.

Rosenfield, Geraldine. 1982. "Attitudes Toward American Jews." *The Public Opinion Quarterly* 46:431–443.

Sarna, Jonathan D. 2004. *American Judaism: A History.* New Haven: Yale University Press.

Smedley, Brian, Adrienne Stith, and Alan Nelson. 2003. "Unequal Treatment: Confronting Racial and Ethnic Disparities in Health Care." Washington DC: Institute of Medicine: National Academies Press.

Svonkin, Stuart. 1997. *Jews against Prejudice: American Jews and the Fight for Civil Liberties.* New York: Columbia University Press.

Waters, Mary C. 1990. *Ethnic Options: Choosing Identities in America.* Berkeley: University of California Press.

Waters, Mary C. 2009. "Social Science and Ethnic Options." *Ethnicities* 9:130–135.

Zuberi, Tukufu. 2001. *Thicker than Blood: How Racial Statistics Lie.* Minneapolis: University of Minnesota Press.

# READING 9

Bowles, Samuel, and Herb Gintis. 1990. "Contested Exchange: New Microfoundations for the Political Economy of Capitalism." *Politics and Society* 18(2):165–222.

Gouldner, Alvin W. 1970. *The Coming Crisis of Western Sociology.* New York: Basic Books.

Parkin, Frank. 1979. *Marxism and Class Theory: A Bourgeois Critique.* London: Tavistock.

Wright, Erik Olin. 1985. *Classes.* London: Verso Press.

Wright, Erik Olin. 1997. *Class Counts: Comparative Studies in Class Analysis.* Cambridge: Cambridge University Press.

Wright, Erik Olin, Andrew Levine, and Elliott Sober. 1992. *Re-Constructing Marxism: Essays on Explanation and the Theory of History.* London: Verso Press.

# READING 10

Acker, Joan. 1994. "The Gender Regime of Swedish Banks." *Scandinavian Journal of Management* 10(2):117–30.

Acker, Joan and Donald Van Houten. 1974. "Differential Recruitment and Control: The Sex Structuring of Organizations." *Administrative Science Quarterly* 19:152–63.

Amott, Teresa and Julie Matthaei. 1996. *Race, Gender, and Work: A Multi-cultural Economic History of Women in the United States.* Boston: South End Press.

Beneria, Lourdes. 1999. "Globalization, Gender, and the Davos Man." *Feminist Economics* 5(3):61–83.

Brodkin, Karen. 1998. "Race, Class, and Gender: The Metaorganization of American Capitalism." *Transforming Anthropology* 7(2):46–57.

Brown, Michael K., Martin Carnoy, Elliott Currie, Troy Duster, David B. Oppenheimer, Marjorie M. Shultz, and David Wellman. 2003. *White-Washing Race: The Myth of a Color-Blind Society.* Berkeley, CA: University of California Press.

Burris, Beverly H. 1996. "Technocracy, Patriarchy and Management." In *Men as Managers, Managers as Men,* edited by David L. Collinson and Jeff Hearn. London: Sage.

Cockburn, Cynthia. 1991. *In the Way of Women: Men's Resistance to Sex Equality in Organization.* Ithaca, NY: ILR Press.

Cohn, Samuel. 1985. *The Process of Occupational Sex-Typing: The Feminization of Clerical Labor in Great Britain.* Philadelphia: Temple University Press.

Collins, Patricia Hill. 2000. *Black Feminist Thought.* New York and London: Routledge.

Collinson, David L. and Jeff Hearn. 1996. "Breaking the Silence: On Men, Masculinities, and Managements." In *Men as Managers, Managers as Men*, edited by David L. Collinson and Jeff Hearns. London: Sage.

Connell, R. W. 2000. *The Men and the Boys*. Berkeley, CA: University of California Press.

Connell, R. W. 1995. *Masculinities*. Berkeley, CA: University of California Press.

Connell, R. W. 1987. *Gender and Power*. Stanford, CA: Stanford University Press.

Figart, Deborah M., Ellen Mutari, and Marilyn Power. 2002. *Living Wages, Equal Wages*. London and New York: Routledge.

Foner, Philip S. 1947. *History of the Labor Management in the United States*. New York: International Publishers.

Frankel, Linda. 1984. "Southern Textile Women: Generations of Survival and Struggle." In *My Troubles Are Going to Have Trouble with Me*, edited by Karen Brodkin Sacks and Dorothy Remy. New Brunswick, NJ: Rutgers University Press.

Glenn, Evelyn Nakano. 2002. *Unequal Freedom: How Race and Gender Shaped American Citizenship and Labor*. Cambridge, MA: Harvard University Press.

Goldin, Claudia. 1990. *Understanding the Gender Gap: An Economic History of American Women*. New York and Oxford: Oxford University Press.

Gutman, Herbert G. 1976. *Work, Culture, and Society in Industrializing America*. New York: Alfred A. Knopf.

Hartmann, Heidi. 1976. "Capitalism, Patriarchy, and Job Segregation by Sex." *Signs* 1(3):137–69.

Hearn, Jeff. 1996. "Is Masculinity Dead? A Critique of the Concept of Masculinity/Masculinities." In *Understanding Masculinities: Social Relations and Culturals Arenas*, edited by M. Mac An Ghaill. Buckingham, England: Oxford University Press.

Hearn, Jeff and Wendy Parkin. 2001. *Gender, Sexuality, and Violence in Organizations*. London: Sage.

Janiewski, Dolores. 1985. *Sisterhood Denied: Race, Gender, and Class in a New South Community*. Philadelphia: Temple University Press.

Kanter, Rosabeth Moss. 1977. *Men and Women of the Corporation*. New York: Basic Books.

Keister, Lisa. 2000. *Wealth in America: Trends in Wealth Inequality*. Cambridge: Cambridge University Press.

Kessler-Harris, Alice. 1982. *Out to Work: A History of Wage-Earning Women in the United States*. New York: Oxford University Press.

Kilbourne, Barbara, Paula England, and Kurt Beron. 1994. "Effects of Individual, Occupational and Industrial Characteristics on Earnings: Intersections of Race and Gender." *Social Forces* 72:1149–76.

McDowell, Linda. 1997. "A Tale of Two Cities? Embedded Organizations and Embodied Workers in the City of London." Pp. 118–29 in *Geographies of Economics*, edited by Roger Lee and Jane Willis. London: Arnold.

Middleton, Chris. 1983. "Patriarchal Exploitation and the Rise of English Capitalism." In *Gender, Class, and Work*, edited by Eva Gamarnikow, David H. J. Morgan, June Purvis, and Daphne E. Taylorson. London: Heinemann.

Milton, David. 1982. *The Politics of U.S. Labor: From the Great Depression to the New Deal*. New York: Monthly Review Press.

Omi, Michael and Howard Winant. 1994. *Racial Formation in the United States*. New York: Routledge.

Padavic, Irene and Barbara Reskin. 2002. *Women and Men at Work*. Thousand Oaks, CA: Pine Forge Press.

Perrow, Charles. 2002. *Organizing America*. Princeton and Oxford: Princeton University Press.

Reed, Rosslyn. 1996. "Entrepreneurialism and Paternalism in Australian Management: A Gender Critique of the 'Self-Made' Man." In *Men as Managers, Managers as Men*, edited by David L. Collinson and Jeff Hearns. London: Sage.

Reskin, Barbara F., Debra B. McBrier, and Julie A. Kmec. 1999. "The Determinants and Consequences of Workplace Sex and Race Composition." *Annual Review of Sociology* 25:335–61.

Royster, Deirdre A. 2003. *Race and the Invisible Hand: How White Networks Exclude Black Men from Blue-Collar Jobs*. Berkeley, CA: University of California Press.

Seidler, Victor J. 1989. *Rediscovering Masculinity: Reason, Language, and Sexuality*. London and New York: Routledge.

Smith, Dorothy E. 1999. *Writing the Social: Critique, Theory, and Investigations*. Toronto: University of Toronto Press.

Taylor, Paul F. 1992. *Bloody Harlan: The United Mine Workers in Harlan County, Kentucky, 1931–1941*. Lanham, MD: University Press of America.

Wacjman, Judy. 1998. *Managing Like a Man*. Cambridge: Polity Press.

Williams, Eric. 1944. *Capitalism and Slavery*. Chapel Hill, NC: University of North Carolina Press.

## READING 11

Acker, Joan. 1990. "Hierarchies, Jobs, and Bodies: A Theory of Gendered Organizations." *Gender & Society* 4:139–58.

Almaguer, Tomas. 1994. *Racial Faultlines: The Historical Origins of White Supremacy in California.* Berkeley: University of California Press.

Barrera, Mario. 1979. *Race and Class in the Southwest.* Notre Dame, IN: University of Notre Dame Press.

Barrett, Michèle. 1980. *Women's Oppression Today: Problems in Marxist Feminist Analysis.* London: Verso.

———. 1987. "The Concept of 'Difference.'" *Feminist Review* 26 (July):29–41.

Blauner, Robert. 1972. *Racial Oppression in America.* New York: Harper & Row.

Bonacich, Edna. 1972. "A Theory of Ethnic Antagonism: The Split Labor Market." *American Sociological Review* 37:547–59.

———. 1976. "Advanced Capitalism and Black/White Relations in the United States: A Split Labor Market Interpretation." *American Sociological Review* 41:34–51.

Bose, Chris, Roslyn Feldberg, and Natalie Sokoloff, with the Women and Work Research Group, eds. 1987. *Hidden Aspects of Women's Work.* New York: Praeger.

Braverman, Harry L. 1974. *Labor and Monopoly Capital.* New York: Monthly Review Press.

Butler, Judith. 1990. *Gender Trouble: Feminism and the Subversion of Identity.* New York: Routledge.

———. 1993. *Bodies That Matter: On the Discursive Limits of "Sex."* New York: Routledge.

Chaplin, David. 1978. "Domestic Service and Industrialization." *Comparative Studies in Sociology* 1:97–127.

Collins, Patricia Hill. 1990. *Black Feminist Thought: Knowledge, Consciousness, and the Politics of Empowerment.* New York: Routledge, Chapman & Hall.

Connell, R. W. 1989. *Gender and Power.* Stanford, CA: Stanford University Press.

Cowan, Ruth Schwartz. 1983. *More Work for Mother.* New York: Basic Books.

Crenshaw, Kimberlé. 1989. "Demarginalizing the Intersection of Race and Sex: A Black Feminist Critique of Antidiscrimination Doctrine, Feminist Theory, and Antiracist Politics." *University of Chicago Legal Forum,* 139.

———. 1992. "Whose Story Is It Anyway? Feminist and Anti-racist Appropriations of Anita Hill." Pp. 402–40 in *Race-ing Justice, En-gendering Power: Essays on Anita Hill, Clarence Thomas, and the Construction of Social Reality,* edited by Toni Morrison. New York: Pantheon.

Davis, F. James. 1991. *Who Is Black?* College Park: Pennsylvania State University Press.

Degler, Carl. 1980. *At Odds: Woman and the American Family from the Revolution to the Present.* New York: Oxford University Press.

Deutsch, Sarah. 1987. *No Separate Refuge: Culture, Class and Gender on an Anglo-Hispanic Frontier in the American Southwest, 1880–1920.* New York: Oxford University Press.

Dominguez, Virginia. 1986. *White by Definition: Social Classification in Creole Louisiana.* New Brunswick, NJ: Rutgers University Press.

Dyer, Richard. 1988. White. *Screen* 29, no. 4: 44–65.

Echols, Alice. 1989. *Daring to Be Bad: Radical Feminism in America, 1967–1975.* Minneapolis: University of Minnesota Press.

Epstein, Barbara. 1981. *The Politics of Domesticity: Women, Evangelism and Temperance in Nineteenth Century American.* Middletown, CT: Wesleyan University Press.

Espiritu, Yen. 1992. *Asian American Panethnicity: Bridging Institutions and Identities.* Philadelphia: Temple University Press.

Fields, Barbara J. 1982. "Ideology and Race in American History." Pp. 143–78 in *Region, Race and Reconstruction,* edited by James MacPherson and M. Morgan Kousser. New York: Oxford University Press.

———. 1990. "Slavery, Race and Ideology in the United States of America." *New Left Review* 181:95–118.

Forbath, William. 1996. "Race, Class and Citizenship." Unpublished manuscript.

Foucault, Michel. 1977. *Discipline and Punish: The Birth of the Prison.* Translated by Alan Sheridan. New York: Pantheon.

———. 1978. *The History of Sexuality.* Vol. 1, *An Introduction.* Translated by Alan Sheridan. New York: Vintage.

Fuchs, Lawrence H. 1983. *Hawaii Pono: An Ethnic and Political History.* Honolulu: Bess.

Garcia, Mario. 1981. *Desert Immigrants: The Mexicans of El Paso, 1880–1920.* New Haven, CT: Yale University Press.

Glenn, Evelyn Nakano. 1986. *Issei, Nisei, Warbride: Three Generations of Japanese American Women in Domestic Service*. Philadelphia: Temple University Press.

———. 1992. "From Servitude to Service Work: Historical Continuities in the Racial Division of Paid Reproductive Labor." *Signs* 18:1–43.

Gramsci, Antonio. 1971. *Selections from the Prison Notebooks*. Edited and translated by Quintin Hoare and Geoffrey Nowell Smith. New York: International.

Haney Lopez, Ian F. 1996. *White by Law: The Legal Construction of Race*. New York: New York University Press.

Harris, Angela. 1990. "Race and Essentialism in Feminist Legal Theory." *Stanford Law Review* 42:581–616.

Harris, Cheryl I. 1993. "Whiteness as Property." *Harvard Law Review* 106:1707–91.

Hartmann, Heidi I. 1976. "Capitalism, Patriarchy, and Job Segregation by Sex." *Signs* 1:137–69.

Higginbotham, Evelyn Brooks. 1992. "African American Women's History and the Metalanguage of Race." *Signs* 17:251–74.

Hull, Gloria T., Patricia Bell Scott, and Barbara Smith, eds. 1982. *All the Women Are White, All the Blacks Are Men, but Some of Us Are Brave: Black Women's Studies*. Old Westbury, NY: Feminist Press.

Ignatiev, Noel. 1995. *How the Irish became White*. New York: Routledge.

Jordan, Winthrop. 1968. *White over Black: American Attitudes toward the Negro, 1550-1812*. Chapel Hill: University of North Carolina Press.

Kaminsky, Amy. 1994. "Gender, Race, Raza." *Feminist Studies* 20:3–32.

Kaplan, Elaine Bell. 1987. "'I Don't Do No Windows': Competition between the Domestic Worker and the Housewife." In *Competition: A Feminist Taboo?* edited by Valerie Minor and Helen E. Longino. New York: Feminist Press.

Katzman, David. 1978. *Seven Days a Week: Women and Domestic Service in Industrializing America*. New York: Oxford University Press.

Laslett, Barbara and Johanna Brenner. 1989. "Gender and Social Reproduction: Historical Perspectives." *Annual Review of Sociology* 15:381–404.

Lind, Andrew W. 1951. "The Changing Position of Domestic Service in Hawaii." *Social Process in Hawaii* 15:71–87.

Liu, Tessie. 1991. "Teaching Differences among Women from a Historical Perspective: Rethinking Race and Gender as Social Categories. *Women's Studies International Forum* 14, no. 4.

Lorber, Judith. 1994. *Paradoxes of Gender*. New Haven, CT: Yale University Press.

MacKinnon, Catharine A. 1989. *Toward a Feminist Theory of the State*. Cambridge, MA: Harvard University Press.

Omi, Michael and Howard Winant. 1986. *Racial Formation in the United States from the 1960s to the 1980s*. New York: Routledge.

———. 1994. *Racial Formation in the United States: 1960-1990*. 2nd ed. New York: Routledge.

Ong, Aiwa. 1996. "Cultural Citizenship as Subject Making: Immigrants Negotiate Racial and Cultural Boundaries in the United States." *Current Anthropology* 37:737–61.

Palmer, Phyllis Marynick. 1989. *Domesticity and Dirt*. Philadelphia: Temple University Press.

Pascoe, Peggy. 1990. *Relations of Rescue*. New York: Oxford University Press.

———. 1991. "Race, Gender, and Intercultural Relations: The Case of Interracial Marriage." *Frontiers* 12, no. 1:5–18.

Reich, Michael. 1981. *Racial Inequality*. Princeton, NJ: Princeton University Press.

Roediger, David. 1991. *The Wages of Whiteness: Race and the Making of the American Working Class*. London: Verso.

———. 1994. *Towards the Abolition of Whiteness*. London: Verso.

Rollins, Judith. 1985. *Between Women: Domestics and Their Employers*. Philadelphia: Temple University Press.

Romero, Mary. 1992. *Maid in the U.S.A*. New York: Routledge.

———. 1995. "Class Formation and the Quintessential Worker." Unpublished manuscript.

Rubin, Gayle. 1975. "The Traffic in Women: Notes on the Political Economy of Sex." Pp. 157–210 in *Toward an Anthropology of Women*, edited by Rayna R. Reiter. New York: Monthly Review Press.

Rubin, Lillian Breslow. 1994. *Families on the Fault Line*. New York: HarperCollins.

Ryan, Mary P. 1981. *Cradle of the Middle Class: The Family in Oneida County, New York, 1790-1865*. Cambridge: Cambridge University Press.

Sacks, Karen Brodkin. 1989. "Toward a Unified Theory of Class, Race and Gender." *American Ethnologist* 16:534–50.

Scott, Joan W. 1986. "Gender: A Useful Category of Historical Analysis." *American Historical Review* 91:1053–75.

Stigler, George J. 1946. "Domestic Servants in the United States, 1900–1940." Occassional Paper 24, National Bureau of Economic Research, New York.

Stoler, Ann. 1996. "Carnal Knowledge and Imperial Power: Gender, Race and Morality in Colonial Asia." Pp. 209–66 in *Feminism and History*, edited by Joan W. Scott. New York: Oxford University Press.

Strasser, Susan. 1982. *Never Done: A History of American Housework*. New York: Pantheon.

Thorne, Barrie. 1993. *Gender Play: Girls and Boys in School*. New Brunswick, NJ: Rutgers University Press.

U.S. Department of Labor, Bureau of Labor Statistics. 1993. *Occupational Outlook Quarterly* (Fall).

Ware, Vron. 1992. *Beyond the Pale: White Women, Racism and History*. London: Verso.

Watson, Amey. 1937. "Domestic Service." In *Encyclopedia of the Social Sciences*. New York: Macmillan.

West, Candace and Sarah Fenstermaker. 1995. "Doing Difference." *Gender & Society* 9:8–37.

West, Candace and Don Zimmerman. 1987. "Doing Gender." *Gender & Society* 1:125–51.

## READING 12

Anzaldua, G. 1999. *Borderlands La Frontera: The New Mestiza*. Second edition. San Francisco: Aunt Lute Books.

Baca Zinn, M., and Dill, B. T. (Eds.). 1994. *Women of Color in U.S. Society*. Philadelphia: Temple University Press.

Bell, D. 2004, April 2. The Real Lessons of a "Magnificent Mirage." *Chronicle of Higher Education*.

Brodkin, K. 1998. *How Jews Became White Folks and What That Says about Race in America*. New Brunswick, NJ: Rutgers University Press.

Bonilla Silva, E. 2006. *Racism without Racists: Color-Blind Racism and the Persistence of Racial Inequality in the United States*. Second Edition. Lanham: Rowman & Littlefield Publishers, Inc.

Chin, M. H., and Humikowski, C. A. 2002. "When Is Risk Stratification by Race or Ethnicity Justified in Medical Care?" *Academic Medicine, 77*(3): 202–208.

Cole, E. S., and Donley, K. S. 1990. "History, Values, and Placement Policy Issues in Adoption." Pp.273–294 in D. M. Brodzinsky & M. Schechter (Eds.), *The Psychology of Adoption*. New York: Oxford University Press.

Collins, P. H. 2000. *Black Feminist Thought: Knowledge, Consciousness, and the Politics of Empowerment*. New York: Routledge Press.

Collins, P. H. 1998. *Fighting Words: Black Women and the Search for Justice*. Minneapolis: University of Minnesota Press.

Crenshaw, K. W. 1993a. "Beyond Racism and Misogyny: Black Feminism and 2 Live Crew." In M. J. Matsuda, K. W. Crenshaw, R. Delgado, & C. R. Lawrence (Eds.), *Words That Wound: Critical Race Theory, Assaultive Speech, and the First Amendment*. Boulder, Colorado: Westview Press.

Crenshaw, K. W. 1993b. "Mapping the Margins: Intersectionality, Identity Politics, and Violence against Women." *Stanford Law Review, 43*: 1241–1299.

Davis, A. 1983. *Women, Race, and Class*. New York: Vintage Books.

Day, C. 1979. Access to Birth Records: General Register Office Study. *Adoption and Fostering, 98*:17–28.

Dill, B. T. 1983. "Race, Class and Gender: Prospects for an All-Inclusive Sisterhood." *Feminist Studies, 9*(1):131–150.

Dill, B. T., and Johnson, T. 2002. "Between a Rock and a Hard Place: Mothering, Work, and Welfare in the Rural South." In S. Harley (Ed.), *Sister Circle: Black Women and Work*. New Brunswick, NJ: Rutgers University Press.

Dill, B. T., Baca Zinn, M., and Patton, S. L. 1999. "Race, Family Values and Welfare Reform." Pp. 263–286 in L. Kushnick and J. Jennings (Eds.), *A New Introduction to Poverty: The Role of Race, Power and Politics*. New York: New York University Press.

Essed, P. 1991. *Understanding Everyday Racism: An Interdisciplinary Theory*. Thousand Oaks, CA: Sage.

Frankenberg, R. 1993. *White Women Race Matters: The Social Construction of Whiteness*. Minneapolis: University of Minnesota Press.

Guinier, L. 2004, June 24. "Top Colleges Take More Blacks, but Which Ones?" *New York Times* (Rimer & Arenson).

Gardiner, J. K. (Ed). 2002. *Masculinity Studies and Feminist Theory: New Directions*. New York: Columbia University Press.

Gordon, L., 1994. *Pitied but Not Entitled: Single Mothers and the History of Welfare, 1890–1935*. New York: Free Press.

Higginbotham, E., and Romero, M. (Eds.). 1997. *Women and Work: Exploring Race, Ethnicity, and Class*. Thousand Oaks, CA: Sage.

hooks, b. 1992. *Black Looks: Race and Representation*. Boston: South End Press.

Hull, G. T., Bell, S. P., and Smith, B. (Eds.). 2003. *All the Women Are White, All the Blacks are Men, but Some of Us Are Brave*. New York: The Feminist Press.

Kimmel, M. 2000. *The Gendered Society*. Oxford University Press.

LatCrit. 2006. Retrieved June 18, 2007, from www.arts. cornell.edu/latcrit/PortfolioOfProjects/ LCPortfolio9_29_2006.pdf.

Lipsitz, G. 1998. *The Possessive Investment in Whiteness*. Philadelphia: Temple University Press.

Lorber, J. 1994. *Paradoxes of Gender*. New Haven, CT: Yale University Press.

Lorber, J. 1998. *Gender Inequality: Feminist Theories and Politics*. Los Angeles: Roxbury.

Massey, D., and Denton, N. 1993. *American Apartheid*. Cambridge, MA: Harvard University Press.

Moraga, C., and Anzaldua, G. 2002. *This Bridge Called My Back: Writings by Radical Women of Color*. Third edition. Berkeley, CA: Third Woman Press.

Morgan, J. 1999. *When Chickenheads Come Home to Roost: My Life as a Hip-Hop Feminist*. New York: Simon & Schuster.

Myers, K. A., Anderson, C. D., & Risman, B. J. (Eds.). 1998. *Feminist Foundations: Towards Transforming Sociology*. Thousand Oaks, CA: Sage Publications.

The Declaration and Programme of Action, NGO Forum of the United Nations World Conference against Racism, September 3, 2001.

Oliver, M., and Shapiro, T. M. 1995. *Black Wealth/White Wealth: A New Perspective on Racial Inequality*. New York: Routledge Press.

Omi, M., and Winant, H. 1994. *Racial Formation in the United States: From the 1960s to the 1990s*. Second edition. New York: Routledge Press.

Portes, A. 2000. "The Resilient Significance of Class: A Nominalist Interpretation." *Political Power and Social Theory*, 14:249–284.

Pough, G. D. 2004 *Check It While I Wreck It: Black Womanhood, Hip-hop Culture, and the Public Sphere*. Boston: Northeastern University Press.

Roediger, D. R. 1991. *The Wages of Whiteness: Race and the Making of the American Working Class*. New York: Verso Books.

Rose, T. 1994. *Black Noise: Rap Music and Black Culture in Contemporary America*. Hanover, NH: University Press of New England.

Silliman, J., Gerber Fried, M., Ross, L., & Gutierrez, R. (2004). *Undivided Rights: Women of Color Organize for Reproductive Justice*. Cambridge, MA: South End Press.

Solinger, R. 1992. *Wake up Little Susie: Single Pregnancy and Race Before* Roe v. Wade. New York: Routledge Press.

Waters, M. C. 1990. *Ethnic Options: Choosing Identities in America*. Berkeley: University of California Press.

Weber, L. 2001. *Understanding Race, Class, Gender, and Sexuality: A Conceptual Framework*. New York: McGraw-Hill Higher Education.

Williams, D., and Collins, C. 1995. "U.S. Socioeconomic and Racial Differences in Health: Patterns and Explanations." *Annual Review of Sociology, 21*, 349–386.

Zambrana, R. E., and Dill, B. T. 2006. "Disparities in Latina Health: An Intersectional Analysis." In A. J. Schulz & L. Mullings (Eds.), *Gender, Race Class & Health*. San Francisco, CA: Jossey-Bass.

Zambrana, R. E., Mogel, W., and Scrimshaw, S. C. M. 1987. "Gender and Level of Training Differences in Obstetricians' Attitudes towards Patients in Childbirth." *Women & Health, 12*(1):5–24.

## READING 13

Brodkin, Karen. 1998. *How Jews Became White Folks, and What That Says about Race in America*. New Brunswick: Rutgers University Press.

Buchanan, Patrick. 2006. *State of Emergency: The Third World Invasion and Conquest of America*. New York: St Martin's Press.

Buck, Pem Davidson. 2001. *Worked to the Bone: Race, Class, Power and Privilege in Kentucky*. New York: Monthly Review Press.

Buck, Pem Davidson. 2008. "Keeping the Collaborators on Board as the Ship Sinks: Toward a Theory of Fascism and the U.S. "Middle Class." *Rethinking Marxism*, 20(1):68–90.

Building a North American Community. 2005. Report of the Independent Task Force on the Future of North America. Sponsored by the Council on Foreign Relations.

Bush, George W. 2005. President's Radio Address. Oct 22. http://www.whitehouse.gov/news/releases/2005/10/ print/20051022.html.

Bush sneaking North American super-state without oversight? 6/13/2006. World Net Daily www .worldnetdaily.com/news/article.asp?ARTICLE_ID=50618.

Du Bois, W. E. B. 1995 [1935]. *Black Reconstruction in America, 1860–1880*. New York: Free Press.

Fluehr-Lobban, Carolyn. 2005. *Race and Racism: An Introduction*. Walnut Creek: AltaMira Press.

Giddens, Anthony. 1987. *The Nation-State and Violence: Volume Two of a Contemporary Critique of Historical Materialism*. Berkeley: University of California Press.

Goldberg, David Theo. 2002. *The Racial State*. Malden MA: Blackwell Publishing.

Haney-Lopez, Ian. 2006. *White by Law: The Legal Construction of Race* (revised and updated). New York: New York University Press.

Harris, Chery. 1993. "Whiteness as Property." *Harvard Law Review* 106 (8):1707–1791.

*Hidden Slaves: Forced Labor in the United States*. 2004. Free the Slaves and Human Rights Center, University of California, Berkeley.

Hill, Jonathan. 1996. "Introduction: Ethnogenesis in the Americas." Pp. 1–19 in *History, Power, and Identity: Ethnogenesis in the Americas, 1492–1992*. Jonathan Hill, ed. Iowa City: University of Iowa Press.

Kapferer, Bruce. 2004. "Introduction: Old Permutations, New Formations? War, State, and Global Transgression." Pp. 1–15 in *State, Sovereignty, War: Civil Violence in Emerging Global Realities*. Bruce Kapferer, ed. New York: Berghahn Books.

Klinker, Philip with Rogers Smith. 1999. *The Unsteady March: The Rise and Decline of Racial Equality in America*. Chicago: University of Chicago Press.

McMichael, Philip. 1999. "The Global Crisis of Wage-labour.: *Studies in Political Economy* 58 (Spring):11–40.

Mills, Charles. 1997. *The Racial Contract*. Ithaca: Cornell University Press.

Mullings, Leith. 2005. "Interrogating Racism: Toward an Antiracist Anthropology." *Annual Review of Anthropology* 34:667–693.

Nordstrom, Carolyn. 2004. "Invisible Empires." Pp. 46-55 in *State, Sovereignty, War: Civil Violence in Emerging Global Realities*. Bruce Kapferer, ed. New York: Berghahn Books.

North American merger topic of secret confab. 2006. World Net Daily 9/20. www.worldnetdaily.com/news/article.asp? ARTICLE_ID=52063.

Olson, Joel. 2004. *The Abolition of White Democracy*. Minneapolis: University of Minnesota Press.

Ong, Aihwa. 2006. *Neoliberalism as Exception: Mutations in Citizenship and Sovereignty*. Durham: Duke University Press.

Roediger, David. 2005. *Working Toward Whiteness: How America's Immigrants Become White. The Strange Journey from Ellis Island to the Suburbs*. New York: Basic Books.

Santa Ana, Otto. 2002 *Brown Tide Rising: Metaphors of Latinos in Contemporary American Public Discourse*. Austin: University of Texas Press.

Shklar, Judith. 1991. *American Citizenship: The Quest for Inclusion*. Cambridge, MA: Harvard University Press.

Southern Poverty Law Center. c. 2006. "Close to Slavery: Guestworker Programs in the United States."

Stevens, Jacqueline. 1999. *Reproducing the State*. Princeton: Princeton University Press.

Swain, Carol. 2002. *The New White Nationalism in America: Its Challenge to Integration*. New York: Cambridge University Press.

Tafoya, Sonya. 2007 [2004]. "Shades of Belonging: Latinos and Racial Identity." Pp. 218-221 in *Race, Class, and Gender in the United States*, Paula Rothenberg, ed. New York: Worth Publishers.

Turner, Terrence. 2003. "Class Projects, Social Consciousness, and the Contradictions of "Globalization"." Pp. 35-66 in *Globalization, the State, and Violence*, Jonathan Friedman, ed. Walnut Creek: AltaMira Press.

Trouillot, Michel-Rolph. 2001. "The Anthropology of the State in the Age of Globalization: Close Encounters of the Deceptive Kind." *Current Anthropology* 42 (1):125–138.

Twelve Percent of U.S. Population Is Foreign Born. 2004. http://usinfo.state.gov/xarchives/display. html?p=washfile-english&y=2004&m=August&x2004 0809150255cmtrop0.7581903.

U.S. Department of Homeland Security. 2003. Endgame: Office of Detention and Removal Strategic Plan 2003–2012: Detention and Removal Strategy for a Secure Homeland. Form M-592 (8/15/03).

Vogel, Richard. 2007. "Transient Servitude: The U.S. Guest Worker Program for Exploiting Mexican and Central American Workers." *Monthly Review*. January. http://monthlyreview.org/0107vogel.htm.

Warren, Jonathan and France Winddance Twine. 1997. "White Americans, The New Minority? Non-Blacks and the Ever-Expanding Boundaries of Whiteness." *Journal of Black Studies*, 28 (2): 200–218.

Whitaker, Mark. 2007. *Learning Politics from Sivaram: The Life and Death of a Revolutionary Tamil Journalist in Sri Lanka.* London: Pluto Press.

Williams, Brackette. 1989. "A Class Act: Anthropology and the Race to Nation Across Ethnic Terrain." *Annual Review of Anthropology* 18:401–444.

Williams, Joseph and Kevin Baron. 2007. Military Sees Big Decline in Black Enlistees; Iraq War Cited in 58% Drop Since 2000.

Yancy, George. 2003. *Who Is White? Latinos, Asians, and the New Black/Non-Black Divide.* Boulder: Lynne Rienner.

## READING 15

Alcoff, Linda Martin. 2006. *Visible Identities: Race, Gender and the Self.* New York: Oxford University Press.

Alcoff, Linda Martin, and Eduardo Mendieta, eds. 2003. *Identities: Race, Class, Gender and Nationality.* Malden, MA: Blackwell.

Cooley, Charles Horton. 1922. *Human Nature and the Social Order* (rev. ed.). New York: Charles Scribner's Sons.

Erikson, Erik H. 1968. *Identity: Youth and Crisis.* New York: Norton.

Fredrickson, George. 2002. *Racism: A Short History.* Princeton, NJ: Princeton University Press.

Kanagawa, Chie, Susan E. Cross, and Hazel Rose Markus. 2001. "Who Am I?" The Cultural Psychology of the Conceptual Self." *Personality and Social Psychology Bulletin* 27(1):90–103.

Kyrsan, Maria, and Amanda E. Lewis. 2005. "The United States Today: Racial Discrimination Is Alive and Well." *Challenge* 28:34–49.

Markus, H., and Sentis, K. 1982. "The Self in Social Information Processing." In *Social Psychological Perspectives on the Self,* ed. Jerry Suls. Hillsdale, NJ: Erlbaum.

Massey, Douglas S., and Nancy A. Denton. 1992. "Racial Identity and the Spatial Assimilation of Mexicans in the United States." *Social Science Research* 21:235–260.

McIntosh, Peggy. 1997. "White Privilege: Unpacking the Invisible Knapsack." Pp. 120–126 in *Race: An Anthology in the First Person,* ed. B. Schneider. New York: Three Rivers Press.

Mead. George Herbert. 1934. *Mind, Self and Society.* Chicago: University of Chicago Press.

Moya, Paula M. L. 2002. *Learning from Experience: Minority Identities, Multicultural Struggles.* Berkeley: University of California Press.

Oyserman, Daphna. 2008. "Racial-Ethnic Self-Schemas: Multidimensional Identity Based Motivation." *Journal of Research in Personality* 42:1186–1198.

Oyserman, Daphna, Markus Kemmelmeier, Stephanie Fryberg, Hezi Brosh, and Tamera Hart-Johnson. 2003. "Racial-Ethnic Self-Schemas." *Social Psychology Quarterly* 66:333–347.

Prentice, Deborah, and Dale Miller. 1999. *Cultural Divides: Understanding and Overcoming Group Conflict.* New York: Russell Sage Foundation.

Tatum, Beverly. 2002. "The Complexity of Identity: 'Who Am I?'" In *Why Are All the Black Kids Sitting Together in the Cafeteria?* (rev. ed.). New York: Basic Books.

## READING 16

Blumstein, Philip. 1991. "The Production of Selves in Personal Relationships." Pp. 305–322 in *The Self-Society Dynamic: Cognition, Emotion, and Action.* J. A. Howard and P. L. Callero (eds.). New York: Cambridge University Press.

Brines, Julie. 1993. "The Exchange Value of Housework." *Rationality and Society,* 5:302–340.

———. 1994. "Economic Dependency, Gender, and the Division of Labor at Home." *American Journal of Sociology,* 100:652–688.

Duerr Berrick, Jill. 1995. *Faces of Poverty: Portraits of Women and Children on Welfare.* New York: Oxford University Press.

Givhan, Robin. 1998. "Dramatic Make-over Gives Jones a More Modest Look." *Eugene Register-Guard,* January 18, p. 9A.

Goffman, Erving. 1959. *The Presentation of Self in Everyday Life.* New York: Doubleday.

———. 1961. *Asylums: Essays on the Social Situation of Mental Patients and Other Inmates.* Garden City, NY: Anchor.

Herrnstein, Richard J. and Charles Murray. 1994. *The Bell Curve.* New York: Free Press.

Howard, Judith A. and Jocelyn Hollander. 1997. *Gendered Situations, Gendered Selves: A Gender Lens on Social Psychology.* Thousand Oaks, CA: Sage.

Hwang, David Henry. 1988. *M. Butterfly*. New York: Penguin.

Kessler, Suzanne J. and Wendy McKenna. 1978. *Gender: An Ethnomethodological Approach*. New York: John Wiley.

Lopata, Helena Z. and Barrie Thorne. 1978. "On the Term 'Sex Roles.'" *Signs: Journal of Women in Culture and Society*, 3:718–721.

Stryker, Sheldon. 1987. "Identity Theory: Developments and Extensions." Pp. 89–103 in *Self and Identity: Psychological Perspectives*. Krysia Yardley and Terry Honess (eds.). New York: John Wiley.

Thorne, Barrie. 1993. *Gender Play: Girls and Boys in School*. New Brunswick, NJ: Rutgers University Press.

West, Candace and Don Zimmerman. 1987. "Doing Gender." *Gender and Society*, 1:125–151.

Woolf, Virginia. 1928. *Orlando*. New York: Harcourt Brace Jovanovich.

# READING 17

Almaguer, T. 1993. "Chicano Men: A Cartography of Homosexual Identity and Behavior." Pp. 225–273 in H. Abelove, M. Barale, and O. Halperin, editors, *The Lesbian and Gay Studies Reader*. New York: Routledge.

Anzaldua, G. 1990. *Haciendo Caras, Una Entrada. Making Face, Making Soul*. San Francisco: Aunt Lute Books.

Barrett, S. E. 1990. "Paths toward Diversity: An Intrapsychic Perspective." Pp. 41–52 in L. S. Brown & M. P. P. Root (Editors), *Diversity and Complexity in Feminist Therapy*. New York: Harrington Park Press.

Berkhofer, R. F. Jr. 1978. *The White Man's Indian*. New York: Vintage Books.

Blackwood, E. 1984. "Sexuality and Gender in Certain Native American Tribes: The Case of Cross-gender Females." *Signs: Journal of Women in Culture and Society*. 10: 27–42.

Brant, B. 1985. *Mohawk Trail*. Ithaca, NY: Firebrand Books.

Brant, B. Editor. 1988. *A Gathering of Spirit: A Collection by North American Indian Women*. Ithaca. NY: Firebrand Books.

Brant, B. 1991. *Food and Spirits*. Ithaca, NY: Firebrand Books.

Brant, B. 1993, Summer. "Giveaway: Native Lesbian Writers." *Signs: Journal of Women in Culture and Society*. 18: 944–947.

Brant, B. 1995. Lesbian Writers. *Aboriginal Voices*. 2(4): 42–42.

Brant, C. 1990. Native Ethics and Rules of Behavior. *Canadian Journal of Psychiatry*, 35: 534–539.

Cardinal, H. 1969. *The Unjust Society: The Tragedy of Canada's Indians*. Edmonton: M. G. Hurtig.

Chrystos. 1988. *Not Vanishing*. Vancouver: Press Gang.

Chrystos. 1991. *Dream On*. Vancouver: Press Gang.

Chrystos. 1993. *In Her I Am*. Vancouver: Press Gang.

Coleman, E. 1982. "Developmental Stages of the Coming-out Process." Pp. 149–158 in W. Paul, J. Weinrich, J. Gonsiorels, and M. Hotvedt (Editors). *Homosexuality: Social, Psychological, and Biological Issues*. Beverly Hills: Sage.

Cross, W. E., Parham, T., and Helms, J. 1991. "The Stages of Black Identity Development: Nigrescence Models." Pp. 319–338 in R. Jones (Editor), *Black Psychology*. Berkeley: Cobb and Henry.

Deloria, V. Jr. 1969. *Custer Died for Your Sins: An Indian Manifesto*. Norman: University of Oklahoma Press.

D'Emilio, J. and Freedman, E. B. 1988. *Intimate Matters: The History of Sexuality in America*. New York: Vintage Press.

Falco, K. 1991. *Psychotherapy with Lesbian Clients: Theory into Practice*. New York: Brunner Mazel.

Fife, C. 1992. *Beneath the Naked Sun*. Toronto: Sister Vision Press.

Fife, C. Editor. 1993. *The Colour of Resistance*. Toronto: Sister Vision Press.

Ing, N. R. 1991. "The Effects of Residential Schooling on Native Child Rearing Practices." *Canadian Journal of Native Education, 18* (Supplement):65–118.

Jacobs, S. and J. Cromwell. 1992. "Visions and Revisions of Reality: Reflections on Sex, Sexuality, Gender, and Gender Variance." *Journal of Homosexuality* 23: 43–69.

Jacobs, S.and W. Thomas. 1994. "Native American Two-spirits." *Anthropology Newsletter, 7* (November 8, 1994). Arlington, VA: American Anthropological Association.

Kroll, I. and I. Warneke. 1995. *The Dynamics of Sexual Orientation and Adolescent Suicide: A Comprehensive Review and Developmental Perspective*. Calgary, Canada: University of Calgary.

Medicine, B. 1983. "Warrior Women": Sex Role Alternatives for Plains Indian Women." Pp. 267-280 in P. Albers and B. Medicine (Editors), *The Hidden Half: Studies of Plains Indian Women*. Lanham, MD: University Press of America.

Miller, J. R. 1989. *Skyscrapers Hide the Heavens: A History of Indian-White Relations in Canada*. Toronto: University of Toronto Press.

Robinson, T. and J. V. Ward, J. V. 1991. "A Belief in Self Far Greater than Anyone's Disbelief: Cultivating Resistance among African American Female Adolescents." Pp. 87-103 in C. Gilligan. A. Rogers, and D. Tolman (Editors). *Women, Girls and Psychotherapy: Reframing Resistance.* New York: Harrington Park Press.

Roscoe, W. Editor. 1988. *Living the Apirit: A Gay American Indian Anthology.* New York: St. Martin's Press.

Roscoe, W. 1991. *The Zuni Man-woman.* Albuquerque: University of New Mexico Press.

Ross, R. 1992. *Dancing with a Ghost: Exploring Indian Reality.* Markham, Ontario: Octopus.

Sioui, G. 1992. *For an Amerindian Autohistory: An Essay on the Foundations of a Social Ethic.* Buffalo, NY: McGill–Queen's University Press.

Spanbauer, T. 1991. *The Man who Fell in Love with the Moon.* New York: Harper Perennial.

Tafoya, T. 1989. "Dancing with Dash-Kayah." Pp. 92-100 in D. M. Dooling & P. Jordan-Smith (Eds.). *I Become Part of It: Sacred Dimensions in Native American Life.* New York: Parabola Books.

Tafoya, T. 1990. "Pulling Coyote's Tail: Native American Sexuality and AIDS." Pp. 280-289 in V. Mays (Editor). *Primary Prevention Issues in AIDS.* Washington, DC: American Psychological Association.

Tatum, B. 1992. "Talking about Race, Learning about Racism: The Application of Racial Identity Development Theory in the Classroom." *Harvard Educational Review* 62: 1–24.

Tatum, B. 1993. *Racial Identity Development and Relational theory: The Case of Black Women in White Communities* (Work in Progress Series). Wellesley, MA: Stone Center for Research on Women.

Weston, K. 1993. "Lesbian/gay Studies in the House of Anthropology". *Annual Review of Anthropology* 22: 339–367.

Whitehead, H. 1981. "The Bow and the Burden Strap: A New Look at Institutionalized Homosexuality in Native North America." Pp. 80-115 in S. B. Ortner and H. Whitehead (Editors), *Sexual Meanings.* Cambridge, England: Cambridge University Press.

Williams, W. L. 1986. *The Spirit and the Flesh: Sexual Diversity in American Indian Culture.* Boston: Beacon Press.

York, J. 1990. *The Dispossessed: Life and Death in Native Canada.* Boston: Little, Brown.

## READING 18

Alba, Richard D. 1990. *Ethnicity in America: The Transformation of White America.* New Haven, CT: Yale University Press.

Chan, Sucheng. 1991. *Asian Americans: An Interpretative History.* Boston: Twayne Publishers.

Espiritu, Yen Le. 1992. *Asian American Panethnicity.* Philadelphia: Temple University Press.

Gans, Herbert J. 1979. "Symbolic Ethnicity: The Future of Ethnic Groups and Cultures in America." *Ethnic and Racial Studies* 2:1–19.

Jiobu, R. M. 1988. *Ethnicity and Assimilation: Blacks, Chinese, Filipinos, Japanese, Koreans, Mexicans, Vietnamese, and Whites.* Albany, NY: State University of New York Press.

Kellogg, Susan. 1990. "Exploring Diversity in Middle-Class Families: The Symbolism of American Ethnic Identity." *Social Science History* 14(1):27–41.

Lowe, Lisa. 1996. *Immigrant Acts.* Durham, NC: Duke University Press.

Nagel, Joane. 1994. "Constructing Ethnicity: Creating and Recreating Ethnic Identity and Culture." *Social Problems* 41:152–176.

Nishi, S. M. 1989. "Perceptions and Deceptions: Contemporary Views of Asian Americans." Pp. 3–10 in *A Look Beyond the Model Minority Image: Critical Issues in Asian America,* edited by Grace Yun. New York: Minority Rights Group, Inc.

Onishi, N. 1996. "New Sense of Race Arises among Asian Americans." *New York Times* 5/30/96, p. A1.

Waters, Mary C. 1990. *Ethnic Options: Choosing Identities in America.* Berkeley, CA: University of California Press.

## READING 20

Aboud, Frances E. 1977. "Interest in Ethnic Information: A Cross-Cultural Developmental Study." *Canadian Journal of Behavioral Science* 9:134–46.

Clark, Kenneth B. and Mamie P. Clark. 1939. "The Development of Consciousness of Self and the Emergence of Racial Identification in Negro Preschool Children." *Journal of Social Psychology,* SPSSI Bulletin 10:591–99.

———. 1940. "Skin Color as a Factor in Racial Identification and Preference in Negro Children." *Journal of Negro Education* 19:341–58.

Corsaro, William A. 1979. "We're Friends, Right?" *Language in Society* 8:315–36.

——. 1987. "A Two-Factor Theory of Black Identity: Implications for the Study of Identity Development in Minority Children." Pp. 117–33 in *Children's Ethnic Socialization: Pluralism and Development*, edited by J. S. Phinney and M. J. Rotheram. Newbury Park, CA: Sage.

Damon, William. 1977. *The Social World of the Child*. San Francisco, CA: Jossey-Bass.

Danielewicz, Jane M., Dwight L. Rogers, and George Noblit. 1996. "Children's Discourse Patterns and Power Relations in Teacher-Led and Child-Led Sharing Time." *Qualitative Studies in Education* 9:311–31.

Derman-Sparks, Louise. 1989. *Anti-Bias Curriculum: Tools for Empowering Young Children*. Washington, DC: National Association for the Education of Young Children.

Donaldson, Margaret. 1978. *Children's Minds*. London, England: Fontana.

Dunn, Judy. 1993. "Young Children's Understanding of Other People: Evidence from Observations within the Family." Pp. 97–114 in *Young Children's Close Relationships: Beyond Attachment*, edited by J. Dunn. Newbury Park, CA: Sage.

Goodman, Mary E. 1964. *Race Awareness in Young Children*. New York: Crowell-Collier.

Holmes, Robyn M. 1995. *How Young Children Perceive Race*. Thousand Oaks, CA: Sage.

Katz, Phyllis A. 1976. "The Acquisition of Racial Attitudes in Children." Pp. 125–54 in *Towards the Elimination of Racism*, edited by P. A. Katz. New York: Pergamon.

Menter, Ian. 1989. "'They're Too Young to Notice': Young Children and Racism." Pp. 91–104 in *Disaffection from School? The Early Years*, edited by G. Barrett. London, England: Falmer.

Porter, Judith D. R. 1971. *Black Child, White Child: The Development of Racial Attitudes*. Cambridge, MA: Harvard University.

Ramsey, Patricia A. 1987. "Young Children's Thinking about Ethnic Differences." Pp. 56–72 in *Children's Ethnic Socialization: Pluralism and Development*, edited by J. S. Phinney and M. J. Rotheram. Newbury Park, CA: Sage.

Schofield, Janet W. and William D. Francis. 1982. "An Observational Study of Peer Interaction in Racially-Mixed 'Accelerated' Classrooms." *Journal of Educational Psychology* 74:722–32.

Spencer, Margaret B. 1987. "Black Children's Ethnic Identity Formation: Risk and Resilience of Castelike Minorities." Pp. 103–16 in *Children's Ethnic Socialization: Pluralism and Development*, edited by J. S. Phinney and M. J. Rotheram. Newbury Park, CA: Sage.

Spencer, Margaret B., Geraldine K. Brookins, and Walter R. Allen. 1985. *Beginnings: Social and Affective Development of Black Children*. New York: Erlbaum.

Strayer, Janet. 1986. "Children's Attributions Regarding the Situational Determinants of Emotion in Self and Others." *Developmental Psychology* 22:649–54.

Thorne, Barrie. 1993. *Gender Play: Girls and Boys in School*. New Brunswick, NJ: Rutgers University Press.

Williams, John E. and John K. Morland. 1976. *Race, Color, and the Young Child*. Chapel Hill, NC: University of North Carolina Press.

Willis, Paul. 1990. *Common Culture: Symbolic Work at Play in the Everyday Cultures of the Young*. Buckingham, England: Open University Press.

# READING 21

Alarcón, Norma. 1990 "The Theoretical Subject(s) of *This Bridge Called My Back* and Anglo-American Feminism." Pp. 356-369 in *Making Face, Making Soul/Hacienda Caras: Creative and Critical Perspectives by Women of Color*, edited by Gloria Anzaldúa. San Francisco: Aunt Lute Books.

Anzaldua, Gloria. Editor. 1990. *Making Face, Making Soul/Hacienda Caras: Creative and Critical Perspectives by Women of Color*. San Francisco: Aunt Lute.

Bourdieu, Pierre. 1984. *Distinction: A Social Critique of the Judgment of Taste*. Cambridge, MA: Harvard University Press.

Bourdieu, Pierre, and Jean-Claude Passeron. 1977. *Reproduction in Education, Society and Culture*. London: Sage.

Eckert, Penelope. 1989. *Jocks and Burnouts: Social Categories and Identity in the High School*. New York: Teachers College Press.

Foley, Douglas. 1990. *Learning Capitalist Culture: Deep in the Heart of Tejas*. Philadelphia: University of Pennsylvania Press.

Fuss, Diana. 1989. *Essentially Speaking: Feminism, Nature, and Difference*. New York: Routledge.

Gray, Herman. 1995. *Watching Race: Television and the Struggle for "Blackness."* Minneapolis: University of Minnesota Press.

Holland, Dorothy C., and Margaret Eisenhart. 1990. *Educated in Romance: Women, Achievement, and College Culture.* Chicago: University of Chicago Press.

Howell, Joseph. 1973. *Hard Living on Clay Street: Portraits of Blue-Collar Families.* Garden City, NY: Anchor.

Lamont, Michele, and Annette Lareau. 1988. "Cultural Capital: Allusions, Gaps and Glissandos in Recent Theoretical Developments." *Sociological Theory* 6 (Fall):153–68.

Lesko, Nancy. 1988. "The Curriculum of the Body: Lessons from a Catholic High School." Pp. 123-142 in *Becoming Feminine: The Politics of Popular Culture,* ed. Leslie G. Roman, Linda K. Christian-Smith, and Elizabeth Ellsworth. London: Falmer.

Long, Elizabeth. 1989. "Feminism and Cultural Studies." *Critical Studies in Mass Communication* 6(4):427–35.

Luttrell, Wendy. 1993. "The Teachers, They All Had Their Pets: Concepts of Gender, Knowledge, and Power." *Signs* 18(3):505–46.

———. 1991. *Feminism and Youth Culture.* London: Macmillan.

———. 1994. *Postmodernism and Popular Culture.* London: Routledge.

Omi, Michael, and Howard Winant. 1994. *Racial Formation in the United States: From the 1960s to the 1980s.* 2nd edition. New York: Routledge.

Ortner, Sherry. 1991. "Preliminary Notes on Class and Culture." In *Recapturing Anthropology: Working in the Present,* ed. Richard G. Fox. Santa Fe, NM: School of American Research Press.

Pipher, Mary. 1994. *Reviving Ophelia: Saving the Selves of Adolescent Girls.* New York: Putnam.

Skeggs, Beverley. 1997. *Formations of Class and Gender: Becoming Respectable.* London: Sage.

Wagner, Venise. 1996. "Crossover." *San Francisco Examiner Magazine,* November 10: 8–32.

Williams, Raymond. 1965. *Marxism and Literature.* New York: Oxford University Press.

Bourdieu, Pierre. 1984. *Distinction: A Social Critique of the Judgment of Taste.* Cambridge, MA: Harvard University Press.

Brint, Steven. 1985. "The Political Attitudes of Professionals." *Annual Review of Sociology* 11:389–414.

Brooks, Clem and Jeff Manza. 1997. "The Social and Ideological Bases of Middle-class Political Realignment in the United States, 1972 to 1992." *American Sociological Review* 62:191–208.

Collins, Randall. 2000. "Situational Stratification: A Micro-Macro Theory of Inequality." *Sociological Theory* 18:17–43.

Daniels, Arlene. 1987. "The Hidden Work of Constructing Class and Community: Women Volunteer Leaders in Social Philanthropy." In *Families and Work,* edited by N. Gerstel and H. E. Gross. Philadelphia: Temple University Press.

Ferree, Myra Marx. 1987. "Family and Job for Working-class Women: Gender and Class Systems Seen from Below." In *Families and Work,* edited by N. Gerstel and H. E. Gross. Philadelphia: Temple University Press.

Halle, David. 1984. *America's Working Man.* Chicago: University of Chicago Press.

Ostrander, Susan. 1984. *Women of the Upper Class.* Philadelphia: Temple University Press.

Rosen, Ellen I. 1987. *Bitter Choices: Blue-collar Women In and Out of Work.* Chicago: University of Chicago Press.

Rubin, Lillian. 1976. *Worlds of Pain.* New York: Basic Books.

———. 1995. *Families on the Fault Line.* New York: Harper Perennial.

Warner, W. Lloyd and Paul S. Lunt. 1941. *The Social Life of a Modern Community.* New Haven, CT: Yale University Press.

## READING 23

Anderson, Elijah. 1976. *A Place on the Corner.* Chicago: University of Chicago Press.

## READING 24

Anderson, Kristin L. 1997. "Gender, Status, and Domestic Violence: An Integration of Feminist and Family Violence Approaches." *Journal of Marriage and the Family* 59:655–69.

Bourgois, Philippe. 1996. *In Search of Respect: Selling Crack in El Barrio.* New York: Cambridge University Press.

Brines, Julie. 1994. "Economic Dependency, Gender and the Division of Labor at Home." *American Journal of Sociology* 100:652–88.

Collins, Patricia Hill. 1990. *Black Feminist Thought: Knowledge, Consciousness, and the Politics of Empowerment.* New York: Routledge.

———. 1998. *Fighting Words: Black Women and the Search for Justice.* Minneapolis: University of Minnesota Press.

Connell, R. W. 1987. *Gender and Power.* Stanford, CA: Stanford University Press.

Cose, Ellis. 1995. *The Rage of a Privileged Class: Why Do Prosperous Blacks Still Have the Blues?* New York: Harper Perennial.

Disch, Estelle. 1997. "General Introduction." Pp. 1–18 in *Reconstructing Gender: A Multicultural Anthology,* edited by Estelle Disch. Mountain View, CA: Mayfield Publishing.

Domhoff, G. William. 1979. *The Powers That Be: Processes of Ruling Class Domination in America.* New York: Random House.

———. 2002. *Who Rules America Now? Power and Politics.* 4th edition. Boston: McGraw-Hill.

Feagin, Joe R., and Eileen O'Brien. 2003. *White Men on Race: Power, Privilege, and the Shaping of Cultural Consciousness.* Boston: Beacon Press.

Fine, Michelle. 1994. "Working the Hyphens: Reinventing Self and Other in Qualitative Research." Pp. 70–82 in *The Handbook of Qualitative Research,* edited by Norman K. Denzin and Yvonna S. Lincoln. Thousand Oaks, CA: Sage Publications.

Gordon, Ted, and Wahneema Lubiano. 1992. "The Statement of the Black Faculty Caucus." Pp. 249–250 in *Debating P.C.: The Controversy over Political Correctness on Campuses,* edited by Paul Berman. New York: Dell.

Hays, Sharon. 1996. *The Cultural Contradictions of Motherhood.* New Haven, CT: Yale University Press.

Hertz, Rosanna, and Susan M. Reverby. 1995. "Gender, Gentility, and Political Protest: The Barbara Bush Controversy at Wellesley College." *Gender and Society* 9:594–611.

Hochschild, Arlie, with Anne Machung. 1989. *The Second Shift: Working Parents and the Revolution at Home.* New York: Viking Penguin.

Hondagneu-Sotelo, Pierrette, and Michael A. Messner. 1994. "Gender Displays and Men's Power: The 'New Man' and the Mexican Immigrant Man." Pp. 200–218 in *Theorizing Masculinities,* edited by Harry Brod and Michael Kaufman. Thousand Oaks, CA: Sage.

Huber, Joan and William Form. 1973. *Income and Ideology: An Analysis of the American Political Formula.* New York: Free Press.

Messner, Michael A. 2003. "Men as Superordinates: Challenges for Gender Scholarship." Pp. 287–298 in *Privilege: A Reader,* edited by Michael S. Kimmel and Abby S. Ferber. Boulder, CO: Westview Press.

Mills, C. Wright. 1956. *The Power Elite.* New York: Oxford University Press.

Morris, Martina, and Bruce Western. 1999. "Inequality in Earnings at the Close of the Twentieth Century." *Annual Review of Sociology* 25:623–57.

Myers, Kristen A. 2004. "Ladies First: Race, Class, and the Contradictions of a Powerful Femininity." *Sociological Spectrum* 24:11–41.

Nader, Laura. 1969. "Up the Anthropologist: Perspectives Gained from Studying Up." Pp. 285–311 in *Reinventing Anthropology,* edited by Dell Hymes. New York: Vintage.

Oliver, Melvin L., and Thomas M. Shapiro. 1995. *Black Wealth/White Wealth: A New Perspective on Racial Inequality.* New York: Routledge.

Ostrander, Susan A. 1993. "'Surely You're Not in This Just to Be Helpful': Access, Rapport, and Interviews in Three Studies of Elites." *Journal of Contemporary Ethnography* 22:7–27.

———. 1984. *Women of the Upper Class.* Philadelphia: Temple University Press.

Pyke, Karen D. 1996. "Class-Based Masculinities: The Interdependence of Gender, Class, and Interpersonal Power." *Gender and Society* 10:527–49.

Rich, Adrienne. 1983. "Compulsory Heterosexuality and Lesbian Existence." Pp. 460-468 in *Powers of Desire: The Politics of Sexuality,* edited by Ann Snitow, Christine Stansell, and Sharon Thompson. New York: Monthly Review.

Schumer, Fran. 2003. "A Peek Inside the Country Club." *New York Times,* March 16, 2003. (http://www.nytimes.com).

Schwalbe, Michael, Sandra Godwin, Daphne Holden, Doug Schrock, Shealy Thompson, and Michele Wolkomir. 2000. "Generic Processes in the Reproduction of Inequality: An Interactionist Analysis." *Social Forces* 79:419–52.

Schwartz, Pepper. 1994. *Peer Marriage: How Love Between Equals Really Works.* New York: Free Press.

Zinn, Maxine Baca. 1982. "Chicano Men and Masculinity." *Journal of Ethnic Studies* 10:29–44.

Zweigenhaft, Richard L., and G. William Domhoff. 2006. *Diversity in the Power Elite: How it Happened, Why it Matters*. Lanham, Md.: Rowman and Littlefield.

## READING 27

Blumer, Herbert. 1969. *Symbolic Interactionism*. Englewood Cliffs, NJ: Prentice Hall.

Brunsma, David L. and Kerry Ann Rockquemore. 2001. "The New Color Complex: Appearance and Biracial Identity." *Identity: An International Journal of Theory and Research* 1:225–46.

Conyers, James E. and T. H. Kennedy. 1963. "Negro Passing: To Pass or Not to Pass." *Phylon* 24:215–23.

Cooley, C. H. 1902. *Human Nature and the Social Order*. New York: Scribner.

Daniel, Reginald G. 1992. "Passers and Pluralists: Subverting the Racial Divide." Pp. 91–107 in *Racially Mixed People in America*, edited by Maria P. P. Root. Newbury Park, CA: Sage Publications.

———. 2002. *More Than Black?* Philadelphia, PA: Temple University Press.

Davis, James F. 1991. *Who Is Black? One Nation's Definition*. University Park, PA: Pennsylvania State University Press.

Gecas, Victor and Michael Schwalbe. 1983. "Beyond the Looking-glass Self: Social Structure and Efficacy-based Self-Esteem." *Social Psychology Quarterly* 46:77–88.

Goffman, Erving. 1963. *Stigma: Notes on the Management of Spoiled Identity*. Englewood Cliffs, NJ: Prentice Hall.

Harris, Cherise A. 2004. *In a Space No One Could Share: Race, Class, and Identity among the New Black Middle-Class*. Unpublished doctoral dissertation, The University of Georgia.

Kaufman, Joanne M. and Cathryn Johnson. 2004. "Stigmatized Individuals and the Process of Identity." *The Sociological Quarterly* 45:807–33.

Kennedy, Randall. 2003. *Interracial Intimacies*. New York: Vintage Books.

Khanna, Nikki. 2004. "The Role of Reflected Appraisals in Racial Identity: The Case of Multiracial Asians." *Social Psychology Quarterly* 67(2):115–31.

———. 2010. "'If You're Half Black, You're Just Black': Reflected Appraisals and the Persistence of the One Drop Rule." *The Sociological Quarterly* 51:96–121.

Killian, Caitlin and Cathryn Johnson. 2006. "'I'm Not An Immigrant!': Resistance, Redefinition, and the Role of Resources in Identity Work." *Social Psychology Quarterly* 69:60–80.

Korgen, Kathleen. 1998. *From Black to Biracial: Transforming Racial Identity Among Biracial Americans*. New York: Praeger.

Marvasti, Amir. 2005. "Being Middle Eastern American: Identity Negotiation in the Context of the War on Terror." *Symbolic Interaction* 28:525–47.

McCall, George J. 2003. "The Me and the Not-Me: Positive and Negative Poles of Identity." Pp. 11–25 in *Advances in Identity Theory and Research*, edited by Peter J. Burke, Timothy J. Owens, Richard T. Serpe, and Peggy A. Thoits. New York: Plenum.

Mead, George Herbert. 1934. *Mind, Self, and Society*. Chicago, IL: University of Chicago Press.

Rockquemore, Kerry Ann and Patricia Arend. 2002. "Opting for White: Choice, Fluidity, and Racial Identity Construction in Post–Civil Rights America." *Race and Society* 5:49–64.

Rockquemore, Kerry Ann and David L. Brunsma. 2002. *Beyond Black: Biracial Identity in America*. Thousand Oaks, CA: Sage Publications.

Russell, Kathy, Midge Wilson, and Ronald E. Hall. 1992. *The Color Complex: The Policies of Skin Color Among African Americans*. New York: Harcourt Brace Jovanovich.

Snow, David A. and Leon Anderson. 1987. "Identity Work among the Homeless: The Verbal Construction and Avowal of Personal Identities." *American Journal of Sociology* 92(6):1336–71.

Storrs, Debbie. 1999. "Whiteness as Stigma: Essentialist Identity Work by Mixed-Race Women." *Symbolic Interaction* 23:187–212.

Williams, Theresa Kay. 1996. "Race as a Process: Reassessing the 'What Are You?' Encounters of Biracial Individuals." Pp. 191–210 in *The Multiracial Experience*, edited by Maria P. P. Root. Thousand Oaks, CA: Sage Publications.

Williamson, Joel. 1980. *New People: Miscegenation and Mulattoes in the United States*. New York: The Free Press.

## READING 29

Brown, Nicola. 2009. "'I'm in Transition Too': Sexual Identity Renegotiation in Sexual-Minority Women's Relationships with Transsexual Men." *International Journal of Sexual Health* 21:61–77.

Butler, Judith. 1990. *Gender Trouble: Feminism and the Subversion of Identity.* New York: Routledge.

———. 1993. *Bodies That Matter: On the Discursive Limits of "Sex."* New York: Routledge.

Connell, Raewyn. 2009. "Accountable Conduct: 'Doing Gender' in Transsexual and Political Retrospect." *Gender & Society* 23:104–11.

Harris, Cheryl I. 1993. "On Passing: Whiteness as Property." *Harvard Law Review* 106:1707–91.

Hollibaugh, Amber. 1997. "Gender Warriors: An Interview with Amber Hollibaugh." In *Femme: Feminists, Lesbians, Bad Girls,* edited by Laura Harris and Elizabeth Crocker. New York: Routledge.

Hutson, David. 2010. "Standing OUT/Fitting IN: Identity, Appearance, and Authenticity in Gay and Lesbian Communities." *Symbolic Interaction* 33:213–33.

Irvine, Janice M. 1994. "A Place in the Rainbow: Theorizing Lesbian and Gay Culture." *Sociological Theory* 12:232–48.

Joslin-Roher, Emily and Darrell Wheeler. 2009. "Partners in Transition: The Transition Experience of Lesbian, Bisexual, and Queer Identified Partners of Transgender Men." *Journal of Gay and Lesbian Social Services* 21:30–48.

Kennedy, Elizabeth L., and Madeline Davis. 1993. *Boots of Leather, Slippers of Gold: The History of a Lesbian Community.* New York: Penguin.

Kessler, Suzanne J., and Wendy McKenna. 1978. *Gender: An Ethnomethodological Approach.* New York: Wiley.

Krieger, Susan. 1983. *The Mirror Dance: Identity in a Women's Community.* Philadelphia: Temple University Press.

Levitt, Heidi M., Elisabeth A. Gerrish, and Katherine R. Hiestand. 2003. "The Misunderstood Gender: A Model of Modern Femme Identity." *Sex Roles* 3:99–113.

McFarland, Daniel A. 2004. "Resistance as a Social Drama: A Study of Change-Oriented Encounters." *American Journal of Sociology* 109:1249–1318.

Munt, Sally R., ed. 1998. *Butch/Femme: Inside Lesbian Gender.* London: Cassell.

Mustanski, Brian S. 2001. "Getting Wired: Exploiting the Internet for the Collection of Valid Sexuality Data. "*Journal of Sex Research* 38:292–301.

Namaste, Viviane. 2000. *Invisible Lives: The Erasure of Transsexual and Transgendered People.* Chicago: University of Chicago Press.

Nyamora, Cory M. 2004. "Femme Lesbian Identity Development and the Impact of Partnering with

Female-to-Male Transsexuals," Psy.D. dissertation, Alliant International University, California School of Professional Psychology.

Patton, Michael Q. 1990. *Qualitative Evaluation and Research Methods.* Newbury Park, CA.: Sage Publications.

Pfeffer, Carla A. 2008. "Bodies in Relation—Bodies in Transition: Lesbian Partners of Trans Men and Body Image." *Journal of Lesbian Studies* 12:325–45.

———. 2010. "'Women's Work?' Women Partners of Transgender Men Doing House work and Emotion Work." *Journal of Marriage and Family* 72:165–83.

———. 2012, "Normative Resistance and Inventive Pragmatism: Negotiating Structure and Agency in Transgender Families." *Gender and Society* 26:574–602.

Renfrow, Daniel G. 2004, "A Cartography of Passing in Everyday Life." *Symbolic Interaction* 27:485–506.

Rosser, B. R. Simon, Michael J. Oakes, Walter 0. Bockting, and Michael Miner. 2007. "Capturing the Social Demographics of Hidden Sexual Minorities: An Internet Study of the Transgender Population in the United States." *Sexuality Research and Social Policy: Journal of NSRC* 4:50–64.

Shapiro, Eve. 2004. "'Trans'cending Barriers: Transgender Organizing on the Internet." *Journal of Gay and Lesbian Social Services* 16:165–79.

Taylor, Verta, and Nancy E. Whittier. 1992. "Collective Identity in Social Movement Communities: Lesbian Feminist Mobilization." In *Frontiers in Social Movement Theory,* edited by Aldon D. Morris and Carol M. Mueller. New Haven, CT: Yale University Press.

Ward, Jane. 2008. *Respectably Queer: Diversity Culture in LGBT Activist Organizations.* Nashville: Vanderbilt University Press.

———. 2010. "Gender Labor: Transmen, Femmes, and Collective Work of Transgression." *Sexualities* 13:236–54.

## READING 30

Andersen, Margaret L. 1991. "Feminism and the American Family Ideal." *Journal of Comparative Family Studies* 22(2):235–46.

Anthias, Floya, and Nira Yuval-Davis. 1992. *Racialized Boundaries: Race, Nation, Gender, Colour and Class in the Anti-racist Struggle.* New York: Routledge.

Collier, Jane, Michelle Z. Rosaldo, and Sylvia Yanagisako. 1992. "Is There a Family?: New Anthropological Views." In *Rethinking the Family.* See Thorne and Yalom 1992.

Collins, Patricia Hill. 1990. *Black Feminist Thought: Knowledge, Consciousness, and the Politics of Empowerment.* New York: Routledge, Chapman and Hall.

———. 1998. *Fighting Words: African American Women and the Search for Justice.* Minneapolis: University of Minnesota Press.

Combahee River Collective. 1982. A Black Feminist Statement. In *But Some of us are Brave*, ed. Gloria T. Hull, Patricia Bell Scott, and Barbara Smith. Old Westbury, NY: Feminist Press.

Coontz, Stephanie. 1992. *The Way We Never Were: American Families and the Nostalgia Trap.* New York: Basic Books.

Crenshaw, Kimberle. 1991. "Mapping the Margins: Intersectionality, Identity Politics, and Violence against Women of Color." *Stanford Law Review* 43(6):1241–99.

Daniels, Jessie. 1997. *White Lies.* New York: Routledge.

Davis, Angela Y. 1981. *Women, Race, and Class.* New York: Random House.

Dill, Bonnie Thornton. 1988. "Our Mothers' Grief: Racial Ethnic Women and the Maintenance of Families." *Journal of Family History* 13(4):415–31.

Frankenberg, Ruth. 1993. *The Social Construction of Whiteness: White Women, Race Matters.* Minneapolis: University of Minnesota Press.

Glenn, Evelyn Nakano. 1992. "From Servitude to Service Work: Historical Continuities in the Racial Division of Paid Reproductive Labor." *Signs* 18(1):1–43.

Goldberg, David Theo. 1993. *Racist Culture: Philosophy and the Politics of Meaning.* Cambridge, MA: Blackwell.

Gordon, Linda. 1994. *Pitied but not Entitled: Single Mothers and the History of Welfare.* Cambridge: Harvard University Press.

Gould, Stephen Jay. 1981. *The Mismeasure of Man.* New York: W. W. Norton.

Haller, Mark H. 1984 [1963]. *Eugenics: Hereditarian Attitudes in American Thought.* New Brunswick: Rutgers University Press.

Haraway, Donna. 1989. *Primate Visions: Gender, Race, and Nature in the World of Modern Science.* New York: Routledge, Chapman and Hall.

Heng, Geraldine, and Janadas Devan. 1992. "State Fatherhood: The Politics of Nationalism, Sexuality and Race in Singapore." In *Nationalisms and Sexualities*, ed. Andrew Parker, Mary Russo, Doris Sommer and Patricia Yaeger. New York: Routledge.

Jackson, Peter, and Jan Penrose. 1993. "Introduction: Placing "Race" and Nation." In *Constructions of Race, Place and Nation*, edited by P. Jackson and J. Penrose. Minneapolis: University of Minnesota Press.

Kuumba, Monica Bahati. 1993. "Perpetuating Neo-colonialism through Population Control: South Africa and the United States." *Africa Today* 40(3): 79–85.

Lorde, Audre. 1984. *Sister Outsider.* Trumansberg, NY: Crossing Press.

Massey, Douglas S., and Nancy A. Denton. 1993. *American Apartheid: Segregation and the Making of the Underclass.* Cambridge: Harvard University Press.

McClintock, Anne. 1995. *Imperial Leather.* New York: Routledge.

Nsiah-Jefferson, Laurie. 1989. "Reproductive Laws, Women of Color, and Low-income Women." In *Reproductive Laws for the 1990s*, edited by Sherrill Cohen and Nadine Taub. Clifton, NJ: Humana Press.

Oliver, Melvin L., and Thomas M. Shapiro. 1995. *Black Wealth/White Wealth: A New Perspective on Racial Inequality.* New York: Routledge.

Omi, Michael, and Howard Winant. 1994. *Racial Formation in the United States: From the 1960s to the 1990s.* New York: Routledge.

Parker, Andrew, Mary Russo, Doris Sommer, and Patricia Yaeger, eds. 1992. *Nationalisms and Sexualities.* New York: Routledge.

Proctor, Robert N. 1988. *Racial Hygiene: Medicine under the Nazis.* Cambridge: Harvard University Press.

Quadagno, Jill. 1994. *The Color of Welfare: How Racism Undermined the War on Poverty.* New York: Oxford University Press.

Raymond, Janice. 1993. *Women as Wombs: Reproductive Technologies and the Battle over Women's Freedom.* San Francisco: Harper San Francisco.

Slack, Jennifer Daryl. 1996. "The Theory and Method of Articulation in Cultural Studies." In *Stuart Hall: Critical Dialogues in Cultural Studies*, edited by David Morley and Kuan-Hsing Chen. New York: Routledge.

Stacey, Judith. 1992. "Backward toward the Postmodern Family: Reflections on Gender, Kinship, and Class in the Silicon Valley." In *Rethinking the family.* See Thorne and Yalom 1992.

Thorne, Barrie. 1992. "Feminism and the Family: Two Decades of Thought." In *Rethinking the Family: Some Feminist Questions*. See Thorne and Yalom 1992.

Thorne, Barrie and Marilyn Yalom. 1992. *Rethinking the Family: Some Feminist Questions*. Boston: Northeastern University Press.

Young, Robert J. C. 1995. *Colonial Desire: Hybridity Theory, Culture and Race*. New York: Routledge.

Zinn, Maxine Baca. 1989. Family, Race, and Poverty in the Eighties. *Signs* 14(4):875–84.

## READING 31

Andersen, M. 2005. "Thinking about Women: A Quarter Century's View." *Gender & Society* 19: 437–55.

Beauboeuf-Lafontant, T. 2007. "'You Have to Show Strength': An Exploration of Gender, Race, and Depression." *Gender & Society* 21:28–51.

Bordo, S. 1993. "Feminism, Foucault, and the Politics of the Body." Pp. 170-202 in *Up Against Foucault*. Ed. C. Ramazanoglu. New York: Routledge.

Brennan, D. 2001. "Tourism in Transnational Places: Dominican Sex Workers and German Sex Tourists Imagine One Another." *Identities* 7:621–63.

Chappell, D. 2000. "Active Agents versus Passive Victims: Decolonized Historiography or Problematic Paradigm?" Pp. 205-228 in *Voyaging Through the Contemporary Pacific*, edited by D. Hanlon and G. White. Oxford: Rowman and Littlefield.

Collet, C. 2005. "Bloc Voting, Polarization, and the Panethnic Hypothesis: The Case of Little Saigon." *The Journal of Politics* 67:907–33.

Collins, P. H. 1990. *Black Feminist Thought*. New York: Routledge.

Constable, N. 2003. *Romance on a Global Stage: Pen Pals, Virtual Ethnography, and "Mail Order" Marriages*. Berkeley: University of California Press.

Crenshaw, K. 1993. "Mapping the Margins: Intersectionality, Identity Politics, and Violence Against Women of Color." *Stanford Law Review* 43:1241–99.

Glodava, M., and R. Onizuka. 1994. *Mail Order Brides: Women for Sale*. Fort Collins, CO: Alaken.

Hirakawa, H. 2004. "Give Me One Good Reason to Marry a Japanese Man: Japanese Women Debating Ideal Lifestyles." *Women's Studies* 33:423–51.

Kelsky, K. 2001. *Women on the Verge: Japanese Women, Western Dreams*. Durham, NC: Duke University Press.

Kim, N. 2006. "'Patriarchy is So Third World': Korean Immigrant Women and 'Migrating' White Western Masculinity." *Social Problems* 4:519–36.

Lee, S., and M. Fernandez. 1998. "Trends in Asian American Racial/Ethnic Intermarriage: A Comparison of 1980 and 1990 Census Data." *Sociological Perspectives* 41:323–42.

Matsuda, M. 1996. *Where Is Your Body?* Boston: Beacon Press.

Mohanty, C. T. 2002. "Cartographies of Struggle: Third World Women and the Politics of Feminism." Pp. 195–219 in *Race Critical Theories*. Ed. P. Essed and D. T. Goldberg. Malden, MA: Blackwell.

Narayan, U. 1995. "'Male-Order' Brides: Immigrant Women, Domestic Violence and Immigration Law." *Hypatia* 10:104–19.

———. 1998. "Essence of Culture and a Sense of History: A Feminist Critique of Cultural Essentialism." *Hypatia* 13:86–106.

Nemoto, K. 2009. *Racing Romance: Love, Power, and Desire among Asian American/White Couples*. New Brunswick, NJ: Rutgers University Press.

Ong, A. 1994. "Colonialism and Modernity: Feminist Re-presentations of Women in Non-Western Societies." Pp. 372–381 in *Theorizing Feminism: Parallel Trends in the Humanities and Social Sciences*, edited by A. C. Hermann and A. J. Stewart. Oxford: Westview Press.

Padilla, L. 2001. "'Dirty Mexican': Internalized Oppression, Latinos and Law." *Texas Hispanic Journal of Law and Policy* 7:61–113, 65–73.

Pyke, Karen. 2000. "'The Normal American Family' as an Interpretive Structure of Family Life among Grown Children of Korean and Vietnamese Immigrants." *Journal of Marriage and Family* 62:240–55.

———. 2007. "Defying the Taboo on the Study of Internalized Racism." Pp. 101–120 in *Global Migration, Cultural Transformation, and Social Change*, edited by E. Elliott, J. Payne, and P. Ploesch. New York: Palgrave Macmillan.

Pyke, K., and D. Johnson. 2003. "Asian American Women and Racialized Feminities: 'Doing' Gender across Cultural Worlds." *Gender & Society* 17:33–53.

Pyke, K., and K. Nemoto. 2009. "Racialized Romantic Desires of White Women Students: Does the Racial

Composition of Universities Matter?" Paper presented at the 80th Annual Meeting of the Pacific Sociological Association, San Diego, CA, April 2009.

Said, E. 1978. *Orientalism.* New York: Pantheon.

Schaeffer-Grabiel, F. 2004. "Cyberbrides and Global Imaginaries: Mexican Women's Turn from the National to the Foreign." *Space & Culture* 7:33–48.

———. 2005. "Planet-Love.com: Cyberbrides in the Americas and the Transnational Routes to U.S. Masculinity." *Signs* 31:331–56.

Yu, E., P. Choe, and S. Han. 2002. "Korean Population in the United States, 2000: Demographic Characteristics and Socio-Economic Status." *International Journal of Korean Studies* 6:71–107.

Yuh, J. 2002. *Beyond the Shadow of Camptown: Korean Military Brides in America.* New York: New York University Press.

Lewin, Ellen. 1993. *Lesbian Mothers: Accounts of Gender in American Culture.* Ithaca, NY: Cornell University Press.

Luttrell, Wendy. 2000. "Good Enough Methods for Ethnographic Research." *Harvard Educational Review* 70(4):499–515.

Roberts, Keith A. 2004. *Religion in Sociological Perspective.* Belmont, CA: Thompson-Wadsworth.

Rubin, Gayle. 1993. "Thinking Sex: Notes for a Radical Theory of the Politics of Sexuality." Pp. 3–44 in Abelove, Barale, Halperin, (Ed.), *The Lesbian and Gay Studies Reader.* New York: Routledge.

Silvera, Makeda. 1995. "Confronting the I in the Eye: Black Mothers, Black Daughters." Pp. 311–320 in Arnup (Ed.), *Lesbian Parenting: Living With Pride & Prejudice.* Charlottetown, Canada: Gynery Books.

Smith, Barbara. 1983. "Introduction." Pp. xox-lvi in Smith (Ed.), *Home Girls: A Black Feminist Anthology.* New York: Kitchen Table: Women of Color Press.

Stacey, Judith. 1998. "Gay and Lesbian Families: Queer Like Us." Pp. 117–143 in Mason, Skolnick, and Sugarman, (Ed.), *All Our Families: New Policies for a New Century.* New York: Oxford University Press.

Stein, Arlene. 1997. *Sex and Sensibility: Stories of a Lesbian Generation.* Berkeley, CA: University of California Press.

Sullivan, Maureen. 2004. *The Family of Woman: Lesbian Mothers, Their Children, and the Undoing of Gender.* Berkeley, CA: University of California Press.

Weston, Kath. 1991. *Families We Choose: Lesbians, Gays, Kinship.* New York: Columbia University Press.

## Reading 32

Barlett, Jane. 1994. *Will You Be Mother? Women Who Choose to Say No.* London, England: Virago Press.

Cabaj, R. P. 1998. "History of Gay Acceptance and Relationships." Pp. 1–28 in Cabaj and Purcell (Ed.), *On the Road to Same-Sex Marriage: A Supportive Guide to Psychological, Political, and Legal Issues.* San Francisco, CA: Jossey-Bass Publishers.

Clarke, Cheryl. 1983. "The Failure to Transform: Homophobia in the Black Community." Pp. 197–208 in Smith (Ed.), *Home Girls: A Black Feminist Anthology.* New York: Kitchen Table: Women of Color Press.

Connell, Robert W., M. D. Davis, and G. W. Dowsett. 1993. "A Bastard of a Life: Homosexual Desire and Practice among Men in Working-Class Mileux." *Australian and New Zealand Journal of Sociology* 29(1):112–135.

Espín, Olivia M. 1997. *Latina Realities: Essays on Healing, Migration, and Sexuality.* Boulder, CO: Westview Press.

Greene, Beverly. 1994. "Ethnic-Minority Lesbians and Gay Men: Mental Health and Treatment Issues." *Journal of Consulting and Clinical Psychology* 62:243–251.

Hartman, Ann. 1999. "The Long Road To Equality: Lesbians and Social Policy." Pp. 91–120 in Laird (Ed.), *Lesbians and Lesbian Families: Reflections on Theory and Practice.* New York: Columbia University Press.

hooks, bell. 1989: *Talking Back: Thinking Feminist, Thinking Black.* Boston, MA: South End Press.

## Reading 33

Anderson, J. D. 1988. The Education of Blacks in the South, 1860–1935. Chapel Hill: University of North Carolina Press.

Armor, D. 1998. Expert Report to the Court in the Case of Capacchione et al. v. Charlotte-Mecklenburg Schools.

Brown v. Board of Education I, 347 U.S. 483 (1954).

Charlotte-Mecklenburg Schools. (1970–1999). Monthly Reports. Author.

Charlotte-Mecklenburg Schools. 1996–1999. Class Counts. Author.

Coleman, J., et al. (1996). Equality of Educational Opportunity. Washington, DC: U.S. Government Printing Office.

Crain, R., and Mahard, R. E. 1972. Desegregation Plans that Raise Black Achievement: A Review of the Research. Santa Monica, CA: rand.

Crain, R., and Mahard, R. E. 1983. "The Effects of Research Methodology in Desegregation Achievement Studies: A Meta-analysis." American Journal of Sociology 88(5):839–854.

Douglas, D. M. 1995. Reading, Writing, and Race. The Desegregation of the Charlotte Schools. Chapel Hill: University of North Carolina Press.

Gardner, D. 1998. Expert Report to the Court in the Case of Capacchione et al. v. Charlotte-Mecklenburg Schools.

Hobson v. Hansen, 269 F. Supp. 401 (DC Cir. 1967).

Lord, D. 1999. Expert Report to the Court in the Case of Capacchione et al. v. Charlotte-Mecklenburg Schools.

Mickelson, R. A. 1998. Expert report to the Court in the Case of Capacchione et al. v. Charlotte-Mecklenburg Schools.

Mickelson, R. A. 1998–1999. Interviews with CMS Principals. Palo Alto, CA.

Mickelson, R. A. 2001. "Subverting Swann: First- and Second-generation Segregation in the Charlotte-Mecklenburg Schools." American Educational Research Journal 38:215–252.

Mickelson, R. A. 2003. "Achieving Equality of Educational Opportunity in the Wake of Judicial Retreat from Race Sensitive Remedies: Lessons from North Carolina." American University Law Review 52(6): 152–184.

Peterkin, R. 1998. Expert Report to the Court in the Case of Capacchione et al. v. Charlotte-Mecklenburg Schools.

Smith, S. S. 1998. Expert Report to the Court in the Case of Capacchione et al. v. Charlotte-Mecklenburg Schools.

Smith, S. S. and Mickelson, R. A. 2000. "All That Glitters Is Not Gold: The Outcomes of Educational Restructuring in Charlotte, North Carolina." Education Evaluation and Policy Analysis 22: 101–127.

Swann v. Charlotte-Mecklenburg, 402 U.S. 1, 15 1971.

Trent, W. 1998. Expert Report to the Court in the Case of Capacchione et al. v. Charlotte-Mecklenburg Schools.

Walker, V. S. 2000. "Valued Segregated Schools for African American Children, 1935–1969." Review of Educational Research 70:253–286.

Walsh, M. 2002, April 24. "High Court Closes Historic Desegregation Case." Education Week. Available: http://www.edweek.com/.

Wells, A. S., and Crain, R. L. 1994. "Perpetuation Theory and the Long-term Effects of School Desegregation." Review of Educational Research 64(4): 531–556.

# READING 34

Allington, R., and Haley, W. J. 1999. "The Politics of Literacy Teaching." Educational Researcher 28(8): 4–12.

Brisk, M. E. 1998. Bilingual Education. Mahwah, NJ: Erlbaum.

Cabán, L. 1999. Constructing a Colonized People. Boulder, CO: Westview.

Carrasquillo, H., and Sánchez-Korrol, V. 1996. "Migration, Community, and Culture." Pp. 98–109 in Origins and Destinies, ed. S. Pedraza and R. G. Rumbaut. Belmont, CA: Wadsworth.

Children Now. 1999. California County Data Book. Los Angeles, CA: Children Now.

Crawford, J. 1999. Bilingual Education, 4th ed. Los Angeles: Bilingual Educational Services.

Delgado-Gaitán, C. 1990. Literacy for Empowerment. New York: Falmer.

Fradd, S. Editor. 1999. Creating Florida's Multilingual Global Workforce. Gainesville, FL: Institute for the Advanced Study of Communication Processes.

García, E. 1995. "Educating Mexican American Students." Pp. 372–387 in Handbook of Research on Multicultural Education, ed. J. Banks and C. McGee Banks. New York: Macmillan.

Gibson, E., and Ogbu, J. Editors. 1991. Minority Status and Schooling. New York: Garland.

Goldenberg, C. 1996. "Latin American Immigration and U.S. Schools." Social Policy Report: Society for Research in Child Development 10(1):1–30.

Goldenberg, C., and Gallimore, R. 1995. "Immigrant Latino Parents' Values and Beliefs about their Children's Education." Pp. 183–228 in Advances in Motivation and Achievement, edited by P. R. Pintrich and M. Maehr. Greenwich, CT: JAI Press.

Goldenberg, C., and Sullivan, J. 1994. Making Change Happen in a Language-minority School (EPR #13). Washington, DC: Center for Applied Linguistics.

Gutiérrez, R. 1995. "Historical and Social Science Research on Mexican Americans." Pp. 203–222 in *Handbook of Research on Multicultural Education*, edited by J. Banks and C. McGee Banks. New York: Macmillan.

Gutiérrez, K. D., Baquedano-López, P., and Alvarez, H. H. (In press). A Cultural-Historical Approach to Collaboration. *Theory into Practice.*

Hubbard, L., and Mehan, H. (In press). Race and Reform. *Journal of Negro Education.*

Kontra, M., Phillipson, R. Skutnabb-Kangas, T., and Varady, I. Editors. 1999. *Language: A Right and a Resource.* Budapest: Central European University Press.

Krauss, M. 1992. "The World's Languages in Crisis." *Language* 68:4–10.

Lee, V., and Smith, J. 1999. "Social Support and Achievement for Young Adolescents in Chicago." *American Educational Research Journal* 36(4):907–945.

López, D. 1999. "Social and Linguistics Aspects of Assimilation Today." Pp. 212–222 in *The Handbook of International Migration*, edited by C. Hirschman, P. Kasinitz, and J. DeWind. New York: Russell Sage Foundation.

Mehan, H., Villanueva, I., Hubbard, L., and Lintz, A. 1996. *Constructing School Success.* Cambridge: Cambridge University Press.

Mercado, C., and Moll, L. C. 1997. "The Study of Funds of Knowledge." *Centro* 9(9):26–42.

Moll, L. C., and González, N. 1997. "Teachers as Social Scientists." Pp. 89–114 in *Race, Ethnicity and Multiculturalism*, ed. P. M. Hall. New York: Garland.

Nieto, S. Editor. 1999. *Puerto Rican Students in U.S. Schools.* Mahwah, NJ: Erlbaum.

Ong, P., and Blumenberg, E. 1996. "Income and Racial Inequality in Los Angeles." Pp. 311–335 in *The City: Los Angeles and Urban Theory at the End of the Twentieth Century*, edited by A. Scott and E. Soja. Berkeley: University of California Press.

Ortíz, V. 1996. "The Mexican-origin Population: Permanent Working Class or Emerging Middle Class?" Pp. 247–278 in *Ethnic Los Angeles*, edited by R. Waldinger and M. Bozorgmehr. New York: Russell Sage Foundation.

Pedraza, S. 1996. "Cuba's Refugees: Manifold Migrations." Pp. 263–279 in *Origins and Destinies*, edited by S. Pedraza and R. G. Rumbaut. Belmont, CA: Wadsworth.

Rivera, M., and Pedraza, P. 2000. "The Spirit of a Latino/a Quest: Transforming Education for Community Self-determination and Social Change." Pp. 223–243 in *Puerto Rican Students in U.S. Schools*, edited by S. Nieto. Mahwah, NJ: Erlbaum.

Rodríguez, C. 1995. "Puerto Ricans in Historical and Social Science Research." Pp. 223–244 in *Handbook of Research on Multicultural Education*, edited by J. Banks and C. McGee Banks. New York: Macmillan.

Ruiz, R. 1997. "The Empowerment of Language Minority Students." Pp. 319–328 in *Latinos and Education*, edited by A. Darder, R. Torres, & H. Gutiérrez. New York: Routledge.

Rumbaut, R. 1998. *Transformations.* Paper presented at the Annual Meeting of the Eastern Sociological Society, Philadelphia, PA. March 21.

Rumbaut, R. 1999. "Assimilation and Its Discontents." Pp. 172–195 in *The Handbook of International Migration*, edited by C. Hirschman, P. Kasinitz, and J. DeWind. New York: Russell Sage Foundation.

Santoro, W. 1999. "Conventional Politics takes Center Stage: The Latino Struggle Against English-only Laws." *Social Forces* 77(3):887–909.

Skutnabb-Kangas, T. 1999. "Linguistic Diversity, Human Rights and the "Free" Market." Pp. 187-222 in *Language: A Right and a Resource*, edited by M. Kontra et al. Budapest: Central European University Press.

Smith, P. 2000. *Community as Resource for Minority Language Learning.* Ph.D. diss., University of Arizona.

Spring, J. 1997. *Deculturalization and the Struggle for Equality.* 2d ed. New York: McGraw-Hill.

Taylor, D. 1998. *Beginning to Read and the Spin Doctors of Science.* Urbana, IL: National Council of Teachers of English.

Valenzuela, A. 1999. *Subtractive Schooling.* Albany, New York: State University of New York Press.

Vásquez, O. 1994. "The Magic of La Clase Mágica." *Australian Journal of Language and Literacy* 17(2):120–128.

Vélez-Ibáñez, C. 1997. *Border Visions.* Tucson: University of Arizona Press.

Walsh, C. 1998. "Staging Encounters": The Educational Decline of U.S. Puerto Ricans in [Post]-colonial Perspective." *Harvard Educational Review* 68(2):218–243.

Warner, S. L. N. 1999. "Kuleana: The Right, Responsibility, and Authority of Indigenous Peoples to Speak and Make Decisions for Themselves in Language and Cultural Revitalization." *Anthropology and Education Quarterly* 30(1):68–93.

Young, B. 1999. *Characteristics of the 100 Largest Public Elementary and Secondary School Districts in the United States: 1997–98*, NCES 1999-318. Washington, DC: U.S. Department of Education, National Center for Education Statistics.

# READING 36

Acker, Joan. 1989. *Doing Comparable Worth: Gender, Class and Pay Equity*. Philadelphia: Temple University Press.

———. 1990. "Hierarchies, Jobs, and Bodies: A Theory of Gendered Organizations." *Gender & Society* 4:139–58.

———. 1991. Thinking about Wages: The Gendered Wage Gap in Swedish Banks. *Gender & Society* 5:390–407.

———. 2006. *Class Questions: Feminist Answers*. Lanham, MD: Rowman & Littlefield.

Acker, Joan, and Donald Van Houten. 1974. "Differential Recruitment and Control: The Sex Structuring of Organizations." *Administrative Science Quarterly* 19:152–63.

Barker, James R. 1993. "Tightening the Iron Cage: Concertive Control in Self-managing Teams." *Administrative Science Quarterly* 38:408–37.

Burawoy, Michael. 1979. *Manufacturing Consent*. Chicago: University of Chicago Press.

Charles, Maria, and David B. Grusky. 2004. *Occupational Ghettos: The Worldwide Segregation of Women and Men*. Stanford, CA: Stanford University Press.

Cockburn, Cynthia. 1985. *Machinery of Dominance*. London: Pluto.

———. 1991. *In the Way of Women: Men's Resistance to Sex Equality in Organizations*. Ithaca, NY: ILR Press.

Collins, Patricia Hill. 1995. "Comment on West and Fenstermaker." *Gender & Society* 9:491–94.

Collinson, David L., and Jeff Hearn, eds. 1996. *Men as Managers, Managers as Men*. London: Sage.

Crenshaw, Kimberlé Williams. 1995. "Mapping the Margins: Intersectionality, Identity Politics, and Violence against Women of Color." In *Critical Race Theory: The Key Writings that Formed the Movement*, edited by K. Crenshaw, N. Gotanda, G. Peller, and K. Thomas. New York: New Press.

Davis, Angela Y. 1981. *Women, Race & Class*. New York: Vintage.

Ely, Robin J., and Debra E. Meyerson. 2000. "Advancing Gender Equity in Organizations: The Challenge and Importance of Maintaining a Gender Narrative." *Organization* 7:589–608.

Enarson, Elaine. 1984. *Woods-working Women: Sexual Integration in the U.S. Forest Service*. Tuscaloosa, AL: University of Alabama Press.

Featherstone, Liza. 2004. *Selling Women Short: The Landmark Battle for Workers' Rights at Wal-Mart*. New York: Basic Books.

Ferguson, Kathy E. 1984. *The Feminist Case against Bureaucracy*. Philadelphia: Temple University Press.

Ferree, Myra Max, and Patricia Yancey Martin, eds. 1995. *Feminist Organzations*. Philadelphia: Temple University Press.

Figart, D. M., E. Mutari, and M. Power. 2002. *Living Wages, Equal Wages*. London: Routledge.

Forsebäck, Lennart. 1980. *Industrial Relations and Employment in Sweden*. Uppsala, Sweden: Almqvist & Wiksell.

Glass, Jennifer. 2004. "Blessing or Curse? Work-family Policies and Mother's Wage Growth over Time." *Work and Occupations* 31:367–94.

Glenn, Evelyn Nakano. 2002. *Unequal Freedom: How Race and Gender Shaped American Citizenship and Labor*. Cambridge, MA: Harvard University Press.

Hearn, Jeff, and Wendy Parkin. 2001. *Gender, Sexuality and Violence in Organizations*. London: Sage.

Hochschild, Arlie Russell. 1997. *The Time Bind: When Work Becomes Home & Home Becomes Work*. New York: Metropolitan Books.

Holvino, Evangelina. 2001. "Complicating Gender: The Simultaneity of Race, Gender, and Class in Organization Change(ing)." Working paper no. 14, Center for Gender in Organizations, Simmons Graduate School of Management, Boston.

hooks, bell. 1984. *Feminist Theory: From Margin to Center*. Boston: South End.

Hossfeld, Karen J. 1994. "Hiring Immigrant Women: Silicon Valley's "Simple Formula." In *Women of Color in U.S. Society*, edited by M. B. Zinn and B. T. Dill. Philadelphia: Temple University Press.

Jacobs, Jerry A., and Kathleen Gerson. 2004. *The Time Divide: Work, Family, and Gender Inequality*. Cambridge, MA: Harvard University Press.

Joseph, Gloria. 1981. "The Incompatible Ménage á Trois: Marxism, Feminism and Racism." In *Women and Revolution: The Unhappy Marriage of Marxism and Feminism*, edited by L. Sargent. Boston: South End.

Kanter, Rosabeth Moss. 1977. *Men and Women of the Corporation*. New York: Basic Books.

Kelly, Erin, and Frank Dobbin. 1998. "How Affirmative Action became Diversity Management: Employer Response to Antidiscrimination Law, 1961 to 1996." *American Behavioral Scientist* 41:960–85.

Martin, Joanne, and Debra Meyerson. 1998. "Women and Power: Conformity, Resistance, and Disorganized Coaction." In *Power and Influence in Organizations*, edited by R. Kramer and M. Neale. Thousand Oaks, CA: Sage.

———. 2005. "The Complexity of Intersectionality." *Signs: Journal of Women in Culture and Society* 30:1771–1800.

McIntosh, Peggy. 1995. "White Privilege and Male Privilege: A Personal Account of Coming to See Correspondences through Work in Women's Studies." In *Race, Class, and Gender: An Anthology*, 2nd ed., edited by M. L. Andersen and P. H. Collins. Belmont, CA: Wadsworth.

Mishel, L., J. Bernstein, and H. Boushey. 2003. *The State of Working America 2002/2003*. Ithaca, NY: Cornell University Press.

Morgen, S., J. Acker, and J. Weigt. n.d. *Neo-liberalism on the Ground: Practising Welfare Reform*.

Nelson, Julie A. 1993. "The Study of Choice or the Sstudy of Provisioning? Gender and the Definition of Economics." In *Beyond Economic Man: Feminist Theory and Economics*, edited by M. A. Ferber and J. A. Nelson. Chicago: University of Chicago Press.

Perrow, Charles. 1986. A Society of Organizations. *Theory and Society* 20:725–62.

———. 2002. *Organizing America*. Princeton, NJ: Princeton University Press.

Pierce, Jennifer L. 1995. *Gender Trials: Emotional Lives in Contemporary Law Firms*. Berkeley: University of California Press.

———. 2003. "Including Mechanisms in Our Models of Ascriptive Inequality." *American Sociological Review* 68:1–21.

Ridgeway, Cecilia. 1997. "Interaction and the Conservation of Gender Inequality." *American Sociological Review* 62:218–35.

Royster, Deirdre A. 2003. *Race and the Invisible Hand: How White Networks Exclude Black Men from Blue-collar Jobs*. Berkeley: University of California Press.

Salzinger, Leslie. 2003. *Genders in Production: Making Workers in Mexico's Global Factories*. Berkeley: University of California Press.

Scott, Ellen. 2000. "Everyone Against Racism: Agency and the Production of Meaning in the Anti-racism Practices of Two Feminist Organizations." *Theory and Society* 29:785–819.

Vallas, Steven P. 2003. "Why Teamwork Fails: Obstacles to Workplace Change in Four Manufacturing Plants." *American Sociological Review* 68:223–50.

Wacjman, Judy. 1998. *Managing Like a Man*. Cambridge, UK: Polity.

Weber, Lynn. 2001. *Understanding Race, Class, Gender, and Sexuality*. Boston: McGraw-Hill.

Wharton, Amy S. 2005. *The Sociology of Gender*. Oxford, UK: Blackwell.

Willis, Paul. 1977. *Learning to Labor*. Farnborough, UK: Saxon House.

## READING 37

Becker, Gary S. 1961. *The Economics of Discrimination*, 2nd Ed. Chicago: University of Chicago Press.

Council of Economic Advisers. 1998. *Changing America: Indicators of Social and Economic Well-being by Race and Hispanic Origin*. September 1998, http://w3.access.gpo.gov/eop/ca/pdfs/ca.pdf.

Darity, William A., Jr. and Mason, Patrick L. 1998. "Evidence on Discrimination in Employment: Codes of Color, Codes of Gender." *Journal of Economic Perspectives* 12(2): 63–90.

Jones, Melinda. 2002. *Social Psychology of Prejudice*. Saddle River, NJ: Pearson Education.

Mullainathan, Sendhil. 2003. "Thinking Through Categories." Mimeo, Massachusetts Institute of Technology.

## READING 38

Bakan, Abigail B., and Daiva Stasiulis. 1997. "Foreign Domestic Worker Policy in Canada and the Social Boundaries of Modern Citizenship," Pp. 29-52 in Abigail B. Bakan and Daiva Stasiulis (eds.), *Not One of the Family: Foreign Domestic Workers in Canada*, Toronto: University of Toronto Press.

Constable, Nicole. 1997. *Maid to Order in Hong Kong: Stories of Filipina Workers*. Ithaca and London: Cornell University Press.

Cornelius, Wayne, 1998. "The Structural Embeddedness of Demand for Mexican Immigrant Labor: New Evidence from California." Pp. 113-144 in Marcelo M. Suárez-Orozco (ed.), *Crossings: Mexican Immigration in Interdisciplinary Perspectives*. Cambridge, MA: Harvard University, David Rockefeller Center for Latin American Studies.

Coser, Lewis. 1974. "Servants: The Obsolescence of an Occupational Role." *Social Forces* 52:31–40.

Hochschild, Arlie. 1997. *The Time Bind: When Work Becomes Home and Home Becomes Work*. New York: Metropolitan Books, Henry Holt.

Hondagneu-Sotelo, Pierrette. 2001. *Domestica: Immigrant Workers and Their Employers*. Berkeley: University of California Press.

Hondagneu-Sotelo, Pierrette, and Ernestine Avila. 1997. "'I'm Here, But I'm There': The Meanings of Latina Transnational Motherhood." *Gender & Society*, 11:548–571.

Lan, Pei-chia. 2000. "Global Divisions, Local Identities: Filipina Migrant Domestic Workers and Taiwanese Employers." Dissertation, Northwestern University.

Laslett, Barbara, and Johanna Brenner. 1989. "Gender and Social Reproduction: Historical Perspectives." *Annual Review of Sociology* 15:381–404.

Menjivar, Cecilia. 2000. *Fragmented Ties: Salvadoran Immigrant Networks in America*. Berkeley: University of California Press.

Waldinger, Roger, and Mehdi Bozorgmehr. 1996. "The Making of a Multicultural Metropolis." Pp. 3–37 in Roger Waldinger and Mehdi Bozorgmehr, (eds.), *Ethnic Los Angeles*. New York: Russell Sage Foundation.

## Reading 39

Acevedo-Garcia, Dolores, Mah-J Soobader, and Lisa R. Berkman. 2005. "The Differential Effect of Foreign-Born on Low Birth Weight by Race/Ethnicity and Education." *Pediatrics* 115(1):20–30.

Acevedo-Garcia, Dolores, Theresa L. Osypuk, Nancy McArdle, and David R. Williams. 2008. "Toward a Policy-Relevant Analysis of Geographic and Racial/Ethnic Disparities in Child Health." *Health Affairs* 27(2):321–333.

American Cancer Society. 2003. "Cancer Facts and Figures 2003." Retrieved May 4, 2008. www.can cer.org/downloads/STT/CAFF2003PWSecured.pdf.

American Psychiatric Association. 1994. *Diagnostic and Statistical Manual of Mental Disorders*, 4th ed. Washington DC: American Psychiatric Association.

Aronowitz, Robert. 2008. "Framing Disease: An Underappreciated Mechanism for the Social Patterning of Health." *Social Science and Medicine* 67(1):1–9.

Bhatia, Subhash and Shashi Bhatia. 1999. "Depression in Women: Diagnostic and Treatment Considerations." *American Family Physician* 60 (July):225–240. www.aafp.org/afp/990700ap/ 225.html.

Burris, Scott. 2008. "Stigma, Ethics and Policy: A Commentary on Bayer's "Stigma and the Ethics of Public Health: Not Can We but Should We." *Social Science and Medicine* 67(3):473–475.

California Newsreel and the National Minority Consortia of Public Television. 2008. *Unnatual Causes: Is Inequality Making Us Sick?* Retrieved May 14, 2008. www.unnaturalcauses.org.

Centers for Disease Control and Prevention. 2008a. "Age-Adjusted Prevalence of Diagnosed Diabetes by Race-Ethnicity and Sex, United States, 1985–2005." Retrieved May 2, 2008. www.cdc.gov/diabetes/statistics/prev/national/figraceethsex.htm.

———. 2008b. "HIV/AIDS Surveillance Report." Retrieved May 20, 2008. www.cdc.gov/hiv/resources/factsheets/us.htm.

Currey, Aaron, Carl Latkin, and Melissa Davey-Rothwell. 2008. "Pathways to Depression: The Impact of Neighborhood Violent Crime on Inner-city Residents in Baltimore, Maryland, USA." *Social Science and Medicine* 67(1):12–30.

Institute of Medicine. 2003. *Unequal Treatment: Confronting Racial and Ethnic Disparities in Health Care*. Washington, D.C.: National Academy of Sciences.

Kaiser Family Foundation. 2008. "Black Americans and HIV/AIDS." *HIV/AIDS Policy Fact Sheet*. Retrieved June 22, 2008. www.kff.org/hivaids/upload/6089_05.pdf.

Kennedy, Steven, James Ted McDonald, and Nicholas Biddle. 2006. "Healthy Immigrant Effect and Immigrant Selection: Evidence from Four Countries." *Social and Economic Dimensions of an Aging Population*. Retrieved May 24, 2008. http://socserv2.socsci.mcmaster.ca/~sedap/p/sedap164.pdf.

Kimbro, Rachel Tolbert, Sharon Bzostek, Noreen Goldman, and Germán Rodriquez. 2008. "Race, Ethnicity, and the Education Gradient in Health." *Health Affairs* 27(2):361–372.

Lincoln, Karen. D., Linda M. Chatters, Robert Joseph Taylor, and James S. Jackson. 2007. "Profiles of Depressive Symptoms among African Americans and Caribbean Blacks." *Social Science and Medicine* 65(2):200–213.

Link, Bruce G. and Jo C. Phelan. 2001. "Conceptualizing Stigma." *Annual Review of Sociology* 27:363–385.

Mayo Clinic. 2008. "Mayo Clinic Study Reveals Rural, Unmarried Women at Higher Risk for Depression." Retrieved June 22, 2008. www.eurekalert.org/pub_releases/2008-06/mc-mcs061108.php.

Mead, Holly, Lara Cartwright-Smith, Karen Jones, Christal Ramos, Kristy Woods, and Bruce Siegel. 2008. *Racial and Ethnic Disparities in U.S. Health Care: A Chartbook.* NY: The Commonwealth Fund.

Meara, Ellen R., Seth Richards, and David M. Cutler. 2008. "The Gap Gets Bigger: Changes in Mortality and Life Expectancy, by Education, 1981–2000." *Health Affairs* 27(2):350–360.

Mechanic, David and Jennifer Tanner. 2007. "Vulnerable People, Groups, and Populations Societal View." *Health Affairs* 26(5):1220–1230.

Moen, Phyllis and Kelly Chermack. 2005. "Gender Disparities in Health: Strategic Selection, Careers, and Cycles of Control." *The Journals of Gerontology. Series B, Psychological Sciences and Social Sciences* 60(2):99–108.

National Center for Health Statistics. 2007. *Health, United States, 2007 with Chartbook on Trends in the Health of Americans.* Hyattsville, MD. Retrieved February 27, 2008. www.cdc.gov/nchs/data/hus/hus07.pdf.

National Institute of Mental Health. 2008. "The Numbers Count: Mental Health in America." Retrieved June 1, 2008. www.nimh.nih.gov/health/publications/the-numbers-count-mental-disorders-in-america.shtml#Intro.

Office of Minority Health and Health Disparities 2007. "Eliminating Racial and Ethnic Health Disparities." Retrieved May 1, 2008. http://cdc.gov/omhd/About/disparities.htm.

———. 2008. "American Indian – Alaska Native Profile." Retrieved May 20, 2008. www.omhrc.gov/templates/browse.aspx?lvl=2&lvlID=52.

Organization of Economic Co-Operation and Development. 2008. "OECD Health Data 2008: How Does the United States Compare." Retrieved July 9, 2008. www.oecd.org/dataoecd/46/2/38980 580 .pdf.

Pescosolido, Bernice A., Jack K. Martin, Annie Lang, and Sigrun Olafsdottir. 2008. "Rethinking Approaches to Stigma: A Framework Integrating Normative Influences on Stigma (FINIS)." *Social Science and Medicine* 67(3):431–440.

Phelan, Jo C., Bruce G. Link, and John F. Dovidio. 2008. "Stigma and Prejudice: One Animal or Two?" *Social Science and Medicine* 67(3): 358–367.

Riolo, Stephanie A., Tuan Nguyen, John F. Greden, and Cheryl A. King, 2005. "Prevalence of Depression by Race/Ethnicity: Findings from the National Health and Nutrition Survey III." *American Journal of Public Health* 95(6):998–1000.

Singh, Gopal K. and Mohammond Siahpush. 2006. "Widening Socioeconomic Inequalities in U.S. Life Expectancy, 1980–2000." *International of Epidemiology* 35:969–979.

Stuber, Jennifer, Ilan Meyer, and Bruce Link. 2008. "Stigma, Prejudice, Discrimination and Health." *Social Science and Medicine* 67(3): 351–357.

Turnbull, Andrew and Mark Serwotka. 2008. *Work, Stress and Health: The Whitehall II Study.* Retrieved May 28, 2008. www.ucl.ac.uk/whitehallII/findings/Whitehallbooklet.pdf.

U.S. Department of Health and Human Services. 1999. *Mental Health: A Report of the Surgeon General—Executive Summary.* Rockville, MD: U.S. Department of Health and Human Services. Substance Abuse and Mental Health Services Administration. Center for the Mental Health Services. National Institutes of Health. National Institute of Mental Health. Retrieved March 1, 2008. www.surgeongeneral.gov/library/mentalhealth/summary.html.

———. 2003. *New Freedom Commission on Mental Health: Achieving the Promise—Transforming Mental Health Care in America.* Rockville, MD: Department of Health and Human Services No. SMA-03-0832.

———. 2008. *Healthy People 2010.* Retrieved January 7, 2008. www.healthypeople.gov/About/goals.htm.

Williams, David R., Hector M. Gonzalez, Stacey Williams, Selina A. Mohammed, Hashim Moomal, and Dan J. Stein. 2008. "Perceived Discrimination, Race and Health in South Africa." *Social Science and Medicine* 67(3):441–452.

Women's Health, U.S. Department of Health and Human Services. 2003. "The Health of Minority Women." Retrieved June 22, 2008. www.womenshealth.gov/owh/pub/minority/concerns.htm.

World Health Organization. 2008. "Gender and Women's Mental Health." Retrieved May 5, 2008. www.who.int/mental_health/prevention/genderwomen/en/.

Yancy, Clyde W. 2008. "Race-Based Therapeutics." *Current Hypertension Reports* 10:276–285.

## READING 42

Aesop. "The Fox and the Grapes." www.pagebypagebooks.com/Aesop/Aesops_Fables/The_Fox_and_the_Grapes_p1.html (accessed December 4, 2003).

"Alabama: Mobile A Prostrate City, Alarming Decline in the Value of Real Estate, Two Hundred and Fifty Stores without Occupants, Poverty and Depression Some of the Causes." *New York Times*, October 21, 1974, 1.

"All in the Family." Classicsitcoms.com, 2004. classicsitcoms.com/shows/family.html (accessed March 21, 2004).

"All in the Family." TVLand.com, 2004. www.tvland.com/shows/aitf (accessed March 21, 2004).

Andrews, Edmund L. 2003. "Plan Gives Most Benefits to Wealthy and Families." *New York Times*, January 8, 2003, A17.

"A New Kind of Poverty." 2003. *Newsweek*, November 22, 2003. www.msnbc.msn.com/id/3540672 (accessed April 2, 2004).

Archibold, Randal C. 2001. "A Nation Challenged: St. Patrick's City Celebrates Its Heroes and Grieves Over Their Loss." *New York Times*, September 18, 2001, B8.

Ard, Ben J., Jr. 1972. "Are All Middle Class Values Bad?" *Family Coordinator* 21:223–24.

Arenson, Karen W. 2002. "Gates to Create 70 Schools for Disadvantaged." *New York Times*, March 19, 2002, A16.

Armour, Stephanie. 2003. "Homelessness Grows as More Live Check-to-Check." *USA Today*, August 12, 2003, A1.

Arnett, Alison. 2003. "Counter Culture." *Austin American-Statesman*, December 18, 2003, E1, E10.

Aristotle. 2000. *Aristotle's Poetics*. Translated by S. H. Butcher. Introduction by Francis Fergusson. New York: Hill and Wang, 2000.

"Arrested Development." FOX.com, 2003. fox.com/schedule/2003/ad.htm (accessed January 10, 2004).

Associated Press. 2004. "New Poverty Guidelines Unveiled." KATU News, Portland, Oregon, February 13, 2004. www.katu.com/news/story.asp?ID=64558 (accessed February 29, 2004).

Biagi, Shirley. 2003. *Media Impact: An Introduction to Mass Media*. Belmont, CA: Wadsworth.

De Coster, Karen and Brad Edmonds. 2003. "TV Nation: The Killing of American Brain Cells." http://www.lewrockwell.com/decoster/decoster78.html (accessed July 4, 2004).

Delaney, Tim and Allene Wilcox. 2002. "Sports and the Role of the Media." Pp. 199–215 in *Values, Society and Evolution*, edited by Harry Birx and Time Delaney. Auburn, NY: Legend.

DeNavas-Walt, Carmen and Robert W. Cleveland. 2002. "Money Income in the United States 2001." *U.S. Census Bureau: Current Population Reports*, P60–218. Washington, D.C.: U.S. Government Printing Office.

hooks, bell. 2000. *Where We Stand: Class Matters*. New York: Routledge.

Mantsios, Gregory. 2003. "Media Magic: Making Class Invisible." Pp. 99–109 in *Privilege: A Reader*, edited by Michael S. Kimmel and Abby L. Ferber. Boulder, CO: Westview Press.

Nocera, Joseph. 1994. *A Piece of the Action: How the Middle Class Joined the Money Class*. New York: Simon and Schuster.

Perrucchi, Robert and Earl Wysong. 2003. *The New Class Society*. Lanham, MD: Rowman and Littlefield.

Proctor, Bernadette D. and Joseph Dalaker. 2003. "Poverty in the United States: 2002." *U.S. Census Bureau: Current Population Reports*, P60–222. Washington, D.C.: U.S. Government Printing Office.

Schor, Juliet B. 2004. *Born to Buy: The Commercialized Child and the New Consumer Culture*. New York: Scribner.

Sternheimer, Karen. 2003. *It's Not the Media: The Truth about Pop Culture's Influence on Children*. Boulder, CO: Westview Press.

Uchitelle, Louis. 2004. "We Pledge Allegiance to the Mall." *New York Times*, December 6, 2004, p. C12.

## READING 48

Bowen, William G., Martin A. Kurzwell, and Eugene M. Tobin. 2005. *Equality and Excellence in American Higher Education*. Charlottesville: University Press of Virginia.

Danziger, Sheldon and Peter Gottschalk. 1995. *America Unequal*. New York: Russell Sage Foundation.

Donato, Katharine M., Douglas S. Massey, and Brandon Wagner. 2006. "The Chilling Effect: Public Service Usage by Mexican Migrants to the United States." Paper Presented to the annual meeting of the Population Association of America. Los Angeles (March 30–April 1).

Golden, Daniel. 2006. *The Price of Admission: How America's Ruling Class Buys Its Way into Elite Colleges—And Who Gets Left Outside the Gates.* New York: Crown.

Jacobs, Jerry A. 1996. "Gender Inequality in Higher Education." *Annual Review of Sociology* 22:153–85.

Karabel, Jerome. 2005. *The Chosen: The Hidden History of Admission and Exclusion at Harvard, Yale, and Princeton.* New York: Houghton Mifflin.

Kozol, Jonathan. 2005. *The Shame of the Nation: The Restoration of Apartheid Schooling in America.* New York: Crown.

Levy, Frank. 1998. *The New Dollars and Dreams: American Incomes and Economic Change.* New York: Russell Sage Foundation.

Massey, Douglas S. 1996. "The Age of Extremes: Concentrated Affluence and Poverty in the Twenty-first Century." *Demography* 33(4):395–412.

Massey, Douglas S. 2003. "The American Side of the Bargain." In *Reinventing the Melting Pot: The New Immigrants and What It Means to Be an American,* edited by Tamar Jacoby. New York: Basic Books.

Massey, Douglas S. and Margarita Mooney. Forthcoming. "The Effects of America's Three Affirmative Action Programs on Academic Performance." *Social Problems.*

Orfield, Gary and Susan E. Eaton. 1996. *Dismantling Desegregation: The Quiet Reversal of Brown V. Board of Education.* New York: New Press.

Shaw, Kathleen M., Sara Goldrick-Rab, Chrisopher Mazzeo, and Jerry Jacobs. 2006. *Putting Poor People to Work: How the Work-First Idea Eroded College Access for the Poor.* New York: Russell Sage Foundation.

Smeeding, Timothy M. 2005. "Public Policy, Economic Inequality, and Poverty: The United States in Comparative Perspective." *Social Science Quarterly* 86(5):955–83.

Western, Bruce. 2006. *Punishment and Inequality in America.* New York: Russell Sage Foundation.

Wright, Erik O. 1997. *Class Counts: Comparative Studies in Class Analysis.* New York: Cambridge University Press.

# READING 49

Alaimo, Katherine, Ronnette R. Briefel, Edward A. Frongillo, Jr., and Christine M. Olson. 1998. "Food Insufficiency Exists in the United States: Results from the Third National Health and Nutrition Examination Survey (NHANES III)." *American Journal of Public Health* 88:419–426.

Alba, Richard D., John R. Logan, and Paul E. Bellair. 1994. "Living with Crime: The Implications of Racial/ethnic Differences in Suburban Location." *Social Forces* 73:395–434.

Baker, John. 1987. *Arguing for Equality.* London: Verso.

Bales, Kevin. 1999. *Disposable People: New Slavery in the Global Economy.* Berkeley: University of California Press.

Barber, Benjamin. 1984. *Strong Democracy: Participatory Politics for a New Age.* Berkeley: University of California Press.

Barnes, Sandra. 2005. *The Cost of Being Poor: A Comparative Study of Life in Poor Urban Neighborhoods in Gary, Indiana.* Albany: SUNY Press.

Bernhardt, Annette, Martina Morris, and Mark S. Handcock. 1995. "Women's Gains or Men's Losses? A Closer Look at the Shrinking Gender Gap in Earnings." *The American Journal of Sociology* 101:302–328.

Bhattacharya, Jayanta, Thomas Deleire, Steven Haider, and Janet Currie. 2002. "Heat or Eat? Cold Weather Shocks Nutrition in Poor American Families." NBER Working Paper No. W9004.

Blau, Francine D., and Lawrence M. Kahn. 1997. "Swimming Upstream: Trends in the Gender Wage Differential in the 1980s." *Journal of Labor Economics* 15:1–42.

Blau, Judith R., and Peter M. Blau. 1982. "The Cost of Inequality: Metropolitan Structure and Violent Crime." *American Sociological Review* 47:114–129.

Broadbent, Edward. Editor. 2001. *Democratic Equality: What Went Wrong?* Toronto: University of Toronto Press.

Brooks-Gunn, Jeanne, Greg J. Duncan, Pamela Kato Klebanov, and Naomi Sealand. 1993. "Do Neighborhoods Influence Child and Adolescent Development?" *The American Journal of Sociology* 99: 353–395.

Browne, Irene. 1999. "Latinas and African American Women in the U.S. Labor Market." Pp. 1–31 in I.

Browne, editor, *Latinas and African American Women at Work: Race, Gender, and Economic Inequality.* New York: Russell Sage Foundation.

Budig, Michelle J., and Paula England 2001. "The Wage Penalty for Motherhood." *American Sociological Review* 66: 204–225.

Bureau of Justice Statistics. 2002. "Homicide Trends in the U.S.: Trends by Race." Online: http://www.ojp.usdoj.gov/bjs/homicide/race.htm.

Bureau of Justice Statistics. 2003. "Victim Characteristics: Annual Household Income." Online: http://www.ojp.usdoj.gov/bjs/cvict_v.htm.

Caplovitz, David. 1967. *The Poor Pay More: Consumer Practices of Low-income Families.* New York: The Free Press.

Chung, Chanjin, and Samuel L. Myers, Jr. 1999. "Do the Poor Pay More for Food? An Analysis of Grocery Store Availability and Food Price Disparities." *The Journal of Consumer Affairs* 33: 276–296.

Coleman, James S., Ernest Q. Campbell, Carol F. Hobson, James M. McPartland, Alexander M. Mood, Frederic D. Weinfeld, and Robert L. York. 1996. *Equality of Educational Opportunity.* Washington, D.C.: U.S. Government Printing Office.

Costanzo, Mark. 1997. *Just Revenge: Costs and Consequences of the Death Penalty.* New York: St. Martin's Press.

Cotter, David A., Joan M. Hermsen, and Reeve Vanneman. 1999. "Systems of Gender, Race, and Class Inequality: Multilevel Analyses." *Social Forces* 78: 433–460.

Coverman, Shelley. 1983. "Gender, Domestic Labor Time, and Wage Inequality." *American Sociological Review* 48: 623–637.

Crane, Jonathan. 1991. "The Epidemic Theory of Ghettos and Neighborhood Effects on Dropping Out and Teenage Childbearing." *The American Journal of Sociology* 96: 1226–1259.

Currie, Elliott. 1998. *Crime and Punishment in America.* New York: Metropolitan Books.

Danziger, Sheldon, and Peter Gottschalk. 1995. *America Unequal.* New York: Russell Sage Foundation.

Davis, Karen. 2000. "Health Care for Low-income People." Pp. 311–320 in Marshal, R. (Ed.), *Back to Shared Prosperity: The Growing Inequality of Wealth and Income in America.* Armonk, NY: M. E. Sharpe.

De Nardi, Mariacristina, Liqian Ren, and Chao Wei. 2000." Income Inequality and Redistribution in Five Countries." Federal Reserve Bank of Chicago. *Economic Perspectives* 24:2–20.

DeNavas-Walt, Carmen, Bernadette D. Proctor, and Robert J. Mills. 2004. "Income, Poverty, and Health Insurance Coverage in the United States: 2003." U.S. Census Bureau, Current Population Reports, P:60–226. Washington D.C.: U.S. Government Printing Office.

Evans, Gary W., and Elyse Kantrowitz. 2002. "Socioeconomic Status and Health: The Potential Role of Environmental Risk Exposure." *Annual Review of Public Health* 23:303–331.

Firebaugh, Glenn. 2003. *The New Geography of Global Income Inequality.* Cambridge: Harvard University Press.

Frank, Robert H., and Philip J. Cook. 1995. *The Winner-take-all Society.* New York: The Free Press.

Frydman, Carola, and Raven E. Saks. 2004. "Historic Trends in Executive Compensation, 1936–2002." Harvard University, unpublished paper.

Furstenberg, Jr., Frank F., S. Philip Morgan, and Paul D. Allison. 1987. "Paternal Participation and Children's Well-being after Marital Dissolution." *American Sociological Review* 52:695–701.

George, Vic, and Paul Wilding. 2002. *Globalization and Human Welfare.* Houndmills, Basingstoke, Hampshire: Palgrave.

Geronimus, Arline T., John Bound, Timothy A. Waidmann, Cynthia G. Colen, and Dianne Steffick. 2001. "Inequality in Life Expectancy, Functional Status, and Active Life Expectancy Across Selected Black and White Populations in the United States." *Demography* 38: 227–251.

Green, Philip. 1998. *Equality and Democracy.* New York: The New Press.

Gutmann, Amy. 1980. *Liberal Equality.* Cambridge: Cambridge University Press.

Hallinan, Maureen T. 2001. "Sociological Perspectives on Black-White Inequalities in American Schooling." *Sociology of Education* 74:50–70.

Harer, Miles D., and Darrell Steffensmeier. 1992. "The Differing Effects of Economic Inequality on Black and White Rates of Violence." *Social Forces* 70:1035–1054.

Hedges, Larry V., and Amy Nowell. 1999. "Changes in the Black-White Gap in Achievement Test Scores." *Sociology of Education* 72:111–135.

Herrnstein, Richard J., and Charles Murray. 1994. *The Bell Curve: Intelligence and Class Structure in American Life.* New York: The Free Press.

Hoffman, Kathryn, Charmaine Llagas, and Thomas D. Snyder. 2003. *Status and Trends in the Education of*

*Blacks.* (Report No. NCES-2003-034). Washington, D.C.: National Center for Education Statistics. (ERIC Document Reproduction Service No. ED481811)

Hughes, Michael, and Melvin E. Thomas. 1998. "The Continuing Significance of Race Revisited: A Study of Race, Class, and Quality of Life in America, 1972–1996." *American Sociological Review* 63:785–795.

Human Rights Watch. 2002. *Race and Incarceration in the United States.* Human Rights Watch Backgrounder, February 27.

Jacobs, Jerry A. 1996. Gender Inequality and Higher Education. *Annual Review of Sociology* 22: 153–185.

Jones, Arthur F., and Daniel H. Weinberg. 2000. "The Changing Shape of the Nation's Income Distribution." U.S. Census Bureau, Current Population Reports, P60–204. Washington D.C.: U.S. Government Printing Office.

Kingston, Paul W. 2000. *The Classless Society.* Stanford, CA: Stanford University Press.

Krieg, Eric J. 1998. "The Two Faces of Toxic Waste: Trends in the Spread of Environmental Hazards." *Sociological Forum* 13:3–20.

LeClere, Felicia B., Richard G. Rogers, and Kimberley D. Peters. 1997. "Ethnicity and Mortality in the United States: Individual and Community Correlates." *Social Forces* 76:169–198.

Lichter, Daniel T., and David J. Eggebeen. 1993. "Rich Kids, Poor Kids: Changing Income Inequality among American Children." *Social Forces* 71: 761–780.

Lin, Nan. 2000. "Inequality in Social Capital." *Contemporary Sociology* 29: 785–795.

Marshall, Ray. 2000. *Back to Shared Prosperity: The Growing Inequality of Wealth and Income in America.* Armonk, NY: M. E. Sharpe.

Massey, Douglas S., and Eric Fong. 1990. "Segregation and Neighborhood Quality: Blacks, Hispanics, and Asians in San Francisco Metropolitan Area." *Social Forces* 69:15–32.

Massey, Douglas S., and Nancy A. Denton. 1993. *American Apartheid: Segregation and the Making of the Underclass.* Cambridge, MA: Harvard University Press.

Massey, Douglas S., Andrew B. Gross, and Kumiko Shibuya. 1994. "Migration, Segregation, and the Geographic Concentration of Poverty." *American Sociological Review* 59:425–445.

McCall, Leslie. 2001. *Complex Inequality: Gender, Class, and Race in the New Economy.* New York: Routledge.

McLanahan, Sara, and Karen Booth. 1989. "Mother-only Families: Problems, Prospects, and Politics." *Journal of Marriage and the Family* 51: 557–580.

McPherson, J. Miller, and Lynn Smith-Lovin. 1982. "Women and Weak Ties: Differences by Sex in the Size of Voluntary Organizations." *The American Journal of Sociology* 87: 883–904.

Merva, Mary, and Richard Fowles. 2000. "Economic Outcomes and Mental Health." Pp. 69–75 in R. Marshal (Ed.), *Back to Shared Prosperity: The Growing Inequality of Wealth and Income in America* . Armonk, NY: M. E. Sharpe.

Mishel, Lawrence, Jared Bernstein, and Heather Boushey. 2003. *The State of Working America 2002/2003.* Ithaca, NY: Cornell University.

Moore, Elsie G. J. 1987. "Ethnic Social Milieu and Black Children's Intelligence Test Achievement." *The Journal of Negro Education* 56:44–52.

Mullahy, John, and Barbara L. Wolfe. 2001. "Health Policies for the Non-elderly Poor." Pp. 278–313 in S. H. Danziger and R. H. Haveman (Eds.), *Understanding Poverty.* New York: Russell Sage Foundation.

Munch, Allison, J. Miller McPherson, and Lynn Smith-Lovin. 1997. "Gender, Children, and Social Contact: The Effects of Childrearing for Men and Women." *American Sociological Review* 62:509–520.

NAACP Legal Defense Fund. 2004. *Racial Statistics of Executions and Death Row in the United States.* Online: http://www.naacpldf.org/deathpenaltyinfo.

Narayan, Deepa (with Raj Patel, Kai Schafft, Anne Rademacher, and Sarah Koch-Schulte). 2000. *Voices of the Poor: Can Anyone Hear Us?* New York: Oxford University Press.

Oliver, Melvin L., and Thomas M. Shapiro. 1997. *Black Wealth/White Wealth: A New Perspective on Racial Equality.* New York: Routledge.

Pearson, Dale F. 1994. "The Black Man: Health Issues and Implications for Clinical Practice." *Journal of Black Studies* 25:81–98.

Pong, Suet-ling. 1998. "The School Compositional Effect of Single Parenthood on 10th-grade Achievement." *Sociology of Education* 71:23–42.

Portes, Alejandro. 1998." Social Capital: Its Origins and Applications in Modern Sociology." *Annual Review of Sociology* 24:1–24.

Rank, Mark Robert. 2004. *One Nation, Underprivileged: Why American Poverty Affects Us All.* New York: Oxford University Press.

Rasmussen, David. 2003. "Annual Estimates of the Population by Sex, Race, and Hispanic or Latino Origin for the United States: April 1, 2000 to July 1, 2003." University of Arkansas at Little Rock, Institute for Economic Advancement. Online: http://www.aiea.ualr.edu/research/demographic/population/NC-EST2003-03.pdf.

Roemer, John E. 1994. *Egalitarian Perspectives: Essays in Philosophical Economics.* Cambridge: Cambridge University Press.

Roscigno, Vincent J., and James W. Ainsworth-Darnell. 1999. "Race, Cultural Capital and Educational Resources: Persistent Inequalities and Achievement Returns." *Sociology of Education* 72:158–178.

Sampson, Robert J., Steven W. Raudenbush, and Felton Earls. 1997. "Neighborhoods and Violent Crime: A Multilevel Study of Collective Efficacy." *Science* 277:918–924.

Spratlen, Thaddeus H. 1973. "Financing Inner-city Schools: Policy Aspects of Economics, Political and Racial Disparity." *The Journal of Negro Education* 42:283–307.

Thompson, Becky Wangsgaard. 1992." 'A way outa no way': Eating Problems among African American, Latina, and White Women." *Gender & Society* 6:546–561.

Tilly, Charles. 1998. *Durable Inequality.* Berkeley: University of California Press.

United Nations Statistics Division. 2000. "Statistics and Indicators on Women and Men: The World's Women 2000." Online: http://unstats.un.org/unsd/demographic/products/indwm/edu 2000.htm.

United Nations Statistics Division. 2004a. Millennium Indicators Database. Online: http://unstats.un.org/unsd/mi/mi_series_list.asp.

United Nations Statistics Division. 2004b. "Demographic and Social Statistics: Social Indicators." Online: http://unstats.un.org/unsd/demographic/demographic/products/socind/socind2.htm#edu.

U.S. Census Bureau. 2001. "Historical Income Tables—People." Tables P-2, P-40, and P-54. Online: http://www.census.gov/hhes/income/histinc/histinc/incperdet.html.

U.S. Census Bureau. 2003. "Historical Income Tables—Households." Table H-3. Online: http://www.cen sus.gov/hhes/income/histinc/h03.html.

Walters, Pamela Barnhouse. 2001." Educational Access and the State: Historical Continuities and Discontinuities in Racial Inequality in American Education." *Sociology of Education* 74:35–49.

Walzer, Michael. 1983. *Spheres of Justice: A Defense of Pluralism and Equality.* New York: Basic Books.

Williams, David R., and Chiquita Collins. 1995. "US Socioeconomic and Racial Differences in Health: Patterns and Explanations." *Annual Review of Sociology* 21:349–386.

Wilson, William J. 2000. "Jobless Ghettos: The Social Implications of the Disappearance of Work in Segregated Neighborhoods." Pp. 85–94 in R. Marshal (Ed.), *Back to Shared Prosperity: The Growing Inequality of Wealth and Income in America.* Armonk, NY: M. E. Sharpe.

The World Factbook. 2004. Central Intelligence Agency. Online: http://www.cia.gov/cia/publica tions/factbook/index.html.

Xu, Wu, and Ann Leffler. 1996. "Gender and Race Effects on Occupational Prestige, Segregation, and Earnings." Pp. 107–124 in E. Ngan-Ling Chow, D. Wilkinson, and M. B. Zinn (Eds.), *Race, Class, and Gender: Common Bonds, Different Voices.* Thousand Oaks, CA: Sage Publications.

Yates, Michael D. 2003. *Naming the System: Inequality and Work in the Global Economy.* New York: Monthly Review Press.

Yinger, John. 1986. "Measuring Racial Discrimination with Fair Housing Audits: Caught in the Act." *The American Economic Review* 881–893.

Young, Iris Marion. 2000. *Inclusion and Democracy.* New York: Oxford University Press.

## READING 50

African American Policy Forum. 2009. "A Primer on Intersectionality." http://aapf.org/wp-content/uploads/2009/03/aapf_intersectionality_primer.pdf.

Blumenfeld, W. 2006. "Christian Privilege and the Promotion of 'Secular' and Not-So 'Secular' Mainline Christianity in Public Schooling and in the Larger Society." *Equity and Excellence in Education* 39:195–210. doi: 10;1080/10665680600788024.

Blumenfeld, W. J., and K. Jaekel. "Exploring Levels of Christian Privilege Awareness among Preservice Teachers." *Journal of Social Issues* 68:128–144.

Blumenfeld, W. J., K. Y. Joshi, and E. E. Fairchild (2009). *Investigating Christian Privilege and Religious Oppression in the United States.* Rotterdam, Denmark: Sense Publishers.

Bonilla-Silva, E. 2010. *Racism without Racists: Color-Blind Racism and the Persistence of Racial Inequality in the United States.* 3rd ed. Lanham, MD: Rowman and Littlefield.

Bonilla-Silva, E. (2003). "'New Racism,' Color-Blind Racism, and the Future of Whiteness in America." Pp. 271–284 in *White Out: The Continuing Significance of Race,* edited by A. W. Doane & E. Bonilla-Silva. New York: Routledge.

Brown, C., & T. Augusta-Scott. 2007. *Narrative Therapy: Making Meaning, Making Lives.* Thousand Oaks, CA: Sage.

Case, K. (2012). "Discovering the Privilege of Whiteness: White Women's Reflections on Anti-Racist Identity and Ally Behavior." *Journal of Social Issues* 68(1):78–96. doi: 10.1111/j.1540-4560.2011.01737.x.

Cole, E. R., L. R. Avery, C. Dodson, and K. D. Goodman. 2012. "Against Nature: How Arguments about the Naturalness of Marriage Privilege Heterosexuality." *Journal of Social Issues* 68(1):46–62. doi: 10.1111/j.1540-4560.2011.01735.x.

Collins, P. H. 2000. *Black Feminist Thought: Knowledge, Consciousness, and the Politics of Empowerment.* 2nd ed. New York: Routledge.

Collins, P. H. 2004. *Black Sexual Politics: African Americans, Gender, and the New Racism.* New York: Routledge.

Coppock, V., D. Haydon, and I. Richter. 1995. *The Illusions of "Post-Feminism."* London: Taylor and Francis.

Coston, B. M., and M. Kimmel. 2012. "Seeing Privilege Where It Isn't: Marginalized Masculinities and the Intersectionality of Privilege." *Journal of Social Issues* 68(1):97–111. doi: 10.1111/j.1540-4560.2011.01738.x.

Crittenden, A. 2001. *The Price of Motherhood: Why the Most Important Job in the World Is Still the Least Valued.* New York: Henry Holt.

Cunnigen, D., and M. Bruce. 2010. *Race in the Age of Obama.* Bingley, UK: Emerald Group Publishing.

Doane, A. W. 2003. "Rethinking Whiteness Studies." Pp. 3–18 in *White Out: The Continuing Significance of Race,* edited by A. W. Doane and E. Bonilla-Silva. New York: Routledge.

Douglas, S. 2010. *Enlightened Sexism: The Seductive Message That Feminism's Work Is Done.* New York: Times Books.

Faludi, S. 1991. *Backlash: The Undeclared War against American Women.* New York: Doubleday.

Feagin, J. R. 2001. *Racist America: Roots, Current Realities, and Future Reparations.* New York: Routledge.

Ferber, A. L. 1998. *White Man Falling: Race, Gender and White Supremacy.* Lanham, MD: Rowman and Littlefield.

Ferber, A. L. 2003. "Defending the Culture of Privilege." Pp. 319–329 in *Privilege: A Reader,* edited by M. S. Kimmel and A. L. Ferber. Boulder, CO: Westview Press.

Ferber, A. L. 2007. "Whiteness Studies and the Erasure of Gender." *Sociology Compass* 1:265–282. doi: 10.1111/j.1751-9020.2007.00014.x.

Ferber, A. L., C. Jimenez, A. H. O'Reilly, and D. Samuels, eds. 2008. *The Matrix Reader: Examining the Dynamics of Privilege and Oppression.* New York: McGraw Hill.

Ferber, A. L. 2009. "Please Don't Wish Me a Merry Christmas." *Huffington Post.* Retrieved January 10, 2012 (http://www.huffingtonpost.com/abby-ferber/please-dont-wish-me-a-mer_b_389824.html).

Ferber, A. L., and D. Samuels. 2010. "Oppression without Bigots." *Factsheet, Network News* (Winter). Sociologists for Women in Society.

Glenn, E. N. 2010. *Forced to Care: Coercion and Caregiving in America.* Cambridge, MA: Harvard University Press.

Hardiman, R., and B. Jackson. 1997. "Conceptual Foundations for Social Justice Courses." Pp. 16–29 in *Teaching for Diversity and Social Justice Courses,* edited by M. Adams, L. A. Bell, and P. Griffin. New York: Routledge.

Hartigan, J., Jr. 2010. *Race in the 21st Century: Ethnographic Approaches.* New York: Oxford University Press.

Irons, J. 2010. *Reconstituting Whiteness: The Mississippi State Sovereignty Commission.* Nashville, TN: Vanderbilt University Press.

Kendall, F. E. 2006. *Understanding White Privilege: Creating Pathways to Authentic Relationships across Race.* New York: Routledge.

Kimmel, M. S., and A. L. Ferber, eds. 2009. *Privilege: A Reader.* 2nd ed. Boulder, CO: Westview Press.

Kincheloe, J. L. 2009. "Selling a New and Improved Jesus: Christotainment and the Power of Political Fundamentalism." Pp 1–22 in *Christotainment: Selling Jesus through Popular Culture,* edited by S. Steinberg and J. L. Kincheloe. Boulder, CO: Westview.

Lewis, A. 2003. *Race in the Schoolyard: Negotiating the Color Line in Classrooms and Communities.* New Brunswick, NJ: Rutgers University Press.

McRobbie, A. 2004. "Post-Feminism and Popular Culture." *Feminist Media Studies* 4:255–264. doi: 10.1080/1468077042000309937.

Nelson, J. 2009. "Christian Teachers and Christian Privilege." Pp. 135–149 in *Investigating Christian Privilege and Religious Oppression in the United States,* edited by W. J. Blumenfeld, K. Y. Joshi, and E. E. Fairchild. Rotterdam, Denmark: Sense Publishers.

Pincus, F. L. 2003. *Reverse Discrimination: Dismantling the Myth.* Boulder, CO: Lynne Reinart.

Plaut, V. C. 2010. "Diversity Science: Why and How Difference Makes a Difference." *Psychological Inquiry* 21:77–99. doi: 10.1080/10478401003676501.

Pratto, F., and A. L. Stewart. 2012. "Group Dominance and the Half-Blindness of Privilege." *Journal of Social Issues* 68:28–45.

Ryan, W. 1971. *Blaming the Victim.* New York: Pantheon Books.

Steinberg, S. 1995. *Turning Back: The Retreat from Racial Justice in American Thought and Policy.* Boston: Beacon Press.

Steinberg, S. R., and J. L. Kincheloe. 2009. *Christotainment: Selling Jesus through Popular Culture.* Boulder, CO: Westview.

Stewart, T. L., I. M. Latu, and H. T. Denney. 2012. "White Privilege Awareness and Efficacy to Reduce Racial Inequality Improve White Americans' Attitudes toward African Americans." *Journal of Social Issues* 68(1):11–27.

Sutton, B. 2010. *Bodies in Crisis: Culture, Violence, and Women's Resistance in Neoliberal Argentina.* New Brunswick, NJ: Rutgers University Press.

Tehranian, J. 2009. *Whitewashed: America's Invisible Middle Eastern Minority.* New York: New York University Press.

Todd, J. 2010. "Confessions of a Christian Supremacist." *Reflections: Narratives of Professional Helping* 16:140–146.

Van Ausdale, D., and J. R. Feagin. 2001. *The First R: How Children Learn Race and Racism.* Lanham, MD: Rowman and Littlefield.

Villalon, R. 2010. *Violence against Latina Immigrants: Citizenship, Inequality, and Community.* New York: New York University Press.

## READING 53

Amparano, Julie. 1997. "Brown Skin: No Civil Rights? July Sweep on Chandler Draws Fire." *Arizona Republic* August 15:B1.

Benitez, Humberto. 1994. "Flawed Strategies: The INS Shift from Border Interdiction to Internal Enforcement Actions." *La Raza Law Journal* 7:154–79.

Breen, Thomas, Sergio Murueta, and John Winters. 1998. *Report of Independent Investigation into July 1997 Joint Operation Between Patrol and Chandler Police Department.* Vol. I, II, and III, Chandler, Arizona: The City of Chandler.

Calavita, Kitty. 1992. *Inside the State, The Bracero Program, Immigration, and the I.N.S.* New York, NY: Routledge.

Chang, Robert S. 1999. *Disoriented: Asian Americans, Law, and the Nation-State.* New York, NY: New York University Press.

Chang, Robert S., and Keith Aoki. 1997. "Centering the Immigrant in the Inter/National Imagination." *California Law Review* 85:1395–1447.

Fletcher, Michael A. 1997. "Police in Arizona Accused of Civil Rights Violations; Lawsuit Cites Sweep Aimed at Illegal Immigrants." *Washington Post* August 20:A14.

Georges-Abeyie, Daniel E. 1990. "Criminal Justice Processing of Non-White Minorities." Pp. 25–34 in *Racism, Empiricism and Criminal Justice,* edited by Brian D. MacLean and Dragan Milovanovic. Vancouver, BC: The Collective Press.

Johnson, Kevin. 2000. "The Case Against Race Profiling in Immigration Enforcement." *Washington University Law Quarterly* 78(3):676–736.

———. 2004. The "Huddled Masses" Myth: Immigration and Civil Rights. Philadelphia, PA: Temple University Press.

Office of the Attorney General Grant Wood. 1997. *Results of the Chandler Survey.* Phoenix, State of Arizona.

Sáenz Benjamin Alire. 1992. *Flowers for the Broken: Stories.* Seatle, WA: Broken Moon Press.

Smith, Dorothy E. 1990. *Texts, Facts, and Femininity: Exploring the Relations of Ruling.* New York, NY: Routledge.

———. 1999. *Writing the Social: Critique, Theory, and Investigations.* Toronto, ON: The University of Toronto Press.

Vargas, Jorge A. 2001. "U.S. Border Patrol Abuses, Undocumented Mexican Workers, and International Human Rights." *San Diego International Law Review* 2(1):1–92.

## READING 55

Bernstein, R. 1994. "Guilty If Charged." *New York Review of Books*, 13 January.

Bowman, C. G. 1993. "Street Harassment and the Informal Ghettoization of Women." *Harvard Law Review* 106:517–80.

Buckwald, A. 1993. "Compliment a Woman, Go to Court." *Los Angeles Times*, 28 October.

Bumiller, K. 1998. *The Civil Rights Society: The Social Construction of Victims*. Baltimore: Johns Hopkins University Press.

Butler, J. 1990. *Gender Trouble: Feminism and the Subversion of Identity*. New York: Routledge.

Chen, A. S. 1999. "Lives at the Center of the Periphery, Lives at the Periphery of the Center: Chinese American Masculinities and Bargaining with Hegemony." *Gender & Society* 13:584–607.

Cleveland, J. N., and M. E. Kerst. 1993. "Sexual Harassment and Perceptions of Power: An Under-articulated Relationship." *Journal of Vocational Behavior* 42(1):49–67.

Cockburn, C. 1983. *Brothers: Male Dominance and Technological Change*. London: Pluto Press.

Collinson, D. L., and M. Collinson. 1989. "Sexuality in the Workplace: The Domination of Men's Sexuality." In *The Sexuality of Organizations*, edited by J. Hearn and D. L. Sheppard. Newbury Park, CA: Sage.

———. 1996. "'It's Only Dick': The Sexual Harassment of Women Managers in Insurance Sales." *Work, Employment & Society* 10(1):29–56.

Conley, F. K. 1991. "Why I'm Leaving Stanford: I Wanted My Dignity Back." *Los Angeles Times*, 9 June.

Conley, J., and W. O'Barr. 1998. *Just Words*. Chicago: University of Chicago Press.

Connell, R. W. 1987. *Gender and Power*. Stanford, CA: Stanford University Press.

———. 1995. *Masculinities*. Berkeley: University of California Press.

Estrich, S. 1987. *Real Rape*. Cambridge, MA: Harvard University Press.

Gardner, C. B. 1995. *Passing By: Gender and Public Harassment*. Berkeley: University of California Press.

Giuffre, P., and C. Williams. 1994. "Boundary Lines: Labeling Sexual Harassment in Restaurants." *Gender & Society* 8:378–401.

Glaser, B., and A. L. Strauss. 1967. *The Discovery of Grounded Theory: Strategies for Qualitative Research*. Chicago: Aldine.

Guccione, J. 1992. "Women Judges Still Fighting Harassment." *Daily Journal*, 13 October, 1.

Gutek, B. A., and M. P. Koss. 1993. "Changed Women and Changed Organizations: Consequences of and Coping with Sexual Harrasment." *Journal of Vocational Behavior* 42(1):28–48.

Gutek, B. A., B. Morasch, and A. G. Cohen. 1983. "Interpreting Social-sexual Behavior in a Work Setting." *Journal of Vocational Behavior* 22(1):30–48.

Hearn, J. 1985. "Men's Sexuality at Work." In *The Sexuality of Men*, edited by A. Metcalf and M. Humphries. London: Pluto Press.

Hopkins, P. 1992. "Gender Treachery: Homophobia, Masculinity, and Threatened Identities." In *Rethinking Masculinity: Philosophical Explorations in Light of Feminism*, edited by L. May and R. Strikwerda. Lanham, MD: Littlefield, Adams.

Johnson, M. 1988. *Strong Mothers, Weak Wives*. Berkeley: University of California Press.

MacKinnon, C.A. 1979. *The Sexual Harassment of Working Women*. New. Haven, CT: Yale University Press.

Malovich, N. J., and J. E. Stake. 1990. "Sexual Harassment on Campus: Individual Differences in Attitudes and Beliefs." *Psychology of Women Quarterly* 14(1):63–81.

Murrell, A. J., and B. L. Dietz-Uhler. 1993. "Gender Identity and Adversarial Sexual Beliefs as Predictors of Attitudes toward Sexual Harassment." *Psychology of Women Quarterly* 17(2):169–175.

Popovich, P. M., D. N. Gehlauf, J. A. Jolton, J. M. Somers, and R.M. Godinho. 1992. "Perceptions of Sexual Harassment as a Function of Sex of Rater and Incident Form and Consequent." *Sex Roles* 27 (11/12):609–625.

Pronger, B. 1992. "Gay Jocks: A Phenomenology of Gay Men in Athletics." In *Rethinking Masculinity: Philosophical Explorations in Light of Feminism*, edited by L. May and R. Strikwerda. Lanham, MD: Littlefield Adams.

Pryor J. B. 1987. "Sexual Harassment Proclivities in Men." *Sex Roles* 17(5/6):269–290.

Quinn, B. A. 2000. "The Paradox of Complaining: Law, Humor and Harassment in the Everyday Work World." *Law and Social Inquiry* 25(4):1151–1183.

Reilly, M. E., B. Lott, D. Caldwell and L. DeLuca. 1992. "Tolerance for Sexual Harassment Related to Self-reported Sexual Victimization." *Gender & Society* 6:122–138.

Rogers, J. K., and K. D. Henson. 1997. "'Hey, Why Don't You Wear a Shorter Skirt?' Structural Vulnerability and the Organization of Sexual Harassment in Temporary Clerical Employment." *Gender & Society* 11:215–238.

Schwalbe, M. 1992. "Male Supremacy and the Narrowing of the Moral Self." *Berkeley Journal of Sociology* 37:29–54.

Smith, D. 1990. *The Conceptual Practices of Power: A Feminist Sociology of Knowledge.* Boston: Northeastern University Press.

Stockdale, M. S. 1993. "The Role of Sexual Misperceptions of Women's Friendliness in an Emerging Theory of Sexual Harassment." *Journal of Vocational Behavior* 42(1):84–101.

Tagri, S., and S. M. Hayes. 1997. "Theories of Sexual Harassment." In *Sexual Harassment: Theory, Research and Treatment,* edited by W. O'Donohue. New York: Allyn & Bacon.

Thorne, B. 1993. *Gender Play: Girls and Boys in School.* Buckingham, U.K: Open University Press.

U.S. Merit Systems Protection Board. 1988. *Sexual Harassment in the Federal Government: An Update.* Washington, DC: Government Printing Office.

West, C., and D.H. Zimmerman. 1987. "Doing Gender." *Gender & Society* 1:125–151.

Wood, J. T. 1998. "Saying Makes It So: The Discursive Construction of Sexual Harassment." In *Conceptualizing Sexual Harassment as Discursive Practice,* edited by S.G. Bingham. Westport, CT: Praeger.

Yount, K. R. 1991. "Ladies, Flirts, Tomboys: Strategies for Managing Sexual Harassment in an Underground Coal Mine." *Journal of Contemporary Ethnography* 19:396–422.

## READING 57

Ezorsky, Gertrude. *Racism and Justice: The Case for Affirmative Action.* Ithaca, NY: Cornell University Press, 1991.

## READING 58

Allport, Gordon W. 1958. *The Nature of Prejudice.* Abridged ed. Garden City, NY: Doubleday Anchor Books.

Ani, Marimba. 1994. *Yurugu: An African-Centered Critique of European Cultural Thought and Behavior.* Trenton, NJ: Africa World Press.

Bendick, Marc Jr., Mary Lou Egan, and Suzanne Lofhjelm. 1998. *The Documentation and Evaluation of Anti-Discrimination Training in the United States.* Geneva: International Labour Office.

Bittker, Boris. 1973. *The Case for Black Reparations.* New York: Random House.

Brooks, Roy, ed. 1999. *When Sorry Isn't Enough: The Controversy over Apologies and Reparations for Human Injustice.* New York: New York University Press.

Carr, Leslie. 1997. *"Color-Blind" Racism.* Thousand Oaks, CA: Sage.

Department of Public Information, United Nations. 1995. *The United Nations and Human Rights, 1945–1995.* New York: United Nations.

King, Martin Luther, Jr. 1971. "I Have a Dream." In *Black Protest Thought in the Twentieth Century*, edited by August Meier, Elliot Rudwick, and Francis L. Broderick. New York: Bobbs-Merrill.

Lincoln, C. Eric and Lawrence H. Mamiya. 1990. *The Black Church in the African American Experience.* Durham, NC: Duke University Press.

O'Brien, Eileen. 1999. "Whites Doing Antiracism: Discourse, Practice, Emotion and Organizations." Ph.D. dissertation. Gainesville: University of Florida.

Rutstein, Nathan. 1993. *Healing Racism in America* Springfield, MA: Whitcomb.

Tajfel, Henri. 1982. *Social Identity and Intergroup Relations.* Cambridge: Cambridge University Press.

## READING 59

Acker, John. 1988. "Class, Gender, and the Relations of Distribution." *Signs* 13:473–97.

Acker, John. 1990. "Hierarchies, Jobs, and Bodies: A Theory of Gendered Organizations." *Gender & Society* 4:139–58.

Brown, Wendy. 1992. "Finding the Man in the State." *Feminist Studies* 18:7–34.

Cockburn, Cynthia. 1991. *In the Way of Women: Men's Resistance to Sex Equality in Organizations.* Ithaca, New York: ILR Press.

Connell, Robert w. 1987. *Gender and Power: Society, the Person, and Sexual Politics.*

Stanford, CA: Stanford University Press.

———. 1990. "The State, Gender, and Sexual Politics: Theory and Appraisal." *Theory and Soceity* 19: 507–544.

Draper, Elaine. 1993. "Fetal Exclusion Policies and Gendered Construction of Suitable Work." *Social Problems* 40: 90–107.

Haraway, Donna. 1995. "A Manifesto for Cyborgs." *Socialist Review* 15(2):65–107.

Hertz, Rosanna. 1986. *More Equal than Others: Women and Men in Dual-Career Marriages.* Berkeley, CA: University of California Press.

Higginbotham, Elizabeth and Lynn Weber. 1992. "Moving Up with Kin and Community: Upward Social Mobility for Black and White Women." *Gender & Society* 6:416–40.

Higginbotham, Evelyn Brooks. 1992. "African American Women's History and the Meta-Language of Race." *Signs* 17:251–74.

Holcombe, Lee. 1983. *Wives and Property: Reform of the Married Women's Property Law in Nineteenth-Century England.* Toronto: University of Toronto Presss.

Hunter, Andrea G. and James Earl Davis. 1992. "Construcruting Genter; An Exploration of Afro American Men's Conceptualization of Manhood." *Gender & Society* 6:464–79.

Jaggar, Alison M. 1983. *Feminist Politics and Human Nature.* Totowa, N J: Rowman & Allanheld.

Jagger, Alison M. 1990. "Sexual Differenced and Sexual Equality." In *Theoretical Perspectives on Cultural Difference,* edited by Deborah L. Rhode. New Haven: Yale University Press.

Johnson, Kay Ann. 1983. *Women, the Family and Peasant Revolution in China.* Chicago: University of Chicago Press.

Kay, Herma Hill. 1985. "Models of Equality." *University of Illinois Law Review,* 1985(1):39–88.

Lorber, Judith. 1075. "Beyond the Equality of the Sexes: The Question of the Children." *Family Coordinator* 24:465–72.

MacKinnon, Catharine A. 1989. *Toward a Feminist Theory of the State.* Cambridge, MA: Harvard University Press.

Martin, Patricia Yancey. 1993. "Feminist Practice in Organizations: Implications for Management." *In Women and Management: Trends, Issues and Challenges in Managerial Diversity,* edited by Ellen A. Fagenson. Newbury Park, CA: Sage.

Nochlin, Linda. 1988. *Women, Art, and Power and Other Essays.* New York: Harper and Row.

Rossiter Margaret L. 1986. *Women in the Resistance.* New York: Praeger.

Soble, Alan. 1986. Pornography: *Marxism, Feminism and the Future of Sexuality.* New Haven, CT: Yale University Press.

Stacey, Judith. 1991. *Brave New Families: Stories of Domestic Upheaval in Late Twentieth Century America.* New York: Basic Books.

Weitzman, Lenore J. 1985. *The Divorce Revolution: The Unexpected Social and Economic Consequences for Women and Children in America.* New York: Free Press.

## READING 60

Agres, Bob. 2005. "Community Building in Hawai'i." *The Nonprofit Quarterly.* Summer 2005.

Anderson, Sarah, John Cavanagh, Scott Klinger, and Liz Stanton. 2005. *Executive Excess 2005.* Boston and Washington, D.C.: Institute for Policy Studies and United for a Fair Economy. http://www.faireconomy.org/press/2005/EE2005.pdf.

Boshara, Ray, Reid Cramer, and Leslie Parrish. 2004. *Policy Options to Encourage Savings and Asset Building by Low-Income Americans.* New America Foundation, discussion draft. January 28, 2004. (From www.newamericafoundation.org).

Brown, Michael K. 1999. "Race in the American Welfare State: The Ambiguities of 'Universalistic'" Social Policy since the New Deal." *Without Justice for All: The New Liberalism and Our Retreat from Racial Equality,* edited by Adolph L. Reed. Boulder, CO: Westview Press.

Collins, Chuck and Felice Yeskel. 2000. *Economic Apartheid in America: An Economic Primer on Economic Inequality and Insecurity.* New York: The New Press.

Ginsberg, Thomas and Paola Ochoa. 2003. "Immigrants Pool Money, Find Success." *Philadelphia Inquirer.* November 17, 2003.

Henry J. Kaiser Family Foundation. 2004. "New Report Provides Critical Information about Health Insurance Coverage and Access for Racial and Ethnic Minority Groups." Washington, D.C. August 1, 2000. http://www.kff.org/uninsured/upload/13342 1.pdf.

Isbister, John. 1994. *Thin Cats: The Community Development Credit Union Movement in the United States*. Davis, CA: Center for Cooperatives, University of California.

Moreno, Ana. 1998. *Mortgage Foreclosure Prevention: Program and Trends*. Minneapolis, MN: Family Housing Fund.

Muhammad, Dedrick, Attieno Davis, Meizhu Lui, and Betsy Leondar-Wright. 2004. *The State of the Dream 2004: Enduring Disparities in Black and White*. Boston: United for a Fair Economy.

Orr, Doug. 2004. "Social Security Isn't Broken." *Dollars & Sense*, 256.

Policy Link. 2003. "Community Reinvestment Act: Why Use the Tool?" http://www.policylink.org/ EquitableDevelopment/content/tools/56/20-all?

Price, Derek. 2003. *Inequality in Higher Education: The Historic and Continuing Significance of Race*, Panel on Colorlines Conference, Harvard Law School Civil Rights Project, August 30, 2003.

Root Cause. 2003. *Community Impact Report*. Miami, FL: November 11, 2003. http://users.resist.ca/~mangus/ CIR_eng.pdf.

Shapiro, Thomas. 2004a. *The Hidden Cost of Being African American: How Wealth Perpetuates Inequality*. New York: Oxford University Press.

Shapiro, Thomas. 2004b. "Power Point Presentation at Center for American Progress Panel on Wealth Inequality." September 23, 2004.

Sherradan, Michael. 1991. *Assets and the Poor: A New American Welfare Policy*. New York: M. E. Sharpe.

Sklar, Holly, Laryssa Mykyta, and Susan Wefald. 2001. *Raise the Floor Wages: Wages and Policies that Work for All of Us*. New York: Ms. Foundation for Women.

Spriggs, William E. 2004. "African Americans and Social Security: Why the Privatization Advocates Wrong." *Dollars & Sense* 256 (2004):18.

United for a Fair Economy. 2002. Annual Report.http:// www.faireconomy.org/.

Woo, Deborah. 2000. *Glass Ceilings and Asian Americans: The New Face of Workplace Barriers*. Walnut Creek, CA: AltaMira Press.